HANSARD'S

PARLIAMENTARY DEBATES.

THIRD SERIES:

COMMENCING WITH THE ACCESSION OF

WILLIAM IV.

47° & 48° VICTORIÆ, 1884.

VOL. CCXCI.

COMPRISING THE PERIOD FROM

THE TWENTY-SECOND DAY OF JULY, 1884,

TO

THE FIFTH DAY OF AUGUST, 1884.

EIGHTH VOLUME OF THE SESSION.

LONDON:

PUBLISHED BY CORNELIUS BUCK,

AT THE OFFICE FOR "HANSARD'S PARLIAMENTARY DEBATES,"

22, PATERNOSTER ROW. [E.C.]

1884.

TABLE OF CONTENTS

TO

VOLUME CCXCI.

THIRD SERIES.

LORDS, TUESDAY, JULY 22.

TABLE OF CONTENTS.

TABLE OF CONTENTS.

TABLE OF CONTENTS.

[*July* 24.] *Page*

TABLE OF CONTENTS.

[*July* 24.] **Page**

ORDERS OF THE DAY.

—o—

TABLE OF CONTENTS.

TABLE OF CONTENTS.

[July 25.] Page

ORDERS OF THE DAY.

TABLE OF CONTENTS.

LORDS, MONDAY, JULY 28.

TABLE OF CONTENTS.

[*July* 28.] *Page*

[*July* 28.] *Page*

ORDERS OF THE DAY.

—o—

TABLE OF CONTENTS.

QUESTIONS.

[July 29.] Page

ORDERS OF THE DAY.

SUPPLY—*considered* in Committee—CIVIL SERVICE ESTIMATES—

(In the Committee.)

CLASS III.—LAW AND JUSTICE.

TABLE OF CONTENTS.

[*July* 29.] *Page*

COMMONS, WEDNESDAY, JULY 30.

PRIVATE BUSINESS.

—o—

QUESTION.

ORDER OF THE DAY.

LORDS, THURSDAY, JULY 31.

TABLE OF CONTENTS.

COMMONS, THURSDAY, JULY 31.

QUESTIONS.

TABLE OF CONTENTS.

[*July* 31.] *Page*

TABLE OF CONTENTS.

[*July* 31.] *Page*

PARLIAMENT—BUSINESS OF THE HOUSE—COMMITTEE OF SUPPLY—STANDING ORDER 425A—Postponement of Motion, Mr. Gladstone; Questions, Lord Randolph Churchill; Answers, Mr. Gladstone 1188

PALACE OF WESTMINSTER — HOUSE OF COMMONS—VENTILATION OF THE HOUSE—Question, Mr. Borlase; Answer, Sir Charles W. Dilke .. 1188

PARLIAMENT—BUSINESS OF THE HOUSE—BURGH POLICE AND HEALTH (SCOTLAND) BILL—Question, General Sir George Balfour; Answer, The Lord Advocate 1188

EGYPT (EVENTS IN THE SOUDAN)—MAJOR KITCHENER—Question, Mr. Ashmead-Bartlett; Answer, Lord Edmond Fitzmaurice 1189

INDIA—REVENUE SETTLEMENT DEPARTMENT—NATIVE APPOINTMENTS—Question, Mr. Thorold Rogers; Answer, Mr. J. K. Cross 1189

ORDERS OF THE DAY.

—o—

SUPPLY—*considered* in Committee—CIVIL SERVICE ESTIMATES—

(In the Committee.)

CLASS III.—LAW AND JUSTICE.

(1.) Motion made, and Question proposed, "That a sum, not exceeding £49,031, be granted to Her Majesty, to complete the sum necessary to defray the Charge which will come in course of payment during the year ending on the 31st day of March 1885, of Criminal Prosecutions and other Law Charges in Ireland, including certain Allowances under the Act 15 and 16 Vict. c. 83."

Whereupon Motion made, and Question proposed, "That a sum, not exceeding £45,031, be granted, &c.,"—(*Mr. Small*) 1190

After debate, Question put, and *negatived.*

Original Question put, and *agreed to.*

(2.) £7,561, to complete the sum for the Court of Bankruptcy, Ireland.—After short debate, Vote *agreed to* 1218

(3.) Motion made, and Question proposed, "That a sum, not exceeding £12,670, be granted to Her Majesty, to complete the sum necessary to defray the Charge which will come in course of payment during the year ending on the 31st day of March 1885, for the Salaries and Expenses of the Office for the Registration of Deeds in Ireland" 1220

After short debate, Motion made, and Question proposed, "That a sum, not exceeding £11,670, be granted, &c.,"—(*Mr. Findlater*:)—After further short debate, Question put:—The Committee *divided;* Ayes 28, Noes 45; Majority 17.—(Div. List, No. 198.)

Original Question put, and *agreed to.*

(4.) Motion made, and Question proposed, "That a sum, not exceeding £83,430 (including a Supplementary sum of £25,340), be granted to Her Majesty, to complete the sum necessary to defray the Charge which will come in course of payment during the year ending on the 31st day of March 1885, for the Salaries and Expenses of the Office of the Irish Land Commission" 1241

After debate, Motion made, and Question proposed, "That a sum, not exceeding £82,680 (including a Supplementary sum of £25,340), be granted, &c.,"—(*Colonel King-Harman*:)—After further short debate, Question put, and *negatived.*

Original Question put, and *agreed to.*

(5.) Motion made, and Question proposed, "That a sum, not exceeding £86,094, be granted to Her Majesty, to complete the sum necessary to defray the Charge which will come in course of payment during the year ending on the 31st day of March 1885, for the Salaries and Expenses of the Commissioners of Police, the Police Courts, and the Metropolitan Police Establishment of Dublin" 1308

Motion made, and Question proposed, "That a sum, not exceeding £85,094, be granted, &c.,"—(*Mr. Healy*:)—After short debate, Motion, by leave, *withdrawn.*

Original Question again proposed 1324

Motion made, and Question put, "That a sum, not exceeding £25,094, be granted, &c.:"—The Committee *divided;* Ayes 19, Noes 73; Majority 54.—(Div. List, No. 199.)

Original Question put, and *agreed to.*

Resolutions to be reported.

Motion made, and Question proposed, "That a sum, not exceeding £51,944, be granted to Her Majesty, to complete the sum necessary to defray the Charge

TABLE OF CONTENTS.

TABLE OF CONTENTS.

[*August* 1.] *Page*

PARLIAMENT—STANDING ORDERS—AMENDMENT—*continued.*

Amendment proposed, to add at the end thereof, the words—

"The Notices shall also state what power it is intended to employ for moving carriages or trucks upon the Tramway,"—(*Mr. Holms.*)

Question proposed, "That those words be there added:"—After short debate, Question put, and *agreed to;* words *added* accordingly.

Remaining Amendments *agreed to:*—*Ordered,* That the said Orders be Standing Orders of this House.

QUESTIONS.

TABLE OF CONTENTS.

ORDERS OF THE DAY.

—o—

TABLE OF CONTENTS.

COMMONS, MONDAY, AUGUST 4.

Page

QUESTIONS.

TABLE OF CONTENTS.

[*August* 4.] Page

ORDERS OF THE DAY.

—o—

TABLE OF CONTENTS.

COMMONS, TUESDAY, AUGUST 5.

QUESTIONS.

TABLE OF CONTENTS.

[*August* 5.] **Page**

ORDERS OF THE DAY.

TABLE OF CONTENTS.

HANSARD'S

PARLIAMENTARY DEBATES,

IN THE

Fifth Session OF THE *Twenty-Second Parliament* OF THE UNITED KINGDOM OF *Great Britain* AND *Ireland*, APPOINTED TO MEET 29 APRIL, 1880, IN THE FORTY-THIRD YEAR OF THE REIGN OF

HER MAJESTY QUEEN VICTORIA.

EIGHTH VOLUME OF SESSION 1884.

HOUSE OF LORDS,

Tuesday, 22nd July, 1884.

MINUTES.]—PUBLIC BILLS—*First Reading*—Contagious Diseases (Animals) Act, 1878 (Districts)* (205); Turnpike Acts Continuance* (206).

Second Reading—Local Government Provisional Orders (No. 6)* (189); Naval Discipline Act (1866) Amendment* (199); Reformatory and Industrial Schools (Manx Children)* (200); Sheriff Court Houses (Scotland) Amendment (193), *adjourned;* Oyster Cultivation (Ireland) (197).

Committee — Local Government Provisional Orders (No. 4)* (163); Local Government Provisional Orders (No. 7)* (164); Local Government Provisional Orders (No. 8)* (165); Local Government (Ireland) Provisional Orders (Labourers Act) (No. 2)* (138).

Committee—Report—Prisons (Ireland) (Cost of Conveyance of Prisoners)* (196).

Third Reading—Local Government Provisional Orders (No. 2)* (132); Elections (Hours of Poll)* (179); Summary Jurisdiction (Repeal, &c.)* (202); Revision of Jurors and Voters Lists) (Dublin County)* (178), and *passed.*

SHERIFF COURT HOUSES (SCOTLAND) AMENDMENT BILL.—(No. 193.)

(*The Earl of Dalhousie.*)

SECOND READING.

Order of the Day for the Second Reading read.

THE EARL OF DALHOUSIE, in moving the second reading of the Bill, explained that certain changes were proposed by it in the interests of the Treasury, and certain others in favour of the local authorities, but that, on the whole, the Bill was favourable to the latter.

Moved, "That the Bill be now read 2ª."—(*The Earl of Dalhousie.*)

LORD ABINGER, in moving that the Bill be read a second time that day six months, said, there was a very strong feeling against the Bill amongst the landed proprietors of Scotland, who were the Commissioners of Supply of the counties. Under the Act in force, passed in 1860, the Government paid one-half and the counties one-half of the expenses of the Court Houses. The county of Inverness had expended a large sum of money under the Act of 1860, and he saw no reason why the Treasury should not pay one-half of that sum. That was the arrangement—*i.e.*, the Government to pay one-half, and the other half to be provided by the Commissioners of Supply. He could not see on what principle of justice the Government now attempted to throw over the counties of Scotland, when an Act so recently as 1860 was passed for the purposes which he had mentioned. Unless the Government consented to strike out the clauses containing these provisions, he considered the Bill so objectionable that he should press his Motion for its rejection.

Amendment *moved*, to leave out ("now") and add at the end of the Motion ("this day six months.")—(*The Lord Abinger.*)

LORD ORANMORE AND BROWNE said, he concurred in the remarks of the noble Lord, and might add that many Court Houses had been built on the faith of the Government guarantee, and it would be very unfair now to withdraw it.

LORD ABINGER said, he understood the Bill, being a Money Bill, could not be altered in Committee; and, therefore, he felt obliged to go on with the Division.

On Question, That ("now") stand part of the Motion? Their Lordships *divided*:—Contents 24; Not-Contents 26: Majority 2.

CONTENTS.

Selborne, E. (*L. Chancellor.*)
Somerset, D.
Camperdown, E.
Derby, E.
Granville, E.
Kimberley, E.
Morley, E.
Northbrook, E.
Sydney, E.
Powerscourt, V.
Boston, L.
Boyle, L. (*E. Cork and Orrery.*) [*Teller.*]
Bramwell, L.
Carlingford, L.
Carrington, L.
FitzGerald, L.
Kenmare, L. (*E. Kenmare.*)
Monson, L. [*Teller.*]
Ramsay, L. (*E. Dalhousie.*)
Saye and Sele, L.
Strafford, L. (*V. Enfield.*)
Sundridge, L. (*D. Argyll.*)
Thurlow, L.
Waveney, L.

NOT-CONTENTS.

Leeds, D.
Sutherland, D.
Leven and Melville, E.
Mar and Kellie, E.
Powis, E.
Romney, E.
Selkirk, E.
Hawarden, V.
Abinger, L. [*Teller.*]
Blantyre, L.
Brabourne, L.
Clanwilliam, L. (*E. Clanwilliam.*)
Colville of Culross, L.
Donington, L.
Ellenborough, L.
Hartismere, L. (*L. Henniker.*)
Ker, L. (*M. Lothian.*)
Lamington, L.
Leconfield, L.
Norton, L.
Oranmore and Browne, L.
Silchester, L. (*E. Longford.*)
Stratheden and Campbell, L.
Tweedmouth, L.
Wemyss, L. (*E. Wemyss.*) [*Teller.*]
Wynford, L.

Resolved in the *negative.*

Moved, "That the Bill be read 2ª this day six months."—(*The Lord Abinger.*)

EARL GRANVILLE said, with reference to the result of the Division, that he did not remember any purely Money Bill having been rejected by that House on the second reading, without any Notice whatever having been given.

THE EARL OF HARDWICKE said, he was in no way responsible for the result, as he did not vote; but if the Bill was one of great importance, why did not the noble and learned Earl on the Woolsack, or another Member of the Government give some explanation to the House; but no noble Lord got up to make any protest against the Amendment. Even if it were a small matter, the Government might have offered some explanation to the House.

THE EARL OF KIMBERLEY said, no doubt it was a small matter; but still it was most unusual to oppose, without any Notice, the second reading of a Money Bill. The opposition not being expected, no explanation was given further than by his noble Friend who represented the Department of the Government. It was not a comfortable thing that such a Motion could be carried without Notice, and the inconvenience of such an occurrence would be excessive.

LORD ELLENBOROUGH asked how they could have amended the Bill, as it was a Money Bill?

LORD ABINGER said, there was a strong feeling in Scotland against the Bill, and the Bill had only been set down on the Paper for that day.

THE DUKE OF ARGYLL said, that was purely and absolutely a Money Bill, and no doubt it would be against Parliamentary usage to amend it in Committee; but Notice should have been given if it were wished to reject it on the second reading. He would mention this—that Money Bills were always closely discussed between the Lord Advocate and the Scotch Members; and as regarded this Bill, so far as he had observed, there had been no opposition to it in the other House. If there had been, he should have made himself acquainted with all the details of the measure. He thought it was objectionable to move the rejection of a Money Bill without any Notice.

THE MARQUESS OF LOTHIAN said, that what had occurred was another proof of the necessity for having a Secretary for Scotland. The noble Earl (the Earl of Kimberley) had complained of the inconvenience of rejecting the Bill; but he would refer the noble Earl to the inconvenience occasioned by the failure on the part of any Member of the Government to get up and answer the statements of his noble Friend. As the Bill could not be amended in Committee, noble Lords took advantage of this opportunity to record their votes in support of his noble Friend, whose statements had not been answered.

EARL GRANVILLE said, that, as this was a small Bill, there was not the slightest idea that it was to be opposed. It had been done suddenly, and entirely without Notice. The provisions of the Bill were explained by his noble Friend, who had charge of the Bills in that Department of the Government. It was against all precedent to throw out a Money Bill without Notice.

LORD ORANMORE AND BROWNE remarked that a great many of these Bills came on suddenly, and at the end of the Session, without anyone knowing when they were to be discussed.

THE EARL OF DALHOUSIE said, that this Bill had been down for second reading for some days, and everyone had had an opportunity of studying it.

LORD ABINGER said, he considered that the Bill had been brought in in a very improper way as far as the landed proprietors, who were Commissioners of Supply in Scotland, and who were interested in it, were concerned. It was introduced after the April meeting of the Commissioners of Supply; it was practically brought in surreptitiously. When it passed through the House of Commons, he received the strongest representations from his own county, Inverness-shire, regarding its provisions. He considered it was a very objectionable Bill, and its rejection would give great satisfaction to the Commissioners of Supply in Scotland.

THE LORD CHANCELLOR said, that the noble Lord appeared, from his own observations, to have meditated opposition to the Bill for some time. In that case he ought to have given Notice that he intended to move its rejection. But the noble Lord had neither given Notice of his Motion nor asked for a further postponement of the second reading. If the Motion that the Bill be read a second time that day six months were rejected, the only result would be that the Bill would be put down for second reading on another day.

On Question? Their Lordships *divided*:—Contents 29; Not-Contents 32: Majority 3.

CONTENTS.

Leeds, D.
Sutherland, D.

Exeter, M.
Winchester, M.

De La Warr, E.
Leven and Melville, E.
Mar and Kellie, E.
Powis, E.
Selkirk, E.

Abinger, L. [*Teller.*]
Bagot, L.
Bateman, L.
Blantyre, L. [*Teller.*]
Clanwilliam, L. (*E. Clanwilliam.*)
Colchester, L.
Colville of Culross, L.
Denman, L.
Donington, L.
Hartismere, L. (*L. Henniker.*)
Inchiquin, L.
Lamington, L.
Leconfield, L.
Middleton, L.
Norton, L.
Oranmore and Browne, L.
Silchester, L. (*E. Longford.*)
Stratheden and Campbell, L.
Wemyss, L. (*E. Wemyss.*)
Wynford, L.

NOT-CONTENTS.

Selborne, E. (*L. Chancellor.*)

Grafton, D.
Somerset, D.

Camperdown, E.
Derby, E.
Granville, E.
Hardwicke, E.
Kimberley, E.
Macclesfield, E.
Milltown, E.
Morley, E.
Northbrook, E.
Sydney, E.

Powerscourt, V.

Boston, L.
Boyle, L. (*E. Cork and Orrery.*) [*Teller.*]
Bramwell, L.
Carlingford, L.
Carrington, L.
FitzGerald, L.
Kenmare, L. (*E. Kenmare.*)
Monson, L. [*Teller.*]
Mount-Temple, L.
Ramsay, L. (*E. Dalhousie.*)
Rosebery, L. (*E. Rosebery.*)
Saye and Sele, L.
Strafford, L. (*V. Enfield.*)
Sudeley, L.
Sundridge, L. (*D. Argyll.*)
Thurlow, L.
Tyrone, L. (*M. Waterford.*)
Waveney, L.

Resolved in the *negative*.

Bill to be read 2ª on *Thursday* next.

OYSTER CULTIVATION (IRELAND) BILL.—(No. 197.)

(*The Lord President.*)

SECOND READING.

Order of the Day for the Second Reading read.

LORD CARLINGFORD (LORD PRESIDENT of the COUNCIL), in moving that the Bill be now read a second time, said, that the measure was intended for the further promotion of the cultivation of oysters in Ireland. It was founded on the English Act of 1868, and would enable the Irish Commissioners of Fisheries to do what the Board of Trade could do in this country. He believed it would prove a useful measure.

Moved, "That the Bill be now read 2ª."—(*The Lord President.*)

THE MARQUESS OF WATERFORD said, he had much pleasure in supporting the second reading of the Bill, which he thought a very useful measure. But there was one proposal which he should like to make, and which he hoped that his noble Friend would accept in Committee. He did not know whether the noble Lord was aware that in the cultivation of oysters American and Portuguese varieties were laid down on the coast of Ireland. Now, there was a law in Ireland which made the sale of oysters illegal in the months of May, June, July, and August; but he believed that those oysters were totally different from the English oyster, and were not only fit to eat, but were at their best during those months, and were sold largely in London. He, therefore, desired to see a clause inserted in the Bill to enable Portuguese and American oysters to be sold in Ireland during that period. They could be easily distinguished, and there would be no difficulty in a Fishery Inspector giving an order for the sale of those particular oysters. If that were done it would encourage the growth of those beds of oysters which seemed to have taken to the shores of Ireland, and additional employment would thus be given to the people.

THE EARL OF COURTOWN said, he thought there might be some danger in carrying out the proposal of the noble Marquess. He hoped that nothing would be done which would in any way interfere with the preservation of the native oyster beds.

THE MARQUESS OF WATERFORD pointed out that the kind of oysters to which he had alluded were now allowed to be sold in London.

Motion *agreed to*; Bill read 2ª accordingly, and *committed* to a Committee of the Whole House on *Thursday* next.

PRIVATE BILLS (RAILWAYS) — NEW STANDING ORDER.—RESOLUTION.

LORD HENNIKER, in rising to move to resolve—

> "That where a Chamber of Commerce or Agriculture, or other similar body sufficiently representing a particular trade or business, in any district to which any Railway Bill relates, petition against the Bill, alleging that such trade or business will be injuriously affected by the rates and fares proposed to be authorized by the Bill, or is injuriously affected by the rates and fares already authorized by Acts relating to the railway undertaking, it shall be competent for the Select Committee to whom the Bill is referred, if they think fit, to hear the petitioners or their counsel or agents and witnesses on such allegation against the Bill, or any part thereof, or against the rates and fares authorized by the said Acts or any of them;"

and to move that the said Resolution be made a Standing Order of the House, said, that last year he brought forward a Motion which referred indirectly to that he now placed before the House. He need not trouble their Lordships with very lengthened remarks, as the subject had been fully discussed "elsewhere." The history of the case was, shortly, that last year a Resolution was carried in the House of Commons without objection. This year a Resolution, nearly the same as the one now submitted, was discussed in that House on May 21. It was objected to by the President of the Board of Trade, on the ground that it was only part of the question dealt with in the Report of the Railway Fares and Rates Committee, and the debate was adjourned in order that he might bring in a complete measure. However, there was no chance of this Bill passing—now, of course, it had been given up; and on July 9 the adjourned debate ended in that Standing Order being carried by a majority of 10. What he wished to do was to make the practice in both Houses alike. The

Resolution was framed on the recommendation of the Committee to which he had referred, and on the Resolutions passed in the House of Commons last year and this. Its object was to place farmers and traders in a fair position with respect to the Railway Companies as to rates. Their Lordships were aware how powerless a trader or a farmer was against a great Company with a permanent staff to conduct their case. The Companies had all the experience gained by being very often before a Committee; and, as a rule, individuals were afraid to attack large Companies. They were not only handicapped heavily to begin with; but the question of expense was a serious consideration. It was difficult even for a body of men to deal with a Company. He had some experience of this, for some years ago he joined in a combination to ask for reduced rates. The large traders were aggrieved; but the moment the Company found the organization strong against them they offered the principal traders preferential rates, and so, in fact, did away with the general demand for a reduction of rates. This showed the power of a Railway Company. In fact, it might be said that Companies might almost paralyze an industry if they chose. On public grounds, as well as in the interests of single traders, therefore, he thought it a wise thing to give Chambers of Commerce and Agriculture a *locus standi*. They were public bodies, and if they took up a case merely to annoy a Railway Company they would lose credit at once. Again, they could not be subject to the operation of an offer of preferential rates to certain individuals. Such a provision as this would at any time be a great advantage; but just now, when trade and agriculture were suffering so much, the boon would be a very great one, particularly as there was a tendency to favour foreign trade as to rates to the injury of the home trade. The most important objection appeared to him to be that the Resolution would open the door to the whole of the rates of a large railway like the Great Northern being revised if they merely applied for some small power, which most large railways did every year. They were asked whether this would be fair. His answer was certainly not. There should be [illegible] for such a course; but he must remind the House that it could not be fairly said that rates once introduced into a Bill should never be altered. On the contrary, a clause had always been inserted in Railway Bills for the last 30 or 40 years to give power to revise. It was admitted, too, that many rates were obsolete, were injurious to various industries, and required revision. Their Lordships would observe, too, that the Committee had power under the proposed Order only if they thought fit. The Business of that House was deservedly praised for the manner in which it was done; and he could not picture to himself any Chairman recommending a Committee to open the vast question of the rates of a great railway because some particular rates were objected to. Surely it was but fair that when a Company asked a boon from Parliament, when they applied for fresh powers, that others who paid these rates should have an opportunity of asking for a revision, particularly in some cases where the antiquated rates he had referred to were as injurious to the railways as they were to trade. A great deal was said about interference with Companies which had such an immense capital invested. But were not traders, who provided the dividends, to be considered? Railway Companies could ask for increased rates, but traders could not put the contrary case. It might be said that this Resolution would lead to frivolous Petitions. He thought this would not be so. The expenses of a Petition were too great, and the penalty of bringing forward anything frivolous too heavy. Again, it was said that this was only one recommendation, that they would be legislating piecemeal, and that they should wait till all the rates could be revised. How long might they wait for such a measure? Meanwhile, why should not the weaker party be protected? He had applied his remarks to existing rates, as he supposed there would be no objection to an appeal against new rates. All he could say was that he made a strong appeal to their Lordships to pass this Resolution. Mr. Chamberlain's Bill was no longer in existence; why not take a step in the right direction—a step acknowledged to be a good one by all except the railways? It was only optional to a Committee to hear a Petition; it was most important to trade and agriculture at all times to have fair rates; but just now, when they were suffering so much, of paramount importance; and any step in this direction would be received as a boon. They had heard a great deal lately of opening the door to agreement between the two Houses. If they could not agree in all things, yet he thought he might fairly appeal—and appeal strongly—to their Lordships to make the practice as much the same as possible in both Houses in a case of this kind. The noble Lord concluded by moving his Resolution.

Moved to resolve—

"That where a Chamber of Commerce or Agriculture, or other similar body sufficiently representing a particular trade or business, in any district to which any Railway Bill relates, petition against the Bill, alleging that such trade or business will be injuriously affected by the rates and fares proposed to be authorised by the Bill, or is injuriously affected by the rates and fares already authorised by Acts relating to the railway undertaking, it shall be competent for the Select Committee to whom the Bill is referred, if they think fit, to hear the petitioners or their counsel or agents and witnesses on such allegation against the Bill, or any part thereof, or against the rates and fares authorised by the said Acts, or any of them."—(*The Lord Henniker.*)

LORD BRABOURNE said, he thought it was rather hard at this period of the Session, when their Lordships' minds were occupied with other important matters, that they should be asked to pass one of the most confusing and involved Standing Orders that it had ever been his lot to read. He pointed out to the noble Lord that Mr. Chamberlain had stated, when a similar Standing Order was brought forward in the House of Commons, that to pass such a Standing Order would be most unfair to the railway interest, and also that if anything was to be done in the direction indicated it should be done only as part of a large scheme. Indeed, he must apologize for rising so soon, as he could not doubt that the Government would take the same view as their Colleagues in the other House, and would oppose this Motion. It was quite true that, owing to a Cabinet Council being held at the time and other circumstances, the other House had passed the Standing Order by a very small majority; but, while he had great respect for the de- [illegible] the other House, their Lord- [illegible] not in the habit of always [illegible]llowing their example, and he desired to point out one or two considerations that ought to weigh with their Lordships in the matter. In the first place, a Select Committee of the House of Commons had sat and fully inquired into all the circumstances of the rates and fares of railways, and had made a great number of recommendations. He thought it was a little too hard that his noble Friend should have embodied in his Standing Order one provision hostile to the railway interest, while at the same time he had omitted those provisions which were favourable to it. His noble Friend also made light of the objection to the Standing Order on account of its innovating character; but he would point out to him that it had hitherto been in both Houses of Parliament the wise and salutary rule that when a Private Bill had been brought forward for consideration in their Lordships' Committees or in those of the other House, the only thing that should be inquired into and decided and legislated upon was the contents of that Bill; that things extraneous to the Bill should not be brought in. His first objection to this Standing Order was that it violated that salutary provision. He asked, moreover, whether it was a just thing on the part of their Lordships, whether it was a wise or fair thing towards the Railway Companies to pass a Standing Order which, in the event of a Company merely desiring powers to alter a station or effect some trifling improvement would, expose them to the risk of having their whole system of rates and fares revised and possibly lowered? It frequently happened that the public desired a Railway Company to afford them some particular accommodation; but, if this Standing Order passed, the answer would be plain—namely, that the Company would have been very willing to grant the request, but that they could not run the risk of having their whole system of rates attacked. This could be done under the new Standing Order, although the Bill introduced by a Company had no connection whatever with rates and fares, and inevitably its effect would be to deter Railway Companies from coming to Parliament with the view of accommodating the public. In all these questions it was the fashion to talk about powerful Companies and Boards of Railway Directors; but it was not the power of Companies or the salaries of officials which were affected by anything which lowered the value of railway property—it was the dividend of the shareholders. Their Lordships must recollect that they were dealing in this legislation with a very large body of railway shareholders, and that while these men did not at all wish to avoid a fair fulfilment of the duties they had undertaken in seeking what was called a boon from Parliament, they at the same time asked, having sank a large amount of capital in these undertakings, that faith should be kept with them. He would, moreover, say that in all their complaints against legislation recently proposed, the railway shareholders had never objected to having enforced the obligations they had undertaken; but they had insisted upon their right to have their causes tried by a competent legal tribunal, and to be treated like any other class of the community. If the rates granted to them by Act of Parliament were to be revised let it be by such a fair and competent tribunal acting upon definite principles; but do not let the whole system of a Railway Company be exposed to the will of such a fluctuating tribunal as a Parliamentary Committee. Some change might possibly be required with respect to the persons having a *locus standi* to oppose Private Bills in that House; but that change ought to be effected by some general legislative enactment, and not by a Standing Order such as this, only dealing with a portion of the subject. It was, no doubt, an advantage to have the practice with regard to Private Bills similar in both Houses; but a Standing Order carried in July by a narrow majority was not a circumstance that should lead that House to adopt it also. Possibly the House of Commons would be glad to recede from its position, and he hoped that their Lordships would reject this Standing Order instead of giving a *locus standi* to new Bodies, and would give the House of Commons a *locus pœnitentiæ*.

LORD SUDELEY said, this Resolution stood in a very peculiar position. When it came before the other House of Parliament, the President of the Board of Trade opposed it; but notwithstanding that the House of Commons determined that the Resolution should become one of its Standing Orders. The position, therefore, was entirely changed. The Government had considered the question very carefully, and they saw that if the Standing Order were not passed in this House, it might, on various occasions, place their Lordships in a very difficult position. At the same time, it was a subject on which great difference of opinion existed, and they thought it a question that the House should deal with entirely on its own responsibility, and that their Lordships were the best judges of the case. The Government had, therefore, come to the conclusion that it would be far better that they should not express any further opinion on the matter, but leave each Member of their Lordships' House to vote as he thought right.

LORD BRAMWELL said, he should oppose the Standing Order. The effect of its adoption would be to injuriously affect the railway rates and fares already authorized. It was said that the Railway Companies came to ask for a boon, and that, therefore, they could not complain if the boon which they asked was never granted unless it was also for the benefit of the public. Suppose Petitioners against a Bill made out that the railway rates and fares were, in some instances, excessive, and the Railway Company made out what they sought—perhaps an additional piece of land—was right and reasonable, what would the Committee do? Would they say that what the Railway Company sought in their Bill was very moderate indeed? But unless they made some sacrifice of the rates and charges they were entitled to levy by former Acts of Parliament, they could not grant the Bill. This Standing Order would give Chambers of Commerce and Chambers of Agriculture a *locus standi*; but such bodies were unknown to the law. Any gentlemen who associated themselves together might, if they pleased, call themselves a Chamber of Commerce, and ask to be heard. If there was some provision for inflicting costs on people who unreasonably, and on frivolous grounds, put Railway Companies to unnecessary trouble and expense, and for thus punishing the aggressors, he should not so much mind.

THE EARL OF MILLTOWN pointed out that the Committee already possessed the power of imposing costs on the promoters of frivolous or vexatious opposition.

THE EARL OF CAMPERDOWN thought the House was entitled to more information as to the position and mind of the Government with regard to this matter. The Government opposed this Standing Order in the House of Commons. The House of Commons adopted it; but that was no reason why the Government should alter their opinion with regard to it. By the practice of their Lordships' House a great deal more power was given to Committees than in the House of Commons, and Chairmen of Committees did habitually decide questions as to whether persons should, or should not, be heard. It seemed to him quite right, when a Bill was put forward which contained new proposals and new rates, that a Chamber of Commerce, or a Chamber of Agriculture, should be entitled to be heard against it. Therefore, he did not himself see that his noble Friend was proposing anything objectionable in itself; but he would suggest that the words relating to existing rates should be left out.

LORD COLVILLE OF CULROSS wished to say a few words, as representing a great Company, against the Resolution. Notwithstanding what had fallen from the noble Lord who had spoken on the part of the Government, he really must ask the Members of the Government in the House to pay a little more attention to what had fallen from their Colleague, Mr. Chamberlain, in the other House. Remembering what had happened in the other House, and how the Resolution had been carried there, he really could not support the Resolution, which he regarded as a Motion to overturn Acts of Parliament passed years ago.

LORD HENNIKER said, he had, of course, expected to have considerable opposition from his two noble Friends near him, who represented the Railway Companies. With respect to what had been said about bringing on this Motion at the end of the Session, he had only to say that Private Bills were dealt with in November; and he thought that it would be more convenient to settle what was to be done now than at the beginning of a Session, and, as the House of Commons Standing Order existed, the position would be awkward. The difficulty with regard to public bodies becoming parties to the opposition to a Bill could be got over by mentioning the President or Secretary of a Chamber of Agriculture or Commerce in the Standing Order, for they were always men of position, and who would be admitted as opponents in their individual capacity. However, one point was to follow the Rule, as nearly as possible, laid down by the House of Commons, and the Standing Order there did not make this distinction. The noble and learned Lord opposite (Lord Bramwell) made a point of the power of raising the general question of rates over a large railway system. He thought that had been answered by the fact that the discretion was left to the Committee to hear the parties when they thought fit. The case put forward was, in fact, an almost impossible one. As to the power to appeal to the Railway Commission, the fact was that this power was not used. Parties did not apply to the Commissioners in the way suggested. With reference to the suggestion of his noble Friend opposite (the Earl of Camperdown) to take out the words affecting existing rates, he did not think there was any objection on the part of Railway Companies to allow new rates to be questioned; but the Motion would be valueless if it were not made retrospective, and did not affect existing rates. He made, again, a strong appeal to their Lordships to pass the Standing Order.

THE EARL OF KIMBERLEY said, although he did not in every particular approve of the Resolution, he would still support it, as it had passed the House of Commons. He had not for some time attended Select Committees; but his experience was that the great defect in the procedure of the House was that the public were never heard. It was all very well for Railway Companies to defend themselves; but there could not be the slightest doubt that the trade in this country did suffer most seriously from the nature of the rates now levied. The injustice of them was such that it pressed upon the trade of the country, and, in some cases, they were so injurious as actually to handicap our own trade in favour of foreign. On these grounds he should vote for the Resolution.

THE DUKE OF SOMERSET considered the Resolution most unjust, and he very much regretted that the Government had not acted in their Lordships' House as they had in the other House.

LORD WINMARLEIGH said, he thought it would be better that the Order should not be retrospective; and, therefore, he begged to move an Amendment to leave out all the words which would have that effect, so as to confine the proposed Standing Order to rates to be levied in the future.

Amendment *moved*,

To leave out ("or is injuriously affected by the rates and fares already authorised by Acts relating to the railway undertaking.")—(*The Lord Winmarleigh.*)

THE EARL OF REDESDALE (CHAIRMAN of COMMITTEES) said, he could not acquiesce in the Resolution. He did not think that a Select Committee was a fit tribunal to settle the question of railway rates all over the country.

EARL FORTESCUE said, that when he was a Member of a Committee appointed many years ago to consider the Private Business of the House of Commons he was much struck by the inadequacy of the representation accorded to public interests as compared with private. Apart from the difficulty of getting individuals, each personally as one of the public but slightly aggrieved, to engage at short notice, either isolatedly or in a hastily-formed combination, in a costly conflict with a rich, powerful Company or confederation of Companies, the requirement of a *locus standi* he considered worked great injustice, and he welcomed any proposal which enlarged the representation of the interests of the public before Committees. He did not like, therefore, to vote against the Resolution, and, if it were amended so as not to have a retrospective character, he should have no difficulty in voting for it.

EARL GRANVILLE said, that, so far as he was concerned, he was prepared to vote for the Resolution if it were amended in the sense suggested by the noble Lord (Lord Winmarleigh).

LORD HENNIKER said, he thought the proposal now made to limit the Standing Order to new rates would not be accepted as a boon to the interests in question; but after what had been said by the noble Earl opposite (Earl Granville), and from the general opinion of the House, he would not trouble their

On Question, *agreed to.*

Then it was *moved* to leave out ("authorised by the said Acts, or any of them") and add at the end of the resolution ("proposed to be authorised by the same"): *agreed to.*

Resolved, That where a Chamber of Commerce or Agriculture, or other similar body sufficiently representing a particular trade or business, in any district to which any Railway Bill relates, petition against the Bill, alleging that such trade or business will be injuriously affected by the rates and fares proposed to be authorised by the Bill, it shall be competent for the Select Committee to whom the Bill is referred, if they think fit, to hear the petitioners or their counsel or agents and witnesses on such allegation against the Bill, or any part thereof, or against the rates and fares proposed to be authorised by the same.

Ordered, That the said resolution be declared a Standing Order; and that it be entered on the Roll of Sanding Orders, and be *printed.* (No. 207.)

REPRESENTATION OF THE PEOPLE BILL—THE AUTUMN SESSION.

OBSERVATIONS.

THE EARL OF REDESDALE (CHAIRMAN of COMMITTEES): My Lords, I have given Notice of the following:—

"To call the attention of the House to the proposed autumnal session, and to the only manner in which the extension of the franchise question can be satisfactorily dealt with."

I think it is desirable, in calling your Lordships' attention to this subject, to refer to the position in which the House stands, in which the Government stands, and in which the question of the extension of the franchise stands. Now, I believe that the relative positions are imperfectly understood throughout the country generally; and I think it very desirable, therefore, that something should be done to let us know the course to be proposed and the way in which the matter is to proceed. In the first place, I would refer to what took place yesterday. There was a great demonstration made in the Park, which was supposed to have some great effect on the conduct of this House. I was delighted to hear that a large number of persons assembled, and that the proceedings passed off in a satisfactory manner, and that those who came—some of them, I understand, were paid for their attendance—had a very pleasant day. And as all passed off so quietly I am induced the more to believe that those who attended will be induced to listen a little to reason on the subject, and that after all they will come to see that the real issue is very different from that which they are asked to countenance and support. The real truth, which has never been fairly brought before the country, is that this House has in no way refused the extension of the franchise. On the contrary, I believe it is generally conceded that this House has accepted the principle of the extension of the franchise. In fact, the persons who are really responsible for the non-adoption of the extension of the franchise in the present Session of Parliament are the Government, who presented a measure so imperfect that it was impossible for this House to agree to such a proposal. It is, my Lords, really much the same thing as a gentleman inviting you to dinner and then saying—"I have a capital haunch of venison and some excellent joints; but unfortunately my cook is away, and I cannot get them prepared, so you must eat them raw." The answer to that would be "No, thank you. I am glad you have an excellent dinner provided; but I must decline your invitation to eat it raw." In the same way the Government give your Lordships an excellent dinner, but ask you to eat it raw. This demonstration, as I have said, was to have had a great effect upon this House by informing us of the opinion of the country on the subject, and leading us to change our opinion, and bow to that of the Government on the subject. My Lords, I have been a long time a Member of this House, and I have seen a great deal of political life, extending over the whole period of the Reform Question, and I should just like to remind your Lordships of what took place in 1832. The question then was a very different one. Parliament met expressly for the purpose of considering that very question. The Bill was passed by large majorities, and it came down to this House perfect and complete in all its details, and it was rejected by this House. The consequence was popular feeling was extremely excited on this subject, and excited to a degree of which no one who has not witnessed it could form the smallest idea. Your Lordships all recollect what took place at Bristol, Nottingham, and other places where there was destruction of property and life, and altogether there was a feeling in the country of the strongest possible kind. Well, in the next Session the Bill was brought in again, and ultimately this House gave way to the popular feeling, and upon that Bill being passed a Parliament was returned which gave only about 150 Members to the Conservative Party, which had opposed the franchise. The consequence was that the whole command of the other House was in the hands of the Government of the day, and a great demonstration in favour of Radicalism was made, the effect being that in the course of another year some of the leading Members seceded from the Government. I refer to the late Lord Derby, the late Duke of Richmond, and Sir James Graham. In the next year after that the King became a little alarmed at the way things were going on, and he exercised the powers given him by the Constitution of changing his Ministers, which led to a Dissolution of Parliament, when it was found that the majority was materially changed. I mention this to show what was the effect of public opinion at that time. After the passing of the Reform Bill this House had continued carefully to watch legislation, and made frequent changes both by the Amendment and the rejection of measures; and, so far from losing in public favour in consequence, the Dissolution proved that it had gained by the attitude of perfect independence which it assumed. Sir Robert Peel, however, finding that the power which he had obtained in the House of Commons was not sufficient to enable him to carry on the government of the country, resigned. Three years after, the death of the King caused another Dissolution, and a Parliament was returned, in which Sir Robert Peel had a still increasing majority of his supporters; and after another Dissolution in 1841 the Government was turned out by a majority of 91 on a Vote of Want of Confidence on the Address in the Commons. Now, my Lords, that only shows how completely public opinion changes, and how little this House has to fear, if it is independent, and carries out its objects in a definite and just manner, from an assemblage of people such as that of yesterday. Depend upon it, my Lords, you have nothing to fear from the body which assembled in London yesterday. I believe they were, for the most part, a respectable body, and that when they come to consider the matter in an impartial manner they will find that the House of Lords has done perfectly right in rejecting an imperfect Bill. I remember that in 1832 the cry was "The Bill and the whole Bill." I hope that when we next meet Parliament may have "the whole Bill," and that this House will join with the other in considering the matter in a fair spirit. Now, my Lords, as to the question of the Autumn Session. I have no objection to it if, in the opinion of the Government, it is desirable to have one. Extension of the franchise is a subject which requires to be treated in the most careful way, and I think it is possible that an Autumn Session may be useful for that purpose, in order to insure that plenty of time be given to this question—namely, the question of the franchise, coupled with redistribution. The question of redistribution cannot be thought of until you have a measure before you; you must know in what manner it is proposed to treat the question of redistribution before you can express a decided opinion upon it. It is most objectionable to separate the two portions of the subject. It has always been the practice that the two subjects should be treated together; it is practically the same, and all you have to do is to introduce the Bill in two parts. Suppose Parliament meets in November, or whenever it may please the Government to call it together; the Bill would be brought in in the House of Commons, and the first portion would be the extension of the franchise. From the manner in which that has been treated in the other House, and from the really kindly way in which it was received in this, I do not think that the consideration of that portion of the Bill would give rise to any very lengthened debate, but would be settled before Parliament adjourned for Christmas. After Christmas the House would meet for the consideration of the other portion of the Bill. That will just allow about three months both for the country and for the House of Commons to consider the question of redistribution; and I think it will be absolutely necessary to have that time allowed to enable them to come to a fair conclusion connected with that most important subject. I may say that I expect that the question of redistribution will be fairly undertaken by the Government—I shall be extremely disappointed if it is not, and that such a measure will be proposed as may be fairly considered in both Houses of Parliament and accepted—and in that way I think the measure would certainly receive the approval of Parliament before [illegible] of the Session. I believe there is not one noble Lord opposite, who is a Member of the Cabinet, who is not fully sensible of the extreme importance of this question of redistribution—not merely upon the next Parliament which may be returned, but upon the position of the country hereafter, and on the character of the Government who propose it. I trust, also, that the Members of the Government in the other House will be willing to give the same consideration to the public interest; above all, I hope and believe that my right hon. Friend the Prime Minister will himself be most desirous that whatever the proposals on that subject may be, they may be of a character that will reflect upon his Government, and upon his political career, a reputation for judgment and success in doing that which will be for the interests of the country at large, and for his own character as a legislator. I think it is desirable that we should know the course the Government are about to take with regard to the Autumn Session before Parliament rises; and I think the Government should be satisfied before they have an Autumn Session as to the manner in which they intend to carry out the question of redistribution; and if, as it seems to me, it is hardly possible to do that in the interval before the Autumn Session, they should postpone it until the ordinary time for the meeting of Parliament. It is most desirable that this question should be settled in the next Session; and I trust that noble Lords opposite will be induced to adopt this view, and to take care that they lay their proposals before Parliament in a manner which is likely to meet with the general acceptance of all Parties.

EARL GRANVILLE: My Lords, the noble Earl who has just sat down speaks with very great authority, not only from the Office which he holds in this House, but from the personal qualities he possesses in the estimation of your Lordships. I am always desirous of carefully considering anything which he says which at all affects the character of this House; and I am bound to add that the remarks he has just made have been characterized by great moderation. But, my Lords, I am sorry to say that his speech has somewhat disappointed me. I was rather in hopes, from the Notice he gave, he was going to suggest some mode of adjustment of the differences which exist between the two Houses which has not occurred to either of the two sides of the House up to this moment. The noble Lord made a becoming allusion to the character of that remarkable demonstration which took place in the Metropolis yesterday. I believe that that demonstration, and others which are likely to follow, are very much owing to the observations of the noble Marquess, who is not here to-night, that there is indifference in the country on this question of the Representation of the People Bill. The noble Earl went on to give us a history of the first great Reform Bill, which I and other Members of your Lordships' House remember, and which all of us have read about. I doubt whether any of the details he mentioned are new to any of us, and I hardly understand the drift of those remarks. He spoke of demonstrations, not orderly and peaceable, as that of yesterday, but of great violence, all over the country. He talked of the concession this House subsequently made to the feeling of the country, and then he explained to you very clearly that the result was not so revolutionary as the opponents of the Government of that day sincerely believed to be the case. But then the noble Earl goes on to suggest that we should give up at once what I know is the opinion of the majority of your Lordships, because that very question has been discussed twice and voted upon twice within this month, and that we should go against what is the opinion of the Government and of the enormous majority of the other House. I have spoken in the two debates, and I do not think that I am called upon on this occasion — and I think I can gather from the disappearance from the Front Opposition Bench of all the noble Lords who usually occupy it that they are of my opinion—I do not think that I am called upon to re-enter, or that there would be any great advantage in recommencing, a debate on exactly the same subject. The noble Earl speaks of redistribution, and appeals to us as to the manner in which we should undertake it. I assure him that he is not mistaken in believing that we all feel that a great responsibility lies upon us in regard to it; but when he makes this allusion I cannot help reminding your Lordships that Mr. Gladstone, on the very first stage of the Representation of the People Bill, speaking then for himself, gave the general character of the principles which ought to govern a Redistribution Bill—a Bill of a very different character from that which has sometimes been advocated by the Members of extreme Parties in this country. No Member of the Government objected to it, and Mr. Chamberlain took an early opportunity of expressing his accordance with those principles. On the other hand, we heard some vague objections to what may be done; but we have not heard one word as to the lines on which redistribution should take place. Therefore, I hope that the noble Earl, while giving us advice, which we will carefully consider, will, at the same time, weigh that advice and give it to his own political friends, in order that we may be enlightened a little more than we are now as to the character of the redistribution to which they look forward. The noble Earl stated that there was a misunderstanding in the country as to the position of this House and the Government. Is it really a misunderstanding that it is the House of Lords and not the Government who have delayed this Bill? I am very much afraid that there is not much chance of the country in general thinking that it is the fault of the Government and not of your Lordships' House when exercising that kindness to the Bill which has been so nearly fatal to it, and has been practically fatal to it this Session. I trust I have said nothing that will lend excitement or unnecessary vigour to the agitation which is going on. The duty of the Government is, I think, very clear, and I cannot depart from it.

THE DUKE OF ARGYLL: My Lords, I am not surprised that the noble Earl has paid the compliment which he has done to the noble Earl the Chairman of Committees for the able and conciliatory manner in which he has spoken to-night. I came down to this House to-night with very great curiosity; because the noble Earl proposed to call the attention of your Lordships to the only manner in which the extension of the franchise question can be satisfactorily settled. Now I have a much less ambitious object in view in the few words I wish to address to your Lordships to-night. But I think that it is not an unfitting occasion to point out to both sides of the House the nearness of the position of the two Parties, with a view to conciliatory action. In the first place, I ask myself what the Government gained as a result of the action of the two Houses. The common impression seems to be that the Government have been defeated in the main object of their policy. I cannot accept that view. It appears to me that the Government have gained their main object. They have secured from this House a distinct and emphatic assent to the principle of the Franchise Bill. I must say that I do not at all share in any doubts, hinted at or expressed, as to the sincerity of my noble Friends opposite. My noble Friend the Secretary of State for Foreign Affairs referred the other night to the contrast between the earnestness of the Prime Minister and the want of earnestness shown on the other side. I must say that there are very few who can rise to the enthusiasm of my right hon. Friend. I must point out to the House that in the eminently able speech in which the Franchise Bill was introduced in this House there were no wild or extravagant views expressed as to the immense advantage to be gained by this great addition to the franchise. I am not quite sure, if I were to examine closely the interior feelings and sentiments of my noble Friends on the Liberal Benches, whether I should not find simply that assent and consent which men of business give in important matters of this kind to a great movement for the public benefit. I believe that most of us accept it, some as an act of justice, but more as an act of obvious political necessity. It was pointed out in the introduction of this Bill that when Mr. Disraeli introduced his Bill extending the franchise to all rateable householders in the boroughs all saw that it was merely a question of time before its extension to the counties. I myself have always said that the population of the country were quite as fitted for the franchise as those of the towns. Well, this great principle having been admitted and accepted by all sides of this House, I say that the Government have gained immensely in the course of action which they have taken. They must not consider, and the country must not consider, that they have been defeated in the measure they have brought forward. That is a great point; but there is another point which, in my opinion, has not been sufficiently looked at. I think that the Government have not only gained in that particular matter; but I think that they have gained the main object which Mr. Gladstone had when he separated the two Bills. I think that great misunderstanding has prevailed with respect to the language of Mr. Gladstone. My right hon. Friend has been quoted by the noble Marquess (the Marquess of Salisbury) as having, in his speech in Downing Street, admitted that the separation of the two Bills was a preconcerted scheme, as if it were a trap for the Opposition. If you will look at the words of the Prime Minister you will find that that is by no means a just construction to put upon them. In his speech in Downing Street he wished distinctly that all Parties, and not only the Opposition, should be placed under pressure to accept a fair Redistribution Bill if the Franchise Bill passed. The passage which was considered by the noble Marquess as a trap for the Opposition was distinctly and candidly explained in the speech which the Prime Minister made in the House of Commons, a corrected report of which has been published. What the Prime Minister said was simply this—a Redistribution Bill is a Bill which, of necessity, touches personal interests, while the Franchise Bill does not necessarily touch the personal interests of anybody. In the House of Commons there are those who represent small boroughs which are likely to be disfranchised; there are those to whose constituencies other boroughs may be added; and others who may be affected by any Boundary Bill that may be introduced. Mr. Gladstone's argument is that so many are the persons on all sides of the House whose interests will, of necessity, be touched by the Redistribution Bill, that nothing can be easier than for the various sections of the House to combine to defeat such a Bill unless they know that the Franchise Bill is practically passed. That is an avowal of tactics on the part of the Leader of a great Party. But it refers not only to the professional opposition, but to the necessary opposition which must arise on so difficult and complicated a measure. It appears to me that by the action of this House in accepting the principle of the Bill the Government have practically gained their object as regards redistribution. What is the effect? We are now sitting in a room with the doors ajar, and 2,000,000 of eager faces are looking into the Chamber for admission. Does any Member of this House think that any power or Party in the State can long leave that door ajar? No; it is not possible. And what would be the effect of it? Many of your Lordships will remember a celebrated phrase of Lord Palmerston, who was himself personally opposed for many years to any great extension of the franchise. Somebody was arguing that it would have a very small result, and that the same class of men would come in as before. "Yes," said Lord Palmerston, "the same men will get in, as before; but they will play to the 1s. gallery instead of to the boxes." That was a somewhat rude and rough expression; but most of your Lordships will recognize the truth of it. Members of Parliament who are now sitting for the present constituencies will, undoubtedly, be affected by the admission of these 2,000,000, their conduct, their language, and their votes will no longer be the same as before. Therefore, the pressure which you wish to put on Members of the House of Commons upon all sides towards a compromise on the question of redistribution is a pressure which you have already secured. That is a consideration which I wish to point out to my noble Friends on the Treasury Bench. There is another point to which I wish to direct the attention of the House, and all the more because it was touched by my noble Friend who has just sat down, and that is the language which Mr. Gladstone held in regard to the principles of redistribution. And I am bound to say that I myself feel strong confidence—although it is impossible for me to convey to other Members of the House that confidence—in the reasonable and moderate opinions of the Prime Minister on this particular question. I have that confidence as strongly as any man may feel it who looks merely at the character of the Franchise Bill, because it is eminently moderate and conservative as far as it is possible to make any Bill conservative which makes such an enormous addition to the electoral body. But Mr. Gladstone has gone to a very great extent in indicating what are his opinions as to redistribution. As his speech has been carefully republished and edited, I took the trouble this morning to extract from it the propositions which he has laid down in regard to redistribution. They are these — First, that the change which is to be made is to be inside the magnitude of the great change of 1832; but, nevertheless, it is to be large in order to secure permanence and stability. The second is that it is not to be based upon, and is not to include, the principle of electoral districts. The third is that there is to be no pure population scale. I cannot sufficiently impress on the House the immense significance of that principle. The element of population must always, of course, be of importance; but what Mr. Gladstone laid down is the negative proposition, that as to the basis of redistribution there is to be no pure population scale. The fourth is that the old Constitutional distinction between town and shire is to be retained. The fifth is that individualities are to be respected. Here, again, is a principle of extensive significance. And I beg the House to observe that in this principle of redistribution you are acting strictly on the ancient lines of the British Constitution, and following precedent. Mr. Gladstone says individualities are to be respected—that is to say, where a town or a borough has been long regarded and represented as an individuality it is not to be dealt with loosely on a mere population scale. The sixth principle which he laid down is this—that the great cities are not to have quite so high a proportional share of representation as the rural dispersed population. Here, again, we have a principle that is eminently moderate and Conservative; and I say I believe that there is no Member of this House who might set himself to devise a scheme of redistribution who would not gladly accept that principle as one which ought reasonably to guide us. Then Mr. Gladstone says—and on this there may be considerable difference of opinion—that in your redistribution the total number of the Irish Members is not to be disturbed—is not necessarily to be disturbed; but, then, that was coupled with another principle—namely, that some addition might be made to the total number of Members of the House of Commons with the view of considering the claim of Scotland to some additional representation. The last proposition was that the small boroughs must be the places from which the new seats are to be obtained. You can hardly expect the Prime Minister, who has not actually drawn up a Redistribution Bill, to go much further than he has done in these declarations on the subject; and I would point out to noble Lords on both sides of the House, and also on the Cross Benches, that this is a basis of redistribution as regards principle, on which I believe it to be perfectly possible for the two sides of the House to agree. My Lords, I will only add that the two Houses of Parliament, having agreed in respect to the extension of the franchise, and having had outlined to them a plan of redistribution which, at least in respect to principles, will, I am satisfied, be generally accepted, I think it would be a great failure of Constitutional government—a great scandal to the Constitution of England—if some scheme could not be devised by which this great reform of Parliament may be peaceably accomplished.

LORD DENMAN said, a fear had been expressed that if a Redistribution of Seats Bill were placed before Parliament before the Franchise Bill was read a second time, or even passed, that a combination of parties interested might defeat it in "another place;" but in the Reform Bills of 1831-2, drawn by Sir Thomas Denman, the whole of the schemes were complete; and one Member (Mr. Hawkins) gave up his exclusive interest in a borough and his seat, for the more just representation of the people, and the present Members of the House of Commons might be trusted by frankness. In 1859 the Franchise Bill was debated separately, and an hon. and learned Member, a relative of his own, was afraid of an education franchise, and then believed that "Jem Penman," capable of forgery, might command votes by voting papers; also in one debate the present Premier said notice might be given for the payment of rates by a certain day, and if they were unpaid the householders should be incapable of voting—from his neglect, after one Government had been beaten on Reform, and another formed. Reform was mentioned in the Queen's Speech; but it was dropped, on which he (Lord Denman), on the 12th of August, promised to bring in the rejected Reform Bill, if not revived by the Government. In 1860, however, Reform was again mentioned in the Speech from the Throne, and a Bill was framed containing a redistribution of seats, and the franchise was reduced in counties from £50 to £10 rental, and in boroughs from £10 rental to £6 rental; but it was withdrawn by the Mover of the Amendment and author of the new Reform Bill (Lord John Russell), in consequence of the large number of Amendments and the lateness of the Session. Lord Palmerston had asked—"Is the House prepared to say there shall be no reform in the representation of the people? It is impossible." In 1866 a Redistribution Bill was forced on the Government, who were only in a majority of 5 (against Earl Grosvenor's Amendment); and the present Premier, in his (Lord Denman's) presence and hearing, in answer to Lord John Manners's quotation from Tennyson's poems—

"A land of settled government,
A land of just and old renown,
Where Freedom broadens slowly down
From precedent to precedent."

said—"It did not suit the noble Lord to go on; he ought to have said—

'And statesmen at her Councils met,
Who knew the seasons when to take
Occasion by the hand, and make
The bounds of Freedom wider yet,
By shaping some august decree
Which kept her Throne unshaken still,
Broad-based upon her People's will,
And compassed by th' inviolate sea.'"

That appeared in *Hansard*, June 4, and in *The Times*, June 5, 1866; but the quotation was from a poem, "You ask Me why, though ill at ease," in page 70; and the passage required to follow was in the epistle dedicatory to the Queen. As the truth only appeared in *Hansard* some time after the debates, he (Lord Denman) expressed his belief that two Bills dealing with the subject of Parliamentary Reform might be brought in early in the Session, six months from the present time, and that then all parties would clearly understand what was best to be done in the matter by reading all the debates on the subject.

ARMY—PAY, PROMOTION, AND NON-EFFECTIVE PAY—THE REVISED ROYAL WARRANT.—QUESTION.

THE EARL OF LONGFORD asked the Under Secretary of State for War,

When the revised Royal Warrant for pay, promotion, and non-effective pay of the Army (which has effect from 1st April 1884) will be issued and be available for reference?

THE EARL OF MORLEY said, the Warrant in question would be printed and circulated early next month. He was afraid it could not be got ready before. Although there had been delay, there had been practically little inconvenience caused. The Warrant was a consolidating Warrant, and it repealed all the Warrants in force up to the present time.

House adjourned at Seven o'clock, to Thursday next, a quarter past Ten o'clock.

HOUSE OF COMMONS,

Tuesday, 22nd July, 1884.

MINUTES.]—SELECT COMMITTEE—*Report*—Harbour Accommodation [No. 290].

SUPPLY—*considered in Committee*—CIVIL SERVICE ESTIMATES—CLASS II.—SALARIES AND EXPENSES OF CIVIL DEPARTMENTS, Votes 37 to 39.

Resolutions [July 21] *reported*.

PUBLIC BILLS—*Ordered*—*First Reading*—Military Pensions and Yeomanry Pay [302]; Cholera, &c. Protection * [303]; [Chartered Companies * [304].

First Reading—Naval Enlistment * [305].

Second Reading—Education (Scotland) Provisional Order * [285]; Public Works Loans * [299].

Committee—Infants [14]—R.P.

Committee—*Report*—Indian Marine * [291].

Considered as amended—*Third Reading*—Trusts (Scotland) * [279], and *passed*.

Withdrawn — County Courts (Ireland) (*re-comm.*) * [104-258].

QUESTIONS.

——o——

CONTAGIOUS DISEASES (ANIMALS)—SWINE FEVER—CIRCLES OF ISOLATION.

MR. R. H. PAGET asked the Chancellor of the Duchy of Lancaster, If he will consider the propriety of granting to local authorities the power to create infected circles in cases of swine fever, immediately after the outbreak, in order to obviate the delay which would be caused in making separate application to the Privy Council for the setting up of an infected area in each case?

MR. DODSON: An Order in Council is in preparation, and will be issued almost immediately, which will give effect to the suggestion of my hon. Friend.

FISHERY PIERS AND HARBOURS (IRELAND)—AUGHRIS PIER, COUNTY SLIGO.

MR. SEXTON asked the Secretary to the Treasury, with regard to the erection of a pier at Aughris, county Sligo, Whether, as appears by the Schedule, at page 28 of the current Annual Report of the Irish Commissioners of Public Works, the request for survey was made by the Fishery Piers Commission on the 4th of October last, and the plan and specification were forwarded by the Board to the Commission on the 12th of February last; whether the plan and specification have been returned to the Board, and how long they have lain in the hands of the Board since the Commission last heard of them, and what department is responsible for the delay of nearly half-a-year since the plan and specification were completed; whether new boats and nets purchased by Aughris fishermen in the expectation of the prompt erection of the pier are being seriously damaged by want of proper accommodation; how soon the work will be begun; whether any of the 39 piers recommended by the Fishery Piers Commission up to the close of the year ended 31st of March last have yet been put in course of construction; and, if not, what explanation can be given?

MR. COURTNEY: Since the Board of Works sent the plans in this case to the Fisheries Commission on February 12, there have been at least three references from the latter to the former suggesting alterations; the last one, received about four weeks ago, refers to a letter which never reached the Board, and suggests a new design. The Board of Works have always answered the references to them with reasonable promptitude; and the delay in this case, which I join with the hon. Member in regretting, can certainly not be laid to their charge. A telegram just received states that the plan is in hand; but the Board have not yet received from the Commission the limit of cost to be sanctioned. With regard to the general Question put by the hon. Member, I have to point out to him that only two cases were finally settled by the Fisheries Commission before March 31, and both of these are now under construction. They are Ballinagaul, in County Waterford, and Inniscrone, in County Sligo.

THE ROYAL UNIVERSITY OF IRELAND.

MR. KENNY asked the Chief Secretary to the Lord Lieutenant of Ireland, Whether the Senate of the Royal University (Ireland) allow medical men who studied in Ireland, and were qualified before the passing of the Royal University Act, but were prevented from obtaining University degrees owing to the state of things which the Royal University was created to remove, to present themselves on condition of their matriculating for the final M.B. examination; and, if not, whether steps will be taken to institute this measure of reform ?

MR. TREVELYAN : The statutes of the University empower the Senate to act as suggested in the case of gentlemen who have passed a course in arts and medicine in certain institutions; and the Senate have, in several cases, exercised the power given to them, and allowed gentlemen who had gone through a course of arts in the Catholic University, prior to the establishment of the Royal University, to obtain the degree in medicine upon passing the matriculation and degree examinations in the Royal University. The Senate have not thought it right to grant any such privilege to medical men who had not pursued arts studies in some University or College, or other cognate institution.

ARREARS OF RENT (IRELAND) ACT—JAMES FARRELL.

MR. KENNY asked the Chief Secretary to the Lord Lieutenant of Ireland, Whether James Farrell, Poor Law Guardian of the Mohill Union, a tenant of the Earl of Granard, obtained the benefit of the Arrears Act in virtue of a joint application made by himself and his landlord; whether, in support of the application, he made and lodged an affidavit declaring that he did not hold land of the annual value of more than £30; whether, at the time of making this affidavit, he held two farms in the Mohill Union, fully stocked and of the annual value of £58; one under the Earl of Granard, the other under Mr. Webber, of Mitchelstown Castle; and, what action the Government propose to take consequent on this state of facts ?

MR. TREVELYAN : Two of the Earl of Granard's tenants, each named James Farrell, obtained the benefit of the Arrears Act. Their applications were supported by the usual affidavits. The Land Commissioners were not previously aware that either of them possessed another holding; but they have made inquiry, and have been informed that it is a fact that one of the tenants in question holds a farm under Mr. Webber, and that the valuation of both holdings, taken together, is in excess of £30. In these circumstances, they will feel it their duty to make a Report of the case for the consideration of the Law Officers.

POST OFFICE (IRELAND)—THE DUBLIN POST OFFICE—SUBSTITUTION OF GAS FOR STEAM ENGINES.

MR. SEXTON asked the Postmaster General, Whether gas engines are being substituted for steam engines for working the pneumatic system in the Dublin Post Office; whether the condemned steam engines did the work to the satisfaction of the Post Office authorities; whether the Technical Department is opposed to the alteration, and whether Mr. Preece, the chief electrician, upon being consulted, reported against the change; what is the cause assigned by the Board of Works for the alteration; were any experts consulted; and, if so, would he state their names; what is the estimated cost of the work, and was it regularly advertised or given away by private tender; and, whether the condemned engines and boilers are already sold; and, if so, who are the purchasers, and what is the price ?

MR. FAWCETT, in reply, said, that there were gas engines used in the Post Office, as additional room was very much wanted. The steam engines did their work very well, and the experiment with the gas engines would be, therefore, to see how they would work. Steam engines were still being used, and it was not the case that they had been sold, as supposed by the hon. Member.

THE IRISH LAND COMMISSION (SUB-COMMISSIONERS)—SITTING AT TUAM.

VISCOUNT CRICHTON asked the Chief Secretary to the Lord Lieutenant of Ireland, If it is the fact that the Sub-Commissioners, on the 18th June last, ordered the police to clear the Court House at Tuam, county Galway, in spite of the remonstrances of the secretary to the grand jury, who was holding a special sessions for the barony of Clare, for the purpose of taking tenders for eighteen roads that were out of contract, and perfecting bonds for those who were accepted as contractors; whether it is the fact that at least a hundred road contractors who attended to put in tenders had to go home without having done their business, and were consequently put to great expense and inconvenience; whether the grand jury for the county Galway pay rent, taxes, and insurance for this Court House and a salary to the Court House keeper; and, whether the Sub-Commissioners had any legal right to take such a course, and to disarrange the fiscal business of a large portion of the county?

COLONEL NOLAN said, he would like to ask the right hon. Gentleman, whether any complaint had been made by the cesspayers, or whether any great inconvenience had been experienced; and also if he had any authentic information as to the number of contractors concerned?

MR. TREVELYAN: It is the fact that an unfortunate difference occurred between the Presentment Sessions and the Sub-Commissioners Court as to the occupation of the Court House at Tuam. This matter had already engaged the attention of the Government before the noble Viscount gave Notice of his Question, and an explanation was received from the Chairman of the Sub-Commissioners, from which it appeared that, although the Sub-Commissioners did decline to yield to the representations of the Secretary of the Grand Jury, it is not a fact that they ordered the Court to be cleared. When they entered the Court House the Bench was unoccupied, and they believed the persons present to be the usual assemblage at their Courts. The persons whom they ordered to move were occupying the seats usually occupied by professional men, and the Commissioners thought that they were farmers who had cases in their Court. The Government think that the use of the county Court House for county purposes ought not, in any circumstances, to be interfered with, and that the Sub-Commission ought not to have continued to occupy the Court until assured by the Secretary of the Grand Jury that arrangements could be made for the transaction of the county business. The Government have expressed to the Land Commissioners their hope that steps will be taken to prevent any similar misunderstanding occurring in future, and they trust that no serious derangement of the county business will result from the present occurrence. I have not heard of any representation from the cesspayers, such as was referred to by the hon. and gallant Member.

THE MAGISTRACY (IRELAND)—THE REV. J. B. FRITH.

MR. SEXTON asked the Chief Secretary to the Lord Lieutenant of Ireland, If the Rev. John Brien Frith, of Enniskillen, against whom a charge of having acted partially and corruptly in his capacity as a magistrate, has been maintained by the verdict of a jury at Derry, and whose motion for a new trial has been refused by the competent tribunal, has yet been superseded from further acting in the Commission of the Peace?

MR. TREVELYAN: This case, I understand, is still *sub judice*, and while it is so no action can be taken by the Government in respect to it. If, however, during the next Sessions no steps be taken to prosecute the appeal, it will be properly considered whether the case can be referred to the Lord Chancellor.

MR. GIBSON: Does the right hon. Gentleman accept the statement in the Question, that any jury has ever maintained a charge against the rev. gentleman that he has acted partially and corruptly? Was not the verdict upon the plea of fair comment? I have made that correction before.

MR. TREVELYAN: The finding of a jury in civil cases might have too much weight given to it with regard to persons against whom the finding is given. The Rev. Mr. Frith, in the whole business, is open to possible exception in other respects than as to his conduct as a Judge on the Bench, with regard to which I express no opinion at all; but there are certain other elements in the business to which I have previously referred, which might possibly be brought before the notice of the Lord Chancellor. The real fact of the jury having found as they did in a civil case, undoubtedly by no means is in itself sufficient ground for referring to the Lord Chancellor.

MR. GIBSON: That is not an answer to my point. I put a precise question to the right hon. Gentleman. It is the second or third occasion I have put it. Is or is it not a fact that there was no plea of justification, and only a plea of fair comment, and it was upon that plea the jury found?

MR. TREVELYAN: I do not in the least say I approve of the wording of the question. In saying Mr. Frith's conduct might ultimately have to be referred to the Lord Chancellor, I do not by any means say it is on the same grounds as the hon. Member for Sligo thinks it should be referred.

MR. SEXTON: I wish to ask the hon. and learned Solicitor General for Ireland, who has a knowledge of this case, whether it is not the fact that Captain M'Ternan swore that the Rev. Mr. Frith had acted corruptly and partially, and that his conduct was a pollution of the justice seat; and, whether, upon the issues raised, the jury found for the defendant; whether it is not the fact that the time allowed by law for appeal has not now lapsed, and that it is impossible to reopen the question?

THE SOLICITOR GENERAL FOR IRELAND (Mr. WALKER): The time has not passed by for appeal. The way the matter stood was this. The issue was not whether Mr. Frith had acted corruptly, but whether a public journalist, on the information before him, was justified in statements which he had made. Captain M'Ternan, in cross-examination, did state that Mr. Frith acted corruptly and partially. That was forced from him on cross-examination; but that was not technically the issue before the jury.

MR. GIBSON: Was it the issue at all?

THE SOLICITOR GENERAL FOR IRELAND (Mr. WALKER): No.

VISCOUNT CRICHTON: Is it the fact that the Judge before whom the case was heard, and the two Judges who heard the appeal, expressed themselves strongly to the effect that there were no grounds for the charge of corruption and partiality?

THE SOLICITOR GENERAL FOR IRELAND (Mr. WALKER): I heard the Charge of the Judge; but I cannot confirm what the noble Viscount has said regarding the appeal. I was not there, and I have not read it.

MR. GIBSON: Oh; everyone has read it.

MR. SEXTON: Is it a fact that a Judge wept on the Bench on that occasion?

[No reply.]

LAW AND JUSTICE (IRELAND)—CASE OF JOHN DONOGHUE, A LUNATIC.

MR. HARRINGTON asked the Chief Secretary to the Lord Lieutenant of Ireland, Whether it is a fact that a young man named John Donoghue was in May last committed to Mullingar Gaol on a charge of murdering his father; whether the verdict of the coroner's jury stated that this young man was a lunatic; whether, notwithstanding, the governor of the gaol allowed him to exercise and work with other prisoners; if it is true that, while so engaged, he made an attack with a spade upon the life of another prisoner, named Dillon, and inflicted upon him injuries so severe that he was confined to hospital for several weeks; has the Prisons Board taken any action to ascertain what official is responsible for allowing a dangerous lunatic, committed on a charge of murdering his father, to associate freely and without restraint with other prisoners; and, will any compensation be given to the young man Dillon, whose health was so seriously impaired by this neglect of the prison officials?

MR. TREVELYAN: John Donoghue was committed to Mullingar Prison on the 25th of April, under a Coroner's warrant, charged with the murder of his father. The warrant contained no reference to the prisoner's being insane, though it is a fact that the verdict of the Coroner's Jury did contain such a reference. For a month following his committal, the prisoner was associated for two hours daily at exercise with the other prisoners of his class, and always conducted himself quietly up to the 27th of May, when he made an attack on the prisoner Dillon. The Prisons Board, at the time, conveyed to the Governor of the prison, who was the responsible official, an expression of their disapproval of a prisoner with such antecedents as Donoghue's having been placed in a position which enabled him to commit the assault. No permanent injury was inflicted on Dillon, and no question of compensation has ever been raised or considered.

MR. HARRINGTON asked, was the young man Dillon at present a prisoner?

MR. TREVELYAN was understood to reply in the affirmative.

THE BOARD OF WORKS, (IRELAND)—CASE OF M'HUGH, OF BOLINTAFFY.

MR. DEASY asked the Secretary to the Treasury, If Patrick M'Cue, a tenant farmer, of Coolaght, Claremorris, county Mayo, made, about half-a-year since, an application to the Board of Works for a loan; whether his landlord is Mr. John P. Ormsby; whether the landlord's son, Mr. Charles C. Ormsby, is the Inspector for the Board of Works in the barony in which his father's property is situate; and, whether the Board will transfer Mr. C. C. Ormsby to another district?

MR. COURTNEY: If the hon. Member alludes to the case of M'Hugh, of Bolintaffy, I beg to inform him that his loan has been sanctioned, and an issue can be made when M'Hugh has produced his rent receipts subsequent to May, 1883. The Board of Works do not know whether their Inspector, Mr. Charles Ormsby, is son to Mr. John Ormsby; and I do not see that it matters whether he is so or not, as there is no conflict between the interests of landlord and tenant in these cases.

ROYAL IRISH CONSTABULARY—PROMOTIONS—SUB-INSPECTOR FRENCH.

MR. DEASY asked the Chief Secretary to the Lord Lieutenant of Ireland, Whether any facts have come to the knowledge of the Irish Government recently such as to lead them to deem it advisable to institute an inquiry into the cases of promotion in the force at the instance of James Ellis French since he held the rank of Sub-Inspector?

MR. TREVELYAN: The Inspector General informs me that no facts have come to his knowledge which would render it advisable to institute such an inquiry. Very strong grounds would be required to justify such a course. The period embraced by the Question would be about 20 years.

OVERHEAD TELEGRAPHIC WIRES—LEGISLATION.

SIR ALEXANDER GORDON asked the Secretary to the Local Government Board, Whether Her Majesty's Government will next year introduce a Bill to give to the Local Authorities of the Metropolis and other towns such a power of inspection and control over the construction and maintenance of overhead telegraphic wires as will tend to protect the public using the streets from the dangers incident to such aerial fabrics?

MR. GEORGE RUSSELL: The Government cannot at present give any undertaking as to Bills to be introduced by them next Session. There would probably be an advantage in the appointment of a Select Committee to inquire into the subject of overhead telegraphic wires, and the question whether such a Committee shall be moved for next Session will be considered.

VACCINATION ACT, 1867—EVESHAM BOARD OF GUARDIANS.

MR. HOPWOOD asked, Whether, legislation or discussion being impossible this Session, it is intended to take any measures, by circular to guardians or otherwise, to discourage the repetition of prosecutions and the infliction of cumulative penalties upon parents declining to submit their children to vaccination?

MR. GEORGE RUSSELL: The letter of the Local Government Board of September, 1875, addressed to the Evesham Guardians, sets forth the considerations which it appears to us should be weighed by Boards of Guardians in determining whether or not they should take further proceedings in any particular case where a penalty has already been imposed under Section 31 of the Vaccination Act, 1867. That letter was issued as a Parliamentary Paper, and has been widely circulated. We have no doubt that Boards of Guardians, generally, are aware of the views expressed in it; and we do not propose to issue any circular letter as suggested.

NAVY—THE DOCKYARDS—THE VISITING TIMBER INSPECTOR.

MR. PULESTON asked the Secretary to the Admiralty, Whether the office of Visiting Timber Inspector is vacant; and, if so, how long it has been vacant, and for what reason; whether the amount of pay attached to it has been regularly appropriated; and, whether it is proposed to fill it?

MR. CAMPBELL-BANNERMAN: The office has been for some time vacant, pending the settlement of the reorganization of the Constructive Department of the Admiralty. As now decided, the office will not be filled up. During the vacancy the amount of the pay has not been appropriated, but merged in the general saving on the Vote.

NAVY—THE DOCKYARDS—COMMISSION ON DOCKYARD WORK.

MR. PULESTON asked the Secretary to the Admiralty, Whether the Report of the Commission on Dockyard Work has been presented; and, when it will be laid upon the Table of the House?

MR. CAMPBELL-BANNERMAN: I presume my hon. Friend refers to the Committee recently appointed to advise the Admiralty on certain matters connected with shipbuilding. The Report of that Committee has not yet been forwarded to the Board; but I am told that it will be finished very shortly.

PUBLIC HEALTH — IMPORTATION OF BUTTERINE AND OLEOMARGARINE.

MR. GUY DAWNAY asked the Chancellor of the Duchy of Lancaster, Whether the Return of the Imports, under the head of Butter, in Table 10, Group 2, of the Agricultural Returns for Great Britain for 1883, includes also the substances termed Butterine and Oleomargarine; and, whether, in view of the disclosures contained in the Copy of Correspondence lately issued by the Privy Council Office in Paper No. 275, steps will be taken for the future to give separate Returns of the Imports of Butter and of the spurious and often deleterious and poisonous compounds of fat and acids imported into this Country under the name of Butter, to the detriment both of the health of the consuming population and of the prosperity of the home butter trade?

MR. DODSON, in reply, said, the Return to which the hon. Member referred included spurious butter under the head of butter. Oleomargarine was not included under that head, being classified by the Customs Department under the head of animal fat. The Customs were now, at the request of the Treasury, endeavouring to secure a separate classification of butterine and other imitations of butter, and they hoped to be able to distinguish them.

LAW AND POLICE (METROPOLIS)—THE REFORM DEMONSTRATION.

MR. GUY DAWNAY asked the First Commissioner of Works, Whether the iron hurdles, posts, and seats in Hyde Park were removed by his orders in order to facilitate the so-called Reform Demonstration on Monday the 21st; and, if so, by whom the expense of such removal and subsequent restoration will be defrayed?

MR. SHAW LEFEVRE: The posts in question were removed by my orders. It was represented to me by the organizers——

MR. WARTON: Who were the organizers?

MR. SHAW LEFEVRE: It was represented to me by the organizers of the demonstration that there would be serious injury and damage to the individuals forming the procession if the posts were allowed to remain, resulting from the crushing of so large a body of people through the posts. Acting upon that representation, I gave the necessary order, and the posts were removed by the ordinary labourers of the Park. There will be no expense caused to the public. I may add that many other demands were made upon me by the organizers of the demonstration, such as were made recently in the case of the meeting at Edinburgh; but I declined to admit them, on the ground that they were contrary to the Regulations of the Park.

MR. WARTON: Would the right hon. Gentleman be good enough to say who were the organizers?

MR. J. LOWTHER: Do I understand the right hon. Gentleman to say that the workmen whose time is paid for out of the Estimates were employed in this service for political purposes?

[No reply.]

MR. TATTON EGERTON asked the First Commissioner of Works, Under what head in the Civil Service Estimates the expenses came, incurred in preparing Hyde Park for the reception of the mass meeting of 21st July, and repairing and restoring the Park in a proper condition for Her Majesty's peaceable subjects?

MR. SHAW LEFEVRE: I think I have already answered that question. There will be no Estimate under which it will be necessary to vote money for the purposes mentioned. I think the House will be glad to know that no damage has been done to the Park.

MR. J. LOWTHER: The right hon. Gentleman has not answered my question which I asked him just now. I do not know whether he caught it, owing to the rather disorderly cries of Members below the Gangway on the other side of the House. [*Cries of* "Order!" *and* "Withdraw!"]

MR. JESSE COLLINGS: I rise to Order. I wish to ask you, Mr. Speaker, whether it is in Order for a right hon. Gentleman to describe certain Members of Parliament as being "disorderly?"

MR. J. LOWTHER: Before you reply, Mr. Speaker, to the point of Order, I wish to state that I am prepared to name the hon. Gentlemen below the Gangway who did make a disorderly cry.

MR. SPEAKER: The word "disorderly" is relative. I think the right hon. Gentleman meant to complain of the noise which may have prevented his being heard.

MR. J. LOWTHER: The question which I asked the right hon. Gentleman was, whether I was to understand his answer as meaning that the workmen employed by his Department, which is connected with the Public Service, were engaged for these special purposes; and whether, that being so, they were not really paid for out of the Estimates?

MR. GLADSTONE: For political purposes.

MR. J. LOWTHER: Very well—political purposes; that is to say, they were employed in work which the right hon. Gentleman told us he was requested to undertake by organizers of a demonstration which has been avowedly—rightly or wrongly—of a political character. I must ask the right hon. Gentleman to answer the question.

MR. BROADHURST: Before the right hon. Gentleman answers that question, I should like to ask him whether the men employed in removing the hurdles for public convenience yesterday are the same men who are employed constantly in keeping a special track of a large portion of the Park for a special and select class of horse-riders?

MR. SHAW LEFEVRE: I have already explained that I ordered the work because I considered it to be necessary for the public safety.

MR. TATTON EGERTON: I should like to ask whether, in any future demonstration, the First Commissioner of Works will be prepared to arrange the Park for political meetings?

MR. SHAW LEFEVRE: That is a hypothetical question which I really cannot undertake to answer.

MR. TATTON EGERTON: I beg to ask the Secretary of State for the Home Department, Whether the police guarding a procession on Sunday passing through Onslow Place were employed on special duty, and by whom paid; and, whether he approves of the Metropolitan Police being employed for the protection of mendicity?

SIR WILLIAM HARCOURT: As to this affair in Onslow Place, if the hon. Member will give me further information, I will make inquiries. All I know is that no special police were employed, and that no special cost was incurred.

MR. TATTON EGERTON: That only shows the ignorance of the Secretary of State as to his work. I wish further to ask the right hon. and learned Gentleman, whether the refusal of a superintendent of police to enable a Member of the House of Commons to cross Piccadilly in the crowd, before any passage of the procession of 21st July, is in accordance with the pledge given by Her Majesty's Government?

MR. R. N. FOWLER (LORD MAYOR): Before the right hon. and learned Gentleman answers, may I ask him whether it was by his orders that Members of Parliament were prevented from passing through the Strand on their way to the House yesterday?

SIR WILLIAM HARCOURT: No, Sir, certainly not; more particularly, I should never have thought of stopping the Lord Mayor. As regards the question of the hon. Member for Cheshire (Mr. T. Egerton), I must have some

further information on that matter before I can answer it. I really do not know who the person was, or the time or the place. If he will give me particulars, I will inquire into the matter. I have received an amusing letter from a gentleman as to a scene of that kind; but I will not read it to the House. With reference to these various charges as to the conduct of the police, I would suggest to hon. Members opposite that, as a right hon. Gentleman on the Front Opposition Bench has given Notice that he intends to move the rejection or the reduction of the Vote for the payment of the Metropolitan Police, these questions should be reserved until then. Of course, a Motion of that kind, coming from the Front Opposition and Conservative Bench, is a very serious matter; and when the Conservative Opposition proposes to refuse the pay of the Metropolitan Police, I shall be prepared to meet the charges against the police, and to maintain that they deserve the approbation, and not the censure or punishment, of this House.

MR. J. LOWTHER: Can the right hon. and learned Gentleman give any indication when that Vote is likely to be reached? I would also ask whether he misunderstands me in saying that I propose the rejection of the Vote?

SIR WILLIAM HARCOURT: No; the reduction.

MR. J. LOWTHER: I undertook, in a formula well known to the House of Commons, to move the reduction of the Vote solely for the purpose of putting myself in Order. If the right hon. and learned Gentleman will put me in a position to move the reduction of the Home Office Vote, that would really meet my views much better.

MR. TATTON EGERTON: I will give the Home Secretary, categorically and in writing, the cases mentioned in my two Questions, and I shall expect to get a categorical answer.

MR. R. N. FOWLER (LORD MAYOR): Is the right hon. and learned Gentleman aware that a Member of this House was stopped yesterday in the Strand when on his way to the House by the police, and that when the hon. Gentleman said he was a Member of Parliament, and was going to the House of Commons, the answer was—"I do not care who you are; my orders are to stop the Queen if she comes this way?"

MR. J. LOWTHER: Will it suit the right hon. and learned Gentleman's convenience to make some fixed arrangement for taking the Metropolitan Police Vote? As the Home Secretary appears to consider it a mattter of importance, as no doubt it is, it will perhaps be for the convenience of the House that some definite arrangement should be made. Will he take it at the beginning of a Sitting?

SIR WILLIAM HARCOURT: Certainly, Sir; if I understand that this is an organized attack on the Metropolitan Police by the right hon. Gentleman opposite, I will take very good care that the Vote is not decided without sufficient Notice.

MR. J. LOWTHER: I must have some explanation of this. Does the right hon. and learned Gentleman still misunderstand me, and say that I mean to attack the Metropolitan Police when I have more than once disclaimed it? My attack is really on the Home Secretary.

PARLIAMENT — BUSINESS OF THE HOUSE—ROYAL COURTS OF JUSTICE BILL.

MR. WHITLEY asked the Secretary to the Treasury, What course the Government intend to pursue in reference to the Royal Courts of Justice Bill?

MR. COURTNEY, in reply, said, the matter was under consideration, and he hoped very shortly to be able to inform the hon. Member of the result.

NAVY—COLLISION BETWEEN IRON-CLADS IN BANTRY BAY.

MR. W. H. SMITH: I wish to ask, Whether the Secretary to the Admiralty can give any information as to the alleged collision between two of Her Majesty's ships off the coast of Ireland?

MR. CAMPBELL-BANNERMAN: Information has reached the Admiralty of the circumstances referred to by my right hon. Friend; but the information does not extend much beyond what appears in the newspapers. The ships are proceeding to Plymouth, where an investigation by court martial will be held into the cause of the collision.

EGYPT (EVENTS IN THE SOUDAN)—GENERAL GORDON.

LORD EDMOND FITZMAURICE: I have to inform the House that Mr.

MR. TATTON EGERTON asked the First Commissioner of Works, Under what head in the Civil Service Estimates the expenses came, incurred in preparing Hyde Park for the reception of the mass meeting of 21st July, and repairing and restoring the Park in a proper condition for Her Majesty's peaceable subjects?

MR. SHAW LEFEVRE: I think I have already answered that question. There will be no Estimate under which it will be necessary to vote money for the purposes mentioned. I think the House will be glad to know that no damage has been done to the Park.

MR. J. LOWTHER: The right hon. Gentleman has not answered my question which I asked him just now. I do not know whether he caught it, owing to the rather disorderly cries of Members below the Gangway on the other side of the House. [*Cries of* "Order!" *and* "Withdraw!"]

MR. JESSE COLLINGS: I rise to Order. I wish to ask you, Mr. Speaker, whether it is in Order for a right hon. Gentleman to describe certain Members of Parliament as being "disorderly?"

MR. J. LOWTHER: Before you reply, Mr. Speaker, to the point of Order, I wish to state that I am prepared to name the hon. Gentlemen below the Gangway who did make a disorderly cry.

MR. SPEAKER: The word "disorderly" is relative. I think the right hon. Gentleman meant to complain of the noise which may have prevented his being heard.

MR. J. LOWTHER: The question which I asked the right hon. Gentleman was, whether I was to understand his answer as meaning that the workmen employed by his Department, which is connected with the Public Service, were engaged for these special purposes; and whether, that being so, they were not really paid for out of the Estimates?

MR. GLADSTONE: For political purposes.

MR. J. LOWTHER: Very well—political purposes; that is to say, they were employed in work which the right hon. Gentleman told us he was requested to undertake by organizers of a demonstration which has been avowedly—rightly or wrongly—of a political character. I must ask the right hon. Gentleman to answer the question.

MR. BROADHURST: Before the right hon. Gentleman answers that question, I should like to ask him whether the men employed in removing the hurdles for public convenience yesterday are the same men who are employed constantly in keeping a special track of a large portion of the Park for a special and select class of horse-riders?

MR. SHAW LEFEVRE: I have already explained that I ordered the work because I considered it to be necessary for the public safety.

MR. TATTON EGERTON: I should like to ask whether, in any future demonstration, the First Commissioner of Works will be prepared to arrange the Park for political meetings?

MR. SHAW LEFEVRE: That is a hypothetical question which I really cannot undertake to answer.

MR. TATTON EGERTON: I beg to ask the Secretary of State for the Home Department, Whether the police guarding a procession on Sunday passing through Onslow Place were employed on special duty, and by whom paid; and, whether he approves of the Metropolitan Police being employed for the protection of mendicity?

SIR WILLIAM HARCOURT: As to this affair in Onslow Place, if the hon. Member will give me further information, I will make inquiries. All I know is that no special police were employed, and that no special cost was incurred.

MR. TATTON EGERTON: That only shows the ignorance of the Secretary of State as to his work. I wish further to ask the right hon. and learned Gentleman, whether the refusal of a superintendent of police to enable a Member of the House of Commons to cross Piccadilly in the crowd, before any passage of the procession of 21st July, is in accordance with the pledge given by Her Majesty's Government?

MR. R. N. FOWLER (LORD MAYOR): Before the right hon. and learned Gentleman answers, may I ask him whether it was by his orders that Members of Parliament were prevented from passing through the Strand on their way to the House yesterday?

SIR WILLIAM HARCOURT: No, Sir, certainly not; more particularly, I should never have thought of stopping the Lord Mayor. As regards the question of the hon. Member for Cheshire (Mr. T. Egerton), I must have some

further information on that matter before I can answer it. I really do not know who the person was, or the time or the place. If he will give me particulars, I will inquire into the matter. I have received an amusing letter from a gentleman as to a scene of that kind; but I will not read it to the House. With reference to these various charges as to the conduct of the police, I would suggest to hon. Members opposite that, as a right hon. Gentleman on the Front Opposition Bench has given Notice that he intends to move the rejection or the reduction of the Vote for the payment of the Metropolitan Police, these questions should be reserved until then. Of course, a Motion of that kind, coming from the Front Opposition and Conservative Bench, is a very serious matter; and when the Conservative Opposition proposes to refuse the pay of the Metropolitan Police, I shall be prepared to meet the charges against the police, and to maintain that they deserve the approbation, and not the censure or punishment, of this House.

MR. J. LOWTHER: Can the right hon. and learned Gentleman give any indication when that Vote is likely to be reached? I would also ask whether he misunderstands me in saying that I propose the rejection of the Vote?

SIR WILLIAM HARCOURT: No; the reduction.

MR. J. LOWTHER: I undertook, in a formula well known to the House of Commons, to move the reduction of the Vote solely for the purpose of putting myself in Order. If the right hon. and learned Gentleman will put me in a position to move the reduction of the Home Office Vote, that would really meet my views much better.

MR. TATTON EGERTON: I will give the Home Secretary, categorically and in writing, the cases mentioned in my two Questions, and I shall expect to get a categorical answer.

MR. R. N. FOWLER (LORD MAYOR): Is the right hon. and learned Gentleman aware that a Member of this House was stopped yesterday in the Strand when on his way to the House by the police, and that when the hon. Gentleman said he was a Member of Parliament, and was going to the House of Commons, the answer was—"I do not care who you are; my orders are to stop the Queen if she comes this way?"

MR. J. LOWTHER: Will it suit the right hon. and learned Gentleman's convenience to make some fixed arrangement for taking the Metropolitan Police Vote? As the Home Secretary appears to consider it a mattter of importance, as no doubt it is, it will perhaps be for the convenience of the House that some definite arrangement should be made. Will he take it at the beginning of a Sitting?

SIR WILLIAM HARCOURT: Certainly, Sir; if I understand that this is an organized attack on the Metropolitan Police by the right hon. Gentleman opposite, I will take very good care that the Vote is not decided without sufficient Notice.

MR. J. LOWTHER: I must have some explanation of this. Does the right hon. and learned Gentleman still misunderstand me, and say that I mean to attack the Metropolitan Police when I have more than once disclaimed it? My attack is really on the Home Secretary.

PARLIAMENT — BUSINESS OF THE HOUSE—ROYAL COURTS OF JUSTICE BILL.

MR. WHITLEY asked the Secretary to the Treasury, What course the Government intend to pursue in reference to the Royal Courts of Justice Bill?

MR. COURTNEY, in reply, said, the matter was under consideration, and he hoped very shortly to be able to inform the hon. Member of the result.

NAVY—COLLISION BETWEEN IRON-CLADS IN BANTRY BAY.

MR. W. H. SMITH: I wish to ask, Whether the Secretary to the Admiralty can give any information as to the alleged collision between two of Her Majesty's ships off the coast of Ireland?

MR. CAMPBELL-BANNERMAN: Information has reached the Admiralty of the circumstances referred to by my right hon. Friend; but the information does not extend much beyond what appears in the newspapers. The ships are proceeding to Plymouth, where an investigation by court martial will be held into the cause of the collision.

EGYPT (EVENTS IN THE SOUDAN)—GENERAL GORDON.

LORD EDMOND FITZMAURICE: I have to inform the House that Mr.

of May, when he made an attack on the prisoner Dillon. The Prisons Board, at the time, conveyed to the Governor of the prison, who was the responsible official, an expression of their disapproval of a prisoner with such antecedents as Donoghue's having been placed in a position which enabled him to commit the assault. No permanent injury was inflicted on Dillon, and no question of compensation has ever been raised or considered.

MR. HARRINGTON asked, was the young man Dillon at present a prisoner?

MR. TREVELYAN was understood to reply in the affirmative.

THE BOARD OF WORKS (IRELAND)—CASE OF M'HUGH, OF BOLINTAFFY.

MR. DEASY asked the Secretary to the Treasury, If Patrick M'Cue, a tenant farmer, of Coolaght, Claremorris, county Mayo, made, about half-a-year since, an application to the Board of Works for a loan; whether his landlord is Mr. John P. Ormsby; whether the landlord's son, Mr. Charles C. Ormsby, is the Inspector for the Board of Works in the barony in which his father's property is situate; and, whether the Board will transfer Mr. C. C. Ormsby to another district?

MR. COURTNEY: If the hon. Member alludes to the case of M'Hugh, of Bolintaffy, I beg to inform him that his loan has been sanctioned, and an issue can be made when M'Hugh has produced his rent receipts subsequent to May, 1883. The Board of Works do not know whether their Inspector, Mr. Charles Ormsby, is son to Mr. John Ormsby; and I do not see that it matters whether he is so or not, as there is no conflict between the interests of landlord and tenant in these cases.

ROYAL IRISH CONSTABULARY—PROMOTIONS—SUB-INSPECTOR FRENCH.

MR. DEASY asked the Chief Secretary to the Lord Lieutenant of Ireland, Whether any facts have come to the knowledge of the Irish Government recently such as to lead them to deem it advisable to institute an inquiry into the cases of promotion in the force at the instance of James Ellis French since he held the rank of Sub-Inspector?

MR. TREVELYAN: The Inspector General informs me that no facts have come to his knowledge which would render it advisable to institute such an inquiry. Very strong grounds would be required to justify such a course. The period embraced by the Question would be about 20 years.

OVERHEAD TELEGRAPHIC WIRES—LEGISLATION.

SIR ALEXANDER GORDON asked the Secretary to the Local Government Board, Whether Her Majesty's Government will next year introduce a Bill to give to the Local Authorities of the Metropolis and other towns such a power of inspection and control over the construction and maintenance of overhead telegraphic wires as will tend to protect the public using the streets from the dangers incident to such aerial fabrics?

MR. GEORGE RUSSELL: The Government cannot at present give any undertaking as to Bills to be introduced by them next Session. There would probably be an advantage in the appointment of a Select Committee to inquire into the subject of overhead telegraphic wires, and the question whether such a Committee shall be moved for next Session will be considered.

VACCINATION ACT, 1867—EVESHAM BOARD OF GUARDIANS.

MR. HOPWOOD asked, Whether, legislation or discussion being impossible this Session, it is intended to take any measures, by circular to guardians or otherwise, to discourage the repetition of prosecutions and the infliction of cumulative penalties upon parents declining to submit their children to vaccination?

MR. GEORGE RUSSELL: The letter of the Local Government Board of September, 1875, addressed to the Evesham Guardians, sets forth the considerations which it appears to us should be weighed by Boards of Guardians in determining whether or not they should take further proceedings in any particular case where a penalty has already been imposed under Section 31 of the Vaccination Act, 1867. That letter was issued as a Parliamentary Paper, and has been widely circulated. We have no doubt that Boards of Guardians, generally, are aware of the views expressed in it; and we do not propose to issue any circular letter as suggested.

NAVY—THE DOCKYARDS—THE VISITING TIMBER INSPECTOR.

MR. PULESTON asked the Secretary to the Admiralty, Whether the office of Visiting Timber Inspector is vacant; and, if so, how long it has been vacant, and for what reason; whether the amount of pay attached to it has been regularly appropriated; and, whether it is proposed to fill it?

MR. CAMPBELL-BANNERMAN: The office has been for some time vacant, pending the settlement of the reorganization of the Constructive Department of the Admiralty. As now decided, the office will not be filled up. During the vacancy the amount of the pay has not been appropriated, but merged in the general saving on the Vote.

NAVY—THE DOCKYARDS—COMMISSION ON DOCKYARD WORK.

MR. PULESTON asked the Secretary to the Admiralty, Whether the Report of the Commission on Dockyard Work has been presented; and, when it will be laid upon the Table of the House?

MR. CAMPBELL-BANNERMAN: I presume my hon. Friend refers to the Committee recently appointed to advise the Admiralty on certain matters connected with shipbuilding. The Report of that Committee has not yet been forwarded to the Board; but I am told that it will be finished very shortly.

PUBLIC HEALTH — IMPORTATION OF BUTTERINE AND OLEOMARGARINE.

MR. GUY DAWNAY asked the Chancellor of the Duchy of Lancaster, Whether the Return of the Imports, under the head of Butter, in Table 10, Group 2, of the Agricultural Returns for Great Britain for 1883, includes also the substances termed Butterine and Oleomargarine; and, whether, in view of the disclosures contained in the Copy of Correspondence lately issued by the Privy Council Office in Paper No. 275, steps will be taken for the future to give separate Returns of the Imports of Butter and of the spurious and often deleterious and poisonous compounds of fat and acids imported into this Country under the name of Butter, to the detriment both of the health of the consuming population and of the prosperity of the home butter trade?

MR. DODSON, in reply, said, the Return to which the hon. Member referred included spurious butter under the head of butter. Oleomargarine was not included under that head, being classified by the Customs Department under the head of animal fat. The Customs were now, at the request of the Treasury, endeavouring to secure a separate classification of butterine and other imitations of butter, and they hoped to be able to distinguish them.

LAW AND POLICE (METROPOLIS)—THE REFORM DEMONSTRATION.

MR. GUY DAWNAY asked the First Commissioner of Works, Whether the iron hurdles, posts, and seats in Hyde Park were removed by his orders in order to facilitate the so-called Reform Demonstration on Monday the 21st; and, if so, by whom the expense of such removal and subsequent restoration will be defrayed?

MR. SHAW LEFEVRE: The posts in question were removed by my orders. It was represented to me by the organizers——

MR. WARTON: Who were the organizers?

MR. SHAW LEFEVRE: It was represented to me by the organizers of the demonstration that there would be serious injury and damage to the individuals forming the procession if the posts were allowed to remain, resulting from the crushing of so large a body of people through the posts. Acting upon that representation, I gave the necessary order, and the posts were removed by the ordinary labourers of the Park. There will be no expense caused to the public. I may add that many other demands were made upon me by the organizers of the demonstration, such as were made recently in the case of the meeting at Edinburgh; but I declined to admit them, on the ground that they were contrary to the Regulations of the Park.

MR. WARTON: Would the right hon. Gentleman be good enough to say who were the organizers?

MR. J. LOWTHER: Do I understand the right hon. Gentleman to say that the workmen whose time is paid for out of the Estimates were employed in this service for political purposes?

[No reply.]

MR. TATTON EGERTON asked the First Commissioner of Works, Under what head in the Civil Service Estimates the expenses came, incurred in preparing Hyde Park for the reception of the mass meeting of 21st July, and repairing and restoring the Park in a proper condition for Her Majesty's peaceable subjects?

MR. SHAW LEFEVRE: I think I have already answered that question. There will be no Estimate under which it will be necessary to vote money for the purposes mentioned. I think the House will be glad to know that no damage has been done to the Park.

MR. J. LOWTHER: The right hon. Gentleman has not answered my question which I asked him just now. I do not know whether he caught it, owing to the rather disorderly cries of Members below the Gangway on the other side of the House. [*Cries of* "Order!" *and* "Withdraw!"]

MR. JESSE COLLINGS: I rise to Order. I wish to ask you, Mr. Speaker, whether it is in Order for a right hon. Gentleman to describe certain Members of Parliament as being "disorderly?"

MR. J. LOWTHER: Before you reply, Mr. Speaker, to the point of Order, I wish to state that I am prepared to name the hon. Gentlemen below the Gangway who did make a disorderly cry.

MR. SPEAKER: The word "disorderly" is relative. I think the right hon. Gentleman meant to complain of the noise which may have prevented his being heard.

MR. J. LOWTHER: The question which I asked the right hon. Gentleman was, whether I was to understand his answer as meaning that the workmen employed by his Department, which is connected with the Public Service, were engaged for these special purposes; and whether, that being so, they were not really paid for out of the Estimates?

MR. GLADSTONE: For political purposes.

MR. J. LOWTHER: Very well—political purposes; that is to say, they were employed in work which the right hon. Gentleman told us he was requested to undertake by organizers of a demonstration which has been avowedly—rightly or wrongly—of a political character. I must ask the right hon. Gentleman to answer the question.

MR. BROADHURST: Before the right hon. Gentleman answers that question, I should like to ask him whether the men employed in removing the hurdles for public convenience yesterday are the same men who are employed constantly in keeping a special track of a large portion of the Park for a special and select class of horse-riders?

MR. SHAW LEFEVRE: I have already explained that I ordered the work because I considered it to be necessary for the public safety.

MR. TATTON EGERTON: I should like to ask whether, in any future demonstration, the First Commissioner of Works will be prepared to arrange the Park for political meetings?

MR. SHAW LEFEVRE: That is a hypothetical question which I really cannot undertake to answer.

MR. TATTON EGERTON: I beg to ask the Secretary of State for the Home Department, Whether the police guarding a procession on Sunday passing through Onslow Place were employed on special duty, and by whom paid; and, whether he approves of the Metropolitan Police being employed for the protection of mendicity?

SIR WILLIAM HARCOURT: As to this affair in Onslow Place, if the hon. Member will give me further information, I will make inquiries. All I know is that no special police were employed, and that no special cost was incurred.

MR. TATTON EGERTON: That only shows the ignorance of the Secretary of State as to his work. I wish further to ask the right hon. and learned Gentleman, whether the refusal of a superintendent of police to enable a Member of the House of Commons to cross Piccadilly in the crowd, before any passage of the procession of 21st July, is in accordance with the pledge given by Her Majesty's Government?

MR. R. N. FOWLER (LORD MAYOR): Before the right hon. and learned Gentleman answers, may I ask him whether it was by his orders that Members of Parliament were prevented from passing through the Strand on their way to the House yesterday?

SIR WILLIAM HARCOURT: No, Sir, certainly not; more particularly, I should never have thought of stopping the Lord Mayor. As regards the question of the hon. Member for Cheshire (Mr. T. Egerton), I must have some

further information on that matter before I can answer it. I really do not know who the person was, or the time or the place. If he will give me particulars, I will inquire into the matter. I have received an amusing letter from a gentleman as to a scene of that kind; but I will not read it to the House. With reference to these various charges as to the conduct of the police, I would suggest to hon. Members opposite that, as a right hon. Gentleman on the Front Opposition Bench has given Notice that he intends to move the rejection or the reduction of the Vote for the payment of the Metropolitan Police, these questions should be reserved until then. Of course, a Motion of that kind, coming from the Front Opposition and Conservative Bench, is a very serious matter; and when the Conservative Opposition proposes to refuse the pay of the Metropolitan Police, I shall be prepared to meet the charges against the police, and to maintain that they deserve the approbation, and not the censure or punishment, of this House.

MR. J. LOWTHER: Can the right hon. and learned Gentleman give any indication when that Vote is likely to be reached? I would also ask whether he misunderstands me in saying that I propose the rejection of the Vote?

SIR WILLIAM HARCOURT: No; the reduction.

MR. J. LOWTHER: I undertook, in a formula well known to the House of Commons, to move the reduction of the Vote solely for the purpose of putting myself in Order. If the right hon. and learned Gentleman will put me in a position to move the reduction of the Home Office Vote, that would really meet my views much better.

MR. TATTON EGERTON: I will give the Home Secretary, categorically and in writing, the cases mentioned in my two Questions, and I shall expect to get a categorical answer.

MR. R. N. FOWLER (LORD MAYOR): Is the right hon. and learned Gentleman aware that a Member of this House was stopped yesterday in the Strand when on his way to the House by the police, and that when the hon. Gentleman said he was a Member of Parliament, and was going to the House of Commons, the answer was—"I do not care who you are; my orders are to stop the Queen if she comes this way?"

MR. J. LOWTHER: Will it suit the right hon. and learned Gentleman's convenience to make some fixed arrangement for taking the Metropolitan Police Vote? As the Home Secretary appears to consider it a mattter of importance, as no doubt it is, it will perhaps be for the convenience of the House that some definite arrangement should be made. Will he take it at the beginning of a Sitting?

SIR WILLIAM HARCOURT: Certainly, Sir; if I understand that this is an organized attack on the Metropolitan Police by the right hon. Gentleman opposite, I will take very good care that the Vote is not decided without sufficient Notice.

MR. J. LOWTHER: I must have some explanation of this. Does the right hon. and learned Gentleman still misunderstand me, and say that I mean to attack the Metropolitan Police when I have more than once disclaimed it? My attack is really on the Home Secretary.

PARLIAMENT — BUSINESS OF THE HOUSE—ROYAL COURTS OF JUSTICE BILL.

MR. WHITLEY asked the Secretary to the Treasury, What course the Government intend to pursue in reference to the Royal Courts of Justice Bill?

MR. COURTNEY, in reply, said, the matter was under consideration, and he hoped very shortly to be able to inform the hon. Member of the result.

NAVY—COLLISION BETWEEN IRON-CLADS IN BANTRY BAY.

MR. W. H. SMITH: I wish to ask, Whether the Secretary to the Admiralty can give any information as to the alleged collision between two of Her Majesty's ships off the coast of Ireland?

MR. CAMPBELL-BANNERMAN: Information has reached the Admiralty of the circumstances referred to by my right hon. Friend; but the information does not extend much beyond what appears in the newspapers. The ships are proceeding to Plymouth, where an investigation by court martial will be held into the cause of the collision.

EGYPT (EVENTS IN THE SOUDAN)—GENERAL GORDON.

LORD EDMOND FITZMAURICE: I have to inform the House that Mr.

Egerton, in an important telegram, dated yesterday, states that a merchant has arrived at Assouan, 60 days from Kordofan, and 17 days from Dongola. He reports that Gordon left Khartoum and got as far as Shendy, but had to return, as there was not enough water. Khartoum had been surrounded by the Mahdi's followers; but they had been utterly defeated by Gordon, and their leader killed. Letters passed regularly between Gordon and the Mahdi; and there are many of the Mahdi's people round Khartoum, but his influence is on the wane. Major Chermside also reports that he learns from his spies that Arabs are much afraid of Gordon, who has defeated four tribes between Khartoum and Berber.

ORDERS OF THE DAY.

——o——

SUPPLY—CIVIL SERVICE ESTIMATES.

SUPPLY—*considered* in Committee.

(In the Committee.)

CLASS II.—SALARIES AND EXPENSES OF CIVIL DEPARTMENTS.

(1.) £1,337, to complete the sum for the Charitable Donations and Bequests Office, Ireland.

(2.) Motion made, and Question proposed,

"That a sum, not exceeding £109,544, be granted to Her Majesty, to complete the sum necessary to defray the Charge which will come in course of payment during the year ending on the 31st day of March 1885, for the Salaries and Expenses of the Local Government Board in Ireland, including various Grants in Aid of Local Taxation."

MR. SEXTON said, he was under the necessity of asking the Committee to agree to postpone this Vote, because it was desirable, in the public interest, that time should be given for the Local Government Board to consider and for the Government to announce the decision they arrived at in the case of Mr. Elliott, a servant of the Board. Mr. Elliott was a rate collector in the service of the South Dublin Union, and in that capacity he held office under the Local Government Board. The greater part of a year had passed since the auditor of the Local Government Board in Dublin discovered that, in his capacity as rate collector for the Blackrock Commissioners, Mr. Elliott had misappropriated moneys to the amount of between £2,000 and £3,000. Of course, if the ratepayers of Blackrock and the Commissioners were willing that their money should be misapplied, he would not ask the Committee to interfere; but what he did ask was, that the official who had committed this misappropriation of public money should be dismissed from the service of the Local Government Board, and deprived of his position of rate collector. It appeared that the misappropriations had extended over a series of years, and for some months the Commissioners had been holding private inquiries, and had been endeavouring to realize the assets of Mr. Elliott, in order to make good the deficiency of public money which had been discovered. The Lord Lieutenant had asked the Commissioners whether their attempt to realize Mr. Elliott's assets had been rendered necessary by any misappropriation or malversation of money on his part? Up to the present moment the Commissioners had not returned an answer. They were continuing their private inquiries. Neither Earl Spencer, as Viceroy, nor himself, as a Representative of the public, asking for information, in that House, had been able to obtain any satisfactory explanation from the Commissioners. It was not necessary, for a moment, to point out how desirable it was that the purity of the Public Service should be maintained in Ireland, especially in regard to the character of officials intrusted with the collection of public money; and the President of the Local Government Board had himself admitted that if an officer was untrustworthy in one capacity, it must be assumed that he would be dishonest and untrustworthy in all. The Chief Secretary, when the matter was mentioned the other day, named the 23rd instant as the day upon which he would explain the course the Local Government Board proposed to take in regard to Mr. Elliott. They had now reached the 22nd, and he should like to hear if the material for enabling the Government to arrive at a decision had yet come into the hands of the Chief Secretary, and, if not, how soon such material might be expected? As the question was one of principle, affecting the whole character of the Public Service, and the nature of the terms upon which trusted officials would be allowed to continue to hold their offices, it would be for the convenience of the House and of the Department if the Vote were postponed until the decision of the Government was announced. If the decision of the Local Government Board should be such as they had a right to expect, discussion on the Vote would be greatly shortened; but if, on the other hand, it were unfavourable, or unjust, it would be necessary for him to go into the case of Mr. Elliott at length, and with a particularity of detail which he would otherwise desire to spare the Committee.

MR. TREVELYAN said, they would all cordially agree with nearly all the hon. Member had said, except that in the present stage of the investigations he was unwilling to declare confidently that Mr. Elliott had misappropriated the public money. He thoroughly agreed with and approved of the canon the hon. Member had laid down—although there were not many occasions on which he did agree with him—that where a public servant had proved himself to be untrustworthy in matters connected with Public Business, he should not be continued in the Public Service. He could hardly accede to the proposal of the hon. Member to postpone this Vote in order that they might await the reply of the Blackrock Town Commissioners, for this reason—that the hon. Member and he were perfectly at one upon the action which it would be necessary for the Local Government Board to take, if that reply was unfavourable to Mr. Elliott. The long and the short of it was this—it appeared to him a very simple case, either that Mr. Elliott had misappropriated the public money, or he had not. Defalcations of this nature were very simple to ascertain. If he had, he would not be continued in office by the Local Government Board—if he had not, of course they should take no notice of his conduct. The hon. Member for Sligo (Mr. Sexton) had no reason to doubt, from his (Mr. Trevelyan's) previous action in matters to which he and his Friends had called attention, that if a charge of malversation or fraud was proved against a public servant, however slight the sum of money concerned, he had invariably acted with rigour. The case of Mr. Byrne was as strong a case as could possibly be brought forward. Mr. Byrne had, by gross irregularities, to say the least, put into his pocket the sum of a few shillings, and, in consequence of having done that in his private capacity, he was deprived of a position which brought him in £1,200 a-year of the public money. Painful as his (Mr. Trevelyan's) duty was in the matter, he felt that his course was perfectly clear. On that principle he had acted then, and on that principle he should act now. Undoubtedly, if he did not fulfil his intentions in this particular, the hon. Member would have a right to complain, and to call him to task. He thought the Blackrock Commissioners had not shown a proper sense of the gravity of the position. If their ordinary meetings were not sufficiently frequent to enable them to consider this matter promptly, they ought to have met specially to consider it. He had every reason to believe that on the 23rd instant the Government would have the Commissioners' final answer. If they did not get a final answer, he should certainly be prepared to take extraordinary means, because the circumstances were extraordinary. He hoped, after that statement, hon. Members would allow the Vote to proceed.

MR. T. P. O'CONNOR pointed out the importance and seriousness of the case. The short sketch which had been given of it by his hon. Friend had been practically corroborated by the Chief Secretary. Of course, the right hon. Gentleman would not admit the actual charge—that a public officer, who was supposed to have been guilty of misappropriating large sums of money, was at present retained in his position. The facts more than suggested the idea that someone connected with the Local Government Board, who had supervision over this gentleman, had not performed his duty in such a manner as to make Mr. Elliott responsible for the acts of which he had been accused. Upon the actual facts of the case, the right hon. Gentleman and his hon. Friend were agreed. The right hon. Gentleman said the Blackrock Commissioners were acting in a sluggish way, and he (Mr. T. P. O'Connor) thought the right hon. Gentleman would agree with him that their action in the matter ought to be stimulated. He had not the smallest doubt as to what the intentions and inclinations of the right hon. Gentleman were in regard to it. The right hon. Gentleman had always distinguished himself by the rigidity of his judgments upon improper conduct such as this, and in all offences against the public morality by officers in the Public Service; but the right hon. Gentleman, being President of the Local Government Board, asked the Committee to pass the Vote for that Department before he had declared his ultimate decision upon a most important question of policy. That demand was most unreasonable, and it was made more unreasonable by the right hon. Gentleman reiterating the statement that he expected to be able to announce his decision on the 23rd.

Mr. TREVELYAN: No, no.

Mr. T. P. O'CONNOR: That is what I understood the right hon. Gentleman to say.

Mr. TREVELYAN: The Board have called a meeting for the 23rd. I suppose we shall get their answer on the 24th. Suppose they give very clear proof that there was no suspicion of defalcation, or, on the other hand, suppose they thoroughly admit that there was malversation, in that case the matter might be settled in two or three days; but suppose there are still delays and doubts, the Local Government Board would then be entitled to take action of their own. The probable action we should take would be to call upon Mr. Elliott for an explanation.

Mr. T. P. O'CONNOR said, the impression in Ireland was that the Blackrock Commissioners were determined to keep Mr. Elliott in his office, at all risks and at all hazards, by every possible means in their power. He thought the Committee ought to insist on retaining its control over the matter, by postponing the Vote until it had been decided. That was the single point between his hon. Friend and the right hon. Gentleman, and there ought not to be two opinions about it, for his hon. Friend had proved to the hilt that the House of Commons ought to retain this power. The only objection of the right hon. Gentleman was, that there were well-known principles which guided the action of the Local Government Board in such cases, and the Committee would be justified in assuming that the course the Board finally took would be the proper one. No one had a higher opinion of the right hon. Gentleman than he had; but, under the circumstances, he hoped his hon. Friend would press his objection to a Division.

Mr. MOORE said, he desired to make a few remarks upon the Vote generally. There was no doubt an opinion, gathering in all quarters and increasing in volume and size every day, that there must be some radical change in the administration of the Irish Poor Law. He, for one, was inclined to attribute the existing undesirable state of things very much to the action of the Local Government Board, who always displayed a narrow-minded spirit in administering this Vote, and he was satisfied that the present workhouse system worked most unsatisfactorily in the case of the really deserving poor.

Mr. T. P. O'CONNOR expressed a hope that the hon. Gentleman would postpone his remarks upon the general question until the Committee had disposed of the case of Mr. Elliott.

Mr. MOORE said, he had no objection to do so; but it would be absolutely necessary that he could refer to the defects of the present Poor Law administration in Ireland before the Vote was disposed of.

Mr. COURTNEY wished to point out that no Motion for the postponement of the Vote could be made. When the Vote had once been put from the Chair, there were no means of proceeding in the way suggested by the hon. Member for Sligo (Mr. Sexton). What the hon. Member would have to do would be to induce the Government to withdraw the Vote. As he understood the issue between the hon. Member and the right hon. Gentleman the Chief Secretary, it was that the House of Commons should not lose its control over the Vote until it was assured what action the Department intended to take. But what was at present in doubt was not the action of the Department. That had already been fully explained by the Head of the Department; but what was in doubt was the action which might be taken by the Blackrock Commissioners. If the Vote were deferred, it would only be because there was some uncertainty in that respect. He thought the statement of his right hon. Friend on the part of the Local Government Board was perfectly plain and clear, and the course now suggested to be taken was not only inconvenient, but displayed a certain amount of distrust in the *bonâ fides* of the Head of the Department. It was practically contended that the Vote ought to be withdrawn until that distrust was removed; but he failed to see why any distrust whatever should be felt.

MR. T. P. O'CONNOR said, he had not expressed any distrust of the Chief Secretary. What he had said was, that he had no doubt the right hon. Gentleman entertained proper ideas of his duty in the matter, and would be prepared to deal with it rigorously; but he had pronounced no opinion as to the steps which ought to be taken with regard to compelling the Blackrock Commissioners to come to an early decision on the subject of the alleged defalcations, and that in that respect he had displayed a want of energy. The right hon. Gentleman himself, in the course of his remarks, had neither directly stated nor hinted that he was prepared to act with such energy as to compel the Blackrock Commissioners to come to a decision at once.

MR. COURTNEY said, the explanation of the hon. Gentleman was to the effect that he was perfectly satisfied with the *bonâ fide* intentions of the Chief Secretary in dealing with the case on its merits; but, of course, the steps to be taken must depend upon the action of the Blackrock Commissioners. If they reported against Mr. Elliott, of course he would be removed from the Public Service. His right hon. Friend had distinctly assured the Committee that unless all suspicion of defalcation was removed from this public officer, he would at once be informed that his services would not be retained. After a declaration of that kind, and having informed the hon. Member for Sligo (Mr. Sexton) what would be the action of the Local Government Board, he trusted the withdrawal of the Vote would not be persisted in.

MR. SEXTON said, he was obliged for the explanation the Secretary to the Treasury had given on the point of Order—namely, that the postponement of the Vote could not be moved. It was, however, all the same to him (Mr. Sexton) if it were decided that the Vote itself should not be passed at the present moment. He thought the argument of the hon. Gentleman was a somewhat specious one. The right hon. Gentleman said the Local Government Board were committed to the principle on which they would act, and that nothing remained but to ascertain the facts to which that principle was to be applied. Now, he (Mr. Sexton) thought there was something more than that to be considered. The right hon. Gentleman spoke of "defalcation" and "fraud;" but he (Mr. Sexton) did not feel quite sure that he and the Chief Secretary would attach to the word "defalcation" the same meaning. If Mr. Elliott, in the course of a few years, had collected moneys from the Blackrock ratepayers and had given receipts for them, and instead of lodging such sums to the credit of the township in the bank he had put them in his own pocket, and used them for his own purposes, even if he had not forged or falsified any entry or receipt, if he retained in his own possession the moneys of the township and appropriated them to his own use, and was unable to make them good when called upon, he would, in the opinion of hon. Members, be guilty of defalcation. He did not know whether the Chief Secretary so understood defalcation. What was the course which the Blackrock Commissioners had taken? They had made themselves partizans. They had referred the case to a Committee who were carrying on a private investigation. They had converted themselves into a Committee of Liquidators in regard to Mr. Elliott, which they certainly ought not to have done; they had taken over his stocks and shares and houses, and they were now engaged in a vain and futile attempt to realize the amount of his defalcations. There was, therefore, no reason for postponing a decision on the case. Indeed, it ought to have been given long ago. The public proceedings of the Commissioners already revealed the fact that Mr. Elliott owed them £2,600, and that they had only been able to realize from his assets £1,300. That was the broad and glaring fact—that after all Mr. Elliott's assets were realized, £1,300 still remained due to the Commissioners. What more was there necessary to prove defalcation? Was not the fact abundantly proved? What was the meaning of this delay and this shilly-shallying on the part of the Local Government Board? The Local Government Board and the Lord Lieutenant were the only parties who remained unconvinced. The Lord Lieutenant had allowed half-a-year to go by without action, and the Blackrock Commissioners for weeks and weeks had withheld a reply to the question of the Local Government Board whether there had been defalcations or not. He, therefore, felt no confidence that the authorities had the power, even if they had the will, to drag a truthful answer from them; and he certainly had no confidence as to what the result would be if the House of Commons gave up their control over this Vote. This was the only Constitutional occasion for raising the grievance, and as the right hon. Gentleman refused to answer the direct question put to him, he (Mr. Sexton) felt that he had no alternative but to resist the Vote. If he sacrificed the present opportunity, however shameful the ultimate decision in regard to Mr. Elliott might be, he would have surrendered for 12 months the right of raising the question. As they were, in a few days, to have the answer of the Blackrock Commissioners, no practical inconvenience would result from deferring the Vote.

Mr. TREVELYAN said, that, after the speech of the hon. Gentleman, he could not consent to postpone the Vote. The hon. Gentleman had given a colour to the transaction which compelled him to take issue with him regarding the action of the Irish Executive. In the first instance, the hon. Member put a Question upon the Paper containing several important allegations. The Irish Executive referred it to the Blackrock Commissioners, stating they were aware they could not call upon them officially for an answer, but that as it concerned the honour of one of their officers they ought to reply. The Commissioners sent a letter answering the questions categorically, and in the course of their letter it was stated that they had been endeavouring to realize the assets of Mr. Elliot. That was the first intimation which the Irish Executive had implying that Mr. Elliot had been guilty of defalcation. The Commissioners then wished the Government to wait for the Report of a Committee which was then sitting; but as the Report of this Committee did not appear likely to be forthcoming, the Government thought it better to call attention to this statement about the realization of the assets, and to ask what was the meaning of it, and what had been the conduct of Mr. Elliot, in regard to public money, that it should require the Commissioners to realize his assets? That letter was now before the Blackrock Commissioners, and was the letter to which the Government now awaited reply. They had decided that, if a proper answer did not come, they would act on the information they had already received, and call upon Mr. Elliot to explain. He did not understand how the Government could have acted in a more rapid manner. Unquestionably, in doing what they had done they had broken through the usual rules which guided the action of independent Departments. Instead of waiting until the case was brought before them, they had put it forward themselves, and had insisted upon having an answer to the specific charges made against Mr. Elliot. With regard to the course which the hon. Member wished the Local Government Board to take in reference to this Vote, he must ask the hon. Member what it implied? There were a large number of Votes in the Estimates which concerned the salaries paid in various Departments, which had an enormous amount of business to do. But take the Department of the Local Government Board in Ireland. There had been no time in which, in the House of Commons, the proceedings of Public Departments were so carefully watched, and there had been no time when so many controversies were pending between certain persons and the Department. For instance, the hon. Member for Monaghan (Mr. Healy) was taking a great interest in the action of a Board of Guardians in Donegal. A letter of his (Mr. Trevelyan's) was now before that Board, and whatever the answer to that letter might be, he should have to take some action upon it. There was no period when they could not find a subject of pending controversy between private Members of the House and the Local Government Board, with regard to nearly every Public Department; and if they consented to tie up this Vote because a certain controversy was pending, in a few days they would be asked to tie it up on account of another. Therefore, when they approached the consideration of the Vote again, some other pretext would be put forward for putting it off; it would be said that there was some other question to be settled, which hon. Members wished to have settled in a particular way. No good object could be attained by deferring the present Vote, because he had already explained, in the clearest manner, the line of action the Local Government Board intended to take.

MR. MOORE said, that as he understood it would not be in Order to postpone the Vote, it would simplify matters if he were to move the reduction of the Vote by the sum of £1,000.

THE CHAIRMAN: Does the hon. Member make that proposition?

MR. MOORE: I have no wish to interfere with the action of my hon. Friends.

MR. T. P. O'CONNOR said, he would appeal to his hon. Friend not to interpose at present. As the Government were disinclined to give way, it was desirable that a distinct and definite understanding should be arrived at. When this matter had been fully discussed, there would be nothing to prevent his hon. Friend from making his Motion. He (Mr. O'Connor) wished to say a few words in answer to the Chief Secretary. When the Secretary to the Treasury addressed the Committee, he confined himself to the difference of opinion between the Irish Members and the Chief Secretary as to whether the Vote should be postponed or not. The Chief Secretary seemed to entertain the same view they did as to the principle upon which the charges against Mr. Elliott should be decided; but the conversation which had since taken place showed that there was even an element of uncertainty as to whether the Chief Secretary and the Irish Members really did agree upon the important question which had been raised by the hon. Member for Sligo (Mr. Sexton). He distinctly challenged the right hon. Gentleman to give his idea of what constituted defalcation.

MR. TREVELYAN: I quite agree with the definition of the hon. Member for Sligo (Mr. Sexton) on that point. Defalcation is a definite crime, and it has been extremely well put by the hon. Member.

MR. T. P. O'CONNOR said, he might, then, assume that his hon. Friend's idea was satisfactory, and a correct definition. What his hon. Friend insisted upon was that defalcation meant the withholding of money by a rate collector, even though he might have made it good afterwards. That was his hon. Friend's definition; and, therefore, it had already been proved that defalcation had occurred. The whole action of the Chief Secretary dated from the time the Blackrock Town Commissioners were attempting to realize the assets of this gentleman; and, therefore, it was admitted on all sides, according to the interpretation of his hon. Friend and the right hon. Gentleman, that defalcation must have taken place. His hon. Friend had accused the Commissioners of sluggishness, and he joined his hon. Friend in reiterating the charge, and in applying it to the Government as well. Elliott was a rate collector of the South Dublin Union, and, therefore, immediately under the control of the right hon. Gentleman. If, therefore, the Chief Secretary had no power over him as collector for the Blackrock Commissioners, he had perfect power to dismiss him as collector of the South Dublin Union; yet, though the right hon. Gentleman knew Elliott's position for two or three months, he had taken no action whatever. The right hon. Gentleman knew, at least, two months ago that there was a *primâ facie* case of defalcation against this man, according to his own definition of that offence, and the officer was directly at the disposal of the right hon. Gentleman.

MR. TREVELYAN: Not two or three months ago. I had no knowledge of the matter before the Question addressed to me by the hon. Member for Sligo (Mr. Sexton). That was the first occasion on which the attention of the Local Government Board was called to the matter.

MR. SEXTON: The Local Government Board had knowledge of the essential facts at a date long anterior to my Question.

MR. T. P. O'CONNOR said, he thought it was perfectly clear that for two or three months, at least, this man was retained in a position under the control of the Local Government Board, although a *primâ facie* case of defalcation rested against him. Elliott held two positions—one as rate collector of the South Dublin Union, which placed him directly under the control of the right hon. Gentleman and the Local Government Board, and the other as rate collector for the Blackrock Town Commissioners. Therefore, as rate collector for the South Dublin Union, he could be dismissed at any moment by the Chief Secretary, although, as collector for the Blackrock Commissioners, he was, of course, independent of the right hon. Gentleman. The right hon. Gentleman had, however, fully accepted the canon that an official who misconducted himself in one office thereby incapacitated himself from serving in another; and, therefore, if Mr. Elliott had been guilty of defalcation in connection with Blackrock, he ought not to be retained for the South Dublin Union. It was an admitted fact that the charge of defalcation against this gentleman had been brought indirectly before the attention of the Local Government Board months ago, and even two months ago in the House of Commons; and yet the right hon. Gentleman asked his hon. Friend to give up the only Constitutional means he had of questioning the propriety of retaining this man in the Public Service by allowing the Vote to pass, and thus removing the matter from the supervision and control of the House of Commons before the right hon. Gentleman gave his decision finally upon a most important question of principle, which could only be raised in connection with the Vote. He thought it was utterly unreasonable for the right hon. Gentleman to expect them to forego their right to pronounce an opinion upon this important question; and he therefore thought that his hon. Friend was justified in pressing the point.

MR. MOORE said, he had no wish to interrupt his hon. Friends in this interesting discussion, and he hoped the question might be brought to an issue between the Treasury Bench and the hon. Member for Sligo (Mr. Sexton). He had risen, however, to move the reduction of the Vote by the sum of £1,000, in order that he might be in a position to make a general statement as to the working of the Poor Law in Ireland, and the treatment of sick, aged, and infirm paupers, especially lunatics, whose condition was the most pitiable of all. The general feeling throughout Ireland was that the institutions known as workhouses were rapidly degenerating into cesspools of crime, vice, laziness, and hereditary pauperism, instead of being suitable asylums for those who had a legitimate claim upon society for support. What they in Ireland wanted was that these workhouses should be made vastly more strict and penal in their administration as regarded the idle, worthless, and dissolute classes, and that they should be made more useful and humane for those who had a legitimate claim upon the community for support and assistance. According to a Return which had just been presented, the total number of inmates in the workhouses was 56,572; and the Committee would be astonished to hear that 20 per cent were described as able-bodied persons. He thought that was a fact well worthy of attention. The number of men whose misconduct was sheltered within these institutions was not only very large, but absolutely monstrous. Many of them were brought up in pauperism; they went out of the workhouses for a short time, but invariably returned again; and when asked what it was that brought them back, they said that they had come to regard it as their old home. Even men, who had gone out as soldiers to India, on their return to Ireland re-entered the workhouses. They had been so accustomed to lead an idle, worthless life, that the moment honest toil and honourable labour become irksome, they returned to their old home, although it might appear extraordinary that they would desire, of their own accord, to return to short rations and uncomfortable accommodation. He presumed that a disinclination to work was at the bottom of it, and that after a very short time they relapsed into habits of idleness. Out of the total of 56,000 inmates, 12,000 were entered as able-bodied. As the figures were taken in the winter—namely, in February, 1883—of course, that would indicate a time of year when the weather was severe, and a good many people were out of work; but, at the same time, during the winter in question there was abundance of food to be obtained, and, therefore, the one fact would counterbalance the other. He strongly objected to the way in which the workhouses were made to shelter vice and profligacy. The number of women of bad character who inhabited them was perfectly astounding. Out of 30,000 women in the workhouses, 20,000 were returned as the mothers of illegitimate children. He believed that by far the great majority of women who visited these institutions were women of bad character; and he was of opinion that in cases of such gross immorality the ratepayers ought not to be bound to provide for them in the way they were provided for now. He felt that some stronger obligation of the law to throw the burden of these illegitimate children upon the fathers was necessary; and there ought to be some provision to prevent the pauper class from constantly converting the workhouses into a refuge in the winter, and going out of them in the summer. In the Northern workhouses the number of women of bad character who made use of them was very extraordinary; they went into them only for a few days. He remembered a case in connection with the Belfast Workhouse where one of these women was reported to have been an inmate of the workhouse 57 times. Persons of that class were called "revolvers;" they were kept and maintained at the expense of the public, and they treated the workhouses simply as lodging-houses. He complained of the laxity and want of vigour displayed in the administration of the Poor Law in Ireland. Idle people were allowed to frequent the workhouses, and to throw themselves on the rates, without any attempt being made to discriminate between their cases and those of the deserving poor. He had spoken of the large number of able-bodied persons who became inmates of the workhouses. A few years ago he visited the South Dublin Union, and noticing a powerful man passing into the house, he asked who he was. He was told that he was a pauper, who was engaged in some manual work in the workhouse, and that he had never been out of it during his life, although he was 45 years of age. He asked if there were many more men in the same position, and he was told that there were many who had never been out of the workhouse, but who had been born, bred, and reared there. He thought there could not be a more striking illustration of the evils of the system than the fact that persons were allowed to grow old in the workhouses, and to become a burden all their lives to the ratepayers, many of whom were in circumstances very little above pauperism themselves. He believed the hospitals of Ireland were very much behind what they ought to be, although they had made considerable advance; and with regard to the religious institutions in many of the workhouses, they had the assistance of religious persons who undertook the care of the children. He was sorry to say that they had not had very much assistance from the Local Government Board in that direction; and, indeed, as far as his experience went, he never remembered the Local Government Board doing anything whatever for the benefit of the poor. He complained, further, of the want of classification. Young persons were constantly placed in the common room with idlers and criminals. There was no other room they could frequent; and although the deserving poor were invariably treated with scant courtesy, he thought that some such provision ought to be made for the aged poor as that which was made in France. In France, when an aged person fell into poverty, and was unable to provide for himself, the State undertook to make provision for him. The principle acted upon was that these persons had a right to relief unless they had brought their pauperism upon themselves by vice or laziness. When once a man fell into a condition that he was no longer able to help himself, he ought to be supported at the expense of the State. Then, as regarded pauper lunatics, there was much room for reform. Their condition was more distressing than that of any other class. There were 1,800 of these lunatics who were inmates of the workhouses. Their treatment was a matter upon which more than one Commission had reported. He remembered a person who gave up the best part of his life to visiting these institutions, and in trying to do something for the benefit of his fellow-men, finding one of these poor idiots chained to a pillar.

MR. KENNY: In what district?

MR. MOORE said, the incident he referred to occurred in the county of Clare some years ago, and the condition of the lunatics who were inmates of the workhouses generally was such as to call for immediate attention and reform. There was a wide distinction to be drawn between the lunatics in the county lunatic asylums and those in the workhouses. No institutions in the Kingdom were better managed than the Irish county asylums, and he had known frequent cases in which persons had been recovered from what was supposed to be a perfectly hopeless state of lunacy.

The provision, however, which was made for the lunatics received in the Irish workhouses was most defective. There was no attempt whatever to cure them, and they were left to live their wretched lives in a hopeless state of imbecility. Of course they were harmless, because if a pauper lunatic attempted a crime he was at once transferred to the county lunatic asylums. He came next to the instruction given in the Irish workhouse schools. According to the last Return, which, however, was not very recent, there were 42 teachers engaged in instructing the children in the workhouse schools, the whole of whom were unclassed and uncertificated, notwithstanding the ready means provided by the law for ascertaining the capability and qualifications of these persons to tecah. He thought the matter was one for inquiry at the hands of the Local Government Board, who had a right to see that no unqualified teacher was appointed. They ought to refuse their sanction to such appointments; but he was sorry to say that he had witnessed in his own district the slowness of the Local Government Board in dealing with proved cases of incapacity. Where the teacher was incapable of performing the duties required of him, the Local Government Board ought to come forward and imperatively put an end to his employment. As to the inspection of the workhouse schools, it was of a two-fold character, and consequently came to nothing. The inspection of the school building came under the Poor Law, whereas the inspection of the educational qualifications of the children came under the National Board. The Inspector of the National Board went down to inspect the schools; but he had no authority to enforce his orders, and therefore the standard of education was below par, and the condition of the children was one of entire neglect; because there was no authority whatever, either direct or indirect, to enforce a better state of things. Very numerous complaints had been made to the Local Government Board, but without effect. If the inspection of the workhouse schools was was not to be an absolute farce the Inspector ought to have power to enforce his orders. As he had said, the inspection was of a two-fold character. The school buildings and materials, and the condition of the children were under the Local Government Board, whereas the educational arrangements were under the National Board; and the result of this two-fold inspection was that the interests of the children were altogether neglected. No doubt, the great defect in the Irish workhouses was that the children were brought up in idleness from the very first day they entered the house; and hence it was found that, even in the case of men who had served the Queen with distinction, it was almost impossible to make them respectable members of society, and they consequently returned to what they regarded as their home. Some of the children were occasionally employed in picking a few weeds, or in some of the minor branches of agricultural labour; but there was no pretence of teaching them any industrial work whatever. The children were brought up in idleness, and this idleness acted upon them in a most deplorable manner, owing to the associations among which they were thrown. There was only one corridor and one recreation ground, and the morals of the children were corrupted by requiring them to mix with able-bodied paupers, whose whole life had been spent in vice and immorality. It was impossible to keep the whole of the pauper inmates of a workhouse in the same building without some contamination; but in the Irish workhouses there was little or no classification at all. He had watched the matter himself and had inquired into it closely, and he was prepared to say that there was no real classification whatever. He was only talking the other day to the manager of one of the reformatory schools in Ireland. That gentleman spoke of the satisfaction and pleasure his work gave him, when he found that many of those who passed through his hands were brought to a better state of mind and became useful members of society; but he added, that of all the classes which came under his hand, the most difficult to deal with, or inspire with any sense of self-respect, were the pauper criminals. When the children were hired out to farmers for a month or two in the summer time they were lost sight of, and nobody seemed to care what became of them afterwards. The Local Government Board had given statistics to show the number of children who had been hired out to farmers in that manner; but there was no confidence to be placed in them. The children themselves were sent out recklessly—hired out for short periods to persons who had no interest in the children themselves, and who could not be expected to place them in such a position in life as would make provision for their future. The Vice President of the Local Government Board not long ago told a Royal Commission that out of 300 children sent out from the South Dublin Union 78 per cent did not return. The right hon. Baronet the Member for East Gloucestershire (Sir Michael Hicks-Beach) asked the witness what reason he had for supposing that that 78 per cent of the children were doing well; and his only explanation was that as they did not turn up at the workhouse it might safely be presumed that they were going on all right. The right hon. Baronet asked if it were not equally possible that this 78 per cent, in regard to whose future such confident hopes were entertained, might be in prison; and this gentleman representing the Local Government Board, after having made a statement that 78 per cent turned out satisfactorily, was bound to confess that his whole reason for believing they had become good citizens was that he knew nothing whatever about them. That showed the extent to which the bigotry of officialism would descend in order to bolster up a bad system. He did not wish to press the Committee further. The House had been saved from an infliction from him on the same subject last year by a "Count-out." He had now had an opportunity of laying the matter before the Committee, and he trusted they would turn their attention to this great social question. He believed that so long as they required these poor people to be brought up in a common life with adult paupers the consequence would inevitably be that they would become criminals. What he wished and hoped was that, sooner or later, the Government would take up the question of the reform of the workhouse system in Ireland. If necessary, he trusted that a Royal Commission would be issued, so that they might get at the bottom of the Poor Law question. The feeling was very strong in Ireland that something ought to be done. They did not ask the Treasury for anything; but it was their own money which they proposed to spend in bettering the condition of these poor people. Surely they ought to be entrusted with the expenditure of their own money.

THE CHAIRMAN: Does the hon. Gentleman move the reduction of the Vote?

MR. MOORE: Yes; by the sum of £1,000.

Motion made, and Question proposed,

"That a sum, not exceeding £108,544, be granted to Her Majesty, to complete the sum necessary to defray the Charge which will come in course of payment during the year ending on the 31st day of March 1885, for the Salaries and Expenses of the Local Government Board in Ireland. including various Grants in Aid of Local Taxation."—(*Mr. Moore.*)

MR. KENNY admitted that the administration of the Irish workhouses was not satisfactory; but he could not altogether agree with the hon. Member in the charge of immorality which he had brought against the female inmates of workhouses. He was well aware that there were many young men in the workhouses whose moral character was not irreproachable; but the vast majority of the women in the workhouses were old women who were there through poverty, against whom no reasonable charge of immorality could be brought. The hon. Member had cited an instance of a Union in the North of Ireland—in the county of Tyrone; but he should be sorry to take that Union as a criterion, as it was well known that that was the most immoral part of the country. It must be borne in mind that these workhouses were the only refuges for women in Ireland who were forced to betake themselves to them for a time; and it was unfair to draw a conclusion of general immorality from a single instance. There was, however, another offence which was, to a great extent, perpetrated in connection with the Irish workhouses—namely, the practice of smuggling whisky into them. Friends who came to visit the pauper inmates constantly brought whisky with them. It was also a fact that many of the *employés* in the workhouses were persons of objectionable character; and, owing to the introduction of whisky, and a neglect of duty on the part of the officials, no doubt scenes of drunkenness did take place. He was glad to find that in the South of Ireland, at any rate, the introduction of nuns as nurses into the workhouses had caused a beneficent change in the morals of the inmates. It was a practice which could not be too highly recommended and too warmly advocated, and he urged upon all the Boards of Guardians in Ireland the desirability of securing the services of nuns as ordinary nurses. He had no doubt it would remove a good many of the very discreditable scandals which were not unfrequently brought to light in Ireland. A very important question had been raised by the hon. Member in regard to the manner in which the children in these workhouses were brought up; but although the teachers employed in the workhouse schools might not have received class certificates, he did not think that any serious charge of incapacity could be brought against them. He had seen a number of workhouse children in a variety of places who had been remarkably well educated as far as reading, writing, and arithmetic were concerned; but he complained of the absence of technical education. The children were taught to read and write, and so on; but the idea of teaching them a trade never appeared to enter the mind of the Local Government Board; and when they went from the workhouses the only employment they were fit for was that of farm servants. All the deserving boys went out as farm labourers; very few of them going into the cities, and the girls were either sent into the country as farm servants or into the towns as housemaids. He thought the workhouses in Ireland were institutions which afforded excellent facilities for the establishment of technical schools. If these young lads were taught trades which they could turn to account afterwards, it would go a long way towards defraying the expense of their maintenance in the workhouses, because they would be learnt how to occupy a very useful future life, instead of being consigned to the miserable fate of a farm servant until they could scrape some money together to take them away to America or one of the Colonies, there to be nothing more than hewers of wood and drawers of water. It was an undoubted fact that children who were brought up in the workhouses had a direct stigma attached to them. They were neglected by the Guardians, or by the Local Government Board, who really directed the actions of the Guardians. Their technical education was altogether neglected. They were taught nothing but to read and write, and nothing was left for them but the most menial occupations when they left the workhouse. He thought the subject of the technical education of the children in the Irish workhouses was really most important; and he was of opinion that the Government ought to take it in hand, and that the Chief Secretary, as President of the Irish Local Government Board, and those gentlemen who acted with him, should take into consideration some scheme for the technical education of these children which would give them a better chance of future success in life.

Colonel COLTHURST said, he agreed with the last speaker as to the bad state of technical education; but he desired to express his opinion that a great deal could be done by the Guardians as the law now stood in Ireland. Where the law was at fault was in not empowering the Local Government Board to act where the Guardians would not act. It was very well known that the Guardians had power to board out the children, and boarding out had been found to be the best way of disposing of orphan and deserted children from the workhouses. But what were the facts of the case? In more than one-half of the Unions of Ireland the Guardians did not board out a single child; but they kept them in the workhouses in the state in which the hon. Member for Clonmel (Mr. Moore) had described. That was the fault of the Guardians, who had full power to board them out. He thought the hon. Member had misunderstood the evidence of the Vice President of the Local Government Board before the Commission of which he (Colonel Colthurst) was a Member. The evidence of Mr. Robinson was to this effect—that, as far as his experience went, where the boarding out system was practised the results were invariably good, and the children in many cases had been adopted by the families to which they were sent. He did not know any reason why the system should not be adopted in every Union in Ireland. As to industrial training, it was difficult to carry it out in the small Unions; but he saw no reason why there should not be Poor Law Schools in Ireland as well as in England, where the children could be collected and taught trades. In the large Union of North Dublin some years ago, a real attempt was made to give industrial training to the children; but the master—a man of great experience—told him himself that, in spite of all he did, he never wished to see a child placed in the workhouse. There could be no doubt that boarding out was the proper thing to do. It stood to reason that if they were boarded out among the people from whom they sprung, they would be restored to the condition which Providence intended them to occupy. He hoped his right hon. Friend the Chief Secretary would at least do what he could to give effect to some of the suggestions which had been made by the hon. Member for Clonmel. Among other things, he would ask the Government, when they dealt with the question of Union rating in Ireland next Session, to give effect to the recommendations of the Committee, so as to give unadulterated Union rating, and not the Union rating proposed in the Bill submitted to Parliament two years ago, in which the administration of out-door relief was excluded from the operation of the Bill. If his right hon. Friend would give a satisfactory answer on that subject, he might spare him (Colonel Colthurst) the necessity of bringing forward a Motion which stood in his name for Friday.

COLONEL NOLAN expressed a hope that the Chief Secretary would answer the questions which had been brought before the Committee in the valuable speech of his hon. Friend the Member for Clonmel (Mr. Moore). He (Colonel Nolan) only proposed to discuss the workhouse system in connection with one particular point. Of course, his hon. Friend knew a good deal about the poor, having paid considerable attention to the subject, and having brought in two or three Bills to remedy the position of children in workhouses; but he thought that there had been one omission in all the speeches which had been delivered upon the question—namely, that no one had gone into the question of pounds, shillings, and pence. Special education and training for workhouse children, together with looking after them when they left the workhouse, would be a very excellent plan if they had unlimited funds to draw upon; and he believed his hon. Friend had brought in a Bill to make provision for deaf and dumb children, by which they were to be sent to institutions specially provided and paid for. No doubt they would be liberally treated and properly looked after there; but they would become extremely expensive to the Unions, and he hoped that in any scheme which might be put forward, and any pressure that might be placed upon the Chief Secretary, the question of the ratepayers would not be altogether neglected. At the present moment the rates were exceedingly heavy; and he had no desire to rush hastily into any project which would largely increase the rates. He thought that was a point which it was quite possible to reconcile with the good administration of the workhouse system. He did not think that many of these children would be better off if they had more opportunities for learning a trade. He did not agree with the hon. Member for Ennis (Mr. Kenny), or the hon. Member for Clonmel, that their employment as herds or farm labourers was bad work for these children. On the contrary, he thought it was proper work for them in the agricultural districts. The great bulk of the community in those districts had to herd stock, or attend to farming operations; and he did not see why these children should not be put out to the same occupation in an agricultural community. Certainly, they ought not to be made pets of, or put in a better position than the children of people who managed to keep out of the workhouse. During the last six or seven years, instead of increasing the industrial schools in Ireland, the Government had limited them. That was not the policy of the present Government alone, but in their action they had merely followed the policy of their Predecessors. Six or seven years ago it was announced that no contribution from the Treasury would be given except to certain existing schools; and the Government had carefully limited the contributions which they gave even to existing schools. He had himself applied for an industrial school in Clifden—at least, he had been made the medium of communication on several occasions between the district and the Government; but he was sorry to say that, although that district was very much in want of an industrial school for boys, the necessary assistance had been repeatedly refused by the Government. He thought if the Local Government Board would extend the system of industrial schools in Ireland, a great many of the objections which were now urged by different Members would be met. Not only might they extend the system, but it was also desirable that they should change the law. The law which at present existed was absolutely absurd. It was necessary that a child should commit some offence, even if it were only begging, before he could be sent to an industrial school; and it was perfectly well known that the solemn farce of committing a child for some trifling offence was frequently gone through in order to get him admitted into one of the existing industrial schools. He did not think it right that the committal of a crime should be a qualification for admission to an industrial school, and he regretted to say that it was exactly the same in regard to the lunatic asylums. Criminal lunatics were sent to the county asylums, but other lunatics were not; and perfectly harmless lunatics suffered in consequence. He was strongly of opinion that this foolish rule ought to be abolished. There was one point in which he differed from the hon. and gallant Member for the County of Cork. (Colonel Colthurst)—namely, that the Local Government Board should have power, in an ordinary case, to override the decision of the Guardians. Of course, if there was a case in which religious prejudices had been allowed to operate, or a pauper had been unfairly treated in regard to his religion, the Local Government Board should have power to demand explanations, and even to override the decision of the Guardians. But for the decisions of a Board of Guardians, who, as a general rule, looked after the finance of a district, to be overridden by the Local Government Board, sitting at a great distance from the Union, was absurd, and would be so great a reflection upon the Guardians, that he hoped no Government would adopt the suggestion. There was another point in which he should like to receive an explanation from the Chief Secretary, and it had reference to the possibility of Ireland being visited by cholera. He trusted that precautions would be taken to prevent the spread of disease, and he hoped Parliament would not be allowed to break up before hon. Members were told exactly what was intended to be done in Ireland. Had the Local Government Board any policy in regard to the rural workhouses? Did they intend that the cholera patients should go into the workhouse hospitals, or be placed in detached hospitals? He was in favour himself of having them placed in detached hospitals as far as possible. He believed that in many cases it would be a good policy to erect temporary huts at a distance from the Union Workhouse, and such temporary huts could be so arranged as to prevent the affection from being communicated through bad water or otherwise, and thus of reducing the chance of the disease spreading to a minimum. He should be glad to know from the Chief Secretary what it was intended to do with the hospital question? What he was afraid might happen was this—that if the cholera visited Ireland, many clever letters and minutes might be written with the object of throwing the responsibility upon the Guardians, and of avoiding the responsibility themselves. He did not care who was responsible—whether the Local Government Board or the Guardians—but his idea was that if the cholera came into the country it must be met by some Central Body, who would be in a position to obtain every kind of knowledge and information, and the Local Government Board would certainly be the best Body for such a purpose. What he would propose to the Local Government Board, in reference to the rural districts, was that they should have one or two temporary hospitals. He would not say what kind of hospitals; but they ought to be cheaply erected, as the expense would be a serious matter for consideration. The merest hut would be quite sufficient. He thought a model ought to be erected at some central station in Dublin, and that some mechanic should be told off, who knew how to put the buildings up. There were more than 160 Unions in Ireland, and if they were required to go to the expense of erecting temporary hospitals, probably nothing might be done by the time the emergency arose. What he asked was a very simple matter, which would cost the Government very little. The cholera might not visit Ireland after all; but if it came a little nearer, he hoped the Government would make some arrangement of that kind;

and, therefore, he trusted that the Chief Secretary would answer the question he had put.

MR. H. H. FOWLER wished to put a question or two in regard to this Vote; but before he did so he would express his regret that the hon. Member for Clonmel (Mr. Moore) had moved the reduction of the Vote before they had exhausted the discussion on the subject introduced by the hon. Member for Sligo (Mr. Sexton). He thought the feeling on that side of the House was that his right hon. Friend the Chief Secretary should withdraw the Vote for the present; and if it was impossible to do so, that the discussion would be allowed to go on fairly upon its merits, so that the Irish Members should retain their control over the very unpleasant issue which had been raised. He was sure his right hon. Friend would not misunderstand him. He did not put it as a question of confidence in the Irish Executive. He thought there was no man in that House who had the slightest doubt that the Chief Secretary was actuated in all these things by the highest and most advanced standard of official honour, and any decision arrived at by him would command the confidence of the House. But he wanted to tell his right hon. Friend—he did not know whether his right hon. Friend was aware of it—that there was growing up in the House, as well as in other quarters, a distrust of the permanent Irish Executive; and he should be sorry that any question should arise which should put hon. Members in conflict with the right hon. Gentleman himself, or with Lord Spencer. He thought the time was arriving when the action of the permanent Irish Executive would be exposed to the very serious criticism, not only of the House, but of the country. Let him take the case they had heard to-night. He knew nothing whatever of the case; but here was a man charged with defalcation—in England they would call it embezzlement. Whether the man was guilty or not he did not know—he knew nothing about the facts of the case—but he was charged with having appropriated the public money, from time to time, during a period which extended over a series of years. When the fraud was found out, the deficiency amounted to between £2,000 and £3,000; and a certain body of Commissioners in Ireland, adopting a course of action which, in England, would be regarded as compounding a felony, still retained the services of the defaulter, and proceeded to realize his assets. No prolonged discussion of the matter was needed. By return of post it would be known—aye or no—whether this collector had those rates or had paid them to the authorities, or whether he was short in his accounts; and if he had retained them for 48 hours beyond the proper time, he ought not to be allowed to remain in the Public Service. He would say no more than to suggest that the right hon. Gentleman should postpone the Report on the Vote until the decision of the Government could be made known, so that not only the Irish, but the English Members, might have a full discussion if they were not satisfied. He desired now to ask for a few items of information as to what he might call the extraordinary amount of this Vote. He could not help contrasting the Irish Local Government Board with the Local Government Board in England. The English Local Government Board had to deal with 25,000,000 of people; the Irish Local Government Board with 5,000,000. In England the highest official, after the President—who was a Cabinet Minister—was a Permanent Secretary, at £1,500 a-year; but in Ireland there was a Vice President with £2,000, a Medical Commissioner with £1,200, another Commissioner with £1,200, a Secretary with £900, and an Assistant Secretary with £600. The difference between the cost of the permanent staff in England and Ireland was almost inappreciable, although the amount of the work done in England was at least three times as much. The time had arrived when attention should be called to the growing extravagance of the Irish Administration in all its parts. He would now take another point. In Ireland there were 14 Inspectors, while in England there were 23; but look at the disproportion in the amounts about to be voted for the personal and travelling expenses of these gentlemen. In England 23 Inspectors took £4,698 as their expenses, while 14 Inspectors in Ireland required £4,020. Then, if he came to the salaries of the Medical Inspectors, in England 3,520 Medical Officers cost £143,000, while 1,064 Medical Officers, or about one-third in

Ireland, cost £74,000. The same thing prevailed through all these Irish Votes; and, in his opinion, the whole Irish Administration was economically and financially, but he hoped not morally, in an unsatisfactory state.

Mr. MOORE protested against the statement of the hon. Member for Wolverhampton (Mr. H. H. Fowler) that he had stepped in between the Committee and the hon. Member for Sligo (Mr. Sexton). He thought nobody could have gone further than he did, seeing that on three occasions he had broken off his speech and discontinued his statement, in order to allow hon. Members an opportunity of going on with the previous subject. Even when his hon. Friend the Member for Galway (Mr. T. P. O'Connor) made a last appeal to the Chief Secretary to postpone the Vote, he positively waited in his seat for a reply. The complaint, therefore, of the hon. Member for Wolverhampton had no foundation whatever.

Mr. SEXTON said, that the moment the reduction of the Vote was moved all chance of the withdrawal of it was put aside. He wished to thank the hon. Member for Wolverhampton (Mr. H. H. Fowler) for the frank and effective speech he had delivered. In a few words he had applied the common sense of an English Member to the narrative he (Mr. Sexton) had given to the House, and he had swept away the cobwebs with which the Chief Secretary sought to cover the case of Mr. Elliott. He hoped the suggestion of the hon. Member would be adopted, and that the Report of the Vote would be postponed until the decision of the Local Government Board was made known. In the meantime he hoped the Chief Secretary would rigidl insist upon the principle he had laid down being carried out—namely, that the Executive should suffer no further delay to take place in eliciting the real facts of the case; and if they found that this officer had appropriated the money of the public that they would remove him at once from the public service. So far the case rested entirely with the right hon. Gentleman. He quite agreed with the several speakers who had recently addressed the Committee as to the neglect of the industrial training of children in the Irish workhouse schools. Indeed, industrial training was neglected in all the primary schools in Ireland, although there was no country where it was so much required. It was of no use to depend upon those whose duty it was to provide the rates, because a good many of them were in very little better condition than the paupers themselves. No matter how urgent the need for reform, they must always consider it as an equation they had to deal with; and however desirous they were of improving the administration of the Poor Law they must take care that the financial burden was not made too heavy a load for the ratepayers to bear. There was another matter in relation to the management of workhouses, to which he wished to call attention. He referred to the decency of religious worship, and the religious training of the young. He had more knowledge of the South of Ireland than the North; and in his opinion, where the Catholics had a controlling power on the Boards, the interests of the Protestant minority were wisely and generously cared for; but in the North of Ireland, where the Catholics on the Boards were in a helpless minority, the treatment given to Catholic adults and children was far different. In the case of the Newtownards Workhouse, there was a Protestant chaplain, and the Protestant and Presbyterian inmates had religious instruction and worship provided for them. But there was no Catholic chaplain, and the consequence was that the children were put out of the school into a yard while religious instruction was given to the rest; and at night in the dormitories, when the Protestant and Presbyterian children were going through their prayers, the Catholic children were locked outside the door until the operation was over. It often happened that, on leaving the workhouse, the children were placed with Protestant masters, the result of which was the complete uprooting of their religious faith. He submitted that the Local Government Board ought to apply themselves to this question of providing for the religious instruction of youth and the common decencies of religious worship. In the same Board, although the Rubric of the Catholic religion required decent order for the celebration of Mass, the base economy of the Board was such that the priest was obliged to celebrate it with an old table furbished up as an altar. The Local Government Board had power, if they were inclined to exercise it, to provide for religious worship in the workhouse schools and for the decent religious instruction of the young. He wished, next, to say a word as to the action of the Local Government Board in dealing with contested elections under the Poor Law. At a contested election at Drumcliff, in the county of Sligo, it was reported to the Board that the candidate who obtained the largest number of votes, in defiance of the law, went to the houses of two of the voters and took possession of the voting papers which had been left by the police, which he kept in his possession for 24 hours. It was an illegal act for which the law provided a penalty. The right hon. Gentleman told the House that because the gentleman in question had a majority of votes sufficient to seat him on the Board of Guardians the Local Government Board had not interfered. No matter how great the majority was which that candidate obtained, he ought not to have been allowed to sit on the Board, as he had committed an illegal act, for which the Local Government Board ought to have prosecuted him. It was no answer to say that the defeated candidate could have brought an action against him. The Department charged with the conduct of the election was the Department which ought to have taken the initiative. He asked the right hon. Gentleman upon what ground of common sense he justified the action of the Local Government Board in refusing to interfere, and in refraining from exacting the full penalty for such an offence? In the case of another contested election, it was proved at the inquiry held by the Inspector that forged proxy papers were issued. The Returning Officer distinctly reported that forged papers were sent in to him, and there had been needless delay in reporting upon it. Before the debate closed, he hoped the Chief Secretary would explain whether the Local Government Board were exercising their powers in finding out how the proxy papers came to be forged, so that the forger, whoever he might have been, might be prosecuted and punished. Turning next to the Gweedore evictions, he wished to point out that 200 men, women, and children had been recently evicted on the estate of Mr. Wybrant Olpherts, in some cases for one, and in others for two years' rent, and were allowed to lie in the ditches for three days and three nights; and although he was contradicted in that House, he had the authority of the parish priest for saying that it was not until the fifth day that the relieving officer came with some vehicles to take the unfortunate people to the workhouse. For the purpose of embarrassing the tenants, the landlord took his proceedings in one of the Superior Courts, and by so doing materially added to the amounts due. The same relieving officer filled the double office of relieving officer and gombeen man, or seller of meal, exacting from the poor people who were driven to the verge of ruin the highest rates. He would like to know whether that was a combination of officers that the Local Government Board were prepared to tolerate; and whether the man who supplied the people with meal at excessive rates should be the same man who was to represent a public Department in relieving them the moment they were turned out-of-doors? The law allowed six months for redemption. These poor people had crops in the land from which they were evicted, and their only hope lay in selling those crops and redeeming their holdings within the statutory six months, by scraping enough together to satisfy the demands of the landlord. In order to watch the crops which were growing in the ground it was necessary that some member of the family should be left on the spot. The Legislature allowed that the persons evicted might get four weeks' outdoor relief; but the evicting landlord, being also Chairman of the Dunfanaghy Board of Guardians, refused to accept a motion to that effect. The Board refused, in the first place, to give any outdoor relief, and even went farther, and decided that no wife should be admitted to the workhouse unless her husband was admitted also, thereby preventing the poor men from taking care of their holdings during the period when they might be redeemed. The law said that the husband might remain outside for the purpose of watching the farm, and seeing that the crops were not destroyed; but the Board of Guardians made themselves the instruments of the tyrannical will of the landlord, and said the husband must come in also, and leave the farm unattended, or the wife and children would be turned out on the roadside to starve. What happened?

When a motion was made to give four weeks' relief to these unfortunate people, Mr. Wybrant Olpherts, this evicting landlord, taking advantage of some quibble which the right hon. Gentleman had endeavoured to explain, ruled that the motion could not be put. He accused the Local Government Board of being supine and neglectful in the discharge of their duties. He contended that when the poor people in Ireland, driven to despair and penury, were unable to meet their engagements, by reason of oppressive rents, the least the Local Government Board could do was to compel their own officials to act impartially, and neither allow the gombeen man to be the relieving officer, or the evicting landlord to preside at the Board of Guardians, with power to refuse the dole which the Guardians were willing to give.

Mr. T. P. O'CONNOR concurred with his hon. Friend the Member for Sligo (Mr. Sexton) in thanking the hon. Member for Wolverhampton (Mr. H. H. Fowler) for adding to the charge they had made against this Department regarding Mr. Elliott the force of his deserved reputation in the House. He had risen now, however, upon another point, as he presumed it would be convenient for the Chief Secretary to reply upon every question that might be submitted to him. He hoped, when the right hon. Gentleman came to deal with the case of Mr. Elliott, that he would be able to give assurances that it would be dealt with not only justly, but promptly. The subject to which he desired to call the attention of the Committee was the working of the Labourers' Act of last year. A Committee was at present engaged in investigating the operation of that Act; and although it had only sat for one day, and there were only two witnesses examined, and those two witnesses officials of the Department—its Vice President and Legal Adviser—the evidence given established every demand which had been made for the amendment of the Act. Their claims that the matter should be promptly dealt with, and dealt with at the Autumn Session, were irresistible, after the evidence given before the Select Committee. They had the broad fact admitted that, while a labourer could only be expected to pay 1*s.* a-week, or £2 12*s.* for his house and plot, that house and plot would cost the Guardians £100, or £5 7*s.* 6*d.* a-year. Thus they had the astonishing fact that these cottages could only be built for the labourer on the condition that the ratepayers of the district paid more than half the sum annually which they had cost. What had been the result? A question was asked in the Committee that day, not by an Irish Member, but by the hon. Member for Peterborough (Mr. S. Buxton), which showed a startling result. Evidence had been given by the Vice President of the Local Government Board that the Act had been confined in its operation to the two Provinces of Leinster and Munster, and there had not been a single attempt in the Province of Connaught to carry out the provisions of the Act, nor in the Province of Ulster. The hon. Member who put the question naturally remarked that it had been stated in evidence that the labourers of Connaught were in a much worse plight than in any other Province, and the reply was, "Certainly." Therefore, the only deduction to be made from the facts was that this Act for the relief of the labourers had not once been carried out in the Province in which it was most required. He believed that the representation he made would be corroborated by every Member of the Committee.

The CHANCELLOR of the EXCHEQUER (Mr. Childers) rose to Order. It was not in Order to discuss the evidence given before a Committee that had not yet reported.

The CHAIRMAN: That is so. Such a discussion is out of Order. If the Committee has not reported, the hon. Member is not entitled to refer to the evidence before it.

Mr. T. P. O'CONNOR said, he was sorry that the right hon. Gentleman the Chancellor of the Exchequer should have felt it his duty to stand upon a technical point as to the propriety of bringing these facts before the Committee. He had been simply anxious to point out one or two facts with regard to the position of the labourers in Ireland upon which the operation of the Labourers' Act could be discussed. He was also anxious to discuss the subject on the present occasion, which was probably the only opportunity that would present itself. He had no wish to add to the already heavy burdens on the shoulders of the right hon. Gentleman the Chief Secretary to the Lord Lieutenant of Ireland; and, considering the time that this discussion would occupy, he should certainly not exceed the limits of propriety. In accordance with the ruling of the Chairman, he should not, of course, refer to the evidence given before the Committee, but would merely put the Committee in possession of facts which were matters of notoriety. It was perfectly well known that as long as the Government continued to charge this high rate of interest the Labourers' Act would be a dead letter. He would submit this point to the right hon. Gentleman the Chief Secretary.

MR. NEWDEGATE rose to Order. It had always been considered contrary to the courtesy due to a Committee of that House that a subject should be taken out of their hands and made a matter for discussion in that House before the Committee had reported. It was a rule of courtesy which the House had always observed during the many years he had occupied a position in the House, and he hoped it would continue.

MR. T. P. O'CONNOR said, there was scarcely anything he would not do for the hon. Member who had just spoken, except vote for a Motion which he had dropped for some years. He would reserve the observations he was about to make until the Committee had reported; but he would ask the right hon. Gentleman the Chief Secretary to the Lord Lieutenant of Ireland to put the Committee in possession of facts that were within his knowledge, and to controvert his statements if he found them to be incorrect. He would ask the right hon. Gentleman whether it was not a fact that, up to the present, not a single house had been built under the Labourers' Act of last year? He asserted that this was the case, and that, perhaps, very good reasons could be given for it. He also asked him to controvert this statement—that a large number of the Unions in Ireland refused to carry that Act into operation, because they considered that the expense of doing so would be excessive; and he would further ask him to state whether or not it was correct that a large number of the Unions which had carried their schemes so far as to have obtained the signature of the Local Government Board and the sanction of both Houses of Parliament—whether he was not strongly of opinion that a large number of Boards of Guardians, although they had carried the matter to the final stage, would not go to the expense of putting their schemes into operation? As a matter of fact, the Boards of Guardians shrank, owing to the excessive cost imposed by the Government, from applying for money to carry out a work which had been sanctioned by both Houses of Parliament, and the consequence was that a large number of houses would not be built which would have been built had the rate of interest been less. What did that mean? It meant that the 12 months which had elapsed since the Labourers' Act was passed had been to a large extent wasted, and that another 12 months would be wasted likewise, because, as the hon. and gallant Member for the County of Cork (Colonel Colthurst) would know, with regard to the practical operation of the Act, that notices under the existing law must be published in the months of September, October, and November. The initiatory step was to publish the notices in those months, and unless those notices were so published no further steps could be taken with regard to the erection of cottages, not only with respect to this year, but also with respect to next year. But was it not a fact that the Chief Secretary could not controvert the statement which he (Mr. T. P. O'Connor) made most positively—namely, that all the probabilities pointed out that not a single Board of Guardians in Ireland would publish any notice during the months of September, October, and November, and that all the facts pointed to not a single cottage being built, either this year or the next, in consequence of such notices not being given? The right hon. Gentleman the Chief Secretary knew the cause as well as he (Mr. T. P. O'Connor) did. The cause was that the people of Ireland could not imagine that the Treasury would be so extortionate, or that the Treasury would be so foolish, as to charge a rate of interest which practically prevented the carrying out of an Act upon the necessity of which all parties were agreed. That being so, the people of Ireland expected further legislation; they had a right to expect it, and it was the expectation of that legislation which suspended and paralyzed the operation of the Act. He could assure the Committee that if new legislation was not brought in the Act would practically remain a dead letter. Owing to circumstances which he dared not allude to, a great and extraordinary opportunity had occurred to Her Majesty's Government of giving that prompt legislation which was necessary for the carrying out of the Act. If Her Majesty's Government were to bring in an amending Bill during the Autumn Session, which had been promised, to deal with points on which there was unanimity of opinion, he felt sure the Bill would pass through the House without any opposition, and that it would become law in time for the different Boards of Guardians throughout the country to carry out the Act this year. Finally, he most earnestly urged the right hon. Gentleman the Chief Secretary to the Lord Lieutenant of Ireland to take the matter into his favourable consideration, so that the Boards of Guardians might proceed with their work; and, still more, that the labourers who, at the end of the Autumn Session, would, in all probability, be added to the political forces of the country, should feel that their grievances had impressed themselves on the mind of the Government, and that the Autumn Session would bring them practical relief.

COLONEL NOLAN said, he should only detain the Committee for a few moments while he made some remarks upon a single point. The hon. Member for Wolverhampton (Mr. H. H. Fowler) in the course of his speech had made one observation with reference to a part of this Vote, which he (Colonel Nolan) was unable to agree with, and which he thought required an answer. The hon. Member for Wolverhampton bad spoken of that portion of the Vote which related to the Medical Department as being too high, as compared with the amount expended in England under the same head. He thought, however, that the hon. Member had been led into a mistake, so far as this item was concerned, by the difference in the manner in which the Votes of the two countries were framed. As a matter of fact they were drawn up quite differently. The items of the medical portion of the Vote relating to Ireland were drawn up under one or two heads, whereas in the English Vote they were spread out under several heads, and it was that circumstance which he believed had misled the hon. Gentleman. If hon. Members would look at the Irish Vote it would be seen that the total amount for medical purposes was £96,400; and if they took the English Vote, including registration, it was £33,854. He did not know why it was, but the medical expenditure under the same Vote was £143,500.

MR. H. H. FOWLER said, he had not alluded to the Medical Vote at all. He had referred to the salaries of the Medical Officers, cost of drugs, &c., and compared them with the corresponding items in the English Vote.

COLONEL NOLAN said, he still thought the hon. Gentleman had fallen into an error, because the Irish Vote undoubtedly included a number of extraneous items. There was, for instance, to be taken into account the expenditure on public vaccination, and travelling expenses in connection with the Medical Department, which were not charged in the same way in the English Estimates. The only fair mode of comparison was to add up all the English medical items and all the Irish medical items and then consider the balance; to deal with them in any other way would only lead to needless dispute. The hon. Member would find he was correct in stating that the whole of the Irish medical items were £96,000, and that the whole of the English medical items amounted to £33,854, adding, as he had before mentioned, the registration charge, which it was only fair to include. The proportion was, therefore, as three to one between the Irish and English Votes. It might be said that the Irish population was one-third of the English population; but he thought that the Medical Service of a country should be to a certain extent regulated by area, and that it should not rest upon population alone. There was another consideration to be kept in view in comparing the Medical Votes of England and Ireland. Ireland was the poorer country of the two, and amongst the reasons why she was poor was the fact that almost all the great public establishments, the prisons, dockyards—in fact, most of the good things out of which the people could earn money—were in England. Finally, although in respect of this Vote he would allow that *primâ facie* the Irish people were better off than the English people, yet, for the reasons he had advanced, he contended that they enjoyed no undue superiority.

COLONEL COLTHURST said, the hon. Member for Sligo (Mr. Sexton) had called the attention of the right hon. Gentleman and the Committee to a very important point in connection with the Catholic children in one of the Northern Irish Unions. He might also mention another Union in which the Board of Guardians had persistently refused, up to within the last few weeks, to do their duty in this respect. He rose for the purpose of saying that if these things occurred in the various Unions it showed the necessity of giving some power to the Local Government Board to deal with matters of this kind. He thought his hon. and gallant Friend the Member for Galway (Colonel Nolan) was not quite fair in his strictures on what he (Colonel Colthurst) had said on the subject. He did not say that the Local Government Board were to over-ride the Boards of Guardians either in England or in Ireland; but he did think that some Central Body should have the power of redressing the grievances of any helpless class of people who had not the means of redressing those grievances themselves. He thought that the Local Government Board should have the power to compel the Boards of Guardians to bring up Catholic children in the manner desired; and he had always regretted that his right hon. Friend the Chief Secretary did not use the power which he undoubtedly possessed in the direction indicated. If the right hon. Gentleman were to supersede Guardians who did not do justice to the Catholic children in the workhouses, he believed that it would have the effect of remedying the evil complained of, and that the power would only have to be exercised once or twice.

MR. DEASY said, he quite agreed with the hon. and gallant Member for the County of Cork (Colonel Colthurst) that it was desirable that the Local Government Board should possess the powers necessary to compel Boards of Guardians to do their duty with respect to Catholic children in workhouses. There were several Boards of Guardians in Ireland who were not disposed to act properly towards the poor; and it was a fact that those Boards of Guardians were mainly composed of persons belonging to the class who were against the people—that was to say, they were mainly composed of landlords and agents. It would be well, under such circumstances, that the Local Government Board should use its powers impartially, and that, if the powers which they at present possessed were found to be insufficient for the object in view, further powers should be given. He maintained, however, that at present the balance of opinion in Ireland was that the Local Government Board exercised the powers vested in them in an arbitrary and despotic manner, and unduly hampered Boards of Guardians in the discharge of their duties. He was of that opinion himself; it was the result of his own experience, because, when he was a Poor Law Guardian, he had often been involved in controversies with the Local Government Board, who were constantly interfering with and overthrowing the work of the Nationalist Guardians. If the Guardians wanted to change their rules, the Local Government Board was sure to send down an order to prevent their doing so. The case of the Cork Board of Guardians, he believed, had engaged the attention of the right hon. Gentleman the Chief Secretary to the Lord Lieutenant of Ireland. On a recent occasion a matter of importance was brought before that Board, and it was proposed by the Guardians to institute a necessary reform in connection with the administration of out-door relief. It had been found that the question of out-door relief was becoming very important, and more pressing year by year, and that it was impossible, under the system in force in Ireland, to keep anything like an adequate check upon the relieving officer. The amount of out-door relief in the Cork Union was increasing at the rate of £2,000 or £3,000 a-year, which so alarmed the Guardians that they appointed a small Committee to consider the matter and report to the Board the advisability of altering the existing arrangement. He remembered that, after many days of labour, the Committee brought in an important Report which was submitted to the Board, and adopted by them unanimously after two days' consideration. The Local Government Board were then asked to give their sanction to the recommendation of the Committee; but they refused to do so, without giving any adequate reason.

Memorials were addressed to them asking them to reconsider their decision in the interest of the ratepayers; but they refused to agree to the proposal. He said that the Local Government Board unduly exercised their powers on the occasion he had referred to. There were several other cases of a similar character which he might draw attention to; but he would abstain from so doing, because he had no desire unnecessarily to prolong the present discussion. With regard to the industrial training of children in workhouses, which the hon. and gallant Member for Cork County had just alluded to, the question was perhaps of more importance than any which could be brought before the attention of the Committee on that Vote. Unquestionably, it was impossible to train these children properly in the workhouses, the Guardians having no facilities for giving them an industrial education, because there was no power to compel pauper children in Ireland to learn any particular trade. Even if a boy were put to a trade in an Irish workhouse, and he desired at the end of a week or a fortnight to give it up and lead a life of idleness, the Board of Guardians had no power to make him go to work; they were obliged to let him have his own way, and the result was that the boy grew up to become a burden on the community. He believed, then, that if increased powers were given to the Boards of Guardians in Ireland, the desire of the hon. Member for Clonmel (Mr. Moore) would be met, and a large number of boys taught to earn their living. In that way the able-bodied men, whom, under the existing system, it was impossible to keep out of the workhouses, would no longer be found seeking admission. If those men had, in their childhood, been sent to some school altogether removed from the evil influences of the workhouses, he believed they would have become useful members of society instead of what they were, merely burdens on the ratepayers. Unfortunately, the people he was speaking of constituted a very large class, of whom it might be said that, whenever they were not in the workhouse, they were in gaol; and he believed that until Parliament gave facilities to board out children, or to purchase and endow schools for the industrial training of pauper children, this unfortunate state of things would continue. There was another matter to which he should like to call the attention of the Committee, and that was the position of able-bodied women in the workhouses in Ireland. The Guardians had it in their power to separate fallen and abandoned women from those who were innocent and virtuous, and this was done in a number of workhouses, although it was neglected in others. Now, he said there was no reason why the Local Government Board should not insist upon the Boards of Guardians throughout the country carrying out the rule of separation; and he believed that if it were done it would at once put a stop to the demoralization amongst women which went on in certain workhouses in Ireland. He complained that the Local Government Board exercised their powers in a manner which was not conducive to the interests of the ratepayers, and which did not lead to the Boards of Guardians having any confidence in the Local Government Board. Let the Committee consider a case in connection with the Kinsale Workhouse which occurred a short time ago. It was proposed that nuns should be introduced into the workhouse for the purpose of taking charge of the hospital, and a resolution was unanimously carried by the Board of Guardians to that effect; but the Local Government Board refused to sanction the arrangement unless a separate building was erected for their accommodation outside the workhouse; though there was ample room within the building, as would be seen when he stated that the Kinsale Workhouse was built for 600 inmates and only contained 120 at present. He would like to know why one rule was made for the workhouse he was referring to, and another rule for the workhouse at Cork, where the nuns had been admitted and had given satisfaction to everyone? It was clear that the Local Government Board had no reason but an imaginary one for refusing to admit the nuns in the first case he had mentioned. He had had some experience himself of the powers of the Local Government Board; and he thought that the way in which they performed their duties generally, with regard to the Poor Law, was extremely objectionable. Further, he contended that some rules should be laid down both for the guidance of the Department, of Boards of Guardians, and of the Auditors When some of the best men in the land were thrown into prison on suspicion by the right hon. Gentleman the Member for Bradford (Mr. W. E. Forster), at that time Chief Secretary to the Lord Lieutenant of Ireland, it was found necessary in some cases to relieve the families of many of those men; and resolutions were passed in the usual manner, at several Boards, authorizing the Guardians to give 15*s*. or £1 a-week for that purpose. The Local Government Board had those resolutions before them; they never made any objection to them; they did not object to the amount of money voted, nor did they give the Guardians the slightest intimation that they were likely to be surcharged for any portion of the item of relief in question. But when the auditing of the accounts had taken place, the Guardians unexpectedly found themselves surcharged to a very considerable amount. In Cork Union the sum was not very large; but in Middleton Union the Chairman was surcharged to the amount of £44. A resolution was sent to the Local Government Board, asking that the influence of the Department might be used with the Auditors to have the surcharge remitted; but the Local Government Board answered that it was not in their power to influence the Auditor. He (Mr. Deasy) was surcharged for a small sum himself. He believed, then, that they had no influence with the Auditor; if he had known at first as much as he knew then, he would have allowed the Sheriff to proceed against him for the recovery of the money claimed. When all the Poor Law Guardians had paid the amount with which they had been surcharged, on account of the families of "suspects," the Local Government Board thought it expedient to exercise that power which before they had disclaimed, and they actually induced the Auditors not to surcharge certain gentlemen belonging to the Orange Society on account of other matters. What had occurred in Cork Union was a case in point. A gentleman, a member of the Orange Lodge and well known to the hon. and gallant Member for the County of Cork (Colonel Colthurst), was surcharged for having given relief to persons who were not legally entitled to receive it; he knew at the time he gave the relief that it was given illegally; he knew that it was distinctly laid down as unlawful, and that the Auditors could surcharge him with the amounts. But the Local Government Board having interfered in his behalf, the surcharge was not enforced. Their action in reference to that affair showed that the statement that they had no control over the Auditor was not true. He would give another instance in support of his argument. Three Governors of the Cork District Lunatic Asylum were surcharged £33 by the Government Auditor, which they refused to pay; and, although the Middleton magistrates gave a decree for the amount, the surcharge was not enforced. Those gentlemen were, of course, Orangemen. He ventured to say that the Local Government Board would do well to lay down some rule for the guidance of Boards of Guardians in the administration of the rates, so that they might know when they were acting legally or otherwise. It was monstrous that the Local Government Board, which had the resolution of the Board of Guardians in question before them week after week, should have left those Guardians to act in an illegal manner, without informing them of the fact. If they had had any notion that the relief they were giving was illegal they would have adopted some other means; but the Local Government Board gave them not the slightest intimation that their action was illegal. There was another matter of great importance, and that was the way in which the pauper lunatics were treated in the lunatic wards in the workhouses in Ireland. He did not think any question more important, because of the helplessness of these people, could occupy the attention of the House. Harmless lunatics were invariably sent to the workhouses, and there was practically no provision made for them. There was a kind of classification; but it was not at all what it ought to be. The nurses knew nothing about the treatment of such people, and there were no doctors whose profession it was to attend them; and, on the whole, the chances of their recovery in these workhouse wards, to say nothing of comfort for them, were hopeless. In 1879, a Report was presented by, he believed, a Select Committee appointed by the late Conservative Government, which recommended that certain workhouses in certain districts should be set aside altogether for the treatment of these unfortunate people. There was no reason why that recommendation should not be carried out, because the workhouses in some parts of the country—Kinsale, for instance—were not filled to one-seventh, or even one-tenth of their capacity. If that plan was adopted, these poor people would be treated properly, and he had no doubt there would more cases of recovery than otherwise. It was one of the most disgraceful things conceivable that these people should not be properly treated, but should be huddled together with no proper provision being made for their treatment. This was a matter which he would ask the Chief Secretary to consider, for it was really one of great importance. He did not wish to say anything on the subject raised by the hon. and gallant Member for Galway (Colonel Nolan) as to cholera patients, except that it was of great importance that hospitals should be provided for them. In the City of Cork there was a hospital set aside for cholera patients should an epidemic break out; but that was not the case in Bandon and other places in the county, and should there be an epidemic in Ireland, no provision having been made for the treatment of the patients, results of a serious nature would follow. He hoped the right hon. Gentleman would consider the few points he had ventured to place before the Committee, and particularly that with regard to the pauper lunatics. There were several other matters to which he would not now advert; but he could not avoid reference to the appointment of Inspectors under the Explosives Acts. The Boards of Guardians had to pay these Inspectors; but the Inspectors were appointed by the magistrates of Petty Sessions, who got one of their own friends to apply for the office, then appointed him, and no sooner was he appointed than they raised his salary; but the Guardians had to pay; and, should they refuse to do so, all the magistrates had to do was to make an order on the Treasurer of the Union, who should regard such an order as a first charge on the balance to the credit of the Guardians, and if there was no balance at the time the order was presented, he was bound to pay it out of the first monies received by him. He referred to this matter, because much irritation had been caused to the Cork Guardians by the manner in which these Inspectors had been appointed, and their salaries increased. They knew that this had been done in the interests of a class; and if the Local Government Board permitted the injustice to continue, they would forfeit altogether what little confidence the Irish people had in them. He did not wish it to be understood that he objected to the Local Government Board as a Central Controlling Authority. It was absolutely necessary to have some such Central Authority; but what he did object to was that in the last three or four years, particularly in Unions where Nationalist Guardians held the balance of power, the Local Government Board had increased their authority in an objectionable manner. He hoped the Government would lay down some rule which would check the action of the Department; if they did, they would find that the Boards of Guardians throughout the Southern counties, and particularly if the Election of Guardians Bill then before the House was passed, would do their duty fairly.

Mr. TREVELYAN said, the remarks of the hon. Member (Mr. Deasy) were very interesting in several particulars, and not the least to him in the sentence with which the hon. Member concluded. Standing on the threshold of the discussion of this Bill, to which some little time had been devoted, he must earnestly express the hope that it would become an Act that Session; because if it did, not only would great benefits be conferred on the Irish people, but some of the most critical and intricate controversies to which allusion had been made would be closed once and for ever. The hon. Member had discussed at some length the questions started by other hon. Gentlemen; but towards the end of his speech he referred to the position of the Explosives Acts, and to the inefficient manner in which they were carried out. It was impossible for him to come provided with papers and statistics for all these points, and he had no time to inform himself as the discussion went on; but upon this point he remembered that the Local Government Board had considerable powers, and that complaints had frequently been made—in private, he must say—of the expensive character of the Inspectors under the Explosives Acts. He should be glad to receive hints from hon. Gentlemen, and to confer with them either in private or in public; but the direction which recommendations lately made to him had taken was the control of the police in this matter. Whether that was the view of the hon. Member he should be curious to learn; but there were many hon. Members who were inclined to think it would, perhaps, be the most economical and the most efficient system. The hon. Member for Clonmel (Mr. Moore), touching point after point which were afterwards filled in by the hon. and gallant Member for Cork County (Colonel Colthurst), argued against the present workhouse system, which he thought was too favourable to those persons who he considered ought not to be in workhouses at all, but should be supporting themselves by their own labour, and which, on the other hand, bore too hardly upon people who ought to be in the workhouses at the public expense. Idlers, he said, were allowed to frequent the workhouses; and, on the other hand, others who ought to be supported by the public on account of their infirmities were neglected. He could not, however, but think that the arrangements made were not far off the mark, and the proper mediums had been struck. The main principle upon which these workhouses were conducted, and the arrangement drawn up was, that idlers who could support themselves by sound labour should be deterred from applying for relief to the workhouses by the restrictions imposed. These restrictions must be uniform. If there was to be a real test of whether a person should or should not be supported by the public, it must be a uniform test; and a uniform test would always admit some persons who ought not to be admitted, and, at the same time, perhaps, bear a little hard on others who deserved better treatment; but he thought it was not yet proved that the workhouses of Ireland, any more than those of England, encouraged a great number of idlers to throw themselves on the public charge; or, on the other hand, that the personal discomforts and vexations of being supported in the workhouses were of such a character as to bear hardly on persons who were pauper inmates. The hon. Member referred to the lunatic wards, and in that respect undoubtedly it would be well if some remedy could be applied. It was a most painful sight to see these unfortunate people collected in small bodies—with the air of depression which such persons usually bore—where they were a small isolated section of the larger body, the great majority of whom were sane. The lunatics were few, and were probably in the charge of persons who were not professionally acquainted with the manner in which they ought to be treated, and their condition was certainly hopeless and distressing. With regard to the pauper children, the same remarks applied, and, to a certain extent, in many cases, must apply necessarily, and in this case it was yet more painful. It was a sad sight to see 8 or 10, or 15, or 20 poor little children being taught with few of those appliances which could be obtained in larger establishments. Their number, and the distressing character of their condition were, no doubt, painful. In this case, and in the case of the lunatics, it would be better if they could in the one case adopt the English system, and have large workhouse schools; while in the case of the lunatics it was well worth considering whether they could be congregated in a central workhouse. But it must be allowed that in all these cases the consideration came in that the contributions of the Treasury were rigorously applied, and that every alteration of system in the direction of a more pleasant life, and more efficient training, and more healthy maintenance was liable to cost money, and they must be very careful that in their desire to obey the dictates of philanthropy, they did not put on the ratepayers a burden which people who had a right to be represented might be unwilling to adopt. The hon. Member had spoken of the inferior class of teachers in the Irish workhouses; but unfortunately the supply of qualified teachers had long been very deficient in Ireland. It was most distressing in the elementary schools to see how few of the teachers at that moment really had such qualifications as would be considered necessary in England, and even, perhaps, in Scotland; but upon that point the Government had clean hands, because the real prime cause of this depression in Irish education was the want of training. The causes of that want of training were well known to all Irish Members, and those causes the Government had done their very best to remove. As time went on, he thought the steps that had been taken would cause an improvement, and they might hope that after the elementary schools had been supplied the Standard might go on improving lower down the scale, and the workhouses might get supplied with better teachers. But the hon. Member likewise spoke of the industrial training, and on that point he charged the Local Government Board with not having furthered it. The Board might not, perhaps, have done all in their power to further it; but they had not prevented the Guardians in any case from establishing industrial training. He was unwilling to anticipate whatever discussion there might be on the Vote for Industrial Schools; but the hon. and gallant Member for Galway (Colonel Nolan) had spoken of the extreme parsimony of the Government for a good many years past, in refusing to allow more industrial schools to be started in Ireland. The hon. and gallant Member was well aware that the parsimony he complained of had not resulted in Ireland being ill-used, as compared with the Sister Island, because in England and in Wales the proportion of money per head for industrial schools was only 3 to 1, as against the proportion in Ireland; whereas the proportion in population was, roughly speaking, twice as large, and more probably 6 to 1, as compared with Ireland. The hon. and gallant Member, as he understood him, proposed to largely relax the conditions under which children might be sent to industrial schools. That was a very serious question indeed. It would result, he could see, in industrial teaching, at the public expense, being extended over almost the whole of Ireland; and it was quite obvious that many hon. Members, including the hon. Member for Wolverhampton (Mr. H. H. Fowler), would certainly have something to say about the great body of Irish children being educated on a system which, in England, was only applied to those who, from the unfortunate circumstances of their homes, had no chance of the least education. The hon. and gallant Member for Cork had said he would not inflict on the Committee a speech on Union rating if he (Mr. Trevelyan) would state what the views of the Government were on that subject—whether they proposed to make the Union Rating Bill a measure for encouraging indoor relief, and discouraging outdoor relief in Ireland; or whether they would adopt the English system of applying Union rating to every species of relief. He could see that it would be impossible to pass a Bill through Parliament for a limited and partial system of Union rating. In all questions in which the two countries could have their affairs managed on the same system, it was very important that the greatest possible amount of similarity should be aimed at. The Union Rating Bill in England, which was passed some 20 years ago, had been, on the whole, a very great success; and the tendency in England during those 20 years had certainly not been in the direction of excessive and dissolute outdoor relief, but rather the opposite; and he had no doubt that although by an artificial system of having Union rating for indoor relief, and divisional rating for outdoor relief, when once they should pass the Bill that would be a system he could not ask Parliament to adopt. The hon. and gallant Member for Galway (Colonel Nolan) had referred to a question upon which he had said something at Question time, and asked what measures were being taken by the Local Government Board to provide hospitals in case of cholera. In that matter there had been a good deal of activity, and the policy of the Local Government Board was this—they proposed first to rely upon the existing hospitals. Wherever fever hospitals existed they were of opinion that it would be well if the Guardians were to use them as cholera hospitals. Where no such hospital existed, or where it was inconveniently or dangerously placed, or where, by any evil chance, the cholera should fall upon Ireland severely, and the hospitals were over-filled, and room was wanting—with a view to that they had carefully examined what measures had been adopted in England. In England advice had in one case been given by the English Local Government Board in the shape of a Memorandum with regard to temporary hospital accommodation. That was, he believed, in the year 1876, and the advice given was that the authorities should resort to huts or tents. The Local Government Board for Ireland had been adopting measures for ascertaining where temporary hospitals might be most rapidly procured; and they had ascertained that one English firm had a sufficient number of tents in store. But they were anxious to have these temporary hospitals on the spot, and they had applied to an Irish firm for the plan of a hospital with the intention of at once furthering the provision of hospitals should they be needed. For immediate purposes he might state that the Government had in store 16 Constabulary huts at Phœnix Park, which had been inspected by Inspector Mackay, and he had found them admirably suited for temporary hospitals. They would accommodate five patients each, and could be erected in a few hours. The Government proposed to hold them at the disposal of any Sanitary Authority that might require them, and they would be willing to leave the question of payment to arbitration; but he would see that this most necessary service was pushed forward quickly, because he quite agreed with the hon. and gallant Member that when troubles arose, whether through the inroad of disease, or war, or famine, the difference was very great between having provision actually made and the question settled of authority and responsibility for the arrangements made, and these things not being settled. Going back to the question with which this discussion commenced, the hon. Member for Wolverhampton (Mr. H. H. Fowler) made some general observations as to the conduct of permanent officials in Ireland. He did not acknowledge the justice of those observations, because he doubted whether the hon. Member could find a case resembling that which they had been now discussing, in which any Government, English, Scotch, or Irish, had acted with more decision than the Irish Government had in the case referred to. He did not know what measure of public spirit his hon. Friend had; but he thought he was present when he described the action of the Irish Government in that case as an earnest of what they would do in similar cases, and he should be very much surprised if the hon. Member could pick any hole in the action of the Irish Government in that matter. The hon. Member said that when an allegation was made two days would be sufficient to settle the matter. The hon. Member had not studied the case sufficiently; he had not paid sufficient attention to the great principle that no man should be condemned untried. The Executive had not had the opportunity yet of writing to Mr. Elliott, to ask him what colour he placed upon the charge. Till the Board had had its meeting, and until the Executive got a reply from them, they would not have that opportunity, because his (Mr. Trevelyan's) recollection of the matter was that the first official intelligence they had that anything that could be construed into defalcations had existed was contained in the answer which the Board of Blackrook Commissioners returned to their first letter, and it was immediately on the heels of that answer that they sent their second letter, to which the Board must return a reply after their next meeting.

MR. MOLLOY: What is the date of that letter?

MR. TREVELYAN said, he had not got the papers with him; he was not aware the subject was going to be started. But the letters of the Executive, whenever they were written, were written very soon after the communication was received from the Blackrock Commissioners. As he had already stated, the Blackrock Commissioners had been exceedingly sluggish, and, consequently, in the last resort, he should propose that the matter be dealt with by two independent bodies. However, as a practical result of this discussion, he was perfectly prepared to accept the suggestion of the hon. Gentleman the Member for Wolverhampton (Mr. H. H. Fowler) to defer the Report. The hon. Gentleman had done much good by comparing the Estimates of the one country with those of the other, and he (Mr. Trevelyan) would be extremely glad if his hon. Friend could, on some future occasion, give them his ideas as to whether a Public Office was better managed by a Board or by a Permanent Secretary. But when the hon. Gentleman spoke of the salary of the Vice President, he (Mr. Trevelyan) must own that Mr. Robinson's responsibilities and duties were not more than adequately represented by a salary of £2,000 a-year. It must be borne in mind that in the English Local Government Board there were two Parliamentary officers who had nothing to do except to look after that Board. In the Local Government Board in Ireland there was only one Parliamentary official, and he was the Chief Secretary; and it was pretty plain that an official who had to be for the best part of seven months in each year in constant attendance in Parliament at Westminster, occupied with the business of many different Departments, and with an amount of what might be called Home Office Business that alone would be enough to keep a Minister actively employed, would not in any sense be able to undertake the duties of a Permanent Supervisor of a Department. Under those circumstances, he could not say that the Vice President of the Local Government Board was at all overpaid. His hon. Friend spoke of the very large expenditure on medical relief, and he (Mr. Trevelyan) did not think that the answer of the hon. and gallant Member for Galway (Colonel Nolan) covered the whole ground. The hon. and gallant Member for Galway put it down to the great territorial size of Ireland as compared with her population. That made some difference, no doubt; but he (Mr. Trevelyan) should say that the difference in the expenditure on medical relief in the two countries was due in great measure to the different habits of the English and Irish populations. The dependence of the Irish people upon medical relief provided by the public went undoubtedly in very much higher classes, and was very much more general, than in England, and was at least one main cause of the very great proportionate expenditure upon medical relief. An indication of that was the difference in the position which was occupied by the public dispenser in England and that occupied by the public dispenser in Ireland. The dispenser in Ireland depended to a great extent upon a public salary; but in England he depended chiefly upon his private practice. The hon. Member for Sligo (Mr. Sexton) referred to several cases of elections in which he considered the Local Government Board had not acted justly. Now, the Local Government Board was extremely anxious to be relieved of its functions in regard to elections. Some 80 or 90 contested elections were brought to be tried and supervised by the Local Government Board every year. The duty was one that was extremely invidious and extremely difficult to perform, and he should be only too glad if it could be transferred by the Bill, which had now gone to "another place," to a tribunal which was well fitted to examine into the questions at issue. But he was bound to say that whenever a Question had been asked in the House with regard to the position of the Local Government Board respecting a contested Poor Law election, he had always gone into the case, and he had generall found that this idea governed the decisions of the Board—that as little as possible should be done to disturb the result of elections unless what had taken place was of a nature to falsify the elections. The Board were of opinion that defects of technical legality should not be pressed too hard unless there was some reason to believe they occurred of malice aforethought, or unless the result of the elections was affected by them. He could not say he had found any case in which the Returning Officer was seriously to blame in which he was not reprimanded, in one case he was even dismissed; and he had not known any case in which an election was turned by illegality. He could not expect hon. Gentlemen to agree with the judgment of the Board in all the cases; but the Board had performed their duty to the best of their ability. He earnestly hoped this would be the last year the Board would have to decide election disputes. The hon. Member for Sligo (Mr. Sexton) spoke of the Gweedore evictions. He should not follow the hon. Gentleman into that part of his speech in which he referred to the relations between the landlord and the tenants. He did not want to enter into controversial questions, which were not essential to the Vote; but with regard to the conduct of the relieving officer, and the conduct of the Local Government Board, he had a word to say. The hon. Member said that the evictions took place on the 1st or the 2nd of July, but that the relieving officer did not transfer the people to the workhouse until a good many days had passed. The relieving officer was specially sent by the direction of the Board of Guardians on Saturday, the 5th of July. Up to that time he conceived that he was performing his duty by remaining at home, ready to be sent over in case he was wanted; and, in so doing, he (Mr. Trevelyan) was informed he was acting strictly legally. The relieving officer had been long resident in the district, he knew well the circumstances of the people, and he was not out of sympathy with the people. The character given him by those who knew him locally, including, he (Mr. Trevelyan) was informed, the Catholic clergy of the parish, was that he was a kindly and honest man, and was upright and generous in his dealings with the people. The Local Government Board were alive to what was going on; from the very first they were in correspondence with the relieving officer, reminding him of the great responsibility he would incur by any neglect of duty. They sent an Inspector down to the locality to make a special Report, and they reminded the Guardians of their power to give outdoor relief; but at that point the powers of the Local Government Board ceased. The Local Government Board, as the hon. Gentlemen well knew, had no power whatever to order outdoor relief in a particular case. Well, on Saturday, the 5th of July, the relieving officer was directed by the Guardians to proceed without delay to the scene of the evictions, and to afford, at his own instance, provisional relief, either in or out of the workhouse, according to the circumstances of each case. He went accordingly, and offered meal in one case where he thought it was immediately wanted, and he offered to provide conveyances to the workhouse. The latter offer was refused by all the people.

MR. HARRINGTON: Will the right hon. Gentleman give the date the officer visited the place?

MR. TREVELYAN: It was the 5th of July.

MR. HARRINGTON: He got the order on the 5th; did he go the same day?

MR. TREVELYAN said, the relieving officer went on the day that he got the order. The offer to provide conveyances to the workhouse was refused—that was to the best of his (Mr. Trevelyan's) belief.

MR. HARRINGTON said, that the orders of Boards of Guardians were not given to relieving officers until after their meetings.

MR. TREVELYAN said, the 5th of July was a long day; but he would not absolutely say the relieving officer visited the scene on the day he got the order; but, at any rate, it was not on the Monday he went. The relieving officer offered to take the people to the workhouse; but his offer was declinod by the people, who were evidently acting under the advice of Father M'Faddy, who said they were all to go in together; and on the Monday following 141 did go into the workhouse, conveyances being provided for them by the priest, though the relieving officer would have provided them if application had been made to him. Then, with regard to no women or children having been allowed to go to the workhouse unless the father of the family went with them, on that point no complaint had hitherto been made to him. He saw, from the Report, that of the persons who went to the workhouse, 72 had been amongst those evicted on the Gweedore estate, and the remainder were the wives and children of tenants on neighbouring estates, who had been evicted, but reinstated as caretakers; so there could not have been a general system forbidding wives and children to go to the workhouse unless the husbands and fathers went in also. The hon. Member for Galway (Mr. T. P. O'Connor) spoke on the subject of the Labourers' Act, with regard to which he was interrupted once by the Chancellor of the Exchequer (Mr. Childers), and once by the hon. Member for North Warwickshire (Mr. Newdegate). The hon. Member for Galway accepted the interruptions in a very cheerful spirit, and he said nothing from that moment forward to which anybody could take exception. But he (Mr. Trevelyan) could not help thinking that the general sense of the Committee would be with the hon. Gentleman (Mr. Newdegate) who appealed to the Chairman; because, when a Committee was sitting upstairs, it was altogether out of reason that the evidence should be the subject of comment in the House. The hon. Member (Mr. T. P. O'Connor) was so ingenious, however, that, though he was obliged to obey the ruling of the Chair, he was not at all disconcerted, but was able to put forward his opinions and views on other grounds than on the evidence of the Committee sitting upstairs. The hon. Gentleman asked him several questions—for instance, whether any houses had been built under the Labourers' Act; and whether any Boards of Guardians had objected to burden their ratepayers in the matter? He (Mr. Trevelyan) was not aware that any houses had been built; but he did not think that, under the schemes which were being put forward, any houses could very well have been built by this time. It was only in the latter part of the Session that the

Provisional Orders were passed; besides, it was extremely unlikely that, with a Committee now sitting, and with further legislation so freely talked of by hon. Members, the present Bill would be put into any very active use. And when he was asked whether any Boards of Guardians had objected to burden their ratepayers, he should be inclined to think it was extremely probable that they had objected. The very principle of the Bill introduced by the hon. Member himself was that pressure should be imposed upon Boards of Guardians from the outside, and that they themselves should have the power to say whether they would burden the rates by building houses. The hon. Member required from him (Mr. Trevelyan) two pledges, neither of which he was able to give. The first pledge was that the Committee now sitting should report this year. On that point he had no power whatever. It was for the Committee themselves to say how much evidence they wished to take, how long they wished to sit; and it would be impertinent in him even to express a wish on the subject. The next pledge was that the Government should, in the Autumn Session, bring forward an amending Bill. On that rested a question of extreme gravity; a question which could only be settled by an appeal to the Prime Minister, and upon which he (Mr. Trevelyan) would not have the courage to express any opinion. He knew that the idea of the Prime Minister was that the Autumn Session should be devoted exclusively to the Representation of the People Bill. One hon. Member mentioned his desire that the Local Government Board should interfere to see that the children in workhouses received the advantages of a religious education. At that moment a question was impending with the Donegal Board of Guardians, with regard to which he (Mr. Trevelyan) was extremely anxious. A controversy had arisen between the Local Government Board and the Donegal Board of Guardians, and he was bound to say there had been faults on both sides; but the difficulty occasioned at present appeared to lie with the Board of Guardians. The Local Government Board had made up their minds to settle the question; and, in the course of the next week, he had no doubt that settled it would be. He was quite certain that they never could permanently allow the children of the poor people in workhouses to be deprived of religious instruction and consolation. Having done his best to deal with the different points which had been started by hon. Members during the discussion, he earnestly hoped they would now be allowed to take the Vote.

Mr. MOORE said, the right hon. Gentleman the Chief Secretary had exhibited great patience and care in going through the many subjects which had been referred to by different Members of the Committee; and he did not intend to reward the right hon. Gentleman's patience by putting the Committee to the trouble of a Division, especially as his hon. Friends sitting on the Irish Benches opposite did not think it wise to do so. He desired, however, before he asked leave to withdraw his Amendment, to thank the Chief Secretary for the pointed way in which he alluded to the condition of lunatics. Of course, he considered the condition of the children was of paramount importance; but he was pleased to find the right hon. Gentleman took a deep interest in the condition of the lunatics. Speaking of the children, the Chief Secretary alluded to the fact that he (Mr. Moore) had said there were 42 unclassed teachers; and the right hon. Gentleman stated that that was owing to the absence of training schools, a defect which the present Government were taking means to remedy. But that did not meet the case at all, because none of the teachers, roughly speaking, were trained. He should be sorry to terminate any of the appointments already made; but what he complained of was that the Local Government Board sanctioned the appointment of any unclassed teachers. Another point upon which he laid stress was that there was a clashing of authority; that the Local Government Board Inspector came down to the schools with certain powers, and then the Inspector of the Education Department came down with other powers, and as a consequence the education of the children suffered. The two points he had mentioned were points of administration with which the right hon. Gentleman the Chief Secretary might very properly deal, with a view to an improved state of things. There was only one more remark he wished to make, and that was that nothing that hon. Members opposite could say could increase his desire to keep down undue expenditure. He had always been a consistent advocate of economy, and he anticipated that, by a wise reform, or modification of the existing system, a very large saving would accrue. He believed that some workhouses might be wholly closed, or only kept open so far as they were required for sanitary purposes. He asked leave to withdraw his Amendment.

MR. HARRINGTON said, he did not wish to travel over the ground that had been so fairly and exhaustively covered by the right hon. Gentleman the Chief Secretary; but he desired to make a few remarks with regard to the observations of the hon. Member for Clonmel (Mr. Moore). The opinion of Irish Members was not absolutely unanimous on some of the questions the hon. Gentleman had referred to. For instance, he could not agree with the hon. Gentleman that it would be an advantage to the educational training of children in workhouses that the duties of inspection should be delegated to the ordinary Poor Law Inspectors. In the first place, the technical knowledge which Poor Law Inspectors had to acquire to enable them to discharge their Poor Law duties was altogether different to that technical knowledge which they should possess to fit them for Inspectors of Schools. It would be a distinct disadvantage, in his opinion, to the education imparted in workhouse schools if the duty of inspecting those schools were taken out of the hands of the Inspectors of National Education in the country. His idea was that the best means of improving the education of children in workhouse schools was to subject them to the same system of inspection as the children of ordinary schools were subjected to. A Poor Law Inspector, from his very position, knew nothing of the system and method of primary education which necessarily must be present to the mind of the man who came into contact with children for the purposes of education. The right hon. Gentleman the Chief Secretary had referred in a very detailed manner to the administration of the Local Government Board. The details rather surprised him (Mr. Harrington), because he knew that government by the Local Government Board was perhaps the most intricate problem in Ireland, and he could conceive the difficulties anyone who had the management of the Department must experience. Now, there was one point connected with the operation of the Labourers' Act to which he wished to draw special attention. The 10th section of that Act provided that where a representation was made to a Sanitary Authority, the Sanitary Authority was to report forthwith to the Local Government Board, and they must see whether the Sanitary Authority had devised a scheme under that representation to put the Labourers' Act into operation; in other words, if the local Sanitary Authority refused to put the Act into operation, the Local Government Board were empowered by this section to do so. The right hon. Gentleman the Chief Secretary had admitted that there were numerous instances where the Boards of Guardians had refused to put the Act into operation. Could the right hon. Gentleman give the Committee a single case where the Local Government Board had used the powers which the 10th section of the Act gave them—namely, to call upon the Sanitary Authority to devise a scheme, or themselves devised a scheme, by which the Act should be put in force? He (Mr. Harrington) had watched the operation of the Act pretty carefully, and he had found that whatever had been done under the Act to improve the dwellings of the labourers had been due altogether to the willingness of the majority of the ratepayers, or to the action of the Boards of Guardians, in which the elected Guardians had been in the ascendancy. He had failed to find a single instance in which the Local Government Board had endeavoured to give effect to the 10th section of the Act by stepping in and compelling the Local Authorities to devise a scheme. Now, from the observations of the hon. Member for Galway (Mr. T. P. O'Connor), it was evident that the Act had had no operation at all in two of the Provinces of Ireland. Only two efforts had been made to put the Act in operation in Connaught, where the condition of the people most required it. He believed that not a single scheme had been devised by the Boards of Guardians in what was called "the loyal Province of Ulster," "the Conservative Province of Ulster." The labouring classes in that Province were as badly housed as those in any other Province. In respect to the two Provinces in which no effort had been made by the Local Authorities to give effect to the Act, it was worth the consideration of the right hon. Gentleman the Chief Secretary whether the Local Government Board, over which he presided, should not themselves put the Act into operation.

MR. WARTON said, he did not propose to enter into any of the purely Irish questions which had been discussed.

Notice taken, that 40 Members were not present; Committee counted, and 40 Members being found present,

MR. WARTON said, he had no intention of entering into the comparison between the work of the Local Government Board in Ireland and England, with which the hon. Member for Wolverhampton (Mr. H. H. Fowler) had threatened them. There was, however, one item in the Vote to which he desired to call attention—namely, the item for the pay of Inspectors. It amounted to £2,100, and what struck him was the small amount of work which appeared to be done by the Inspectors for their salaries. Their labours appeared to be confined to the neighbourhood of the Parks, and the item was exactly the same as it was in the previous year. It was made up of the personal expenses of six Inspectors at £1 1*s.* a-day for 163 days, and the personal expenses of seven Sub-Inspectors at the same rate; but although there were 313 working days in the year, these officers appeared to have been employed in one case for 166 days, and in the other for only 143. He did not know what the explanation was, and it might be that they were only paid when they were actually employed. It certainly appeared that there were more Inspectors than were absolutely necessary, or else they did not perform half work enough.

MR. COURTNEY said, the Inspectors received a guinea a-day when they were employed on the work of inspection.

MR. HEALY wished to ask the Chief Secretary if there were any Unions in Ireland in which Vice Guardians were employed? He would also ask him what the intention of the Government was with regard to the Union of Newport, in the County Mayo? For a long time this district had been subjected to heavy rates, at which the greatest dissatisfaction was expressed, as they were paying no less than 4*s.* 6*d.* in the pound. They had passed a resolution to the effect that they were totally unable to pay 4*s.* 6*d.* in the pound, and they had recommended that there should be an amalgamation between them and the Westport or Belmullet Union in order to lessen these high and grievous expenses. The poor people had resolved that they would pay no higher rate than 2*s.* in the pound. That, however, he thought, would be a foolish step for them to take, as they subjected themselves to political disability, and deprived themselves of their votes. If they wanted not to pay so much, it would be much more preferable that they should come to a resolution to decline to pay county cess, because it would be better to strike against a tax which did not entail the loss of the vote or any political disability. Non-payment of the poor rate did, of course, involve political disability. The Local Government Board had held an inquiry into the case, which had been adjourned to the 7th of August; but he did not see why three weeks should be taken up by Mr. Robinson, the Inspector, in this way. The valuation of the entire district was only £14,000, and it was absolutely absurd that there should be such charges made for such a poor district. He trusted that they would have some assurance from the Chief Secretary that the Government were willing to concur with some scheme of amalgamation of Unions which would relieve the people. He was entirely opposed to the present system for the management of the Poor Law districts in Ireland, although he admitted that there might be a difficulty in regard to the medical authorities. He did not think, however, that the difficulty was an insuperable one; and where they had dispensary districts they could, by an arrangement in regard to the staff of doctors, obviate much of the evil. He also wished to ask a question with regard to the Donegal Union, and he certainly thought that the Chief Secretary had not dealt with the Guardians of that Union as he would have done if it had been a Union further South. The Catholic clergyman was still divorced from his flock, because the Guardians would not comply with the suggestions of the Chief Secretary, and had chosen to get rid of every Catholic official who had been connected with the administration of the affairs of the Union. He had raised the question last year, and was sorry to find that no progress had been made in the matter since. The Guardians were still recalcitrant. It was unjust that, because the Guardians were almost all Protestants or Presbyterians, the paupers, who were almost entirely Catholics, should be shut off from the administrations of their clergy. In the case of the old sick poor this was peculiarly unjust. In the case of the old sick, who were on the verge of the grave, they found themselves shut out from the consolations of their religion. Even in England, where the religious grievance could hardly be realized because it was practically non-existent, any distinction of this kind would be held to be an intolerable grievance. It might be said that the young people were able to attend the Catholic churches in the towns; but in the event of being attacked with small-pox, scarlatina, or any of the complaints to which children were subject, they were cut off from the ministrations of the priest. He asked the Chief Secretary to deal with the Boards of Guardians in the North of Ireland as he had done with the Union of Carrick-on-Suir in the South. Why had not the Guardians of the Donegal Union been dealt with in the same manner? If a similar defiance of the regulations of the Local Government Board had occurred anywhere else, the Chief Secretary would have suspended the Guardians from the exercise of their functions, and appointed Vice Guardians. It was monstrous that hundreds of these unfortunate paupers professing the Roman Catholic faith were allowed to die without Christian ministration simply because they were paupers. In Ireland, where religion was strong, there was a very widespread feeling on the subject, and he trusted that the Committee would have some statement from the Chief Secretary that would be satisfactory, instead of being put off again with promises never intended to be performed. For more than 12 months this kind of thing had been going on, and the Irish Members had been unable to obtain satisfaction. In England such a scandal would be settled immediately. Time after time they had been told that the question was on the verge of settlement, but it had not been settled yet. So dogged were the gentlemen who officiated as Guardians in the Donegal Union in their religious prejudices that they would defer dealing with the question until they were absolutely driven to do so. Unless there was something in the shape of a menace from the Government, he did not believe for a moment that the Guardians would consent to come to terms. He hoped to hear from the Chief Secretary some statement as to the nature of the steps which the Local Government Board intended to take.

MR. GRAY said, the Chief Secretary in the course of his speech had touched upon various important subjects, and one of the matters which had been alluded to by the right hon. Gentleman was of special importance at the present moment—namely, the provisions which the Local Government had made or were making in view of the contingency of a possible outbreak of cholera in Ireland? He was aware that this was a subject to which the right hon. Gentleman and the Vice President of the Local Government Board should have their attention directed to; and he would ask if they were alive to the responsibility, and were prepared to accept it? There was no reason to assume that the United Kingdom would escape a visitation of this kind, for the history of previous epidemics pointed to the almost certainty of the disease visiting these shores in a more or less virulent form. It might not be at first in the most virulent form; but, judging from past experience, the visitation next year would be much more serious and severe. The right hon. Gentleman had told them what provision was intended to be made in regard to the hospitals, and so on; but there was one highly essential precaution which ought to be taken. He believed that it would be necessary to make a regular revolution in the present system of cleansing and scavenging. Cholera was essentially a disease which became dangerous and even fatal wherever filth existed, and he was of opinion that every precaution should be taken to insure cleanliness, for where that was done there was little to fear from the disease. Cleansing and scavenging, to be efficacious, required time; and he believed that no time should be lost in taking measures to prevent the disease from spreading. So far as medical assistance was concerned, it could not be necessary until the very moment of the attack and visitation; but it was very different with scavenging, cleansing, and disinfection, which, although very humble methods of prevention, were, perhaps, the most efficacious, although they undoubtedly took up the most time. He did not gather from the statement of the right hon. Gentleman that he had in his mind the propriety of urging upon the Local Government Board the necessity of making these regulations. It was all very well to tell them that he had in view preparations which would be available when the visitation came; but it was desirable to do a great deal more. A fortnight ago, he had asked the right hon. Gentleman under what circumstances the Local Government Board would feel themselves called upon to issue an Order, and he was told that it would be issued under the provisions of the 149th section of the Irish Act. Yesterday, the Chief Secretary repeated something to the same effect. He thought it was time the Local Government Board told them distinctly what the nature of the arrangements was. All the Continental cities had taken precautions; and even America, which was 3,000 miles away from any centre of the contagion, had made preparations to prevent its inroads. Probably they would be told that the Local Government Board were fully alive to the necessities of the case; but that they would refrain as long as possible from issuing their Orders, for fear of producing a panic. Now, he did not believe in any person dying of panic, and nothing effective would be done until the Local Government Board issued a sealed Order. If there were any persons who were likely to die of panic, he did not think it of much importance whether they lived or died. He would urge on the right hon. Gentleman himself not to be panic-stricken in regard to the effect of panic on other people. It was his duty, and that of the Local Government Board, to take timely precautions, and to issue Orders at once under which the Sanitary Authorities would be able to act. Scavenging and cleansing could not be accomplished in a moment, and after the Orders were issued weeks and months would elapse before their cities could be thoroughly purified and cleansed, and justify the people in regarding the approach of the disease with comparative equanimity. Scavenging and cleansing could not be carried on without great danger if the disease were actually to visit these shores, as it would be in that case a most serious thing to stir up the festering accumulations of filth which were known to exist. What would be thought of anyone stirring up the mud of the Thames, or the accumulations of refuse in the back yards, if the disease were actually amongst them? Everyone who had a nose had palpable evidence that the streets of London required effective cleansing. He would urge upon the right hon. Gentleman the necessity of taking timely precautions in this matter. He should remember that, if the case of cholera which had been discovered in the Mersey the other day had been introduced into Liverpool, the disease would have been in Dublin within three days. He did not believe there was the least danger of the people becoming panic-stricken if the necessary Order was made by the Local Government Board to have steps taken to institute precautionary measures. It would be folly to defer their action until cholera was actually in their midst. If the provisions of the Public Health Act were to have any effect at all, now was the time for putting them in force. The Irish people would prefer having their streets cleansed under a sealed Order rather than having them left in a state of filth. He considered this a matter of enormous importance. The right hon. Gentleman had alluded to an Act passed last year which materially affected Ireland, the object of the Act being to concentrate the responsibility in a single Sanitary Authority. In the peculiar conditions of Irish law, up to last year the duty in one district would be divided between the two Sanitary Authorities; but the Act of last year enabled the Local Government Board to concentrate the authority in the hands of one Body, and so far the measure was a useful one. Unless the evil he would point out was mitigated, the Act would be found inoperative. The authorities called on in the urban districts in Ireland to carry out the special provisions which might be made whenever the Local Government Board mustered up courage enough to issue a sealed Order were the Poor

Law Guardians. The duty of carrying out the work was vested in that Body, even in Dublin City, and the financial effect of that was, that the expense was divided between the owners and the occupiers, as all Poor Law charges were in Ireland. The Act of last year enabled the responsibility to be handed over to the Urban Sanitary Authority, which in ordinary cases was, of course, the Corporation. The taxes payable to the Corporation were payable solely by the occupiers, so that the financial result would be that, if the Local Government Board availed themselves of the Act of last Session, they would take the cost, so far as one-half was concerned, from the shoulders of the owner, who was certainly best able to bear it, and whose life, in his own opinion at any rate, was more valuable than that of the poor occupier, and to transfer it to the shoulders of the occupier solely, who might be presumed, in most cases, to be the poorer man, and less able to bear a sudden impost, and less likely to submit to it with willingness. Now, that was an effect which he believed was not contemplated by the Act. He was not quite certain that the Local Government Board had any power in the matter; but if the Urban Sanitary Authorities, or any of them, were to be selected to undertake this grave responsibility, a responsibility which would probably bring on them, under any circumstances, a great amount of odium, and nothing else, they might also be saddled with the responsibility of transferring to the occupier liabilities which the occupier would not otherwise incur. He would ask the right hon. Gentleman to give his consideration to this matter, or else he might find that, when the rules came to be enforced, they would all be dislocated by the financial difficulty that so often cropped up. With regard to the Labourers' Act, he (Mr. Gray) quite recognized the difficulty, and, in fact, the inexpediency, of generally discussing the subject pending the Report of the Select Committee. He trusted that the Committee would see its way to reporting that Session; but he acknowledged that the right hon. Gentleman would not be justified in seeking to put any pressure upon that Body to express its opinion on the subject just now. It was suggested that, in consequence of the Act not having been put into effective operation either in Connaught or in Ulster, it might be the duty of the Local Government Board to exercise the powers conferred upon them by Section 10, and to endeavour to force, to a certain extent, the putting of the Act into operation in extreme cases. Of course, the Local Government Board might consider it their duty to act in that way; but he, for one, must dissent from the opinion of his hon. Friends to this extent—that he believed they would be only justified in taking action of that kind in extreme cases. He thought it would be very much better for the interests of the labourers, and the success of the Act in the end, that the local Representative Bodies should be permitted to take the initiative. He did not believe in spurring on Local Bodies too energetically. He thought that where a Body was really representative of its constituency it was the best judge, and it was even better to let it make a mistake, and allow experience to put it right, than to suppress it and put matters in such a state that they would go back to their former position. The true remedy against the apathy, and even the hostility, which characterized a certain number of Boards of Guardians in Ireland was to make them more representative of the people. As his hon. Frend had pointed out, wherever the elected Guardians had a majority on the Board, wherever really the popular party had had the preponderance of votes upon the Board, they had shown their willingness to carry out the Act; and it was only where the *ex officio* element, or the sympathizers with that element, had been too strong for the truly local element, that the Act had been rendered nugatory. He thought that the remedy for that was to strengthen the representative element on the Boards. They knew that the Labourers' Act was in its very essence a Sanitary Act. How was it that sanitary matters had attracted, during the last 10 or 15 years, such an enormously increasing amount of attention in England? Why, it had only been since the time when Parliament had vested in the householders of cities and boroughs the franchise that those higher up in the social scale, statesmen and others, had found the necessity of directing their attention practically to sanitary matters. It was the last Reform Act which, by giving the people power in this country, had really brought about the important and valuable legislation which they had had in recent years in connection with all sanitary matters. Now, if in the same way in Ireland they gave the people more power on their local Representative Boards, they would insure their awaking in a very short time to the necessity for sanitary reforms, even to the extent of putting into operation the Labourers' Act. That would be a healthy, wholesome, and natural movement. But the Local Government Board in Ireland did not command the entire confidence of the Irish people, and pressure from that Board might have a deleterious effect. As he was on the sanitary question, he wished to call the attention of the right hon. Gentleman to the fact that, while he deprecated any pressure from the Local Government Board in this respect, he thought that Board could do a great deal to instruct and encourage the local Sanitary Authorities, whether Corporations, or Boards, or Poor Law Guardians, in their duties under the sanitary laws. Now, the Local Government Board in England was ceaseless in its efforts in this direction; but the Local Government Board in Ireland never did anything at all. The Local Government Board in England, immediately after the passing of the Public Health Act of 1875, set to work in the most careful manner, and, under the highest possible professional advice, drafted a series of model Poor Laws, circulated them amongst the Sanitary Authorities, and got them to adopt them with such modifications as might be required in certain localities. The Local Government Board in Ireland had done nothing of the kind. Not only had the Local Government Board in England issued a set of bye-laws, but after a certain number of years they had issued a revised and more valuable set. He would ask the right hon. Gentleman the Chief Secretary to the Lord Lieutenant whether the Local Government Board of Ireland would do anything to stimulate the Local Bodies in a legitimate way to a more healthy and vigorous action. The Sanitary Authorities in Dublin had adopted a set of bye-laws framed on the English model; but they got in the matter no assistance whatever from the Local Government Board, and that Board would not, even when they were framed, adopt them as a model and see how they could be applied to all the other Sanitary Authorities of Ireland. He had put a Question on this matter to the right hon. Gentleman, and the right hon. Gentleman had informed him vaguely that the Local Government Board of Ireland did not see the necessity for the bye-laws. He (Mr. Gray) failed to see why the Local Government Board in Ireland ought not to be as zealous in instructing and encouraging the local Sanitary Authorities, who naturally could not be expected to be informed on these subjects—why they should not, in fact, become as much interested in their work as did the officials of the Local Government Board in England. Possibly the secret of it was to be found in the fact alluded to by the right hon. Gentleman in connection with an observation which he made as to the salary of the Vice President of the Local Government Board. He (Mr. Gray) respectfully agreed with him, that in the case of an official occupying so responsible a post as Mr. Robinson, and performing his duties on the whole so well, he was not too highly paid by a salary of £2,000 a-year. He did not think they could get a good man to do the work for much less. In England, the Local Government Board was represented by two Parliamentary officers, one of them a Minister of Cabinet rank. The right hon. Gentleman, in the speech he had made, touching on a variety of subjects, had shown a marvellous amount of industry and a splendid memory; but no sane man could expect that the Chief Secretary could possibly make himself acquainted with all the details of the Local Government Board in Ireland in the manner in which the two Gentlemen who represented the English Local Government Board, and who were charged solely with those duties, and no others, could make themselves acquainted with the details of their Office. Compared with the enormous number of duties which the right hon. Gentleman had to discharge, his functions as President of the Local Government Board were merely nominal. All he could possibly be expected to do was to act as a species of funnel to submit to the House information which he received from the officials in Ireland. He was not like either of the English Representatives of the Department, who were responsible officials, and not merely nominal Heads, but Parliamentary Heads of the Office, able to answer Questions, and go into subjects from their own knowledge. He (Mr. Gray) was amazed at the amount of knowledge which the right hon. Gentleman (Mr. Trevelyan) had shown; but the right hon. Gentleman did not profess to have the same knowledge of the Department as the officials of the Local Government Board in England were legitimately expected to have, seeing that they were more responsible and had more knowledge in the matter. He wished to call the attention of the right hon. Gentleman to the difficulty which sometimes arose in connection with the functions of auditors under the Local Government Board and local Representative Bodies in Ireland. The clauses of the Irish Act appointing them, and giving them their powers of surcharge, were not precisely the same as the corresponding clause of the English Act. Still, in substance they were the same. But he did not think that the Auditors in Ireland took as broad a view of their duties as did the Auditors in England. He knew that sometimes Local Bodies in Ireland had serious reason to complain that the Auditors inflicted upon them surcharges for money really *bonâ fide* expended in the interests of their constituents, and sometimes on public objects. He did not think that, in giving this power to surcharge, the object was that it should be used in a narrow, technical manner, and that the Auditors should have power to charge an individual doing an important public duty without any kind of fee or reward—that he should be really able to fine them if they stepped out of the technical limit of their powers, as they sometimes happened to do, for the public benefit, although the action was technically *ultra vires*. He would call attention to one case of surcharge, not important as to the amount, but very important as to principle—a case which occurred within the last few years in the Dublin Corporation. The Dublin Corporation had been in the habit of constantly sending deputations to England in connection with such matters as Royal marriages, Royal christenings, and Royal what-nots. Usually, the Lord Mayor and certain members of the Corporation came over, attended by the civic officers, to add *éclat* to the occasion. The custom was for the Lord Mayor, and the members of the Corporation who attended him, to pay their own expenses; but for the expenses of the civic officers to be paid out of the rates. That, he believed, was a common habit in England. The Local Government Board Auditor invariably allowed these expenses, thus showing that, in his opinion, they were legal expenses, and that it was within the discretion of the Local Body to spend the rates under their control for congratulating Her Majesty whenever any auspicious event occurred in connection with the Royal Family. Well, last year, a matter which, perhaps, some of the Irish people deemed to be of almost as much importance to them as the advent of a new Royal Infant, occurred in Ireland. An Exhibition, a National Exhibition, was opened in Cork for the purpose of seeking to encourage Irish local manufacturing enterprize and industry. It partook, in no sense, of a rebel or revolutionary character. The chief movers in it were strong Conservatives. All parties in Cork joined to make it a success; and it actually enjoyed the patronage and presence in bodily form of the Lord Lieutenant, which was an abundant guarantee of the useful and loyal character of the undertaking. Well, the Corporation of Dublin considered it their duty to encourage the Exhibition by all the means in their power; and they passed a resolution for the then Lord Mayor of Dublin to attend in state, and ordering the civic officers to accompany him. The Lord Mayor, as usual, paid his own expenses; but the expenses of the officers—their travelling expenses—were paid, by order of the Common Council, out of the funds of the Municipality. Twelve months afterwards, when the Auditor came to audit the accounts, he surcharged, not the individuals who had ordered the payment, but the persons who, by the routine of the service, had to sign the cheques. Now, what distinction was there in law between the Corporation sending their Lord Mayor and officers to England for the purpose of carrying an Address of sympathy or congratulation to the Royal Family, and their sending their officers to Cork for the purpose of attending the opening of a National Industrial Exhibition? Why, in the one case, were individuals to be made to pay out of their private purses, and, in the other, the ratepayers be held liable by the auditor?

He would ask the attention of the right hon. Gentleman the President of the Irish Local Government Board to that particular point. He (Mr. Gray) had given the right hon. Gentleman briefly the facts of the case. As to the general system of audit, it would be worthy of the right hon. Gentleman's attention whether some improvement should not be made. The system both in England and Ireland was very extraordinary, but particularly so in Ireland. Resolutions were come to at one meeting, and were usually acted upon at the next. It saved time, and was the most convenient course. For instance, at a meeting of the Poor Law Guardians a number of payments would be ordered to be made to-day, and at the next meeting the formal operation of signing the cheques would be gone through. In the event of one unlawful payment being made, and the auditor surcharging it, it was not the individuals who ordered the payment to be made who were held liable, but the individuals who happened to go through the purely mechanical act of signing the cheque—individuals who might have had no connection whatever with the operation of ordering the payment. The Act said that the Auditor, under the circumstances, should be entitled to surcharge the illegal or improper payment on the person making or authorizing the illegal payment. If the payment were illegal, or such as should be surcharged, it was right to surcharge the person authorizing it; but the fact that the mechanical operation of signing a cheque rendered the person so signing liable to the surcharge struck him as something like an absurdity. He himself had known many cases in which individual members of a Corporation voted against a certain payment; in a week or a fortnight cheques in connection with that payment came up; they were signed in the ordinary routine, the resolution of the Corporation being thought to be a sufficient guarantee to those who signed them that the payments were justifiable; subsequently the Auditor surcharged the amount, and the persons who signed the cheques, although they might have been opposed on the Council to the illegal payment, had to pay the surcharge. This was an absurdity. Where thousands of cheques had to be signed, it would be impossible for the persons signing them to consider whether each payment authorized by the previous action of the Body was legal. Though the matter was a small one, he would ask the right hon. Gentleman to consider it in order to see whether it could not be placed on a better footing. He did not deny that there might be legitimate surcharges; but where they existed, they should be enforced upon the proper individuals, because, as he had pointed out, at the present time they were very often put upon the wrong people. As to the Auditors and the Inspectors of the Local Government Board, he wished to mention to the right hon. Gentleman that he believed a great amount of dissatisfaction existed amongst officers of the Local Government Board in consequence of the way in which the prizes of the Office were frequently given away by the Heads of the Departments. Officers who had served long in any Department looked forward to promotion—to Inspectorships, or to Auditorships—as the rewards of their services; and when some outsider, comparatively ignorant of the work of the Department, without any kind of qualification except merely that of being a relative of this person, or the pet of that individual who might have influence, was pitchforked over the heads of those who were entitled to promotion from long and faithful services, the result was to discourage the officials of the Department. He did not wish to drag forward the names of individuals; but it would possibly be in the recollection of the right hon. Gentleman himself how many times during the last few years outsiders had been taken in and presented to lucrative offices, while competent individuals, who had been for considerable periods in the Service, had had their claims passed over. He did not make any complaint against the right hon. Gentleman, because he believed that under the late Government the system was, if anything, worse. He (Mr. Gray) did not see why, if they could find an efficient officer in the Department, they should go outside it to fill vacancies; and even if a man happened to be a captain, a colonel, or the relative of a Lord, he did not see why he should have £600 or £700 a-year presented to him for doing work in order to learn how to perform which it was necessary that he should have a man under him. There was another matter to which attention had been very frequently directed. It was a matter which did not affect the Chief Secretary so much as the Secretary to the Treasury; but he would call attention to it, although he had not the least hope that what he said would have any effect upon the hon. Gentleman. They would find in this Vote a considerable sum for the salaries of sanitary officers. By the Public Health Act of 1874, as well as he remembered, the Treasury, in order to encourage the appointment of sanitary officers, paid the Sanitary Authorities in Ireland—and he believed that the same thing was done in England—half the salaries of these persons; but, in consenting to do that, they inflicted what he considered to be a very great injustice upon those Sanitary Authorities, and he had already taken action for the purpose of bringing about sanitary improvement before it was compulsory upon them to do so. Prior to the passing of the Act of 1874, under the former Public Health Acts, it was open to the Sanitary Authorities to appoint sanitary medical officers, and a sanitary staff or not, as they thought fit. Some of them thought fit, but most of them did not. Now the Treasury, which, after the passing of the Act of 1874, had rendered these appointments compulsory on all Local Bodies, said—"We will give to those who, up to 1874, had neglected their duties and made no appointments, half the salaries of the new officers; but as an encouragement to those who did their duty, and did make appointments, we will offer no assistance whatever." That seemed to him very [illegible] the ratepayers who did their duty and rewarding those who neglected it. How could they expect that Local Authorities would put into effective operation [illegible] legislation if they treated them in that way? Was it not natural that [illegible] the circumstances, the Boards of Guardians should hang back and say—"The Treasury will do the same in connection with the Labourers' Act as they are doing in connection with the Public Health Act. We will wait [illegible] they do." These Bodies [illegible]—"If we do not put [illegible] provisions of the Act [illegible] we shall receive some [illegible] the Treasury; whereas, if we do put the Act into operation we shall have to bear the whole expense [illegible] receive any assistance." The action of the Government in this matter was certainly not just. And it did not seem to him (Mr. Gray) to be good policy. He could understand the Treasury even saying that in the lifetime of the individuals already appointed they would not make contributions to their salaries; but to say that for ever they would make this distinction between officers performing the same duties, and between similar Public Bodies—to say that they would pay a contribution of half the salaries to one set, where they neglected their duty, and refused to another, where they performed their duty, was to give a premium to sluggishness, and a punishment in perpetuity to the progressive districts in Ireland. The Government did not seem to have a defensible position; although he had no doubt the Financial Secretary to the Treasury would have some excellent reasons to give for maintaining the existing state of things. The system appeared to him (Mr. Gray) to be hardly compatible with justice or common sense; and certainly it tended to encourage Sanitary Authorities in future to refrain from doing what they should for the carrying out of the Labourers' Act. The right hon. Gentleman had alluded to the case of the man Elliott of Balbriggan [illegible] South Dublin Union. [illegible] arrive at official knowledge of the fact? Supposing the case were published in all the newspapers, and were made the subject of discussion for months. Would it not suggest itself to the right hon. Gentleman to make some inquiries concerning the individual, and to question the man himself? Would he not take that course in the case of one of his own servants? Would he not ask him what he had done with the money that was missing? Supposing anyone in that House had an *employé* against whom such a charge was made; would he not ascertain by the best means in his power what truth there was in that charge? Would not the simple way of obtaining information be either to write or to send to the man, asking whether it was a fact that he was short in his accounts? The *employé* would have to reply yea or nay. If this course were pursued in the case of Elliott, and if the latter said neither yes nor no, it would then be sufficiently manifest to the common sense of the right hon. Gentleman that the man was guilty. Everyone knew that he was guilty. It had been the subject of discussion on the Board day after day. The Board had taken his property. He had been under their vigilance day by day, and they estreated his belongings. Surely, this was not a man who ought to be allowed to remain in the Public Service, handling public money. The right hon. Gentleman did not seem to think that there was anything for him to do; but there was a simple thing for him to do. In the first place, he should cause a letter to be written to Mr. Elliott, as to an *employé*, asking for an explanation, and should give Mr. Elliott to understand that if he did not send one he would be dismissed from his office; but that, under any circumstances, in the meantime he would be suspended. Saying this much could not be attended with any kind of injustice or hardship. In connection with the Local Government Board Vote there was such a variety of topics, all of them of considerable interest and importance, that once he (Mr. Gray) had commenced, he found some difficulty in stopping. He thanked the Committee for the patient attention they had given to him.

Mr. DAWSON said, that with regard to the last question mentioned by the hon. Member who had just sat down, he would remind the Chief Secretary of the answer which the Secretary to the Treasury had given to him (Mr. Dawson) as to the steps to be taken in the case of Mr. Elliott, because he was sorry to say that the Local Government Board would ride off on the excuse that the difficulties in the defalcations of Mr. Elliott were matters for the Sanitary Board, and not for the Local Government Board. He had asked what course they would pursue if they found a man in the Government employ, but in another capacity of a municipal kind, had been guilty of defalcations? He had asked how they would proceed; and the Secretary to the Treasury had told him that the Home Secretary would take cognizance of the matter in England. Well, the right hon. Gentleman the Chief Secretary stood, so far as Ireland was concerned, not only in the position of President of the Local Government Board, but also in the position of Secretary of State. He (Mr. Dawson) therefore maintained that he was bound, not only as Head Official of the Local Government Board, but as the Chief Secretary of State for Ireland, to take cognizance of Mr. Elliott's defalcation, and to institute, as a Secretary of State would do in England in the case of an English official, a full inquiry into the matter. Then, as to the Auditor, he begged to ask the Chief Secretary if he would give them, if not of his own knowledge, at least on the authority of the officials with whom he was associated, some categorical answer to this plain question? If the Auditor of the Local Government Board should say that it was legal to spend the public funds of Dublin in coming to the Bar of the House to congratulate Her Majesty on an auspicious event, how could they draw the line and say it was illegal for the same Corporation to send their officer to open in state an enterprize that was for the national benefit and the general progress of the community? They certainly did not find in the Act any definite instruction as to where to draw the line. The phraseology of the law which directed the Auditor in the two countries was typical of all the other legislation which was passed for the two countries. In the first article of the Instructions to the Poor Law Officers in England, the conditions under which they should surcharge were detailed in a comprehensive manner; but what was the wonderful power given, unfortunately, by the Act applying to Ireland? It was to surcharge everything contrary to law, or anything they deemed to be not according to law. He thought that the right hon. Gentleman the Chief Secretary to the Lord Lieutenant of Ireland, or the hon. and learned Solicitor General for Ireland, should give the Committee a plain statement as to the liability of officers who administered the public funds in a city like Dublin in respect of money spent by them in sending an Address to Her Majesty and in respect of other public events. He was of opinion, and he trusted the right hon. Gentleman the Chief Secretary would be able to say, that as soon as possible some legislation should be introduced to define the power of Auditors of the Local Government Board in Ireland in respect of surcharges. What the Committee looked for from the right hon. Gentleman now was that he should answer the legal point raised with regard to the two species of deputations, and also that he should state whether he intended to take proceedings against Mr. Elliott.

MR. KENNY said, it would be superfluous for him to follow the hon. Member for Carlow County (Mr. Gray) into the question of the sanitary arrangements at Dublin, because he had so thorough a knowledge of the subject, and had spoken upon it so ably and fully, that it would be almost impossible to add anything of value to what he had stated. But the hon. Member had also called the attention of the right hon. Gentleman and the Committee to the appointments of Sanitary Inspectors; and, in doing so, he had pointed out an extraordinary anomaly with regard to them—namely, that, whereas the Medical Inspectors and Officers of Health who were appointed under the Act of 1874, had the half of their salaries paid by the Treasury, those who were appointed previously to that Act coming into operation had no portion of their salaries paid out of the Consolidated Fund. He was bound to say that he regarded the existence of those officers as a complete fraud—an imposition. They did nothing for their pay. Notwithstanding the large salaries they received nothing was done by them to preserve the health of the people. In cases where they were employed by people, it was not likely that they would report adversely to those who supported them, because they depended more upon their practice than they did upon their salaries as Officers of Health. This office, which was so necessary, was made such a fraud on the public that when the present Amendment was disposed of, he should feel it his duty to move the reduction of the Vote by the sum of £7,400 which represented half the salaries of the Sanitary Officers. But he rose mainly for the purpose of addressing the right hon. Gentleman on a subject which was closely connected with the question of the health and sanitary condition of a town in Ireland. Some time since, owing to a variety of circumstances, the existence of the Ennis Town Commissioners ceased. Now the Town Improvement Act had ceased to be enforced, and it was sought to have that Act re-adopted, a proposal which was agreed to by the ratepayers at a public meeting. On the 9th of April last, a deputation of townspeople went to the Board of Guardians and asked them to take charge of the water and sewage works, and also of the lighting of the town; a deputation was then deputed to beg the consent of the Local Government Board. The deputation, having attended the Local Government Board with reference to the sewage and water works, informed them that the Board desired to know what their powers were, and whether they were authorized to undertake the duty of contracting for the supply of the town; and, in regard to the question of lighting, what power they had to supply gasworks, or of contracting for the supply of gas from the present Company; and also whether the Board of Guardians could assume the functions which formerly had had belonged to the Town Commissioners? The letter sent in reply stated that the Board of Guardians could not undertake the lighting of the town, and that the opinion of the Law Officers would be obtained on the other point. But three months had elapsed since that time, and yet no answer had been given, notwithstanding that repeated communications had passed asking for a reply to the inquiry of the Board of Guardians. It appeared that the Local Government Board found it impossible to prevent the Board of Guardians taking charge of the water works, as the rates would have to be divided between the landlords and the tenants. Of course, there was a feeling amongst a certain portion of the population of the town that it would be adverse to their interest to have the Board of Guardians appointed for the purpose, because the adjustment of taxation might be different under the Board of Guardians from what it was under the Town Commissioners. He need not point out that at the present moment it was exceedingly desirable that the sanitary arrangements at Ennis should be looked after and made as complete as possible; that the town should be lighted; that the water works should not be allowed to fall into a defective state owing to there being no person to look after them, and that there should be some authority appointed who should be responsible for their proper management. It appeared that when the water works were originally constructed, there was a little stream near them which was shut off by the engineer responsible for the management of the works. But owing to the present unsatisfactory state of affairs this stream had broken through the barrier and entered the reservoir which supplied the town. The Committee would at once perceive the very serious consequences which were likely to follow from the town being supplied with bad water, especially if there were an epidemic of cholera. He would venture to put this matter before the Solicitor General for Ireland. It appeared to him that under the Public Health Act there were strong reasons for supposing that the Board of Guardians had power to assume the responsibility for supplying water to and lighting the town, which the Town Commissioners previously possessed. It was stated in the reply which the Board of Guardians received from the Local Government Board, on the 28th of April last, that there was no power in them to light the town, which, by the Public Health Act, was confined solely to the Local Authorities. But Section 80 of the Act gave power to the Sanitary Authority to contract for lighting, and even to purchase gas works, and, therefore, he was of opinion that the Board of Guardians were entitled to contract for the lighting of the town. He would also call the attention of the hon. and learned Gentleman to the words "duly authorized" in the connection in which they stood in the 232nd section of the Act, which clearly implied that the Board of Guardians had power to light the town. For his own part, he thought that, under various provisions of the Public Health Act, it was clearly established that the Board of Guardians could assume the exact functions which the Town Commissioners had ceased to exercise. He could quite understand that it might be inconvenient for the hon. and learned Gentleman to reply upon this question at the present time, because he (Mr. Kenny) had introduced the subject without any previous Notice. He understood that the question was rather an involved one, and that the cases which had arisen under the Act of Parliament were very intricate and complicated, and therefore the hon. and learned Gentleman would probably prefer to reply on the point he had raised on a future occasion. Still, as his constituents were extremely anxious to know in what position they stood in reference to this matter, he should be obliged if the hon. and learned Gentleman would state the day on which it would be convenient that such reply should be given.

THE SOLICITOR GENERAL FOR IRELAND (Mr. WALKER) said, this was probably the first time that the question brought forward by the hon. Member for Ennis (Mr. Kenny) had been raised since the Act was passed under which the Town Commissioners ceased to exist. *Primâ facie* he did not think the Board of Guardians had power to light the town. However, he was aware that some difference of opinion existed on the matters to which the hon. Member had referred, and if the hon. Member would place a Notice on the Paper, he would undertake to answer it in detail on Friday next.

MR. DAWSON said, he must ask the Solicitor General for Ireland, as the Legal Representative of the Irish Government, to give an opinion on the power of the auditor to make a distinction with regard to surcharging public officers in cases where they expended money on different public objects. What powers had they to distinguish between money spent on presenting an Address to Her Majesty, and money spent, say, upon opening an important public Exhibition?

THE SOLICITOR GENERAL FOR IRELAND (Mr. WALKER) said, it was the duty of the Auditor to exercise his discretion and legal knowledge in striking out payments that he deemed to be illegal. The auditor might be right, or he might be wrong, in deciding on a particular charge; but he would point out that a two-fold remedy was provided—first, by an appeal to the Local Government Board, who, after consultation with their legal advisers, might decide whether an auditor was right or wrong; and, secondly, by an appeal from the Local Government Board to the Court of Queen's Bench by writ of *certiorari*. It was clear, therefore, that the law provided ample remedy in case of error on the part of the auditor.

MR. GRAY said, with all respect to the hon. and learned Gentleman the Solicitor General for Ireland, he did not think he was quite right in the view he had taken of the remedy open to public officers who were surcharged by the auditor of the Local Government Board. The hon. and learned Gentleman had described that remedy as two-fold; but his recollection was that the exercise of one part of the remedy precluded the use of the other. They might appeal to the clemency of the Local Government Board with reference to the question of law, or, at their own instance, they might seek to have the question decided at law; but they could not first appeal to the consideration of the Local Government Board, and then, if the result were unfavourable, proceed in the Queen's Bench. He was anxious to make the position clear with reference to this point. His opinion was that the remedy was not two-fold, as the hon. and learned Gentleman had described it to be, but alternative. The hon. and learned Gentleman said that the auditor was entitled to exercise his discretion as regarded the legality of certain payments, and that the word "unfounded" meant unvouched, not unjustifiable; that was to say, the auditor was only entitled to consider whether the payments made were illegal payments or not. For instance, one might conceive it to be perfectly proper on the part of the Local Authorities to send a deputation, at their own expense, to congratulate Her Majesty under certain circumstances, or to open an Exhibition; on the other hand, it might be, in the opinion of other persons, improper to send a deputation for any trifling pupose. Now, he said that if the auditor was not to have regard to the test of the discretion of the body in question, but was solely to be restricted to the consideration as to whether the expenditure was legal or not—if that were so, he contended that nothing could well be more unsatisfactory, because the auditor was found often to forget that he was a public official, to seek to place himself in the position of the elected representatives of the ratepayers, and to say whether such or such an expenditure was or was not extravagant and imprudent, besides occasionally surcharging, not because he thought the expenditure illegal, but because he did not like it. For instance, the auditor, on one occasion, surcharged the fees paid by the Dublin Corporation to Messrs. Ellis and Sons, solicitors, for appearing, on behalf of the Council, before the Recorder of Dublin, on the ground that they had a regular law agent, although that gentleman was then engaged upon important legal business in London. Now, he felt sure that the legal mind of the Solicitor General for Ireland would revolt from that exercise of the auditor's discretion. There was an appeal, undoubtedly, to the Local Government Board, and that appeal might decide the matter, not on the point of law, but on the point of whether the expenditure was one which they approved, or otherwise; and there was an appeal to the Court of Queen's Bench, in which a great deal of money might be unsuccessfully spent. But there ought, he contended, to be some means by which a local body, without expense or formality, could obtain a legal decision with regard to the legality of surcharges by auditors of the Local Government Board. It was not sufficient that the Local Government Board should, in some cases of surchage, be able to tell the auditor to say no more about the matter. There ought to be more than that; there ought to be responsibility on the part of the auditor. The law, as it stood, would amply provide against any absolutely improper application of the funds. There ought to be such a remedy as an application to the Court of Queen's Bench for a *mandamus* or some other means of recovering the money. Further, he thought that a Government official should not have the right to interfere at all between the ratepayers and those who expended the public money. He was of opinion that there ought to be a double remedy—first, an application on the merits of the case to the Local Government Board, and, failing that, an application to the Court of Queen's Bench. With regard to the case put by his hon. Friend the Member for Carlow (Mr. Dawson). Here was an instance in point. Money had been spent by a public body on two objects—in the one case upon a deputation to congratulate Her Majesty upon certain circumstances, and in the other upon the opening of an important public Exhibition, and the auditor stepped in and said—"I will allow the charge for the Queen; I will not allow it for the Exhibition." He did not think that the answer of the hon. and learned Gentleman met the case put by his hon. Friend.

MR. ARTHUR ARNOLD said, having listened for some time to the complaints of Irish Members opposite, he felt bound to commiserate the state of their affairs. He rose on that occasion to say a few words with reference to what had fallen from the hon. Member for Carlow (Mr. Dawson), and other hon. Members, in regard to the question of surcharges by auditors of the Local Government Board. He had understood the hon. Gentleman the Secretary to the Treasury to wish to lead the Committee to suppose—["No, no!"]—at all events, the hon. Gentleman had led him to suppose that, in some circumstances, in England it was possible for such a matter to occur as the hon. Member for Carlow had alluded to. But no such thing had ever happened in England. There was no Government audit of the Corporation accounts of any municipal borough in England; and if the Corporation of any borough in England thought fit to come up to London at that time to congratulate the Prime Minister on the passing of the Representation of the People Bill through the House of Commons there was no power to surcharge the expense of such a visit upon those who incurred it. The auditors of Municipal Corporations were appointed by the Corporations themselves, their functions were clearly defined, and were limited to investigating whether or not the expenditure was met by the vouchers that were produced to them at the audit. He assured the hon. Gentleman that no such case could occur, with regard to any Corporation in England, as that described by the hon. Member for Carlow; and he did not see why the Corporation of the City of Dublin should labour under a disability which did not apply to any Municipal Corporation in England.

MR. DAWSON said, he felt it his duty to press this question further upon the hon. Gentleman the Secretary to the Treasury. He could assure the hon. Gentleman that the circumstances he had alluded to had created a very strong interest amongst the people of Dublin and of Ireland generally. In this matter of audit they complained that power was left to the auditor, who was not a lawyer, to decide upon his own judgment what he would and what he would not allow; in other words, it was left to him to say whether he would irritate and annoy the whole Corporation of Dublin, and put the people into a state of discontent with the law of the land. He was sorry to trouble the President of the Local Government Board, whose duties were so constant and multifarious; but he would be glad to know distinctly from him whether it was a fact that the Department had issued a request to the auditors who were engaged in carrying out the law in England that they would only surcharge what was not accounted for? The Irish Act contained the words with reference to surcharges "which he deems to be unfounded," and those words he (Mr. Dawson) contended ought to be restricted. The result of the present action of the auditors might well be that if the Corporations in Ireland could not send their officers to open a public Exhibition, which in the case in question, he believed, was under the patronage of Her Majesty the Queen and of the Lord Lieutenant of Ireland, they could not send deputations of the other kind indicated—they might say they could not send deputations to condole with Her Majesty in her domestic bereavements, or to congratulate her on having escaped from the hand of an assassin, because they would have to bear the expense themselves. If they were told they must not employ their officers to open an Industrial Exhibition, as they would have to pay for it, why that wholesome custom would have to be discontinued. The point was, that the Dublin Corporation were allowed to send a deputation to London to present an Address of Congratulation to Her Majesty because the auditor said the expenditure was legal; but when they sent to Cork to open an Exhibition that would be useful to the people of Ireland the case was entirely different. This high-minded man said—"We will allow you to come to London and spend £50 on an Address to the Queen; but if you go down to Cork to open an Exhibition for the purpose of facilitating the development of Irish industry we will surcharge you every farthing." He therefore appealed to the painstaking President of the Local Government Board to take this matter up, and to prevent the further irritation of public opinion which the action of the auditors had produced throughout Ireland. Under the Irish Act an incompetent man often got to be auditor, and, in the matter of allowing expenses and expending the funds of the Municipality, took upon himself to tell the people what they should do and what they should not do, in spite of his want of knowledge on the subject.

Mr. COURTNEY said, he took part in the debate with great reluctance, and at the outset he felt it necessary to take exception to expressions made use of by the hon. Member for Salford (Mr Arnold).

Mr. ARTHUR ARNOLD said, he would withdraw any expression the hon. Gentleman thought out of place.

Mr. COURTNEY said, the hon. Member for Salford was not correct when he stated that any of these expenses could be borne out of the borough fund in England.

Mr. ARTHUR ARNOLD: I said that any expense out of the borough funds could not be made subject to surcharge.

Mr. COURTNEY: I do not say those were the hon. Member's very words. I say the argument of my hon. Friend was that the excessive expenditure at the discretion of Town Councils in England could not be questioned by the auditor.

Mr. ARTHUR ARNOLD: Not questioned in the same manner.

Mr. COURTNEY: It was asserted that in England the authority of the Town Council was not sufficient to cover the expense incurred by the Town Council. The question was opened in England, although in a different manner, as was seen in the case of the Corporation of Sunderland.

Mr. GRAY: The action of the Town Council was questioned in a Court of Law.

Mr. COURTNEY: Precisely. No doubt the auditor in Ireland is able to question the accounts and surcharge illegal expenditure; but is his action final?

Mr. GRAY: Yes.

Mr. COURTNEY said, the statute which created the auditor's duties provided two means of redress and getting the auditor's decision corrected—one way by applying to the Local Government Board for a reconsideration of the auditor's decision, and asking that, if necessary, the auditor should be superseded, and the other way precisely as in England—by applying to the Court of Queen's Bench for a writ of *certiorari*. Those were the remedies afforded by the Statute. The first seemed very simple—namely, to appeal to the Local Government Board—and it involved no expense whatever. In the case in question no remedy had been resorted to. It was not for him to question the consistency of the decisions in the matter of the various expenses of the Dublin Corporation, some having been surcharged and the others allowed. Possibly the Corporation would come to the conclusion, after what had occurred, that if they were not to be permitted to spend money for one purpose they would not spend it for another.

Mr. JESSE COLLINGS said, one was struck by such speeches as they had just heard with the want of knowledge of the Members of the Government as to the nature of local business. He thought it should be necessary for a man before he became a Minister to serve an apprenticeship of not less than three years in one of their local Municipal Corporations, or that Parliament should occasionally meet in one of their large Provincial towns, in order to get out of the miserable atmosphere of London and acquire some knowledge of local affairs. There was nothing worse—there was nothing more irritating than this auditorship in large towns. An auditor came down to Birmingham, or Manchester, or Liverpool, to audit the School Board accounts, and took off, say 1*s.* 6*d.*, for a cab which some unfortunate individual had seen fit to hire in the peformance of his duty in connection with the School Board. His hon. Friend (Mr. Courtney) talked about "a remedy." But the hon. Gentleman must remember that an appeal, if unsuccessful, involved great expense to those who made it. He must also remember that election to a position on the Town Council no doubt carried with it a great deal of honour. ["Oh, oh!" *and a laugh.*] He expected cheers of that kind from Gentlemen who did not know the dignity of their municipal institutions; but he could assure them that the position was regarded by the leading citizens in their municipal boroughs as a high honour. That was to say, it was the highest position within their reach — the highest position in which they could serve their fellow-citizens and secure good local government. As he was saying, the position of Town Councillor, although it involved a great deal of honour, at the same time involved considerable responsibility. Added to these drawbacks, the responsibilities and sacrifices of public municipal life, they were asking by the remedy the hon. Gentleman suggested that men should get themselves out of a position of difficulty in which they had been placed by some official knowing nothing about the circumstances by appealing to London, very possibly getting themselves into expense. Take the Corporation of Birmingham, for instance, which had upon it a large number of men unable to bear heavy expense. Surely, it was a very hard position to place such men in, to hold them responsible for the repayment of the cheques required, if one of these auditors should come down and surcharge the expenditure. In his opinion no audit at all was required. Corporations were required to furnish accounts periodically—once a year—and they were scrutinized by the ratepayers, and that was a sufficient check. In Birmingham they had two local auditors who, so far as vouchers and so far as expense was concerned, were very considerate. It was necessary to get out of the minds of the Government and their law-makers this idea of centralization. That a man or two or three men shut up in a room in London could understand the wants or do justice to a particular locality in these matters of expenditure was absurd, and it should be get out of the minds of the Government. He on one occasion had been engaged in regulating a public meeting for a public object, and an action was brought against him. The Town Council decided to defend him. One or two individuals moved the Queen's Bench, or whatever it was in London, to prevent the charge for his defence being levied on the ratepayers; and the result was that the costs, amounting to £200 or £300, were put upon him. What right had anyone in London to say to the people of Birmingham, represented by their local Parliament—"You shall not do this thing; and your Chief Magistrate, who for no purpose of his own, but in order to secure good order in an action which the inhabitants compelled him to undertake to preside over, shall bear the expense of defending himself." What right had anyone in London to say that the people of the Muncipality should not bear the expense of defending that Chief Magistrate? He thought the tendency of the House should be to leave the localities to help themselves, and to manage their own affairs. At present the state of things was simply like a nurse saying to a child—"I will never let you walk until you can walk properly." At least, let a child learn to walk. It must always have its falls and bumps; but they would teach it experience that would cease when it began to stand well. In the same way it was most foolish to keep Corporations continually in leading strings. He did not know Irish Corporations were subjected to indignities that English Corporations were free from, and if they were it was time the arrangement was altered. All bodies elected by the people should be let alone. The House might depend upon it that if they went wrong once or twice they would not go wrong a third or fourth time, for the ratepayers, or those who had to supply the money, would very soon insist upon those who had the spending of it awaking to a sense of their duty. To his mind they had quite enough to do in that House instead of meddling in all these little ridiculous things connected with subjects which they could not possibly understand. If hon. Members could see the ridicule in the locality itself attached to the proceedings of auditors sent down to audit the affairs of a Municipality they would be amused. For instance, the manner in which the expenditure of the School Boards was audited was regarded as a perfect farce. The expense of the salaries of these officers was regarded as an absolute waste of money, and he had no hesitation in saying that where £100 was spent on these officials they did not effect a saving of as many shillings. He knew cases where there had been grave doubt and serious reflection as to the accounts of a Municipality, and where in the end there had been about 2*s.* 6*d.* struck off for some simple matter. As to the remedy pointed out, that in a very small degree, if at all, alleviated the difficulty. It added to the expense, no doubt; and if those who appealed were unsuccessful the expense fell upon them—the poor Town Councillors. In this case there was no allegation of any fraud or mal-administration. But in cases where the representatives of the people spent money with the full approval of the constituents, and in the interest and for the benefit of the locality, if the auditor when he came down should happen to disagree with the item, possibly because of his over-officiousness, such representatives of the people would have to bear the expense. The ratepayers had a remedy in their own hands if anything wrong was going on with the accounts. They had the power of turning out the Town Councillors at the next election. The ratepayers knew what was going on—the auditor knew nothing about the borough. They wanted a species of Home Rule in England in these matters as well as in Ireland. Let the people in their boroughs manage their own affairs—it would satisfy the localities, and enable Parliament to devote more time to more important Imperial matters. He earnestly hoped the Government would take this matter into their consideration, and would move in the direction of putting a stop to all this waste and expense of auditing. He was conscious that there was a difficulty in the way of such a proceeding—namely, the idea the various Departments had of the advantages of creating new offices. The Departments were always anxious for an opportunity of creating a new office—they readily availed themselves of any pretence for such a proceeding. They all liked creating offices to which salaries of some hundreds a-year were attached, and in connection with which there were some duties to perform which they endeavoured to persuade the country were useful. All this sort of thing caused great dissatisfaction in their municipal boroughs; and it was a matter which when they had time, and when the Parliamentary atmosphere was clear of present legislation, the Government would have greater pressure put upon them to deal with.

MR. DAWSON said, the Secretary to the Treasury, who was nothing if not critical, in this case had exercised his criticism on matters with which he had not the slightest acquaintance. They had not taken action against the decision of the auditor in the case of Dublin, but they had in the case of Limerick. Limerick, in order to give effect and solemnity to the Industrial Exhibition, had also sent up to Cork their civic officers, and when the expenses of these officers were surcharged upon the Town Council an appeal *ad misericordiam* was made to the Local Government Board. This appeal met with no satisfactory response—the mission was not recognized as one for which the ratepayers should be allowed to pay, however they might desire to, because it was not a toadying affair. Limerick had applied to the Queen's Bench; but their surcharge was confirmed in a much more Governmental manner than it had been by the Local Government Board itself. The Municipality of Dublin, therefore, had been forewarned and forearmed. They had heard upon this subject a very powerful appeal from the hon. Member for Carlow (Mr. Gray)—a much more powerful description than they had heard in the interest of the Government on the other side. If English Members would only take the interest in these matters which they took in the affairs of the Soudanese and the Basutos, no doubt some satisfactory issue might result. If the Prime Minister said one word about the South African Natives, or the inhabitants of the Soudan, he raised a discussion at once, and the London papers teemed with the subject. He (Mr. Dawson) told them that Ireland was of more consequence to them than the Basuto tribes. He told them that the peace and goodwill of Ireland, which was set at nought, was of more importance to England than what occurred in the Soudan, or in the fate of General Gordon. He did not blame the English people at all for the attitude assumed by English Members in that House. If the English people were as thoroughly informed about the real *status quo* as they were about the remote and unimportant Colonies of the Empire, they would care more about the security, safety, and prosperity of Ireland. Therefore it was that the hon. Member for Carlow (Mr. Gray) and he (Mr. Dawson) had drawn this matter out of the small area of the Metropolis of Ireland, in which it originally rested. They had drawn the matter out of the small question as to the jurisdiction of the officer who supervised the accounts of Dublin for the time being, and who told the Corporation where they should go with their civic officers, and where they should not go with municipal deputations. He would ask the Secretary to the Treasury to secure, not only that knowledge of the Provinces of England which it was desirable that such an official should possess, but also a knowledge of the Municipalities of Ireland. The hon. Member might look upon these things as trifles, but he should not shut his mind to trifles, particularly where Ireland was concerned. Trifles were at the bottom of many human affairs, and trifles made the whole history of Ireland. He trusted that the discussion which the hon. Member for Carlow had raised would initiate a system of local and municipal government in Ireland which would be of vast value, not only to that country, but to the United Kingdom.

MR. GRAY said, he had scarcely hoped, when he mentioned this small matter, that the discussion would have blossomed into a Home Rule debate. He hoped some benefit would accrue to Ireland therefrom. He would like to give to those Gentlemen who had the experience of English municipal life a few examples, which were in his own recollection, as to the working of the present municipal system in Ireland. Some years ago they were building in Dublin a new bridge. At that time it was in contemplation, as it was needed at the present time, to carry out in the Irish capital a system of main drainage, something on the same principle, though on a more modest scale, as that which obtained in London; and, by the advice of the engineers, it was determined that culverts should be made when the bridge was built. The engineers advised them that if in connection with the building of the new bridge they were to make culverts in the main sewers, which they contemplated carrying along each side of the river, those culverts could be made at a very small expense; but that if they built their bridge, which was to be of stone, and subsequently attempted to tunnel under it, it would involve enormous expense, and possibly endanger the stability of the structure. They accordingly determined that, at the cost of £4,000 or £5,000, they would make the culverts while the new bridge was building. Anyone acquainted with municipal affairs would see that that was a wise determination to come to; but it did not commend itself to the Local Government Board official. They happened to have a capital fund at the time on account of this main drainage expenditure. Having that capital fund, and not having any immediate occasion for its expenditure, they decided to expend some portion of it in the construction of these culverts. That expenditure amounted to some £6,000. Well, the Local Government auditor, when he came to consider the various bearings of the matter, decided the legal point in his non-legal mind. This gentleman happened originally to have been a clerk—a very good clerk—but nothing but a clerk. This gentleman having read up certain Acts of Parliament, and having somewhat forced himself into the process, came ultimately to the conclusion that the Municipality ought to have levied a tax instead of spending the capital sum they had lying by useless at the time. This gentleman accordingly surcharged these individuals, not those who had authorized the payment, but those who had signed the cheques—surcharged them to the amount of some £6,000. It was within his (Mr. Gray's) knowledge that one of the gentlemen—a man of good social position and high personal character—there was no harm in talking about the matter now, for it was many years ago—happened to be in some temporary financial embarrassment. It became noised abroad that he had been surcharged, not with a share of the £6,000, but with the whole of it; an it was owing to the merest chance that, by reason of the surcharge of the sum expended in the interest of the citizens, this gentleman was not made bankrupt. For months, metaphorically speaking, this gentleman had to go on his knees to the Local Government Board to obtain, not freedom altogether from the charge, but a promise from the Local Government Board that they would not take legal steps to enforce the charge until they knew what the Municipality would do. He (Mr. Gray) wanted to know how long such a thing would have been tolerated in England—how long would hon. Members have been "loyal" if such a thing had taken place? In another case, the local Gas Company was endeavouring to obtain an increase of capital. The Municipality of Dublin was against it; but there was some difficulty in their petitioning against the Bill as citizens of Dublin, or as representatives of the citizens. The Gas Company asked for the increase of capital for some new purpose outside the City limits, and that was the reason for the opposition of the Corporation. The Company proposed to spend a considerable sum at the Port of Bray, where they had small gas works, and the money for the new operations would have come out of the general gas capital of the Company. The new works were to be the erection of piers at Bray. The Company had not reached their maximum charge, being 6*d.* under what they were entitled to charge by their Dublin Gas Acts. The Corporation argued in this way. They said that the expenditure of these thousands of pounds at Bray would be comparatively unproductive; they declared that the township of Bray, being a very small place, the consumption of gas would be very limited, and that the Gas Company, whether they made an unproductive gas expenditure or not, would take good care to maintain the 10 per cent interest they were paying their shareholders, and the only way they could do that, if they wasted money on Bray, was either by increasing or maintaining the existing prices of gas in Dublin. They, therefore, thought the Bill a dangerous one, and made up their minds to oppose it. They did oppose it, and opposed it successfully. Well, though they took that course, and, in their opinion, preserved the interests of their constituents, this clerk, to whom he had already referred, again examining into the law of the case, decided that they had no power to oppose the Bill, because the expenditure the Gas Company had proposed to incur would have taken place outside the city limits. This gentleman surcharged the members of the Corporation. That was more than they could stand, and they determined that they would fight him in the case. They considered it a most insulting surcharge, and determined to fight the auditor. They defeated him on this absurd point. It chanced that the Dublin Corporation ran a water pipe through the township of Bray; and they argued that because of that pipe they were citizens of the township, and entitled to a *locus standi*. Was this not absurd? He would only give one more instance. On one occasion a Lord Mayor of Dublin—a Mr. Bulgin—died in office. The Corporation were anxious to pay his memory as much respect as was in their power, and they voted that the Corporation and the officers of the Corporation should attend his funeral in State. The small expense they decided to go to was for black scarves for the official drivers and footmen, and to place black rosettes on the horses. The thing cost, he thought, 25*s.*, and the auditor surcharged them all. Now, was that a thing to be surcharged? If the representatives of the citizens were sufficiently respectful to the right hon. Gentleman the President of the Local Government Board and to his officials as to go down on their knees and beg them to be good enough not to surcharge them out of their own money, the probability was that they would remit the surcharge. But that was not a position in which the representatives of the citizens should be placed; and if they did not do that, they had to fight the matter in the Queen's Bench. The Secretary to the Treasury seemed to think that the position in England and Ireland was practically the same. In the one case what happened was this—There was an auditor—not a nominee of the Crown, but a man elected by the ratepayers—who had no power of surcharge, but, as he understood, only power of report. The auditor in England might report on any improper or extravagant expenditure, and say—"In my opinion, this was an expenditure which ought not to have been incurred;" and, therefore, any ratepayer who thought proper to do so could, at his own risk, go to the Queen's Bench. If the ratepayer be defeated, he would be required to pay his own costs and the costs of his opponents as well. What happened in the case of Ireland? The authorities must themselves go to the Queen's Bench if they wished to be relieved, and even if they were successful they must pay the expenses, not only of the appeal, but of the unsuccessful auditor; if they proved the auditor to be in the wrong, they were rewarded by being permitted to pay his expenses. Such was the difference between the systems which prevailed in the two countries. He trusted that the system of auditing in Ireland would be reconsidered by the Government, and that the present irritating and vexatious badgering would be removed. He believed that members of Corporations and of other Local Bodies in Ireland endeavoured to do their duty with regard to public funds as well as corresponding authorities in England did; and there was no reason why Parliament, by its laws, should declare its want of confidence in the authorities in one country, and its confidence in the authorities of the other country. Parliament should leave the ratepayers and their representatives to settle matters of this kind between themselves. Of course, if there be any improper charge, one involving anything of the nature of fraud or of solid and real illegality, a ratepayer should have his remedy by going to the Queen's Bench. A ratepayer had that remedy in England, but not in Ireland. But that the auditor should be the nominee of a Board of nominees, and generally a partizan, and, at the same time, to add insult to injury by compelling the local authorities to pay his salary, was rather too bad. It was, to say the least, irritating to a Corporation that they should be obliged to pay the man who surcharged them in sums not amounting, on the average, to £50 in the year. The Corporation of Dublin were required to pay a man £500 a-year for coming down and insulting them with these surcharges whenever he thought fit. That was not a system calculated to encourage healthy political life in Ireland; it was not a system calculated to encourage the best men to enter local representative bodies. Men of position and of self-respect would not tolerate these petty insults, they would not be bothered to go to the Local Government Board to make appeals to their mercy, or to go to the Court of Queen's Bench to fight, at their own peril, local points. As a matter of fact, the tendency of the system was to encourage the advent of inferior men, men who, far from doing what was required in the interests of the ratepayers, were likely to take an opposite course.

MR. KENNY said, that, when speaking earlier, he omitted to move a reduction of the Vote by £6,400.

THE CHAIRMAN: There is an Amendment already before the Committee. It must be disposed of before the hon. Member can move his.

Motion, by leave, *withdrawn.*

Original Question again proposed.

MR. KENNY moved to reduce the Vote by the sum of £6,400. His reasons for wishing a reduction of the Vote he had already stated.

Motion made, and Question put,

"That a sum, not exceeding £102,144, be granted to Her Majesty, to complete the sum necessary to defray the Charge which will come in course of payment during the year ending on the 31st day of March 1885, for the Salaries and Expenses of the Local Government Board in Ireland, including various Grants in Aid of Local Taxation."—(*Mr. Kenny.*)

The Committee *divided*:—Ayes 21; Noes 105: Majority 84.—(Div. List, No. 174.)

Original Question again proposed.

MR. DAWSON said, that, owing to the fact that they had got no promise whatever from the Head of the Local Government Board as to whether he would take any steps to restrict the arbitrary power of auditors in Ireland, he (Mr. Dawson) now proposed to reduce the Vote by £500. Some English Members, as well as the Irish Representatives, had appealed to the right hon. Gentleman the Chief Secretary, but, up to that point, fruitlessly. The right hon. Gentleman professed to have very great intimacy and knowledge of the various Departments; and he had displayed it that night in a remarkable manner. The hon. Member for Carlow (Mr. Gray) had pointed out that the auditors in Ireland had surcharged Corporations for undertaking patriotic work for the benefit of the citizens, and for no personal object whatever; he had told them that the Corporation of Dublin had been surcharged 25*s*., which they had expended in rosettes to be worn by the officials of the Corporation when attending the funeral of the Lord Mayor. The Committee had been told that whereas the Corporations of Dublin and Limerick were permitted without surcharge to send deputations to congratulate Her Majesty upon certain events, and to condole with her upon others, they were surcharged when they sent representatives to the Exhibition at Cork, an Exhibition which was destined to promote the industry and trade and commerce of the country. He would like the Chief Secretary, as the Head of the Irish Local Government Board, to tell them whether his Department had issued any order to the auditors in Ireland analogous to the orders which had been issued to auditors in England by the English Local Government Board? The orders to the auditors in this country were distinctly to the effect that they were only to surcharge in cases of negligence, or fraud, or matters obviously contrary to law. Would the right hon. Gentleman give an undertaking that he would cause the Local Government Board in Ireland to issue orders to the auditors in Ireland that would confine their actions within the limits of reason and prudence, in which the actions of the auditors in England were confined?

MR. TREVELYAN assured the hon. Gentleman that if the case he had just brought forward of the check which was put on the patriotic tribute paid to the Cork Exhibition by the Dublin Corporation had been brought before him at the time there was not the slightest doubt what decision he should have given in the matter. Indeed, he would look most carefully into the system of audit. The hon. Member had asked him whether the Local Government Board were prepared to issue instructions similar to those issued in England. The Board would examine those instructions, and if it was found that they were based upon just principles, they would have no objection to issue such instructions to the auditors in Ireland. His own desire was to leave, as far as possible, the discretion of all the local bodies unfettered; but he could not go so far as to say off-hand, in the course of a debate on the Estimates, that he disapproved altogether of a central audit on every occasion. He was inclined to believe that it would be a very great evil for the ratepayers in Unions if there was no system of central auditing. It was extremely probable that ratepayers might suffer very much what shareholders of Companies frequently suffered; their business might get into the hands of men who were not to be trusted, and who totally disregarded the interests of the ratepayers. Such things had occurred. Everyone would allow that if, in some of the Southern States of America, there had been in past years a more rigorous audit, the financial condition of those States would be very different from what it was now. The question of the abrogation of the Act of 1871—of the emancipation of Municipalities from audit—was one which he would like to consider very carefully. He should like to consider to what extent the English Municipalities were satisfied with the system of audit to which they were subjected before he removed the audit which in 1871 was imposed on Irish Municipalities.

MR. RYLANDS heard with great surprise that the Corporations in Ireland were subject to an audit. He was persuaded that a proposal to subject English Municipalities to a central audit would be looked upon with the greatest disfavour; and he should be glad to join in the expression of opinion that in Ireland it was desirable that Municipalities should be allowed to exercise their own discretion in the administration of local funds.

MR. ILLINGWORTH said, that what was claimed on behalf of Municipalities was that they should have absolute power over their own affairs. Members of Town Councils in the English Municipalities were elected by the entire body of ratepayers; they were as truly representative, and even more so, than the Members of the House of Commons. If there was no appeal against the decision of the House in matters of Imperial expenditure, he wanted to know why there should be an appeal from the decision of municipal authorities, and that appeal to a man who might be utterly ignorant of the policy of certain expenditure? The security against extravagance was that every three years the members of Town Councils had to go before their constituents. It must be borne in mind that there were always two parties in a Corporation, and that there was the greatest vigilance exercised by one party over the other. That also was a very great security against any corrupt expenditure. A Government audit would result in irritation and annoyance, and would afford no security against improper expenditure. It was not to be for one moment supposed that a Government auditor could understand the merits of large expenditure incurred by a Corporation on water, gas, sewerage, or other great works. He hoped his right hon. Friend's (Mr. Trevelyan's) mind would soon be disabused of the idea that any good could come from such interference in municipal financial affairs as took place in Ireland.

MR. RAMSAY said, he thought it right to remind his hon. Friends who were conversant with affairs in England that the school boards, which were representative bodies, were subjected to Government audit. It appeared to him somewhat strange that his hon. Friends (Mr. Rylands and Mr. Illingworth), who condemned a Government audit in Ireland, should themselves have sanctioned the same rule in the case of the English school boards.

MR. DAWSON said, he was sorry that such a venerated Member of the House (Mr. Ramsay) should have stumbled into a mistake. In England an auditor could only surcharge in cases where there was negligence, fraud, or something contrary to law. That was quite fair; but in the Dublin and other Irish Corporations the auditor's power of surcharge was not so restricted.

MR. GRAY said, he thought his hon. Friend (Mr. Dawson) ought to be satisfied with the assurance which the right hon. Gentleman the Chief Secretary had given him. He (Mr. Gray) was satisfied that when the right hon. Gentleman looked into the question, he would see there was a substantial grievance which ought at once to be remedied. The right hon. Gentleman had made a very long and interesting speech, touching upon a good many points; but, still, he might have spared three or four minutes to deal with the points he (Mr. Gray) raised, and which, to his mind, at least, were worthy of attention. He did not expect that the Secretary to the Treasury (Mr. Courtney) would have told them anything about the remission of these half salaries; but it was a grievance which, one day, would have to be remedied. They could not have in perpetuity a different system with regard to two practically identical bodies. It would be very much better that the Treasury should give the same sum in a different manner than give it as at present—namely, paying half the salaries of one set of officers of one Corporation, and paying nothing at all for a similar set of officers of a similar Corporation, simply because the one set were appointed at a certain date, and the other set not until after that date. It was a system which did not bear examination, and he trusted that, at least, between this and next year, the right hon. Gentleman (Mr. Trevelyan) would give the matter his consideration. He (Mr. Gray) would certainly bring the question up again when the Vote again came on for discussion. With reference to the cost of the police he had nothing further to say, and should not press for a reply from the right hon. Gentleman, supposing the right hon. Gentleman did not see his way to giving a reply at once. But there was one matter which he felt bound to urge on the attention of the right hon. Gentleman, and that was, whether he would not consider the propriety of issuing a sealed order to the proper authorities, in view of a possible outbreak of cholera in Ireland? He put it to the right hon. Gentleman whether it would not be much better to issue such an order at once than to wait until the cholera made its appearance? A sealed order need not deal with all the subjects mentioned in the 49th section of the Act of Parliament. Such an order might be supplemented afterwards by another sealed order if, unfortunately, the necessity should arise. He would, at any rate, beg the right hon. Gentleman to consider the matter. He did not want a positive assurance upon it at the present moment, but merely an intimation that he would carefully consider the point he had thus raised, which, to put it briefly, was this—that, inasmuch as the Sanitary Authorities of Ireland would require time to carry the order into effect, and there would be little use in waiting until such time as the disease should actually make its appearance, if, unfortunately, that eventuality should come to pass—because any attempt to carry the order into effect by setting about the cleansing and scavenging of the different towns and cities when the disease was rife among the people, instead of being beneficial, would be the most dangerous thing possible—it would be infinitely wiser and more prudent to deal with the matter in advance.

MR. TREVELYAN: I entirely agree with the hon. Member who has just addressed the Committee. I think we have the power, and that we ought to exercise it, to separate the classes of subjects to which he has called attention, under the 49th section of the Act of Parliament; and I may state that the Local Government Board are prepared to issue at once to all the Sanitary Authorities throughout Ireland a Circular pointing out the necessity of exercising vigorously the powers already possessed in regard to the treatment of nuisances in their respective districts. That will be done under the ordinary law. But with regard to the Public Health Act, the 49th section of the Act of 1876, the first step has already been taken by communications that have been sent to all the large cities—such as Dublin, Cork, Belfast, and Waterford; and if the answers should be favourable, the policy to be pursued ought obviously to be to prepare and issue the instructions we are empowered to issue under the Act of 1866 with regard to the abatement of nuisances. With reference to the three other heads, it is also obvious that they must be kept in view. I was specially impressed with the hon. Gentleman's remarks with regard to appointments and promotions to Auditorships and Inspectorships. I think he did not speak especially of what has happened during the last two years. Since I went to Ireland I have always taken great interest in these proposals; and if the rule has not been absolutely unbroken, my desire would be to carry out what I think to be for the absolute security and efficient administration of the Department.

Original Question put, and *agreed to.*

(3.) Motion made, and Question proposed,

"That a sum, not exceeding £39,997, be granted to Her Majesty, to complete the sum necessary to defray the Charge which will come in course of payment during the year ending on the 31st day of March 1885, for the Salaries and Expenses of the Office of Public Works in Ireland."

CAPTAIN AYLMER said, there were one or two points to which he wished to call the attention of the right hon. Gentleman the Chief Secretary to the Lord Lieutenant. The increase in the amount of the arrears of loans appeared to be very great, especially with regard to Ireland. On the present amount outstanding — namely, £777,000 — the amount of arrears had increased from £60,000 to £95,000 during the past year. That he regarded as very serious, especially as the increase of those arrears had been getting larger from year to year. The arrears under the Land Improvement Act had been raised from £30,000 in 1880 to £56,000 last year. That was a matter which required to be attended to. The subject, however, on which he had risen to speak was one which he thought required the special attention of the Chief Secretary's Department. The Commissioners of the Board of Works had specially to do with loans for the drainage of land in Ireland, and they had to see to these matters under the provisions of no fewer than 19 different Acts of Parliament. Seeing that the whole system of land in Ireland had been changed by the present Parliament, and that the owners of land in that country had no longer the same interest as formerly in borrowing money for drainage, now that the land was in the hands of the tenants, it was obvious that these loans were no longer in request on the part of the landlords. The Chief Secretary to the Lord Lieutenant had this year brought in a Bill, because it was evident that the Irish Board of Works would not be able, in future years, to carry out the complete business of encouraging the drainage of Ireland as they had done under the old Acts. When the right hon. Gentleman brought in that Bill this Session, many of those who were specially interested in the subject looked forward to the prospect of its being passed with some satisfaction. It was founded on the Report of the Commission of which the noble Viscount the Member for Fermanagh (Viscount Crichton) was a Member. The Bill was blocked by the hon. Member for Cavan (Mr. Biggar) and another Member, and the consequence was that it was now among the numerous measures that had been dropped. It had been announced as the intention of the Chief Secretary to endeavour to get the Bill read a second time, and then to refer it to a Royal Commission; and he (Captain Aylmer) wished to ask the right hon. Gentleman whether he would not now consent to the appointment of a Royal Commission to consider the question of the arterial drainage of Ireland, and how the 19 Acts of Parliament, of which he had just spoken, could be consolidated, so that the Irish Board of Works, or whoever might hereafter be interested in the carrying out of a measure on the subject, would have an Act that would work well with the present system of land tenure? If the right hon. Gentleman assented to the appointment of this Royal Commission, he hoped it would not confine itself to the Report of the Committee to which reference had been made, nor to the various Acts that were in operation, but would go to what was the real point of the whole question—the arterial drainage of the country. If it did that, it would give great satisfaction, not only to the landlords, but to the tenants, and would add many millions of pounds to the value of land in Ireland. He hoped the Chief Secretary would consent to this proposal on behalf of Her Majesty's Government.

COLONEL COLTHURST desired to support the recommendation made by the hon. and gallant Member who had just spoken. Last year his hon. Friend the Secretary to the Treasury (Mr. Courtney) had brought in two Bills; but unfortunately they had not reached a second reading. At the beginning of the Session he (Colonel Colthurst) had, almost from day to day, called the attention of the House to the question; but in deference to his hon. Friend (Mr. Courtney), who had made a very reasonable request, his Motion was withdrawn, on the understanding that the Bills which had been introduced should be referred to a Select Committee. Those Bills were, however, unfortunately dropped. Next Session, no doubt, the hon. Gentleman would re-introduce them; but the probability was that they would again be blocked, and the whole Session would again be lost. No one conversant with the question of arterial drainage could do otherwise than admit that the matter was one of the most pressing importance, and that without legislation on the subject nothing could be done. The conditions of the tenure of land in Ireland had undergone a complete change, and a new definition of owners was required, otherwise all operations under the Acts would be suspended, though he believed that the Report lately issued by the Commissioners of Public Works showed that five districts had been established this year. As far as it went, this was a great improvement on what had been going on during the last few years; but still improved legislation was required in order to render effective the legislation already existing. As far as his own opinion went, he did not consider that the Bills which his hon. Friend the Secretary to the Treasury had brought forward would have met the case. He thought they must have a Royal Commission. In such a body there would be a certain number of experts, and if they were to investigate the matter during the approaching autumn they might have their Report ready by February next, and a Bill could then be brought in giving effect to their recommendations. He knew that a very general consensus of opinion existed on this subject among all parties in Ireland, and he hoped his hon. Friend would see his way to giving his assent to the appointment of the Commission.

COLONEL NOLAN said, he did not altogether concur in the remedies which had been suggested. Five-and-twenty years ago there were immense arterial drainage works established in different parts of Ireland, and these works had done a great amount of good, having completely changed the face of the country. They all knew what advantages were derived from such works in Ireland. No doubt some of them were very expensive; but certainly many fully recouped themselves, and there was no doubt that if the system were further extended much good would be done to the country. Not only ought they to extend the arterial drainage of Ireland, but in the case of many properties a good deal more was required, as the drainage works stood in need of extensive repairs, such as were wanted about every 15 or 20 years. These were very costly. Under the present state of the law, two-thirds of the landowners must act together in order to form a Board; but at the present moment it was absolutely impossible to get them to do this. A great many would not answer the letters that were sent to them. He had made particular inquiries on the subject, and, as far as he could ascertain, not a single landowner would agree to act in the matter, although half the money was to be found by the Government. Recent legislation had intensified the unwillingness of the landowners to join in the carrying out of large drainage operations. In fact, the situation had become such that it was necessary to find some remedy. The hon. and gallant Member for Maidstone (Captain Aylmer) had reminded them of one remedy, which was, perhaps, not a bad one—namely, that the tenants should agree, and that they should form a Drainage Board. There was a great deal of good sense in that suggestion, and he (Colonel Nolan) believed that, in a great many cases, it would work well; but he would go further than that, inasmuch as it might be said that the proposition was too Democratic a one. Whether that was so or not, the present state of things was one of despotism. What he would propose was this. Whenever a sufficient number in a particular district should petition for the appointment of a Drainage Board, a qualified engineer should be sent down by the Board of Works, and that officer should be charged with the investigation as to whether it was or was not desirable that effect should be given to the Petition. This Petition might be preseen ed either by a certain number of individual residents in the district, or by the District Board of Guardians, or any other recognized public body, and upon their Petition the investigation should take place. When the Report of the Engineer, sent down by the Board of Works, had been received, it would then be for the Board itself to decide whether a Drainage Board should be constituted. Some such system was now at work in Ireland. He would not say it was the only system; but he would repeat that it was now impossible to get a sufficient number of landowners to agree to act together for the reasons he had already stated. He would mention a case in point; it related to a small drainage work in his own district. They had dealt first with his own property, he having no objection to that being done, and the tenants being willing to pay the expenses; but the agent of one owner—a lady—said—"No; I will not advise the owner of the property to accede to what is proposed, as she has really no interest in the land." The tenants came forward, all of them agreeing in the matter. They stated that all they asked was that the lady should give her name; but she would not do so. The land in that neighbourhood was extremely wet, and the tenants were very much impoverished, because there were no means of efficient drainage. Nothing, however, could be done, and that was one of the results of the operation of the Land Act in Ireland. What, he would ask, had the Government been doing? During the last two years they had made the most abortive attempts to bring in a Bill; but they had not been able to pass one. The consequence was that many districts in Ireland were being kept in a wet and swampy state, like a sponge, because the Government could not find the time to attend to the drainage, or in consequence of their busying themselves so much about the affairs of Egypt and other matters to which they gave almost their entire attention. The hon. Member for Newcastle (Mr. J. Cowen) once said the best thing they could do with Ireland was to dry it; and, for his own part, he (Colonel Nolan) had always considered that a most sensible remark; but, unfortunately, the Government would not take the advice. They had been asked to issue a Royal Commission to consider this subject. Let them do so, although the Committee knew very well what frequently came from the appointment of Royal Commissions. In the first place, they could not be got to report within a month or so; but the House had to wait for a year or a year and a-half before the Report was presented, and then, very frequently, nothing came of it. However, they might as well have a Royal Commission; it would be quite as good as the Government bringing in a Bill and then giving the House no time to discuss it in. A Royal Commission would be quite as good as that. Why the Government should act in so ridiculous a manner with regard to this important subject no one who had not been in the House of Commons, as he had been for a number of years, could understand. They never thought of asking the assistance of Members of Parliament, like his hon. Friend the Member for the City of Cork (Mr. Parnell), or the hon. Member for Tyrone (Mr. T. A. Dickson), who could render valuable service; but they went to someone connected with the Board of Works, and the Board of Works, naturally enough, considered what was likely to give them the least trouble. All they did was to talk very wisely, and then suggest some impracticable scheme; and the Government were really showing that they were totally unfit to develop the material interests of Ireland in a matter which, to that country, was of vital importance. He did not confine this remark to the present Government.

The Conservative Government had been quite as bad, as they had never done anything to improve the drainage laws. The Shannon measure was perfectly ridiculous. The Government were warned by the Irish Members, and they found time to debate the Bill; but it was, as he had just stated, a ridiculous Bill. There was another point connected with this subject which had relation to the question of small ownership in Ireland. Her Majesty's Government were about to use their utmost efforts to pass a Household Franchise Bill, which was to apply to Ireland as well as to England and Scotland; and, at the same time, they were proving to the small landowners in Ireland that they were to be totally and entirely neglected. This was totally absurd, and just the sort of thing which led the country into all sorts of trouble, and tended to foster revolutionary ideas. They were going to give these men a vote, and yet leave them in this ridiculous position. A rich man could get a large loan with but little difficulty, and the position of the Government was that under the system which was now being carried out they were saving trouble. No doubt they were. But why should not several small tenants who wanted loans obtain them by combination. The Government would not grant loans of less than £50; and it was said that one of these small loans gave as much trouble as a loan of £1,000. He admitted that that was so; but there was a remedy, and if eight or ten men wanted small loans of from £10 to £20, the cost of inspection would not be more than in the case of a loan of £200. Why, therefore, should not eight or ten men be allowed to combine together? That, however, was refused at the present time. It was simply a question of the Government officials wishing to save themselves trouble. Why should the Government not consult the Irish Members on this matter? He would defy the Government to show where the difficulty would be in allowing 10 or 20 men to join together for the purpose of obtaining a loan for the improvement of property in the same district. The result was that where a small tenant paying £8 or £10 a-year wanted to execute some useful work, and went to his landlord in order to get the money, the landlord said to him—"You can hardly give security for a loan of £50;" and the man was very often unable to get the money, whereas if he were allowed to join with others he would be able to execute the works that were necessary for the improvement of his holding. Then there was another and a minor point connected with this subject. When a man was able to obtain a loan of £50 or £100, he was not allowed to spend the whole of it for drainage and building. He might get £50 for drainage or for building; but he would not be allowed to spend half of it in drainage and half in building. In old times, when loans were obtained by large landowners, it was extremely convenient to have one loan for drainage and another for building; but, nowadays, when they came to the case of the small owners who only wanted sums of about £50 to aid them in improving their farms it was a totally different thing. If a man only had a small farm, he might wish to spend £20 on buildings and £30 on drainage; but in that case he would not be allowed to have a loan at all. That was a point on which he thought the Government, looking to the altered circumstances of the country, might very well consider whether they could not provide some such remedy as he had pointed out. The proposition had nothing revolutionary in its character, but simply appealed to the common sense of the Government; and they could hardly wonder at the feelings induced in the minds of a large number of respectable men when they found that their wants were disregarded, and they were not allowed to acquire the means of carrying out essential improvements under any circumstances. He really thought the Government might do something to meet the wishes of the Irish people in this respect. He had never entertained any great amount of admiration for the Government of the day. At the present moment they were in want of demonstrations, and wished to see large numbers of men marching from place to place, in order that they might carry out a particular line of policy. He was only putting before them a reasonable argument in pointing out these things, although he must say he did not expect very much from them. His hon. and gallant Friends (Captain Aylmer and Colonel Colthurst) wanted the Government to appoint a Royal Commission; but if they did so it would be found that they would not get the Irish Members there. He should support the hon. and gallant Member for Cork (Colonel Colthurst) if he divided the Committee on the subject, for he feared that under the very bad Government they had in Ireland it would not be found possible to get the most common-sense proposals properly considered.

MR. LABOUCHERE desired to call attention to a few points which he deemed worthy of consideration. In England they had a Board of Works with the right hon. Gentleman then in the Chair (Mr. Shaw Lefevre) at its head. The cost in Ireland was, altogether, a sum of £57,000, or, exclusive of the Land Act loans, £24,000. He would now ask the Committee to look at a few details. The First Commissioner of Works had a salary of £2,000 per annum; but in the case of Ireland they had a Chairman of the Board—the First Commissioner of Works in England having no Commissioners to act with him—receiving a salary of £1,500 a-year, and having the assistance of two Commissioners, who together received £2,400 per annum. That was to say, that what the First Commissioner of Works did for £2,000 was done in Ireland at a cost of nearly £4,000. Going further into detail, the first thing he came upon was the fact that there were in Ireland two classes of bookkeepers and clerks, including, as he perceived by a note at the foot of the page, one who was paid a special allowance of £50 for injured prospects. Could the hon. Gentleman the Secretary to the Treasury tell the Committee what this absurdity really meant? The hon. Gentleman could not. For his own part, he (Mr. Labouchere) had not the most remote idea of what this item referred to. In England the First Commissioner had no architect under him. The work was done, probably under the right hon. Gentleman's own supervision, by clerks and surveyors; but in Ireland they had an architect; and he saw, by a note below, that this architect, who was put down as receiving a salary of £1,039, also received a second salary of £100 a-year as architect for the national monuments. Then there were chief surveyor and surveyors of buildings, principal draftsman and furniture clerk, and a superintendent of fuel and light, a gentleman who received an allowance to cover the cost of offices. Then they had a Board of Control for Lunatic Asylums, and there was also an architect receiving a salary of £300 per annum and a pension of £300 a-year in addition, as was stated in a foot note, on account of his having been late architect to the Poor Law Board in Ireland. What did that gentleman do for his salary of £300 per annum? Why did he get the large pension of £300 a-year? Probably he did nothing in either office. If some Irish Member would be kind enough to move a reduction of the Vote, he (Mr. Labouchere) would be most happy to support him. Everybody must see that these sums were perfectly preposterous. In all probability those officials were Englishmen, and, therefore, were not worth much; and in Ireland, no doubt, it was true that Satan found some work for idle hands to do.

MR. COURTNEY said, the central point of the hon. Member's speech was the comparison between the Irish Board of Works and the English Board of Works, over which the First Commissioner presided. He would ask anyone who knew anything about the two Boards whether there was a single function that was common to the two. The functions of the two Boards were not at all similar, and had nothing in common. The Board in Ireland had to look after loans to railways, loans for tramways, land improvement loans, business with respect to drainage and piers, and a hundred other matters, with not one of which he suspected the hon. Member was familiar. The hon. and gallant Member for Maidstone (Captain Aylmer) had called attention to the question of arrears of loans, and in that matter the appearance was very much worse than the reality. The total indebtedness had not increased; but, instalments of principal having become due and not been paid, there was an apparent alarming increase in the amount of arrears. The matter had been under the consideration of the Government; but it was difficult to enforce the payment of the instalments. The Government would, however, spare no effort to reduce the total of the arrears. With respect to the appointment of a Royal Commission to inquire into the question of arterial drainage, he was afraid he could not share the anticipations as to the great advantages to be derived from such a

Commission. If the Government had only to consult themselves and their own convenience, nothing would be easier or simpler than the appointment of a Royal Commission. That would mean the postponement of the question for a year; but this year the Government had introduced two Bills, one dealing with the powers of the Board of Works, embodying the recommendations of a Royal Commission. Had they advanced with that Bill because it was founded on the Report of a Royal Commission? On the contrary, it had been immovable, in consequence of objections of two Irish Members representing two sections of the House. He had agreed to let the Bill be read a second time, and to be referred to a Select Committee upstairs; and if that had been carried out, he should have been glad to have listened to the representations of the Irish Members with the greatest respect. As to arterial drainage, the Bill contained something which might be accepted if it were sent upstairs. Why did not Irish Members exert themselves so as to get this question dealt with upstairs? He did not believe that if a Royal Commission were appointed the Bill would be passed; but he hoped that next year something might be done.

Mr. SEXTON said, he thought the hon. Gentleman must admit that the Irish Members applied themselves as actively to their Parliamentary duties as hon. Gentlemen who received salaries for doing so; and if the hon. Gentleman would take some steps to advance the interests of Ireland, he would find that they would assist him. The hon. Gentleman prided himself upon accurate knowledge; but he thought the conclusions of the hon. Member for Northampton (Mr. Labouchere) were more accurate than those of the hon. Gentleman the Secretary to the Treasury, with all his knowledge. He greatly sympathized with the conclusions and the contention of the hon. Member, as he did with any hon. Member, whether English, Scotch, or Irish. The English Department of Works was much more important than the Irish; but, although a great many of the powers of the Government had been gathered in the hands of the Irish Board, and although its functions were very important, and its cost was very considerable, he believed the Board did very little good for the country. The hon. Member invited some Irish Members to move a reduction, and if he were now as he was four years ago he might be deluded by the hon. Member's suggestion; but he should not adopt the suggestion, for two reasons—first, he believed the hon. Gentleman's Radical mind was not robust enough to follow him into the Lobby; and, secondly, with regard to this Board of Works, he did not believe that any proposal for a reduction would be Radical enough for him; but if the hon. Member would move to abolish the institution altogether he should be glad to support him, and to go in for a cheaper institution. If any hon. Member wished to satisfy himself as to the defined functions of this Board, he would find that the Board was authorized to lend £920,000 for loans to Local Boards, Grand Juries, public buildings, harbours, railways, labourers' dwellings, drainage works, land improvement, repairs of fishery piers, lunatic asylums, and emigration. Emigration was an inevitable dish in every bill of fare for Ireland. If this Department, instead of being supine, cold, and callous, went energetically to work, it might do a great deal to lessen the pressure of poverty on the Irish people. There were vast tracts of land in Ireland which, at a moderate expense, might be reclaimed. But what had been done in the past year? One loan of £60,000 for reclamation. Why was there only one loan for that purpose in the year? Was it because of some impediment of the law? If it was not, then the Government stood self-condemned. If it was, they were almost equally condemned, because they ought to propose an amendment of the law. Then, with regard to National School teachers, 6,000 out of 7,500 were at that moment without suitable residences attached to the schools. He knew that many of them walked many miles; and many lived in houses, not in homes, but in rooms in a condition ruinous to morals and health. It was most difficult for them to live with that external respectability which was essential with anybody having to instruct children. The Local Government Board never troubled themselves to induce the Government to erect teachers' residences, and for these 6,000 teachers only 40 residences had been erected in the past year. Then, again, the Labourers' Cottages Act had been abortive; but if the Department had exerted itself, at least some labourers' cottages might have been erected. Again, as to the Sea Fisheries Act, the Commission, headed by the hon. Member for Waterford (Mr. Blake), had set to work, but too near the end of the financial year, and, as far as he was aware, not a stone had been laid towards the construction of any harbour or pier on the coast of Ireland. The Department admitted that there were 200,000 holdings in Ireland occupied by solvent tenants at an annual value of £7 who were entitled to come in under the Act and obtain loans up to £200,000; but how many loans had been advanced? If there were 200,000 persons entitled to have loans, the Department must advance more than £200,000 a-year if they were to make any real progress; but instead of encouraging these poor people, and explaining the regulations and conditions, the Department took pride in multiplying obstacles in the way of these men. If a tenant applied for a loan, at the end of three months' waiting he got a form to be filled up and sent somewhere; but if there happened to be a mistake in the paper it was sent back to him, and then he entered upon a ceremonial during which he was deluged by forms of all sorts. He had known men withdraw from application, after several months, utterly bewildered and broken-hearted. But there was no lack of zeal on the part of the Department when it was called upon to send people out of the country. Although there were only 163 Boards of Guardians in Ireland, the Board had sanctioned during last year no less than 62 loans and spent £11,000 for this purpose. They were empowered to spend £100,000 for that purpose under the Act, and so eager had the Board been to use that power, that, although only two years had elapsed since the Act was passed, no less than £87,132 had been allotted. He should like to have some information as to how many people had been sent away; whether any care was taken to provide the people with the means of living when they arrived in America; and whether it was true that the other day 600 men were sent back as assisted paupers? He would like to know, also, whether it was a fact that a capitation grant was still allowed to the Poor Law Officers in Ireland, and whether they still received 5*s.* a-head as a bribe from the country for every person emigrated?

MR. H. H. FOWLER said, he thought there was a consideration underlying this question which the Chief Secretary had passed over. The question raised by the hon. Member for Northampton (Mr. Labouchere) was not the amount of work the Board did in Ireland compared with what the English Board did, but the extravagance of the Board in Ireland in doing their work. That was an important question. It had been brought forward for several Sessions—namely, the question of national expenditure. If the present Government came in upon any question it was that of national economy; but he was bound to say that their promises had not been fulfilled. Every attempt made by hon. Members to reduce the national expenditure was ridiculed, and they were treated as if they were a set of foolish fanatics. They were led to believe that the Estimates were everything they could be; but the Government would find that the people of the country had not forgotten this question of national economy. The Conservative Party were working it up throughout the land, and the Government would find that this question would have to be faced, and that if they came back to Parliament with a majority it would make itself heard. He felt compelled to make these observations because of the statements which had been made. Every item in the Vote indicated wanton extravagance which ought to be explained, and he wished Irish Members to understand this. Everybody was extravagantly paid, and yet Members were expected to defend this before their constituents. He felt exceedingly aggrieved by the view which the Secretary to the Treasury had taken; and although he felt it was impossible to attempt economy in this Parliament, he hoped the time would soon come, under this or some other Government, when the national expenditure could be reduced.

MR. DAWSON said, he wished to draw the attention of the hon. Gentleman the Secretary to the Treasury to several items in the Estimate which required some explanation. There were, under the head of Salaries of the Staff, a number of discrepancies with regard to which he would like to hear a statement from the hon. Gentleman. For instance, in the case of the Secretary to the Board of Works, Ireland, the minimum salary of that official was stated to be £800, with an annual increment of £25. Now, that gentleman's salary stood last year at the minimum amount of £800, and, according to the scale of increase stated in the Vote, the amount of this year's salary ought to have been £825. It was, therefore, a matter of surprise to him that in one year—that was to say, since 1883-4—the salary should have sprung up to the maximum of £1,000, which sum was now asked for. The item certainly baffled his comprehension, and as no information whatever upon the subject was furnished in the Estimate, he must ask the hon. Gentleman by what extraordinary process of computation this sudden jump from £800 to £1,000 in one year had occurred? Then with regard to the first class clerks, there were three clerks of that class with minimum salaries of £320, rising by an annual increment of £20 to a maximum of £500. In their case it appeared that an operation entirely the reverse of that which had taken place with regard to the Secretary's salary had occurred. The salaries of the three first class clerks stood for the year 1883-4 at the total amount of £1,357, to which, if the increment of £20 each were added, or £60 in all, the amount would be £1,417; but the actual amount of their salaries, according to the Estimate, was £1,377 only. Here, again, was a remarkable discrepancy, and he would ask the hon. Gentleman the Secretary to the Treasury to explain why it was that the Secretary to the Board of Works, Ireland, suddenly jumped up, as regarded his salary, to £175 more than his annual increment appeared to warrant, and why the three first class clerks had not advanced at the rate at which they were entitled to advance?

MR. COURTNEY said, in answer to the hon. Member for Carlow (Mr. Dawson), he believed he could satisfy the hon. Member with regard to the points raised in connection with the salaries of the Secretary and the first class clerks in the Department. The gentleman occupying the position of Secretary was formerly in charge of the accounts of the Office; he was the person who, as appeared on the next page, 181 of the Estimates, received £850 a-year in 1883-4 as Clerk in Charge of Accounts; on his retirement from that position he was promoted to the position of Secretary, which he now held. That being so, having been in receipt of £850 a-year as accountant, it was felt necessary to put him at once at the maximum salary of £1,000, at which he would remain. Then, with regard to the salaries of the three first class clerks, which the hon. Member had referred to, although he was not at the present moment able to give the actual details, he would point out that the apparent inconsistency might be explained—he could not, however, vouch for the accuracy of the explanation—on the supposition that two of the first class clerks were at the maximum of their salaries, or £500 each. That would make up £1,000 of the amount of £1,377, the rest of which might possibly be the salary of the one remaining clerk. With regard to the observations of the hon. Member below the Gangway, the question was whether the subjects he had drawn attention to were proper work for the Committee to be engaged upon in connection with this Vote. The suggestion of the hon. Member was that the work done by the Office of Public Works in Ireland was identical in character with that done by the Board of Works in England; but anyone who had heard the long list of items for the last year which had been read out by the hon. Member for Sligo (Mr. Sexton) a short time back must at once perceive that the two Boards were absolutely dissimilar. Any comparison of the two Boards was, therefore, misleading; and hon. Members were not, in his opinion, entitled to make any such comparison, unless they were at the same time prepared to examine the nature of the work done. Then, with regard to the argument made use of by hon. Members opposite, and reiterated by the hon. Member for Northampton (Mr. Labouchere). The hon. Member had imputed to the Board of Works in Ireland the duty of taking the initiative. But that was an entirely erroneous view of the matter; because the Board of Works took action on the applications made to them by certain persons, and it was a justification of their conduct if it were proved that the applications made to them had been dealt with. It was, therefore, no fault on the part of the Board of Works, Ireland, that they had made only one loan for the reclamation of land; and no case could be established against them until it was proved that a great many persons entitled to claim did make applications, and were refused. In the same way, with regard to the tenants who were supposed to have a right to receive loans under the Land Act of 1881, the question was not how many tenants were entitled to ask for loans, but how many had actually applied; and how many of those applications had been accepted or rejected. Looked at in that light, the case wore an entirely different aspect to that presented to the Committee by the hon. Member. The Board had started necessarily with an imperfect knowledge of the work to be done, and in the earlier part of the time considerable arrears, no doubt, accrued; but those arrears had, during the last year, been very considerably reduced. The number of applications under inquiry last year had been 1,486; but the number had since been very considerably brought down. The total number received to 31st March last was 6,600, and out of those applications 6,100 had been sanctioned. The effect, therefore, of the action of the Board of Works, Ireland, last year, had been considerably to reduce the arrears, to bring the new cases under consideration down to a smaller number, and to sanction a large number of loans. Hon. Members might ask whether the money had been paid, to which he replied that the money was issued as the work was done and certified. He did not think it necessary to go through every item touched upon by the hon. Member for Sligo (Mr. Sexton). He would simply express his opinion that the action of the Board of Works, Ireland, had been reasonably efficient in dealing with the applications made to them; and, further, he had great satisfaction in testifying to the energy shown in conducting the work of the Department generally. There was, however, one branch of the work of the Office on which he felt it his duty to say a few words—namely, that in relation to the Fishery Commission. The hon. Member had referred to what had been done in respect of that branch, and he had blamed the Board of Works for not responding more readily to the action of the Fishery Commission. But what did the Report say? It showed that out of 39 applications for survey made up to the 31st of March last, 35 cases had been considered by the Board of Works, and that plans and specifications had been forwarded by the Board of Works to the Fisheries and Harbours Commission. On the 15th of February eight plans had been sent out, and the rest by the 15th of April, the interval having been, of course, occupied with surveys and work of that kind. The rest of the cases were referred back for change of plans, &c. Then with regard to the action of the Board with reference to another subject. An hon. Member had complained of the action of the Board of Works in respect of the Labourers' Act of last Session, and founded that complaint upon the Report which brought up their work to the 31st of March last. But the hon. Member must be aware that it was impossible for the Board of Works to have taken any action at all under the Act of last year, and that inability on their part formed a material point in the Report. The other reference of the hon. Member with regard to emigration related to the Local Government Board, not to the Board of Works, Ireland.

MR. T. P. O'CONNOR said, he did not consider that the Office of the Board of Works were in any way to blame on account of the delay which had occurred in connection with the Labourers' Act of last year. The facts of the matter were—the Bill did not receive the Royal Assent until the month of August, and therefore even preliminary steps could not be taken under the Act at the very earliest until the month of September. He believed that he should be more correct in saying that no proceedings at all could take place before November, because the Boards of Guardians were not actually seized of the plan and purposes of the Act itself until that month. At an earlier stage of the discussion of that evening he had felt it his duty to call the attention of the right hon. Gentleman the Chief Secretary to the Lord Lieutenant of Ireland to the very serious vexational difficulties which stood in the way of the operation of the Act in almost every particular. The hon. Gentleman the Secretary to the Treasury was, he presumed, familiar with the details of carrying out the Act in question; and he would, therefore, repeat to him his apprehension that there was very great danger, in the case of many of the proposed schemes which had already reached their final stage so far as the Board of Works and the Boards of Guardians were concerned, that those schemes would not be carried out at all owing to the difficulties placed in their way. For his own part, he was perfectly convinced that the Treasury would not insist in forcing upon the authors of these schemes an amount of taxation which rendered the erection of labourers' cottages practically impossible; and, therefore, he had reason to hope that the hon. Gentleman the Secretary to the Treasury would add his valuable assistance to his (Mr. T. P. O'Connor's) endeavour to impress upon Her Majesty's Government the desirability of taking this matter immediately into their consideration. He would just make one or two observations with regard to the general question upon which the Secretary to the Treasury had spoken in reply to the hon. Member for Northampton (Mr. Labouchere). He did not think the Committee should be surprised or irritated by the amount of warmth displayed by the hon. Gentleman in this matter; the hon. Gentleman had only followed good example, and he would add that the Head of any Department who did not stand up to defend that Department with some vehemence was not worth his salt. The hon. Gentleman said he differed from hon. Members on those Benches. There was nothing in that to cause surprise to the Committee; nor did he at all blame the hon. Gentleman for being tempted into an unusual display of vehemence out of zeal for his subordinates. But there had been a sight witnessed by the Committee that evening which he thought was extremely significant and interesting. For the first time during the last four years there had been something like earnest assistance on the part of English Members given to Irish Members in their efforts to restrain extravagance in Irish Departments. Now, it was this which had caused the vehemence which the hon. Gentleman vented on the innocent observations of the hon. Member for Northampton. The moment the discussion of these Irish Estimates ceased to be the monopoly of Irish Members and was taken up by Members on the other side of the House, that moment the present system was doomed, and the hon. Gentleman the Secretary to the Treasury knew it very well. It was during the Russo-Turkish difficulty, the parent of the present Liberal majority, that the Duke of Argyll made use of the expression—"My Lords are beginning to be found out." Let the hon. Gentleman the Secretary to the Treasury consider that the phrase by which his Department was designated was—"My Lords, your Department is being found out;" and that the Offices under its control in Ireland were being conducted on a scale of extravagance that would not be tolerated for one moment in this country. But this Department was only one of many Departments where the same extravagance existed. There were more Judges than were wanted; more Secretaries, Presidents, and Vice Presidents than were necessary; throughout every Department the same vicious system ran—namely, that of tempting English officials into the ranks of the Irish Civil Service.

Mr. LABOUCHERE said, he did not complain of the remarks of the hon. Gentleman the Secretary to the Treasury, who, if he were not a Government official, he had no doubt would have supported his hon. Friends and himself in pressing this matter on the consideration of the Government. Situated, however, as the hon. Gentleman was, he had to give some reason, good, bad, or indifferent, for every job perpetrated by the Government. He was not in the least surprised that Irishmen knew more about what went on in Ireland than the Secretary to the Treasury, and Irishmen who lived in Ireland had one and all protested against the general extravagance in regard to the pay of all Irish officials, and particularly in regard to those whose salaries the Committee were now engaged in considering. And yet the hon. Gentleman came forward and, in defiance of the wishes of Irish Members, said that the system was a proper one under which large sums of money were spent upon officials in Ireland who were not wanted in Ireland, and whose salaries were higher in proportion than those of the officials who did the same work in England. The hon. Gentleman did not answer that complaint of hon. Members, and why? Because he knew absolutely nothing about the matter. He asked the hon. Gentleman why there should be an architect appointed to the Board of Control and the Board of Lunacy at a salary of £300 a-year, when there was an architect appointed for the whole Board of Works who received a salary of £900 a-year, and a special allowance of £200, as well as another £100 a-year a sarchitect for National Monuments. And he further asked the hon. Gentleman why he received the latter salary obviously for doing nothing, and if he also received £300 per annum for another office which he once held under the Poor Law Board? He had been under the impression that the official in question was not to receive a pension; but it now appeared that he was getting £300 a-year in respect of an office with which he had nothing to do. It was in that way these things were done, and if the matter in question were looked into, it would, no doubt, be found that this person was a relation of someone who had done something in the interest of the Government, and that giving him the office was an act of mere Party bribery. He did not say that the present occupants of the Treasury Bench were one whit worse than the Gentlemen who sat opposite them. He could see exceedingly little difference between Parties in that respect; but his great objection was that whenever a job, be it big or little, was perpetrated it was done at the expense of the nation.

MR. KENNY said, it would appear from the statement of the hon. Gentleman the Secretary to the Treasury that the officers of the Board of Works in Ireland were perfect individuals. The hon. Gentleman defended each item, and he endeavoured to prove that in every respect the officials whose actions had been questioned on both sides of the House discharged their duties perfectly. But he ventured to say that if each item were examined in the light of the Report which had been presented to the House for the year it would be found that there had been a deplorable failure on the part of the officials in question to meet the reasonable expectations of the people, with regard to the question of the Fishery Boards and Harbours Act of last year. The statement of the hon. Gentleman the Secretary to the Treasury a few minutes since, that of 39 schemes sent forward only two were in course of being carried out at the present time, was, in his opinion, the most eloquent condemnation that could possibly be passed on the Board. He was obliged to say that the boast of the Secretary to the Treasury, that with regard to 35 of these schemes plans and specifications had been forwarded, was somewhat premature and misleading, because he (Mr. Kenny) perceived that of eight of those schemes specifications had not been sent on; so that he apprehended there was a mistake somewhere. For his own part, he should be sorry to admit that the hon. Gentleman's estimate was accurate. He passed now to page 28 of the Report, on which it appeared that £13,275 had been advanced this year to a Mr. Drinkwater for reclamations. It appeared from the Report that the works were commenced in 1873, and the Report went on to say—

"We are now engaged in making such arrangements as will facilitate the execution of the works."

What did that mean? Did it mean that Mr. Drinkwater had broken his contracts? It would appear so, and that the Treasury had no satisfaction whatever for his having done so. The Secretary to the Treasury had given the Committee nothing in the nature of an explanation of this extraordinary transaction, which certainly had the magnitude of a public scandal. Hon. Members on those Benches would like to know whether Mr. Drinkwater was still responsible for the loan; how much money had been expended on the works, and what security the Treasury had that this money would be repaid? Passing from this transaction, which required to be cleared up, there was another matter to which he desired to refer. What was the extraordinary expenditure in connection with the Labourers' Act of last year? They had the following items:—One Assistant Commissioner, £800; one Examiner, £300; three Draftsmen, £240; 36 Inspectors at £300, £10,675; travelling expenses of Inspectors, £6,500; advertising, £3,000; registry of loans, £1,500. It was the function of these gentlemen to prepare Reports as to loans amounting to £200,000. It appeared, therefore, that the preliminary expenses made a charge of 7 per cent on each loan before it was granted. Such a waste was to be deplored. The manner in which the Labourers' Act had been, so to speak, paralyzed by the extraordinary demands of voracious officials was a thing they ought to have some explanation of. There was nothing more deplorable than the manner in which the public officials in Ireland ate up enormous slices out of the money that was granted in the shape of loans by Parliament for the purpose of carrying on public works. He hoped the Secretary to the Treasury would be able to give them further information as to fisheries, though he did not think he would be able to do so. Whether or not, he trusted the hon. Member would be able to give them some information as to the other matters to which he had drawn attention. There was another question to which he would like to advert—namely, the inspection the Government were bound to make of those schemes which were prepared under the Tramways Act of 1861. He saw a lot of bogus schemes on the Paper, that from the commencement had never had a chance of being carried to a successful issue. These schemes were prepared by men of straw, by men who were nothing but swindlers who came from England. Such practices should not be allowed to go on. As he said, they were nearly all Englishmen who came over to Ireland to carry on their swindles, and it was a scandal that they should be allowed to thrive with impunity on the unsophisticated people of Ireland.

Mr. WARTON said, he did not want to go into these questions as to the Poor Law Board of Ireland; but he desired to call attention to the persistency with which the Secretary to the Treasury insisted upon putting into the Estimates arithmetical puzzles and absurdities, and the innocent manner in which he offered explanations. He (Mr. Warton) was not going fully into these questions, because they had been gone into by the hon. Member for Carlow (Mr. Gray); and he had no doubt that everything the Secretary to the Treasury had said in reply to that Gentleman, with regard to the persons promoted from one post to another, was, from his point of view, perfectly right. That was not the question. Because the hon. Gentleman could give a reasonable account of the promotion of an official he thought he was answering the whole question; but that was not so. These Estimates should be arithmetically correct, and no explanation as to the virtues or excellence of a certain official was a reason for financial absurdities. They had an item of four second-class clerks with maximum salaries of £300, rising by annual increments of £15. The total was £1,239, or £39 more than the maximum of the four clerks, which would be £1,200. The item for 1883-4 was £1,204, and he should like to know how the difference between that sum and £1,239 could be made up by any increment of £15? Then they had an item showing that in 1883-4 the minimum salary of the Secretary was £800. It should have risen to £850, the increment being £25; but here they had an item of £1,000 put down for 1884-5. The Secretary to the Treasury should be ashamed of putting such absurdities in the Estimates, and he (Mr. Warton) felt it his duty to protest against the system. That was not the first time or the second they had had such Estimates prepared.

Mr. COURTNEY said, he was sorry the hon. and learned Gentleman the Member for Bridport was not satisfied with the explanation he had given. He (Mr. Courtney) might be open to censure; but the explanation was that the person appointed to the post of Secretary was a gentleman receiving a salary already above the minimum of the post —he was a gentleman transferred from one post to another, of course on full pay. With regard to the question put by the hon. Member for Ennis (Mr. Kenny) as to the cost of working the Land Act of 1881, he was afraid that the expenditure was necessary in the nature of things. It was necessary that they should have Inspectors to visit the localities, in order to ascertain the nature of the proposed improvments, and report upon them. It was obvious, therefore, that the expense of the Commissioners must be considerable in proportion to the work they did. They still took security for the due execution of the work. The hon. Gentleman put a question as to the Clare slob reclamation. He (Mr. Courtney) thought he had explained how that stood. The scheme as originally promoted was promoted by private individuals, and promised to be a great improvement and a work financially profitable. It was eventually ascertained, however, that it would be much more expensive than had been supposed. The works did not go on, and further loans were necessary to carry it through. Even after further loans were granted the work was not completed, and then an additional payment of three-fourths was granted. An Inspector of the Board of Works was sent down to see that the work was done.

MR. KENNY: Was the Inspector constantly there?

MR. COURTNEY said, he was not there every day; but week by week he went down to examine the work done. Finally, the Board of Works had been obliged themselves to take the work over. The operation had proved to be a loss; but it was one of those things they had been constantly urged to undertake—that was to say, in this case, as in many others, they had been constantly invited to grant loans for the reclamation of land which was covered with water at high tide. These things were often recommended as profitable reclamations, but frequently turned out to be a loss. In this case the work was carried out at the expense of English capitalists.

MR. ARTHUR O'CONNOR: How much capital was invested?

MR. COURTNEY: £20,000; the figures have been given over and over again in answer to the hon. Member for Ennis.

MR. ARTHUR O'CONNOR: Did they not become bankrupt?

MR. COURTNEY said, they liquidated, and the whole matter was inquired into. There were many cases of precisely the same character, and the Government had to be continually on their guard. In the matter of the tramways, the Board of Works was executing the duty thrown upon it by Parliament. When the scheme for the construction of the tramways was brought under their notice they had no option but to proceed to make an inspection for themselves, and to estimate the cost of the work, so as to be ready to satisfy the Grand Jury, and to put the case before the Committee of Council. The action of the Board of Works might have been imprudent; but it was altogether due to the Act of last Session, which the hon. Member himself had heartily supported.

MR. HARRINGTON said, the right hon. Gentleman the Chief Secretary, with considerable ingenuity, made himself out to be completely innocent of Irish feeling as to this Vote. He did not know whether the right hon. Gentleman would feel offended with him for saying so; but "where ignorance is bliss 'tis folly to be wise." Certainly, if the right hon. Gentleman found it his duty to defend the system carried on by this Board for so long, he (Mr. Harrington) could only say that it must be a matter of bliss to the right hon. Gentleman if he did not know that the functions of the Board towards the Irish nation were of the highest importance. The right hon. Gentleman was ignorant of the fact that, if the Board moved with anything like the progress they had a right to expect, it would be of immense advantage to the country, instead of being, as it was, a drag on every movement for its real improvement. When a scheme of any kind passed through that House, no matter how urgent was the necessity for it, and how pressing was the case which had been made out—however great the necessity in Ireland might be—the administration of the scheme was at once confined to that Irish limbo called the Board of Public Works. It was practically many years after a scheme had obtained the sanction of Parliament that it began to show its head above the surface of social and political life in Ireland. Last year, by the energy and zeal of the hon. Member for Waterford (Mr. Blake)—whose services he (Mr. Harrington), as an humble Member of the Party, regretted extremely to hear they were about to lose—a very excellent Bill was passed through the House for the erection of fishery piers. It was provided that a sum of £50,000 or £70,000 for the first year, and not more than £50,000 each succeeding year, should be expended on fishery piers and harbours. What was the story the right hon. Gentleman had to tell them? Why, that not a single stone of any pier had yet been laid. Only two schemes had been prepared—two efforts had been made; he supposed he might say that two stones had been laid; perhaps the divers in these cases had gone down and sounded the bottom. He would appeal to the hon. Gentleman who had charge of the passage of the Bill, and who had taken upon himself, without remuneration, the onerous and important duties of Chairman of the Commission for the carrying out of the work, and to which, to his (Mr. Harrington's) knowledge, the hon. Member had devoted a great deal of energy and labour—he would appeal to him, in his position as Chairman of the Commission, to know whether anything had been done on these important schemes which had occupied the consideration of Parliament last year. The hon. Member might not find himself free to stand up and take part in a debate; but he (Mr. Harrington) would challenge him to say whether anything had been done. Why was the time of Parliament occupied with this matter last Session, if there was not immediate and urgent necessity for the passing of the Bill; and why was it that this scheme, to obtain its first growth and sanction in Ireland, had been for the past 12 months winding its way through the circuitous route of the routine of this Board? If there was anything in the whole system of government in Ireland which excited the ridicule of the Irish people, who were peculiarly sensitive on matters of this kind, it was this same Board. They knew perfectly well that when a man applied for a loan under it his hair grew grey, practically, before he could succeed in getting the first instalment; and that, when he did succeed in getting one, the work which he wished to carry out, and part of which he might have carried out, was utterly useless, because of the period which elapsed before he got a second instalment. The circumlocution which was practised as to the first instalment was practised as to the second. He found that after he had laid a foundation he was struck idle, waiting until the lethargic officers of this public Body found it convenient to set themselves again in motion in order to give him a second instalment. The right hon. Gentleman, of course, had quite a style of his own of meeting charges of this kind—a style which seemed to be satisfactory to a great many Members. It was well for him that he had only the British House of Commons to deal with, and that it was not necessary for him to put himself before the people of Ireland. In this matter, however, the right hon. Gentleman would find that, if he were confronted, not only by that House, but by the people of Ireland on this question, the laugh would be all on the other side. Everyone had condemned the existing system in Ireland. A few petrified officials had been allowed to continue in office after they had grown unfit for their duties a decade at least. It was admitted by the Board that these officials were unfit to discharge their duties, and yet the Government left them in possession of them. A Commission was appointed in 1878 to inquire into the working of the Board, and he found in the Report of that Commission certain comments made upon the action of this Board. Hon. Members opposite seemed to be paying some attention to this subject, much more than they generally paid to questions raised by the Irish Members; and he would, therefore, invite their attention to this. It appeared that up to 1860 the Report, which the right hon. Gentleman had quoted, said the Commissioners had held four meetings with tolerable regularity. The minute book was duly kept, and the minutes received the counter signature of the Secretary in the usual way. During the next two years, according to the Report, the new minutes entered were minutes of transactions in the Office rather than transcriptions of the Board, and such formalities as the attesting signature of the Secretary were dispensed with, though on what ground those who made the Report were unable to say. The Report went on to say that at last traces of Board meetings disappeared, and it had not been customary for the Commissioners to hold formal sittings. He did not know how much weight that Report had had with the Government, or what effect was given to the recommendations of the Commission; but with regard to some of their recommendations the House was in a position to judge in the matter, and hon. Members knew that though the Commission had suggested the retirement of the Chairman, a length of time was allowed to elapse before he could be removed out of the way. The retirement of the Secretary was suggested; but he was allowed to remain in office for eight years after the Commission had suggested his retirement, and had practically pointed out that he was unable to fulfil the duties that he was entrusted with. If this Commission had to discharge a merely formal routine business, there would not be much ground for complaint; but that was not the case. There were many such bodies as this in Ireland. The Government was in the habit of rewarding its servants with payments of this kind, and hon. Members from Ireland would not object so much if they did not happen to be a drag on every movement for the improvement of the people, and for the improvement in the resources of the country. He had touched upon the action of the Board with regard to the Fishery Commission. The right hon. Gentleman had certainly given extremely scant satisfaction with regard to that; he had not in any manner explained to the Committee why it was that of the £70,000 which they had been allowed to believe the Government would have expended, scarcely 1*d*. had been expended up to the present time.

An hon. MEMBER: £6,000 has been spent.

MR. HARRINGTON said, he was told that £6,000 had been spent; but what was that out of £70,000? Was this supineness and lethargy owing to the fact that the Board had too many duties placed upon its shoulders? If it had too many duties imposed upon it, why was not that stated to the House, and why did not the Board refuse to do the duties, and why were not those duties handed over to some other Department? But if, as was believed in Ireland, the whole system was wrong, and that the men at the head of it were unable to discharge the duties entrusted to them through not having been trained to the work, and if they had no means of grasping or dealing with the difficulties of their position, why was not some effort made by the Government to clear them all away, bag and baggage, and establish in their place some cheap and fast method of dealing with this matter? As to the system of inspection in connection with the improvement works carried on, he remembered that large loans were obtained from the Treasury through that Board in 1879-80, when the landlords in Ireland were so exceptionally favoured as to get at a nominal interest very large loans, ostensibly for the purpose of giving some employment to people in the country, but really for the purpose of improving their own property. Cases were numerous where people could point out that landed proprietors in Ireland were taking large sums of money from this Department to effect certain improvements on their land, and that not a single 1*d*. of the money had ever been expended for the purpose for which it had been obtained. They were able to get from the Treasury money at the rate of 1 per cent; but they used it for whatever purposes they chose. He challenged the right hon. Gentleman the Chief Secretary to deny that half the money that had been so raised was applied to the purposes for which it was lent by the House. There was not a county or district in Ireland where the people could not tell them that landlords living there had obtained loans for the drainage and improvement of their properties; but that not a single 1*d*. of the loans had been expended with that object. Sometimes a slight pretext was made of doing something; a few holes were dug in the ground here and there in which to plant trees; but the trees were never planted, the holes remaining unfilled. Everything that the Board touched it corrupted. There was no Board in Ireland more odious to the people, not because of the political influence it had, not because of any objection, personal or otherwise, they had to the men—they were mere nobodies, so far as the people were concerned—but because any measure which passed through the House of Commons, and which had any connection with money, was sure to be consigned to limbo by the Board of Works.

MR. ARTHUR O'CONNOR asked the Secretary to the Treasury if he could now say what had been the result of the survey of the basin of the Barrow, which had been in the hands of the Board of Works for a long time? The valuation had now been received, and the Secretary to the Treasury had promised that it should be laid on the Table almost immediately.

MR. PARNELL: Can the hon. Gentleman state the substance of the Report?

MR. COURTNEY was sorry to say that the matter was in a very unsatisfactory position. Mr. Fitzgerald had not done all the work expected from him. He had a letter from that gentleman addressed to the Secretary of the Office of Public Works, and dated the 15th of this month. Mr. Fitzgerald said—

"In reply to your letter received on the 14th instant, I can only repeat what I have before informed you—namely, the impossibility of my naming the time for the completion of my valuation."

The fault, therefore, was not with the Office of the Board of Works, but with Mr. Fitzgerald, who was not a Government official, as the hon. Gentleman knew. It would be impossible to have the Report ready to lay before the House before the end of the Session. The Board of Works were pressing the matter forward; but the situation was most unfortunate.

Mr. ARTHUR O'CONNOR asked whether the Board of Works would still continue to defer action until they got the completion of the valuation by Mr. Fitzgerald, or whether they would take some steps to prevent the devastation by the autumn floods, which were very often more injurious to the property of the river side population than the winter floods themselves? The amount of devastation last year and the year before along the Barrow was almost incredible to those who did not actually see it; and, therefore, it seemed a little unreasonable that important work should be delayed for a mere valuation Return.

Mr. COURTNEY said, he ought, in justice to Mr. Fitzgerald, to say that in his letter he explained that he had been interrupted in the preparation of his valuation; he had had, for instance, to attend before a Committee of the House of Lords, and do other things. The hon. Member (Mr. A. O'Connor) asked him (Mr. Courtney) whether they could not take action before the valuation was completed. He (Mr. Courtney) was afraid the question of money was an essential matter, a more essential element than what should be done. What should be the range of the work, and, of course, what contracts should be accepted towards doing the work, depended entirely upon the cost of the work.

Mr. ARTHUR O'CONNOR said, the hon. Gentleman knew the range of the work, because the survey was complete.

Mr. COURTNEY said, that the survey had, no doubt, been completed; but if the work would involve the expenditure of a considerable sum of money, it might be necessary to submit a smaller plan. He said this, however, to show that, in the absence of a valuation, it was impossible to take action. He regretted the situation extremely.

Mr. DAWSON said, that in this Vote there was an item of £300, which represented the salary of "the superintendent of fuel and light." Was this superintendent the man who looked after the fires?

Mr. COURTNEY explained that the Board supplied the fuel and light for all the Government Establishments.

Mr. DAWSON thought that a salary of £300 for a man to keep an account of the coals used, and to attend to the lights of the offices, was rather exorbitant.

Mr. COURTNEY said, the man was in charge of a very large Department. If the Committee considered that the Board of Works had to look after the Viceregal Lodge, and all the Public Departments in Dublin, they must come to the conclusion that this superintendent had very considerable functions. He had to see that the contracts for coals were fairly carried out, and generally had to superintend the lighting and firing.

Mr. DAWSON pointed out that under the Chief Secretary's Vote £4,455 was allowed for fuel and light. Why, he asked, should a man be paid £300 a-year for keeping an account of the Chief Secretary's coal?

Mr. COURTNEY said, that the superintendent's duty was to see to the supply of coals and light.

Mr. KENNY noticed an item in the Vote arising out of the Report of the Board of Works upon the piers on the Shannon. A Bill dealing with those piers was before the House; but he saw that Notice of opposition to it had been given. He would like to know whether the Secretary to the Treasury (Mr. Courtney), who, he understood, had been in communication with the hon. Member for Limerick (Mr. Synan) in regard to the matter, would consent to refer the Bill to a Select Committee, in the event of the Notice of opposition being withdrawn?

Mr. COURTNEY said, he had been in communication with the hon. Member for Limerick as to referring the Bill to a Select Committee. The hon. Gentleman wanted half the Members of the Committee to be Irish Members, and he (Mr. Courtney) expressed his willingness to agree to that arrangement. The hon. Gentleman, however, told him that he had been in communication with the hon. Member for Cavan (Mr. Biggar), and he refused to remove his block to the Bill.

Mr. KENNY asked whether the hon. Gentleman (Mr. Courtney) would send the Bill to a Select Committee if the hon. Member for Cavan were induced to withdraw the block?

MR. COURTNEY said, he would do so if the Session were not too far advanced.

MR. ARTHUR O'CONNOR said, he did not wish to detain the Committee unduly; but the question of the Barrow drainage was one of immense importance to half of the people he represented. Tens of thousands of acres were devastated year after year by reason of the neglect of the authorities to take this matter in hand. Months ago the Board of Works came to an agreement with a number of representative gentlemen in Kildare, King's County, and Queen's County; and according to that agreement several hundreds of pounds were collected which were to go in part payment of the expenses of the survey, with a view to some action being taken by the Board of Works to mitigate the damage done by the floods. The collection of the money was a very serious tax upon the people impoverished by these annual losses. At any rate, the money was collected, the survey was completed, and a Report with regard to it had been sent in. The valuation which Mr. Fitzgerald was making was not at all essential to the carrying out of the work. It might be very interesting, in a financial point of view, to the officials of the Treasury; but it did not at all go to the essence of the claim. The decision of the surveyors, as to the mode in which the drainage should be carried on, was altogether independent of the valuation to be made by Mr. Fitzgerald. He asked the hon. Gentleman the Secretary to the Treasury to state, for the satisfaction of the tenants and the landowners of the three counties—Kildare, King's County, and Queen's County—what was the scheme which the surveyors advised; what was the system of drainage to be adopted, and what was the area to be affected by the scheme, apart altogether from the valuation of Mr. Fitzgerald?

MR. MOLLOY said, he had several times brought the matter before the House by Question and otherwise, in the hope of inducing the Government to settle the matter. He fully endorsed all his hon. Friend the Member for Queen's County (Mr. A. O'Connor) had said regarding it. Up to the present nothing whatever had been done; but he (Mr. Molloy) and his hon. Friend were inundated year after year with complaints from the tenants of the district. It was only fair that some satisfactory answer should be given to the question of the hon. Member for Queen's County.

MR. COURTNEY said, he had told the Committee with the utmost frankness how the matter stood. As far as the survey had been made it had come before him; but until the matter was complete he could not give the information as to the scheme which the hon. Member for Queen's County (Mr. A. Connor) asked for. The hon. Gentleman must admit that the blame could not be put on the Board of Works, or on the Government. The Government were quite conscious of the importance of the work, and it should be pressed forward. As he had already explained, the delay rested with Mr. Fitzgerald; but he still hoped to be able, before the end of the Session, to make a definite statement. At present he could not say what would be done.

MR. ARTHUR O'CONNOR said, that all he would ask the hon. Gentleman was, whether he would lay on the Table of the House the Report sent in by the surveyor of the Board of Works without waiting for the valuation by Mr. Fitzgerald?

MR. COURTNEY said, he would communicate with the Board on the subject.

MR. HARRINGTON wished to ask a question with regard to the Inspectors. There were 36 Inspectors charged for at a salary of £300 each. Had the hon. Gentleman (Mr. Courtney) any knowledge of the disposition of the Inspectors? Were they merely gentlemen who lived in different parts of the country, away from the control of the Office, or had they certain districts assigned to them, or did they go from one part of the country to another according as they were ordered?

MR. GRAY said, that within the last two or three months 15 additional Inspectors had been appointed. The hon. Gentleman the Secretary to the Treasury was asked some Questions in the House about the appointments which attracted some attention at the time in Dublin. He believed that 15 young gentlemen were appointed at a salary of £300 a-year each. Perhaps the Secretary to the Treasury would say what the Inspectors were supposed to do.

MR. COURTNEY said, he had not the tables by him; but the number of Inspectors was increased to meet the demands made by hon. Members on that side of the House that the working of the Land Act of 1881 should not be in arrear. Thirty-six was the full number of Inspectors, and it was sufficiently large to prevent any arrear in the consideration of the applications for loans. The Inspectors were placed in different parts of the country in a way that there should be no overlapping of jurisdiction.

MR. GRAY said, that, as to the new appointments, he wished to ask the hon. Gentleman whether any public notification was made, so as to ensure, as far as possible, that the most competent men would apply? Was any test of fitness applied to the candidates? If so, what? Had the gentlemen appointed any professional qualification? Was there any examination, or any test of any kind, beyond the religious test?—because, as a matter of fact, the gentlemen appointed were Protestants. Was it true that professional men, having, by accident, heard of the vacancies, applied, but were rejected, while unqualified men were appointed? Were the appointments so urgent that no public notification could be given?

MR. COURTNEY said, he was afraid he could not answer what qualifications were required. He did not make the appointments, as the hon. Gentleman (Mr. Gray) well knew. He (Mr. Courtney) knew, however, that a very large number of applications were sent in, and he thought the appointments were made by the Board of Works; but he was not sure.

MR. GRAY said, he was rather anxious to ascertain something about the matter, and he had not got at the bottom of it yet. Was there any public notification given of the vacancies? Was there any test applied, either the test of professional qualification or the test of examination? What were the special qualifications for the post of Inspectors? Were the appointments thrown open in any way to the public? Was the list of applications a private list? How could one get at the list? And when the hon. Gentleman (Mr. Courtney) said he did not make the appointments, were not the appointments, as a matter of fact, subject to the approval of the Treasury? With regard to the Board of Works, he did not intend to go into the details which had been fully discussed by other hon. Members; but he thought this debate had shown the anomalous position of this most important, perhaps the most important Irish Department which had the administration of a large number of important Acts of Parliament, the good administration of which was almost vital to the welfare of the country. The Board was not represented in the House of Commons, except by an official of the English Treasury, who, when he was asked as to certain appointments, said he did not make them. Who did make the appointments? Could the Board of Works perform the smallest administrative act without sending over to the Treasury and getting the sanction of "my Lords?" The Board was used as a mere buffer of the Treasury to keep off important Irish demands. It was, and is at this moment, an off-shoot of the English Treasury; it had no real power, no Representative in the House of Commons; it had no kind of responsibility. The Secretary to the Treasury would not pretend seriously that he could be conversant with all the details of this great Irish Department. As to the cost of the Board, the hon. Gentleman had justly enough said it was impossible to compare the Irish Board of Works with the English Board of Works, because the Irish Board was so enormously more important and had so much greater duties to perform. Yet the English Board of Works was invariably represented in the House by an official ready to answer for every act of the Department; but the Irish Board of Works, which the hon. Gentleman (Mr. Courtney) very truly contended was so much more important, was not represented in the House except by an official of the Treasury, who told the Committee he had nothing to do with certain appointments. Who had to do with them; and why were the appointments made in such an extraordinary fashion? The mode of the appointments created the greatest possible discontent and the greatest possible disgust in Ireland; and, therefore, the Committee were entitled to some explanation. The question did not come on the hon. Gentleman the Secretary to the Treasury by surprise, because it had been raised in the House once before during the Session. Of course, as usual, the hon. Gentleman did not know anything about the religion of the gentlemen appointed: but he (Mr. Gray) knew that they were all, as he had described, Protestants. He could not understand why, if the appointments were intended to be properly made, they were made in such a hurry, with no notification given, with no fair play given to those who might desire to compete upon their individual merits.

MR. COURTNEY said, the hon. Gentleman was perfectly entitled to ask these questions; but he was not in a position to answer them. He did not think there was any ground for the imputation made in the selection of the Inspectors; but he would make inquiries and give the hon. Gentleman the fullest information if he would put a Question down for Monday next. [MR. HEALY: Postpone the Vote.] He knew that a large number of the Inspectors were necessarily appointed on short notice in order to fulfil the condition of working the business with expedition, which no one was more energetic in demanding than the hon. Member for Monaghan (Mr. Healy).

MR. HARRINGTON said, the hon. Gentleman (Mr. Courtney) had just touched on the question which he (Mr. Harrington) raised a few moments ago—namely, the question of the position of the Inspectors. It was quite evident from the hon. Gentleman's reply that he did not know what the precise position of the Inspectors was. He would tell the hon. Gentleman why it was he asked the question. In all there were 36 Inspectors, or in other words, more Inspectors than there were counties in Ireland. If the men were distributed over the districts of Ireland and controlled by some Central Authority in Dublin it would be very easy for them to inspect the country. But what was the fact? He happened to know a few of the gentlemen who had been appointed. They were young gentlemen just fresh from school. They were sons of landowners in Kerry; and he had never known them to discharge the duty in connection with the work of the Office. Possibly when they went out to hunt they might take a valuation in the way; but, for all the people knew of them, while they were receiving a salary from the Board of Works, they were living at home in their fathers' houses. Their absence from home was certainly never noticed by those who lived in the locality. If it was a fact that there was no control over the movements of these men, if there was no system for employing their industry and directing their energies, could not the Chief Secretary to the Treasury take the Department in hand and devise some means by which it could be shown what value in work was given for the amount expended? From the manner in which the appointments were made, it was apparent that they were used for political purposes merely; they were mere jobs, they were not open to public competition, there was no test by examination, no special knowledge, and, so far as he knew, no education required; if a man could write a letter, then, to all intents and purposes, he was deemed able to discharge the duties of the post. He was not aware that the Department exacted any duties at all from some of them. Surely the Secretary to the Treasury might well be asked to demand some test of qualification from those who sought employment in the Department, and some security that those appointed should really perform their duties.

MR. COURTNEY said, to the question of the hon. Member for Carlow (Mr. Gray), as to the method of appointment, he had only to answer that he would make inquiries; but upon the point raised by the hon. Member for Westmeath (Mr. Harrington) he could throw some light—namely, the amount of work. During 1883 applications were received steadily at the average rate of 86 per week; 614 cases were sent up for inquiry, and in the result about 135 cases on an average went through the hands of each Inspector in the course of the year, added to which were 106 cases of works in progress for which certificates were issued. An average of 436 visits to different holdings had to be made; and taking this into consideration with the large amount of office work, several visits to different works had to be made by an Inspector each day, so the amount of work was considerable—in fact, there was rather the fear that the work would be scamped through the amount having to be done than that the work was insufficient to occupy the men's time.

Mr. GRAY said, this scarcely indicated the amount of work, because, in a great many cases, the inspection had reference only to the building of a cottage or the draining of a field, and such matters as would occupy a competent man only a few minutes on a visit, during which he would see, in a very short time, if the work was practical or not. Why, a professional architect, in large practice, could make a score of visits to buildings in progress during a day. So there was not much information in the hon. Gentleman's answer. But, so far as he was concerned, he was quite content with the assurance that the information he had asked for should be forthcoming. He would ask the Committee to observe, as an example of the different manner in which two great Departments were conducted in England and in Ireland, how readily an English Member could obtain information in regard to matters connected with the Department over which the First Commissioner of Works (Mr. Shaw Lefevre) presided. Upon a question of a glass door in any part of the building, upon the trimming of a lamp, upon a question of drainage in the neighbourhood, or if there was a fear the head of the statue of the Duke of Wellington would be turned the wrong way, the First Commissioner of Works could give a reasonably full explanation, because he was possessed of personal knowledge of the facts; but matters of great importance in Ireland could only be known to officials by way of mere report; they had no personal knowledge at all. There was no person in the House who was prepared with the knowledge to give Irish Members satisfactory information on matters, perhaps, of quite as much importance as the head of the Duke of Wellington, or an evil smell in the neighbourhood of the House of Commons.

Mr. HEALY said, he thought the Secretary to the Treasury had made a good suggestion in proposing to postpone the Vote for a few days.

Mr. COURTNEY said, Oh, no; he had not done so.

Mr. HEALY said, he was sorry to find himself mistaken, for the suggestion struck him as being an admirable one; and he did not exactly see how they could arrive at a solution of the difficulty without a postponement. The hon. Member for Carlow (Mr. Gray) had asked for information, which the Secretary to the Treasury said should be supplied on Monday; but he should like to know of what avail would it be when they had lost all grip of the Vote? With all respect, he ventured to say English Members would not be treated in that way; he should like to see such an attempt made. His hon. Friend (Mr. Gray) had done extremely good service in calling attention to the Vote. On a former occasion it had been pointed out how the staff expenses were £1 to give 10*s*. to a farmer; and, for all that was known, it was costing £1 10*s*. for each 10*s*. advanced. In all these systems there was always one class gained largely, the Irish officials; in fact, it was a system of outdoor relief of officials from the Orange class; it was nothing less than so much money spent to keep them from the poorhouse. The money was voted, and these gentlemen got the benefit of the jobs. The new head of the Department, General Sankey, was as completely in the hands of the permanent officials of Ireland as his predecessor was, and played into the hands of the worst gang of such there could be. Why should not officials be appointed with some regard to the general condition of classes in Ireland? Was it not the fact that all these particular appointments fell to men of one particular class, notwithstanding the large majority of the population were Catholics and Nationalists? If in using the dice a player turned up sixes 19 times out of 20 they naturally suspected the gentleman who had such extraordinary good luck. Let the Secretary to the Treasury be reasonable and postpone the Vote. How could they vote money with calm consciences knowing how the money was wasted? In one instance recently brought to light, in reference to a contract for building a pier, the work done was 80 feet when the contract was for 100 feet. The contractor found the work more difficult than he expected, that the ground was soft, that there was a bog, or an earthquake, or something else in the way; he told his tale to the Department, and the reply was—"All right, by boy, never mind; here is the money for the whole 100 feet!" This was the case with the Teelin Pier in Donegal. And having shoved out the pier into the sea no roads were made to approach it, and there was some £600 or £700 put into the sea and useless, £1,000 of it from the Canadian Fund, and £1,000 advanced by an unfortunate neighbouring land owner. Why, if such a state of things existed in relation to an English Vote there would be a revolution in the Committee, and, in spite of the Caucus, Radical Members would vote against the Government. That was a strong statement, but the facts were strong. Here was a great institution like the Board of Works absolutely irresponsible, governed by a gentleman imported from Bombay, administered by a staff of members of Orange Lodges, of greater age than would be allowed in any other Department, and with officials who could spend their time attending Emergency sales when they ought to be at work in Dublin Castle. One gentleman was secretary to an Orange Lodge, local secretary for two Insurance Associations, and painted over his door "auctioneer and valuer," and as such attended to buy cattle at Emergency sales. In point of fact, the office was an official Orange Lodge as much as that presided over by Mr. De Carlyn at Belfast, members attended their Lodge for convivial purposes at night, and attended the official Lodge for which they were paid in the day. Why was this not reformed? Years ago a Committee made inquiry and recommendations, then, after six years, Colonel M'Kerlie was got rid of—he was Sir Something M'Kerlie now, though why he was knighted it was difficult to conceive—and now there was General Sankey in his place. But only the men were changed, not the system. The Department had important duties to discharge under the Land Act. It could give enormous assistance to the fishing industry in regard to the erection of piers; but it continued in creating irritation to fester all over the country. He had a correspondence between a solicitor and the Board of Works which was sufficient to make a horse laugh. It had reference to some application for a loan by a tenant; but the correspondence was too long to read it to the Committee. In the first place there was the application for the loan, and the applicant waited six weeks, and no reply came. Then he wrote again saying he had sent a letter. The Board after a week or two replied, asking for a copy of the letter. A week or two more passed and the solicitor wrote again, and after another interval the Board of Works asked for the date of the communication, and, that being furnished, they again replied saying the letter had been mislaid and asked for another copy. This was so absurd, so altogether ridiculous, that people would scarcely believe it; but he had the very correspondence sent to him by the solicitor. This was the state of things, and the Secretary to the Treasury asked for the Vote for these most efficient officers, Colonels, Generals, Grand Masters of Orange and Masonic Lodges, who did nothing. Every year was the Vote asked for, year by year was the same "hue and cry" raised, and there was no more suggestion of reform than there was years ago.

Question put.

The Committee *divided*:—Ayes 61; Noes 12: Majority 49.—(Div. List., No. 175.)

Motion made, and Question proposed, "That the Resolutions be reported to the House."—(*Mr. Courtney.*)

Mr. WARTON asked when the next Vote in the Class was proposed to be taken? It seemed to have relation to a similar subject—Irish buildings.

Mr. COURTNEY said, he had hoped to take it immediately after the Vote just passed, discussion would range over the same topics; but he was afraid objection would be taken to proceeding further now. To-morrow he proposed to resume at the point the Committee left off.

Mr. ARTHUR O'CONNOR said, he proposed to make some observations upon the next Vote, which he would not have been in Order in making on the Board of Works Vote.

Motion *agreed to*.

Resolutions to be reported *To-morrow*.

Committee to sit again *To-morrow*.

SUPPLY.—REPORT.

Resolutions [July 21] *reported*.

Resolutions 1 to 5, inclusive, *agreed to*.

Resolution 6—

"That a sum, not exceeding £23,518, be granted to Her Majesty, to complete the sum necessary to defray the Charge which will come in course of payment during the year ending on the 31st day of March 1885, for the Salaries and Expenses of the Board of Supervision for Relief of the Poor and for Expenses under the Public Health and Vaccination Acts, including certain Grants in Aid of Local Taxation in Scotland."

MR. FRASER-MACKINTOSH said, he had intended to call attention under this Vote to the case of an Inspector in the Highlands, who had been dismissed under circumstances which had given rise to great dissatisfaction. This man was dismissed not for incompetency or irregularity; but at that late hour he would not enter on the subject. He wished, however, to ask the Lord Advocate whether he would agree to give as an unopposed Return, a list of all who had been dismissed by the Board of Supervision from the office of Inspector of the Poor, together with the reasons for such dismissals, from the formation of the Board to the present date?

THE LORD ADVOCATE (Mr. J. B. BALFOUR) replied, that at that moment he did not see any reason for objecting to give the Return; but he had not known until that evening that it was to be moved for, and perhaps the hon. Member would not hold him absolutely bound to what he had said.

Resolution *agreed to.*

Remaining Resolutions *agreed to.*

MAGISTRATES (IRELAND) SALARIES BILL.—[BILL 292.]

(*Mr. Courtney, Mr. Trevelyan.*)

SECOND READING.

Order for Second Reading read.

MR. HEALY said, he observed that this Bill was on the Paper to-night, and he wished to ask whether the Government intended to proceed with it; and whether the Government would give some information with respect to Mr. Clifford Lloyd, without which they could not proceed with the Bill?

MR. COURTNEY said, he could not give any date as to proceeding with the Bill, nor the hour, until he had consulted with the Chief Secretary for Ireland; but it would not be taken at an unreasonable hour.

Second Reading *deferred* till *Thursday.*

INFANTS BILL.—[BILL 14.]

(*Mr. Bryce, Mr. Horace Davey, Mr. Anderson, Mr. Staveley Hill.*)

COMMITTEE.

Bill *considered* in Committee.

(In the Committee.)

MR. TOMLINSON moved that Progress be reported on the ground of the importance of the Amendments to be introduced into this Bill, and the fact that several Members who proposed Amendments were not present.

MR. WARTON seconded the Motion on the grounds given by the hon. Member, and also because it was now after 2 o'clock, and the House had to meet again at 12 o'clock.

Motion made, and Question proposed, "That the Chairman do report Progress, and ask leave to sit again."—(*Mr. Tomlinson.*)

MR. BRYCE said, he hoped the Committee would go on with the Bill, for a large number of Members had come down and stayed until that late hour to assist in bringing the Bill to a close, and he should be sorry that they should be put to the same trouble again. If it was found that the Bill was likely to take much time, Progress could then be reported.

THE ATTORNEY GENERAL (Sir HENRY JAMES) said, he was quite sensible of the difficulty of proceeding with the Bill at that hour; but he could not help feeling that there were many Members who had come down for that express purpose, and he hoped the Committee would go on with the Bill to some extent.

MR. R. N. FOWLER (LORD MAYOR) said, the hon. and learned Gentleman knew that this Bill had been put down night after night, and had brought him down every night, together with other Members. He did not complain of that, but he thought they were entitled to some consideration.

Question put.

The Committee *divided:* — Ayes 5; Noes 60: Majority 55.—(Div. List, No. 176.)

Clause 1 *agreed to.*

Clause 2 (Father and mother to be joint guardians).

MR. INCE moved the omission of the clause, believing it to be inexpedient to have a system of double control during the lifetime of both parents. At that hour he refrained from repeating the argument which had been brought forward on the second reading.

Motion made, and Question proposed, "That the Clause stand part of the Bill."

MR. BRYCE objected to the proposed omission, on the ground that the provision would be of use in promoting domestic happiness by giving the mother a better status in the family, that of full equality, and also because the principle of the clause had received a considerable amount of support from the public. As many as 150 Petitions, with 15,000 signatures, had been presented to Parliament in favour of the principle of equal rights between husband and wife in the custody of their children. Having regard to that, he should be bound, in spite of the hostility manifested to the clause in the House, to take a Division upon the Motion; and he hoped that many hon. Members would give him their support.

THE ATTORNEY GENERAL (Sir HENRY JAMES) said, he would ask the hon. and learned Member whether that was a wise course to pursue? If he took a Division he would place the Bill as a whole in great peril· They should not discuss the principle of the Bill now, the Bill having been read a second time.

Question put.

The Committee *divided*:—Ayes 19; Noes 43: Majority 24.—(Div. List, No. 177.)

Clause 3 (Surviving parent to be guardian).

MR. INCE said, he proposed to amend this clause in order to carry out what had been the prevalent feeling of the House on the second reading. The effect of the clause would be that after the death of the father or the mother the survivor would be the guardian both of the estate and of the person of the infant. He proposed to add a Proviso the object of which was that if there was any property belonging to the infant the father should have power to appoint a guardian of the estate who would not interfere in any way with the mother's appointment of a guardian of the person, or with the mother being such guardian herself. The appointment of a guardian by the father he proposed, however, should only come into effect in case the mother married again. He thought that even the hon. and learned Member who had charge of the Bill would admit that he was not unduly interfering with the rights of the mother. In a case where there was property and the mother married again he thought it was desirable that there should be some independent person acting in the father's interest in regard to the estate.

Amendment proposed,

In page 1, line 12, after "Guardian," add "Provided, That it shall be lawful for the father of an infant, by deed or will, to appoint a guardian or guardians of the estate of such infant, but such appointment shall only take effect after the father's death, and as against the mother or any guardian appointed by her under the powers of this Act (if she shall be the surviving parent) in the event of her marrying again."—(*Mr. Ince.*)

Question proposed, "That those words be there added."

MR. FINDLATER said, that although he did not go as far as his hon. and learned Friend, yet he supported the principle of the Bill; but what he desired was that the wife should not be the guardian of the property. Neither the training nor the education of the wife qualified her for a position of that kind, and he thought it would be very undesirable that she should have its management. He was quite sure that the husband, if he appointed a guardian, would not be able to get anyone who would act with the wife; because those who had had experience in such matters knew that it was very difficult to work with a woman in business affairs of this nature. As the Bill stood it went very far indeed. In every case the wife was to be the guardian of the infant's fortune, and it seemed very hard indeed that the only privilege left to the husband should be to appoint a guardian associated with his wife. The husband in most cases provided the property, and certainly one would think that he should have the power of disposing of that property as he wished, and of appointing any person he chose to manage it. At all events, it should not be left as the Amendment proposed, and he thought in no case should the wife be made the guardian of the fortune.

Amendment proposed to proposed Amendment, to leave out all after "infant," in line 3.—(*Mr. Findlater.*)

MR. ARTHUR O'CONNOR said, it seemed to him that the Amendment of the hon. and learned Gentleman as amended, or without the Amendment last moved, would introduce a change in the law of some importance, but which appeared to have escaped notice. By the Wills Act testamentary power was taken from all infants, although he believed that under the Statute of Charles II. infants had the power of appointing guardians over their children. The Bill, if it became law, would make an alteration in respect of the Wills Act. He did not know whether the hon. and learned Gentleman who proposed the Amendment had noticed the point; but it was one which he thought might have an important bearing beyond the Amendment.

MR. WARTON presumed that the hon. Member for Queen's County referred to the position of an infant father.

THE SOLICITOR GENERAL (Sir FARRER HERSCHELL) said, that under the Amendment whatever appointment a man might wish to make by his will might apply, as far as he could see, even if the husband and wife were living separate. Personally, he should prefer the Amendment of the hon. Member for West Aberdeenshire (Dr. Farquharson).

MR. HEALY said, he should like to know in what way, under the clause or under the Amendment, the religious difficulty was to be dealt with? It appeared to him that in the case of mixed marriages under the clause, in the case of the death of a Protestant father, the Catholic mother would become guardian of the children, and *vice versâ*. He would like some little information as to how this matter would be affected by the clause. He was afraid that as the Bill was drawn it would lead to some difficulty in the case of mixed marriages.

MR. TOMLINSON said, he thought that the case the Committee ought primarily to consider was that of parents living in harmony, and bringin up their children as they ought to be brought up. He believed that the mother in that case would wish that in the guardianship of her infant children someone should be associated with her. That opinion, he thought, would be shared by most hon. Members who had had an opportunity of considering what the ordinary feelings of a mother were. There could be little doubt that she would desire someone to be associated with her where there was personal property concerned. He certainly preferred the clause of the hon. Member for West Aberdeenshire (Dr. Farquharson), with which Amendment he was willing to support the clause.

MR. BRYCE said, that personally he rather preferred the Amendment of the hon. and learned Member for Hastings (Mr. Ince) to that of his hon. Friend the Member for West Aberdeenshire; but he felt there was great force in what had fallen from the Solicitor General with regard to the Amendment of the latter hon. Member, and he believed he should meet the views of the Committee by saying that he was prepared to accept that Amendment. With regard to the observations of the hon. Member for Monaghan (Mr. Healy), he believed the question raised by him would, at any rate, be simplified by the adoption of this clause. His own opinion was that a number of the difficulties at present raised in law in connection with this subject of the religion of minors would be got rid of by enlarging the discretion of the Court; if not altogether got rid of, they would be considerably diminished under a later clause of the Bill. Some of these difficulties were such as must arise under any system; neither this Bill nor any other could dispose of them: it was enough if it mitigated them.

Motion made, and Question proposed, "That the Chairman do report Progress, and ask leave to sit again."—(*Mr. Findlater.*)

MR. WARTON said, the question he had to consider was not the danger of agreeing to either Amendment; the danger was in the clause itself, and that the Bill had been brought on at a time in the morning when it could not be considered at all. The wording of this clause was the vice of the Bill, and he was afraid it would not make much further progress in that House unless it was altered. He begged to second the Motion of the hon. Member opposite.

MR. HEALY suggested that the clause should be postponed, and that the Committee should proceed with the other clauses of the Bill. That would give the Committee time for further consideration.

MR. ILLINGWORTH said, he hoped his hon. and learned Friend the Member for the Tower Hamlets (Mr. Bryce) would consent to the Motion for reporting Progress. No one could doubt for one moment the high motives of his hon. and learned Friend He thought that some gratuitous errors had been made in the preparation of the original Bill; and the present position was that his hon. and learned Friend had whipped up a few Members, and was prepared to see the Bill carried, even at the sacrifice of discussion. How was it possible that this far-reaching question could be reported, and submitted to the decision of their constituents at that hour? It was true that some persons had written to their Members about the Bill; but the general public knew nothing of what was going on. When he considered that this proposed change in the law would set up a new condition of things in every household in the country, he, for one, protested against going any further with the Bill on that occasion. Seeing that they had reached a point of fundamental difference, he hoped his hon. Friend would agree to the Chairman reporting Progress.

MR. HORACE DAVEY said, he hoped the Committee would, at least, consent to go on until they had passed the clause. [MR. WARTON: No, no!] Although, no doubt, his hon. and learned Friend the Member for Hastings (Mr. Ince) was quite right in saying that considerable objections were expressed in different parts of the House to Clause 2 on the second reading of the Bill, yet, so far as his recollection went, Clause 3 was then regarded with, he might say, almost universal favour. Although he did not deny that the clause was capable of improvement—and capable of improvement in the direction indicated by the Amendment of the hon. Member for West Aberdeenshire (Dr. Farquharson)—still, he thought the clause did command the general approval of the House.

MR. SEXTON supported the Motion for reporting Progress, because he felt that if the Committee went on, most of the clauses would be carried. It appeared to him that hon. Members were considering the Bill with a very imperfect knowledge of the changes in the law which it proposed to effect. But those ignorant of the law might see that the Bill introduced a very doubtful and dangerous state of things. He did not know that for Ireland it would be beneficial.

MR. BRYCE said, he should not oppose the Motion of the hon. Member for Monaghan (Mr. Findlater) to report Progress, in the hope that when the Bill again came forward it would be agreed to by those hon. Gentlemen who now objected to it.

MR. HARRINGTON: Exclude Ireland.

Question put, and *agreed to.*

Committee report Progress; to sit again upon *Thursday.*

MOTIONS.

—o—

MILITARY PENSIONS AND YEOMANRY PAY BILL.

LEAVE. FIRST READING.

SIR ARTHUR HAYTER, in moving for leave to bring in a Bill to make further provision with regard to the Pensions of Soldiers, and to the Pay and Pensions of the Yeomanry, said, he might be permitted to say that the changes which had been made in the proposed measure since last year had completely satisfied the Chelsea Commissioners, who had withdrawn their opposition to the scheme. He might further observe that a Memorandum would be laid on the Table of the House by the Secretary of State for War before the second reading was taken, in which the provisions of the Bill would be fully explained.

MR. ARTHUR O'CONNOR asked if it was the intention of the War Office to make any alteration in the constitution of Chelsea Hospital, and whether they proposed to do away with the Hospital, and to transfer the Staff; or whether they had other proposals in view?

SIR ARTHUR HAYTER: No, Sir; we have no intention of the kind.

MR. ARTHUR O'CONNOR: Has the War Office abandoned that idea?

SIR ARTHUR HAYTER: That is not the intention of the Bill at all.

Motion *agreed to.*

Bill to make further provision with regard to the Pensions of Soldiers, and to the Pay and Pensions of the Yeomanry, and for other purposes, *ordered* to be brought in by The Marquess of HARTINGTON and Sir ARTHUR HAYTER.

Bill *presented,* and read the first time. [Bill 302.]

CHOLERA, &C. PROTECTION BILL.

On Motion of Mr. GRAY, Bill to make better provision against Cholera and other dangerous epidemic diseases, *ordered* to be brought in by Mr. GRAY and Mr. DAWSON.

Bill *presented*, and read the first time. [Bill 303.]

CHARTERED COMPANIES BILL.

On Motion of Mr. ATTORNEY GENERAL, Bill to declare the Law relating to the Incorporation of Chartered Companies, *ordered* to brought in by Mr. ATTORNEY GENERAL, Mr. CHANCELLOR of the EXCHEQUER, and Mr. SOLICITOR GENERAL.

Bill *presented*, and read the first time. [Bill 304.]

House adjourned at a quarter after Three o'clock.

HOUSE OF COMMONS,

Wednesday, 23rd *July*, 1884.

MINUTES.]—SUPPLY—*considered in Committee*—CIVIL SERVICE ESTIMATES—CLASS II.—SALARIES AND EXPENSES OF CIVIL DEPARTMENTS, Votes 40 to 42; CLASS III.—LAW AND JUSTICE, Votes 1 and 2.

PUBLIC BILLS—*Second Reading*—Superannuation* [146]; Ulster Canal and Tyrone Navigation [244].

ORDERS OF THE DAY.

SUPPLY—CIVIL SERVICE ESTIMATES.

SUPPLY—*considered* in Committee.

(In the Committee.)

CLASS II.—SALARIES AND EXPENSES OF CIVIL DEPARTMENTS.

Sir LYON PLAYFAIR in the Chair.

(1.) £4,416, to complete the sum for the Record Office, Ireland.

MR. SEXTON asked the Secretary to the Treasury who was in charge of the Vote for an explanation of an item of £160 with reference to the editing of facsimile manuscripts? He had recently addressed a Question to the hon. Gentleman in regard to the recording and indexing of Irish papers; and he wished to know how long the Department would be engaged upon this work, and what results had been attained? There was also a charge for the Keeper of the State Papers of £500. He assumed that the Keeper of the State Papers performed useful functions and that he was not overpaid; but he observed that the same gentleman also received a sum of £750 for the Office of Ulster King-at-Arms. He appeared, therefore, to be a gentleman who received one salary for doing something, and another salary for doing nothing at all. He would like to know how long this pluralism of Office was to be allowed to continue; and whether, in the case of Ulster King-at-Arms, there was any possibility that this Office, in the fulness of time, would be abolished? He believed the time had come when those who wished to flourish before society with coats of arms, alleged to have belonged to their ancestors, should pay for the social honour which thereby accrued to them; and if this gentleman was to be retained for the purpose of providing a pseudo-aristocracy, those persons who wished to assume heraldic arms and mottoes should pay for the honour. He also thought there must now be crowds of officials so well acquainted with the State ceremonials at Dublin Castle, that there was no necessity for the guests to be led by the hand by the Ulster King-at-Arms as children were led by their nurses. If it was necessary to keep up this State official, he ought to be paid by those who derived pleasure or profit from his performances.

MR. COURTNEY said, the case was not so bad as had been represented by the hon. Member. If the hon. Member would look at another Vote for the Household of the Lord Lieutenant, he would see that the sum of £650 had been received in fees, so that, in point of fact, those who desired new coats of arms did pay for them. The Office of Keeper of the State Papers was, he assured the hon. Member, no sinecure. It had been an Office established in the year 1715.

MR. T. P. O'CONNOR asked if the hon. Gentleman would be good enough to state the duties of the Keeper of the State Papers?

MR. COURTNEY said, the duties were regulated by 31 *Vict*. c. 70. It was his duty to collect and classify the State Papers, and remove them to the Record Tower in Dublin Castle. After they had been examined, they were allowed to remain under the care of Sir Bernard Burke, or whoever might happen to be Keeper, for a period of 50 years, after which they were transferred to the Record Office, where they were under the care of the Master of the Rolls. The Keeper of the State Papers arranged the documents, and saw that they were were kept in safe custody, and that they were forthcoming whenever they might be required, or whenever it was necessary to examine them. When they were placed under the care of the Master of the Rolls they were catalogued.

MR. T. P. O'CONNOR: From day to day?

MR. COURTNEY said, they were catalogued as they were sent in. The facsimile work in connection with the Irish national manuscripts had now been in progress for 10 or 12 years, and certain volumes had been published. It would be completed by the publication of one additional volume, which was now passing through the Press, and was expected to be issued in the course of a few weeks. Mr. Gilbert, the Secretary of the Record Office, was the person who was paid for editing these manuscripts, and he had been engaged on the work since 1872.

MR. T. P. O'CONNOR asked whether they were to understand that the publication of these facsimiles, in regard to which the hon. Gentleman had given them such interesting information, was to be continued; and whether there were not other Irish ancient manuscripts which were worth being reproduced? There had been no complaint from that quarter of the House as to the manner in which the present volumes had been prepared; and he thought the feeling of the Irish people would be grossly misrepresented if a word was said to imply that they had not a right to the reproduction of these records in the best possible form. He should be glad to learn what manuscripts were represented by the volumes already published.

MR. KENNY quite agreed with his hon. Friend that the sum required for editing these manuscripts was not exorbitant. On the contrary, he believed it to be very small. As the translation of these manuscripts was said to be approaching a conclusion, it would be of some interest to the Irish people to learn from the Secretary to the Treasury whether there was any intention of translating into English any of these Irish volumes, which were of great interest. In particular, he should be glad to learn whether it was intended to continue the translation of the Brehon Laws. The late Dr. O'Donovan had translated four volumes, and there still remained something like six volumes to be translated into English. He did not know whether there was any person in Ireland who was competent to continue the translation of the Brehon Laws and other old works; but it was quite possible that there might be. It was a matter of great interest. Very few people in Ireland had so complete a knowledge of the Celtic language as to be able to read these old MSS., even if they succeeded in deciphering them. The old manuscript form of the Brehon Laws was in the Royal Irish Academy; but the existence of these works was of no practical value, except to those competent to decipher them. He believed that it would be of the greatest possible interest for the people of Ireland to learn what were the laws of their country many centuries ago. He believed there was only one edition in existence, so that the study of them was clearly restricted. It would be a matter of general satisfaction if these volumes were translated into English, so as to afford a better insight into the ancient laws.

MR. SEXTON agreed with his hon. Friend the Member for Ennis (Mr. Kenny) that the sum for editing these manuscripts was a small and beggarly item. He saw by the English Estimates that £3,000 was spent in translating the records of foreign countries; and, therefore, he thought the sum of £160 very inadequate for this purpose in Ireland. If it was necessary to expend £3,000 for editing and translating the political remains of England in foreign countries, surely £160 for editing the Irish MSS. was a very inadequate sum. He hoped the work would not be brought to a conclusion until the Government had thoroughly ascertained and satisfied the Irish Members whether any further work of the kind remained to be done. He felt great satisfaction in knowing that this work was under the direction of so competent and enthusiastic an Irish scholar as Mr. Gilbert, who had written one or two of the ablest historical works of the time. Any work of this kind would be read with interest; and he quite agreed with the hon. Member for Ennis that it would be desirable to have the Brehon Laws translated, in order to show that Irishmen many centuries ago were able to make very much better laws for themselves than Englishmen could now.

Mr. COURTNEY said, he did not understand that the hon. Member for Ennis (Mr. Kenny) complained of the amount included in the Vote.

Mr. KENNY : Certainly not.

Mr. COURTNEY said, that the right hon. and learned Member for the University of Dublin (Mr. Gibson) had complained, not that the work had been undertaken of publishing these facsimiles of ancient Irish MSS., but of the expensive way in which they had been brought out, which rendered them inaccessible to the people generally. The item for editing and translating of the English records, to which reference had been made, related to chronicles and State Papers of a totally different kind from those now in question. The Vote related to certain MSS. written in Irish, the reproduction of which was now coming to an end. The cost of translating the Brehon Laws would be included in the Royal Irish Academy Vote. He believed that a gentleman named Mahoney, now dead, had been engaged in the translation of these Brehon Laws. Some four volumes had been completed.

Mr. KENNY said, that the work was not now in progress, but had been arrested.

Mr. COURTNEY: Yes; by the death of Mr. Mahoney.

Mr. KENNY: Are there not other people capable of continuing the work?

Mr. COURTNEY: I will ascertain how the matter stands; and, if possible, the work will be continued.

Mr. DAWSON said, he was glad that the Vote afforded an opportunity, in reference to this question of the translation and preservation of ancient Irish MSS., of calling the attention of the Government to a very lamentable case in connection with this matter in Dublin. The brother of the late Professor Eugene O'Curry, an eminent scholar who had spent his life in the practical work of translating these documents, died some time ago. Anthony O'Curry, whose knowledge of Irish was even more extensive than that of his great brother, assisted his brother Eugene O'Curry, and had been untiring in his labours during his lifetime. He died at an advanced age, and had left a widow, and a large family of daughters, almost entirely unprovided for, and they were frequently in circumstances of the direst poverty. He had himself, in Dublin, several times started a private subscription to help these poor people; but periodically they fell into the deepest poverty, and were continually waiting upon him and others to assist them with a few shillings towards the payment of their rent. He would ask the Secretary to the Treasury to consider the case of this poor old lady, the wife of a distinguished scholar, who really might have been better provided for but for her husband having given up the whole of his time for the benefit of the public. Mr. O'Curry, by his distinguished labours in the field of Irish literature, had left a name which would not soon be forgotten; and while he was living he had been of much assistance to his brother and other Irish scholars.

Mr. COURTNEY said, he was afraid that the hon. Member was in error in addressing him. He had no power whatever to interfere in any case of this kind. It would have to be done by communication directly with the Prime Minister, who had charge of the Royal Pension List.

Mr. DAWSON said, he would take the course suggested. He was quite sure, from the well-known kindness of heart of the right hon. Gentleman, that an appeal would not be made to him in vain.

Vote *agreed to*.

(2.) £11,126, to complete the sum for the Registrar General's Office, Ireland.

Mr. DAWSON wished to ask the Chief Secretary how it was that the Secretary, or Chief Clerk of this Office, assumed the title of "Assistant Registrar General," for which he had not the slightest legal authority? He had heard as a fact that this official made use of this pompous title in order, in the most insolent and supercilious manner, to lord it over the other subordinate officials. When a Question was put to the right hon. Gentleman the other day, he said this gentleman was entitled to use the name by law, because the section of the Act of Parliament allowed the Registrar General to appoint an assistant during his absence or illness. That was part of the truth, but not the whole of it. The section of the Act no doubt permitted the Chief Clerk to use the title of Assistant Registrar when the

Registrar General was ill or absent; but at no other period had he authority to assume the title and that insolence in office which was the predominating character of Government officials in Ireland. He did not know whether the Registrar General, who had £1,000 a-year, was supposed to be ill or absent for the entire year; but, as a matter of fact, the Chief Clerk used the title of "Assistant Registrar" regularly, and he had no right to it except in the absence of his Chief. He hoped that they would get an assurance that he would be obliged to discontinue a title to which he had no claim except in the illness or absence of the Registrar General. If he (Mr. Dawson) failed to get such an assurance, he would certainly move the reduction of the Vote.

MR. HARRINGTON said, there was another small matter connected with this Vote which he would call attention to. In this Office, in addition to a permanent staff, a number of gentlemen had for years been employed as task writers. They were only engaged in daily service; but from their long service they were as much identified with the Office as any of the permanent officials. Lately, however, a system had grown up of giving the task work to the permanent clerks; and so men who had been practically for periods of 20 or 30 years in the Public Service, and had given up every other pursuit, because they were not regularly on the staff, were by this course deprived of their means of livelihood. They found themselves at the end of their days, when they were unfit to seek for any other position of emolument, practically deprived of the means of livelihood which the Office had supplied them with for so many years. As a matter of fact, they were in reality dismissed from the Public Service. It was not that there was any want of work in the Department, for the work was as great as formerly, and, if anything, increasing; but whoever had the distribution of the task work now gave it to the permanent clerks employed in the Office. It was all very well to assist the permanent clerks of the establishment as much as they could, and to give them the opportunity of increasing their salaries by extra labour; but everybody knew that in an Office of this kind, where strict supervision did not exist, the clerks did this work in addition to their ordinary work, not at home, but in the Office during office hours. Of course, they received extra pay for it, although it could be easily done by the gentlemen whose case he was advocating. He desired to know what the arrangements of the Office were. If the task work was not paid for, he would not mind; but it was a great grievance that these men, who had spent their lives in the Public Service, but were not salaried officials, should see their work handed over to the permanent clerks, many of whom did the greater portion of their work during their official hours.

MR. TREVELYAN said, that he had as great a feeling of sympathy as anybody who had been connected with public work must have for the class of men called "writers," whose position had been brought before the Committee by the hon. Member for Westmeath (Mr. Harrington). He should be very sorry, indeed, that anything should be done to injure their position, and, in some sense, they had a just claim for consideration. Of course, if the work were done by the clerks in the Office without payment the hon. Member would not wish to interfere.

MR. HARRINGTON: Oh, no.

MR. TREVELYAN said, he would inquire into the matter, as he understood it was the impression of the hon. Member that the work was done by the clerks of the establishment for payment. Certainly, with reference to Mr. Matheson, the Deputy Registrar General, he found that he was entitled to have that title during the absence of the Registrar General. He was informed that it was a matter of convenience that he should be appointed once for all. He would, however, look into the matter. He was told that Mr. Matheson never signed himself Deputy or Assistant Registrar General, except in the absence of his Chief; and it would be necessary to appoint him every time the Chief was absent. That would be a greater concession than any Member of Parliament had a right to demand.

MR. SEXTON said, he was glad to see that the right hon. Gentleman treated the matter in a playful spirit; but no one would think of putting the right hon. Gentleman to the trouble of appointing Mr. Matheson every time the Head of the Office was absent. That would be a reduplication of appointments which none of them would desire; but he could not see the necessity for this official to assume a superior title in order to carry on the work of the Department. He was sure that when the Prime Minister was away his work was capably performed by the hon. Gentleman the Secretary to the Treasury; but the hon. Gentleman did not find it necessary to assume the title of Prime Minister. Nor was it necessary, when the Chief Secretary was away from Dublin, for the second official to assume his title. He was thankful to the right hon. Gentleman for the manner in which he had responded to the appeal which had been made to him in reference to the case of the task writers. He (Mr. Sexton) was closely acquainted with the grievances under which they laboured; and he would say that there never had come under his notice a meaner or shabbier instance of the conduct of officials in Ireland than the treatment of these poor and almost worn-out task writers. It ill became the permanent officials, who were in receipt of large and luxurious salaries themselves, to take out of the mouths of these poor task writers their small crust of bread. The Registrar General he saw had £1,000 a-year, the Secretary £600, the Superintendent £450, the first, second, and third clerks £400, £300, and £200, and yet he found that it was their policy to take from some two or three old public servants the miserable £1 or £2 a-week with which they endeavoured to maintain themselves. There could be no difficulty in finding employment for these men in the Office; and all his hon. Friend desired was that, in future, the work, if done for pay, should not be done by permanent members of the establishment. The functions of the Office were being daily augmented, and constant employment could be given to the three or four men who had been attached to the Office for so long a period, and it was the merest pretence to say that the functions and details of the work of the Office were now such as to prevent constant employment from being found. He knew one man who had been attached to this Office for 21 years, and now, at the end of his days, he found himself deprived of employment. He had known him to rise at 4 or 5 in the morning, and work till midnight on work farmed out to him by officials who only paid half the price to which he would be entitled himself. He would be ashamed to say what he believed to be the motive for this treatment; but he would, if the right hon. Gentleman desired, inform him privately what he believed to be the motive for the meanness and malignity of the conduct which this man had been exposed to by the officials. He was sure if the right hon. Gentleman knew it that he would not tolerate it for a moment. But unless some steps were taken to provide these men with suitable employment at the end of their days, as long as he remained in Parliament he would never cease from bringing the question forward when the Estimates came on for discussion. He had no desire to see the Estimates increased, or 1*d.* spent which could be avoided; but he did say that when a man had served the public, in whatever humble capacity, for 20 or 30 years blamelessly and efficiently, it was cruelly unjust that in the end he should be deprived of his means of livelihood, even although some paltry question of economy might arise. He sincerely hoped that when they reached the Estimates next year this cause of complaint would have disappeared.

Mr. COURTNEY remarked that the question of the position of the class of persons known as writers had been raised some time ago, and a promise had been given that it should be inquired into.

Mr. HARRINGTON wished to point out that in this matter of task work there was no possibility of the Head of the Department being able to deal with it as readily as if the men were engaged in the Office. The emoluments received for task work were in accordance with the amount of work done, and if the task writer were not able to do the work he received no payment at all.

Mr. ARTHUR O'CONNOR said, he had no wish to find fault with the Head of the Office. He was inclined to think that if the Heads of Departments were aware of the position of many of their subordinates, that position would be very materially ameliorated. As the right hon. Gentleman had intimated that he would institute an inquiry into the condition of the men employed under the Registrar General, he would ask him to direct special attention to the position of the men described as transcribers. He found that they had been employed now for some 16 years. Ten years ago they were required to pass a qualifying examination; and in every respect they had discharged their duties faithfully and well. From that time to the present they had been employed in work] for which they received very inadequate remuneration, although a similar class of public servants in this country received £210, £280, and £320 respectively. One of the transcribers was actually doing the work of one of the senior clerks who received £400 a-year. It would also be found that some of these men were employed as permanent officials at a time when many of the second, third, and fourth class clerks had not entered the service at all. In the year 1873-4 a Commission sat to inquire into their position, consisting of Earl Percy, Mr. Blackwood, and Mr. Hamilton. The Commission reported in favour of an amelioration of the condition of these men; but all that came of the matter was a miserable increase of £3 a-year for five years, raising the ultimate remuneration to £160 a-year as the maximum. Whereas it would appear from the present Vote that a man employed temporarily as a transcriber on the agricultural statistics rose as a fourth class clerk from £86 by annual increments to £200 a-year. The consequence was that transcribers who were employed on much more important work were in the position of seeing their juniors by many years promoted over their heads as officers of the permanent official staff, and paid much more liberally. He desired to submit the case of these men to the Secretary to the Treasury; and he was sure that, if it were found to be as he had stated, the hon. Gentleman would be glad to do something to improve their condition.

MR. T. P. O'CONNOR said, he had a personal knowledge of the facts of the case to which the hon. Member for Sligo (Mr. Sexton) had referred, and he could confirm what his hon. Friend had said on the subject—that all the circumstances pointed to some motive which was not creditable on the part of certain individuals who had compelled him to occupy his present position. The poor man in whose behalf his hon. Friend had spoken could not be described as past his work, because, as a matter of fact, he was employed in doing the same kind of work farmed out to him by other officials. Therefore, it could not be from any dissatisfaction at the manner in which he did the work that he had been dismissed. With reference to the matter to which the hon. Member for Carlow (Mr. Dawson) had called attention—namely, the assumption by the Chief Clerk in the Registrar General's Office of the title of Assistant Registrar General, he wished, in speaking of the temporary character of the appointment, to refer them to *Thom's Almanack*, which was a sort of Court Guide and general *vade mecum* to those interested in official matters in Dublin. In that volume Mr. Matheson was described as Assistant Registrar General. He believed that *Thom's* was supplied with its information in the same way as *Dod's* Parliamentary information was obtained—namely, directly from those whose names were inserted. An hon. Friend informed him that *Thom's Almanack* was a good deal more authoritative than *Dod's Parliamentary Companion*; and he certainly hoped its casual information was a little more accurate than that which sometimes appeared in *Dod*. Perhaps, however, the inaccuracies in the latter work arose from the fashion which Members of Parliament, as well as ladies, had of understating their ages.

GENERAL SIR GEORGE BALFOUR believed that the last Government had inquired into the position of these men, and given promises that their position should be improved. Some years ago he had asked the Financial Secretary to see what could be done; but nothing satisfactory had yet resulted. The same complaints as those which were made in Ireland were made by the Scotch writers.

Vote *agreed to*.

(3.) Motion made, and Question proposed,

"That a sum, not exceeding £16,593, be granted to Her Majesty, to complete the sum necessary to defray the Charge which will come in course of payment during the year ending on the 31st day of March 1885, for the Salaries and Expenses of the General Valuation and Boundary Survey of Ireland."

MR. SEXTON said, he observed, under this head, an item of £400 for the salary of the Solicitor to the Valuation and Boundary Survey in Ireland. He was bound to ask who this solicitor was? Was it Mr. George Bolton, a gentleman whose name had been frequently before the House? He also found by a foot note that the holder of this office in 1883-4 received an annual salary of £400 as Crown Solicitor for the County of Tipperary, paid out of the Vote for Law Charges in Ireland. They had, therefore, upon that record the fact that Mr. George Bolton received £800 in the course of last year from the public purse. He would like to know how, if Mr. George Bolton was Solicitor to this Department of the Valuation and Boundary Survey, and also Crown Solicitor for the County Tipperary, he found time to leave Tipperary and Dublin to go down to a gaol in the West of Ireland in company with a policeman in order to see a prisoner in his cell, who was said to have turned approver in a murder case? It was also remarkable that immediately after Mr. George Bolton's and the policeman's visit to that man he committed suicide, and was found hanging dead in his cell next day. He wished to know what connection this visit had with the functions of Mr. George Bolton as Solicitor to the Valuation and Boundary Survey Department, or as Crown Solicitor of the County of Tipperary? He would further ask for an explicit statement of the amount which this gentleman actually received per year from the public purse. It was said that his income amounted to some £2,000 or £3,000 a-year, besides which he received sums for law charges in criminal prosecutions. Probably his income was presented in such a shape that it was impossible to ascertain the actual amount of it. It was a matter of notoriety that he had contracted debts to the large amount of about £90,000, and that he was unable to offer his creditors a satisfactory composition. He had been fooling and deluding the Bankruptcy Court for a considerable time. He had repeatedly obtained leave to let some lands of his, and had pocketed the rents without giving the Court any security whatever. The Sheriff in Dublin had endeavoured without effect to levy a decree which had been obtained against this broken-down defaulter and evader of his duties and financial obligations, who was not only retained in the Public Service, but retained as a pluralist, and sent on a secret mission to an approver which resulted in suicide. This was the same gentleman who some years ago defrauded his own wife after he had deluded her into marrying him. He was reported and denounced by Mr. Justice Fry to the Lord Chancellor; but no notice was taken of it. It was sworn that he had drawn up a marriage settlement on his own behalf, the validity of which was impugned, and which was a gross attempt to defraud. This man, who had repeatedly deluded the Bankruptcy Court, conducted his domestic affairs in such a manner that the Sheriffs and Law Officers were utterly unable to seize even a chair or a table in order to execute one of the decrees obtained against him. He (Mr. Sexton) and his hon. Friends near him would have to press for an answer to the question as to how much this man received from the public purse every year. He observed that the hon. and learned Solicitor General smiled.

The SOLICITOR GENERAL (Sir Farrer Herschell): I was not smiling at the observations of the hon. Member.

Mr. SEXTON said, he thought that if the hon. and learned Gentleman knew the full facts of the case all his influence—which undoubtedly was very great—would be brought to bear upon the case in order to free the Public Service from the stain of any connection with such a man. The reason he mentioned these facts was that he thought it would be desirable that the Government should take steps to allocate some of the money received from the public purse, in order to satisfy the creditors of a man who had perverted the administration of justice and made his own wife the victim of his frauds. It was, indeed, a remarkable thing that the chief engine for compelling other men to continue in the paths of legality and honesty should be himself the very embodiment of illegality and dishonesty. He had to ask how long would this system of dealing be allowed to last? Would the Government allow such a shameful parody upon public justice to continue, and allow such a man to pocket his salary as Crown Solicitor for Tipperary and all the special fees, and to evade payment of his debts by numerous discreditable ingenuities? Would no arrangement be made for the benefit of his creditors, for he maintained that the scandal had reached a height that could no longer be permitted. As a protest, he begged to move the reduction of the Vote by £400, and, unless he received an assurance as to the arrangements which would be immediately made for the satisfaction of Bolton's creditors, it was the intention of the Irish Members to press the Motion with all the force they could. He believed when the action of the Bankruptcy Court in Dublin the other day was considered, it would be only reasonable that the Government should withdraw this portion of the Vote from the consideration of the Committee until the question of the character of Mr. George Bolton was decided in the same way that that of Gustavus Cornwall had been decided. Bolton had commenced an action against his hon. Friend the Member for Mallow (Mr. O'Brien) in Belfast, and the trial was to come on in a day or two. The other day, when Bolton's case came before the Bankruptcy Court in Dublin, the Judge, after there had been numerous evasions of the orders of the Court, and after Bolton's ingenuity had been exerted to the utmost, instead of making him disgorge some of his ill-gotten gains for the benefit of his creditors, postponed e investigation of his affairs, becausethhe thought that Mr. George Bolton would probably obtain damages in Belfast against his hon. Friend. The Solicitor General for England looked surprised; but his hon. Friend the Member for Queen's County (Mr. A. O'Connor) remarked that, however easy it might be to surprise the learned Solicitor General for England in regard to the administration of the Irish law, the Irish Members were too well acquainted with the matter to be surprised at anything. Suppose that a public official in England contracted debts to the extent of £90,000, that his action was impugned and stigmatized by questionable proceedings, that the time came when a public Court called upon him to make a disclosure of his debts and assets, and his capability of meeting his obligations, what would the learned Solicitor General think of that individual, having, at the dictation of his superiors, brought an action against a public journalist for an accusation well known to be true? Suppose that in such a case he had been allowed to delay the examination of his affairs, and to keep a veil closely drawn over his repulsive character, because the Judge said he had brought an action and might probably obtain damages. He thought the learned Solicitor General would say that the Judge had departed from that impartiality which was to have been expected from his office in order to prejudice the minds of the jury unfavourably, and to put a gloss upon the merits of the case which were not consistent with a fair trial. He thought that they had a strong claim to call for the postponement of the payment of such a person's salary until his character was decided, and until it could be shown that he was entitled to be retained as a public servant. He begged to move the reduction of the Vote by the sum of £400.

Motion made, and Question proposed,

"That a sum, not exceeding £16,193, be granted to Her Majesty, to complete the sum necessary to defray the Charge which will come in course of payment during the year ending on the 31st day of March 1885, for the Salaries and Expenses of the General Valuation and Boundary Survey of Ireland."—(*Mr. Sexton.*)

MR. HARRINGTON said, he hoped the right hon. Gentleman would consider the point raised by his hon. Friend the Member for Sligo with regard to the postponement of this Vote until the trial. The trial would probably take place during the present week, and certainly before the Vote was likely to come up upon Report, even if it were passed now, and the House would then be in a position to judge what the nature of certain circumstances in connection with this official was. As a matter of fact, Mr. Bolton's character was about to be tried by a jury of his own selection. He had lodged an affidavit that there was only one county in Ireland in which he could hope to obtain a fair trial. This immaculate official, this manipulator of juries, this wire-puller in connection with all the trials by jury under the Prevention of Crime Act in Ireland, had himself deposited an affidavit, in which he declared upon oath that there was only one county in which he could obtain a fair trial of the action between himself and the hon. Member for Mallow (Mr. O'Brien), and that county happened to be the one in which it was well known the hon. Member had no influence whatever, and where the case would be tried by an Orange jury. He (Mr. Harrington) believed that upon that fact alone Bolton stood condemned. It showed that his character had fallen so low, that his depravity was so notorious, and his public life so well known and condemned, that he himself declared that in 31 out of 32 counties of Ireland he could not hope to obtain a verdict; and that the only chance he had was to go to a place where the hon. Member for Mallow was personally disliked. To-morrow they would be in a position to have Bolton's character decided by a jury of his own selection; and he submitted that, under the circumstances, they had an unanswerable claim to have the Vote postponed. Until they were in a position to know what the allegations made against Bolton were, and what the nature of his defence was, the House of Commons ought to withhold the payment of his salary. His hon. Friend the Member for Sligo had stated the amount of this man's liabilities. As a public official he had been receiving some four or five different salaries, including £400 a-year as Solicitor to the Boundary and Valuation Survey, £400 a-year as Crown Solicitor for the County of Tipperary, with very large pickings through his friend Mr. Anderson, under the Prevention of Crime Act, which brought up his income to at least £1,500 or £2,000 a-year. He was the one man in whom the whole system of Crown prosecutions in Ireland was vested. His case was somewhat similar to that of James Ellis French, the late Head of the Criminal Detective Department of Ireland. That immaculate public servant was required to hunt out criminals, and, in order to do so, he reduced himself to the level of the lowest of them by the commission of the most horrible crimes. George Bolton was the man upon whom the Crown rested for the prosecution of criminals; and he (Mr. Harrington) would appeal to the fairness of English Members whether, seeing that, in the course of a few days, there would be a definite judgment as to this man's personal character from the one jury in Ireland with whom he dared to intrust his reputation—a jury selected and manipulated by himself—it was desirable, to pass this Vote? How did it come to pass that the House were compelled from time to time to listen to the history of the private lives of Irish officials? No doubt, it was a most unpleasant thing, but it was a duty to be obliged to call attention to the private character of officials; but, unpleasant though it was, it was a duty which they owed to that House and to their constituents, for so long as men of Bolton's character were retained in the Public Service in Ireland so long would the people of that country have a hearty contempt for the character of the administration there by Her Majesty's Government. With salaries amounting to £1,500 or £2,000 a-year, this man, with no family, and without even a residence of his own, had become involved in debts to the extent of £90,000. And how did he propose to meet his engagements? For nearly 12 months past a suit had been pending against him in the Court of Bankruptcy, and day after day motions had been made to delay the proceedings. Bolton was simply dodging, just as James Ellis French attempted to dodge, the accusations made against him by the hon. Member for Mallow (Mr. O'Brien). The affidavit he had submitted to the Court of Bankruptcy was a most singular document. If such an affidavit had been presented in this country by a Government official, he did not think that such Government official would have been allowed to remain in the Public Service for 24 hours. His liabilities were £90,000, and on what did he ground his application for delay? He said, in his affidavit, that he had an action pending for libel against the hon. Member for Mallow, and that he hoped that action would bring him in such damages as would enable him to be in a better position to meet the claims of his creditors, and to make a better offer. Why, anything more monstrous, anything more ruffianly, he might almost say, than that affidavit had never been presented to a Court of Justice. In no country in the world would a Judge listen to, much less act upon, such an affidavit outside Ireland. It was really insulting the intelligence of hon. Members in that House to ask for a Vote for Mr. Bolton under the present circumstances, because he had brought his battered character into Court, and hoped, by a jury of his own selection, to get such a verdict as would enable him to make his creditors an offer of a few shillings more in the pound. To whom were they to vote this salary of £400? Was it to Mr. Bolton? In his (Mr. Harrington's) opinion, it ought to be voted to Mr. Bolton's creditors. Were they to vote money to a man who had hitherto failed to lead a decent or Christian life in order to enable him to defraud his creditors? This man did not deny that he had defrauded his wife; he did not deny the allegation that he had led an infamous life while married; but he said that, though he was guilty of every crime in the Decalogue, there was one crime of which he was not guilty, but it was a crime with which he was never charged; and yet upon that point he appealed to a jury of his own selection to give him damages, so that he might do something in order to satisfy his creditors. He was surprised that that Government had not long ago taken steps to expunge this man's name from the Votes. It was scandal enough that he should be connected with one Government Department; but there was scarcely a Vote in connection with the Irish Administration in which the name of George Bolton did not turn up. They knew very well that much they had to say against the Government of Ireland was due to the action of this man. They knew that he had been selected as the man to manipulate the juries whose panelling had given such great dissatisfaction—that he was a man who, standing up in a Court of Justice as Crown Solicitor, dared to insult men of the highest and best position in Dublin because he knew them to be possessed of religious feelings and a conscience. The very moment a Roman Catholic presented himself in the jury-box this was the moral man, this immaculate Government official, this man with a high sense of conscience, who insulted him and ordered him to withdraw, no matter how law-abiding a citizen he might be, no matter how high his social position, or even if he were in the Commission of the Peace. The reason was that he hesitated at nothing in order to secure his victim. But how could it be expected, when he displayed no conscientious scruples in his dealings with his own wife or his creditors, that he would manifest any in the discharge of his public duties? He did so because he wanted a verdict, he cared not how; because he wanted results, however obtained; and it was not surprising that he did so when his antecedents were borne in mind. No matter what complaints were made of the Government; no matter what charges they made against public officials in Ireland, and no matter how strong the evidence upon which they rested them, it would have no effect upon Members in that House, who by their votes practically said that the Irish Members were liars, until, after sacrificing time, energy, and money, like his hon. Friend the Member for Mallow (Mr. O'Brien), they forced the truth of their statements upon reluctant English minds. They had a definite set of grievances to complain of. They were told of corruption under the American system of Government. No person could now be surprised at the statement of the hon. Member for Leeds (Mr. Herbert Gladstone), when he said that Ireland was the worst governed country in Europe. The hon. Gentleman might even have used stronger language to describe the state of things which prevailed; but he promised the hon. Member that as the Party to which he (Mr. Harrington) belonged grew in strength, and were able to grasp all that was occurring, they would drag into light a state of things that the hon. Member little dreamt of when he made that statement. The hon. Gentleman was proceeding to reiterate the special charges against Mr. Bolton when he was called to Order by

THE CHAIRMAN (Sir LYON PLAYFAIR), who said: The hon. Member is repeating the argument which he has already several times used in the course of his speech.

MR. HARRINGTON said, he was putting to the Secretary to the Treasury a question as to whether he would apply himself in this case to ascertaining whether the moral character of this man was such as reflected credit on the Department to which he belonged; whether the Department had taken any steps to mark the sense of their disapproval of his conduct; and whether they approved of the extraordinary affidavit which Bolton had made in the Bankruptcy Court? He asked the hon. Gentleman whether an official who was in debt to so large an extent, an official who had brought an action for libel against a Member of that House in order that, if he succeeded, he might be able to make a composition with his creditors, ought to remain in the Public Service? He asked if the hon. Gentleman had taken any steps to make known his sense of, or his disapproval of, the conduct of an individual who had presented such an affidavit as had been described? He hoped that a statement would be forthcoming from the Government Bench which would show to every official in the Public Service, whose character and whose conduct was as discreditable as that of Mr. Bolton's, that he would not be shielded by the Government.

MR. COURTNEY said, he thought that, whatever else might be said with regard to this Vote, it was to be regretted that it afforded another opportunity of introducing the name of Mr. Bolton. It was unfortunate that the manner in which the Civil Service Estimates were made out caused his name to be so often referred to.

MR. ARTHUR O'CONNOR: Unfortunate — unfortunate for the Government.

MR. HARRINGTON: Strike his name out of the Estimates.

MR. COURTNEY said, he would appeal to hon. Members, in view of the circumstance that the salary of this gentleman as Crown Solicitor for Tipperary was coming forward next week on the Vote for Law Charges, that this was a reason for deferring any observations they had to make with respect to Mr. Bolton until that Vote was reached. As the hon. Member for Westmeath (Mr. Harrington) said that this official was bringing an action against the hon. Member for Mallow (Mr. O'Brien) to vindicate his character—[Mr. KENNY: He has no character.]—and as that action was coming on that day or to-morrow, he would put it to hon. Gentlemen opposite whether, in view of that fact, it would not be well to follow the course he had suggested? He asked hon. Gentlemen opposite whether, seeing that this action was pending, it was making a judicious use of the time of the House to say, as the hon. Member for Sligo (Mr. Sexton) had said, that every charge against Mr. Bolton was true; and again to say, as the hon. Member for Westmeath had said, that this official had broken every article of the Decalogue except in respect of some crime which he (Mr. Courtney) believed was not included in the Decalogue? He could not but think, in reference to some remarks that had been made, that the course then being pursued by hon. Gentlemen opposite was highly inconvenient. There were two aspects of the case which were really pertinent to the discussion of the question; first of all, there was the question whether Mr. Bolton was or was not to be retained in the Public Service. And he thought that hon. Members ought to consider whether judgment on that question should not, at all events, await the decision of the action then pending, and whether the taking of any action in that House would not prejudice the decision of the jury, or prejudice any action which the Government might think fit to take after the conclusion of the trial. The second point was as to the relations existing between this official and his creditors. The hon. Member opposite said that Mr. Bolton had presented a Petition to the Court of Bankruptcy, and he asked him (Mr. Courtney) whether he had not received official notice of the affidavit filed by Mr. Bolton in the Court of Bankruptcy. He had not received any official notice on the subject, nor did he see how such notice could have been given to him. Had the matter come before him it might have been officially considered; but no such step, as far as he was aware, had been taken. But he must point out that this was a matter for the consideration of the Judge in Bankruptcy, who would in due course determine what Mr. Bolton must do in respect of his debts—what portion of his salary he must assign for his debts—but it was not the business of the Treasury to go into that question; they could not constitute themselves liquidators to Mr. Bolton's estate, or direct him in any way to make some arrangement with his creditors. The Treasury, it was true, might have to consider the question of retaining Mr. Bolton in office; they might have to consider the necessity of obeying an order of the Court of Bankruptcy with regard to his income if that order were made. But it was obviously a question for the Judge in Bankruptcy; and it was not for that House or for the Treasury to do anything that would prejudice the action-at-law which was then pending. Again, he would point out that this was a Vote of money for an Office, not necessarily for Mr. Bolton personally. It was a Vote of money for an Office, and it did not follow that it would be paid to Mr. Bolton. If he continued in the office the money might be paid to him; but he might have to resign his office, and the question might arise as to whether the money should be paid to his creditors. Further, the question as to retaining Mr. Bolton in the Public Service or dismissing him was one which might be raised, as he had before pointed out, on the Vote for Irish Law Charges, which would come on at the end of the week, or more probably at the beginning of next week, by which time the Government would be in possession of the view of Mr. Bolton's character taken by a Court of Law, which must necessarily command more respect than *ex parte* statements of hon. Members made in that House.

MR. ARTHUR ARNOLD said, he thought there was no ground whatever for the postponement of this Vote, which might be interpreted and used at the trial as an *ex parte* expression of opinion by the Committee. He rose, however, for the purpose of putting a question to the hon. Gentleman the Secretary to the Treasury with reference to the Public Service, of which he had had at one time the honour of being a member. He (Mr. Arnold) held that the rule of the Public Service was that when a man presented a Petition in Bankruptcy he ceased to be a member of the Public Service, and he asked the hon. Gentleman whether that rule was still in force; because he was of opinion that if the rule did not now exist the sooner it was re-established the better it would be for the public interest. He did not hesitate to say that the character of the Public Service demanded that this should be the case. Further, he would take that opportunity of expressing his opinion that hon. Members on both sides of the House had abstained during that day's discussion very properly from any matters relating to the question at issue in the action now pending. He laid it down as a principle that if Mr. Bolton had presented a Petition in Bankruptcy, that fact ought to be sufficient to cause his suspension from the Public Service. The character of the Public Service demanded that the rule which existed in England should be carried out in Ireland; and if any hon. Member would move for the omission of Mr. Bolton's salary on that ground he should be happy to support him.

MR. GIBSON said, the hon. Member who had just sat down had pointed out that it would not be reasonable to ask for the postponement of this Vote, because it might be used at the trial as a partial expression of opinion by that Committee. But he (Mr. Gibson) thought that neither would it be reasonable to ask for a declaration of opinion on the part of the Committee on a Motion to reduce the Vote by the amount of Mr. Bolton's salary, which might with equal possibility be made use of in the course of the trial to-morrow. As far as he had read the papers, it appeared that no adjudication of bankruptcy had yet taken place.

MR. ARTHUR ARNOLD: I understand that he has himself presented the Petition.

MR. GIBSON asked the hon. Member for Salford to take his statement. He had read the report of the case in the public Press pretty closely, and from what had occurred he was not aware that Mr. Bolton's status before the law had been in the slightest degree altered in any respect whatever. Proceedings had been taken—no doubt those proceedings were pending; but no adjudication of bankruptcy had taken place.

MR. ARTHUR ARNOLD: Is there a Petition in Bankruptcy, or is there not?

MR. GIBSON said, he wished to record his own opinion of what had taken place, and, having said so much, he desired to make a few more remarks in support of what had fallen from the hon. Gentleman the Secretary to the Treasury. It had been mentioned by those hon. Members who had spoken prominently in reference to this Vote that a trial of an important character would take place to-morrow in Belfast, in which trial Mr. Bolton was the plaintiff. Now, surely that was a circumstance which should make hon. Members in all parts of the House anxious to do nothing and to say nothing which might by a hair's-breadth affect the result of that trial. For his own part, he offered no opinion with reference to that trial one way or the other. It was an action for libel, in which Mr. Bolton claimed large damages for what was obviously, if it were well founded on fact, a grave and terrible charge. As to whether that charge was made he offered no opinion, and as to what should be the result of the trial he expressed no opinion whatever; it was obvious that all these questions should be left to the constituted tribunals. Much had been said in the course of the discussion which he thought might better have been left unsaid. With regard to the venue, which had been placed in Belfast, it was alleged that Mr. Bolton stated that in 32 counties in Ireland he could not get a fair trial. He (Mr. Gibson) was not aware that Mr. Bolton said anything of the kind. The question of venue was argued before the Court of Queen's Bench in Ireland; and the Court, having heard the arguments, stated that the case of Mr. Bolton was that the defendant was editor of a newspaper which had a large circulation, and circulated much more in Dublin than in other parts of Ireland.

Mr. HARRINGTON: As I read the report, Lord Justice Barry said that Mr. Bolton stated he could not get a fair trial in 32 counties.

Mr. GIBSON said, however that might be, it was not the point. He had read the reports of these legal proceedings in the Queen's Bench. When the Motion came on for hearing, the Judges decided that under the circumstances they were not at all at liberty to interfere with the plaintiff's selection of the venue in Belfast. The defendant was not satisfied, and he appealed to the Court of Appeal in Ireland, which consisted of so many able and eminent Judges, and the ruling of the Court was that they concurred in the judgment of the Court of Queen's Bench, and that they were not called upon in the interest of justice to interfere with the venue being changed from Belfast. It was said by the hon. Member for Westmeath (Mr. Harrington) that Lord Justice Barry made an observation in the course of the proceedings with reference to the number of counties in which it was alleged that Mr. Bolton could not obtain a fair trial. He was quite willing to accept any statement as to what occurred; but that eminent Judge did not in any way whatever dissent from the jud men of the Appeal Court, which, without question, sanctioned the exercise of the plaintiff's discretion in placing the venue in Belfast. Then it was alleged against Mr. Bolton that he had sworn a certain affidavit in the Bankruptcy Court, which affidavit had been described as infamous. He would not go into the question in detail; but he was bound to say in passing that it did not seem to him to be necessarily or in any respect infamous that a man should make a statement that a verdict was pending which might place him in possession of more funds than he had at present, and consequently enable him to make a better settlement with his creditors. But why was Mr. Bolton so obnoxious to attack on the part of Members below the Gangway? Was it because he was Crown Solicitor? Why, he had for years been a solicitor in Ireland; and he ventured to say that if he had been merely Crown Solicitor, getting not a large salary, or even Solicitor to another Department with a moderate salary for discharging the duties of his office, not one word would have been said against him in that House. He (Mr, Gibson) had had official relations with Mr. Bolton for many years; he had been directly connected with him as Crown Solicitor, and his experience was that Mr. Bolton was an able, energetic, and a judicious public servant, who endeavoured to perform his duty to the public without bringing any unfair pressure to bear against prisoners. That being so, he should be wrong if he withheld his testimony on the subject. Why was it, then, at that hour of the day, that this attack had been made on Mr. Bolton? Was it not largely because Mr. Bolton's services had been used by the present Government in the exercise of their official discretion to aid and assist them in most of the important prosecutions which had arrested public attention in Ireland during the last two or three years? He believed that was the case, and that Mr. Bolton's name as Crown Prosecutor had won for him an amount of unpopularity which but for that circumstance would not have attached to him. ["No, no!"] He believed that to be a fair observation, at the same time he should be very ready to accept any statement that proceeded from minds unprejudiced on the subject. He asked whether it was wise, reasonable, or just, having regard to the fact that a trial was about to take place in which Mr. Bolton was plaintiff, and in which the hon. Member for Mallow (Mr. O'Brien) was defendant, that anything should be done on either side of the House which would convey to the public the idea that there was a desire to prejudice the case in any way whatever. Mr. Bolton had not brought his action without advice and consideration. That must be clear to everyone. If it were a well-founded action, he was entitled to get a fair hearing; and if it were unfounded, and the jury were satisfied, the defendant was entitled to get his case heard with every impartiality. He did not discuss the merits of various observations made with reference to Mr. Bolton. He had alluded to them before, and it was not necessary to go into them again. But the hon. Gentleman the Secretary to the Treasury had pointed to one circumstance which was worthy of notice. It was said that this Vote should not be allowed to pass before the trial, because there might not be any other opportunity of discussing it after the trial, in the event of its being thought right, having regard to the result of the pending litigation, to take certain action. That point had, he thought, been met by the circumstance that there would be a Vote taken in the course of the next four or five days which included the salary of Mr. Bolton as Crown Solicitor, and which would afford ample opportunity of discussing the whole matter. He had, of course, no right to regulate the action of anyone in that House but himself, nor did he seek to do so; but he did not think it unreasonable, without expressing any feeling one way or the other, to say that it was not in consonance with the requirements of the position to have a discussion on the present Vote which might be calculated to lead to opinions being formed and expressed one way or the other on the very eve of the trial. The discussion then taking place would be reported in all the newspapers of to-morrow morning, amongst others the newspapers in Belfast, and for his own part he should be very sorry if anything should escape him to the prejudice either of the plaintiff or defendant, whose case would be decided very shortly upon the evidence given before a Judge and jury.

MR. RYLANDS rose to speak——

MR. COURTNEY: As I foresee another flood of easy declamation——

MR. ARTHUR ARNOLD: I must protest against this statement of the Secretary to the Treasury.

MR. RYLANDS: I certainly protest against it.

MR. ARTHUR ARNOLD: It is monstrous.

MR. COURTNEY said, the question had been raised by the hon. Member for Salford (Mr. Arnold) as to the practice in the Civil Service under certain circumstances.

MR. ARTHUR ARNOLD: The question was raised as to whether Mr. Bolton had or had not presented the Petition in Bankruptcy?

MR. COURTNEY said, he had understood the hon. Member for Salford to ask if it were not the rule in the Civil Service that a person who presented a Petition in Bankruptcy ceased *ipso facto* to be a member of the Civil Service? Further, he understood the hon. Gentleman to state that if that were not the rule at present, the sooner it was made so the better. He (Mr. Courtney) wished to state what was the practice in the Civil Service with respect to both England and Ireland. The rule was that if a person became bankrupt in England, Ireland, or Scotland, it did not matter which, he at once became liable to dismissal. But it was also the case that his dismissal depended entirely on the character of his bankruptcy. If the bankruptcy appeared to be the result of riotous living and extravagance, and if there was any suspicion of fraud, the man was, of course, dismissed. But the hon. Member would know that there were bankruptcies which involved no kind of moral guilt on the part of the individual. For instance, a person holding bank shares as a Trustee who became personally liable for a large amount of money through the failure of the bank might become bankrupt, and on the supposition that that gentleman was a member of the Civil Service, it would be monstrous to dismiss him under such circumstances. It remained to him to allude to an observation which had escaped him in jest, and for which he offered his apologies to his hon. Friend the Member for Burnley (Mr. Rylands).

MR. RYLANDS said, he readily accepted the apology of his hon. Friend; but he was bound to say that he could not accept with satisfaction the statement with which he had met the complaints of the hon. Member for Salford (Mr. Arnold). He had a strong impression that the course taken by the Secretary to the Treasury had certainly led to a great waste of public time. They all knew that hon. Gentlemen from Ireland occupied a very different position in that House to that occupied by English Members. He regretted the necessity under which Irish Members lay of constantly calling attention in that House to grievances connected with

Irish officials. They were in a peculiar position in that respect, for if any scandals such as hon. Members from Ireland had brought under the notice of the House were to occur amongst public officials in England, the Press of the country and the public opinion of the country would crush the offenders. In this case it was the voice of a few Irish Members who represented public opinion in Ireland that the Government had to listen to. He asked whether public opinion in Ireland affected Dublin Castle? Not at all. Was it not a fact that Irish Members had only that House in which to make their complaints, and was it not a fact that they came down night after night and brought to the knowledge of the House evidence that the whole of the Public Service in Ireland was honeycombed with influences which were calculated to create a bad impression? They were told to wait the result of the trial pending. That, he supposed, was the action against the hon. Member for Mallow (Mr. O'Brien); but he would point out that, in all probability, there would be other actions brought against the hon. Member for Mallow by Government officials, and surely it could not be contended that hon. Members were to refrain from expressing their opinions upon the charges against Mr. Bolton until those actions had been decided. From their experience of what had already occurred, were they not to anticipa e that the charges made by the hon. Member for Mallow had some foundation? He did not wish to prejudice the case in the slightest degree; he knew nothing about it; but he was bound to say that he had heard Questions put in that House over and over again with regard to Mr. Bolton's conduct, and that he had heard answers from the Treasury Bench which had impressed his mind with the belief that if any public official in England were made the subject of the imputations cast upon Mr. Bolton, the Government would have been bound to investigate those charges, and to have dismissed him in the event of their being found to be true. The hon. Gentleman the Secretary to the Treasury said it was an unfortunate circumstance that this gentleman's salary appeared on the Votes in such a way as to afford an opportunity of frequently raising this question with regard to Mr. Bolton. Why, if it were not for that, there would be no opportunity of discussing Mr. Bolton's conduct as a public servant.

MR. COURTNEY: I only said that in a humorous sense. I said it was unfortunate that the name should appear twice.

MR. RYLANDS said, if his hon. Friend considered the expression "unfortunate circumstance" was humorous, it did not give him that impression. He said that hon. Members from Ireland had no other chance than that which was offered by the discussion of the Estimates of controlling these matters in Ireland. They had no Parliament of their own; and, therefore, they came to that House and had to take advantage of the Votes to raise questions which deeply interested them and their constituents. He had felt constantly that English Members of the Imperial Parliament laboured under a serious disadvantage, from the fact that there was ground—serious ground—for the endeavours of Irish Members to direct attention in England to the state of affairs existing in Ireland. Now, he regretted that his right hon. Friend the Chief Secretary to the Lord Lieutenant of Ireland was not present. He thought his right hon. Friend ought to have been in his place when this Vote was under discussion. His hon. and learned Friend the Solicitor General for Ireland also was absent, although he had been in his place a short time ago. His hon. Friend the Secretary to the Treasury could not be expected to answer the questions put to him with regard to Mr. Bolton's position; he could not answer the question of the hon. Member for Salford (Mr. Arnold) as to whether the Petition in Bankruptcy had been presented by Mr. Bolton himself or by others. Well, his hon. Friend said that that did not affect the question. If a man were simply dragged into the Bankruptcy Court by having a Petition filed against him, there were answers which could be made to such a Petition, and it might, perhaps, be that the Court would refuse the application; but this was a very different position from that occupied by a man who went to the Court and proclaimed his own bankruptcy, and petitioned as a bankrupt. It was a fact that his hon. Friend the Member for Salford asked for information with regard to the presentation of the Petition in Bankruptcy. The right hon. and learned Gentleman opposite the Member for the University of Dublin (Mr. Gibson) gave his own impression of what had taken place; but the Secretary to the Treasury could not say whether any Petition had been presented by Mr. Bolton or not. Well, he (Mr. Rylands) had the best reasons for knowing that a Petition was presented by Mr. Bolton himself. But, whether that was so or not, what struck him was that from time to time a great deal had been brought before the House touching the conduct of this public official; and although he knew nothing personally about the matter, the impression he derived from the answers given to the Questions of Irish Members from the Treasury Bench was that it was the duty of the Executive to consider whether Mr. Bolton should be retained in office or not. His hon. Friend the Secretary to the Treasury told the Committee that there would be another opportunity after the trial had taken place of raising and discussing this question. So far, he was willing that the matter should remain over until the Vote for Irish Law Charges was reached. But although he did not dispute the argument of the hon. Gentleman that this £400 was required for the purposes of the Office, and that it would not necessarily be paid to Mr. Bolton, yet he could not agree that the Vote should be taken on that ground without discussion, because hon. Gentlemen who protested against the conduct of an *employé* would have no opportunity of making their voice heard unless they took advantage of the Votes as they came forward, for that was the only means of making known their grievances. He repeated that he should be willing to allow the matter to remain until the other Vote referred to had been reached, which, he believed, would afford an opportunity of deciding the question; and then, if the charges against Mr. Bolton were made good, he believed it would be quite possible to get the Committee to strike out the Vote for his salary. In conclusion, he deeply regretted that there should be a necessity for these constant representations on the part of hon. Gentlemen from Ireland, which they were perfectly justified in bringing under the notice of the House, with regard to officials in Ireland who appeared to conduct themselves in a manner that was neither creditable to themselves nor for the advantage of the people of Ireland.

MR. SEXTON said, he thought it was unfortunate that they should be obliged to carry on a discussion involving the conduct and character of an important Irish official in the absence of the Minister who was chiefly acquainted with and responsible for affairs in Ireland—that was to say, in the absence of the right hon. Gentleman the Chief Secretary to the Lord Lieutenant of Ireland. He thought the absence of the right hon. Gentleman was all the more regretable because the hon. Gentleman the Secretary to the Treasury had pleaded, in the course of the discussion, that he had not been officially informed as to the position of Mr. George Bolton before the Court of Bankruptcy. The Chief Secretary to the Lord Lieutenant of Ireland was, as the Parliamentary Head of the Department, officially informed of Mr. Bolton's affairs, and there could be no doubt that had he been in his place on that occasion he would have been able to enlighten the Committee with regard to them; but, as he was not present, he thought there was an additional reason for the postponement of the Vote. Notwithstanding that he knew the right hon. Gentleman was very much overworked by his labour in that House, he was bound to say that he considered his absence greatly to be regretted. Although he had a serious objection to the speech of the right hon. and learned Gentleman the Member for the University of Dublin (Mr. Gibson), he took the liberty to point out that it would be well if the Secretary to the Treasury would induce himself to imitate the Parliamentary method of the right hon. and learned Gentleman. The hon. Gentleman the Secretary to the Treasury, whenever he had anything to say, made his argument needlessly offensive. There were circumstances, of course, in which the phrase "easy declamation" might be used; but it should be remembered that the retention of Mr. Bolton in his official position was well calculated to excite in the minds of Irish Members indignation; and before the hon. Gentleman accused them of indulging in "easy declamation" on that subject, he thought he should consider the propriety of retracting his ill-considered phrase about "unfortunate conscientiousness" with which the Estimates were drawn up. Perhaps the hon. Gentleman would have preferred a system under which Mr. Bolton's salary could be buried out of sight, and not appear on the Estimates at all. He thought the phrase unfornate, and one which could not be explained away by any reference to humour. It was a very unfortunate humour, which misled the House of Commons. The right hon. and learned Gentleman the Member for the University of Dublin had accused them of want of impartiality and want of due regard for the raising of the character of debate in that House, by their attacking the character of a man who was a party to the action to be tried to-morrow. The right hon. and learned Gentleman was a skilful debater, and was accustomed with great force to urge his advice upon that House; but his (Mr. Sexton's) complaint was that his whole speech was saturated with the effort to defend the character of Mr. Bolton. He had accused hon. Members on those Benches because they brought forward what they claimed to be facts, while he spoke of the industry, zeal, and energy of Mr. Bolton in such a manner as by oblique means to convey to the jury that a verdict should be found in his favour. Well, the right hon. and learned Gentleman asked why Mr. Bolton had been singled out for attack, and he said it was on account of the manner in which he had conducted certain prosecutions. He (Mr. Sexton) repelled with all his force the accusation that any man on those Benches had attacked Mr. Bolton because of any special energy or vigour that he had displayed in the discharge of his duties. There were plenty of other men in Ireland who displayed energy and ability. Was Mr. Cornwall singled out, because he had energy and ability, which he displayed in the interest of the State? No. Mr. Bolton had been singled out, as Mr. Cornwall had been singled out because he had committed offences which rendered his retention in a Public Office a scandal; and he (Mr. Sexton) asserted for himself and his hon. Friends that so long as any official in Ireland conducted himself properly he would never be attacked from those Benches, but that when such official misconducted himself he would be made the object of attack in the manner which he deserved, and in that manner only. The fact was left out of view that for many years the main features of Mr. Bolton's life had been matter of notoriety. It mattered little whether a Petition to the Bankruptcy Court had been presented by him or against him, the fact being notorious that he owed £90,000, that he would not or could not pay 1*d.* of that money, that the Sheriff of Dublin could not execute a decree of 6*d.* against him, and that he had repeatedly evaded the order of the Court with respect to the land which he possessed. Hon. Members on those Benches were blamed for anticipating the merits of the trial which would take place to-morrow. Upon that he desired to make two observations. First, they were there as the Representatives of the people, and they said that the public interest concerned in the retention of a man of this character in an important office in the Public Service was infinitely greater than the interests either of the plaintiff or defendant in the case to be tried to-morrow. If there were any obligation upon them to be discreet and reserved in their language, how much greater was that obligation upon the Judges on the Irish Bench? But had they set an example of discretion and reserve? Why, on the very motion for changing the venue in the action against his hon. Friend the Member for Mallow (Mr. O'Brien), when his hon. Friend pleaded that his life would not be safe in Belfast, one of the Judges observed that he would be as safe in Belfast as at church—that was to say, if he ever went to church. That was the impartiality, that was the reserve of the Judicial Bench in Ireland, exhibited by a Judge when he was sending his hon. Friend, a Catholic in creed, to be tried by a Protestant jury in a Protestant Court at Belfast; when it was known that there was no man who stood higher in social character and with regard to the observances of his creed than the hon. Member for Mallow. So much for one of the Judges. Again, when this Petition came before Judge Walsh, the other day, although in the ordinary course of law the affairs of Mr. Bolton should have been laid before the public at that moment, the Judge granted him delay and gave him immunity until the trial was over, because, as he said, Mr. Bolton had brought an action against Mr. O'Brien, and there was a probability that he might obtain a verdict. That was another example of judicial impartiality and reserve on the par of the Irish Bench. When Judges behaved in that manner, were they, the Irish Members, to be accused for taking advantage of an occasion when it arose for denouncing an individual in the interests of the public? It appeared to him extraordinary on the part of the Government that they should expect Irish Members to forego discussion on Mr. Bolton's salary in this Vote on the ground that a trial was to take place. It was no fault of theirs that the trial had been fixed for to-morrow; the succession of time and events was not the work of Irish Members, and if the Government did not want the discussion with regard to Mr. Bolton to come on they could very easily have avoided it. Nothing more was necessary than to withdraw the Vote. But they had not done that, and therefore he said that if the interests of justice were involved in what had occurred or would occur in the course of the discussion, upon the Government, and not upon hon. Members on those Benches, rested the blame. The hon. Gentleman the Secretary to the Treasury said he was not officially informed on the subject of Mr. Bolton's affairs. He thought the hon. Gentleman should be ashamed of such an admission.

MR. COURTNEY said, his statement was that the Treasury had no official information with regard to the affidavit of Mr. Bolton in the Court of Bankruptcy.

MR. SEXTON contended that, when the salary of an official in Ireland was brought before the House, it was not creditable that an official charged with defending the Vote should be unable to inform hon. Members with respect to a transaction intimately connected with the character of the individual for whom the money was asked, and consequently intimately connected with the question as to whether that individual should be retained in the Public Service. He asked upon what principle of justice, when hon. Gentlemen on those Benches requested to be informed whether or not George Bolton had petitioned to be made a bankrupt, and whether or not his creditors had petitioned the Court against him, they were to be told that his salary was to be passed in that Committee without their questions being replied to, and without any answer to the question of the hon. Member for Salford (Mr. Arthur Arnold) and the remarks of other hon. Members as to whether a man would any longer be retained in the Civil Service who had presented a Petition, or against whom a Petition in Bankruptcy had been presented? He said they were entitled to receive from Her Majesty's Government the fullest information as to the state of Mr. Bolton's affairs. He could assure the hon. Gentleman the Secretary to the Treasury that no sarcasm of the right hon. and learned Gentleman the Member for the University of Dublin (Mr. Gibson), no specious pleas delivered in sympathetic language, would prevent him or his hon. Friends taking advantage of every Constitutional opportunity that presented itself for criticizing the conduct of officials in Ireland. There might be another Vote to come forward next week, on which this question of Mr. Bolton could be raised; but Irish Members were so used to the manipulation of these matters by the Government, and to the devious course which they were in the habit of pursuing, when the conduct of their officials was called in question, that he would not be surprised, when the Vote for the Crown Solicitors came on next week, if they were told that Mr. George Bolton had been promoted for distinguished services; that he was no longer a Crown Solicitor, and that his conduct must not be discussed on the Vote at all. They were, he repeated, so accustomed to the procedure of the Government in cases of this kind, that, no matter how they were accused, they should do their duty, as Representatives of the people, and ask for no excuse for their mode of criticizing the personal conduct of officials in Ireland.

MR. ARTHUR ARNOLD said, he could not congratulate the hon. Gentleman the Secretary to the Treasury on the method of his replies. He had himself put a simple question to the hon. Gentleman as to whether Mr. George Bolton had or had not presented a Petition to the Court of Bankruptcy? He had asked the hon. Gentleman, also, whether he had any authority for believing that he had done so, and had added that if Mr. George Bolton had presented a Petition to the Court of Bankruptcy, he ought, like any other public servant, to be immediately suspended, and probably dismissed. But the hon. Gentleman the Secretary to the Treasury had presumed to meet that statement by a reference to "easy declamation," and by what he ventured to call humour. Now, he (Mr. A. Arnold) had a very strong opinion that the present was not an occasion for humour; and, moreover, although he had the highest respect for the character of his hon. Friend, he should have thought he would have been the last man in that House, when the conduct of a public servant was called in question, to attempt a *rôle* for which he was singularly unfited—namely, that of humourist. Apparently, the hon. Gentleman could not give him an answer to the simple question as to whether this official, Mr. Bolton, had petitioned the Court of Bankruptcy? From information he (Mr. A. Arnold) possessed, he believed that was the case; and feeling, as he did, that in this matter Her Majesty's Government had acted with neglect in not immediately suspending Mr. Bolton from the Public Service, he should vote on the Division with hon. Gentlemen opposite.

MR. WARTON said, he did not very much like the manner of the hon. Member for Salford (Mr. A. Arnold) in wishing to go to a Division immediately after his attack on the hon. Gentleman the Secretary to the Treasury. He (Mr. Warton) was no friend of the Government, or of the Secretary to the Treasury; but he was bound to say that the hon. Gentleman had on that occasion been unfairly attacked by the hon. Member for Salford and others in the course of the debate. He (Mr. Warton) felt, with regard to the hon. Gentleman's allusion to humour, that it was a harmless and pleasant joke. He was surprised that Irishmen should have failed to perceive the harmless little jest of the Secretary to the Treasury—their minds, it would seem, having for the occasion sunk to a Scotch level. There were, of course, exceptions to the rule, and the perception of a joke was not given to all; but there was no excuse for Irishmen in a matter of this kind, and he thought it was wrong for them to take hold of an innocent observation which must have been so understood by almost everyone who heard it. With regard to the attitude assumed towards this question by the hon. Member for Burnley (Mr. Rylands), he must say that he had never listened tdha more unblushing Electioneering speec made by anyone in the prospect of a Dissolution. He thought there must be a great number of Irish voters in Burnley, or the hon. Member would not have said he regretted that Ireland had not a Parliament of her own. He believed that all English Members were in favour of the Union.

MR. RYLANDS said, he had expressed no regret that Ireland had not a Parliament of her own.

MR. WARTON said, it was true that the hon. Member for Burnley had not used the word regret; but he had asked what the Irish people could do, and said that Ireland had no Parliament of her own. That certainly was as much as to say that he regretted the fact that Ireland had no Parliament of her own; and he supposed the hon. Member's remark was intended for the Irish electors of Burnley. It was the first time during the present Session that they had heard the hon. Member announce his intention of voting against the Government in view of the approaching Election. With regard to Mr. Bolton's case, he was strongly of opinion that he ought to be retained as Public Prosecutor, because he held the threads of so many conspiracies in his hands. And he thought Her Majesty's Government would be justified in retaining him even if he had presented a Petition to the Court of Bankruptcy, which men often did with a view to arranging their affairs, after they had time to look around them, and especially on the ground that against Mr. Bolton, as Public Prosecutor, no charge had been or, he was convinced, could be made.

MR. T. P. O'CONNOR said, he wished, on behalf of himself and other hon. Gentlemen on those Benches, to protest against the suggestion of the hon. and learned Member who had just sat down that Mr. Bolton should be retained in the office under discussion, because, as the hon. and learned Member for Bridport had alleged, there was no charge against him as Crown Prosecutor. They were not discussing in Committee that day Mr. Bolton's conduct as Crown Prosecutor. If that question were to be raised, it would be raised at the proper time. Their whole case at that moment was whether Mr. Bolton's personal character was such that he could no longer be continued with decency as a servant and official of Her Majesty's Government. That was the whole point under discussion. He did not deem it necessary to go into the rather unworthy suggestions of the hon. and learned Member for Bridport with regard to the attitude taken up on this question by the hon. Member for Burnley (Mr. Rylands) and the hon. Member for Salford (Mr. A. Arnold). He would simply express his conviction that it was no small personal matter, such as the hope of securing a few votes, that made those hon. Gentlemen speak as they had done that day on the Vote before the Committee. He wished to call the attention of the Committee to the fact that they had witnessed that afternoon an opposition of a serious kind, indeed, to the attitude of the Government towards their subordinates, started by hon. Members opposite, and not by hon. Members on those Benches. That, he said, was a most significant fact. He knew it was a circumstance which would be marked with considerable satisfaction in Ireland, and he thought it was one which ought to act as a warning to the Head of Her Majesty's Government, who happened to be present on that occasion. Whenever a Napoleonic demonstration took place in Paris, the Republican journals took care to point to the fact that there were certain absentees from the demonstration, the reason being that most of those gentlemen had found their way inside the walls of gaols for conduct which, at other times, would perhaps have secured them reward. If any similar demonstration were hereafter to take place in Ireland, it might be that a large number of highly-rewarded officials in power there would find themselves in gaol for misconduct which had been allowed to pass unchecked. Apart from their strong political differences, Irish Members had a strong personal regard for the Chief Secretary to the Lord Lieutenant of Ireland. For his own part, he considered him an official who acted indiscriminately, and often unwisely; but with regard to the right hon. Gentleman himself, most persons would agree with him when he said that they had for him the greatest respect as an honourable and high-minded gentleman. What was the position in which the right hon. Gentleman was placed? When he (Mr. T. P. O'Connor) saw the right hon. Gentleman in that House haggard, and weary, and distressed every day of his life, because of the association he was brought into with loathsome criminals, he maintained it was a position in which a gentleman like himself ought never to be allowed to be dragged into; but the uprising of hon. Gentlemen on that (the Irish) side of the House against the right hon. Gentleman as to his contact with officials in Ireland, was to save him, and other Englishmen in Ireland, from the stain and stigma of associating with these evil criminals in Ireland. The Vote was £400 for George Bolton, and the statement of Irish Members was this—that George Bolton ought not, and could not, be retained as an official of any Government who had a respect for itself, or a respect for the decencies of life. That was their whole case. What were their proofs in favour of that position? The Secretary to the Treasury must think that the House had been asleep for the past four years. The hon. Gentleman rose up and raised a question as to facts which he (Mr. T. P. O'Connor) thought had passed altogether into the domain of historical and undisputed facts. The charges the Irish Members brought against George Bolton were supposed by the hon. Gentleman to be supported merely by their *ipse dixit*. The hon. and learned Gentleman who had just spoken, and the right hon. and learned Gentleman the late Attorney General for Ireland (Mr. Gibson), supposed that the attacks of the Irish Members on Mr. Bolton were because of his efficiency as a Crown Solicitor. Why, the main charge on which they relied was with regard to what had happened in 1876, before the present Irish Party in the House was thought of. The charge brought against Mr. Bolton was not made by a politician or an Irishman, but made by the deliberate judgment of an Englishman in an English Court of Law—in a judgment by Mr. Justice Fry, who charged Mr. Bolton in two characters—namely, as a solicitor and as a husband. These charges had not been, and could not be, denied by Mr. Bolton, either in one character or the other; and they should at once have disqualified him from any further employment under a decent and self-respecting Administration. What were the charges? Why, George Bolton married a lady of considerable fortune;

she asked him to draw up a deed that would give her control of her property; but betraying his trust as a solicitor, and also the more sacred duty of a husband, this man drew up a deed giving himself the disposal of her property, denuding her, in fact, of all she possessed. He drew up a deed giving himself the right of disposing of her property, and the right he so obtained he had carried to the extent of dissipating a very considerable amount of that unfortunate lady's wealth. There were several other charges against Mr. Bolton's moral character, but into these matters he (Mr. T. P. O'Connor) did not wish to go—charges affecting the character of the man which his official superiors were now considering, and which, in the case of an English official, they always did consider on the earliest possible occasion. He (Mr. T. P. O'Connor) contended that no Government, however much stronger than the one which at present controlled the destinies of this country, would dare to keep in office, for one week in England, an official against whom a Judge of the land had pronounced such a damning opinion as that pronounced by Mr. Justice Fry, in 1876, against Mr. Bolton. Take the second point. The Irish Members said that a man who had presented a Petition in Bankruptcy had no right to remain in the service of the Government. On the other side, it was declared that a Petition had not been presented by Mr. Bolton. The right hon. and learned Gentleman (Mr. Gibson) had, he thought, made a strong point of that—that the Petition was not presented by himself, but by some of his creditors. But, as a matter of fact, the Petition was presented by Mr. Bolton himself, and at that moment that man was in the position of being liable for £90,000, the debts for which he was unable to make anything like a decent provision. The hon. Member for Salford (Mr. Arnold) had got up and asked this very simple question, to which aye or no could have been easily given—namely, whether in this country an official who presented a Petiton in Bankruptcy would not have been at once suspended until the case was decided? The Secretary to the Treasury could not deny that that was the rule.

MR. COURTNEY: I beg pardon; I stated exactly what the situation was. Whether Mr. Bolton presented the Petition himself, or whether the Petition was presented by others, I stated that the fact of a declaration of bankruptcy rendered a person liable to instant dismissal.

MR. HEALY: Why do not you dismiss him then?

MR. COURTNEY: Allow me to finish my sentence. I say, whoever presents the Petition, the fact of a declaration of bankruptcy against a public official renders him liable to instant dismissal. That applies to England and Ireland. There is an official examination into the affairs of such a public servant to determine the character of the bankruptcy. If it appears that the bankruptcy results from riotous living and improvidence, or, still more, if there is anything of fraud in the case, dismissal is absolute; but if, as may happen, a man became bankrupt through no fault of his own, but who, for instance, is in the unfortunate position of holding shares in an unlimited bank which has failed, and become liable to the extent of all he possesses for the debts of the bank, it would be a cruel and unjust thing to dismiss him. In the present case, we are waiting for the decision as to the character of the bankruptcy before we decide upon what course to follow.

MR. T. P. O'CONNOR said, he had a clear recollection of what the right hon. Gentleman had said, and he now merely repeated what he had said before. No doubt, the rule laid down by the hon. Gentleman as to the dismissal of public servants, an their retention in ffice in cases of bankruptcy, was a thoroughly just and equitable rule for the conduct of the Heads of Departments in dealing with their subordinates. Lest he should misrepresent the hon. Gentleman, he wished to ask him whether it was not the fact that, pending the decision of Bankruptcy Petitions, officials were not subject to suspension from the performance of their duties?

MR. COURTNEY: Not necessarily.

MR. T. P. O'CONNOR: But as a rule?

MR. COURTNEY: I do not think any rule could be laid down upon this subject; it is a matter for the discretion of the Heads of Departments.

MR. T. P. O'CONNOR said, the hon. Member for Queen's County (Mr. A. O'Connor), who had a larger experience of the Civil Service even than the hon. Gentleman the Secretary to the Treasury, informed him that the rule and practice was that when an official had presented a Petition in Bankruptcy, he was suspended until the character of the Petition was decided. Well, had George Bolton been suspended?

MR. COURTNEY: No.

MR. T. P. O'CONNOR said, that that being so, he accepted the very just and honourable distinction the hon. Gentleman had drawn of different forms of bankruptcy. A man might be innocent, and a man might be guilty; everyone knew that. He would take the definition of the hon. Gentleman. The hon. Gentleman had said that a bankruptcy which arose from riotous living would be a kind of bankruptcy which would compel the Head of a Department to get rid of his subordinate. Riotous living! That was exactly the charge which had been established up to the hilt against George Bolton; a charge which had been established over and over again—which had been established judicially by the Judgment of Mr. Justice Fry as far back as 1876. Mr. Justice Fry delivered such a philippic against the character of Mr. Bolton, which, if any Irish Member had uttered in that House, would have caused the Chairman to call him to Order. Riotous living was the real cause of the bankruptcy of George Bolton; and yet this man, with all these charges on his head, was defended by an English Gentleman like the Secretary to the Treasury in that House, because it was supposed to be a canon in Ireland that every English official, however dirty he might be, was a tool clean enough to perform the function of administering in Ireland. That appeared to him (Mr. T. P. O'Connor) to be a discreditable and disgraceful state of things. The Irish Members were quite willing to discuss the present relations between England and Ireland in their purely political aspect; but he declared this, that if they were as strong friends of the existing relations between England and Ireland as the bitterest Tory in this country, nothing could be produced more calculated to engender amongst them disgust of the Administration than the unfortunate attitude taken by the Government with regard to the action of officials in Ireland. He would go back to the illustration with which he commenced. If there were an overflow of the existing political relations between England and Ireland similar to the overflow which occurred in France some 14 years ago, where would be the troop of officials who were now screened, defended, and protected by English Gentlemen sitting on the Treasury Bench? From Cornwall to French, down to Bolton and one or two others he could name, they could produce in Ireland a gallery of celebrities in infamy who would form a most worthy addition to Madame Tussaud's "Chamber of Horrors."

MR. LABOUCHERE said, that considering the strong feeling that existed in Ireland on this subject, it seemed to him most desirable that all officials in this country should be entirely above suspicion. Now, what was the case with respect to Mr. Bolton? In 1876 or 1877 a Judge had himself reported, in respect to a trial to which Mr. Bolton was a party, that that gentleman had thoroughly misconducted himself. That report was made to the Lord Chancellor; and, that being so, one would suppose that Mr. Bolton would have been at once dismissed from the Public Service. He was not dismissed, however; he was retained; and what was the consequence? Why, the consequence was that Mr. Bolton, who at that time was stated by the Judge to have got into difficulties, and very serious difficulties, owing to riotous living, had now presumably spent more than he possessed, and had presented a Petition in Bankruptcy. It was said on the one side that he had presented it himself, and on the other that it had been presented by his creditors; but that was not the question. The question was, whether he was in a state of bankruptcy or not? Mr. Bolton had to admit himself that he was. If, therefore, the Committee were to vote this salary, they would be presenting a Bill of Indemnity to Mr. Bolton. Looking at the fact that he was Crown Solicitor, he ought, at least, to be suspended from his important duties until the question of bankruptcy was decided in a Court of Law. The Secretary to the Treasury told them that Mr. Bolton could not be suspended until a decision was come to, and the man was declared a bankrupt in the Court. Bu they all knew how proceedings were det layed in the Bankruptcy Court. The proceedings in this case might be delayed for five years.

MR. COURTNEY: No, no.

MR. LABOUCHERE: They may be delayed two years.

MR. COURTNEY: The estate may be in course of winding up for many years; the settlement of the assets may occupy a considerable period; but the question of bankruptcy may be tried in a few weeks and settled in a few months.

MR. LABOUCHERE: Then, are we to understand that during these few weeks this gentleman, who occupies the position of Crown Solicitor in Ireland, and who, by his own admission, is a bankrupt, will not be superseded? I believe he ought to be.

MR. JESSE COLLINGS said, that hon. Gentlemen on that (the Ministerial) side of the House were put in a considerable amount of difficulty at that moment. If these charges were true—they had no means of judging as to whether they were or not; but they were so notorious, that surely the Government should know whether they were true or not—and if they were true, what were they asked to do? They were asked to vote £400 to this gentleman; and if, as he said, the charges were true and the Vote were passed, it would be one of a most immoral character; and certainly Radical Members, friends of the Government though they were, ought not to permit themselves to be dragged through the mire as to vote a sum of money to a man who had been guilty of such conduct. A man who had been guilty to only half the extent described by hon. Members taking part in that debate ought not only to be superseded now, but he ought to have been superseded long ago. He ought to have been superseded in 1876. He did hope that the Government would take them into their confidence. The only way out of the difficulty was for the Government to promise now that Mr. Bolton should be suspended—he did not think, on grounds of common morality, any other course was open to them. Suppose a report of such a transaction as that came from America or some other country, they would take it as an example of the character of the Government of such country; and he, therefore, as a matter of common respectability, as a question of vindicating the purity of the administration of the Government, asked that someone in a responsible position should now give a promise that this gentleman should be superseded until the result of the bankruptcy proceedings was known. He trusted that the Government, for the sake of their supporters on that (the Ministerial) side of the House, to say nothing of the Irish Members, would agree to that course. If they did not, they who were in the habit of hearing these charges brought against officials by Irish Members, and were in the habit of hearing them denied by the Treasury Bench, and who had no means, speaking generally, of knowing which side was right, would have to give credence to the case submitted by the Irish Representatives. As a rule, when cases of this kind came up, there was a difficulty of judging which side was right, and English Members were apt to believe in the Government case; but unless the Government acted in the interests of decency and morality in this case, for the future English Members would be apt to believe there was an equal amount of truth in all the charges brought against Irish officials. He earnestly hoped that the Secretary to the Treasury would treat this as a serious matter, and would give the desired pledge.

MR. COURTNEY said, the hon. Member for Ipswich (Mr. Jesse Collings) was not in the House when he (Mr. Courtney) had made his statement a short time ago. He must apologize to hon. Members who were present at the time for any repetition he might make; but he would very succinctly state what his view of the matter was. The Vote was for the Valuation and Boundary Survey, and included an item for the Solicitor to this Department. It did not at all follow, by sanctioning this Vote, that this money, or any part of it, would go to Mr. Bolton. The question to the Government really was the payment of the salary to the Office, and the money might go to Mr. Bolton's successor. He admitted that that in itself would not be a sufficient plea for asking for a suspension of action on this Vote; but he had put two other circumstances before the Committee. The affairs of Mr. Bolton were now really before two Courts of Law—one the Bankruptcy Court, and the other the Court of Nisi Prius, before which an action would be tried to-morrow. Moreover, Mr. Bolton's name would come before the Committee again in relation to the Vote for Law Charges. It would come before the Committee either at the end of this week or the beginning of next; and what he put to hon. Members opposite, and what he put, with great confidence, to the Committee now, was that they should let this Vote pass, as it did not imply any payment to Mr. Bolton, but merely a payment to the office-holder, whoever he might be. The holder of the office, to whom the money would have to be paid, might not necessarily be Mr. Bolton. Mr. Bolton might be superseded or dismissed, and, in that case, the money would be paid to his successor. The mere voting of this money was no sanction on the part of the Committee of the retention of Mr. Bolton in the Public Service. They would have an opportunity of considering this question, as he pointed out, at the end of this week or the beginning of next, when the Vote for Law Charges was brought forward, and when Mr. Bolton's salary as Crown Solicitor of Tipperary was proposed. B the time that Vote was reached there would, at least, have been a decision given in the case now pending in the Nisi Prius Court.

MR. HEALY said, he must point out to the Committee that the statement of the hon. Gentleman who had just sat down was altogether beside the question. What would be tried in the Nisi Prius Court to-morrow? Why, the issue was this—William O'Brien had made a series of charges against George Bolton. He had said to him—"You are a thief; you are a forger; you are a swindler; you are an adulterer." Mr. Bolton says—"You have coupled me with the name of French and Cornwall, and that is tantamount to an accusation of being guilty of unnatural offences;" therefore, the question to be tried to-morrow was not whether Mr. Bolton was a thief, a swindler, and so on, but whether his name being coupled with those of French and Cornwall meant, in addition to his other crimes, that he was guilty of unnatural offences. That was the only issue that would be submitted to a jury to-morrow. He (Mr. Healy) was surprised to see the Secretary to the Treasury attempting to prejudice the minds of English Gentlemen, who could not be so well acquainted with the matter as were the Irish Members, by a miserable shift of this kind. They were told it was not certain that Mr. Bolton's Petition had been presented by him.

MR. COURTNEY: The question does not turn on that.

MR. HEALY said, what did the Chief Secretary answer when he had put the matter to him? Why, that the Government had driven Bolton into bankruptcy. So that it was the Government who had compelled him to arrange a settlement with his creditors; and there being no other way of arrangement, he had taken refuge in bankruptcy. He (Mr. Healy) would warn the Government of this. The Chief Secretary had brought upon himself grave censure for the manner in which he had winked at the delay in bringing the case of French to an issue; the evidence had turned out to be of a terrible character; if the right hon. Gentleman had known what that evidence was, he would not have made the bold statement he did in reply to the Motion of the hon. Member for Queen's County (Mr. Arthur O'Connor). What was the case of the Secretary to the Treasury now? Why, his position was this—that George Bolton might succeed, before a jury of Orangemen, in securing a verdict for £30,000 against William O'Brien. That would be accepted by his creditors, and then there would be no bankruptcy at all. They had had the experience of the Cornwall and French case. The Government would not suspend or dismiss these officials, and they would not allow a discussion, because there was a libel action pending, and because they said it would prejudice the case; but, in spite of that, a jury of Dublin, on which there were five Orangemen, had found it impossible to go beyond the facts, and had been obliged to give a verdict for his hon. Friend the Member for Mallow (Mr. O'Brien). The Secretary to the Treasury now placed himself in exactly the same position as the right hon. Gentleman the Chief Secretary with regard to Cornwall and French. He said—"I have the assurance of Judge Walsh that the defendant has a good case—wait till he has had his 'pound of flesh'—wait until the Orange jury has given him £30,000, and there will then be no necessity for Bolton to go into the Bankruptcy Court." The hon. Gentleman was making himself to that extent an accomplice of George Bolton, because, by insisting upon this

Vote in the House of Commons, in the face of a Belfast jury, who would be only too willing to take a wink from hon. Gentlemen on the Treasury Bench, he would be practically giving a vote of whitewash to George Bolton. They were supposed in that House of Commons to be all honourable men. Some people said they were not—he was not referring to hon. Gentlemen opposite; but it was said that hon. Members on those (the Irish) Benches were not honourable men. But the Belfast jury would say—"Are we to suppose that the House of Commons, composed of the first Gentlemen in England, knowing the character of Mr. Bolton—are we to suppose that, though it is said this man is stamped with the brand of infamy, the House of Commons, having able debaters amongst them, and having discussed this question, would have passed this Vote unless they knew this man was maligned by these Nationalists?" What stand had the Government to take? The Prime Minister had rebuked him (Mr. Healy) last year for what he had said on a Vote somewhat similar to this. He had said, with regard to Crown prosecutions in Ireland, that it was a great misfortune that the Government could get no one to give evidence for them, except persons of a discreditable character. The Prime Minister had declared that he was very wrong in pointing that out, as he ought to have known that no one would think of deciding cases on the evidence of people of disreputable character. But what were they to think when the very founts of justice were poisoned by such scoundrels as Bolton? The Government wanted Irish Members to admire their administration, and to proclaim themselves at one with them, and yet, from their Detective Director and Post Office Secretary, down to George Bolton the Crown Solicitor, they chose the most infamous scoundrels and rascals they could lay their hands on for the transaction of official business in Ireland. They had divided on this Vote last year. The Irish Members had got no satisfaction from hon. Gentlemen opposite; but he was glad to think that, after all, the words of the Irish Members had not been wasted. It was consoling to them to know that even now, at the eleventh hour, the consciences of hon. Gentlemen opposite were stricken. The Irish Members had spent many an hour in vain in urging these cases on the attention of the House. They had not, in the past, obtained a single vote in support of their proposals; but even water wore away stones, and at last the Irish Members had succeeded in making some impression on the hearts and consciences of hon. Gentlemen opposite. When the Government's own followers began to repudiate and become ashamed of the officials of the Government, it was time for the Administration to take warning. The Secretary to the Treasury told them that the name of this man Bolton would come up again. Yes, it would come up again and again, because there was scarcely a penny of money voted in the Irish Departments but George Bolton had a finger in the pie; he was a pluralist of the most alarming description. There was an item for him in the Vote under discussion; he was Crown Prosecutor for the county of Tipperary; he was Under Crown Prosecutor for the county of Dublin—wherever there was a dirty job to be done in Ireland, George Bolton was there to do it. Probably, that was on the principle that, wherever dirty work was to be done they should have a dirty man to do it. But, however that was, such was the fact. Was it possible that the Government of Ireland, the British Government, the Government of the Queen had sunk so low that they could not get a decent man connected with any other Irish Department? Was that their position? Was Irish official nature absolutely fallen so low that out of the multitude of West Britons in the country they could not get one single man with a decent, honest, and sweet reputation? Was that the position of the Government, and, if it were, why were hon. Members obliged to make these references? Ought they not rather to be delighted to have the opportunity of clearing out their nest of vipers which was looked upon with the deepest hatred in the country—that nest of vipers which had stung the people to madness, and who, to a large extent, were responsible for the way in which the Government was regarded in Ireland? What was the last act they had heard of in connection with these men? Why, an unfortunate creature who had been driven to accept the position of informer had absolutely hanged himself, through remorse, in his cell. That unhappy occurrence had taken place immediately after Bolton's visit to him; like Judas, immediately the man had betrayed his friend, he hanged himself. This man Bolton went round prosecuting his dark designs, setting father against son, and husband against wife; arresting whole families, playing upon the remorse of human nature and the ties of family affection. He went like a serpent from one person to another, getting up cases, caring nothing so long as he pocketed the blood-money. By retaining such a man in the Service, they were putting a premium on crime, they were rewarding the man whose interest it was to keep up the harvest of crime in Ireland. So long as it was profitable to a man like Bolton to have criminal trials so long would these criminal trials continue. George Bolton made money out of them. It was as much a portion of his trade to obtain this blood-money as it was of any honest handycraftsman to obtain a day's work. Crime! Bolton gloated over it, delighted in it. When the country was happy, George Bolton was miserable; when the country was criminal, George Bolton was delighted. That was the man the Government employed; that was the person who swindled his creditors out of £90,000, who was condemned by an English Judge as a ruffian and as a person who ought not to be continued in any Public Department—that was the man whom an English Judge had recommended to be struck off the rolls. And yet for that man the Government asked them not only to vote this £400, but to come down some days later and vote him some further hundreds. He was not surprised that the Chief Secretary had fled from the Treasury Bench; it was convenient for him to leave this case to Gentlemen who knew less about George Bolton than he did. The right hon. Gentleman had already burned his fingers in defending Cornwall and French. He (Mr. Healy) ventured to say that the next time an Irish official was attacked in that House the right hon. Gentleman would not be so keen to come forward in his defence. Not a single representation that the Irish Members had made had ever received the slightest attention from the Government. They had pointed out again and again the state of corruption in which Dublin Castle was steeped; but it was some satisfaction to them to know that English Radicals at last had had their consciences touched, and whatever the Government thought about it, they and their constituencies would support the Irish Members in this matter.

MR. NEWDEGATE said, no man in that House disliked despotic government more inveterately than the humble Member who now addressed them, yet the hon. Members from Ireland who sat near him must forgive him if he asked them for a moment to consider whether they had not contributed to the state of things in Ireland which had compelled Parliament to supersede the operation of the Common Law by investing the authorities in Ireland with despotic power, one instrument of which was this Mr. Bolton, the Public Prosecutor, whose character and conduct those hon. Members had vied with each other in painting in the blackest colours? It was, indeed, a pretty pass, according to their version, to which they had brought matters in Ireland. Bad as the state of things might have been and might be, he (Mr. Newdegate), who had often been accused of supporting too severe laws for Ireland, preferred the government by law to the abuses of despotic power, which he, in common with the hon. Members near him, deprecated. The case of Mr. Bolton, however, involving matters touching his character, was before two Courts of Law. Both cases were now pending; and if there was one thing more than another, in defence of government by law, that he (Mr. Newdegate) held to be essential, it was abstinence from interference or interception on the part of that House in cases pending before the Courts of Law. It was upon that broad principle that he (Mr. Newdegate), without expressing any opinion upon the character or the conduct of Mr. Bolton, would vote against the Amendment before the Committee.

THE SOLICITOR GENERAL FOR IRELAND (Mr. WALKER) said, he did not expect that any discussion on this matter would have come before the Committee on the particular Vote before them. The Committee had been informed, an was thoroughly well aware, that this £400 which appeared now in the Estimates was in no way connected with Mr. Bolton's position as Crown Solicitor, but was merely the salary of the Solicitor to the Valuation and Boundary Survey of Ireland. Hon

Members must not take him as complaining of this discussion, but merely as pointing out that if the discussion had taken place at all, it would be much more convenient that it should occur on a Vote which was to be proposed—namely, the Irish Law Charges. In this matter they were dealing with a public servant who had been 33 years in the Public Service. Mr. Bolton had entered the Public Service in 1852, and since that time he had discharged his duties satisfactorily; and he (the Solicitor General for Ireland) was not aware that there was anything against him in his capacity as public servant.

MR. ARTHUR O'CONNOR: Is there nothing against him as a solicitor?

THE SOLICITOR GENERAL FOR IRELAND (Mr. WALKER) said, he only wanted to say a few words on the two subjects referred to. They had two matters to consider—one was the Vote which was asked for, and the other was what was the effect of that Vote. The passing of this Vote did not put £400 into the pocket of Mr. Bolton; but the refusal of it would do this—it would condemn him before an opportunity had been given for the case now pending before the Court at Belfast to be tried. If the Vote were refused by that House, it would amount to——

MR. HEALY: Why do not you postpone it?

THE SOLICITOR GENERAL FOR IRELAND (Mr. WALKER) said, the refusal of the Vote would amount to a condemnation by the House of Commons of the conduct of Mr. Bolton before two actions now pending before legal tribunals relating to that conduct were tried. What were the charges made against Mr. Bolton? Why, one of them, as had been stated by an hon. Member opposite, was so old that it dated back to 1876. Its nature, which had been glanced at by some hon. Members, was this. It was alleged that Mr. Bolton, being a solicitor, had prepared his wife's marriage settlement, which was a thing no solicitor should do. If Mr. Bolton did that, and if the settlement so prepared departed from the rules which ought to have characterized it, it would follow that the settlement would be altered and placed in the proper form. That question had come before an English Court; and the English Court, as it was bound to do, had, he should say, set aside that settlement. Well, what followed? The charge brought against Mr. Bolton was investigated by the late Government in a most careful and anxious manner, and the opinion of the then Lord Chancellor, and the Law Officers of the Crown, was that, as Mr. Bolton's case had not been heard, and as it involved equitable considerations, they could not come to the conclusion that there were grounds on which they could dismiss him, and year after year since that period his salary had been put in the Estimates, and the Vote had been passed. Was it reasonable, or was it fair, now to ask the Committee, in regard to a transaction which had taken place so many years ago, that a Government succeeding the Government which had inquired into the subject should reverse the decision of its Predecessor? That would be an altogether unprecedented act, and an act of great unfairness. Further, what position were they now in with regard to Mr. Bolton's alleged Bankruptcy Petition? Let him remind the Committee of the position that Petition was in. This was not a bankruptcy in the ordinary sense of the term. It was a Petition—whether by himself or not he (the Solicitor General for Ireland) did not care.

MR. ARTHUR ARNOLD: As a matter of fact, was the Petition presented by himself?

THE SOLICITOR GENERAL FOR IRELAND (Mr. WALKER) said, that if he could answer that question he would; but, as a matter of fact, he did not know. Assuming, however, that he did present it himself, he (the Solicitor General for Ireland) did not think it would make much difference. The case stood in this way. Mr. Bolton, at a period when he, like other men, did not anticipate a fall in the price of land in Ireland, made large purchases of land, and gave a mortgage on the property which he had so bought. These mortgages amounted to £50,000, or thereabouts. They were debts, no doubt, in the legal sense of the term—every mortgage was a debt; but if it were argued that they were debts in the moral sense of the term—namely, debts which ought to be held as justifying the Court in condemning him for being a bankrupt—that would raise a very large question. Mr. Bolton was in debt to the extent of £80,000 or £90,000, as he himself estimated, of which some £50,000 were secured. Under these circumstances, he brought a Petition for arrangement, stated the debts, and showed the condition of his property. No doubt, there were unsecured debts.

MR. HEALY: What are they?

THE SOLICITOR GENERAL FOR IRELAND (Mr. WALKER) said, he had the surplus of his landed property, and also his salary, every farthing of which could be taken, and not 1*d*. paid to himself; and it was said that, under these circumstances, when the matter stood in that way that he was guilty of such gross misconduct in making that arrangement that the House ought to condemn him before his Petition was heard. He was speaking in the hearing of many Members who knew what bankruptcy proceedings were. If it should turn out in the course of the proceedings that Mr. Bolton had been guilty of fraud or misconduct, the Petition might be at once turned into a bankruptcy. The fullest power was vested in the Court, and the bankruptcy could be declared in the course of a week—there was no reason why there should be a moment's delay. Well, the Bankruptcy Court, having cognizance of the whole facts, would decide the question of the bankruptcy, and say whether or not Mr. Bolton had been guilty of fraud; but if the House passed a vote refusing Mr. Bolton's salary, would not that be virtually telling the Judge that he was bound by the declaration of the House of Commons to say that Mr. Bolton was a bankrupt? ["No, no!"] Yes; he maintained that it would. The mere suspension of this Vote would go a great way towards prejudicing the mind of a Judge against the Petitioner. This Vote did not give any money to Mr. Bolton; but the effect of refusing it would be to pass on Mr. Bolton a condemnation before the proper period had arrived. They were told, and they believed it was the fact, that to-morrow an investigation was to take place before another Legal Court as to Mr. Bolton's conduct.

MR. HEALY: On another issue altogether.

THE SOLICITOR GENERAL FOR IRELAND (Mr. WALKER) said, that charges had been made against Mr. Bolton, not only of complicity in terrible offences, but also coupled with that—or, as Mr. Bolton's accuser put it—"We do not charge him with that, we charge him with being a forger, a swindler, a defrauder of his own flesh and blood."

MR. HEALY: He did not deny that.

THE SOLICITOR GENERAL FOR IRELAND (Mr. WALKER) asked whether anyone would tell him that, if this case were investigated before a jury, this very charge against Mr. Bolton would not be gone into? The man's whole life and his whole character, every act of his career since he entered the Public Service, would become public property, and would be for a jury to decide upon. If the Committee took the action proposed by hon. Members opposite, it would prejudice the action of a Court of Law—it would have taken over a function that only a jury should exercise. He (the Solicitor General for Ireland) did not desire now—he thought it would be unreasonable—that they should go into these matters while a trial was pending affecting a man's most solemn interests; that was to say, affecting a man's life and character. What he (the Solicitor General for Ireland) asked the Committee to do was to pass this Vote without expressing any opinion as to Mr. Bolton's conduct.

MR. H. H. FOWLER said, he quite agreed with the hon. and learned Gentleman who had just sat down that it would be most unfair and most unjust for the Committee to condemn Mr. Bolton on either one or the other of the issues; but what he (Mr. H. H. Fowler) objected to was that they should acquit him on either of the issues. There were two questions *sub judice*—first, whether Mr. Bolton's bankruptcy, or his financial embarrassments, were such as to disentitle him to remain in the Service of the Government; and, secondly, the more serious question as to his moral character, which was coming on for trial to-morrow. Now, he (Mr. H. H. Fowler) objected to be called upon to say whether Mr. Bolton was guilty or innocent. They had no facts before them. He did not know whether the man was a saint or a sinner; but what he did say was, that if the House of Commons, after this discussion, voted £400 towards Mr. Bolton's salary, the House would be expressing an opinion that Mr. Bolton was innocent of these charges, and that he ought to be retained in the Public Service. If they did such a thing as that they would be putting themselves in an entirely false position. He certainly regretted the attitude the Secretary to the Treasury had taken up, both last night and to-night, on these two unfortunate Votes, with a view of compelling them to come to a decision while these matters were pending. The course adopted by the Secretary to the Treasury had not facilitated the despatch of Public Business. The Vote which they had discussed last night was again to be discussed on Report, and to-day they had spent four hours in the discussion without having made any progress. He objected very strongly to the Constitutional theory which the hon. Member the Secretary to the Treasury had laid down—namely, that the House of Commons must not object to vote the salary of an official because it was possible that the Executive Government of the day might dismiss him after his salary had been voted. That would simply mean ousting the jurisdiction of the House of Commons altogether. The House of Commons had a right to declare itself a Court of Appeal, and they had a perfect right to say—"This is not a man who should belong to the Public Service." It was simply hair-splitting to say that the money voted was not for the man actually in office at the time. He now repeated, in presence of the Prime Minister, what he had already stated as to the growing distrust of the administration of affairs in Dublin Castle. He was satisfied that complaints so constantly made must ere long form the subject of a most searching and vigorous inquiry. In conclusion, he wished merely to say that he expressed no opinion as to this man's acts, but he would not vote that he was innocent.

MR. BROADHURST said, he appealed to the Government, as one who had voted steadily with them throughout on Irish affairs, to make some satisfactory statement to the Committee that would enable that (the Radical) portion of the House at least to give a vote in their support, if possible. He had heard the statements on the opposite side, and had heard the speeches from the Treasury Bench—both the speeches of the Secretary to the Treasury and of the hon. and learned Gentleman the Solicitor General for Ireland—and he was prepared to say that, in his mind, there was not one sentence in either of those statements that at all relieved them from the very grave responsibility in voting any money for the salary of a person about whom it was possible for such statements to be made, when he was holding such an important position as that of Crown Prosecutor in Ireland. Surely a legal officer, occupying such an important post as that occupied by Mr. Bolton in Ireland, should be altogether above suspicion; and he (Mr. Broadhurst), for one, should certainly vote with the Irish Members on that occasion if they went to a Division, unless some promise were made by the Government to suspend the Vote until inquiries could be made.

MR. WILLIAMSON said, the speeches he had heard from the Treasury Bench had now convinced him that he ought not to vote for the proposed reduction. He did not agree with the hon. Member for Wolverhampton (Mr. H. H. Fowler) in thinking that if he did vote for the salary of Mr. Bolton, it would be tantamount to voting a sentence of acquittal; but, at the same time, in view of what had been said, and in view of all that was notorious in this case, though he certainly could not vote for the payment of the money, he did not see why the Vote should not be postponed. No good argument, or reason, or statement had been advanced to show why the Vote should not be postponed. He urged that course as the reasonable solution of the present difficulty; but, for one, if compelled to vote, he should be obliged to vote against the payment of this salary.

SIR HENRY HOLLAND desired to state why he should support the reduction of the Vote. He should do so as a protest against the refusal of the Government to postpone the Vote as requested, and he thought on good grounds, by the Irish Members below the Gangway. He did not offer any opinion as to the character or proceedings of Mr. Bolton. He considered that it would be most improper to do so while these questions were before the Courts of Law. But he did not consider that the proposed postponement of this Vote could be taken in any way to prejudice Mr. Bolton in those proceedings. The Committee had been informed by the hon. and learned Solicitor General for Ireland that these cases would be heard in a few days; indeed, he gathered that one case might possibly be heard to-morrow, and he could not understand why the Government in these circumstances should not postpone this Vote for a short time.

MR. GLADSTONE: It is with great reluctance that I approach a question of this kind, in which I do not feel myself well qualified to give a judgment, and in regard to which I have some difficulty in ascertaining, from the speeches of hon. Gentlemen below the Gangway on the opposite side of the House, what is the precise ground on which they desire this Vote to be refused or to be postponed—I am not quite sure what their desire is.

MR. HEALY: That it should be postponed.

MR. GLADSTONE: Technically, they desire to postpone it. I have heard the speeches, which undoubtedly partook, as it appeared to me, of a warmth that ought not to be imported into a matter of this kind, which is most strictly judicial in its character. I assure Gentlemen on that side of the House that, however I may differ from them on many important matters, any allegation of fact made by them is entitled at my hands, and at the hands of the Government, to precisely the same attention as if it proceeded from persons in entire accord with us; but in this case I have much difficulty in determining what is the exact ground on which hon. Gentlemen opposite demand the postponement of this Vote. For example, there was great excitement in that part of the House when the Solicitor General for Ireland referred to the transactions which occurred in 1876, and when presumptions were raised of a character most adverse to Mr. Bolton; and, undoubtedly, the plain meaning of the various manifestations from that quarter of the House is that those transactions of the year 1876 of themselves constituted a reason why this Vote should be withheld.

MR. HEALY: There was another Judgment in 1882 to which the Solicitor General for Ireland did not allude at all.

MR. GLADSTONE: I am dealing with the Judgment of 1876. My knowledge of this case is confined to what I have heard on the present occasion; I am dealing with the indications of opinion from many Gentlemen in that portion of the House. I say it is quite impossible for this House, consistently with its own character, to go against Mr. Bolton in respect of the transactions of 1876. It is not merely because those transactions were examined by the Executive Government—whether the late Government or this Government, makes no matter—I pay the same respect to their examinations as to our own. The House, I admit, as the hon. Member for Wolverhampton (Mr. H. H. Fowler), I think, very justly said, is not in the slightest degree bound to respect the acquittal which this Government or that Government may have pronounced; but in this instance the time for considering that question has passed by. It is plain that if the House had chosen, after the investigation by the late Government, to withhold the salary of Mr. Bolton, it was entitled to do so. It did not do so, therefore that matter cannot be stirred. The House has committed itself on that subject by repeated acts of voting this salary; and even allowing, though I am not qualified to give an opinion, that it might have been a righteous thing to reverse the decision of the late Government, yet it would be most unrighteous to stir any question on that matter now. Therefore, I must say to hon. Gentlemen that I would give greater weight to what they say on this case, if it did not appear to me they were carried away by a kind of feeling with which most Members must have some sympathy, so that the balance of the judicial faculty was in their minds considerably disturbed. Well, now, Sir, I have heard, I am bound to say, three speeches with regard to which those observations of mine could have no application whatever—the speeches of the hon. Member for Wolverhampton (Mr. H. H. Fowler), the hon. Member for Stoke-on-Trent (Mr. Broadhurst), and the hon. Baronet opposite (Sir Henry Holland).

MR. SEXTON: And the hon. Member behind the Treasury Bench (Mr. Williamson).

MR. GLADSTONE: Quite so. But he did not adduce any arguments upon the subject. He stated an opinion, as he was qualified to do, and I meant no reproach by not mentioning him. I take the speech of the hon. Baronet opposite (Sir Henry Holland). I am quite satisfied he approaches this question in a perfectly judicial spirit, so that his judgment carries weight. I wish to test it, however, and ascertain whether he is right. What he says is, if I understand him, that there is a possibility that the result of the legal proceedings now pending in Ireland may be unfavourable to Mr. Bolton.

SIR HENRY HOLLAND: Not quite so. I expressed no such opinion. I understood the hon. and learned Solicitor General to say that those proceedings might be taking place now, and I stated that I would say nothing favourable or unfavourable to Mr. Bolton, but would postpone the Vote, as those proceedings were now about to take place.

MR. GLADSTONE: I am glad to receive the explanation, because I must vary what I was going to say. There are two questions before us, and I presume this discussion has reference principally to the action which is to come on to-morrow. The hon. Baronet (Sir Henry Holland) is aware that there are two cases before us, one of them the case in which Mr. Bolton has brought an action in vindication of his own character, the other the case in which a Petition has been presented to the Court of Bankruptcy, and apparently, for the sake of argument, the Petition is stated to be Mr. Bolton's own. I must consider the two cases apart, and I must first take the case of the charge which is to be tried to-morrow; and I think the hon. Baronet had that case principally in his mind. Now, I want to know whether the hon. Baronet is correct—that he is just in his intentions I have no doubt—but is he right, going strictly according to justice, in contending that, because an action is coming on to-day or to-morrow, in which a public servant is prosecuting another individual who has made awful charges against him, that, therefore, the salary of that official should be withheld? I do not mean withheld finally, but for one day. I am disposed to admit that if there were proceedings by the Government against Mr. Bolton—if there were a *primâ facie* case depending upon the credit of some public authority, and that was the matter that was going to issue—I could then well understand the contention in this House that it was right to suspend any act whatever bearing upon that individual person. But, Sir, that is not so. Upon the facts of this case I have no right to listen to the rhetoric of the hon. Member for Monaghan (Mr. Healy). Every word he speaks may be true, or every word may be untrue; but I have no right to take it into view. So far as I know, this gentleman is protecting his own character. If he is protecting his own character——

MR. HEALY: On only one point.

MR. GLADSTONE: I am quite aware of that. I am now addressing myself very much to the hon. Baronet (Sir Henry Holland), and what was evidently weighing on his mind. If Mr. Bolton is protecting his own character by an action at law, is the general proposition to be adopted that public servants, whose salaries have to be voted in the regular course of business, and who are so endeavouring to protect themselves by an action at law in which they themselves are the movers—not in which they are to be charged by some responsible authority, but in which they are the movers—will the hon. Baronet (Sir Henry Holland) say deliberately and advisedly that the fact of their so moving to protect themselves is a reason why the voting of their salary should be postponed? I can only say I cannot adopt that view; I think it is quite necessary that the Committee should consider this bearing of the case for that reason. My hon. Friend the Member for Wolverhampton (Mr. H. H. Fowler) took occasion to repeat what he stated last night with respect to what he believed to be the tainted character and general unsatisfactory condition of the Irish Civil Service. [*Cries of* "Dublin Castle!"] Dublin Castle I am always accustomed to hear cited as the synonym for the centre of the Irish Civil Service. That is a most important subject, and one which ought to be probed to the bottom. I put it to the candour of my hon. Friend (Mr. H. H. Fowler) to say when a case, difficult and delicate, and requiring the utmost accuracy of view on our part is raised, whether it is wise or altogether just to associate that case with charges against the Irish Civil Service in general? It is our duty to put that matter entirely aside. Let the Irish Service be the best in the world, or let it be the worst, we would be guilty of injustice, and would be incurring just discredit and disparagement, if we allowed ourselves to be biassed one hair's breadth in the course we take in this matter by any consideration of the general character of that Irish Service. I have endeavoured distinctly to lay down in answer to the hon. Baronet (Sir Henry Holland), differing from him with great respect, the ground on which I proceed. My contention is this—that if a Civil servant is bringing an action in protection of his own character, and if that action is going to be tried on the day or on the morrow of the day when the House is asked to vote the salary of that Civil servant, that is no reason why the Vote should be postponed, because the postponement of the Vote involves this—that the House believes there is some presumption against the Civil servant. Is it a sin in a man to protect his own character by an action at law? Is it a thing for which he should be made the subject of foul and loathsome reproach, and is a man to be put under the slightest prejudice or suspicion because he so defends himself? If upon that ground you put aside the Vote, you imply a certain amount of presumption against that individual. Then comes the other question—that of bankruptcy. I did not understand that to weigh so much upon the mind of the hon. Baronet (Sir Henry Holland). It is not a matter, I think, upon which anyone who is a civilian or layman can speak with great confidence. These transactions in bankruptcy are transactions with which I have no personal acquaintance; but my hon. and learned Friend the Solicitor General is acquainted with these matters, and upon his professional character and reputation I understand him to say distinctly, and as a responsible Officer of the Crown to assure the House, that there is nothing in the facts as they are before us which warrant a presumption adverse to Mr. Bolton of such a character as, if proved, would require or justify his dismissal from office. If that be so, then, again, I submit that although this may not be a very agreeable duty to perform, and although I know I am compelled to go against gentlemen in whose sense of justice and integrity I have confidence, yet, if that be the fact, it is our duty, through good report and through evil report, to stick to the strict lines of justice. The time will soon come when this matter can be discussed. I am sure I will never be the man to find fault with hon. Members who call upon the Government to execute strict justice upon delinquent Civil servants. But it is our duty to avoid the passing of any opinion whatever with regard to the existence of adverse presumption, unless the facts warrant adverse presumption. As I understand they do not in this case warrant such a presumption, I am exceedingly sorry this debate has taken place, because it is hardly possible to expect that the issue of the debate will not bear, in some way or other, upon the minds of some of the jury in the trial that is about to take place. I hope it will not. I trust it will not. But our duty in the matter is absolutely simple —to look to the demands of justice to a particular individual. And as I believe the Committee can only in that way avoid expressing an opinion on the subject, I hope they will support the Vote.

MR. SEXTON acknowledged with gratitude the assurance given by the right hon. Gentleman the Prime Minister, in the closing passages of his speech, that he would not blame or consider questionable the conduct of any Member on the Irish Benches who endeavoured to do justice in respect of delinquent officials in Ireland. The various signs of growing keenness and awakening consciousness upon the subject of the Public Service in Ireland, which had been shown by hon. Gentlemen above and below the Gangway, on the Ministerial side of the House, and by the hon. Baronet the Member for Midhurst (Sir Henry Holland), who possessed a knowledge of the obligations of public life inferior to none, entitled him (Mr. Sexton) to attach more importance to the constructive pledge of the right hon. Gentleman the Prime Minister that justice would be done, than he would have been entitled to attach to similar pledges given in former days. The right hon. Gentleman had spoken of the heat of some of the speeches which had been made on this subject; but he, in the same breath, admitted he was unacquainted with the facts of the case of Mr. Bolton. The Irish Members were acquainted with those facts. The facts of Mr. Bolton's official career were burnt into their minds, and if they had displayed some heat, it was not because their judicial faculties had been warped, but because their feelings had been excited by the long delay of the Government. There was an action to be tried to-morrow. The right hon. Gentleman had said that the character of Mr. Bolton was at stake. The question involved in the action to-morrow was whether Mr. Bolton had committed unnatural offences, and, whatever the result might be, the question whether Mr. Bolton should remain in the Public Service would still be in suspense. So long as *United Ireland* called him a forger, adulterer, swindler, Mr. Bolton made no reply. For weeks and months these accusations were showered upon him; but he maintained the silence of the coward, whose conscience was stricken by the truth. It was only when unnatural offences were attributed to him that he went into a Court of Law. The character of Mr. Bolton was not to be judged by the issue of the trial to-morrow, but by the issue of the two proceedings—the one in Belfast, and the other before the Bankruptcy Judge. What did the Committee do if they agreed to vote Mr. Bolton's salary? Why, every man who was a party to that agreement would declare his belief that there was no evidence or presumption that George Bolton was a person unfit to be in the Public Service. Because he felt that presumption was inevitable, and because he felt a supreme obligation of conscience in the matter, and because he felt every man who voted a single 1*d*. to this disgraceful swindler would be guilty of a moral offence, he should put the Committee to the trouble of dividing.

MR. GIBSON desired to offer a few observations to the Committee before this Vote was taken. It was very necessary indeed that the Committee should appreciate and understand exactly what the Vote was on which they were asked to arrive at a decision. When he reached the House, he was under the impression that the question before the Committee was whether the Vote should be postponed or decided now; but he had since learned that that was not the issue; neither was the question that pointed out by his hon. Friend (Sir Henry Holland), whose opinion he so highly valued. It was not a question whether the Vote should be kept over until later, and discussed with fuller knowledge and with greater appreciation—with the knowledge of what took place during the Belfast trial; but whether in advance, after a discussion which few anticipated would take place that day, and on the eve of the trial, a Vote should be taken which would unquestionably prejudice the trial. He put it to every fair-minded man in the House—was it reasonable, was it in accordance with the most elementary principles of justice, on the eve of a trial, that the Committee should be asked to arrive at a vote which, if it should be against Mr. Bolton's salary, would be an argument that must be used with considerable power in the trial to-morrow for the benefit of the hon. Member for Mallow (Mr. O'Brien), and against Mr. Bolton? That was a circumstance which he ventured to think the hon. Member for Mallow, if he were present, would not press upon the attention of the Committee. ["Withdraw the Vote!"] That was not the question before the Committee. If he understood the hon. Member for Sligo (Mr. Sexton) aright, the question before the Committee was that the salary of Mr. Bolton should be disallowed.

MR. SEXTON said, he had desired to move the postponement of the Vote; but the Rules of the House would not permit him to do so. He, therefore, moved to reduce the Vote; but, subsequently, he appealed to the Government to withdraw the Motion.

MR. GIBSON said, he would not pursue his observations with reference to that point. He intended to say only one or two short sentences more—as he had spoken earlier in the debate, he was not going to abuse his privilege. As the decision of the late Government had been referred to, he would make one observation upon that point. Some of the matters which had been referred to came under the attention of the Lord Chancellor of the Conservative Government. Dr. Ball was a man of the highest personal character and of the highest legal attainments, and he investigated the matter fully in 1879, and arrived at the conclusion, with the concurrence of the then Law Officers of the Crown, that there was nothing to call for the interference of the Executive. That was now five or six years ago, and the matter had been continuously before the public ever since. Parliamentary and Executive sanction had been given to Mr. Bolton's continuance in the Public Service from that time to the present. The late Lord Chancellor, Mr. Law, had the matter before him; he went into it fully, and saw no reason to dissent from the opinion of his Predecessor. He (Mr. Gibson) need not give Mr. Law any character in the House of Commons. If ever there was a man worthy of being spoken of with the highest respect, it was Mr. Law; everyone knew that he approached his Judicial as well as Executive duties with an earnest and anxious desire to do what was just in the interest of the Public Service. The matter came before others, and the opinion of all the Executive in Ireland was that the decision arrived at in 1879 ought not to be disturbed. That was a circumstance which was entitled to very substantial weight. Surely, the decision ought not to be disturbed on the eve of the trial of the action which Mr. Bolton had brought in vindication of his own character. He (Mr. Gibson) had said all he desired to say with reference to the action for libel which it was understood would come on for hearing in Belfast to-morrow. He offered no opinion one way or the other upon that action; the trial of the action was a matter for the Judge and jury before whom it came; but, in the name of common justice, he asked that the Judge and jury be given an opportunity of deciding the case upon its merits, and not have their minds warped by a vote of the House of Commons.

MR. HEALY pointed out that Mr. George Bolton had been appointed to the office he now held since he was attacked in 1876 by Mr. Justice Fry, an English Judge. ["No!"] Two years ago, Bolton attempted to upset his wife's will, and a second English Judge attacked him, and showed that he had acted in a most audacious manner. If his impression was wrong as to his first assertion, the hon. and learned Gentleman the Solicitor General for Ireland (Mr. Walker) totally failed to deal with the second case in which Bolton was attacked by an English Judge.

MR. COURTNEY said, that, as a matter of fact, Mr. Bolton held his present office for a considerable time before 1876.

THE SOLICITOR GENERAL FOR IRELAND (Mr. WALKER) thought it was necessary to explain the legal proceedings to which the hon. Member for Monaghan (Mr. Healy) had just referred. Mr. Bolton's dispute of his wife's will came before the Court of Probate, and the learned Judge who tried the case came to the conclusion that, under all the circumstances, it was not unnatural Mrs. Bolton should make a will unfavourable to her husband.

Question put.

The Committee *divided*:—Ayes 58; Noes 116: Majority 58.—(Div. List, No. 178.)

Original Question again proposed.

MR. HARRINGTON said, that from time to time Questions had been put to the hon. Gentleman the Secretary to the Treasury (Mr. Courtney) with regard to the action of the valuators, and one case of injustice had just been brought under his (Mr. Harrington's) notice. The hon. Member for Wicklow (Mr. Corbet), by a Question he asked in the House about 12 months ago, pointed out that the system of bracketing two farms together in the rate book had existed in the county he represented for some time past with the object of depriving the tenants of their votes. One man in Wicklow farmed 51 acres, 2 roods, and 18 perches, and his valuation was £31 10*s*., and another farmed 30 acres, 3 roods, and 13 perches, and his valuation was £16 10*s*. Because the official valuator chose to bracket the farms together in his book, the men were disqualified from voting. A Question was asked about the cases of these men, and the Secretary to the Treasury assured the House that he would attend to the matter. Twelve months had now elapsed, but nothing had been done. The season was approaching, but the men were in precisely the same position they were in a year ago. A constituent of the hon. Member for Wicklow wrote to him (Mr. Harrington) as follows:—

"There are two men in this district who have been deprived of their votes for years on account of their valuations being bracketed in the rate book. Last year Mr. Corbet was present in the Rathdrum Revision Court when they were struck off the Register, and I believe he brought the case before the House of Commons. The result of Mr. Corbet's action was that the Revising Valuer was instructed to survey these and other cases of a similar nature. He has reported to the Rathdrum Board of Guardians that he cannot survey all in time this year, although he had over six months to do so, and, strange to say, the very two about whom the question was asked are among the number not dealt with yet. Please let me know as early as possible what steps should be taken to secure these two votes."

Why men holding independent farms, and being valued at a high figure, should be bracketed together in the rate book, and thus deprived of the franchise, he could not understand. He was persuaded the hon. Gentleman the Secretary to the Treasury must acknowledge the gravity of the matter. There was an impression in Ireland that such men as the two to whom he referred had, for purely political purposes, been illegally and unconstitutionally deprived of the franchise. In order to show the importance of the subject, he would read a resolution which was passed at a recent meeting of the Rathdrum Board of Guardians. It was proposed by Mr. J. Byrne, seconded by Mr. M. Byrne, and carried unanimously—

"That this Board desire to bring to the notice of the Revising Officer that, owing to the lumping of areas held separately by and rated separately on the occupiers, it appears that the Revising Barrister has held that these occupiers cannot claim their vote, because they appear jointly on the books as to area although separately as to their rating. Under these circumstances, the Board of Guardians consider the areas should now be entered separately, and beg that the matter receive the consideration of the Revising Officer at the next revision."

It was with the official valuator that the onus of separating the two names in the rate book rested. The Clerk of the Union had refused to separate the names, and could refuse to separate them. It was not his duty, and he would refuse to do it until the official valuator recommended that that course should be adopted. He (Mr. Harrington) trusted that an effort would immediately be made to do justice to the two men, at least, whose case had now for the second time been brought before the House.

MR. KENNY said, his hon. Friend (Mr. Harrington) had reasonable ground of complaint, because there seemed to be a system of "jerrymandering" in force to deprive men of their votes. That was a very deplorable state of facts, and it was very desirable there should be some explanation from the hon. Gentleman the Secretary to the Treasury (Mr. Courtney). There were a number of items in the Vote which, although they appeared trivial, required explanation. He saw that the minimum salary of the Commissioner of the Valuation and General Boundary Survey was £1,000, and the maximum salary £1,200. The present Commissioner received £1,300, including a personal allowance of £100. Perhaps the hon. Gentleman (Mr. Courtney) would explain why it was necessary to make this allowance. He (Mr. Kenny) noticed also that there was a personal allowance to nearly all the officials, no matter how small their office might be. There were 13 first class valuers and surveyors getting a personal allowance of £50 a-year each; one valuer received in addition to his salary a temporary allowance of £200 a-year, paid from the Vote for the Irish Land Commission, to which his services had been transferred temporarily; an allowance of £10 a-year was paid to one of the second class valuers during the absence of the above-mentioned valuer. There was an allowance of £50 each to the chief clerk and one of the first class valuers, and an allowance of £25 to one of the first class clerical. It appeared to him that all these additional allowances were given for no reason whatever. There was another point on which he should like to obtain some information from the Secretary to the Treasury — namely, what steps had been taken to carry into effect the recommendations of the Boundary Commission? The Commissioners furnished a Report in 1882; but nothing had been done to carry out their recommendations. The tendency of the recommendations was to increase the area of the boroughs in Ireland. It was very desirable that the area of the small boroughs in Ireland should be increased. At the present time the geographical formation of the Irish boroughs was most peculiar, and it was plain to any-one that the boundaries had been circumscribed for certain purposes. It would be very interesting to the people of the different boroughs to know what steps the Government intended to take to give effect to the wishes of the Commission.

MR. HEALY said, the Irish Representatives had never been satisfied with the condition of the Valuation Department in Ireland, and a Return had been presented to the House which threw a flood of light upon the subject. There was a £12 franchise in the Irish counties, and he found that there were in Ulster 3,448 valuations between £11 10*s.* and £12, in Munster 1,616, in Leinster 1,507, and in Connaught 987. In point of fact, out of the 4,110 persons who were valued between the disqualifying and the qualifying figure, 3,448 were in Ulster. Above £12 it was needless to go. The Return showed very clearly how the people were cheated out of their votes. If a farm was valued at £11 17*s.* or £11 18*s.*, the custom in all the Provinces except Ulster was to make it even money—say £11 15*s.* or £12. But in Ulster what did they find? Why, that whereas in Munster there were only 640 farms valued at £11 11*s.*, in Leinster 582, in Connaught 363, in Ulster there were 1,354. Therefore, for the sake of 5*s.* in the valuation, which would probably not make a 1*d.* difference in the rating 1,354 persons in Ulster, no inconsiderable number under the present franchise, were cheated out of their votes. Valued at £11 18*s.*, there were 12 in Ulster, 7 in Munster, 1 in Leinster, and 10 in Connaught. He wanted to know how this state of things arose? Could they find anything administratively clean in the whole country? His hon. Friend the Member for Westmeath (Mr. Harrington) had shown that there was a system of lumping two men together, and thus depriving them of a vote, and in the Province of Ulster, where the Nationalists and Whigs ran neck and neck, the monstrous system he (Mr. Healy) had pointed out existed. This system of chicanery was proved by the Government's own Return, and in order to mark his sense of the way the Department had acted he moved to reduce the Vote by £3,000.

Motion made, and Question proposed,

"That a sum, not exceeding £16,293, be granted to Her Majesty, to complete the sum necessary to defray the Charge which will come in course of payment during the year ending on the 31st day of March 1885, for the Salaries and Expenses of the General Valuation and Boundary Survey of Ireland."—(*Mr. Healy.*)

MR. COURTNEY said, that the hon. Gentleman, in order to prove his charge, would have to show that the unusual proportion of valuations between £11 10*s.* and £12 in the Province of Ulster, as compared with other Provinces, was not parallel with the valuation between £12 and £12 10*s.* With respect to the question brought forward by the hon. Member for Wicklow (Mr. Corbet) some time ago, and which was revived this afternoon by the hon. Member for Westmeath (Mr. Harrington), he was at a loss to understand how the Revising Barrister struck these persons off the list; but, as had been revealed by the hon. Member to-day, these had been valued jointly for many years.

MR. HARRINGTON said, the valuations were separate, but the acreage had been jointly entered by the clerk.

MR. COURTNEY said, he believed that, as a matter of fact, these people had not been struck off the Register.

MR. HARRINGTON said, he thought the hon. Gentleman did not understand the manner in which the lists were presented to the Revising Barrister. There was a supplemental list presented every year——

MR. COURTNEY said, the point he was making was that the valuation system had not been changed for years. He would make inquiries about the matter; and as to the other matter with respect to the proportions, he found that the graduation of the valuation was fairly distributed from top to bottom, and there was no one unduly punished. If the hon. Member for Westmeath would write him a letter and explain the matter he would look into it.

MR. HARRINGTON said, he did not wish to detain the Committee long upon this matter; but he thought it was only just that he should read the letter from which he had quoted an extract. The letter was written to one of his constituents, and put the case strongly—

"Cloneen, Feb. 19th, 1884.

"Dear Sir,—I received yours of the 16th on last night.

	a.	r.	p.		£	s.
Thomas Neill, Ballard,	61	2	18	val.	31	10
James Butler . . .	30	3	13	val.	16	10

The above T. Neill sold one of two farms he held in Ballard to Mr. Butler in 1882. At the revision in said year Dr. Darley refused him, Neill, his vote, on the ground that he was not one year without the second farm, though the two farms was (*sic*) a quarter of a mile asunder (*sic*). In the spring of 1883, when the revising valuator came to Rathdrum, they went to him to have themselves separately (*sic*) rated, the valuer to all appearance regulated their acres and valuation, and Neill's vote was registered at last revision. However, on examining the books this season, I discovered the bracket to their names as you see on the other side. This season, when the revisory valuer came to Rathdrum, I brought them to him and pointed out their case. He said it was all right. I asked him what brought the bracket there (pointing to it). He said it was done in the office in Dublin, and that it should not be there, at the same time bloting (*sic*) it with his pen. The town of Ballard is in the electoral division of Ballinaclash, and polling district of Rathdrum. The second case is that of James Clancy, Sheanamore, in the Ballinacor electoral division, and polling district of Aughrim.

	a. r. p.		£ s.
James Clancy . .	23 1 11	val.	10 10
Jas. Clancy . . .	48 0 34	val.	5 10
Terns Clancy . .		val.	5 10
William Corter . .		val.	5 10

The two James Clancys (*sic*) above is (*sic*) the same man; but by lumping a portion of his land with the other two to the value of £5 10*s*., it brought his upper value down to £10 10*s*.; there (*sic*) by braking (*sic*) his vote according to Dr. Darley's plan at last revision, he was not objected to last revision and escaped. In 1883, said Jas. Clancy, being sick, sent his son and a young man named Brien to the revising valuator at Rathdrum to have his land and valuation put together (as in reality it was). When the boys told their story to the valuator, he said he supposed that was all right—the clerk (Mr. B. Manning) interfered, and said there was a political motive in that. They (*sic*), boys, denied there was, and pointed to Mr. Manning a mistake the collector of the poor rates made with him some time before, and stated he, Mr. Manning, had to write to the collector to refund the money. Mr. Manning then said to the officer he should go to see the ground, which he did not. Clancy thought his case was all right till I discovered it this year. The above Jas. Clancy was objected to in 1881, on the ground of the bracket and lumping as above, and when he swore that he never was in partnership with the other two, Dr. Darley registered his vote. Had he been objected to last revision, his vote would surely be broken. You can see Dr. Darley's ruling in 1881 in the above case, and compare it with his ruling in 1883 in the case of Michael Lambert, junr., Cappagh, in the electoral division of Ballinacoa, and polling district of Aughrim. Lambert was not objected to; but Mr. B. Manning read him out as bracketed with two others, and Dr. Darley, without a moment's hesitation, struck his name off the register, though I am told he is not in partnership with them. I have several other cases of bracketing, as you know; but we cannot tell now long they are so. I understand some of them was (*sic*) bracketed in the time of Griffith going round valuing. However, I see by advertisement in *The People* that Mr. Manning (*sic*) has got back the revised valuation, and we will soon (*sic*) see how the bracketing and lumping is disposed of.

"I remain, dear Sir,

"Faithfully yours,

"John Byrne."

Mr. HEALY said, he thought it would be a very bad case upon which the hon. Gentleman would not be able to say something for himself; but it was only with the greatest difficulty that he had been able to get this Return from the hon. Gentleman, and he was sure that if he had asked for fuller particulars, they would have been refused him. Indeed, it was refused in the form in which he originally asked for it, and it was only after some correspondence that the Lord Lieutenant, who was extremely ready to give information whenever he could, that the Return was granted. The position he took was this—that between £11 10*s*. and £12 there ought not to be 8,000 people disfranchised in a small country like Ireland. This would not happen in England, because in England there was not the same valuation. Of these 8,000 people more than half were in Ulster. This was a remarkable state of things, and one which required to be investigated. He did not wish to put the Committee to the trouble of a Division, and if the hon. Gentleman could give some assurance that steps should be taken to prevent this injustice he would not persist in his Motion.

Mr. COURTNEY said, that the complaints made by hon. Members opposite in connection with the valuation of tenements in counties would be no longer possible when the Representation of the People Bill should have passed. He would, however, inquire whether there was any real reason for suspecting a misuse of the present powers of valuators.

Mr. DEASY said, he did not think the hon. Gentleman could have the least doubt as to the way in which these valuations ought to be made. The present improper policy had been carried out for a very long time. In the town of Bandon, the representation of which was for many years in the hands of the family of the Earl of Bandon, there were 300 or 400 voters; but it had been found a few years ago that there were 50 houses valued at between £3 15*s*. and £4. Now, that number of votes would turn the scales at an election in favour of the Nationalists, and he had no doubt that if an impartial valuer inspected those houses, he would raise the valuation of each to over £4. The result of the present system was that a small minority returned Members of their own political leaning. Representations were made to the valuation officer, in Dublin, last year, to the effect that improvements were made in a large number of houses, and that, therefore, the valuations of those houses should be increased, and the result was that 25 or 30 new voters were put on the list, which proved that this was a matter that ought to be dealt with. Another important question had been touched upon, but no satisfactory answer had been given by the Secretary to the Treasury. It was asked when the

Boundary Commissioners would present their Report, and when the Government intended to carry out its recommendations? A few weeks ago it was proposed that the city of Cork should be re-valued; but, on consideration, it was found advisable that that should not be done until the Boundary Commission, who were to inquire into the matter, had presented their Report. The effect of this delay on the part of the Commissioners was the suspension of improvement works, because it was found, in the City of Cork, that large and wealthy districts lying outside the border of the borough boundary, which should bear a large proportion of the taxation of the city, could not be taxed under the present arrangement. An unfair proportion of the cost of such work would, therefore, fall on the occupiers within the present area of taxation, and press heavily on the poor people who would derive least benefit from such expenditure. He hoped the Government would lose no time in carrying out the recommendations of that Commission when they were presented. With regard to the manner in which Clerks to Unions discharged their duties in putting electors on the valuation lists, he knew that in consequence of their action a great number of people who were clearly entitled to the franchise in the county of Cork were prevented from having it. The same thing prevailed in other counties, he believed, to a great extent. He did not say that this was intentional on the part of the Clerks; but it certainly happened, and it was important that the Government should take some steps to remedy it.

MR. HEALY said, it was very invidious to divide against the salary of a person like Mr. Green, and, after the promise of the hon. Gentleman, he would withdraw his Motion. Mr. Green, by a stroke of the pen, had struck off nearly 20,000 persons, and he did not think it would do any harm to give Mr. Green a good warming up.

Motion, by leave, *withdrawn*.

Original Question put, and *agreed to*.

CLASS III.—LAW AND JUSTICE.

(4.) £54,651, to complete the sum for Law Charges.

GENERAL SIR GEORGE BALFOUR called attention to the inadequacy of the annual Index to the Statutes, and to the fact that there was no Index to the Scotch Statutes.

THE ATTORNEY GENERAL (Sir HENRY JAMES) said, that there was a considerable amount of work going on from time to time in the revision of the Statutes. For instance, a Bill before the House with respect to Summary Jurisdiction involved the repeal, either in part or altogether, of no less than 153 Statutes. Different persons were employed on the revision, and each editor prepared his own headings, which might lead to some amount of difficulty. He would inquire whether any alteration could be made so as to make the Index to the Statutes more simple for those who were not lawyers.

MR. GREGORY remarked, that he had experienced the same difficulties as the hon. and gallant Member with regard to this Index. One improvement, of which he would urge the adoption, was that the Statutes should be numbered not only by the years of the Reign, but also by the year in which they had been passed. If that could not be managed, the Index at least might be so arranged. He believed that the Commissioners were doing their work very well, and that the public was very much indebted to them.

GENERAL SIR GEORGE BALFOUR said, that, as far as he could make out, there had been no great advance in the work recently.

MR. ARTHUR O'CONNOR asked whether it was not the case that the Ushers in the Courts were in the habit of levying fees which they had no right to demand; and also of paying special jurors only a sovereign instead of a guinea, thus gaining 12*s*. on each trial, unless the jurors insisted on being paid a guinea?

THE ATTORNEY GENERAL (Sir HENRY JAMES) said, that he would inquire into the matter.

Vote *agreed to*.

(5.) £2,707, to complete the sum for the Public Prosecutor's Office.

MR. RYLANDS asked whether it was to be understood that there was to be an entire change in the system adopted with regard to public prosecutions? He was of opinion that there should be no charge upon public funds arising out of these charges. It seemed to him that, as this system of public prosecutions had not turned out at all as satisfactory as had been expected, the Government would have to find the Public Prosecutor other employment; but if they could not do that, they were not entitled to come to Parliament so early for power to compensate Sir John Maule, the Public Prosecutor. He hoped to hear from the Secretary to the Treasury that there would be no compensation given; but if that assurance could not be given, the only course would be to oppose the arrangements proposed by the Government.

THE ATTORNEY GENERAL (Sir HENRY JAMES) pointed out that the question raised by the hon. Member for Burnley did not arise upon that Vote. There was a Bill before the House for the purpose of carrying out what had been suggested by the Committee in regard to the Public Prosecutor. There was a clause in that Bill relating to compensation, and that clause would afford an opportunity of discussing the point mentioned by the hon. Member.

MR. LABOUCHERE observed, that his hon. Friend had raised the point simply with a view to obtaining an explanation; and unless some satisfactory explanation was given as to this gentleman, who received £2,000 a-year for doing very little, the Bill would probably not pass this Session.

SIR HENRY HOLLAND begged the Committee to observe that the observations of the hon. Member for Burnley (Mr. Rylands) had really little or no bearing upon the question before the Committee. That hon. Member argued against giving any compensation to the present Public Prosecutor, in case the office was abolished; and that argument would be very properly urged when the Bill before the House for altering the office of Public Prosecutor had obtained a second reading, and when the clause providing for compensation came before the Committee on the Bill. But at the present time they did not know that that Bill would become law; and they could not assume that it would do so, as much opposition was threatened to it, and as it was blocked by the hon. Member for Kirkcaldy (Sir George Campbell). They must, therefore, provide for the continuance and working of the office during the present financial year; and to do so, they must vote the proposed Estimate, and whether they should do so was the question before the Committee, and not the question whether, if the office was abolished, Sir John B. Maule should receive any or what compensation. He (Sir Henry Holland) had more than once strongly advocated a change in the existing office of the Public Prosecutor, and the amalgamation of that office with the Solicitor of the Treasury's office. The Committee, of which he was a Member, had recommended that change, and the Bill was introduced to give effect to their recommendations. He had always understood that the hon. Member for Burnley advocated the same view; and, if such were the case, he would beg him to let the Bill have a second reading and go into Committee, when the question of compensation could be fully discussed. By opposing the Bill, he would only help to make it necessary to vote this Estimate, not only for the present financial year, which was absolutely necessary, but for the next and, possibly, other succeeding years.

MR. WARTON was glad to find that the Government at last intended to get rid of this atrocious sham. The Government seldom saw things until too late; but they ought to have seen three years ago that this office was a farce. With regard to the Bill itself, the hon. Member for Wolverhampton (Mr. H. H. Fowler) was wrong in supposing that he had blocked the Bill. He thought this sham ought to be put and end to, and he would press the Government to endeavour to carry that out.

MR. GREGORY desired to know what were the relations between this office and the Board of Trade in regard to bankruptcy proceedings? He had taken some part in the Bankruptcy Bill of last year, and he had always contemplated that one of the great advantages of it would be the public examination of a bankrupt with a view to the disclosure of his affairs; but a great many disclosures had been avoided by bankrupts absconding. So there had been an entire concealment of the state of affairs, and the whole matter was left in a state of suspended animation. He wished to know whether the Public Prosecutor had been put in motion with respect to these cases? So far as he knew, no attempt had been made to trace these people. He admitted that they had gone beyond the jurisdiction of our Bankruptcy Court; but there would have been no difficulty in tracing them and putting in force the law applicable to such cases; and he ventured to think that the proper person to do that was the Public Prosecutor, on the initiation of the Board of Trade. He was most anxious that the working of the Act should be efficient; but that depended on the way in which it was put in operation by the Board of Trade. It was contrary to all acknowledged principles that facilities should be given to these people to get out of the way, and that the Court should have no notion as to what their conduct had been, or how their liabilities stood. He thought some steps ought to be taken to enforce their attendance, and to make them submit to the examination provided for under the Act.

Sir GEORGE CAMPBELL said, the observations of the hon. Member showed that this matter ought not to be disposed of in a hole-and-corner manner. This sham offies ought to be abolished, and not allowed to remain a burden on the British taxpayer. But it was proposed not only to abolish the office, but to give statutory power to compensate those who had received appointments. Could the Government give the Committee some assurance that by the course they proposed they would not be tying their hands with regard to such compensation as they might think equitable?

Vote *agreed to.*

ULSTER CANAL AND TYRONE NAVIGATION BILL.—[Bill 244.]

(*Mr. Courtney, Mr. Herbert Gladstone.*)

SECOND READING. [ADJOURNED DEBATE.]

Order read, for resuming Adjourned Debate on Question [14th July], "That the Bill be now read a second time."

Question again proposed.

Debate *resumed.*

Question put, and *agreed to.*

Bill read a second time, and *committed* for *Monday* next.

MOTION.

VENTILATION OF THE HOUSE.

Ordered, That the Committee appointed to inquire into the Ventilation of the House have power to inquire as to the noxious smells which occasionally pervade the House, and into the cause of the same.—(*Mr. William Henry Smith.*)

House adjourned at Five minutes before Six o'clock.

HOUSE OF LORDS,

Thursday, 24*th July*, 1884.

MINUTES.]—Public Bills—*First Reading*—Trusts (Scotland) * (209); Arbitration (210).

Second Reading—Strensall Common * (195); Poor Law Guardians (Ireland) (201), *negatived;* Sheriff Court Houses (Scotland) Amendment * (193).

Committee — Tramways (Ireland) Provisional Order (168-211); Tramways (Ireland) Provisional Order (No. 2) * (144); Local Government Provisional Orders (No. 6) * (189).

Committee—Report—Naval Discipline Act (1866) Amendment * (199); Reformatory and Industrial Schools (Manx Children) * (200); Oyster Cultivation (Ireland) * (197).

Report—Local Government Provisional Orders (No. 4) * (163); Local Government Provisional Orders (No. 7) * (164); Local Government Provisional Orders (No. 8) * (165); Local Government (Ireland) Provisional Orders (Labourers Act) (No. 2) * (138).

Third Reading—New Parishes Acts and Church Building Acts Amendment * (171); Prisons (Ireland) (Cost of Conveyance of Prisoners) * (196), and *passed.*

ARBITRATION BILL.

BILL PRESENTED. FIRST READING.

Lord BRAMWELL, in presenting a Bill to consolidate the law relating to arbitration, said, he was aware that the Bill could not be proceeded with that Session; but it was considered desirable that the measure should be introduced. It had been prepared under the auspices of the London Chamber of Commerce; and, from his reading of it, he thought it deserved a favourable reception from their Lordships.

Bill *presented;* read 1ª; and to be *printed.* (No. 210.)

STANDING ORDERS—LABOURING CLASS DWELLINGS.

MOTION FOR PRINTING.

The Marquess of SALISBURY, who had on the Paper a long Notice of Motion, the object of which was to amend the Standing Orders of the House of Lords relating to Labouring Class

Dwellings, by a series of Amendments, so as to provide that "in the case of any Private Bill which proposed to take compulsory, or by agreement, in the Metropolis, twenty or more houses, or in any city, borough, or other urban sanitary district, ten or more houses, occupied wholly or partially by persons belonging to the labouring class, the promoters of such Bill should deposit at the Office of the Local Government Board before the end of November a statement of the number, description, and situation of such houses; and no such Bill should be read a second time, until the Local Government Board had reported with respect to the housing of the people thus displaced; and, further, that the Committee on any such Bill should insert such clauses as would secure the provision of suitable accomodation within a distance of one mile from their place of residence for such number of persons as the Local Government Board should specify in their Report, unless they (the Committee) should see fit, either with or without condition, to modify or waive such requirements," said, that in rising to move that the said Amendments be printed, he would intimate that they had been finally approved by two Royal Commissions, including the one which was now sitting, and had been accepted by the Government. There had been a delay, which their Lordships might have observed. of a considerable time, during which they had been retained on the Paper, because it was thought very desirable to hear all the objections which Parliamentary agents, representatives of Railways, and other persons, might have to make, before adopting the ultimate form which the Standing Order was to take. He believed the Standing Order, as it was now proposed to be amended, would meet with scarcely any opposition from these persons. The main object of the Amendment was one of extreme importance—namely, that in the construction of any railway, through the Metropolis or elsewhere, there should not only be compensation given to the poor and working classes who were evicted from their houses, but that the amount of house accommodation that was available for persons of that class should not, as far as possible, be diminished by works of that kind. Hitherto, it had been imagined that if the existing tenant were sufficiently compensated, all had been done that was necessary to do; but there was a further and larger and much more important consideration —that the houses available for the working classes were scantily supplied, and that the number of them was liable to constant diminution; while the working classes—those who required accomodation—were, of course, constantly increasing with the growth of the population, and the increased industry and prosperity of the country. It was, therefore, very desirable that all works which were authorized by Parliament should, as far as it was practicable, be prevented from diminishing the amount of accomodation for the working classes which now existed. That was really the object of the Standing Order as proposed to be amended. This would be carried into effect by bringing in the Secretary of State or the Local Government Board to supervise the action of the Railway Companies or other promoters of Bills; and the Committee was charged to see that wherever working class accommodation was destroyed, a corresponding quantity should be provided. He begged to move that the Order, as proposed to be amended, be printed with a view to its being taken into consideration on Tuesday next.

Moved, "That the proposed Amendments to the House of Lords Standing Orders on Labouring Class Dwellings be printed."—(*The Marquess of Salisbury.*)

THE EARL OF WEMYSS said, he apprehended that the Orders would work in this way—that accommodation within one mile should be found.

THE MARQUESS OF SALISBURY: "Found" hardly expresses it—"dwellings shall be provided" are the words in the Orders.

THE EARL OF WEMYSS said, he did not see how that was to be done except by turning others out.

THE MARQUESS OF SALISBURY said, there was scarcely a district in London in which accommodation could not be found by making buildings taller; but the Orders were not intended to work in an iron manner. It was not desirable to insist on unreasonable conditions.

Motion *agreed to*.

Ordered, That the said Amendments be taken into consideration on Tuesday next.

TRAMWAYS (IRELAND) PROVISIONAL ORDER BILL.—(No. 168.)

(*The Lord President.*)

COMMITTEE.

House in Committee (according to Order).

LORD INCHIQUIN said, agreeably to his Notice, he would move the insertion in the Bill of the clause he had placed upon the Paper. He had withdrawn the Motion which he moved on a previous occasion, as he considered that the new clause which he now proposed would effect the object he had in view—namely, the protection of the ratepayers of the different counties who guaranteed the capital of these tramway undertakings. He thought that some provision of this character was really required.

Moved, to insert the following Clause:—

"The capital authorised by this Act shall not be issued save as said capital may from time to time be required for the actual construction and carrying out of the said undertaking, and the certificate of the Board of Trade in that behalf shall be the evidence of such requirement: Provided that the Board of Trade shall reserve their final certificate in respect of not less than five per cent. of the whole capital until twelve months after the line has been opened and worked for traffic."—(*The Lord Inchiquin.*)

LORD CARLINGFORD (LORD PRESIDENT of the COUNCIL) said, he was sorry that the noble Lord opposite (Lord Inchiquin) should persevere with this Amendment. It really would have a very hard and, possibly, a fatal effect on these tramway undertakings. It would prevent local capital being invested in the tramway lines constructed under the Act of last year, and would throw the promoters of those lines entirely into the hands of financiers. As he had previously stated, he was quite ready to insert in this Bill the provision which had been inserted in the West Clare Bill by the Irish Privy Council.

LORD INCHIQUIN said, that as the noble Lord the Lord President of the Council did not think it prudent to insert this clause in the Bill, he would withdraw it. He really thought, however, that the Government should insert some protective clauses in all Provisional Orders, and send out a Memorandum to Grand Juries, calling attention to the matters which should be inserted in the Presentment for the protection of the county interests.

Clause (by leave of the Committee) *withdrawn.*

On the Motion of The LORD PRESIDENT, Amendment made by inserting Clause 9 of the Tramways (Ireland) Provisional Order (No. 2) Bill in the Bill.

Further Amendments made.

The Report of the Amendments to be received on *Monday* next; and Bill to be *printed* as amended. (No. 211.)

POOR LAW GUARDIANS (IRELAND) BILL.—(No. 201.)

(*The Lord President.*)

SECOND READING.

Order of the Day for the Second Reading read.

LORD CARLINGFORD (LORD PRESIDENT of the COUNCIL), in rising to move that the Bill be now read a second time, said, that it had been several times before the House of Commons, and almost made its way through that House; but it had reached the House of Lords now for the first time. It was a Bill upon which there had been a large amount of agreement in the other House amongst Irish Members as to its main provisions, which he would call the second reading portion of the Bill; although, upon other and minor points, there had been a difference of opinion. The Bill was not a Government measure, and it did not reach that House as a Government measure; but as no independent Member of their Lordships' House had taken it up, and as it appeared to him that it was a Bill of considerable importance to Ireland, he thought it ought to be brought under the notice of the House. He had, therefore, undertaken to move the second reading. What he would call the main provisions of the Bill were contained in the first and second parts of it. The main object of the Bill was to put an end to the present system of voting at Poor Law elections for Guardians in Ireland, by substituting for the voting papers, at present in use, vote by ballot. That was a change which, in his opinion, would be one of great value in that country. He could not conceive any much worse system than the present system of voting for Poor Law Guardians. The unfortunate voter

—as everyone who knew Ireland must be aware—was exposed to every kind of the most contrary influences—to the influence of the landlord, the agent, the bailiff, the local Land League, the red-hot Nationalist, who might be his next-door neighbour, the priest, and the curate; and he was pressed and pulled in all directions by these various forces. Such a state of things was thoroughly objectionable; and under such pressure, and such contrary motives and passions, the system of voting papers was liable to great abuse, and it was pretty well known that great abuse had taken place. He could not doubt that it would be a great improvement to substitute vote by ballot for that system; and if a general measure were introduced dealing with local government in Ireland, he had no doubt that this provision would form part of it. Then there were improvements, as concerned registration, in the way of constructing a Register of Voters; and the Bill also proposed a great improvement in the way of giving proper means and facilities for the hearing of Petitions against elections of Guardians. It was proposed, under the Bill, that Petitions should be referred to the County Court Judge. At present, nothing could be more objectionable than the way in which these points were decided—namely, by means of inquiries held by Poor Law Inspectors. It was left to the Local Government Board to hold an inquiry as to whether a particular Guardian had been properly elected or not. The result was, that there were constant collisions between the Boards of Guardians and the Local Government Board, whose duties in this respect were very onerous and invidious. His right hon. Friend the Chief Secretary for Ireland had informed him that, since the Spring Poor Law elections, the return of 127 Guardians had been disputed. Eighty of these cases had been decided; the rest remained still to be considered, and of those considered, 10 had been set aside. That was a state of things which would be cured at onec hy the provisions of this Bill. Then there was a clause providing that the elections should be held triennially, instead of annually, which, he considered, would be a great improvement. That, in his view, was the main part of the Bill that he would ask their Lordships to read a second time. There were other points of considerable importance.

There was a provision with regard to the rateable qualifications of Guardians. That qualification, which now varied in Unions, at the discretion of the Local Government Board, it was proposed to fix at £12. At present, in many Unions it was higher, and in many others lower than that sum. Another provision fixed the maximum number of votes which any one voter might give at 18. That number had been taken, under the advice of the Law Officers, as that which was intended by the existing law—that was to say, six votes might be given by the same person in each of three different capacities—namely, as owner, as occupier, and as holding a beneficial interest. There were other points which were those mainly in dispute in the other House, and which would, no doubt, be mainly in dispute in this. One provision proposed to reduce the number of *ex officio* Guardians from one-half to one-third of the whole body. That, he believed, was now the legal proportion of *ex officio* Guardians in England, and it was also the proportion fixed in the original Irish Poor Law, although it was afterwards raised to one-half, he did not know why. Again, at present, any Resident Magistrates became *ex officio* Guardians, and if the number of Resident Magistrates was not sufficient, it was filled up from owners within the Union who resided elsewhere; but it was a chance, of course, who these gentleman might be. The Bill proposed, while reducing the legal number to one-third, that the Justices should themselves elect the members to constitute that one-third from their own body. It was found, by experience, that gentlemen so elected for the express purpose of attending the Boards of Guardians were far more likely to act than those who found themselves on those Boards by haphazard, so to speak. By this change it was hoped they would get magistrates who would regularly attend the Boards. But the proposal which had been most objected to was that which provided for the abolition of proxy voting. At present, the owner could hand over his proxies to his agent, as was often done, in blank, leaving him to vote for whatever Guardian he pleased. The owner might be living out of Ireland, and, knowing nothing about the persons who were candidates, left it to his agent to vote for him. Of course, he knew the ground on which such a system would be defended—that of the due representation of property; but he submitted that on principle, and on its merits, it was very difficult to defend such a system. He quite admitted, however, that that was a question which was very well open to discussion; but it was a question which could be very well discussed in Committee, if the House read the Bill a second time. He observed, indeed, that in the other House, several prominent Members of what was called the "Popular Party" thought there were other possible modes of dealing with that particular question. There was, at all events, great objection to the exercise of the voting power by a mere absentee landlord, who sent over a proxy which lasted from one election to another. The proxy was not even required to be exercised for a particular election, but it would last for a considerable time.

THE MARQUESS OF WATERFORD: For one election only.

LORD CARLINGFORD (LORD PRESIDENT of the COUNCIL) said, he very much doubted that statement of the noble Marquess; anyhow, the system was much objected to. That, however, was a matter which was quite open for consideration in Committee; but he might say that the Local Government Board had the power, and would be prepared, as far as they could, to exercise the power, of so fixing the elections in the different Unions that owners of property might be able personally to exercise their right of voting in Unions in which they were interested on different days. That was how that matter stood. He had said that these last points, though of considerable importance, were not the essential principle of the Bill; and he would ask their Lordships to read the Bill a second time, because he held that, in the present circumstances of Ireland, the change in the present system of voting to vote by ballot would be of great advantage as preventing much abuse and a vast amount of the harassing and undue pressure to which voters were subject. Further than that, the question of a change in the system of proxy voting to which he had alluded was a matter very well worth discussing, and it could be discussed in Committee. No doubt, there was very much to be said about the due representation of property in these elections, and it was often urged that the argument in favour of the case in Ireland was much stronger than in England, because, in Ireland, the rates were divided—one-half falling on the landlord and one-half on the tenant—while in the case of holdings under £4 the rates were paid wholly by the landlord. That was a consideration which their Lordships would bear in view. On the other hand, he thought it right to say that, in his opinion, it was very doubtful whether this attempt to divide the rates between landlord and tenant in Ireland had been very successful; and as to the comparison with the payment of poor rates in England, he thought it was a matter of great doubt whether, in the long run, the landlord in England did not pay more than the landlord in Ireland. The question had often been discussed how far the rates were thrown on the landlord in this country. Certainly, in present circumstances, an English tenant in taking a farm would take the rates into account, and make the fullest allowance for them; and if, on the expiration of his lease or agreement, matters were not arranged to his satisfaction with the landlord, in connection with his rent, the tenant would throw up his farm and look for another. The case, however, was different in Ireland. A diminution of the rent in proportion to the rates was not so easily made in Ireland, inasmuch as freedom of contract entered so little into the question of the settlement of rent, a fact which he considered one of those elementary truths that were plain to everyone who had learned to open his eyes to the conditions of Irish life. He very much doubted, therefore, whether, in spite of the artificial division of the rate between the landlord and the tenant in Ireland, the rates did not, in fact, fall to a larger extent on the landlord in this country than they did in Ireland. That, however, was a matter of argument; and he now asked their Lordships to read the Bill a second time, on the ground that the main object of the Bill was a good one—that of substituting for the present system of voting papers vote by ballot.

Moved, "That the Bill be now read 2ª."—(*The Lord President.*)

THE EARL OF LONGFORD, in rising to move that the Bill be read a second time that day three months, said, that he did not think the reform proposed at all such a pleasant one as the noble Lord opposite (Lord Carlingford) had seemed to regard it, and there were good reasons why it should be postponed for a certain time. The measure, in the first place, did not come from aggrieved Guardians or ratepayers, but from the politicians who had been organizing the Irish Boards of Guardians into amateur political debating societies for their own purposes. The noble Lord the Lord President of the Council had not quite correctly described the parentage of the Bill, nor the circumstances of its passage through the other House. He (the Earl of Longford) found that the names which originally appeared on the back of it, were Mr. O'Brien, Mr. Gray, Mr. Mayne, Mr. O'Sullivan, and Mr. Marum. Now, he desired to speak of those Gentlemen with all respect as Representatives of considerable constituencies; but they were members of an extreme political Party, and one of their articles of faith, according to their own utterances, was to bring the landlords to their knees If this Bill were passed, it would have an effect in that direction. The noble Lord, in moving the second reading of the Bill, mentioned its passage through the House of Commons; but he scarcely gave an idea of how the Government had treated the opponents of the Bill. He (the Earl of Longford) found that the Bill had been introduced by private Members early in the year. It came on for second reading on the 2nd of July, and then Mr. Trevelyan, on behalf of the Government, smiled upon it and spoke favourably of it. He (the Earl of Longford) thought the right hon. Gentleman had adopted it; but the noble Lord the Lord President of the Council said that the Bill was not regularly in his hands. It was adopt by him, however, so far as speaking favourably of it; and he showed his approval of it by indicating certain Amendments to which he would consent, and which would remove some of the objectionable features of the Bill. The result was, the Irish Members and the Government having joined, the opponents of the Bill were helpless, and did not divide against it. Here he might observe that a majority supporting the Government in the other House were described as an intelligent representation of the will of the nation; whereas, in their Lordships' House, a majority against the Government were spoken of in altogether different terms. With this indication of Mr. Trevelyan's view on the part of the Government, the Bill went to the next stage, which came on the 15th of July. The Amendments which Mr. Trevelyan had referred to were then adopted, and the Bill was toned down by the omission of some of the conditions to which the opponents had strongly objected. The Report stage of the Bill was taken on the 17th of July; and on that occasion, to the astonishment of the opponents of the measure, the same Amendments to which Mr. Trevelyan had acceded two days before were cancelled, and the objectionable conditions were reinstated in the Bill with no further notice than the insertion in the Votes of that morning. The third reading of the Bill was low down on the Orders of the Day, and did not come on until 2 o'clock; and, notwithstanding the earnest protests of the few opponents of the Bill who were present, by a Division at close on 4 o'clock in the morning the Bill passed in its present objectionable state. That was the mode in which the Bill had passed through the House of Commons, and in which it had come to their Lordships for consideration. He was far from charging any Member of the Government with sharp practice in the matter; but he scarcely knew in what other way to characterize what had occurred; and, if he were not to say another word, he thought he was justified in asking their Lordships to reject such a slippery Bill in such slippery hands. However, he had a few words to say about the merits of the Bill, in regard to which he took a somewhat different view from the Lord President. This Bill, if passed, would be the means of creating further sources of ill-will between the different classes living in Ireland. As regarded election of Guardians by ballot, and for a term of three years, if they were considering a new mode of constructing the Poor Law system, there might be something to say on those points; but the present system was not, by any means, open to the objections to which the noble Lord had referred. The conditions of the Poor Law in England and in Ireland were quite different. The proposed change was really a theoretical rather than a practical one, and it might very well wait for consideration hereafter. The owners of property had great reason to view this Bill with suspicion; and when he said this, he did not in any way take an exaggerated view of the rights of property. As regarded himself, he lived a good deal in Ireland, and generally on good terms with his neighbours, except sometimes. The Poor Law was a very heavy burden indeed upon the owners of property; and in the construction of the Poor Law system one-third *ex officio* Guardians were placed upon the Board. Subsequently that proportion was increased to one-half, as it now remained; and, considering the amount owners of property contributed to the rates, they were fully entitled to the representation they at present enjoyed. They paid more than half the poor rate, and they were entitled to half of the representation. There was certainly no pretence for the assertion that the elected Guardians were habitually overborne by the *ex officio* Guardians. The circumstances of the case made it impossible; because the elected Guardians, being always resident in the Union, available at all times, the contrary being the case with the *ex officio* Guardians. Those gentlemen having occupations at a distance were rarely all available at one time. On such occasions as the election of Chairman—or to resist political questions which had no concern with the Poor Law administration—on such occasions, though rarely, the *ex officio* Guardians might be able to assert themselves in favour of something like order. In four Unions with which he was connected the elected Guardians had recently displaced *ex officio* officials in favour of members of their own body. He did not think that the proposal in the Bill to reduce the proportion of *ex officio* members from a-half to one-third could be reasonably defended. A change on which the noble Lord (Lord Carlingford) had spoken, and about which he thought he appeared to be a little uncertain, was the matter of the abolition of the proxy. Upon that point, if the noble Lord wished for further information, he could refer him to the speech which Mr. Trevelyan delivered in June, 1883, and in which he would find himself most completely refuted in almost everything he had said. There was no real abuse in this matter of voting by proxy. It was not the case of a standing authority handed over by an absent man to a deputy. The proxy form filled up was an elaborate one, must be signed in the presence of a witness, and could only be used on one occasion. A further clause in the Bill reduced the qualification for the Guardians in many cases. This was really most unwise. The policy of Parliament now was to impose upon Boards of Guardians new and additional duties, and it was not desirable at all to reduce their status. If their status was reduced, they would become a chorus to be worked by the wire-pullers as political agents. The central clauses of the Bill were elaborate arrangements for raising disputes as to elections of Guardians, and for deciding disputed cases. The Land Act had created disputes in almost every parish in Ireland, and it was unnecessary to introduce these further differences of opinion. On the whole, he would say that the Bill was not required for the better administration of the Poor Law. It was brought forward for altogether different purposes, and he trusted their Lordships would reject it. Therefore, in order to give them an opportunity of doing so, he would move its postponement for three months.

Amendment *moved*, to leave out ("now") and add at the end of the Motion ("this day three months.")—(*The Earl of Longford.*)

LORD FITZGERALD said, there were provisions in the Bill to which he also entirely objected. He particularly referred to the clause providing for a reduction in the proportion of the *ex officio* Guardians to the elected from one-half to one-third. Whether such a change might be wise eventually he did not presume to say; but, in his judgment, it certainly was not wise at the present time. If the Bill should reach Committee, and if the noble Earl opposite (the Earl of Longford) moved the rejection of that clause, he promised that he would support him. He could not support the proposal to abolish proxy voting. It would be unfair, and to do so would be to create a further divergence between the law of England and Ireland to which he objected. One of the main principles of the Bill was voting by ballot, and to that he was favourable; but he contended that it was not necessary to protect tenants from the landlords as had been suggested. They required no protection in that direction; but he did think they required protection from certain other external influences, and he therefore approved of the clause providing for voting by ballot. The Bill contained a great deal of useful matter, such as the provision for making an elected Guardian a Guardian for three years, and for trying all questions as to disputed elections of Guardians before a County Court Judge without a jury. He thought that a cheap and very Constitutional mode of settling such disputes. He hoped the House would accept the second reading of the Bill, seeing, as he had said, that it contained a great deal of very useful matter, and that they could then go into Committee, where all proper Amendments could be made. It would then be for the House of Commons to accept them, or to take the responsibility of rejecting them.

THE MARQUESS OF WATERFORD said, he was glad to find that the noble and learned Lord opposite (Lord Fitzgerald) agreed that the greater part of the Bill was most objectionable. The only two points which he appeared to approve were the povisions for making the election of a Guardian last for three years, and for trying election petitions in regard to Poor Law matters before a County Court Judge. As far as he (the Marquess of Waterford) himself was concerned, there was only one thing in the measure which he believed was good, and that was that the elections should take place every three years. The law, both of England and Ireland, had worked very well, and he maintained that the new machinery was entirely unnecessary. But the Bill bristled with various other proposed changes in the law, and it was not worth while reading the Bill a second time, merely for the purpose of passing into law two such provisions as those of which the noble and learned Lord approved. The Bill was entirely different from any other that had ever been proposed in the House of Commons. No previous Bill destroyed the *ex officio* element. He could not make out where the noble Lord (Lord Carlingford) found the agreement of which he spoke as to the provisions of the Bill. He (the Marquess of Waterford) was satisfied that the Conservative, and he believed a great portion of the Liberal Members in the House of Commons were entirely opposed to a great number of its provisions.

LORD CARLINGFORD (LORD PRESIDENT of the COUNCIL): I spoke of the principle of vote by ballot.

THE MARQUESS OF WATERFORD said, the Bill would take away from those who contributed, to a large extent, to the payment of rates all control over the disbursement of those rates. In Ireland the landlord paid half his tenant's poor rates, and the whole of his poor rates if he was rated under £4. The landlords of Ireland thus paid about five-eighths of the whole rates of Ireland, and this Bill would take from them the power which they now possessed over the expenditure of Boards of Guardians. He thought their Lordships had every right to reject the Bill. He was advising them to do so, not on his own authority, but on the authority of a Gentleman who ought to know better than anyone else at this moment what should be done in Ireland. He meant the authority of the Chief Secretary for Ireland, who said last year that the number of owners to occupiers was most disproportionate, and that in the richest Unions they were in the proportion of seven or eight to one. Yet the Chief Secretary for Ireland supported such a Bill as this, which would still further reduce the number of *ex officio* Guardians. They were to be, according to the clause in the Bill, not one-third of the Board, as had been stated by the Lord President, but one-third of the elected Guardians, which was one-fourth of the Board.

LORD CARLINGFORD (LORD PRESIDENT of the COUNCIL): No, no.

THE MARQUESS OF WATERFORD said, the Bill proposed that the *ex-officios* should be one-third of the elected Guardians, and therefore one-fourth of the whole. It was a very easy calculation. He believed that in Ireland the *ex officio* Guardians were at one time only a third; but that the proportion was raised to a half in 1847 by Lord John Russell, a Liberal Minister, on account of the jobbery and extravagance that existed. Mr. Trevelyan had entirely changed his tactics since last year. He then stated that, having regard to the fact that the owners paid one-half of the rates, it would be extremely unjust if, practically, the whole election was handed over to the occupiers. He (the Marquess of Waterford) could not make out the influence that had been at work since then. The right hon. Gentleman entirely forgot that if the Bill passed it would have the effect of abolishing proxy voting, for owners who had property in various districts and Unions in Ireland could not be travelling about for three weeks, as would probably be necessary to record their vote, especially as the elections might in many cases take place on the same day.

LORD CARLINGFORD (LORD PRESIDENT of the COUNCIL) said, the Chief Secretary for Ireland also said that the present system of proxy voting was detestable.

THE MARQUESS OF WATERFORD said, he would admit that Mr. Trevelyan did say that; but he did not show why it was detestable. That he should have changed his opinion on the subject was perfectly extraordinary. The whole measure showed an intention to oust the owners from managing the money which they themselves paid. It was a monstrous proposal which reduced the *ex officio* Guardians to one-fourth of the Board. He must say that it was an extraordinary thing that his noble Friend should bring up to their Lordships a Bill that was passed through the House of Commons in such a way as this Bill. Last year Mr. Trevelyan said he was in favour of continuing the *ex officio* Guardians; but this year the clause had been knocked out in Committee in the House of Commons by the Government themselves, and on Report Mr. Trevelyan came forward and re-inserted it. That change spoke volumes for the pressure that could be brought to bear on the Government and on Mr. Trevelyan by 30 Members acting together. The provisions of the Bill would entirely revolutionize the whole system of the Poor Law in Ireland. Some of them might not be as vicious as others; but there was only a single point of which he could approve. If the law in Ireland was assimilated to that in England, and the occupiers paid their own rates, there might be no such objection to the Bill; but when in no case the occupier paid more than half the rates, and in many instances no rates at all, he could not conceive how so iniquitous a Bill could ever have been brought before their Lordships' House. He would give an instance of how the Boards of Guardians in Ireland carried on their work. Mr. Sexton, speaking two years ago in Ireland, suggested how the expenditure of the landlords might be increased by making them pay rates for the families of suspects and evicted tenants; and on looking over a Return of the Tralee Board of Guardians he found that that Board allowed £1 15*s.* each to the families of suspects, while they only allowed from 1*s.* 6*d.* to 5*s.* for the same number of a family of other distressed persons. That was the way in which the rates were disbursed by elected Guardians in Ireland; and, of course, this came much heavier upon the landlords. He had a letter that morning from a gentleman in Ireland, a Catholic, and a strong Liberal, who said that if this Bill passed he and his friends, as *ex officios*, would never go into the Board of Guardians again, because they would only be laughed at and insulted. The Bill would give a most frightful impetus to jobbery of every description. Last year the Carrick-on-Suir Guardians had to be disbanded, and paid Guardians were sent down. If the Bill was allowed to pass, this would soon have to be the case in almost every instance in Ireland, for the extravagance of Boards elected as these would be could hardly be described. He therefore trusted the Bill would be rejected.

On Question, "That ('now') stand part of the Motion?" Their Lordships *divided*:—Contents 41; Not-Contents 110: Majority 69.

CONTENTS.

Selborne, E. (*L. Chancellor.*)

Ailesbury, M.
Normanby, M.

Derby, E.
Granville, E.
Innes, E. (*D. Roxburghe.*)
Kimberley, E.
Morley, E.
Northbrook, E.
Spencer, E.
Sydney, E.

Eversley, V.

Aberdare, L.
Belper, L.
Boyle, L. (*E. Cork and Orrery.*) [*Teller.*]

Breadalbane, L. (*E. Breadalbane.*)
Calthorpe, L.
Carlingford, L.
Carrington, L.
Dormer, L.
Ettrick, L. (*L. Napier.*)
FitzGerald, L.
Hammond, L.
Hothfield, L.
Kenry, L. (*E. Dunraven and Mount-Earl.*)
Methuen, L.
Monson, L. [*Teller.*]
Ramsay, L. (*E. Dalhousie.*)
Ribblesdale, L.
Robartes, L.
Sandhurst, L.
Saye and Sele, L.
Sefton, L. (*E. Sefton.*)

Somerton, L. (*E. Normanton.*)
Strafford, L. (*V. Enfield.*)
Sudeley, L.
Thurlow, L.
Vernon, L.
Wenlock, L.
Wolverton, L.
Wrottesley, L.

NOT-CONTENTS.

Grafton, D.
Northumberland, D.
Rutland, D.

Abercorn, M. (*D. Abercorn.*)
Abergavenny, M.
Exeter, M.
Hertford, M.
Salisbury, M.
Winchester, M.

Abingdon, E.
Annesley, E.
Ashburnham, E.
Bradford, E.
Cairns, E.
Caledon, E.
Clarendon, E.
Clonmell, E.
Dartrey, E.
Ellesmere, E.
Feversham, E.
Fortescue, E.
Hardwicke, E.
Harrowby, E.
Howe, E.
Ilchester, E.
Kilmorey, E.
Lanesborough, E.
Lathom, E.
Leven and Melville, E.
Lucan, E.
Macclesfield, E.
Milltown, E.
Nelson, E.
Powis, E.
Radnor, E.
Redesdale, E.
Romney, E.
Rosse, E.
Rosslyn, E.
Selkirk, E.
Sondes, E.
Stanhope, E.
Zetland, E.

Clancarty, V. (*E. Clancarty.*)
Gough, V.
Hawarden, V.
Templetown, V.
Torrington, V.

Abinger, L.
Amherst, L. (*V. Holmesdale.*)
Ardilaun, L.
Bagot, L.
Balfour of Burley, L.
Blantyre, L.
Boston, L.
Brabourne, L.
Brodrick, L. (*V Midleton.*)
Carysfort, L. (*E. Carysfort.*)
Castletown, L.
Clanwilliam, L. (*E. Clanwilliam.*)
Clifford of Chudleigh, L.
Clonbrock, L.
Cloncurry, L.
Colchester, L.
Cottesloe, L.
Crofton, L.
Denman, L.
Digby, L.
Donington, L.
Ellenborough, L.
Forbes, L.
Forester, L.
Gage, L. (*V. Gage.*)
Gerard, L.
Harlech, L.
Hawke, L.
Howard de Walden, L.
Inchiquin, L.
Keane, L.
Kenlis, L. (*M. Headfort.*)
Ker, L. (*M. Lothian.*)
Lamington, L.
Langford, L.
Leconfield, L.
Lyveden, L.
Middleton, L.
Minster, L. (*M. Conyngham.*)
Moore, L. (*M. Drogheda.*)
Mostyn, L.
Norton, L.
Oranmore and Browne, L.
Oriel, L. (*V. Massereene.*)
Penrhyn, L.
Rodney, L.
Rossmore, L.
Saltersford, L. (*E. Courtown.*)
Saltoun, L.
Shute, L. (*V. Barrington.*)
Silchester, L. (*E. Longford.*) [*Teller.*]
Stanley of Alderley, L.
Stratheden and Campbell, L.
Strathnairn, L.
Templemore, L.
Trevor, L.
Tyrone, L. (*M. Waterford.*) [*Teller.*]
Wemyss, L. (*E. Wemyss.*)
Winmarleigh, L.
Worlingham, L. (*E. Gosford.*)
Wynford, L.
Zouche of Haryngworth, L.

Resolved in the *negative.*

Bill to be read 2ª *this day three months.*

SHERIFF COURT HOUSES (SCOTLAND) AMENDMENT BILL.—(No. 193.)

(*The Earl of Dalhousie.*)

SECOND READING.

Order of the Day for the Second Reading read.

Moved, "That the Bill be now read 2ª."—(*The Earl of Dalhousie.*)

THE EARL OF WEMYSS said, that his noble Friend (Lord Abinger), who had opposed the Bill on Tuesday, had given Notice of his intention to renew that opposition. He (the Earl of Wemyss) would venture very humbly to suggest to him, having supported him on the previous occasion, whether it might not be desirable for him to withdraw his opposition, because, from information he had got from Scotland, he believed that, upon the whole, the arrangement which had been come to was a very fair one, so far as the Treasury was concerned. This Bill, as it now stood, would give advantages to Scottish counties which had already gone to expense in the erection of Court Houses, the cost and maintenance of which up to the present time had mainly fallen on the rates. These counties were at present entirely out in the cold, as they did not come under the provisions of the Act of 1860. As regarded the security which the Treasury hoped to obtain against undue expenditure, he thought there was nothing unreasonable in that. Indeed, looking at the Bill as a whole, he ventured to think that it was one in the interests of the Scottish counties, and that it should pass into law.

LORD ABINGER said, that, since he put the Motion for the rejection of the Bill on the Notice Paper, he had been in communication with the Lord Advocate and several noble Lords from Scotland on both sides of the House; and, upon the whole, he thought the general opinion seemed to be that they had better come to a compromise, rather than fight the measure. He thought some points of the measure were very objectionable; but, after all, in matters of compromise, they could not expect to have everything their own way. Some of the counties would benefit by it, and others would suffer by it; but, on the whole, he thought it was the general feeling of the Peers from Scotland that the Bill should pass.

THE EARL OF ROSEBERY said, he wished to call their Lordships' attention to the fact that the Bill was read a third time in the other House four days after the "Massacre of the Innocents." The "Massacre of the Innocents" included, as their Lordships knew, the Secretary for Scotland Bill, whilst this Bill, which was one of much less advantage to Scotland, was allowed to proceed. He confessed he should like to be able to give his friends in Scotland some explanation of this.

THE EARL OF KIMBERLEY said, it appeared to him that the explanation was extremely simple. This was a very small and unimportant Bill, while the Secretary for Scotland Bill, as his noble Friend (the Earl of Rosebery) would himself admit, was one of great importance, and in a different category altogether.

LORD BALFOUR said, he was glad his noble Friend (Lord Abinger) had not persisted in his opposition to the Bill, because he thought, on the whole, it was a Bill which could fairly be accepted. The point, however, he wished to represent to the House was this—he thought the Scottish counties were not fairly treated in the way in which this Bill was introduced. The Members of the Government knew perfectly well that the principal meetings of the Scottish counties—of Commissioners of Supply, and such meetings—were held towards the end of April and the beginning of May. The Government must by that time have made up their minds to introduce this Bill, because it was introduced very soon afterwards in the other House. In a matter of this kind, so closely affecting the administration of counties and the laying on of assessments, it was surely only natural that the Commissioners of Supply should have been given an opportunity of expressing their opinion on the matter; but by the course which the Government took in introducing the Bill towards the end of May, it was very likely to slip through without any notice being attracted to it. It was read a second time in the other House very soon after its introduction, and slipped quickly through several stages, and, being a Money Bill, no Amendment could have been put into it in this House. Therefore he must say he thought the time chosen by the Government for introducing the Bill was a most unfortunate one. He had only this further to say—that if the Secretary for Scotland Bill had passed, they might have been insured against such procedure on the part of the Treasury in future. He thought the only cure against their being treated in this way in Scotland was to have a responsible Department to look after the affairs of that country; and, for his own part, he sincerely trusted that Bills of this kind, so much affecting the administration of counties as this did, would be introduced at an earlier period of the Session, and before the principal meetings of those having charge of the administration of the counties.

Motion *agreed to;* Bill read 2ª accordingly, and *committed* to a Committee of the Whole House *To-morrow.*

House adjourned at a quarter past Six o'clock, till To-morrow, a quarter past Ten o'clock.

HOUSE OF COMMONS,

Thursday, 24th July, 1884.

MINUTES.]—SELECT COMMITTEE—*Special Report*—Police and Sanitary Regulations [No. 298]; Agricultural Labourers (Ireland), Mr. Rathbone *disch.*, Mr. Cheetham *added.*

SUPPLY—*considered in Committee*—CIVIL SERVICE ESTIMATES—CLASS III.—LAW AND JUSTICE—Votes 3 to 13.

Resolutions [July 22, 23] *reported.*

PUBLIC BILLS—*Ordered*—*First Reading*—Expiring Laws Continuance* [306].

First Reading—Supreme Court of Judicature Amendment* [307].

Referred to Select Committee—Ulster Canal and Tyrone Navigation* [244].

Special Report of Select Committee—Church Patronage* [No. 297]; Church Patronage (No. 2)* [251].

Committee — Superannuation [146] — R.P.; Public Works Loans [299]—R.P.

Committee—*Report*—Pier and Harbour Provisional Orders (*re-comm.*)* [259].

Committee—*Report*—*Third Reading*—Prisons* [293]; Teachers' Residences (Ireland)* [268], and *passed.*

Considered as amended—Third Reading—Municipal Elections (Corrupt and Illegal Practices) [252], and *passed*.
Third Reading—Indian Marine * [291], and *passed*.
Withdrawn—Marriages Legalisation * [237].

QUESTIONS.

—o—

POOR LAW (IRELAND)—DR. CALAGHAN, MEDICAL ATTENDANT, NENAGH UNION DISPENSARY.

MR. LEAHY asked the Chief Secretary to the Lord Lieutenant of Ireland, What action the Local Government Board have taken upon a request made to them by Mr. John M'Cormack, carpenter, of Nenagh, county Tipperary, to the effect that Dr. Calaghan, the medical attendant of the Nenagh Dispensary District of the Nenagh Union, having been served with a red ticket on Friday the 29th May last, which made it his duty to visit immediately Alice M'Cormack, the daughter of the complainant, a girl who was lying at that time dangerously ill, the said Dr. Calaghan allowed four days to elapse, and did not visit the girl until Monday the 2nd of June?

MR. TREVELYAN: In this case the Local Government Board called upon the dispensary doctor for an explanation; and it appears that, though he admits the red ticket may have been left with him, he can find no trace of it. There was no neglect or forgetfulness on his part. He passed the house of the sick child's parents twice on the day on which the ticket is believed to have been left with him, and could have called without any inconvenience to himself, if aware that he was wanted. The doctor had previously to this occurrence, and also after it, prescribed for the child, who is now quite well.

ROYAL IRISH CONSTABULARY—THE LICENSED TRADES OF KILLESHANDRA.

MR. BIGGAR asked the Chief Secretary to the Lord Lieutenant of Ireland, If he has received a memorial from the licensed trades of Killeshandra, complaining of the constabulary bringing quite a number of charges before the Petty Sessions Court which Mr. T. D. Gibson, R.M. decided were unsupported by evidence; and, if so, will he say whether he proposes to take any, and, if so, what action in the matter?

MR. TREVELYAN: Sir, several complaints have been made, and are being inquired into. The matter is one which requires and shall receive full investigation.

SALE OF INTOXICATING LIQUORS ON SUNDAY (WALES) ACT—OPERATION OF THE ACT.

MR. WARTON asked the Secretary of State for the Home Department, Whether it is a fact, as reported in the last number of *Truth*, that the Mayor of Wrexham has stated that drunkenness had trebled since the Sunday Closing Act (Wales) came in force; and, whether a Police Inspector there stated that, on the previous Sunday, nearly half the people were drunk?

SIR WILLIAM HARCOURT: I have received two letters on this subject—one from the Mayor, who says he expressed a personal opinion much to the effect stated in the Question; the other from one of the Justices to say that the other Justices present did not concur; and they seem to think that the Mayor's views were not unnaturally influenced by his own professional pursuits.

INDUSTRIAL SCHOOLS (IRELAND).

COLONEL COLTHURST asked the Chief Secretary to the Lord Lieutenant of Ireland, Whether his attention has been called to the refusal of the County Tipperary Grand Jury of the South Riding at the recent assizes to grant any contributions towards the maintenance of children in industrial schools?

MR. TREVELYAN: The secretary to the Grand Jury informs me that no application was made for a presentment under the Act; but that a gentleman asked the Grand Jury to give some assurance that money would be granted at a future Assizes to a school which is not yet in existence. The reply was that the Grand Jury could not pledge any future Grand Juries, and the foreman declined to pledge himself personally.

POOR LAW (IRELAND)—ELECTION OF GUARDIANS, CARMEEN DIVISION, COOTEHILL UNION—THE INQUIRY.

MR. HEALY asked the Chief Secretary to the Lord Lieutenant of Ireland, If it has come under his notice that, at the sworn inquiry in Cootehill Workhouse on the 8th instant, relative to the validity of the late election for Carmeen Division, Mr. Armstrong, Local Government Board Inspector, formally ruled that the solicitor for Mr. Owen McCabe, defeated candidate, had no right to an inspection of the claims under Form A 1 to the votes given to which he objected; will any steps be taken to remedy the injury done to the case of Mr. McCabe by their non-production; is it the fact that, at the same inquiry, it transpired that Vaughan Montgomery, Esq. J.P., Crilly, Aughnacluy, county Tyrone, lodged a claim to vote as lessor of Patrick McCabe, Mountain Lodge, on a valuation of £19 10*s*., and that, by the sworn evidence of Mr. P. McCabe, his lease, and rent receipts, it was proved that Mr. Montgomery had no interest, directly or indirectly, in this holding; and, will he ask this magistrate for an explanation of the filing of this claim.

MR. TREVELYAN: The Local Government Board consider that their Inspector was wrong in refusing to permit an inspection of the claims referred to. They have so informed the Inspector; and they have told Mr. M'Cabe that, if he desires it, the inquiry shall be reopened to afford him an opportunity of inspecting them. Mr. Montgomery has been written to on the subject of his claim; but his explanation has not yet been received. On such an inquiry I presume that it will be competent for anyone to proceed, and make of Mr. Montgomery any inquiries desired.

MR. HEALY: There are two points in the Question—the first that of forgery, which is one for the Government; and I presume there is a question for the Lord Chancellor as to whether he will supersede Mr. Montgomery.

MR. TREVELYAN said, that he believed if an offence was proved the party would be open for prosecution and a fine of £10.

POOR LAW (IRELAND)—ELECTION OF GUARDIANS—EDENDERRY UNION, KING'S COUNTY.

MR. ARTHUR O'CONNOR asked the Chief Secretary to the Lord Lieutenant of Ireland, Whether the attention of the Local Government Board has been called to the fact that, at the Poor Law election held in March for Edenderry Division, Edenderry Union, King's County, Lord Arthur Hill was allowed to record six votes, although the name of Lord A. Hill does not appear on the rate book, or in any of the legal documents used in the Land Commission Court in the proceedings with the tenants living on that part of the estate out of which Lord A. Hill claims to vote; whether the clerk of the Union, who acted as returning officer, allowed the Trustees of the Marquess of Downshire to record ten votes more than they were entitled to; whether the clerk compelled the rate collector to give a receipt to a son of one of the candidates, who was then allowed to vote out of a portion of his father's land, not being an occupier, and still living in his father's house, and having no more claim than the other children; whether the votes of several tenants were disallowed on the ground that they owed seed rate, although all the seed rate due to the Union was, long before the election, wiped out by a Resolution of the Board of Guardians; whether the Local Government Board have arrived at any decision yet after four months' consideration; and, whether they will grant a sworn investigation, or allow the same person to act as returning officer at future elections?

MR. TREVELYAN: I am informed that the proxy of Lord Arthur Hill was allowed votes on a statement of claim in respect of rent from property of which he is owner in fee. It is not necessary that he should be rated. The tenants and occupiers are the persons rated in such cases. On the 12th of last month I informed the hon. Member, in reply to a former Question, of the facts as to the excess votes allowed to Lord Downshire's trustees. The allegation in the third paragraph of the Question is being inquired into. The votes of several persons were properly disallowed, on the ground that they owed seed rate. The Board of Guardians have no power to wipe out seed rate legally due. The Local Government Board have come to a decision on the matter complained of in respect of this election, and have set aside the election of one of the Guardians returned. They have fully instructed the Returning Officer as to the several points raised, and they see no sufficient ground to supersede him in his office.

MR. ARTHUR O'CONNOR asked whether those persons who had not paid the seed rate would be permanently disfranchised while the seed rate was not paid?

MR. TREVELYAN, in reply, said, he believed that the non-payment of the seed rate, like the non-payment of any other poor rate, was permanent in its effect so long as the rate was not paid.

MR. ARTHUR O'CONNOR: The Guardians having wiped out the seed rate, will they be disfranchised for a sum which is no longer demanded from them?

THE SOLICITOR GENERAL FOR IRELAND (Mr. WALKER), in reply, said, that the same effects applied to this rate as any ordinary poor rate. It was really a portion of the poor rate.

POST OFFICE (IRELAND)—THE GENERAL POST OFFICE, DUBLIN—THE STAFF OF THE SECRETARY'S OFFICE.

COLONEL KING-HARMAN asked the Postmaster General, If a revision and additions to the staff of the Dublin Secretary's Office of the General Post Office was promised in February last, and which revision and additional staff was rendered imperatively necessary owing to the large increase in the correspondence arising out of telegraph and parcels post business, and, if so, why it has not been carried out; if it is the fact that the corresponding office in Edinburgh, though performing fully a third less work than the Irish Department, has been revised and additions made to its staff; and, if he will state what has been the cost of the hands temporarily employed in the Dublin Secretary's Office to meet the pressure arising out of the increased duties there?

MR. FAWCETT: In reply to the hon. and gallant Member, I have to say that there is no intention to revise the establishment of the Dublin Secretary's Office, and there has been no promise to do so; but it is possible that some slight addition may be made to the existing numbers. The cost of two officers temporarily lent from London is 15*s*. a-day each; but these gentlemen will shortly return to their ordinary duties. Four additional lower division clerks at Edinburgh have been authorized.

IRISH LAND COMMISSION (SUB-COMMISSIONERS)—MR. JOHN M. WEIR.

COLONEL KING-HARMAN asked the Chief Secretary to the Lord Lieutenant of Ireland, If he will state the grounds upon which Mr. John M. Weir, who is a shopkeeper at Cookstown, and is believed to have no practical knowledge of land or farming, is to be reappointed a Sub-Commissioner under the Land Act?

MR. HEALY: Mr. Speaker, I wish to ask you, on a point of Order, whether the hon. and gallant Member is in Order in putting a Question of this sort, which contains matter of a contentious character, inasmuch as it states that Mr. Weir "is believed to have no practical knowledge of land or farming." As the belief is one which is only in the mind of the hon. and gallant Gentleman, I wish to know whether a Notice of that kind ought to be allowed to appear on the Paper?

MR. SPEAKER: I think the Question, as it stands, is not out of Order, as it inquires whether a gentleman in a certain office is or is not unfit to be reappointed?

MR. HEALY: Then, before the right hon. Gentleman answers the Question, I would like to ask whether he will be prepared to state the grounds on which all the other Sub-Commissioners, to whom I and my hon. Friends objected, were reappointed?

MR. TREVELYAN: I should be exceedingly unwilling to promise that. As to the Question on the Paper, I can only say that the Lord Lieutenant, after consultation with the Land Commissioners, made such selections for reappointment as it was thought would be most conducive to the Public Service, and Mr. Weir would not have been selected if his work had shown that he had no practical knowledge of land or farming.

SALMON FISHERIES PROTECTION.

MR. SEXTON asked the Secretary to the Admiralty, If vessels of the Royal Navy are used for the protection of salmon fisheries anywhere on the coast of Great Britain; whether applications made to the Admiralty for vessels of the Royal Navy to protect salmon fisheries in Lough Foyle, in the River Lee, county Cork, in the Youghal River, county Cork, and in other places in Ireland, were uniformly refused, on the ground that it was the duty of the Conservators and other persons interested in the salmon fisheries to afford the necessary protection; whether it was agreed between the Admiralty and the Irish Inspectors of Fisheries that no vessel of the Royal Navy should be used for such a purpose unless in case when the inspectors apprehended a breach of the peace; whether, in the absence of any statement of such an apprehension, and without any reference to the Inspectors of Fisheries, the Admiralty have quartered a gunboat on the coast of Sligo and Donegal, in the Ballyshannon Fishery District; why this course has been adopted; whether the gunboat will be withdrawn, and the protection of the fisheries be left, as in every other case throughout Great Britain and Ireland, to the Conservators and other persons interested; and, whether a Copy of Correspondence between the Admiralty and other Departments of the Public Service, as to the employment of vessels of the Royal Navy in protecting salmon fisheries, will be laid upon the Table?

MR. CAMPBELL-BANNERMAN: Before I reply to the series of Questions addressed to me by the hon. Member, I would beg to refer him to the answer given on the 30th of June last to a Question put to me by the hon. Member for Monaghan (Mr. Healy), which covered the whole ground, with the exception of the individual case in Donegal Bay. Vessels of the Royal Navy have been formerly used for the protection of the salmon fisheries in Great Britain; but it may be understood generally that they are no longer so employed. The answer to both parts of the second paragraph of the Question is in the affirmative. No definite arrangement such as is indicated in the third paragraph of the Question has been come to; but the subject is still under consideration. With regard to paragraphs 4, 5, and 6 of the Question, it is the case that on a requisition to the Lord Lieutenant a Coastguard cruiser was ordered into Donegal Bay, owing to the fact that a large number of Coastguardsmen were withdrawn for a few weeks for the purpose of undergoing their annual drill in the Reserve Squadron. That vessel will no longer be required when the men return. The general policy of the Government has been to leave the duty of protecting all the fisheries, except the sea fisheries, to the Conservators of the respective districts. I stated on the previous occasion to which I have referred that the Correspondence on the subject cannot well be produced, it being of a confidential character between the two Departments.

FISHERY LAWS (IRELAND)—CLERK AND INSPECTOR OF SALMON FISHERIES, BALLYSHANNON.

MR. SEXTON asked the Chief Secretary to the Lord Lieutenant of Ireland, If it is a fact that the salaried Clerk and Inspector of Salmon Fisheries for the district of Ballyshannon, county Donegal, is also the lessee of a salmon fishery in that district; whether, as such Clerk and Inspector, he is the legal agent of the Board of Conservators of the District, and charged with the duty of prosecuting for breaches of the Fishery Laws, and in the event of any breach of the Fishery Laws by himself, as lessee of a salmon fishery in the district, or by his *employés*, his duty as Clerk and Inspector would be to prosecute himself; whether the Irish Inspectors of Fisheries have remonstrated against the existence of this state of facts; and, whether it will be permitted to continue?

MR. TREVELYAN: The Inspectors of Fisheries report that they have been informed that the fact is as stated in the first paragraph of the Question; and, that being so, the possibility of such an anomalous state of affairs as is suggested in the second paragraph would appear to arise. The law gives the Inspectors of Fisheries no control over the action of the Board of Conservators in this matter. It is possible, however, that, nevertheless, a remonstrance on the part of the Inspectors might have some effect, and I shall ask them to communicate with the Conservators with regard to this office.

PUBLIC HEALTH—VACCINATION.

MR. HOPWOOD asked the Secretary to the Local Government Board, Whether the Department has revised and sanctioned the issue of a pamphlet called "Facts Concerning Vaccination;" whether the following statements, among others, appear:—

> "No risks of injurious effects from it need be feared;" "The fear that a foul disease may be implanted is an unfounded one;"

whether the Department has been informed by the Committee of medical experts appointed to report on Dr. Cory's case that it is possible for syphilis to be communicated in vaccination from a syphilitic person—

"Notwithstanding that the operation be performed with the utmost care to avoid the admixture with blood;"

and, whether such statements will be allowed to be made under the authority of the Board?

MR. GEORGE RUSSELL: The National Health Society have published a pamphlet under this title. It was revised by the medical officer of the Local Government Board, and the Board have stated that it might be used with advantage in house-to-house visitation. The quotations given in the hon. and learned Member's Question are taken apart from the context. The pamphlet points out—

"That with due care in the performance of the operation no risk of any injurious effects from it need be feared,"

and that such mischief as the communication of a foul disease by vaccination—

"Could only happen through the most gross and culpable carelessness on the part of the vaccinator."

These statements are in no way inconsistent with the Report of the medical experts respecting Dr. Cory's case. The Committee reported expressly that—

"The infants from whom Dr. Cory took lymph for his experiments on his own arm were in such a condition of obvious syphilitic disease as would certainly have precluded their use as vaccinifers by even an inconsiderate and reckless vaccinator. Indeed, they were selected by Dr. Cory for his self-vaccination because they were unquestionable syphilitic cases. It is a rule of practice in the profession not to use in vaccination lymph taken from a child in whom there is any suspicion whatever of syphilitic taint, or, indeed, in whom there is any skin disease although of a character known to be harmless; and the observance of this professional rule is strictly enjoined by the Local Government Board in its instructions to public vaccinators throughout the country."

The Board see no reason to alter their views with regard to the pamphlet in question.

PALACE OF WESTMINSTER—WESTMINSTER HALL (WEST FRONT).

SIR GEORGE CAMPBELL asked the First Commissioner of Works, Whether, since the Report on Westminster Hall (just presented) shows that, from the time it was built, and "divers lodgings" were attached on the west side, till the Law Courts were demolished the other day, the space on the west side of the Hall always has been occupied by useful buildings, he will fully consider the growing wants of Parliament, and provide for them?

MR. SHAW LEFEVRE: Sir Charles Barry intended to erect an additional wing to this building, running from St. Stephen's porch and meeting another wing from the Clock Tower. This extension, however, was abandoned some years ago, and I can hold out no prospect of the proposal being revived.

SIR GEORGE CAMPBELL: I beg to give Notice that, considering the strong opinion expressed by the Prime Minister in regard to the delegation of the duties of this House, I shall take an early opportunity of asking him, whether he will use his influence with the First Commissioner of Works not to make such delegation physically impossible by devoting the only available space to a piece of sham ancient architecture?

MR. DICK-PEDDIE asked, whether there was to be a Supplementary Estimate proposed this Session for the buildings in Westminster Hall?

MR. SHAW LEFEVRE: Yes.

LAW AND POLICE (METROPOLIS)—THE REFORM DEMONSTRATION.

MR. DIXON-HARTLAND asked the Secretary of State for the Home Department, By whose authority Members of Parliament were prevented by the police from passing through the Strand on Monday afternoon on their way to this House?

SIR WILLIAM HARCOURT: I have received the following answer from the Chief Commissioner of Police:—

"The orders given to the police were that they were to afford every facility in their power to Members of Parliament; and, if any mistake was made, it was not from want of instruction. I do not understand how a Member was stopped in the Strand, unless by the procession itself, and, if particulars are given, I will inquire into the cause."

MR. DIXON-HARTLAND: I wish to ask, whether the police had any orders to draw a cordon across Westminster Bridge and refuse everyone passage, stating that, Members or no Members, no one was allowed to pass. I was stopped myself in the same way, and I should like to ask what steps the right hon. Gentleman will take if that were done contrary to his orders?

SIR WILLIAM HARCOURT: I will take no steps at all. My orders were these. I was very anxious that Members should not be interrupted, and when I originally saw the plans of the police, I found there had been no provision made for keeping open the main access to the Houses of Parliament. I directed, therefore, that a clear road should be kept from Charing Cross down to the Houses of Parliament, and that was done, as everyone knows, most efficiently. Of course, I could not go all over London looking where Members of Parliament might be. I could not instruct the police to do that. The general instructions were to give every facility they could. I also consideredywhether it was possible, so as not to interfere more than was necessary with the traffic, to break at intervals the procession, in order to allow the traffic to go through; but, on consideration with the police, it was seen that such a course would lead to great confusion—that the procession would fall into confusion, and that it would lead to that interruption which it was most desirable to avoid. Therefore, we determined that could not be done. In these circumstances, of course, a certain amount of personal inconvenience was inevitable. That always happens, and must happen, whenever there is a crowd—whether there is a Volunteer Review, whether there is a procession, an entrance of Garibaldi into London, a triumphal return from Berlin, or anything of that kind. There is always a certain amount of inconvenience caused by a crowd in London. The only thing the police can do is to minimize the inconvenience as much as possible; and I think the general opinion of London, and England, and of Europe is that the police did their duty admirably on this occasion, and that the public suffered as little inconvenience as possible.

MR. WARTON asked the Postmaster General, Whether he is aware that a Post Office van was delayed for two hours, standing in front of the Army and Navy Club, on the occasion of the so-called "Demonstration" of last Monday; and, whether, should any similar "Demonstrations" be announced, he will take such steps as he can to insure the free passage of vans and carts in Post Office employ?

MR. FAWCETT: I find that a Post Office van, and also a mail cart, were detained on the spot referred to for about two hours last Monday afternoon, and a communication has been addressed to the Commissioner of Police upon the subject. Generally speaking, I am informed that the police exerted themselves to prevent delay to the mail vehicles.

Subsequently,

VISCOUNT FOLKESTONE said, he wished to ask the Secretary of State for War a Question of which he had been unable to give him Notice—namely, Whether it was true, as stated in a letter to *The Times*, that three Yeomanry bands in uniform took part in the Reform Demonstration on Monday; whether that act was not an infraction of the Queen's Regulations; and, whether the authorities intended to take any notice of such infraction, and to take steps to prevent such conduct in the future?

THE MARQUESS OF HARTINGTON: I cannot answer that Question without Notice. It is extremely improbable that any such thing occurred.

VISCOUNT FOLKESTONE: I will put the Question again to-morrow.

LABOURERS (IRELAND) ACT, 1883—BALLYMENA BOARD OF GUARDIANS.

MR. SEXTON asked the Chief Secretary to the Lord Lieutenant of Ireland, Whether it is a fact that the agricultural labourers of the electoral divisions of Ahoghill and Portglenone, county Antrim, applied last year, immediately after the passing of the Labourers (Ireland) Act, to the local sanitary authority, the Ballymena Board of Guardians, to make an Improvement Scheme in virtue of the Act, and that the application was attended with no result; whether, towards the end of March this year, a representation, in conformity with the statute, was laid before the Ballymena Board, in the interest of the labourers above mentioned, together with a report from Alexander Young, M.D., Ballymena, describing the houses of the labourers in question as being—

"In a truly wretched condition," "evidently unfit for human habitation," "covered with scanty and decayed thatch, the walls in numerous instances split and rent, in many cases ready to come down, in all more or less saturated with moisture,"

and whether the Report declared an Improvement Scheme to be requisite; whether the Ballymena Board adjourned the question twice, on the third occasion refused to make a Scheme, and held back the Report of Dr. Young until the meeting after that at which they had resolved upon such refusal; whether the Board, in compliance with section ten of the Act of 1883, have sent to the Local Government Board a copy of the representation, accompanied by their reasons for not acting upon it; and, what steps the Local Government Board will take in reference to the matter?

MR. TREVELYAN: Sir, I am informed that a Memorial relating to the two electoral divisions referred to was put forward in October last, and the Guardians appointed Committees to inquire into the matter. The Portglenone Committee reported that, in their opinion, action was not necessary in that division. It was subsequently agreed that a scheme should be formulated for Ahoghill; but the matter was delayed too long to admit of anything being done this Session. In March last, a Memorial was addressed to the Guardians, asking them to adopt a resolution in favour of an improvement scheme, and to receive a deputation on the subject, which they did. I am informed that it is not a fact that these representations were accompanied by any Report from Dr. Young, or that the Report, when subsequently received, was in any way kept back. The clerk states that, on his return from the Board's meeting on the 7th of June, he found a Report from Dr. Young, who is not the medical officer of health, without date, in his private office, and that he submitted it to the Board at their next meeting on the 14th of June. A proposal to formulate a scheme was several times before the Guardians, and was finally rejected on the 7th of June. This was reported to the Local Government Board on the 15th of July, the reasons stated being, that in the divisions specified, as well as throughout the entire Union, there are numbers of cottier houses unoccupied for which tenants cannot be procured. The Local Government Board are not empowered to take any very practical steps in the matter. It rests with the sanitary authority to prepare a scheme, and submit it if they see fit to do so. The hon. Member has called my attention to a matter in the 5th paragraph; and I will see whether an inquiry can be ordered.

MR. SEXTON asked, would the right hon. Gentleman call upon the Local Government Board to remonstrate with the Ballymena Board of Guardians for the delay in dealing with the scheme of the 7th of June?

MR. TREVELYAN: I will see about it.

POST OFFICE (IRELAND)—THE CLONMEL MAILS.

MR. MOORE asked the Postmaster General, Whether he has come to any decision as to the acceleration of the Mails between Dublin and Clonmel; whether it is a fact that the Inspector of Mails in Ireland has recommended that the Mails for Clonmel be thrown out and taken up at Thurles; and, whether the only objection to this course is the exorbitant price demanded by the Limerick and Waterford Company for carrying the Mails between Thurles and Clonmel?

MR. FAWCETT: I have not yet been able to come to any decision as to the acceleration of the day mail to Clonmel. The question of delivering and taking up the Clonmel mail at Thurles by the mail trains while in motion is still open to consideration; but, even if no difficulty existed on that point, I fear that I should not be justified in calling for a train to be run from Thurles to Clonmel solely for the Mail Service. The circumstance would be different if the Company were running a train for passenger purposes at hours suitable for the Mail Service.

In reply to a further Question from Mr. MOORE,

MR. FAWCETT said, that further inquiry should be made.

TOWNS IMPROVEMENT (IRELAND) ACT —FINES FOR DRUNKENNESS.

MR. HEALY asked the Chief Secretary to the Lord Lieutenant of Ireland, If it is the fact that the Inspector General of Constabulary has, since 1878, directed the police, where a local town court is established under the Act of 1854, that persons arrested for drunkenness within the town limits, but residing outside the town, are not to be brought before the Town Justices; whether this has the effect of diverting the fines from the Borough Fund to the Constabulary

Fund, which latter receives one-half of all such fines at Petty Sessions; whether this is excused on the allegation that the warrant of a Town Justice cannot be executed outside the boundary; whether, if this be so, the Lord Chancellor will appoint the Town Justices to the County Commission; if not, will any steps be taken to amend the powers of Town Justices as to trans-boundary warrants; is it the case that at present the Inspector General is empowered to indorse town warrants under section seventy-seven of the Act of 1854, as well as under the Petty Sessions Act; and, whether, as many towns complain of the great loss caused to their funds by the rule of the police, a change will in future be made?

MR. TREVELYAN: The Constabulary have been informed that the effect of a recent decision, in a case tried in the Court of Common Pleas, is that they are entitled to take proceedings in their own names as complainants at Petty Sessions against persons found drunk in the public streets of towns under the Towns Improvement Act, and that only one moiety of the fines recovered in such cases is payable to the Town Commissioners. They are also directed to take that course in the cases of persons residing outside the town. In these cases the Constabulary Force Fund receives one-half the fines imposed at Petty Sessions; but I am advised that it is not right to represent such half as diverted from the Borough Fund, inasmuch as the legal title of the Constabulary Force Fund to its share is equally clear with that of the Borough Fund. The practice of not bringing before the Town Justices persons arrested for drunkenness within the town limits, but residing outside the town, is not justified on the ground stated in the Question—namely, "that the warrant of a Town Justice cannot be executed outside the boundary"—but on this—that the Constabulary maintain order and act as guardians of the peace in these towns; and that although the Town Commissioners have statutory power to utilize the services of the Constabulary as night watchmen (on paying for them), yet they do not do so, but leave the work of watching the town and maintaining order, and suppressing drunkenness to the Constabulary without making any payment. If the Constabulary were employed as night watchmen, they would take out summonses in the name of the Commissioners, and then the whole of the fines would go to the Borough Fund. The Government are advised that the present arrangement is not unreasonable or unlawful.

POST OFFICE (IRELAND)—DELIVERY OF LETTERS AT DALKEY, CO. DUBLIN.

COLONEL KING-HARMAN asked the Postmaster General, Whether he will take steps to remedy the very great inconvenience suffered by persons residing at Dalkey and the adjoining districts, in the county of Dublin, by the non-delivery of their letters until nearly ten o'clock in the morning, the consequence of which is that a great number of persons who have daily business avocations in the city of Dublin cannot receive their letters before leaving home; whether this inconvenience, and also the annoyance caused by the unnecessarily late delivery of letters in the evening, are wholly attributable to a want of a sufficient number of letter-carriers and assistants; whether it is true that the already overworked postmen have had their labours increased by the means of transport for the Parcel Post having been reduced; whether a promise was given to the residents of Dalkey that their grievances in this particular should be remedied after the acceleration of the Irish Mail; and, whether he will consider the propriety of having the mails sent direct to Dalkey, instead of keeping that office as a sub-office to Kingstown, having regard to the very large number of business and professional men who reside at Dalkey and its neighbourhood, especially during the summer and autumn months?

MR. FAWCETT, in reply, said, he had ascertained that the first delivery at Dalkey was finished at 9 o'clock in the morning, and he thought that was not an inconvenient time. If the hon. and gallant Member opposite (Colonel King-Harman) had any special case to complain of, he would have inquiries made about it. He regretted to find that Dalkey did not profit as yet by the accelerated mail service to Dublin, because it was necessary to keep the hour of delivery at its former point, in order to include letters arriving from the Irish provincial towns. He would inquire whether anything could be done to accelerate the delivery in this respect. Letter-carriers at Dalkey only took light parcels, which did not delay the delivery.

COLONEL KING-HARMAN asked, whether the means of transport had been reduced by the taking away of a horse and cart from the district? He could give a great many instances of delay in the matter.

MR. FAWCETT said, the horse and cart were found expensive, and no harm was done by discontinuing them. People were able to get their letters quicker by the present arrangement.

AFRICA (WEST COAST)—CONSULAR JURISDICTION.

MR. BUCHANAN asked the Under Secretary of State for Foreign Affairs, Whether the Order in Council to extend British consular jurisdiction on the West Coast of Africa, so as to insure the more speedy and economical apprehension of criminals, is now prepared; and, when it will be laid upon the Table of the House?

LORD EDMOND FITZMAURICE: The Order in Council referred to is not yet completed; but it is expected to be ready shortly, and will be laid in due course.

PARLIAMENT—PALACE OF WESTMINSTER—WESTMINSTER HALL—THE BRITISH MUSEUM.

MR. NEWZAM-NICHOLSON asked the Chief Commissioner of Works, Whether his attention has been called to the last paragraph of the interesting Report of Mr. J. L. Pearson, R.A., on Westminster Hall, which states that by the rules of the British Museum he has been unable to obtain some important tracings to accompany his Report, especially from the Crace Collection; and, whether he can suggest a method by which such important drawings and information, for a National purpose, can for the future be obtained, without difficulty, from a National establishment like the British Museum?

SIR JOHN LUBBOCK, in reply, said, that as one of the Trustees of the British Museum, he trusted he might be allowed to answer the Question. The answer was that, according to the rules of the Museum, tracings were not allowed to be taken from drawings or prints without the permission of the keeper. No application was made by Mr. Pearson to the present keeper; and if any was made in the time of his predecessor there is no record of it in the office. The permission is given in special cases, when no injury is apprehended; but the general rule is a necessary precaution for the protection of these valuable documents.

OVERHEAD TELEGRAPH AND TELEPHONE WIRES—LEGISLATION.

SIR HENRY TYLER asked the Secretary to the Local Government Board, Whether he is aware of the number of wires now stretched overhead in various portions of the Metropolis, of which about 230 may be counted between the Royal Exchange and St. Michael's Church, Cornhill, and about 200 between the Mansion House and Queen Street, over Queen Victoria Street; and, whether, having regard to the danger thus occasioned to persons using the streets, especially in thunder-storms, snow-storms, and in high winds, he will consider if the time has arrived when some means should be taken to deal with this question?

MR. GEORGE RUSSELL: We are aware that there is a large number of wires stretched overhead in the Metropolis, and have no reason to doubt the statement as to the number of such wires in the localities mentioned. In replying to the hon. and gallant Member for East Aberdeenshire (Sir Alexander Gordon) I stated that we would consider whether a Select Committee shall not be moved for next Session for the purpose of inquiry and report on the subject. I am advised by the Postmaster General that of the 230 wires mentioned by the hon. Member only six belong to the Post Office, and of the 200 only four.

MERCHANT SHIPPING—PILOTAGE—PORT OF SLIGO.

MR. SEXTON asked the President of the Board of Trade, Whether, in consequence of the action of the Board of Trade, in granting pilots' licences to two masters of steamers trading to and from the port of Sligo, and the action of the Sligo Harbour Board, in granting pilots' licences to four other masters of steamers trading to and from the port of Sligo, the regular outside pilots of that port, who gained their licences after apprenticeship, and have acted in connection with the port for many years, are now almost deprived of their means of living, their average incomes having fallen from £35 to about £12 a-year; and, whether any steps will be taken to give them compensation?

MR. CHAMBERLAIN: It is the duty of harbour authorities, and in their default of the Board of Trade, under the Statute, to grant, after examination, certificates to masters and mates, enabling them to pilot the ships in which they serve. This has been done by the Board of Trade in two cases at the Port of Sligo. I do not know what licences have been granted by the Harbour Board. There is no provision for giving compensation to persons who had been acting as pilots before such certificates were granted. No funds are at my disposal for this purpose.

PALACE OF WESTMINSTER—HOUSE OF COMMONS—TELEGRAPHIC NEWS-RECORDING INSTRUMENT FOR USE OF MEMBERS.

MR. GRAY asked the First Commissioner of Works, If he has yet come to a decision whether he will allow a telegraphic news-recording instrument to be erected in the House for the use of Members; whether, immediately after the subject was last mentioned in the House, the Company which supplies such instruments offered him to erect one in the House on payment of the cost of erection only; if he can state how many hours it would take to put up one of these instruments; and, whether he can hold out any hope of one being at work this Session, or during the proposed Autumn Session, or during the Session of 1885?

MR. SHAW LEFEVRE, in reply, said, he had consulted with the Serjeant-at-Arms, who had charge of the arrangements for supplying telegraphic news to the House, and he was of opinion that the proposal of the hon. Member did not offer any facilities over the present system to hon. Members which would justify a change. The Company would propose to supply the instrument at a rental of £50 a-year, with certain occasional charges; whereas the present Telegraph Company supplied its news free.

PUBLIC HEALTH—THE UPPER AND LOWER THAMES.

MR. LABOUCHERE asked the President of the Local Government Board, Whether he will take into consideration the expediency of obtaining full powers to deal at once with the dangers to which the inhabitants of the Metropolis and of the Lower Thames Valley are exposed, owing to the absence of land water in the Thames, and to the pestiferous nature of the water that circulates between Bailey Creek and Teddington, and to obtain money for carrying into effect such a scheme as he may deem necessary to mitigate these dangers? In putting the Question, he would ask leave to read the following extracts from the Report of the principal Dockmaster of the East and West India Dock Company to the Directors of the Company:—

"This half-year we have raised 73,100 tons what we considered a good year's work before 1881. The river is in a fearful condition, the stench from the sewage is very bad, and the water very thick and black. It is awfully sickening, and we have had during last week high tides, and through having to draw down after every high tide water to Trinity datum for the protection of the lockgates, causes a strong tide to rush in before the following high water at Blackwall entrance and Eastern Dock entrance, bringing in an enormous amount of sewage. I reckon in four days last week not less than 400 tons entered each tide, for as fast as I dredged in Blackwall Basin I found almost the same water the next day. The banks of the basin are covered with a green slimy substance, and smell very bad. Some steps should be taken by correspondence through the daily newspapers, or by direct reference to the Chairman of the Royal Commission, to keep the question open, or it will have the same fate as other Royal Commissions when the excitement dies out."

Minute of Board—

"The condition of the water is such as tends to the enervation of the staff, and would be a factor in inducing cholera. The matter should be pressed upon the notice of the Board of Works and the Government, with a view to the river being dealt with, not only in the interest of the Docks, but of the citizens at large."

SIR CHARLES W. DILKE: I have had this subject under consideration; but the matter is not one with regard to which I can propose legislation during the present Session. I have, however, instructed Mr. Harrison, one of the Inspectors of the Board, to report to me as to the condition of the part of the Thames on which the Lower Thames

Valley abuts, and whether, in his opinion, any temporary arrangements can be made by the Local Authorities with the view of removing the evils which are stated to exist, and providing a remedy.

EMPLOYERS' LIABILITY ACT—MINING ACCIDENTS.

MR. MACFARLANE asked the Secretary of State for the Home Department, If it is true that the Reports of the Official Inspectors of Mines, in cases of explosions, are refused to persons suing for damages under the Employers' Liability Act, and to the counsel in such cases, and that such officers can refuse to give evidence when summoned in support of a case; and that, in consequence, the strongest and most reliable evidence of negligence is unavailable for suitors; and, if he proposes to remove this obstacle to the requirements of justice?

SIR WILLIAM HARCOURT: I am not aware, nor have I been able to discover, that any Reports have been so refused; but, speaking generally, I concur in the spirit of the Question, and will take care that instructions are given that if Reports are applied for they shall not be refused, unless under special circumstances.

EDUCATION DEPARTMENT—COMPULSORY SCHOOL ATTENDANCE.

MR. RANKIN asked the Vice President of the Committee of Council, Whether during the recess he will take into his consideration the advisability of altering the age of compulsory school attendance from five years to seven years of age, with a view to prevent children from leaving school by passing the fourth standard at so early an age as many do at present, and also with a view to lessen the great difficulty experienced by magistrates in having to convict parents for not sending young children of five and six years of age regularly to school?

MR. MUNDELLA: Considering that there are 1,345,196 children of all classes between five and seven years of age, of whom 920,000 are on the registers of public elementary schools, I am not prepared to adopt the suggestion of the hon. Member. What ought to be done, and what I hope will be done very soon, is to follow out the recommendation of the Royal Commission on Technical Instruction, and enact that Standard V. shall be the minimum for total exemption.

EGYPT (EVENTS IN THE SOUDAN)—EXPEDITION FOR RELIEF OF GENERAL GORDON—VOTE OF CREDIT.

LORD EUSTACE CECIL asked the Secretary of State for War, Whether any Supplementary Estimate or Vote of Credit will be presented to the House, before the Prorogation, to defray the cost of any expedition that may be necessary for the relief of General Gordon and the defence of Egypt?

THE MARQUESS OF HARTINGTON: The Government have arrived at no decision to present a Supplementary Estimate before the Prorogation to defray the expenses of any expedition that may be necessary for the relief of General Gordon. It is probable, however, that a Supplementary Estimate will be required in connection with expenses being incurred in preparations for the defence of Egypt; and I shall probably be able to give the noble Lord a definite answer to-morrow.

MR. W. E. FORSTER asked the Under Secretary of State for Foreign Affairs, Whether he can give the House any information with regard to General Gordon's present position; whether the rewards which the Government have offered for information are now in force, or whether they lapsed in the month of June; and, whether it is true that the Nile will be at its lowest at Khartoum by the end of September, so that it will then be more difficult to send relief to General Gordon up the Nile, and also more difficult for him to leave Khartoum by the river, especially by the White Nile, than it is at present?

LORD EDMOND FITZMAURICE: I have from time to time given the House all the information in the possession of the Foreign Office in regard to General Gordon's position. The rewards have not lapsed except in the case of the messenger mentioned at page 67 of "Egypt (No. 25) 1884;" but complete discretion as to money rewards has been given to Mr. Egerton, as stated in No. 43. It is high Nile at Khartoum about the beginning of September, and this lasts about a month. The river begins to fall early in October, and is half Nile by the end of that month. Above Khartoum the Nile attains its greatest height early in September.

MR. LABOUCHERE asked the noble Lord whether steps are still being taken with a view to convey to General Gordon instructions to withdraw, if possible, from Khartoum and the Soudan without further bloodshed; and, whether steps will be taken to inform, if possible, the Mahdi that Her Majesty's Government has already recognized the independence of the Soudan, and that, as messengers have been despatched to General Gordon ordering him to withdraw from that country, he was acting contrary to those instructions if he slaughters Soudanese, unless in self-defence?

LORD EDMOND FITZMAURICE: The answer to the first part of the hon. Member's Question is in the affirmative; to the second, in the negative.

EGYPT—COLLECTION OF TAXES—USE OF TORTURE.

MR. LABOUCHERE asked the Under Secretary of State for Foreign Affairs, Whether instructions have been sent to Her Majesty's Representatives in Egypt to inquire into the alleged use of torture in levying taxes from the fellahs, and to see that, if such is the present habit, it will no longer be pursued?

LORD EDMOND FITZMAURICE: If my hon. Friend will refer to the Papers on Egyptian affairs which have just been distributed, he will find from the Report of Sir Evelyn Baring, dated June 28, that he is of opinion that the use of torture by the courbash in the collection of taxes has practically ceased. Her Majesty's Government, after consulting Sir Evelyn Baring, did not consider that further instructions were necessary, as those already given are quite distinct. The use of torture and the courbash is illegal, as will be seen on reference to the Proclamation given at page 36 of "Egypt (No. 6) 1883." and since that the Penal Codes have been enacted, which put an end to any punishment except those specifically there mentioned.

CRIME AND OUTRAGE (IRELAND)—ATTACK ON THE RESIDENT MAGISTRATE, CO. SLIGO.

COLONEL KING-HARMAN asked the Chief Secretary to the Lord Lieutenant of Ireland, If he has received any information as to an attack having been made upon the Resident Magistrate for Sligo on the 13th instant?

MR. TREVELYAN: I am informed that, about 10 days ago, the Resident Magistrate, while taking a walk after dusk, was struck by a stone, which was thrown over the fence from an adjoining field. He chased and secured a man who, he believed, threw the stone, and, having demanded his name and address, he let him go. It was subsequently ascertained that the name and address given were false. Mr. Molony does not himself consider that the affair was an outrage.

MR. SEXTON: Where did this happen?

MR. TREVELYAN: While the magistrate was taking a walk along the river side near the town.

LOWER THAMES VALLEY MAIN SEWERAGE BOARD.

MR. BARRAN asked the President of the Local Government Board, Whether, having regard to the importance of the sewage of the Lower Thames Valley being diverted from the river at the earliest moment, to the applications made to the Local Government Board by Heston and Isleworth, Kingston-on-Thames, and Richmond, for the severance of those places from the Lower Thames Valley Main Sewerage Board, and to the Report of the Select Committee on the Bill of this Session—

"That the continuance of the Joint Board is not only unnecessary, but operates as a hindrance to the several authorities purifying the sewage of their respective districts,"

he will now give facilities for the dissolution of the Joint Board and sub-division of its district as recommended by the Committee; whether those objects could be effected by a short Bill passed during the present Session; and, if he is not prepared to bring in such a Bill, what other steps does he propose to take in the matter in the interest of the public and the localities?

SIR CHARLES W. DILKE: The Lower Thames Valley Main Sewerage District, as I have already stated in reply to a Question of the hon. Baronet the Member for Finsbury (Sir Andrew Lusk), was constituted by a Provisional Order, which was issued by the Board after local conferences and inquiries, and was subsequently confirmed by Parliament, after very full consideration by a Select Committee. It is true that the Select Committee on the Bill of this Session recommended the dissolution of the Joint Board and the setting up of new districts. But that recommendation was made after hearing the evidence of two only out of the 11 constituent authorities, and without hearing any evidence whatever on the part of the other nine constituent authorities, or the Main Sewerage Board on the subject. The Board have received communications from Heston, and Isleworth, and Richmond as to separation from the district; but no similar application has been made by the Kingston-on-Thames Sanitary Authority since 1881. I am not in a position to dissolve the district and set up other districts without giving those interested full opportunity of making their representations on the subject at a local inquiry. I am, as I stated in reply to the Question of the hon. Member for Northampton (Mr. Labouchere), obtaining a Report as to whether any temporary arrangement can be made by the Local Authorities with the view of mitigating the evils stated to exist.

VISCOUNT FOLKESTONE said, he wished to say that the Select Committee heard the promoters of the scheme.

SIR CHARLES W. DILKE said, if he was wrong on that point, he was right in stating that the Committee did not hear nine out of the 11 opponents.

VISCOUNT FOLKESTONE said, that the Committee, having heard two of the opponents, considered that they had sufficient evidence before them.

ARMY — MILITARY BARRACKS AT LONGFORD—RESIDENCE FOR THE MEDICAL OFFICER.

MR. JUSTIN M'CARTHY asked the Secretary of State for War, Whether it is intended to buy or take on lease a house for the Army Medical Doctor outside the Military Barracks in Longford; and, whether there is not ample accommodation within the barracks, there being now twelve quarters unoccupied there?

THE MARQUESS OF HARTINGTON: No proposal of the nature indicated in the Question has been made to the War Office; and if such a proposal had been made, careful inquiry would be made before it was sanctioned.

ARREARS OF RENT (IRELAND) ACT—COLONEL DIGBY, J.P.

MR. HARRINGTON asked the Chief Secretary to the Lord Lieutenant of Ireland, Whether it is true that Colonel Digby, J.P. Westmeath, obtained from the Land Commissioners, under the provisions of the Arrears of Rent (Ireland) Act, certain arrears of rent alleged by him to be due of a tenant of his named James Rickard; whether this James Rickard had actually parted with the interest in his tenancy to a man named James Egan, who paid to the landlord all arrears due of the holding; whether, after this payment was made, Colonel Digby received, and he and Rickard divided between them, the money thus obtained from the Land Commission; and, whether, if these allegations are well founded, he will order fresh proceedings to be taken against Colonel Digby, and take steps to secure the due hearing of the charge before a competent tribunal?

MR. TREVELYAN: I am informed that, on the joint application of the landlord and tenant, the Land Commissioners extinguished arrears of rent amounting to £5 15*s*., and that a sum of £2 17*s*. 6*d*. was paid to the landlord. The tenant, Rickard, alleges that Colonel Digby gave him £2 7*s*. 6*d*. of this sum—from which it would appear that he retained 10*s*. of it for himself—under what circumstances does not appear. I am also informed that it is a fact that Rickard sold the interest of his farm in November, 1882, to a man named Egan, and that of the price given—£40—a sum of £21 10*s*. was paid to Colonel Digby for rent and costs. Whether this included all arrears I cannot say. An explanation will be written for, and, on receipt of that explanation, these Reports shall be laid before the Law Officers for directions whether these Reports disclose an offence, or a case for further inquiry.

MR. HARRINGTON: Will the right hon. Gentleman communicate with the tenant Egan, who purchased the holding, and who may have valuable information to give?

MR. TREVELYAN said, there was enough information on the subject to satisfy the Law Officers.

MR. HEALY: Is it usual, when a person is charged with theft, for the

Government to write to him for an explanation?

CONTAGIOUS DISEASES (ANIMALS) (IRELAND) ACT—CATTLE INSPECTOR, KILMACTHOMAS UNION.

MR. LEAMY asked the Chief Secretary to the Lord Lieutenant of Ireland, If the Lord Lieutenant recently refused to sanction the appointment of a gentleman to the post of Cattle Inspector to a Southern Poor Law Union, on the ground that he was not a fully qualified veterinary surgeon; and, if so, whether in future only qualified veterinary surgeons will be appointed to the post?

MR. TREVELYAN: It is presumed that this Question relates to the Kilmacthomas Union, County Waterford, in which the Lord Lieutenant refused, in April last, to sanction the appointment of an Inspector who was not a qualified veterinary surgeon, on the ground that the Local Authority could procure the services of a duly qualified veterinary surgeon for the office. The Order in Council dealing with the subject requires that the persons appointed shall be veterinary surgeons, unless the Lord Lieutenant is satisfied that it is impossible to procure, or that for other sufficient reason it is undesirable to appoint, a person so qualified.

PRISONS (IRELAND)—THE LATE GOVERNOR OF LIMERICK PRISON—SUPERANNUATION.

MR. O'SULLIVAN asked Mr. Solicitor General for Ireland, Under what Act of Parliament had the grand jury of the county Limerick power to alter and increase the retiring allowance of the late Governor of the County Limerick Prison by thirty-three pounds ten shillings per annum over and above the amount fixed by a previous grand jury in that county?

THE SOLICITOR GENERAL FOR IRELAND (Mr. WALKER): Mr. Eagar, the late Governor, was appointed prior to the Prisons Act, 1877, and his position was continued under the Prisons Board till last year, when he was retired consequent on the abolition of Spike Island. The superannuation allowance is regulated by the Superannuation Act, 1859, and a Treasury Minute of 14th January, 1879, and the Prisons Act, 1877, provides for an apportionment of the allowance on the county in respect of services prior to April, 1878. The power of the Grand Jury, to make a presentment for this is retained by the Prisons Act. The portion payable by the county would have been *primâ facie* £160 18*s*. per annum; but the Grand Jury, in the summer of 1883, passed a resolution that, on account of Mr. Eagar's good and long services, the allowance should be £194 15*s*. 6*d*. This was the first and only resolution passed by the Grand Jury, and it was founded on the authority I have mentioned.

POST OFFICE (IRELAND)—DAY MAIL TO CORK.

MR. LEAMY asked the Postmaster General, If he is aware that about five-sixths of the passengers from Dublin to Waterford travel viâ Maryburgh, and if, under the proposed agreement for the acceleration of the mails from Dublin to Cork, the Great Western mail will not stop at Maryburgh, these passengers will be compelled to travel viâ Carlow; whether such an arrangement will give an unfair advantage to the Great Southern and Western line over the Central Ireland Railway, which would thereby lose a large share of its present passenger traffic; and, whether he will bear this fact in mind when considering the proposed agreement?

MR. FAWCETT, in reply, said, that, in carrying out the acceleration of the day mail to Cork, Limerick, &c., it was not intended to alter the present day mail train from Dublin at 9 A.M., which would continue to stop at Maryburgh; but the new special train would not call there, a stop being unnecessary for mail purposes. He regretted that the effect of the new arrangement should be in any way unfavourable to the Waterford and Central Ireland Railway Company; but, so far as the day mail to Waterford was concerned, he saw no reason why such an improvement of the service by the present route *viâ* Carlow should not be affected as should secure as long an interval for replies by return of post as an accelerated service *viâ* Maryburgh. Inquiries on this point were being made.

INDIA—THE SALT TAX.

MR. JUSTIN M'CARTHY asked the Under Secretary of State for India,

Whether his attention has been drawn to an article in *The Lancet*, published two months ago, in which that high medical authority asserts that—

"As the diet of the Hindoo is almost entirely farinaceous and vegetable, it is a cruel injustice to impose a tax that renders a physiological necessary a high-priced luxury;"

and, whether the Government will take into account the opinion of *The Lancet* in arranging their future policy with regard to the Salt Tax in India?

MR. J. K. CROSS, in reply, said, that the Government of India was fully aware of the objections which might be urged against the Salt Tax, and bore them in mind when considering its fiscal changes.

UNION RATING (IRELAND).

COLONEL COLTHURST asked the Chief Secretary to the Lord Lieutenant of Ireland, Whether it is the intention of the Government to give effect to the recommendation of the Select Committee of 1871-2 with regard to Union Rating in Ireland; and, if so, whether such legislation will embrace outdoor as well as indoor relief?

MR. TREVELYAN, in reply, said, the Government were very anxious to give effect to the recommendation referred to. The system in Ireland should be assimilated to the system in England, both with regard to indoor and outdoor relief.

JAMAICA—IMPORTATION OF COOLIES.

MR. A. PEASE asked the Under Secretary of State for the Colonies, Whether, in view of the large amount of debt which the importation of Coolies has already entailed upon Jamaica, and also, in view of the despatch of Her Majesty's Secretary for the Colonies of the 29th September 1877, relieving the people of the Island from future taxation for this purpose, Her Majesty's Government have any intention of adopting the proposal of the Commissioners, that the importation of Coolies shall be renewed, and supported from the general taxation of the Island?

MR. EVELYN ASHLEY: No decision has yet been arrived at on the proposals of the Royal Commissioners relative to Coolie immigration into Jamaica; and, indeed, it is a question on which the Government would not think it right to give any definite directions until the new Jamaican Legislative Council had an opportunity of considering it at their meeting in September next. I may point out, however, as to the terms of my hon. Friend's Question, that the importation of Coolies has never been stopped, and that, under present arrangements, the expense of hospital treatment for the Coolies is maintained from the general taxation of the island.

AFRICA (SOUTH)—BECHUANALAND.

SIR HENRY HOLLAND asked the Under Secretary of State for the Colonies, Whether he can give to the House any information as to the condition of affairs in Bechuanaland; and, whether he will lay upon the Table further Papers relating to that Country, before the Supplemental Estimate is considered?

MR. EVELYN ASHLEY: Further Papers on Bechuanaland are in preparation, and will be laid on the Table before the end of the Session; but not, I fear, in time for the Supplementary Estimate. It would be impossible, within the limits of an answer to a Question, to give the general account asked for; but when the Supplementary Estimate is moved, I shall be ready to state any information we may be in possession of. Meanwhile I may say that we have received a telegram from the Governor of the Cape, in which he informs us that the following Resolution has been carried in both Houses of the Legislature of the Cape Colony—namely,

"That, in the opinion of this House, it is expedient, pending the ratification of the London Convention of 1884 by the Volksraad of the South African Republic, that the Colonial Government be authorised to open communications with the Imperial Government, with a view to submitting to Parliament, next Session, a measure for the annexation to the Cape Colony of the territory of the south-western border of the South African Republic, now under British protection—that is to say, Bechuanaland."

SIR HENRY HOLLAND: That will include the so-called Republic of Stellaland and Göschen?

MR. EVELYN ASHLEY: Yes; all these territories.

ARMY—LOSS OF LIFE IN EGYPT.

MR. STANLEY LEIGHTON asked the Secretary of State for War, Whether his attention has been drawn to the following approximate estimate of loss of life in Egypt since the English occupation appears in trustworthy sources of information, to wit:—

	Number of Killed.
1882. Destruction of Alexandria (Ann. Reg. 1882, p. 368)	2,000
Tel-El-Kebir (ditto, ditto) . .	1,000
1883. Massacre of Hick's Army (ditto, 1883, p. 389)	11,000
Attempt to relieve Sinkat (ditto, p. 391)	760
1884. Massacre of Baker's Army (Despatch to Sir E. Baring, Blue Book, Egypt, No. 12, 1884, p. 36)	2,346
El Teb (Graham's Despatch, ditto, p. 121)	900
Tamasi (ditto, ditto, p. 161) .	2,000
Total . . .	20,000

and, whether he will submit the above statement to official inspection for correction and amplification, and lay the amended statement upon the Table of the House?

THE MARQUESS OF HARTINGTON: I have referred to the authorities which are quoted in the Question, and the numbers which are given in the hon. Member's statement appear to be correctly stated from these authorities. However, except in the case of Baker Pasha's force, and the Battle of El Teb, they appear to be estimates only. We have no means in the War Office of correcting or amplifying these estimates. I do not see there would be any advantage in embodying the estimates referred to in a Parliamentary Return; but it would, of course, be open to the hon. Member to make any use he thinks fit of the information which he has compiled.

SCOTLAND—THE MUSEUM OF SCIENCE AND ART, EDINBURGH.

MR. BUCHANAN asked the First Commissioner of Works, Whether, inasmuch as by the munificence of a private benefactor all difficulties as to the allocation of the space in the new wing of the Edinburgh Museum of Science and Art are obviated, he will give instructions for the work to be begun at once?

MR. SHAW LEFEVRE: Yes, Sir; tenders will be invited for this building in a few days.

IRELAND—THE MUSEUM OF SCIENCE AND ART, DUBLIN.

MR. DAWSON asked the Secretary to the Treasury, Whether any further progress has been made in the selection of the design for the Science and Art Museum, Dublin, and how soon the arrangements are likely to be complete?

MR. COURTNEY, in reply, said, the hon. Member knew that the recommended design proved, on valuation, to involve an expenditure much above the prescribed limit. They had, therefore, been driven, in justice to the other competitors, to inquire into the other designs. Two of these could not be entertained under any circumstances; valuations were in progress as to the other two, which the Committee of Advisers had placed in order of merit. The Board of Works were considering what preliminary work could be done in anticipation of the final decision.

MR. DAWSON: What is the difference between the cost of the selected design and the sum which the Government is prepared to give?

MR. COURTNEY: I do not think it would be fair to state that until the other designs have been examined.

MR. DAWSON: Is not the hon. Gentleman aware that it is a matter of a very few thousand pounds?

MR. COURTNEY: No.

MR. DAWSON: Will the hon. Gentleman state what it is, if he knows it?

MR. COURTNEY: It is not fair to other competitors to state what this difference is.

MR. GRAY: Is it the fact that the competitors, whose designs are now under consideration, are Englishmen, and that the competitor whose design has been set aside is an Irishman? And more particularly, I wish to ask the hon. Gentleman, whether he hopes to be able to state the decision of the Treasury in this important matter before the House rises?

MR. COURTNEY: I have no information as to the nationalities of the competitors. I hope the examinations will be completed in time to announce them to Parliament.

MR. DAWSON: I wish to ask the hon. Gentleman, whether it is not the fact that this question, which concerns the education of the Irish people, has been, for the sake of a few thousand pounds, 16 years in contemplation, and has not yet been settled?

MR. COURTNEY: I have already told the hon. Gentleman that it is not a matter of a few thousand pounds.

MR. DAWSON: I ask, is it a fact that it has been 16 years in contemplation by the Government?

[No reply.]

SHIP BROKERAGE (FRANCE).

MR. CHARLES PALMER asked the Under Secretary of State for Foreign Affairs, Whether he will lay upon the Table of the House a Return of the Correspondence with Shipping Associations and Reports from the British Embassy at Paris, on the question of Ship Brokerage in France (in continuation of Parliamentary Paper, Commercial, No. 12, 1883)?

LORD EDMOND FITZMAURICE: There will be no objection to lay upon the Table the Correspondence to which my hon. Friend refers, and it will be at once prepared for publication.

MR. CHARLES PALMER asked, Whether the noble Lord would state that any more energetic steps would be taken to bring this matter, in which the commerce of this country took so great an interest, to a satisfactory conclusion?

LORD EDMOND FITZMAURICE: I can hardly admit that more energetic steps are necessary, because these negotiations have been carried on in Paris by Mr. Crowe with great ability. No doubt the matter is one of importance. It is now before the Secretary of State, and it may be advisable, if no satisfactory result is soon arrived at, to take some further steps.

METROPOLIS—STATE OF THE STREETS AT NIGHT.

MR. SAMUEL SMITH (for Mr. CROPPER) asked the Secretary of State for the Home Department, Whether his attention has been drawn to remarks made at a meeting last week of the "Central Vigilance Committee," at which His Grace the Duke of Westminster stated that the condition of certain streets of the Metropolis was "notoriously scandalous and disgraceful," for utter shamefulness "not to be equalled in the whole world;" that tradesmen "in some of the principal streets" live under what is really "a Reign of Terror," and, if they took "individual . . . . . or isolated action," they would be in fear of being boycotted; whether the powerlessness of the police in regard to this nuisance is owing to a difference of opinion on the part of the magistrates in regard to the evidence necessary to support convictions for the offence specified in Sub-Section 11 of 2 & 3 *Vict.* cap. 47, sec. 54; and, whether it may not be possible to obtain a consensus of magisterial opinion on this point?

MR. PULESTON asked, whether, in view of the unfortunate state of things arising from the suspension of the main provisions of the Contagious Diseases Act, the Government would not restore those provisions, pending the introduction of the long-promised Bill on the subject?

MR. ONSLOW asked, if the right hon. Gentleman was aware of the extent to which innocent young men and innocent old men were accosted by females in the streets?

SIR WILLIAM HARCOURT: My attention has long been directed to this subject, and I think it one of very great importance. I am glad to see, by the Question of my hon. Friend behind me (Mr. S. Smith), that he attributes a great part of the evil to the helplessness of the police in the matter. That is entirely my opinion. I believe the condition of the streets will never be made what it ought to be unless further powers are given to the police, as in Glasgow and other towns. Clauses to that effect were introduced into a Bill which passed the House of Lords, and I deeply regret that that Bill cannot pass into law this Session. It is not necessary for the Government to consider the question, because they have embodied their views in the clauses of that Bill. I am glad to see, from the Questions on the Paper, that those views will have the support of the Vigilance Committee; and, with their support, I have very little doubt that the Bill will pass into law, and will have the effect desired.

SIR R. ASSHETON CROSS said, the right hon. Gentleman had expressed the opinion that the police ought to have further powers. He entirely agreed with the right hon. Gentleman; and he wished to ask, whether he could not give effect to that view in a short Bill this Session?

SIR WILLIAM HARCOURT said, he wished he could think that a short Bill would involve a short discussion on this subject. The information he had on that point hardly encouraged him in such a hope. Short Bills sometimes took a long time in passing.

MR. PULESTON said, that the right hon. Gentleman had not answered his Question, whether something could not be done in the way of restoring the suspended powers of the Acts he had referred to, so as to prevent that condition of things which arose from the withdrawal of the police?

SIR WILLIAM HARCOURT said, that the Government did not propose to do anything of the kind referred to. They considered that the police in towns had ample powers, which they might put into operation if they chose so to do.

MR. ARTHUR O'CONNOR asked whether the right hon. Gentleman was aware that there were several large establishments in which the girls employed slept on the premises five nights in the week, but were not allowed to do so on Saturday and Sunday nights?

SIR WILLIAM HARCOURT said, he had no cognizance of that.

MR. SAMUEL SMITH asked the Secretary of State for the Home Department, Whether his attention has been called to the following extracts from a speech made by the Right honourable the Earl of Shaftesbury, at the Annual Meeting of the "Central Vigilance Committee" at Willis's Rooms on July 16th 1884:—

"There are hundreds and thousands of poor girls, as honest, good girls as ever lived, engaged in their daily occupations in London at a distance from their homes. Often, in the winter season, especially, they have to return home after dark, and they are exposed to every form of temptation. Unless you could hear from their own lips, as far as they dare communicate it to you, what they see or hear, it would seem almost too monstrous to believe. A gentleman called upon me the other day who had been in Regent Street. He said he was at the head of a very large firm, and he had in his establishment from 200 to 300 married women and young single women. He said, 'I am obliged constantly to go as far as I can with these women when they leave their work to see them safe beyond a certain point, because there are people waiting in the neighbourhood for the purpose of alluring them away, and perhaps indulging their horrid inconceivable taste by pouring the most filthy wickedness into the ears of these young girls.' That is the case with reference to one large establishment, and I have heard it with regard to others. If you want to correct the evil you must go to this male solicitation, as well as female solicitation (applause). You must create a strong public opinion, which will prevent the evil practices of these men, many of whom are in a decent position in society, and have ample means. You must prevent these men going out night by night as they do, indulging their beastly proclivities, and corrupting and dishonouring society to the utmost extent possible. You must know that circumstances have very much altered now in respect to the work of these young women, who, as I say, have to work some two or three miles away from their homes. A short time ago the hours of labour were very much limited, in some of the workshops, and they managed to get home in decent time, but now, by the permission of the Secretary of State, with the view to the relief of certain trades, the hours of labour are so prolonged that many of these poor girls cannot leave their workshops until nine or ten o'clock at night. Then they have perhaps three or four miles to go from their work to their homes. What they say is, 'so long as we can keep together we are tolerably safe, but the time comes when we must separate to go in different directions to our homes, and that is the time when we are exposed to these annoyances, too dreadful to describe.' That is the state of things in our streets;"

and, whether he is prepared to consider, during the recess, some remedy for this deplorable state of things?

SIR WILLIAM HARCOURT said, he thought he had substantially answered the Question already.

ARMY—MARRIED SOLDIERS' QUARTERS AT WOOLWICH.

BARON HENRY DE WORMS asked the Secretary of State for War, with reference to his statement that the overcrowding of the married soldiers' quarters in the Cambridge Cottages at Woolwich would at once be remedied, Whether it is the fact that, although negotiations have taken place for renting sixteen houses, in order to afford proper accommodation for the married soldiers, no result has been arrived at, and the overcrowding still continues, causing much inconvenience and danger to the health of the troops and of the inhabitants of the adjacent districts?

THE MARQUESS OF HARTINGTON: Authority has been given to the General Officer Commanding at Woolwich to hire cottages for the purpose of relieving the married soldiers' quarters; but it is necessary that the sanitary conditions of the cottages should be carefully examined before they are actually taken over. This inspection, and the consequent repairs, will be pushed on as rapidly as possible.

POST OFFICE—THE TELEPHONE COMPANIES.

Mr. JACOB BRIGHT asked the Postmaster General, When he will be able to return an answer to the Telephone Companies in regard to matters in discussion between them and the Post Office Department?

Mr. FAWCETT: The United Telephone Company and its affiliated Companies have submitted to me three different proposals, the consideration of which involves many complicated and difficult details; and I am sure it is of great importance that these proposals should be carefully considered in all their bearings. I have personally devoted all the time to their investigation I could spare, but have not yet been able to complete it. I may add that from four other licensed Companies I have not received any statement; but I have informed them that if they do not at once furnish me with one, I must decide without having their views before me. Although I cannot fix the precise day, I can but repeat the promise that there shall be no unnecessary delay; and I can assure my hon. Friend (Mr. Jacob Bright) that no one can be more anxious than I am that the question should be speedily settled.

Mr. GRAY asked whether the right hon. Gentleman expected that his decision would be pronounced before the Post Office Estimates were taken?

Mr. FAWCETT said, he should do everything he could to speedily arrive at a decision; but he felt that the interest not only of the Post Office and the public, but of the Telephone Companies themselves, required that that decision should not be a hasty one; and, therefore, he should not like to give the hon. Member a pledge.

Mr. GRAY said, that on Monday he would address a Question on the subject to the Prime Minister. He would ask whether the right hon. Gentleman was aware that a question was in dispute as to the respective rights of this House and of a Government Department to override the House's decision?

POST OFFICE (IRELAND)—THE MAILS IN CAVAN.

Mr. BIGGAR asked the Postmaster General, Is it a fact that in the town of Cavan the mail closes at six o'clock in the evening, although the train which carries it on does not start from Clones, twelve miles distant, until fifteen minutes past nine p.m. in consequence of the bags from Cavan being now sent, as they were a century ago, by a one-horse car taking two and a-half hours to make the journey, although there is direct communication between both towns by rail which could be accomplished in twenty minutes; is it also a fact that by this arrangement the towns of Arva, Killeshandra, Ballynagh, and Carrigallen have to post their evening letters in the middle of the day, from three to half-past three o'clock p.m., several other minor offices in the district being also equally inconvenienced; whether, within the past two years, the Town Commissioners of Cavan, and representative meetings of merchants, traders, bankers, and other inhabitants of the different towns mentioned, have not by memorials pointed out this great grievance more than once to him, and requested a remedy; his reply being, in one case, that the Railway Company for this short journey claimed an exorbitant price; and in the other, that the matter "would have attention;" whether it is not a fact that a train arrives from Dublin and the west at eight p.m. each evening, by which passengers cannot proceed further because of the breach in the service at this point; and, whether it is in the power of the Government to compel the Great Northern Railway Company to supply this great public service by running a train from Cavan at a quarter-past eight p.m., for mails and passengers, at a reasonable price, in connection with the arrival of the Midland Great Western train each evening, there being no difficulty in arranging for the return morning service, a train being already running, which, by a slight attention to time, can be utilized for this purpose?

Mr. FAWCETT: It is the fact that the night mail between Cavan and Clones is conveyed by cars, there being no existing trains at hours suitable for the mail service. I will have further inquiry made as to the possibility of coming to some arrangement with the Railway Company; but unless the trains could be utilized for ordinary traffic I fear the cost of running them specially for the mails would be greater than the correspondence for the district affected would warrant.

POST OFFICE (IRELAND)—THE LETTER CARRIER BETWEEN BALLYCONNELL AND DERRYLIN.

MR. BIGGAR asked the Postmaster General, Whether it is a fact that a few months ago a person named M'Mullen, who acted as letter-carrier between Ballyconnell and Derrylin, committed several breaches of trust in opening letters containing cheques, coin, etc.; whether, since M'Mullen absconded, a person named M'Garvey has for three months performed the duties; whether there was any cause of complaint against M'Garvey; and, whether it is now proposed to give the appointment to a brother of the former *employé* M'Mullen?

MR. FAWCETT: In reply to the hon. Member's Question, I beg to say that George M'Mullen, the postman referred to, was employed under an allowance to the sub-postmaster of Ballyconnell to provide for the work, and that his services were dispensed with in consequence of his not performing it satisfactorily. The suspicion which had previously fallen on M'Mullen of tampering with letters was not the cause of his losing his situation. M'Garvey has been employed by the sub-postmaster as a temporary arrangement only, pending the appointment of a permanent postman in M'Mullen's place. William M'Mullen, who has been nominated and who is about to be appointed, was strongly recommended. So far as I am able to ascertain he bears a very good character, and I do not think that the fact of his brother's performing his work unsatisfactorily ought to stand in his way.

In reply to a further Question from Mr. BIGGAR,

MR. FAWCETT said, he did not know whether the two brothers had lived in the same house; but, in consequence of the misconduct of one brother, he made special inquiries as to the conduct of the younger brother, and people in the neighbourhood informed him there was nothing whatever against his conduct.

ARMY (AUXILIARY FORCES)—MILITIA OFFICERS.

SIR FREDERICK MILNER asked the Secretary of State for War, Whether it is a fact that there are 792 vacancies for Officers in the Militia, and that some Regiments want more than half their establishment of Officers; and, whether, under these circumstances, the rule will be enforced by which Officers are retired under the age clause, particularly in Regiments where the forced retirement of Officers would cause another vacancy?

THE MARQUESS OF HARTINGTON: The actual vacancies for officers of Militia amount to 795; and in 11 regiments the vacancies amount to half the number of officers. As regards the forced retirement of Militia officers, I can only repeat the answer I gave on the 16th June to the hon. Member for Clare (Mr. O'Shea)—

"Under the Regulations now in force lieutenant-colonels retire at 55, majors and captains at 50 years of age; but in all cases officers are permitted, on the recommendation of the General Officer commanding, to serve five years longer. Having regard to the efficiency of the service and the maintenance of a fair flow of promotion, it would not, in my opinion, be desirable to suspend these Regulations."

I am not aware of any present reason for changing the opinion I then expressed. This serious deficiency is, however, under the consideration of the Department, with a view to the suggestion of some remedy if possible.

SIR FREDERICK MILNER asked whether it was worth while to spend so much money on the Militia if they were not to be maintained in an efficient state?

[No reply.]

LAW AND POLICE—ARMED BURGLARS.

SIR FREDERICK MILNER asked the Secretary of State for the Home Department, Whether, in view of the dastardly outrages recently committed by armed burglars, he will consider the advisability of immediately introducing a short Bill, giving the Judges power, on conviction, in all cases where weapons, dangerous or destructive to human life have been used, or, (if thought advisable) where they have been found on the person of the burglar, to order flogging, in addition to the punishment already provided; and, whether the punishment of flogging has been found to have a most salutary and deterrent effect, in cases of garotting and robbery with violence?

SIR WILLIAM HARCOURT: Sir, this is a matter which has often been considered, and a great deal is to be said on both sides; but I would rather not commit myself to an opinion in the negative. Certainly, the last time when it was proposed to extend to various offences the punishment of flogging, the opinion of Parliament was decidedly adverse.

GIBRALTAR AND SPAIN—EXPULSION OF SPANISH SUBJECTS.

MR. WODEHOUSE asked the Under Secretary of State for the Colonies, Whether the statement reported to have been made by the Spanish Home Minister, in the Spanish Senate, that 5,000 Spaniards had been expelled from Gibraltar in retaliation for the measures adopted by the Spanish Government to prevent an invasion of cholera, is correct?

MR. EVELYN ASHLEY: No, Sir; the action taken by the Gibraltar Government was in nowise one of retaliation, but one of necessity. There would have been, and is, no objection to admit the Spaniards as usual, did the Spanish Government allow them to return each night to Linea. This, however, the Spanish officials will not allow. They have, therefore, been kept out, as, if once admitted, they would not be allowed to return to Spanish territory, and the Government of Gibraltar would be compelled to lodge, feed, and employ these aliens, and in the event of a visitation of cholera would find the city, which is already crowded, saddled with the addition of thousands of Spanish subjects.

LAW AND JUSTICE (ENGLAND AND WALES)—ISLE OF WIGHT PETTY SESSIONS.

MR. ARNOLD MORLEY (for Mr. SEELY) asked the Secretary of State for the Home Department, Whether his attention has been called to a paragraph in the *Hampshire Independent* of the 16th instant, which states that, on the preceding Saturday, the whole business of the Isle of Wight Petty Sessions was brought to a standstill, and great inconvenience thereby sustained by the refusal of two magistrates to take their seats on the Bench, although they were within the building at the time; and, whether, if this allegation is true, he will, either himself or through the Lord Chancellor, convey to these gentlemen his disapproval of their conduct?

SIR WILLIAM HARCOURT: Before I take any official action, I should have more authentic information of the matter than is contained in a newspaper paragraph. When the circumstances are brought before me, then I shall see what should be done.

EGYPT—THE CONFERENCE.

SIR H. DRUMMOND WOLFF asked the Prime Minister, Whether the labours of the Conference had arrived at such a point that he could inform the House whether application was likely to be made to Parliament to sanction any official arrangement?

MR. GLADSTONE: No, Sir; I cannot give any information at present. The Conference met to-day, and meets again on Monday. I cannot say positively, but I am not without hope, that after that meeting on Monday I may be able to give more definite information on the subject.

ABYSSINIA—THE TREATY.

MR. M'COAN said, he wished to ask a Question as to the non-appearance of the Abyssinian Treaty. The other documents were published that morning, but the actual Treaty was not. When would it appear?

LORD EDMOND FITZMAURICE, in reply, said, he believed that Paper would be distributed in the course of the day.

LOCAL GOVERNMENT BOARD (IRELAND)—MR. J. D. ELLIOTT, RATE COLLECTOR FOR THE BLACKROCK TOWNSHIP COMMISSIONERS.

MR. SEXTON: I wish to ask the Chief Secretary to the Lord Lieutenant of Ireland, in reference to the debate which took place in Committee of Supply on Tuesday evening, during which certain pledges were given by the right hon. Gentleman, If he can now inform the House whether the Local Government Board have arrived at any decision; and, if so, what decision, as to the further employment of Rate Collector Elliott?

MR. TREVELYAN: Sir, the following letter has been received by the Under Secretary from the Blackrock Town Commissioners:—

"Blackrock Township, Secretary's Office, Town Hall, Blackrock, July 23, 1884.—Sir,—In reply to your letter of the 13th ultimo, I am directed by the Commissioners of Blackrock to state, for the information of His Excellency the Lord Lieutenant, that the reason which led the Commissioners to realize the securities given by Mr. Elliott at the time of his appointment was as follows:—Finding the rates much in arrear, the Commissioners called on Mr. Elliott for an explanation. He at once informed them that relying upon the practice which had existed ever since Blackrock became a township—namely, that a period of two years was allowed to the collector for the collection of the rates, he had retained in his hands money belonging to the Commissioners which he had collected and was then unable to pay them in cash. He made a full disclosure of the sums so retained, and handed over to the Commissioners house property, which they have reason to believe will, together with the securities referred to, cover the amount, and they obtained from him additional securities to replace those realized, and to provide for his punctuality in future. I am directed to add that the Commissioners have, of course, altered this vicious system of collection which led to these irregularities.—I have the honour to be, Sir, your obedient servant, J. M. PORTER, Secretary. To the Right Hon. G. O. Trevelyan, M.P., Chief Secretary for Ireland."

The Irish Government and the Local Government Board have no doubt whatever that Mr. Elliott ought to be removed from his office. This can be done at once by issuing a Sealed Order, under the 33rd section of the 1 & 2 *Vict.*, c. 56; but the Board of Guardians might complain of such a mode of dealing with one of their officers without communicating first with them. The Board of Guardians will accordingly be requested at their next meeting to call upon Elliott to resign, and to inform him that the Local Government Board has determined not to allow him to retain a position of trust in the Poor Law, and that they will be prepared, under the section above referred to, to remove him if he does not resign. I am sorry to make what would otherwise be a premature statement; but considering that the Blackrock Town Commissioners have practically refrained from answering our letter from the 13th June to the 23rd July, and then only did it under pressure, I should hardly be justified in taking any other course, and therefore I think Parliament is entitled to hear, at the earliest moment, our decision.

MUNICIPAL ELECTIONS (CORRUPT AND ILLEGAL PRACTICES) BILL.

MR. GLADSTONE: I wish to state, for the convenience of the House, that we are desirous of going forward with the Municipal Elections (Corrupt and Illegal Practices) Bill; and I shall therefore ask the House to go out of Committee soon after half-past 11 this evening.

MR. GRAY: I beg to ask the right hon. Gentleman, whether it is still intended to proceed with the Medical Act Amendment Bill?

MR. GLADSTONE: I hope to be able to state that to-morrow.

SIR STAFFORD NORTHCOTE: The Bill is down for Monday.

MR. GLADSTONE: Yes; but I hope to be able to state the intentions of the Government regarding it to-morrow.

ORDERS OF THE DAY.

—o—

ULSTER CANAL AND TYRONE NAVIGATION BILL.—[BILL 244.]

(*Mr. Courtney, Mr. Herbert Gladstone.*)

BILL REFERRED TO SELECT COMMITTEE.

MR. COURTNEY said, he had to inform the House that he had two alterations to make in reference to this Bill. The first was simply a Resolution, authorizing the insertion of money clauses. That was a matter of course. The other matter was—it had been found that the Bill must be referred to a mixed Committee—three Members to be nominated by the House, and two by the Committee of Selection. He should, therefore, propose to discharge the Order for Committee on next Monday, and move that it be referred to this Hybrid Committee. It would not prejudice the important provision asked for by the hon. Member for Monaghan (Mr. Healy)—prohibiting the sale of the Canal to any Railway Company—as to which he hoped to be able to arrange satisfactorily.

MR. HEALY asked if the hon. Gentleman would give any assurance as to who the Members of the Committee would be, or would this proposal in any way withdraw from the House the power of Amendment?

MR. COURTNEY, in reply, said, that when the Bill had been reported from the Committee it would be competent for the House to recommit it. As the number of the Committee was so small, no assurance could be given as to who the Members would be.

Order for Committee upon Monday next read, and *discharged.*

Bill referred to a Select Committee of Five Members, Three to be nominated by the House and Two by the Committee of Selection.

Ordered, That all Petitions against the Bill presented two clear days before the meeting of the Committee be referred to the Committee; that the Petitioners praying to be heard by themselves, their Counsel, or Agents, be heard against the Bill, and Counsel heard in support of the Bill:—Power to send for persons, papers, and records; Three to be the quorum.

SUPPLY—CIVIL SERVICE ESTIMATES.

SUPPLY—*considered* in Committee.

(In the Committee.)

CLASS III.—LAW AND JUSTICE.

(1.) £105,764, to complete the sum for Criminal Prosecutions, Sheriffs' Expenses, &c.

MR. WEST said, he wished to call attention to a matter which properly arose under this Vote. In the first place, he thought there ought to be a diminution in the amount of the Vote, seeing that there had been a considerable diminution of crime in the country during the last few years; and he thought, if certain steps were taken, which he intended to point out, the amount of the Vote might be still further reduced. The Committee would be aware that, in accordance with the recent decision which they had come to among themselves, the Judges now thought it their duty, when on Circuit, to deliver the gaols of all the Sessions' prisoners who might be in prison at the time they went on Circuit. The operation of that rule had, no doubt, very considerably increased the expense to which the country was put in connection with criminal prosecutions; and he would ask his hon. Friend the Secretary to the Treasury (Mr. Courtney) to state, if he was able to do so, what the difference was in the average charge of cases tried at the Assizes as compared with those tried at Sessions. The way in which the new rule operated was this. When a Judge went into an Assize town—and he might mention Manchester, because, as hon. Members knew, he was connected with the administration of justice in that city, and, therefore, was acquainted with what occurred there, although he had no doubt that the same thing occurred in other towns—when a Judge went into Manchester, whether the number of prisoners in gaol was large or small, he had to try them all, and the practice involved a considerably increased charge under the present rule, although he was not aware what the actual increase of expense was. His opinion, however, was that the cost of the trial of prisoners at Assizes was almost double the cost of trial at Sessions. It was obvious that it must be so. The Assize fees were heavier than those at Sessions, and the witnesses, both for and against the prisoners, were engaged for a much longer time. There was another matter which he thought deserved the attention of the Committee, and it was this—even the innovation to which he objected did not involve alone an increased expense to the Imperial Exchequer, but it also inflicted a very great hardship upon prisoners. He would give, as an illustration, a case which occurred the other day, and which happened over and over again. By the practice which the Judges adopted of trying all these prisoners at the Assizes, accompanied by the power they possessed of trying them at a central station, prisoners were frequently taken from very long distances to the Assize towns, and it was often very difficult for them to bring up their witnesses. The other day, under this arrangement, a prisoner was sent from Barrow-in-Furness all the way to Manchester to be tried. It appeared to him (Mr. West) that it was a very grea hardship upon the prisoner, even if he were guilty—for he was only a boy, and sentenced to a few days' imprisonment—to be tried in another and a distinct Division of the county of Lancaster, after having been sent, on a charge of committing some trifling offence, all the way from Barrow-in-Furness to Manchester, a distance of more than 70 miles. If he wished to call witnesses, how could he bring them up, when they might have to remain in Manchester for a week or 10 days before the trial came off? These were difficulties which arose from the new practice which had been adopted by the Judges. He was not complaining of the Judges at all, nor would he say that, under the present system of administering the law, they were not right in what they did. But the evil of which he complained was a great one; and he could not help thinking that the Government and the House of Commons ought to look into the matter, and devise some remedy for a state of things that ought not to be allowed to continue. The gentlemen serving upon the jury were also complaining of the fact that the duty of trying such offences was thrown upon them; and that was not all. The Judges themselves who had adopted this new practice were frequently found making public declarations that a great hardship was thrown upon them when they were called upon to try such cases. He, therefore, could not help thinking that some remedy ought to be considered and, if possible, adopted; for, as the matter went on, it would become more and more important. It was known that the Judges had lately entered into a bargain with the Treasury as to the scale upon which they were to be paid their Circuit expenses. What that bargain was he did not know; but he hoped to hear something about it in the discussion of the present Vote. If the newspapers were right, the public were given to understand that the expenses of the Judges during the time they were on Circuit were to be paid by the day. He was afraid that the tendency of that arrangement would be to throw a good deal of unnecessary work upon the Judges. He was not prepared to say that the Chairmen of Court of Quarter Sessions or the Recorders would shirk their own part of the duty; but where there were a body of men paid for the discharge of certain duties, and another body either not paid at all, or at a very diminished rate, somehow or other the paid body very generally got a larger share of the work than the unpaid body. Whether that would be the result in this case he was unable to say; but such a scheme would tend towards an increase of the duties of the Judges; and on the part of the Chairmen of the Courts of Quarter Sessions and the Recorders there would be no indisposition to allow the Judges to do a little more of the work, so that those who were not quite so well paid for it might do a little less. He hoped his hon. Friend the Secretary to the Treasury would be able to tell the Committee what was the difference in the average cost of trying cases at the Sessions and at the Assizes. He further trusted that his hon. and learned Friend the Attorney General (Sir Henry James) would be able to hold out some hope that a remedy would be applied to this undoubted evil, both in regard to the juries, the public, and the Judges themselves.

MR. COURTNEY said, he would leave it to his hon. and learned Friend the Attorney General to reply to the hon. and learned Gentleman (Mr. West) upon the legal aspect of the case, while he himself (Mr. Courtney) would only deal with the financial part of it; and he was afraid that, even upon that point, he was able to give his hon. and learned Friend very little information. The present system had only been in operation for little more than a-year; and, consequently, there was not much experience to go upon. Further experience, therefore, was needed, in order to ascertain how it would work. The only way in which the financial effect could be ascertained would be by comparison with the relative number of prisoners tried at the Sessions and at the Assizes, and then comparing the average cost at the Sessions with what the cost of trying prisoners at the Assizes was, together with the length of the sittings.

MR. WEST said, he did not wish to trouble his hon. Friend with the average expense; but what he would like to get at was the difference between the cost of trials at the Sessions and at the Assizes.

MR. COURTNEY said, he was afraid he was not in possession of the figures which his hon. Friend asked for. The actual cost of trials might depend very much upon various circumstances. For instance, there was the case, to which his hon. Friend had referred, in which a prisoner had been sent from Barrow-in-Furness for trial in Manchester. It was a very difficult matter to ascertain the cost of a trial, seeing that a prisoner might be detained at the Assizes for a much longer time before his trial came on than he would be at the Sessions. He would endeavour to ascertain whether any calculation of this kind could be made.

The ATTORNEY GENERAL (Sir Henry James) said, he could only state, in reference to the legal portion of the matter, that, as far as he was personally concerned, he was in favour of remitting the trial of all smaller classes of offences to the Court of Quarter Sessions. He saw no reason why they should not be tried there, instead of being sent to the Assizes. It was most important, not only in regard to the expense, but in consideration of the other important functions the Judges had to perform, that their time should not be unnecessarily wasted in the trial of trivial offences on Circuit. At present there were four Assizes, instead of the two they had formerly; and if the trials at they Court of Quarter Sessions took place immediately before the trials at the Assizes, the duties of the Judges might be relieved. If that were not so, prisoners might be left over for trial for a considerable period.

Sir R. ASSHETON CROSS said, he thought the suggestion was worth consideration whether, if there were four Assizes in the year, as he hoped there always would be now, the holding of the Quarter Sessions just before the Assizes might not be important in order to prevent what was little short of a scandal under the present arrangement? No doubt, it would be improper for the Judges to leave prisoners in gaol awaiting trial for a long period; and at present it was necessary, as a matter of law, that the Judges should effect an entire clearance of the gaols as far as possible; but if the Sessions were going to be held very shortly after the Assizes, would it be absolutely necessary, as it was under the present terms of the Commission, to effect an entire delivery of prisoners from the gaols? Was it not possible to alter the terms of the Commission, and thus get rid of the evil?

The ATTORNEY GENERAL (Sir Henry James) said, it was a moot point whether it was absolutely necessary or not that the Judges should effect an entire clearance of the gaols. He thought that the Judges had come to the conclusion that it was not absolutely essential; but the practice had been to deliver the gaols, and leave no prisoner awaiting trial.

Sir WALTER B. BARTTELOT said, that if that were the opinion of the hon. and learned Gentleman the Attorney General (Sir Henry James), he would call his attention to what happened at the Spring Assizes at Lewes this year. A certain learned Judge went down to deliver the gaols at the Assizes, and prisoners were sent to be tried both from East Sussex and West Sussex. But what happened? The Judge got through a certain portion of his work, and he then stated that he had to go somewhere else, and all the prisoners who were untried had to be taken back to gaol without trial—a thing unheard of before. From his neighbourhood all the prisoners were sent to Lewes, and the witnesses had, of course, all to attend there; and the cases ought, therefore, to have been disposed of at once. He did not blame the learned Judge, because he had no doubt that he was obliged to go somewhere else; but the fact remained that the gaols were not delivered, the cases were not tried, and the prisoners had to be taken back to Lewes again some one or two months later. He thought it a circumstance which ought not to have happened; and, therefore, he had called attention to it.

The SOLICITOR GENERAL (Sir Farrer Herschell) said, he entirely agreed with his hon. and gallant Friend opposite (Sir Walter B. Barttelot) that it was most undesirable—and he might even use a stronger expression than that—that the trial of prisoners should have been delayed in the manner described. He hoped the recent arrangements would prevent such an occurrence in future. The new arrangement prescribed that if there happened to be more work in a particular town than was expected, or more than the Judge could satisfactorily get through in the time fixed for holding the Assizes, another Judge should be sent down to his assistance from London in order to secure that the whole of the work should be got through.

Mr. H. H. FOWLER said, the recent arrangement, as they were told by the hon. and learned Attorney General (Sir Henry James), did not touch the grievances of the Judge's time being occupied in trying Court of Quarter Session cases. A scandal occurred at Wolverhampton some years ago in consequence of a Judge considering it his duty to clear the gaols. In some of the cases the parties were not ready to proceed with the prosecution; and, therefore, the Judge discharged all the prisoners, and let them loose upon society. He had in his possession a letter from the late Lord Chief Justice Cockburn, in which that learned Judge stated that in his opinion, when prisoners were sent for trial to the Court of Quarter Session, it was not the duty of the Judge of Assize to deliver the gaols. The remedy he (Mr. H. H. Fowler) would suggest was that the prisoners committed for trial to Quarter Sessions should only be tried at Quarter Sessions, and that it should not be imperative on the Judges to interfere in any way whatever. He would ask whether the Commission could not be altered so as to set the question at rest? The Commission was altered once, and altered so as to remove the difficulty; but, subsequently, on account of some difference of opinion among the Judges, it was altered back again to the old form, thus bringing about the same difficulty and expense.

MR. WEST said, that the difficulty just alluded to by his hon. Friend the Member for Wolverhampton (Mr. H. H. Fowler) reminded him (Mr. West) that before the Judicature Act was passed the Commission issued for the county of Lancaster was in a different form from that issued for the other counties in the country. It was issued in such form that the Judges were not required to deliver the gaols. He might call to the attention of his hon. and learned Friend the Attorney General a circumstance which had happened within his own knowledge. Within the last year an Assize had been put off because the Sessions had been fixed for two days after the date proposed for the Assizes; and if the Assizes had been held on the proposed day, the Judges would have had to have tried all the Sessions' prisoners.

GENERAL SIR GEORGE BALFOUR asked for information in reference to the examination of the accounts under this Vote before the Comptroller and Accountant General.

MR. COURTNEY said, it was impossible for the Treasury to enter into a detailed examination of the accounts which were sent in by the local authorities, when payment of the expenses actually incurred was ordered.

GENERAL SIR GEORGE BALFOUR said, he knew that perfectly well; but he wanted to know how the various charges in the accounts were examined, and by whom?

MR. COURTNEY said, he could only state that the gross amount paid over to the local authorities would be about £150,000.

Vote *agreed to.*

(2.) £289,822, to complete the sum for the Supreme Court of Judicature.

MR. ARTHUR ARNOLD said, that he was himself in full sympathy with the proposal for continuous sittings, and he also agreed with the doctrine laid down by Jeremy Bentham—and he was glad to see a strong disciple of Bentham on the Treasury Bench in the person of his hon. Friend the Financial Secretary (Mr. Courtney)—that a law tax—that was an undue cost of law—was the worst of all forms of taxation. He did not propose to move the Amendment for the reduction of this Vote which stood in his name; but he would now address himself to a statement recently made by the Lord Chancellor in reply to a deputation from the county of Lancaster. The Lord Chancellor, referring to the Chancery Court of the Duchy of Lancaster, expressed an opinion that it might be possible to constitute that Court a portion of the Supreme Court of Judicature; but that a material element in the case would be the disposition, on the part of the locality, to find the necessary funds. A Return moved for last year had been produced, showing the surplus fees of the Palatine Court; and he would ask his hon. and learned Friend the Attorney General (Sir Henry James) whether he could say what the position of the public in the county of Lancaster was in regard to the surplus fees, which amounted to about £80,000? The Lord Chancellor, in reference to the Supreme Court, said that the matter was going to be made clear by a new Order as to the process of trying Admiralty and Chancery cases on the spot. He wished to know if the hon. and learned Gentleman the Solicitor General or the Attorney General could give any explanation of that new Order, and what would be the arrangements after it was issued in reference to the Assizes held at Manchester and Liverpool, because the Lord Chancellor did not make it clear whether, in the event of the business not being completed, for instance, at Manchester, the Judge would return from Liverpool to Manchester in order to deal with the unfinished business. He understood that morning that the Judge now sitting at Manchester had ordered a delay of the Commission for Liverpool, until he had completed the business at Manchester. He thought that was a perfectly fair arrangement, and he had no question to put in regard to it; but he hoped the hon. and learned Solicitor General would be able to give some information on the other point.

THE SOLICITOR GENERAL (Sir FARRER HERSCHELL) said, he was unable to state what form the Order would take. He knew, however, that it was proposed to provide for the hearing, both at Manchester and Liverpool, of Chancery cases that were entered for trial locally, and the Judges would go to Manchester and Liverpool to try Chancery cases at certain stated times. With regard to Admiralty cases, they often involved a great deal of expense; and it was frequently found that the arrangements that were found suitable for the hearing of Chancery cases were not at all suitable for the hearing of Admiralty cases, inasmuch as it was desirable to fix a day for the latter cases, when it was possible to get the witnesses to attend. There would always be a difficulty, therefore, in sending anyone down to try Admiralty cases locally; and he was unable to say how it was proposed to deal with them; but, as regarded Chancery cases, it was proposed that the Judges should go both to Manchester and Liverpool in order to to try them in those cities.

SIR HENRY HOLLAND said, he wished to call the attention of the Committee to the Writ Department of the Central Office of the Supreme Court. Last year a complaint was made by the hon. Member for Burnley (Mr. Rylands) that the number of clerks in this Department was too large, and the expense too great, for the work that had to be done; and he (Sir Henry Holland) was disposed to concur in that view. It was then stated, in reply, that new arrangements were to be made, which would tend to reduce the Staff, at all events, the expense of the Department. But he observed that the contrary was the case; for, in the present Estimate, there was an increase of £494 in respect of the first and second class clerks, and, admitting the decrease of £200 in respect of the third class clerks, there still remained an increase of £294 in lieu of the promised decrease. He desired to know the reason of this increase; and whether it was probable that the new arrangements would soon lead to a decrease? He desired to put another question to the Government in respect of this Vote. It was stated last year, during a discussion, that the reason why the arrears in the Chancery Division of the Supreme Court were so much larger than in the Common Law Division was that the business was greater because the scale of costs in the Chancery Division was 30 per cent higher than in the Common Law Divisions, but that new rules were being made, or to be made, to equalize the scale of fees in all the Divisions. He wanted to know whether such rules had been made; and whether, if they had been made, they had been sufficiently long in operation to enable the Government to judge whether the effect of them has been to equalize the business and arrears in the Chancery and Common Law Divisions?

MR. R. T. REID said, he would suggest that Probate and Divorce cases, as well as Chancery and Admiralty cases, might be tried in Lancashire, and also in other centres throughout the country. It was notorious to those who were familiar with the practice of the Probate and Divorce Court that the expenses were very heavy, and that a great part of them were incurred by reason of the large number of witnesses who were brought up to London and kept in attendance for a long time. If they were about to send Judges to such centres as Lancashire, to try Chancery and Admiralty cases, he did not see why they should not extend the jurisdiction to other classes of cases. If it was desirable to try Chancery and Admiralty cases at Manchester and Liverpool, there was no reason why Probate and Divorce cases might not also be tried, and the expense of sending witnesses to London saved; nor did he see why the number of centres should not be increased, and, for example, jurisdiction given to try cases at Bristol, Plymouth, and York. It seemed to him that a considerable amount of economy might be produced by increasing the number of centres they now had.

MR. GREGORY said, that in regard to the question raised by the hon. Member for Salford (Mr. Arthur Arnold), he was in favour of trying cases on the spot, and of allowing the Judges to sit until all the cases were disposed of, making provision that, as far as possible, they should be tried locally; but, although that applied to Chancery as well as Common Law cases, there was very considerable doubt whether Admiralty cases should not be exempted from the general rule of trying cases locally. Admiralty cases required a special jurisdiction. There were very few Judges who were qualified to try Admiralty cases, and there were only a limited number of the members of the Bar who were qualified to conduct them. They required a special training, and a special knowledge. Therefore, he thought the Admiralty jurisdiction would form an exemption to the general rule, although he admitted that facilities should be given for trying Chancery cases locally. He had not risen, however, to make a comment upon that question, but upon the more general one which was involved in the present Vote. The Vote itself was one of very considerable magnitude and of great importance; and what he wished to call the attention of the Committee to was the very large contributions to the Vote which were received from the suitors. He thought the Committee were hardly aware of how much of the expense fell upon the suitors. It would be found that the total Vote amounted to £492,000; and if hon. Members would look at the foot-note they would find that no less a sum than £409,000 was contributed by suitors towards that expenditure; so that, practically, the suitors provided nearly the whole of the expenditure they were now dealing with. He confessed that he was one of those who very much agreed with the principle that the administration of justice was a matter of common right to which everyone was entitled; and it was hard enough for a man to come into Court to defend his rights, without being subjected to a heavy pecuniary fine. A suitor, in many instances, was not only fighting his own cause, but was very frequently engaged in getting a general principle of law laid down and in settling a case for the public advantage. He was afraid it was a little too late to alter the principle which guided the general admininistration of the country now, because for many years past the suitors had been dealt with in a different way; but, at all events, he had a right to ask, on behalf of the suitors, that they should not be subjected to any further burdens. He called attention to this question because, very recently, a very considerable imposition had been put upon the suitors in the shape of the increased fees they were required to pay. He did not wish to trouble the Committee with details of the figures. A Return had been laid upon the Table of the House, and from that Return it would be seen that it amounted to something like £30,000 or £40,000 a-year. It was provided, under the new Rules, that when any discovery was required, or any interrogatories made, the parties requiring the information should be bound to deposit £5 for costs. He had protested against the Rule on more than one occasion. No doubt, it was all very well to limit interrogatories or frivolous applications; but he thought that might be done if proper attention were paid to the nature of them, and he did not think that the imposition of a heavy fine upon the suitor was the proper way of limiting such applications. It was found that for every £5 deposited there was an average expenditure of £2 15*s*. for paying in the amount and obtaining a payment of it out of Court; so that every suitor who deposited £5 for a discovery or an interrogatory, had to pay £50 per cent of that amount for the information he required. He trusted that some alteration would be made, so that the practice might be got rid of altogether. He had reason to think that it was altogether unnecessary. With regard to the alteration of the fees generally by the Commission appointed to revise them, their principle with respect to these fees had been to place all of them upon what was called the higher scale. There were formerly two scales of fees, according to the amount involved—one in regard to claims under £1,000, and the other to claims above that amount. But recently, under the new Rules, all these fees had been levelled up, and all of them assessed upon the higher scale. That, however, was not all, because fees *ad valorem* were levied on sales under this Court; and any property sold, purchased, or mortgaged under an Order of the Court became subject to a new imposition of this nature. He hoped these matters would receive attention and correction, and he protested most earnestly against any additional fees being thrown upon the suitors. He thought they were already sufficiently heavily taxed for the administration of justice. No doubt, the Judges' salaries were thrown upon the Consolidated Fund, and the suitors were not called upon to pay for their services; but, as the question now stood, all the rest of the cost was thrown upon the suitors. It was an unduly heavy tax upon the administration of justice, which was a common interest, and ought to be borne in some measure by the community at large. He did not see why the accumulations of the fees contributed by suitors might not be made use of in cheapening the cost of the administration of justice, and he hoped to have some assurance from the Law Officers of the Crown that the matter would receive attention. He saw no reason why the accumulated fund should not be permitted to be used for the benefit of suitors in the Court, which would put an end to a considerable amount of that taxation which, at the present moment, was found to be extremely onerous.

MR. H. H. FOWLER said, he would not attempt to follow his hon. Friend the Member for Salford (Mr. Arthur Arnold) in discussing whether Jeremy Bentham was right or wrong in regard to imposing the cost of justice upon the country. A good deal had happened since Bentham wrote upon that question, and he did not think the Committee would be prepared to accept Bentham's views on many questions, and especially in reference to the administration of justice. He thought the latter part of his hon. Friend's speech answered the former part of it. He did not see, upon principle, why the general taxpayer should pay for the litigation into which other people entered. Why should a man who wanted a divorce get it for nothing, and throw the expense upon the public, who already contributed something towards the general expense of keeping up the admininistration provided by the Divorce Court? A very large sum was charged upon the Consolidated Fund in the shape of salaries, which did not fall upon the suitors at all. Although that sum did not appear in the present Vote, there was a Memorandum which showed what it was; so that it was evident the fees did not balance themselves as accurately as the hon. Member for East Sussex (Mr. Gregory) thought; and he (Mr. H. H. Fowler) was not prepared to urge upon his hon. Friend the Secretary to the Treasury (Mr. Courtney) the propriety of decreasing the fees. He had great confidence, however, that the hon. Gentleman would not decrease them; and he was sure that if he attempted to impose the burden upon the taxpayers he would meet with a strong, vigorous, and successful opposition. Much of the business of the Courts was administrative, and not contentious, and it was absurd to contend that the persons interested should not bear the burden. He wished to ask for information upon a point which had been referred to by the hon. Baronet the Member for Midhurst (Sir Henry Holland)—namely, the staff of the Central Court. He had a letter in his pocket which he would not trouble the Committee by reading; but if the statements contained in it were true, it was quite clear that a vigorous investigation was required into the whole of the administration of the Central Court. He had understood his hon. and learned Friend the Solicitor General to promise last year that such an investigation should take place. He did not know whether the hon. Gentleman the Secretary to the Treasury had had his attention called to the Return which appeared in *The Times* almost week by week in reference to bills of sale. Two years before the Act of 1882 they reached about 60,000 a-year. That Act was passed under the recommendations of a Committee over which the hon. and learned Gentleman the Attorney General presided, and last year the number was reduced from 60,000 to 11,000; but he did not see that there had been any reduction in the cost of the Bills of Sale Office. On the contrary, he found it was costing just as much now there were only 11,000 bills of sale registered, as it did when there were 60,000 to register. He would also ask what control there existed over what might be called the inner life of the Courts of Justice? If hon. Members turned to Page 212 of the Estimates, they would find that there was an extrardinary staff of ushers, messengers, porters, &c.; altogether, about 200 persons were engaged in the Courts of Justice, costing the country nearly £20,000 a-year. He believed there were about 19 or 20 Courts. No doubt the building was a very large one; but he found that there were 10 ushers and messengers attached to the Central Office; 21 to the Chancery Division; 21 to the Queen's Bench Division; 29 to the Probate, Divorce, and Admiralty Office; seven to the Bankruptcy Department; while the sub-divisions had also a large draft of their own. Who was responsible for the employment of so many persons about the Courts? Who saw that they discharged their supposed duties? And who controlled the time they devoted to them? He thought the whole of the Central Courts ought to be placed under the control of some Department of the Government—the First Commissioner of Works, or some other person, who should be responsible for the work done and for the salaries paid. It was also desirable that something more should be known as to the intentions of the Government in regard to the working of the Judicature Act, which had now been in force for something like 10 years, and for the carrying out of which £500,000 had been voted. He was expressing almost the unanimous opinion of the Legal Profession, when he said that the administration of justice was never in a more unsatisfactory state than it was at present. In fact, they were in a perfect state of general chaos. What was wanted was economical justice, and quick justice; but they got neither. Matters were getting daily worse and worse; they were continually trying fresh experiments, but they did not go to the matter root and branch. They were always trying stop-gap Acts of Parliament—trying to put new wine into old bottles, with the result that the bottles burst and the wine was wasted. That had been the course pursued during the last 10 years. There was no man more capable or more competent than his hon. and learned Friend the Attorney General to deal with the matter, and if he would deal with it in the same manner as he had dealt with corrupt practices, he would find that the House of Commons were prepared to support him. He was quite aware of the opposition that would be raised; but their forefathers had surmounted the opposition of Lord Eldon and those who agreed with him in those days, and he thought the hon. and learned Gentleman would receive general support now. The business of Law Reform at the present moment was increasing the cost of law and delaying the administration of justice.

THE ATTORNEY GENERAL (Sir HENRY JAMES) thanked the hon. Member for Wolverhampton (Mr. H. H. Fowler) for the complimentary way in which he had spoken of him; but he could not quite admit that the present state of things in respect of legal procedure was worse than it had ever been.

MR. H. H. FOWLER said, his remarks applied principally to the Chancery Division.

THE ATTORNEY GENERAL (Sir HENRY JAMES) said, they were apt to conclude that things never could have been so bad as they found them. They were apt to forget evils which had been got rid of; and he imagined that if they could go back to the state of things which existed under Lord Eldon's rule in the Chancery Courts, and in regard to the administration of justice generally, it would be found that a much greater cause of complainst existed than could be found now. He did not for one moment suggest that the present system was by any means perfect, and that there were not considerable causes of complaint; but his hon. Friend would agree with him that changes made for the sake of change were in themselves to be avoided. If they unsettled procedure, or unsettled existing regulations, out of consideration for the suitors and the expenses which had to be borne by them, they might bring about evils greater than those which they remedied. They had lately introduced new Rules, the operation of which had not yet been tested, and it would be somewhat premature, therefore, to hold out a promise of any further change at present. No one knew the difficulty of effecting changes in their legal procedure unless they had practically undertaken them. Unless they could get a concurrence of opinion among those who were intrusted with the responsibility of administering justice, the introduction of small changes would not only be dangerous in itself, but were very apt to be overborne. He did not think that any great change could now be introduced in the direction of legal reform with any beneficial result. As far as he could ascertain, the Lord Chancellor and the Judges were doing their best to increase the public satisfaction with the administration of the law. As for the minor officials about the new Law Courts, there was not one person too many for the work that had to be done. Any person who was in the habit of constantly attending the Courts would know that there was not one person employed there more than was absolutely required. The interests of the public required protection. There was an immense number of rooms in the Courts containing very valuable property and valuable papers, which it was impossible to leave unguarded. The public and the juries needed protection and direction. Formerly, they had great assistance from the police. The police in Westminster Hall acted in aid of the ushers of the Court, and gave most valuable assistance. They took charge of the passages leading to the Courts, and directed persons who were required to be in attendance upon the Courts. All that was now done away with, and all the work was thrown upon the official staff. Therefore the number, large as it appeared to be upon the Paper, was impossible to be reduced.

Mr. WARTON said, he wished to call the attention of the hon. and learned Attorney General to a matter to which he (Mr. Warton) had already directed attention, but unfortunately without success. He alluded to the want of economy in regard to Clerks of Assize. At Page 209 of the Estimates, he found that there was a clerk appointed to the South-Eastern Circuit at £950 a-year. They knew perfectly well that what was called the South-Eastern Circuit was a combination of four out of five counties in the Home Circuit and part of the Norfolk Circuit. It was quite natural that so long as the old clerk of the Norfolk Circuit lived, he should be continued to be paid his salary; but he thought there should be an undertaking that, in the event of the death or resignation of either one or the other of these gentlemen, one clerk would in future be sufficient for the whole Circuit. He found that one Associate did for the whole Circuit, and one Clerk of Indictments, and why should there be more than one Clerk of Assize? As a matter of fact, the counties were taken in a certain regular order following one after another. There was, consequently, no clashing of places, and the same gentleman could go from town to town throughout the whole Circuit. When the question was last raised the hon. and learned Attorney General seemed to think that this reckless expenditure should be continued for ever; but his hon. and learned Friend might have changed his opinion since, and he would therefore ask him whether, in the event of a vacancy arising, he would arrive at the conclusion that there was only a necessity for retaining the services of one officer? The other point he wished to refer to, was the secret bargain between the Judges and the Treasury. Whether it was a dignified matter to enter into a bargain at all, he would not venture to inquire; probably, the Judges knew what was best for them to do. It had not been formally stated to the House, but it had leaked out somehow or other, that the sum of £15 15*s.* a-day was to be paid to each Judge on account of his expenses on Circuit. As an ordinary rule, the Judges received £4,500 a-year, and, being allowed £500 for their Circuit expenses, they had in reality £5,000. Then putting the salary at £5,000 a-year, why, in addition, should they have £15 15*s.* a-day? The bargain might be a fair and honourable one both for the Judges and the Treasury to enter into; but when he came to Page 215 of the Estimates, he could not find any item that led him to suppose that any allowance of this kind was made. The Estimate appeared to have been passed without any consideration of the effect of the change. There seemed to be an addition in the aggregate of £350; and he should like to know if that item went in any way to make up this increase, or, if not, where the increase was explained? It was possible that the Estimate was drawn up before the arrangement was made, and, if that were so, they might probably be told that there would be a Supplementary Estimate. He certainly did not see in the Vote any sort of an Estimate for this £15 15*s.* a-day. Therefore, he should be grateful for an explanation.

Mr. LABOUCHERE said, he had no doubt that all this legal work could be done for about one-half of the present charge, not because the Judges objected to any reform, but because there were a great many lawyers in the House, and so long as the House contained so large a number of legal Gentlemen they would naturally get up to defend almost any abuse which gave a salary to a lawyer. He was agreeably surprised to find his hon. Friend the Member for Wolverhampton (Mr. H. H. Fowler) suggest that there should be an inquiry. He could assure his hon. Friend that he was quite a *rara avis* among the legal Gentlemen of the House, who naturally looked after "NumberOne." He wanted to know something about Masters in Lunacy and the Visitors in Lunacy. He believed that last year there was a sum of £80,021 spent on the Masters in Lunacy; and, besides that, two sums of £10,275 and £5,895 for the Commissioners of Lunacy. There was a strong feeling in the country that something ought to be done in regard to the law affecting supposed lunatics. He did not know if the Visitors in Lunacy visited private asylums; but recent events showed that persons could be taken up upon what he might term "bogus" certificates, put in asylums, and kept there without being visited by any independent official. He did not complain that the Vote was too large; he almost thought it was too small, considering the large number of lunatics there were about. He thought that, if necessary, some kind of legislation should take place. He should also like to have some information with reference to the Petty Bag Office. The salaries and expenses of that Office amounted to £1,400, and, recently, when he put a Question to his hon. and learned Friend the Attorney General, he was informed that the hon. and learned Gentleman knew nothing about it. Perhaps the hon. and learned Gentleman the Solicitor General would be able to enlighten the Committee on the subject? It was perfectly true that a year or two ago some moderate services were performed by these officials; but he understood that they were not performed now, as they had been abolished by the changes introduced into the law. Nevertheless, the salaries were still being paid. He also desired to know why the item of £225 for the Preacher of the Rolls Chapel was allowed to appear on the Estimates? What did this Preacher do? He had never heard of the Rolls Chapel, and he had never heard of a Preacher until he found that the country was called upon to pay £225 a-year for him. There was an Established Church in this country, possessing very large funds, and he did not see that it was for the benefit or good of anyone that they should vote money in order that this Preacher should preach in the Rolls Chapel, probably to no congregations.

MR. TOMLINSON said, he wished to make a few observations in reference to the question of fees. The charge for the administration of justice amounted to £490,852; whereas £409,000 were received from fees, in addition to other items, which brought the total sum up to £464,000. The charge upon the Consolidated Fund included the whole cost of the Judges for criminal as well as civil business; and the Vote now under consideration included a sum of £41,000 from the District and Probate Registries. He thought he was correct in saying that those District and Probate Registries were kept chiefly engaged on work connected with the proving of wills. He did not think they undertook any contentions matters, or any work that corresponded with the usual work of the Registrars of the Courts of Justice. Therefore, that sum of £41,000, together with half the judicial charge on the Consolidated Fund, as representing the criminal portion of the duties of the Judges, ought to be deducted; and he found that there would still be a profit upon the administration of justice, which, he thought, was a state of things which ought not to exist. Certainly, if the country allowed its administrative work in connection with justice to be paid for by fees, it was not desirable that they should make a profit out of it. The form in which the Estimates were produced afforded them no opportunity of knowing what portion of the fees belonged to the different branches of the administration of justice; but he noticed that the Chancery fees came to £380,000, so that a very large portion of the contributions towards the cost came from the Chancery Division. He was strongly impressed by the fact that the country derived a considerable profit out of the business of the Chancery Division. This was not a state of things that ought to be allowed, and, at all events, they ought to have some mean of ascertaining whether it was so or not. If it were really the fact, regulations ought to be carried out to diminish the fees in that branch of legal procedure It certainly could not be fair to charge the Chancery suitors with any portion of the cost of Common Law business. Another serious grievance on the part of the Chancery suitors was the great delay which arose in the conduct of business. He believed the main cause was the excessive amount of work in the Chief Clerk's office, and he would suggest that, where necessary, additional Chief Clerks should be appointed. He believed that additions might be made without any actual cost to the country. The fees from the additional amount of business transacted would pay for the extra cost. With reference to the proposal to allow Chancery cases to be heard locally in the county of Lancashire, he thought it would be regarded as a satisfactory one as far as it went. He would, however, reiterate what he had said before on the Bill of the hon. Member for Liverpool (Mr. Whitley), that the only satisfactory way of dealing with the Chancery business of Lancashire would be to incorporate in some way the Chancery Court of the County Palatine with the High Court of Justice. The County Palatine Court had, at present, its local Registries, and a perfect establishment for administration. Its only defect was, that it was limited by localities. If that limit were abolished, and if the cases could be dealt with in that Court, either in London or in the locality, he believed a great advantage would arise.

Mr. ARTHUR O'CONNOR said, the hon. Member for Northampton (Mr. Labouchere) seemed to think that lawyers in that House were always in favour of increasing legal charges. He had said that they did that in the interest of "Number One," and then the hon. Gentleman went on to propose that there should be an increase in the cost of the administration of the Lunacy Law. He (Mr. Arthur O'Connor) did not know whether the hon. Member, in regard to that, was actuated by the same sort of motive. With regard to several subjects which had already been brought before the Committee, he believed they furnished good and substantial grounds for carefully discussing the Vote from beginning to end. He remembered three years ago, when he was able to obtain a detailed examination of the Vote, that after a long struggle, he succeeded in inducing the Government to reduce the Vote, because it was discovered that they had actually charged for some office that did not exist. They had charged, for instance, for four Official Referees, when only three were in existence. He believed there four Official Referees in existence now; but whether the hundreds of officers who were charged for in the present Vote were really in existence, he very much doubted. Before the Judicature Act was passed, and before the fusion of the Court of Common Pleas, the Court of Queen's Bench, and the Court of Exchequer, there was a Master in each Division respectively in charge of the discipline of the Office; but since the fusion into one Central Court, it was very hard, indeed, to find out who was responsible for the discipline and for the official staff. The official staff was now enjoying an independent and easy life, which was very remarkable. He was credibly informed that the number of officials who were present in the Court at the present day were very much below the establishment. A large number were constantly on leave, thus reducing the staff to such an attenuated form, that those who had occasion to go to the different offices, found it difficult to get their business transacted. He also thought that the distribution of officials in the different offices since the fusion might, with advantage, be revised. Some observations had been made in reference to the Writ Appearance and Judgment Department; but although the charge in the Vote for the officials in that Department was high in proportion to their number, he did not think the number of officials was too great. In fact, he fancied that that particular Department was undermanned and short-handed. They were not paid enough for the work they had to do; but in regard to the other Departments, he certainly thought the staff ought to be overhauled and reduced. He could not see what the Chief Remembrancer's Department wanted with two first and two second class clerks. He did not see what work there was for so many officials, and he thought the Office might be advantageously inquired into and recast. Last year he had directed the attention of the hon. and learned Gentleman the Attorney General to the Taxing Officers. Every year there was a large number of cases which might be closed, but which were kept open for months, because the taxing of the costs could not be proceeded with, owing to the fact that the Taxing Officers were away during the Vacation. He thought it was not too much to ask, in the interests of the great body of suitors, that there should be some continuation of sittings in the Taxing Office, so that costs might be taxed without the suits being kept open for months after the close of the sittings. He could not help feeling, in regard to the arrears in the Courts, that more Judges ought to be appointed. If the Government were not inclined to increase the number of Judges, he would venture to suggest a very easy and cheap expedient that would relieve the difficulty, without increasing the expense. In England, there were not enough Judges; whereas, in Ireland, there were too many. If they would increase the English Judges by three, four, or five, the Irish people would make no complaint whatever if they availed themselves of the existing staff in that country.

MR. MACFARLANE said, that some three years ago he had called the attention of the hon. and learned Gentleman the Attorney General to the question of the Taxing Masters in Chancery, and the delay which took place in the taxation of costs. The hon. and learned Gentleman admitted the grievance, and promised that the matter should be inquired into. He supposed the matter had been looked into; but no change had been made. He had had cases sent to him in which sometimes the taxing of the costs took up a longer period of time than the original suit. The Taxing Master appointed an hour, say, at the beginning of May, and half of the hour was wasted while the parties awaited the arrival of the Taxing Master. Then, after six weeks or two months, he appointed another hour; and so matters went on with the result that the life was worried out of the poor suitor before he succeeded in having the case settled. This was a question in which the lawyers themselves had no direct interest. He did not think they cared anything about it, and therefore he did not think they would oppose a reform in this particular branch. He was sure that if the hon. and learned Gentleman the Solicitor General could see his way to facilitating the taxing of costs, he would do a great deal to benefit the wretched suitors who were kept in suspense under the present system. He saw in the Vote an item of £20,000 for the fees of Taxing Masters, and he was afraid that either their attendance was insufficient, or that they were too few in number. If they required more men to do the work effectively, he did not think it was good economy to grudge the money. He did not understand that that was really the case; but if, on the contrary, it was the system that was in fault, the hon. and learned Solicitor General would do good service by looking into the mattter.

MR. WAUGH said. he had to complain of the cost of the Bankruptcy Division. Last year they voted for that purpose £34,537, and this year the Vote amounted to £94,712, being an increase of more than £60,000. They would shortly be required to vote a further sum of £40,000, making the total increase £100,000, together with £20,000 for Non-Effective Services, owing to the changes which had formerly and lately been carried out in the Court of Bankruptcy. He thought that was a most extraordinary charge, considering that the Court of Bankruptcy in Ireland only cost £10,000, the Supreme Court in Ireland £90,000, and that the charge for Law and Justice in Scotland was £62,000, making altogether £162,000; whereas, in England, the Court of Bankruptcy cost nearly as much. It certainly appeared to be extraordinary that in Ireland and Scotland the Court of Bankruptcy and the administration of Justice together, could be maintained for a sum little more than the cost of the Bankruptcy Court in this country.

MR. GREGORY said, that the Taxing Masters were a very highly qualified and hard-worked class. They did the work not only in their offices, but a good deal of it at home, in order to facilitate the interests of the public. If there was more delay than was desired, it was not the fault of the Masters, nor was it due to any want of exertion on their part. At certain periods of the year there was very great pressure upon them, but they were most anxious to facilitate the work.

MR. COURTNEY stated that the next vacancy in the Office of the Petty Bag would not be filled up. He did not say that the Office would be abolished, but there would be a re-arrangement of the duties. The hon. and learned Member for Bridport (Mr. Warton) had called attention to what he called the "secret bargains" between the Judges and the Exchequer with respect to their expenses while on Circuit. He thought the hon. and learned Member must have overlooked a Memorandum which was laid on the Table some months ago, giving full particulars of this arrangement. The sum, however, was not £15 15*s.* a-day, but very much less. As to the Masters in Lunacy, the remarks of the hon. Member for Northampton (Mr. Labouchere) ought to have been addressed to the Lunacy Commissioners. He was astonished at the ignorance of the hon. Member in regard to the Preacher of the Rolls Chapel. One of the greatest of English Divines had been Preacher at the Rolls Chapel. It was there that Bishop Butler preached his great sermon on Human Nature. He might say for himself that he had very frequently attended that Chapel and listened to this Preacher, when Sir John Romilly was Master of the Rolls. The hon. Members for Carlow (Mr. Macfarlane) and Queen's County (Mr. Arthur O'Connor) had spoken of the action of the Taxing Masters, to which the hon. Member for East Sussex (Mr. Gregory) had given a reply. He could only add that some improvement in the working of that Office might be looked forward to. The functions of the Queen's Remembrancer were not so light as were imagined, but a considerable amount of work occupying a considerable amount of time was transacted in that Office.

MR. J. W. LOWTHER said, he had a few remarks to make on the items for the payment of the Marshals. He was aware that, under a Treasury Minute of the 26th of June this year, a new arrangement had been entered into with respect to those officers which, as far as he knew, was a satisfactory one. It was rather to the manner of payment than the amount of the charge that he took exception. He understood that the Judge who took his Marshal with him, made a Return to the Treasury, and that the Treasury on receipt of it gave him a warrant. Now, he believed it was notorious that in the case of one Judge on the Bench, it was his habit to give the appointment of Marshal to his son or some relative, and to take some other person with him on Circuit to do the work. That, in his opinion, was a state of things which ought not to be allowed to continue, and he thought that the Treasury ought to make it obligatory upon the Marshals to state that the payment made was to the person who had done the work. If that rule were established, he believed that the practice to which he had alluded would cease.

THE SOLICITOR GENERAL (Sir FARRER HERSCHELL) said, with reference to the inquiries of the hon. Member for Wolverhampton (Mr. H. H. Fowler) and the hon. Baronet the Member for Midhurst (Sir Henry Holland) as to the salaries of the clerks in the central office and the amount of work done there, he would recall to the recollection of those hon. Members what he had stated last year upon the subject, and on an occasion prior to that. A Committee had been appointed by the late Lord Chancellor, of which he (Sir Farrer Herschell) was a Member, to consider the question as to what would be done in respect of the central office under the Judicature Act. That Committee made such recommendations as appeared to them right upon the knowledge which they then possessed. But their view on the whole was, that it would be impossible to determine what would be the real number of clerks required in the central office, until experience had shown the amount of work and how the subject ought to be dealt with, which could only be arrived at when the whole establishment was at work. That being so, he would, in due course, call the attention of the Lord Chancellor to the question whether the time had not arrived for inquiry, in order to ascertain the extent of the duties performed in the central office. He pointed out to the Committee that where it was necessary to deal with a number of offices of this description, it was impossible, until the old officials ceased to exist, to get the arrangements into the shape desired—a condition of things which could only be reached at a more remote period. With regard to the observations of the hon. Gentleman the Member for East Sussex (Mr. Gregory), he begged to remind him that the matter to which he had referred was brought forward on the Courts of Judicature Bill, when he had stated that the question as to some of the fees should be considered, because he thought that a case had been made out for inquiry. The question was, whether the fees were not dealt with too much as a whole in certain matters; whether a more careful classification might not be made; whether fees, which in one class of cases might be reasonable, were not equally reasonable in another class of cases; and whether fees might not be separated, instead of being, as was now the case, classed together? He was prepared to admit that there might be some inequality existing in this matter, and he quite agreed with his hon. Friend that it would be possible, without diminishing the amount raised by taxation of the suitor, to make some readjustment by which a more equitable arrangement could be arrived at. With regard to the work of the Taxing Masters, he at once admitted that there was delay in the case of some of those officers, at all events. There had come within his own observation delays which ought not to have occurred. Very recently, a case had come under his observation in which an altogether inordinate time was consumed in the taxation of a bill of costs which the solicitor was most anxious to get taxed as soon as possible. He agreed that such delays should not take place, and he would urge the matter on the attention of the Lord Chancellor.

MR. TOMLINSON said, he should like the hon. and learned Gentleman the Solicitor General to answer one question. Were the Government going to take into consideration the block in the Chancery Division, with a view to remedying it, either by increasing the number of clerks to the Judges, or by other means?

THE SOLICITOR GENERAL (Sir FARRER HERSCHELL) said, that the Government had taken one step—a considerable one—in the direction indicated by the hon. Member for Preston. They had relieved the Chancery Judges from going Circuit, and retained them exclusively for the duties of the Chancery Division. He believed that arrangement would be found to constitute a considerable addition to the power of the Court. The increase of the number of Chancery clerks was another matter, and it deserved consideration, because he thought that the block in Chambers was, perhaps, more pressing than in the Court itself.

MR. LABOUCHERE said, he must ask the hon. Gentleman the Secretary to the Treasury (Mr. Courtney) why such considerable differences existed in the amount of salaries paid in respect of the various District Probate Registries? It appeared by the Estimate that, amongst others, the salary of the Registrar at Birmingham was £800; at Carlisle, £700; at Exeter, £1,000; at Lichfield, £800; at Northampton, £250; and at Wakefield, £1,200. The assignment of these salaries appeared to him to be made quite irrespective of the size of the places where the District Registries were situated, because, for some of the smaller districts, more money was paid than for the larger districts. For instance, Birmingham was a large district. [Mr. COURTNEY: No.] Was he to understand that the Birmingham district was smaller than the Wakefield district? The arrangement appeared to be most extraordinary.

MR. COURTNEY said, that the amount of the salaries was according to the work to be done. Lichfield, for instance, was the centre of a considerable district in which there was a large amount of work.

MR. ARTHUR O'CONNOR said, there was one point on which he desired to have some information from the hon. and learned Gentleman the Solicitor General. That hon. and learned Gentleman had mentioned what was undoubtedly a fact—namely, that a great deal of the existing block in the Chancery Division was due to the block in Chambers. The question he wished to ask was, why there were some Masters who never sat in Chambers?

THE SOLICITOR GENERAL (Sir FARRER HERSCHELL) said, the reason was, probably, because they sat in Court. He did not know to whom the hon. Member for Queen's County (Mr. Arthur O'Connor) referred. He supposed that the work was better done under the arrangement referred to; but he could not give a more precise answer without knowing the Masters to whom the hon. Member alluded.

MR. ARTHUR O'CONNOR said, that in order to make a set-off for the other expenditure, two of the clerks had been asked to give up the post of Marshal which they held, and that they declined to do so, although they offered to surrender their position as second class clerks. Was it arranged that the second class clerks were to be transferred to the central office; and, if so, would the consent of the Commissioners be obtained in some special manner to the arrangement if they did not pass the examination which would otherwise be required to be passed by the appointees?

MR. COURTNEY said, he could hardly be expected to enter into the question of what was proposed and what was not proposed to be done.

MR. ARTHUR O'CONNOR: It is with regard to what is being done.

MR. COURTNEY said, the arrangement rested with the Judges.

Vote *agreed to.*

(3.) £9,078, to complete the sum for the Wreck Commission.

(4.) £376,726, to complete the sum for the County Courts.

MR. R. T. REID said, he had a very few words to say in connection with this Vote. He would be glad to know whether there was any Return or means by which the Committee could ascertain whether there was any truth in the statement that some of the County Court Judges, especially those in the crowded districts in the North of England, were accustomed to work seven, eight, or nine hours a-day; and whether it was true that the County Court Judges in the agricultural districts, especially in the West, had such an excellent time of it that they did not work more than 120 or 150 hours out of the year? There was a large number of County Court Judges; and, without saying one word in regard to the proper salaries which they enjoyed, or without wishing in any way to interfere with their position or number, he was bound to ask whether some table of the kind indicated could be obtained, in order that upon it might be based some more equal distribution of the work than existed at the present moment, and under which some of the Judges were undoubtedly very much harder worked than others? He hoped the hon. and learned Gentleman the Solicitor General would be able to give some information on this subject.

MR. WEST said, he had a few figures to lay before the Committee with regard to the number of days in the course of a year on which the County Court Judges, held their sittings. He wished to say, at the commencement of his remarks, that he could find nothing in the Returns about the hard work which the hon. and learned Gentleman who had just sat down (Mr. R. T. Reid) said was cast upon County Court Judges in some districts in the North, as compared with the comparatively light duties of other County Court Judges in the Western agricultural districts. He found that the County Court Judges in the country did not sit on the average three days a-week. Still, he agreed with his hon. and learned Friend in what he had said with regard to not diminishing the salaries of the County Court Judges, because, although their salaries had been increased within the last few years, he did not think them an undue remuneration for the work they had to perform. But there was a very serious matter in connection with this Vote, to which he desired to call the attention of Her Majesty's Government. There sat, in 1873, a Committee, which went into this question at considerable length, but which Committee, in consequence of the Dissolution of 1874, never reported. The question of the number of County Court Judges was considered, and, although he had no right to anticipate what the Report would have been, he could not help thinking that the Committee were of opinion that the number of the County Court Judges was much too great. Little or nothing had been done in the direction of reducing the number of the County Court Judges; the rate at which they improved in these matters was so exceedingly slow. He would give one or two illustrations with regard to this subject. In 1874, the Legal Department Committee sat to consider this very question among others. That Committee comprised Lord Bramwell and other persons of experience and distinction, and they made an unanimous Report to Parliament in favour of the reduction of the number of County Court Judges. But to show the energy and zeal of the Government, he would point out that they had reduced the number of the County Court Judges by one, since that Committee reported. Now, if these Judges were to be reduced in number from 60 to 30, at that rate the country would probably have to wait 300 years before that result was arrived at. After careful and exhaustive inquiry into the question, the Committee said—

"The number of Judges is limited by Statute (21 & 22 Vict. cap. 74) to 60, and there are at the present time 57, so that some absorption of circuits has taken place; but Mr. Nicol is of opinion that there is room for further consolidation. We find that, although the days of sitting of some Judges occupy nearly half the year, the annual average attendance of the whole number in the last ten years has not exceeded 135 days, so that it is not unreasonable to suppose that more work might fairly be required of them without unduly tasking their powers or risking that the business should be done too quickly or slurred over. We observe from the same Return that the attendance in Court and at Chambers of the Common Law Judges averages 200 working days in the year. . . . We are of opinion that the remuneration now prescribed by statute 28 & 29 Vict. cap. 99, for the Judges, viz., £1,500 a-year, is not excessive, although the extension of equitable jurisdiction to these Courts which was the reason for granting the increase of salary does not seem to have materially added to the duties of the Judges. Since then, however, they have had increased work given to them in Bankruptcy, and in a few instances in Admiralty suits; and it appears to us that even if future Judges are required to undertake enlarged circuits, the salary now received would be sufficient."

It was clear, from a comparison of the time occupied in former days with that at present given to the performance of their duties by the County Court Judges, that although a large addition—an addition of 25 per cent—had been made to most of the salaries, the number of days which they gave to the public had considerably diminished. In the year 1883, the number of days for the whole of the Judges was 8,034, according to the last Return. Now, people said that the County Court Judges did not do sufficient work. He did not say that they were under or over paid; he gave no opinion upon that point; but he did say that since their salaries had been increased, the number of days on which they worked for the public had diminished. He did not mean to say that the diminution had occurred exactly contemporaneously; but the figures were as follows:—In 1857, the County Court Judges sat altogether 9,019 days; in 1871, only 8,041 days; in 1879, 8,283 days; in 1880, 8,268 days; in 1883, 8,034 days. Therefore, it could not be said that they sat fewer days in consequence of their having small salaries. The real cause was that they had comparatively little work to do. The total cost of the County Court system was £600,000 a-year—a very considerable item in the administration of the country—and he should like to know from Her Majesty's Government whether the recommendation of the Committee for the reduction of the number of the Judges would be acted upon, and whether they considered that that recommendation was satisfied by the fact that the number of the County Court Judges had been reduced by one?

MR. H. H. FOWLER said, that the amount named by the hon. and learned Gentleman who had just sat down (Mr. West) represented the whole expense in connection with the County Courts. The Return which had been laid on the Table of the House in the course of the last month, showing the actual number of days which the County Court Judges sat in 1883, was, in his opinion, of that importance and gravity that he wished to direct the attention of the Government to it. In order to appreciate that Return, it was only necessary for hon. Members to adopt the most elementary principles of calculation. For instance, the Committee would be aware that there were 365 days in the year; if Sundays, holidays, some days at Christmas were deducted, there remained 305 working days during the year. Then came the question as to the number of days' holiday which a person discharging these important functions in the State required, and which would have to be taken out of the 305 working days. He ventured to think that 12 weeks was a handsome holiday for any public servant. He doubted if hon. and right hon. Gentlemen on the Treasury Bench had as long; he was quite sure the Prime Minister did not. However, he was prepared to allow 12 weeks, which, when deducted from the 305 working days, left 230 days available for the Public Service in the course of the year. His hon. and learned Friend who spoke last had told the Committee that the Judges in the Superior Courts sat on the average 200 days in the year, and he (Mr. H. H. Fowler) need not remind them that the number of days on which those Judges sat did not at all represent the time and labour which they devoted to their duties. They had to prepare their judgments, and consider a number of matters out of Court; and, therefore, he considered that 200 days was a very fair number for Judges of the Superior Courts to sit.

Several of the Superior Judges sat 197 days in the year; the Judges of the Court of Appeal sat 193 days. Now, what did the Return which he held in his hand show? It showed that there was only one County Court Judge who sat on 190 days in the year; that one sat on 186 days, one on 184 days, and one on 181 days. He found that there were Judges who sat on less than 100 days; one 99 days, and one on 93 days, the salaries being precisely the same in each case—namely, £1,500 a-year—irrespective of the number of days on which they sat. He found also that 10 County Court Judges sat for less than 120 days; 27 sat from 120 to 150 days; 10 for 160 to 170 days; and eight only sat on 180 days in the year. He put it to the Committee, in view of these figures, whether the time had not arrived for reconsidering the whole of the County Court system? Either they were bound to reduce the number of Judges, or to increase the amount of work they had to do. Personally, he was in favour of re-grouping the County Courts, so that they might do the same amount of work as the Judges of the Superior Courts, and do it to the satisfaction of the people. The hon. and learned Gentleman the Attorney General gave it as an excuse, the other day, that these County Court Judges had to travel some distance to their labours; but he (Mr. H. H. Fowler) had the impression that the distance which they had to travel had nothing to do with the matter. He could put his finger on a case of a Judge who sat 128 days in the year; he had to attend three Courts, all of which were within a distance of six or seven miles from his residence, and there were trains to the locality every quarter of an hour. The case of the Judge who sat 93 days was, he thought, in a locality not far from London. [An hon. MEMBER: No; it was a Lancashire case.] Yes; it was the Bacup, Bolton, Rochdale, &c., Judge. The places in which this Judge had to sit were close together, and were within easy reach of each other, so that it could not be said that a great deal of time was occupied in travelling. If they were to allow 25 per cent of the Judge's time for travelling all round, it seemed to him that it would be quite ample. He thought the time had quite come when they should consider this question as to grouping of places to be attended by the single Judge, or the increasing the duties of each individual. So far as he was concerned, he preferred increasing. Last year it appeared that 25 per cent of the civil cases tried in the Superior Courts were under £50. These were cases which the County Court Judges could very well dispose of; and if the House would only adopt the recommendation of Committee after Committee which had sat to consider the matter, and would give a County Court jurisdiction up to £100, instead of having to increase the number of Superior Judges, they would find it possible to make a decrease. He would ask the hon. Gentleman the Secretary to the Treasury to look at Page 221 of the Estimates, where he would find an item, "Conveyance of Persons committed to Prison, £2,680." That item astonished him very much, as he had thought that if they had done anything at all in the matter of Bankruptcy in the Grand Committee last year, that which they had prided themselves upon having done was having abolished imprisonment for debt in small cases. They had inserted provisions in the Bill to enable persons who went through the Bankruptcy Court, owing less than £50, to make an application to the Court to get freed without difficulty. The right hon. Gentleman the President of the Board of Trade (Mr. Chamberlain) was in this matter very ably assisted by the hon. Member for Stoke (Mr. Broadhurst), and it was certainly the impression of that hon. Member, and that of the Committee, that they had put an end to this imprisonment for debt in County Court cases. He was, therefore, unable to understand that item of £2,680, which looked very much as though the old system was still in existence. He trusted they would get some assurance from the Government that the whole system of the administration of justice by the County Courts would be inquired into; that they would endeavour to find some method either of reducing the cost, or increasing the work, of the County Courts.

THE SOLICITOR GENERAL (Sir FARRER HERSCHELL) said, he was quite sure the Committee would feel that those who had called attention to this matter had done a useful service. Every one, he thought, must agree that it had been shown that in particular County Court districts, experience had established the fact that those districts, as now arranged, did not afford sufficient employment to occupy the entire time of the Judges. His hon. Friend the Member for Wolverhampton (Mr. H. H. Fowler) had made a suggestion with regard to the question of increased jurisdiction, and changes in the allocation of the districts of County Court Judges, and he (the Solicitor General) thought that, even if they were desirous of increasing that jurisdiction, the matter would really require careful consideration. They would find that there would still be particular districts where there would be very little work, while in others there would be a great deal. He admitted the question was one deserving very considerable consideration. It was obvious they had now obtained an experience as to the relations of the different districts, one to another, in regard to the amount of work to be done, which they had not before, and everyone would agree it was desirable, as far as possible, to distribute the work so that no Judge should cover a district in which there was really an insufficient amount of work properly to occupy the whole of his judicial time. This question of re-grouping districts must, he was sure, be felt to be one of considerable difficulty; because when they were dealing with an existing Judge, who had been accustomed to the district in which he was now working for a long period, they could not approach a change as easily as though they were working new ground. It was not easy to make a change, except when the time came for a change in the Judge. He might say, however, in regard to certain districts in the neighbourhood of the Metropolis, the Lord Chancellor was now considering the question of re-arranging the business. He could assure his hon. Friend the Member for Wolverhampton that the matter would not be lost sight of by the Lord Chancellor and the Government, and that the noble and learned Earl and his Colleagues would direct their attention, as far as possible, to re-arranging the districts, so as to distribute the business in a better and more economical manner. There was one matter that the hon. Member had not taken into consideration, and although it was very trifling, he desired just to call attention to it. With regard to some districts, no doubt, there was very little travelling to be done by the Judges; but in connection with other districts, that was not the case—it was necessary for the Judge to take long journeys from town to town. He did not say that this proposal was universally applicable; but, at any rate, in the case of some County Courts, a considerable amount might be added to the work of the Judges in consideration of the small amount of time they lost in travelling. No doubt, there were some districts where the work was not at all sufficient to occupy the time of the Judge.

MR. WARTON said, he thought it right to call attention to a point in the discussion upon which some correction was needed. The hon. Member for Wolverhampton (Mr. H. H. Fowler) always put cases before the Committee with clearness and force; but the hon. Member could not have taken into consideration the importance of this matter to which he (Mr. Warton) was about to refer. He (Mr. Warton) had had considerable experience of County Court Judges, and he thought it was hardly fair to look merely at the number of days on which they sat. The Judges of the Superior Courts came late to Court, and rushed away early; whereas County Court Judges came early to Court, and sat late—he had over and over again known them to sit until 7 or 8 o'clock in the evening. He (Mr. Warton) put it to the Committee whether the County Court Judge was not exercising a very wise discretion when he said he would rather have two or three days in one place, when all persons connected with the cases were ready, and all witnesses were in attendance, than sit for a much longer time going leisurely through the business. With regard to travelling, there were many cases, particularly in Wales, where there were long distances between the places in which the County Court was held, and which were visited by the Judge only once in two or three months. In these cases, as well as those cases where the places were close together, it would be desirable for the Judges to get through the work in a more business-like way, and with greater expedition than was the case at present. It would be far better to have a sitting over in two or three days than to have seven days occupied over it. If the County Court Judges had their wits about them, they would endeavour, if the opportunity were given to them, to sit as long as the Judges of the Superior Courts, but to sit late in the day. It was far better, both for themselves and the suitors, to get good long days, and to finish the list before them, rather than to spin it out to an inordinate length. The Judges of the Superior Courts, even the Lord Chief Justice, lounged into Court at half-past 10 or a quarter to 11 o'clock, and were anxious to get to a meeting of Judges, say, by a quarter to 4 o'clock; but, on the contrary, County Court Judges were in the habit of sitting to 7 or 8 o'clock in the evening. The latter practice was highly to be commended. Many judical functionaries did not by any means perform a sufficient amount of duty, and it was somewhat remarkable to hear the expressions of opinion which were given, sometimes coming from very high sources, on these subjects. It was remarkable to observe that just recently a Bill had been passed to relieve from a certain portion of his functions a judicial functionary who only sat 160 days in the year. He did not consider that a sufficient amount of work for such a person to perform. On this point he was quite sure of what he said, and he should not speak with such confidence if he had not experience of many County Courts.

MR. MOLLOY asked whether the hon. and learned Solicitor General was able to state how many County Judges held the double position of County Court Judge and Recorder? The position of Recorder was one which in many cases carried with it no emolument, or very little emolument.

THE SOLICITOR GENERAL (Sir FARRER HERSCHELL): There is nothing to prevent a County Court Judge from holding the position of Recorder.

MR. MOLLOY asked whether some arrangement could not be made by which a Judge, when he obtained his Judgeship, might be given to understand that it was necessary for him to resign the position of Recorder? As he had said, the emolument in many cases was not a matter worth much consideration. In some cases it was very small—in Sandwich, for instance, it was only some £10 or £15 a-year. The position of County Court Judge, to which a Recorder might be nominated, was a much higher one of the two, and yet in many cases the titular position of Recorder was retained in addition to the Judgeship. He knew amongst members of the Bar there was a strong feeling of objection to the present system; and it was generally felt when a Recorder had been raised to the dignity of a County Court Judge, he ought to abandon the other titular position, and that the Recorderships vacated in that way should be distributed amongst the members of the Bar, who, from their position, were entitled to some recognition of that kind. He had stated that the Recordership of Sandwich was only worth some £10 or £15 a-year; therefore, it could not be said that the title of Recorder was retained because of the addition it made to the salary of the County Court Judge. In some cases, the County Court Judges received salaries of £1,500 a-year; and, seeing the small number of days which they sat, he did not think it right that they should also retain the Recordership which might bring in some £200 or £250 a-year. Some explanation could be given of the shortness of the sittings of some of the County Court Judges by referring to the number of days occupied in their situations as Recorder. When the fees of the County Court Judges were first established, it was supposed that the whole time of the gentlemen employed in that capacity would be given up to the work, and it was certainly never anticipated that any of them would be in addition receiving the salary and discharging the functions of Recorder. On the broad ground, it seemed only fair that when a Recorder was appointed a County Court Judge he should resign the former titular position for the benefit of other members of the Bar. He (Mr. Molloy) had been requested to bring this matter forward by a large number of barristers, and he placed it before the Government hoping that the point would not escape their attention.

SIR WILLIAM HARCOURT said, he agreed very much with what had fallen from the hon. Member who had just sat down (Mr. Molloy), and he would call the special attention of the Lord Chancellor to his suggestion in regard to the Recorderships held by County Court Judges. It might be made a condition on a man being appointed a County Court Judge that he should give up his office as Recorder.

Vote *agreed to*.

(5.) Motion made, and Question proposed,

"That a sum, not exceeding £3,442, be granted to Her Majesty, to complete the sum necessary to defray the Charge which will come in course of payment during the year ending on the 31st day of March 1885, for the Salaries and Expenses of the Office of Land Registry."

MR. ARTHUR ARNOLD said, the history of the Land Registry Office was so well known that he need not detain the Committee more than a minute or two in making the Motion with regard to it which stood in his name. The Office was established, as the Committee were aware, not for limited districts, but for the whole of the country, and to carry out Earl Cairns' Land Transfer Act of 1875. The failure of that Act had been long seen and well understood, and, unfortunately, it was a progressive failure. The Act continued to fail more and more every year; and he (Mr. Arthur Arnold) wished particularly to impress on the Committee the fact that, in the year 1883, the failure of the Act seemed to have reached almost the lowest possible depth. Well, he was able to state that in that year the number of new estates registered in the Office of the Land Registry was, in the last six months of the year, two, whilst in the preceding six months it was four; so the total number of new estates registered in the course of the year 1883 was six. When he stated that the probable number of transfers of real property which took place in this country amounted to about 360,000 a-year, the Committee would easily understand that an Office which was registering new estates at the rate of six per annum, was not exactly fulfilling an important function in the State, and not giving them the slightest hope that at any conceivable period they would have a complete Registry of Titles. It would be seen, from the item in the Estimate, that the Office of the Land Registry at the present moment cost about £1,000 for each new estate registered. That was, probably, the greatest scandal in the whole of the Civil Service Estimates; and when he considered the smooth words used not long ago by the right hon. Gentleman the Chancellor of the Exchequer, who was a master of smooth words, in informing the House that he and the Secretary to the Treasury had made careful investigation of the whole of the Civil Service Estimates, and that they—probably two of the very ablest administrative servants of the Crown connected with the Treasury—had been unable to find a single item on which they could recommend a reduction of the Public Expenditure—when they considered these smooth words of the Chancellor of the Exchequer, all they could say was, that it was very much to be regretted that the right hon. Gentleman and his Colleague had not been more successful in their search. He (Mr. Arthur Arnold) certainly thought they might have recommended such a reduction as he was about to ask the Committee to consider this evening. But, before he advocated that reduction, he would allude to the fact that, during the present Session, the hon. Gentleman the Secretary to the Treasury (Mr. Courtney), in connection with the hon. and learned Gentleman the Attorney General, had introduced a Bill proposing to remove the Middlesex Land Registry into the Land Registry Office. Now, the Secretary to the Treasury had been distinctly challenged upon that point. He had been asked by the hon. and learned Member for Hastings (Mr. Ince) and himself (Mr. Arthur Arnold) whether the Bill proposed to effect any economy whatever in regard to Public Expenditure? The hon. Member, unless he (Mr. Arthur Arnold) was much mistaken, was silent when that challenge was made; but, at all events, he did not give a hope that the passing of the Bill would save the Public Expenditure one single farthing; and, under these circumstances, holding the strong opinion that a Registry of Titles was what they wanted, and not a Registry of Deeds, he had opposed the shovelling of the Middlesex Land Registry into that Office. It appeared the Treasury would have given the countenance of the Government to that transfer, without any proposed improvement of the system of registry; it was simply, no doubt, an attempt to avoid the scandal of bringing forward this Vote year after year. He (Mr. Arthur Arnold) was about to suggest another and more equitable method of reducing this most scandalous Vote. It was not uncommon for civil servants in this country, when there was an excess of work in their Departments, to come to the Government, or to the Members who represented them in Parliament, and ask for an increase of pay. That being so, it appeared to him (Mr. Arthur Arnold) to be only fair and just, that when in their Department there was absolutely nothing to do, or next door to nothing to do, the civil servants should submit to a reduction in their salaries. He thought it ought to have been plain to those two Officers of the Treasury—namely, the Chancellor of the Exchequer and the Secretary to the Treasury—when they entered into that very careful investigation of the Civil Service Estimates, to which the right hon. Gentleman the Chancellor of the Exchequer had referred, that they could save at least £2,000 a-year in connection with this Vote by reducing the salaries. Why should the Chief Registrar of this absolutely abortive and wasteful Office receive £2,500 a-year? No doubt, the gentleman who held the office was not to blame. It must be admitted that it was not that gentleman's fault that the office was practically a sinecure; but he (Mr. Arthur Arnold) certainly did contend that, inasmuch as that gentleman was very little worked—in fact, that he had almost nothing to do—he should submit to a reduction of his salary. He thought the Government would be justified, on the same ground on which they sometimes granted an increase of pay to civil servants, in ordering a reduction in this case. A reduction might also be made in the case of nearly all the servants in this Office. He had nothing personally to complain of with regard to these gentlemen, or the way in which they performed their duties; but he certainly thought it would be right and just to say that their salaries should be reduced, considering that their positions had become sinecures. There were seven gentlemen connected with the Office, the total salaries of whom amounted to £5,430. It would be perfectly right and just—nay, more, it seemed to him it would be the duty of the Treasury—to enforce such a revision as he had stated. He should have been very glad if the Government had displayed a greater disposition, during the life of the present Parliament, to promote measures of Land Law Reform, and specially to promote measures making the system of registration of titles effective throughout the country. He complained, and he was entitled to do so, that this had not been done. He believed that measures had been promoted in this Parliament of far less value to the public than such a measure would have been. He admitted there had not been very much time wasted by the Government with regard to legislation; but, looking at the importance of this subject, he should have thought preference would have been given to it. However, in moving the reduction of the Vote by the sum of £2,000, he desired not only to call attention to the urgency of reform as to this matter of the registration of titles, than which he could not conceive a reform more calculated to benefit the public at large, but he also desired most emphatically to express his own opinion that it was the duty of the Government to, at all events, reduce the salaries of the officials in this Office. It could not be contended that a man should continue to receive £2,500 a-year, another £1,500, and others £400, £350, £250, and so on, in an Office in the condition of the Land Registry Office; therefore, on the grounds he had stated, he begged to move that the Vote be reduced by the sum of £2,000.

Motion made, and Question proposed,

"That a sum, not exceeding £1,442, be granted to Her Majesty, to complete the sum necessary to defray the Charge which will come in course of payment during the year ending on the 31st day of March 1885, for the Salaries and Expenses of the Office of Land Registry."—(*Mr. Arthur Arnold.*)

MR. W. FOWLER said, he felt very much for the hon. Gentleman the Secretary to the Treasury (Mr. Courtney) and other hon. and right hon. Gentlemen opposite on this question, seeing that they had to support a Vote which was practically unsupported elsewhere. The Committee generally must feel very much for gentlemen who had given up, in order to accept these posts, good practices—who had accepted their situations on the faith that they would continue to receive their salaries. It was extremely difficult in a matter of this kind to vote a reduction, and he (Mr. W. Fowler) most readily admitted it. But year after year they had heard the same story that nothing was doing in this Office, and he did not know what his hon. Friends had said in support of the Vote, or could say, except that which he had just pointed out—namely, that they could not, without compensation, take away an office from a man who had given up a large practice and very good prospects, to fill it. But, for his own part, he would rather give a man handsome compensation than require him to remain in a place of this kind. It was a great pity for gentlemen like these to have nothing to do, and to be obliged to go day after day to the office. [An hon. MEMBER: The Chief Registrar never goes.] He was not aware of that; but he should doubt it very much. At any rate, he would suggest to the hon. Gentleman the Secretary to the Treasury that some of the subordinate officers should have some other work given to them to do, seeing there was no work for them to discharge in connection with their own department. The clerks, for instance, might have other employment in the State so as to enable them to earn their salaries, so that it would not be necessary to dismiss them altogether from the Civil Service. Something of the kind might be done. The question was certainly a very curious one. His hon. Friend (Mr. Arthur Arnold) had pointed out that it had been considered by Committee after Committee and Commission after Commission, and yet they were no nearer a satisfactory conclusion than they ever were. They had gone through the process of appointing a highly-paid gentleman to do nothing, and that simply because, it seemed to him (Mr. W. Fowler), they had missed altogether the true principles on which they ought to have acted. He thought they would never have a Registry of Deeds worth having until registration was compulsory, not directly but indirectly compulsory. If after a certain date no transactions affecting land were valid unless the land was registered it would be found that a large amount of land would be registered. They must import something in the way of indirect compulsion if they expected people to go on the register? Why should a man go on the register. He knew a gentleman who had an excellent title, and yet it cost him a year's rent to get his land registered, and very sorry indeed he was that he registered, because he had to pay a very considerable sum for what really amounted to nothing; his friend was no better off now than he was when he was off the register. If a man did not want to do anything with his land, he could not understand why registration should be necessary. If they made it the law that a landlord could not sell his land or mortgage it unless it were registered, they would soon find him on the register. He (Mr. W. Fowler) knew there were people who denied the value of registration and said they were just as well off without it; but he thought that if there was a registration of titles and not of deeds, and the provision he had mentioned was the law, they would soon find that the expense of inquiring into titles would be very greatly diminished. His hon. Friend the Member for East Sussex (Mr. Gregory) approved of a registration of deeds, rather than of titles. Now, when he (Mr. W. Fowler) was in America, he inquired as to the system adopted there. He found that even in America, where transactions in land were very numerous, but not, he supposed, in some parts as numerous as in a great city like London, the experience was that registration of deeds led to great complication as to indexes and maps; indeed, private Companies now registered titles. A great business was carried on in Baltimore in the registration of titles by private Companies, because the public system was so imperfect. He, however, thought that if there was in this country a proper registration of titles, the difficulty experienced in America might be avoided. His impression was that they ought not to ask a man to register an indefeasible title. Some people had an idea that putting land on the register would not simplify matters; because, in their opinion, complications began to arise directly they got on the register. But the Committee had not now to decide all these details. The question before them was—What should they do with this Vote; should they pay this money or not? He should certainly listen with great curiosity to hear what his hon. Friend the Secretary to the Treasury (Mr. Courtney) had to say in defence of the Vote. He should not commit himself to any course of action until he had heard what his hon. Friend had to say; but he protested against them continuing, year after year, the sham and farce of voting £5,400 to men who absolutely did nothing at all. He thought his hon. Friends on the Treasury Bench were ingenious enough to invent some way of getting out of the difficulty. He should be glad if some of this money could be used in establishing a real system of registration if they were to have one at all. The present system had proved to be an utter absurdity. If they did register, let the register be something worth having. What they had got now was not worth having, and he did not think the register ever would be worth having if they stuck to the idea of only registering indefeasible titles. He could not imagine why any man should be so stupid as to go on the register, unless he was going to divide his land into small lots. He earnestly hoped his hon. Friend (Mr. Courtney) would be able to tell them something which would get them out of the present difficulty, and prevent them going through the process of again voting this large sum of money for nothing at all.

SIR HENRY HOLLAND said, he had hoped that the hon. Member for Cambridge (Mr. W. Fowler) was going to remain faithful to the opposition to this Vote which had been expressed by hon. Members who now sat on the Government side of the House; but his hopes were somewhat dashed by the concluding observation of the hon. Member, that he trusted the Government would give some satisfactory explanation which would enable him to vote against the proposed reduction. That was the course taken by many other hon. Members after they had crossed from one side of the House to the other, as he should presently show. He would not now attempt to discuss the important question of the registration of deeds or titles. That had been argued at great length in that House for years, and had been reported upon by Committees and Commissions, and would not now be properly discussed in the few observations with which he would trouble the Committee. He would, however, express his entire concurrence in one part of the hon. Member's speech, in which he admitted that if the Office was abolished or reduced, compensation must be awarded to the officers who had done their duty faithfully, and given effect to such powers as were vested in them. This was necessary in the interests of the Public Service, for good men could not be got to leave their professions, unless compensation were to be awarded to them if the office which they were induced to enter was abolished. The only alternative would be to offer them very largely increased salaries, which the Committee would hardly be prepared to grant. But this alternative would fail, in his opinion, to secure good and able men. He would prefer to face the compensation question rather than keep an useless Office on the Votes. Certainly, the history of this Office was peculiar. In 1879 an attempt was made to reduce the salaries, and he had then argued that it would be unfair, without notice, as it were, to take such a step, though he would not continue to vote for it unless improved. But the present Secretary of State for the Home Department, then in Opposition, would not hear of such an argument. He wanted to know what the House was sitting in Committee for, if salaries could not be altered? He said the duty of the Committee would be a farce if this argument were to apply; and his name appeared in the Division List for the reduction. The right hon. Gentleman the present Chancellor of the Exchequer expressed much the same view. The majority was only obtained that year in the belief and on the understanding that more work would be found for the Office, if it was to be continued. But then came the change of Government, and with it an apparent change of opinion and votes. It was true that the present Chancellor of the Exchequer still held that the constitution and working of the Office was unsatisfactory, and the hon. and learned Gentleman the Attorney General agreed; but they voted for the salaries. In 1881 no Division took place. In 1882 again the Office was attacked, and the hon. and learned Attorney General stated that it was proposed to add to the work by adding the work of the Middlesex Registry Office to it. In 1883 the hon. and learned Attorney General said this attempt had failed; and this year another attempt had been made to take the same step. But this plan, even if sufficient, had not met with the approval of the House; and, as far as he (Sir Henry Holland) knew, no other attempt had been made to increase in any other way the duties of the Office. And now the Committee were asked again to vote in support of this Office, which had been proved to be practically useless. It could hardly be contended that, at all events, some considerable reduction might not be made in it, and he should support the proposed reduction as a protest against this continued waste of money.

MR. COURTNEY said, his hon. Friend the Member for Cambridge (Mr. W. Fowler) had remarked that this Vote was insupportable, and then immediately proceeded to give an argument in support of it. He (Mr. Courtney) had to point out that the gentleman who took this Office had enjoyed a large practice at the Bar previous to his acceptance of the post. It was, therefore, rather unreasonable to expect that a reduction of salary should be made in the case of an official who had sacrificed a large practice to take a post of this kind on the faith of Parliament, even granting that the amount of work at present was not sufficient for the Staff. It was said, however, that they should abolish the Office altogether and pension the office-holders; but if they were to do that, they would practically make up their minds to do without land registry altogether. They could not keep those officials at the Office and reduce their salaries, on the faith of which they were induced to give up their practice; and if it was intended to develop this Office, it would be very rash and very false economy to retire them.

MR. HASTINGS said, there could be no doubt that the present position of the Office was very little short of a public scandal. As a matter of fact, they were asked to vote £5,000 a-year for an Office which really did no work at all. Personally, he was of opinion it would be better to develop the Office, if possible; and what he complained of was that things should go on, year after year, in the same make-shift fashion. There was a great work to be done in registration, and this Office ought to be put to do it. Not many weeks ago he was one of a deputation who submitted to the hon. and learned Gentleman the Attorney General (Sir Henry James) a Memorandum from the Law Amendment Society dealing with the subject; and he (Mr. Hastings) thought that anyone who would take the trouble to read that Memorandum would see that there was a great work to be done in connection with land registration. There had been for many years a system of land registration in force in the whole of our Australian Colonies; and he believed that, at the present moment, there was an effort being made to extend the system to Canada. The system had been extended to other parts, and wherever it had been put in force it had proved a great success. What he and others asked was that the Government should turn their attention to the subject, and that if they found that the system had not succeeded, or was not applicable to this country, they should, at least, tell Parliament why they came to that conclusion. They had a right to know why, when there was a Land Registry Office which cost £5,000 a-year, no effort was made to extend to England the system of land registration which had conferred such great benefit on many parts of Her Majesty's Dominions. He had not the least doubt that a similar land registration was perfectly feasible in this country, all the more feasible now that a Cadastral Survey was being carried out in the Kingdom. The whole of the difficulties in the way of registration vanished as soon as that Survey was made. The question of Land Law Reform was really dependent upon thoroughly good land registration. He trusted that Her Majesty's Government would show, in some future Session of Parliament, that they were alive to the question, and that they would endeavour, either by the adoption of the Torrens' system now in force in Australia, or some other system, to give the people of this country the benefit of land registration.

MR. GREGORY said, he did not propose to enter into a discussion of the whole system of land registration; but as he had been referred to by the hon. Member for Cambridge (Mr. W. Fowler) he felt bound to offer a few remarks. He might say, at once, that he was in favour of a registration of deeds, and that he believed the failure of this Office to be due to the fact that it was an Office for the registration of titles, and not of deeds. What the Government could do was to convert the Office into one for the registration of deeds, and of that he was entirely in favour. The Government had introduced a Bill for that purpose, and the hon. and learned Gentleman the Member for Launceston (Sir Hardinge Giffard) had introduced a Bill of the same character, though carrying the object somewhat further. Both the Bills had been read a second time, and his suggestion, adopted by the hon. Gentleman the Secretary to the Treasury (Mr. Courtney), was that they should be referred to a Select Committee. In the event of those Bills, or either of them, becoming law, the Office would be necessary. In his opinion, it would be absurd to abolish the Office now; besides they could not do so without full compensation to the present officials. It was requisite, in the public interest, that they should weigh very carefully such a step, because it was evident that no one would accept an Office on the contingency of its success or failure. It was quite true that the present Registrar had given up a very valuable practice to take the Office. Under the circumstances, the hon. Gentleman the Member for Salford (Mr. Arthur Arnold) would do well not to press his Motion.

MR. ARTHUR ARNOLD said, the hon. Gentleman (Mr. Gregory) had fallen into a slight error. The hon. Gentleman stated that Her Majesty's Government proposed to convert the Office into an Office for the registration of deeds. That was not the case. Under the Bill of the Government, the Office would remain an Office for the registration of titles; but there would be a registration of deeds as well as of titles in the same Office. He feared that would result in great complication. His hon. Friend the Member for East Worcestershire (Mr. Hastings) had spoken of the development of the Office; but the Office could not be developed through the present Registrar. He desired to speak of the Registrar with great respect; but he was bound to say it was absolutely impossible to develop the Office, and make it a really effective registry of titles through the gentleman who now held the chief Office. The hon. Gentleman the Secretary to the Treasury (Mr. Courtney) had spoken of the opinion of Parliament on this subject. His hon. Friend had laid it down that Parliament would not sanction a Bill for the compulsory registration of titles. Considering that that was the only Parliament in which the hon. Gentleman had held Office, it would only have shown respect to the independence of private Members if he had not given utterance to so confident an opinion. The opinion of this Parliament had never been taken on the subject. A proper registration of titles to land was absolutely necessary before there could be any satisfactory settlement of Land Law Reform. He entertained one deep regret, and it was that that great lawyer, Earl Cairns, was not a Liberal statesman, because, in that event, he was persuaded the question of Land Law Reform would not have been so long delayed.

MR. BARRY said, that, although this Office was one of the greatest scandals in the Civil Service, it would be a distinct breach of faith if the Committee were to reduce the salaries of the officials. He regretted the Secretary to the Treasury (Mr. Courtney) had no proposal to make which would put an end to the scandal. Was it not possible to give the gentlemen in the Land Registry Department some other appointment? There were a large number of appointments in the Civil Service. Surely, in the course of the year, opportunities would be found of placing the Land Registry officials in positions in which they would earn their salaries. It was very strange that the Government should say they were utterly helpless in this matter. He remembered the time when the sweets of Office destroyed the appetite for reform; but in this case it seemed an extremely simple matter to find some other work for the officials in question. If it happened that in one department of a large commercial concern there was a lack of work, and there was nothing whatever for the *employés* of that department to do, the common sense of the managers would prompt them to find work for the *employés* in some other department. He put it to the Secretary to the Treasury (Mr. Courtney) why common sense should not operate in this case, and employment be found for the officials in some other branch of the Civil Service.

MR. COURTNEY said, the Middlesex Land Registry Bill was before the House, and under that Bill a great deal more work would be thrown upon the Office.

MR. BARRY asked if it was likely any change would be made in the immediate future?

MR. COURTNEY said, the Middlesex Land Registry Bill had been referred to a Select Committee, and the whole object of that Bill was to put the Office on a different footing, and give it additional work.

MR. HASTINGS said, that the business of the Middlesex Land Registry was altogether a great mistake, being a registration of deeds and not of titles; and he entertained a strong objection to hand over the Land Registry to any such body.

MR. MOLLOY said, he hoped that his hon. Friend (Mr. Arthur Arnold) would divide. The second reading of the Bill referred to had not obtained the assent of the House in reality, although it had done so nominally; and it was perfectly certain the measure would neither pass this year, next year, nor the year after that. The hon. Gentleman the Financial Secretary to the Treasury (Mr. Courtney) simply asked to continue this sum in the Votes, because it was intended to combine with the Middlesex Registry another useless Office. His own opinion was that it was objectionable, in getting rid of one scandal, to create another just as great. He would request his hon. Friend to continue his opposition to the Vote, notwithstanding the defence of it by the Financial Secretary to the Treasury, which was really not of the slightest value.

Question put.

The Committee *divided*:—Ayes 32; Noes 41: Majority 9.—(Div. List, No. 179.)

Original Question put, and *agreed to*.

(6.) £18,690, for Revising Barristers, England.

(7.) Motion made, and Question proposed,

"That a sum, not exceeding £10,023, be granted to Her Majesty, to complete the sum necessary to defray the Charge which will come in course of payment during the year ending on the 31st day of March 1885, for the Salaries and Expenses of the Police Courts of London and Sheerness."

MR. H. H. FOWLER said, he intended to take the sense of the Committee upon this Vote, as a protest against the charge for the London Police Courts being thrown upon the Imperial Exchequer. The cost ought to be borne by the Local Authorities, as it was in Manchester, Liverpool, and other towns. If the London Government Bill had passed, the Metropolitan Government would have had to meet the charge out of the rates. He begged to move the rejection of the Vote.

SIR WILLIAM HARCOURT said, he was not prepared to argue against the principle of the proposal of his hon. Friend (Mr. H. H. Fowler), because he quite agreed with it, and was of opinion that the charge should be defrayed out of the Metropolitan rates. But his hon. Friend was, above everything, a practical man; and he (Sir William Harcourt) would ask his hon. Friend what would happen if he succeeded in rejecting the Vote? There would then be no Police Courts in London, and no one to carry on the administration of justice. Under the circumstances, he hoped his hon. Friend would not press the Motion to a Division.

MR. ALDERMAN W. LAWRENCE said, that his hon. Friend the Member for Wolverhampton (Mr. H. H. Fowler), in moving the rejection of the Vote, had done so because he considered that charges of this kind ought to be paid by the Metropolis, and that they should not come out of the Imperial Exchequer. The objection of his hon. Friend did not apply to the City of London, because the City paid for its own Police Courts. Those of the Metropolis outside the City had, however, always been paid for by the country; and if a charge of this nature were struck out of the Votes, it must not be forgotten that the Metropolis paid a considerable number of charges out of the local rates, such as the rates for the Royal Parks, Palaces, the Foreign Office, Home Office, Admiralty, War Office, Somerset House, the Barracks, the Tower of London, the Post Office, and other public buildings, which ought to fall upon the public generally. A large number of institutions of this kind were spread over the Metropolis; and if they were rated as other property was for drainage, sanitary precautions, and for the poor and general rates, the taxation of the inhabitants of London would be considerably relieved. At present, these public buildings escaped from contributing their fair share to local taxation, and the consequence was that the Metropolis had to pay a much larger sum than it ought to pay. He had very little doubt that the inhabitants of London paid in this way a much larger sum than they were relieved from in consequence of the cost of the Metropolitan Police Courts being defrayed by the Imperial Exchequer. Take the Fire Engine Establishments. A small and inadequate sum was contributed towards their maintenance by the large Government establishments, although a regular sum was charged upon every other description of property for their support, and the Government establishments enjoyed the full share of the protection which they afforded. The sum paid by the Government towards local taxation, on behalf of the Government establishments, was simply ridiculous compared with the value of the property and the services rendered; and the question raised by the hon. Member for

Wolverhampton (Mr. H. H. Fowler) was, consequently, a very large and important one. He (Mr. Alderman Lawrence) maintained that, at the present moment, if the country paid its fair share of its local rates on account of the public establishments in London, they would have to bear a much larger burden than they now bore for the expense of the Metropolitan Police Courts, and, probably, one or two other small matters. It could not be said that his hon. Friend had brought forward any arguments for throwing the cost of these Courts upon the ratepayers of London; and he understood that his hon. Friend simply wished to take a division. But it was impossible to allow the matter to pass altogether without notice, because the charge made amounted to an allegation that the Metropolis was robbing the country. [An hon. MEMBER: Certainly.] He did not agree with the hon. Member; but, on the contrary, he contended that the Metropolis paid much more than its fair share of the cost of the public establishments. It contributed largely towards the expense of keeping up the Royal Palaces and Parks, the barracks, and other public buildings, and much more largely than there would be any necessity for, if these public establishments paid, as other establishments were obliged to do, towards the local taxation of the Metropolis.

MR. H. H. FOWLER said, he did not propose to take up the time of the Committee with any lengthened remarks. The question was a very simple one, and was thoroughly understood. But after the peculiar position which had been taken up by his hon. Friend (Mr. Alderman W. Lawrence) in defence of the Metropolis, he desired to point out that the arrangements under which the Government establishments paid local rates did not apply to London alone, but to every borough in England. In Manchester, Leeds, Birmingham, and other towns, there were large public establishments, as well as in London, and the same arrangement was applied to all of them. He should be quite ready, whenever the day came, to strike a balance between the Imperial and local expenditure. He did not anticipate any great accession of Members to the Metropolis; but he had no doubt that whoever might be sent to the House of Commons to represent the Metropolitan constituencies would, as soon as they got there, endeavour to protect the pockets of the ratepayers of London at the expense of the rest of the country. At the same time, he was satisfied that, whenever the question was raised at the hustings of the Kingdom generally, there would be a strong expression of opinion that London should bear its own local burdens exclusively, and that the country should bear theirs. His right hon. Friend the Secretary of State for the Home Department had said that he (Mr. H. H. Fowler) was a practical man. He was obliged to his right hon. Friend for the compliment, and it was simply upon that ground that he intended to take issue upon his Motion for the rejection of the Vote. No difficulty would arise, even if the Vote were rejected. The salaries of the Metropolitan Police Magistrates were not included in the Vote, but were provided by the Consolidated Fund. The expenses of the Courts were also provided for until next October. He, therefore, intended to take a division as a protest against the present state of things. If the Vote were rejected, he had no doubt that his right hon. Friend would at once bring in a Bill, which could be disposed of in a few days, imposing upon the Metropolitan Board of Works the charge that was necessary for keeping the Police Courts of London in order. He was not at all sanguine that he would be able to carry his Motion; but he should certainly take a division as a protest against the principle of London—he would not use the word "robbing," suggested by his hon. Friend the Member for the City (Mr. Alderman Lawrence)—but confiscating the property of the country for the benefit of the wealthy ratepayers of London.

Question put.

The Committee *divided*:—Ayes 50; Noes 24: Majority 26.—(Div. List, No. 180.)

(8.) £279,875, to complete the sum for the Metropolitan Police.

(9.) Motion made, and Question proposed,

"That a sum, not exceeding £968,298, be granted to Her Majesty, to complete the sum necessary to defray the Charge which will come in course of payment during the year ending on the 31st day of March 1885, for certain Expenses connected with the Police in Counties and Boroughs in England and Wales and with the Police in Scotland."

MR. SEXTON said, he had given Notice some days ago, chiefly for the information of the right hon. Gentleman the Secretary of State for the Home Department, that he intended to move the reduction of this Vote. He rose now, accordingly, to move that the Vote be reduced by the sum of £5,000; and he did so in order to call the attention of the Secretary of State and of the Committee to some circumstances connected with an Orange riot and fatal affray which occurred at Cleator Moor, near Whitehaven, in the County of Cumberland, on the 12th of the present month. He would state in a few words what happened. The town of Cleator Moor had a population of about 10,000. It was the centre of a mining district, and one-half of the population of the town and a large part of the surrounding population were comprised of persons of Irish nationality and of the Roman Catholic faith. For that reason the Orange leaders in the North of England had, until the present ear, for some years abstained from holding any of their national meetings or festivities in the vicinity of Cleator Moor; but, unfortunately, this year the evil counsels of some of the local leaders resident in the town of Cleator Moor were allowed to prevail, and a desire to violate the peace of the town and to insult the Catholicinhabitants took the ascendancy, and had the effect of counteracting the prudent course which had hitherto been taken. It was resolved to hold a public meeting this year in the vicinity of Cleator Moor. There were, however, local reasons why the Orange leaders should have avoided holding a demonstration in this particular district; because the right hon. Gentleman the Secretary of State for the Home Department would remember that some years ago a person named Murphy, describing himself as a convert from the Roman Catholic Church, gave a series of public lectures, and issued a number of insulting handbills, the staple of his lectures consisting of foul and exasperating attacks upon the doctrines of the Roman Catholic Church. At last, in the town of Whitehaven, this person's harangues produced such an effect that a serious riot occurred, in which the unhappy man received such injuries that he subsequently died of them. This event produced an excited and dangerous state of feeling between persons of different creeds in this part of the North of England; and, therefore, it ought to have suggested itself to those who were responsible for the Orange demonstration on the 12th of the present month that if they desired to vindicate or advance Orange principles in the North of England, they ought to have selected a different place. On this part of the case he thought there would be no difference of opinion. He now came to consider the conduct of the local magistrates and police in reference to this meeting. The Orange Society was not a thing of yesterday. Its principles, its methods of proceeding, and its objects were well ascertained, and were familiarly known. They all knew that the Society had been founded for the purpose of commemorating certain events in Ireland, which had had the effect of placing the Roman Catholic people of that country for more than a century under the merciless heel of Protestant ascendancy, which led the way to those Penal Laws which formed the most disgraceful chapter in the history of English rule in Ireland, and which no man in these days attempted to justify or defend. To go no further back than the past year, the magistrates and the police in the North of England knew well what had been the course pursued by the Orange leaders in Ireland, and what fatal results had followed on different occasions when they had assembled the Orange Party together. They knew that the Orangemen had been told to keep powder in their revolvers, and not to fire them off in the gaiety of their hearts, nor to shoot unless they had somebody in front of their weapons. They knew that wherever the Orangemen had assembled in Ireland they had used deadly weapons; that they had used them on the occasion of the right hon. Gentleman's (Sir Stafford Northcote's) visit to Belfast and Dromore; on the occasion of Lord Rossmore's mock heroic demonstration in Derry, at Rosslea, and at a public meeting only a few days ago at Newry. On all those occasions, the two distinguishing features which marked the attempts made by the Orangemen against the lives of those who differed from them in religious creed were, first of all, the ferocious deadliness of the attempt to take away human life; and, secondly, the cowardliness of those who made them. They planted themselves on the roofs of houses, or concealed themselves behind walls, or wherever they could find a safe ambush, and then made a deliberate attack, with deadly weapons, upon the lives of their opponents. They knew what had happened in the county of Tyrone. Only the other day, in order to prevent the holding of a peaceful and perfectly legal meeting, the Orangemen poured in from distant places carrying sacks full of revolvers. Their sole object was to prevent, by intimidation and acts of violence, the citizens from exercising their Constitutional rights; and as they persistently refused to obey the orders of those who were intrusted with the execution of the law, and the preservation of the peace, the Constabulary found themselves obliged to eject them from the scene by force of arms; and in the pursui one misguided youth, brought in from at distance, met with his death at the hands of the police. This having been the prelude, and these being facts that were familiar in the minds of everyone in the country, he respectfully submitted that when the members of the same Orange Society, distinguished in Ireland by their violence and lust of blood, notified their intention of holding a public meeting on English soil, and of transferring these violent and fatal feuds to this country, it was the duty of the magistrates and of the police, who were paid under the present Vote, to take special steps to prevent a breach of the peace. That was his first contention—namely, that if the magistrates had no information, further than their knowledge, of the notorious purposes and methods of the Orange Society, as proved by recent events in Ireland, and emphasized by debates in that House, of their own motion they ought to have taken steps to prevent the loss of life or any violation of the law. But the magistrates of themselves did nothing. The next step in his argument was that the magistrates and the police were fruitlessly moved to take effective action. The Catholic priest of Cleator Moor, the Rev. Father Burchall, went before the bench of local magistrates and informed them of his desire to swear an information that he apprehended a breach of the peace; that an Orange meeting could not be held in the midst of an excited people without great danger; and that he had reliable information that the Orangemen were instructed to attend the meeting armed. Surely, the magistrates ought not to have needed such information, after the firing at Newry and the successful use of revolvers at Dromore. But, far from accepting the statement of the Rev. Father Burchall, far from permitting him to lay the information he desired to make, the magistrates took no action whatever in regard to his statement; and he (Mr. Sexton) claimed that in treating with disregard and contempt the appeals of a gentleman who, by his position, by his local knowledge, by his interest in the people, and the high responsibilities of his sacred office, was entitled to peculiar consideration, were guilty of a gross dereliction of duty. The Rev. Father Burchall did not stop with the police and the magistrates. He wrote to the right hon. Gentleman the Secretary of State for the Home Department; and if it was necessary to fix the date of the fruitless appeal to the magistrates, it must have been at least a week before the unfortunate man, Tumelty, lost his life, because the letter to the Home Secretary was written on the 8th instant, at least a couple of days after the application to the magistrates. Having failed in his application to the magistrates on the 8th of July, Father Burchall posted a letter to the Secretary of State; but it was only several days after the fatal affray took place that the fact became known. As soon as it came to his (Mr. Sexton's) knowledge, he questioned the right hon. Gentleman, and it was not until he did so that the right hon. Gentleman made any acknowledgment of the fact that a letter had been addressed to him by Father Burchall. The right hon. Gentleman stated that it was received at the Home Office on the 9th—that was to say, that the Home Office had at least three full days, if they believed the information of the Catholic priest of Cleator Moor, for taking effective steps for the preservation of the public peace and the prevention of loss of life. He would ask the right hon. Gentleman who received that letter on the 9th; who opened it; who read it, and what became of it? Why was no action taken upon it? Was it opened by some subordinate clerk? Was it tossed aside by some careless official, or did it only come to the right hon. Gentleman's knowledge when Henry Tumelty was lying dead with an Orange bullet through his brain? The right hon. Gentleman said that it would have made no difference if the letter of Father Burchall had reached his hands in due course. [Sir WILLIAM HARCOURT assented.] The right hon. Gentleman nodded assent. Surely, if the letter had come to his knowledge on the 9th, it would have been within his competency, and would have been part of his duty, as one of Her Majesty's Principal Secretaries of State for Great Britain, to have suggested, at least, to the magistrates of Cleator Moor that it was their duty to obtain information, to ascertain if the fact was well founded, that the Orangemen proposed to attend the meeting armed; and, if so, that they were called upon to exert their powers as conservators of the public peace for the protection of life. He, therefore, held it to be a most calamitous circumstance, whatever the cause of it might have been, that the letter of Father Burchall, received on the 9th, in reference to a danger apprehended on the 12th, had become submerged in the Correspondence of the Home Office, and was only brought to light when the fatal event had occurred. The Home Office did not listen to Father Burchall. The right hon. Gentleman did not reply to him; the 12th of July arrived, and the Orangemen, to the number of 1,500, appeared on the scene, having been mostly conveyed by special train from various parts of the county. They were decorated with the regalia of the Order, and, accompanied by bands and banners, they marched to the place of meeting. Now, however trifling it might appear to be to Englishmen who were unacquainted with the internecine wars in Ireland, the mottoes upon these banners were of the most exasperating type; the Orangemen themselves were armed with swords and pikes, conspicuously displayed, while most of them carried hidden, but loaded, revolvers. They came with a deadly purpose in their hearts, and that murder was their intention from the outset could be made clear by their conduct from the earliest moment; because, on passing the Roman Catholic church, where religious services at the time were proceeding, instead of behaving themselves as men would behave who were desirous of avoiding all wanton acts of provocation, they uttered all manner of offensive cries, and played insulting Party tunes. The playing of Party tunes might seem to the right hon. Gentleman a trifle; but to Irish Catholics they brought to remembrance attacks upon their personal liberty, and of a long series of outrages upon an unoffending people. The Orangemen, as he had said, uttered exasperating cries, and, having proceeded to the place of meeting, delivered speeches of the usual character. The meeting being over, they left the field, and returned to the town towards the railway station, along a route about a mile in length. On several occasions when the Orange Societies in Ireland had issued placards, the Government had decided that they were not to be abridged in their rights, and police were collected in considerable numbers to protect them. At Dromore there had been a meeting of the same description as that at Cleator Moor, and there, also, a large number of Catholics opposed the aggressive tactics of the Orange Party. The whole of the circumstances were, to a large degree, analogous to those at Cleator Moor. The Executive assembled 800 Cavalry, 200 Infantry, and a force of police, all of whom were employed, not to separate opposing crowds, but to render a collision impossible. Did the right hon. Gentleman mean to tell the Committee that a body of men were likely to be able to march through the streets of a town carrying swords and spears without a probability of bloodshed? What the police at Cleator Moor ought to have done was to have instructed the Orangemen to take a different route to the station, and so have prevented a collision. This was how the fatal collision occurred, according to the report. The Orange Party were armed with pistols, swords, and spears; they were dressed in the Orange costume, carried flags and banners, and were accompanied by bands of music. One of the Orangemen thrust a flag in the faces of some of e crowd, whereupon the opposing crowd, consisting of about 6,000 people, rushed in on the Orange Party; several blows were struck, and the encounter resulted in the death of the boy Tumelty. The police only numbered 45, instead of 500 or 1,000, and they contented themselves with walking in the rear of the procession, allowing the collision to take place, the peace to be broken, and life to be taken; and now the right hon. Gentleman argued that the police should be acquitted, because, after the collision, and after life was taken, and after dangerous wounds had been inflicted upon several persons, they separated the parties. He maintained that the collision ought to have been absolutely prevented, as was frequently done in Ireland. The course taken by the Irish Executive for preventing collisions in Ireland was far more intelligent than that pursued by the English police. The general effects of the methods, and purposes, and acts of the Orange Society were sufficient to have caused the magistrates to have provided a special force of sufficient strength to prevent a collision. In the second place, the local magistrates, on the request of the Rev. Father Burchall, ought to have invited him to lay an information, and on his doing so, and swearing that the Orangemen would come armed, they ought to have considered whether it was their duty to prevent the meeting. In the third place, it appeared that some of the officials were guilty of the most grave and deplorable neglect of duty in allowing the solemn letter of the priest, who wrote with a view of preserving the public peace, and of preventing loss of life, to remain unnoticed for a week. Further, the police ought to have provided a sufficient force to prevent the two crowds coming together, and instead of allowing the excited Orangemen to go along the high road until they came into collision with the Catholics, they should have directed them to go by some other route, or else should have compelled the Roman Catholic crowd to keep back. With regard to the matter of arrests, it was clear that the Orangemen were the only Party armed, and that they alone gave deliberate provocation; the Catholics were victims of Orange ferocity; and yet the energy of the police was ironically illustrated by the fact that they arrested five or six of the Orange Party, but subsequently arrested, at 5 o'clock in the morning, six or seven of the Catholics, whom they took out of their beds. He threw upon the Government the responsibility of the violent death of this unfortunate youth Tumelty; and for the vindication of justice against those who caused his death, and inflicted wounds upon other persons, he begged to move the reduction of the Vote by £5,000.

Motion made, and Question proposed,

"That a sum, not exceeding £963,298, be granted to Her Majesty, to complete the sum necessary to defray the Charge which will come in course of payment during the year ending on the 31st day of March 1885, for certain Expenses connected with the Police in Counties and Boroughs in England and Wales and with the Police in Scotland."—(*Mr. Sexton.*)

SIR WILLIAM HARCOURT: I am obliged to speak upon this subject with more reserve than the hon. Member for Sligo (Mr. Sexton); because, although he has stated, with great confidence, the facts of this case, which are now necessarily under the consideration of the Courts of Law, I cannot take the same licence that he has taken. With regard to the history of this matter, I shall not offer any plea in vindication of these wretched Party processions. I could give no encouragement to Party processions, especially to those which are embittered by the *odium theologicum*, which are the worst of all. All I have to do in the matter is to consider whether these processions are unlawful or not. When I first came to the Home Office I found a tradition well established in that Office—a very sensible tradition. I am bound to say that, in England, we have little trouble with Party processions, except those which the hon. Member has called Irish religious processions. They do not involve English antagonism of feeling; but in Liverpool and Glasgow, and some other towns, these Orange processions have given a great deal of trouble and caused riots; and I found that the Law Officers had laid down the doctrine that if an information were sworn that a procession was likely to lead to a breach of the peace, the magistrates should declare such procession to be unlawful. That was a good and sensible doctrine, I thought, and I wished it had turned out to be the law. But, unfortunately, the law does not always turn out to be as we could wish; and this doctrine—which served us very well in regard to Salvation Army disturbances, which have sometimes approached in severity Orange riots, for we had, with good effect, advised the magistrates that when they thought there would be a breach of the peace they should put a stop to these meetings by proclamation — this doctrine the Courts of Law decided could not be sustained, and that magistrates had no power to proclaim such meetings. From that moment the situation became extremely difficult for local magistrates. When the magistrates anticipated a row, and had only a small force of police, they did not know what to do when there was a gathering of the Salvation Army and the Skeleton Army. I regret that state of things very much. With regard to these occurrences at Cleator Moor, I must say that I think the Orangemen were foolish to go to Cleator Moor; but the hon. Member seems to think that the magistrates ought to have declared their meeting unlawful; but, after the decision of the Courts of Law, the magistrates could not have undertaken to declare the meeting unlawful. The hon. Member says the meeting should have been declared unlawful, because the Orangemen were to carry arms; but I am not prepared to say that the mere possession of arms on the part of those going to a meeting constitute an unlawful meeting. With respect to the Rev. Father Burchall, what was it that he asked the magistrates to do? He asked them to prohibit the meeting, and he asked me to do so. Why did he ask this? Because he knew that his own flock would attack the Orangemen. He did not believe the Orangemen had brought these arms with the intention of using them; but he knew that the Catholic Party would be so offended that they would attack the Orangemen. That is an exactly similar case to the case of the Salvation and Skeleton Armies. In some cases the friends of the Salvation Army have said that they knew that if the Army held a meeting the Skeleton Army would attack them; but the magistrates have held that the Salvationists were not to be treated as aggressors, because the Skeleton Army were likely to attack them. That is exactly the case here. The Orangemen arrived on Cleator Moor. I have no doubt they were absurdly dressed, and may have carried absurd emblems; but if they had been left alone no harm would have been done. As to their having these arms with them, this is not a case like the Derry riots, in which Orangemen are armed to attack other people. If the Orangemen had been left alone, nothing would have happened, and nobody anticipated that anything would happen. The Catholics, however, were determined to attack the Orangemen. The hon. Member says that the magistrates despised the warning of the Rev. Father Burchall, and did nothing; but there he was altogether misinformed.

MR. SEXTON: He told the magistrates that he desired to swear an information.

SIR WILLIAM HARCOURT: He wanted to swear an information that he was under the impression that the meeting would lead to a disturbance; but the magistrates told him that it was of no use to swear an information, because they could not prevent the meeting. The hon. Member is wrong in supposing that the magistrates did nothing. The magistrates thought the matter a very grave one, and gathered together 45 police constables. The hon. Member may not think that a large force. The ordinary force in that district would not have been more than half-a-dozen constables; but, on this occasion, they had the Chief Constable on the spot, and magistrates ready to read the Riot Act, if any disturbance occurred. Therefore, so far from their having neglected the warning of the Rev. Father Burchall, they expected that something serious might take place, and they collected a large force of police. I very much regret that the rev. gentleman's letter to me should have been treated in what must appear to him a discourteous manner. I do not like to throw the blame on other people, but would rather take it upon myself. What happened was, that the letter was put into the letter-box by my Private Secretary. When I get a number of letters, those which I do not answer myself are answered by my Secretary; and others, which I have not time to dispose of, are put into the box to be dealt with by him. By some error —and I should wish it to be supposed to be my own, rather than someone else's—it was imagined that I had seen this letter, and on the day after that it arrived I found it endorsed—"Seen by the Secretary of State." If I had thought that the neglect of that letter had produced any serious consequences, I should be the first to confess it; but it produced no such effect. I will say at once what I should have answered. I should have said that I was sorry that Mr. Burchall's application for the stoppage of the meeting could not be granted; because the law had declared that the magistrates could not prevent such a meeting, but that I would forward the letter to the magistrates, although I observed that he had already written to them, as well as to myself. I could not have instructed them as to what force to send, or as to what they were to do. So much, therefore, for my part in this matter. But I am prepared to maintain that the magistrates acted perfectly properly in the matter. They got together all the constabulary they could, and the force was one which was competent to deal with the case. The magistrates were there ready to read the Riot Act; but it was not necessary to do that, because, after the first collision, the police overpowered the mob. Therefore, the magistrates did collect a sufficient force to deal with the matter; and if it had not been for the unfortunate fact that the Orangemen were armed, nothing serious would have taken place. But I cannot allow this matter to be treated entirely from a one-sided point of view. The Orangemen may have been very foolish; but the Catholics were totally unjustified in attacking them with stones. They were four times the strength of the Orangemen. The hon. Member says that the Orangemen were the aggressors, and gave the provocation; but what provocation is proved? One man thrust a flag in the faces of some others. That is a thing which happens every day or so; but it would not justifiy 6,000 men in attacking another party. That is a thing which happens at every election, and for a mob of 6,000 men to throw stones at another party for such an act is a proceeding totally unjustifiable. To talk of thrusting a flag in the faces of several people as a serious provocation and as a justification of an attack of the kind which took place in this case is unreasonable. Therefore, I cannot say, much as the occurrence is to be deplored, especially the death of this boy, who took no part in the transaction, that the magistrates were to blame. What does the hon. Member say ought to be done in a case of this kind? He says the Government, or the magistrates, ought to have summoned a force of 800 or 1,000 men. But that is totally impossible. In Ireland, where thereyis a constant state of semi-civil warfare going on, there are plenty of police available; but in England we are not in the habit of having 1,000 men constantly ready to deal with a Salvation Army, or a Skeleton Army, or with processions of Catholics or Orangemen. ["Hear, hear!"] A small body of police is quite sufficient to deal with disturbances, and it cannot be held that whenever a row is expected 800 men are to be gathered together. This is really introducing into England from Ireland ideas with which we are not familiar. I cannot condemn the magistrates on this account. As far as I can see, they acted with prudence, and collected an adequate force, and very soon put an end to the difficulty, although an unfortunate shot produced a fatal result. No serious charge, therefore, I think, is to be brought against either the magistrates or the police. And now, what has taken place since? I wrote to the magistrates telling them that the proper thing to do was to get hold of the principal offenders without partiality, and that they have done. They have been active in arresting the ringleaders on both sides. The hon. Member says that only one Party was guilty, and that that was the Party which it appears was attacked. The Orangemen had attacked nobody. The whole row arose from the Catholics attacking the Orangemen. [Mr. SEXTON: No.] The hon. Member may say No; but, so far as the facts are stated in the Papers we have received, there was no attack with the exception of this waving of flags in somebody's face. We do not in England call waving a flag in a man's face an attack. If a man waves a flag in my face, I do not call it an attack, and I should not feel justified in throwing stones at him in consequence. If a man waves a flag in another man's face, and the other man throws a stone back, I should call the man who threw the stone the attacking party. So far as I can see, the magistrates have been perfectly impartial in endeavouring to seize all the leaders who were guilty of violence on this occasion. Whether one party was more in the wrong or used more violence than the other must be decided before the tribunal before which the case must come. But I do not see that the hon. Member has made out any case against the magistrates or the police.

MR. PARNELL said, that however the right hon. Gentleman opposite (Sir

William Harcourt) might suppose that he had made out his case, he had not made it out with regard to one point on which he chiefly relied—namely, that the magistrates had no legal power to proclaim the meeting in question. He thought the right hon. Gentleman unduly under-estimated the proceedings of the Orangemen on that day, and also the gravity of that movement, which appeared to have been transferred from Ireland—having been put down by the magistrates in that country—and to have come within the jurisdiction of the right hon. Gentleman himself. He (Mr. Parnell) was sorry to listen to the speech of the right hon. Gentleman, because he could not help thinking that it would be taken by Orangemen as an indirect incitement to continue these deplorable proceedings. That was not the first time in which the right hon. Gentleman had taken the side of the aggressor in attacks upon Roman Catholics by Orangemen in England. He (Mr. Parnell) recollected that, in 1882, an English village was cleared out of the whole of its Irish population under circumstances of great barbarity towards these unfortunate people. The right hon. Gentleman, on the occasion in question, in his remarks in that House, did as much as he could to excuse the doings of the malefactors, and to render the position of the Irish labouring population still more difficult with regard to earning their bread. Now, he protested against the tone of the right hon. Gentleman's speech, and he believed it would lead to further proceedings of the same character on the part of Orangemen. It must be borne in mind that these were not all Irishmen—they were chiefly Englishmen. The right hon. Gentleman was good enough to say that he would not regard the waving of a flag in his face as any provocation to him; but the mere waving of a flag was not what took place on the occasion in question. According to the Report of the Chief Constable of the district, which had been read out by the right hon. Gentleman the Secretary of State for the Home Department in the House a few nights ago, the disturbance commenced in this way—One of the Orangemen thrust a flag in the faces of some of the crowd. It was well known that flags were attached to poles, the ends of which projected several inches, if not a foot, beyond the drapery which composed the flags. He did not know whether the right hon. Gentleman had ever had a flag thrust in his face—that was to say, whether he had had a pike thrust in his face; but, if so, he (Mr. Parnell) was inclined to think that he would have been very much disposed to gain possession of the flag-staff, and retaliate in kind, and that he would not treat the occurrence with such levity as he had done that evening. But, entirely apart from the question as to who commenced the disturbance, although from the Report of the Chief Constable there could be no manner of doubt about that, the right hon. Gentleman had received full warning by letter from the Rev. Mr. Burchall, that the Orangemen intended to go to Cleator Moor to attend a meeting of the character of which the local magistrates had also full, due, and timely notice from the same source. He was inclined to ask hon. and learned Gentlemen present, with the greatest respect to the Secretary of State, whether a procession armed with revolvers, and known to be armed with revolvers and other weapons, was not an illegal procession; and whether it did not constitute an illegal assembly? The decision which was given by the Courts, and quoted by the right hon. Gentleman the other day, was with regard to an illegal assembly of an entirely different character, because it had reference to an assembly of persons not armed; but a number of men proceeding in a disciplined body with deadly weapons in their possession, and vowing their determination to use those weapons, as his hon. Friend (Mr. Sexton) had described, and going out of their way to meet persons upon whom they might use them—such persons could not be held to constitute a peaceable, orderly, or legal assembly, and as an illegal assembly there was surely some power in the Secretary of State to have prohibited it. And he wished to draw attention to another question. The right hon. Gentleman had been asked some days ago, before this occurrence took place, whether a constable could not arrest, search, and take proceedings against any persons whom he supposed to be carrying a revolver without a licence?

SIR WILLIAM HARCOURT: The hon. Member is mistaken; I do not remember any such Question being put to me.

MR. PARNELL: If it was not asked of the right hon. Gentleman, it was asked of one of his Colleagues; and the reply was that the constable had the power to do that.

SIR WILLIAM HARCOURT: I think the answer must have been that, in case of suspicion of intent to do bodily harm, a constable would have power to arrest. That would be the more legal form of answer.

MR. PARNELL said, he did not think there was any qualification in the case in question. He should be within the remembrance of the Committee, who could correct him; and if his memory served him aright, he believed the Question put was with regard to the carrying of arms without a licence simply as a breach of the Excise Law, and that the answer was that any person could search or take proceedings against a person whom they suspected of carrying weapons contrary to the Excise Law. Well, then, the carrying of revolvers without licences involved a breach of the Excise Law. The magistrates were warned that this assembly of Orangemen were going to carry deadly weapons; and, moreover, on their march, they flourished some of these within sight of the police. He submitted that, under the law, even supposing that the right hon. Gentleman had made out his contention—that it was impossible, under the recent decision of the Courts in 1881, for the magistrates or the Home Office to stop these processions—he submitted that, under the law, it was possible for the police to have surrounded the procession, and for them to have arrested and disarmed the people, carrying these weapons as was done in Ireland under the ordinary law, when people were searched, and revolvers taken from them in sackfuls. That, he said, was the plain course which ought to have been followed; it was a course which would have prevented loss of life, and it was a course which could have been taken within the law. Surely, the right hon. Gentleman the Secretary of State for the Home Department did not mean to say that he regarded the prospect of processions and meetings of Orangemen in England with equanimity. Was that what the right hon. Gentleman intended to convey to the Committee? Because he would have to face the question what would be done on the other side. Did the Government suppose that the other side could not buy revolvers as well as Orangemen? Did they suppose that when the next procession which came into an Irish district in England, where a vast proportion of the population were Irish, that the latter would wait for the Orangemen to shoot them down? That seemed to be the idea which underlay the speech of the right hon. Gentleman. [*Cries of* "No, no!"] Well; but the right hon. Gentleman had offered those people, under the circumstances, no hope of protection; he declared that the law was powerless to assist them, which was equivalent to saying that they must protect themselves. Now, he had pointed out the way in which processions, either of Orangemen or of Irish Nationalists, if they took to the use of arms, which the latter had never done either in Ireland or in England, could legally have their arms taken from them. If those arms could not be legally taken from them in the way he had pointed out, he should be glad if the Secretary of State, with his superior legal knowledge, would point out the way in which it was possible to prevent persons attending these meetings and processions, when there was reason to believe they had deadly weapons in their possession. He pretended to no legal knowledge in this matter himself, and he had only given the reply of a responsible Minister to a Question recently put to him in that House. He asked the right hon. Gentleman whether it was not possible to direct the magistrates to take some steps such as he had indicated, the next time a procession of the kind went into their district, whether Irish Nationalists or Orangemen, when there was reason to suppose that they had deadly weapons in their possession, would be stopped; and whether those who carried such weapons in defiance of the Excise Law would be deprived of them? It seemed to him that both the magistrates and the right hon. Gentleman had the matter entirely within their own power, and that the right hon. Gentleman had no excuse, on the ground of the failure of the law, to supply him with the necessary means for this purpose. Well, he wished to go a little further, and he would say this—the Secretary of State seemed to think that there was an excuse for the resort to deadly weapons on the occasion in question, because, as he had alleged, an assault had been first committed by the National Party on the Orangemen, y the throwing of some stones. He (Mr. Parnell) had shown by the Report of the Chief Constable that the assault, legally and morally, first came from the ranks of the Orangemen. However, passing that by, he contended, notwithstanding the statement of the right hon. Gentleman, that no man was justified in resorting to the use of deadly weapons, unless he supposed that his own life was in danger.

SIR WILLIAM HARCOURT: The hon. Member must have misapprehended me. I never intended to convey any such impression. Far from it; I am of opinion that such conduct is most improper, and most to be condemned. But I will say no more upon the subject, because the matter is under investigation.

MR. PARNELL said, he was bound to defer to the statement of the right hon. Gentleman. He accepted it fully, and to the utmost extent; but, certainly, the impression made by his statement the other day upon his mind was such as he had described. But he wished to reiterate that nobody was entitled, even under circumstances of great provocation, to resort to deadly weapons, except for the purpose of protecting his own life, and when he fully believed that he would lose his life if he did not do so. He believed that was the law; and he believed the result of these proceedings would be to show the Orangemen that they were not entitled to resort to the use of deadly weapons, even though children might hiss them, or even throw stones at them. He should be glad to hear from the right hon. Gentleman the Secretary of State, or some other Minister, a statement on this point. He would repeat that the reply of the Secretary of State had produced a most unfavourable impression on his mind. The right hon. Gentleman had his hands sufficiently full of Salvation Army riots, and other disorderly proceedings, without incurring additional riots of an Orange or Nationalist character. The right hon. Gentleman might depend upon it that if a little firmness were displayed the whole thing would be put down. Immediately the Irish Executive used the powers which they had for dealing with such business in Ireland the whole thing melted away like snow before the sun. He sincerely hoped that the right hon. Gentleman would not allow that wretched religious antagonism to come to a head in this country. He submitted that the Irish labourers and artizans living in England and Scotland, who were toilfully earning their living, were entitled to some protection from the law. In the days when they first came over to England, driven by famine from their native country, they were treated as outcasts, and not entitled to the consideration given to their fellow-men. But that time had gone by, and he trusted the right hon. Gentlemen would not allow the condition of things to be repeated under which these unfortunate men had dragged out their existence. Poverty-stricken they might be, many of them without education; but the Government should remember that the poverty and other evils which surrounded them in England were due to English misgovernment of Ireland in times past. He submitted that these people had a special claim on the Government for protection, and that the Government should see that its duty lay in affording them that protection by putting an end to the infamous attacks to which they had been subjected.

SIR WILLIAM HARCOURT said, he desired to make a few remarks in answer to the moderate and reasonable speech of the hon. Member for the City of Cork (Mr. Parnell). He entirely agreed with the hon. Member that the Irish population in this country deserved all the protection which could be given to them by Parliament and by the Government. England derived great advantage from their labour, which constituted a considerable portion of the national wealth, and they were entitled to quite as much protection and consideration from the Government as any other part of the population. He should deeply regret if, holding the scales as it were between the two Parties, any words of his could be considered as giving the smallest encouragement to that bitter feeling which he thought the Orangemen had displayed towards their opponents on the occasion in question. He repudiated the idea of such a thing, which he believed would be productive of considerable evil in England, as well as in Ireland. The hon. Member for the City of Cork had suggested several ways in which this matter could be dealt with. He asked whether the Secretary of State for the Home Department considered the present state of things satisfactory. His (Sir William Harcourt's) answer to that was, that he thought it most unsatisfactory, inasmuch as it placed the population and magistrates, in towns where there was not an overpowering body of police, in an almost helpless position on occasions such as these.

MR. SEXTON: Would not the Secretary of State for War send a regiment, if application were made by the magistrates?

SIR WILLIAM HARCOURT said, that was a last resort; not one to be used every day. The Secretary of State for War, had it been deemed necessary to do so, would have been able at once to place a military force at the disposal of the magistrates, there having been a force at Carlisle. But he did not think the present state of the law satisfactory, and he would very much like to establish what he believed would be a beneficial change in it—namely, that the magistrates should have power, upon well-founded apprehension of a breach of the peace, to prevent such breach of the peace. He had believed that power already existed; but the Judges had recently decided otherwise, and he was quite willing to introduce a Bill declaring that to be the law. He knew there might be a certain amount of jealousy, on the ground that this power might be used to prevent legitimate meetings; but he did not believe that result would follow. In his opinion, the magistrates, where the police force was not overpowering, and where the public peace was endangered, should have this power. Such was the remedy he proposed. But as to the remedy suggested by the hon. Member for the City of Cork, he did not think it would be efficient. In the first place, the Excise Law could do nothing as against the pikes; and, secondly, it could do nothing against persons who had an Excise licence, because any man could get a licence, and he should not wonder if these people had Excise licences at the time of the occurrence. Therefore, he did not think the proposal of the hon. Member would be effectual. He entirely agreed with the hon. Member that it was not because people were attacked that they were justified in using firearms. Such an act was most cowardly and monstrous. But he did not wish, seeing that the case was before the proper tribunals, to say more upon this subject than that he deeply deplored what had taken place, and that he hoped, from what had been said that evening, that he should be encouraged in introducing a measure to give power to the Local Authorities to prevent meetings when there was a well-founded apprehension of a breach of the peace.

SIR R. ASSHETON CROSS said, he agreed with much that had fallen from the right hon. Gentleman the Secretary of State for the Home Department. He had himself, in former times, been placed in a position of some difficulty, under circumstances similar to those which had been the subject of discussion that evening. They were not accustomed to see these disturbances in England as they were in Ireland; they were happily unknown here, and he need not say how deeply he regretted that anything in the nature of a demonstration on either side should have occurred which tended to produce a breach of the peace. The magistrates in this country were really in a very difficult position under such circumstances, because they very often had not at their disposal sufficient physical force to help them in case of disturbance. But the reason was obvious; because, as he had remarked, it was not the habit of the people in this country to have such meetings; they did not want them, and when they did occur it was on special occasions only. He had taken much pains to make himself acquainted with what had occurred at Cleator Moor, because he was naturally largely concerned and interested in an event which had taken place in a county adjacent to his own. Before concluding, he desired to pay a tribute to the judgment and excellent qualities of the Chief Constable in the district, than whom he believed there was no officer who more thoroughly knew, or more conscientiously acted up to, his duty. He was also bound to say that the observations of the right hon. Gentleman the Secretary of State for the Home Department with reference to legislation on this subject were worthy of the fullest consideration; and he begged to assure him that any Bill which he might bring forward for strengthening the hands of magistrates in the direction indicated, should receive his conscientious attention, quite irrespective of Party views. No one could deplore more than he did the growing custom of carrying arms, and he should indeed be glad to see a stop put to it; for the danger connected with the practice in large towns, politically and otherwise, was extremely great. Finally, the remarks made upon this practice by the hon. Member for the City of Cork (Mr. Parnell), were, in his opinion, worthy of the consideration of the House and of the country, and he trusted sincerely that they would be acted up to in their spirit.

MR. WILLIS said, he was sorry that the right hon. Gentleman the Secretary of State for the Home Department had not condemned, with all the authority of his position, the conduct of those persons in Cumberland which had brought this calamity on the district. It was true the right hon. Gentleman had condemned the spirit shown; but he (Mr. Willis) failed to hear any condemnation of the men who had weapons in their possession for the purpose of shooting down those who interfered with them. There was no justification for their carrying weapons for any such purpose; and, although it was well known that arms were at one time carried by English gentlemen, and although the Bill of Rights recognized the right of carrying arms, he did not believe that the law had ever sanctioned, or recognized, the right of a man to carry arms, with the intention of using them for the destruction of life in case another person interfered with him. This assembly, having been armed, was, in his opinion, an unlawful assembly from the first. When the Orangemen went out with the intentention of using these weapons, in case they were assailed, they acted unlawfully; and, although he was opposed to anything that would interfere with the right of public meeting, properly so called, he was in favour of the magistrates putting down every meeting assembled under the circumstances described. He was sorry that the Secretary of State for the Home Department had not said that any person having a weapon in his possession, and being ready to use it if assaulted, was guilty of murder, if he happened to kill anyone. The right hon. Gentleman, he thought, dissented from that view. If he (Mr. Willis) accidentally had a revolver in his possession, and hastily used it, if he were assaulted, the killing of a man under these circumstances would only be manslaughter; but if, when he went out, he had put a weapon in his pocket with the intention of using it if he were assaulted, and while out he did use it, and unfortunately killed anyone, the crime would be that of murder. Nothing grieved him more than the growing indication they saw of the desire on the part of some members of the community to resort to force. He was glad to be able to say that he had never had a weapon in his hand in his life. Nothing would ever induce him to take one, and, as a consequence, his personal liberty and safety were secured. It was time to put down such scandalous proceedings as those under discussion; they were not to be compared for a moment with the proceedings of the Salvation Army; because, in that case, the people had gone out without weapons, and simply for the purpose of walking the streets, and it was only when violent and indefensible attempts of other processionists to interfere with them were made that riots were brought about. The men in the case under discussion had gone out with weapons in their possession, and with the determination to take advantage of any momentary exhibition of temper to provoke a breach of the peace and to use violence.

MR. SYNAN said, that the magistrates of the district in which the disturbance had occurred were informed, several days before the meeting, that if the Orange demonstration took place there would be danger to human life. A similar notice had been sent to the Home Office. What was it the duty of the magistrates to do on that occasion? Why, their duty plainly was this—either to act on the evidence they had received, or to call on their informants to make sworn informations. If they had acted on the evidence they had received, they could have obtained sufficient force to prevent any serious bodily injury being inflicted. The right hon. Gentleman the Secretary of State for the Home Department seemed to take the view that the Salvation Army case was a precedent for this. That, however, he (Mr. Synan) could not agree with, because the Salvation Army meeting was a lawful meeting—it was a "lawful assembly," the people simply gathering together to sing hymns and recite prayers. He had never heard that a such an assembly was likely to injure human life, or that there was any danger of an exhibition of physical force in connection with it. What precedent was there in connection with such a meeting for another assembly of men armed with swords and spears and revolvers—what precedent could a Salvation Army gathering be for an assembly of 1,000 or 2,000 men armed in this manner on one particular day? Why, it had been established law for very many years that an assembly of that kind was an "unlawful assembly," and if the right hon. Gentleman had any doubt upon it he should have instructed someone to prosecute members of the assembly for the purpose of having the question decided, once for all, in a Court of Law. The right hon. Gentleman had said that the only authority to decide the matter was a Court of Law; but had he put it in such a course of training that a decision of a Court of Law would be taken upon it? The mere fact of the assault being brought before a magistrate, or before a Judge, would not decide the question of law as to whether the assembly was lawful or not; but if the right hon. Gentleman caused any member of the armed assembly to be arrested and taken before a Court of Law, the question would then be decided whether the armed gathering at Cleator Moor was an assembly similar to the Salvation Army, which collected in a village for the purpose of singing songs or reciting prayers. If an ordinary member of the Cleator Moor assembly were prosecuted, the Court of Law would then decide the matter, and, to his mind, hon. Members would find that the result would be a declaration that the Salvation Army case was no precedent for the other. His belief had been that the law of England, as established by all the authorities and all the books, was that an armed assembly which was likely to prove dangerous to any person or any body of men was an unlawful assembly, and that it ought to be put down by force, or that there should be such a force present as would prevent the assembly from using its arms against any innocent person. Was there such a force at present at Cleator Moor? Was a body of 45 policemen a sufficient force to prevent thousands of armed men from using their weapons against other men who rose up when they came into their village? The attack made by the villagers was no justification for the firing of arms. As his hon. and learned Friend (Mr. Willis) had said, the firing of arms and the killing of any person, if the arms were carried without premeditation, would amount to manslaughter only; but if the arms were carried with premeditation, such shooting might amount to murder. He asked, therefore, why, under these circumstances, the magistrates had not brought together a sufficient force to prevent this large armed assembly from meeting? Why did not the magistrates take this course, having a full knowledge that the meeting was to take place, and that the men were to be armed? It seemed to him to be a very plain case, and he was astonished the right hon. Gentleman the Secretary of State for the Home Department, being a lawyer himself, should have any doubt at all about it. If the right hon. Gentleman had a doubt at all about it, he (Mr. Synan) would put it to him that it was his duty to settle the law and settle the doubt by prosecuting members of the meeting for being members of an "unlawful assembly." On a former occasion, the right hon. Gentleman had stated that he had caused some of the inhabitants of the village who threw stones to be arrested—he had insinuated that the guilty persons were the inhabitants of Cleator Moor. The right hon. Gentleman had said—"If I went out armed, and shot a man who threw a stone at me"—but he (Sir William Harcourt) would not form an "assembly," though he might be a host in himself. A man had a right to go armed for the protection of his own life. No one had a right to assault him, and if anyone did, and he used the weapon he happened to have about him for the purpose of protecting himself, he was adopting a course which he had a perfect right to adopt; but that was not the case with each individual member of an "unlawful assembly," which entered a town or a village of an unarmed people with the intenion of using their arms against those unarmed people, if in the excitement of the moment they came out for the purpose of making a protest against the invasion of their

disorder, whose fault was it? Who kept up the Orange disorder in Ireland? Who, in 1848, distributed thousands upon thousands stands of arms to the Orangemen of Belfast? Of course, he did not intend to enter into that subject; but even Earl Spencer, a Member of the present Cabinet, some 10 years ago, when he was last in Office, and when there was some little difficulty in the country, took occasion to go to the North, where he was more welcome than he was at the present moment, to arouse the spirit of Orangeism, and to incite Orangemen against the general body of Catholics. The Secretary of State, knowing that that was the state of things in Ireland, that the Orangemen had had the approval of the Government for centuries, that the Catholic population, not having Grand Juries to throw out bills against them for murder, usually got the worst of it, and that the law had been in favour of Orangemen, the hangman only being on the side of the Catholics, provoked the laughter of certain London Aldermen by congratulating the House on the smug contentment of England, which could afford to be content, not having been conquered itself, or, at least, having put up with its conquering. The right hon. Gentleman congratulated himself upon the fact that Englishmen could be oblivious to these demonstrations. He (Mr. Healy) believed that what would happen would be this—that the people of Cleator Moor, seeing that Orangemen could shoot with immunity, and could come down with force of arms without, so far as he could judge, any strong disapproval being manifested by the Secretary of State, would also bring arms, and, if they were again insulted in this way, would very probably feel inclined to use them; and if this did occur, the Government of Her Majesty the Queen, through the mouth of the right hon. Gentleman, would be distinctly responsible for that position of affairs. If the law in the Sittingbourne case had failed, how was it, he asked, that the Government in Ireland found no difficulty in preventing these assemblies? Before the Crimes Act was passed, the Government, as a matter of course, found no difficulty in putting a stop to any meeting that they found inconvenient. In Drogheda, for instance, two years ago, a meeting which had not been proclaimed was dispersed by Mr. Clifford Lloyd, who brought down by special train 200 policemen from Dundalk and a body of Cavalry. He brought his men down at the double, drew them across the streets, and levelled their bayonets at the breasts of the people, declaring, without reading a proclamation, that if they did not disperse, they would be shot down. If such a thing could be legally done in Ireland, where was the difficulty of dealing with the question in this country? If the Sittingbourne case tied the hands of the Government, why not prosecute the leaders of the assembly for riot? If the leaders knew that they would be indicted for holding an illegal assembly and for riot, he ventured to think they would soon give up the system of coming armed into a district where they knew that their presence would be provocative of disorder. But as to the statement made by the right hon. Gentleman, with regard to the necessity for a change in the law, he (Mr. Healy) could not follow him. To his (Mr. Healy's) mind, the law was sufficiently strong if it were only put into force. So far as the Irish people had been able to judge of it—and they had quite enough experience of it—the law was sufficiently strong. They could put down meetings without the Crimes Act, and they had their Constabulary, and they could give the order—"If you do not march, we will shoot you." He ventured to say that had the 45 constables at Cleator Moor displayed the same amount of vigour that the Royal Irish Constabulary would have displayed against the Nationalists, this murder would not have taken place. But the Government, who were so gingerly in dealing with these matters in England, found no difficulty in dealing with them in Ireland. If the Secretary of State for the Home Department were transplanted to Dublin Castle—[Sir WILLIAM HARCOURT: No, no!]—well, he joined with the right hon. Gentleman in protesting against such an event as that ever happening; but if the right hon. Gentleman, by any chance, should be transplanted, he would have no difficulty in learning how to deal with these assemblies. The right hon. Gentleman had told them that England not being in a state of semi-civil war, they did not want a large body of policemen. That might be so; but they always had large

sulting the people—insulting the Catholics by smashing the panes of glass in their chapel—the people were to do nothing. The people did do nothing until this act of violence was offered. Hon. Members knew very well that where they had a powder magazine it only needed a spark to cause an explosion. Therefore, the right hon. Gentleman was wrong to make so little of an event which had led to a collision on the occasion in question. Let them suppose that, instead of being an assemblage of Orangemen, brought from a distance to march through a Catholic district, this had been a Fenian procession marching through the streets of London. Supposing the Fenians were to meet openly, as the Reformers met on Monday last on the Embankment; and supposing they carried swords and guns with them, and supposing that they marched on, waving flags and insulting the general population by whom they were surrounded, and supposing the excited crowd through which they proceeded was calm enough not to attack them, notwithstanding the insults they showered around, and notwithstanding the waving of their flags bearing devices insulting to the English people, if they thrusted one of these flags in the face of an Englishman, how would the right hon. Gentleman have treated the riot, supposing that assault had been resented by the knocking down of a Fenian, and had led to that Fenian drawing a revolver and shooting one of the citizens? Why, he would have treated it in a very different manner. The speech of the right hon. Gentleman would arouse many evil passions in this country. The Irish Members had been accused of never having denounced violence and disorder. Well, the Irish Members, at least, had not the responsibility of Ministers of the Crown. They never had that responsibility, and they were never likely to have it; but here was a Minister of the Crown, who was practically, to a large extent, the conservator of peace in the country, getting up and speaking of a riot in which one man was killed, and scores had been wounded, without saying one single word against the practice of carrying arms. ["Oh, oh!" *and* "He did refer to it!"] Well, at any rate, the right hon. Gentleman had not mentioned it until it had been dragged out of him by the hon. Member for the City of Cork (Mr. Parnell). In this initial speech the right hon. Gentleman had not one word to say about the carrying of arms; and it was not until the hon. Member for the City of Cork said—"If you do not defend these people, they will have to defend themselves," that the right hon. Gentleman, seeing to what conclusion his speech had led hon. Members, was obliged to utter some academic words against the practice of carrying arms. [Mr. GLADSTONE dissented.] But the right hon. Gentleman took great care to add—and he (Mr. Healy) would have the Prime Minister, who was shaking his head, to bear this in mind—"if they carry an Excise licence, I do not see how we could prevent them." In other words, dealing with an Orange demonstration—dealing with a body of men with hundreds of pounds at their command, and who, therefore, could easily obtain licences to carry arms—the right hon. Gentleman says—"The law may be against you, if you assemble with arms under ordinary circumstances; but, if your funds are large enough to procure licences, then you may go down and shoot Catholics, and no one will be able to punish you." The Catholics of Cleator Moor—a population of 6,000 people—had a foreign body brought from a distance amongst them, for the purpose of assembling and provoking them; and the right hon. Gentleman the Secretary of State, knowing that, and that there were only 45 police, brought, as the right hon. Gentleman had said, from far afield for the purpose of protecting the law, gave it to be understood that these were the only officers who could be got together to keep the peace between 1,200 armed men and 6,000 or 8,000 Catholics. If that were the case, it was surely a very regretable state of things. How did they deal with these matters in Ireland? The right hon. Gentleman the Secretary of State had made great capital, and had evoked the somewhat sneering cheers of his Friends by saying that in England they were not in the constant state of semi-civil war that they were in Ireland. The right hon. Gentleman had produced great laughter when he told them that in this country people were of a very calm and pacific habit of mind, and that it was only in Ireland that the people were of a wild and riotous disposition. But if in Ireland they were occasionally provoked to disorder, whose fault was it? Who kept up the Orange disorder in Ireland? Who, in 1848, distributed thousands upon thousands stands of arms to the Orangemen of Belfast? Of course, he did not intend to enter into that subject; but even Earl Spencer, a Member of the present Cabinet, some 10 years ago, when he was last in Office, and when there was some little difficulty in the country, took occasion to go to the North, where he was more welcome than he was at the present moment, to arouse the spirit of Orangeism, and to incite Orangemen against the general body of Catholics. The Secretary of State, knowing that that was the state of things in Ireland, that the Orangemen had had the approval of the Government for centuries, that the Catholic population, not having Grand Juries to throw out bills against them for murder, usually got the worst of it, and that the law had been in favour of Orangemen, the hangman only being on the side of the Catholics, provoked the laughter of certain London Aldermen by congratulating the House on the smug contentment of England, which could afford to be content, not having been conquered itself, or, at least, having put up with its conquering. The rig t hon. Gentleman congratulated himself upon the fact that Englishmen could be oblivious to these demonstrations. He (Mr. Healy) believed that what would happen would be this—that the people of Cleator Moor, seeing that Orangemen could shoot with immunity, and could come down with force of arms without, so far as he could judge, any strong disapproval being manifested by the Secretary of State, would also bring arms, and, if they were again insulted in this way, would very probably feel inclined to use them; and if this did occur, the Government of Her Majesty the Queen, through the mouth of the right hon. Gentleman, would be distinctly responsible for that position of affairs. If the law in the Sittingbourne case had failed, how was it, he asked, that the Government in Ireland found no difficulty in preventing these assemblies? Before the Crimes Act was passed, the Government, as a matter of course, found no difficulty in putting a stop to any meeting that they found inconvenient. In Drogheda, for instance, two years ago, a meeting which had not been proclaimed was dispersed by Mr. Clifford Lloyd, who brought down by special train 200 policemen from Dundalk and a body of Cavalry. He brought his men down at the double, drew them across the streets, and levelled their bayonets at the breasts of the people, declaring, without reading a proclamation, that if they did not disperse, they would be shot down. If such a thing could be legally done in Ireland, where was the difficulty of dealing with the question in this country? If the Sittingbourne case tied the hands of the Government, why not prosecute the leaders of the assembly for riot? If the leaders knew that they would be indicted for holding an illegal assembly and for riot, he ventured to think they would soon give up the system of coming armed into a district where they knew that their presence would be provocative of disorder. But as to the statement made by the right hon. Gentleman, with regard to the necessity for a change in the law, he (Mr. Healy) could not follow him. To his (Mr. Healy's) mind, the law was sufficiently strong if it were only put into force. So far as the Irish people had been able to judge of it—and they had quite enough experience of it—the law was sufficiently strong. They could put down meetings without the Crimes Act, and they had their Constabulary, and they could give the order—"If you do not march, we will shoot you." He ventured to say that had the 45 constables at Cleator Moor displayed the same amount of vigour that the Royal Irish Constabulary would have displayed against the Nationalists, this murder would not have taken place. But the Government, who were so gingerly in dealing with these matters in England, found no difficulty in dealing with them in Ireland. If the Secretary of State for the Home Department were transplanted to Dublin Castle—[Sir WILLIAM HARCOURT: No, no!]—well, he joined with the right hon. Gentleman in protesting against such an event as that ever happening; but if the right hon. Gentleman, by any chance, should be transplanted, he would have no difficulty in learning how to deal with these assemblies. The right hon. Gentleman had told them that England not being in a state of semi-civil war, they did not want a large body of policemen. That might be so; but they always had large bodies of troops to rely on, and there could not be the slightest doubt that the use of a troop or two of the soldiery, or the mere sight of the soldiery, would have induced the Orangemen to disperse without the slightest delay. But he (Mr. Healy), in the present attitude of the Government, saw the snake of the Reform agitation lurking in the grass. It might be necessary for men in the Irish towns to demonstrate against the House of Lords. Englishmen might have to meet with pikes and swords, and some anti-Reformer might get a prod in the back, and it might not be convenient to indict his assailant for unlawful assembly. He would put it to the Government, in conclusion, whether, looking at the fact that this Orange organization in every phase only excited the disturbing element, it was not time that steps should be taken to put a stop to it? They should look at what was done in Ireland, America, and Newfoundland, where 30 or 40 men were indicted for murder and riot. He would put it to the Government, that when they found an organization like that of the Orangemen, only showing itself in one phase, and that phase being brutality and outrage, it was not time for them to take some prompt and vigorous action to put it down?

COLONEL COLTHURST said, he should like to approach the subject from another point of view, though without detracting from the merits of the observations of the hon. Member who spoke last (Mr. Healy)—he should like to take up the subject where the hon. Member for Limerick (Mr. Synan) had left it. The hon. Member had made an appeal to the law. If the law was in the uncertain state that the Secretary of State for the Home Department had declared it to be in, his hon. Friend (Mr. Synan) had pointed out how it could be ascertained—namely, by indicting some of the persons who took part in the assembly, which, according to the opinion of his hon. Friend, was an unlawful one. He had always been under the impression that it was in the power of magistrates or of the Government, at any rate in Ireland, to proclaim any meeting or procession, no matter how lawful the purpose might be, if there was reasonable apprehension of a breach of the peace. It seemed, however, that that was not the law, and he thought the Government ought to take such steps as were necessary to ascertain the exact state of the law.

MR. JUSTIN M'CARTHY said, he wished to ask for further information as to the condition of the law in this country; for the statement of the right hon. Gentleman (Sir William Harcourt) was most unsatisfactory, and the law seemed to be in a most barbarous condition. As he understood the right hon. Gentleman, a number of men might assemble and march out for a purpose not in itself unlawful and might go armed to the teeth, every man carrying some sort of weapon, and that so long as they paid the licence for carrying arms, they were entitled to go to any part of a city and make a demonstration against the citizens. Was that actually the law? Was it the law that a number of men—say, a number of anti-Reformers—might march to Chelsea, or promenade in Mid Lothian, armed with guns and swords, and sword-bayonets, and be protected in doing so? If that was the law, it was unworthy of any civilized country. Speaking not as a lawyer, nor professing to know much about the law, he could hardly believe that that was the law in any civilized country; but if it was the law, and if any number of men might publicly parade in what he would call battle array, armed to the teeth, whenever they pleased, then it was time that an improvement in the law should take place. If he (Mr. Justin M'Carthy) were Secretary of State for the Home Department, he would bring in a short Bill declaring that, in this country, as in every civilized country, it was not legal for men to march, in battle array, menacing, with weapons of all kinds, through the heart of a peaceable town. He did not know whether his hon. Friends would agree with him; but he hoped the Secretary of State for the Home Department would bring in a short Bill giving the magistrates further powers. The business of the law in a civilized country was to protect meetings which had nothing directly illegal in them. The Orangemen had a perfect right to hold their meetings and have their processions, and he thought the duty and business of the law was, at any cost, to protect all men in their right to meet and hold demonstrations. He must say he thought the right hon. Gentleman, in one part of his speech, had treated rather too lightl the manner in which this matter began. He spoke of someone thrusting a flag in the face of someone else, and asked if anyone would seriously resent such a trifle as that? The right hon. Gentleman had further said that the magistrates did not suppose there would be any chance of a serious disturbance; but he did not agree with the right hon. Gentleman that they knew so little of Orange riots as that came to. Those magistrates must have been very young, indeed, if they could not remember the Orange riots in Manchester and Liverpool. Some years ago this House was driven again and again into discussions upon the prevention of the annual outbreaks in Liverpool and Manchester. Why had not these magistrates foreseen that an armed procession of Orangemen through this place would lead to bad temper and the chance of some disturbance? The Secretary of State for the Home Department might bring in a measure to prevent armed demonstrations of this kind; and he should also see that a sufficient force of military or police was got together to secure to men the right of meeting, and to prevent their meetings being turned into armed demonstrations.

MR. HARRINGTON said, he wished to support the remarks of his hon. Friend (Mr. Justin M'Carthy) upon what he considered the unnecessary course pursued by the Secretary of State for the Home Department in regard to giving additional powers to magistrates for the suppression of public meetings. He did not think it was just to the people of England, who wished to enjoy, to the fullest extent, the right of public meeting, that because disturbances might occasionally take place between different bodies of Irishmen, therefore the right of public meeting in England should be curtailed. The people were entitled, to the fullest extent, to hold public meetings, and he thought his hon. Friend would agree with him that the Irish Members had no desire whatever to curtail that right. But he submitted that there was no necessity whatever for any curtailment of that right; and he thought the right hon. Gentleman would agree with him that the magistrates had not been quite so active as they might have been. It was quite possible that they might not have apprehended that consequences of such a serious character might arise from the demonstration, and it was also possible that the representation of a Catholic clergyman might have been looked upon by them as only a partizan declaration, and as intended to prevent what was a legitimate right of the Orangemen to hold a meeting. They had no desire, either in England or Ireland, to curtail the right of Orangemen to hold meetings; but what they did object to was that when they met they should assemble with arms. That was *primâ facie* evidence, that if there was any hostility whatever shown, they were prepared to shoot down those who expressed any opinion opposed to theirs. In the next place, they contended that a meeting of that kind, with Party emblems, was calculated to excite bitter feeling and to endanger the peace; and, although they did not wish to interfere with or curtail their right of meeting, they held that it was the duty of the authorities wherever such meetings were held to have a sufficient force to prevent a collision between those who met and those who objected. He was very glad the right hon. Gentleman had had a second opportunity of speaking on this subject; because, undoubtedly, his second speech had, to a very large extent, done away with the unhappy impressions created by his first speech. He did not think the right hon. Gentleman had intended to convey that impression, and he was confirmed in that belief by the answer which the right hon. Gentleman had given to a Question immediately after the riots took place. In that answer the right hon. Gentleman had given an assurance—and he (Mr. Harrington) thought his hon. Friend might be satisfied with that assurance—that, in future, cases of this kind would be dealt with more vigorously than in this instance. He did not at all anticipate any danger arising from the purely Orange demonstrations in England; but what he regarded as the chief element of danger in this matter was, that where a body of Orangemen lived in England among people who sympathized with them as English people, it was possible that the demonstrations might be used for trade or Party purposes. If they were not more vigorously dealt with than they had been in the past, greater danger might arise in connection with them in future. He did not believe there was any necessity for an amendment of the law in the direction of giving further powers to the magistrates. As the law now was they could call in the military when necessary, and could summon to their assistance special constables; and, therefore, they had ample powers for dealing with these meetings.

Mr. PERCY WYNDHAM said, that though they had had knowledge of such demonstrations as this in Cumberland for the last 18 years past, they had never been of any great size, and had never attracted any particular attention, and they had never caused anything approaching to a disturbance. Therefore, he did not think the magistrates could naturally have expected that, on this occasion, anything would take place more than had usually occurred. But, as this question was being considered, he should like to raise the point as to whether something could be done to discourage the practice of carrying revolvers. What did anyone in this country, who was not a soldier or a policeman, want with a pistol? When the present Lord Sherbrooke was Chancellor of the Exchequer, he proposed that a high duty should be put upon pistols. It was not only Orangemen or Catholics who used revolvers, but it was the habit of all the mining population in the North to carry pistols, and what he would suggest was that a duty of one guinea should be put upon the carrying of a revolver.

Mr. DAWSON said, the question was whether there had been justice in the course pursued in this matter? If the matter were reversed, and the Catholics of Cleator Moor went into the Orange district, and a Protestant rector or clergyman wrote a letter to the magistrates, as a Catholic clergyman had done in this case, would that warning have been overlooked? Would the magistrates have taken no steps whatever to prevent a disturbance? Would they have allowed these people to gather together when they had the power to search them for arms carried without a licence? The Secretary of State for the Home Department was begging the question when he said these people probably had licences. No one knew whether they had or not; but they could have been prevented from carrying arms. He was strongly impressed by the idea that there was no fair play in dealing with Orangemen. Some time ago, he was in Omagh when some Orangemen used arms quite recklessly. It was, therefore, clear that there was one law for Orangemen and another for the Nationalists; and by this country, which had ever been distinguished for exercising justice between contending parties, favouritism was shown to the Orangemen. He quite agreed with the hon. Member for Monaghan (Mr. Healy) that there was no desire on the part of Irish Members to interfere with the right of public meeting in England or in Ireland; but they wanted fair and even-handed justice, and that Orangemen should not be treated with favouritism. But the Secretary of State had not shown any evidence of a spirit of fair play in his own mind in his answer to the questions of the hon. Member for Limerick (Mr. Synan). Would he indict these people, and prevent their carrying arms as they had hitherto done? It would be very satisfactory if the right hon. Gentleman would give an assurance to that effect.

Sir WILLIAM HARCOURT said, he was sorry if he had not answered the questions put to him precisely. He might indict the Orangemen for being members of an unlawful assembly and carrying arms; but in this country he could not indict people simply for carrying arms. The Government could not enter upon indictments without reasonable grounds for believing them to be well-founded. Unless they were well-founded, he could not enter upon them.

Mr. KENNY said, no hon. Member on that side would object to the right of meeting; but people ought not to be allowed to go about with offensive weapons to the terror of Her Majesty's subjects. He knew Cleator Moor, and he was the principal speaker at the last Catholic meeting held there. The majority of the people in that part of Cumberland were Irishmen and Catholics, and they came some distance from the town to meet him, with bands, but no arms. There was no violence and no bloodshed; but the origin of these demonstrations in Cumberland he believed lay in the fact that, something like 18 years ago, a certain notorious preacher named Murphy, who went about insulting Catholic gentlemen, and making absurd and mischievous charges against the monasteries and members of that religion, met with his death at the hands of a Whitehaven mob of Catholics. The population of Cleator Moor was mainly Catholic; but Whitehaven was almost exclusively Protestant. There were a number of small mining towns in that district, and for the last 17 years those towns had been exclusively selected as the scenes of these annual celebrations of the victory of the Battle of the Boyne; but, for the first time, Cleator Moor had been selected this year, because a small body of Orangemen, who belonged to an Orange Lodge there, threatened to secede from the Lodge unless Cleator Moor was selected. The Orangemen naturally expected that there would be considerable opposition if they went to Cleator Moor. The arrival of a great body of men from the different mining towns and villages had, no doubt, the effect of attracting a great crowd of Catholics. The Secretary of State for the Home Department had expressed some surprise that the thrusting of a flag in a person's face had stirred up a riot, and he also spoke of the *odium theologicum;* but he seemed to forget that it was easier to provoke a breach of the peace when the subject was religion. Without going into the question of the rights of the Home Office, he certainly thought that Department was to blame for not having directed special constables to be sworn in. It was an extraordinary thing that human life should have been sacrificed owing to the culpable neglect of the officials, and he was satisfied that if these complaints had come from a different source, the Home Office would not have been so remiss in its duty as it had been in this instance.

MR. SEXTON said, that, having listened attentively to the statement of the Secretary of State for the Home Department, he felt justified in hoping that the results of this debate would be salutary, not only with regard to the vindication of justice in this case, but to the preservation of the peace in similar cases. He therefore did not feel called upon to put the Committee to the trouble of a Division.

Motion, by leave, *withdrawn.*

Original Question put, and *agreed to.*

(10.) £285,109, to complete the sum for Convict Establishments in England and the Colonies.

(11.) £374,869, to complete the sum for Prisons, England.

MR. HARRINGTON said, he had intended to move a reduction of this Vote, because he had fruitlessly drawn attention to the scant pay of prison officials in Ireland, and he thought that if officials could be got cheaply to perform onerous duties in that country, there was no reason why cheap labour should not be got in England.

SIR WILLIAM HARCOURT said, that if there was any serious objection to this Vote, he would move to report Progress. He did not know whether the hon. Member (Mr. Harrington) meant to oppose the Vote; but, perhaps, it would meet his views to defer his discussion until they came to the Irish Prisons Vote.

MR. HARRINGTON said, it was impossible to move to increase the Irish Estimate; indeed, they had no means of drawing attention to the poor salaries paid to the Irish prison officials except by moving to reduce the Vote for the English prison officials.

SIR R. ASSHETON CROSS said, this question was one which had been specially referred to the Royal Commission, and therefore he thought it would be better to defer the discussion upon it until, at all events, they had received the Report of the Commissioners.

MR. HARRINGTON said, he should be glad to agree to the suggestion, if the right hon. Gentleman (Sir R. Assheton Cross) could hold out any hope that before the Irish Estimates came on for consideration, the Report of the Commissioners, together with the recommendations which they, no doubt, would make, would be laid before the House. If the right hon. Gentleman would undertake that his Report should be laid on the Table before the end of the Session, he (Mr. Harrington) would be glad to postpone his Motion.

SIR R. ASSHETON CROSS said, he would do all he could to publish the Report before the end of the Session. He really thought that to discuss the subject on the present Vote, with the Report of the Commissioners pending, would be a useless waste of time. He hoped the hon. Gentleman would postpone his Motion.

MR. HARRINGTON said, he had only been prompted to move in the matter now, because the question had been so very frequently raised, so many recommendations had been made, and so much reluctance to do justice in the matter had been shown by the Members of the Treasury Bench. Last year the hon. Gentleman the Secretary to the Treasury (Mr. Courtney) based his argument on the fact that the officials of the Irish prisons could live more cheaply than similar officials in England; but that, to his (Mr. Harrington's) mind, was no valid argument at all.

MR. R. N. FOWLER (LORD MAYOR) said, he hoped the Government would now consent to report Progress. Hon. Members had been brought down, night after night, to consider the Municipal Elections (Corrupt and Illegal Practices) Bill. That was the fourth or fifth night that Members had been brought down for that purpose, so that he hoped Progress would now be reported, or that an assurance would be given that the Bill would not be proceeded with to-night.

MR. HARRINGTON said, he understood that the Government intended to move to report Progress. Failing such a disposition on their part, he would move to report Progress.

Motion made, and Question proposed, "That the Chairman do report Progress, and ask leave to sit again."—(*Mr. Harrington.*)

SIR WILLIAM HARCOURT said, he hoped the hon. Gentleman (Mr. Harrington) would allow them to take this Vote, reserving any discussion he might wish to raise until the Irish Prisons Vote was brought on. Of course, if the hon. Member declined to do that, there was no course open to the Government but to consent to report Progress.

MR. HARRINGTON said, he would raise a discussion on the Irish Vote, and would, therefore, ask leave to withdraw his Motion.

Motion, by leave, *withdrawn.*

Original Question again proposed.

MR. BARRY said, that for two or three years proposals were made with the object of making prison labour more remunerative than it was at present. At that time, an agitation was got up against the manufacture of cocoa-nut matting, and in consequence, he believed, the manufacture was discontinued in seven or eight prisons. Had any other manufactures been discontinued?

MR. HIBBERT said, that what the hon. Member (Mr. Barry) had stated had been carried out to a great extent. Mat-making was carried on to some extent in most prisons, though the manufacture had been limited on the ground that it was injuriously affecting the trade. He had, in his possession, a Return of the prison labour for the last five years, and it showed a considerable increase upon the amount received therefrom. In 1879, the total amount received for manufactures and work upon buildings was £41,000; but, in the year 1884, the amount had increased to £68,800. Though the number of prisoners in local prisons had decreased by something like 2,700, the increase in the sum received from prison labour was such as he had mentioned. In the ordinary service of the prison, the value of the work done was—In 1879, £74,000; in 1884, £78,000; so that the total value of prison labour was, in 1879, £115,000, and in 1884, £147,000. The Prison Commissioners were endeavouring to increase the number of trades in prisons, in order to do away with interference with one particular trade, such as mat-making.

MR. BARRY said, he was glad to hear there had been an increase in the amount received from prison labour, yet the amount received might be much larger.

MR. RANKIN asked, if there was any intention to further reduce the number of prisons?

SIR WILLIAM HARCOURT said, the number of prisons was being gradually reduced. The desirability of closing two other prisons was now under consideration. He was merely carrying out the policy laid down in the Prisons Act, of consolidating prisons so far as consolidation might be compatible with the convenience of the localities, which must be regarded in the matter.

Vote *agreed to.*

Resolutions to be reported *To-morrow.*

Committee to sit again *To-morrow.*

MUNICIPAL ELECTIONS (CORRUPT AND ILLEGAL PRACTICES) BILL.

(*Mr. Attorney General, Secretary Sir William Harcourt, Sir Charles W. Dilke, Mr. Solicitor General.*)

[BILL 252.] CONSIDERATION.

Further Proceeding on Consideration, as amended, *resumed.*

Bill, as amended, *further considered.*

MR. WARTON, in moving, as an Amendment, the insertion of the following Clause:—

(Interpretation of "The Corrupt and Illegal Practices Act, 1883.")

"In construing 'The Corrupt and Illegal Practices Act, 1883,' the words 'Solicitor to the Treasury' shall be deemed to be substituted for 'Director of Public Prosecutions,'"

said, it would be in the recollection of the hon. and learned Gentleman the Attorney General (Sir Henry James) that, for many years past, he (Mr. Warton) had pressed upon him very strongly the utter impropriety of maintaining the office of Director of Public Prosecutions. A Committee had been appointed to consider the subject, and it had reported that, as far as possible, the office should be amalgamated with, or absorbed in, the office of Solicitor to the Treasury. A Bill had been brought in to carry out the recommendation of the Committee. That Bill ought to make its way through the House; but an obstinate Scotch Member, who wanted to force the Scotch system on the English people, had blocked the Bill. There was, therefore, little chance of the measure passing this Session; but with regard to prosecutions for electoral corruption, he (Mr. Warton) had endeavoured, by this Amendment, to give effect to the recommendation of the Committee. The Public Prosecutor had been found wanting. The Solicitor to the Treasury was a very good official, and that was an additional reason why the Amendment should be accepted.

New Clause (Interpretation of "The Corrupt and Illegal Practices Act, 1883,")—(*Mr. Warton,*)—*brought up*, and read the first time.

Motion made, and Question proposed, "That the Clause be read a second time."

THE ATTORNEY GENERAL (Sir HENRY JAMES) said, he was sorry he could not accept the Amendment, the effect of which would be to alter the whole of their work of last year by substituting Solicitor to the Treasury for Public Prosecutor. So long as the Public Prosecutor existed the duties they had placed on him by the original Act ought to be continued by this Act. If the gentleman in question ceased to be Director of Public Prosecutions, and his place was taken by the Solicitor to the Treasury, this clause was unnecessary, because they would transfer the duties from the one to the other. He did not think they ought to take away from the Public Prosecutor the duties he had under the original Act, still leaving him in existence for all other purposes. He (Sir Henry James) hoped the hon. and learned Gentleman (Mr. Warton) would not press his Amendment.

Question put, and *negatived.*

Clause 2 (Definition and punishment of corrupt practice at municipal election).

THE ATTORNEY GENERAL (Sir HENRY JAMES) moved, as an Amendment, in page 1, line 10, after "set forth in," insert "Part One of."

Amendment *agreed to.*

Words *inserted* accordingly.

MR. WARTON moved, as an Amendment, in page 1, to insert, after "election," in line 14—

"Other than the offence of aiding, abetting, counselling, and procuring the commission of the offence of personation."

The object of this Amendment was to reduce, to a certain extent, the penalty for the offence of aiding and abetting personation, for the Amendment must be read with the next one which stood in his name, which was to add at the end of the clause—

"A person guilty of the offence of aiding, abetting, counselling, and procuring the commission of the offence of personation, shall be liable to the like punishment, and subject to the like incapacities, as a person guilty of bribery."

It would, no doubt, be in the recollection of the House that, at the time the Ballot Act was introduced, it was imagined that it would lead to a great amount of personation. As a matter of fact, bribery had been reduced and personation had not increased. At the time terrible penalties were provided for persons who were found impersonating; indeed, the penalties were made much heavier than those for bribery under influence, and so forth. It seemed to him that it was not right to inflict heavier penalties for personation than for bribery, especially now that the working of the Ballot Act had shown that personation was not carried on to any great extent.

Surely, it was unnecessary to have extraordinarily high penalties for one particular offence. Personally, he was afraid that the effect of high penalties would be to defeat the object of the Bill.

Amendment proposed,

In page 1, line 14, after "election," insert "other than the offence of aiding, abetting, counselling, and procuring the commission of the offence of personation."—(*Mr. Warton.*)

Question proposed, "That those words be there inserted."

THE ATTORNEY GENERAL (Sir HENRY JAMES) said, they discussed this matter very fully last year, when they were in Committee upon the Parliamentary Elections (Corrupt and Illegal Practices) Bill; and he believed his hon. and learned Friend (Mr. Warton) made the same suggestion then that he made now. He (Sir Henry James) did not wish to make any difference between the law affecting Parliamentary elections and that affecting municipal elections. It seemed absurd to say they would pass one sentence for the offence of personation if committed at a Parliamentary election, and another sentence if the offence was committed at a municipal election. Inasmuch as they had taken one course in relation to Parliamentary elections, he wished to adhere to it in cases of municipal elections. The Amendment amounted to this—that if a person procured another person to personate 100 voters, he should receive a milder punishment than the person who really committed the personation. It seemed to him (Sir Henry James) that the originator of the act ought to receive the same punishment as the man who committed the act. He had not the slightest sympathy with a man who procured the act of personation, for it must be an intentional act. In his opinion, the procurer of the act was far more guilty than the person who became a victim to his persuasion. He hoped the House would reject the Amendment.

Question put, and *negatived.*

Clause 4 (Certain expenditure to be illegal practice).

THE ATTORNEY GENERAL (Sir HENRY JAMES) moved, as an Amendment, in page 2, line 32, leave out from "ward" to end of sub-section (1), and insert—

"And if the number of electors in such borough or ward exceeds two thousand, one additional committee room for every two thousand electors and incomplete part of two thousand electors over and above the said two thousand."

Amendment *agreed to.*

Words *substituted* accordingly.

MR. WARTON moved, as an Amendment, in page 2, line 37, to leave out the word "either," and insert the words "within two months." Now, if the hon. and learned Gentleman the Attorney General (Sir Henry James) was determined, whether with reason or without reason, to keep everything in this Bill exactly as it was in the Act of last year, he would resist this Amendment. But had not the experience of the Act of last year shown that in a great many cases people were getting frightened at the refusal made last year to fix any period of time during which an election lasted? He supposed hon. Gentlemen who intended to contest again the constituency for which they now sat might take it that the next Election had already begun. Certainly the right hon. Baronet the Member for Chelsea (Sir Charles W. Dilke) and his hon. and learned Colleague (Mr. Firth), who had asked him (Mr. Warton) to subscribe towards their election expenses, ought to consider that the election in which they intended to take a part had begun. The object of the Amendment was to insure something like certainty as to the time an election began. He hoped hon. Members would pay a little attention to what they were doing, and not let the Bill pass in a defective state. It was very necessary that people should know when an election began, and he now proposed what seemed to him a very moderate limit of time. This Amendment, and the one which stood next in his name—namely, to insert "or" after "before," would have the effect of making the clause read "payment," &c., "within two months before or during or after an election." Now, if hon. Members saw the force of what he said, they would, he was sure, support him. If the hon. and learned Attorney General wished it to be supposed that they were never to act wisely, but that everything they put in the Bill of last year was to be put in the Bill of this year, there was very little hope of the most rational Amendment being adopted. It was out of all reason that a sitting Member, for instance, should be liable to have all the terrible penalties of this Bill inflicted upon him, because he did not know when an election began.

Amendment proposed, in page 2, line 37, to leave out the word "either," and insert the words "within two months," —(*Mr. Warton*,)—instead thereof.

Question proposed, "That the word 'either' stand part of the Clause."

THE ATTORNEY GENERAL (Sir HENRY JAMES) said, this Amendment brought him back to the recollection of this time last year. Twelve months ago they agreed it was impossible to define or limit the time an election lasted. If they did, the law was sure to be evaded. If they put in one month, or two months, or three months, and said, "You may do what you like outside the limit," they would have a great deal done that ought not to be done. The House came to the conclusion, after full discussion, that it would be very dangerous to fix a limit of time.

Question put, and *agreed to.*

MR. WARTON moved, as an Amendment, in page 2, line 40, to leave out "a party," and insert "privy." It seemed to him that this was an Amendment in the interest of purity of election. He knew the hon. and learned Gentleman the Attorney General (Sir Henry James) supposed he (Mr. Warton) was standing up for corruption; but the hon. and learned Gentleman was quite mistaken. There might be other persons engaged in an improper payment besides the person who made the payment or the person who received it. A third party might suggest corruption; therefore, it would be better to substitute here the word "privy" for "a party." The alteration would cover the case of any person who concealed an act of corruption. He hoped that if hon. Gentlemen sitting on the Ministerial Benches were sincerely actuated by a desire to put down electoral corruption, they would not oppose an Amendment moved in the interest of purity of election, although it might happen to be proposed by a Member of the Opposition.

Amendment proposed, in page 2, line 40, leave out "a party," and insert "privy."—(*Mr. Warton.*)

Question proposed, "That the words 'a party' stand part of the Clause."

THE ATTORNEY GENERAL (Sir HENRY JAMES) said, that by this Amendment the hon. and learned Gentleman (Mr. Warton) would increase, no doubt unwittingly, the stringency of the Bill, because he would make it an offence for anybody to be "privy" to an act of corruption. Anyone who received knowledge of corruption accidentally would be privy to the offence. If they made a person "a party" to an offence he must be guilty of some substantial act. A person who read of corruption in a newspaper would be privy to it. He (Sir Henry James) would prefer to be a little lenient in this instance, if the hon. and learned Gentleman would allow him.

Question put, and *agreed to.*

MR. WARTON said, he had an Amendment to move to the clause for the purpose of making the phraseology of the various clauses of the Bill consistent. He wished to call the attention of the House and the hon. and learned Attorney General to the fact that the expression which he was about to move in substitution of the words "contravention of this Act," in line 41, occurred in Clause 13, page 6, line 30 of the Bill. The expression which there occurred was "contrary to law," and he proposed to move the insertion of those words in place of the words now in the clause. If the hon. and learned Gentleman was so consistent with regard to certain words in the Parliamentary Elections Act of last year, he trusted he would be consistent in regard to this Bill, and not have one expression in one clause, and a different expression to convey the same idea in another clause of the Bill. He would give the hon. Gentleman his choice of the two phrases; but he hoped that one or e other of them would be adopted. Fothhis own part, he thought "contrary to law" the better expression, and he should also prefer it, because, in the place he had indicated, it was used in connection with a very similar matter. Moreover, the words "contrary to law" were words of limitation, and words of limitation were generally good.

Amendment proposed, in page 3, line 41, to leave out the words "in contravention of this Act," and insert the words "contrary to law,"—(*Mr. Warton*,)—instead thereof.

Question proposed, "That the words 'in contravention of this Act,' stand part of the Bill."

THE ATTORNEY GENERAL (Sir HENRY JAMES) said, he was unable to agree to the Amendment of the hon. Member, because he thought it would not improve the wording of the clause. He considered "in contravention of this Act" the better wording.

Question put, and *agreed to.*

MR. WARTON said, he proposed, as an Amendment, to move the insertion of the words "or otherwise," after the word "agent," in page 3, line 2. He thought these words should be inserted, because a person might be engaged to stick bills on a wall, and it did not follow that he was strictly an advertising agent. The clause ought to extend its provisions to persons who might carry on the business of exhibiting bills for payment, and he did not think such persons would be included in the words "advertising agent." He thought that the words "or otherwise" tended in the direction of purity of election, which the hon. and learned Attorney General seemed alternately to care for and to reject. He urged the Amendment on the favourable attention of the House, because it was quite possible to contentemplate the case of a man exhibiting an election bill, and yet not being what was known as an advertising agent.

Amendment proposed, in page 3, line 2, after the word "agent," to insert the words "or otherwise."—(*Mr. Warton.*)

Question proposed, "That those words be there inserted."

THE ATTORNEY GENERAL (Sir HENRY JAMES) said, he could not adopt this Amendment. This matter had been fully discussed last year, when Clause 7 of the Parliamentary Elections (Corrupt and Illegal Practices) Bill was under the consideration of the House, and it was then decided that the words "advertising agent" should stand without the addition of the words "or otherwise." He thought it better to adopt the same wording with regard to the present Bill which it was decided to retain in the Act of last year. If they did not keep this distinction in favour of the advertising agent, by saying, "doing the ordinary business of advertising agent," every publican and every greengrocer, who sometimes exhibited a bill at election time, might claim to be paid for it. The intention was to make an exception in favour of the advertising agent only, and not in favour of those persons who sometimes exhibited bills.

Question put, and *negatived.*

MR. WARTON said, he regarded the words "deemed to be," in page 3, line 4, of the Bill, as an absurd expression, and one which was only intrduced for the sake of euphony. He would, therefore, move their omission from the clause.

Amendment proposed, in page 3, line 4, to leave out the words "deemed to be."—(*Mr. Warton.*)

Question proposed, "That the words proposed to be left out stand part of the Bill."

THE ATTORNEY GENERAL (Sir HENRY JAMES) said, he was reluctantly obliged to say "No" to the hon. and learned Member's proposal to strike out these words. It was better, perhaps, sometimes to be consistently wrong, than inconsistently right. However, that might be, he would point out that the Act of last year, with regard to Parliamentary elections, contained these very words, "shall be deemed to be illegal," a circumstance which it would seem had escaped the hon. and learned Member's acute attention when that measure was passing through the House. If they escaped the hon. and learned Member then, he thought they might have been allowed to escape him now for the sake of consistency.

Amendment, by leave, *withdrawn.*

Clause 5 (Expense in excess of maximum to be illegal practice).

MR. WARTON said, there was a great desire on the part of the hon. and learned Attorney General to retain in the Bill useless phrases, for no other reason, that he (Mr. Warton) could discover, than that they were in the Parliamentary Elections (Corrupt and Illegal Practices) Act of last year. He would ask the hon. and learned Gentleman whether he intended to maintain in the Bill the principle embodied in this clause? He believed the great majority of the House had never heard the reasons which induced the hon. and learned Gentleman to adopt the words of this clause. They were, of course, in ignorance of what had taken place in the Grand Committee, and no one seemed to know exactly what had been going on with regard to the Bill. Whatever reason there was for the clause in the Act of last year with regard to Parliamentary elections, he was satisfied that it would be very injudicious to fix the proposed maximum with regard to these minor elections in municipalities, and he should, therefore, move that the clause be struck out. The great absurdity which ran through this Bill was that it treated these little elections as if they were of the same importance as Parliamentary Elections. He trusted the hon. and learned Gentleman would be able to explain to the House why he had changed front so completely since the debate on the Motion for the second reading of the Bill—why he had changed his views in Committee.

Amendment proposed, in page 3, to leave out Clause 5.—(*Mr. Warton.*)

Question proposed, "That the words proposed to be left out stand part of the Bill."

MR. WHITLEY said, he also should like some explanation from the hon. and learned Attorney General of the reasons which had induced him to take up a position with regard to the principle of this clause entirely different from that which he occupied when the Bill was introduced to the House. The view of the hon. and learned Gentleman at that time was certainly against the introduction of a maximum expenditure in the case of municipal elections. He (Mr. Whitley) was certainly in favour of the opinion then expressed by the hon. and learned Gentleman, and he was bound to express his surprise that the hon. and learned Gentleman did not now hold the same opinion with regard to this subject. It must be obvious to the House that this clause affected the various constituents in different ways. In the constituency which he had the honour to represent (Liverpool), for instance, there were no less than 23,000 electors who had the right of voting at municipal elections; and, therefore, the arrangements in connection with such elections for polling rooms, polling clerks, and their assistants, were necessarily very extensive. The House would perceive that the maximum expenditure sought to be imposed by this clause would be absolutely insufficient for the purposes of municipal elections in Liverpool. The case would be entirely different with regard to towns in which there were, perhaps, 200 electors, and even a smaller number than that—but in Liverpool and other towns in Lancashire, he believed there was no municipality with a smaller electorate than 1,000. He could assure the hon. and learned Gentleman that it was impossible that this maximum could be maintained in the case of municipal elections in those places. It would be far better, in his opinion, to have no maximum at all, if it was to apply to all places without distinction. He maintained that the retention of the clause in its present form would constitute a great injustice in the case of large constituencies. It was a question of the magnitude of the electorate, and he was convinced that it would be utterly impracticable to carry out municipal elections in large towns within the limit of expenditure prescribed by the clause. He was sure that that was not the intention of the hon. and learned Gentleman, and he was equally satisfied that the Members of the Grand Committee had not fully considered the bearing which the proposed maximum would have upon important municipal elections. The question was a large and serious one, and he hoped the hon. and learned Gentleman would agree to the Motion of the hon. and learned Member for Bridport (Mr. Warton) to strike out the clause. If his hon. and learned Friend went to a Division, he should, for the reasons given, feel it his duty to vote with him.

MR. SAMUEL SMITH said, he believed it would be extremely difficult, if not actually impossible, to conduct municipal elections of any importance upon the very small scale of expenditure proposed in this clause. For his own part, he had considerable misgivings with regard to the fixing of a maximum scale in these cases. He was, of course, aware of the wisdom of surrounding municipal elections with all possible safeguards for purity; but he ventured to doubt whether the effect of the principle contained in the clause upon large municipal elections had received sufficient attention at the hands of the Grand Committee.

He should be glad to see the Bill passed without any scale at all.

THE ATTORNEY GENERAL (Sir HENRY JAMES) said, he had endeavoured to obtain the best information upon this subject before he introduced the Bill to the House, and at the time when the Bill was introduced, he thought it would be, on the whole, better to strike out the maximum Schedule, and to insert a minor Schedule. He stated, in Committee, that objections had been expressed to that plan, but that he thought it was better to adopt it, and he was met by a considerable amount of criticism; the hon. and learned Member for Chatham (Mr. Gorst) and others told him that he was entirely wrong in having taken that course. He adhered, however, to his former opinion, and a Division being taken, he found there was scarcely a working majority in favour of his view. Every Conservative Member voted against it—a circumstance which he hoped the hon. and learned Member for Bridport (Mr. Warton) would take to heart—and those who spoke on the question contended that there ought to be a maximum Schedule, while many opinions were expressed that he ought not to give way on the point. The proposal which he laid before the Grand Committee having been carried by a very narrow majority, he thought it best to meet the views of the minority half-way. Having got rid of the election agent, he hoped the fears of the hon. Member for Liverpool (Mr. Whitley) would not be realized. They had simplified the matter very much; but there still appeared to be a certain amount of doubt on the subject, and if the hon. and learned Member for Bridport (Mr. Warton) took a Division on his Motion, the actual opinion of the House would appear.

SIR R. ASSHETON CROSS said, he thought much credit was due to the hon. and learned Gentleman the Attorney General for the course he had taken in this matter throughout the whole proceedings. The hon. and learned Gentleman had, in the first instance, formed the opinion in his own mind that it was not wise to introduce a maximum scale. It was quite true that he (Sir R. Assheton Cross) had made some severe comments in the course of the debate on the second reading of the Bill as to the difference which existed between this Bill and the Act of last year with regard to corrupt and illegal practices at Parliamentary elections; but, no doubt, strong opinions were expressed in the Grand Committee, not by Conservative Members alone, but by a large number of Liberal Members, who had had experience of the working of the Act of last year, in favour of a maximum scale, and the result was that, when the Committee went to the Division on the question, there was but a narrow majority in favour of the proposal of the hon. and learned Attorney General, which led the hon. and learned Gentleman to reconsider the question, and to place the matter on a different footing. The hon. and learned Gentleman thought it wise to reconsider the decision at which he had arrived, and he (Sir R. Assheton Cross) believed that in the proposal he had made, he carried with him, if not an absolutely unanimous, yet a very general concurrence of opinion on the part of hon. Members. The hon. and learned Gentleman consented to introduce a maximum scale of expenditure into the Bill, a perfectly proper provision, so far as the election agent was concerned, and to that extent he entirely agreed with the hon. and learned Attorney General. But when he came to consider the maximum scale that had been introduced into the Bill, that appeared to him an entirely different matter, and he quite agreed with his hon. Friend near him the Member for Liverpool (Mr. Whitley), and the hon. Gentleman opposite (Mr. Samuel Smith), that the proposed maximum scale ought to be decidedly enlarged. He was perfectly satisfied that no municipal election could be carried on within the limits of such a scale. The matter was of such importance that he was in some doubt as to whether its discussion ought not to be deferred to a later period. They were, of course, all agreed that bribery and corruption ought not to take place at these or any other elections; but there was nothing of the kind involved here. The amount had been placed at a figure altogether too low, and he was of precisely the same opinon as his hon. Friend (Mr. Whitley), that it was insufficient to pay for the persons who could be legally employed under the Bill for the purposes of municipal elections.

Question put, and *agreed to*.

Amendment proposed, in page 3, line 6, to leave out the words "subject to such exception as may be allowed in pursuance of this Act."—(*Mr. Warton.*)

Question, "That the words proposed to be left out stand part of the Bill," put, and *agreed to.*

MR. H. S. NORTHCOTE said, it was evident that if the matter was to be dealt with in the way that the hon. and learned Gentleman the Attorney General wished the scale of expenditure fixed by the Bill as it stood at present was insufficient. He proposed, therefore, to move that the maximum of £20 should be increased to £25. It was obvious that if municipal contests were to be conducted on non-political lines, the electors ought to have the fullest information of the views of the local representatives before them. Although it was impossible to say that an expenditure of £25 could have any great effect in corrupting the boroughs, yet its expenditure on printing, &c., might have a great effect in affording the electors of the borough full information with regard to the questions at issue. He should like to suggest to the hon. and learned Gentleman the Attorney General a possible compromise. He did not know whether the hon. and learned Gentleman would be able to see his way to accept it; but it had been suggested to him (Mr. Northcote) by a municipal agent, who had devoted great attention to the matter. This municipal agent proposed that in wards of under 500 voters, £15 should be allowed; in wards between 500 and 1,000 voters, £25; and in wards over 1,500, £30, with a scale of 4*d.* for each voter over the initial number.

Amendment proposed, in page 3, line 13, to leave out the words "twenty pounds," and insert the words "twenty-five pounds,"—(*Mr. H. S. Northcote,*)—instead thereof.

Question proposed, "That the words 'twenty pounds' stand part of the Bill."

THE ATTORNEY GENERAL (Sir HENRY JAMES) said, the hon. Gentleman (Mr. Northcote) had stated the case very fairly, and he quite felt that there was a great deal in what he had said. This was really a practical matter, and he hoped that every Member would vote exactly as he thought right. The question was, whether £25 should be the initial expenditure, and 3*d.* or 4*d.* per head the subsequent amount? As far as he (the Attorney General) could judge, whether they adopted the £25, or maintained the £20 limit, or whether they had 4*d.* instead of the 3*d.* for subsequent expenditure, either sum would take elections out of the area of corrupt practices. He would state to the House briefly why he should prefer to adhere to the £20 limit and the smaller sum per head. In the first place, they had discussed this matter in the Grand Committee, and if there was any question which it was desirable that such Committee should determine, it was this. It was eminently a question to be intrusted to such a body. The question was one very materially depending upon the information obtained by those interested in the matter. Information had been obtained by many Members of the Grand Committee from the districts they represented, and the majority of the Committee had been in favour of maintaining the maximum at £20 instead of £25. The majority of the constituencies had thought that £20 would be quite sufficient to pay all legitimate expenses. He agreed with the hon. Member for Liverpool (Mr. Whitley) that they would not be able to carry on municipal elections for this sum if those elections were to be conducted in the future as they had been in the past—that was to say, if they were to carry them on by giving all sorts of useful information to the electors as to the merits of particular candidates by addressing placards and advertisements to them. In that event, neither sum now proposed would be sufficient. He did not think it was necessary to give information of this kind to the electors. Whether a ward was a small one, or whether it was composed of 1,600 electors, he believed that every morning, when a ratepayer arose from his bed, he would get all the information he required about the candidates, if there was anything he did not know, in the local papers. The electors would know all they were wanted to know without putting the candidates to the necessity of advertising. If they had a committee room at all, it would do for 1,000 as well as for 500 electors, and in the same way a clerk would be able to manage a large number as conveniently as he could a small number. It was necessary that they should form an opinion upon this matter upon detailed information they received from the constituencies; and though he did not for a moment say that he would supersede the responsibility of individual Members in this matter, at the same time he must point out that they would not obtain any advantage by going into a lengthy or detailed debate on the question. The only expression of opinion necessary for him to give was a general one; and, as a matter of fact, he believed that if £25 was inserted in the place of £20, it would be just as useful in putting an end to corrupt practices.

Sir R. ASSHETON CROSS said, he was very glad the hon. and learned Gentleman the Attorney General had done two things. In the first place, he was pleased to hear him say that any Member of the House could vote exactly as he thought fit, without any pressure, because he happened to sit on one side of the House instead of the other. He (Sir R. Assheton Cross) agreed that this was not a Party question. In the second place, he was glad to hear the hon. and learned Gentleman say that the acceptance of the higher sum instead of the lower would be equally efficacious in putting a stop to bribery and corruption. He (Sir R. Assheton Cross) had gone carefully into this question to find out whether the £20 would be sufficient, and the result of his inquiries was that in large boroughs like Liverpool it would be far from sufficient. He would ask the House, as there was no question of corruption in the matter, whether a man had a fair chance of giving his constituents to understand his qualifications and his reasons for desiring to be put upon the Municipality, when his initial expenses were limited to £20; or, at any rate, whether he would have as good an opportunity as he would if he were enabled to spend £25? He was not speaking of a man who could get up and make a speech at a meeting of his constituents, but of a man who, without the opportunity of attending meetings, desired to let his constituency know what he felt, and why he stood. The question was, could a man do this for the smaller sum? And his (Sir R. Assheton Cross's) opinion was that in such places as Liverpool and Manchester he could not do so. No man who wished to stand at the municipal elections at these places should be debarred; and he was sure that, if the smaller sum were adopted, many persons would be prevented from availing themselves of the advantages they wished to possess, and of the advantages they wished their constituents to have. He would appeal to the hon. Member for Liverpool on that (the Opposition) side of the House (Mr. Whitley) and to the hon. Member for Liverpool on the other side of the House (Mr. Samuel Smith), and to the hon. Member for Manchester, whether his view was not the correct one? The hon. Member for Manchester who sat on that (the Conservative) side of the House(Mr. Houldsworth) had spoken to him very strongly upon the matter.

Mr. WHITLEY said, he wished to point out that the hon. and learned Gentleman the Attorney General had not addressed himself to the real difficulty. He did not think the hon. and learned Gentleman at all realized what it was to contest a ward in a Municipality containing so many thousand electors as Liverpool. The hon. and learned Gentleman proposed to give them 18 polling places. They must have two polling places in each ward, and then they must have a polling clerk at each station; and he would, therefore, ask how was it possible to work such a constituency as this with the money proposed to be allowed? In the ward he (Mr. Whitley) represented, it was essential that there should be a large number of polling places, and it was impossible that they could get them for the amount proposed to be allowed in the Bill. The hon. and learned Gentleman the Attorney General had intimated that he had consulted various interests on this matter; and he (Mr. Whitley) would like to ask him if he had consulted anyone, no matter of what politics, or even those who had no political bias at all, in the large towns, without coming to the conclusion that it would be impossible to work an election in a place like Liverpool with this money? No doubt, it would be possible to do it in small boroughs; but supposing they had a constituency of 23,000 to send an address to, their money would be almost gone at once. He was talking of a constituency with an area of seven miles. The hon. and learned Gentleman the Attorney General could have no idea of the difficulty candidates in Liverpool would be placed in if his proposal were accepted; and he (Mr. Whitley) would ask hon. Members representing large constituencies whether, if they consulted their constituents, they would not find them all against the proposal of the Bill? He trusted the House would support the Amendment.

MR. WARTON said, that as the hon. and learned Gentleman the Attorney General was kind enough to say that they might all vote as they liked, he would ask right hon. Gentlemen sitting on the Treasury Bench not to put forward the Government Whips as Tellers in the Division.

Question put.

The House *divided*:—Ayes 95; Noes 42: Majority 53.—(Div. List, No. 181.)

MR. H. S. NORTHCOTE: I have another Amendment on the Paper; but after the Division we have just taken I do not propose to proceed with it. I refer to my proposal to leave out in line 15 the words "three pence," and insert "four pence."

Clause 6 (Voting by prohibited persons and publishing of false statements of withdrawal to be illegal).

Amendment proposed, in page 4, line 16, after the word "election," to leave out "for the purpose of promoting or procuring the election of another candidate."—(*Mr. Warton.*)

Question proposed, "That the words proposed to be left out stand part of the Bill."

THE ATTORNEY GENERAL (Sir HENRY JAMES) said, he had not caught the object of the hon. and learned Member (Mr. Warton) in moving this Amendment, and he certainly thought it would be better to adhere to the words in the Bill.

Question put, and *agreed to.*

Clause 7 (Punishment on conviction of illegal practice).

MR. WARTON said, the next Amendment, he trusted, would meet with the approbation of the hon. and learned Gentleman the Attorney General. He thought that the £20 he proposed would be quite a sufficient disability, without adding a greater incapacity; and he would therefore move to leave out "one hundred" and insert "twenty."

Amendment proposed, in page 4, line 24, to leave out the words "one hundred," and insert the word "twenty,"—(*Mr. Warton,*)—instead thereof.

Question proposed, "That the words 'one hundred' stand part of the Bill."

THE ATTORNEY GENERAL (Sir HENRY JAMES) said, he could not accept the Amendment, as £100 had been accepted after a long discussion. The clause said "not exceeding one hundred pounds;" therefore, it seemed to him that it would meet any very gross case.

MR. TOMLINSON said, he could not imagine anything more likely to discourage respectable men from becoming candidates than such a thing as this. If such a provision as that in question were retained, the effect would be to throw elections into the hands of an inferior class of men. That would be the effect of imposing too heavy a penalty for what might not be very distinctly an illegal act.

Question put, and *agreed to.*

Clause 10 (Employment of hackney carriages, or of carriages and horses kept for hire).

MR. WARTON said, the next Amendment he had on the Paper might appear to some hon. Members a very trifling one; but it really was not trifling, because, if they looked at the phraseology of the Bill, they would find in its nomenclature "illegal hiring and illegal practices." If the hon. and learned Gentleman the Attorney General would look at the provision before the one he (Mr. Warton) wished to amend, he would see the words used in another sense. In the present clause the phrase "illegal hiring" was not used in its proper sense, because it was used both in the sense of hiring and letting for hire. He objected to this use of new phraseology—this introduction of a new phrase altogether. They would find the words "guilty of illegal hiring" in Clause 16, not only in the clause, but in the marginal note also. It was not "an illegal hiring." He wished to know whether the hon. and learned Attorney General would have "an illegal hiring" as he had in one part of the Bill, or "illegal hiring" as he had in others?

Amendment proposed, in page 5, line 25, leave out "an."—(*Mr. Warton.*)

Question proposed, "That the word proposed to be left out stand part of the Bill."

THE ATTORNEY GENERAL (Sir HENRY JAMES) said, the striking out of this word did not make the slightest difference in the Bill. As, however, it would bring about greater uniformity, he was much obliged to the hon. and learned Member for having pointed it out, and he had much pleasure in accepting the proposal.

Question put, and *negatived.*

Word *struck out* accordingly.

On the Motion of Mr. WARTON, further Amendment made in line 30, by striking out the word "an."

Clause 12 (Certain expenditure to be illegal payment).

MR. WARTON said, that in page 6, line 7, he wished to move an Amendment which affected rather an important matter of principle, with regard to which he was afraid that the hon. and learned Gentleman the Attorney General would give him the same answer as he had done when they were discussing the Parliamentary Elections (Corrupt and Illegal Practices) Bill of last year. The object of the Amendment was to leave out that part of the clause which was against the use of cockades and ribbons, which, to his (Mr. Warton's) mind, were quite harmless things. These municipal elections were not of the same gravity as Parliamentary elections; and, therefore, even if it was desirable to put a stop to the use of these things at Parliamentary elections, which he did not believe it was, it was not necessary to put a stop to their employment in connection with these elections. It was not necessary to go into the same *minutiæ* in this Bill as they had in the Parliamentary Elections (Corrupt and Illegal Practices) Bill.

Amendment proposed, in page 6, line 7, after the word "flags," to insert the word "or."—(*Mr. Warton.*)

Question proposed, "That the word 'or' be there inserted."

THE ATTORNEY GENERAL (Sir HENRY JAMES) said, he must adhere to his banner. This provision was contained in the 12th clause of the Parliamentary Elections (Corrupt and Illegal Practices) Act of last year, and it was discussed at some length. If they allowed banners to be used in a municipal election and not in Parliamentary elections, he was afraid people would be prone to make mistakes.

Question put, and *negatived.*

Clause 13 (Certain employment to be illegal).

MR. WARTON said, he would not move the next two Amendments which stood in his name, as they were similar to those rejected on Clause 4; but he did hope to have the support of the hon. and learned Attorney General, now that he had to propose to leave out in page 6, line 36, "contrary to law," and insert "in contravention of this Act." Honestly and fairly he called the hon. and learned Gentleman's attention, when they were on Clause 4, to the inconsistency in the Bill, and he gave him his choice of the phrases "contrary to law," or in "contravention of this Act." It would be well that, as they were creating new crimes by this Bill, the expression "in contravention of this Act," which the hon. and learned Attorney General required in a previous clause, should be required now.

Amendment proposed, in page 6, line 36, to leave out "contrary to law," and insert "in contravention of this Act"—(*Mr. Warton,*)—instead thereof.

Question proposed, "That the words 'contrary to law' stand part of the Clause."

THE ATTORNEY GENERAL (Sir HENRY JAMES) said, he did not see much difference between the two phrases, and, therefore, he would agree to the Amendment.

Question put, and *negatived.*

Question proposed, "That the words 'in contravention of this Act' be there inserted" put, and *agreed to.*

MR. WARTON proposed the omission of the clause. The hon. and learned Attorney General spoke with great force in respect to this clause when he moved the second reading of the Bill. The hon. and learned Gentleman said it was very proper that they should prevent public-houses being engaged for election purposes; but perhaps the hon. and learned Gentleman would not consider it unkind in him (Mr. Warton) if he said that in his speech the hon. and learned Gentleman gave excellent reasons why the same provision should not be applied to municipal as to Parliamentary elections. They knew that in Parliamentary elections it was very easy to get committee rooms, because all sorts of peculiar places could be obtained; but in municipal elections it was not so easy to get rooms for the purposes of committees. It seemed to him (Mr. Warton) that there should be no stigma placed on a really respectable trade. The licensed victuallers only wished to do what was proper; but they were supervised by the police and restricted in every way. He proposed to omit the clause.

Amendment proposed to leave out Clause 16.—(*Mr. Warton.*)

Question, "That the words 'any premises' stand part of the Bill," put, and *agreed to.*

MR. H. S. NORTHCOTE proposed, as an Amendment, in page 7, line 17, after "association," to insert—

"Not being a *bonâ fide* club, society, or association, which shall have been in existence for the period of 12 months prior to the passing of this Act."

He said he need not detain the House for many moments in submitting this Amendment to its judgment. Although the hon. and learned Attorney General (Sir Henry James) was at one time not disinclined to accede to the principle of allowing *bonâ fide* clubs to be used for political election purposes, ultimately he failed to make a proposal which was satisfactory to the great majority of the House. The Amendment he (Mr. H. S. Northcote) submitted in Committee on this subject was rejected, on the ground that municipal elections should not be conducted on political lines. As a matter of fact, however, municipal contests, in a great majority of the boroughs of the United Kingdom, were fought on political grounds, and he did not see any immediate prospect of a cessation of the practice. If such contests were to be fought on political grounds, it was desirable that the legitimate political machinery should be used. It appeared to him that these *bonâ fide* political clubs were necessarily the places where a great part of the work attending municipal elections was done; and, therefore, their use as committee rooms should be formally legalized. He was afraid, if that was not the case, a great deal of indirect and underhand work must necessarily be done at the clubs. He was quite certain that if working men belonged to the clubs they would go in the evening and talk over the election, and it was impossible to avoid a certain amount of objectionable work being done in an informal way. If his Amendment were adopted, there would be an assimilation, as far as possible, of the mode of conducting Parliamentary and municipal elections. It was clear that the legalization of the use of political clubs would not make any difference in the conduct of municipal elections upon political grounds; because the men who became candidates for seats in Town Councils were, as a rule, not the working men who habitually used the club, and who became thoroughly saturated with political Party principles, but leading tradesmen, who might join clubs with the view of encouraging the Liberal or the Conservative cause, and who would stand for positions in the Town Council entirely independent of their membership of a club. Under these circumstances, and wishing that if municipal elections were to be fought on political grounds, they should be fought in a legitimate manner, he had ventured to submit this Amendment to the House. If he might make a verbal alteration in his Amendment it would be to substitute "permanent" for "*bonâ fide.*" "Permanent" was a better word, and more completely expressed his meaning. His only object in saying "*bonâ fide*" was to guard against the employment of mere drinking shops, which were sometimes called clubs.

Amendment proposed,

In page 7, line 17, after the word "association," to insert the words "not being a permanent club, society, or association, which shall have been in existence for the period of 12 months prior to the passing of this Act."—(*Mr. H. S. Northcote.*)

Question proposed, "That those words be there inserted."

THE ATTORNEY GENERAL (Sir HENRY JAMES) said, he would suggest to the hon. Gentleman (Mr. H. S. Northcote), that he should withdraw his Amendment in favour of the one standing in the name of the hon. Gentleman the Member for Mid Lincolnshire (Mr. E. Stanhope), on which Amendment the question could be more appropriately raised. He (Sir Henry James) had only to trouble the House with a few sentences in expressing his views upon this subject. He had to ask the House even more strongly than before to take upon itself the entire responsibility of dealing with this proposal. As he was in the novel condition of finding himself differing with some of his Colleagues on the question, he wished to state briefly why he desired to see this Amendment rejected. Would the House see what they were discussing? It really was not the question of the convenience of a particular candidate; but a very broad question they were discussing. Many persons wished to take municipal elections out of the area of Party politics; they wished to get, as members of municipal bodies, men of moderate views, who would not run on political lines; but who would be willing and anxious to serve the localities without being tied to one side or the other. What was proposed was to give to the club managers to decide who should be elected. Let the House take into its view a practical condition of things. Suppose there were three candidates for one seat, a Tory, a Liberal, and an independent. The Tory and the Liberal would have the use of their respective clubs for committee rooms; but what would become of the independent candidate? Take the case where they had two Tories and no Liberal standing for one seat. The Tory who placed himself in the hands of the Tory managers had a great advantage over his opponent, because he obtained the support of the club, as well as of those who were of the same political opinion. By the use of a club they did not only save the expense of a committee room, but the whole weight of the club was given to the candidate the club espoused. If a political club took up the cudgels of one of its partizans and gave him the whole weight of the Party organization and the club management, what chance had any other candidate, even though he might hold the same political views? He (Sir Henry James) considered that if the House accepted this Amendment they would give great strength to those who desired to see Party politics control municipal elections; they would give to municipal contests greater political weight than, in the interest of the public, they ought to have. These were his own opinions, from which many with whom he generally agreed differed.

Mr. E. STANHOPE said, he would admit there was something in what the hon. and learned Gentleman the Attorney General (Sir Henry James) had said; but he thought the hon. and learned Gentleman did not attach sufficient importance to the fact that many clubs had been established for the purpose of promoting electoral purity. ["Oh, oh!"]. That was his opinion—indeed, he was quite certain it was a fact that, in a good many boroughs where previously corrupt practices had prevailed, pure elections had been the outcome of the establishment of political clubs. One reason why he had framed his Amendment in the form in which it appeared on the Paper was that many clubs had been formed in which intoxicating liquors could not be sold, and the clause now under consideration would prevent such clubs being used for political purposes. That, in his opinion, was unreasonable and unfair. If his hon. Friend (Mr. Northcote) would allow him to submit his Amendment to the House, he hoped it would meet with the approval of hon. Gentlemen.

Mr. H. S. NORTHCOTE asked leave to withdraw his Amendment.

Amendment, by leave, *withdrawn*.

Mr. E. STANHOPE moved, as an Amendment, to add, at end of the clause—"Provided also, That nothing in this section shall apply to any permanent political club."

Amendment proposed,

In page 7, line 32, to insert at the end of the sub-section, the words "Provided also, That nothing in this section shall apply to any permanent political club."—(*Mr. E. Stanhope*.)

Question proposed, "That those words be there inserted."

Mr. ARTHUR ARNOLD said, with regard to the remark made by the hon. and learned Attorney General (Sir Henry James), that if they did not allow political clubs to be used for election purposes, they would certainly not prevent municipal elections being more or less political. His hon. and learned Friend dwelt upon the fact that politics did enter into municipal contests. He said—"You give to the Liberal or Tory candidate all the club organization."

He (Mr. Arthur Arnold) replied to the hon. and learned Gentleman—"You cannot take it from him." In every large borough these clubs existed—in all the Lancashire boroughs they existed to a great degree, and it was impossible to deprive a Party candidate of the support a club could give him. The hon. and learned Attorney General asked what was to become of the independent candidate. Unless he was a man of great personal weight he would stand very badly at any time; if he was a man of great weight and standing he would probably succeed. Considering that every Member on the Grand Committee who represented a large borough constituency voted for this Amendment he hoped the proposal of the hon. Member for Mid Lincolnshire (Mr. E. Stanhope) would be adopted by the House.

MR. CAUSTON said, he hoped the Amendment would not be adopted. When the House was in Committee on the Parliamentary Elections (Corrupt and Illegal Practices) Bill of last year, he and his hon. Friend the Member for Bedford (Mr. Whitbread) spoke strongly against such a proposition as the present. If all the clubs which would be affected were *bonâ fide* political clubs, he should have no objection to the proposition; but what he contended was that in nearly all the boroughs of the Kingdom clubs had been started which were not *bonâ fide* Liberal or Conservative clubs. The rank and file of some clubs paid very small contributions, while the richer members of the Party to which the club was attached provided funds which enabled the poorer members to enjoy the luxuries of eating and drinking, but not at their own expense. That, in his opinion, was corruption in its worst form. It was quite unnecessary that clubs should be used for municipal election purposes. He hoped the House would support the hon. and learned Attorney General in his endeavour to put down what really amounted to a very corrupt practice.

SIR R. ASSHETON CROSS said, it was quite clear the hon. Member for Colchester (Mr. Causton) knew nothing of the independence of feeling and action of the working men of Lancashire.

MR. DILLWYN said, he entirely agreed with the view of the hon. and learned Attorney General. The more they eliminated political matters from municipal elections the better. He desired to see independent men taking an active part in the local concerns of a borough; and, in his opinion, the prohibition of the use of political clubs for election purposes would greatly contribute to such an end.

MR. H. H. FOWLER said, his hon. and learned Friend the Attorney General (Sir Henry James) had said he was very anxious to prevent the introduction of the political element into municipal conflicts. The hon. and learned Gentleman seemed to forget that that element already existed very largely in some of the principal boroughs of the Kingdom. He asserted that, as a matter of fact—and he challenged contradiction on the point—municipal elections in some of the largest boroughs were invariably fought on political lines—just as much on political lines as any Parliamentary election. He did not intend to argue whether it was right or wrong. It was a very taking argument in favour of the view of the hon. and learned Attorney General, that they should, if possible, get the best men to perform the work of our Municipalities. But it was contended that the best way of getting the best men was the introduction of the political element. The experience of many Gentlemen, who knew a great deal more about municipal life than he did, was that the best men of the different Parties came forward when they received the sympathy and influence of their Parties. But whether it be right or wrong, he did not think the House of Commons, in passing a Municipal Elections (Corrupt and Illegal Practices) Bill, was justified in endeavouring to introduce some new principle into municipal elections which did not exist already. They had to try to prevent bribery and corruption, and not to try to introduce any new principle into municipal elections. Last year, when considering the Parliamentary Elections (Corrupt and Illegal Practices) Bill, they came to the conclusion that they ought to allow candidates the advantage of the use of permanent political clubs for committee purposes. If it was right to use clubs in Parliamentary elections, it was equally right to use them in municipal elections. The observations of the hon. Member for Colchester (Mr. Causton) would apply with as much force to Parliamentary as to municipal elections. The Legislature did not adopt the view of his hon. Friend, but had allowed clubs to be used for political purposes. He (Mr. H. H. Fowler) could not see why the House should apply one rule to one class of elections and another rule to another class of elections. When a Liberal and Tory stood for any municipal constituency, it was useless to talk about an independent candidate. In boroughs where the Liberal and Tory elements were strong, elections would be fought on Party lines. He should certainly vote with the hon. Member for Mid Lincolnshire (Mr. E. Stanhope); because what the hon. Gentleman proposed was a wise provision to introduce, and it would fairly carry out the legislation of last year.

Mr. MONK said, that, with all respect to the hon. Member for Wolverhampton (Mr. H. H. Fowler), he could not agree with him that municipal elections ought to be fought strictly on political grounds.

Mr. H. H. FOWLER said, he should be sorry to be misunderstood. He did not say municipal elections ought to be fought on political lines; but he said, as a matter of fact, they were fought on political grounds. He must not be quoted as having said that municipal elections ought to be so fought.

Mr. MONK said, he entirely agreed with the hon. Member for Wolverhampton that, in the majority of instances, municipal elections were fought on political grounds; but he thought the House should do all it could to discourage such elections being so fought. He took exception to what had fallen from the hon. Member for Salford (Mr. Arthur Arnold). That hon. Gentleman had said that in the Grand Committee, of which he was a distinguished Member, all the Members for the large municipal boroughs voted in favour of this Amendment. Now, there was a Division in the Committee; but there was a majority of three to one against the view of the hon. Member for Salford —there were 26 against the proposal, and nine for it, and by far the larger number of Members who sat for large municipal boroughs voted against the proposal. His hon. Friends the Member for Salford and the Member for Oldham were the principal Representatives of large boroughs who voted for the proposal, while the hon. Member for Bristol, the hon. Member for Dundee, the hon. and learned Member for Stockport, and others—by far the greater majority of Representatives of large constituencies—were opposed to it. He hoped the House would support the hon. and learned Attorney General (Sir Henry James) in rejecting this proposal.

Mr. AGNEW said, he should certainly vote for the Amendment of the hon. Gentleman the Member for Mid Lincolnshire (Mr. E. Stanhope), because he was convinced that the agency of clubs had largely resulted in inducing the best men, be they Liberals or Conservatives, to become candidates at municipal elections. He was of opinion, too, that the clubs so largely established in the North of England had, in their operation, resulted in not only providing a better class of candidates for municipal elections, but in elections being conducted in a much more orderly manner than formerly.

Question put.

The House *divided*:—Ayes 48; Noes 78: Majority 30.—(Div. List, No. 182.)

Clause 19 (Report exonerating candidate in certain cases of corrupt and illegal practice by agents).

Mr. WARTON, in moving, as an Amendment, to insert after "character," in page 8, line 27, "and could not reasonably have been supposed to have affected the result of the election," said, the hon. and learned Attorney General (Sir Henry James) would know, of course, whence the words he proposed to insert came. Parliament had already laid down the principle that, where corrupt practices extensively prevailed, it was reasonable to suppose they affected the result of the election. He (Mr. Warton) thought, however, that if the corrupt practices were of a trivial character they ought not to be held to invalidate the election. It was quite possible that in the case of a very closely-contested election—an election which turned, for instance, on one or two votes — the offences committed might be of a very trivial and unimportant nature. This Amendment he proposed in the interest of purity of election, and he confidently submitted these words to the approval of the hon. and learned Attorney General.

Amendment proposed,

In page 8, line 27, after the word "character," to insert the words "and could not reasonably have been supposed to have affected the result of the election."—(*Mr. Warton.*)

Question proposed, "That those words be there inserted."

THE ATTORNEY GENERAL (Sir HENRY JAMES) said, he could not assent to the Amendment, because it was evident, if any offences affected the result of the election, they could not be trivial or unimportant.

Question put, and *negatived.*

Clause 20 (Power of High Court and Election Court to except innocent act from being illegal practice, &c.).

MR. WARTON, in moving, as an Amendment, to insert after "same," in page 9, line 12, "a corrupt practice or," said, this Amendment also he moved in the interest of purity. He wanted to have corrupt practices provided for, as well as illegal practices.

Amendment proposed, in page 9, line 12, after the word "same," to insert the words "a corrupt practice or."—(*Mr. Warton.*)

Question, "That those words be there inserted," put, and *negatived.*

Clause 21 (Sending in claims and making payments for election expenses).

MR. WARTON, in moving, as an Amendment, to leave out line 24 in page 9, said, it seemed to him perfectly absurd to retain this line in the clause. The same idea was expressed twice over in two consecutive lines—"Any person who makes a claim except where the payment is allowed." How could a payment be made in contravention of the section if it was allowed by the section?

Amendment proposed, in page 9, to leave out line 24.—(*Mr. Warton.*)

Question proposed, "That line 24 stand part of the Bill."

THE ATTORNEY GENERAL (Sir HENRY JAMES) said, he must confess that the hon. and learned Gentleman (Mr. Warton) had been rather ingenious in finding opportunities to move Amendments. Payment might be in contravention of the section, as the hon. and learned Gentleman would see in the next page, although, in contravention of the section, certain payment was to be allowed. This line was quite necessary.

Question put, and *agreed to.*

Amendment proposed, in page 10, line 13, to leave out the word "an."—(*Mr. Warton.*)

Question, "That the word 'an' stand part of the Bill," put, and *agreed to.*

Clause 24 (List in burgess roll of persons incapacitated for voting by corrupt or illegal practices).

MR. WARTON, in moving, as an Amendment, to leave out "other," in page 11, line 29, said, he wished to explain that this Amendment must be considered in conjunction with the others he had put down to the same clause. It appeared to him it would be far better not to have the phrase "or an election to any public office." It would also be shorter and simpler to say "continuing or amending this or that Act." The phrase employed in the clause was rather roundabout; and as they were dealing with corrupt practices and other crimes, it was needless to say "under any Act continuing or amending this or that Act."

Amendment proposed, in page 11, line 29, to leave out the word "other."—(*Mr. Warton.*)

Question, "That the word 'other' stand part of the Bill," put, and *agreed to.*

Amendment proposed,

In page 11, line 29, to leave out from the word "Act" to the word "office," in line 30, inclusive, in order to insert the words "continuing or amending this or that Act,"—(*Mr. Warton,*)

—instead thereof.

Question, "That the words proposed to be left out stand part of the Bill," put, and *agreed to.*

Amendment proposed, to leave out the word "and," in page 11, line 32, and insert the word "or,"—(*Mr. Warton,*)

—instead thereof.

Question, "That the word 'and' stand part of the Bill," put, and *negatived.*

Question, "That the word 'or' be there inserted," put, and *agreed to.*

Mr. WARTON proposed, as an Amendment, to insert after "Parliamentary," in page 11, line 41, "or municipal."

Amendment proposed, in page 11, line 41, after the word "Parliamentary," to insert the words "or municipal."—(*Mr. Warton.*)

Question proposed, "That those words be there inserted."

The ATTORNEY GENERAL (Sir Henry James) opposed the Amendment because the words "or any public office" covered "municipal."

Mr. WARTON said, he agreed with what the hon. and learned Attorney General had said; but it would be better and shorter to have "Parliamentary or municipal."

The ATTORNEY GENERAL (Sir Henry James) said, the word "municipal" did not carry into effect what was wished. There were offices such as Boards of Guardians and Local Boards which did not come under "municipal," but which did come under "other public office."

Question put, and *negatived.*

Clause 25 (Time for presentation of petition alleging illegal practices).

The ATTORNEY GENERAL (Sir Henry James) moved, as an Amendment, to insert Clause 26 as sub-section (1) of Clause 25.

Amendment proposed,

In page 13, line 10, at beginning of Clause, to insert Clause 26 as Sub-Section (1).—(*Mr. Attorney General.*)

Question, "That the said Clause be there inserted as sub-section (1)," put, and *agreed to.*

Mr. WARTON moved, as an Amendment, to leave out "an," in page 13, line 11.

Amendment proposed, in page 13, line 11, to leave out the word "an."—(*Mr. Warton.*)

Question proposed, "That the word 'an' stand part of the Bill."

The ATTORNEY GENERAL (Sir Henry James) said, he was sorry he could not give way to his hon. and learned Friend's "an" on this occasion.

Question put, and *agreed to.*

Clause 27 (Withdrawal of election petition).

Mr. WARTON, in moving, as an Amendment, to leave out "on special grounds," in page 13, line 39, said, it seemed to him that these words were quite unnecessary. Why not say, "which seem just to the Court," as they had said before?

Amendment proposed, in page 13, line 39, leave out the words "on special grounds."—(*Mr. Warton.*)

Question, "That the words proposed to be left out stand part of the Bill," put, and *agreed to.*

Mr. WARTON, in moving, as an Amendment, in page 14, line 1, to leave out all after "state," to end of subsection, and insert—

"Fully the terms of any agreement or undertaking made or entered into respecting the withdrawal of the petition, to which agreement or undertaking the deponent may have been party or privy."

said, it appeared to him that the provision in sub-section (2) was extremely long and unnecessary, and he trusted the hon. and learned Attorney General would see his way to omit it.

Amendment proposed,

In page 14, line 1, to leave out all the words after the word "state" to the end of sub-section, and insert the words "fully the terms of any agreement or undertaking made or entered into respecting the withdrawal of the petition, to which agreement or undertaking the deponent may have been party or privy,"—(*Mr. Warton,*)

—instead thereof.

Question, "That the words proposed to be left out stand part of the Bill," put and *agreed to.*

Mr. WARTON, in moving, as an Amendment, to leave out "(whether lawful or unlawful)" in page 14, line 18, said, he would ask what did the phrase mean? Did it mean that the person making the affidavit was to state whether, in his opinion, the grounds were lawful or unlawful, or did it mean all the grounds? If it meant all the gronnds, it would not be necessary to say whether lawful or unlawful.

Amendment proposed, in page 14, line 18, to leave out the words ("whether lawful or unlawful.")—(*Mr. Warton.*)

Question, "That the words '(whether lawful or unlawful)' stand part of the Bill," put, and *agreed to.*

MR. WARTON said, he should not move any of the following 10 or 12 Amendments which stood in his name on the Paper.

Clause 30 (Power to election court to order payment by borough, or individual, of costs of election petition).

MR. INDERWICK said, he proposed, as an Amendment, to insert at the end of the clause—

"No witness on the trial of any municipal election petition presented after the passing of this Act shall be liable to be asked, or bound to answer, any question for the purpose of proving, or tending to prove, the commission of any corrupt practice at or in relation to any Parliamentary or municipal election prior to the passing of this Act."

There were two modes of inquiring as to the existence of corrupt practices at a Parliamentary election—either Commissioners were appointed by the Crown to make an inquiry, or an Election Petition was presented against the return of a Member to the House. The 49th section of the Parliamentary Elections (Corrupt and Illegal Practices) Act was as follows:—

"Provided that in all cases where the Commissioners have been appointed to inquire into corrupt practices, the Commissioners shall not inquire into any corrupt practices with regard to any elections which have taken place before the passing of the Act;"

and then the Act further provided—

"That no witnesses called before such Commissioners, and no witnesses called on any election petition after the passing of this Act, shall be allowed to be asked, or bound to answer, any question for the purpose of proving the commission of corrupt practices in relation to any election prior to the passing of this Act."

Of course, the Amendment he proposed had no reference to a Commission, because a Commission was not issued for the purpose of inquiring into corrupt practices at municipal elections. But there were such things as election petitions in regard to municipal elections, as there were in regard to Parliamentary elections; and he proposed, therefore, to add words to assimilate this Act with the Act of last year in regard to the mode in which election inquiries should be conducted. The House would recollect that this matter was discussed at great length when the Parliamentary Elections (Corrupt and Illegal Practices) Bill was before the House. A clause, similar to the one he (Mr. Inderwick) now moved, was proposed by the hon. Member for Glasgow (Mr. Anderson), and received the universal assent of the House. The hon. and learned Attorney General (Sir Henry James) gave his assent to the clause, and said, in his opinion, it would be a very valuable addition to the Bill; and added—

"With regard to these matters, byegones should be byegones; and when this Act passed, there should be no one who should be in fear of coming forward."

Such was the feeling entertained by every Member of the House, and accordingly the clause received general assent. There was only one other observation he had to make. When the Act was passed last year, it was said it was very proper to pass an Act of Parliament which would prevent any Member's past misdeeds being inquired into. He was bound to say the House of Commons would stand in a somewhat invidious position if they failed to consider in the same tone and temper a question of this kind as affecting Municipalities and municipal electors of the country. He begged to move the Amendment which stood in his name.

Amendment proposed,

In page 18, line 13, at the end of the sub-section, to insert the words—"No witness on the trial of any municipal election petition presented after the passing of this Act, shall be liable to be asked, or bound to answer, any question for the purpose of proving, or tending to prove, the commission of any corrupt practice at or in relation to any Parliamentary or municipal election prior to the passing of this Act." (*Mr. Inderwick.*)

Question proposed, "That those words be there inserted."

MR. EDWARD CLARKE said, that though he was partly responsible for the form of the clause adopted by the House last year, he could not support his hon. and learned Friend (Mr. Inderwick) in the proposal he now made. The two cases were essentially different. It was felt that unless some such clause as this were inserted in the Parliamentary Elections (Corrupt and Illegal Practices) Bill, there were a good many boroughs in the country in which Petitions would not be presented from the fear that the evidence given concerning past elections might have the effect of bringing about a disfranchisement of the constituency. He (Mr. E. Clarke), and the majority of the House, thought it was desirable to remove that fear, and so enable boroughs to start entirely free from the check upon petitions which existed in the memory of past misdeeds. But that did not apply to municipal elections at all. There was no danger of the revelations made upon one petition leading to a Commission and the disfranchisement of the place. The only thing that this clause would do, if it were put in the Bill, would be to enable people who had been guilty of bribery in past times to go into the witness-box and present themselves on the trial of an election petition absolutely free from any danger of having their character attacked, or of having their evidence discredited by their past actions. He hoped the hon. and learned Attorney General (Sir Henry James) would not consent to introduce this clause, which would not produce the good results which they hoped and expected from the clause inserted in the Bill of last year, but which would result in putting the man unclean in municipal matters on exactly the same footing as the man who had been clean all his life.

THE ATTORNEY GENERAL (Sir HENRY JAMES) said, he could not vote for the clause. An inquiry into a Parliamentary election was very different to that into a municipal election. In the case of a Parliamentary election, Royal Commissioners were appointed whose duty it was to inquire into past elections. In the case of municipal elections, they had no such inquiries. They had only inquiries as to particular elections, and the result of this clause would be simply to prevent cross-examination as to a man's credit. As a matter of fact, the clause would give a good character as regarded corrupt practices to every witness who came into the box. A man might have been a briber all his life, and yet nothing could be asked him as to his credibility. That would be the only effect of the clause; and, therefore, he (Sir Henry James) hoped it would not be approved by the House.

MR. SYDNEY BUXTON said, he could not agree with his hon. and learned Friend the Attorney General (Sir Henry James) and the hon. and learned Member for Plymouth (Mr. E. Clarke) in their attempt to discriminate in this matter between Parliamentary and municipal elections. The object of this Bill and of the Parliamentary Elections (Corrupt and Illegal Practices) Bill was, as he understood it, to promote purity of election, and the only way in which that could be done was to encourage Petitions. The hon. and learned Gentleman the Member for Plymouth had argued that they would discourage Parliamentary Petitions, but not municipal petitions, by not accepting this clause. It appeared to him (Mr. S. Buxton) that they would just as much discourage municipal election petitions as they would Parliamentary Election Petitions, for the borough was as corrupt in municipal matters as in Parliamentary. It would be just in those boroughs where corruption had taken place at past municipal elections that a petitioner would be afraid to petition, not through fear of disfranchisement, but through the fear that he himself, or his friends, would be exposed to the obloquy of having taken part in past acts of bribery. He (Mr. S. Buxton) could not agree with the hon. and learned Attorney General that that fear would be entirely done away with by the fact that the town would not be disfranchised. He agreed with his hon. and learned Friend (Mr. Inderwick) that, in this matter, the law relating to municipal elections should be assimilated to that affecting Parliamentary elections; and, therefore, he very heartily supported the clause the hon. and learned Gentleman proposed.

Question put, and *negatived*.

Clause 36 (Application to City of London of Act and of Part IV. of 45 & 46 Vict. c. 50).

MR. R. N. FOWLER (LORD MAYOR) said, he proposed, as an Amendment, to leave out, in page 20, line 34, "in the case of an election by liverymen in Common Hall, and." The City of London had no wish to be exempted from the provisions of the Bill; but the elections with which this and the subsequent Amendments he had on the Paper had to deal were very different from any other municipal elections—they were, in fact, rather of the character of Parliamentary elections. The Liverymen formed a very large constituency, many of them residing considerable distances from the City. Under the circumstances, he did not see how it was possible the provisions of the Bill could apply to the elections by Liverymen. As regards the Lord Mayor's election, in any contest the merits of the candidates would be well known, more or less; but in the case of an election for the office of Chamberlain that would not be the case, and candidates might not be very much known. Politics, he was happy to say, did not enter much into City elections; but that made it all the more necessary to make oneself known to the electorate by circulars and advertisements, and any candidate must be put to very considerable expense. So that they had a claim to have a reasonable sum allowed for expenses that must necessarily be incurred under the circumstances. The sum he had named was quite as little as it was possible to conduct an election upon, and it was only two-thirds of what would be allowed in a Parliamentary election. In many respects, the election for Lord Mayor bore more analogy to a Parliamentary election than anything else, and, certainly, he did not see how it was possible to conduct an election on the small sum allowed in the Bill; and he, therefore, hoped his hon. and learned Friend the Attorney General would see his way to allowing the Amendment. Contested elections to the offices of Lord Mayor and Sheriff were rare—still they occasionally arose; and he did not see how they could be properly conducted as the Bill stood.

Amendment proposed, in page 20, line 34, to leave out the words "in the case of an election by liverymen in Common Hall, and."—(*Mr. R. N. Fowler.*)

Question proposed, "That the words proposed to be left out stand part of the Bill."

MR. ALDERMAN W. LAWRENCE said, he was sorry the discussion of this Amendment had been driven to such a late hour, for this was a very important clause in the Bill. At first, the City was not included in the Bill; but the civic authorities thought the City ought to be included, for they did not think their elections should be so expensive as they had been. The elections in Common Hall were different to any other elections in the country. In Common Hall, the Lord Mayor, Sheriffs, the Chamberlain, and two or three less important officers were elected; and, under the present system, if a poll was demanded, it was open for seven days, the Liverymen living at a distance to which there was no limit, though there was a limit of distance, if they voted as Liverymen for a Member of Parliament. Now, the object was not to encourage an extravagant expenditure—the object was to prevent an evil in the other direction. The office of Chamberlain was one of high position, power, and emolument; and it was the desire of many to occupy it. The citizens wished to have one of their number in that position of whom they could be proud; they wished to have a man who would uphold the honour and dignity of the City, and be a credit to his position. But it would be possible to adopt tactics by which a man might be put forward, with sufficient support to carry an election, before the great body of Liverymen could be informed on the facts and merits of the case; and what was wanted was the opportunity of allowing information to be distributed among the Liverymen. Considering the cost of sending 10,000 circulars, and the cost of advertising, the amount allowed in the Bill was quite insufficient. The Corporation asked that this should be altered, so as not to debar them from the means of getting the best man to fill an important position. Any idea that the money might be used for furthering corruption was absurd; the amount, in itself, gave no opportunity for it. He would not go into the question whether the system was the best; but it had existed for four or five centuries; and now, when altering a seven days' poll to one, it was the more necessary to have the claims of candidates made well known to the electors. Not the same difficulty would arise in the election of a Lord Mayor, as the Liverymen elected two, and the Aldermen made the selection. That was done last year, and was the subject of much criticism at the time; but he believed that it was now generally admitted that the selection by the Aldermen of Alderman Fowler for Lord Mayor was wise and discreet. It was a different thing in the election of Chamberlain; whoever was elected to fill that position must spend money previously, in some shape or form, to inform the Liverymen of his claims. He hoped his hon. and learned Friend the Attorney General would grant the request of the City.

THE ATTORNEY GENERAL (Sir HENRY JAMES) said, his only desire was to act in a manner most acceptable to those most concerned. In the Grand Committee this question was left open for the decision of the House; for, as he said when the proposal was made, then they had not sufficient information. He felt the force of that which his right hon. Friend the Lord Mayor had said. These elections were quite distinct from those under ordinary circumstances, the Liverymen having the privilege of living out of the borough. At the same time, while willing to make the concession, he thought that £400 was a rather larger sum than was really necessary. He thought that £250 would be a sufficient and reasonable sum.

Question put, and *negatived.*

Amendment *agreed to.*

MR. R. N. FOWLER (LORD MAYOR) said, as regarded the third Amendment he had on the Paper, he would accept the proposal of the hon. and learned Gentleman the Attorney General, and substitute £250 for £400. First, however, he would move the Amendment in line 35.

Amendment proposed, in page 20, line 35, after "Alderman," insert "and Common Councilman."—(*Mr. R. N. Fowler.*)

Question, "That those words be there inserted," put, and *agreed to.*

Amendment proposed, in page 20, after line 37, insert the following subsection:—

"(1.) In the case of an election by liverymen in common hall a sum may be paid and expenses incurred, if a poll be not demanded, not exceeding forty pounds, and, if a poll be demanded, then not exceeding two hundred and fifty pounds, and in the event of a poll being demanded, such poll shall take place on the third day after the demand for a poll be made, unless such third day be a Sunday, in which case the poll shall take place on the fourth day, and the poll shall last for one day only, and commence at the hour of eight in the morning and close at six in the evening.—(*Mr. R. N. Fowler.*)

Question, "That those words be there inserted," put, and *agreed to.*

Clause 41 (Act not to extend to Scotland).

THE ATTORNEY GENERAL (Sir HENRY JAMES) said, he would propose, as an Amendment, that the Bill should not extend to Ireland. The election of Guardians in Ireland was the only class of election, he believed, which required the application of this Bill, and such elections would be dealt with in another Bill.

Amendment proposed, in page 23, line 11, after "Scotland," insert "or Ireland."—(*Mr. Attorney General.*)

Question, "That those words be there inserted," put, and *agreed to.*

On the Motion of Mr. ATTORNEY GENERAL, Clause 42 (Application of Act to Ireland), *struck out* of the Bill.

SCHEDULES.

On the Motion of Mr. ATTORNEY GENERAL, the following Amendments made.

Schedule 1, page 25, line 23, leave out from end of line to end of Schedule; Schedule 2, page 26, line 29, leave out from end of line to end of Schedule; Schedule 3, page 29, line 11, at end of Part I., insert—

Enactment defining the offences of bribery, treating, undue influence, and personation.

"The Municipal Corporations Act, 1882."
(45 and 46 Vic. c. 50, s. 77.)
(Definitions.)

"S. 77. 'Bribery,' 'treating,' 'undue influence,' and 'personation,' include respectively anything done before, at, after, or with respect to a municipal election, which, if done before, at, after, or with respect to a parliamentary election, would make the person doing the same liable to any penalty, punishment, or disqualification for bribery, treating, undue influence, or personation, as the case may be, under any Act for the time being in force with respect to parliamentary elections."

Bill read the third time, and *passed.*

ROYAL COURTS OF JUSTICE BILL.

(*Mr. Courtney, Mr. Herbert Gladstone.*)

[BILL 139.] COMMITTEE.

Order for Committee read.

Motion made, and Question proposed, "That this House will, upon Monday next, resolve itself into the said Committee."—(*Mr. Courtney.*)

MR. WARTON, in moving, as an Amendment, to substitute "Monday 4th August" for "Monday next," said, he should like to know whether there was any real intention to proceed with the Bill, after the important decision of the House a few weeks since, when the Government were defeated? The effect of that was to leave the Bill a mere shell, a wreck. Did the Government mean to proceed with it in that state; or did they wish to seize an opportunity when the attendance of hon. Members was small to restore the Bill to its original shape? The latter would certainly not be a right thing to do.

Amendment proposed, to leave out the words "Monday next," in order to insert the words "Monday 4th August,"—(*Mr. Warton*,)—instead thereof.

Question proposed, "That the words 'Monday next' stand part of the Question."

Mr. COURTNEY said, no; they did not intend to seek to restore the clause; but they were not without hope of getting the Bill through.

Question put, and *agreed to*.

Committee *deferred* till *Monday* next.

SUPERANNUATION BILL.—[Bill 146.]

(*Mr. Herbert Gladstone, Mr. Courtney.*)

COMMITTEE.

Order for Committee read.

Mr. BOORD said, he did not want to oppose the Bill; but he wished to have it extended to certain classes of workmen engaged in the manufacturing departments of the War Office. He had explained this to hon. Gentlemen opposite, and he hoped to have some assurance that the matter had received consideration.

Mr. HERBERT GLADSTONE said, this question had been raised before; and his hon. Friend the Surveyor General of Ordnance (Mr. Brand), on the part of the War Office, was ready to make further inquiries. At the same time, he did not think the inquiry would result in altering the opinion of the Treasury, which was adverse to the views of the hon. Member opposite. Further inquiry, however, would be made, and he would suggest that they should now go into Committee. He would then move to report Progress at once, and defer the Bill to Monday.

Bill *considered* in Committee.

Committee report Progress; to sit again upon *Monday* next.

PUBLIC WORKS LOANS BILL.

(*Mr. Courtney, Mr. Herbert Gladstone.*)

[BILL 299.] COMMITTEE.

Order for Committee read.

Mr. MARJORIBANKS said, in moving the Motion he had given Notice of, he would briefly refer to the Harbours and Passing Tolls Act of 1861, and the provisions therein. That Act was passed as the consequence and result of two inquiries that were held—one by the Select Committee of 1857-8, and one by the Royal Commission of 1859-60. Among the recommendations that resulted from these inquiries was one that loans to trading harbours should be granted at a low rate of interest. To give effect to this a Bill was introduced by the right hon. Gentleman the late Mr. Milner Gibson, the then President of the Board of Trade, and the present Prime Minister, then Chancellor of the Exchequer, which enacted that loans should be granted at 3¼ per cent to trading harbours. The Bill passed, and the Act worked fairly well down to 1879, when a change was introduced by a Bill similar to the one now before the House—a "Public Works Loans Bill," which left it at the discretion of the Treasury to raise the rate of interest on advances under the Harbours and Passing Tolls Act, and any other Acts sanctioning loans at a special rate of interest, to whatever rate under 5 per cent the Treasury thought desirable. In consequence, a Treasury Minute was issued, which changed the 3¼ per cent to a sliding scale of interest of 3½ per cent under 20 years; 3¾ per cent between 20 and 30 years; 4 per cent between 30 and 40 years; and 4¼ per cent between 40 and 50 years. This had the effect of raising the rate of interest 1 per cent on all harbour loans; for, naturally, such loans were required for the longest term that could be granted, the works requiring a long time for completion and to fructify. The intention, in the passing of the Act of 1861, was very well expressed in evidence recently given before his Committee by Sir Thomas Farrer. He said—

"The policy of granting loans to harbours was adopted in place of making harbours of refuge at the expense of the public funds. You must not look at loans to trading harbours as if they stood quite alone, or were to be considered on the bare principle of political economy. The fact was the loans were not merely for the improvement of harbours, but were for staving off or preventing a larger expenditure on the construction of harbours of refuge."

He (Mr. Marjoribanks) said that the raising of the rate of interest was practically a breach of faith with Harbour Trusts of the Kingdom. The Select Committee, over which he had had the honour to preside, was so thoroughly convinced of that, that, when reporting last year to the House, they made a special recommendation with regard to the rate of interest charged on advances under the Harbours and Passing Tolls Act, 1861. He believed that immediate effect could be given to that recommendation; and from a private conversation which he had had with the right hon. Gentleman the Chancellor of the Exchequer (Mr. Childers), and also from an answer which the right hon. Gentleman had given him in that House, he gathered that he was by no means prepared to meet this recommendation of the Select Committee with entire hostility. He had, therefore, hoped and expected that some change would have been arranged for in this Bill; and he was bound to say that he felt somewhat surprised and disappointed when he found, on Tuesday morning, that no change whatever was proposed. Under those circumstances, having had to consider the best course to pursue, he had arrived at the conclusion that the proper course to be taken was to put a Notice on the Paper of a Motion for an Instruction to the Committee to give effect to the recommendations of the Select Committee on Harbour Accommodation. He would not trouble the House with a lengthened argument at that hour of the night; he would merely appeal to hon. Members to support him in the Division he intended to take upon the Motion standing in his name, and which he now begged to move.

Motion made, and Question proposed,

"That it be an Instruction to the Committee on Public Works Loans that they have power to give effect to the recommendations of the Select Committee on Harbour Accommodation in their Report of 1883, having reference to the reduction of the rate of interest charged on advances made under 'The Harbours and Passing Tolls Act, 1861.'"—(*Mr. Marjoribanks.*)

MR. COURTNEY: Sir, I am sorry to have to ask a question with reference to a point of Order. I ask, whether it is in Order to move an Instruction of this kind to the Committee, when the Committee is already able to give effect to the object of the Motion without such Instruction? I understand that an Instruction is only permissible where the Committee about to be appointed is unable to report without that Instruction.

MR. SPEAKER: The hon. Gentleman has rightly stated the Rule on this point. Instruction is only permissible when it is necessary for the purpose of giving powers to a Committee to do that which otherwise they would have no authority to do.

MR. HEALY: How are we to know what view the Chairman of the Committee of Ways and Means will take of an Amendment embodying the terms of the Motion? We may have the Chairman of the Committee of Ways and Means ruling that such an Amendment does not come within the scope of the Bill. I ask, whether it is intended to inform the Chairman of Ways and Means that the Amendment may be moved?

MR. SPEAKER: The terms of the Motion will be a matter entirely for the Committee, and not for the Chairman of the Committee of Ways and Means, to decide.

MR. HEALY: But with regard to an Amendment; it will be competent for anyone in Committee of Ways and Means to ask the Chairman whether the proposal which the hon. Member for Berwickshire (Mr. Marjoribanks) has moved would be in Order; and it might be part of the tactics of other hon. Members to defeat the object of the hon. Member by some other means, just as they were trying to defeat it at the present moment. I wish to know, whether we have any guarantee that the Chairman of the Committee of Ways and Means will not give a ruling in favour of the Resolution not being moved?

MR. SPEAKER: It is a question of Order that has arisen, not a question of the ruling of the Chairman of the Committee of Ways and Means.

MR. HEALY: Then I understand that you have given no ruling on the point with regard to the Resolution in the Committee?

MR. SPEAKER: I am quite willing to hear the arguments on that point.

MR. COURTNEY: Sir, I am sorry there is another point which must be raised, as to whether it is competent to move the Resolution at all.

MR. MARJORIBANKS said, that in the Public Works Loans Act, 1879, certain authority was given to the Treasury, and the Treasury, using that authority, had issued a certain Minute, and it was that Minute which he desired to take the power of altering in this Bill.

Mr. COURTNEY: This Committee derives authority from the Public Loans Act, 1879, which deals with the whole question of public loans. I submit that the Motion for going into Committee on the Public Works Loans Bill of this Session would not be the proper place in which to introduce a Resolution of this nature. It would be irregular to move an Instruction to the Committee to do that which they already have the power to do under the Act. From the nature of the aim which my hon. Friend has in view, I believe it is within the competence of the Committee to deal with the question.

Captain AYLMER said, he thought the position taken by the hon. Member for Monaghan (Mr. Healy) had not been clearly understood. It seemed to him that the point of the hon. Member was, that if Mr. Speaker ruled that this Resolution could be put in Committee without Instruction, the hon. Gentleman the Secretary to the Treasury might nevertheless rise in Committee and object to the Amendment being inserted, on the ground that a money question was raised.

Mr. HEALY said, he would submit a point in support of what had fallen from the hon. and gallant Gentleman who had just sat down (Captain Aylmer). It was that it was not competent to any Member of the House to move a Resolution of this kind in Committee, and therefore an objection taken by the Government would completely upset any such Motion. They were taking the only course open to them on a Money Bill—that was to say, they were appealing to the Government, by Resolution of the House, to give effect to the recommendations of the Select Committee; and it was because, as private Members in Committee, they had no power to proceed by way of Amendment, that they appealed to the Government to carry out their object by Instruction to the Committee.

Mr. COURTNEY said, the argument of the hon. Member for Monaghan (Mr. Healy) was fatal to the Motion. A private Member could not move the House to do that which he could not move in Committee.

Mr. HEALY said, it was not necessary at all that, because they were asking that effect should be given to the Resolutions of the Select Committee, they should go into the recommendations of the Select Committee. They were simply asking that the Resolution passed by the Select Committee should be given effect to, and they were not called upon to go into the question raised by the hon. Gentleman.

Mr. SPEAKER: It would be clearly competent to the Committee to undertake this duty without Instruction from the House. It has already competence to do so.

Mr. HEALY: Will you, Sir, supplement that by a statement to the effect that it would be competent for a private Member to move the Resolution?

Mr. SPEAKER: It would not be proper to move in this House an Instruction to the Committee to do that which the Public Works Loans Act already empowers the Committee to do. The Question, therefore, cannot be put.

Mr. INDERWICK said, he would be glad to hear what course the Government intended to pursue in this matter. His hon. Friend the Member for Berwickshire (Mr. Marjoribanks) had given Notice of this Motion, for the purpose of obtaining a statement from the Government on this question of interest. He was not himself a Member of the Select Committee; but he had some knowledge of the smaller harbours on the South Coast of England, many of which were silted up and quite useless for the purpose for which they were intended. They had drifted into that condition, because the money was lent to the Trustees at such a high rate of interest that it was impossible for them to borrow the money necessary to keep them in an efficient state. For the purpose of giving the Secretary to the Treasury an opportunity of stating what course the Government proposed to follow in this matter, he begged to move the adjournment of the debate.

Motion made, and Question proposed, "That the Debate be now adjourned."—(*Mr. Inderwick.*)

Mr. COURTNEY said, he was about to make a statement on the subject. Perhaps the hon. and learned Member would withdraw his Motion for the adjournment of the debate.

Motion, by leave, *withdrawn*.

Mr. COURTNEY said, that this Resolution had been brought on by his hon. Friend the Member for Berwickshire (Mr. Marjoribanks) rather suddenly. He did not mean to say that the question was a new one.

Mr. MARJORIBANKS said, he begged the hon. Gentleman's pardon; his Notice had been on the Paper during the whole of the Session.

Mr. COURTNEY said, his meaning was that the Motion had been brought on rather suddenly, so far as this Bill was concerned. He had to state that only that morning, having had an opportunity of consulting the right hon. Gentleman the Chancellor of the Exchequer (Mr. Childers) upon it, they were in hope that the hon. Gentleman would not have thought it necessary to proceed. In the first place, he would point out that the rates of interest charged on the loans were regulated at present by Treasury Minute, and that the proper form of making an alteration of the rate of interest to be paid hereafter on those loans would also be by Treasury Minute. It was therefore considered undesirable in this Bill to specify any exact terms on which money should be advanced. As an illustration of that, he was bound to point out the inconvenience which would result from the rate of interest being fixed by the Bill. If the rate of interest were fixed by Act of Parliament, instead of by Treasury Minute, they would not be able by Treasury Minute to reduce the rate of interest. It was, therefore, thought desirable that the Executive Government should have power to determine the rate of interest from time to time, as well as the amount of security to be provided. Therefore, he urged upon his hon. Friend the imprudence of bringing this matter within the scope of the Bill, instead of leaving it to be dealt with by a Treasury Minute. It was quite true that this subject had been brought before the Select Committee of last year, and that it formed part of the preliminary Report at the end of last Session; and although it was true that his hon. Friend had, on one or two occasions, put a Notice on the Paper in relation to the question, he had yet never brought it forward. The recommendations of the Select Committee were considered at the beginning of the Session by the right hon. Gentleman the Chancellor of the Exchequer and himself (Mr. Courtney), with a desire to go as far as possible, consistently with, and having regard to, the responsibility of the Treasury, to meet the recommendations of the Committee. They believed they had discovered a way which promised to fulfil that aim. They thought that some form of collateral security should be given for loans of this kind, and that if such were forthcoming a reduction of the rate of interest might be made. Now, he believed that the principle of collateral security was one which had not been very much embodied in Acts of Parliament, so far as England was concerned, although it had been acted upon in Ireland, where loans had been made for the purpose of constructing railways on the security of the rates. It was thought, with respect to recent harbour loans, that collateral security might be offered on the part of the municipalities. There was the idea that the municipalities might come in aid of the tolls, because the tolls of harbours were obviously a very unsatisfactory and risky security. For instance, a harbour might pass out of use, merely by the falling off of the shipping trade at the place where it was situated, and the tolls of the harbour, under such circumstances, would constitute a very unsatisfactory security for the amount of public money which might be advanced. But in the event of adequate collateral security being forthcoming in the neighbourhood, from persons responsible for the harbour, and responsible for its management, and having, probably, a voice in the selection of Trustees for keeping the harbour in a proper condition, under those circumstances, he said, the desire would be to meet the view of the Select Committee of last year with regard to reducing the rates of interest. He appealed to his hon. Friend to leave the matter in the hands of the Treasury; because he believed it was one which should be regulated by Treasury Minute, and not by a strict line embodied in an Act of Parliament, which could not necessarily provide for all the circumstances connected with the harbours for which the loans might be asked. He trusted this statement would be satisfactory to his hon. Friend, and that he would now allow the Bill to go forward.

Mr. MARJORIBANKS said, his hon. Friend the Secretary to the Treasury (Mr. Courtney) had not confined himself to his arguments at all. He spoke of taking collateral security for harbour loans; but he (Mr. Marjoribanks) would remind the hon. Gentleman that that was the very thing recommended in the Report of the Select Committee last year. The recommendation with regard to the reduction of the rate of interest was entirely distinct, and in addition to that recommendation. A number of boroughs had been able to give that security; he knew a case in his own district where the local rates were assigned as collateral security. With regard to the amount of loss supposed to accrue from these harbour loans, he would like to say a few words. The amount of interest actually received on all loans under the Harbours and Passing Tolls Act since 1861 was £897,381; the amount that would have been receivable on the same advances at 3 per cent, the rate at which the Government borrowed money, would have been £822,428, or £74,953 less than the amount actually received. So far, therefore, the Government had made an actual profit of nearly £75,000 on advances in respect of interest alone. There was in arrear on the 31st March, 1883, the sum of £61,270, out of the total sum advanced of £2,561,849, while the total sum remitted amounted to £33,992. He hoped that his hon. Friend the Secretary to the Treasury would have gathered from the observations which had fallen from hon. Members in the course of the discussion that there was a strong desire in the House to make a material reduction in the rate of interest, and he trusted that they would have a reduction made known to them before long in the shape of the Treasury Minute announcing the fact.

MR. HEALY said, it was much to be regretted that, owing to the technical point raised by the hon. Gentleman the Secretary to the Treasury (Mr. Courtney), the House was unable to come to a decision on the question brought forward by the hon. Member for Berwickshire (Mr. Marjoribanks). The principle on which the hon. Gentleman the Secretary to the Treasury wished the House to act was something like this—"Shut your eyes and open your mouth, and see what the Treasury will send you." Having had some experience of Irish loans, he could assure the hon. Gentleman the Member for Berwickshire that the Treasury would not do a single thing after having got the Act passed. When the Act was passed, the hon. Member for Berwickshire might organize as many deputations to the Treasury as he pleased, or he might raise discussions in that House; but the Secretary to the Treasury would only shrug his shoulders and say—"I am very sorry I am quite unable to do anything for you." Such was the experience of Irish Members with regard to the Government in the matter of loans. It might be said that when they had passed their Bill, and fixed the rate of interest by Treasury Minute, their regard for that Minute was much greater than the regard which a poor Mussulman had for the Prophet. The hon. Member for Berwickshire might take it for granted that the hon. Gentleman the Secretary to the Treasury, at the present time, would do absolutely nothing to forward the recommendations of the Committee; and, so far as the Resolution was concerned, when the time came, the hon. Gentleman the Secretary to the Treasury would completely ignore it. The House would have come to a decision on the point that night had it not been prevented by the clever technical device of the hon. Gentleman, who, directly the Bill was passed, would simply say that, having looked into the circumstances, he was quite unable to do anything in the matter.

Bill *considered* in Committee.

(In the Committee.)

Clause 1 *agreed to*.

Clause 2 (Grant of £3,000,000 for Public Works Loans. 38 and 39 Vict. c. 89. 42 and 43 Vict. c. 77.)

MR. MARJORIBANKS said, unless he received some satisfactory statement from the hon. Gentleman the Secretary to the Treasury (Mr. Courtney) he should be compelled to move that Progress be reported.

MR. COURTNEY said, he hoped his hon. Friend (Mr. Marjoribanks) would not think it necessary to move to report Progress. He was very much surprised that the hon. Member for Monaghan (Mr. Healy) should doubt what he had said with reference to the rate of interest.

Motion made, and Question proposed, "That the Chairman do report Progress, and ask leave to sit again."—(*Mr. Marjoribanks.*)

Mr. HEALY said, the hon. Member for Monaghan was extremely obliged to the hon. Gentleman the Secretary to the Treasury, and begged leave to inform him that observations of that kind were not likely to induce the hon. Member for Monaghan to accept the representations of the Secretary to the Treasury, or to facilitate the passing of the Bill.

Mr. WARTON said, there had been so many instances of breaches of faith on the part of the Government that he, for one, was very suspicious of their assurances. He would ask, with regard to this question, whether they intended to perform what they had promised? For his own part, he never trusted the Government at all.

The SOLICITOR GENERAL (Sir Farrer Herschell) said, he would remind the Committee that the remark of his hon. Friend the Secretary to the Treasury (Mr. Courtney) was due to the observations made by the hon. Member for Monaghan (Mr. Healy). His hon. Friend had distinctly assured the hon. Member for Berwickshire (Mr. Marjoribanks) that the matter would be dealt with by Treasury Minute. He had, at the same time, pointed out the advantage of dealing with it in that way, as opposed to dealing with it by Act of Parliament. The hon. Member for Monaghan thereupon said—"Do not give the Government their Bill, because, when it has passed, the Secretary to the Treasury will do nothing."

Mr. HEALY said, if he had understood the hon. Gentleman the Secretary to the Treasury (Mr. Courtney) to give a distinct pledge, he would not have made the remarks to which the hon. and learned Gentleman the Solicitor General referred; but he did not believe that the Secretary to the Treasury gave any pledge whatever.

The SOLICITOR GENERAL (Sir Farrer Herschell) said, he understood his hon. Friend the Secretary to the Treasury (Mr. Courtney) to say that he would deal with the matter in a Treasury Minute, and that he shadowed out the form which the Treasury Minute was to take with reference to the rate of interest. That he understood to be what his hon. Friend intended. The hon. Member for Monaghan (Mr. Healy) said he did not understand that a pledge had been given; but his (the Solicitor General's) hon. Friend certainly thought he had given a strong pledge, and that was why he had spoken so warmly.

Mr. DODDS said, that this was a matter in which he took great interest, and had taken great interest for many years. The Act of 1861 provided that advances should only be made for public harbours. Loans had been refused where adequate security was not provided.

Mr. BUCHANAN rose to Order. He wished to know whether it was competent for the hon. Member for Stockton (Mr. Dodds) to go into this matter, seeing that the Motion before the Committee was that the Chairman report Progress, and ask leave to sit again.

The CHAIRMAN said, the hon. Member for Stockton was scarcely in Order—in discussing the subject-matter of the Bill on the Question to report Progress.

Mr. DODDS said, they were now discussing whether they should report Progress for the reason that they had not received a distinct pledge from the hon. Gentleman the Secretary to the Treasury (Mr. Courtney) as to the rate of interest. He (Mr. Dodds) had listened in vain for a single word from his hon. Friend to the effect that the Government would consent to reduction spoken of. It had been said that these matters would be dealt with by a Treasury Minute; but nothing had been said as to whether the Government would consent to reduction. If the hon. Gentleman the Secretary to the Treasury would give that pledge he would satisfy the Committee; but with anything short of that the hon. Member for Berwickshire (Mr. Marjoribanks) ought not to be satisfied.

Mr. COURTNEY said, he had thought he had given a most distinct pledge that the matter would be dealt with on the Report of the Committee. If he had not absolutely agreed to the figure stated by the Committee, he had, at any rate, stated the figure as near as he could. The only reason he was not in a position to say more was that he had not been able to see his right hon. Friend the Chancellor of the Exchequer that evening. That had probably prevented him from being able to give the exact figure; but he had certainly given a pledge that the matter should be dealt with by way of a reduction of interest. Having, as he thought, given that pledge distinctly, he had felt very much hurt at the remarks of the hon. Member for Monaghan (Mr. Healy).

CAPTAIN AYLMER said, he thought it would be well to report Progress, in order that an opportunity might be given to the hon. Gentleman (Mr. Courtney) to consult with the Chancellor of the Exchequer upon this subject.

MR. SEXTON said, he considered that the hon. Gentleman the Secretary to the Treasury (Mr. Courtney) had given a conclusive and unquestionable reason why the Committee should agree to report Progress. He had given a pledge that the hon. Member for Monaghan (Mr. Healy) was quite entitled to regard as evasive—namely, that the matter would be dealt with by a Treasury Minute. That might mean that the hon. Gentleman intended to deal with the question according to his own pleasure and fancy. The hon. Gentleman had now altered his statement at the Table, and had declared that he could not give a distinct pledge, on account of the absence of the Chancellor of the Exchequer. It was, therefore, desirable that the Committee stage should not be further proceeded with until the hon. Member had had an opportunity of seeing the Chancellor of the Exchequer.

Question put, and *agreed to*.

Committee report Progress; to sit again *To-morrow*.

SAVING BANKS ACTS AMENDMENT BILL.—[BILL 277.]

(*Mr. Fawcett, Mr. Courtney.*)

SECOND READING.

Order for Second Reading read.

Motion made, and Question proposed, "That the Bill be read a second time To-morrow."—(*Mr. Courtney.*)

MR. WARTON said, he wanted to know whether the Government intended to proceed with this Bill? This was one of the measures mentioned by the right hon. Gentleman the Prime Minister on the memorable Thursday when he killed nine of his Bills. The right hon. Gentleman had stated that he would not go on with any measure which was seriously opposed. Well, this was a measure against which there was serious opposition, and they should have a distinct understanding whether the Government were going to go on with it. The Government ought to say exactly what Bills they were going to pass, and what Bills they were going to give up.

MR. COURTNEY said, that one clause in this Bill was very important—namely, the clause enabling the amount to be deposited in the Savings Banks in a year to be increased from £30 to £50. That clause was likely to be opposed, and therefore the Government intended to drop it.

Question put, and *agreed to*.

Second Reading *deferred* till *To-morrow*.

SUPPLY—REPORT.

Resolutions [22nd July] *reported*.

First Resolution *agreed to*.

Second Resolution *postponed*.

Third Resolution *agreed to*.

Postponed Resolution to be considered upon *Monday* next.

MOTION.

EXPIRING LAWS CONTINUANCE BILL.

On Motion of Mr. HERBERT GLADSTONE, Bill to continue various Expiring Laws, *ordered* to be brought in by Mr. HERBERT GLADSTONE and Mr. COURTNEY.

Bill *presented*, and read the first time. [Bill 306.]

House adjourned at half after Three o'clock.

HOUSE OF LORDS,

Friday, 25*th July*, 1884.

MINUTES.]—PUBLIC BILLS—*First Reading*—Municipal Elections (Corrupt and Illegal Practices) * (212); Prisons * (213); Teachers' Residences (Ireland) * (214).

Second Reading—Contagious Diseases (Animals) Act, 1878 (Districts) * (205)

Committee—Report—Local Government Provisional Orders (No. 5) * (183); Sheriff Court Houses (Scotland) Amendment * (193).

Report—Strensall Common * (195); Local Government Provisional Orders (No. 6) * (189).

Third Reading—Local Government Provisional Orders (No. 4) * (163); Local Government Provisional Orders (No. 7) * (164); Local Government Provisional Orders (No. 8) * (165); Local Government (Ireland) Provisional Orders (Labourers Act) (No. 2) * (138); Naval Discipline Act (1866) Amendment * (199); Reformatory and Industrial Schools (Manx Children) * (200), and *passed*.

EGYPT—THE CONFERENCE.

QUESTION.

EARL DE LA WARR: I wish to ask the noble Earl the Secretary of State for Foreign Affairs a Question of which I have given private Notice. I beg to ask him, when it will be convenient for Her Majesty's Government to give some further information to this House relative to the Conference?

EARL GRANVILLE: Her Majesty's Government are anxious that there should be as little delay as possible in making a statement with regard to the Conference; but I can make no definite promise. I can only inform the noble Earl that the Conference met yesterday, and that it will hold a meeting on Monday, and it is possible that on that day I may be able to make a statement. However, as I have said, I can give no positive pledge on the matter.

House adjourned at half past Four o'clock, to Monday next, a quarter before Eleven o'clock.

HOUSE OF COMMONS,

Friday, 25th July, 1884.

MINUTES.]—SUPPLY—*considered in Committee*—CIVIL SERVICE ESTIMATES—CLASS III.—LAW AND JUSTICE—Votes 14 to 19, 21, 23, 25, and 32—CLASS IV.—EDUCATION, SCIENCE, AND ART.

Resolutions [July 24] *reported.*

PUBLIC BILLS—*Ordered—First Reading*—Metropolitan Asylums Board (Borrowing Powers) * [310]; Public Health (Ireland) (Districts) * [311].

First Reading—Bishopric of Bristol * [309].

Second Reading—Military Pensions and Yeomanry Pay * [302]; Naval Enlistment * [305]; Prosecution of Offences [287]; Revenue, &c. * [300]; Building Societies Acts Amendment * [301].

Committee—Report—Public Works Loans [299]; Infants [14-308].

Report — Third Reading — Local Government (Ireland) Provisional Order (Labourers Act) (No. 8) * [283], and *passed.*

Considered as amended—Pier and Harbour Provisional Orders * [259].

Withdrawn—Medical Act Amendment * [207].

QUESTIONS.

METROPOLIS (THAMES CROSSINGS)—BRIDGE AT LITTLE TOWER HILL.

SIR HUSSEY VIVIAN asked the Right honourable the Lord Mayor, Whether it is the intention of the Corporation of the City of London to apply to Parliament next year for power to construct a Low Level Opening Bridge across the Thames at Little Tower Hill, and to apply thereto the surplus funds of the Bridge House Estate?

MR. R. N. FOWLER (LORD MAYOR), in reply, said, that the Bridge Estates Committee had had the subject under their consideration, and had reported in favour of a low level opening bridge. He had summoned a special meeting of the Common Council for Monday, in order to consider the question.

PARLIAMENT — BUSINESS OF THE HOUSE—ATTENDANCE OF MINISTERS.

LORD EUSTACE CECIL, who had given Notice that he would ask the Secretary of State for War,

"Whether he can now state when any Supplementary Estimate will be presented to the House to defray the cost of any expedition that may be necessary for the defence of Egypt?"

said: I think it is unnecessary for us to come down to the House at a quarter-past 4 o'clock to find that Ministers are not present to answer Questions.

MR. COURTNEY said, he was afraid he could give no information on the subject; but he imagined that the matter had been under consideration that afternoon. There was no doubt a Supplementary Estimate would have to be presented; but how far that would have relation to any expedition to Egypt he was not in a position to say.

LORD EUSTACE CECIL (before the Marquess of HARTINGTON'S arrival) said, that in the absence of the Secretary of State for War he would postpone his Question until Monday, unless the President of the Board of Trade was prepared to answer it. He must again protest against the manner in which the Cabinet was treating the House of Commons by Ministers not being present to answer Questions.

SAVINGS BANKS ACTS AMENDMENT BILL.

LORD ARTHUR HILL (for Mr. ION HAMILTON) asked the Secretary to the Treasury, Whether, viewing the great probability of much opposition being offered to the provisions of the Savings Banks Acts Amendment Bill, it is the intention of Her Majesty's Government, to proceed with that measure at the present late period of the Session?

Mr. COURTNEY, in reply, said, everybody seemed to be absent. He had arranged with the Postmaster General to answer this Question, and in his absence he could only repeat what he had already said, that there was no serious opposition to the Bill except with regard to the clause raising the limit of the yearly deposits from £30 to £50, and that clause it was proposed to withdraw.

Mr. MOORE inquired whether the Secretary to the Treasury was going to answer all the Questions addressed to the Postmaster General in the right hon. Gentleman's absence?

Mr. COURTNEY: Oh no, Sir.

CUSTOMS—IMPORTATION, MANUFACTURE, AND SALE OF OLEOMARGARINE AND OTHER BUTTER SUBSTITUTES.

Mr. DUCKHAM asked the President of the Local Government Board, Whether he is aware that large quantities of oleomargarine are manufactured in the United Kingdom; that most obnoxious compounds of fatty matter are used in its manufacture; that it is sent from this Country to Holland and to Norway to be there manipulated with milk and re-imported as butter or butterine; whether he has any power to order a supervision of the oleomargarine and butterine factories in the United Kingdom; and, if not, whether he will be prepared to introduce a Bill during the Autumn Session to provide for such a supervision, in order to guard against the use of impure or deleterious compounds in its manufacture; and, whether he will direct the attention of the local authorities throughout the United Kingdom to the deleterious compounds used in the manufacture of oleomargarine, butterine, and cheese, in countries from whence large quantities are imported, and request them to enforce the provisions of the Food and Drugs Adulteration Acts, in order to prevent the sale of articles so calculated to injure the health of those who consume them?

Mr. HIBBERT: The Local Government Board have no definite information as to large quantities of oleomargarine being manufactured in the United Kingdom. Neither have they any power to order a supervision of oleomargarine and butterine factories. At present the Board have no information that would lead them to suppose that the provisions of the Sale of Food and Drugs Act are not sufficient to meet the case of any deleterious compound being used in the manufacture of these articles. The Board last month issued a Circular letter to the Sanitary Authorities in England directing their attention to the provisions of the Sale of Food and Drugs Acts and urging them to avail themselves of their powers under those Acts of obtaining samples of food and drugs for the purpose of analysis. From the answers already received the Board have reason to believe that those powers will in future be more fully exercised than has hitherto been the case. The samples analyzed will no doubt include the articles mentioned by the hon. Member; and if, as alleged, they are injurious to health, or if they are sold in substitution for the articles asked for, it may be anticipated that prosecutions will follow. There have already been many convictions for the sale of butterine in the place of butter. At present, the Board do not consider that it is necessary to address any special communication to the authorities on the subject, further than the Circular already issued.

SCOTLAND—NORTHERN LIGHTS COMMISSIONERS—LIGHTHOUSE ON FAIR ISLE.

Mr. J. W. BARCLAY asked the President of the Board of Trade, Whether the Trinity House authorities have come to any conclusion as to the erection of a lighthouse on Fair Isle; and, if not, whether, considering the great advantage a light on Fair Isle would be to vessels crossing the Atlantic, the providing of a lighthouse on it might not be considered apart from the general scheme for lighting the Shetland and Orkney coasts?

Mr. CHAMBERLAIN, in reply, said, that the Trinity House authorities had not yet reported on the extensive scheme which had been under their consideration; but the question of dealing with the lighting of the Fair Isle was one which naturally came under the consideration of the Northern Lights Commissioners.

IRELAND—ORANGE PROCESSIONS—THE 12TH OF JULY CELEBRATIONS—ORANGE ARCH AT GLENARM.

Lord ARTHUR HILL asked the Chief Secretary to the Lord Lieutenant of Ireland, Whether his attention has been drawn to a letter which appeared in *The Belfast News Letter* on the 23rd instant—

"The Arch at Glenarm.—Sir, We, the owners and occupiers of the two houses from which the Orange arch was suspended on 12th July last, are very much surprised at the reply given by the Chief Secretary to Lord Arthur Hill in the House of Commons last night;

"We beg to give the statements therein made the fullest and most emphatic contradiction. No arch was ever erected there against our will, nor was there ever any disturbance in Glenarm in connection with an arch;

"We are prepared to make affidavits to this effect;

"In to-days issue of *Morning News* we see that Mr. Sexton insinuated that the arch was attached to the house of the parish priest. All we can say in reply to this is that neither of us is a parish priest:

"(Signed) John Cobain,
"William Hunter;

and, whether he still adheres to the statement which he made on the 22nd instant, or whether he proposes to modify it in any manner?

MR. TREVELYAN: The noble Lord has not given me any opportunity of making the further inquiry which I presume he desires, as he has put down his Question without Notice. I can, therefore, only say that I based my Answer on an explicit statement of the District Inspector of Constabulary as to facts known to the police.

IRELAND—MONEY RETURNED THROUGH THE POST.

MR. HEALY asked the Chief Secretary to the Lord Lieutenant of Ireland, What disposition was made by him of the money recently returned him through the Post; and, will it be refunded to the Secret Service Department?

MR. TREVELYAN: Some time ago I received £15 in notes in a letter without address. Knowing nothing of the matter, I followed the course I always follow with regard to anonymous communications which appear to require notice, and handed the letter and its contents to the police authorities.

MR. HEALY: I beg to inform the right hon. Gentleman that the money belongs to Mrs. Tyler, of the Secret Service Department.

LAW AND POLICE (METROPOLIS)—THE REFORM DEMONSTRATION.

MR. TATTON EGERTON asked the Secretary of State for the Home Department, Whether the police guarding a procession on Sunday passing through Onslow Place were employed on special duty, and by whom paid; whether he approves of the Metropolitan Police being employed for the protection of mendicity; and, whether the refusal of a superintendent of police to enable a Member of the House of Commons to cross Piccadilly in the crowd, before any passage of the procession of 21st July, is in accordance with the pledge given by Her Majesty's Government?

SIR WILLIAM HARCOURT: The police were not employed on special duty on the occasion in question at Onslow Place. The only men present were those on the adjoining beat, and they remained on duty to preserve order, seeing so large a concourse of people. No payment was anticipated. With regard to the second Question, I am bound to say, from the particulars with which the hon. Member has furnished me, I think that the police have fairly done all they could in the circumstances.

MR. TATTON EGERTON: As to my first Question, the police were marching with the procession. I do not think that they were the police on the adjoining beats. The right hon. and learned Gentleman has been misinformed by the heads of his Department.

ARMY—VOLUNTARY RETIREMENT.

COLONEL KINGSCOTE asked the Secretary of State for War, Why voluntary retirement, with pension and gratuity sanctioned by the Pay Warrants, have been partially suspended?

THE MARQUESS OF HARTINGTON: In replying to this Question, Sir, it may probably remove some misconception if I make a short statement on the subject of voluntary retirement. The House is, perhaps, aware that the present system of Army promotion is based on the Report of a Royal Commission, presided over by Lord Penzance. In the Report of the Commissioners the following passage occurred in reference to the voluntary retirement with pension or gratuity which they recommended:—

"The above system, then, is intended as a flexible one, under which the actual rate of promotion can be controlled. It is an inevitable result of the regimental system, and of promotions taking place within the regiment, that the officers of any one regiment may, from time to time, go forward quicker than those of another, by reason of more frequent deaths or other causes of vacancy. This inequality may, to some extent, be rectified in the granting or withholding voluntary retirement in each individual case, according to the state of promotion in the particular regiment. By the exercise of a like discretion the general rate of promotion may be held in check on the one hand, or stimulated on the other, throughout the Army. And further, we may remark that a system of this kind, capable of expansion or contraction in the hands of those who are to administer it, will readily adapt itself to the changes by way of augmentation of the higher ranks or otherwise, which the future development of military organization may render necessary."

This recommendation was given effect to by Article 94 of the Royal Warrant, which runs as follows:—

"Voluntary retirement with retired pay or gratuity shall only be permitted when it shall be deemed expedient by our Secretary of State. Before such voluntary retirement be permitted it shall be specially recommended by our Commander-in-Chief and approved by our Secretary of State."

The contingency contemplated by the Commissioners has arisen. Promotion has for some time been, on the average, very much more rapid than the normal rate; and if no change were made would continue at an undue rate. I have, therefore, partially suspended voluntary retirements, so as to check promotion in regiments where it is unduly rapid, in accordance with the intention of the recommendation of the Royal Commission and of the Royal Warrant. I have thought it fairer to the officers of the Army to do this in the form of a General Regulation, so that they may know their exact position, than to treat each case on its merits, as recommended by the Royal Commission.

EDUCATION (IRELAND)—LEGISLATION.

MR. SEXTON asked the Chief Secretary to the Lord Lieutenant of Ireland, If he will introduce, before the end of the Session, the Bill which he has prepared on the subject of Irish Education, in order that its provisions may be considered during the Recess.

MR. TREVELYAN: No, Sir; the Government cannot bring in any Bills at this period of the Session which they do not see their way to passing. When I promised to bring in the Bill, it was on the distinct understanding that if it was to be passed at all, it was to be passed by common consent, or something approaching. I do not consider it desirable to introduce a Bill merely to have it seen.

MR. HEALY asked the Chief Secretary to the Lord Lieutenant of Ireland, If the Intermediate Education Secretaries edit the questions set at each examination, if they are competent to do so in all the subjects; and, if not, upon what grounds do these officials continue to receive as salaries six per cent. of the entire income of the Board, or, as per the Report of 1883, a very large percentage of the Board's annual expenditure; which of the Secretaries was responsible for editing and correcting the proofs of the papers set in algebra and arithmetic at the recent examination; whether one of the papers set in algebra contained questions extending beyond the prescribed course, and whether the junior grade paper in arithmetic contained an unpardonable error; and, do these mistakes arise from the employment as secretary of an ex-Queen's College professor who is past his labour, and otherwise incapacitated?

MR. TREVELYAN: The Assistant Education Commissioners, in pursuance of the Rules of the Board, approved by the Lord Lieutenant, revise the examination papers except in five special subjects, and are competent to do so. In all cases proofs are submitted to the examiners for correction. One or two letters have been received objecting to two questions in the junior grade algebra paper, on the ground that they were outside the prescribed course. In the opinion of the Assistant Commissioners the objection is not well founded; but the matter awaits the decision of the Board. Dr. Curtis is the Assistant Commissioner who revises the science papers. The error in the arithmetic paper, to which the hon. Member refers, was, I am informed, purely a typographical one—the misplacing of a point, which arose in the process of printing, and did not exist in the proofs corrected by the examiner and revised by the Assistant Commissioner. I am not aware of any grounds for the suggestion that Dr. Curtis is past his work or otherwise incapacitated.

POST OFFICE (IRELAND)—DISPLAY OF PARTY EMBLEMS BY THE LETTER CARRIER AT NEWCASTLE, COUNTY DOWN.

MR. HARRINGTON asked the Postmaster General, Whether it is true that, on July 12th, the Orange anniversary, the letter carrier at Newcastle, county Down, wore an orange sash when delivering the letters through the town; and, whether this was noticed by the Postmaster; and, if so, was any remonstrance addressed to this man for wearing party emblems while engaged in official duties?

MR. FAWCETT: It is the case, as implied in the Question of the hon. Member, that on the 12th instant the man who delivers letters at Newcastle, county Down, wore an orange sash while in the discharge of his official duties. The man in question, who is employed by the local Postmaster, disclaims all intention of giving offence, expresses regret that offence should have been given, and promises not to wear his scarf when on duty again.

LAW AND POLICE (METROPOLIS)—THE REFORM DEMONSTRATION.

MR. J. LOWTHER (for Viscount FOLKESTONE) asked the Secretary of State for War, Whether it is true, as stated in a letter in *The Times* of the 24th, that three Yeomanry bands, in uniform, took part in the Demonstration on Monday last; and, if so, if it is not an infraction of the "Queen's Regulations;" and, whether the Military authorities propose to take any and, if so, what notice of such an infringement of the "Queen's Regulations?"

THE MARQUESS OF HARTINGTON: It would be a grave breach of discipline for a Yeomanry or Volunteer band to take part, in its military capacity, in a political assemblage; and if any case is reported to me, with the name of the offending corps, proper notice will be taken of such an infringement of Regulations. On the other hand, the noble Viscount will perhaps allow me to point out that the letter in *The Times*, to which he refers, is flatly contradicted by a signed letter in the same journal to-day.

MR. WARTON said, he had a letter from a gallant Colonel of the Army and Navy Club confirming the statement of the noble Viscount the Member for South Wiltshire.

THE MARQUESS OF HARTINGTON: It is extremely desirable that particulars of the alleged attendance of the band should be furnished to me. I am inclined to think that no such incident took place.

POST OFFICE (IRELAND)—THE MAILS BETWEEN DUBLIN AND CORK.

MR. LEAMY asked the Postmaster General, Whether, seeing that a stoppage of five minutes would be quite sufficient to allow the Great Southern and Western Mail, under the proposed new service between Dublin to Cork, to drop and take up passengers at Maryborough, and that the Central Ireland Railway is willing to send a special train to meet the Mail at Maryborough, he will, in the interests of the public, require that such stoppage shall be made?

MR. FAWCETT: In answer to the hon. Member, I beg to say that, beyond the detention during the actual stoppage, time is lost in slackening speed and getting it up again; and a stop at Maryborough, which is not required for Post Office purposes, would proportionally shorten the very moderate interval which it is possible to secure for replies at Cork by the accelerated service; by which service also Waterford will largely benefit.

MR. LEAMY asked what time would be lost by stopping the mail train at Maryborough?

MR. FAWCETT said, he believed eight or ten minutes; but there was another application from the hon. Member for Clonmel for stoppage at Thurles. ["No, no!"]

MR. ARTHUR O'CONNOR asked whether the mail train did not now stop at Thurles for water; whether water could not be taken in instead at Maryborough?

MR. MOORE said, it was not a question of stopping the train at Thurles, but of throwing out the mail bags. He begged to ask the right hon. Gentleman at what hour it was anticipated that the accelerated mail train would pass Thurles Station; and, what was the nature of the inconvenience urged by the Limerick and Waterford Railway Company as a reason for not running a train to meet the mail train?

MR. FAWCETT said, there would be no objection whatever to throwing out the mail bags at Thurles, if the local railway would run a train to meet the mail bags; but he understood they did not consider the traffic would justify them in doing that, so that there would be no advantage in throwing out the mails.

DEFENCE OF EGYPT—EXPENSES—SUPPLEMENTARY ESTIMATE.

MR. J. G. TALBOT (for Lord EUSTACE CECIL) asked the Secretary of State for War, Whether he can now state when any Supplementary Estimate will be presented to the House to defray the cost of any expedition that may be necessary for the defence of Egypt?

THE MARQUESS OF HARTINGTON: I have communicated on this subject with my right hon. Friend the Chancellor of the Exchequer, and have come to the conclusion that unless circumstances, at present unforeseen, should arise which would lead to a larger expenditure than is at present going on, it will be unnecessary to present any Supplementary Estimate for the Army in the course of the present Session.

MEDICAL ACT AMENDMENT BILL.

In reply to Mr. J. G. TALBOT,

MR. GLADSTONE said: We have considered as carefully as we could the prospects of this Bill, and, I am sorry to say, with the result which is often arrived at. Our chance of carrying the Bill would be very small; and having regard to the comfort and convenience of the House, and to the circumstances of the period of the Session, although anxious to push it forward, I am obliged to state that the Government do not intend to proceed with the Bill.

IRELAND—MANUFACTURES AND INDUSTRIES—A ROYAL COMMISSION.

SIR EARDLEY WILMOT asked the First Lord of the Treasury, If he will advise Her Majesty graciously to issue a small Royal Commission to inquire into the present condition of manufacturing and productive industries in Ireland, with a view to the more ample development of those industries, and the more effectual promotion thereby of the material wealth and prosperity of the Irish people?

MR. GLADSTONE: I have consulted my noble Friend the Lord Lieutenant, and our opinion certainly is that, even if an inquiry of this kind were desirable, a Royal Commission would not be the best instrument for conducting it, viewing the nature of the subject. It is a subject which would be more fitly considered by a Committee of this House; and with regard to a Committee of this House, that must depend a good deal on the desire and views entertained in this House. But I am bound to say that we do not feel great anxiety for such an inquiry even by a Committee of this House, and for this simple reason—what we are afraid of is, that bringing to bear further public inquiries on this matter would rather tend to weaken what, above all things, we wish to see strengthened in Ireland—namely, the sense of self-reliance, and would raise expectations of aid from a quarter from which it could never effectually come.

POOR LAW GUARDIANS (IRELAND) BILL.

MR. PARNELL asked the First Lord of the Treasury, Whether, in view of the rejection by the House of Lords on the Second Reading of the Poor Law Guardians (Ireland) Bill, he will introduce a similar measure during the Autumn Session with the view of enabling the Upper House to reconsider the subject?

MR. GLADSTONE: We regret very much the loss of this Bill. I have not had the power of communicating with my noble Friend in whose charge it was. But I presume there will be a desire to revive it on the first proper opportunity. I think, however, the hon. Member can hardly expect me to say that a proper opportunity would be found in the Autumn Session. The Autumn Session, according to the advice on which Her Majesty has been pleased to express Her intention to act, will be summoned for a very specific and a peculiar purpose; and it would be a very great mistake on our part if we were—I will not say to allow, because, of course, the House must be the sole judge of what subject it will entertain—but if we were to be parties to mixing up other matters totally distinct from the question of the Franchise with the Business of the Autumn Session. It is obvious that in rejecting the Poor Law Guardians (Ireland) Bill, although we may lament the circumstance, the House of Lords did not go beyond its rights. This Bill has none of those specialities which would entitle it to be taken in the Autumn Session.

MR. T. P. O'CONNOR: In reference to the distinction which the right hon.

Gentleman has just drawn between the Poor Law Guardians (Ireland) Bill and the Franchise Bill, I should like to ask him whether he is aware that whereas the Franchise Bill has only passed a second reading once, the Poor Law Guardians Bill has passed a second reading two or three times?

MR. GLADSTONE: That circumstance does not bear on the conclusion to which we have come.

PUBLIC WORKS LOANS BILL.

MR. MARJORIBANKS asked the Secretary to the Treasury, Whether he would now state what amendment he was prepared to introduce into the Public Works Loans Bill, which stood for Committee that evening?

MR. COURTNEY, in reply, said, he had been in consultation with the Chancellor of the Exchequer on the subject, and his right hon. Friend would be in his place and make a statement when the Order was called.

LAW AND POLICE—ARMED BURGLARS.

SIR FREDERICK MILNER: I wish to ask the Home Secretary a Question, of which I have given him private Notice, in reference to his Answer yesterday to me on the subject of armed burglars. I would ask whether he can conceive any reason why a man who knocks you down, ill-treats you, and robs you in the street, should be visited with a more severe punishment than a man who shoots you in the groin with a revolver, or makes a hole in your skull with a life-preserver?

SIR WILLIAM HARCOURT: My hon. Friend has given me short Notice of the Question. He asks me whether I should prefer one treatment or the other. I have not had time to reflect which of these two operations I should prefer; and, therefore, if he will allow me to think over it during the Autumn Recess, I shall perhaps be able to give him an answer.

BURGH POLICE AND HEALTH (SCOTLAND) BILL.

MR. ANDERSON: I wish to ask the Prime Minister, Whether he has come to any decision as to proceeding with the Burgh Police and Health (Scotland) Bill?

MR. GLADSTONE: We have never wavered in our expectation with respect to that Bill. I cannot say anything with regard to the exact time or date when it will be taken; but we desire to proceed with it this Session.

PUBLIC HEALTH—CHOLERA—RAGS FROM MARSEILLES.

SIR FREDERICK MILNER asked the President of the Local Government Board, Whether it was not a fact that the cargo of rags from Marseilles believed to be infected with cholera, to which allusion had been recently made in that House, had, notwithstanding assurances to the contrary, been actually passed through Goole and landed near Dewsbury, a low-lying district specially liable to infection?

SIR CHARLES W. DILKE: I asked the hon. Member the other day to take a little more trouble in ascertaining the facts before asking Questions of this character. It is not a fact that these rags have been landed near Dewsbury. They have not been landed anywhere at all. The rags which have arrived near Dewsbury are a different cargo, from a different place, and of a very different quality. They have been landed, not at Dewsbury itself, but near Dewsbury, and we have no reason to suppose that any danger attaches to them. A General Order was issued after the difficulty had arisen as to the first cargo, against the landing of any rags from Toulon and Marseilles. The cargo of rags, as to which there was a discussion in this House, was never landed anywhere, and the statement to that effect in the newspapers was absolutely untrue. The rags landed near Dewsbury came, I believe, from Dieppe.

MR. TATTON EGERTON: Will the right hon. Gentleman state where the original rags are now?

SIR CHARLES W. DILKE: They have certainly not been landed. I have received a very satisfactory telegram from the Town Clerk of Hull with regard to them. I do not quite know where they are at this moment; but they certainly have not been landed. They were transferred to lighters; but were not taken up the canal, and they were never put ashore. The probability is they were sent back again.

MR. TATTON EGERTON: Will the right hon. Gentleman give the House an assurance that they will not be landed?

SIR CHARLES W. DILKE: Yes; they certainly will not be landed.

MR. JOSEPH COWEN: May I ask the right hon. Gentleman whether it is not a fact that the cholera never was transmitted by rags, so that all this excitement is entirely unnecessary?

SIR CHARLES W. DILKE: I stated in the House the other day, in reply to a Question, that there was no evidence that cholera had been communicated by rags. Small-pox and wool-sorters' disease have been transmitted by rags; but there is no evidence to that effect with regard to cholera.

ORDERS OF THE DAY.

——o——

SUPPLY.—COMMITTEE.

Order for Committee read.

Motion made, and Question proposed, "That Mr. Speaker do now leave the Chair."

INLAND REVENUE—CARRIAGE TAX.

RESOLUTION.

LORD ALGERNON PERCY, in rising to move—

"That the Taxes on Carriages are exceptional in character, and injurious to trade, and should therefore be abolished,"

said, he would only detain the House for a short while, as that period of the Session was not favourable to a detailed consideration of the question. Great misapprehension prevailed as to the character of the Carriage Tax. It was commonly believed that it was a tax upon luxury, and that it was only paid by those who could well afford to do so. It was also argued that it was too small an amount to seriously affect any trade. He contested all these positions. The real fact was that the tax was not levied upon luxury, but was a tax upon the product of industry. It was the last special trade tax remaining, and was injurious to that trade, and thus affected many artizans and working men—over 26,252 being employed in that trade alone—and there were, at least, 116 collateral trades concerned by the imposition of the tax in coach-building, all of which suffered. The tax had to be paid by many to whom a carriage was not a luxury, but just as much an article of necessity as a chisel or a hammer was an article of necessity to a workman. A carriage was not a luxury to a doctor, a surveyor, or a commercial traveller. It was just as much a necessity to the members of these professions as carts were to farmers, and tools to workmen. The carriage manufacturers had no right to ask for special legislation; but they had a just claim to be put on the same footing as other trades. They had a right to demand fair play; and this they did not obtain as long as their industry was singled out for taxation, and it should be remembered that this tax was an annual tax, such as was imposed on no other trade. The Carriage Tax was the last special trade tax, the Silver Duty being the only other tax of the same kind; but that tax was only paid once, whereas this was an annual tax. All other trade taxes had been repealed. As a matter of justice, it was impossible to defend the maintenance of a tax which pressed injuriously upon a highly skilled and a most important trade. He had said that the Carriage Tax was not a tax upon a luxury. Whatever might have been the case when most travelling was done on horseback, it was evident that even to the rich the carriage was not to the same extent a luxury as formerly. Carriages were now used by medical men, clergymen, hotel-keepers, jobmasters, and others; and it was just as necessary that they should use them in the duties of their calling as the farmer should use the carts on which he did not pay duty. Even if a tax were a tax upon luxury, the House would be cautious about imposing it if it hampered or injured an important trade which if free would give employment to many additional skilled artizans; indeed, the trade taxes had been repealed for that very reason. Even if the carriage were a luxury there was no good ground for a carriage eing singled out as a special article df luxury for taxation. Yachts were built with the greatest care, and fitted up with the greatest luxury, yet a yachtsman might travel all round the world without paying any taxation, while the country doctor could not go his round of two miles without having to a a heavy tax on his carriage, very muphydisproportioned to its value. Billiard tables, pictures, and musical instruments were certainly articles of luxury quite as much as carriages, but these articles were rightly not taxed. Why should a carriage be especially singled out as an object for taxation? If the supporters of the tax defended it on the ground of luxury at least they should be consistent, and subject other luxuries to taxation. But they did not do this, and those interested in the carriage trade had good grounds for complaining that they were not treated impartially. The tax, to a certain degree, was a tax on locomotion. Steamers were not taxed; and although there was a Passenger Duty on railways, it did not press with anything like the severity that the tax on carriages did. Bicycles, tricycles, and train carriages were not taxed and more or less competed with the carriage building trade, and thus the tax rendered it more difficult for the coachbuilding trade to meet this competition. The tax itself was very unfairly apportioned; it was levied with a total disregard either to the value of the article or to the period during which it was employed. For instance, a pony carriage of a certain size and weight paid the same tax as the State coach of the Lord Mayor, the tax often amounting to 5 per cent on the value of the carriage, and in a number of years to half, and more than half, its original cost. A carriage costing £40, supposing it to last for 10 years, during that time would have paid in taxation more than half its cost. The amount paid in tax frequently came to more than the cost of keeping the carriage in repair. A coach-builder had informed him that a brougham taken out of his yard 11 years ago cost £9 to keep it in repair, and the taxation during that time amounted to 22 guineas. Then, again, an old and ricketty carriage paid exactly the same as a new one; and if a carriage was only used for one week, it had to pay the tax for a year. If a man borrowed a carriage from the coachmaker while his own was being repaired, he had to pay duty on the borrowed carriage, thus mulcting him in double duty for what was practically the use of only one vehicle. With regard to the objection that the tax was so small that it could not affect the trade, he might say that the annual turnover of the carriage-building trade was £2,500,000, while the amount raised by the tax was over £550,000, so that the trade was practically taxed to the amount of 20 per cent. It was evident, he thought, that no trade could really prosper under such circumstances. However surprising it might seem, there could be no doubt the existence of the tax prevented many people from purchasing carriages. Some hon. Members had told him that but for the tax they would buy one or two more carriages than they now possessed. The first economy made in an establishment was the discontinuance of the use, of a carriage, and the real fact was that the tax did not fall on the rich, but the rich suited their establishment. In Ireland, where there was no Carriage Tax, many more carriages were in the hands of owners than was the case in England. In Ireland there was no inducement for a man to limit the number of his carriages, and when a carriage was partly damaged, there was no necessity to part with it. In England, however, when a carriage was much worn the owner did not retain it, as he was called upon still to pay duty for it, although the vehicle was unusable. This led to a system of barter in the trade. The carriage dealers, when they got an order for a new carriage, always had to take an old one in part payment. The result was that their premises were crowded with surplus stock. He had received letters from coachbuilders, one of whom said he had 150, and another 500, second-hand carriages on hand. An ordinary carriage occupied something like 60 superficial feet, and anyone could easily estimate how much ground a stock, varying from 150 to 500 carriages, would cover. Rent and rates for these premises had to be paid. The same cause that returned carriages to the coachbuilders' yards tended to keep them there, and often carriages were kept until they largely depreciated in value. This was a very serious inconvenience and loss, which would not arise if the duty were abolished. The whole system, therefore, hampered and harassed a most important industry. If there were no tax, the carriage dealers would be enabled either to let these old carriages at low rates or sell them at small prices. Old carriages might thus be brought into use at country railway stations and other places to the great benefit of the people. If the tax were removed, there was every reason to believe that there would be a great impetus given to the trade. Whenever a tax had been taken off an industry that had always been the result, and there was every reason to believe that in this instance it would be equally as great.

if not greater, than in the case of other trades that had been freed from taxation. In Hungary this tax was removed a short time ago, and the carriage-building trade had revived, in consequence, to an enormous extent. One firm alone had received an order for over 400 carriages. Like results had accrued in other trades in this country. When the duties had been taken off soap, paper, and bricks, vitality had been given to each business; and there had been an immense development in all these trades after they had been freed. The parties directly interested in them had not alone been served, but the entire population had been benefited. He felt sure a like result would spring from the removal of the tax on carriages. He knew it was contended by some that as carriages wore away the roads they should contribute to the highway rates. But it was not the carriages that cut up the roads. It was the farmers' carts, waggons, traction engines, and other heavy vehicles. They did infinitely more damage to the highways than carriages did, and were not taxed as being necessary to their owners for the proper carrying on of their business; he had shown that carriages were employed by many to whom their use was a necessity. He was neither advocating nor condemning the principle of taxing vehicles generally; but if they were to be taxed at all, the most destructive should be taxed as well, and the tax should not be levied in the way it was now. The trade thankfully acknowledged the small relief the Chancellor of the Exchequer had accorded it in his Budget. But it did not affect them much. It was, however, a tacit acknowledgment that the tax was false in principle. The trade had been unusually depressed in recent years, as an illustration of which he might mention that over 14,000 carriages had been returned on the builders' hands within the last three years. That might be owing, in part, to the general depression of the times; but it was also due largely to the great increase of tramways and railways, and they were placed besides in a peculiarly disadvantageous position in comparison with other trades in consequence of special taxation. He had good authority in favour of the cause he was advocating. The tax, according to the Prime Minister, was a remnant of the stupidity of past legislation. In 1879 the right hon. Gentleman told the farmers of Mid Lothian that, in his opinion, "they should be relieved of every unjust and unnecessary restraint," and that "they were entitled to the free sale of all their produce." "And his whole argument applied to all trades they pleased to name." The senior Member for Birmingham had also expressed himself in favour of the abolition of the tax, and had stated that it was totally indefensible. The Chambers of Commerce of London, Newcastle, Bristol, Derby, Worcester, Leicester, and other places had passed resolutions in favour of the abolition of the tax. The combined Chambers, at a meeting held in London, had also passed a similar resolution. There had been upwards of 80 Petitions in favour of this Resolution. The Petitioners felt that in asking this relief from taxation they only asked for justice and fair-play, and he trusted they would not long have to ask in vain. He would only add that he pleaded for the abolition of the duty: first, because it was based on bad principles—principles that did not apply to any other trade; second, because it was a direct hindrance and injury to a skilled and highly-important industry; third, because the incidence of its imposition was inequitable and unjust in operation; and, lastly, because he believed that if it was removed it would give an impetus to trade, and be of great service to a large number of skilled artizans and working men. On these grounds, he commended the proposal to the favourable consideration of the House, and asked for it the support of the Government. The noble Lord concluded by moving the Motion which stood in his name.

MR. JOSEPH COWEN said, he had much pleasure in seconding the Resolution of the noble Lord; but he was not able to add much to what the noble Lord had already said, and so well said. The case was covered by very few facts, and these facts had been so clearly put before the House, that all there was left for him to do was to compress the salient points into a few sentences, and urge the Government to give favourable consideration to the subject. The carriage trade was a highly important one. There were between 25,000 and 26,000 workmen directly employed in it, and there was a large number of others indirectly interested. The annual turnover of the trade was calculated at £2,250,000, and the Carriage Tax amounted to £250,000. The amount of revenue, therefore, that the carriage business yearly contributed to the Exchequer was something like one-fifth of the turnover. This was very large, and it seriously hampered the trade, which, for several years past, had been in a very languishing condition. The depression was something more, he feared, than temporary. There were upwards of 14,000 less carriages in use now than there was a few years ago, and the trade with the Colonies and other countries was declining. He did not mean to contend that this decrease was entirely attributable to the duty; but certainly the duty was principally the cause of it. The tax itself was unsound in principle and inequitable in operation. The noble Lord had quoted the testimony of the Prime Minister and the right hon. Gentleman the senior Member for Birmingham against the tax. But he might have gone further, and quoted the testimony of every Chancellor of the Exchequer since the Reform Bill. All condemned taxes upon industry, and nearly all condemned taxes upon locomotion. The Carriage Duty was a tax on both. It was argued that it was too small an impost to injure the trade; but they all knew that the injury inflicted by a duty was not in proportion to its amount. Sometimes an insignificant tax inflicted considerable injury upon a trade. And that was the case in this instance. It was levied in a very offensive manner. The coachbuilders were required to keep books always open to the Revenue officers, in a way that was both annoying and troublesome. And they had to do this under a penalty of £20. When a carriage left the builder, it continued to pay the tax until it was destroyed; and the result was that when the owner of a carriage wanted a new one, he always gave the old one in part payment for the new one. As a consequence, the carriage-builders' yards were crowded with carriages which they could not dispose of. The rent and rates they were called upon to pay for the extensive premises necessary was a very heavy drain on a depressed trade. Old carriages were often kept for years, and the amount paid in shape of duty equalled the price of the article. It was incorrect to say that this was a tax upon luxury. It was a tax upon industry. It was quite true that the more sumptuous carriages were used only by the most wealthy section of the community; but there was a very large section to whom carriages were a necessary part of their stock and trade. But whether it was a tax upon luxury or upon industry, the fact was that they had abolished nearly every tax on industry except this, and it ought to go also. He knew the Chancellor of the Exchequer was not unfavourable to the proposal in principle; but, of course, it was necessary for him to raise the Revenue. All taxes were objectionable, and he recognized that it was difficult to choose whether this or some other tax should be removed; but, as far as he knew, there was no other tax that for its amount did so large a measure of injury as this one, and he claimed that it should have the first attention of the Government. But even if the tax were not abolished, it certainly might be more equitably levied. A tax upon a carriage when it was made would be better than an annual duty levied in the way this was. He appealed for the liberal and favourable consideration by the Chancellor of the Exchequer of the very reasonable request the noble Lord had made in such very felicitous terms, and in so temperate a spirit.

Mr. Joseph Cowen

Amendment proposed,

To leave out from the word "That" to the end of the Question, in order to add the words "the Taxes on Carriages are exceptional in their character, and injurious to trade, and should therefore be abolished,"—(*Lord Algernon Percy*,)

—instead thereof.

Question proposed, "That the words proposed to be left out stand part of the Question."

THE CHANCELLOR OF THE EXCHEQUER (Mr. CHILDERS), said, that the noble Lord and his hon. Friend had put forward clear and able arguments in very few words, and he must congratulate them on having done so. His hon. Friend had mentioned, frankly enough, the first argument which any Chancellor of the Exchequer would have to use in meeting a proposal to condemn a tax. His hon. Friend said that almost all taxes were objectionable. That was so, though in one or two cases taxes had their good side and were in themselves advantageous. But as to the great mass of taxes, whether direct or indirect, he admitted that they were in themselves, to a very large extent, evils, and it would be much better if they could do without them. There was a series of taxes—he would enumerate some of them—which had been the subject of Parliamentary debate, of a good deal of discussion outside the House, and of deputations to himself and his Predecessors, and which it was acknowledged were open to grave objections. But if the House of Commons passed a Resolution of that character as to a particular tax, it would be held to mean that that tax was to be taken first among those which were to be altered, reduced, or abolished. Now, he could not admit, so far as he was concerned, the doctrine that the Carriage Tax was so bad that it should be repealed before other taxes. He would give instances of one or two taxes which had been the subject of discussion, and which it was said ought to be repealed. They had had an interesting debate on the subject of tobacco not long since; and the argument had been put forward, not without effect, that the time had come when the 4*d.* per pound imposed a few years ago might safely be taken off. It was imposed, the House was told, only as a temporary measure; and the right hon. Gentleman the Member for North Devon said, the other day, that he hoped the time would soon come when it would be possible to take it off. If the Motion of the noble Lord were carried, the tax on carriages would be taken off first. There had been no little discussion lately in the Press about the Railway Duty, and his hon. Friend behind him had a Motion to take off the rest of the duty. On that he expressed no opinion; but certainly, if the Motion of the noble Lord was carried, the Carriage Tax would have precedence of the Railway Duty. There were other taxes which had been the subject of discussion, and as to which strong representations had been made. Take, for instance, the Death Duties. He admitted there were some who thought the Death Duties might be increased; but there were others who thought that a considerable remission in the aggregate amount received ought to be conceded by the Treasury. That remission must give precedence to the Carriage Duty if the Motion of the noble Lord were carried. Then there was a strong feeling on the subject of the Marine Insurance Duty. But the repeal of the Marine Insurance Duty would have to give way, if the Motion of the noble Lord were carried; but there was a more important duty. His hon. Friend the Member for the City of London (Mr. Alderman W. Lawrence) had brought several times before the House the question of the House Tax, and his hon. Friend the Secretary to the Treasury and others had admitted that there were great anomalies in the tax, and it had been urged that in redressing them it might be necessary to sacrifice a certain amount of Revenue. But here, again, they would be unable to deal with the House Tax if this Resolution should be adopted. There was a much more important class of duties still—the duties on tea, coffee, and dried fruits, which a very large section of the House, with which he sympathized, wished to reduce or abolish. Were they to give precedence to the tax on carriages before carrying further the proposals for a free breakfast table? The tax on gold and silver plate was small, and might be expected not to stand in the way. Still, the supporters of its repeal, like those who would deal with patent medicines and the like, must be taken into account. There was another great demand affecting the power of the House to reduce taxes—namely, for aid in relief of local burdens, the charge for which must, to a large extent, whether it was direct or indirect, fall on the Exchequer. Now, was the noble Lord prepared to say that the repeal of this particular tax should take precedence of the measures for giving relief to local burdens, which, whatever form they took, must heavily burden the Exchequer? On these grounds alone, it would be impolitic in Parliament to take one particular tax for remission out of the dozen to which grave objection might be urged, and virtually call on the Chancellor of the Exchequer to deal with that particular tax before adopting any measure of relief. And now a word or two on the tax itself. Nobody would deny that, in the main, the tax fell upon the rich. There were some, no doubt, who could not avoid using carriages — professional people, for example—who might not belong to the rich or the well-to-do classes; but they bore a very small proportion of the tax. If he were to hazard a guess, he should say that about three-fourths at least of the duty was paid by the wealthy. Therefore, by that Resolution they singled out a tax, not like taxes on tea, coffee, and tobacco, which were mainly paid by the poor, but a tax which was mainly paid by the rich; and the House would declare, if it adopted the Resolution, that the first taxpayer to be relieved should be mainly the rich people in Great Britain, for in Ireland, he might remark, no Carriage Tax was paid. On that ground alone, he confessed that he should see grave objection to that Resolution. But the noble Lord said it might be true that the rich in the main paid that duty; but incidentally it fell on those who built carriages. That was true. Every tax on articles of manufacture, although it fell directly on those who had the advantage of the article produced, incidentally fell on the manufacturer, whoever he might be. But that afforded no reason why they should single out a tax that was paid mainly by the rich, merely because it incidentally touched those who were engaged in the trade of making the taxed article. The noble Lord had alluded to some incidents of the tax, and had repeated the figures given by a deputation which waited upon him some months ago. Many of these were doubtless not far wrong; but he must except those of the numbers in the trade and the annual turnover, which, he was satisfied, had not been sufficiently worked out. The turnover, he felt satisfied, was much larger than the amount that was estimated by the deputation to which he had referred, and from the report of which the noble Lord had quoted. Then the noble Lord said—"You select a particular form of locomotion for taxation; but you leave other forms of locomotion untaxed;" and he particularly mentioned railways. The railways, the noble Lord said, paid only a small tax as compared with the owners of carriages. Now, he had read that morning the report of a speech made by a great Railway Chairman, in which he alluded to the incidence of the Railway Duty, and certainly his idea of its incidence was very different from that of the noble Lord. He described it in strong language as very heavy. The produce of the Railway Passenger Duty was something over £400,000 a-year, and that of the Carriage Duty something over £550,000; so that there was no great excess in the Carriage Duty over the Railway Duty. Then the noble Lord said—"Look what a number of second-hand carriages are to be found in all the carriage-builders' shops. That is because persons who want a new carriage before their old one is worn out are driven by the tax to send the latter to the coachmaker, who has to make them an allowance for it in the price of the new carriage." Now, judging from his own experience, the price given for an old carriage was very small indeed; and he did not think the transaction was a very lucrative one for those who kept carriages. The argument was exactly the other way. But the noble Lord had referred to the state of things abroad in connection with that question. On that subject he had a good deal of conversation with the intelligent deputation which waited upon him; and he had since made inquiries as to Carriage Taxes abroad—particularly in France, the country to be compared most properly with our own. Hungary or Austria could bear no comparison with England as to the use of carriages; but in France, especially in Paris, the use of carriages almost approached that of England. Through the kindness of Lord Granville, he had obtained very full information from the French Government as to the Carriage Duties there. He was not speaking now of the municipal charges paid in Paris and other French towns for cabs and other vehicles plying for hire, which were very heavy, but of the Government tax on carriages. That tax was far larger than it was in England. In Paris the Government tax on a four-wheeled carriage was 60 francs per annum, on a two-wheeled carriage 40 francs, and on every horse 25 francs. These were the duties paid in Paris by the owners of carriages as part of the Inland Revenue. In other places in France there was a sort of sliding scale; but in Paris and in France generally the Carriage Tax was far higher than in this country. The state of things in France was far more burdensome on carriage owners than it was here; and yet in France he had heard of no complaint of the large number of second-hand carriages accumulated in the hands of the coachmakers. The fact was, carriages were not the only second-hand articles that accumulated in the hands of the makers. The owners of pianofortes often preferred, after using them a certain time, to send them back into the hands of the maker, and get new instruments; but there was no tax on pianos. That practice in regard to carriages was not the consequence of the tax at all, but the consequence of the habits of the country. He did not think that the smallness of the increase in the number of carriages kept from year to year, as the noble Lord supposed, had practically anything to do with the duty. In point of fact, those who kept carriages had largely benefited by recent legislation. The repeal of the Horse Duty and the abolition of turnpikes had been a great relief to them; but those measures had not led to more carriages and horses being used. Therefore, he could not see that the Carriage Duty had the effect which the noble Lord supposed. The tax constituted a very trifling percentage in the cost of keeping a carriage, and could not be called burdensome to those who had to pay it; and for these reasons he trusted that the House would not adopt the Resolution of the noble Lord.

SIR ROBERT PEEL said, he thought that the statement of the Chancellor of the Exchequer raised an issue altogether foreign to the point raised by the noble Lord. The Motion said that that tax was exceptional in its character and injurious to the interests of a particular trade. The Chancellor of the Exchequer told them that there was a series of taxes open to grave objection, among them being the duty on tobacco, the Tea Duty, the Railway Duty, the Marine Insurance Duty; and he asked whether the Carriage Duty ought to have the precedence over those taxes? Now he would point out that that was the only annual tax on a useful manufactured article in this country. Moreover, there were not only some 26,000 skilled artizans directly interested in that trade; but a vast number of collateral trades depended on the success and the excellence of the work which those 26,000 skilled artizans were employed in perfecting; and he maintained that that tax being very injurious to trade ought to be abolished. A deputation had waited on the right hon. Gentleman a short time ago in connection with this subject. He had given that deputation, he believed, encouragement; but it was a remarkable fact that in addition to that deputation the Chambers of Commerce throughout the country had dealt with the question. He found on inquiry that the Chambers of Commerce of London, Bristol, Derby, Newcastle, Worcester, and Leicester had all passed resolutions in favour of the remission of this tax. Besides these Bodies very important meetings at Bath and Manchester had dealt with the question; and, as had been pointed out, even the Prime Minister himself had advocated some years ago the remission of this tax. The Chancellor of the Exchequer had acknowledged that the complaint of the deputation was well founded. The trade said that the overturn of their business in the year was £2,500,000; the amount of tax it had to pay to the Chancellor of the Exchequer was about £545,000 a-year. He asked the House, therefore, whether the subject was not worthy of consideration? The right hon. Gentleman had said that the tax was one which fell mostly upon the rich. This was a great mistake. Everyone knew that in commercial and industrial districts, where there was hardly any resident gentry, the carriage became almost an article of livelihood to the neighbourhood. He thought there was great force in the Motion of the noble Lord, and he hoped the House would not put it aside merely upon the assertion of the Chancellor of the Exchequer that there were so many other taxes which ought to be considered, and that this tax on carriages ought not to have the preference.

MR. ANDERSON said, he did not agree with the right hon. Gentleman who had just spoken that the manufacturers of carriages paid this tax. He recognized that the tax fell mainly on the rich; but the manner in which it operated against the manufacturers of carriages was to cause the rich people to keep a smaller number of carriages in consequence of the tax. If they freed the trade of this tax, therefore, they would give an impetus to it, and create a larger demand for carriages. There were two ways of looking at the question—first, as a tax upon a luxury, and next as a tax upon industry. So far as the tax was a tax upon luxury paid for by the rich, he approved of it. It was a good tax. So far as it acted as a restraint upon an important manufacture he disapproved of it; it was a bad tax. What the House had to consider was whether it did more good in the one direction or more harm in the other. After fully considering the matter for some years, he confessed his opinion was that the tax did more harm in restraining a trade than it did good as a tax upon luxury; and he thought, therefore, the tax ought as soon as possible to be abolished. The Chancellor of the Exchequer admitted that it was not a good tax—at least, he mildly condemned it; and his answer was practically that he could not afford to take it off, because there were a number of other taxes which competed for his attention when he had any surplus to dispose of. There were, for example, the Tobacco Duty, the Railway Duty, the Death Duties, local burdens, marine insurance, and the duty on gold and silver plate. He (Mr. Anderson) had on previous occasions advocated the taking off of the Marine Insurance Duty and the duty on gold and silver plate, because he thought those duties were in restraint of a manufacturing industry. He maintained, therefore, that the taxes on gold and silver plate, marine insurance, and on carriages were directly in restraint of manufacturing industry, and ought to be taken off. The right hon. Gentleman also mentioned the Tea and Coffee Duties. He had before now advocated the reduction of those duties; and what he complained of was that while the right hon. Gentleman condemned a great many taxes and said they were bad and ought to be taken off, he did not avail himself of his opportunities to take them off when he could. The right hon. Gentleman had this year no less a sum than £5,000,000 dropping into his hands by the expiry of Terminable Annuities. Why could not the right hon. Gentleman have used some part of that surplus in removing these most objectionable taxes. That could have been done, and a large part of the sum used for the reduction of the Debt. Instead of doing that the right hon. Gentleman kept on all these objectionable taxes, however bad they might be, in order that he might use the whole amount of the expired Terminable Annuities to make a great flourish about the reduction of the Debt. Instead of relieving the present generation of manufacturers and taxpayers, the Chancellor of the Exchequer threw the relief on to some future generation, about which they knew nothing at all. There was another way in which the right hon. Gentleman might make a very considerable amount of money that would help him a good deal. He was glad the proposal to issue bogus half-sovereigns had been dropped. If the right hon. Gentleman, instead of issuing bogus half-sovereigns, would issue a reasonable quantity of paper money —both £1 notes and 10*s.* notes— the Chancellor of the Exchequer and the country also would obtain great benefit. The right hon. Gentleman had missed one golden opportunity for removing these taxes, and it was impossible to say when he would find another.

Mr. MACFARLANE said, he did not think the tax affected the coachbuilder to anything like the extent which had been stated. He looked upon the tax as strictly a rich man's tax, and therefore it was one of the best taxes in use. He believed that no man who could afford to keep a carriage was deterred from doing so by this impost. A reference had been made to the Tea and Coffee Duties; but what, he asked, was the actual comparison between the old woman who drank tea and the old gentleman who rode in his carriage? The old woman paid 100 per cent on every pound of tea she drank, while the Carriage Tax only amounted to 2 or 3 per cent. The working man, too, paid a duty of 600 to 700 per cent on his tobacco. If the question were pressed to a Division he would vote against the Motion.

Mr. FRANCIS BUXTON expressed a hope that the Chancellor of the Exchequer would see his way to abolishing the Passenger Duty, which affected far more people than the Carriage Tax. He (Mr. F. Buxton) was in favour of the abolition of all duties on locomotion; but if the effect of passing this Resolution were to be to abolish the Carriage Duty rather than the Railway Passenger Duty, he must vote against the Motion of the noble Lord.

Mr. ILLINGWORTH said, he thought the grievance of the carriage makers was more fancied than real. He did not believe that it affected the carriage industry. No doubt there was stagnation in the trade, but there was depression all over the country, and carriages being a luxury were naturally one of the first things that people gave up. There were many taxes that the Chancellor of the Exchequer ought to have taken the opportunity before now of abolishing or reducing, instead of indulging in an heroic plan for the reduction of the National Debt. He agreed with the hon. Member for Glasgow (Mr. Anderson) that the Chancellor of the Exchequer was doing rather too much for posterity in his endeavours to reduce the interest on the National Debt. He thought there was no case to be urged for the abolition of the Carriage Taxes in comparison with the claims of tea and tobacco. Tea was consumed to an enormous extent, and the duty on it was disproportionately large. He would urge that it was to the advantage of the country, consumers, producers, and taxpayers, that we should lessen the proportion of indirect taxation, and go to the more scientific principle of direct taxation. That system would be far preferable to the present crude and unjust system of levying taxes not in proportion to the ability to pay, but on the amount of the article actually consumed.

MR. DUCKHAM said, he did not consider that the Carriage Tax seriously affected an important industry. It was a tax paid by those who used the vehicles, and its effect upon the manufacturers, he thought, must be very infinitesimal. As a Local Taxation Reformer, he considered it to be a tax that should be transferred from Imperial to Local Authority. Upon the removal of the turnpike gates the Chambers of Agriculture strongly urged that the horse and vehicle tax should be so transferred; but, unfortunately, one of the first acts done by the late Government was to repeal the Horse Tax, although that repeal was comparatively unasked for; and the overburdened ratepayers had their burden most seriously increased, the gates being removed without any equitable provision being made for the future maintenance of the roads. And now an attempt was made to obtain a further repeal, and that of a tax yielding upwards of £500,000 annually, and that, too, a tax borne principally by the wealthy. He (Mr. Duckham) hoped that the right hon. Gentleman would consider the cry of the heavily taxed urban and rural ratepayers. They had been promised substantial relief. The transference of Imperial taxes had been shadowed forth by the Government as the source from whence to expect that relief; but he failed to see how that promise could be carried into effect if such taxes were frittered away.

MR. WHITLEY said, he did not think the Chancellor of the Exchequer had met the real question—namely, that that tax was the only existing tax upon industry. The interests of this country were suffering in every direction; and though hon. Members had spoken of the other classes who were suffering from an excess of taxation, it had been forgotten that those taxes affected the whole section of citizens, whereas the Carriage Tax was put upon a class who were also subject to other taxes. He had never heard that the rich scrupled to pay the tax; but there was a very strong feeling on the part of those engaged in the trade, on the part of a large number of workmen who were struggling for their living, that the tax being the only one which pressed on industry and labour was one which ought to be repealed at the earliest possible moment. The Chancellor of the Exchequer had avoided that question, and had never alluded to the exceptional nature of the tax, that it was one dealing entirely with labour, and therefore essentially different from other taxes. On those grounds he should support the Motion of his noble Friend.

Question put.

The House *divided*:—Ayes 93; Noes 38: Majority 55.—(Div. List, No. 183.)

Main Question proposed, "That Mr. Speaker do now leave the Chair."

PARLIAMENT — PUBLIC BUSINESS — PROCEDURE—HOUSE OF LORDS BILLS.—OBSERVATIONS.

MR. WARTON, in whose name the following Notice stood upon the Paper:—

"To call attention to the procedure in this House with respect to Bills brought from the House of Peers; and to move the following Resolution:—'That all Bills brought from the House of Peers be read the first time by announcement from the Chair, and that one clear day at the least intervene between the first and second readings of such Bills. That this Resolution be a Standing Order of this House,'" said, there was, in the procedure of the House, an evil with regard to Bills brought from the Lords, and that was that they were read a first time as a matter of course. A Bill might be brought down one evening, read a first time, and the very next morning might be down for second reading. With regard to the first part of his Resolution, an improvement had been made in the practice, because Mr. Speaker had been careful to announce from the Chair Bills coming from the Lords; and, therefore, the first evil seemed to have been remedied. What he would ask, however, was that, when a Bill came down from the Lords, Notice of that fact might be put upon the Papers distributed to Members in the morning. The Prime Minister, who always spoke of the majority in that House as a thing to be regarded as sacred, was in the habit of characterizing a majority of the House of Lords as a mere majority or a sheer majority. Although the Forms of the House would prevent him from moving the Resolution of which he had given Notice, he trusted that, as he had on a former occasion withdrawn his Notice on this subject to facilitate progress being made with the Franchise Bill, the Prime Minister would give him an assurance that he would give the matter his favourable consideration.

MR. GLADSTONE: I beg to assure the hon. and learned Member that I retain a full recollection of his courtesy on a former occasion in allowing us to proceed with other matters, and I hope that a recollection of such Parliamentary goodwill will not easily be effaced from my mind. I am afraid, however, that I should fail in my duty if I were to permit a grateful recollection of that courtesy and of my obligation to the hon. and learned Member to give a bias to my view of the merits of any particular question; and, therefore, I feel bound to look at his proposition in a spirit of rigid impartiality, and in the result I cannot say that I regard it altogether with favour. In dealing with this question we must fall back upon the principle which men necessarily apply to a great portion of the transactions of this life, which is not to make an alteration in an established Rule without good cause being shown. The hon. and learned Member seeks to introduce an exception into the established proceedings of this House, and I must presume that in practice the Rule which he seeks to alter has been found convenient; and neither my Colleagues nor myself have ever heard that any inconvenience has arisen from the mode of procedure adopted by this House in reference to Bills coming down to us from the House of Lords. That mode of procedure simply implies the existence of a certain amount of courtesy between the two Houses of Parliament, and that the fact that a measure has passed through one of the Houses of the Legislature affords a presumption favourable to a Bill, not as regards its merits, but merely that it should receive an early introduction into the other. That is a principle which I regard as being reasonable in itself; and if we were to depart from it, it might possibly follow that counter projects "elsewhere" might diminish the facilities which Bills coming from this House receive "elsewhere." The difference between the practice as regards a Bill originally introduced into this House and a Bill coming down from the House of Lords is that the latter Bill gains a single day, in consequence of its having passed through the House of Lords by reason of no Notice of the intention to move for leave to introduce it being required. I do not see how any more limited privilege can be accorded to a measure coming down to us from the House of Lords if there is to be any privilege at all in the matter. But then the hon. and learned Gentleman puts forward another argument derived from the half-past 12 o'clock Rule. He says that the indulgence accorded to Bills coming from the House of Lords prevents the sweeping application of that Rule. Perhaps I do not take so high a view of that Rule as the hon. and learned Gentleman does. I am not a decided opponent of it by any means; but the hon. and learned Gentleman seems to idealize and to worship it, and to be desirous of elevating it into the Magna Charta of Parliament. He appears to think that it is a principle of such wide scope and so consecrated in its character that on no account must anything be allowed to limit its application to any measure to which it is capable of being applied. I must say that I am not able to accompany the hon. and learned Member in his view of the matter. The amount of the hon. and learned Gentleman's grievance is that, in consequence of the system adopted in regard to Bills coming from the House of Lords, the blocking of such Bills cannot be made applicable to the second reading if the Bill goes forward *de die in diem*, except in the single case where the Member has not happened to perceive the announcement of the introduction of the Bill. I admit that very often a Member may not be present, or the announcement of the Bill may take place, as it does sometimes, at the close of the proceedings, in which case he loses the opportunity of blocking Bills on the second reading. But what does that amount to? The hon. Member may, if he thinks fit, block the Bills at their Committee stage——

MR. WARTON: That is not enough.

MR. GLADSTONE: That exactly illustrates what I was just saying. The hon. and learned Gentleman's enthusiasm on this subject is well calculated to inspire sympathy; but we must be upon our guard against the too great indulgence of that kind of sympathy; and, on the whole, I think that the hon. and learned Member ought to rest content with his power of blocking these Bills at their Committee stage, if by chance the fact of the announcement of their introduction has escaped his vigilance. Upon these grounds I feel bound to say that I cannot concur in the proposal of the hon. and learned Member.

CENTRAL ASIA — RUSSIAN ADVANCE. OBSERVATIONS.

MR. MACFARLANE, who had given Notice of his intention to call attention to the advance of Russia in Central Asia, with the view of moving a Resolution to the effect that the advance of Russia to Merv and Sarakhs endangers the safety of Herat, threatens the independence and integrity of Afghanistan, and is deserving of the most serious consideration of Her Majesty's Government, said, that there were many reasons why he should not proceed with his Resolution. In the first place, the House being occupied with things near at hand would pay no attention to matters which were occurring at a distance. He was not one of those who held that the British lion should go growling about the world, wagging its tail, and seeking matters of quarrel on every side; but, at the same time, he conceived that where this country really possessed interests, the British lion should let it be generally known that he was prepared to defend them. In the next place, he believed that at length the Indian Government had become alive to the importance of this question, and that the policy of masterly inactivity, or, as he should rather say, of dastardly inactivity, which they had followed with regard to it had come to an end. As he believed that the Government of India were now alive to the importance of this question, he should be content to leave it in their hands until next Session.

MR. J. K. CROSS said, that he could assure the hon. Gentleman that he was not wrong in supposing that the Government of India were fully alive to the importance of the matter referred to; and after that assurance he hoped the hon. Gentleman would not further press it upon the attention of the House.

POOR LAW (IRELAND)—ELECTION OF GUARDIANS, NEWRY UNION — ILLEGAL ACTION OF RETURNING OFFICER.—OBSERVATIONS.

MR. SMALL, who had a Motion on the Paper in the following terms:—

"That, in the opinion of this House, the action of the Local Government Board in Ireland in neglecting to hold an inquiry into the charges made against the Returning Officer of Newry Union is most unsatisfactory,"

rose to call attention to the subject. He complained that he and his colleague were not allowed to inspect the voting papers, which were inspected at an advanced hour. The Returning Officer did not show the smallest favour to himself (Mr. Small) or his colleagues at the late election; but, on the contrary, showed the most unfair partizanship towards their opponents. They applied, on the 31st March last, to the Local Government Board for an inquiry into the charges which they had preferred; but notwithstanding all their efforts that inquiry had never yet been held, although the result of it had been to deprive them of their seats. They had not obtained the smallest satisfaction. The entire majority of the Board of the Newry Union had been changed at the election; and, although they had made charges against the Returning Officer, not the smallest notice had been taken of it. They had repeatedly specified these charges; but all their complaints had been of no avail. The Returning Officer had, on the occasion of the scrutiny of the votes in the Division, showed the most marked animus against himself and his colleagues, and said three days before that he knew what the result of the election would be. He and his colleagues had been told that at the scrutiny of the votes there had occurred what was very seldom done in the country—namely, the counting in of the votes of political friends and the rejection of the votes of those who did not happen to be political friends. It was, considering all these allegations, a most extraordinary thing that the Local Government Board would not grant an inquiry, or even send down an Inspector in order to investigate the matter. He would not ask the Chief Secretary to prejudge the matter; but he would ask him, as President of the Local Government Board in Ireland, to have an inquiry granted into these charges.

Mr. TREVELYAN said, he had read the very voluminous Papers in this case, and he should say that they appeared to him to bear in a very marked manner on the events of the past few days. He was impressed by the reading of the documents with the enormous advantage to the public at large of the proposals contained in the Poor Law Guardians (Ireland) Bill, which was unfortunately rejected in "another place" last night. He was quite satisfied that the great abuses, the enormous waste of time of the Local Government Board, and the extreme uncertainty of the law relating to claims to vote at Poor Law elections would be obviated, and thoroughly obviated, by that Bill. The whole process of election was in an unsatisfactory state. When the election approached, instead of having a register of electors, it was left to a clerk to settle who should vote. Then voting papers were left at houses to be filled up in circumstances which lent themselves, in a most remarkable degree, to fraud. It was impossible that an election could be quite fairly conducted on such methods as those. Then it was not satisfactory that the inquiring into questions arising out of elections should rest with an Inspector of the Local Government Board, which was not a judicial, but an administrative body. He regretted very much indeed, therefore, that a Bill which proposed to establish an excellent tribunal—namely, the County Court, to hear disputes arising out of these elections—a tribunal to which no objection had been raised there or in "another place"—had been so summarily rejected; and he foresaw that, as a result of that rejection, they would have to again enter into a wilderness of mutual recrimination and mutual distrust, and go on with labours that were simply Herculean when every election of Guardians arose. But, in the present case, he did not think, on such an examination of the Papers as he had been able to make, that the charge of personal animus against the Returning Officer had been made out. That officer, so far as he could judge, was a painstaking man, who had done his best in the circumstances. He was not, however, satisfied that the question of the return of the Guardians had been satisfactorily ascertained. He was much struck by the magnitude of the contest, and the narrow margin of majority by which it was decided. On the whole, he had come to the conclusion that an inquiry from head-quarters ought to be instituted into the conduct of the election, although he could not then specify what would be the exact character of the inquiry. He trusted, however, that no personal charges would be brought forward, unless really substantial grounds for such charges could be furnished. The personal charges, in this instance, appeared to him to be somewhat frivolous in their nature. ["Oh!"] He was of that opinion after having carefully read the Papers. He should communicate with the Local Government Board in order to see what course should be taken. Poor Law inquiries were not so easy as the hon. Member seemed to think, and the Inspectors at present had their time fully occupied.

Mr. MOLLOY said, he was unacquainted with the particular case in question; but so many complaints were made of a similar character, that it seemed evident that the present system required amendment. The election of Mr. Farrell, of Edenderry Union, had been conducted in an equally unsatisfactory manner. Votes had been received from persons on a property qualification who had really possessed no property in the neighbourhood. If the Chief Secretary admitted that injustice existed, it was his duty to see that justice was done. Was he prepared to use the powers invested in him?

MR. O'SULLIVAN said, he hoped that some Inspector of experience would be sent down to Newry to hold the inquiry, as questions of great difficulty would arise, and that there would be no delay in dealing with the matter.

MR. WILLIAM REDMOND said, that many ratepayers were deprived of the right of voting at Poor Law elections simply because they were not at home at the time the policeman called with the papers. He had received a letter on this matter from the County Carlow, where it appeared that persons, who had not received voting papers on the days appointed for distributing them, applied to the Clerk of the Union for them, but were told that the police of the district had already sent papers to all voters. It afterwards turned out that the police had called at the houses, but that, not finding anyone there, they brought back the papers, so that some of these persons had no opportunity of voting.

Notice taken, that 40 Members were not present; House counted, and 40 Members being found present,

LAW AND JUSTICE (IRELAND)—THE TUBBERCURRY PRISONERS.

OBSERVATIONS.

MR. SEXTON, who had given Notice that he would call attention to the course pursued by the Crown in the case of the Tubbercurry prisoners; and to move—

"That, in the opinion of this House, the practices growing in Ireland, of delaying magisterial action in criminal cases by repeated remands, and of postponing, by adjournment of trials, the right of the accused to have his case decided by a jury, are unconstitutional, and prejudicial to the interests of justice, and therefore ought to be discontinued,"

said, he had grievous ground of complaint against the Legal Officers of the Crown. Several months had passed away since these 11 men, who were connected with the county he had the honour to represent, were arrested by the police and thrown into prison. They were all persons of respectability. The gravity of the charges against them — treason-felony and conspiracy to murder—made it the more important that they should be speedily brought to trial. What course did the police pursue? They began, and continued from week to week, an unconstitutional system of private remands in gaol; and when attention was called by him in that House to that proceeding, they resorted to a system of eight-day remands in public, doling out the evidence on each occasion in driblets. It appeared quite plain that the Crown was acting not so much from a sense that they had evidence in their possession to entitle them to get a committal, as from a hope that chance circumstances would enable them to eke out their case. A promise was at length made on behalf of the Crown that these men should be tried at the next ensuing Sligo Assizes. That promise was not fulfilled, and he was informed the other day by the Solicitor General that an application was made by the Crown to postpone the trial, and that it was granted. In the report of what took place, he found it stated that a circular, appealing for funds in aid of the defence of the prisoners, had been distributed in the County of Sligo, and that the document was calculated to interfere with the fairness of the trial. He quite admitted that the circular indicated a strong feeling on the part of those who sent it out; but he desired to point out that it was dated the 16th of June, and that the Attorney General for Ireland might have used the power he had of changing the venue some weeks before the date fixed for the Sligo Assizes. The application to postpone the trial was not made until the last moment, and the result was that some of the men had to be detained in prison for a further period. He had to-day received a letter from one of these unfortunate men, who was a Poor Law Guardian, and occupied a respectable position in Tubbercurry. He had now been in prison four months, separated from his family, his business ruined, his health impaired. Writing from prison on the 23rd instant, he said—

"I have seen the Solicitor General's reply to your question. The appeal he referred to appeared immediately after we were sent for trial seven weeks ago, and we never heard a word about it interfering with our trial until we were put into the dock last Saturday. Was there not time enough during these seven weeks to have the venue changed? But was it not one of those flimsy excuses the Crown resort to in cases like this? I believe they are ashamed to bring us to trial on the evidence."

Three of the prisoners were charged with treason-felony and conspiracy to murder; but, notwithstanding that serious charge, they were admitted to bail in the sum of £25 each. That fact, in his opinion, showed the real character of the case, and indicated that the Crown had no hope of obtaining a conviction. The men were anxious to be brought to trial, and they were confident that they would be able to prove their innocence. The general opinion in Sligo was that the informer in this case was a person of such a character that it would be an injustice to keep a dog one hour in a kennel upon his oath. It was neither reasonable nor constitutional to arrest men, and then find a reason for keeping them in prison. No man ought to be arrested without reasonable evidence having been obtained beforehand against him. He protested against the system under which these men were kept in prison for months together without being brought to trial. This whole system was a scandal. There was nothing in the present condition of Ireland to justify it. The country was now peaceable and law-abiding, and this sinister and vindictive method of prosecution ought to be abandoned by the Government. As Representative of the county to which these prisoners belonged, he deemed it his duty solemnly to call upon the Solicitor General to place these men in the dock without delay, and to produce his evidence against them.

THE SOLICITOR GENERAL FOR IRELAND (Mr. WALKER) said, he extremely regretted that the Tubbercurry prisoners were not tried at the last Sligo Assizes. When they were first brought before the magistrates, he himself gave directions that there should be as few remands as possible. In a case of this kind, however, it was obvious that there should be remands from time to time, and it was considered desirable that the whole of the evidence should be produced before the prisoners were committed for trial. The men were charged with conspiring to murder an official of Tubbercurry Workhouse, and also with treason-felony. He would not comment upon the case beyond saying that the charge was a very serious one, and that there was *primâ facie* evidence against the 12 men in question. It was the desire of the Crown that the prisoners should be tried at the Sligo Assizes, and the Attorney General for Ireland went down for the purpose of conducting the prosecution. A document, however, had been circulated, dated the 16th of June, among the special jurors who were to try the men, and he was of opinion that the Attorney General was right in the conclusion at which he arrived—namely, that that document would affect the fairness of the trial. The document said that the only crime of the accused men was undying attachment to their country, that their liberty had been bartered away for lucre; and it contained the strongest reflections upon their accusers. The District Inspector made an affidavit that that document had been widely circulated among the class of special jurors, some of whom would have to try the case, and that a widespread feeling existed among them that their lives would not be safe if they were to convict. Therefore, an application was made, but with the greatest reluctance, for the postponement of the trial, and the learned Judge consented to postpone it. The hon. Member said that three of the prisoners had been admitted to bail. That was because the Attorney General, as the trial was to be postponed, out of a kindly feeling, consented that they should be allowed out on bail. [Mr. SEXTON: £25 bail.] Surely the hon. Gentleman could not complain that the bail was so small. He was informed that the Attorney General would consider whether he could not let out more. It was never intended that the prisoners should remain in gaol until the March Assizes. The trial would take place about the 1st of October, so that they would be left in gaol only for two months more.

MR. PARNELL said, that he had read the proceedings, and he was surprised that the learned Judge should have agreed to the postponement of the trial on so flimsy a pretext. The circular was not issued by the prisoners; it was an appeal to raise a fair trial fund; and it furnished no grounds whatever for depriving the men of their right to be tried in their own district by people among whom they had spent their lives, and by whom the informers also were well known—probably too well known in the opinion of the Crown officials. The issue of the circular was no reason why the men should be taken off to Dublin, far from their own residences, to be tried by jurors prejudiced by appeals daily made to them by the English Press to convict and 'hang those who came before them. If there was intimidation involved in the issue of the circular it was not within the control of the prisoners in any respect whatever. Why was not Mr. Devine, who put his name to it, proceeded against under the Intimidation Clauses of the Prevention of Crime Act, or why was he not punished by the Judge, with the enormous powers he possessed, for contempt of Court? Instead of that the cause of the prisoners was prejudiced and their prospects imperilled. He had taken a special interest in this case from the beginning, particularly in connection with the arrest of one of his constituents—Mr. Fitzgerald—whom he had known for years. He (Mr. Parnell) had come to the conclusion that it was a "fishing" prosecution. All the proceedings had been dictated by a desire to get further evidence, which, in all probability, did not exist in a case which was bound to break down in present circumstances. The Prime Minister, when the Prevention of Crime Act was passing, promised that no proceedings should be taken against persons on stale charges of treason-felony, and it was upon that condition that the Irish Members modified their opposition to the clauses. But after the Irish Members had been forcibly driven from the House, other and different clauses were brought forward. Mr. Fitzgerald had been arrested, and would be tried upon as stale a charge of treason-felony as ever entered the head of an Attorney or a Solicitor General. He protested against the action of the Government in this case, which was bringing law and order into contempt. In the district of Tubbercurry crime had ceased; it had ceased in Sligo, and nearly all through the country. He would ask the Chief Secretary whether it was desirable to go on in such circumstances with a case against respectable men on the testimony of the most abandoned informers that could be collected throughout the country? The district was now, and had been for some time past, perfectly safe; but these people were bandied about from place to place and from week to week, and their trial delayed. Nothing could be more injudicious and foolish on the part of the Government than the venomous way in which prisoners were persecuted, and he hoped they might hear that the Chief Secretary would consider the whole question of bail. Persons having a stake in the country ought clearly to be allowed out on bail, so that they might return to their avocations and to that breadwinning which their families stood so much in need of.

MR. HARRINGTON called attention to the conviction of the policeman Muldowney, and pointed out the fact that the policemen present in Court all declared him innocent. Equally, in his opinion, had other innocent people been convicted and hanged in Ireland. In no other country in the world, he believed, would a case be trumped up on the evidence of a man who had, first of all, got seven years' penal servitude for highway robbery, then 12 years' penal servitude for an attempt upon the life of Mr. Justice Lawson in the streets of Dublin, and then penal servitude for life for complicity in the Phœnix Park murders. Great injustice was also done by the Irish authorities by delaying the trial of prisoners. They were thus prevented from proving their innocence, because their witnesses often left the country and could not be called when their trial at length was called on.

MR. HEALY said, he was astonished at the action of the Government in these trials. It had been stated in the House that they had no intention of postponing them to any subsequent Assizes; and what reliance could be placed upon any assurance of the Government or Ministers of the Crown after this pledge had been broken? They were to be kept in gaol seven months longer. He thought that no better training could be had for a Solicitor General or a Chief Secretary for Ireland than a few months in gaol, and a little oakum picking, in order that they might realize what unfortunate prisoners had to endure through their neglect. He wondered how the Chief Secretary would like having to spend the next three months in a cell 8 feet by 5 feet in extent. He ventured to think that if he had a little experience of that kind he would have more commiseration for unfortunate prisoners remanded from week to week and month to month at the quibble of some lawyer, and in spite of Constitutional practice. Now, they were to be transferred to Dublin, in order to be tried by grand jurors of the class of the gentlemen now in Kilmainham awaiting trial for unnatural offences. The Crown would have no difficulty in a county where there were at least 100 magistrates like Sligo in packing a jury of 12 men and true, excluding every Catholic, or even fair-minded Protestant. No Catholic prisoner against whom the Crown had any animus had a chance of getting off. What was the pretence for postponing the trial until October? Plenty of other Assizes were going on in the country. Why must Government rely upon the tainted jurors of the City of Dublin? Were they to be told that there was no body of men to be trusted except the corrupt jurors of Dublin, against some of whom the Government had been obliged to bring most frightful charges? This continual reliance upon the City of Dublin bore, to his (Mr. Healy's) mind, a very extraordinary complexion. The Freemasons met in their offices in Dublin, and decided who should be acquitted and who should be hanged. James Ellis French had been made Prime Mason on the very day that the charge was brought against him by the hon. Member for Mallow. It should be remembered that the organization of Freemasonry, as it existed in Ireland, was imbued with political virus, and was not to be compared with the order of English Freemasonry. Were Irishmen to be subjected to indictments sworn, for anything they knew, in these secret Lodges on the night before a trial? That secret body controlled verdicts. Delaney had been arraigned for attacking Judge Lawson and for other serious offences, and yet there was no objection to his being brought forward as a Government witness; and one would have thought that a living Chief Secretary would have hesitated before making use of man as a witness on behalf of the Crown who had been convicted of the murder of the right hon. Gentleman's Predecessor. In no other country in the world had there been an instance in which a Government had availed themselves of such testimony. By a careful process of picking and choosing the Government might succeed in getting 12 men of a class who would believe any story which the Crown might choose to tell them. But the children and friends of the men whom the Government unjustly hanged and imprisoned would yet constitute a form of danger to the Government of Ireland and to the peace and order of the country. He (Mr. Healy) did not say he approved of it; but retaliation would assuredly come, and would throw the country into turmoil and disorder. The Government were doing their best to bring about that state of things. A trial was to take place in Belfast on Monday. The plaintiff was Mr. George Bolton. Evidence was requisite, and that very day he understood the Government had again placed themselves in partizanship with men of Bolton's class. He had here a telegram detailing how the solicitor and detective of his hon. Friend the Member for Mallow (Mr. O'Brien) had been to-day arrested in Dublin. He should read the telegram to the House, and ask why the Government lent their policemen to Bolton any more than to French? ["Question!"] If that ignorant Gentleman on the Ministerial side understood his business he would perceive that the Question was that the Speaker do leave the Chair. He trusted he should be free from interruptions for the remainder of his address. He had here a telegram from Mr. Chance with regard to his arrest, and if the Government spared him from the interruptions of their ardent supporters he would read it—

"Meiklejohn and I went to see Alice Carroll, a witness *re* Bolton, to-day. While talking to her mother, Constables 79 D and 149 D entered, and requested us to go to the station (a polite way of saying 'We arrest you'). I asked upon what charge. Constable 79 D replied being there for unlawful purposes (exactly the charge made by Head Constables Cottingham and Irwin against Meiklejohn in regard to French). The constable said, 'I must take you into custody.' This they did. Both constables refused to make any charge. Alice Carroll and her mother were asked by the police to make a charge. They refused. We were brought to the North Circular Road Station, and interrogated. I required the charge to be be entered. Both constables refused to make any. No warrant was shown or produced. This deprives us of important evidence against Bolton."

Now, when the Government, which had not hesitated to enlist its detectives on behalf of French, were likewise throwing its ægis over Bolton, the chaste and virtuous, he wanted to know what guarantee was there for fair play or law and order in Ireland? They had got two of their police constables to obstruct the solicitor for Mr. William O'Brien, and to prevent him getting evidence against one of the Crown prosecutors. Was such a thing ever heard of before?

What did English Members say to that? They were told there was trumped-up evidence in the case of French. The Government were now relying upon that "trumped-up evidence." It was upon "trumped-up evidence" that the reporters were being excluded from the Police Court in Dublin, because, he presumed, French wanted to "round" upon Colonel Hillier and other high officials; yet the Government to-day had sent two constables to arrest Mr. Chance and Mr. Meiklejohn because they were getting up evidence against Bolton. Matters were coming to a serious pass in Ireland. They had the Government, on one hand, changing venues and arresting innocent men, delaying trials for months, and visiting prisoners in their cells; and, upon the other hand, using the same machinery to shield Bolton, the swindler and forger, whom they persisted in keeping in their employment. What were they to think of such a Government? They said they were anxious to convict criminals. If so, why would they not put Bolton on his trial? And, above all, why did they use Government machinery to obstruct the obtaining of evidence against them? There never was a more flagrant instance of the use of the machinery of Dublin Castle than these arrests to-day for the purpose of preventing justice being done in the Bolton case. Whatever the verdict in this case now, it would go forth to the world that the Constabulary of Dublin, under the advice of the Chief Secretary, had been employed to prevent witnesses being brought forward. When they found the circumstances he had mentioned, they were entitled to say that this thing in Ireland which was called the Government was simply a prostitution, which was not entitled to any respect from any honest man, but which ought to be covered with scorn and shame by every man who had the interest of his country and his race at heart.

MR. TREVELYAN: I can only speak now by the indulgence of the House. I rise simply for the purpose of saying that the hon. Gentleman, before stating that what has been done in Dublin to-day was done at the instigation of the Chief Secretary, ought to have asked me whether that was so?

MR. HEALY: What I said was this. After what occurred in French's case, after Cottingham and Irwin had been used by the Government on behalf of French to prevent the witnesses of Mr. O'Brien coming forward, I did not believe that these constables would have acted except at the direct instigation of high officials of whom the Chief Secretary is the Head.

MR. TREVELYAN: I will not dispute the words of the hon. Member. The hon. Member has left the impression upon the House that he believed this was done by my orders. I know nothing about it. I was not aware whether Mr. Chance and Mr. Meiklejohn were in Dublin or Belfast, or where they were, or what connection with this case they had. I do not enter into these minute points in legal cases. I do not think it is the business of the Chief Secretary of Ireland to do so, as it is not of the Home Secretary in this country. If the police have exceeded their duty, I will ascertain that after due inquiry, and I will see that proper means are taken that they shall not do so again. I will look into the case, and do what is just and right in the matter. If the story turns out to be incorrect, of course, there will be an end of the case. I have no further observation to make, except this—that I agree generally with the views put forward by my hon. and learned Friend the Solicitor General for Ireland; and I would remind the hon. Member who introduced this discussion of his assurance that the Attorney General was considering at this moment whether two more of the Tubbercurry prisoners could not be let out on bail.

MR. DEASY remarked, that when the Government arrested these men they had no idea of the charge they were about to bring against them, but trusted entirely to chance. The witnesses against them were of the lowest class; and no credence ought to be given to their evidence as against that of respectable persons. He hoped these men would either be unconditionally released, or be brought to trial at once. Mr. Fitzgerald, one of the men charged, happened to be one of his constituents; and he was convinced that the Government only arrested him because he was a troublesome person whom they were determined to get rid of at any cost.

Main Question, "That Mr. Speaker do now leave the Chair," put, and *agreed to*.

SUPPLY—CIVIL SERVICE ESTIMATES.

SUPPLY—*considered* in Committee.

(In the Committee.)

CLASS III.—LAW AND JUSTICE.

(1.) £134,957, to complete the sum for Reformatory and Industrial Schools, Great Britain.

Notice taken, that 40 Members were not present; Committee counted, and 40 Members being found present,

MR. WARTON said, the law as it now stood provided that no child should be sent to a reformatory school unless it had been previously convicted by magistrates. He believed he was correct in saying or supposing that there was some disposition on the part of the Government in favour of a change of the law in this respect. He (Mr. Warton) believed there was a general feeling that there ought to be some change in the law; that there ought to be some reformatory or other to which children could be sent who had not proper homes, and who had not become criminals in the strict sense of the word.

MR. HIBBERT said, he quite agreed with the hon. and learned Member for Bridport (Mr. Warton) that it was very desirable that a child could be sent to a reformatory without first of all being sent to prison. He was, however, not aware that there was any proposal now before the House to obviate that, though it was very desirable such a proposal should be made. He had no doubt that when the Report of the Commissioners who sat upon industrial and reformatory schools was being considered, this question would be considered along with others.

MR. RANKIN asked whether, under the Industrial Schools Act, it would be possible to make grants to those schools which had been formed for the sake of taking in children of the same class and character which supplied the present industrial schools, but destined to train children for emigration to the Colonies? He thought that the making of grants to those schools would be one of the most useful ways in which money could be spent; and, on the whole, it would be a most economical way. He knew that what he suggested would meet with the approval of the Colonial agents and other persons connected with the Colonies. He would be glad to know whether, if the Government thought it was not possible to make the grants under the present Act, they would consider the advisability of making some alteration in the law by which grants could be made?

MR. HIBBERT said, that under the present law it was not possible to make grants to the schools established for the purpose the hon. Gentleman (Mr. Rankin) had indicated. It was no doubt a very desirable object, and might be considered when a reconsideration of the subject took place. He would take care the matter was considered by the Home Office during the Recess.

MR. HARRINGTON said, he did not know whether the same system with regard to industrial schools prevailed in England as they had to complain of in Ireland. The system was practically this—that before a child could go to an industrial school he must place himself in the position of a criminal; before a child could be got into an industrial school in Ireland it must first be proved before a magistrate that he had been seen begging, for instance. The system was abused to such an extent that a child was very often sent into the streets to beg by those who were interested in his removal to an industrial school.

THE CHAIRMAN (Mr. RAIKES) called the attention of the hon. Gentleman to the fact that Ireland was not included in this Vote.

MR. HARRINGTON said, he had no desire to discuss the custom in Ireland; but simply wished to ask the hon. Gentleman (Mr. Hibbert) if the system in this country was the same as that in Ireland? If it was he intended to move for its abolition.

MR. HIBBERT said, the system was very much the same in England as in Ireland. It was not necessary that in all cases a child should be sent on the streets to beg before it could be sent to an industrial school. There were many reasons why a child should be sent to an industrial school, and no doubt one of the reasons was that it should be found begging in the streets. That was one way of getting a child out of the hands of parents who did not behave properly to it. There were many instances in which, in consequence of the neglect of the parents, it was to the interest of children that they should be sent to some industrial school.

MR. HARRINGTON said, he was not referring to the case of children whom it was necessary to take away from the charge of negligent parents; but he was referring to cases of frequent occurrence where children had no parents or guardians able to provide for them. He had known the magistrates refuse to admit orphan children to industrial schools until they had been found begging in the streets. He regarded that as a great grievance, and one which required a remedy. Possibly the law was a desirable one where it became necessary to take children out of the charge of negligent parents; but, in the case of orphans, it was really leading children into hypocrisy at the very commencement of life, to send them into the streets to beg in order that they might, therefore, be sent to an industrial school. Surely such children might be admitted without their first of all committing some criminal act.

MR. HIBBERT assured the hon. Gentleman (Mr. Harrington) the subject should be fully considered.

Vote *agreed to.*

(2.) £19,772, to complete the sum for the Broadmoor Criminal Lunatic Asylum.

MR. WARTON said, he had a question to ask which seemed to him to be one of considerable importance. There was a large increase in the number of patients provided for this year—namely, 550 against 515 last year. The increase was thus very nearly 7 per cent. He would like to know to what cause the increase was to be attributed? They were told that, upon the whole, crime was on the decrease; and, therefore, it was well they should be told whether the increase in the number of criminal lunatics arose from any increasing tendency on the part of the Judges and others to agree with what might be called the medical, rather than the legal, theory of insanity. There was no disguising the fact that lawyers and doctors had been at variance with regard to the theory of insanity. It was quite possible that a man might know that what he did was wrong, and yet not be morally responsible for his actions. The only other question he had to ask was, whether it was expected that any difference would be made in the expenses of the Broadmoor Asylum owing to the operation of any Bill which might now be before the House, and which had been introduced in consequence of the recommendation of the Committee that investigated this subject?

MR. HIBBERT said, the increase in the number of patients at Broadmoor arose very much from the fact that no criminal lunatics were now sent to licensed houses; and he thought the Committee would agree that it was very desirable no more criminal lunatics should be sent to houses of that character. Another reason of the increase was that strong representations were made by the Local Authorities against the practice of sending dangerous criminal lunatics to county and borough asylums. More criminals of that class, therefore, were now confined at Broadmoor. With regard to the second question of the hon. and learned Gentleman, he was bound to say that if the Criminal Lunatics Bill became law, there would be a considerable increase of the Vote, because the Bill relieved the Local Authorities of very considerable burdens they had at the present time. The matter had been very fully considered by a Departmental Committee. They went fully into the question, and recommended a change to meet the views of the Local Authorities. Of course, the alteration would not come into operation just yet, so it was not necessary to make any provision for it in the present Estimates. Perhaps it might be necessary to provide for the additional expense by a Supplementary Estimate, which would be submitted, not in the present Session, but later on in the year.

Vote *agreed to.*

(3.) Motion made, and Question proposed,

"That a sum, not exceeding £38,801, be granted to Her Majesty, to complete the sum necessary to defray the Charge which will come in course of payment during the year ending on the 31st day of March 1885, for the Salaries and Expenses of the Lord Advocate's Department, and others, connected with Criminal Proceedings in Scotland, including certain Allowances under the Act 15 and 16 Vic. c. 83:"

DR. CAMERON said, that this Vote included the salaries of the Procurators Fiscal. He had some time ago brought forward the anomalies, and worse than anomalies, of the existing system with regard to Public Prosecutors in Scotland. Since then a number of new cases had come into his hands. For instance, the Chief Constable of an important burgh complained that the Procurator Fiscal of that burgh refused, in a case which the Chief Constable considered most clear, to prosecute a man who was his private client. He (Dr. Cameron) was not going to enter into cases of this kind; but since he brought his Motion before the House, the Crofters' Commission had reported in favour of the proposition he then made; and he would now ask the Government whether they would be prepared to carry out the recommendations of that Commission, and forbid Procurators Fiscal in Scotland to act as agents in private cases, or as land agents? Unless he got a satisfactory answer with regard to the case of the Procurator Fiscal of Dumfries, he should move to reduce the Vote by £670, which was the amount of his salary. Some time ago a young man in Dumfries applied for a licence, but the licence was refused by the magistrates on the ground that he was under 21 years of age; but they told him that if he overcame that difficulty by living for another six months they would probably grant him a certificate. In the meantime, he went to the Excise, and got permission to carry on a public-house without a certificate or licence. The law provided that a penalty of £500 should be imposed on any official of the Crown who permitted liquor to be sold without a licence; but when he mentioned this matter in the House, the Secretary to the Treasury lightly suggested that he (Dr. Cameron) might enrich himself by recovering that amount. He had no ambition to figure as a common informer; and he thought the best course was to move a reduction of the Vote, and allow the country to profit, not by £500, but by £670, which was the amount of the salary of the Public Prosecutor, whose business it was to enforce the law, and who had not enforced it in this case. The law distinctly laid down that any person shebeening in Scotland should be prosecuted. Recently, in Glasgow, some extraordinary arrests for shebeening were made; but at the very time these arrests were being made in Glasgow the Lord Advocate was allowing shebeening to take place in Dumfries with perfect equanimity. The right hon. and learned Gentleman the Lord Advocate had perfect confidence in the Secretary to the Treasury (Mr. Courtney), and said that if the Excise Authorities had not seen fit to interfere he did not see how he was called upon to do so. However great might be the iniquity of the Excise Authorities, who seemed to do almost anything for money, he held that the Lord Advocate, as the Head of the Department which had to administer justice, was bound to obey and to administer the law; and it was no excuse for him to appeal to the Secretary to the Treasury. What he (Dr. Cameron) and others wanted was to see the law properly administered in these matters by the Lord Advocate and the Procurators Fiscal. Numerous instances had come under his notice in which the law had not been enforced by these officials. He had taken one case, in which there was no room for quibbling, and he asked the Lord Advocate why he had failed to put the law in operation in that case, and why he allowed shebeening to go on for six months even? For the purpose of bringing the matter to an issue, he moved to reduce the Vote by £670, being the amount of the salary of the Procurator Fiscal of Dumfries.

Motion made, and Question proposed,

"That a sum, not exceeding £38,131, be granted to Her Majesty, to complete the sum necessary to defray the Charge which will come in course of payment during the year ending on the 31st day of March 1885, for the Salaries and Expenses of the Lord Advocate's Department, and others, connected with Criminal Proceedings in Scotland, including certain Allowances under the Act 15 and 16 Vic. c. 83."—(*Dr. Cameron.*)

THE LORD ADVOCATE (Mr. J. B. BALFOUR) said, he understood that the case to which the hon. Member for Glasgow (Dr. Cameron) referred, was one which he brought under the notice of the House on two previous occasions by way of Question. If he (the Lord Advocate) recollected aright, it related to a hotel or inn called the "Ship" Hotel, at Dumfries. The facts, as far as they were present to his mind, were that the application for licence had been made in the usual way, when it appeared that, on the ground of minority, or some similar ground, the Licensing Magistrates did not feel that at that moment they should grant the licence to the applicant, but they unanimously recommended that the matter should be kept in a state of suspense, and, he thought, indicated that when the next licensing period came round they would grant the licence, they were so well satisfied of all the qualifications being possessed by the applicant. The point then came to be what course the Revenue authorities should follow—whether they should treat this as a case of what his hon. Friend (Dr. Cameron) had called "shebeening," which he (the Lord Advocate) did not at all admit to be a correct description; or whether they had not the power to consider that, in the circumstances of a particular case it was intended to meet, it would not be an act of oppression to apply a stringent law? The Revenue authorities came to the conclusion that it would be stretching the law to put in force the power of suing for penalties in such a case. In that state of matters, he apprehended that the Procurator Fiscal was guilty of no neglect of duty—on the contrary, that he would have been guilty of something like improper meddlesomeness in a Revenue matter if, when the authorities who were more directly charged with the conduct of the Department said they considered this was not a proper case for a prosecution, it not being one, in their opinion, in which a statutory offence against the Inland Revenue had been committed, he had presumed to override the Department, and, against their directions and wish, instituted a prosecution. He (the Lord Advocate) was perfectly willing to leave it to the judgment of the House whether the Procurator Fiscal so acting was guilty of any wrong; or whether, where the Licensing Magistrates and the Department charged with the matter considered that it would not have been a right use of the statutory powers to apply them in such a case, there was anything blameworthy on the part of the Procurator Fiscal? As regarded the more general request which his hon. Friend (Dr. Cameron) had raised, and which he brought under the notice of the House on a previous occasion, he (the Lord Advocate) had nothing to add to what he then said. He then explained the plan on which the present Government, at all events, had been acting with regard to the appointment of Procurator Fiscals. His hon. Friend, he was afraid, forgot that this was a matter that stood on the Statute Law of the country. Procurators Fiscal were not appointed by the Government, but under an Act of Parliament only six or seven years old, by the Sheriff, and all the Home Secretary had to do was to give his assent or withhold it; in fact, he had a power of veto, but not a power of appointment. It was not an element in the qualification for a Procurator Fiscalship that the person should not engage in private practice. He knew that was a point as to which there was great difference of opinion. He was perfectly familiar with the recommendations, by no means unanimous, of the Crofters' Commission on the poin. Anyone who had read and studied the Report must have been struck with certain weighty observations made by a very respectable and eminent Member of the House on that point. That hon. Gentleman called attention to the fact that it was only by some large interpretation of the Reference to the Commission that the Committee took cognizance of such matters as law and justice at all. He (the Lord Advocate) welcomed anything that came from that Commission; but, at the same time, he was not aware that the Commission took evidence on the point that they called before them those who were best qualified to give an opinion upon it; and it was impossible for anyone who was familiar with the course of inquiry into this branch of the administration of law to forget that a very influential Commission, composed of distinguished lawyers of the two countries, of chief magistrates of various burghs, of conveners of a number of counties, and of many of the most eminent and best informed laymen, reported so lately as 1871 against the restriction of Procurators Fiscal from private practice. That matter was now under the consideration of the Government, like all the other points in the Report of the Crofters' Commission; but he was not prepared, until the matter had been fully matured, to say that the Government would legislate against the recommendations of a Commission appointed to inquire into Law and Justice in Scotland because of the recommendations of another Commission, before which the matter had come only incidentally. The Government had always gone on the principle of seeing that the private duties of an official should never be allowed to come in collision with his public duties.

SIR WILFRID LAWSON said, he did not consider the answer of the Lord Advocate was at all satisfactory. He should like to know whether the man to whom his hon. Friend (Dr. Cameron) referred was selling drink illegally or not? If the man was selling drink illegally, who ought to see he did not continue to do so? He (Sir Wilfrid Lawson) asked this question, because whenever anybody in the House got up and tried to amend the law relating to the sale of drink, it was said—"Oh, the great thing is to carry out efficiently the laws that you have."

THE LORD ADVOCATE (Mr. J. B. BALFOUR) said, that, as put by his hon. Friend the Member for Carlisle (Sir Wilfrid Lawson), there was a charming simplicity about the question, and he supposed the hon. Baronet wished a "Yes" or a "No" to it. This person was selling drink without a licence; but the licensing authority recommended that he should not be interfered with, and practically promised he should have a licence; and the Department of the Government charged with the administration of the matter said that the circumstances were not such as to warrant a prosecution. As to who was responsible, he should perhaps say that the Department was responsible. Whether they were right or wrong, he left the House to judge. It rather seemed to him that the suggestion involved in the question was, that if anybody was to be prosecuted it should not be the man, but somebody connected with the Department.

MR. FRASER-MACKINTOSH said, he was rather disappointed at the answer of the Lord Advocate with regard to Procurators Fiscal. The right hon. and learned Gentleman always showed a disposition to throw in their faces the fact that several years ago a Commission upon Law and Justice reported that the position of Procurators Fiscal should remain as it was; but the Lord Advocate must recollect that there was a very considerable minority in that Commission in favour of the change. In the recent Commission on the Highlands and Islands, five out of six Commissioners were perfectly unanimous for the change. Some years ago this question was brought to a Division in the House; and among those who voted for limiting the duties of Procurators Fiscal, were five Members of the present Administration, including the Secretary to the Treasury, the Home Secretary, and the Judge Advocate General. That Division took place years after the Commission, to which the Lord Advocate referred, reported. The Vote under consideration included the expenses of the whole of the administration of justice in Scotland, both civil and criminal; and, as he understood that the Lord Advocate was responsible for that administration, he wished to bring before the Committee two points—one affecting criminal and the other affecting civil law in Scotland. With reference to criminal administration, the Lord Advocate was assisted in his duties by four Advocates-Depute, appointed mainly, as commonly reported, for political services. Be that as it might, he wished to ask the right hon. Gentleman for an explanation of a very extraordinary case which recently occurred in the High Court of Justiciary. The parties accused of serious offences, from the counties of Orkney and Shetland, were obliged to appear in Edinburgh.

THE CHAIRMAN (Mr. RAIKES): I must point out to the hon. Member, that although he is in Order in discussing any part of the present Vote at the present moment, he is not in Order in anticipating the next Vote, which includes the Court of Justiciary.

MR. FRASER-MACKINTOSH said, he was about to refer to the action of one of the Advocates-Depute whose salary was included in the present Vote. He was informed that in a recent case a great number of witnesses came up from the remote Islands of Orkney and Shetland—some for the Crown, and some for the prisoner. When the case was called, an objection was stated on behalf of the prisoner to the relevancy of the indictment. The Judges threw out the libel very summarily, indulging in some plain observations on its construction; and the consequence was that the whole matter fell to the ground, and that a great deal of expense fell upon the Crown and inconvenience upon the prisoner. He also understood that it was not an uncommon occurrence for criminal indictments framed by this Advocate to be cast; and, therefore, he should like to receive some explanation of the matter from the Lord Advocate. The next point to which he wished to refer was connected with Sheriff Courts. The Lord Advocate was aware, no doubt, that the question of double Sheriffships had been frequently brought before Parliament. It was complained by many persons that there was great expense and delay, and he was obliged, with great hesitation, to bring his own county (Inverness) before the attention of the Lord Advocate. He held in his hand a letter just received, with regard to his own county, in which the writer said—

> "The state of our local Sheriff Court has become intolerable, and calls for immediate attention on the part of those at head-quarters. The Sheriff cannot be got to decide the cases before him, and most of the cases in Court are lying at *avizandum*—some of them for one year. This causes a great loss to the parties."

Some years ago there used to be complaints that in the Supreme Courts of Scotland there were considerable delays; but of late years the despatch of the business in those Courts had been satisfactory. But with regard to the other Courts, where double Sheriffships prevailed, delays were becoming greater and greater.

MR. DICK-PEDDIE said, there could be no doubt that the selling of beer without a licence was clearly an illegal act. It was an illegal act under the Statute, and if an act were illegal, it could not be made legal by the Department condoning it. He would like a further explanation of this matter, because he understood it was one of the functions of a Procurator Fiscal to prosecute whenever an illegal act was committed. With regard to the complaint made by his hon. Friend (Mr. Fraser-Mackintosh) of dilatoriness on the part of the Sheriff of Inverness, he was bound to say that if there had been any dilatoriness, it, no doubt, arose from the circumstance, which was within his own knowledge, that the gentleman in question had been for several months in an indifferent state of health.

MR. KENNY said, one point struck him as being rather peculiar in connection with this Vote. The Committee would observe a discrepancy in line 3 of Page 256, which, he thought, ought to be explained or removed from the Estimate. He perceived that the First Clerk to the Crown Agent had a minimum salary of £500 a-year, and a maximum salary of £650, rising to that amount by an annual increment of £25. Now, the amount voted for this official last year was the minimum salary of £500, whereas the amount asked for this year was the maximum sum of £650. He should like to know how the amount of £125 paid in excess was accounted for?

THE LORD ADVOCATE (Mr. J. B. BALFOUR) said, if there were no other reasons for the amount of salary asked for in this case than appeared on the face of the Estimate, the charge would, of course, be open to objection; but the gentleman who now occupied the position of First Clerk to the Crown Agent, did so with very great advantage to the public, and when, about six months ago, there was a re-arrangement in the Office, it was deemed right to make this addition to his salary.

MR. KENNY said the right hon. and learned Gentleman had not accounted for the excess.

THE LORD ADVOCATE (Mr. J. B. BALFOUR) said, with respect to the points raised by the hon. Member for Inverness (Mr. Fraser-Mackintosh), he did not know on what authority or evidence he had arrived at the conclusion that the Advocates-Depute were appointed for political reasons, and not because of their fitness for the office. His experience of these gentlemen was that they were exceedingly well qualified for their office; and during the time he had held his present position, he had uniformly received from them the most devoted and valuable assistance in the duties of the Office. He hoped the hon. Member for Inverness did not want to cast any imputation upon them in respect of the manner in which they discharged their duties. The hon. Member had not indicated the particular Advocate-Depute to whom he referred; but he seemed to be under the impression that it was ground for complaint against a public official, that an indictment which he had framed or supported was found to be irrelevant—a thing which happened when the matter set out did not sustain a valid criminal charge. It must be evident to all concerned in the administration of the law in this country and in Scotland that there were very many acts which it was difficult to bring under the category of any particular crime. There was, consequently, great difficulty and nicety in framing an indictment, and indictments were often found irrelevant upon strictly technical rules of construction; acts had been committed which it would be a misfortune not to make the subjects of criminal charges, but with respect to which it was found on strict examination that an indictment would not hold. That was what hon. Members would see in the public Press every day, and he was satisfied that the mere fact of a particular charge having failed, was by no means evidence of any incompetence or carelessness on the part of those who were concerned in its preparation. He did not think his hon. Friend alleged that there was anything of that nature involved in this question; but he clearly appeared to think that the fact of the indictment having failed, constituted ground of complaint. However, he felt sure that, on reflection, his hon. Friend would feel that it was not so, and that it would appear to him that there was no ground for the suggestion which it seemed to him (the Lord Advocate) he was ready to make. With regard to the Sheriff Courts, the hon. Member had raised a question which everyone acquainted with the administration of the law in Scotland knew to be a very vexed and difficult one—that was to say, the question of double Sheriffship, and with regard to it he was compelled to differ from the view taken by his hon. Friend. But his hon. Friend must see that it was a very large question, and one involving many considerations, and with which Her Majesty's Government had no power to deal without an Act of Parliament. He quite agreed that there were many matters connected with the administration and with the framework of the judicial system which did admit of remedy, and if there were more Parliamentary time, he thought such remedial legislation would be a very fitting subject to take up. But at the present time the double Sheriffship did exist; and although he could not say he was particularly favourable to it himself, still it was a point on which there was considerable divergence of opinion. But he did not see, looking at the present state of Public Business, that Her Majesty's Government had any means of making immediate proposals to Parliament on the subject. Again, his hon. Friend had read a letter which seemed to reflect on the Sheriff-Principal of the county of Inverness. He could only say that he had known that gentleman for many years—since the time he (the Lord Advocate) came to the Bar, and previously—and he had never, until that time, heard any suggestion made against him of the nature which he understood to be implied by the statement of his hon. Friend. The delay alleged in this case was perfectly new to him; he had never heard of it before; and having known the gentleman in question for so many years, it was not what he should have expected, nor was he prepared to accept it on a mere passage from a letter which, in his judgment, was insufficient to sustain a complaint of this kind. If there existed any ground for the complaint made, and if the allegation was made in a formal manner, the matter would be investigated. For his own part, he had no doubt that an explanation would be forthcoming of the delay which might have occurred. He was bound to add his belief that the Committee would not expect him to say more than this, having, as he had already pointed out, full knowledge of the personal character of this gentleman, as well as the devotion with which he had discharged his duties. There was no doubt that the Sheriff Courts in Scotland had been generally very efficiently administered, and he did not think there had been much delay in the transaction of their business, although there might, of course, have been some in special cases. He believed that they had shared in the spirit of despatch which his hon. Friend admitted to have very largely pervaded the Supreme Courts during recent years.

Dr. CAMERON said, the Lord Advocate had told the Committee that the proposal of the Crofters' Commission, with regard to the form of appointment of Procurators Fiscal, was under consideration by Her Majesty's Government, upon which he would remark that the proposal had been under consideration for a long time, and that it would be, in his opinion, considerably longer before anything was done to give effect to it. When the Conservatives came into Office, the Lord Advocate would, probably, be ready to deal with the matter, and he would be found, no doubt, supported by the Secretary to the Treasury, the Home Secretary, the Judge Advocate General and others, who would have nothing to say to it when they sat on that side of the House. With regard to the licensing question which had been raised, it appeared to him that the Government acted on the principle on which "Messrs. Spenlow and Jorkins" conducted their business. Deputations innumerable came up to London to see the Lord Advocate. They were received with the utmost politeness; they were assured that nothing was more at the heart of the Government than the carrying out of the legislation thought to be necessary; that none more bitterly deplored the present state of things; and that none were more anxious to give effect to the heart-felt desires of those persons who wished to free themselves from this curse of drink. Thus, the deputation afterwards went away satisfied for the time being. But, to return to his illustration, it was found that "Mr. Spenlow was perfectly willing that the law should be given effect to, but—there is Mr. Jorkins!" And Mr. Jorkins, in this instance, was personified by the Secretary to the Treasury. Of course, he and his hon. Friends could not carry out the law; it was the business of Parliament to make laws; and when a law was made with the most deliberate intention by Parliament, it was the business of the Government to administer that law. The Government were very ready in making promises to the supporters of the Permissive Bill; but it appeared to him that, in this instance, they had been a Permissive Bill unto themselves, having granted this licence in spite of all they could have done to prevent it. On that account, he should take a Division on his Amendment for the reduction of the Vote.

MR. KENNY said, he did not agree with hon. Gentlemen from Scotland opposite, because he believed there was a very wide difference between the case of the individual in question and that of the shebeen man. The difference was that whereas the shebeen man sold liquor without any licence whatever, this individual had received permission to sell liquor. Under those circumstances he did not think he ought to be prosecuted. He was a man who went to the authorities and asked for a licence, and it was said they refused to give him the licence —if so, it was a great shame—but the Excise Department took no steps to interfere with his selling liquor. Therefore, he could not support the Motion of the hon. Gentleman the Member for Glasgow (Dr. Cameron) for the reduction of the Vote by the amount of the salary of the Procurator Fiscal of Dumfries. He observed on Page 254 of the Estimates a charge of £1,100 for the Sheriff of Lanarkshire for salaries of criminal officers in Glasgow. He also observed that there was no Vote under this head last year, and, therefore, he would like to know what this new charge was for, and what were the functions of the so-called criminal officers in Glasgow?

THE LORD ADVOCATE (Mr. J. B. BALFOUR) said, the question of the hon. Member for Ennis (Mr. Kenny) was very fairly raised on this Vote, and the explanation was simply this—that formerly these officers were paid by fees, but latterly every opportunity which presented itself for commuting those fees for fixed salaries had been availed of, and the consequence was the present charge for the salaries of criminal officers at Glasgow. The alteration was one which he believed the Committee would approve.

SIR WILFRID LAWSON said, as the Committee could get no satisfaction out of the Lord Advocate, they might, perhaps, get something out of the Secretary to the Treasury. He would be glad to hear whether that hon. Gentleman approved this breaking of the Law of Excise at Dumfries? His hon. Friends and himself did not want to divide on the Motion of the hon. Member for Glasgow, if they could get an assurance that the law would be carried out. His hon. Friend had told the Committee that this sort of thing was perpetually coming up in Scotland. [The LORD ADVOCATE dissented.] The Lord Advocate shook his head, which showed that he had a bad case. The way the authorities had dealt with the licence in this case reminded him of the old barrel that used to be kept until the heir came of age. The Lord Advocate would only allow the licence to be used when this individual had reached the age of 21. However, he relied much on the Secretary to the Treasury to clear up the difficulty. He desired to put two questions. Was it legal for this young man to be selling drink at the present time? If not, who was responsible for his not being prosecuted?

MR. ILLINGWORTH said, the position taken up by the Government seemed to be that when a young man came of age he should have a licence to sell liquor, and that before he came of age he should have every opportunity of breaking the law. [The LORD ADVOCATE dissented.] The Lord Advocate shook his head, as much as to say that the matter was a very simple one. But a principle of importance was involved, and he should have thought that the state of affairs which had been disclosed would be insupportable in Scotland after the statement of the Lord Advocate. For his own part, he could not see why his hon. Friends on those Benches should be called upon to lower their flag at all; he thought they were bound to go to a Division, otherwise they would be parties to this lax administration of the law. If this young man were to be allowed to sell liquor for profit without a licence, he would like to know where the matter would end. He was bound to say that the right hon. and learned Gentleman had, by his statement on this question, laid himself open to considerable comment. It was of such a character that he hoped his hon. Friend the Member for Glasgow (Dr. Cameron) would divide the Committee on his Motion.

MR. KENNY said, with regard to the payment of the Procurators Fiscal by fees, that he should have expected the Estimate would show exactly the amount of fees in excess of the amounts asked for last year.

MR. COURTNEY pointed out that, in consequence of the present arrangement, the salaries appeared as diminishing, and the fees as increasing.

MR JOSEPH COWEN said, that if the case at Dumfries were exceptional, he thought it might be passed over; but if it were not, the matter assumed a very different form, and it was most important that some steps should be taken.

THE LORD ADVOCATE (Mr. J. B. BALFOUR) said, it was only right to say that his information about this case had come to him exclusively in reply to his inquiries. The case had never been reported to his Department, and he knew nothing about it until, in consequence of Questions in that House, he caused inquiries to be made, with the result stated. That information he had laid before the Committee. He never knew another case like it. He had nothing whatever to do with licences, or the supervision of publicans, or anybody else.

MR. COURTNEY said, he was not at all aware that this was a customary case; he looked upon it, on the contrary, as distinctly abnormal. With respect to the observations of the hon. Member for Carlisle (Sir Wilfrid Lawson), the hon. Baronet knew perfectly well that he was not responsible for the administration of the Law of Licence. He was responsible, to a certain extent, for the collection of the money paid for licences.

DR. CAMERON said, he could assure the Committee that this was not an exceptional case; he should, therefore, go to a Division on his Amendment as a protest against the acquiescence of the legal authorities in the infraction of the law. Last year he had asked Questions with regard to three similar cases in Fraserburgh; and this year, also, he had asked a Question with regard to a case of the kind at Bellshill. Nor were these all the cases that had been brought to his attention, although he had not thought it necessary to make every one of them the subject of a Question in that House. They were of far more frequent occurrence than might be supposed, in spite of the elaborate system of Rules laid down to prevent the sale of liquor without licence; and he felt bound to express his regret and surprise that the Questions he had put in that House had made so little impression upon the Members of the Government to whom they were addressed.

Question put.

The Committee *divided*:—Ayes 19; Noes 58: Majority 39.—(Div. List, No. 184.)

Original Question put, and *agreed to*.

(4.) Motion made, and Question proposed,

"That a sum, not exceeding £42,657, be granted to Her Majesty, to complete the sum necessary to defray the Charge which will come in course of payment during the year ending on the 31st day of March 1885, for the Salaries and Expenses of the Courts of Law and Justice in Scotland, and other Legal Charges."

MR. FRASER-MACKINTOSH said, he desired to have an explanation from the Lord Advocate of one item in this Vote—namely, £350 for the Deputy Keeper of the Signet. Some 20 years ago, a professional man in Edinburgh of great practice was appointed Keeper of the Register of Sasines. This appointment was considered so objectionable, in view of the great private practice of the person appointed, that in the year

1868 an Act of Parliament was passed regulating the registration of writs in Scotland, and by Section 20 of the 30 & 31 *Vict.* c. 64, it was declared that when the office of Keeper of the Register of Sasines became vacant, the next person appointed should hold no other place, either by himself or by deputy. Now, a few years ago, on the death of the holder of the office of the Deputy Keeper of the Signet, a new appointment was made; and who was the person appointed? The House would be surprised to hear that the very individual was appointed who, by the Act of 1868, was declared, inferentially, not to be a suitable person. He understood the patronage of the office rested with the Lord Clerk Register, and not with the Crown; but he wished to know whether, seeing that the Act of 1868 showed that the person who held the office of Keeper of the Register of Sasines had occupation enough to do to keep that office alone, and that some years afterwards he was selected for a second post—he wished to know whether the Lord Advocate or the Crown did, or did not, make any objection to the appointment of this official, and whether or not it was competent now for them to refuse to pay any salary for the service?

THE LORD ADVOCATE (Mr. J. B. BALFOUR) said, he was not aware that the Crown either did or could make any objection to this appointment; and he could only say that, even if it had been in the power of the Crown to make any such objection, if the case had been represented to him he should have advised the Crown not to make it, because the Act referred to did not relate to this matter, but pointed to cases where difference of opinion existed, and provided that, in future, holders of the office of Keeper of the Register of Sasines should not be engaged in private practice. That Act did not, however, make any provision with respect to the present holder. As his hon. Friend (Mr. Fraser-Mackintosh) had made reference to that gentleman, he (the Lord Advocate) could only say that, in the opinion of everyone acquainted with the services he had rendered to the important Department with which he was connected, those services had been most valuable to the Office. A great many changes which had been made in the system of registering and for giving additional security to the Scotch system of land rights and additional facilities for the searching of those rights, were due to this gentleman. He (the Lord Advocate) did not know whether it was suggested that this gentlemen holding the office of Deputy Keeper of the Signet interfered with his proper discharge of the duties of Keeper of the Register of Sasines; but it was certain that such was not the case.

MR. FRASER-MACKINTOSH: May I ask the Lord Advocate if this gentleman discharges the duties of this office in person? Does he ever go near the Office?

THE LORD ADVOCATE (Mr. J. B. BALFOUR): This gentleman does discharge his duties in person most certainly.

MR. FRASER-MACKINTOSH: I mean the duties of Deputy Keeper of the Signet?

THE LORD ADVOCATE (Mr. J. B. BALFOUR): I am not aware of that—I am not so well acquainted with the duties of the Deputy Keeper of the Signet. I should not, however, think them particularly onerous. These duties the present holder of the office, I understand, has discharged with efficiency and great success.

DR. CAMERON said, he thought it would, perhaps, be worth the while of the Secretary to the Treasury to look into the matter, and see whether there was any necessity to pay a salary of £350 a-year for a Deputy Keeper of the Signet. Probably that £350 a-year might be saved to the State. The point, however, he (Dr. Cameron) wished more particularly to call attention to was in connection with the office of Extractor. There had been numerous complaints in this matter. The duty of the Extractor was to extract judgments.

THE LORD ADVOCATE (Mr. J. B. BALFOUR): I rather think my hon. Friend is about to refer to another Extractor—not to the one affected by this Vote.

DR. CAMERON: I rather think the salary of the one I wish to refer to comes under this Vote.

THE LORD ADVOCATE (Mr. J. B. BALFOUR): No; it comes under another Vote.

DR. CAMERON said, he thought he was right in the matter. He wished to refer to the Extractor of the Court of

Session. The Extractor to whom he was referring was complained of very seriously by solicitors and litigants, who complained that they could not get their extracts out of him. Having got their judgments, they were kept a long time, under one plea or another, waiting for what they wanted. There was another complaint. A gentleman who, at one time, was in the Office, had gone very minutely into the whole working of the Extractor's Office, and had compiled a specific list of many hundreds of cases, showing that, in the case of a large percentage of the extracts procured by the public, a charge was made more than the statutory charge. In cases where a number of extracts were taken, the over-charge was considerable. Well, the law provided that if any circumstances of that kind were brought under the notice of the Lord Advocate, there should be a clean sweep made; but specific cases of these over-charges had been brought under the notice of the Lord Advocate by himself (Dr. Cameron), who had told him that the man who had given him his information had been dismissed from the Office under circumstances which were not creditable. He (Dr. Cameron) knew nothing about this man who had drawn up the list of cases. The statement of the Lord Advocate was altogether disputed by him; but, however accurate the right hon. and learned Gentleman might be, it had nothing whatever to do with the question. In the list there were a large number of cases —hundreds of cases given, chapter and verse. Either these allegations were true, or they were not true, and a reference to the books of the Department ought to enable a calculation to be made to show whether there had been over-charges made or not. He (Dr. Cameron) contended that it was in the public interest, and their duty to the public, for those in authority to see whether over-charges were made in connection with any Public Office, and where they were found to exist to put an end to them at once. In addition to this matter of over-charging, he was told that this office of Extractor was one which could well be dispensed with. Unless he had been misinformed, nothing analogous to it existed in England. It was a drawback against litigants enforcing their rights. He was not aware of the precise method adopted in England, but he was assured that it

was quite as satisfactory as the Scotch. Before moving a reduction in the Vote, he should like to hear what explanation the right hon. and learned Gentleman might have to offer on the three points he had mentioned—namely, the over-charges, the delays, and the absence of necessity for the office?

THE CHAIRMAN (Mr. RAIKES): The hon. Member has not moved the reduction of the Vote.

THE LORD ADVOCATE (Mr. J. B. BALFOUR) said, that, no doubt, various questions had been raised as to the office of Extractor, whose duty was to draw up copies of the decrees of justice. No doubt, there had been various complaints and questions raised as to the administration of the Office, and, so far from these complaints not having been effective, they were made the subject of careful examination by the officials of the Treasury and the Crown Agent acting under his direction, so that the matter had been fully gone into. There did appear to have been some irregularities; but he did not think there had been any clear defalcations except on the part of the person whom his hon. Friend (Dr. Cameron) spoke of as his informant in the matter.

DR. CAMERON: No; not my informant.

THE LORD ADVOCATE (Mr. J. B. BALFOUR) said, that, at any rate, this person had been proved to have been guilty of very grave defalcations—defalcations which the Extractor, with great kindness, perhaps, with too great kindness, had overlooked at the time. Then followed the charges to which the hon. Gentleman had referred; but, so far from this person having any cause of complaint, if the Extractor was to blame at all, it was for having treated him with undue leniency. This person had commenced an action in the Courts against the Extractor, but, seemingly, had not gone on with it. The hon. Gentleman the Secretary to the Treasury would bear him (Dr. Cameron) out when he said that, both on the part of the Treasury and his own part, full inquiry had been made into the Extractor's Office, and they had come to the conclusion that the public had no reason to complain in regard to defalcations.

DR. CAMERON said, the Lord Advocate told them there were defalcations in the Extractor's Office in consequence of which the gentleman whom the right hon. and learned Gentleman designated as his (Dr. Cameron's) informant was dismissed. Now, in the first place, the gentleman in question altogether denied the Lord Advocate's statement; and, in the second place, he was not his (Dr. Cameron's) informant. This gentleman had published a volume giving instances in which these over-charges occurred. The Lord Advocate had been questioned about the over-charges, and he said they rested on the statement of the dismissed official. It did not matter whom the charges were made by—whether by Ananias and Sapphira, or anyone else. Chapter and verse of the defalcations were given. The amounts the Office was entitled to charge under the Statute were given, and the amounts actually charged were set forth. The Lord Advocate had not promised to make any investigation into the matter at the time the disclosure was made, and he had not told them whether he had since made any investigation into the specific charges. These were not the matters in regard to which the person who had given the information had been dismissed. If this man had had anything to do with these things, it was not likely that he would have published his defalcations to the world. At any rate, if he had done so, he should have been punished. The dismissal was owing to a dispute between the person dismissed and the Extractor. Personally, he (Dr. Cameron) had not investigated the matter. That duty devolved upon the Lord Advocate. He was bound by Statute to look into the charges, and yet he had not said that he had looked into them. He (Dr. Cameron) did not wish to go into the dispute between this man and the Extractor; but desired simply to know whether the list of alleged over-charges had been investigated, and whether anything had been done to punish the individuals who made them, and to prevent over-charge in future?

THE LORD ADVOCATE (Mr. J. B. BALFOUR) said, he was not in a position to say whether all the particular instances alleged in the pamphlet which this gentleman had published had been gone into individually; but he knew that, with this document and other documents before them, the Treasury officials and the Crown Agent had made the best investigation into the matter they could. There did seem, so far as supervision was concerned, that there had been a certain amount of laxity in looking after the work of subordinate clerks. There had, however, been nothing discovered reflecting on the integrity and honour of the Extractor. So far as he (the Lord Advocate) knew, the only person against whom defalcations appeared to be established was the gentleman the hon. Member referred to. He (the Lord Advocate) had not gone fully into the question of the dismissal. The man denied that he was dismissed on account of the alleged defalcations about which he had given information, and he (the Lord Advocate) did not say he was; but it was, nevertheless, the fact that this person had been guilty of defalcations to a very considerable extent.

DR. CAMERON said, the right hon. and learned Gentleman had again entirely evaded the point. As the volume of over-charges referred to had not been published until after the man was dismissed, it was impossible that he could have been discharged in consequence of an investigation into the over-charges. Every question he (Dr. Cameron) had put had been evaded. It appeared to him that, in the interests of justice, the Lord Advocate, on whom the statutory duty devolved, should look into the matter. The right hon. and learned Gentleman said that, if anyone had been wronged, he should have proceeded against the Extractor. Imagine a man who had been over-charged to the extent of 10*s.* bringing an action to recover the amount. Winking at these over-charges, and permitting them, was a scandal, and he should therefore, move to reduce the Vote by the sum of £500, being the salary of the principal Extractor.

Motion made, and Question proposed,

"That a sum, not exceeding £42,157, be granted to Her Majesty, to complete the sum necessary to defray the Charge which will come in course of payment during the year ending on the 31st day of March 1885, for the Salaries and Expenses of the Courts of Law and Justice in Scotland, and other Legal Charges."—(*Dr. Cameron.*)

Question put.

The Committee *divided*:—Ayes 23; Noes 59: Majority 36.—(Div. List, No. 185.)

Original Question again proposed.

MR. KENNY asked for an Explanation of the item of £1,000 for "Expenses of agents attending to the interests of the Crown." It appeared from this Vote that the Crown appointed the agents, and paid them out of the Consolidated Fund. Further on there was a sum of £450 for "Costs and expenses recovered from the Office of Woods in actions to which the Crown is a party;" and, again, under the heading "Law Agents' bills of charges," £1,000 for the Office of Woods. Perhaps, the Lord Advocate would explain these items?

THE LORD ADVOCATE (Mr. J. B. BALFOUR) said, the £1,000 was the solicitor's charges in certain civil actions. The Agents for Woods and Forests were charged for separately.

MR. RAMSAY said, he voted in the minority in the recent Division with considerable reluctance, because he had hitherto believed that the administration of justice in Scotland was free from the shadow of suspicion. He felt that when charges were made against individuals or Departments employed in the administration of justice, the right hon. and learned Gentleman the Lord Advocate should, whether he was bound by statutory obligations resting upon him or not, in the interest of the public, make such investigations as to whether the individuals or Departments charged were free from the suspicion of defalcations of any kind. It did not appear to him that the right hon. and learned Gentleman had given a satisfactory explanation of the various delays which had taken place in the various Departments connected with the Supreme Court. He felt that any undue delay in any one Department should, in the public interest, be satisfactorily explained. He felt that when any aspersions were cast upon the administration of justice, the Lord Advocate should not rest satisfied until he had obtained full satisfaction in his own mind that the whole administration was perfectly pure, and, as he (Mr. Ramsay) said, free from the shadow of suspicion. He did not regret having voted, apparently, against the right hon. Gentleman, because he failed to see that the right hon. Gentleman gave a satisfactory explanation either as to the delays he (Mr. Ramsay) had referred to, or as to the defalcations which the right hon. Gentleman himself admitted had occurred, and which were a disgrace to the administration of justice in their country.

THE LORD ADVOCATE (Mr. J. B. BALFOUR) said, he fully accepted the responsibility for the duty of making an investigation into such a matter as that alleged; and he thought he stated that he did make an investigation, and that the Treasury, for their own purposes, also made an investigation at the same time. The result of his investigation was, that there did appear to have been some delay in the extracting of judgments on the part of subordinate clerks; but certainly nothing derogatory attached to the integrity or the honour of the gentleman who held the office of Extractor. There had been a certain amount of complaint with regard to the delay, and that was one of the matters investigated. Complaint was also made of delay in the extracting of deeds. The extracting of deeds, however, belonged to the Lord Clerk Register's Department, a Department for which he was in no sense responsible.

MR. ANDERSON asked what was the meaning of the item for investigating Peerages? Was it not the fact that gentlemen who claimed Peerages had to make their own investigations, and pay the cost of such investigations?

THE LORD ADVOCATE (Mr. J. B. BALFOUR) said, that since he had held the Office he had now the honour to hold, there had not been any charge under this head that had actually come against the Crown, because there had not been any Scotch Peerage cases during the last two or three years; but it had always been the practice, both in England and Scotland, for those who represented the Crown, which was the fountain of honour, to see that any claims which were made to Peerages in either country were not allowed to pass unless they were satisfied that the claims had been made out. Accordingly, it had always been the custom that, in Peerage cases in the House of Lords, the Attorney General in the case of England, and the Lord Advocate in the case of Scotland, had appeared in fulfilment of their duty as representing the Crown, from which all honours flowed. He had never had the honour of appearing in such a case; but if a claim to a Scotch Peerage came to be made, it would be the duty of the Crown Solicitors to make certain investigations, so that the Crown might be advised whether the claim was well-founded or not; and the Committee of Privileges, when they came to hear a Peerage case, always expected that counsel representing the Crown should sum up the case, and indicate whether the Committee ought or ought not to grant the title.

MR. RAMSAY said, he should like the right hon. and learned Gentleman the Lord Advocate to say who was responsible for the provision of such an adequate staff as would secure that there should be no delay in any Department with regard to deeds or extracts of deeds? Perhaps the right hon. and learned Gentleman might tell him that it was the Treasury, and not himself personally, who was responsible for the appointment of such a staff as would guard against undue delay. If the Treasury was responsible, the injustice was more aggravated, because the people of Scotland paid fees adequate to secure despatch.

THE LORD ADVOCATE (Mr. J. B. BALFOUR) said, the last question of his hon. Friend (Mr. Ramsay) related not to the Vote applicable to Law and Justice, but to the Vote relative to the Register House. As a matter of fact, it was the Treasury and the Registrar General's Department who were responsible. He did not feel competent to go fully into the subject; but he might point out that it would not be quite just to assume that wherever there was delay there was necessarily blame, because there were certain functions requiring to be performed both in the writing up of registers and in the making of extracts, which, from their very nature, prevented more than a certain number of persons being employed on the work simultaneously. The work would be done, he was sure, with all due despatch, and whatever staff was necessary would be employed.

MR. ARTHUR ARNOLD wished to ask a question with reference to a Department in which he had taken considerable interest—namely, that of Woods and Forests. He noticed that in this Vote there was a charge of £1,000 for "Law Agents' bills of charges for the Office of Woods and Forests." He was speaking from memory; but he thought he was quite correct in saying that the Crown Woods and Forests in Scotland were confined to six farms in Caithness. Was it possible that, under such circumstances, there should be a charge of £1,000 for law agents' charges?

THE LORD ADVOCATE (Mr. J. B. BALFOUR) said, that all the Crown fisheries and teinds, and such things, in Scotland came under this head. It would be satisfactory to the hon. Member (Mr. Arthur Arnold) to know that the law charges of the Department had very largely diminished of late years. There was less litigation than formerly.

MR. ARTHUR ARNOLD said, that fisheries could not come under the head of Woods and Forests.

THE LORD ADVOCATE (Mr. J. B. BALFOUR) said, the public fisheries did not, but the Crown salmon fisheries certainly did; and many of the greatest questions that had arisen in the Department had related to salmon fisheries, and also to foreshores.

MR. ARTHUR O'CONNOR said, the Lord Advocate had not explained how the £1,000 for expenses of agents attending to the interests of the Crown was distributed. All he had given the Committee to understand was, although some years ago a good portion of the money went for investigating Peerage claims, of late years no such work had been done. If that was the case, the Government could not want all the money, and it would be fair to move a reduction of the Vote for that reason alone. But with regard to the Office of Woods, the explanation of the Lord Advocate did not appear to explain anything. They found that £450 was set down for office work in the Office of Woods; but three lines above that £1,000 was charged for the Office of Woods. It would occur to anybody that if £1,000 was charged for the Office of Woods, and if costs and expenses were recovered to the amount of £450, that £450 might well come out of the £1,000; but, instead of that, it was added to it. There must be an error there. If there was not, then an explanation was wanted. Perhaps the right hon. and learned Gentleman could give the Committee further information?

THE LORD ADVOCATE (Mr. J. B. BALFOUR) said, the hon. Member for Queen's County (Mr. Arthur O'Connor) would see that the £1,000 was followed by £500 for "other departments." Then there was an estimated reduction for probable amount to be recovered within the year of £300, and that brought the estimate down to £1,200. The estimate did not seem to him to suggest the difficulty which occurred to the hon. Gentleman.

MR. ARTHUR O'CONNOR said, that if the £300 was deducted, and the £450, was charged on the very same account, there must be, according to the right hon. and learned Gentleman's own showing, an error of £150.

THE LORD ADVOCATE (Mr. J. B. BALFOUR) said, the hon. Member must see that the £300 was set down as the probable amount to be recovered during the year, while the £400 was an absolute charge.

MR. ARTHUR O'CONNOR said, these were estimates, and not actual sums at all, they were dealing with, and the Lord Advocate had not said how it was he asked for £1,000 for agents, the need for whose services he himself admitted no longer existed.

MR. KENNY said, this was a case which the Secretary to the Treasury (Mr. Courtney) would, no doubt, understand. Perhaps he would explain it to the Committee?

MR. COURTNEY pointed out that the amounts recovered were put down in diminution of the sums charged. As to the "expenses of agents attending to the interests of the Crown," the item varied from year to year; it varied to a large extent from the want of regular recurrence of Peerage claims. For instance, the item charged under this head in 1868 was £2,337; in 1879, £648; in 1880, £1,212; and in 1882, £2,609. In that year there were two Peerage claims, including the Annandale case. It was hoped that £1,000 would cover the expenses during the next year. If any expenses were not incurred, of course, the money would not be paid.

MR. ANDERSON said, he did not think the hon. Gentleman's (Mr. Courtney's) answer was quite clear. £300 was set down as the probable amount which would be recovered, and it was deducted; but £450 was the amount actually recovered, and that was charged.

MR. COURTNEY said, that the true explanation of the matter was that in the one case the recovery was from the Crown, and in the other case against the Crown.

MR. RAMSAY said, he had always understood that those who inherited Peerages were made to pay certain sums for the honours they acquired. Why should they not pay this £1,000? He did not see any reason why the expenses connected with the investigation of Peerage claims should fall as a charge on the public. The public took no interest in the Peerages, and, therefore, they should not be required to pay any expenses connected with their investigation.

MR. COURTNEY said, he believed that if a debit and credit account were made out, it would be found that the fees paid by the persons claiming Peerages would very much exceed the fees which were paid to the Law Officers for conducting the investigations. It must be obvious to his hon. Friend (Mr. Ramsay) that when a person made a claim to a Peerage which had been in abeyance, it was necessary that some public officer should attend and watch the case on behalf of the Crown. It could not be expected that the applicant should pay the expenses of his enemy as well as his own.

Question put, and *agreed to.*

(5.) Motion made, and Question proposed,

"That a sum, not exceeding £24,603, be granted to Her Majesty, to complete the sum necessary to defray the Charge which will come in course of payment during the year ending on the 31st day of March 1885, for the Salaries and Expenses of the Offices in Her Majesty's General Register House, Edinburgh."

MR. FRASER-MACKINTOSH said, the administration of the Register House excited a great deal of interest in Edinburgh. There were several grievances in connection with that administration which he would endeavour to explain as briefly as possible. A few years ago, the clerks and other officials in the Register House, Edinburgh, were made Civil servants, and the charge for them put upon the Treasury. Amongst the arrangements that were made, first, second and third class clerks were created. As to the first class clerks, he had no observation to make; but in respect to the second and third class clerks, the complaint of the third class clerks was, that while their rate of remuneration was very much below that of second class clerks, their duties were decidedly the same. In answer to a Question he (Mr. Mackintosh) put some time ago, the Lord Advocate stated that the duties of the two classes were analogous, but that the quality of the work was much better in the one case than in the other. While the second class clerks began at £170 and rose to £240, the third class clerks commenced at £90 and increased to £160. The second class clerks were 12 in number, and the third class 63. The latter thought that, as they had to perform exactly the same duties as the second class clerks, they were very improperly and unfairly treated. He thought it was a matter which ought to be dealt with by the Treasury. The engrossing clerks, also, had a grievance. Those clerks were only paid for the work they did, and he believed that in the aggregate something like £8,000 was paid them. They did important work, because accuracy in the engrossment of the public records was most essential. Some time ago, these clerks sent a Memorial to the Lords Commissioners of the Treasury in which they set forth the most depressing effect which certain recent regulations had had upon them. Amongst others, it was stated that an errors' book was kept, and the result of the audit had been that since the beginning of the year every engrossing clerk had been fined from one month's to 10 weeks' salary. Recently an order had been issued threatening even a more severe punishment; and the Memorialists complained that the suspicions and threatening had a very demoralizing influence upon them, and made them work in daily fear. Now, this was a lamentable state of matters to have in any Public Office. Some of the clerks were obliged to work sometimes 70 hours a-week, and yet their payment was not greater than that made to similar clerks 60 or 70 years ago. He held it was the duty of the Treasury to look into the grievances of these clerks without delay. Another point he had to bring under the notice of the Committee was that the fees for searches charged in the Register House were much larger than necessary, and outsiders took up the business and undersold the Government. It was of importance that the Treasury should look into this matter, and consider whether or not they should any longer permit these high charges to be made, or, on the other hand, should permit outside people to make use of the public records at a very small charge. A further point was that for a great number of years the receipts in this Office had far exceeded the expenses. In the last 10 years, nearly £40,000 had been taken from the pockets of the proprietors of land and houses in Scotland, while the expenses had not reached nearly that amount. Complaints had been made to the Treasury upon this subject, and a Departmental inquiry had been made, but the result had not been satisfactory; and he thought that an inquiry by a Select Committee of that House was the only way of properly dealing with the matter, and no other would be satisfactory to the public, or those more immediately concerned.

MR. J. A. CAMPBELL said, that he had much pleasure in supporting the complaint put forward by his hon. Friend opposite. The grievances of the clerks of the Sasines Office had been frequently brought before the public in recent years, and always in a quiet and temperate manner. He (Mr. J. A. Campbell) thought that the patience and moderation which the clerks of this Office had shown in prosecuting their complaints entitled them to favourable consideration. It was impossible to exaggerate the importance of the Sasines Office to the public; and it was certainly a serious matter that so large a proportion of the staff should be discontented and feel that they had serious grounds for complaint against the Government. The hon. Member for Inverness (Mr. Fraser-Mackintosh) had referred to the number of the third class clerks. These clerks numbered no less than 63, while there were only 12 second class clerks; so that the 63 third class clerks saw little prospect of promotion into the second class. While their remuneration was very much less than that given to the second class clerks, their work was of equal importance. In a Memorial which they presented they stated that the work of the two classes was absolutely the same. It would be seen by reference to the Estimates that the third class clerks began at £90 a-year, and reached no higher salary than £160 a-year, which was £10 less than the minimum salary of second class clerks. In the Treasury Minute, dated March 8th, something like a promise had been made to these third class clerks that their case should be considered, it being stated that the number of the second class clerks would be subjected to revision hereafter when experience had shown to what proportion of the staff it would be necessary to intrust work which they at present performed. These clerks looked upon that as indicating a probability, although it was not an absolute promise, that their case would be reconsidered before much time had elapsed. They felt that now sufficient experience had been obtained of the working of the

Office to enable the Treasury to come to a decision upon their Memorial, and what they asked for was a public inquiry such as was held some years ago with regard to the Deeds Office in Ireland. The hon. Member opposite had also referred to clerks who were described in the Estimates as copyists. Their grievance was that, owing to changes adopted by the Keeper of the Register of Sasines, their power of obtaining emoluments had been reduced, new duties having been imposed upon them which interfered with their opportunities of earning money. Their present rate of pay was the same as it was 70 years ago, but owing to the changes made in the Department they could now only earn 4*d.* for an amount of work for which they formerly received sixpence. The consequence was, that in order to earn a decent livelihood they had to work from 60 to 70 hours a-week. Some time ago there were serious frauds committed in this Office, which were traced to some of the engrossing clerks. It was impossible, of course, to excuse fraud; but, at the same time, when a fraud was committed by an under-paid servant, there was some ground for reflection on the employer as well. The public confidence in this Office had been considerably shaken by the frauds he had referred to, and a very serious reflection was cast upon the general management of the Office. He had no intention of throwing blame on the highly respectable and able gentleman who was Keeper of this Office. He was a man of first-rate position, and great ability, and had introduced many improvements in the administration of the Office. But there was this serious defect, that, being a gentleman in large private practice, he could not devote very much time to the Keepership. He would not say that it might not be the right thing to have a man of his position at the head of the Office, but he would say that if it was, there ought to be a Deputy Keeper also, a professional man of high standing, who could give the whole of his time to the duties of the Office. In answer to the possible objection that this would involve an additional charge, he would repeat what the hon. Member for Inverness had stated, that the Office yielded to Government a large profit—he believed of from £8,000 to £10,000 a-year. There was, therefore, no reason whatever for sparing expense in order to have the work of the Office thoroughly and efficiently done. But in urging on the Government that the Memorial of these clerks should receive favourable consideration, and that a public inquiry into the whole condition and management of this Office should be held, he desired to say that that would be the shortest and the best way of restoring public confidence.

MR. ANDERSON said, that, in supporting what the hon. Member for Inverness had stated, he would like to add that these engrossing clerks had not only complained of the time their duties occupied, but that they were not in any way on the permanent staff. They might go on year after year, but they had no hope of being taken on to the permanent staff. In former years, the permanent staff was open to them; but they were now absolutely debarred from being taken into the third class of clerks, and so from being placed on the permanent staff. That was a great hardship upon them. There was nothing to distinguish them from the other clerks, and there was no reason why they should not have these means of promotion open to them if they were able to pass a Civil Service examination. Some of them, possibly, would not be able to do that, but at least they ought to have the opportunity; and he thought that when vacancies occurred in the third class, preference should be given to these engrossing clerks.

MR. DICK-PEDDIE reminded the Committee that, two years ago, he brought the grievances of these clerks before the House. The grievances of the third class clerks had been well stated by the hon. Member for Inverness, but they had not been stated so fully as they should be. Their chief grievance was not so much that their salaries were inadequate when compared with those of the second class clerks, as that they were inadequate when compared with those of clerks in all other branches of the Civil Service. In this connection it might be well to compare the Register House in Edinburgh with the Registry of Deeds in Ireland. The latter Office contained only 45 first, second, and third class clerks, whose salaries amounted to £12,585; while in the Sasine Department of the Register House in Edinburgh there were 83 clerks, whose salaries amounted to £13,115. If the clerks in Edinburgh were paid at the same rates as the Irish clerks, their salaries should amount to £22,672. The work in the Edinburgh Office was of a very superior kind compared with that in the Dublin Office. In the Edinburgh Office the clerks registered in the public records a great variety of writs affecting land in Scotland, and on the accuracy of those records depended the validity of all titles to land in that country. They were not only required to pass Civil Service examinations, but had to go through a good deal of legal training, and many of them had attended the legal course in the University. In Ireland no such qualification was required. The only qualification there was the passing the Civil Service examination. But the Scotch clerks, doing much more onerous work than those in Ireland, were paid less than two-thirds of the amount paid for inferior work in the Irish Office. In the Sasine Office it was the duty of the third class clerks to prepare minutes of all the deeds presented for registration. In Ireland these minutes were prepared by the solicitors of the persons whose deeds were presented, and thus a large expense fell on the clients of these solicitors from which persons presenting deeds for registration in Scotland were exempt. While all classes of clerks in the Register House in Edinburgh were paid on a much lower scale than that on which the clerks in the Irish Registry of Deeds were paid, the third class clerks in Edinburgh had a special ground for complaint. Not only was the scale of their pay very low, but their chances of promotion were very small. In the Irish Office the third class clerks had a salary beginning at £90 and rising by annual increments of £10 to £170. In the Scottish Office the salary also began at £90, but it rose by annual increments of only £5 to £160. But in Ireland the second and third class clerks were nearly equal in numbers, while in Scotland the second class clerks were 12 in number, and the third class clerks 60. The result was that in Scotland the third class clerks, doing exactly the same work as the second class, had but little chance of promotion, and could hardly look to get into the second class until after 25 to 30 years of service. It might be said that the Irish clerks were overpaid, and that their being so was no reason for overpaying the Scotch clerks; but he did not think the Irish clerks were overpaid, and the Financial Secretary had not, when the Vote was discussed, two years ago, ventured to say that they were. He (Mr. Dick-Peddie) believed that they were underpaid. When he brought this matter forward, two years ago, the Financial Secretary to the Treasury stated, as a justification for this low rate of pay, that the Government could easily find other persons able and willing to do this work at the same rate. If they were to act upon that test, they might, perhaps, be able to effect a large saving in many Departments of the Public Service, and might begin with advantage by applying it to some of the occupants of the Treasury Bench. He cordially supported the suggestion that a Select Committee should be appointed to inquire into this case, as was done in the case of the Irish Deeds Office some years ago.

SIR R. ASSHETON CROSS said, that this was a question which in former years he had considered, and the first conclusion he came to was that these clerks had always put forward their grievances in the best spirit of moderation. He was certain it would be for the public advantage that, if the alleged grievances did exist, the clerks should at least feel that their case had been fully inquired into before a resolution was come to upon the subject. They had sent Memorials to the Treasury; but they felt that those Memorials had never been properly attended to, as similar Memorials from the Irish Office had been some years ago. An Office of such importance as this to the country should be above all suspicion of error in any way, and the clerks should, at all events, be satisfied that there had been a full inquiry into their grievances. They were not satisfied at present, and he thought it rested with the Government to accede to their extremely just claim. This was an Office which returned a large sum of money to the Treasury, and these clerks were not asking for a single farthing beyond what was fair. They were putting a large sum of money into the Treasury; and, while he agreed that the Treasury should see that a proper margin of profit was obtained from this Department, they ought to give the clerks, who earned the money, proper remuneration. But there was no chance of the Treasury suffering, and he believed that before long it would become a fair question whether the fees charged at this Office should not be diminished. That was a matter which would have to be thoroughly discussed; and he hoped that the whole subject would receive the earnest consideration of the Government. He wished to put one question to the Lord Advocate upon another point affecting the Registry of Deeds. There were two systems of working up the arrears, and it was decided that both systems should be kept up, in order that there should not be any arrears. But he could not imagine why the official staff had not been employed in this work? He was perfectly aware of the great services rendered in this Office by Mr. Brodie; but he thought Mr. Brodie's time was so much occupied with other matters that he had not sufficient leisure for the duties of this Office; and he urged that whenever a vacancy occurred in the post which Mr. Brodie held, some person should be appointed to it who would be able to devote very much more time to its duties.

MR. COURTNEY stated that the amount of salary of clerks and payment of copyists came to £25,550 a-year; but there must be added to that amount two items, before it was possible to obtain a just account of profit and loss—namely, the amount for pensions, which was, in fact, deferred pay, and the amount for stationery. The Non-Effective Vote for the whole Office was £4,800. As a matter of fact, this Office only just paid its way. The right hon. Gentleman (Sir R. Assheton Cross) had expressed the opinion that the application of these clerks was a just one. [Sir R. ASSHETON CROSS: A just application for inquiry.] Well, did the right hon. Gentleman know whether there had been an inquiry? This Office was the subject of an inquiry in 1881, upon an application of the Departmental clerks. With regard to the different classes of clerks in this Office, the grievance was that the copyists did not become third class clerks, and the third class clerks did not become second class clerks. The third class clerks were in an enviable position when copyists were talked of, and in a deplorable position when their own claims were urged. He wished to put it to the Scotch Members, whether they were going to pay for what was, to a large extent, only routine work the same rates which prevailed in mercantile offices, or whether they were going to pay some fancy rates fixed by the judgment of the clerks themselves? The appeals made by the Scotch Members were appeals to the benevolence of that House, at the cost of the taxpayers of the United Kingdom. There was nothing that he was aware of to render it necessary to deal with this Office on principles different from those which were applied in the case of other branches of the Civil Service. The claim of these clerks, which the right hon. Gentleman opposite (Sir R. Assheton Cross) said was a just one, had been duly examined at the time when the Office was re-arranged in 1881. Since then, he believed that two Memorials had been received, and in each case the position of the clerks had been reconsidered. The Petition of the clerks, referred to particularly by the hon. Member for Inverness (Mr. Fraser-Mackintosh) and by the hon. Member for the Glasgow and Aberdeen Universities (Mr. J. A. Campbell), had been fully considered two months ago. Application had been made to Edinburgh for further light upon the matter; but in view of the Report received, and of the Memorials themselves, the Treasury had not seen any ground for acceding to the application for an improvement of terms. He very much regretted that the rate of remuneration of writers should be so low; the Treasury would be glad to see an improvement in that respect; but they could not increase the salaries of these individuals at the expense of the taxpayers of the country. Very proper rules had been laid down in the Office to insure the correctness of the copying work, one of which was that the copyists should be fined for errors. It was, in his opinion, perfectly just that the consequences of these errors should, to some extent, be visited on those who made them; the Memorialists, however, asked to to relieved from the consequences of their own carelessness. That application had been fairly considered; it had been judged on its merits; it had been referred and reported upon; and the Government were obliged to say, reluctantly, that it was impossible to accede to the principles set forth in the Memorial. In replying to the appeals of the hon. Member for Inverness, and other hon. and right hon. Gentlemen, he addressed himself to a general principle, and upon that general principle he felt that the common sense of the

House, as well as public opinion, should resist these appplications for increased pay at the expense of the taxpayer.

COLONEL NOLAN said, that there were no less than 12 men in the Registry of Deeds Office, Edinburgh, who got £500 a-year, as compared with four persons in the Irish Office. Then, with regard to the whole number of Curators and Assistant Keepers, with salaries rising to £550 a-year, there was nothing like a corresponding arrangement in the Dublin Office. He thought the hon. Gentleman the Secretary to the Treasury had not gone with sufficient fulness into the case, and that hon. Members on those Benches would require some further particulars. Their contention was that the Civil Service system, as between the two countries, should be the same, and if a Committee were moved for to consider whether the *employés* should be dealt with in the same way he should support the Motion.

DR. CAMERON said, he thought that a great deal more might be done with regard to this Office in the interest of the taxpayer than had been done. He was amused at the facility with which that rigid political economist the Secretary to the Treasury denounced appeals to the benevolence of the House of Commons, and also at his remark that men must be justly punished if they made mistakes. Why, the Keeper of the Registry of Sasines received £1,000 a-year as salary, and Parliament had decreed that he should devote the whole of his time to that important Office. But he and his hon. Friends had heard that he had another Office, and that his present business left him no time to attend to the important duties of the Register House. He asked where was this severe application of the principles of political economy to begin and to end? All they asked was that there should be an inquiry into the condition of affairs at the Register House. He reminded the Committee that in the course of the trial of certain clerks of the Office, one of the counsel declared that the Register House was rotten from top to bottom. Departmental inquiries, under such circumstances, were of no use, because the only desire would be to hush up the bulk of the jobs that were perpetrated. The appointment of a Committee of Inquiry, composed of Members of that House, would, he was convinced, be attended with very different results; and although the conduct of some overpaid officials in connection with the Department might be gone into, the result, in his opinion, could not fail to be of benefit to the public interest. The Secretary to the Treasury had stated that the surplus of the Department derived from the fees was not great; but that was not due to the amount paid for the labour of copyists and clerks. With regard to the alteration in the arrangements to which the hon. Gentleman the Secretary to the Treasury had referred, he reminded the Committee that it was only when the state of things at the Register House became a public scandal, and a lively interest was taken in it by the people, that any reform was introduced, and then all that was done was to adopt the Glasgow system which had been for years in operation with regard to the registration of titles. But there was another point. His hon. Friend the Member for the Inverness Burghs (Mr. Fraser-Mackintosh) had referred to the great difference between the charges made by private and official searchers, and the result this difference had in throwing business into the hands of private searchers. He would ask whether the interest of the taxpayer might not be served by reducing the large official charges? Finally, he thought every reason pointed to the desirability of instituting a public inquiry in order to see whether the working of the Department might be improved, and whether they could cut down the salaries of men who, although highly paid, did not attend to their work. For these reasons, if his hon. Friend divided the Committee on his Amendment, he should certainly support him.

THE LORD ADVOCATE (Mr. J. B. BALFOUR) said, there was one point in the statement of the hon. Member for Glasgow which he could not pass over without reply. His hon. Friend had quoted the observation of counsel in a trial which had taken place, and which observation he was afraid was used with forensic licence, to the effect that the Register House was rotten from top to bottom. That was a statement well known to all acquainted with the Office to be entirely unfounded. It was made in the course of the trial of certain clerks who had been guilty of certain frauds in connection with the charges they made for copying. It appeared, in the course of the inquiry, that in the lower department there was a deficiency of check with regard to the counting of the number of words in each page of work, and the result was that safeguards were introduced for checking the amount of work done. The suggestion that the head of the Department, or the large number of clerks in the Office who had their responsible duties to discharge, should count the words in the copy, was really too extravagant to be seriously treated in the House of Commons. Everyone in the Office was responsible, according to his degree, for the work which he had to do, and for seeing that those below him did their duty.

Mr. RAMSAY said, he had been in expectation that the right hon. and learned Gentleman the Lord Advocate would have been able to favour the Committee with some proofs that the Department was in all respects efficient. The right hon. and learned Gentleman had simply referred to some complaint that had been made with regard to the condition of the work in one of the Departments of the Office; but he had not shown that the Office was in a state of efficiency. It was to have been expected that the Government would take into their consideration the complaints which had been made, and not alone the complaints with regard to the position of the clerks; because his hon. Friend had, in bringing that matter forward, other objects in view than the mere raising of salaries. He agreed with the hon. Gentleman the Secretary to the Treasury that for a number of men to enter an office upon well-understood conditions, and then to make complaints with regard to the salaries they received, was not just. He thought that the fair market value of their services, which the taxpayers of the country were willing to pay, was the proper pay of persons employed in the Public Service; and that, he believed, was the rule which should guide the Treasury when they were dealing with questions of this kind. But he was not satisfied that this establishment was as efficient as it might be made; and, therefore, he agreed that a thorough investigation should take place at no distant period. He considered, also, that there should be no undue distinction with regard to the clerks—that their case should be considered and justice done. He trusted, therefore, that there would be an official investigation which would satisfy those in the Public Service that they were being cared for, and that they were receiving what was a proper return for their services.

Mr. BIGGAR thought that, as a general rule, Government *employés* in Edinburgh or Dublin were not entitled to as much remuneration as if they were employed in London. It was well known that rents were higher in London than in Dublin or in Edinburgh. ["No!"] An hon. Member said "No!" but he had seen houses in London let at much higher rents than those of the same quality and size in Dublin and Edinburgh. There was not the least doubt about that point; and, besides, many things were sold at a higher rate of profit in London than in other cities. Therefore, he said, no argument could be established on that ground for reconsidering these salaries. Again, no account seemed to be taken by hon. Members of the difference of cost of land and building so far as concerned the premises in which the work of these Departments was carried on.

The CHAIRMAN (Mr. Raikes): I would point out to the hon. Member that the Question now before the Committee is that of the expenses of the Register House, Edinburgh.

Mr. BIGGAR said, he merely wished to point out that the value of the premises in which these Departments were placed was an important factor in the calculation. It was argued that the fees exceeded in amount the outlay in payment of officials; and he was drawing attention to the fact that the hon. Gentleman who used that argument lost sight of the value of the houses in which the business was carried on.

Mr. FRASER-MACKINTOSH said, as the Government had held out no hope that an inquiry would be held, he felt it his duty to move the reduction of the Vote by the sum of £500.

Motion made, and Question proposed,

"That a sum, not exceeding £24,103, be granted to Her Majesty, to complete the sum necessary to defray the Charge which will come in course of payment during the year ending on the 31st day of March 1885, for the Salaries and Expenses of the Offices in Her Majesty's General Register House, Edinburgh." — (*Mr. Fraser-Mackintosh.*)

COLONEL NOLAN contended that the only true principle to apply in matters of this kind was that the Civil Service *employés* should be paid the same in the Three Kingdoms. His hon. Friend the Member for Cavan (Mr. Biggar) was, of course, entitled to his opinion on the subject of the relative cost of living in Dublin and London; but he (Colonel Nolan) was also able to form some opinion on that matter, and the conclusion he had arrived at was that there was no difference. It was true that owing to the fact of the Union a large number of old houses in Dublin were let at low rents.

Question put.

The Committee *divided:* — Ayes 19; Noes 64: Majority 45.—(Div. List, No. 186.)

Original Question put, and *agreed to.*

(6.) £79,897, to complete the sum for Prisons (Scotland).

DR. CAMERON said, there was one item in this Vote to which he wished to call attention—attention, he believed, never having been called to it before. He would ask his right hon. Friend the Lord Advocate and the hon. Gentleman the Secretary to the Treasury to look into the matter. In the list of prisons there was the prison of Jedburgh, which was almost entirely useless—that was to say, it would be useless were it not for the number of persons imprisoned in it under the Tweed Fisheries Acts. These were most iniquitous Acts, which enabled persons to be imprisoned on the evidence of a single witness. There was nothing analogous to them in Scotland. Only the other day several persons had been imprisoned on perjured evidence. It was true that when the circumstances were represented to the Home Secretary he instantly had the men released. He need not say, however, that no action had been taken against the perjurers. It was preposterous that this prison should be retained and kept up at the public expense merely for the benefit of the proprietors of the Tweed fisheries, and the maintenance of an iniquitous law. He hoped the matter would be remedied, or, at any rate, that the fishery proprietors would not be allowed to conduct these prosecutions under an entirely exceptional system of law. He trusted the right hon. and learned Gentleman would look into the subject, at least, to the extent of seeing that persons confined in Jedburgh Gaol were confined on the same evidence as was required in the case of any other criminals.

THE LORD ADVOCATE (Mr. J. B. BALFOUR) promised to look into the matter.

MR. RAMSAY asked the right hon. and learned Gentleman to give instructions to the Commissioners to separate the Criminal Lunacy Department from the other Departments. They had had separate accounts prepared for some years, but had not this year; and that he felt to be a defect. The system of separate accounts had enabled them to contrast the expenditure on criminal lunatics at Perth with the charge made for persons of the same class at Broadmoor, and other Criminal Lunatic Asylums. He did not wish to delay the Committee by proposing any reduction of the Vote; but he thought it would be satisfactory to have these separate accounts, and regretted that they were not shown in the present Estimate.

MR. HIBBERT said, he quite agreed that it was better to have the accounts separated; but there was some difficulty in the way of the arrangement. He would see what could be done in the matter in the future.

MR. HARRINGTON said, he saw an item of £648 for the maintenance of prisoners in police cells. He would like to ask the hon. Gentleman for what time, on an average, were prisoners kept in police cells? They saw no such charge in the Irish Prison Estimates. He mentioned this matter, as he wished to ascertain whether prisoners were detained in prison a very long time before being brought to trial. £648 seemed a very large item, and it must either represent a very large number of prisoners detained for a short time in police cells, or a small number detained for a long time.

THE LORD ADVOCATE (Mr. J. B. BALFOUR) said, the charge covered the entire country. There were some places where there were no gaols, but only a certain number of police cells, licensed for giving short terms of imprisonment—terms of 14 days. Licences were given to these places for the detention of prisoners for short periods, so as to avoid the trouble and expense of having to remove them to the more important places of detention, which might be some distance away.

Mr. HARRINGTON asked whether he was to understand that these so-called "police cells" included not only ordinary barrack cells, but also special places of confinement?

The LORD ADVOCATE (Mr. J. B. Balfour): We have no "barrack cells" in Scotland. I cannot say whether the Scotch prison system is in any way similar to the Irish.

Mr. HARRINGTON said, he desired to put a question on another subject—namely, the grants to the Discharged Prisoners' Aid Society. The item was a very small one, and it would seem that it had reference to some one particular prisoner—it would seem that some one prisoner had been aided in a particular town. If the item covered aid to more than one prisoner the amount given in each case must be very small. He (Mr. Harrington) did not wish to be understood as taking exception to the Vote. To his mind it was a Vote for a most laudable purpose, and his desire would be rather to extend the assistance under such a Vote than anything else. Could the right hon. and learned Gentleman the Lord Advocate tell him how the Vote was disposed of—whether it was given to one prisoner or more, and where it was given?

The LORD ADVOCATE (Mr. J. B. Balfour) said, the item covered several grants, no one of them exceeding £2 in amount. He had the details with him if the hon. Member desired to have them. The grants were distributed very widely. With regard to the other subject mentioned just now by the hon. Member, he found, from the details as to the detention of prisoners in Scotland, that the detentions in the police cells varied from one to seven days. In some places the average was four days, in others only one; but nowhere was there a longer detention than seven days.

Vote *agreed to.*

(7.) £60,066, to complete the sum for the Supreme Court of Judicature in Ireland.

(8.) £785, to complete the sum for the Admiralty Court Registry, Ireland.

(9.) £1,513, to complete the sum for the Registry of Judgments, Ireland.

Motion made, and Question proposed,

"That a sum, not exceeding £99,980, be granted to Her Majesty, to complete the sum necessary to defray the Charge which will come in course of payment during the year ending on the 31st day of March 1885, for the Expenses of the General Prisons Board in Ireland, and of the Prisons under their control; and of the Registration of Habitual Criminals."

Mr. HEALY: No, no!

Mr. SEXTON: I must ask the Government to postpone this Vote, as several matters which will have to be discussed arise upon it.

Mr. HEALY: I move that the Chairman do report Progress.

Motion made, and Question proposed, "That the Chairman do report Progress, and ask leave to sit again."—(*Mr. Healy.*)

Mr. COURTNEY: I am afraid if we persevered with this it would lead to some difficulty. I would propose not to go on with it if the Motion for Progress is withdrawn.

Motion, by leave, *withdrawn.*

Original Motion, by leave, *withdrawn.*

Motion made, and Question proposed,

"That a sum, not exceeding £51,944, be granted to Her Majesty, to complete the sum necessary to defray the Charge which will come in course of payment during the year ending on the 31st day of March 1885, for the Expenses of Reformatory and Industrial Schools in Ireland."

Colonel NOLAN said, he did not wish to detain the Committee very long on this Vote; but there was just one matter to which he desired to call the attention of the Chief Secretary to the Lord Lieutenant.

Mr. HEALY: Postpone the Vote.

Colonel NOLAN said, he only desired to draw the attention of the Chief Secretary to the desirability of having an industrial school for boys at Clifden, in Connemara. There was a school for girls, and it was very necessary that there should be one for boys also. The nearest boys' industrial school to the Clifden district at the present time was a long way off, and he, therefore, trusted the right hon. Gentleman the Chief Secretary would bear this appeal in mind.

Mr. SEXTON said, he had an objection to the Vote being taken at all to-night. He had been in communication with some of the Irish officials as to the state of the schools in the Province of Connaught; but as yet had not received all the information he desired. He was now waiting for an answer, and, therefore, would ask for the postponement of the Vote.

MR. TREVELYAN: Does the hon. Member say he has been in communication with the Irish Government?

MR. SEXTON: No; not with the right hon. Gentleman, but with some of the local officials.

MR. HEALY: We have given several Irish Votes without discussion, and I think the right hon. Gentleman ought in fairness to postpone this one.

MR. COURTNEY said, it would not take the Committee very long to dispose of this Vote. The rest might be adjourned.

MR. HEALY: To Monday?

MR. COURTNEY: No; he was afraid the Army Estimates would have to be taken on Monday. The present Vote it would be well to consider to-night, and the Votes postponed now would have a better chance of full discussion if deferred until to-morrow; because, if deferred until any other day, several important Votes already postponed would have to be considered before them.

MR. SEXTON said, it was impossible for Irish Members to assent to the discussion of the Vote for Industrial and Reformatory Schools now. He thought the Irish Members had acted in the matter most reasonably, and that the Government were most unreasonable in now seeking to press the Vote. As he had already stated, he was in communication with certain local officials in Ireland, but had not yet received the full explanation he desired.

MR. MOORE said, he hoped the right hon. Gentleman the Chief Secretary would not press the Vote to-night. He looked upon the policy of the Government on this subject as most questionable, and did not see what object the right hon. Gentleman could have in desiring to embarrass the working of these institutions in Ireland. He (Mr. Moore) found it necessary to make frequent complaints as to the working of these institutions; and he certainly thought a little time should be allowed to enable them to go thoroughly into the matter. He earnestly hoped the Government would not expect or ask them to go on with the Vote at this hour. If the Government insisted, it would be necessary for the Irish Members to resist them.

MR. COURTNEY said, he thought he had given a very reasonable argument when he said that if the Vote were postponed it would only come on some other day after a number of other deferred Votes, when the opportunity for discussion might not be so good as today. However, if hon. Gentlemen opposite did not agree with him, he would withdraw the Vote.

Motion, by leave, *withdrawn.*

(10.) £4,066, to complete the sum for the Dundrum Criminal Lunatic Asylum, Ireland.

MR. COURTNEY: We will go on with Class IV. now.

MR. HEALY: No, no!

Vote *agreed to.*

CLASS IV.—EDUCATION, SCIENCE, AND ART.

Motion made, and Question proposed,

"That a sum, not exceeding £284,825, be granted to Her Majesty, to complete the sum necessary to defray the Charge which will come in course of payment during the year ending on the 31st day of March 1885, for the Salaries and Expenses of the Science and Art Department, and of the Establishments connected therewith."

MR. WARTON said, he would move that the Chairman do report Progress. This was Friday night, at the end of a long week of hard work, and he thought the least the Government could do would be to report Progress.

Motion made, and Question proposed, "That the Chairman do report Progress, and ask leave to sit again."—(*Mr. Warton.*)

MR. HEALY said, the Irish Members had been under the fond delusion that if they allowed the last Class to pass they would no longer be kept there; at any rate, that they would not be kept, as they were yesterday, until 4 o'clock in the morning. The Irish Members had allowed several Irish Votes which they might have discussed to pass—Votes the very reasonable discussion of which would have occupied at least an hour and a-half. The Government themselves had felt the inconvenience of the long night they had had yesterday—they had shown how oppressed they were by being unable to attend in their places at 4 o'clock this afternoon,

They had got a big bunch of Votes to-night; but yet they desired, in the most gluttonous manner possible, to go on still further.

THE CHANCELLOR OF THE EXCHEQUER (Mr. CHILDERS): I think there is something in what the hon. Gentleman says; therefore, we will not press more Votes to-night. The House, however, ought to be aware that it will be very hard work to get the Votes through in good time.

MR. SEXTON: Are we to understand that the Irish Votes in Class III. will be taken on Tuesday?

MR. COURTNEY: Yes.

MR. WARTON: Will the Irish Vote No. 22 in Class I.—which was struck out for some unaccountable reason—be taken then? Why was that Vote kept out?

MR. COURTNEY: Yes; that Vote will be taken. As hon. Gentlemen acquainted with the matter are aware, there was great difficulty in going on with the Vote in question.

Resolutions to be reported upon *Monday* next.

Committee also report Progress; to sit again upon *Monday* next.

PUBLIC WORKS LOANS BILL.

(*Mr. Courtney, Mr. Herbert Gladstone.*)

[BILL 299.] COMMITTEE.

Bill *considered* in Committee.

(In the Committee.)

MR. MARJORIBANKS said, he rose for the purpose of moving a new clause, to come in after Clause 2. The clause ran in this way—

(Advances to be made at three and a-half per cent.)

"Notwithstanding anything in the Public Works Loans Act, 1879 (42 & 43 Vic. c. 77), the rate of interest on loans granted by the Public Works Loan Commissioners under the authorisation of the Harbours and Passing Tolls Act 1861 (24 & 25 Vic. c. 47) shall not exceed the rate of £3 10*s*. per annum on each £100 where the aggregate amount of principal money due to the said Commissioners from any one harbour authority, in pursuance of the said Harbour and Passing Tolls Act, does not exceed £100,000."

The object of this clause was simply to place the conditions under which Harbour Authorities could obtain loans on exactly the same footing as they were prior to 1879, with this one exception—that the rate of interest he now proposed was 3½ per cent instead of 3¼. He thought it quite possible that 3¼ per cent might not leave sufficient margin to enable the Treasury to recoup itself for expenses of management or losses; but he was perfectly certain that 3½ would leave quite sufficient margin, and that no loss could possibly accrue to the Treasury. His contention was that loans for harbours should not be treated as ordinary loans. The Harbours and Passing Tolls Act was passed in order to relieve the country from making large grants for the purpose of harbour construction. The Act was to enable works to be carried out by means of loans which were going to be of national use and profit; and it was a hard thing that faith should be broken with Harbour Authorities, and that they should be treated on the same footing as borrowers for purposes of much less national importance in regard to the rate of interest they had to pay. He was quite aware that a very considerable loss had accrued from these various loans which had been made by the State. These figures had been given. In 1879 the amount of interest receivable at 3 per cent on all the loans which had been granted up to that time was £10,095,000, whereas the actual amount received was only £9,361,000, being a loss, on the whole, of £734,000; but no such loss had occurred with regard to harbour loans. The amount of interest received on loans under the Harbours and Passing Tolls Act since 1861 was £897,381; the amount that would have been receivable at 3¼ per cent was £890,964, being £6,427 less than the sum actually received, whereas, if the rate of interest had been calculated at 3 per cent, there was a balance of £75,000. Therefore, so far as interest was concerned, there had been no loss on these harbour loans; so that, in all probability, were a uniform rate of 3½ per cent charged, there would be enough margin to enable the Treasury to recoup itself for expenses of management or such losses as might possibly occur. He hoped the right hon. Gentleman the Chancellor of the Exchequer would show some pity towards the harbours, and would accept the small proposal he was venturing to make.

New Clause (Advances to be made at three and a-half per cent,)—(*Mr. Marjoribanks*,)—*brought up*, and read the first time.

Motion made, and Question proposed, "That the Clause be now read a second time."

THE CHANCELLOR OF THE EXCHEQUER (Mr. CHILDERS): My hon. Friend has taken a course which I think is without precedent, and which very nearly approaches to a violation of the Rule under which our financial Business is conducted. I do not think there has been, on any previous occasion, a proposal made by a private Member to introduce into a Bill of this kind, which does not deal with questions of interest at all, a clause amending, for the purpose of this Act, the Act of 1879, and thereby imposing a charge on the public. If my hon. Friend's clause is passed, the consequence will be that in future there will be a diminution of interest on these loans, which will thereby become an additional charge on the taxpayers. At the same time, I cannot say that, although that is the effect of my hon. Friend's proposal, it is distinctly a breach of the Standing Order; so I do not take exception to it on that ground. But, whether it is so or not, it is undoubtedly opposed to the spirit and the custom which regulates our financial transactions; and I hope that on that account it will not receive the support of the Committee. Under the Act of 1861, these loans below £100,000 paid 3½ per cent; but it soon became evident that those loans did not leave such a margin as would relieve the Government and the taxpayer from loss, and the result was that in 1879 the right hon. Baronet the Member for North Devon, who was then Chancellor of the Exchequer, introduced a general Act fixing the rates of interest to be paid on loans of all kinds, but giving, at the same time, to the Treasury a relaxing power with reference to them. That proposal cannot be said to have been lightly discussed in this House, for it raised considerable debate, and no little difference of opinion. [Mr. SEXTON: What was the rate you first mentioned?] The rate was 3½ per cent for sums under £100,000, and for sums above £100,000 a rate not exceeding £5 per cent. The right hon. Gentleman the then Chancellor of the Exchequer introduced, therefore, into the Act of 1879 a provision putting all loans upon the same footing, assigning a scale of from 3½ to 4½ per cent with reference to the duration of the loan. I was saying that that proposal was fully discussed in this House; and although there was much difference of opinion upon certain questions, I remember that the House was distinctly in favour of the proposal laying down a general rule, and giving the Treasury a relaxing power; and now my hon. Friend proposes to take loans for harbours out of the general category, to take away the power of the Treasury under the Act of 1879, and to lay down a hard-and-fast line for all loans made with regard to harbours.

MR. MARJORIBANKS: Under £100,000.

THE CHANCELLOR OF THE EXCHEQUER (Mr. CHILDERS): Under £100,000, whatever their duration may be.

MR. MARJORIBANKS: That only refers to loans under the Harbours and Passing Tolls Act, and they cannot be for a longer period than 50 years; therefore, it is not for any undefined period whatever.

THE CHANCELLOR OF THE EXCHEQUER (Mr. CHILDERS): My hon. Friend has not looked at the construction of his clause. He proposes that 3½ per cent should be charged, whether the term is 25, 30, or 40 years. Before I come to the manner in which I propose to deal with my hon. Friend's proposal, let me put to the Committee what are the facts in reference to the risks which the taxpayer runs in making these loans to harbours. Up to the present time, we have advanced to harbours, under the Act of 1861, the sum of £2,600,000, roughly. Of that amount £34,000 have been written off, and about £70,000 of principal are in arrear at the present moment, so that, instead of receiving 3½ per cent interest, we have actually been paid £25,00 to £30,000 less on the amounts advanced. The House must thus remember that there is a considerable amount of money, in connection with these loans, either lost, or in danger of being lost. Now, my hon. Friend seems to think that there is something peculiar in harbours, which makes advances for harbours more secure than advances for other purposes. I am bound to say that the fact is just the reverse. The operations of the sea are so uncertain and so destructive that these works are subject to great and perilous influences to which other works are not exposed; and I find that at the present time harbour loans are by no means secure; for instance, at Wick and Port Erin; and, therefore, so far from making special exceptions in favour of harbour loans, if any exception were to be made at all, I think it should be in an opposite direction. Under these circumstances, I think that the Committee would do very unwisely to run counter to the position which was taken by the late Government in 1879, when the scale of rates was fixed by the Bill brought in by the right hon. Gentleman the Member for North Devon (Sir Stafford Northcote), when he was Chancellor of the Exchequer. But my hon. Friend would expect something more from me than that. I have said that I think it would be unwise to take from the Treasury the power they have under this Act of 1879; and I think I can give reasons why that should not be done, and why a hard-and-fast line of 3½ per cent, whatever may be the duration of the loan, would not be wise; and I will state to the Committee how I should propose to deal with this question, if the matter is still left, as I hope the House will allow it to be, to the discretion of the Treasury. What I would ask of the House is not to disturb the discretion of the Treasury in dealing with these loans, and not to take from the general category of the Act of 1879 these particular loans, but to allow the Treasury to retain their powers under that Act. But I will state, at the same time, what, if that is the case, we hope to do before the House meets in 1885, in dealing, not with these loans only, but with the whole of the loans made by the Public Works Loans Commissioners. The present scale, under the Act of 1879, is that interest shall be calculated for a period not exceeding 20 years at 3½ per cent; for a period not exceeding 30 years, at 3¾ per cent; and for a period not exceeding 40 years, at 4 per cent, or, exceeding 40 years, 4½ per cent, What we hope to do is this. Whenever collateral security is offered, as will be the case with respect to many of these works, we will deduct something from these rates—I do not say how much. Then, in addition to that, I think the time has come when we may revise the basis of the rate at which the Government can advance money; so that the scale now in force under the Act of 1879 would be subject to two deductions—one in respect to the cheaper rate of interest, and one in respect to the rate at which, when there is collateral security, these loans should be made to Local Authorities. The effect of this would be perceptibly to reduce the rate of interest charged for these loans. What I will promise my hon. Friend and the Committee is that during the Recess I will take this question into consideration, not only with regard to harbours, but with regard to other advances which should receive attention. I will undertake to apply the two modifications of the scale which I have explained; and I will undertake, before the Session of 1885, that special arrangements shall be completed, and that the new scales shall come into operation. I hope that after that promise the Committee will not adopt the clause fixing one single line as to interest.

Mr. SCLATER-BOOTH said, that, of course, the House was anxious that these public works should be carried out, if with public money, at a moderate rate of interest. Parliament had committed itself to the view that a considerable risk should be run; but, from the manner in which he had spoken, it would seem that the right hon. Gentleman thought the whole House was in favour of a reduction of the rates of interest on public loans. All that Members wished was that the interest should be moderate, and that the loans should be safe. He thought the right hon. Gentleman might have gone a step further, and explained that this Motion had been made without Notice. He had never heard of a question of so much importance being raised at 2 o'clock in the morning without Notice. When public finances were in question, it was only reasonable that proper Notice should be given of the terms of the proposal. Certainly, many Members would have left the House but for the fact that, by the accident of a mere question, they had learnt from the Chancellor of the Exchequer that the Vote was to be brought on. He should, therefore, support the Chancellor of the Exchequer in resistiug this Motion; and, indeed, he should hope that, after what had occurred, the hon. Member would not divide upon the Motion. By this Motion the hon. Member came very near violating the wholesome principle that private Members could not be allowed to propose Motions of this kind.

THE CHAIRMAN (Mr. RAIKES): I understood from the hon. Member that this proposition was intended to apply only to future loans; but the clause appears to me to be retrospective, and to apply to existing loans. The hon. Member must put himself in Order by making the clause apply to future loans.

MR. MARJORIBANKS said, he only intended the clause to apply to future loans.

THE CHAIRMAN (Mr. RAIKES): The hon. Member must make that clear. In my opinion, the clause as it stands is retrospective.

MR. MARJORIBANKS said, he would amend the clause by inserting before the word "granted," in line 2, the words "to be."

Question, "That those words be there inserted," put, and *agreed to.*

MR. ARTHUR ARNOLD said, his hon. Friend had presided over a Committee of this House of which he had been a Member, and every Member of the House must be indebted to him for his labours. But after the frank and conciliatory statement of the Chancellor of the Exchequer, he hoped the hon. Member would see fit not to proceed with his Motion, but would wait for a future debate on the subject, when the Report of the Committee on Harbours had been presented.

MR. SEXTON said, that this subject had come under the consideration of, and had given rise to some unsatisfactory remarks by, the Secretary to the Treasury. The hon. Member for Berwickshire was entitled to speak with some authority on this subject. The Chancellor of the Exchequer had mentioned a sum of £600,000, of which he said £30,000 had been written off, so that in a quarter of a century there had been a very heavy loss on the capital sum. It was too early to assume anything as to the remainder; but the right hon. Gentleman had said that the Treasury were now able to borrow money at 2¾ per cent, so that their position had improved something like ½ per cent. As to harbour loans being particularly perilous, he thought the argument was as much in favour of the hon. Member as of the Government; because, considering the national utility and a ue of these harbours and the great difficulty of prosecuting them to a successful conclusion, if the Government pursued a generous policy, the very fact that these harbours were perilous investments showed that they were entitled to special attention from the Government. What was the difference between the hon. Member and the Government? The right hon. Gentleman acknowledged that the Government had power to do what the hon. Member asked. They had a maximum scale, so that they could do what the hon. Member asked. Between the letter of the Act of Parliament and the discretion of the Treasury, he preferred the letter of the Act, so far as Ireland was concerned, because they had always found in Ireland that where the discretion of the Treasury operated, a harsh, rather than a generous, system was applied. The discretion of the Treasury meant a harsh policy towards Ireland, and he should prefer to have a rate of 3½ per cent under the clause proposed by the hon. Member, than 3½ or 4½ per cent under the Treasury. In the County Sligo the Harbour Authorities laboured under great difficulties; and he would recommend the Government not to pursue a stingy policy, but to advance these loans at as low a rate as they could. He considered that the hon. Member had taken a proper course, for this was a Bill dealing with public loans, and he simply proposed a clause fixing the rate of interest. A more proper occasion could not have been taken for bringing this matter before the House, and he was surprised at any objection being raised by a Radical Cabinet. He would conclude with one remark—namely, that they had reduced the rate of interest by 1 per cent on railway loans.

MR. MARJORIBANKS said, Harbour Trusts did not need to come to the Government at all to borrow money at 4½ per cent, because they could raise it at that rate in the open market. In order to carry out the Act of 1861, they should be able to borrow money at the lowest possible rate of interest—not more than 3½ per cent. He much regretted that he should have to trouble the Committee to divide on his Motion.

MR. DAWSON said, that the right hon. Gentleman the Chancellor of the Exchequer had argued that the danger to which the works were exposed was a reason why the Committee should support him in opposing the Motion of the hon. Member for Berwick ; but he would remind the right hon. Gentleman that these works were not constructed for individual benefit, but in the interest of the nation. The right hon. Gentleman must be aware of what the Colonial Governments had done in matters of this kind; they had carried out the works knowing that, owing to the great peril to which they were exposed, private persons could not undertake them. That, he said, was a reason *à fortiori* why the Government should come forward and assist in the construction of harbours in the three Kingdoms. But there was this difference between the Government and the hon. Member for Berwickshire—if the Motion of the hon. Member were carried, the reduction of the rates of interest would be effected by Act of Parliament at once, instead of remaining dependent upon the chances referred to by the right hon. Gentleman. He trusted the Committee would support the Motion for the second reading of the clause.

Question put.

The Committee *divided*:—Ayes 27; Noes 45: Majority 18.—(Div. List, No. 187.)

Bill *reported*, without Amendment; to be read the third time upon *Monday* next.

ULSTER CANAL AND TYRONE NAVIGATION [COST OF REPAIRS].

Considered in Committee.

(In the Committee.)

Motion made, and Question proposed,

"That it is expedient to authorize the payment, out of moneys to be provided by Parliament, of the Costs of Repairs of the Canals, which may become payable under the provisions of any Act of the present Session to transfer the Ulster Canal and the Tyrone Navigation to the Lagan Navigation Company."

COLONEL NOLAN wished to know whether the Government intended to bring in a Bill to provide compensation for the lowering of the value of the land which might be flooded in consequence of the canals not being efficiently kept up? He was prepared to draw up and submit a clause to the Government, which he would ask them to insert in the present Bill.

MR. COURTNEY said, he was not in a position to give any promise of the kind asked for by the hon. and gallant Member for Galway. In the present case there was nothing before the Committee but a Resolution. Another opportunity would present itself for discussing the question to which the hon. and gallant Member referred.

MR. HEALY said, they were anxious that no power should be given to the Company taking over this canal that would have the effect of damaging the interests of the district.

Question put, and *agreed to*.

Resolved, That it is expedient to authorise the payment, out of moneys to be provided by Parliament, of the Costs of Repairs of the Canals, which may become payable under the provisions of any Act of the present Session to transfer the Ulster Canal and the Tyrone Navigation to the Lagan Navigation Company.

Resolution to be reported upon *Monday* next.

MAGISTRATES (IRELAND) SALARIES BILL.—[BILL 292.]

(*Mr. Courtney, Mr. Trevelyan.*)

SECOND READING.

Order for Second Reading read.

Motion made, and Question proposed, "That the Second Reading be deferred."—(*Mr. Courtney.*)

MR. SEXTON asked when the Government intended to proceed with the Bill?

MR. COURTNEY said, the Bill would be taken after the Army and Navy Estimates had been disposed of on Monday next. He was afraid it would come forward at a late hour.

MR. SEXTON: Not after midnight, I hope.

MR. COURTNEY: I cannot say that at this period of the Session.

Question put, and *agreed to*.

Second Reading *deferred* till *Monday* next.

PROSECUTION OF OFFENCES BILL.

(*Mr. Courtney, Secretary Sir William Harcourt, Mr. Hibbert.*)

[BILL 287.] SECOND READING.

Order for Second Reading read.

Motion made, and Question proposed, "That the Bill be now read a second time."—(*Mr. Courtney.*)

MR. WARTON said, he had brought forward a series of Amendments to the Municipal Elections (Corrupt and Illegal Practices) Bill on the occasion of its passing the third reading, which would be suitably introduced in this Bill also—namely, to substitute the words "Solicitor to the Treasury" for the words "Public Prosecutor." It was quite clear that the Government accepted the principle of those Amendments. His object in drawing attention to this was to point out that if the Government proceeded with reasonable speed, both these Acts might be made consistent with each other.

MR. COURTNEY said, he was afraid that the course suggested by the hon. and learned Member for Bridport was not a convenient one. The Bill considered last night was not the only other Bill in which the Public Prosecutor was mentioned.

Question put, and *agreed to.*

Bill read a second time, and *committed* for *Monday* next.

REVENUE, &c. BILL.—[BILL 300.]

(*Mr. Courtney, Mr. Herbert Gladstone.*)

SECOND READING.

Order for Second Reading read.

Motion made, and Question, "That the Bill be now read a second time,"—(*Mr. Courtney,*)—put, and *agreed to.*

MR. COURTNEY said, he proposed to put down the Committee stage for Tuesday next. The Bill had now been before the House for some time.

Motion made, and Question proposed, "That this House will, upon Tuesday next, resolve itself into Committee on the Bill."—(*Mr. Courtney.*)

MR. WARTON said, it was, in his opinion, wrong to put down the Committee stage of a Bill of this nature so soon after the second reading. There was a great virtue in the "&c." included in the title of the Bill; and, as he thought hon. Members should have more time to consider what Amendments were necessary, he hoped it would not be brought forward before Thursday next.

MR. WHITLEY said, he thought that Clause 6, which made great alterations in the law, should be further explained.

MR. COURTNEY said, he was compelled to put down the Bill for Tuesday; but if there was difficulty in the way he might be able to reconsider the matter.

MR. WARTON said, there were four or five distinct matters to be considered. The House had no time to go into them at that hour (2.5 A.M.), and the Secretary to the Treasury had moved the second reading of the Bill without a word of explanation. He moved that "Thursday" be substituted for "Tuesday" in the Motion of the hon. Gentleman.

Amendment proposed, to leave out "Tuesday," and insert "Thursday,"—(*Mr. Warton,*)—instead thereof.

Question put, "That 'Tuesday' stand part of the Question."

The House *divided*:—Ayes 53; Noes 2: Majority 51.—(Div. List, No. 188.)

Committee upon *Tuesday* next.

INFANTS BILL.—[BILL 14.]

(*Mr. Bryce, Mr. Davey, Mr. Anderson, Mr. Staveley Hill.*)

COMMITTEE. [*Progress 22nd July.*]

Bill *considered* in Committee.

(In the Committee.)

Clause 3 (Surviving parent to be guardian).

DR. FARQUHARSON said, he begged to move the first Amendment on the Paper—an Amendment depending merely on what would come later on.

Amendment proposed,

In page 1, line 12, at end, add "either alone or jointly with any guardian to be appointed as hereinafter provided."—(*Dr. Farquharson.*)

Question proposed, "That those words be there inserted."

MR. INCE said, he proposed to move an Amendment to this Amendment—a merely formal one to improve the Bill. It was to insert before the word "either" the words "and in the event of the mother being such survivor."

Amendment proposed to the proposed Amendment, before the word "either," to insert the words "and in the event of the mother being such survivor."—(*Mr. Ince.*)

Question proposed, "That those words be there inserted."

MR. BRYCE said, he did not see any objection in point of substance to this Amendment to the proposed Amendment; but, as a matter of drafting, he thought the words were unnecessary. The Amendment was governed by the last three words "as hereinafter provided," and the provision there referred to—which was to be moved in place of Clause 4—dealt with the case of the survivors. The Amendment to be presently moved by the hon. Member for West Aberdeenshire (Dr. Farquharson) said the father of any infant might appoint "a guardian or guardians to act jointly with the mother of such infant," &c.

MR. INCE said, the hon. Member might think the words unnecessary; but he had not so much observed the capacity of the Courts to make mistakes as he (Mr. Ince) had. It seemed desirable to put these words in to prevent the possibility of a mistake.

MR. HORACE DAVEY said, he quite agreed with the last speaker as to the capacity of the Courts to go wrong; but he should think that if they put these words into the clause Courts would be entrapped into going wrong. There did not seem to be any necessity for an addition to the Amendment. The proposal, it was admitted, would not alter the substance of the Amendment; and as the substance appeared quite clear enough, and as it would only tend to obscurity to add anything, he hoped the original Amendment would be accepted without alteration.

MR. WARTON said, he was certainly decidedly in favour of the addition proposed, and for the reason that it would be a safeguard. This Bill was brought in through the influence of strong-minded women over weak-minded men. He would not go into the argument that God had established a distinct inequality between men and women; but he would say that if this Amendment were not inserted the contention of fanatics that men and women were considered in the clause as equal would prevail. This Amendment would show that woman was not in the same position as man.

Question put, and *negatived.*

Original Question put, and *agreed to.*

Motion made, and Question proposed, "That the Clause, as amended, stand part of the Bill."

MR. WARTON said, the Amendment they had just agreed to was very good so far as it went; but the clause was wrong altogether, being a material part of a very bad Bill. He, therefore, moved its rejection altogether. It was very hard that, at this period of the Session, they should be engaged in discussing a Bill of such importance—a measure for altogether revolutionizing our domestic relations. Besides, all these discussions were useless—a sheer waste of time—as the Bill was certain to be thrown out in the House of Lords.

Question put, and *agreed to.*

Clause 4 (Parents, or survivor of them, may appoint guardians).

Motion made, and Question proposed, "That the Clause stand part of the Bill."

MR. WARTON rose to Order. He said there was an Amendment lower down on the Paper in the name of the hon. Gentleman the Member for West Aberdeenshire (Dr. Fa quharson) commencing in this way—"Page 1, leave out Clause 4, and insert the following Clause." He (Mr. Warton) wished to know whether, if they passed Clause 4 now, it would be competent for the hon. Member, later on, to move his clause? They would have passed Clause 4 before the hon. Member's proposal came before them. A similar question would arise on Clause 5; therefore, he asked at once for the decision of the Chairman to settle both questions.

THE CHAIRMAN: It will be competent for the hon. Member for West Aberdeenshire to negative this clause. If he does so he can then move the clause standing in his name when it is reached.

Question put, and *negatived.*

Clauses 5 to 7, inclusive, *agreed to.*

Clause 8 (Interpretation of terms).

MR. BRYCE said, he had several Amendments to propose to Clause 8. The first three were—page 2, line 15, after "justice," insert "or the County Court of the district in which either of the parents resides;" line 16, after "justice," insert "or the County Court of the district in which either of the parents resides;" line 17, after "Session," insert "or the Sheriff Court within whose jurisdiction either of the spouses resides."

These Amendments were all, practically, the embodiment of the same principle, which was that jurisdiction under the Act should be given not only to the High Court of Justice in England and Ireland, and to the Court of Session in Scotland, but also to the inferior Courts—that was to say, to the County Courts and Sheriff Courts. The object of the Amendments was to meet the case of poor persons who would be unable to afford the expense and time necessary to make application to the Superior Courts. The benefits of the Bill would be confined to woll-to-do persons if these Amendments were not agreed to. In moving the second reading of the Bill, he had intimated that such an extension of the powers conferred by it on the Court would probably be desirable, and what he had heard since had strongly confirmed him in the belief that this ought to be done.

Amendment proposed,

In page 2, line 15, after "justice," insert "or the County Court of the district in which either of the parents resides."—(*Mr. Bryce.*)

Question proposed, "That those words be there inserted."

THE SOLICITOR GENERAL (Sir FARRER HERSCHELL) must say he thought the proposed Amendment suggested some new terrors, because, though his hon. Friend had said it was to meet the case of poor persons, it could not be limited to that case. Every father under the Bill might be dealt with by the County Court in the district in which he resided. This was one of the most delicate jurisdictions one could possibly establish; and he owned he did not himself think it right that the County Court Judges, who, certainly, were not appointed for the discharge of any such function, should be intrusted with it compulsorily as against any person. If the hon. Member were to provide means of appeal from the County Court to a Superior Court the case would be different. In some cases, no doubt, it would be better to have a case heard in the County Court; but, in other cases, it would be necessary to resort to a much higher tribunal.

MR. BRYCE: The hon. and learned Gentleman will see the Amendment says "or the County Court." He will mark the word "or."

THE SOLICITOR GENERAL (Sir FARRER HERSCHELL): But if the County Court is resorted to a person would be bound to submit to the jurisdiction of the Judge presiding over the district in which he resides. Some people might hesitate about submitting themselves voluntarily to the County Court; and I, therefore, think the County Court Judge should have authority to give power to move, on the application of either party.

MR. ANDERSON said, he thought this a most valuable Amendment, and hoped the hon. Member (Mr. Bryce) would persevere with it. The Solicitor General, when he spoke about the County Court Judges, forgot the difference between the County Court Judges in England and the Sheriffs in Scotland. The Sheriff's Court had a much larger jurisdiction.

THE SOLICITOR GENERAL (Sir FARRER HERSCHELL): There is no question as to the Sheriff's Court before the Committee. I am speaking of the English case, and not of the Scotch.

MR. HEALY thought there was a great deal in what the Solicitor General had said. An option should certainly be given to enable persons to go either to a Superior Court or a County Court. In religious cases, especially in Ireland, decisions would not have by any means the same weight, and actions would in no way attract the same amount of attention, if tried before some little local Court, as they would if tried before a Superior Court. The mothers would not have the same amount of protection, nor would the fathers, in cases in which religious differences occurred, in the County Court as they would in a Superior Court. He was content to have the County Courts in the Bill, but thought it necessary that any party, at his or her option, should be able to apply to a Superior Court.

MR. HORACE DAVEY said, the Solicitor General would see at once the necessity of providing for the County Court being a Court within the meaning of the Act, as it would apply to persons without means who could not bear the expense of going to the High Court. He quite agreed that there would be some difficulty in giving jurisdiction to the County Court in every case. It was, unfortunately, impossible to put a limit to the cases to be heard by a County Court Judge by fixing a certain sum, as was done in ordinary mercantile affairs. The hon. Gentleman the Member for the Tower Hamlets (Mr. Bryce) and himself had discussed this question, and had come to the conclusion that some words might be devised, and brought up on Report, to meet the objection of the Solicitor General. Such a provision as "Provided always that either party can apply to the Judge of the County Court to remove the case to the High Court," might meet the objection.

Question put, and *agreed to.*

Motion made, and Question proposed, "That the Clause, as amended, stand part of the Bill."

MR. WARTON said, that on this clause he wished to make one observation. One of the Acts repealed was the Act of Charles II.; but in that matter the section conflicted with Section 6, which had reference to the old Act. If the old Act was repealed here, it should be struck out from Section 6. The whole of the section remained in force in one place, and only part of it in another. He only pointed this out in a friendly way.

Question put, and *agreed to.*

Clauses 9 and 10 *agreed to.*

MR. INCE said, the next Amendment stood in his name in the following terms:—

"Page 1, leave out Clause 4, and insert the following clause:—

(Surviving parents may appoint guardians.)

"It shall be lawful for the surviving parent of an unmarried infant by deed or will to appoint a guardian or guardians of such infant after the death of such survivor."

After what had taken place he proposed to waive his right to move this clause.

On the Motion of Dr. FARQUHARSON, the following new clause was inserted in lieu of Clause 4:—

(Each parent may appoint guardian.)

"1. Each of the parents of any infant may by deed or will appoint any person or persons to be guardian or guardians of such infant after the death of the survivor of such parents (if such infant be then unmarried), and the guardian or guardians so appointed shall act jointly with the guardian or guardians (if any) appointed by the other of such parents.

"2. The father of any infant may appoint a guardian or guardians to act jointly with the mother of such infant in the event of her surviving him.

"3. The mother of any infant may apply to the court for the appointment of some fit person or persons to act as guardian or guardians of such infant after her death jointly with the father of such infant, and the court, if satisfied that, having regard to the character or habits of the father or other grave cause, such appointment is desirable in the interests of such infant, may appoint such guardian or guardians so to act as aforesaid.

"4. In the event of guardians being unable to agree upon a question affecting the welfare of an infant, any of them may apply to the court for its directions, and the court may make such order or orders regarding the matters in difference as it shall think proper in the interest of the infant."

MR. BRYCE said, he wished to propose a new clause in substitution for the 5th clause, which had been struck out, and to enlarge the powers of the Court to some extent. The Court at present had power, to some degree, to give effect to the wishes of the father unless his conduct had been bad. It was proposed by this new clause to admit the wishes of the mother, and the conduct of the parents, as considerations which would affect the Court's discretion, and in that way it was hoped that the more serious existing evils would be removed. The clause practically embodied what was the practice of the English Court, except that it would enable the Court to have regard more than hitherto to the conduct of the parents and the wishes of the mother. In Scotland the Court of Session did not seem to consider itself to have this power.

New Clause—

(Court may make order as to custody of infant.)

"The court may, upon the application of the mother of any infant (who may apply without next friend), make such order as it may think fit regarding the custody of such infant, or the religion in which it is to be brought up, having regard in the first place to the interests of the infant, and then to the conduct of the parents, and to the wishes as well of the mother as of the father,"—(*Mr. Bryce,*)

—*brought up,* and read the first time.

Motion made, and Question proposed, "That the Clause be read a second time."

MR. WARTON said, he could not understand what was meant by the "interests" of the child. How would the matter stand if the child's father was a Protestant owning a family living, and he had the child educated for the Church in order to take that living; but the mother who brought the child up was a Roman Catholic? This Bill would revolutionize society, and some day its supporters would blush for having passed it. The Court of Chancery had exercised the very jurisdiction embodied in this clause for centuries, and had had no difficulty in determining questions of this kind as to the interests of a child.

The SOLICITOR GENERAL (Sir Farrer Herschell) said he viewed this clause with considerable misgiving. In certain cases the Courts had had to consider the question of the religion in which a child had been brought up; and they had had a guide which it was now proposed to take away from them. Hitherto the religion of the father had been the primary rule as to the children, and when it was a question of Protestant or Roman Catholic there was that guide. The Court had followed that guide; but now it was proposed to take away all guide in the matter, and the mother or the father being alive could apply to the Court to determine in what religion the child should be brought up. If the mother applied to the Court and asked that the child should be brought up in a particular religion, what test had the Court to adopt in order to determine what was the interest of the child? It was not, it appeared, to be the worldly interest of the child. That might be one test; but in many instances it would be an unsatisfactory one. Then, if religion was to be taken, what was the guide? He confessed he could not see how this clause was to be worked out. This was a matter subject to extreme differences of view. There might be a difference between Protestants themselves—a difference on ecclesiastical points. How was the Court to determine that, if it was to have regard, in the first place, to the interests of the infant? He did not propose to say what was to be the guide in this matter; but he should look with considerable doubt upon this clause. He did, however, quite agree with one part of the clause, for he thought there should be a greater power in the Court than there now was if an application was made by the mother to the Court with reference to the conduct of the father, because there were, no doubt, cases in which a proper check was put upon the action of the father when he had shown himself unfit to have control. He was quite willing to see some steps taken in that direction; but when it came to dealing with the religion in which the child was to be brought up, having regard, in the first place, to the interests of the child, he felt they were on the horns of a dilemma. If they looked to the temporal interests of the child they would be disregarding what many people considered higher interests; but if they looked to those higher interests, two Judges might determine in exactly opposite directions. He feared that without any such guide as was now provided it would be impossible to work this clause.

Mr. BRYCE said, he thought it would not be possible to avoid dealing with religion at all; because, as they all knew, serious grievances had arisen, and might arise, through forcing a child to follow the religion which was the religion of the father. But this clause would not make the difficulty any greater than it was already; it would rather diminish it by preventing the Court from becoming, in extreme cases, the unwilling agent of cruelty. It must be remembered, in the first place, that no application could be made except upon some ground being shown for the change desired. There must be some ground shown to justify the application; and, in the next place, the striking out of Clause 2 of the present Bill made the Bill leave the Common Law right where it was before—that was to say, in the father. There was nothing in the construction of this new 5th clause to negative or extinguish the permanent Common Law right of the father, and all that was said in this clause with regard to the wishes and conduct of the parents must be taken to be subject to that Common Law right; and, therefore, *primâ facie* the child would be brought up in the religion of its father. The Court would have that Common Law rule as a guide; and it was only where that rule failed to throw light on the subject that it would, in respect to religion, be empowered to have peculiar regard to the interests of the child and wishes of the mother.

Mr. HARRINGTON said, the speech of the hon. Member had strengthened his opposition to the Bill. If there was anything at all that might be taken as consolation for the speech of the Solicitor General, the hon. Member opposite had completely demolished it. There was nothing to guide the Court except the Judge's own discretion; and, looking at the wording of this clause, he failed to see how the Judge could rule otherwise than in accordance with his own view as to what was best in the interests of the child. He could not see how the Judge could say that it would be better for the spiritual interests of the child, having regard to this section, which established no standard whatever, to be brought up in any other religion than that of the parents.

MR. HEALY said, this was a very important matter; and, in his view, the arguments of the Solicitor General had not been answered at all. It would be better to leave the law as it was at present; at least, so far as the religion was concerned. There did exist some guarantee at the present time, and it was needless to enforce the arguments of the Solicitor General; but he thought, at least, they should omit the words—"or the religion in which it is to be brought up." They must have regard to the interests of the child; but "infants" were sometimes of a very mature age, and it would be necessary to consider their wishes also.

THE SOLICITOR GENERAL (Sir FARRER HERSCHELL) suggested that the best course would be to report Progress now, and then they could consider what should be done. This was a most delicate question, and it ought not to be dealt with hastily.

MR. BRYCE said, he thought it might be well to pass by this clause now, and deal with it on the report, going on with the rest of the Bill in the meantime. He was reluctant to report Progress yet.

MR. HEALY proposed that the Bill should be allowed to pass now, and afterwards should be recommitted in respect to clauses that were contentious.

MR. HARRINGTON said, he fully recognized the desire of the hon. Member in bringing forward this measure, and quite believed that the hon. Member was animated by the best intentions; but the best intentions might sometimes lead people astray. A proposal of this kind was likely to considerably affect existing statutes and raise grave and serious complications; and he felt that this was not a time of morning at which to discuss a subject of this nature. He, therefore, hoped that Progress would be reported.

THE SOLICITOR GENERAL (Sir FARRER HERSCHELL) said, the hon. Member was, no doubt, anxious to get this Bill through Committee; and he would advise his hon. Friend to allow the Bill, as amended, to be reported, and then put down this or a similar clause for consideration on Report.

MR. HEALY asked if the Bill would be recommitted?

THE SOLICITOR GENERAL (Sir FARRER HERSCHELL) replied that it would not.

MR. HEALY said, he thought that in such a matter as this it would be very unsatisfactory to bring up a clause on the Report stage, especially at 2 or 3 o'clock in the morning, before which it could not be brought on.

COLONEL NOLAN said, he believed this clause would be most dangerous to the members of any religious community who were in a minority. The clause, if insisted upon, would lead to a question of endurance, and if it was pressed, he should begin at the commencement of the Bill, and put down as many Amendments as he could.

Motion made, and Question put, "That the Chairman do report Progress, and ask leave to sit again."—(*Mr. Warton.*)

The Committee *divided:*—Ayes 10; Noes 42: Majority 32.—(Div. List, No. 189.)

Original Question again proposed.

MR. BRYCE said, he would agree to report Progress now, and bring up his amended clause on Report, and so have this question settled.

COLONEL NOLAN said, he objected to this course being adopted. He had understood that the clause would be altogether withdrawn, or so shaped that those who were in a minority in England and a minority on the Bench in Ireland would be able to obtain guarantees. If that was done, then he should be content to have the clause withdrawn.

MR. BRYCE said, that that was what he intended to do.

COLONEL NOLAN said, he objected to allowing the Bill to go on without some assurance from the Government that they would not consent to a clause like this being passed. If that was given, he should then be satisfied; but if that assurance was not given, he should simply take means to place on the Paper Amendments to every clause in the Bill.

THE SOLICITOR GENERAL (Sir FARRER HERSCHELL) said, he could not give any pledge that the Government would oppose this clause; but he thought he had given indications that he would oppose any clause involving the objections which had been pointed out to this clause.

MR. HARRINGTON said, he could not assent to the proposal of the hon. Member (Mr. Bryce), for it would deprive hon. Members of an opportunity of speaking in the debate. If they had been able to express their views, this miserable and mischievous clause would have been disposed of. In Ireland this clause would give power to a number of County Court Judges to administer the law. It would invest them with an entirely new power; and, from what they knew in Ireland, they could not have the slightest confidence in those Judges. Only a few days ago he had endeavoured to bring before the House the conduct of one of the officials intrusted with the administration of such measures as this. That official had induced Roman Catholic children to join in an excursion given to the inmates of the Protestant Orphans' Home, and he took that opportunity of preaching to the Catholic children. Every member of his family was identified with that Home. This clause would give to that Judge and others of the same kind absolute discretion as to the best interests of the child in regard to its religion; and he and his hon. Friends would, therefore, offer the strongest opposition to the clause.

MR. BRYCE pointed out that the hon. Member would have every opportunity of rejecting this clause, and it was quite clear, from what had been said, that he could not carry this clause in face of the opposition of the Solicitor General. Therefore, hon. Members were perfectly safe; and, for his part, he should be quite willing to omit all reference to religion, if the House preferred that.

MR. HEALY said, he recognized the fact that the hon. Member for the Tower Hamlets had no intention to impose a disability upon Members in this matter; but what they wanted was that when this clause was put down, the Bill should be recommitted in reference to this clause. So far, they had no guarantee as to that; but he thought it was a perfectly reasonable proposition, and such a course need not delay the Bill at all.

COLONEL NOLAN said, he wanted something more than the hon. Member for Monaghan (Mr. Healy) wanted. He wanted to have this clause left out altogether. He did not object to the Bill, except for that clause; but with that clause, he looked on the Bill with the greatest fear, and knew that he should be found fault with if he allowed it to pass without offering it the strongest opposition at this period of the year. The clause would change the whole position of the minority, and unless he could get some assurance, he should oppose the Bill to the utmost.

Notice taken, that 40 Members were not present; Committee counted, and 40 Members being found present,

MR. WARTON said, the objections to taking up this clause again on Report were very strong. If this was an ordinary Bill of only trifling importance, that course might be pursued; but it was too important a matter to be slurred over. It involved a complete change of the rights of husbands and wives, and there could be no greater example of recklessness in regard to Business than the way in which it was proposed to pass this Bill. This Bill was not in accordance with the real sentiment of the House, and it was the duty of those present to protest, in the interests of parents, against this irreligious and immoral proposition.

SIR CHARLES W. DILKE appealed to his hon. Friend to accept the suggestion of the hon. Member for Monaghan (Mr. Healy).

Motion, by leave, *withdrawn.*

Clause *withdrawn.*

Bill *reported;* as amended, to be considered upon *Tuesday* next, and to be *printed.* [Bill 308.]

MOTIONS.

—o—

METROPOLITAN ASYLUMS BOARD (BORROWING POWERS) BILL.

On Motion of Sir CHARLES DILKE, Bill to enable the Managers of the Metropolitan Asylums District to borrow for certain purposes of "The Diseases Prevention (Metropolis) Act, 1883," *ordered* to be brought in by Sir CHARLES DILKE and Mr. GEORGE RUSSELL.

Bill *presented,* and read the first time. [Bill 310.]

PUBLIC HEALTH (IRELAND) (DISTRICTS) BILL.

On Motion of Mr. SOLICITOR GENERAL for IRELAND, Bill to amend "The Public Health (Ireland) Act, 1878," with reference to Sanitary Districts, *ordered* to be brought in by Mr. SOLICITOR GENERAL for IRELAND.

Bill *presented*, and read the first time. [Bill 311.]

House adjourned at a quarter before Four o'clock in the morning till Monday next.

HOUSE OF LORDS,

Monday, 28th July, 1884.

MINUTES.]—PUBLIC BILLS—*First Reading*—Local Government (Ireland) Provisional Orders (Labourers Act) (No. 8)* (217); Education (Scotland) Provisional Order * (218).

Second Reading—Canal Boats Act (1877) Amendment (198); Cholera Hospitals (Ireland) * (204); Trusts (Scotland) * (209); Naval and Greenwich Hospital Pensions * (203); Teachers' Residences (Ireland) * (214).

Committee—Yorkshire Registries (192-219).

Committee—Report—Strensall Common * (195).

Report—Tramways (Ireland) Provisional Order (No. 5) * (211); Tramways (Ireland) Provisional Order (No. 2) * (144).

Third Reading—Local Government Provisional Orders (No. 5) * (183); Local Government Provisional Orders (No. 6) * (189); Oyster Cultivation (Ireland) * (197); Sheriff Court Houses (Scotland) Amendment * (193), and *passed.*

Royal Assent—Licensing Act (1872) Amendment [47 & 48 *Vict.* c. 29]; Royal Military Asylum Chelsea (Transfer) [47 & 48 *Vict.* c. 32]; Great Seal [47 & 48 *Vict.* c. 30]; Newcastle Chapter [47 & 48 *Vict.* c. 33]; Colonial Prisoners Removal [47 & 48 *Vict.* c. 31]; Public Libraries Acts Amendment [47 & 48 *Vict.* c. 37]; Elections (Hours of Poll) [47 & 48 *Vict.* c. 34]; Revision of Jurors and Voters Lists (Dublin County) [47 & 48 *Vict.* c. 35]; Prisons (Ireland) (Cost of Conveyance of Prisoners) * [47 & 48 *Vict.* c. 36]; Indian Marine [47 & 48 *Vict.* c. 38]; Naval Discipline Act (1866) Amendment [47 & 48 *Vict.* c. 39]; Reformatory and Industrial Schools (Manx Children) [47 & 48 *Vict.* c. 40]; Local Government (Ireland) Provisional Order (Labourers Act) (No. 7) [47 & 48 *Vict.* c. cliv]; Benefices (Tiverton Portions) Consolidation Amendment [47 & 48 *Vict.* c. clv]; Local Government (Ireland) Provisional Order (The Labourers Act) (Enniscorthy, &c.) [47 & 48 *Vict.* c. clvi]; Local Government Provisional Order (Salt Works) [47 & 48 *Vict.* c. clvii]; Local Government Provisional Orders (No. 2) [47 & 48 *Vict.* c. clviii].

THE WELLINGTON STATUE.

QUESTION.

LORD DENMAN desired to ask the Government a Question, of which he had given Notice some weeks ago, but which, being out of town, he was unable to put at the time—namely, Whether permission might be given for a photographer, at private expense, to obtain a photograph of the head of the statue of the late Duke of Wellington, removed from Hyde Park Corner? He did so, if possible, to prove that the head of the colossal statue was a strong, but coarse, likeness of the late Duke of Wellington—and more fitted to remain in London, according to the wish of a majority of the House of Lords, which, if the Government had not been too late, might have prevented the removal of the head at all, and have proved that the statue was suitable for its former elevated place, while a refined statue on a smaller scale might be more appropriate for Aldershot.

LORD SUDELEY: In reply to the noble Lord, I have to state that if he had asked this Question three or four weeks ago, when he first placed it on the Paper, the First Commissioner would have been most happy to have considered the matter to see if it could have been carried out. It is now, however, too late in the day, and a photograph of the head could not be made without delaying the removal of the statue to Aldershot, and, therefore, the First Commissioner regrets that he cannot consent to it.

PUBLIC BUSINESS—BURGH POLICE AND HEALTH (SCOTLAND) BILL.

QUESTION. OBSERVATIONS.

LORD BALFOUR said, he wished to ask Whether the Government could name a day after which they would not ask this House to give a Second Reading to the Burgh Police and Health (Scotland) Bill? He knew it would not be in Order to discuss the Bill on this occasion; but in order to make his Question intelligible, he would like to say that the Bill had been printed on the 3rd of April; that it was a Bill of 558 clauses, with 40 pages of Schedules, there being altogether 234 pages. It had been referred to a Select Committee, who, considering it in private, had taken 57 Divisions upon it, had expunged nearly 50 clauses, added a considerable number, and amended 209. They were coming to a period of the Session when there was not likely to be much time for the discussion and consideration of measures; and he wished to ask how it was possible to give adequate consideration to a complicated Bill of this kind unless a reasonable time was allowed? He certainly thought the Bill had been considered for so long a period in the other House that they should not lightly refuse to proceed with it; but the procedure in regard to it showed that it was by no means a Bill about which there was no contention. He therefore hoped that at least a week or 10 days would be allowed to elapse between the second reading and the Committee stage in this House if the Bill was to be persevered with.

THE EARL OF DALHOUSIE said, it was quite true that this was a complicated Bill, and that it had been long delayed in the other House; but it would be premature to say what steps the Government might take with regard to it, because, although it was generally understood that the Prorogation was not far off, still the day was not yet fixed, and he thought it was altogether too soon to decide what course might be taken by the Government with regard to this measure.

EGYPT—THE CONFERENCE.

QUESTION.

THE MARQUESS OF SALISBURY: I wish to ask Whether the noble Earl the Secretary of State for Foreign Affairs has any information to communicate to the House with regard to the Conference? I understood that something passed in the other House as to the day on which a statement would be made.

EARL GRANVILLE: I do not understand that any pledge was given upon the matter; but I am quite ready to give the noble Marquess what information I possess. The Conference met again to-day. An important point arose, which required reference to the Powers. We meet again to-morrow, in the hope of the Plenipotentiaries having received their instructions. This, however, is not certain; but I can assure the noble Marquess that we are making every effort in the Conference to lose no time.

ARMY—ORDNANCE DEPARTMENT—NEW SMALL-BORE RIFLE.

OBSERVATIONS.

THE EARL OF WEMYSS, in calling attention to the proposed manufacture of a new small-bore rifle for the Army, and to the consequent evils of a break of gauge, said, he would ask their Lordships to consider what was the fresh arm, whether it was a good and efficient soldier's weapon, what were its supposed advantages, and whether these outweighed what might be said in favour of the existing arm. By the evidence that they had they had proved distinctly that the Martini-Henry had showed itself to be in all respects a trustworthy and most serviceable weapon. It had been tried in all parts of the world, and the opinions of soldiers proved that it had shown itself a most valuable and effective arm. Mr. Martin Smith, one of the best shots in the world, and for many years a member of the English Eight, had said of it that it possessed a very long range, good trajectory, and moderate recoil. In the Russo-Turkish War it had inflicted losses at so great a distance as two miles, and at 2,000 yards it would penetrate 9 inches of sand. Up to the present time it was far in advance of the men who had to use it; and what possible advantage could there be in giving the soldiers a slightly improved arm at an enormous cost? It was said that the trajectory of the new small-bore rifle proposed to be manufactured would be lower than that of the Martini-Henry. He ventured to think that this question of trajectory might be met in the present arm. The real question was whether they were for the sake of a slight increase in range and accuracy to cast the whole thing adrift again and establish a break of gauge. That, in his opinion, would be an evil so great as to outweigh an increase in these directions. The day might come when the Reserve Forces and the Regulars would be called upon to act together, and the danger of a difference in ammunition would be seriously felt. As to the Reserve Forces, it was said that they must give the Army the best arm, and the inferior arm would do for the inferior troops. He ventured to think that the argument was the other way. In what he had said about this old question he was not giving what was merely his own opinion, but also that of experienced officers, such as Sir Henry Wilmot. This new arm was to be about half-a-pound heavier than the existing arm. Now, anyone who had carried a rifle, either for military purposes or for deer stalking, would know what a difference a few ounces would make. Having himself been for many years Chairman of the National Rifle Association, and having done all in his power to encourage rifle shooting, he was anxious that the Army and the nation should have the best possible weapon; and he would not advocate, he would not say a retrograde step, but a resistance to further advance, if he did not in his conscience believe that the present arm was all that was necessary for the efficiency of the Army.

THE EARL OF MORLEY remarked, that the noble Earl had made a very strong appeal to the House, or rather to the Government, not to adopt a change in the present arm. He might say that a conclusion had not as yet been arrived at. A very strong Committee, consisting of officers and civilians, had been sitting for the last three years, and had finally come to the conclusion to recommend to the Secretary of State for War the weapon to which the noble Earl had called attention. The noble Earl had alluded to the extreme accuracy attained by the present Martini-Henry. He had no desire or reason to controvert the statement. For certain purposes, as compared with other European rifles, the Martini-Henri did not stand badly, especially at long ranges. But since 1871 great improvements had been made in the manufacture of rifles; and yet the whole argument of the noble Earl had been that they were never to make any improvement, because, if they did, they would be obliged to have a certain portion of their whole Forces for a time armed with one rifle, while the rest had another. He quite agreed with the noble Earl that, as far as possible, the whole Force of the country should be armed with the best possible weapon; but the Regular troops had got the Martini-Henry because, unfortunately, they were constantly obliged to use their weapons in actual warfare, and, therefore, it was the obvious duty of the Government to arm them first. As he had said, the matter was still *sub judice;* but he would like to mention a few points in connection with this new weapon. The bore was to be slightly reduced, and a corresponding reduction made in the weight of the bullet. The result of this would be that in a range of 500 yards the trajectory of the new weapon would, at its highest point, be 2 feet lower than that of the present Martini-Henry, with a corresponding difference at longer ranges. With respect to lowness of trajectory, it was not merely of importance at long ranges, but was of even greater importance at short ranges. The great reduction in the height of trajectory was of enormous importance, not only in the case of good shots, but also with regard to the less skilful ones. Another point to which the noble Earl had referred was the increase of weight in the new weapon. It was true that owing to some additions—that of a guard, to prevent the hand from being burnt by the heat, and of an increase of metal in the barrel—the new rifle was heavier than the present one, but the ammunition was lighter; so that taking the new rifle with 60 rounds of its ammunition, a man would only have a few ounces more to carry than with the present rifle and 60 of its rounds. The real argument of the noble Earl, however, had been that it was inadvisable to effec another break of gauge. It was absolütely necessary, to some extent, to go gradually to work. There would, no doubt, be a considerable number of rifles required in a very short period; and it was hoped, if the new rifle was adopted, that all the Infantry of the Line would be at once armed with it. Therefore, the only break of auge would be between the Regular and the Auxiliary Forces. He agreed that no change should be made unless it were necessary; but the inconvenience of which the noble Lord complained was a temporary one. If, however, his advice were followed, it would render other inconveniences permament. His noble Friend had suggested that it would be possible to obtain all the results that were sought to be obtained by the new rifle by using the rifle they now possessed with a smaller bullet. That matter was discussed in 1871 by a Committee over which his noble Friend on the Cross Benches presided, and the Committee rejected the proposal made by his noble Friend, which would involve the very great inconvenience of having two kinds of ammunition for the Army. It was necessary to keep pace with other countries in having the best possible weapons for modern warfare; and the questions for consideration were whether the improvements in the new weapon were sufficiently important to justify the temporary inconvenience which might, to a slight extent, arise from the break of gauge which the noble Lord deprecated.

LORD CHELMSFORD said, he was glad to hear from the noble Earl the Under Secretary of State for War that the question was still *sub judice*, because, although the proposed new rifle might be a superior weapon in firing power to the Martini-Henry, a weapon could easily be produced which would be of the same gauge as the Martini-Henry whilst possessing all the improvements contained in the new one; and thus the disadvantages of having two rifles requiring separate ammunition would be prevented His experience in South Africa showed that it was necessary to have a half-cock weapon; otherwise the men had either to go with their rifles unloaded, and were therefore unprepared for sudden emergencies, or when their rifles were loaded there was always the danger of some nervous man letting his weapon go off and shooting his comrades. Upon sentry and outpost duty it was desirable that the men should always have their weapons loaded.

THE EARL OF WEMYSS, in reply, said, that this new rifle was to be introduced as a "temporary arrangement." The Martini-Henry rifle was brought in as a "temporary arrangement" 15 years ago, and was still in use. He hoped that the result of that discussion would be that the Government would turn their attention to improving the Martini-Henry rifle in every way, and avoid, if possible, the very serious evil of a break of gauge.

ARMY (OFFICERS)—VOLUNTARY RETIREMENTS—THE NEW WARRANT.

MOTION FOR AN ADDRESS.

THE EARL OF POWIS rose to call attention to the new Warrant suspending voluntary retirements for captains and majors of the line; and to move for number of first appointments to cavalry and infantry of the line respectively (excluding household cavalry, foot guards, and colonial corps) in 1880, 1881, 1882, 1883; number of lieutenants promoted captains in cavalry and infantry of the line, respectively, in each of those years; with number of cavalry regiments and line battalions on establishment. The noble Earl said, that at the time when the system of purchase in the Army was abolished, and when objection was made to the introduction of compulsory retirement in the lower ranks of the Service, the War Office laid great stress on the existence of voluntary retirement, and stated over and over again that voluntary retirement would make compulsory retirement a mere fiction. Those declarations answered their purpose at the time; but now within two years they were being considerably modified. He thought it would have been much more simple if so important a change as this, and one which affected so severely the individuals concerned, had been mentioned by the Secretary of State for War when moving the Army Estimates. The plan must have been all digested then, and an explanation of the cause which had led to its adoption would have obviated any apprehensions as to its probable effect. In 1883, excluding Guards, Household Cavalry, and Colonial Corps, in 28 regiments there had only been 24 promotions from lieutenant to captain. In 141 battalions of Infantry, having 15 subalterns each, there had only been 159 promotions. Surely, neither of these rates could be called extravagant. If there were a special run of vacancies in any particular regiment, there were plenty of old subalterns who might be promoted from other regiments. Hart's *Army List* showed that there were enough subalterns of nine years' standing to supply nearly a year's vacancies; and if eight years were taken there would be an infinite number. There was not even the miserable excuse of a money saving, because a series of officers retiring in succession upon gratuities would receive less money than a series retiring upon £200 a-year for the same period, the average duration of such an annuity at 40 years of age being 13 or 14 years by the War Office Tables. The treatment of the majors was still more unjust. An officer, if a captain, was turned out of the Army by the War Office for its own convenience at 40; but if he had the luck to be a major, he was to be kept compulsorily till he was 48, when his health might be failing. While every military *doctrinaire* denounced long service for the soldier as an atrocity, the officer was to be chained to the oar like a Venetian galley-slave. The reservation in the Warrant of a power of suspension was intended only for emergencies — such as an Indian Mutiny, or threat of invasion.

Moved for—

Return of number of first appointments to cavalry and infantry of line respectively (excluding household cavalry, foot guards, and colonial corps) in 1880, 1881, 1882, 1883; number of lieutenants promoted captains in cavalry and infantry of the line, respectively, in each of those years; and number of cavalry regiments and line battalions on establishment.—(*The Earl of Powis.*)

THE EARL OF MORLEY, who was very indistinctly heard, said, that the Secretary of State for War had answered a similar Question fully a few days ago, and had sent a copy of his answer to all the newspapers. The Government would have no objection to granting the Return which the noble Earl asked for. The Warrant, however, to which the noble Earl referred was not a Warrant at all; it was merely an explanatory Regulation under the Warrant long ago issued. The noble Earl accused the War Office of gratuitously and without sufficient reason making changes, and he seemed to blame the War Office for the present system of promotion in the Army. The present system of Army promotion was based on the Report of a Royal Commission presided over by Lord Penzance. In the Report of the Commissioners the following passage occurred in reference to the voluntary retirements with pension or gratuity which they recommended:—

"The above system, then, is intended as a flexible one, under which the actual rate of promotion can be controlled. It is an inevitable result of the regimental system and of promotions taking place within the regiment that the officers of any one regiment may from time to time go forward quicker than those of another by reason of more frequent deaths or other causes of vacancy. This inequality may to some extent be rectified in the granting or withholding voluntary retirements in each individual case according to the state of promotion in the particular regiment. By the exercise of a like discretion the general rate of promotion may be held in check on the one hand or stimulated on the other throughout the Army. And, further, we may remark that a system of this kind, capable of expansion or contraction, in the hands of those who are to administer it will readily adapt itself to the changes by way of augmentation of the higher ranks or otherwise which the future development of military organization may render necessary."

This recommendation was given effect to by Article 94 of the Royal Warrant, which was as follows:—

"Voluntary retirement, with retired pay or gratuity, shall only be permitted when it shall be deemed expedient by our Secretary of State. Before such voluntary retirement be permitted, it shall be specially recommended by our Commander-in-Chief and approved by our Secretary of State."

The Secretary of State pointed out, in the answer to which he referred, that he should deal with every individual case, and not allow the retirement of a major unless the vacancy was to be filled by the promotion of a captain, who must have seen at least 18 years' service, and not to allow the retirement of a captain unless the lieutenant to be appointed had seen nine years' service. Therefore, taking into consideration the recommendation of the Royal Commission, and the fact that the Warrant distinctly laid down that voluntary retirement should be regulated by the Secretary of State, he thought that the Regulations made were fair and reasonable, and that officers had no just grounds of complaint. As a matter of fact, he believed these Regulations would affect them very little.

THE EARL OF LONGFORD said, the noble Earl's explanation was very satisfactory, except to those affected by it. He had before now called attention to the inconvenience caused to officers by the uncertainty that prevailed as to the War Office Warrants and Regulations.

Motion *agreed to.*

CANAL BOATS ACT (1877) AMENDMENT BILL.—(No. 198.)

(*The Lord Carrington*)

SECOND READING.

Order of the Day for the Second Reading read.

LORD CARRINGTON, in moving the second reading of this Bill, said, it was merely for the purpose of amending certain slight defects in the Act of 1877, and incorporating into it certain definitions.

Moved, "That the Bill be now read 2ª."—(*The Lord Carrington.*)

THE EARL OF WEMYSS thought the Bill unnecessary, and said he would explain his reasons on the Motion to go into Committee.

Motion *agreed to;* Bill read 2ª accordingly, and *committed* to a Committee of the Whole House on *Thursday* next.

LANDED ESTATES (IRELAND).

MOTION FOR RETURNS.

THE MARQUESS OF WATERFORD, in moving for Returns with regard to the number of Irish estates in the hands of Receivers, said, that Mr. Trevelyan, in introducing the Land Purchase Bill, which had unfortunately been dropped, made a statement pointing out that they were in Ireland rapidly approaching to that condition of affairs which resulted in the Encumbered Estates Court Act being passed in 1849. At that time there was a rental in the hands of Receivers of £750,000 a-year, and there were 1,000 Chancery suits, in which the rights of the parties had been ascertained, but where it was impossible to realize the property. At the present time, owing to various circumstances, Receivers were collecting a rental of £440,000 a-year, and there were 750 properties ripening for sale, and which at present had no chance of being sold. This was Mr. Trevelyan's statement. He was not prepared to say how this state of affairs might be obviated. It was desirable the expenses should be cut down as low as possible. The reason why he was moving for these Returns was that the expenses were much larger than necessary, and that the work might be done at a much less cost. A great deal of the present expense was needless extravagance. No doubt, it was necessary, after the money was paid into Court, that parties should appear before the Judge to claim the proportions due to them; but the costs in the previous part of the transaction might be materially cut down, and thus relieve those encumbered estates which of all in Ireland were least able to bear this excessive expense. If the Returns were granted, they should see clearly what the expenses under the present system were; and he trusted that Her Majesty's Government would, if he were right in his contention, take measures, by the appointment of a Royal Commission, to inquire into the present system, and see whether a great deal of this official work which at present came before a Judge, thus entailing all the necessary expense of judicial procedure, could not be transferred to an officer of the Court acting under the Judge, who could carry out the work in an equally efficacious but far simpler and less expensive manner; while the Judge's undivided attention could then be given to purely judicial work. The noble Lord concluded by moving for the Returns.

Moved, That there be laid before the House—

"I. Return showing the number of estates under the management of receivers in the High Court of Justice in Ireland—(*a.*) At the close of the year 1877 (seven); (*b.*) At the close of the year 1883 (three); (*c.*) The total gross annual rental of such estates.

"II. Return of—(*a.*) Total amount of the costs of passing receivers accounts taxed in the year 1883; (*b.*) Total amount of receivers miscellaneous costs taxed in the year 1883; (*c.*) Total amount of costs of the petitioner or other the person having carriage of the proceedings in receiving matters taxed in the year 1883."—(*The Marquess of Waterford.*)

LORD CARLINGFORD (LORD PRESIDENT of the COUNCIL) said, the Returns would not be opposed, and he should reserve what he had to say until the figures were before the House.

THE LORD CHANCELLOR said, he should not be surprised to hear that the noble Marquess had been on some points misinformed about the details of the expenses supposed to be necessary to be incu.red in these proceedings. It appeared to him that much of the work referred to which was supposed to involve the expense of application to the Court ought to be done in Chambers. He did not think a Royal Commission would be a proper way of proceeding, and he was afraid the Returns would throw no light on the matter, as it did not go into details.

THE EARL OF LONGFORD said, he was afraid the noble Marquess was not misinformed at all, as he had frequently heard the matter represented in the same terms in Ireland. He hoped the machinery was capable of considerable expansion, as in the present state of the country there would be a great deal more of this work for the Courts to do.

Motion *agreed to.*

Returns *ordered* to be laid before the House.

LAW AND POLICE (METROPOLIS)—THE REFORM DEMONSTRATION.

QUESTION. OBSERVATIONS.

LORD STRATHEDEN AND CAMPBELL: My Lords, I have a Notice on

the Paper to ask Her Majesty's Government, On what ground the different routes to Parliament were blocked up or prohibited on July 21st? To guard myself against misapprehension, let me say that, as a supporter of the Franchise Bill on its second reading, I give no opinion against the demonstration which occurred. I even join in the eulogies which have been rather prodigally lavished on its good organization, and its law-respecting character. Glad should I be if even now it led to a transaction between rival Parties in the State by which excitement in the autumn would be obviated. The Question bears exclusively on the conduct of the Government. To show that it is a proper and a necessary Question, I must refer—however trivial in itself—to my experience on Monday. At 4 o'clock, I left the neighbourhood of Berkeley Square to be here at the time of Public Business. The police turned me from Berkeley Street, and again from Grafton Street—which were not the route of the procession — while they declared St. James's Street to be impassable, and recommended Regent Street, which really was so. By choosing my own path I was able to reach Bridge Street, and there had to remain an hour, as there was no access to Palace Yard except by crossing the procession. To bring the procession at all into that quarter was most superfluous, as it involved a detour, and was not their nearest way to Piccadilly. It was a quarter past 6 before I could join your Lordships. On my part, there is no personal complaint, no personal annoyance. It happened to be immaterial whether I reached the House at one time or another. It is an advantage in some respects to be forced to contemplate at leisure a remarkable display of banners and of bands which may affect the history of the country. But what ought to strike your Lordships, and probably will do so, is that if on an occasion of this kind streets are barred at the discretion of a Government, they may exclude from the two Houses the individuals they desire to exclude, they may rush through the measures they are anxious to precipitate, or negative the Motions they do not wish to be adopted. Now, if a matter of this kind is unnoticed, it is nearly sure to be repeated. If attention is directed to it, it is not likely to become a precedent. It is, therefore, a public duty to address the Question to Her Majesty's Government.

THE EARL OF DALHOUSIE: All I can state, on behalf of the Government, is that they did not arrange the route of the procession. They issued directions to the police so to regulate the traffic as to prevent disorder and to insure that as little confusion and obstruction as possible should arise from the procession. It is, I suppose, impossible for a procession of this magnitude to take place in the City of London without some inconvenience; but I do not see how the Government could have given other orders than they did on this occasion. If the police had failed in their duty, or made their arrangements without any foresight, then, no doubt, the police would be to blame, and the noble Lord would be justified in complaining of the Government; but I am not prepared to admit any failure on the part of the police. Therefore, I have to say that the Government do not consider they have any reason to apologize for what has happened.

THE EARL OF REDESDALE (CHAIRMAN of COMMITTEES): I should like to ask whether the route the procession intended taking was made known to the Government before it actually took place?

THE EARL OF DALHOUSIE: I cannot answer the Question positively; but I have reason to believe that the route was communicated beforehand to the Secretary of State, who gave his directions accordingly. The police, I believe, consulted with the right hon. and learned Gentleman, and he made such modifications in regard to the arrangements as he thought desirable.

THE EARL OF REDESDALE (CHAIRMAN of COMMITTEES): The point I meant was, why the procession was allowed to come by Parliament Street? It met on the Embankment, and its destination was Hyde Park. What earthly reason could the processionists have for going all round the end of Parliament Street, and up that street to Charing Cross, thus making a much longer route, and stopping up a great number of streets?

THE EARL OF DALHOUSIE: That is a Question which should rather be addressed to the leaders of the procession than to the Government. The Government maintain it was not their duty in any way to say what route the procession should take.

THE EARL OF REDESDALE (CHAIRMAN of COMMITTEES): The Government, at any rate, might have told the processionists what route they should not take.

THE MARQUESS OF LOTHIAN: It is generally understood that these processions should not come within some distance of the Houses of Parliament. On this occasion the Government were in communication with the police, and could they not have said that they did not wish the procession to come by Westminster? I am rather sorry the question has been raised; but as it has been put, I agree as to the character of the procession, though I do not think it is likely to have any effect upon anyone. I wish, however, to take this opportunity of asking the Under Secretary for War whether the statement which I have seen in the papers of Volunteer and Yeomanry Calvalry bands being in uniform and taking part in the procession is correct? I am not certain whether the War Office Regulations forbid men to appear in uniform on such occasions; but, if they do, some remonstrance ought, I think, to be addressed to the officers to whose battalions the men belong.

THE EARL OF DALHOUSIE: There is an Act of Parliament in force that processions shall not come within a mile of the Houses of Parliament if they intend to present a Petition; but this procession did not propose to do anything of that kind, and, consequently, there was nothing illegal in what they did.

THE EARL OF LONGFORD: As the matter has been referred to, I would like to know what will be done in the future? If the Government intends to patronize these demonstrations, and looking at what occurred lately, I would suggest that, on similar occasions hereafter, practicable routes should be publicly indicated for Members of Parliament, so that loss of time in gaining access to the two Houses may be obviated.

THE EARL OF MORLEY: I am glad to have the opportunity of denying that any Yeomanry, Volunteers, or Militia bands in uniform took part in the demonstration.

THE EARL OF MILLTOWN: It is clear that a procession can not come within a mile of the Houses of Parliament when a Petition has to be presented to Parliament; but I wish to ask who arranged this procession, for an unfortunate impression has got abroad that the leaders are to be found in the ranks of Her Majesty's Government?

YORKSHIRE REGISTRIES BILL.

(*The Lord Wenlock.*)

(NO. 192.) COMMITTEE.

House in Committee (according to order).

Clauses 1 to 36, inclusive, *agreed to.*

Clause 37 (Appointment of officers, &c.).

THE EARL OF FEVERSHAM moved, as an Amendment, to strike out the words limiting the appointment of Registrar to a barrister or solicitor of seven years' standing.

Amendment *moved,*

In page 19, lines 14 and 15, to leave out the words ("of not less than seven years' standing.")—(*The Earl of Feversham.*)

LORD WENLOCK said, that he was uable to accept the Amendment. The duties of the Registrar would now be more technical and would cause more responsibility than before, and it was necessary that he should have legal knowledge. Strong representations had been made to him by solicitors that they would have more confidence in the Office if the head of it were properly qualified by a knowledge of the law. He hoped that his noble Friend would withdraw his Amendment.

THE LORD CHANCELLOR remarked that it would be impossible for anyone without some qualification of this kind to discharge personally the duties of his office.

Amendment *negatived.*

Remaining Clauses *agreed to,* with Amendments.

The Report of the Amendments to be received *To-morrow;* and Bill to be *printed* as amended. (No. 219.)

PARLIAMENT — PALACE OF WESTMINSTER—WESTMINSTER HALL.

QUESTION. OBSERVATIONS.

LORD NORTON asked Her Majesty's Government, Whether the designs now exhibited in the Library of the House of Commons for battlemented buildings blocking up again the buttresses of Westminster Hall were decided on? He wished to know whether their Lordships would have any opportunity of expressing or even forming an opinion upon those designs before they were decided upon? At present he believed they were exhibited in the Library of the House of Commons, and he did not know whether that was meant to be sufficient for their Lordships intuitively to form an opinion upon them. Duplicates of the designs might have been put in their Lordships' Library, or, at all events, the plans might have been put in a place to which the Members of both Houses had access. The Report of Mr. Pearson, the very eminent architect, had only just been put into his hands, and had not been circulated—it was a most historical and critical document—and upon it they would have to form their judgment.

LORD SUDELEY: In reply to the noble Lord, I have to state that when the designs and plans for carrying out Mr. Pearson's proposals for the reconstruction of the west side of Westminster Hall were placed three weeks ago in the Library of the House of Commons, the First Commissioner stated that unless there was serious opposition to them the Government would submit a Vote for carrying out the works. As regards these plans, it was so late in the Session that it was not thought desirable to make duplicate plans; but I am sure the First Commissioner will endeavour to place them so that your Lordships may be able to inspect them with greater convenience than you are able to do now in the Libary of the House of Commons. The Report of Mr. Pearson has been communicated to this House, and will be printed and distributed forthwith. The cloister which Mr. Pearson suggests is a restoration of that which undoubtedly existed from the time of Richard II. till the beginning of the present century. He worked out on evidence which seems unanswerable, the curious fact that a wall ran between the upright buttresses so as with the roof, which it certainly carried, to compose a cloister. This was removed to make way for the Law Courts, which have now been taken down. The buttresses will not be blocked up, but will be still visible to a very great extent above the cloister, and will stand out 8 feet. Mr. Pearson is confident from old drawings that the parapet of the wall was embattled. So far as can be ascertained these plans have met with general approval, and the Government therefore propose to ask for a Vote to carry out the restoration.

THE MARQUESS OF LOTHIAN expressed a hope that in future some means would be found of exhibiting proposed plans and designs connected with public buildings of interest, in places where they could conveniently be seen by the Members of both Houses of Parliament. He did not complain of the plans themselves.

LORD SUDELEY said, he was sure the First Commissioner would endeavour to carry out the suggestion, so that in future any plans of that nature would be placed in some chamber which would be convenient to the Members of both Houses wishing to inspect them.

House adjourned at a quarter before Seven o'clock, till To-morrow, a quarter past Ten o'clock.

HOUSE OF COMMONS,

Monday, 28th July, 1884.

MINUTES.]—SELECT COMMITTEE—*Second Report* — Kitchen and Refreshment Rooms (House of Commons) [No. 304]; Agricultural Labourers (Ireland), Sir Hervey Bruce *disch.*; Mr. Corry *added.*

SUPPLY—*considered in Committee*—ARMY ESTIMATES—Votes 15 to 25—NAVY ESTIMATES—Votes 12 to 17.

Resolutions [July 25] *reported.*

PUBLIC BILLS—*First Reading*—New Parishes Acts and Church Building Acts Amendment * [312].

Second Reading—Chartered Companies * [304]; Magistrates (Ireland) (Salaries) [292], *debate adjourned;* Supreme Court of Judicature Amendment * [307]; Expiring Laws Continuance [306]; Metropolitan Asylums Board (Borrowing Powers) [310].

Select Committee — Ulster Canal and Tyrone Navigation * [244], *nominated.*

Committee—Report—Military Pensions and Yeomanry Pay * [302]; Prosecution of Offences * [287].

Committee—Report—Third Reading—Naval Enlistment * [305]; Building Societies Acts Amendment * [301], and *passed.*

Report—Third Reading—Education (Scotland) Provisional Order * [285], and *passed.*

Third Reading—Pier and Harbour Provisional Orders * [259]; Metropolitan Board of Works

(Money) [278]; Public Works Loans* [299], and *passed*.

Withdrawn—Board of Works (Ireland) (No. 2)* [165].

PRIVATE BUSINESS.

—o—

CHESTER IMPROVEMENT BILL [*Lords*].

CONSIDERATION.

Order for Consideration, as amended, read.

Motion made, and Question proposed, "That the Bill be now considered."

Message to attend the Lords Commissioners;—

The House went;—and being returned;—

Mr. SPEAKER *reported* the *Royal Assent to* several Bills.

CHESTER IMPROVEMENT BILL [*Lords*].

Question again proposed, "That the Bill be now considered."

MR. COURTNEY said, that one of the objects of this Bill was to transfer certain property and tolls to the Corporation under the 11th and other clauses of it. Now, as a rule, the right of tranferring property could only be carried out under the general law by affixing a stamp, frequently very costly, to the instrument by which the transfer was effected. Such stamp formed part of the receipts of the Inland Revenue Office. It appeared, however, that an Act for the erection of an additional bridge over the River Dee at Chester, and for the construction of convenient roads and approaches, was authorized in the 6th year of the Reign of *Geo.* IV. c. 124, and by that Act, subsequently extended by an Act 2 *Will.* IV. c. 41, certain tolls were authorized for the purpose of maintaining the bridge, and of defraying the interest and repaying the principal of any debt that might be contracted; and after satisfaction of these purposes the tolls were to cease and determine. The Act thus created a public trust, and did not establish any private undertaking with a possibility of surplus revenue and profit. By the present Bill, the Corporation were empowered to purchase the Dee Bridges Undertaking for £15,000; but this was, in fact, the amount of the existing debt, and the real effect of the Bill was simply to transfer the trust from one public body to another without any conveyance of a beneficial interest. The stamp on such a transfer was nominal, and might be neglected; but he had felt it necessary to direct attention to the matter, because there had been other instances in which the Inland Revenue had suffered materially from non-compliance with the law in cases of transfer of property under the authority of an Act of Parliament. He was, therefore, anxious that the present instance should not be passed over *sub silentio*, and an inconvenient precedent established for the future. Some five or six years ago, a bridge which belonged to a certain Company, and from which a revenue, in the shape of tolls, was derived, was transferred by Act of Parliament without the Treasury knowing anything of the matter, and the consequence was that the obligation imposed by the Stamp Duties was evaded. In order to prevent that unfortunate occurrence from being drawn into a precedent he had considered it desirable to trouble the House with these observations.

Question put, and *agreed to*.

Bill *considered*: to be read the third time.

QUESTIONS.

—o—

POOR LAW (IRELAND)—ELY DISPENSARY, DERRYGONNELLY—USE OF BUILDING FOR PARTY PURPOSES.

MR. HEALY asked the Chief Secretary to the Lord Lieutenant of Ireland, Whether anything has been done in reference to the use of the Ely Dispensary, Derrygonnelly, as an Orange Lodge?

MR. TREVELYAN: The Guardians, at their meeting on the 8th instant, appointed some of their number as a Committee to meet the Dispensary Committee, and consider the subject and report to the Boardd The 23rd of is month was appointe as the day ofthmeeting; but I am informed that the Guardians selected did not attend on that day. The Board have again been requested by the Local Government Board to give their attention to the matter. If the Guardians do not at their next meeting afford satisfactory information on the subject, the Local Government Board will direct their Inspector to ascertain how the matter stands.

INDIA (MADRAS)—DIRECTOR OF PUBLIC INSTRUCTION.

MR. GIBSON asked the Under Secretary of State for India, When is the appointment of Director of Public Instruction, Madras, expected to be vacant; will the Government, on the occasion of such vacancy, recognise the preferential claims of officers of the Educational Department, as promised by former Secretaries of State; and, does the Madras Educational Department include graduates in first class honours of the Universities of Oxford, Cambridge, Dublin, and Edinburgh, who have efficiently discharged the duties of their office?

MR. J. K. CROSS: The India Office has no information as to when this office will be vacant. The appointment rests with the Governor of Madras, by whom, I have no doubt, when a vacancy occurs, the claims of the members of the Education Department will be fully considered. The rule laid down is that preference is to be given to members of the Department if they are competent to discharge the duties of the office. The Department contains various officers who have taken good University degrees, and who have efficiently discharged the duties of such offices as they have held.

POST OFFICE—THE PARCEL POST—THE EASTERN DISTRICT OF LONDON.

MR. RITCHIE asked the Postmaster General, Whether it is a fact that the letter carriers of the Eastern District are compelled to collect and deliver parcels, regardless of size, weight, and number, and that, owing to this duty having to be performed by them, a serious delay is frequently caused to public correspondence?

MR. FAWCETT: The postmen in this district are not required to collect and deliver parcels regardless of size, weight, and number. The postmen deliver only the smaller parcels; and strict instructions have been given that when parcels from their size, weight, and number are likely to hinder the proper performance of the Letter Service, they are to be specially collected and delivered. I am assured that these instructions are carefully attended to, and that no complaint of delay has arisen from the public.

AUSTRALIAN COLONIES (NEW SOUTH WALES)—IMPORTATION OF FRENCH RECIDIVISTS FROM NOUMEA.

MR. ERRINGTON asked the Under Secretary of State for the Colonies, Whether the attention of the Secretary of State has been called to the fact that, in addition to the influx into our Australian Colonies of casually escaped convicts from the French penal settlements, against which the Colonists are constantly protesting, in April last the French Messageries Steamer *Dupleix* landed openly at Sydney nine expirees, the nature of whose sentence imported that they were only released from Noumea conditionally on their never returning to France; whether any, and what, steps are being taken to remonstrate with the French Government against the deliberate importation into the Territories of a friendly Power of a class of criminals whom their own Country will not receive, and among whom according to the Colonial authorities—

> "Are found the criminals commonly known as recidivists, and undoubtedly the worst of their kind;"

and, whether, to put a stop to this practice, Her Majesty's Government will approve or recommend to the Colonial Governments legislation making it penal for the captain of any vessel, Home or Foreign, to land released convicts in any of the Australian Colonies?

MR. EVELYN ASHLEY: The attention of the Colonial Office has been called to the incident mentioned. Her Majesty's Government have been for many months in communication with the French Government on the general subject, and have reason to believe that their earnest representations are receiving serious consideration. It is, therefore, hoped that the necessity for legislation in the Colonies may not arise; but Her Majesty's Government would not interfere with any reasonable measure that they might feel compelled to take for their own protection.

PREVENTION OF CRIME (IRELAND) ACT, 1882—EXTRA POLICE, CO. TYRONE.

VISCOUNT CRICHTON (for Mr. MACARTNEY) asked the Chief Secretary to the Lord Lieutenant of Ireland, Whether fifty police, a District Inspector, and a Resident Magistrate were sent to Coagh, county Tyrone, and a similar number of police to Cookstown, in the same county and neighbourhood, on the 12th July last; whether such police were sent in opposition to the strongly expressed and unanimous opinion of the local magistrates; whether both these districts are, and have been for some time, peaceful, and entirely free from Party disturbances; and, whether the Government will consent to relieve the county from the heavy charge thus imposed upon it?

MR. TREVELYAN: Sir, the extra police were not sent to both places in opposition to the wishes of the magistrates, but at the express request of the District Inspector, who consulted with the magistrates at Cookstown, and they confirmed the recommendation that 50 men be sent; but at the other place they did not think so many were required. Party feeling was very strong in the district, and there were serious disturbances there on a former occasion. Party feeling runs very high in the district, and there is no intention to depart from the usual practice in this matter.

THE MAGISTRACY (IRELAND)—ENNIS QUARTER SESSIONS—MR. C. KELLY, Q.C., CHAIRMAN.

MR. KENNY asked the Chief Secretary to the Lord Lieutenant of Ireland, If the Irish Government has had under its consideration a Petition from Mr. H. B. Harris, of Ennis, complaining of insulting and violent language used towards him in Court by Mr. Charles Kelly, Q.C., Chairman of Quarter Sessions; if Mr. Harris, acting as juror in a larceny case, stated that—

"He should like to have evidence of someone who could prove the actual theft;"

and thereupon Mr. Kelly interfered, and told the juror to keep silent; if Mr. Harris claimed a right to make such an observation, and that Mr. Kelly immediately threatened to send him to prison if he spoke another word; if Mr. Harris in his Petition also states that—

"Unfortunately for all who have to attend the Quarter Sessions Court, they are obliged to submit to the insulting and disparaging remarks Mr. Kelly makes, and to witness the scenes that are enacted in Court from day to day, which it is painful for a nervous person to be an observer of, while another would consider the Court a burlesque;"

if, upon another occasion on which Mr. Harris was witness in a case, Mr. Kelly told him that he did not believe a word he swore, and if this expression is constantly being used by Mr. Kelly towards witnesses, from the most respectable to the most humble; if he is aware that Mr. Harris is a gentleman occupying a most respectable and valuable commercial position in Ennis; and, if the Lords Justices have the power to interfere to prevent the recurrence of painful scenes in a Court of Justice, or to inquire into Mr. Kelly's fitness to discharge the duties of a County Court Judge; and, if not, what course is open to aggrieved persons to obtain redress?

MR. TREVELYAN: The Irish Government have had before them a Memorial from Mr. Harris to the effect stated, and informed him that the Lords Justices have no power to interfere with a Judge in the discharge of his judicial duties. But although a Judge is only accountable to Parliament for his conduct, yet, as it was in his capacity as a juror that Mr. Harris complained, the Lords Justices considered that they might reasonably and properly ask the Judge for any explanation he might wish to offer in this matter, and a letter in this sense was accordingly sent to Mr. Kelly on Saturday last. His reply has not been received.

CONFEDERATION OF THE COLONIES (AUSTRALIA)—THE SYDNEY CONVENTION.

SIR HERBERT MAXWELL asked the Under Secretary of State for the Colonies, Whether it is true that the Legislative Assembly of Queensland has unanimously passed the Convention in favour of the Confederation of the Colonies, of the Annexation of New Guinea and other Western Pacific Islands, and of combined legislation against criminal aliens; and, if so, what is the attitude of Her Majesty's Government towards this policy?

MR. EVELYN ASHLEY: The facts are as stated in the hon. Member's Question. Her Majesty's Government have already signified their readiness to confirm and carry out by any necessary Imperial legislation the Confederation Scheme of the Sydney Convention, if, and when, it is adopted by the different Colonial Legislatures, and Her Majesty's Government would not interpose should they combine in any well-considered legislation to protect themselves against criminal aliens. As to the other questions, all I can say at present is general, and that is that the whole matter is being considered by the Cabinet.

ATTORNEYS AND SOLICITORS (IRELAND) ACT, 1866—MR. ROBERT D. O'BRIEN.

MR. HEALY asked Mr. Solicitor General for Ireland, Whether Mr. Attorney General will give the necessary sanction, under "The Attorneys and Solicitors (Ireland) Act, 1866," to the Incorporated Law Society to recover the penalty of £50 incurred by Robert D. O'Brien, 2, Lower Glentworth Street, Limerick, for having, without professional status, on the 21st July, conducted an eviction case before the Rathkeale Bench, in absence of plaintiff or solicitor; and, whether the conduct of the magistrates, in allowing a non-professional person to appear in the case, in spite of the protest of a solicitor in court, will be brought under the notice of the Lord Chancellor?

THE SOLICITOR GENERAL FOR IRELAND (Mr. WALKER): No application to sanction any proceeding has been received by the Attorney General for Ireland from the Incorporated Law Society. He will carefully consider any such application if made. Mr. Robert O'Brien is the brother of the complainant, and, as such, might come within the definition of his "agent" in the Petty Sessions Act, 1882; and, if authorized by his brother, he might, with leave of the Court, appear and be heard. There seems no ground for imputing misconduct to the magistrates if they took another view.

MR. HEALY: Might I ask if the hon. and learned Gentleman is aware that the Attorney General for Ireland has given an opinion that the word "agent" signifies either a solicitor or barrister, and no one else?

THE SOLICITOR GENERAL FOR IRELAND (Mr. WALKER): I am not aware of any such decision?

MR. HEALY: Then, I may tell the hon. and learned Gentleman that a written opinion to that effect by the right hon. and learned Attorney General for Ireland (Mr. Naish) exists.

LAW AND JUSTICE (IRELAND)—THE MAGHERAFELT PRISONERS.

MR. HEALY asked the Chief Secretary to the Lord Lieutenant of Ireland, What is the cause of the delay in replying to the memorial of the people of Magherafelt, county Derry, forwarded on 24th June to His Excellency, for a remission of sentence on three prisoners; whether the memorial is signed by two local magistrates, by the parish priest, the Protestant rector, the Presbyterian minister, and many respectable inhabitants; and, whether, as the men's sentences must expire at a comparatively near period, the Executive will give it consideration without further delay?

MR. TREVELYAN: A Memorial was received on the 1st of July, and was laid before the Recorder. His Report has not yet been received, though asked for; and until this Report is received the Lords Justices cannot decide upon it.

COMMITTEE OF PUBLIC ACCOUNTS—THE SECRET SERVICE FUND.

MR. GRAY asked the Chief Secretary to the Lord Lieutenant of Ireland, Whether his attention has been called to the Letter of the Exchequer and Audit Department to the Secretary to the Treasury, dated March 22nd last, and printed on page 169 of the Appendix to the Report from the Committee of Public Accounts, wherein complaint is made that, amongst others, the Chief Secretary for Ireland does not vouch the expenditure of that portion of the Secret Service Fund expended by him, "by the solemn declaration which the statute prescribes;" and, whether he is prepared to make this declaration in future?

MR. TREVELYAN: I understand that on receipt of the letter in question the Treasury took the opinion of the Law Officers of the Crown upon the points raised in it, the Audit Office letter being set out *in extenso* in the case. The opinion has been communicated to the Comptroller and Auditor General, and is now under his consideration.

MR. GRAY: I may point out to the right hon. Gentleman that he has not answered my Question.

MR. GRAY asked the Secretary of State for the Home Department, Whether his attention has been called to the Letter of the Exchequer and Audit Department to the Secretary of the Treasury, dated 22nd March last, and printed on page 169 of the Appendix to the Report from the Committee of Public Accounts, wherein complaint is made that, amongst others, the Secretary of State for the Home Department does not vouch the expenditure in that portion of the Secret Service Fund expended by him, "by the solemn declaration which the statute prescribes;" and, whether he is prepared to make this declaration in future?

SIR WILLIAM HARCOURT: Although I believe and am advised that, as regards the money disposed of under my authority, I am not called upon to make a statutory declaration, I always like to be on the safe side; and, therefore, I did make a statutory declaration two months before the letter of the Comptroller and Auditor General was written.

MR. GRAY asked the Secretary to the Treasury, Whether he is prepared to act for the future on the recommendation of the Exchequer and Audit Department contained in the following paragraph of the letter addressed to him by the Chief Clerk of that Department on March the 22nd last, and printed on page 170 of the Appendix to the Report from the Committee of Public Accounts:—

"I am to take this opportunity of calling their Lordships attention to the sum of £10,000 charged upon the Consolidated Fund, under the authority of Act 1 Vic. chap. 2, sec. 15, for Secret Service, but at present admitted to the account of the Consolidated Fund upon the simple receipt of the Parliamentary Secretary to the Treasury, and I am to state that in the Comptroller's and Auditor General's opinion there should be in this case, as in the case of voted money, a certificate of actual expenditure within the year, and surrender of any unexpended balance, and the declaration before the High Court of Justice required under the Act."

MR. COURTNEY: The point was included in a case laid before the Law Officers of the Crown, and their opinion upon it has been communicated to the Comptroller and Auditor General, and is still under his consideration. The matter will necessarily come before the Public Accounts Committee next year, and it is not for me to say what view they will take of it. In the meanwhile, it would premature to suggest any alteration in the existing practice, which is, I believe, of long standing.

MR. GRAY asked the Parliamentary Secretary to the Treasury, Whether he is prepared in future to vouch by solemn declaration before the High Court of Justice, as required under the Act, the Secret Service money received by him, as recommended by the Auditor General in his letter to the Secretary to the Treasury, printed on page 170 of the Appendix to the Report from the Committee on Public Accounts, and to surrender any unexpected balance, as recommended in the same letter?

LORD RICHARD GROSVENOR: I cannot give any more definite answer than has been given by my Colleagues. I think the answer that has just been given by the Secretary to the Treasury covers the ground.

MR. GRAY asked whether the Secretary to the Treasury was prepared to make the statutory declaration if required?

[No reply.]

CENTRAL ASIA—DELIMITATION OF THE AFGHAN FRONTIER.

MR. ONSLOW asked the Under Secretary of State for India, Whether he can now give full particulars regarding the arrangements made by Her Majesty's Government for the fixing of the boundaries of Afghanistan and the neighbouring Countries; and, whether the officers appointed for this duty are to have any escort during the time they are so employed?

MR. J. K. CROSS: The communications between Her Majesty's Government and the Government of Russia, and between the Viceroy and the Ameer of Afghanistan, on the subject of the proposed delimitation of the Afghan Frontier, are not yet complete; and, therefore, it is not possible to give the full particulars for which the hon. Member asks. I may say, however, that Major General Sir Peter Lumsden has been appointed British Commissioner to examine and report on the boundaries in question, in association with a Russian colleague, and it is hoped that the Commission will begin work in October next. The party will be accompanied by a moderate escort, the details of which are under consideration.

MR. BOURKE asked if the escort was to be provided by the Ameer of Afghanistan, or was it to be a British escort?

MR. J. K. CROSS replied, that he had stated that these details were under consideration. He could not state the exact numbers or the composition of the escort.

MR. BOURKE asked if the Commission had received the assent of the Ameer of Afghanistan?

MR. J. K. CROSS said, it had received the assent of the Ameer; but

ATTORNEYS AND SOLICITORS (IRELAND) ACT, 1866—MR. ROBERT D. O'BRIEN.

MR. HEALY asked Mr. Solicitor General for Ireland, Whether Mr. Attorney General will give the necessary sanction, under "The Attorneys and Solicitors (Ireland) Act, 1866," to the Incorporated Law Society to recover the penalty of £50 incurred by Robert D. O'Brien, 2, Lower Glentworth Street, Limerick, for having, without professional status, on the 21st July, conducted an eviction case before the Rathkeale Bench, in absence of plaintiff or solicitor; and, whether the conduct of the magistrates, in allowing a non-professional person to appear in the case, in spite of the protest of a solicitor in court, will be brought under the notice of the Lord Chancellor?

THE SOLICITOR GENERAL FOR IRELAND (Mr. WALKER): No application to sanction any proceeding has been received by the Attorney General for Ireland from the Incorporated Law Society. He will carefully consider any such application if made. Mr. Robert O'Brien is the brother of the complainant, and, as such, might come within the definition of his "agent" in the Petty Sessions Act, 1882; and, if authorized by his brother, he might, with leave of the Court, appear and be heard. There seems no ground for imputing misconduct to the magistrates if they took another view.

MR. HEALY: Might I ask if the hon. and learned Gentleman is aware that the Attorney General for Ireland has given an opinion that the word "agent" signifies either a solicitor or barrister, and no one else?

THE SOLICITOR GENERAL FOR IRELAND (Mr. WALKER): I am not aware of any such decision?

MR. HEALY: Then, I may tell the hon. and learned Gentleman that a written opinion to that effect by the right hon. and learned Attorney General for Ireland (Mr. Naish) exists.

LAW AND JUSTICE (IRELAND)—THE MAGHERAFELT PRISONERS.

MR. HEALY asked the Chief Secretary to the Lord Lieutenant of Ireland, What is the cause of the delay in replying to the memorial of the people of Magherafelt, county Derry, forwarded on 24th June to His Excellency, for a remission of sentence on three prisoners; whether the memorial is signed by two local magistrates, by the parish priest, the Protestant rector, the Presbyterian minister, and many respectable inhabitants; and, whether, as the men's sentences must expire at a comparatively near period, the Executive will give it consideration without further delay?

MR. TREVELYAN: A Memorial was received on the 1st of July, and was laid before the Recorder. His Report has not yet been received, though asked for; and until this Report is received the Lords Justices cannot decide upon it.

COMMITTEE OF PUBLIC ACCOUNTS—THE SECRET SERVICE FUND.

MR. GRAY asked the Chief Secretary to the Lord Lieutenant of Ireland, Whether his attention has been called to the Letter of the Exchequer and Audit Department to the Secretary to the Treasury, dated March 22nd last, and printed on page 169 of the Appendix to the Report from the Committee of Public Accounts, wherein complaint is made that, amongst others, the Chief Secretary for Ireland does not vouch the expenditure of that portion of the Secret Service Fund expended by him, "by the solemn declaration which the statute prescribes;" and, whether he is prepared to make this declaration in future?

MR. TREVELYAN: I understand that on receipt of the letter in question the Treasury took the opinion of the Law Officers of the Crown upon the points raised in it, the Audit Office letter being set out *in extenso* in the case. The opinion has been communicated to the Comptroller and Auditor General, and is now under his consideration.

MR. GRAY: I may point out to the right hon. Gentleman that he has not answered my Question.

MR. GRAY asked the Secretary of State for the Home Department, Whether his attention has been called to the Letter of the Exchequer and Audit Department to the Secretary of the Treasury, dated 22nd March last, and printed on page 169 of the Appendix to the Report from the Committee of Public Accounts, wherein complaint is made that, amongst others, the Secretary of State for the Home Department does not vouch the expenditure in that portion

and who ranks as the principal Inland Revenue official in that country, has a salary of only £700, by annual increments to £800, whilst the Chief Clerk of the Stamp and Tax Branch of the same Department, really a subordinate, receives £750; whether it is a fact that the maximum salary and duty pay attainable by a Chief Clerk in the Excise Branch, Custom House, Dublin, is only £250, though a lower division clerk in the Stamps and Taxes may reach £300; whether the superintending clerk, Excise Branch, in the same office, receives only £300, though the ordinary clerks in the Stamps and Taxes, in the next room, are paid at the rate of £450; whether third class surveyors of Customs are paid maximum salaries of £420 and overtime allowances, whilst second-class supervisors of Inland Revenue, performing more numerous and important duties, receive only a maximum of £270, and are paid nothing for overtime or even when doing double duty; whether examining officers of Customs are paid a maximum salary of £300 and overtime pay, though division officers of Inland Revenue of corresponding official rank and duties, and who are in addition accountants and book keepers for their respective stations, are only granted a maximum of £200 and no overtime pay; and, whether if such are the facts, the Chancellor of the Exchequer will take steps to place these officers on a more equal scale of salaries?

MR. COURTNEY (for the CHANCELLOR of the EXCHEQUER) said: The maximum salary of the Collector of Inland Revenue in Dublin is £800, that of the Chief Clerk of the Stamp and Tax Department is £650, and he also receives £50 for special duties. These two Departments are quite distinct, the Head of the latter being the Controller of Stamps and Taxes. The normal maxima for a Chief Clerk in the Excise branch and Lower Division clerk in the Stamps and Taxes are the same—namely, £2[illegible]; and each has a chance of rising to £[illegible] by promotion and duty pay respectively. The only clerks at £450 in the Stamps and Taxes are redundants, who will be replaced on vacancies by Lower Division clerks. Third class Surveyors of Customs, except in London and Liverpool, rise to £[illegible] only. It is true that second class Supervisors of Excise rise to £270 only, and the fluctuating nature of their work does not admit of a system of overtime payments; but I do not know on what ground the hon. Member says their duties are more important than those of the Surveyors of Customs. It is true that Examining Officers get £300 and also overtime for work additional to their regular hours of attendance, while Division Officers rise to £200 only, and could not get overtime allowances, owing to the fluctuating nature of their duties. I do not think it is possible to compare the relative importance of different classes of officers in two services, whose duties are performed under very different conditions; and I may say that each Board would maintain that its service was more economical than the other; but if there be any real inequality, the proper method of correcting it would appear to be a reduction in the cost of the more highly-paid Department.

EVICTIONS (IRELAND)—BARONY OF CASTLEA, CO. LIMERICK.

MR. O'SULLIVAN asked the Chief Secretary to the Lord Lieutenant of Ireland, If he is aware that the three tenants, Messrs. O'Connell, Murphy, and the widow Casey (who were lately evicted off the property of C. John Coote, in the barony of Castlea and county of Limerick), have written to the landlord within the past two months, offering to accept their former farms at whatever terms the Land Court may fix for rent and arrears; and, if he is aware that there are no other farms in that district from which tenants have been evicted but those on Mr. Coote's property; and, if so, under those circumstances, whether it is just to the public taxpayers to continue six police in charge of those farms?

MR. TREVELYAN: The alleged communications of the evicted tenants to their landlord are not matters of which any official record would exist; and in the absence of the landlord and his agent the police have not been able to make any inquiry. I may mention, however, that the number of police on these farms is two, not six, as stated in the Question.

MR. O'SULLIVAN: May I ask whether any crimes have ever been committed in the county to render the police necessary?

[No reply.]

the Afghan representatives had not yet been appointed.

MR. ONSLOW: Considering the great importance of this subject, I will, on this day week, put the following and, perhaps, other Questions:—Under whose protection the Commission recently appointed to fix the Afghan Boundaries will be; will the Ameer be represented; if so, by how many officers; what will be the duties of the Commission, and what orders have been given to them; in case of difference of opinion between our officers and the Russian officers, or those of the Ameer, to what Government will our officers refer; is the escort to be provided to consist entirely of Native Troops; and, what arrangements have been made for constant communication between our officers and either the Home Government or the Government of India?

MR. BOURKE: In consequence of the answer of the hon. Gentleman, I wish to give Notice that, on going into Committee of Supply, I will move—

"That it is inexpedient for Her Majesty's Government to incur such obligations as those which the proposed arrangement for fixing the boundaries of Afghanistan must necessarily impose upon this Country."

Subsequently,

MR. ONSLOW: I beg to ask the Prime Minister a Question, of which I have not been able to give him private Notice, Whether, before the Prorogation of Parliament, the Government will give the House and the country full opportunity of discussing the contemplated mission of British officers for the delimitation of the Afghan frontier?

MR. GLADSTONE: That is a Question of great importance, and one upon which the House will be glad to be informed; but I am not able to say, without Notice, whether particulars can be communicated in advance.

MR. ONSLOW: I will put the Question down for Monday.

ARMY (ORDNANCE DEPARTMENT)—COLONEL MONCRIEFF'S GUN-CARRIAGE.

COLONEL KING-HARMAN asked the Secretary of State for War, Whether it is true that the experiments lately made at Woolwich with the Moncrieff hydro-pneumatic disappearing carriage-gun were carried on without the inventor having had any notice or any opportunity of being present?

THE MARQUESS OF HARTINGTON: The War Department has not obtained any hydro-pneumatic carriages for permanent works from Colonel Moncrieff himself. They purchased a hydro-pneumatic carriage from Messrs. Easton and Anderson, Colonel Moncrieff's engineers, which was delivered in September last year; and it is believed that this carriage was manufactured by Messrs. Easton and Anderson upon designs furnished by Colonel Moncrieff. A representative of Messrs. Easton and Anderson attended the trial on January 9, 1884, and again on May 20, 1884. Messrs. Easton and Anderson had had notice of every trial, and might, if they had so desired, have secured the attendance of their client, the inventor, on every occasion.

In reply to Sir WALTER B. BARTTELOT,

THE MARQUESS OF HARTINGTON said, he believed the Committee was the Ordnance Committee; it was not a Constructive Committee, but only a Judicial Committee.

GRAND JURY ACT—COUNTY CESS—MR. DOWLING, CAPPAWHITE.

MR. MAYNE asked the Chief Secretary to the Lord Lieutenant of Ireland, Whether it is true that County Cess for a period of two or more years remain due of Mr. Dowling, Inchinquillip, Cappawhite; and, have the Poor Rates been regularly collected off this property during that time by another collector; and, if so, why is it that the County Cess has not been regularly collected?

MR. TREVELYAN, the Secretary of the Grand Jury reports that he is not aware that there are any arrears of county cess due on Mr. Dowling's property, as the barony collector has paid up the amount of his warrant regularly. The Clerk of the Union reports that there is a balance of about £10 of poor rates outstanding, which has been transferred to this year's rate.

INLAND REVENUE OFFICE, DUBLIN—SALARIES.

MR. ARTHUR O'CONNOR asked Mr. Chancellor of the Exchequer, Whether it is true that the Collector of Inland Revenue for Dublin, and Receiver General of Stamp Duties for Ireland,

and who ranks as the principal Inland Revenue official in that country, has a salary of only £700, by annual increments to £800, whilst the Chief Clerk of the Stamp and Tax Branch of the same Department, really a subordinate, receives £750; whether it is a fact that the maximum salary and duty pay attainable by a Chief Clerk in the Excise Branch, Custom House, Dublin,' is only £250, though a lower division clerk in the Stamps and Taxes may reach £300; whether the superintending clerk, Excise Branch, in the same office, receives only £300, though the ordinary clerks in the Stamps and Taxes, in the next room, are paid at the rate of £450; whether third-class surveyors of Customs are paid maximum salaries of £420 and overtime allowances, whilst second-class supervisors of Inland Revenue, performing more numerous and important duties, receive only a maximum of £270, and are paid nothing for overtime or even when doing double duty; whether examining officers of Customs are paid a maximum salary of £300 and overtime pay, though division officers of Inland Revenue of corresponding official rank and duties, and who are in addition accountants and book-keepers for their respective stations, are only granted a maximum of £200 and no overtime pay; and, whether, if such are the facts, the Chancellor of the Exchequer will take steps to place these officers on a more equal scale of salaries?

MR. COURTNEY (for the CHANCELLOR of the EXCHEQUER) said: The maximum salary of the Collector of Inland Revenue in Dublin is £800; that of the Chief Clerk of the Stamp and Tax Department is £650, and he also receives £50 for special duties. These two Departments are quite distinct, the Head of the latter being the Controller of Stamps and Taxes. The normal maxima for a Chief Clerk in the Excise branch and Lower Division clerk in the Stamps and Taxes are the same—namely, £250; and each has a chance of rising to £300, by promotion and duty-pay respectively. The only clerks at £450 in the Stamps and Taxes are redundants, who will be replaced on vacancies by Lower Division clerks. Third class Surveyors of Customs, except in London and Liverpool, rise to £340 only. It is true that second class Supervisors of Excise rise to £270 only, and the fluctuating nature of their work does not admit of a system of overtime payments; but I do not know on what ground the hon. Member says their duties are more important than those of the Surveyors of Customs. It is true that Examining Officers get £300 and also overtime for work additional to their regular hours of attendance, while Division Officers rise to £200 only, and could not get overtime allowances, owing to the fluctuating nature of their duties. I do not think it is possible to compare the relative importance of different classes of officers in two services, whose duties are performed under very different conditions; and I may say that each Board would maintain that its service was more economical than the other; but if there be any real inequality, the proper method of correcting it would appear to be a reduction in the cost of the more highly-paid Department.

EVICTIONS (IRELAND)—BARONY OF CASTLEA, CO. LIMERICK.

MR. O'SULLIVAN asked the Chief Secretary to the Lord Lieutenant of Ireland, If he is aware that the three tenants, Messrs. O'Connell, Murphy, and the widow Casey (who were lately evicted off the property of C. John Coote, in the barony of Castlea and county of Limerick), have written to the landlord within the past two months, offering to accept their former farms at whatever terms the Land Court may fix for rent and arrears; and, if he is aware that there are no other farms in that district from which tenants have been evicted but those on Mr. Coote's property; and, if so, under those circumstances, whether it is just to the public taxpayers to continue six police in charge of those farms?

MR. TREVELYAN: The alleged communications of the evicted tenants to their landlord are not matters of which any official record would exist; and in the absence of the landlord and his agent the police have not been able to make any inquiry. I may mention, however, that the number of police on these farms is two, not six, as stated in the Question.

MR. O'SULLIVAN: May I ask whether any crimes have ever been committed in the county to render the police necessary?

[No reply.]

RAILWAY REGULATION ACT AMENDMENT—LEGISLATION.

MR. CRAIG-SELLAR asked the President of the Board of Trade, Whether he intends to re-introduce the Railway Regulation Act Amendment Bill next Session; and, if so, whether he will consider the expediency of extending the functions of the Superior Court of Record under that Bill, so as to enable it to relieve the Committees of this and the other House of Parliament of the duty now imposed upon them of investigating and dealing with questions of fact relating to Railway Bills?

MR. CHAMBERLAIN, in reply, said, he was afraid he could not give his hon. Friend any definite reply to his Question. In his judgment, the matter his hon. Friend suggested for consideration was hardly one that would come properly within the scope of the Bill introduced this Session. His hon. Friend asked whether that Bill would be reintroduced next Session. If by that he meant the Autumn Session, certainly not. If he meant the Session of next year, all he could say was that it would be quite premature at present to consider what legislation would be proposed for that Session.

GRAND JURY ACTS—COLLECTION OF COUNTY CESS—CO. KERRY.

MR. HARRINGTON asked the Chief Secretary to the Lord Lieutenant of Ireland, Whether his attention has been directed to the following passages in the report of the auditor presented to the Grand Jury of the county of Kerry at the present assizes:—

"In previous reports I have drawn attention to the delay on the part of some of the barony constables in collecting the amount of Cess, for which they are respectively responsible. Not only, however, has no improvement taken place, but the position of affairs has been getting from bad to worse, and all of which would have been avoided if the provisions of the 148th section of the Grand Jury Act had been enforced—that section requiring each barony constable to pay the entire amount of his warrant to the treasurer two days before the first day of the next Assizes, in default of which he should, according to the 7th section of the Act, Geo. 4, c. 33, lose and forfeit all poundage claimed by him.

"The result of this serious omission, in not carrying out the Law, is accordingly the accumulation of arrears of county cess up to March last, amounting to the large sum of over £4,600.

"Another grave circumstance is the delay which continues to take place on the part of some of the barony constables in the lodgment of their respective collections, the gentlemen referred to persistently acting as if in total disregard both of the terms of the Order in Council and of the Grand Jury Acts, by which they are required to make regular lodgments to the credit of the county, and are prohibited from at any time retaining in hand more than £100.

"The collectors to whom I refer are Messrs. C. E. Leahy, Arthur Hutchins, and F. M'G. Denny. With the exception of £65, lodged by Mr. Leahy in December last, no other sum was paid into the credit of the county by any of the gentlemen named from the time they got their warrants, in September last, until within a few days of the Assizes in March;"

and, what steps he proposes should be taken to remedy this state of things?

MR. TREVELYAN: It is a fact that the auditor reported to the Local Government Board to the effect described, and the Board sent a copy of the Report to the Secretary of the Grand Jury, and have no power to interfere further in the matter. The county cess collectors are appointed at each Assizes by the Grand Jury. They are entirely the officers of the Grand Jury, and the Government have no control over them. It was, therefore, for the Grand Jury to take such action as they might deem necessary in the circumstances brought to their knowledge; and I understand that at the late Assizes they appointed a Committee to inquire into the matter, and received an explanation from the Inspectors which they deemed satisfactory.

STATE OF IRELAND—ORANGEMEN AT LISBURN.

MR. GRAY asked the Chief Secretary to the Lord Lieutenant of Ireland, Whether complaints have been made to the police that Orange drumming parties at Lisburn systematically annoy Catholics by playing outside or near the chapel on Saturday nights at the hour when Catholics are at confession therein; whether the police paid any attention to these complaints; and, whether the police permitted Orange arches to be erected in the Catholic quarter in such positions as to render it impossible for Catholics to attend their places of worship without passing under these arches?

MR. TREVELYAN: I am informed that some of the Roman Catholic clergy at Lisburn have complained of drumming parties passing the chapel. It has been the practice for many years past for drumming parties to pass up and down the streets of Lisburn on Saturday nights, and the practice does not appear to have caused any ill-feeling. The drumming parties never interfere with their Roman Catholic neighbours; and as they are peaceable and commit no offence, the police have not thought it prudent, in the interest of the peace of the town, to attempt to stop them. On the occasion of the recent anniversaries Orange arches were erected in several places; but they cannot be said to have been placed in a Catholic quarter, as there is no Catholic quarter in the town. Catholics and Protestants live in every part of it, and on good terms with each other.

MR. GRAY: May I ask the right hon. Gentleman if he is aware whether it is a fact that the Catholics could not go to their church on Sunday without passing under them?

MR. TREVELYAN: As the Catholics and Protestants live indiscriminately about the town, I am afraid that that would be the case.

LAW AND JUSTICE (IRELAND)—PETTY SESSIONS COURT AT CASTLE-WELLAN, CO. DOWN.

MR. GRAY asked the Chief Secretary to the Lord Lieutenant of Ireland, Whether the same room is used at Castlewellan, county Down, for an Orange Hall, a Freemasons' Hall, for Protestant religious instruction, and for Petty Sessions and Road Sessions?

MR. TREVELYAN: I am informed that the fact is as stated in the Question. I think the hon. Member will have to ask me more particular Questions on this point, as I do not know enough of the state of the case at present. I do not quite see what the objection is. The cost of a hall would be heavy, and, besides, it would be difficult to get a convenient place, whilst this place is hired for various purposes. In this case the rent of £10 a-year is paid for this matter.

PUBLIC HEALTH (IRELAND) — THE PROTESTANT EPISCOPAL GRAVE-YARD AT DROMORE.

MR. GRAY asked the Chief Secretary to the Lord Lieutenant of Ireland, as President of the Local Government Board, Whether he is aware that in hot weather there is an objectionable effluvium from the Protestant Episcopal Graveyard at Dromore; whether it is a fact that coffins interred there are sometimes only covered with a few inches of earth; whether it is true that a large business is done in this graveyard by cheap interments of persons dying in Belfast, sometimes four or five in a day; and, whether there was a serious epidemic last year in the town?

MR. TREVELYAN: The Executive Sanitary Officer of the district reports that there is not the slightest evidence of any effluvium from the graveyard, and that it is not the fact that interments are carried out in the objectionable manner described. He states that the interments which take place are few in number, and take place only in cases where rights of sepulture exist. The epidemic which occurred last year was scarlatina, and the Medical Officer of Health, who himself lives within 50 yards of the graveyard, states that there was not the remotest connection between the two. Scarlatina was at the same time prevalent in adjoining towns.

THE MAGISTRACY (IRELAND)—KILDY-SART PETTY SESSIONS, CO. CLARE.

MR. KENNY asked the Chief Secretary to the Lord Lieutenant of Ireland, How many magistrates usually attend the Kildysart, county Clare, Petty Sessions Court; if some time ago the board of guardians of the Kildysart Union recommended the names of two gentlemen for appointment to the Commission of the Peace; if the valuation of one was about £500 per annum, and the other over £200; if he will state how many of the magistrates have been appointed in Clare by the present Lord Chancellor, and how many of them are Catholics, and how many recommendations have been forwarded by the Lord Lieutenant of the county; and, whether it is proposed to give effect to the recommendations of the Kildysart Board of Guardians?

MR. TREVELYAN: I am informed that the usual attendance is one, or sometimes two. There are three or four local Justices in the neighbourhood, one or other of whom occasionally attends, with the Resident Magistrate of the district. The Board of Guardians did send a Memorial to the Lord Chancellor, naming two gentlemen for appointment to the Commission of the Peace. Their valuation was given in the Memorial as £454 and £123 respectively. The Lord Chancellor has the recommendation in their behalf under his consideration. Five gentlemen have been recommended by the Lord Lieutenant of the county of Clare. Two have been placed in the Commission. They are believed to be Protestants. The other recommendations have not yet been disposed of.

THE MAGISTRACY (IRELAND)—MR. CLIFFORD LLOYD.

MR. SMALL asked the Chief Secretary to the Lord Lieutenant of Ireland, Whether Mr. Clifford Lloyd is at present in receipt of £125 per annum service pay, or of any other sum out of the Revenues of the United Kingdom; and, if not, up to what time was the last payment of any kind made to him?

MR. TREVELYAN: Mr. Lloyd is not at present in receipt of any sum from any Irish Vote, nor, so far as I am aware, from the Revenues of the United Kingdom. The last payment made to him from the Vote, out of which the salaries of Resident Magistrates are provided, was up to the 15th of September last.

EGYPT (RE-ORGANIZATION)—THE POLICE LAW.

MR. HEALY asked the Under Secretary of State for Foreign Affairs, Is it true that Mr. Clifford Lloyd initiated the Police Law in Egypt without even submitting it to the Egyptian Legislative Council, in accordance with the Constitution accorded by Lord Dufferin; if not, why did the Chamber cause a protest to be inserted in *The Journal Officiel*; is it the case that Mr. Clifford Lloyd threw every obstacle in the way of the working of the Native tribunals instituted by Lord Dufferin; and, is it the case that, although no formal order was issued by him suppressing the Conseil d'Etat, it ceased to meet after Mr. Lloyd's arrival?

LORD EDMOND FITZMAURICE: Mr. Clifford Lloyd drew up a Minute for the organization of the police. This Minute was issued in the form of a Decree by the Egyptian Ministry, who appeared to have considered that it was not necessary to submit it to the Legislative Council. The responsibility lay with them. I have no reason whatever to suppose that Mr. Clifford Lloyd threw any obstacle in the way of the work of the Native Tribunals. The circumstances relating to the suspension of the functions of the Council of State are given in Egypt, No. 12, 1884, pages 24 and 103. Mr. Clifford Lloyd had nothing to do with the matter. I have not seen in *The Journal Officiel* any protest from the Chamber respecting the Police Law; but I understand that there was some expression of opinion. Whether it took an official shape or not I cannot say.

ARMY (INDIA)—GENERAL LIST OF INDIAN OFFICERS.

SIR EARDLEY WILMOT asked the Under Secretary of State for India, Whether his attention has been drawn to Petitions recently presented to this Honourable House by officers of the General List of the Indian Army, complaining that they have been compulsorily placed on Staff Corps scale of promotion, while debarred from equal privileges as to retiring allowances; and, whether Her Majesty's Government will give favourable consideration to those Petitions, in order that General List Indian officers may be placed on an equal footing, as regards those allowances, with officers who joined the Staff Corps prior to September 1866?

MR. J. K. CROSS: The subject of these Petitions has been considered by the Secretary of State; but, in his opinion, there is no ground for extending to the Officers of the General List the actuarial scale of additional pensions awarded to those officers who joined the Staff Corps prior to 1866, and to whose special conditions of service this scale is alone applicable.

ROADS AND BRIDGES (IRELAND)—DRUMHERIFF BRIDGE, CO. LEITRIM.

COLONEL O'BEIRNE asked the Chief Secretary to the Lord Lieutenant of Ireland, If he will give instructions to have the works now in progress in the construction of the piers and abutments of Drumheriff Bridge, county Leitrim, immediately stopped, in order to protect the interests of the cesspayers, as these works are not carried out in accordance with the specification, drawn up by the county Roscommon surveyor, and the late county surveyor of the county Leitrim, the stones not having the required dimensions, or laid in Portland cement and rubble stone, mortar being substituted for backing; and will an inspection of the above works be ordered by a county surveyor on behalf of the county Leitrim; and, if it is a fact that the assistant county surveyor for the county Leitrim refuses to certify that the work is being done in accordance with the specification, and has cautioned the contractor to discontinue building the piers and abutments of the Leitrim portion of the bridge with the materials he is at present using?

MR. TREVELYAN: The bridge is in course of construction between the counties of Leitrim and Roscommon, and the work is being carried on under the direction of a joint Committee appointed by the Grand Juries under the statutory powers vested in them. The Government have no power over the work, nor has any grant been made in aid of it. There is no power in the Government to have the works stopped, or to order an inspection by a County Surveyor on behalf of the county of Leitrim. I am informed that the estimate prepared was for an outlay of £1,900; and that as the presentment passed was only for £700 from each county, the plans had to be departed from in some particulars relating to masonry in order to keep within the estimate. There seems to be a difference of opinion between the officials of the two counties. The joint Committee of the Grand Juries already appointed is the proper tribunal to adjust them, and I hope this Question will have the effect of inducing them to take prompt action. I am aware that the matter has been specially brought to their notice by the Assistant County Surveyor, who raised the objection on the County Leitrim side.

ARMY (AUXILIARY FORCES)—MILITIA QUARTERMASTERS—RETIREMENTS.

COLONEL KING-HARMAN asked the Secretary of State for War, Whether, with reference to the Parliamentary Return respecting Retired Militia Quartermasters, dated on the back 15th March 1884, his attention has been drawn to the case of six retired officers of this rank now living who served 20 years as such, and were allowed on retirement in 1875, 1876, and 1877, a Militia pension less by a shilling a-day than what was allowed in 1817 for only 15 years' service; and also to the case of 13 officers of the same rank and longer service now living, who were compulsorily retired in 1878 on a pension of no higher rate than what was allowed in 1817 for less service; and, whether he intends to propose any arrangement by which these pensions will be in accordance with precedent, and with the position and requirements of these officers?

THE MARQUESS OF HARTINGTON: The Warrant under which the Militia Quartermasters referred to were granted retirement was very carefully considered, and they received the full benefit of its provisions. Moreover, their claims have been repeatedly examined, and it has on each occasion been decided that they have no just cause for complaint. I am not prepared to revise the previous decisions.

NAVY—NAVAL OPERATIONS IN THE SOUDAN—EXTRA PAY.

LORD RANDOLPH CHURCHILL (for Sir H. DRUMMOND WOLFF) asked the Secretary to the Admiralty, Whether the officers and men of the Navy employed in the late Soudan expedition are to receive the same batta as that given to the Army, for the exceptionally hard work imposed on them by recent operations?

MR. CAMPBELL-BANNERMAN: I am not sure that the word "batta" can properly be applied in this case. But a gratuity on the same basis as that awarded for the operations in 1882 will shortly be payable to the Naval and Marine Forces employed in the operations during the spring of this year in the Soudan; the portion for the Navy being distributable according to the Navy prize scale, and that for the Marines under the Army scale.

SIR JOHN HAY: Will there be a Supplementary Estimate?

MR. CAMPBELL-BANNERMAN: I cannot say what will be required; but certainly it is not necessary at present.

SIR JOHN HAY: Under what Vote will this be taken?

MR. CAMPBELL-BANNERMAN: Under Vote 1, Wages to Seamen and Marines.

EGYPT (EVENTS IN THE SOUDAN)—THE TREATY WITH ABYSSINIA.

MR. STANLEY LEIGHTON asked the Under Secretary of State for Foreign Affairs, If any guarantee has been taken by Her Majesty's Government that the cruel methods of savage warfare will not be practised by the Abyssinians in their invasion of the Soudan as the allies of the English, under the Treaty with the Negoosa Negust of Ethiopia?

LORD EDMOND FITZMAURICE: There is no question of an "invasion" of the Soudan by the Abyssinians as the allies of this country; and I may add, what I have already stated in this House, that Her Majesty's Government have no reason to suppose that King John intends to ravish and lay waste the country.

MR. STANLEY LEIGHTON: Do I understand that the Abyssinians are not about to occupy Kassala?

LORD EDMOND FITZMAURICE: That is a totally distinct Question, of which Notice has not been given.

MR. STANLEY LEIGHTON: Is there any understanding that King John is not to invade the Soudan?

LORD EDMOND FITZMAURICE: The Abyssinian Papers are before the House. The agreement with the King of Abyssinia is that he is to assist the withdrawal of the Egyptian garrisons from the three places mentioned, of which Kassala is one.

MR. STANLEY LEIGHTON: Then, Sir, I repeat, have any guarantees been taken that in this invasion of the Soudan by the Abyssinians the cruel methods of savage warfare will not be practised?

LORD EDMOND FITZMAURICE: I have just stated that Her Majesty's Government have no reason to suppose that what the hon. Member calls "cruel methods of warfare" are going to be pursued.

POOR LAW (IRELAND)—MR. R. MOORE, CLERK OF INNISHOWEN UNION, COUNTY DONEGAL.

MR. DEASY asked the Chief Secretary to the Lord Lieutenant of Ireland, Whether Mr. Robert Moore, Returning Officer and Clerk of the Innishowen Union, county Donegal, is also agent for several landlords holding property within the Union; and, whether, if that be so, the Local Government Board will take steps to compel Mr. Moore either to give up his agencies or to resign his office as Clerk of the Union?

MR. TREVELYAN: The Clerk of the Innishowen Union states that he receives rent for four landlords in the Union, and that he has acted in that capacity for the last 30 years. The Local Government Board see no reason to require him to give up this employment, unless it is shown that it causes him to neglect his duties. There is nothing recorded against this officer in the Local Government Board's Department.

POOR LAW (IRELAND)—ELECTION OF GUARDIANS, BANDON UNION.

MR. DEASY asked the Chief Secretary to the Lord Lieutenant of Ireland, Whether a sworn inquiry into the late election for Poor Law Guardian in the Innishannon Electoral Division, in the Bandon Union, county Cork, was demanded on the ground that Mr. George Stanley, the candidate declared elected by the returning officer, was guilty of bribery; whether the Local Government Board have decided to grant such an inquiry; whether the said Mr. Stanley has been elected to the office of rate collector in the Bandon Union at a poundage of sixpence, though a Mr. Dineen tendered to collect the rates at fourpence in the pound; and, whether the Local Government Board approve of Mr. Stanley's appointment; and, if not, what steps they propose to take in reference to it?

MR. TREVELYAN: A resolution requesting a sworn inquiry into the conduct of a collector named Edward Stanley in connection with the election of Mr. George Stanley was proposed at the Guardians' meeting on the 28th of May—but was not passed. The complainants applied to the Local Government Board for a sworn inquiry, and the collector was called on for an explanation; but he died before the matter was disposed of. Mr. George Stanley, having previously resigned his office of Guardian, was elected Poor Rate Collector on the 9th of this month; but, protests having been lodged against his appointment by the majority of the Guardians, the Local Government Board have the matter now under consideration.

PREVENTION OF CRIME (IRELAND) ACT, 1882—EXTRA POLICE AT LIMERICK.

MR. SYNAN asked the Chief Secretary to the Lord Lieutenant of Ireland, Whether Mr. Felix M'Carthy, resident magistrate for the city of Limerick in 1880, 1881, and 1882, applied for an extra police force in those years; whether Mr. Forster, then Chief Secretary to the Lord Lieutenant, visited the city of Limerick in the year 1882; whether he then saw or was permitted to see Mr. M'Carthy; and, whether Mr. Clifford Lloyd was then at Limerick, as resident magistrate for the province of Munster?

Mr. TREVELYAN: On various special occasions in the years mentioned Mr. M'Carthy applied to have the Police Force of the city temporarily strengthened. In May, 1882, he signed a requisition for 25 extra men, which he considered wanted at the time. I understand from my right hon. Friend the Member for Bradford (Mr. W. E. Forster) that he paid no special visit to Limerick; but that on his way to the county of Clare, and again, a few days later, when returning, he spent an hour or two in the city. Mr. M'Carthy, R.M., had no interview with him, nor did he seek one. The suggestion that any hindrance was placed in the way of such a meeting is without foundation. Mr. Clifford Lloyd was then at Limerick, in charge of the counties of Limerick and Clare.

POST OFFICE—NEWSPAPERS.

Mr. GRAY asked the Postmaster General, Whether for years the Post Office made an extra charge for newspapers that were "stitched;" whether, after a long agitation, this charge was abandoned; whether it is true, as stated in a Letter of Mr. H. Trueman Wood to *The Times* of the 22nd instant, that the Department still charges extra for a supplement to a newspaper, if stitched; and, whether, in the case mentioned, the Department made a demand for five pounds on account of its forbearance in not surcharging all copies of last week's *Journal of the Society of Arts*, because it had a stitched supplement?

Mr. FAWCETT, in reply, said, that the regulation with regard to not allowing supplements to be stitched was maintained with the view of placing some limitation on the size and weight of supplements. With regard to the particular journal referred to by the hon. Member, an insufficient amount of postage had been paid; and, in order to obviate the inconvenience of making a separate charge to all the persons to whom copies had been sent, it was arranged that the sender of the journal should pay the insufficient postage, which amounted to exactly £5.

POST OFFICE (IRELAND)—GENERAL POST OFFICE, DUBLIN—FEMALE SUPERVISORS.

Colonel KING-HARMAN asked the Postmaster General, If it is true that female "supervisors" are appointed on the Telegraph staffs of the Leeds, Edinburgh, Glasgow, Newcastle on Tyne, Liverpool, and Manchester Post Offices; why such appointments have not been made on the Dublin Telegraph staff; and, whether there are not three such supervisors appointed at Edinburgh, the female staff of that office numbering 53, whilst, although 70 females are employed in the Dublin Post Office, there are no supervisors appointed?

Mr. FAWCETT, in reply, said, he would inquire whether a better system than that which at present prevailed could be found for the appointment of supervisors.

PUBLIC HEALTH—ALLEGED DEATH FROM VACCINATION.

Mr. HOPWOOD asked the Secretary to the Local Government Board, Whether it be the fact that a child named Horace Best was vaccinated at Hull on June the 9th, and died on the 30th of June after great suffering, and that the cause of death was certified as "erysipelas;" whether there was any cause but vaccination; whether any other case of injurious effects from the same vaccine matter occurred at the same time; whether the parents have requested an inquiry to be conducted by some other person independent of the doctor who operated; and, whether any order has been given in consequence?

Mr. GEORGE RUSSELL: We learn that the child was vaccinated on June 9, and that in the course of the second week after vaccination it contracted erysipelas, which began on the child's neck and extended down the unvaccinated arm and side, affecting the vaccinated arm last and least. This information was communicated to Dr. Walton, the public vaccinator, by the medical attendant, Mr. Cooper, who saw the child until its death on the 30th. He saw no special connection between the erysipelas and the vaccination, and told the parents so. We learn that erysipelas was the cause of death; that it appears to have been certified by Mr. Cooper as "general erysipelas;" that there is no reason for believing that vaccination had anything to do with the production of it; and that the other children vaccinated from the same lymph as the child Best had nothing (beyond regular vaccination) the matter with them. The parents asked for an inquiry as to the death of the child; but at present no action has been taken.

BANKRUPTCY ACT, 1869—WINDING-UP OF PROCEEDINGS.

MR. ARTHUR O'CONNOR asked the President of the Board of Trade, Whether he proposes to take any steps, in accordance with the suggestion of the Acting Controller in Bankruptcy, to enforce the prompt winding up of old bankruptcy proceedings under the Act of 1869?

MR. CHAMBERLAIN, in reply, said, he was inclined to agree with the official referred to; but he had been advised that it would require fresh legislation to effect the object, and, of course, fresh legislation on the subject at the present time could not succeed.

EGYPT (FINANCE, &c.)—ARREARS OF TAXES.

MR. M'COAN asked the Under Secretary of State for Foreign Affairs, Whether there is any, and what, truth in the following statement, telegraphed from Alexandria to a morning paper:—

"The Minister of Finance, directed by the English Government, has just issued a circular insisting on immediate payment of arrears of taxes. This measure forces the cultivators to sell their crops standing—in the case of cotton, three months before the harvest—to speculators, who take advantage of the scarcity of money to pay only about 60 per cent. of the normal value. The circular is disapproved by all the authorities here, and will vastly increase the misery and embarrassment of the fellaheen."

LORD EDMOND FITZMAURICE: No, Sir; Her Majesty's Government has not directed Mr. Egerton to issue any Circular to the above effect, and I am not aware that any such Circular has been issued.

BANKRUPTCY ACT, 1883—BANKRUPTCY OF R. B. SCARBOROUGH.

MR. DIXON-HARTLAND asked the President of the Board of Trade, Whether, at a meeting held at the Official Receiver's (Mr. Cecil Mercer) under the bankruptcy of R. B. Scarborough (Receiving Order, 25th May 1884, Greenwich) the following facts were elicited from the bankrupt—namely, that he had not handed over his books and papers to the Official Receiver, nor disclosed a mortgage he had executed on his property; and whether the chairman of such meeting did express his opinion that it was a case that required the fullest investigation; whether, notwithstanding, the Official Receiver declined to examine the bankrupt when he came up for public examination; and whether the solicitor of one of the creditors specially sent for the purpose was refused permission to do so upon the ground that he had no written authority from his client; whether the Incorporated Law Society, on the 30th day of June last, obtained a Rule Nisi calling upon the Registrar to show cause why the solicitor should not be allowed to examine the bankrupt on behalf of his client; and, whether, notwithstanding the Rule is still pending, the Official Receiver has not consented to the bankrupt passing his public examination without being publicly examined as to his affairs; whether the attention of the Board of Trade has been called to the fact that the words "or his representative authorised in writing," in sub-section four of section seventeen of the Act, are being applied to barristers and solicitors; and, what steps he proposes, under the circumstances, to take?

MR. CHAMBERLAIN: I have made inquiries with respect to the Question of the hon. Member, and have received the following Report:—

"In the bankruptcy of R. B. Scarborough in the County Court of Greenwich—It is not the fact, as implied in the Question, that the bankrupt's books and papers had not been handed over to the Official Receiver at the date of the meeting referred to; but it is quite true that the representative of the Official Receiver who presided at the meeting did express his opinion that it was a case requiring investigation. The Official Receiver did accordingly institute a full investigation into the debtor's affairs prior to the public examination, and having satisfied himself regarding them, he did not decline to examine the bankrupt, but limited such examination mainly to a verification upon oath of certain questions and answers which had previously been reduced to writing and signed by the bankrupt. It is understood that the Court refused to allow a solicitor, who professed to be acting for a creditor, to take part in the examination, because he was not authorized in writing as required by the Act. The Board of Trade have no knowledge of the action of the Incorporated Law Society in the matter. The passing of the public examination and the declaring it concluded is a matter entirely within the jurisdiction of the Court, which the Official Receiver can neither interfere with nor prevent. The attention of the Board of Trade has not been called to the fact referred to in the last clause of the Question. No steps appear to be either necessary or desirable."

The Board of Trade are extremely desirous, as the hon. Member is aware, to have the fullest inquiry made into the conduct of the debtor in all cases.

INDIA—THE POST OFFICE (MADRAS).

MR. JUSTIN M'CARTHY asked the Under Secretary of State for India, Whether he has noticed the assertions repeatedly made of late in the Madras newspapers that the Government of Madras have opened in the post office letters addressed to private individuals; whether he has noticed the fact that one gentleman has officially informed the postal authorities that he has evidence that his letters are regularly copied while in the Post; and, whether it is true that the members of the Governor's Staff, Madras, are allowed by the Governor to send letters Home at soldiers' rates of postage in a special bag from Government House?

MR. J. K. CROSS: The India Office has no official information on this subject, and I have been unable to find in recent numbers of the Madras papers the assertions to which the hon. Gentleman called my attention. It would save great trouble if hon. Members asking Questions about newspaper statements would give the references. As regards the last paragraph of the Question, I have to say that the Governor General and the Governors of Madras and Bombay have the privilege of franking a special bag.

EGYPT—MR. BLUNT.

MR. JUSTIN M'CARTHY asked the Under Secretary of State for Foreign Affairs, Whether the Government intend to make any amends to Mr. Blunt for the treatment he received from Egyptian officials and English officials in Egypt?

LORD EDMOND FITZMAURICE: No, Sir; I am not aware that Mr. Blunt has undergone any treatment which would entitle him to receive amends.

MR. JUSTIN M'CARTHY gave Notice that he would call attention to the subject on the Foreign Office Vote.

INDIA (MADRAS)—SETTLEMENT OF TAXATION.

MR. JUSTIN M'CARTHY asked the Under Secretary of State for India, Whether the Secretary of State will cause inquiries to be made into the complaints made by the Badaga and other native cultivators of lands on the Nilgiri Hills, Madras, against the settlement of taxation now being effected in their district; and, whether this settlement, dating from 1882, is of a novel character?

MR. J. K. CROSS: The settlement in question is not of a novel character. Its object is to ascertain titles, to demarcate forest reserves, and to define areas available for sale under the Waste Lands Rules. The Settlement Officer has reported that the definition of village boundaries is not p pular with the some of the people, who have long been at feud with their neighbours as to grazing and other rights; but that they will soon become accustomed to it, especially as all the rights and privileges they have hitherto enjoyed are secured to them. In these circumstances, the Secretary of State sees no necessity for ordering an inquiry.

EMIGRATION (IRELAND)—THE TUKE EMIGRATION FUND.

MR. HEALY asked, Whether any Government officials audited or vouched the expenditure of the £46,000 of public money granted to the Tuke Emigration Fund; where can the accounts be seen; upon whose recommendation was this large sum given; and, will the Government explain who Mr. Tuke is, or on what grounds he was entrusted with such a disbursement, and if there is any precedent for it?

MR. TREVELYAN: The lists of persons sent out by Mr. Tuke's Committee have always been submitted to a member of the Emigration Committee acting under the Local Government Board, and the Government grant was never recommended until he was satisfied that the emigration had been carried out. There is no other audit of the actual disbursement of each grant, nor has it been considered necessary. The cost of emigration is considerably in excess of the grant, and proof of each emigrant having left the country is sufficient evidence of the fact that the Government grant has been properly appropriated. The Government made their grants under the provisions of Section 20 of the Arrears Act, which provided that grants for emigration purposes might be made to such body or persons as the Lord Lieutenant might approve. The Lord Lieutenant had every confidence in the gentlemen forming Mr. Tuke's Committee.

Grants have in the same manner been made to four other Committees formed in Ireland under the provisions of the section referred to.

Mr. T. P. O'CONNOR asked whether the attention of the right hon. Gentleman had been called to the list of paupers at Castle Garden sent out by Mr. Tuke's Committee?

Mr. TREVELYAN: I have seen a notice in the newspapers about it. I will make inquiries on the subject.

Mr. HEALY: Would the right hon. Gentleman answer that part of the Question as to who Mr. Tuke is?

Mr. TREVELYAN: Mr. Tuke is a man of great benevolence, who has done great service.

LAW AND JUSTICE (IRELAND)—THE DUBLIN SCANDALS.

Mr. HEALY asked the Chief Secretary to the Lord Lieutenant of Ireland, If there is any foundation for the following statement of *The Freeman* in regard to the French-Cornwall case:—

"It is stated that Chief Superintendent Mallon has been relieved from the duties of Chief Superintendent of the Dublin Metropolitan Police pending the termination of the present inquiries and probable trials. His duties will be temporarily carried out by Superintendent Laracy, of the B Division;"

if so, on what grounds and by whose orders was Mr. Mallon suspended; and, have the Government made any inquiry into the charges of neglect brought against Colonel Bruce, Inspector General, in regard to the French case?

Mr. TREVELYAN: The statement quoted has no foundation beyond the fact that Mr. Mallon's time is so much occupied at present that it has been found necessary to give him some assistance in his ordinary duties; and by the desire of the Commissioner of Police this assistance is afforded by Superintendent Laracy. The Government see no ground for reviewing the conduct of Colonel Bruce.

RAILWAYS—CHEAP TRAINS ACT, 1883 —THE MIDLAND RAILWAY.

Mr. THOROLD ROGERS asked the President of the Board of Trade, On what principle the fares on the Midland Railway from Kentish Town to Upper Holloway are charged a Passenger Tax of five per cent, although the line has on both sides masses of houses, and although there is a street Railway (called a Tramway) from Kentish Town to Upper Holloway which pays no Passenger Duty, and therefore competes unfairly with this part of the Midland Railway?

Mr. CHAMBERLAIN: According to the recommendation of the officer appointed to report on the applications under the Cheap Trains Act, 1883, the district to which the hon. Member refers is stated not to be one which in the opinion of that officer complies with the conditions specified in Clause 2, subsections 2 and 3, of that Act. If, however, the Railway Company consider themselves aggrieved by this decision, I shall be very happy, on receiving further application, to reconsider the matter.

LAW AND POLICE—COUNTY OF WATERFORD.

Mr. O'DONNELL asked the Chief Secretary to the Lord Lieutenant of Ireland, How many police form the regular free force in the county of Waterford; how many of this force have been on service outside the county during the past six months; and, how many police have been charged as extra police to the county of Waterford in the same period?

Mr. TREVELYAN: The free force is 219. The present extra force is 66. Without time for inquiry, I cannot say how many men, if any, have been sent out of the county during six months. If the hon. Member will repeat his Question on a later day I shall be happy to answer it.

STRAITS SETTLEMENTS—THE RAJAH OF TENOM—CREW OF THE "NISERO."

Mr. STOREY asked the Under Secretary of State for Foreign Affairs, Whether the Dutch have yet given a definite reply to Earl Granville's Despatch of July 19th, so as to obviate further delay in the active operations for the release of the crew of the *Nisero*?

Lord EDMOND FITZMAURICE: Yes, Sir. Identical instructions have been agreed upon and despatched telegraphically, both by Her Majesty's Government and the Netherlands Government. They will be laid before the House.

Mr. PULESTON asked if the noble Lord was aware that the Paper presented to Parliament on this subject was published in Holland four or five days before it was given to the Members of that House?

LORD EDMOND FITZMAURICE: I do not know what Paper the hon. Member alludes to, because the Blue Books published here and in Holland were at short intervals.

MR. PULESTON: The last Blue Book.

LORD EDMOND FITZMAURICE: I do not think that is possible. The last Papers published are up to date.

MR. STOREY asked whether our officials on the spot have altered their oft-expressed opinion that action through or with the Dutch Government, for securing the release of the crew of the *Nisero*, is calculated to insure failure; and whether our officials on the spot have been consulted as to the proposed joint action of the British and Dutch Governments for the release of the crew of the *Nisero*?

LORD EDMOND FITZMAURICE: The action to which the officials on the spot expressed an adverse opinion was not the present plan, which contemplates the use of joint action by the two Powers should the Rajah refuse to release the crew. There have been frequent communications with the Governor of the Straits Settlements and the Acting Governor on the whole subject; and if the hon. Member will refer to page 68 of the Papers recently laid (Netherlands, No. 3) he will see that the plan now about to be carried out was communicated on July 12 to the Acting Governor, who has offered no objection to it.

MR. SLAGG: May I ask whether any further information has been received as to the condition of the crew?

LORD EDMOND FITZMAURICE: No; not since the last statement I made.

MR. STOREY: The noble Lord states that our officials on the spot have not objected to the present procedure. To-morrow I will refer him to page 53 of the Blue Book, where the Acting Commissioner states that unless some compromise were effected between the Dutch and the Natives the lives of the crew would be sacrificed; and I will ask whether our Representatives in those parts have not consistently held to the opinion that action through the Dutch is sure to result in the death of the men?

POOR LAW (SCOTLAND) — APPOINTMENTS UNDER THE BOARD OF SUPERVISION—MESSRS. A. M'KINNON AND A. MARTIN.

DR. CAMERON asked the Lord Advocate, Whether it is true that Mr. Angus M'Kinnon has been appointed Inspector of Poor for the parish of Snizort, in Skye; whether it is true that Mr. M'Kinnon is also Inspector of Poor for the parish of Kilmuir, and lives at a distance of twenty-two miles from one district of the parish of Snizort, and seven miles from the nearest district; whether the Mr. Alexander Martin, who has been appointed collector of poor and school rates for the same parish, is correctly described as a boy of fifteen; and, whether the attention of the Board of Supervision has been called to these appointments?

THE LORD ADVOCATE (Mr. J. B. BALFOUR): It is true that Mr. Angus M'Kinnon has been appointed Inspector of Poor for the parish of Snizort. He is also Inspector of Poor for the parish of Kilmuir; but it was arranged at the time of his appointment that he should for the future reside at Uig, which is a place in the parish of Snizort, and is, in the opinion of the Board of Supervision, a convenient centre from which the two parishes can be worked. The Board of Supervision do not discourage the appointment of the same Inspector for two parishes, as it is often possible by this means to secure the services of a better class of Inspectors than could be obtained for the salary which one parish could afford to give. Mr. M'Kinnon's salary for his recent appointment is £31 10*s.* In such cases, however, the Board of Supervision require that the Parochial Board should appoint some person to receive applications in the parish where the Inspector does not reside; and, on receiving notice of Mr. M'Kinnon's appointment, the Board of Supervision called the attention of the Parochial Board to this rule. I am informed that Mr. Alexander Martin is a youth of 16 years of age; that he has been unanimously appointed by the Parochial Board as collector of rates in succession to his deceased father, for whom he had been doing work for some time past, and he has found security for his intromissions. Mr. Martin's appointment was not intimated to the Board of Supervision, the collector being exclusively the officer of the Parochial Board, removable at their pleasure.

PUBLIC HEALTH—CONDITION OF THE THAMES.

MR. THOROLD ROGERS asked the Secretary of State for the Home Department, Whether he can inform the House as to the communications which have passed between him and the Metropolitan Board of Works as to the present condition of the Thames between London Bridge and Erith or thereabouts; and, whether he will be willing to lay upon the Table of the House the Correspondence which has passed between the parties who have called and paid attention to the facts, and the Metropolitan Board of Works and himself?

SIR WILLIAM HARCOURT: I have been for more than two years in communication with the Metropolitan Board of Works as to the very serious injury caused by the pollution of the Thames through .the outfall of the London sewage. I have addressed several letters to the Board on the subject, and have received replies from them. If my hon. Friend will move next week I should be very happy to present the Correspondence to the House.

PARLIAMENT—PUBLIC BUSINESS—IRISH BILLS IN THE HOUSE OF LORDS.

MR. PARNELL asked the First Lord of the Treasury, Whether his attention has been called to the fact that five Bills, relating exclusively to Ireland, have been rejected during the present Parliament by the House of Lords after having passed the House of Commons, viz. the Limitation of Costs Bill, the Registration of Voters Bill, and the Compensation for Disturbance Bill in the Session of 1880; in the Session of 1883 the Registration of Voters Bill, and, in the present Session, the Poor Law Guardians Elections Bill; that, during the same period, only one Bill relating exclusively to Great Britain, viz. the Local Government Board (Scotland) Bill, was rejected by the Lords under similar circumstances; that, during the same period, the only Irish Bills of a contentious nature, other than Coercion Bills, which have received the Royal Assent, were the Land Act and Arrears Act, passed in the Sessions of 1881 and 1882; and, whether, in view of these facts, and that five Irish Bills have been thus rejected to one Scotch and no English Bill, he will introduce the Poor Law Guardians Bill as a Government measure during the Autumn Session, or send it back to the Lords by tacking it to the Appropriation Bill this Session.

MR. O'DONNELL: I beg to supplement the Question of the hon. Member by asking the right hon. Gentleman whether his attention has been called to the fact that during the present Parliament upwards of 20 measures of reform for Ireland, introduced by Irish Members, have been rejected by Government majorities in the House of Commons; whether he has taken into consideration the fact that in the present Session alone two most important measures—one amending the Land Law Act, and the other amending the Labourers' Dwellings Act—were summarily rejected on second readings in this House; and that a third measure—the Purchase of Land (Ireland) Bill—was withdrawn by the Government, merely, I believe, to produce some political scenic effect; and, whether there is any possibility of the Irish people being relieved from the constant obstruction to Irish domestic interests by both Houses of the Imperial Parliament?

MR. GLADSTONE: I assure the hon. Member, who has put his Question for the purpose of what he calls scenic effect, if he wishes to call my attention to any matter, I must request that some Notice shall be given to enable me to give my attention to the very elaborate query such as that he has now framed. With respect to the Question on the Paper, I have no doubt that the recitals of the hon. Member are accurately made; but I have not had them under consideration except in connection with this particular subject. As regards the last paragraph of the Question, I regret extremely, in company with my right hon. Friend the Chief Secretary for Ireland, the loss of the Bill to which the hon. Member for the City of Cork refers. The Question divides itself into three parts—one whether the Bill can be introduced as a Government measure; another, whether it can be introduced at the Autumn Session as a Government measure; and a third, whether it can be tacked on to the Appropriation Bill? Now, taking these in the reverse order, it cannot be tacked on to the Appropriation Bill; that is a practice contrary to Parliamentary usage.

MR. ARTHUR O'CONNOR: The Paper Duties Bill.

MR. GLADSTONE: I cannot undertake it. Moreover, if it were open to us to tack anything to the Appropriation Bill I am not sure that another measure would not take precedence over this. However, we cannot entertain that subject at all. Neither, at the present moment, can the Government entertain a proposal for the re-introduction of the Bill during the Autumn Session. The House, of course, will exercise its own discretion as to what it shall entertain during the Session; but if the Government were to go beyond this particular Bill —setting aside the case of urgent necessity—with reference to which they have advised Her Majesty to call Parliament together, it is quite evident that they would find it very difficult to stop the addition of other measures. There is one, for instance, to which the hon. Member (Mr. O'Donnell) just referred. The most important practical part of the Question of the hon. Member for the City of Cork I conceive to be whether it will be a Government measure. I cannot give a positive answer to that at the present moment. No doubt the hon. Member heard the reply of the Chief Secretary for Ireland the other day as to the keen regret with which he viewed the rejection of the Bill; and certainly we shall carefully consider whether it can be made a Government measure. A Bill of this kind, as Parliamentary Business used to be conducted—a Bill which was not opposed—not very seriously opposed in this House——

MR. GIBSON: The conduct of the Chief Secretary compelled opposition.

MR. HEALY: It was not divided against at any stage.

MR. GLADSTONE: I believe it was passed without occupying a very great deal of the time of the House. In former times it was practicable to send Bills of this kind to the House of Lords within two or three weeks at the beginning of the Session; but they are now occupied by the debate on the Address. Supply has then to be taken, and the opportunities of discussing such a Bill as this are indefinitely postponed. All I can say is that the Government will take into their careful consideration the question whether the Bill can be made a Government measure; and, if so, it will be put forward in that light.

TOWNS IMPROVEMENT (IRELAND) ACT—THE ENNIS TOWN COMMISSIONERS.

MR. KENNY asked Mr. Solicitor General for Ireland, If his attention has been directed to the fact that the Towns Improvement Act has ceased to be in force in Ennis consequent upon the lapse of the Town Commissioners; if a Resolution of the Ennis Board of Guardians, dated April 9th, was sent to the Local Government Board asking for instructions how to act under the new duty thrown upon them as Sanitary Authority, desiring to know if it was competent for them to take over the waterworks and to undertake the lighting of the town, and to levy the necessary taxation; if the questions sent were submitted to the Law Officers, and when will the answer of the Law Officers be given; if, under the Public Health Act, it is provided (see Clauses 80 and 232) that the lighting and cleansing of the town may be carried on by the Sanitary Authority; upon what grounds it is stated that the waterworks under existing circumstances vest in the Crown; and, if it is not perfectly legal for the Local Government Board to direct the Board of Guardians to assume control of them?

THE SOLICITOR GENERAL FOR IRELAND (Mr. WALKER): Sir, my attention has been drawn to the fact that the Towns Improvement Act has ceased to apply to Ennis, by reason of the Town Commissioners ceasing by their own default to exist as a Corporate Body. A case was submitted to the Law Officers, and they have advised that on the Town Commissioners ceasing to exist the waterworks vested in the Crown as *bona vacantia*. I think the lighting cannot be carried on by the Guardians under Clauses 80 and 232, nor a rate be levied by them for the purpose; nor is it competent for the Local Government Board to direct the Guardians to assume control over the lighting and existing waterworks. The case does not appear to have been contemplated by the Public Health Act; and I have brought in a short Bill to meet this and similar cases.

POOR LAW (IRELAND) — COLLECTOR OF POOR RATES, RATHKEALE UNION, CO. LIMERICK.

MR. JOHN REDMOND asked the Chief Secretary to the Lord Lieutenant of Ireland, Whether his attention has been called to the election of Mr. Michael Slattery as collector of poor rates for No. 1 District of Rathkeale Union, county Limerick; whether, on June 25th, the Poor Law Board fixed July 9th as date for holding the election; whether, on July 2nd, a meeting of the said Board, largely composed of *ex-officio* Guardians, passed a resolution postponing said election until 23rd July; whether resolutions negativing former decisions of the Board are not illegal, according to the Articles provided for guidance of Boards of Guardians by the Commissioners of the Local Government Board without fourteen days' notice, and, consequently, whether the adjournment of said election was not illegal; whether, on the original date fixed for the election, namely, July 9th, a quorum of Guardians assembled and elected Mr. Michael Slattery poor rate collector for the district; and, whether such election was not perfectly legal?

MR. TREVELYAN: The original date fixed for the election of a collector was the 9th of July, as stated; and on the 2nd of July a resolution was unanimously adopted postponing it to the 23rd, on the ground that the majority of the Guardians would be unable to attend on account of the Assizes and the Coleraine Horse Fair. On the postponed date 32 Guardians attended, and a collector was appointed. It is true that Article 13 of the General Regulations as to proceedings of Boards of Guardians provides that no resolution previously adopted shall be rescinded without 14 days' notice; but the Local Government Board do not consider that that was ever intended to apply to a case such as this, in which a Board of Guardians, finding that circumstances would make it inconvenient to hold an election on the day fixed, unanimously adjourned it to another, serving notice on every member, and advertising accordingly. It would, no doubt, have been more strictly regular if the Guardians had received the applications on the date originally fixed, and then postponed the election. With regard to the election of Mr. Slattery, there is no doubt that it was not valid, as he was a sitting Guardian at the time, and therefore ineligible. The circumstances of his election were as follows:—Notwithstanding the fact that all the Guardians were aware of the postponement, four of them —of whom Mr. Slattery was one—attended on the date originally fixed. He handed in his resignation of the office of Guardian to the other three, who proceeded to elect him to the position of collector. The Guardians have no power to accept the resignation of one of their number, and Mr. Slattery was, therefore, still a Guardian until his resignation was accepted by the Local Government Board, who did not receive it until eight days later.

PUBLIC HEALTH (METROPOLIS)—THE DEATH RATE IN LONDON.

MR. RITCHIE asked the First Lord of the Treasury, Whether he has received a letter from the medical officer of health of St. George's-in-the-East on the subject of his late comparison of the death rate in the sub-district of St. John's in that parish with the death rate of St. John's Paddington, to the effect that in St. John's, St. George's-in-the East, 314 out of the total number of 480 deaths registered there occurred in the infirmary of the parish, which is situated in that sub-district, and that 65 acres out of a total area of 98 acres are occupied by the docks with a population estimated at 348 persons, thus making the density of the population, exclusive of the docks, 244 to an acre; and, whether he proposes to make further inquiry into the facts of the case with a view of correcting the statement made by him if he finds his previous statement was based on insufficient information?

MR. GLADSTONE, in reply, said, he had received the letter to which the Question referred; and he assumed that the gentleman who wrote it would take whatever steps he thought fit to give publicity to it. The statement he (Mr. Gladstone) had made was strictly accurate; but there were circumstances which the knowledge of the medical officer enabled him to supply that modified the inferences to be drawn from it.

EGYPT—THE CONFERENCE.

SIR STAFFORD NORTHCOTE: I wish to ask the Prime Minister whether he is in a position to make any statement with regard to the Conference?

MR. GLADSTONE: The Conference met to-day, as I rather think I intimated would be the case when I was last questioned on the subject. A point of considerable importance arose in the course of the discussion to-day on which the Plenipotentiaries found it necessary to refer to their Governments. They all of them undertook to press for an immediate reply; and I should hope that most or all of them will obtain it, even in the short time in which they hope to obtain it—that is to say, by the hour of Business to-morrow. They intend to meet to-morrow, in the hope that they may be in possession of a reply. I cannot say it is quite certain they will be; but I feel perfectly assured they will use every effort to press the matter forward.

SUPPLY—CIVIL SERVICE ESTIMATES—THE FOREIGN OFFICE VOTE.

LORD RANDOLPH CHURCHILL asked the First Lord of the Treasury, When the Vote for the Foreign Office would come on? It would be very convenient to Members if some day for it were fixed; because there were many points of detail which would have to be discussed.

MR. GLADSTONE, in reply, said, that he thought they were sufficiently provided with Business for that night and to-morrow night; but he did not know whether the Business for Wednesday was absolutely settled, and it was a question whether the House should not proceed with the consideration of the first Zulu Vote. To-morrow's Business would be the Civil Service Estimates, and, he believed, the Irish Law Charges.

PALACE OF WESTMINSTER — HOUSE OF COMMONS — VENTILATION OF THE HOUSE.

MR. THOROLD ROGERS: I beg to ask the Secretary of State for the Home Department, Whether the rumour is correct that on a late occasion, when the Houses of Parliament were exceptionally full, and should have been supplied with pure air, sewage gas by some agency was pumped into both Houses by those admirable authorities who manage the Metropolis?

SIR WILLIAM HARCOURT: I believe a Committee has been appointed by you, Sir, to inquire into this matter, and therefore I need not make a statement on the subject.

EGYPT (EVENTS IN THE SOUDAN)—THE TREATY WITH ABYSSINIA.

SIR WILFRID LAWSON: With reference to the answer given by the noble Lord the Under Secretary of State for Foreign Affairs, I beg to ask, Whether, by Article 3 of the Abyssinian Treaty, by which the King of Abyssinia engages to facilitate the withdrawal of the Khedive's troops from the Soudan, he is to allow those troops to pass through his territory, or whether it contemplates the sending of an army to the Soudan?

LORD EDMOND FITZMAURICE: There is a Question on this subject on the Paper for to-morrow, and I shall answer the hon. Baronet's Question then.

NOTICE OF RESOLUTION.

——o——

PARLIAMENT—THE LORDS AND THE REPRESENTATION OF THE PEOPLE BILL.

MR. WILLIS: I beg to give Notice that at the earliest opportunity I shall move the following Resolution:—

"That it is necessary to declare that the House of Lords, in rejecting the Representation of the People Bill for the purpose of forcing the Ministers of the Crown to dissolve Parliament, has abused its authority, encroached upon the prerogative of the Crown, and assailed the independence of this House; and, in refusing its assent to the Second Reading of the said Bill because it did not contain provisions for the redistribution of Electoral Power, has violated the fundamental right and privilege of this House to determine in what order it will redress the grievances that happen within the realm."

MR. NEWDEGATE: I beg to ask the First Lord of the Treasury, Whether Her Majesty's Government will give any facilities for the consideration of the Notice which has just been given?

MR. GLADSTONE: No application has yet been made for the consideration of this subject by the hon. Member who has given Notice; and it is not usual to reply to an application from another Member, even from one so much respected as the hon. and learned Gentleman.

ORDERS OF THE DAY.

—o—

SUPPLY—ARMY ESTIMATES.

SUPPLY—*considered* in Committee.

(In the Committee.)

(1.) £31,600, Miscellaneous Effective Services.

MR. PULESTON said, that upon this Vote he wished to call attention to the subject of the suspension of the Compulsory Clauses of the Contagious Diseases Act. In the course of the Session he had been anxious to obtain an opportunity for saying something on the subject under a little more favourable circumstances than he could have now, at that late period of the Session. However, late as the period of the Session was, he felt it his duty not only to his constituents, but to the public generally, to bring the question forward. Last year the Resolution moved by his right hon. Friend the Member for Halifax (Mr. Stansfeld) was passed by what he would call a sort of snatch vote in the House; and he thought he might say, without his right hon. Friend venturing to contradict him, that the country entertained the confident hope that after the triumph obtained by the right hon. Gentleman, the Government would, as soon as possible, give effect to it by bringing in a Bill based on the lines of the Resolution; no one could have dreamt that the Resolution then passed would have immediate effect given to it by the Government by repealing the existing law. He thought he had a right to say that the course taken by the Government was altogether un-Parliamentary and un-Constitutional. What he had complained of, and what he still complained of, was not that the Compulsory Clauses of the Act should have been suspended, but that they should have been suspended before anything was put in their place. They were promised that a Bill should be introduced. A Bill was laid upon the Table late last Session; but it was afterwards practically withdrawn by the noble Marquess (the Marquess of Hartington), who promised another Bill with some alterations. That Bill was also introduced and withdrawn, and a third Bill promised this Session. Nothing, however, had been done, and they were now at the close of the second year since the Compulsory Clauses of the Act were suspended. A Return had been issued by the War Office, in which the figures strongly indicated the deplorable consequences which had resulted from the suspension of the Acts. It must be borne in mind that those who were in favour of the Acts had not raised an agitation upon the subject. They had no paid Committee, no paid agents, and no paid secretary. They had neither spent hundreds nor thousands of pounds, and therefore they had no opportunity of replying to the enormous quantity of literature which was issued upon this subject day after day, and distributed broadcast throughout the country. Their only course was to bring the matter under the attention of the House; and, although he regretted to occupy the time of the Committee, no other course was open to him. He had received the other day a somewhat important letter, which he was about to quote, from the paid secretary of the Association for the repeal of these Acts, who, condescendingly referring to the answer of the Home Secretary to a Question he (Mr. Puleston) had put, wrote as follows:—

"Apropos of the Home Secretary's prepared answer to your Question yesterday, I beg to call your attention to the inclosed. If, as a superintendent of the police in your borough says—'It is preposterous that the Home Secretary should be hoodwinked in such a manner with the cock-and-bull stories about the much worse state of Devonport; surely it is not only preposterous, but disgraceful, that persons should seek to hoodwink you in a similar manner.'"

Now, he (Mr. Puleston) did not think he was very much hoodwinked in the matter. When he first went to Devonport, he went without prejudice. As far as he knew anything about the working of the Acts, his prejudice was rather against than in favour of them; but having paid, as he considered himself bound to do, a great deal of attention to the subject, having been President of the Royal Albert Hospital, and having gone into the figures and the assumed facts of the right hon. Gentleman the Member for Halifax (Mr. Stansfeld), time after time, he felt himself unable to come to any other conclusion, with due regard to common honesty, than that the Acts, objectionable as they were to some people, were necessary. The noble Marquess the Secretary of State for War had told the House, on more than one occasion, in answer to himself (Mr. Puleston) and other Members, that it was no part of the duty of the Government to protect the morals of the community among whom these Acts were enforced. Perhaps the noble Marquess would bear with him when he said that that was not altogether so, because, if an Imperial Government established barracks, naval depôts, and dockyards in particular localities, they certainly owed it to the community at large to protect the inhabitants of such districts from the consequences of placing large bodies of soldiers and sailors there. He thought that so much, at all events, ought to be readily conceded by the noble Marquess. In view of the statement contained in the letter of the Secretary to the Metropolitan Repeal Association which he had just read to the Committee, he (Mr. Puleston) had taken pains to inquire specially into the condition of the subject at this moment in order that he might not be accused of quoting ancient history. He had, therefore, written last week to friends at Plymouth, Devonport, and Stonehouse, asking them to let him know how the matter stood now. He had received a letter from the Mayor of Plymouth—a gentleman who was known to a good many Members of that House. At one time the Mayor was Chairman of the Liberal Committee in Plymouth, and he was a man very much respected in the borough. Well, the Mayor of Plymouth said—

"I was at one time strongly opposed to the Acts: but, having seen the uniformly judicious action of the Metropolitan Police, and the great improvement that was brought about in our town, I was compelled to admit the beneficial influence of the Acts. Since the Government have ceased to give effect to the Acts, I can only say there is a general testimony as to the sadly altered condition of our streets, and also as to the great increase in the extent and virulence of disease. The magistrates are unanimous in their desire to see the Acts again in operation, and, at the same time, they feel that the local police are not suitable agents to be employed for the purpose. I see much of the opposition comes from Members who are ignorant, or who represent constituents ignorant, of the real working of the Acts; and I believe if they knew something of the places where the Acts have been in operation, not only reducing disease, but lessening prostitution, and, in many cases, leading to reformation, their objections would be withdrawn."

He considered it right to trouble the Committee with these matters, because it was the only way in which he could give an authoritative denial to the leaflets that were constantly issued by the Association of which the right hon. Member for Halifax (Mr. Stansfeld) was the distinguished head. Surely, when he stated in that House, on the evidence of gentlemen of all political Parties, and of the magistrates, that they were unanimous in desiring to see the Acts again in operation, he trusted that hon. Members would accept that statement in preference to the one which was contained in the letter written to him by the Secretary of the Association. He thought the right hon. Gentleman himself, and his hon. and learned Friend the Member for Stockport (Mr. Hopwood) who sat near him, and who took an equal interest in the matter, would feel inclined to repudiate any such authority as that which he had quoted. The ex-Mayor of Plymouth, also a gentleman very well known, and possessing great influence in that part of the country, said—

"The increase of disorder in the streets, the increase of juvenile prostitution, the increase of disease, and the loss of the opportunities for preventive and rescue work, which were afforded and made use of under the operation of the Acts, are now remarkably apparent."

Mr. Shelly went on to say—

"Suspension has had its natural effect, and the streets are still more disorderly than they were when the Acts were in operation. The magistrates are very stern, and do everything they can in order to minimize the effect produced by the suspension of the Acts."

He adds—

"We are greatly shocked and alarmed at the large proportion of very young girls now in the streets. What I may call irregular prostitution —by servant girls, dressmakers, and even by women in a higher position of life—is on the increase. The fear of registration under the Acts was a great deterrent to women of this class, and the police, acting under the Acts, were able to warn them, and to prevent many of them from going astray; but this influence being now removed, there is no check upon them. I have had brought under my notice specially, both in this way and as a magistrate, the great mischief which is done by the large liberty granted to the boys on board the training-ships. This is a matter which ought to be brought to the notice of the Admiralty."

He (Mr. Puleston) had received a great many other letters, with which he would not trouble the Committee; but they brought the question right down to the present day. The letter he held in his hand was one from a very prominent member of his constituency, who was disposed, in the first instance, to look favourably upon the repeal of these Acts, and who had done everything to study the question from a conscientious point of view. He wrote as follows:—

"Notwithstanding these views, with which you are familiar, one thing is very certain, and I am obliged to confess it—namely, that the disease is worse now than it has been for some time; and I may say emphatically that the disease is more prevalent in other places than it was before, and the increased prevalence of the disease is a matter of general remark, but I speak of it as knowing it in my professional practice."

The Town Clerk of Devonport, also, who was not a gentleman who did him (Mr. Puleston) the honour of supporting him politically, but who occupied a very high position in that part of the country, and was not likely to err in any statement he made, because he was constantly on the spot, wrote as follows:—

"There is a general concurrence of opinion in our town that the virtual discontinuance of the operation of the Contagious Diseases Acts, as regards their compulsory powers, has brought about a most remarkable state of things, only too apparent in the condition of our streets, and in the condition and behaviour of women and young girls of loose character. Here, as in other towns, it is found to be practically impossible for the local police to act without the Compulsory Clauses."

He (Mr. Puleston) had taken the liberty of reading the evidence of some of the leading gentlemen in the three towns, and thoroughly well known; and he could not imagine that it was possible for any hon. Member to get up in that House and argue in support of the views enunciated in the leaflets issued and statements made by this Metropolitan Repeal Association, or whatever its name might be. An important Memorial to the Prime Minister from the Association had been placed in his hands that afternoon. It was addressed to the Prime Minister by working men, and was represented to be "The Memorial of the Working Men's National League for the Repeal of the Contagious Acts." There were several statements contained in it which were altogether unwarranted. One was that, under the operation of the Acts, women were set apart for immoral purposes. Of course, that was simply untrue; there was nothing of the kind, either direct or indirect; and it was a remarkable fact that serious men, or a serious Association, should allow themselves to make use of such language, for which there was not the least foundation whatever. Among the papers put in his hands was a translation from a speech by a well-known French Professor, in which the speaker gloated over the action taken in the House of Commons, because he believed that it would help them in France to do away with State-regulated vice. Now, he (Mr. Puleston) would be just as much opposed to State-regulated vice, if it were introduced into this country, as any hon. Member opposite, and he would join cordially with them in preventing the adoption of any such scheme of registration, or anything else in this country which might connect the operation of these Acts with the system now in vogue in France. To assert that there was anything in these Acts in the nature of the French system was simply to mislead the public of this country. He knew that it was a very easy thing indeed to go upon a platform in this country, and place before religious people the enormous evil of State-regulated vice; but the agitation was conducted under a false name by paid agents. The Memorial he held in his hand professed to be signed by working men,; but, on looking over the signatures, he found that they were those of professors of literature, editors of newspapers, and so on. Nevertheless, it was called a Working Man's Association. Against that Memorial he had another which was signed by every magistrate in Plymouth, with the exception of three, and their signatures were not appended to it simply because they happened to be absent at the time the Memorial was drawn up; but they were in agreement with their colleagues. He saw several hon. Members in the House, among others hon. Gentlemen representing Cornwall, who were well acquainted with Plymouth and the three towns, who would be able to judge of the weight to be attached to a Memorial signed, as this was, almost unanimously by the magistrates, and by more than two-thirds of the clergy of all denominations, medical practitioners, and gentlemen belonging to all shades of political opinion. He was glad to mention that fact, because one of the misfortunes connected with the question was that the Resolution of his right hon. Friend the Member for Halifax (Mr. Stansfeld) was carried by the votes of hon. Members on the other side of the House, and, therefore, the appearance of a Party character had been given to the vote. If the right hon. Member for Halifax and his Friends would only visit the three towns, or any other place where these Acts had been in operation, they would find that there was a unanimous opinion against their suspension; and surely the right hon. Gentleman would give the inhabitants of the three towns credit for possessing ordinary intelligence, and for not allowing themselves to be unduly biassed on this important subject. No one desired, naturally, to have Acts like these in operation. He should like to know who could desire them. But he remembered very well his Predecessor, Mr. Delaware Lewis, who represented Devonport in the Parliament of 1868, saying, just before the last Election—

> "If you happen to defeat me there is only one thing I want to say to you, and that is, consider and study well the operation of the Contagious Diseases Acts before you take any stand against them. When I first came here I felt very much disposed to think that they were wrong, but I have given them very careful consideration, and I can only say to you that so far as my opinion may be of any use to you I hope you will act upon it."

He (Mr. Puleston) had gone into the subject as well as he could, and every step he had taken only strengthened his conviction as to the good the acts had done. A Committee of the House of Commons sat upon the subject for four Sessions. His right hon. and learned Friend the Judge Advocate General (Mr. Osborne Morgan) was a Member of that Committee. He had reason to think if the right hon. and learned Gentleman had a bias either one way or the other, it was distinctly against the Acts, and in favour of the views of the right hon. Member for Halifax (Mr. Stansfeld). The right hon. and learned Gentleman, however, signed the Report of the Committee. The right hon. and learned Gentleman was well known in the House, and hon. Members on both sides had a great personal regard for him and for his intelligence, and would not fail to give him credit for desiring to act to the best of his knowledge. Yet the right hon. and learned Gentleman came to the conclusion that these Acts were among the best upon the Statute Book, and that they ought to be retained. The whole of the evidence went to show—after sifting it for four Sessions, and a laborious work it was—that the Acts were necessary; and the Committee, by an overwhelming majority, came to the conclusion that they ought not to have been repealed. But, in the face of all that testimony, Her Majesty's Government, to the astonishment of everybody, upon a Resolution, which might be said to have been snatched in a Division, came down to the House and gave to it, to the amazement of everybody—friend and foe—the sanction of law. Such a thing had never been heard of before. If they had determined that a Bill should be brought forward, and that pending the passing of it the Acts should remain in operation, their course would have been understood. What was more remarkable than all was that the three Cabinet Ministers who alone had to do with the Acts—the First Lord of the Admiralty, the Home Secretary, and the noble Marquess at the head of the War Office—were personally very strongly in favour of the Acts. Why was that the case? It was owing to the fact that of all the Ministers of the Crown they were the three Representatives of the Cabinet who alone had had anything to do with the subject, and they were unanimously in favour of the Acts. The other Members of the Government who were in favour of the Acts were his right hon. and learned Friend the Judge Advocate General and the Secretary to the Admiralty. Only recently, a deputation, headed by the Earl of Mount-Edgcumbe—a deputation composed of gentlemen of the highest character and standing in their respective districts, including the Mayors of every place where the Acts were in force, waited upon the Government in reference to these Acts. The Earl of Mount-Edgcumbe lived in the neighbourhood of Plymouth, and was perfectly well able to understand the operation of the Acts. No one could accuse him of saying anything that was deliberately untrue, and yet the statement issued by the National Association for the repeal of these Acts, with which his hon. and learned Friend the Member for Stockport (Mr. Hopwood) was connected, deliberately denied the statement of the Earl of Mount-Edgcumbe as the mouthpiece of the deputation. [Mr. HOPWOOD: Hear, hear!] His hon. and learned Friend said "Hear, hear!" but he had very little doubt the statements made by the Association were made by men who had no knowledge of the communities among which the

Acts were in operation. Was it reasonable to suppose that any hon. Member, or any individual, who had never paid any attention to the working of the Acts, and who had never lived in the communities in which they were in operation, could be sufficiently good judges of the effects of their working to pronounce that all men were liars who lived in the districts affected, and who were as honourable and as respectable as themselves? He had read a letter from the Secretary of the Association.

MR. STANSFELD: I have called no one a liar.

MR. PULESTON said, that if the right hon. Gentleman imagined for a moment that he attributed such words to him, he might disabuse his mind at once. He might add that he was quite satisfied of the sincerity of the convictions of his right hon. Friend as well as of those of his hon. and learned Friend the Member for Stockport (Mr. Hopwood). The person he referred to was the paid officer and Secretary of the Association of which his right hon. and hon. and learned Friends were active members.

MR. HOPWOOD: I am not a member.

MR. PULESTON begged his hon. and learned Friend's pardon. He had been under the impression that he was a member of the Association; at any rate, he had taken an active part in the agitation for the repeal of the Acts. The right hon. Member for Halifax (Mr. Stansfeld) was, he believed, a member of the Association.

MR. STANSFELD: I am not a member; but, nevertheless, I endorse the acts of the Association.

MR. PULESTON said, this was what the right hon. Gentleman endorsed—that the Home Secretary was hoodwinked with "cock and bull" stories about the moral state of Devonport; and it was not only preposterous, but disgraceful, that other persons should seek to hoodwink him (Mr. Puleston) in a similar manner. His right hon. Friend deliberately endorsed that view after the evidence he (Mr. Puleston) had produced in reference to the feeling of men of the highest character and position in the communities among which the Acts were in operation. What was he obliged to say now, that his right hon. Friend endorsed this statement? He was afraid that he should be obliged to rescind his withdrawal of the expressions complained of. There was no other course left open to him, because those who objected to the compulsory suspension of the Acts had not suffered themselves to be hoodwinked at all. He had already referred to the Memorial to the Admiralty got up by the magistrates, medical practitioners, and others in the boroughs of Plymouth and Devonport, and the township of Stonehouse. In that Memorial was the following statement:—

"We believe that although, if extended, the usefulness of the Contagious Diseases Acts would soon be greatly increased, and more universally recognized, they have been the means of removing a great amount of physical suffering, while they have been the road to reformation to many fallen women, who, were it not for the existence of these Acts, would never have had an opportunity of returning to a respectable course of life."

Therefore, the right hon. Gentleman endorsed a statement which was absolutely untrue. He should be very glad indeed not to have the opportunity of connecting his right hon. Friend with these matters; but if his right hon. Friend endorsed this statement, he gave the lie direct—it was as well to call things by their right names—to the opinion of the magistrates of Plymouth and Devonport, and a large body of clergymen and ministers of religion of every denomination. He (Mr. Puleston) had no hesitation in saying that he believed the Memorialists were thoroughly conscientious in what they did. He was sorry that no one of greater force and weight than himself had undertaken to bring the facts of the case out, because he was entirely convinced that the suspension of the Acts had led to a greatly increased amount of suffering and immorality; and the amount of seduction which had taken place among young girls, now that the powers of these Acts were gone, hon. Members had no notion of whatever. A gentleman in Plymouth, who had taken great interest in the question, had published a correspondence upon the subject. He was a magistrate—Mr. Luscombe—and in answer to statements made by friends of the right hon. Gentleman he quoted a passage from the Report of the Select Committee of the House of Commons—

"That they would call special attention to the fact that in the course of 16 years not a single case has been brought before your

Committee in which any women, alleged to have been wrongfully brought under the operation of the Acts, have brought an action or taken legal proceedings against the police authorities in respect of any act done by them under the Contagious Diseases Acts."

Mr. Luscombe added—

"It is only necessary to look over the evidence given by the opponents, to be convinced that the slightest chance given by the police would have instantly become the basis of proceedings hostile to particular legislation."

The noble Marquess, on more than one occasion, and only the other day the Home Secretary, had pointed out that the local police could themselves enforce the Acts. Mr. Luscombe said—

"I am ready to admit the possibility to some extent; but there are services rendered by the Crown police only, and necessarily so, from the peculiar sources of information open to them. It is not merely the minimizing of a foul disease, but there is a suppression of youthful depravity in the rescue of children from the snares of vice in its most deadly form, and in the assistance ever ready to be given by the parent or guardians when the unexpected and dreaded absence of one of the home group creates a suggestion or terror intelligent enough to those who are familiar with the temptations too rife in a large community."

That statement had been made several times in answer to the remark that other agencies could effect the good which had been going on under the instrumentality of the Metropolitan Police. The local police under the existing Acts did not possess the power necessary to carry out the Acts as they were carried out before the suspension of the compulsory powers. Even if they were a central body, the local police were not competent to deal with the matter on account of their unwillingness. The superintendent of the police at Devonport was deservedly respected, and performed his duty very well; but, surely the statements of the principal people of the town, and the large majority of the most respectable inhabitants, ought to be worth something against the statement of the superintendent of the police. The superintendent of police, however, only referred to the order in the streets. Everybody knew what the condition of the streets in the three towns was, and what the state of morality was before the Acts came into operation; and the fact was, that they had grown greatly and undeniably worse since the suspension of the Acts. No doubt, during the time the Acts had been in operation, now some 16 or 17 years, the state of things had improved; but they were rapidly falling again into their old state. He was sorry the noble Marquess the Secretary of State for War had endorsed the view that it was the duty of the localities to look after their own morals. What had the Societies for the repeal of these Acts done for these poor women? They had spent their money in agitating and in printing; but had they ever done anything to help these poor women by the establishment of voluntary lock hospitals? If they would visit the Royal Albert Hospital in Devonport, they would find that there had been a cessation of voluntary admissions, except in the most severe cases, and the nature of those cases might be taken as a type of an immense mass of disease not under treatment outside the hospital. Was that what hon. Members opposite wanted to promote? [*Cries of* "Oh!"] Hon. Members said "Oh!" but he made this statement on the authority of the Secretary of the Royal Albert Hospital, and if hon. Members doubted it, let them go there and make inquiries. Let them appoint a Voluntary Committee to look into the matter, and sit during the Recess in the three towns. Let them go into the whole question carefully, and let them have all the ministers of every denomination, magistrates, and others before them to examine them for themselves. If they would do that, they would soon become convinced that the consequences of the withdrawal of the Compulsory Clauses of the Act had been deplorable in the extreme. He had no wish to occupy the time of the Committee. Although there was a great deal more which he should like to say in connection with the matter, he thought he had said enough. He hoped that other hon. Members on both sides of the House would advocate a cause like this which had been so neglected by the Government, and which, in spite of all their promises, they had failed to legislate upon. They had admitted that it was necessary to substitute something for what they had taken away; and, notwithstanding the admission, they had allowed, and were allowing, these deplorable consequences of their want of action to go on from month to month. It would be quite an intelligible policy on the part of the Government if they said that nothing was needed. But to suspend the Acts without providing something in their place, although they admitted that something was absolutely and essentially necessary, was a most misguided policy. Not only was it unwise, but in this case it was the most cruel and deplorable policy that could possibly have been pursued by the Government.

SIR EDWARD WATKIN said, he was anxious to say a few words, not because he had not much sympathy with the right hon. Gentleman the Member for Halifax (Mr. Stansfeld) in his notion of the cruelty which might be perpetrated under these Acts, but because what had been reported and proved to him in the borough he represented (Hythe) compelled him to bring the plain logic of facts to bear upon the question. The borough he represented contained the Shorncliffe Camp at one end of it, and the School of Musketry at the other, and the experience of the borough showed that the suspension of the Acts must be looked upon as an unmixed evil. Last year a deputation waited on the Home Secretary, consisting of the principal authorities of Folkestone, Sandgate, and Hythe. He had introduced the deputation to the right hon. and learned Gentleman. What did they say? Sadly enough they informed the right hon. Gentleman that juvenile prostitution was largely on the increase; that as regarded the minor point of disorder in the streets, it was plainly and unmistakably on the increase; that as regarded the increase of disease, lamentable as it was, it was undoubted, and as regarded the virulence of the disease there could be no possible mistake. They, therefore, contended that undoubtedly a curse had been inflicted upon the borough by the abolition of the Acts. He could not find out that there had been a single complaint of abuse on the part of those who had administered the provisions of the Acts in Hythe. There had been no complaint against any of those who had been charged with putting the Acts in operation; and therefore they found themselves in this position—that whereas before the suspension of the Acts they had order, comparative morality, and a very large amount of effort for the reclamation of these unfortunate women, all that had now been reversed. They, therefore, said to Parliament—"Why inflict upon us this evil, when previously, by the operation of these Acts, we were relieved from the evils of which we complain?" He was one of those who thought the question might probably be solved even to the satisfaction of the right hon. Member for Halifax (Mr. Stansfeld) by a simple alteration—namely, by requiring that the examination of women should be conducted by women. He thought that would do away with a great deal of the antagonism to the Acts, and he saw no reason why it should not be done. It was complained that women only were subjected to this treatment; but if that was an objection, why did not the right hon. Member for Halifax bring in a Bill to treat men in the same way? He wanted to know if Parliament had any concern whatever in the future of the rising generation; and, if so, whether they were justified in allowing poison to be spread wholesale? He contended that it was the duty of Parliament to prevent the sowing of the seeds of degradation and of death. He hoped the action of the Government would now be changed, and that they would not allow themselves to be swayed by different sets of opinion. They ought to make up their minds collectively as to what was best for the people of the country, and there would be no difficulty if they would act in accordance with the vast body of opinion before them. The question was a very serious one; and he asked again, why should Parliament or the Government persist in inflicting upon the population evils which were incalculable in their consequences? When he had introduced the deputation to the Home Secretary, the right hon. and learned Gentleman said he agreed with them. On being asked why he did not act, he said that it was because Parliament had of its own account passed a Resolution for the suspension of the Acts. When told that Parliament would yield if the Government took a decided attitude, he then pleaded the Cabinet. He was satisfied that if the right hon. and learned Gentleman, on his responsibility as a Cabinet Minister, supported by the noble Marquess the Secretary of State for War and the First Lord of the Admiralty, were to advise Parliament to re-impose these powers, they would not meet with a refusal.

MR. ACLAND said, he did not know that the question was intended to be raised, or he would have fortified himself with facts. He would, however, mention one fact which he thought he had mentioned before—namely, that many of the clergy, and even the Nonconformist ministers in and about the neighbourhood of the three towns, had expressed a most earnest hope that if the Government were not able to reimpose the Acts as they were before, they would do something to remedy the evils which had been brought about by their suspension. He had been told by one of the leading gentlemen in the three towns that he himself knew the Acts had had the greatest influence in deterring young girls from commencing an immoral career. He had discussed the question carefully with residents in Plymouth, and he must say that he had modified his own opinion to a certain extent since the vote was taken which led to the suspension of the Acts, and he believed there was some ground for the answer given by the Government that it was a question now for the inhabitants of the affected districts. It was, no doubt, in the power of the locality to do a very great deal to remedy these evils, and Glasgow was instanced as a place in which a great deal had already been done. Glasgow, however, was not in the same position as three or four garrison towns like Devonport, Portsmouth, Dover, and others, where it was a matter of necessity to the Government that a large number of soldiers and sailors should be collected. Therefore, although Glasgow had been able to succeed, it did not at all follow that Plymouth, Dover, and other towns would have the same success. At any rate, he thought that if the Government were not prepared to retrace their steps, it was their duty in some way or other to help the inhabitants of the places affected in remedying the evils which were now produced. There were one or two points which he wished particularly to bring to the mind of the Committee; and, first, he would direct attention to the appeal which had been made by the right hon. Member for Halifax (Mr. Stansfeld), the hon. and learned Member for Stockport (Mr. Hopwood), and their friends, for the repeal of the Acts. That appeal had been backed up by opinion wholly outside the affected districts. It was not supported inside those districts, and yet the latter were the only localities which possessed any experience or knowledge of the matter. It might be incumbent on the affected districts to do something for themselves; but, at any rate, it was incumbent on the Government to assist them. In the course of the agitation promoted by the right hon. Member for Halifax it had been frequently urged that every town ought to look after its own immorality; but he would ask whether it was not a highly criminal act for individuals to be constantly spreading disease, knowing perfectly well what the consequences of their proceedings were? In some of the garrison towns cases of the most aggravated character had occurred; and he contended that for any individual knowingly to spread disease was a criminal act. He was of opinion, much as he respected the liberty of the subject, that the Government had a rigbt to prevent the spread of disease by the strongest possible measures. All he wished now to urge upon the Government was that in the interests of the people they could not afford to neglect the inevitable results of the accumulating disease in the affected districts, not only on account of social and moral reasons, but for sanitary reasons also. He quite agreed with the right hon. Member for Halifax that the Government ought not to lend its sanction to the regulation of vice; but he thought that the ordinary laws of the country ought to be directed to a certain extent to the enforcement of those rules of morality which ought to guide the conduct of every individual. There was even more than that in the case now under consideration, and they had a right to appeal to the Government for help. At any rate, the agitation which the right hon. Member for Halifax led was not supported by the districts to which the Acts applied.

THE MARQUESS OF HARTINGTON said, that, as far as the discussion had already proceeded, hardly a word had been said upon the relation of the subject to the Army. A great deal, however, had been said about the effect of the Compulsory Clauses of these Acts upon the order and morality of the owns to which the Acts originally applied; and, although the hon. Member for Devonport (Mr. Puleston) had said in a general way that the statistics laid upon the Table showed the enormous increase of disease that had resulted, he had not used any figures to prove the position he had taken up. He (the Marquess of Hartington) had had to deal with this subject chiefly, of course, with regard to the effects of this legislation upon the health of the Army. He had very little indeed to say on the subject of the indirect benefits supposed to follow from the operation of the Acts. He had been very much confirmed in the opinion he had previously formed that the effects of these Acts on the health of the Army were, owing to the extremely partial character of their operation, very slight, and also extremely fluctuating. That opinion was borne out by a Return which had been laid on the Table since the suspension of the Compulsory Clauses of the Acts. There had been an increase in the amount of disease since the suspension of the Acts; but he thought he would be able to show that it was not a large increase, and that it was one which might be attributable to other causes. Between the first week after the Compulsory Clauses had been suspended and the last week included in the Returns, after the suspension had been in operation for rather more than six months, the difference in the number of men admitted into hospital for this disease was very small, being only 0·86 per 1,000 —that was, in a strength of 1,000 men, there were about 8-10ths of a man more admitted after the suspension had been in operation six months. The number was 3·78 before the suspension, and 4·64 six months after the Act was suspended. A similar, though smaller, increase had been going on in the 14 unprotected stations, in which there had been an increase of 0·18; there was, therefore, an increase of 0·68 due to the suspension, or a little more than half a man per 1,000 per week. The same Return showed that, during the same period, in the number of men remaining in hospital there had been an increase of 2·24 per 1,000, or two and a-fourth of a man. While there had, no doubt, been an increase since the Acts had been suspended, there had been fluctuations during their continuance quite as great. In the 14 protected stations, on the 12th of May, 1882, the ratio per 1,000 was 2·73; but in the month of September in the same year, while the Acts were in full operation, that rate had risen to 5·98, or to a larger rate than even now existed. It was, therefore, very difficult to attribute to these Acts any remarkable effect upon the health of the Army. The hon. Member for Devonport (Mr. Puleston), conscious of the weakness of his case, had not gone into these figures, but had confined himself to the cases adduced by the hon. Member for Portsmouth (Sir H. Drummond Wolff). He (the Marquess of Hartington) thought it was probable that, in consequence of the suspension of these Acts, the severer form of disease had increased in a somewhat greater ratio, though it was not shown to be greater by any figures, and neither himself nor the hon. Member was justified in making use of problematical or hypothetical results if the information was not absolutely before them. The hon. Member had dwelt almost entirely upon the moral effects of the administration of the Acts; but, as the hon. Member himself admitted, he (the Marquess of Hartington) had already reminded the House that with that the War Department had nothing to do. The Acts were not passed for the purpose of improving the morals of the people. Any effect which the Acts might have had in that direction had been purely incidental, and were not within the intentions of those who passed them. The Acts were passed simply and solely in the hope of improving the health of the Army and Navy, and of increasing their efficiency. He did not in the slightest degree underrate the importance of the moral considerations brought forward by the hon. Member and others, but the object of the Acts was what he had stated. If it were possible by any improvement or alteration of the law, or by granting increased powers, to secure morality, by all means let it be done, and that was the object of the Bill introduced in "another place;" but that Bill had shared the fate of a great many other measures which had been abandoned for the present Session. The moral aspect of the question could only be dealt with by special legislation; and he believed it was still the firm intention of the Home Secretary to endeavour to pass a Bill similar to that which had passed the House of Lords. Surely anything that was done in that direction ought to be done upon the responsibility of the Government, and with reference to the whole country. They discussed the question fully last year, and all he could do was to repeat the statement he had then made on behalf of the Government. He denied that the decision on the Resolution of last year was in any sense a "catch" vote; and he did not believe that if the House were to divide on the question of the Compulsory Clauses again the result would be different. He had done all in his power to warn hon. Gentlemen who were in favour of the Acts what the consequence would be. He had, therefore, felt it useless to propose a Vote for the continuance of the compulsory powers exercised by the Government under the Acts. He also believed, and, indeed, he had stated the view of the Government, that the powers conferred on the Government under the Acts were permissive, and not compulsory, and it was entirely within the discretion of Government whether they would ask Parliament to provide the necessary funds for the administration of the Acts, or allow them to remain in abeyance. As he had said before, under the powers of the Acts it was left to the local districts and the local police to exercise the powers if they thought fit. The powers of the Acts still remained, and the only thing that was in suspense was the employment of the Metropolitan Police, in regard to which it would require the action of the Government and the approval of the House in order to provide the necessary funds. He believed that the approval of the House would not be given; and, therefore, the Government had lost no time in acting upon that belief, and in withdrawing, to a great extent, the Metropolitan Police. The effect of the suspension of these Acts upon the health of the Army, as he had shown, had not been considerable, although that there had been a certain effect he did not deny. What was done last year was done with the full knowledge of Parliament—that the decision would, to a certain extent, lead to evils of this kind. Nevertheless, the House voted deliberately in favour of the Resolution of the right hon. Member for Halifax (Mr. Stansfeld), and he believed if the question were put now a majority of the House would be still of that opinion, and would remain of opinion, that even an improvement of the health of the Army was not to be accomplished at the cost of enforcing these unpopular Acts. He had not concealed, and he had not altered his opinion, that these Acts had been beneficial, and he was convinced that the moral objections which were taken to them by his right hon. Friend and those who acted with him had no solid foundation. What he had said, and what he repeated was, that so long as the operation of these Acts was partial, and was limited to a few districts, the effect must be small. It was in vain to suppose that by the limited operation of Acts such as these any considerable effect could be produced upon the health of the Army; and, looking at the question from that point of view, he must admit that he was not surprised that those who entertained very strong moral objections to the operation of these laws should contend that the results which had been obtained, or could be obtained, were not sufficient to justify the continuance of Acts which were opposed to the moral sense of a great number of people in the country. The only other object which had been referred to was the promise which had been given with regard to the introduction of a measure dealing with the subject. It was his firm intention to introduce that Bill as soon as the state of Business in the House afforded an opportunity of doing so; but that opportunity had never yet arisen, and, from circumstances which took place a few weeks ago, it appeared quite impossible to introduce the Bill, or to hope for its second reading this Session. Until, however, that Bill had been introduced, and the House had been able to discuss the principle of the Bill, he contended that the results obtained under the powers conferred by the Compulsory Clauses which had been suspended were not sufficient to warrant the rescinding of the decision of last year.

SIR JOHN HAY said, he had heard with great regret the intimation conveyed by the Secretary of State for War that he had not been convinced of the necessity of reviving the Compulsory Clauses of these Acts. He had always himself supported the Acts, both on the ground of reforming the persons who were unfortunately brought under them, as well as on the ground that they were for the advantage of the Army and Navy and the public generally. He had risen now because the noble Marquess, in quoting the Returns, had alluded to the Navy as well as the Army, and had included the Navy as well as the Marines. He was, therefore, anxious to say a word on the subject. He thought the noble Marquess was wrong in saying that, owing to the great increase of disease in the Navy, there had not been a serious deprivation of the services of a large number of men. Now, the Returns he had consulted put the question in such a light that he would ask the Secretary to the Admiralty whether, in consequence of the Navy being deprived of the services of 12,000 men since the suspension of the Acts, it might not be necessary to increase the Naval Force, in order to render it efficient? At Page 10 of the Returns, the Secretary to the Admiralty would see that the force being the same at Portsmouth—namely, 7,000 men during the year—whereas there had only been 800 in Haslar Hospital previous to the suspension of the Acts, there were now 1,111 men in Haslar Hospital. If they took Plymouth Hospital, they would find that the average number, which was about 500, although it occasionally went down to 360, had now gone up to nearly 900. The same thing had occurred at Plymouth, where the number of men in the hospital had been increased by 133 per cent.

The JUDGE ADVOCATE GENERAL (Mr. Osborne Morgan): Per 1,000, not per 100.

Sir JOHN HAY said, the number had risen to 280, or 133 per 1,000. The figures showed that there were nearly 2,000 men in hospital suffering from contagious disease in the course of last year, as against 1,000 in the last year in which the Acts were in force. In other stations there had been almost a similar increase; and this terrible contrast was also to be drawn, that whereas nearly 2,500 women were admitted into certified hospitals and discharged cured, with many of them reclaimed, during last year only 720 were admitted during the period of the suspension of the Compulsory Acts. This Return was, to his mind, more convincing than anything which could have been placed upon the Table in showing the advantage of the Compulsory Clauses of the Acts. He had always supported the Acts on moral grounds, and in regard to their advantage in preserving the health and strength of Her Majesty's Forces. He trusted that the Government would take his view, and take advantage of the experiment they had themselves made to re-enact the Acts, having already ascertained the evils which resulted from suspending them. He thanked the Government for having given this information to the public, and he thought it would completely justify them in reviving the Compulsory Clauses, which had done so much for all persons concerned. He was glad the question had been raised now, as it would prevent any reference being made to it when they came to the Naval Vote. He would, however, ask the Secretary to the Admiralty whether the Board of Admiralty intended to add to the Naval Forces of the Crown, in order to make up for the increasing number admitted into the hospitals owing to the ravages of disease?

Dr. FARQUHARSON remarked that, although he deplored the result, yet he could not help thinking that the action which the Government had taken in the matter had been forced upon them by the decision of the House, and it appeared to him that they had no alternative but to yield in the way they had done. They were now placed in the curious position of having practically suspended the operation of the Acts without substituting anything for them. It was promised, in the first instance, that a Bill would be introduced to put everything right; but there was not the slightest chance of any measure being introduced during the present Session, and they might have to wait for several Sessions before any fresh legislation took place. He quite agreed with the hon. Member for Devonport (Mr. Puleston) that the suspension of these Acts had been disastrous to the observance of order and decency in the streets. Juvenile prostitution was rapidly on the increase, and a large and influential deputation had waited on the Government the other day, and gave some deplorable facts as the result of the withdrawal of the Acts. They were told that the condition of women in many of these towns was most pitiable; that they were living in a state of misery and wretchedness rapidly approaching the condition they were in before the Acts were originally passed. All this misery, vice, and immorality was being brought about because the Acts were not in force. They were told that the Acts were not introduced in the interests of law and order, although, no doubt, law and order had benefited very much from their operation. They were told, also, that they were not brought forward for the benefit of the women who were principally affected by them, although they had undoubtedly received many benefits under them. Not only had they been early brought under the influence of medical treatment, but large opportunities had been afforded them of escaping from their evil courses and becoming once more respectable and reputable members of society. He maintained that the withdrawal of compulsory examinations was fatal to the efficiency of the Acts. He bore testimony to the admirable and skilful manner in which the Metropolitan Police and the doctors engaged in the administration of the Acts had carried out their duties, and the aid which the police had rendered in rescuing many girls in the streets who were trembling on the verge of vice. He stated that his firm and unalterable opinion was that in the absence of compulsory examination, the administration of these Acts must always prove a failure, and he regretted that this provision had been withdrawn.

Mr. CAMPBELL - BANNERMAN wished at once to respond to the appeal which had been made to him by the right hon. and gallant Gentleman the Member for the Wigtown Burghs (Sir John Hay), although the question the right hon. and gallant Gentleman had raised did not properly come under the Vote they were now dealing with. He entirely agreed with the right hon. and gallant Gentleman that the figures which he had quoted showed a decided increase of disease at Haslar, Plymouth, and Devonport. Anyone, however, who had followed the statistics of this subject must be aware that there were most extraordinary fluctuations in the number of persons affected. He said that by way of caution, although, of course, it was to have been expected that a large increase of disease should have taken place after what had occurred last year. But his right hon. and gallant Friend stated that those Returns showed that more men in the Navy were disabled, and asked whether the Admiralty had taken any steps to supply the places of those men. The figures quoted by the right hon. and gallant Gentleman were admissions to the hospital, and not Returns of men absolutely disabled during the year. There was nothing like the diminution in the strength of the Navy which had been indicated. Instead of 1,200 men being disabled from service, the excess of loss to the Navy throughout the year had been only 110 men. That, he thought, was not a matter sufficiently serious to warrant the Admiralty in taking steps to supply the gap with fresh men. There was really no cause for any such action being necessary, although there was no difficulty whatever in finding a sufficient supply of seamen.

Sir FREDERICK FITZWYGRAM said, that having held a command at Aldershot for many years, he could bear testimony to the beneficial effect of these Acts, which had been very great in one respect at least—namely, in the large decrease in the number of prostitutes since the Act came into operation. Some years ago at Aldershot, before the Contagious Diseases Acts were in force, there were known to be about 400 of these women parading the streets; after the Acts came into operation, the number had decreased, he believed, to slightly under 150; since the suspension of the Compulsory Clauses, the number had increased to 350 two months ago, and it had since probably increased still further. The Contagious Diseases Acts, although many hon. Members might not be aware of the fact, did not render the trade of prostitution legal. The trade was not an offence at Common Law, and the operation of the Acts was to limit a previously existing right. He contended that the beneficial effect of the Acts was shown by the state of their great camp at Aldershot, where, as he had already pointed out, the number of prostitutes had, while they were in force, been reduced from 400 to 150. He, for one, regretted the increased facilities for prostitution now given by the non-enforcement of the Compulsory Clauses.

Mr. HOPWOOD said, he was rather surprised that the hon. and gallant Member who had just sat down should have described the Acts as beneficial in their operation at Aldershot. He had alluded to the reduction in the number of prostitutes. The evidence showed that in Aldershot they would have one regiment side by side with another, under equal conditions in every way—the one seriously affected with disease, the other comparatively free. Now, he doubted whether this law was likely to put the men on a better footing as regarded character. Surely there was something to be said on that question. The character of regiments had been shown to be the cause of the difference between them in respect of the amount of disease. One regiment was absolutely forgetful of decency and of the restraints of good character, when placed in the way of these temptations; while another with the same temptations avoided them. Now, with all respect to the gallant officers of regiments, might they not do more for their men? If they set the necessary example, it might be that they would do much for the reclamation of their subordinates. He had once asked the noble Marquess the Secretary of State for War in that House this Question—he wanted to know why soldiers, more than any other class of Her Majesty's subjects, were to be protected by special laws from the consequences of their acts? And he put the same question now, because he thought that this was the groundwork of the Acts, and it was that which touched the moral sense of the nation. These Acts were passed in 1866-9, while the people were unaware of what was being done. It was said that the vote of the 20th of April, 1883, which condemned them, was a "snap" vote; but he asserted it was the result of a consensus of opinion of the majority of that House. A certain number of hon. Members on the other side who were in favour of the Acts stayed away; they dared not vote for them, and they abstained from doing so. Taking the majority, then, it was a very significant fact that the House was never more representative of the voice of the nation than it was on the occasion referred to, when the Acts were curtailed. But the conversation they were having had shown that a very great improvement had taken place in the conscience of the Government Departments statistically. It was a matter for wonder how that had been secured. For long years his right hon. Friend the Member for Halifax (Mr. Stansfeld) had fought this battle, during which time he had been met over and over again in that House with statistics of the most convincing and overwhelming character—if reliable—from the Departments in favour of the Acts. There had also been paragraphs inserted by authority in *The Times* and other newspapers describing the flood of blessings which this legislation had shed upon the British Army and Navy. But they found now, by the Report of the Committee on which he had had the honour of serving, what had been the actual result during the last 14 or 15 years—a trifling saving, if even that could be accredited to the system. Now they had it on the high authority of the noble Marquess that they must not rely on this sort of figuring, and found upon it these conclusions, because he had discovered for himself that the Acts had not done much good. He and his hon. Friends congratulated themselves on having one of independent judgment to preside at the War Office. The Department of the noble Marquess had given a complete answer to his right hon. Friend opposite (Mr. Cavendish Bentinck). The noble Marquess said that even when the Acts were in force the admissions, taking occasional periods of time, had been more numerous than they were now; and therefore, he said, they could not be too cautious in making use of the statistics. The best test they had were the Returns furnished for the six months which ensued on that very decisive vote that was given on the 20th of April, 1883. It appeared that at the end of that time the admissions per week had increased by a fraction of a man per 1,000. The noble Marquess, he was aware, had dealt with another set of statistics, and had said with regard to the continuance of the men in hospital that for the same period there had been an increase of those remaining in hospital. He did not want to dwell too much upon figures; it had always been their contention that they should not be too much relied upon—at least, his right hon. Friend (Mr. Stansfeld) had always contended for that, and he (Mr. Hopwood) had added his protest; but they were not listened to. But this he would say, if the disease, as was alleged, had so much increased, the admissions into hospital would have increased correspondingly. But it appeared there had been little or no such increase. He had had to ask Questions also in that House with regard to the statistics from the Admiralty. The right hon. and gallant Admiral opposite (Sir John Hay) had been dwelling on the Return relating to the Navy. And what had happened with regard to that branch of the Service? Ever since these Acts had been in force, certain ports had been subjected to them. Some years ago, Sir Harcourt Johnstone had moved for a Return comparing five ports in subjection with five ports not in sub jection to the Acts. Would it be believed that in making that Return the Admiralty ranked 4,000 boys as men, and with regard to the prevalence of disease, gave the benefit of that classification to the subjected districts? That had been over and over again pointed out to the Secretary to the Admiralty as vitiating the Annual Reports; but it was not until last year that the Admiralty were brought to admit that the mode of comparison was misleading. Misleading! He should say it was playing with the House of Commons; he called it making statistics to justify a false conclusion. Last year the Admiralty promised to leave it out of the Navy Report. But they had only left out a portion of it. Their attention had been called to two tables in which the same error existed, and when reproached with it they said it was no error at all; they had the hardihood to say there was no error in ranking 4,000 boys amongst men; but they added that in the next Report, as the operation of the Act had been suspended, the classification would not be presented to the House. He said that the Return in question was an unfair and unjustifiable statement; and, as a matter of figures, he was bound to say that it shook one's confidence in all the official Returns with regard to such things. Now this matter, with regard to the Acts, was a fancy of the Heads of the Departments and of some hon. Members; and it was also a fancy thing with some in society. It was, in his opinion, dangerous that those who advocated the Acts should be trusted to prepare unchecked the statistics which they put before the House. He was not going into the whole of the wide subject that had to be dealt with. He did not think it would be in good taste, because he was exceedingly glad to hear the opinion which the noble Marquess had expressed, and to perceive that he had taken up an important position in relation to the subject. But he (Mr. Hopwood) was anxious to refer to the question of morals. The idea of the hon. Member for Hythe (Sir Edward Watkin) was that those opposed to the Acts relied on fear of disease to deter young men from a departure from virtue, but that, for his part, he advocated protection for them. He would ask the hon. Baronet whether there was any such thing as the Code of Ethics, which he would apply to the conduct of the nation? His only idea was that boys should be kept from disease; and that seemed to be his notion of morality. The idea of the Acts was that greyheaded fathers should say to their boys—"Never mind those who teach that morality is right and self-restraint is necessary; we have thrown aside all that sort of nonsense; we have passed an Act to make vice safe; listen to the teachings of the Legislature, and not of the divines." The public standard of morality was thus altered. Some hon. Members had said that the Acts produced order in the streets. They had been challenged over and over again on that point. There was not a word in the Acts which gave a policeman power even to question loose women; and a great deal that they did under the Acts was perfectly illegal, and ought long since to have been put an end to. It was said that they produced order. In what way? The policeman was made the tutor, the conductor, and the gaoler of women diseased, and he was set over them in command. And that was called preserving order! Why, they had no power under these Acts to interfere with women from the day they were on the register, provi e they came up at the prescribed times for examination. Then it was said—"You know there are a number of people who disagree with you—estimable, religious people, and so on." Of course, he granted that. But what was the explanation? He would take one or two of the clergy thus cited. One gentleman was a Roman Catholic priest, and two or three instances of clergy of different denominations had been cited. Why did clergymen like the Acts? Clergymen were, as a rule, ready, in what they deemed the cause of religion, to pass Acts of Parliament arbitrary and tyrannical; and their idea was that if frail women could be got within the net, and placed under the influence of the clergy, or under other influence which they believed to be good, the legislation would be justified; and that was what they desired to do. Accordingly, they relied upon getting women into hospitals, and upon being then able to set to work to convert them. What could be more striking than the hypocrisy of asserting, on the one hand, that their intention was to reclaim, to guide to holier influences, while, at the same time, they put women on the register, submitted them to inspection, forced them into a hospital, and then went through the mockery of introducing the chaplain to them? They did not, and naturally they could not, expect their opponents to share their sentiments in this matter. But they knew that the majority of their countrymen would not allow these filthy Acts to be continued in any shape, not even by a Bill in the Lords, such as had been brought in for the amendment of the Criminal Law. This legislation, he was glad to say, was doomed. In 1871 a Royal Commission sat to inquire into this matter, and they arrived at the same conclusion that the House had arrived at by its vote. For more than 12 years successive Governments had gone on, in the face of their advisers, imbuing the population with the filth of this legislation, and in spite of the strong efforts made against it. Would they go on in this way? It struck him that their masters would take care they did not, and they would not need a strong appeal to make them come to that conclusion.

MR. CAVENDISH BENTINCK said, he did not think the noble Marquess the Secretary of State for War had much mended his case by what he had said that night. He had not offered what could be called a strong defence of the course which Her Majesty's Government had thought proper to take in this case. He was obliged to join issue with the noble Marquess on one point—namely, that these Acts were originally passed for the benefit of the Army and Navy alone. It was quite true that that was the principal ground of policy on which the Acts were introduced; but at the time that they were carried, there were many Members, amongst whom was himself, who supported the measure as being in the interest of unfortunate women, and who, touched with pity at the miserable condition to which those unfortunates were reduced, were determined to do all that might be in their power to rescue them from the state of degradation into which they had fallen. That had been his motive for supporting the Acts when they were introduced into the House of Commons; and it was perfectly well known that there were many other Members whose motives at the time were the same. The noble Marquess had referred to the Returns of the Army; but he (Mr. Cavendish Bentinck) was bound to say that they were not satisfactory Returns to him in any way. They only came down to the end of last year, when the actual effect of the suspension of the Acts was not plainly visible; and he could not agree with the conclusions which the noble Marquess had drawn from them, for even in the short period referred to of the year 1883, while in the protected stations the average strength was 39,100, there were 6,960 admissions; whereas in the previous year, when there were 40,900 men, there were 5,927 admissions. There was, therefore, upon the noble Marquess's Return, a difference of 1,000 as between the two years. That he regarded as a very considerable amount; and so far as his own information, obtained from general officers, went, and as the result of his own observations, he believed that a great deficiency had occurred in the effective ranks of the Army owing to the suspension of the Acts; and he expected that the next Returns, when brought out, would show a still further diminution in the general efficiency of the Forces. Moreover, the noble Marquess, in this curiously-constructed Return, had not given the various forms of disease; the more severe and the lighter forms were jumbled together; and they were entitled to know whether there had been any increase in the former.

THE MARQUESS OF HARTINGTON: The Returns of the hon. Member for Portsmouth (Sir H. Drummond Wolff) are on the Table, and if the right hon. and learned Gentleman had objected to them, the form could have been amended.

MR. CAVENDISH BENTINCK: That was for the noble Marquess to do, so far as the Army Estimates were concerned. But he (Mr. Cavendish Bentinck) had suggested to his hon. Friend the addition with regard to admissions of women into hospital, and he should also have to refer to that subject again, and bring to bear upon it figures that were absolutely reliable. He was bound to say that Her Majesty's Government had shown great vacillation and inconsistency—that would not be denied—in this matter, because if the Acts were bad they ought to have dealt with them a long time ago. Why had they been allowed to continue in force for 17 years? He remembered the time at which there were very strong local objections to the Acts, but one by one they had fallen off; and now they were told, and most truly, what no one in the House would deny—that in the subjected districts the Acts were most popular, and that there was a strong desire on the part of the majority of the populations there that their provisions should be revised. Then he came to the next point —what was now the policy of Her Majesty's Government? First of all, they had introduced the Detention in Hospitals Bill, which had been practically withdrawn; then, in answer to a deputation the other day, the right hon. and learned Gentleman the Secretary of State for the Home Department said that a remedy in the shape of a Criminal Law Amendment Bill would be forthcoming; but the noble Marquess knew well that that Bill never had the slightest chance of passing in that House, for it was objected to not only by those who shared his (Mr. Cavendish Bentinck's) views, but also by hon. Members below the Gangway opposed to the Acts, and denounced by publications which represented their particular views. It was the general opinion that the Bill never had the least chance of success—certainly not this Session; and, from the nature of the Business which the House would have before it next Session, he did not think there was much likelihood then of its passing, or even being considered. Therefore, he felt justified in making charges of vacillation and inconsistency against Her Majesty's Government on account of their having suspended these useful Acts, and in having proposed one measure which they had not carried forward, and then in having put forward another which was not likely to become law. The result of this vacillation and inconsistency had been, as was generally the case with the policy of the Government in reference to most questions, disaster; at all events, it had proved disastrous to the unfortunate women whom he, for one, desired to be protected by the Acts. Now, if prostitution were not abolished — and he did not think the right hon. Gentleman the Member for Halifax (Mr. Stansfeld), who represented the views of the Repeal Association on the Committee, had ever proposed to abolish it, or make it criminal for a woman to carry on the trade of a prostitute—how were these women to be relieved? They could not be got into hospitals of their own free will; he should be able to show that nothing of the kind could be done. The country had an excellent law on this subject; it had been suspended, and nothing substituted for it; the Government had found order existing, and replaced it by chaos. He had taken some trouble to investigate this matter by the light of what had occurred at the London Lock Hospital, to which he had been for many years a subscriber; he had personally attended upon the House Surgeon and the Secretary, and obtained some statistics which perhaps the noble Marquess might place upon the Table as a Parliamentary Return, for they were very interesting statistics with regard to the condition of women in the hospital. Well, then, in the London Lock Hospital, comparing the year ending on the 30th of June, 1882, with the year ending on the 30th of June, 1884, the total number admitted on the Government side was 464 in the former period; whereas, in the latter, the number had fallen to 207; and the number of cases of gonorrhea, which in 1882 was 183, had dropped to 20. Constitutional or secondary syphilis had risen from 33 per cent to 55 per cent, and the average duration of treatment had extended from 23·31 to 52 days.

MR. PULESTON: The average duration in the Royal Albert Hospital has risen from 30 days to 60 days.

MR. CAVENDISH BENTINCK said, the figures he had quoted showed that while there was the enormous reduction from 464 in 1882 to 207 in 1884, the percentage of cases of constitutional syphilis had risen from 33 to 55. He had a letter from the House Surgeon of the Lock Hospital, who, in forwarding the Return to which he (Mr. Cavendish Bentinck) had just referred, said—

"While the number of women relieved has enormously decreased, the disease under which they suffer is of a very aggravated kind."

He (Mr. Cavendish Bentinck) would now take the noble Marquess (the Marquess of Hartington) to the Chatham Hospital. Miss Webb, writing from Chatham on July 4, 1884, said—

"In answer to your letter received to-day, I consider we may say we are, since the suspension of the police, in about the same position as before 1870: therefore, a fair comparison should date within a short time of that period and now. The admissions to this Hospital, from July 1, 1871, to July 1, 1872, were 614. The number of beds usually occupied, 60 to 68; on one occasion, 73. Detention in hospital, 28·35 days. Owing to the benefits conferred by the 'C. D. Acts' in their entirety the numbers of admissions decreased, and from July 1, 1881, to July 1, 1882, they were 474. The number of beds occupied, 26 to 30. Detention in hospital, 24·58 days. On the suspension of the police, Shorncliffe Hospital was closed, and the patients of that district are received at this Hospital. With that addition, the number of admissions from July 1, 1883, to July 1, 1884, have been 154. The number of beds occupied, 13 to 26; on one occasion, 30. Number now in hospital 20, three of whom have been under treatment for more than seven months, and are still too ill to be discharged, and two came in two days ago likely to want as long treatment; few are able to be discharged under three or four months in the present state of things."

That was the result of the suspension of the Contagious Diseases Acts. In the Chatham Hospital, also, the number of admissions had fallen very much; but the diseases under which the unfortunate women suffered were of a very aggravated kind. Miss Webb also told him that 53 out of the 75 admissions during the last six months were very bad cases of secondary disease, and more of such cases were being admitted. He had a further letter from a gentleman who was well acquainted with the matter. His correspondent wrote—

"You may be assured that the reports you received yesterday from the House Surgeon at the London Lock Hospital, as to the relatively greater number and the increased severity of the cases of secondary syphilis are precisely what you would receive at all the certificated Lock Hospitals. What is worse, at Portsmouth and Devonport especially there are now a much greater number of very young girls between 17 and 20 than there were formerly, many of these affected with the worse forms of syphilis, and the statements made by them in hospital confirm the belief that there must be large numbers of young girls on the streets infected with the most virulent type of syphilis. They will not seek admission until compelled to do so by the severity of their sufferings, and the cases are necessarily much longer under treatment."

These were the results which were always prophesied by the supporters of the Acts. The witnesses who gave evidence before the Committee stated over and over again that women would not go into hospital until they were compelled, or if they did they went in too late and came out too early. It seemed to him that if ever the female sex had been misused, they had been misused by the policy adopted by the right hon. Gentleman the Member for Halifax (Mr. Stansfeld) and by the hon. and learned Gentleman the Member for Stockport (Mr. Hopwood). He (Mr. Cavendish Bentinck) had always endeavoured to befriend the women. [*A laugh.*] The right hon. Gentleman (Mr. Stansfeld) laughed; but did he think it right that these poor unfortunate women u not be admitted to hospital; didshe lthink-it right they should be allowed to rot and starve in the streets? Was the right hon. Gentleman a subscriber to the Lock Hospital? No, Sir. Was the hon. and learned Gentleman the Member for Stockport (Mr. Hopwood) a subscriber to the Lock Hospital? No. They considered it wrong to subscribe to such a place; but it was a great pity they did not visit the hospitals, and see what a great advantage they were to the unfortunate sex whose cause they claimed to espouse. There was a Society opposed to the Acts called the Rescue Society, the Secretary of which was called as a witness before the Committee. The Society had a very limited operation, and one of the pieces of information which the Secretary gave them was that they never, on any consideration, in these later times took in a woman who came from a subjected district. This was an instance of the Christian charity on the part of the Rescue Society; this Society declined to have anything to do with any abandoned woman who had come from where the Acts were in force. He had only that morning received a further letter from Miss Webb, and it was so interesting that he did not hesitate to read it to the Committee. Writing on July 25, 1884, Miss Webb said—

"I have so lately sent you statistics of the number of women who have passed through this hospital at different periods, that I will now only add, what has been brought to my notice lately, by ladies who devote their time to 'rescue work' in these towns; they tell me the state of the place with regard to immorality, is worse than they have ever known it, and two clergymen who I met a few days since, told me they had never known such a sad state of things in all their experience, as it has become since the suspension of the 'C. D. A.' police. I have been asked to help to trace girls gone astray, which I could have done easily when the Acts were in force, but am now powerless. Only two days ago two ladies came to me about a child, not quite nine running about barracks in danger of harm; her mother being in here. Had the 'C. D. A.' police been on duty, that child and many quite as young would have been placed out of danger. I am aware this has been fully represented by the deputations in favour of the 'C. D. A.,' and I am also aware that one argument is that 'rescue work' was not the intention of the Acts, but only incidental. Granted. Take it on sanitary grounds. There are only 20 women in hospital, and that from eight towns, with a radius of 10 miles round each, under (we can no longer say *protected* by) the 'C. D. Acts.' Though I came here solely for the purpose of trying to reform the poor women brought under the 'C. D. A.,' a time has come when the exigencies of the case require I should speak plainly, however painful to myself. The argument that women are injured by these Acts, I, after 14 years' experience, pronounce absurd. These unfortunates make a trade of their passions. Should the Police be restored (which is much to be desired) I would like a clause added to the Acts—namely, that once a doctor has pronounced a woman must be received into hospital, the police should not lose sight of her, on the plea that she 'wants to lock up her house,' etc., etc. Numbers have come in after, semi-intoxicated, and boasted to their companions of the mischief they knew they had done in the two or three hours so gained of liberty. Should such creatures—I cannot call them women—be allowed to go on unrestrained?"

That was the experience of everybody who had had to do with the Acts, and certainly it was his experience of the evidence which was given before the Committee. He was not aware that any witnesses thoroughly acquainted with the working of the hospitals had been brought to contradict the evidence which was given by the persons practically acquainted with the working of the Acts. In fact, almost all the witnesses who were produced by the right hon. Gentleman (Mr. Stansfeld) were witnesses who, when pressed, said the real fact was they knew nothing about the matter. That being so, what answer had been given to the statements of the supporters of the Acts? What was to be said on behalf of those who would deny to these poor women the great benefits they had received from the Lock Hospitals? It was the old argument of superstition which was really at the bottom of the opposition to these Acts—namely, that these diseases were God-made punishments. Such an argument had been repeated to him over and over again at the time of a Parliamentary Election. He attended a meeting at Exeter Hall not long ago. He heard the hon. Member for Liverpool (Mr. S. Smith) make a speech; but he was bound to say that a more superstitious speech he never heard. It was so superstitious that even the audience objected to it. It was argued at the meeting that it was an offence against religion and morality to relieve the sufferings of these unfortunate women. Was that Christian charity? If so, it was not charity he (Mr. Cavendish-Bentinck) cared to practice. He was glad reference had been made to a certain Memorial to the Prime Minister against the Acts. He found, however, that most of the signatures to the Memorial were those of members of Radical Clubs, Trades Unions, and other similar Societies, who for some years had taken an objection to the Acts; but he could not exactly understand why. One of the paragraphs of the Memorial was to the effect that the tendencies of this legislation was to force women into the hands of irresponsible officers. He denied that a policeman was an irresponsible officer, and the hon. and learned Gentleman the Member for Stockport (Mr. Hopwood) would not say, as a lawyer, that a police officer was an irresponsible person. A policeman was responsible to his superior and to the authorities. If ever there had been a case of misconduct brought against a policeman—no case had as yet been brought—he (Mr. Cavendish Bentinck) had not the slightest doubt the man would have been punished. Another paragraph of the Memorial was to the effect that the power given by the Act was abused. A more untrue statement was never made, and he was surprised to see amongst the signatures to the document that of the hon. Member for Stoke (Mr. Broadhurst). The hon. Member had before him all the evidence given before the Committee, and, therefore, it was surprising he should have neglected to examine that evidence before he signed a document which contained statements so deliberately false as the one to which (Mr. Cavendish Bentinck) had called attention. As hon. Members knew perfectly well, there was no instance in which virtuous young women had been hurried into a life of prostitution by the action of the police, as was alleged in the Memorial. If there had been such a case it would have been brought before the Committee, and its merits would have been adjudicated upon by the Committee. Another basis for opposition to the Acts was that of intolerance and prejudice. It was a most surprising thing that so few Scotch Members supported the Acts. He did not know what had become of the right hon. Gentleman the Member for the University of Edinburgh (Sir Lyon Playfair), who used to defend the Acts so energetically; but he knew that the right hon. Gentleman was still a strong advocate of the Acts, and he also remembered that, not long since, a most able speech was made in the House by his hon. and gallant Friend the Member for South Ayrshire (Major General Alexander)—who he regretted not to see in his place—in answer to another very powerful speech against the repeal of the Acts. No doubt, considerable Parliamentary pressure had been put upon Scotch Members to induce them not to vote and speak in support of the Acts. That was one of the reasons why he had always advocated secret voting in the House on occasions of this kind. Under such a system they would really get at the true opinions of Members, because Members would not be afraid of an adverse vote at the next Election. How was it, he repeated, that the Government had allowed the Acts to continue in operation for 16 years without taking any action? Why, last year, when the right hon. Gentleman the Member for Halifax (Mr. Stansfeld) proposed his Resolution, the Government did not make up their minds until the eleventh hour as to which way they would go. The House were always led to suppose that, as three Heads of Departments—the Home Secretary, the noble Marquess the Secretary of State for War, and the right hon. and learned Gentleman (Mr. Osborne Morgan), who represented the Government on the Committee—were in favour of the Acts, the Members of the Government would vote for them; but, at the last moment, the majority were found going the other way. The right hon. Gentleman at the head of the Government appeared to have given the word of command that the wishes of the right hon. Gentleman the Member for Halifax (Mr. Stansfeld) were to prevail, so the Government support melted away like wax, and a vote adverse to the Acts was taken. He (Mr. Cavendish Bentinck) could not congratulate the Government on the course they then took. He thought it was their duty, if they meant to oppose the Acts, to have used their influence, and not to have led hon. Members on the Opposition side of the House to absent themselves, as many did, in the belief that, as this was a Government question taken on the Motion to go into Committee of Supply, there was no need for them to come down to vote. He could not conceive how the right hon. Gentleman the Prime Minister could reconcile the position he had taken up upon this question; because the right hon. Gentleman was Chancellor of the Exchequer when the Acts were passed, allowed the money to be voted for the purpose of carrying out the Acts, supported the Acts all along, and then absented himself on the occasion of the memorable Division on the Motion of the right hon. Gentleman the Member for Halifax (Mr. Stansfeld). If hon. Members looked at the Petitions which had been presented against the Acts they would find that almost everyone of them sprang from one class of society; they came principally from the Dissenting or Nonconformist Bodies of the country. The right hon. Gentleman the Prime Minister had already said that the Nonconformist or Dissenting Bodies of the country were the backbone of the Liberal Party. He (Mr. Cavendish Bentinck) thought it was probably in the desire to keep that backbone in its right position that the extraordinary move or vote against the Contagious Diseases Acts was taken last year. He wished the right hon. Gentleman had announced a more distinct and straightforward policy upon this question; because then supporters of the Acts would have had a better opportunity of holding their own. The right hon. Gentleman the Member for Halifax (Mr. Stansfeld) had said that some ladies demanded a repeal of the Acts. He (Mr. Cavendish Bentinck) attended a meeting at Exeter Hall, and the right hon. Gentleman was present. It was called a religious meeting; but with the exception of a ceremony which occasionally took place at Naples, he thought he never saw any performance which ought more properly to be called rank superstition. There were at that meeting a certain number of half-crazy women—some in the pulpit, some on the ground, and they were preaching and praying and singing. So far as he could see, there was no reason why they should not pray and preach and sing any more than he saw any reason why people should not believe in the liquefaction of the blood of Saint Januarius. Belief in the latter would do no harm, whereas the preaching, praying, and screaming which went on at Exeter Hall did a great deal of harm, because, not only was the health of the Army impaired, but as he had already shown—and he was sorry that the right hon. Gentleman the Prime Minister was not in his place when he was reading the statistics—the admissions of unfortunate women to the Lock Hospitals had been reduced by something like three-fourths; while the severity of the disease from which they suffered had been more than doubled. He presumed that result made no effect upon the mind of the right hon. Gentleman. The right hon. Gentleman cared not whether the women suffered or not, so long as he could keep his Party together and occupy a seat on the Treasury Bench—the unfortunate creatures might rot in the streets and perish without any commiseration on his part. He (Mr. Cavendish Bentinck) had in his possession the copy of a letter written by the Prime Minister to one of the principal performers on the occasion referred to at Exeter Hall. The letter was as follows:—

"10, Downing Street, Whitehall, June 20.

"Dear Mrs. Butler,—I am directed by the Prime Minister to acknowledge the receipt of the Memorial forwarded to him by you praying for the total repeal of the Contagious Diseases Acts. We need hardly assure you that the Government are sensible of its weight; and that, having advisedly adopted a Resolution on the subject, they intend to act to the best of their ability in the spirit of it. I remain, dear Mrs. Butler, yours faithfully, Herbert J. Gladstone."

Now, was that the Resolution which had been now advisedly adopted, or was it advisedly adopted last year when the right hon. Gentleman the Leader of the House was absent, or had it been adopted since? He would like to know whether the right hon. Gentleman's policy was embodied in the Detention in Hospitals Bill and the Criminal Law Amendment Bill? He would like to know, also, whether the Government meant to stick hard and fast by those two measures, and to pass them, if ever a Session came round in which they could pass them? It was said that there were many important members of society who were opposed to the Acts. He had been told that certain Bishops were opposed to the Acts. One Bishop he heard make a speech at Exeter Hall, but the right rev. Prelate knew very little about the subject indeed; he appeared to have never troubled himself at all to understand the alphabet of the subject. His (Mr. Cavendish Bentinck's) impression was that a number of very excellent people did not take the least pains to acquaint themselves with the details of the case, but were too apt to rely on any wild statements they heard. No less a person than the Secretary to the Post Office, Mr. Stevenson Blackwood, presided at a meeting held at Exeter Hall this year on this subject, and he made one statement so astounding and so absolutely incorrect that he (Mr. Cavendish Bentinck) felt it his duty to call the attention of the Home Secretary to it. Mr. Stevenson Blackwood said—

"As citizens of a free country, we denounce and oppose the Acts, because they are a gross and violent outrage upon the liberty of the subject, and that, too, upon the liberty of the weaker and most defenceless portion of the population, whom they hand over to the mercies of the spy police and the danger of imprisonment without trial."

[MR. SAMUEL SMITH: Hear, hear!] He (Mr. Cavendish Bentinck) would ask the hon. Member not to cheer too soon. And then Mr. Stevenson Blackwood went on to say that the Acts must be demoralizing to the agents who enforced them; for there were people ready to put money into the hands of the spy police to send women to hospital. It was an official of the Post Office who made this misleading statement; and when he (Mr. Cavendish Bentinck) called him to account for it, what did the Committee think was his excuse?—

"Oh, I did not refer to the police under the control of the Home Secretary—not to the Metropolitan Police—I referred to something that was done many years ago in Hong Kong."

Mr. Stevenson Blackwood was very angry with him (Mr. Cavendish Bentinck) afterwards, because he did not admit the excuse, and because he said he (Mr. Stevenson Blackwood) had no right to make such a statement to the superstitious and ignorant people who composed his audience at Exeter Hall. He (Mr. Cavendish Bentinck) did not think it right to call any Member of Parliament ignorant, and therefore he would not say the hon. Member for Liverpool (Mr. S. Smith) was ignorant, but that the hon. Member was superstitious, and that his superstition forbade him to examine the law. The hon. Member evidently had not instructed himself in law, or else he would have been aware that no woman could be imprisoned under the Acts without trial. But as to the statement about Hong Kong. If Mr. Stevenson Blackwood meant Hong Kong, why did he not say so? It was all very well to make a misleading statement to a number of ladies gathered together in Exeter Hall, and then withdraw it in a letter which, probably, very few persons saw —a letter printed in an obscure corner of a newspaper. Mr. Wheeler, of Rochester, afforded an instance of the same sort of thing. He did not wish to call anyone bad names; but Mr. Wheeler, who had said there were hundreds of cases of forcible imprisonment — who had repeated the statement in lying leaflets—while he was unable to show even one such case, pretended to describe them. Wheeler was a contemptible person; but he thought it was highly improper for an official holding one of the highest positions in the Service to take the chair at a meeting of this sort at Exeter Hall, and make such grossly misleading and untrue statements. If persons of that position committed themselves in such a way, it was not surprising that persons of an inferior class of society should allow themselves to be deluded. In fact, he himself knew of two cases in which ladies, having been told that Mr. Blackwood had made these statements, said they must be true, for nothing he said could be untrue. This gentleman held a leading position in some places as a preacher, and, he believed, was highly moral and virtuous; but, virtuous and moral and distinguished as he might be as a preacher, he had no right to preside at a meeting at Exeter Hall and give utterance to untrue statements that could not be supported in any way whatever. He felt very grateful to the hon. Member for Devonport (Mr. Puleston) for having brought this matter before the Committee, for that was the only chance there had been that Session of discussing the subject. The discussion, he was sure, had been very wholesome and useful, for it had shown that no argument could be advanced in favour of the policy of the Government except the misleading Returns produced by the noble Marquess the Secretary of State for War. He had had paper after paper sent to him by writers employed by the Society saying how misleading those Returns were, especially by their principal statistician. Therefore, he did not think it could be denied that the Returns were misleading. He had always supported these Acts, with a view to the relief of these unfortunate women. They had obtained relief while the Acts were in force, but since the Acts had been suspended, the reverse had been the case, and it was impossible to consider that the action of the Government had been either for the public good or for the advantage of these unfortunate women.

MR. STANSFELD: I do not propose to follow the right hon. and learned Gentleman at any length or in detail through the points of his very discursive speech. It does not seem to me that I am called upon to do so, and if not it would be a waste of the time of the Committee to do so, the Committee being desirous of proceeding with the Business before them. But there is one statement of the right hon. and learned Gentleman to which I must refer, and that is his statement involving an attack on the truthfulness of Mr. Stevenson Blackwood. Now, Mr. Blackwood is a gentleman well known to a great many Members of this House—well known to Gentlemen who sit on these Benches, and to Members who sit on the opposite Benches; and I will undertake to say that there is no man who has ever met Mr. Blackwood in official relationship, or who has ever met him in public, or private, or social relationship who does not entertain the very highest opinion of the character and the truthfulness and accuracy of the man. The right hon. and learned Gentleman has said of Mr. Blackwood that he made a statement, as chairman of a meeting, which was grossly misleading and untrue. The right hon. and learned Gentleman had a correspondence with Mr. Blackwood, which I have seen, and now I say to the Committee that it is the right hon. and learned Gentleman who is guilty of misrepresentation, and that he has misrepresented to this Committee of the House of Commons the words and actions of Mr. Blackwood as explained by that Gentleman in letters which the right hon. and learned Gentleman had received.

MR. CAVENDISH BENTINCK: I referred to a statement made at the meeting.

Mr. STANSFELD: I will prove my statement, I think, to the satisfaction of the Committee. The purport of the argument and the insinuation of the right hon. and learned Gentleman was that Mr. Blackwood, trading on the supposed ignorance of his audience, induced them to believe that in this country there existed a system of enabling spy police to lead people to offend against the law. I absolutely deny the accuracy of the statement of the right hon. and learned Gentleman. That meeting was called to protest not only against the Contagious Diseases Acts in this country, but against the system of which these Acts are the expression as far as this country is concerned; and one of the Resolutions passed by that meeting referred not only to the Contagious Diseases Acts, but to the system as administered in Hong Kong. I undertake to say that that vast meeting had every reason to understand, and that the vast majority did accurately understand, Mr. Blackwood to refer not to the state of things in this country, but to the possibilities of such principles and such a system as illustrated by the Acts in force in Hong Kong. That was the explanation given by Mr. Blackwood to the right hon. and learned Gentleman; but the right hon. and learned Gentleman does not deal with Mr. Blackwood as we deal with each other as Members of this House; and I want to know what right he has to not treat Mr. Blackwood as his equal, and as the equal of any man on the Benches of this House. Those who know him know there is no truer gentleman or more honourable man in this country than Mr. Blackwood, and I, for one, am proud of the privilege of being able to call him my friend. The right hon. and learned Gentleman sneers at Mr. Blackwood as a religious man; but that is one of the attributes of Mr. Blackwood most to be respected and venerated. Whether a false impression was produced on the mind of the meeting or not—and I do not believe that was so—the right hon. and learned Gentleman had the distinct declaration of Mr. Blackwood that he referred not to England, but to Hong Kong; and I think it would have better become him, knowing the character of Mr. Blackwood, if he had in a frank and manly manner accepted that explanation. I have another reason for wishing to occupy the Committee for a short time to-night, and it is this: I, for one, cannot but feel highly satisfied with the course of this discussion. My noble Friend the Secretary of State for War, it is true, said that he had never agreed with the arguments I have brought forward from time to time to demonstrate, as I thought, the immoral tendency of the Contagious Diseases Acts; but I need not quarrel with my noble Friend for that difference of opinion, because he absolutely testified to the correctness of the arguments I have been advancing for so many years with reference to the hygienic basis of these Acts. My noble Friend remains of opinion that if these Acts could be applied universally they would be of great benefit; but he says that as they are only applied to certain exceptional districts their effect is slight and fluctuating, and hence not very beneficial. If there is no sufficient hygienic argument to advance in support of these Acts, they are lost beyond any possibility of support. The hon. Member for Devonport (Mr. Puleston) and other Members have referred to a certain Return; but I wish to say for myself that, so far as I am concerned, I take the authority of the Government as the highest authority upon this question of hygiene; and when we find Her Majesty's Government, in the Reports of the officials concerned in the administration of these Acts, admitting, as my noble Friend has frankly admitted, and as the hon. Gentleman the Secretary to the Admiralty has also admitted, that their operation has not been of such hygienic value as to justify their retention, I am determined, in future, to take my stand upon that admission on the responsibility of the Government, and I do not feel myself compelled to occupy the time of the Committee by discussing statistics brought forward on the spur of the moment, perhaps privately obtained, and which it would be impossible to discuss. But there is another point upon which I must say a word. The hon. Member for Devonport seemed to think that because I ejaculated across the floor of the House an expression of difference of opinion, I gave him or some other hon. Gentleman the lie. He accepted my explanation that I had no such intention; but I do say this—that I absolutely disbelieve the accuracy of the views represented and believed in by himself and those other hon. Gentlemen. My hon. Friend referred to a deputation to the Home Secretary. He said truly that that deputation consisted largely of magistrates, and that their statements were of a very serious nature. They were of a very serious nature, and I have had a report of that deputation, and I find that the statement of the Memorial was no less serious than this—that the withdrawal of the Metropolitan Police, by whom the Acts were carried out, had conduced to most disastrous effects, which were seen in an increase in prostitution; especially in juvenile prostitution; in more reckless conduct of prostitutes in the streets; in an increase of disease, and in its more virulent character. That was the very serious statement made by the deputation; but the attention of the Earl of Mount-Edgcumbe was shortly afterwards drawn by two of our Associations interested in the repeal of these Acts to statements which he was said to have made, and I have a letter from him in reply. This letter was addressed to the Secretary of the National Association, and he wrote another to another Association, which I also have. He says—

"I have to acknowledge your letter of the 25th instant, referring to my remarks in introducing the deputation to the Home Secretary, in reference to the Contagious Diseases Acts. In reply, I have to say that I was unexpectedly called upon to introduce the deputation, and while commenting on the statements made in the Memorial, I distinctly stated that I myself had no personal knowledge of the facts, which others who were present would be able to confirm."

Therefore, so far as the Earl of Mount-Edgcumbe was concerned, it is perfectly clear that, as spokesman of the deputation, he relied on the statements of the deputation, and had no personal knowledge of the matter. Then the hon. Member for Devonport referred to the fact that a great many Members of that deputation were magistrates. I have something to say upon that question. If they were magistrates, they ought to have known the law, and as magistrates, it was their duty to enforce the law; and the magistrates and mayors of England would surely have command over the local police. It is absolutely undeniable that, if you want to preserve order in the public streets, you must have recourse to the general law, and not to the Contagious Diseases Acts, because they contain no powers for the preservation of order; and, therefore, when this deputation went to the Home Secretary, and entreated him to restore these Acts, and maintained that the suspension of the Acts had increased disorder, they were condemning themselves, because the law still exists which alone is necessary for the purpose of preserving order. No law has been repealed or suspended by which order could be maintained at all; and if these magistrates have not carried out the law the responsibility and fault are theirs. Then as to the facts. The hon. Member cited the Mayor and ex-Mayor of Plymouth; but I will cite the Mayor of Devonport for last year. He is a medical man, and when he had retired last year, and heard these statements by the Earl of Mount-Edgcumbe and others, he denied that there had been any increase of disorder in Devonport, and maintained that there had been no such increase in consequence of the suspension of these Acts. I have been very much accustomed, during the many years in which we have been discussing this subject, to find gentlemen who desired to uphold these Acts glad to receive and rely upon evidence from the police. The police have always been held up to me as great authorities; but what say the police? The chiefs of the police of Plymouth and Devonport contradict every statement made by the Earl of Mount-Edgcumbe and other members of this deputation, and I have their views on record. I have first to quote an extract from *The Western Daily Mercury*, of June 5, that being the Report of the Chief Constable of Plymouth contradicting the statement of increased disorder since the suspension of the Acts. Referring to a statement made at the Local Board of Guardians' meeting, that, since the repeal of the Contagious Diseases Acts, there had been an increase of prostitution, he says—

"I am in a position most confidently to state that such is not the case. There are, in fact, fewer brothels and fewer prostitutes in the town than there were 12 months ago. Neither has juvenile prostitution nor disorder in the streets increased, as is so often stated; and as regards the street more particularly referred to—Summerland Place—there are at present only five brothels, and fewer prostitutes than there were two or three years ago. I and those under my command are ever ready and willing to undertake such prosecutions when taken in the interest of order and morality, and I fearlessly assert that, taking into consideration the large number of people who frequent our streets at night, the streets of Plymouth are as free from disorder as any town of the same size in America or in this country."

That is the evidence of the Chief Constable of Plymouth. Then I have the evidence of the Chief Constable of Devonport. What he says on the 11th of June is this—as to the virulence of the disease he would say nothing; but—

"As to the increase of juvenile prostitution and disorder in the streets, I must emphatically say that that is not the case in Devonport. Some time ago the Earl of Mount-Edgcumbe made a similar statement; but then it was contradicted. Unfortunately, he had not seen the statistics of the town, and it must be in the knowledge of every magistrate in Devonport that there was a marked decrease in the number of loose women brought before them."

The Chief Constable adds—

"There is a wonderful decrease of prostitution, and as to disturbances in the streets, I emphatically contradict the statement of the Earl of Mount-Edgcumbe."

That, at any rate, shows that there are two sides to the question, and that I am as much entitled to rely upon these statements as the hon. Gentleman is to rely on the statements he has laid before the Committee. Therefore, I am entitled to differ *in toto* from his view. The only other word I would say is this—I would like to get my hon. Friend, and some others who have been accustomed to argue that these Acts were very beneficial in reducing disease, and in promoting order and decency, and so forth, to turn back to the Resolution of April 20, last year, to see what it meant and what it has effected. That Resolution simply expressed, in a manner which was unquestionable, and which I think could not be reversed, the deep feeling and conviction of the majority of the House of Commons against the system of compulsory examination of women for the purposes of these Acts. Now, Her Majesty's Government, not able, I believe, to repeal these Acts at the time, and substitute what other legislation they might think necessary, in the exercise of their discretion and judgment, suspended their operation as far as they were, by that Resolution, bound to do. What, therefore, the Government have done is this—they have not withdrawn the police; they have only withdrawn a portion of the police; and the only thing they have stopped is the system of the compulsory examination of women; and what I want to point out is that, if nothing will satisfy hon. Gentlemen but harping upon these Acts, and entreating the Government to go back upon the Acts—which neither this nor any future Government will, I believe, be at all likely to do—the position in which they place themselves will be this—that the compulsory examination of women is not only the best, but the only method which they deem is possible to carry out their views. How can they justify a contention of that kind? So far as hygiene is concerned, we have it on the best medical authority that the effect of these Acts is trivial. So far as order and decency are concerned, they cannot deny that the Acts have done nothing enabling the authorities to preserve order. If they think that the deterrent influence of the system of compulsory examination is the only method of preventing juvenile prostitution, then I beg to say that they are extremely mistaken in point of fact. I deny, as a matter of fact, that juvenile prostitution has increased, and I have given the evidence of the Chief Constables of Plymouth and Devonport to support my case. But I would ask them to take the example afforded by Glasgow, where compulsion has become impossible. Let us accept the alternative of freedom and persuasion; let us strive to make our Army sober and moral, and so to diminish the causes of prostitution. Let us do what we can to save the young, and redeem those who have fallen. That can be done independently of the system of compulsory examination of women, which is odious to the hearts and minds of all people who have given consideration to this subject. I do not believe there is a man who has brought himself to the idea that compulsory examination was necessary, without beginning by disliking it. It is repugnant to every mind. Do not let us, then, despair. Do not let us be so impotent as to imagine that there is no other method of diminishing disease and enforcing order and decency in the streets, and checking prostitution. Do not let us, for a moment, be so feeble as to slip into the foolish conception that there is only one *nostrum* and method, and that is compulsory examination. I am profoundly convinced—and there is, perhaps, no man living who has given so much attention to this subject in all its aspects as I have—that when these Acts have been repealed, and are dead and buried, and when we have ceased to hanker after them; when, in consequence, you have given yourselves to the only other policy of non-compulsion and freedom, education and moral persuasion, charitable hospitals and medical assistance to the diseased of both sexes—I am strongly and completely convinced that you will then arrive at results in the reduction of disease, and vice, and disorder in the streets greater than any you can obtain by such methods as these Acts.

Mr. SAMUEL SMITH said, he did not desire to trouble the Committee with a speech on this subject; but he wished to make one or two observations, because he had been taunted by the right hon. and learned Member (Mr. Cavendish Bentinck) with belonging to a superstitious sect. He did not believe that any good whatever could come from a bad principle, and that was the reason why he objected to these Acts. He hoped the House would never be led by any sophistry into believing that any benefit would ever be derived from legislation that was contrary to the laws of morality. He trusted that the Government would not desist from the course they were now taking, but that they would adhere firmly to the decision of the House of Commons last year.

Mr. WARTON said, he was sorry to see the Government in this position. All the responsible Heads of the Departments most interested knew that these Acts were absolutely essential for the promotion of the health of their soldiers and sailors. The right hon. and learned Gentleman the Judge Advocate General, who had formerly a strong prejudice and leaning against them, had been converted, and now took a favourable view of them, simply from hearing the evidence before the Committee over which he had presided.

The JUDGE ADVOCATE GENERAL (Mr. Osborne Morgan) remarked that he was not Chairman of the Committee.

Mr. WARTON said, that the right hon. and learned Gentleman, if not actually Chairman, was very often in the Chair. He (Mr. Warton) had read the whole of the evidence, and he found that the right hon. and learned Gentleman who had taken a distinguished part in the proceedings was compelled, by the overwhelming weight of the evidence given by doctors, clergymen, priests, matrons of hospitals, and the police, to come to the conclusion that the Acts were beneficial, not only in regard to the health of their soldiers and sailors, but as regarded the reformation of the unhappy women who came under their influence. As a believer in Christianity, he thought it was a Christian act to remove these poor women out of all temptation to sin. One thing which had particularly struck him was the clear evidence that, under the operation of these Acts, juvenile immorality, which once largely flourished, had almost ceased, and that houses of ill-fame had greatly diminished in number. These were facts beyond dispute; and, therefore, he was sorry for the decision of the Government, because he believed that their defeat last year was, to a great extent, accidental. The right hon. Member for Halifax (Mr. Stansfeld) had spoken of the majority of the House. In one sense, it was true that there was a majority of the House in favour of the repeal of the Acts; but, in another sense, it was not true. The actual Division last year showed 170 or 180 in favour of repeal, against 110 or 115 on the other side. But that was very far from being a majority of the House, and those who knew how Divisions were taken in the House, no matter upon what question, knew very well that all those who were actively and tremendously in earnest in pushing on an agitation assembled in the full strength of their numbers, and it was exceedingly doubtful whether, if the whole House had been polled on this particular occasion, they could have got more than the 170 or 180 votes they did. But there were many hon. Members absent who would have been present if they had imagined that such a result would have been brought about. It was by a lucky accident that those who were in favour of the proposal of the right hon. Member for Halifax were present in their full numbers, while others were away who fondly supposed that Her Majesty's Government would stand firm, and would have strength sufficient to insure the rejection of the Resolution. If the Government had freely used their influence, or if a single crack had been opened, a majority composed of two-thirds of the House would have supported them. He thought it showed remarkable weakness on the part of the Government in yielding, under the circumstances, to a scratch majority. He recollected that when another Division took place affecting the contagious diseases of cattle, although there was a clear majority against the Government, they refused to give effect to the wishes of that majority, and took occasion, over and over again, to evade even the repeated decision of the House. The only ground on which he thought the Government could have refused to give effect to the Resolution in this case was that in both cases the same object was to be attained—namely, the prevention of the spread of disease. By giving way in the one case to a majority, and by refusing to give way in the other, the Government had encouraged the spread of disease. The only thing which could justify them was the ground of consistency; but, for his part, he was of opinion, after the careful perusal of the whole of the evidence given before a Select Committee—evidence given by magistrates, and ministers of every creed—that these Acts had worked well for the unhappy women who were affected by them, and had resulted in the restoration of many of them to society, and that they had prevented many poor girls, who were on the borderland between right and wrong, from going astray. The only thing he was able to find in opposition to the Acts was a feeling of sentiment—a sort of *à priori* idea, that nothing should be done which might appear to sanction vice. He hoped that some of the fanatics who had taken part in this agitation would be ashamed to see how far their ideas had carried them, and would ask the Government, once for all, to give up these follies and fooleries. The truest morality was to relieve suffering and misery, to take these poor women off the streets and reform them. He had the firmest conviction that such results would follow from the careful, but strict administration of these Acts.

MR. PULESTON said, that it was quite superfluous for the right hon. Gentleman opposite (Mr. Stansfeld) to inform the Committee that he did not, of his own knowledge, know anything of the state of the streets in Plymouth, Devonport, and Stonehouse. The Earl of Mount-Edgcumbe, however, possessed such knowledge, and he simply lived across the river, and was closely identified with the three towns. The right hon. Gentleman had quoted the ex-Mayor of Devonport, and had stated that he was against the Earl of Mount-Edgcumbe and others, who took a contrary view. Now, he (Mr. Puleston) found that, attached to the Memorial of the magistrates, clergymen, medical practitioners, and others in the boroughs of Plymouth and Devonport, and the township of Stonehouse, an extract from which he had read, was the name of Dr. Rolston. He did not know what evidence could be stronger as to the views of Dr. Rolston than his signature to that very strong Memorial. He fully appreciated the statement of the noble Marquess, who told them that he still firmly maintained his former opinion in favour of the Acts. The arguments of the right hon. Member for Halifax (Mr. Stansfeld) and the hon. and learned Member for Stockport (Mr. Hopwood) were altogether unsound, as were certainly those of the hon. Member for Liverpool (Mr. Samuel Smith), who spoke of the action of the Government, and appealed to them to stand firm by the decision already arrived at; but he (Mr. Puleston) begged those hon. Members not to forget what the views were of the Cabinet Ministers who had had most to do with the working of the Acts. The noble Marquess the Secretary of State for War, who might be presumed to know as much of the matter as an hon. Gentleman who had exercised no control whatever over the subject, was, at least, not of the same way of thinking as the hon. Member for Liverpool, but candidly told them that nothing that as yet had been adduced, either inside or outside the House, had induced him to change his mind. He should not follow the arguments of the Secretary to the Admiralty, who had ingeniously whittled down the number in the hospitals to 110. All he (Mr. Puleston) knew was that since the Acts were suspended, the number of persons in the hospitals suffering from disease were exactly double. He believed that since the suspension of the Acts there had been an influx of immoral women into the towns which had formerly been within the operation of those laws. It was too soon yet to judge fully of the physical degradation which would result both in the Army and Navy from the suspension of the compulsory clauses. Those who advocated those clauses, he would remark, had not the least objection to the adoption of other measures also, such as had been recommended by the right hon. Member opposite (Mr. Stansfeld). What they objected to was that the operation of the Acts should have been suspended before anything else had been provided to take their place. Notwithstanding all the evidence that had been produced, the right hon. Gentleman preferred to rely upon the evidence of one or two men against the positive and unequivocal statements of the editors of all the local newspapers, and three-fourths of the whole population of the towns concerned. If that was the way in which evidence should be tested, it must be apparent that the foundation of most of the legislation of this country was unsound.

MR. CAVENDISH BENTINCK complained that the right hon. Gentleman the Member for Halifax (Mr. Stansfeld) had made an attack upon him, and then run away. Since the right hon. Gentleman had left the House, he (Mr. Cavendish Bentinck) had had an opportunity of referring to printed documents, and he found that they entirely supported his assertion that Mr. Stevenson Blackwood did not mention the "Hong Kong" case either directly or indirectly in his speech at Exeter Hall, and that the audience must, therefore, have construed the charge as referring only to the Metropolitan Police. He (Mr. Cavendish Bentinck) therefore insisted that it was abundantly clear that he had made out his case. As to the way in which the Earl of Mount-Edgcumbe had deluded or hoodwinked the Home Secretary. Devonport and the two other towns were not the only towns which which had received benefit from these Acts. The evidence of his hon. Friend the Member for Hythe (Sir Edward Watkin) was very strong upon that point. He himself (Mr. Cavendish Bentinck) knew a good deal about the City of Canterbury; and there was a very strong opinion there that the city had sustained great injury by the suspension of the Acts. The same might be said of Chatham and Portsmouth. The right hon. Member for Halifax (Mr. Stansfeld) urged that moral suasion would be sufficient to induce people to give up immorality in the Army. Why, then, was not moral suasion tried in reference of the women of London, of whom the hon. Member for Liverpool (Mr. S. Smith) complained so strongly the other day when bringing before the House some extracts from the speech of the Earl of Shaftesbury—why did not the advocates of these Acts try moral suasion there? He thought they ought; and that if ever there was a case for moral suasion it was that; and if it was a failure in London, in all probability it would result in a similar failure elsewhere. He believed himself that, much as the details and principle of the Acts might be objectionable, there was no other mode of meeting the evil. It was with melancholy satisfaction he noticed that neither the right hon. Member for Halifax (Mr. Stansfeld), the hon. Member for Liverpool (Mr. S. Smith), nor the hon. and learned Member for Stockport (Mr. Hopwood) had said one word in regard to the fatal effects which the suspension of these Acts had produced upon the unfortunate women themselves, nor had they expressed one word of pity for their condition. One hon. Member said he would prefer their being placed in an hospital where they might be made accessible to religious instruction and influences. Was it contended that they would be made worse by religious instruction even in a Lock Hospital? The suspension of the Acts had had a most disastrous effect; and he thought he had clearly proved his case that the compulsory clauses of the Acts should again be put in force.

DR. FARQUHARSON asked for an explanation of an item under Sub-head G of £600 for grants made to certain institutions.

SIR ARTHUR HAYTER said, this was a grant of £600 to the Discharged Prisoners Aid Society to enable prisoners who had been, uufortunately, detained for crime to maintain themselves until they could procure work after their release from prison. Acting upon a suggestion which had been made by the right hon. Member for King's Lynn (Mr. Bourke), he had placed himself in communication with the prison authorities, and, in conjunction with the Director of Clothing, he was happy to say that arrangements had been made by which the whole of the clothes of the prisoners and their bedding were now made by the prisoners themselves, instead of being exercised at shot drill, where good conduct justified this relaxation of the rules.

CAPTAIN AYLMER asked for an explanation of an item of £2,700 under Sub-head J for commission granted to local bankers for a supply of specie for the payment of pensioners, &c., residing in the Colonies. It seemed to him that if pensioners chose to reside in the Colonies it was quite sufficient for the Colonial pensioners to charge for providing for that specie; and he did not see why there should be any additional charge for home pensioners.

SIR ARTHUR HAYTER said, that for many years pensioners had resided in the Channel Islands, and this was a payment in connection with such pensioners.

COLONEL NOLAN said, he thought that £2,500 was a large item for providing change for the small amount of money paid in the Colonies. He hoped the Secretary to the Treasury would give some idea of the number of pensioners in the Colonies and the amount of the pensions paid.

SIR ARTHUR HAYTER said, the bankers charged 3 per cent on the amount which passed through their hands, and the payment was sanctioned by the Treasury. It would be difficult to say at that moment how many of these pensioners there were.

GENERAL SIR GEORGE BALFOUR asked if there was any alteration in the rate of commission, so as to make the concession more profitable at one time than another? He wished also to have some information as to an item of £12,000 which appeared under Sub-head O for rewards to inventors.

MR. BRAND said, that the rewards to inventors were given in accordance with the recommendation of a Committee as appointed by the present Chancellor of the Exchequer when Secretary of State for War. The Committee had to decide on various critical questions which arose in connection with the construction of the new steam ordnance, and the Committee held its meeting at Woolwich. Experiments were constantly made, and Reports were presented. The Reports were sent to the Surveyor General, who transmitted them to the Secretary of State. It was not considered to be for the interest of the Service that the Reports should be made public. The rewards during the present year consisted of the sum of £1,000 paid to the inventor of a torpedo, and £200 in rewards for inventions now under the consideration of the Committee.

SIR HENRY FLETCHER said, that under Sub-head M he noticed an item of £500 for medals. It seemed that there was an item last year for a similar purpose which amounted to £600.

SIR ARTHUR HAYTER said the decrease from £600 to £500 was simply because medals for the Admiralty were now paid out of the Admiralty Vote; £500 was the ordinary charge for military medals.

CAPTAIN AYLMER asked what was the scope of the inquiry of the Committee appointed by the late Secretary of State for War? Was it extended to Ordnance generally, or confined to Field Artillery?

MR. BRAND said, the Committee considered all questions relating to Ordnance.

CAPTAIN AYLMER asked if he was to understand that the Committee referred to was a permanent Committee?

MR. BRAND: Yes.

Vote *agreed to.*

(2.) £245,200, War Office.

MR. CAUSTON said, upon this Vote he desired to say a few words on behalf of a very intelligent and deserving body of men—he meant the Military Staff Clerks of the General Staff. No doubt it was for the interest of the Army, with a view of encouraging intelligent and respectable men to join its ranks, to hold out to them the prospect of promotion. In all branches of the Service with this single exception of the Corps of Military Staff Clerks, promotion from the ranks did prevail; but under the existing Regulations commissions were practically closed to Military Staff Clerks. In the following branches of the Service men who joined the Army had a prospect of obtaining commissions:—The Cavalry, the Artillery, the Royal Engineers, the Office of Schoolmaster, the Commissariat Department, the Ordnance, the Household Corps, and Infantry battalions. In the whole of these branches of the Service a man, entering the Army as a private, was able to reach the post of commissioned officer—such as Riding Master, Quartermaster, Inspector, or various other positions in which they ranked as commissioned officers. But in the Corps of Military Staff Clerks there was no promotion at all. Nevertheless, the Staff Clerks, were, he believed, a very intelligent and respectable body of men, and very useful indeed to the Staff officers. They were called upon to guide, as it were, and to act in support of all new Staff officers. The noble Marquess the Secretary of State for War, and hon. and gallant Gentlemen who had served on the Staff of the Army would be in a much better position than he was to speak of the qualifications of these Staff Clerks; but he had been given to understand that it was impossible to find in the entire ranks of Her Majesty's Military Service a more useful and trustworthy body of men. Their position, however, was very different from that of any other soldier. A man in any other branch of the Service, by his ability, attention to his duty, good conduct, and intelligence was capable of being promoted from the ranks; but if he once became a Staff Clerk, when the regiment left the garrison town in which he was stationed, he was left behind, and he and his services, however meritorious, were soon forgotten by the officers connected with the regiment, and everybody else. Unless he happened to misconduct himself the probability was that he never joined his regiment again, and, therefore, he was necessarily passed over in any promotion in the regiment, and such promotion was given to someone actually serving with the regiment, and he did not complain of it. Now, he wished to suggest a remedy for the grievance of which he complained, and it was that these Staff Clerks who were stationed in a garrison town, and did not leave with the regiment like the rest of the soldiers, and had consequently no prospect before them of promotion to commissioned rank —that this Corps of Clerks should be eligible for promotion to the rank of Quartermaster; and that they should be afforded an opportunity of filling the posts now filled by the Civilian Clerks at the War Office, who already possessed salaries equivalent to those paid to Quartermasters. For his part, he could not help thinking that this very useful class of men would make quite as good clerks as civilians, because they would be able to bring their practical knowledge of Staff work to bear at the War Office; and he should imagine that it would be of very great advantage to the Staff officers to know that their communications were being attended to by those who thoroughly understood the technical details of the services required. The action of the noble Marquess with regard to the Quartermasters had been very highly appreciated, and he believed that it would not only be an act of wisdom, but of fairness to hold out to these deserving clerks the prospect of promotion in the same way that promotion was given to those who joined the ranks and served in other capacities. He did not for a moment believe that the omission had occurred wilfully; he had no doubt that it was the result of mere accident. But it was undoubtedly the fact that some of the best men serving in the Army had been debarred from participating in the prospect of obtaining commissoned rank which was open to all other soldiers. He sincerely hoped that the noble Marquess would give him some encouragement, and that he would hold out to the clerks, in whose behalf he (Mr. Causton) had spoken that night, some hope that he would grant the request which he now made.

SIR WALTER B. BARTTELOT wished the hon. Member for Colchester to explain what the corps of clerks was? As long as he had served in the Army he had never heard of a corps of clerks until that moment, and he confessed that he was unable to understand what it consisted of, unless the hon. Member referred to the Staff sergeants and others serving at the different headquarters throughout the country.

MR. CAUSTON said, he referred to the Military Staff Clerks serving with the Staff in different parts of the country.

SIR WALTER B. BARTTELOT said, they would have rank of some sort or other according to their service, and some would belong to certain regiments. But, be that as it might, he wished to call attention to the clerks as organized at the War Office; and after what had been repeatedly said in regard to the employment of non-commissioned officers as clerks in the War Office it was most unsatisfactory to find that only 82 were so employed out of 523 clerks at the War Office. The noble Marquess had said that it was his anxious wish to employ as many non-commissioned officers as he was able in the different posts at his command. Non-commissioned officers in the Army looked forward very much to such employment, and any post that could be given to them, both in the office and elsewhere, would be very well bestowed. These men fought all over the world for their country, and in many instances they received a very inadequate return for their services. It must be remembered that they were the backbone of the Army, and it was desirable that they should attract the best class of men they could obtain for the Service. When he saw so few of them employed at the War Office, although they had been increased by 12 recently, he felt it his duty to impress upon the noble Marquess the desirability of making some greater recognition of the important services rendered by these men. He had ventured to call the attention of the noble Marquess to the matter, because he was quite sure that the noble Marquess was as anxious as he (Sir Walter B. Barttelot) was that these men should receive the reward their long and valuable services deserved.

MR. WHITLEY wished to invite the attention of the Committee to the grievances of another Department—namely, the officers of the Army Pay Department, who were not represented at the War Office. He believed that was the only Department which was not represented at the Horse Guards, and they could only bring their grievances before the House itself. Their grievance was a considerable one; but he had no doubt that it would receive attention at the hands of the Financial Secretary, who was noted at all times for his courtesy. At the present time there was a body of 300 or 400 officers of the Army Pay Department who were debarred from obtaining the rank which was enjoyed by the Commissariat and Medical Department. At present, in consequence of the smallness of the number of Chief Paymasters, men who had been 20 or 30 years in the Army got no promotion, and he asked if it would not be possible to increase the number by 15 or 20? Another grievance was of a different kind—namely, that after serving five years in the Department as Chief Paymasters they were not allowed to retire with the honorary rank of Lieutenant Colonel. He believed at the present moment that there were only one or two officers in the Army Pay Department who were Lieutenant Colonels. From an answer received from his hon. and gallant Friend opposite (Sir Arthur Hayter) some time ago, it would appear that his hon. and gallant Friend was under the impression that if honorary rank were conferred upon these officers they would be placed in a combatant position in case of the absence of a superior officer. He believed there was no ground whatever for that impression, and that honorary rank would not place them in a position to command. He thought that his hon. and gallant Friend had himself discovered that in that respect he had committed an error. He would urge on the Secretary of State for War and the Government the desirability of increasing the number of officers of the Army Pay Department in the position of Chief Paymasters from 15 to 20, and of giving them the rank of Lieutenant Colonel after five years' service. He believed that such a course would strengthen the Department, and produce a feeling of contentment in the minds of the officers. He, therefore, trusted that the grievances of the Army Pay Department would be taken into consideration.

GENERAL SIR GEORGE BALFOUR wished to point out that a transference had been made from this Vote to another which made the Vote appear this year much less than it was in the former year, and for that reason, therefore, he objected to it. This practice of changing items in this Vote was not unusual, and should not be permitted. With regard to the suggestions of his hon. Friend the Member for Colchester (Mr. Causton) regarding the extension of the employment of soldiers as clerks in the War Office, he begged to refer to the Staff Clerks, of whom there were a number of very excellent men liable to be sent abroad who were now serving in different capacities, as efficient clerks in the Army. He was sure that from the ranks of the Army they could get any number of qualified men to do the clerical work which had been referred to. He trusted that the noble Marquess would give his attention to the matter, and see what could be done.

THE MARQUESS OF HARTINGTON: I agree with the hon. and gallant Gentleman the Member for West Sussex (Sir Walter B. Barttelot), and with the hon. Gentleman the Member for Colchester (Mr. Causton), that it is desirable to give as much encouragement as possible to deserving non-commissioned officers in the Army by giving them employment, if possible, in the War Office, and in any similar employment that may be open to them. The subject has not been lost sight of. Military clerks have been introduced from time to time in the War Office; I believe that at one time they were employed to a larger extent than they are now. The number was reduced because it was found that the system was not altogether successful—that the clerical work was not advantageously placed in the hands of men who had had no experience of such employment. Military clerks are employed to some extent under the Adjutant General in connection with Artillery, and they are admirably suited for record work. They are invaluable in connection with work of this kind, and in this kind of duty they will continue to be employed as much as possible; but for other duties, involving a greater amount of education and a greater amount of Departmental training, it has not been found advantageous to employ them. I need not, therefore, add that, however desirable it may be to give encouragement to meritorious non-commissioned officers, it would be false economy to employ them in work which experience has shown they are not familiar with and not qualified for. Attention has been given to the matter, however, and whenever it has been found advantageous to employ the services of non-commissioned officers or pensioned soldiers, they are employed in preference to civilians. For instance, all the messengers of the War Office will, in future, be non-commissioned officers, and not civilians. With regard to the point raised by the hon. Member for Colchester as to transferring Military Staff Clerks from the districts to the War Office, I have to say that the practice has not been found altogether successful, and it has therefore been discontinued. The non-commissioned officers are willing and anxious to be employed; but I have not heard that any improvement in their prospects is required. No representation of any grievance in this matter has been made to me; but now that the subject has been raised, I will make a point of looking into it. Without further inquiry, I cannot pledge myself to any opinion that any improvement in the position of these men is necessary. With regard to what has fallen from the hon. and gallant Gentleman the Member for Kincardineshire (Sir George Balfour)—as to some transfer of expenditure from this Vote to another—I did not quite catch the point to which he adverted; but I may say it is inevitable that from time to time alterations in the formal rendering of the accounts should take place, and, no doubt—as I suppose has occurred in this instance—in the first year in which the alterations in form are made some inconvenience is experienced. I believe that all that is possible will be done to minimize the inconvenience. I do not think my hon. and gallant Friend, or anyone who takes the interest he does in the matter, will find it difficult to discover what the transfers are.

Sir FREDERICK FITZWYGRAM said, he thought the feeling of the Army was more in favour of having better paid employment given to non-commissioned officers in their regiments than increase of pay to Staff Clerks. The great prominence which had been given to these Staff clerkships instead of doing good to the Army had rather had the opposite effect. Regimental appointments had become depreciated in the minds of the men in the regiments. The Army was far from desiring to see these Staff clerkships increased, and wished to see better pay and increased advantages given to regimental appointments. He did not think that non-commissioned officers looked for employment outside their regiments.

Sir GEORGE CAMPBELL remarked that this was the last of the Effective Votes, and he hoped, therefore, he should be in Order in asking one question with regard to the Effective Service in Egypt. He desired to have some explanation as to how the expense of the Army in Egypt was borne—as to who paid the cost of its being moved up and down? They constantly heard of troops being moved from place to place——

The CHAIRMAN: There is no reference whatever in this Vote to the expenses incurred in Egypt.

Sir GEORGE CAMPBELL: I think I am entitled to go into this matter, seeing that this is a Vote for military administration. Of course, I am in your hands, Sir.

The CHAIRMAN: This Vote is for the War Office and the Staff of the War Department; it does not embrace any expenditure of the kind the hon. and gallant Gentleman refers to.

Sir ARTHUR HAYTER said, that in reply to the hon. Member for Liverpool (Mr. Whitley), who had referred to the Paymasters' Department, he should like to offer some explanation. In the first place, the hon. Member had recommended that there should be an increase in the number of Paymasters; and, secondly, he had expressed himself in favour of some revision of the relative honorary rank possessed by these officers. The hon. Member had asked if the Chief Paymasters could not be increased to 20. Well, there had been a careful revision of the whole of the Chief Paymasters' duties, and it had resulted in the issue of a new Warrant under which the number of Chief Paymasters was increased from 12 to 15. He could assure the hon. Member that there was no desire whatever to limit the expense; but they had been bound to consider what were the duties performed. It had been found that it was not the case, as had been contended by the Paymasters themselves, that there should always be a Chief Paymaster in every district where there was a General Officer. Three stations had been found where Chief Paymasters were required—Hong Kong, Aldershot, and one other station which he did not, for the moment, remember. To these places Chief Paymasters had been added; but he was afraid he could not hold out any hope of the number being extended beyond 15. With regard to the second point, which was that the relative rank of Staff Paymasters should be altered, and the rank of Lieutenant Colonel given to them, he would explain the position as to the honorary rank of the officers in the Pay Department after five years' service. At present Chief Paymasters ranked with Lieutenant Colonels, and became Colonels after five years. The Staff Paymasters ranked with Majors, and ordinary Paymasters with Captains. It was only very recently that the higher honorary rank had been given to Chief Paymasters, and the War Office Authorities felt, after consultation with the Military Branch, that it was too much for the Paymasters to expect that the Lieutenant Colonels' rank should be given to the Staff Paymasters as a matter of right after five years' service. The hon. and gallant Baronet the Member for West Sussex (Sir Walter B. Barttelot) would bear him out when he said that it was not to be expected that the non-combatant officers should rank immediately after the officers commanding regimental districts. The Staff Paymaster attached to a regimental district had now the rank of Major; were he given the honorary rank of Lieutenant Colonel he would be the senior officer in the regimental district whenever the officer commanding was absent. It was only recently that the ranks had been revised, and he was sure the Military Authorities would strongly object to granting this honorary rank of Lieutenant Colonel, after five years' service, to Staff Paymasters.

Mr. ARTHUR O'CONNOR said, that this Vote suggested many considerations on different points—so many, in fact, that he would not venture to detain the Committee on more than two or three of them. He should like to offer a few remarks with reference to the observations of one or two hon. and hon. and gallant Gentlemen who had preceded him. With regard to these Military Staff Clerks, the noble Marquess had hardly caught the exact drift of the observations of the hon. Member for Colchester (Mr. Causton). The Vote showed that, whereas there were only 70 of these clerks employed in the War Office last year, there were now 82. So far the Military Staff Clerks had little reason to complain, because the authorities at headquarters had shown a disposition to utilize their services so far as possibly might be. The noble Marquess was quite right in saying that the experiment which had been made in using these men for clerical duties had not been altogether successful; but the complaint which, as he understood it, the Staff Clerks made, was this—They belonged to the Staff Corps, and were unlike non-commissioned officers in Line regiments, in so far as they could not be promoted after having lost their hold upon the regiment. However long a Staff officer of the Line had left his regiment, he had a chance of promotion; but not so with officers of the Staff Corps; and this was all the more hard, because the cause of their leaving the regiment for the positions offered was, as a rule, owing to excellence of character and superior conduct and ability. That was a very just complaint, and he hoped that in any inquiry the noble Marquess instituted it would not be lost sight of. Then, as to the position of the writers. On page 85 an item of £6,500 would be found—

"For Pay of Writers employed from time to time as occasion arises in the several branches of the War Office, at the rate of 10*d.* an hour whilst employed."

Speaking from his own personal knowledge of the Department of the work and of many of the men employed, he was bound to say that this remuneration of 10*d.* an hour was a disgraceful pittance for the services these men rendered. Tenpence, he believed, was the sum originally mentioned in the Report of the Committee which sat upon the general question of the employment of clerks in the Civil Service; but that sum was never intended as a maximum. The original experiment was a payment of 10*d.* or 1*s.* an hour, he forgot which. These men had been employed not merely casually, and from time to time, as one would suppose in reading this description, but many of them had been employed for many years. They had had great experience, and were of great value. He could put his hand on men within the walls of the War Office who were worth twice or three times as much as 10*d.* an hour, and who, nevertheless, had been working on for years with no prospect of an increase of pay, although the cost of living had increased almost daily, and although as time went on they, of course, advanced in years. He certainly did think that in a large Department like the War Office, where so many men were employed as writers in the discharge of useful duties, some attention ought to be given to their claims upon the Treasury for increased remuneration. As to the Civil clerks, as the Committee would observe, they were put in different classes. There were men described as "clerks" with salaries of £500; others described as "clerks, upper division," with salaries of £400; and then there were "supplementary clerks" with £300, and "men clerks" with £250. The men of the lower division were more numerous than those of the upper, and their salaries were limited to £250—that was the maximum. These men had entered the Civil Service on just the same terms as the upper division clerks—men who were receiving two, and sometimes as much as three times their amount of salary. They were every bit as good as the upper division clerks. Although they received such miserably small salaries, they could be trusted to do any work which was done by any portion of the Civil Staff in the War Office. As a rule, the hardest and heaviest part of the work was given them to do. They had less leisure than the clerks above them; they had less leave, and in every respect were treated less favourably. He saw no reason why the upper division of the clerical staff should not be reduced by something over 100; their places, or, at least, half of them, being replaced by the men of the lower division. If this were done, the country would benefit in the matter of economy, and would not in the least suffer in the matter of efficiency. The men of the lower division were quite as able to do the work as the men of the upper division; in fact, in many cases, they were much more fit for superior duties. So much for these clerks. What appeared to him to be the most important aspect of this Vote was this—that the whole of the increase was in the Department of the Commander-in-Chief. On that point he would have to find occasion more favourable for offering some remarks, for at that period of the Session, and in the present mood of the House, it would hardly be advisable to raise the very large question which might well be raised in regard to the position of the Commander-in-Chief. If, as he said before, the occasion were favourable, he should be prepared to submit to the House that the position of the Commander-in-Chief at the War Office was, to a very great extent, the cause of a large number of little wars in which this country had for the last 15 or 20 years been engaged. They had had wars on the Red River, wars on the Gold Coast, wars against the Basutos, wars against the Zulus, in the Transvaal, a raid against Abyssinia, and now this descent upon Egypt. If it were not for the dominant position of the Commander-in-Chief he believed they would have been spared many of these wars. He believed the secret of their entering into these useless and far from honourable enterprizes was to be traced to the fact that military officers, anxious for promotion, anxious for an increase of pay and allowances, tired of inaction and the irksomeness of an idle military life, brought pressure to bear on the Military Authorities at headquarters whenever there was a favourable opportunity for a quarrel, and so launched the country into a line of action which, if the Civil element at the War Office were dominant as it ought to be, would never have been entered upon. But, as he had said before, the present was not a favourable opportunity for the discussion of this matter, and he would not venture to go further into it. With regard to the administration of the noble Marquess the Secretary of State for War, he begged to remind the Committee that when the Army Votes were first taken in Committee hon. Members were not allowed a fair opportunity of discussing many things which they were desirous of having thrashed out. Amongst other questions he had wished to discuss was the question of the Riding Establishment at Woolwich, and this the noble Marquess had promised to look into between that date and this. Earlier on he (Mr. A. O'Connor) had given his reasons for believing that the Riding Establishment at Woolwich—which cost some £5,000 or £6,000 a-year—was perfectly useless, and was a thorough waste of public money, keeping a large number of men in a comparatively idle life. He had shown, in fact, that the establishment had nothing whatever to justify its continuance. The noble Marquess had said he was not acquainted with its details, or even with its *raison d'être*, and had promised to inquire into the matter. But although the noble Marquess had had two or three opportunities of speaking since then, he (Mr. A. O'Connor) had noticed that he had said nothing about the matter. He would ask the noble Marquess to say something upon it now.

THE MARQUESS OF HARTINGTON: The hon. Member says that the increase in this Vote is due to the Commander-in-Chief's Office.

MR. ARTHUR O'CONNOR: Almost all the increase.

THE MARQUESS OF HARTINGTON: That point has been raised and answered already. The increase in the Commander-in-Chief's Department is only a nominal one. It is owing to the transfer of certain of the Commissariat Staff to the Commander-in-Chief's Department from the Department of the Surveyor General of the Ordnance. That has been done because the Staff has been under the Commander-in-Chief. Being under his direction, it is only right that the transfer in the Vote should take place. With regard to the hon. Gentleman's remarks as to the Riding Establishment at Woolwich, immediately after the discussion to which he refers I called for a Report on the subject. That Report has been received, and has been more or less under discussion; but I do not think it would be possible to make any changes until next year's Estimates are under consideration. The subject is not one of pressing importance, and I cannot say that I have examined into it very carefully. I will do so, however, when next year's Estimates are in course of preparation. The hon. Member has referred to the great disparity between the salaries and position of the clerks in the upper division and those of the clerks in the lower division, and he has called attention to the large number of men clerks in the lower division. This disparity is not due to the present War Office, but is owing to the system inaugurated by our Predecessors; besides, it applies to all Departments, and is not peculiar to the War Office. I believe the lower division clerks do not accept service on the same conditions or in the same division as the upper division clerks. I believe these changes were introduced in consequence of the Report of the Commission presided over by the right hon. Gentleman the Member for the University of Edinburgh (Sir Lyon Playfair). Several improvements have been made in the position of the lower division clerks, who are now sometimes allowed to become clerks in the higher division. But this is not their right, seeing that they accepted the positions they hold in the lower division under well-defined terms. The War Office had no control over the appointment or the pay of the writers. Whenever assistance of that kind is wanted, application is made to the Civil Service Commissioners to furnish the War Department with the required number of writers, who are paid according to rule, and in whose rate of remuneration it would be impossible for the War Office to make any alteration.

MR. A. F. EGERTON said the noble Marquess had certainly stated correctly the practice at the War Office with regard to the writers being furnished to the Department by the Civil Service Commissioners; yet he (Mr. Egerton) thoroughly endorsed what had been said by the hon. Member for Queen's County (Mr. A. O'Connor) with regard to that practice not working in a satisfactory manner. No one, he believed, would say that it did work satisfactorily. He agreed also with the hon. Member in saying that the breach, or division, which separated the upper from the lower division clerks was much too wide, and that there ought to be some better and easier means of bridging it over than at present existed. He had heard it said that there were many gentlemen in the lower division perfectly capable of performing higher duties in the Office than those which they had to perform; but that it was under the present system quite impossible for them to jump over the gap between them and the clerks of the higher grade. He ventured to hope that before long there might be a thorough investigation of, and inquiry into, the working of the Playfair system. He thought that inquiry ought to be held as soon as possible, and that it would result in good to the Service. With regard to the pay of the writers, he thought 10*d.* an hour was a very miserable pittance, and that there ought to be some means by which these persons could be advanced by selection. There were some writers perfectly capable of performing much higher duties than those for which they had been engaged, and in some of the Public Offices those higher duties were entrusted to them with advantage. There were many cases of the kind, and from the success which had attended the arrangement he ventured to think that the whole system with regard to the employment of writers would soon have to be carefully considered.

MR. RYLANDS said, he was very much disposed to think, with the hon. Gentleman opposite (Mr. A. F. Egerton), that the whole arrangement between the Civil Service Commissioners and the War Department required reconsideration. He remembered several occasions on which questions relating to Public Offices were before Parliament. It had been urged that by reconsideration and reconstruction in the Office certain economies might be effected; that certain clerks should be removed, and a staff of a more efficient character organized. It was believed that, although some charge might be incurred for pensions, in the long run economy would be effected by reducing the number of officials employed. But those prospects had been falsified. The Vote went on, gradually creeping up in the number of clerks employed, and in the amount paid to them. Now, it was his impression that they did not get as much work out of those in the Public Service as they ought to do; he believed that to be the case as a rule. He referred to gentlemen who were placed in the highest class, favoured servants of the Crown, who had a great many advantages in pay and short hours, and who were allowed to play the part, in short, of the aristocracy of the Public Service. On the other hand, in the lower class there were men who were expected to work more regularly, who had no hope of future advancement, who received less pay, and, no doubt, represented the lower class of the Public Service. He agreed with the hon. Gentleman on the Front Opposition Bench (Mr. A. F. Egerton) that the strong line of demarcation between these highly paid and indulged servants of the higher class and a large number of men of the lower class was open to serious objection. He thought, of course, that the noble Marquess was right in saying that it was very necessary to secure for the Public Service men whose qualifications were fitted to the higher work of the Departments by some such distinctions as those which existed. But the point was that they should give a stimulus to men in the Service to devote themselves with earnestness and zeal to the public interest; and if, combined with that, they showed greater capacity, they ought to be able to rise to the higher positions, if the chance were open to them, no matter what their qualifications were at first, because that was a matter of little consequence, what was to be looked to being the qualities they displayed afterwards. He thought that greater opportunities should be given for the promotion of these men. He should be glad if the whole position of clerks under the Playfair scheme were investigated by a Committee of the House, which he would prefer to a Departmental Committee as being better able to judge whether the arrangements for the Public Service might not be improved, so as to give more hope of advancement to the *employés*, and, at the same time, have a beneficial effect upon the Public Expenditure. The hon. Member for Queen's County (Mr. A. O'Connor) had gone down, not only to the lower, but to the lowest, stratum of the Public Service, the writers, and he complained that those gentlemen were only paid 10*d*. an hour, no doubt a small sum to work for, and it might be said that their position was a hard one. But it must be remembered that the State was not bound to give more than the market value for such work, although he could quite understand, and he should be willing to see, a higher rate, even 3*s*. an hour, paid for work of a certain kind perfectly well done. With regard to the other points, he thought every man in the establishment ought to have a chance of rising to the highest position, if he showed attention, zeal, and ability to discharge the duties; and, therefore, he should be glad to see the whole matter carefully inquired into, first of all, to ascertain whether the Playfair scheme ought to be retained in its integrity; secondly, whether it should be modified; and, thirdly, to ascertain whether the Public Service was not overmanned.

SIR HENRY HOLLAND desired to protest against the statements made by the hon. Member for Burnley (Mr. Rylands), that the first class clerks were too highly paid, and that they were "indulged." He had had some years of official experience, and he could distinctly assert that such allegations were quite contrary to the facts. No class of public servants did their duty more efficiently, and more to the satisfaction of their superiors, than these first class clerks; and he was sure that all the Heads of the Departments would confirm that view. He was not particularly wedded to the Playfair scheme, nor should he object to an inquiry by a Committee as to the working of that scheme, if it should be thought that the time had arrived when such an inquiry might be advantageously made; but he must remind hon. Members who had taken up the case of the second class clerks, and had dwelt upon the hardship inflicted upon them by not allowing them to be promoted into the upper division, that these clerks had entered the Public Service with a full knowledge of their position and chances. Without at all underrating the work done by these clerks, and their zeal, and without affirming that in no case should promotion be made in very deserving cases to the higher class, he doubted very much whether it would be to the interest of the Public Service that there should be any claim or supposed claim on the part of ythese clerks to promotion upon a vacancy in the higher division. Such a claim would necessarily lead to the promotion in every case of a lower division clerk.

MR. ARTHUR O'CONNOR said, he trusted he should not be supposed to disparage the services of the upper portion of the clerks in the War Office. His contention was that the lower class clerks were not treated fairly in respect of having to do the same work and getting less pay for it than others sitting in the same room perhaps. The hon. Member for Burnley (Mr. Rylands) said he would take men into the Office at the market price for their services, and that when they were taken in he would give them every prospect of rising, if their ability and assiduity showed them to be worthy of promotion; but his (Mr. A. O'Connor's) complaint with regard to the writers was that, although they were taken into the Office at a low market price of 10*d*. an hour, if they worked for 15 or 16 years they had no increase of pay, although they gave good and valuable service, and their experience every year became more valuable to the public. Nor had they any chance of promotion, or of improvement in their position. He knew very well that the writers were worth a great deal more than 10*d*. an hour, and that the clerks in the War Office would be very sorry to lose their services; if they were withdrawn they would very soon want to know why they were taken away, and would find it very difficult to get through their work without their assistance. The work they had to do was of an important character, and required a certain amount of official experience for its proper execution; and yet there were men of 14 and 15 years' service having no hope of promotion, and receiving no more pay than they did when they first came into the Office. He considered it unjust on the part of the Treasury to resist the application for improvement in their position on the part of men who, after a long period of service, had become of great value to the public.

Vote *agreed to.*

(3.) £20,300, Rewards for Distinguished Services.

SIR JOHN HAY said, he proposed to move the reduction of this Vote by £1,300, in order that he might call attention to the fact that the reward for meritorious services here proposed was not the only reward bestowed upon such services, nor was it the best mode in which they might be recognized. As a matter of fact, a Vote for money, as a reward for meritorious services, was one very just and proper way of treating them; but there were some kinds of meritorious services which had always been rewarded by a Vote of Thanks in that House. That, in his opinion, was a more excellent way of proceeding in reference to the Army. This was the first occasion, he believed, when the courtesy of the House had not been extended to a private Member who had offered to its consideration a Vote of Thanks to the Army for distinguished services rendered in the field. According to the authority of Sir Erskine May, that courtesy had been extended on two former occasions—in 1803 to Mr. Sheridan, and in 1828 to Mr. Hobhouse; and he believed that if he had been permitted to bring under the notice of the House the services rendered in the Soudan it would have gladly passed a Vote of Thanks.

THE CHAIRMAN pointed out to the right hon. and gallant Gentleman that that Committee had no power whatever to deal with the subject he was discussing, which was one solely for the consideration of the House. The right hon. and gallant Gentleman was not in Order in discussing on this Vote the subject of a Motion he had placed on the Paper.

SIR JOHN HAY said, he proposed to justify his proposal to reduce the Vote by £1,300 by pointing out that this was not the best manner in which reward could be offered for the distinguished services to which he was about to call the attention of the Committee. Very recently in the Soudan certain meritorious services had been performed, and it had been stated that the War Office and the Admiralty had alike proposed to recognize those services by giving sums of money; but he could not find any trace of the sums voted by Parliament for such services rendered. Thus, Members were deprived of any opportunity of expressing their opinion on those services. He believed this was an unusual course, and he could find no parallel case in which a large sum of money had been paid to the Navy or the Army while no charge was submitted to the House. No doubt, the only opportunity which Members of the House had for considering services rendered was on Vote 1. That opportunity was taken for asking the House for a sum of money to bestow on persons who rendered these services; and yet they were informed that money had been paid by the Admiralty and the War Office without any Vote being taken in that House. He ventured to say there were many in that House who would gladly have voted the money, and it was strange that there should be no trace of a Vote for the money which they knew had been paid.

THE MARQUESS OF HARTINGTON: If a Vote had been taken for a gratuity, it would have been in Vote 15 for Miscellaneous Services. It could not possibly come under a Vote for Non-Effective Services.

SIR JOHN HAY said, it was desirable that the House or the Committee should, in some way or other, understand how, where, and when the rewards were to be given for the most distinguished services which had recently occurred in the Soudan. The Army was fighting in a space 50 miles square; within that space nine battles had been fought. Amongst those battles were the two victories gained by General Graham which entitled him, and the officers and men serving with him, to the thanks, not only of the House, but of the country. Those two victories involved the destruction of 20,000 lives, and retrieved the honour of the English name in the Soudan. No doubt, the *prestige* of England had been sadly shaken by previous defeats, and the enormous loss of life which they entailed; but General Graham, with an imperfect force of 4,000 picked up haphazard, was sent down, and he, in the most gallant manner, succeeded in defeating a large force of the enemy in a manner beyond all praise. That was decidedly one of those distinguished services for which the thanks of the House had been formerly given.

THE CHAIRMAN said, he could not understand how the right hon. and gallant Gentleman connected his statements with the reduction of the Vote.

SIR JOHN HAY said, his object was to point out that there was a more excellent way of rewarding these services than that which the War Office had adopted. He, therefore, thought it right to call attention to these distinguished services which were being rewarded in so imperfect a manner.

THE MARQUESS OF HARTINGTON said, those services could not be considered under this Vote. The Vote could have no possible reference to the services to which the right hon. and gallant Gentleman referred, because it was framed before the battles were fought.

SIR JOHN HAY asked on what Vote it would be possible to call attention to rewards which had been given, and were now being given, to the officers and men of the Army and Navy for the distinguished services for which the House had not been allowed to thank them?

THE MARQUESS OF HARTINGTON said, he did not think it was altogether his duty to tell the right hon. and gallant Gentleman under what Vote he would be able to call the attention of the Committee to a particular question; but he imagined that the best plan to adopt would be to move a substantive Motion, or to propose a Resolution on the Motion to go into Committee of Supply. The question of a Vote of Thanks did not appear to be relevant to any particular Vote of the Army Estimates.

SIR JOHN HAY said, he did not wish to interfere with the Chairman's ruling, or to detain the Committee. He had given Notice of a Vote of Thanks; he had been refused by the Government an opportunity of bringing it forward; and it was not his fault if, having given Notice of it, he was not permitted to call the attention of the House or the Committee to the distinguished services recently rendered by the Army and Navy. He would not interfere with the Chairman's ruling; but he should endeavour, upon the last day of the Session, to give effect to the Motion which he now had upon the Paper.

Vote *agreed to*.

(4.) £77,000, Half Pay.

(5.) £1,193,900, Retired Pay, &c.

SIR WALTER B. BARTTELOT said, he had one remark to make upon this Vote, inasmuch as it brought clearly to view the cost of the abolition of purchase. He had in his hand a Return which the House had granted upon his proposition. From that Return it appeared that they had already paid in hard cash £6,444,771 5*s.* 4½*d.* for the abolition of purchase; and it was estimated in that Return what it would cost the country up to the year 1903. In 1883-4 the charge was £287,106 half-pay and retired pay to General Officers; £341,365, half-pay and retired pay to Regimental Officers; £12,000 for rewards for distinguished services, and £118,500 for payments awarded by the Army Purchase Commission, making a total for that year of £758,971. The Return showed that in 1902-3 the half-pay and retired pay of General Officers would be £174,876, the half-pay and retired pay of Regimental Officers £894,208, rewards for distinguished services £10,000, and payments under the awards of the Army Purchase Commissioners £17,800, making a total for that year of £1,096,884, and a grand total from 1883 to 1903, irrespective of the £6,444,771 already paid, of £18,019,398. He merely mentioned that to show the cost the country had been and would be put to by the abolition of purchase. There were, of course, certain payments made before the abolition of purchase; but into those he would not now enter. He could not help thinking that if they had been wiser in their generation, and had returned the regulation money, as was proposed at the time, they would not have had anything like this enormous sum of money to pay. He did not wish to say anything more; but he thought it was right the country should know what it had paid and would have to pay for the abolition of purchase in the Army.

COLONEL NOLAN said, he wished to direct the attention of the Committee to the injustice of the retirement scheme which was introduced by the late Government about seven years ago. He did not mean to say that the present Secretary of State for War (the Marquess of Hartington) was responsible for the scheme; indeed, the noble Marquess went as strongly as he could against the scheme, and took a Division against it. Under the retirement scheme captains were to be compulsorily retired at about 40 years of age, and majors at about 44 or 45. That scheme, if it was unjust and foolish, was consistent; but now the scheme had been made thoroughly inconsistent by the Secretary of State. Under a new Regulation, which he (Colonel Nolan) thought it was very probable had been issued at the instance of the Commander-in-Chief, captains were still to be compulsorily retired at 40; but majors were not to be allowed to retire at 44 or 45. The effect of that, of course, was that they would compel some men to serve beyond 45, while they would compel other men to retire at 40. It might be said that the new Rule would not be operative; but the Secretary of State for War had announced that he had taken the power to himself, and he meant to put it in force in certain cases. The noble Marquess would not allow a major to retire at 44 or 45; but he would compel a captain to retire at 40. It was ridiculous to say there was any difference between captains and majors. There was, practically, no difference between them; and if captains were too old for service at 40, surely majors were too old at 44 or 45. He thought it was very silly to compel officers to retire at 40 or 45; it was an extravagant system, and it had, to a great extent, prevented the Army being as good a Profession as it was formerly. If they had a scheme of retirement, it ought to be a consistent one. The present state of things required amendment, or, at least, an explanation.

Sir ALEXANDER GORDON said, the compulsory retirement of officers at 40 years of age was as injurious to the State as it was unjust to the individual officers of the Service. Under the scheme to which the hon. and gallant Gentleman (Colonel Nolan) had referred, the State lost the services of men at the very prime of their lives—lost the services of the very men who were wanted to fight their battles; men who had seen difficult service were sent about their business in order that their places might be filled by young ensigns and boys. He was aware that up to the present time nothing had been done to alter the new Regulation; but the Regulation was made by the present Chancellor of the Exchequer (Mr. Childers) some few years ago, and it must hold sway for some time. He (Sir Alexander Gordon) was satisfied that the day would come when the country would not allow the Rule to be carried out of compelling men who were of the greatest value to the Service to retire at 40 years of age. His chief object in rising, however, was to draw the attention of the Committee to the large increase in the Vote which they were now considering. The increase over last year was no less than £59,944. There was a steady yearly increase in the Non-Effective Vote for the Army. The Committee would find that for 1877-8 the Estimate for the Non-Effective Services was £1,985,069; this year it was £3,714,274, a difference of £1,700,000. It was really worth the while of the Committee to consider why this increase took place. Perhaps hon. Members who did not follow up the matter were not aware that the taxation of the country had increased steadily by £1,000,000 a-year for the last 10 years. The taxation was now £10,000,000 more than it was 10 years ago, and there was no security that in the next 10 years the taxation would not increase by another £10,000,000. The Committee ought, on occasions like the present, to do all they could to reduce the expenditure of the country. A few years ago he drew the attention of the Committee to the increase in the Non-Effective Vote; and Mr. Gathorne Hardy, who was then the Secretary of State for War, said—"Oh, this is a Vote over which we have no control; and we cannot help the increase." But he (Sir Alexander Gordon) could not accept this dictum. The noble Marquess (the Marquess of Hartington) ought to pay as much attention to the Non-Effective Vote as to the Effective Vote. The year before Viscount Cardwell left the War Office, the Army Estimates amounted to £11,600,000; now they reached £18,500,000. In that short time the Army Estimates had increased by such an enormous amount. Every year the Army Estimates increased by about £500,000; surely something ought to be done in the direction of retrenchment. The Committee met, and talked matters over; but they were actually powerless to check the War Office. The Army ridiculed the discussion on the Army Estimates, because they knew that nothing was ever done either to improve the position or comfort of the Army, or to make any effective reduction. The net increase in this Vote in the last 12 months was £59,000. He trusted that some explanation would be given of that increase.

SIR GEORGE CAMPBELL said, he had always regarded the retirement system as an extravagant system. In his opinion, the country ought to receive something more for its money—something, say, in the shape of Reserve officers. He only rose to make one suggestion, and it was that if the retirement system must go on, the retired officers ought to go to the Reserve. The officers were retired with considerable pay; therefore, why should they not be required to join the Militia, and thus do a modicum of service?

THE MARQUESS OF HARTINGTON said, that, in replying to the observations of his hon. and gallant Friend the Member for East Aberdeenshire (Sir Alexander Gordon), he was afraid he could only repeat what Mr. Gathorne Hardy said years ago—namely, that this was a Vote over which the Government had no control. Whether the present system of retirement was a good one or an extravagant one, it was deliberately introduced by the Government of the day, and sanctioned by the House of Commons; and, therefore, the matter had passed entirely out of the control of the Government. Parliament, of course, must provide the necessary funds. He understood the hon. and gallant Gentleman the Member for Galway (Colonel Nolan) to call attention to a statement he (the Marquess of Hartington) made the other day on the subject of suspension of voluntary retirement, and to make a comparison between the condition of compulsory and voluntary retirement. No alteration could be made in the system of compulsory retirement without very serious consideration. If any change were now made, the officers who had already been compulsorily retired would have very great ground of complaint. They would argue that they had been treated more unfairly than their successors. On the other hand, as he said the other day in answer to a Question, voluntary retirement was still at the discretion of the Secretary of State for War and the Commander-in-Chief, and the system was created for the express purpose of equalizing, as far as possible, the rate of promotion in the different corps of the Army. It was always understood that voluntary retirement would be used, according as it became desirable, either to stimulate or to check promotion in the Army. Under the circumstances he stated the other day, it was now found necessary to check somewhat the undue and abnormal rate of promotion which was going on in the different corps, and that was being done by means of the system of voluntary retirement.

COLONEL NOLAN said, the noble Marquess did not argue that it was better to retire officers compulsorily at 40 years of age than to allow them to remain in the Service longer; he had simply argued that the law would not allow him to change matters; he must retire captains at 40, whether it was right or wrong, though he was allowed to prevent other officers retiring at 45. That was the noble Marquess's case; he did not argue the case on its merits. The noble Marquess virtually contended that he was bound by law to retire captains at 40; but, in order to regulate promotion, he could prevent majors retiring at 44 or 45. Hard cases made bad laws. The noble Marquess was in the minority when the law was passed, and he voted against it. He did not approve of the law; and, therefore, he ought to alter the scheme, if necessary, by legislation. In one way, it would be hard on the men who had been retired at 40; but no injustice would be done if the noble Marquess were now to raise the age of compulsory retirement of captains to 42, 43, 44 or 45. It would be rather cheaper to let captains continue longer in the Service, and let majors retire earlier. The present scheme was extravagant, because 40 years was too young an age to put men out of their Profession. An officer was quite fit for duty at 55, so that it must be extravagant to retire him compulsorily 15 years earlier than was necessary. The nation was the sufferer in every respect; the charge imposed on the nation in consequence of this retirement scheme increased by £15,000 and £20,000 every year. The charge would increase year by year; indeed, it would not find its level for 10 or 15 years to come. This extravagant scheme would have to be remedied sooner or later.

MR. RYLANDS recollected perfectly well that when the retirement scheme in question was before the House some years ago, it was very strongly opposed by several hon. Members. Nothing could be more unsatisfactory than that they should have a Vote which was increasing every year under conditions which even the noble Marquess (the Marquess of Hartington) himself could not say were calculated to improve the efficiency of the Army. It was perfectly unjustifiable on the part of the Committee that they should allow to continue a scheme which was prejudicial to the interests of the Army, and which, at the same time, increased every year the burden upon the taxpayers of the country. When the scheme was before the House originally, he spoke very strongly against it, because he considered at the time it was a scheme which would necessarily lead to very large expenditure, and not only lead to a large expenditure, but have the effect of driving out of the Army some of the very best men they ought to keep. He had known many cases in which officers who were in the prime of life who chose the Army as a Profession, and who were admittedly very efficient officers, had been sent about their business, and for what? To increase the efficiency of the Army? Certainly not. To make a flow of promotion. The public purse and the efficiency of the Army was to be sacrificed in order to gratify a desire that there should be a flow of promotion. The time was not very far distant when people would say that the efficiency of the Army was not at all commensurate with the cost imposed on the country, and they would ask the reason why. When the people discovered that the non-effective charges amounted to such an enormous proportion of the entire cost of the Army, they would not fail to see that the system had been bolstered up. and that a large expenditure was being incurred in the interest of one class. He believed that if all these pensions and superannuations went on increasing year after year, the time would soon come when the difficulties which the noble Marquess the Secretary of State for War now experienced would be dealt with by the people in a manner which would not be pleasant to those who were receiving the pensions and superannuations. ["Oh, oh!"] Hon. Gentlemen might differ from him; but he was saying what he believed from his knowledge of the feeling of the working classes of the country. If these enormous pensions continued to increase, the feeling of the people would be that their taxes were taken from them without justification, that they were being defrauded, and that large sums were being paid for which the country got no advantage whatever. The Members of the present Government were opposed to the retirement scheme now in force; but, of course, they could not be expected to make any change that Session. He was persuaded, however, that they would shortly look seriously at this matter with a view, if possible, of avoiding these constant increases of the non-effective charges of the Army, and of securing that men who were most capable in the Service of the country should not be retired merely to provide a flow of promotion.

THE MARQUESS OF HARTINGTON said, the view taken by the hon. and gallant Gentleman the Member for Galway (Colonel Nolan), and the hon. Gentleman the Member for Burnley (Mr. Rylands), was that he (the Marquess of Hartington) had not defended the retirement system upon its merits. He had not done so, because he did not think it was desirable that they should be constantly altering the terms under which officers served in the Army. He thought that unless there was some absolute necessity for a change, it would be much better to leave the matter alone. The terms under which officers in the Army served were embodied in the Royal Warrant; and unless strong reasons were shown why he should do so, it was not necessary for him to investigate any individual grievances. He was far from saying that some Regulations—he would not say these precise Regulations—were not necessary. When his hon. Friend the Member for Burnley (Mr. Rylands) talked about these Regulations being absolutely unnecessary for the efficiency of the Army, and about their being only initiated for the purpose of providing a flow of promotion amongst the officers, he forgot altogether that a flow of promotion was absolutely necessary for the efficiency of the Army. Did his hon. Friend want battalions of the Army to be commanded by old men of 70 and 80 years of age; or did he think it was expedient for the efficiency of the Service that battalions should be commanded by officers in the prime of life? How were officers to rise in their Profession unless some steps were taken to secure a flow of promotion? When the hon. Gentleman (Mr. Rylands) talked about there being a large expenditure in the interest solely of a class, he altogether forgot that some provisions of this kind were absolutely necessary for the very existence of the efficiency of the Army.

Vote *agreed to.*

(6.) £120,000, Widows' Pensions, &c.

(7.) £17,000, Pensions for Wounds.

(8.) Motion made, and Question proposed,

"That a sum, not exceeding £33,200, be granted to Her Majesty, to defray the Charge for Chelsea and Kilmainham Hospitals and the In-Pensioners thereof, which will come in course of payment during the year ending on the 31st day of March 1885."

COLONEL NOLAN asked whether the question of pensioners came under this Vote?

THE CHAIRMAN: No; under the next Vote.

MR. ARTHUR O'CONNOR said, that on this Vote he wished to submit a point to the noble Marquess the Secretary of State for War. Some time ago there was published a statement of the accounts of the Commissioners of Chelsea Hospital for services other than those voted by Parliament for the year ending 31st March, 1883; and from that account it appeared that there was a balance in the hands of the Commissioners for Army prize money of £76,000 in securities, and some £1,200 or £1,300 in cash. Of all that sum only £121 had been distributed as prize money to the soldiers or their representatives; but a sum of £200 had been granted to the officials in Chelsea Hospital as the expense of the Prize Department—that was to say, the Secretary in the Hospital was allowed £100 a-year, and the principal clerk was allowed another £100 a-year in order to enable them to dispense a total sum of £121. The simple fact was that it cost £200 to pay away £120. The Public Accounts Committee called on the Commissioners of the Chelsea Hospital to say what amount of prize money had been distributed during the past three years, and this was the result. Taking the three years ending 31st March, 1884, the sum annually distributed was respectively £65 11*s.*, £121, and £167, and for each of these years there had been a charge made of £200 to defray the expense of distributing this miserable amount of money. The story of the distribution of prize money through the Chelsea Hospital and the Military Authorities was one of the most disgraceful stories of the whole history of the military arrangement of this country. The very names of Banda and Kirwee must stink in the nostrils of all who were acquainted with the transactions in regard to prize money. The gentlemen who got the salaries to which he had referred had no right at all to them, as they did no work, and as the money was taken from funds that belonged to the soldiers and their representatives. In order to get rid of the balance arising from the prize money, the authorities were obliged to spend £3,361 in the maintenance of grounds and for other purposes at Chelsea. It appeared to him that the Committee was bound to take some notice of the way in which this money was being jobbed away; and, in order to bring the matter to an issue, he would move a reduction of the Vote by the amount of the salary of the Secretary and of the principal clerk, in all £200.

Motion made, and Question proposed,

"That a sum, not exceeding £33,000, be granted to Her Majesty, to defray the Charge for Chelsea and Kilmainham Hospitals and the In-Pensioners thereof, which will come in course of payment during the year ending on the 31st day of March 1885."—(*Mr. Arthur O'Connor.*)

THE MARQUESS OF HARTINGTON: I trust the hon. Member will not persevere in his Motion for the reduction of this Vote. The matter is one with which the War Office has absolutely no concern whatever. So far as this money is concerned, it is true the Chelsea Commissioners, who have to deal with it, are subordinates of the War Office; but, so far as I am concerned, I have nothing whatever to do with their action, and have no knowledge of the working of the prize fund. The Army prize fund accounts are audited by the Auditor General in the ordinary way; I can only promise to ascertain whether the sum is properly spent.

MR. ARTHUR O'CONNOR: After that declaration from the noble Marquess I will rest satisfied; and I can only say that I trust that by this time next year a General Election will have relieved the noble Marquess from the service of the Department. If I then happen to be in my present position, I shall take care to raise the question, and probably I shall not do so without success.

Motion, by leave, *withdrawn.*

Original Question put, and *agreed to.*

(9.) £1,411,000, Out-Pensions.

COLONEL NOLAN said, there was a Question which he had put upon the Paper some two months ago, when the Army Estimates were before them, which he wished now to repeat. He would follow the habit which had now for some time been adopted in the House of putting the Question without reading it from the Paper, as the War Office knew all about it from its being on the Votes. He had repeatedly brought the question under the notice of the War Office, so that no one could plead ignorance of it. He did not wish to have any dispute as to the facts, for he believed his statement was perfectly correct, having gone to the trouble of obtaining from the various Departments of the War Office what information he could of an accurate kind. The case was one of a very gross kind; the individual whose grievance he was representing, who was a very poor man, having been done out of 3*d.* a-day and part of the result of his labours during the greater portion of his life. It seemed to him absolutely necessary that the rights of pensioners of this kind should be carefully protected. These pensioners from the ranks were not like the officers or higher grade pensioners they had been dealing with under Vote 19. The amounts were very humble compared with those voted to the officers; but, however small, they were as important to the poor pensioners, or even more so, than were the large sums granted to people in higher grades, and it was necessary they should be very closely guarded and watched by the House. He could not mention a stronger and more grave case of a man having been absolutely done out of his pension than the present. The case was that of a man who had enlisted very many years ago into the Indian Artillery, the contract of enlistment being different to that for the English Artillery or the Royal Artillery. The question of character was not so much looked into in the case of men enlisted for the Indian Artillery in those days. The character of men enlisted for the Royal Artillery was, of course, a matter of moment; but in the case of men enlisted for the Indian Army they desired to get the white man, and were prepared to give him 1*s.* a-day without taking his character into consideration. He mentioned that with emphasis, because, to a great extent, the point of the whole case turned upon it. This man had contracted, as a great many men from this district did, to join the Indian Artillery on the understanding that at the end of 20 years he was to get a pension. It was customary in those days to enlist nearly the whole of the white contingent of the Indian Artillery in the South of Ireland, the Royal Artillery being recruited from the North of Ireland and England. Well, there happened in India the great Mutiny. The Indian Artillery was amalgamated with the Royal Artillery, not in exactly the same way as the Infantry were amalgamated, but still an amalgamation took place. 8,000 or 9,000 men of the Indian Artillery mutinied—that was to say, the Law Officers of the Crown declared it to be a mutiny. They declined to serve with the new force, but this man did not. These 7,000 or 8,000 men declined to serve, because they thought that their case would not be properly considered by the Government, and no doubt their apprehensions were well founded if the case of this man was at all typical of the action of the English Military Authorities. The artilleryman whose case he was bringing before the Committee went to Lucknow. Two years' service was reckoned off his time on account of the transfer, and having served the requisite number of years he was to have his pension. The original contract, as he (Colonel Nolan) had stated, was that this man was to get 1*s.* a day at the end of his service. He was to have his pension at the end of 21 years, so that when he had served 19 years, having had two years taken off on account of his agreement to be transferred to the English Army, he was entitled to 1*s.* a-day. Within a month of the expiration of the 19 years the War Office said practically—"We do not want to give you this 1s. a-day; we will bring you before a Medical Board and see whether you are fit for service." They brought him up before a Medical Board, and they found that he had varicose veins, and they dismissed him from the Service, striking off 3d. a-day—a small amount no doubt, but to a man in the position of this person a sum as important as £500 a-year would be to a Member of that House. Great blame was to be attached to the Military Authorities who had held out to this man, as an inducement to join the English Service, that they would keep the contract of the Indian Government. In the case of this man they had obviously broken their contract. The officer who applied to the Medical Board might have been ignorant of the rule that an Indian artillerist was in a different position to that of an English artillerist. Just 27 days before this man would have been entitled to his 1s. a-day he was discharged on account of varicose veins. It was perfectly absurd to discharge a man in that way. The man in all probability had got into some difficulty or other, not sufficient to entitle the officers to bring him before a court martial, but still sufficient to render his superiors inclined to punish him. Probably he had been bragging about his pension, saying, perhaps—"You fellows of the Royal Artillery are not so well situated as I am." He might have made himself unpopular in that way, and have got himself disliked; but the fact of a man being disliked was certainly not sufficient to entitle the authorities to deprive him of 3d. a-day for life. The grievance in this case was a most serious one. It was said, as a rule, the men of a regiment were protected by their own officers. No doubt that was so in 99 cases out of 100. Generally it was a most efficient protection, but in this case it was nothing of the kind. The feeling of *esprit de corps* which would have induced the officers to protect the men of the Royal Artillery was wanting in the case of the man who had left the Indian Artillery to join them in time of emergency. As a rule, the men taken over from the Indian Service were not badly treated; but in this case, as he had explained, it was probable that it was seen that the man was about to get an advantage over their own soldiers, and that he was bragging about it, and therefore the officers sought to punish him. The man was discharged for a nominal weakness of health—not that the medical certificate could be challenged—but it was absurd to suppose the man could not do barrack duty for the remaining 27 days of his 21 years. He might have been unfit to go with his battery on service; but it was absurd to suppose that he could not, on account of varicose veins, discharge barrack duty for 27 days. He had gone into this case at some length, and had repeatedly brought it before the notice of the War Office, because it was one of a serious kind to the individual for whom he was pleading. He was very curious to know how the War Office would treat it.

SIR ARTHUR HAYTER said, he was very glad the hon. and gallant Gentleman had brought this case forward; probably it was a case of one of his own constituents?

COLONEL NOLAN: No; it is not.

SIR ARTHUR HAYTER said, then it was the case of a man belonging to that branch of the Service—the Royal Artillery—of which the hon. and gallant Gentleman had been so distinguished a member? He (Sir Arthur Hayter) fully admitted all the statements made by the hon. and gallant Gentleman and those he had placed on the Paper, with two exceptions. He found the fifth paragraph was incorrect, there being no record at Woolwich of the man ever having been employed on active service in the field.

COLONEL NOLAN: He took part in the advance on Lucknow.

SIR ARTHUR HAYTER said, that there was no record of the man having been on active service, nor had he any medal. Again, with regard to paragraph 7, he could not admit that the Government had saved anything or that the man had lost anything, because it could be shown that he had not fulfilled the contract which he had made with the late Indian Government, the fulfilment of which contract alone would have entitled him to full pension. Although that might be thought a hard case, the man having nearly completed his service, it was by no means an exceptional one. There were several cases—four or five at least—in which men had rendered themselves ineligible for full pension a few days or a month or two before the expiration of their period of service. The Chelsea Commissioners had taken into consideration the character of this man—and it was necessary to look into that question for a moment. It was obvious from the statement of the hon. and gallant Gentleman that this man could not have made up his 21 years' service without boon service, because he was enlisted on the 18th of August, 1847, and discharged on the 14th of July, 1866. Even adding the two years' boon service which was given to every soldier who enlisted from the Indian into the Imperial Army, he had not made up his 21 years. The man had lost through his misconduct, and through being twice tried by court martial, 83 days' service; and although, at the end of 21 years' service, he would have had 1*s.* a-day, he was only allowed 9*d.*, because he had not completed his contract of service. His character was returned on his discharge—and it was well known that they were not unduly severe in making that return on a man's leaving the Army—as indifferent. He had been 24 times drunk, twice tried by court martial, 32 times in the regimental report book; and the cause of his discharge was that he was unfit for military service in consequence of varicose veins. However, the case had been taken up, and the Chelsea Board had been referred to on no fewer than five occasions by the War Office; but the Commissioners had always most consistently refused to make any addition to the man's pension. They said they were unable to make any alteration under the terms of their Statute, by which their action was governed, and pointed out clearly that the Statute only allowed them to give 1*s.* a-day pension when a man had fulfilled his contract of 21 years' service, and that for anything less than that they could not give more than 9*d.* a-day. That was the only ground for their decision, and there was none of a special character for the reduction of this pension from 1*s.* to 9*d.* The Bill which the Secretary of State for War had introduced into the House, and which stood for second reading that evening, would enable them to give greater elasticity in the matter of pensions, because for the future they would be given under the Royal Warrant, or under Regulations made by the Secretary of State for the time being. He did not know that he could say more, even if he went more fully into the case; but it did not appear to him to be an exceptionally hard case when the facts were fully gone into.

COLONEL NOLAN said, his contention was still unaltered. The Financial Secretary allowed that the man was within 27 days, deducting 83, of the completion of his 21 years' service. Of course, if the man had had the 83 days, the whole case of the Government would fall to the ground, according to the strict letter of the contract. If this had been the case of a rich man, who could afford to bring an action in a Court of Law, there would have been no hesitation on the part of anyone sitting on such a case to declare that this had been a gross breach of faith. It would be held at once that this was such a flagrant swindle on the side of the defendants that they would be at once required to comply with the terms of the contract, and to pay the costs. The Government were simply eluding the contract. He (Colonel Nolan) was not complaining that the Chelsea Commissioners had not given the man 1*s.* a-day; but what he was complaining of was that the officers had discharged him in the manner in which they did, and for the sake, perhaps, of preventing his getting the 1*s.* a-day to which he was entitled. It was usual, just before the expiration of a man's period of service, to give him a month's furlough—to send him away a month before his time. As to drunkenness and the question of character, as he had already pointed out, the Indian Government had been anxious to get a white-faced man beside a black-faced man, and in securing that they did not care so much about individual character. They wanted a white man, and they got him, because the white man was sure, or thought he was sure, of getting his 1*s.* a-day pension. The British Government, when it took over the Indian Army, had undertaken to carry out the contract of the Indian Government; but it had neglected to do so. As for the man getting drunk, they could not expect all the cardinal virtues for 1*s.* a-day; and as to his having been on active service, he must have been pretty near the campaigning, because he got his two years' boon service for his advance on Lucknow. To his (Colonel Nolan's) mind, this was one of the grossest cases of violation of contract—at any rate in spirit. If, however, he was told by the Financial Secretary that this case could be dealt with under the new Bill, of course he would not go further into it. Otherwise, however, when the next Vote for high pensions came on he should move a reduction, and point out the discrepancy between the award of £800 or £1,000 a-year without question to this or that distinguished man, whilst they defrauded "Tommy Atkins" of his 3*d.* a-day.

SIR ARTHUR HAYTER: This man was discharged by a Regimental Board of Royal Artillery officers.

COLONEL NOLAN: The War Office ordered them to discharge him.

SIR ARTHUR HAYTER: Not in the first instance. Application must have been made for a Board to assemble.

COLONEL NOLAN: The Secretary of State orders the Regimental Board.

SIR ARTHUR HAYTER: Yes; but the Board, when assembled, inquires into the case.

SIR ALEXANDER GORDON said, he wished to call attention to the defective manner in which these Estimates were presented, in consequence of the amalgamation of the Supplementary Votes with the original Votes. The net increase on the total Vote was stated to amount to £91,100; but those who had eyes to see might read in a foot note that there was £50,000 added to the original Vote last year in the Supplementary Estimate for the Egyptian Vote, and the consequence was that the real increase on the Vote of last year was £141,100. That arose from the system of not placing the original Vote of one year in juxtaposition with the original Vote of the subsequent year, which was the only way of forming a proper comparison between the Votes of one year and the Votes of another. The result was that the increase was always minimized and the decrease was magnified, and so a very wrong impression was conveyed. Members at a late hour—say, at 2 or 3 o'clock in the morning—saw "net decrease" so many thousands, and they were satisfied that the amount was less than in the previous year; but, in reality, they might be voting hundreds of thousands more, and that was one of the reasons why the Estimates crept up without their knowing it. He hoped that next year the noble Marquess (the Marquess of Hartington) would consider whether he would not adopt the system adopted in regard to the Navy Estimates, by which this inconvenience might be entirely obviated. In the Navy Estimates the original Votes for one year were placed in juxtaposition with the original Estimates of the following year, so that the House could make an exact comparison between the Estimates of one year and the Estimates of another, and know precisely whether the normal expenditure of the country was being increased or not.

SIR ARTHUR HAYTER said, the increase was owing to £91,000 which was the lesser amount of the Non-Effective Votes.

SIR ALEXANDER GORDON said, he thought the hon. and gallant Gentleman was altogether wrong. It was distinctly in consequence of the Supplementary Vote provided last year for Egypt, and the real increase was £141,100, and not £91,000.

THE MARQUESS OF HARTINGTON said, he would look into the matter and consider the system in regard to the Navy Estimates; but he could not imagine that there could be any difficulty in comparing the amounts in the present form.

Vote *agreed to.*

(10.) £190,000, Superannuation Allowances.

(11.) £50,100, Retired Allowances, &c. to Officers of the Militia, Yeomanry, and Volunteer Forces.

COLONEL KING-HARMAN asked the noble Marquess to give a little more information with respect to Quartermasters of Militia. In an answer to a Question the noble Marquess could not be expected to say much; but he thought a case had been completely made out in regard to these Quartermasters. Their case was simply this. A very small number of deserving officers, who had chiefly risen from the ranks, and had served Her Majesty in every part of the globe faithfully and well, had grievances which the public outside believed to be substantial grievances, involving a small amount to the State, but meaning a large amount to men of this position. He did not think it was sufficient for the noble Marquess to say, as he had said that day, that this matter had been inquired into by previous Secretaries of State for War and decided. He did not wish to say anything offensive; but it seemed to him that this Government rather prided themselves on having a policy entirely different from that of their Predecessors, and he thought this was a matter of justice to men who deserved well of their country. The matter was very small in point of pounds, shillings, and pence; but it was a hard thing that men who had given so many years of their lives to their country should at the latter end of their lives find themselves in an almost penniless position. They were not in the position of ordinary pensioners. They were given the rank of Captains, and they had to keep up a certain position; but their pensions were very small—far less than they imagined they had a right to, and far less than he thought they were entitled to.

THE MARQUESS OF HARTINGTON said, he did not know that he could add anything to what he had said in answer to a Question that day. The fact, he believed, was, that in 1870 the maximum pension for these men was 4*s*. a-day, and in 1877 it was nearly 5*s*. a-day. In 1881, however, the maximum was raised to 7*s*. a-day, as compensation for compulsory retirement. He did not think there was any precedent whatever for giving an increased pension to Quartermasters who had retired under a Warrant, as these men had.

Vote *agreed to.*

SUPPLY—NAVY ESTIMATES.

(12.) £62,500, Medicines and Medical Stores, &c.

(13.) Motion made, and Question proposed,

"That a sum, not exceeding £10,400, be granted to Her Majesty, to defray the Expense of Martial Law, &c. which will come in course of payment during the year ending on the 31st day of March 1885."

CAPTAIN MAXWELL-HERON said, he was sorry to have to trespass on the Committee in bringing before them a question which was raised last year; but he would not travel over the same ground. He must, however, bring the matter up now, first, because he thought there had been a misunderstanding as to the arrangement made by the Prime Minister with the House; secondly, because of certain passages in the speech of the Secretary to the Admiralty on that occasion, which were prejudicial to the interests of the late Commander of the *Clyde*, but to which, as they were then on the Report stage, he had no opportunity of replying; and, thirdly, because this was the only Court of Appeal to which recourse could be had with regard to a Naval court martial. The Committee would recollect that at an early hour on one day in August last he brought the subject of the court martial upon Commander Heron, of Her Majesty's Ship *Clyde*, before the Committee. He then raised three principal points—the first was as to the evidence of the second in command of the *Clyde*, Gunner Fitzgerald; the second was with respect to the corroborative evidence; and the third was the constitution of the court martial itself. To the last-named point he should mainly confine his remarks on this occasion. The Prime Minister agreed to refer the point he raised as to Gunner Fitzgerald to the Law Advisers of the Crown; but, at the same time, the right hon. and gallant Gentleman opposite (Sir John Hay), and also, he believed, the right hon. Member for South-West Lancashire (Sir R. Assheton Cross), asked the Prime Minister whether he would also refer to the Law Officers the point as to the constitution of the court; and he quite understood that the right hon. Gentleman agreed to do so. He was rather astonished at receiving from the Admiralty an official letter containing the opinion of the Law Officers; but that opinion only related to the point as to Gunner Fitzgerald. The circumstances of the case were these —Fitzgerald was second in command of the *Clyde* when Commander Maxwell-Heron had command of that ship; and he was afterwards tried and dismissed from the Service. Last year he drew attention to these facts, and pointed out, first, that Fitzgerald was an interested and prejudiced witness; and next, that this man and another who gave corroborative evidence having been under arrest, were released in order to give Queen's evidence against the Commander of the *Clyde*. He also drew attention to the fact that at the preliminary inquiry these men made certain statements, and when called at the court martial they swore to diametrically opposite statements. One made a statement so prejudicial to the prisoner that the court did not believe him. He could not go over the circumstances of the case again, because the matter had been referred to the Law Officers; but their dictum was this—that after eliminating the evidence of Gunner Fitzgerald, there was still sufficient evidence to justify the decision of the court. But how was this arbitration—if he might so call it—conducted? It was simply a case of submitting the decisions of two courts martial, one on the Commander of the *Clyde* and one on Gunner Fitzgerald, to the Law Officers, the point placed before them being only one of the points he had raised in that House. It was the well-known practice that in an arbitration the two sides should be heard; but in this case only one side had been heard, and none of the points raised in the debate was submitted to the Law Advisers except the one he had mentioned. The only consideration put before them was whether, after eliminating the evidence of Fitzgerald, there was sufficient justification for the decision. He thought this unfortunate and gallant officer ought to have been allowed to put before the Law Officers the points that had been raised in the debate, and the method adopted seemed to him to be a very extraordinary way of carrying out the intentions of the House. As he understood the arrangement made, it had not been carried out, neither the constitution of the court nor the corroborative evidence being referred to the Law Officers. Another point was this. In his speech last year the Secretary to the Admiralty—no doubt without intention—used some words which were very disparaging to the officer in question. Referring to the most serious charge, that of appropriating certain things, the hon. Gentleman said there was doubt in the mind of the court as to the charge made by Fitzgerald against Commander Maxwell-Heron. How could he know whether there was doubt in the mind of the court? The court was sworn to secrecy; but to say there was a doubt in the mind of the court was to say that the accused officer only escaped conviction by a very narrow margin owing to that doubt. The third consideration was that there was no Court of Appeal against decisions of courts martial but the House of Commons. These courts could ruin, condemn, convict, and sentence a man without there being any appeal. But in the Army every decision of a court martial was referred to the Judge Advocate General, and he believed the Judge Advocate General had had many thousands of such decisions sent to him for revision, and that at least 400 or 500 had been altered upon his advice. Why should not the same system be adopted in the Navy? There was at one time a Judge Advocate General in the Navy; but he was disposed of, and his duties were undertaken by the Counsel to the Admiralty. Last year there was a case raised, which he understood the Government would not submit to the Counsel to the Admiralty, though if it had been an Army case they would have submitted it to the Judge Advocate General. He could not see what use the Counsel to the Admiralty was. He received a certain amount from Votes by that House, and the rest was made up by fees; but such a system ought not to be allowed to prevail. There was no appeal against the decision of a Naval court martial, and that was why these cases could only be brought before that House. The constitution of this court martial was the point to which he wished to refer more especially. It was laid down in the Rules under the Naval Discipline Act that no officer should be relieved from attending upon a court martial, except the Admiral of a Royal Dockyard. This court martial was held on December 13th, 1882, on board the *Victory* at Portsmouth. The order of the Service was, that on the signal for a court martial being given, all officers of junior rank to the President must repair to the ship and answer to their names. On this occasion the names were called over, among them being the names of Captain Gordon, captain of the *Vernon* torpedo ship, and Captain Codrington, captain of the *Excellent*. They were reported by the Deputy Judge Advocate General as being absent on leave. But how were they on leave? One of them was reported to be absent on Government duty. Now, it could not be accepted as right by anyone who valued the Services, that a man should be reported absent on leave when he was with his regiment or on board his ship. If he was on board his ship he was on duty, and the same if he was with his regiment, and he could not be relieved of his responsibility. There might be a mutiny or a fire, or any other circumstances might happen; and if this rule was to be accepted, an officer who was supposed to be absent on duty might shelter himself behind that plea. It was absolutely impossible that the captain of a line-of-battle ship should be on board his ship except on duty, and on this morning both Captain Gordon and Captain Codrington were on their ships, although reported absent on leave. Captain Gordon, he believed, had received leave; but it had been cancelled at his own request, and Captain Codrington had been granted leave on Government duty. The primary duty of all Naval officers was to attend courts martial, and he submitted that these two officers ought to have repaired to the *Victory*, and answered to their names. They ought to have been members of the court, and as they were not the court assumed the aspect of having been packed. He did not mean that it was packed for any particular reason; but the order of the Admiralty could not been allowed to contravene an Act of Parliament. On this occasion these were the facts, and the answer he had received from the Admiralty upon this matter was that the Commander of the *Clyde* had an opportunity of challenging the constitution of the court; but he could not possibly know who were the officers who ought to have sat upon that court. He was satisfied with the constitution of the court with regard to the honour, integrity, and ability of the officers who sat there; but being a prisoner he could not possibly know that there were two absent officers who ought to have been present. But supposing he had challenged the constitution of the court, he conceived that if there was a chance he ought to lose no opportunity of trying to relieve this officer from the position in which he was placed by a sentence acknowledged to be very severe by every officer of the Navy of every rank to whom he had spoken. These were the facts, and he could not conceive how they could be controverted. Captain Gordon and Captain Codrington were on board their ships, and if they did not sit on the court then the constitution of the court was illegal. He knew it was a very difficult thing to get a matter such as this discussed at a late hour, and he had had the greatest difficulty in bringing it forward last year; but he knew there were many Members of that House who thought the case a very hard one. The Prime Minister had acknowledged that the case was a very peculiar one. At the court martial not a single Executive officer was examined. All the witnesses called were subordinate Warrant officers, and he was convinced that some day the whole truth of the matter would come out. He believed that his unfortunate relative was the victim of a conspiracy, and that it was a conspiracy in which the witnesses were obliged to take the course they did, and to make the statements they did, to save themselves from the punishment they really deserved. He considered that this unfortunate officer was sacrificed to overweening confidence in the second in command of the *Clyde*. He trusted that officer in every way, and then that officer had turned round upon him. There was one other point he would like to submit to the Committee. After the court martial had dismissed the Commander of the *Clyde* from the Service, the second in command was tried, and though the Commander of the *Clyde* was subpœnaed as a witness, the court absolutely refused to receive him as a witness, although he had been the Commander of the ship, and there were many things stated at the inquiry which he had no opportunity of refuting because he was not represented, and his evidence could not be given. That in itself, he thought, was a very serious matter; but, however that might be, the case he now brought before the Committee was simply that the constitution of the court being illegal its decision was of no value, and went for nothing. He firmly believed that the decision was illegal, for these two officers ought to have sat upon the court martial, and he was quite sure there were many officers in the Navy who were of the same opinion. Every officer he had spoken to took the same view, and one of them who had been and still was one of the greatest friends of Commander Heron was General Gordon, who was now at Khartoum, and had accepted his services on his intended journey to the

Congo. General Gordon was the least likely man in the world to accept the services of a man who he thought had been guilty of the crimes alleged against Commander Heron. He was deprived of every opportunity of vindicating his character before this court, and holding that the constitution of the court was illegal, he felt that he ought to leave no stone unturned on behalf of this unfortunate officer in order to replace him in his former position; and he maintained that if the constitution of the court was illegal the decision at which it arrived must be quashed. He sympathized much with the position in which this gentleman was placed, because, whatever the decision of the court martial might have been, he was satisfied that he had never done anything in his life to discredit himself, or that would raise a blush on the face of any of his friends.

Motion made, and Question proposed,

"That a sum, not exceeding £10,150, be granted to Her Majesty, to defray the Expense of Martial Law, &c. which will come in course of payment during the year ending on the 31st day of March 1885."—(*Captain Maxwell-Heron.*)

SIR JOHN HAY said, his recollection of what had occurred last year entirely confirmed what had fallen from his hon. and gallant Friend opposite. On that occasion the intention of the House was, no doubt, that the whole of the points raised in the debate should be referred to the Law Officers of the Crown. He himself was present on the occasion, and remembered that he had asked the Prime Minister that very question, and the answer of the right hon. Gentleman was that his hon. and learned Friends had had the advantage of hearing the whole of the debate and that all the points raised would be referred to the Law Officers of the Crown. It was, therefore, with considerable surprise that he found that only one point had been referred to the Law Officers of the Crown for inquiry, that point being, in his (Sir John Hay's) opinion, of not much value. The composition of the court martial was, no doubt, satisfactory; but the evidence brought before it had been recognized by many as evidence which ought not to have been relied upon; and although he understood the Law Officers of the Crown to say that there was sufficient evidence to justify the finding of the court martial irrespective of the evidence supposed to be tainted, yet the Committee would perceive how much the mind of the Court would at the time have been influenced by the evidence which would be presented to it, although it was found afterwards that the evidence was such that it ought not to have been received. A court composed of men not of legal mind, but of honourable gentlemen only, having before them evidence which at the time was not properly estimated at its true value, would naturally be influenced in its decision by that evidence; and although it might be true that some subordinate points were not affected by the character of that evidence, yet it must be remembered that the charges most detrimental to the character of this officer were the charges which were not proved. He was bound to say—it was his duty to say—that Commander Heron had served with him during five years, and that he knew him to be an officer of high character, in view of which circumstance it did seem to him that his case was of the hardest. That officer had served with the highest character until he was 45 years of age, originally in the Red Sea, and there he was placed in relation with General Gordon. He held in his hand a letter from that distinguished man to Commander Heron, from which it appeared that he had selected him to accompany him to the Congo, which arrangement would have been carried out had not General Gordon been sent on his present mission to the Soudan. It seemed to him that so distinguished an officer as Commander Heron, whose character when he came home from the Red Sea so highly commended itself to General Gordon, was not the man of whom it ought to be supposed that he would commit an act which he must have known would ruin his name and fortune. He contended that the character of this officer ought not to be ruined entirely for a comparatively trifling mistake. Commander Heron was sent down to the *Clyde*, a vessel fitted up as a dancing saloon, with gas pipes and other appurtenances, and with a gunner in charge. Commander Heron was not expected to superintend the dances, which he believed was the work of sergeants and of this gunner, who had been sentenced to dismissal from the Service with disgrace. Commander Heron, who had been all his life on active service, had so far distinguished himself that when he returned from the Red Sea he was offered promotion to the rank of retired captain, although he preferred service in a lower rank which would afford him occupation. He (Sir John Hay) acknowledged that he had not sufficiently attended to the duties which he was appointed to discharge on board the *Clyde*, and that he thought certainly deserved some punishment; but the amount of punishment in such cases should, in his opinion, be proportioned to the offence. It was perfectly clear that the House of Commons had a right to see that the Act by which courts martial were appointed was correctly carried out, and it was, therefore, their province to inquire into the sentences of courts martial. Now, who were the officers to be excused from sitting on courts martial? There was a special clause in the Act of Parliament by which Admiral Superintendents were so excused. He had served on many courts martial, and knew perfectly well how the Act was to be interpreted; it provided that every officer should appear on board the flagship who was within sight of flag or sound of gun. It was decided by Captain Codrington's superiors that his services were of more value in another capacity. That officer had business to attend to in Portsmouth Harbour; the court martial was held on three successive days; he was present at Portsmouth and was cognizant of the fact that a court martial was being held; but as he had pointed out, through no fault of his own, he did not attend. But then there was the captain of the *Vernon*. He had, it was true, applied for leave of absence, but he had not availed himself of it, and it was his duty to have attended on board the flagship on which the court was held, and to have answered to his name when called upon. The result of the absence of these two officers was, that Commander Heron instead of being tried by a court composed of an admiral and six captains was tried by a court composed only of an admiral and four captains. A court of six was undoubtedly of more value than a court consisting of five officers only. He knew not whether this court martial of five was or was not unanimous, because the members of the court were bound not to reveal what took place beyond the room in which the court was held; so much so, indeed, that a gallant friend of his, overjoyed at the fact that the character of a fellow-officer had been cleared, having told him, when he returned his sword, that he had been unanimously acquitted, was justly reprimanded for breaking the rules. But he would say that a court of six would have had more stability, and its decision carried more weight, especially as the Act of Parliament said that a court martial should consist of nine officers, and that it was only when that number could not be obtained, that it might consist of less. It appeared to him that the court in question was illegally constituted; and, that being so, it was a point which that House and the Committee had a fair right to consider. Well, then, they had the fact that the court was illegally constituted; that the officer tried was a man of high character up to the time at which he joined the *Clyde*; that he joined that vessel when his health was unequal to the discharge of his duties. No doubt, it would have been better had he acted on the proposal of the Admiralty to retire when he came home, in which case he would have been in the enjoyment of retired pay, instead of having lost the reward of his services and the high character he had gained. But, in view of the facts he had set forth, it seemed to him that the Admiralty were bound to give Commander Heron a new trial, or at least that they should not insist upon the carrying out of a sentence of this severity which was not usually passed on officers of rank and good character unless they had committed themselves in a manner which was certainly not attributed to Commander Heron. If his hon. and gallant Friend would allow it, he would prefer to take the sense of the Committee on the words he had himself placed upon the Paper; but in any case he would appeal to the Admiralty not to treat with such extreme rigour an officer of distinction for the first offence, and he appealed to the Committee to join him in insisting that a further trial should take place in consequence of the fact that the court martial which tried Commander Heron was not constituted in accordance with the Act of Parliament.

THE SOLICITOR GENERAL (Sir FARRER HERSCHELL) said, it was, of course, impossible not to sympathize with the interest felt in this case by his hon. and gallant Friend (Captain Maxwell-Heron) and by the right hon. and gallant Admiral opposite, who were relatives of the officer concerned in the finding of the *Clyde* court martial; but it appeared to him, nevertheless, that it would be wrong if the Committee were to allow that feeling to induce them to say that officers or seamen tried by court martial had any such claim as that the House of Commons was a proper Court of Appeal in such cases. His hon. and gallant Friend said that was the only Court of Appeal open to them; but he could conceive nothing worse than a tribunal of that House dealing with cases from courts martial; there was no tribunal more unfit to deal with an appeal of that kind from a court consisting of honourable and upright men who had heard the whole evidence and come to a conclusion honestly and impartially on the facts. How could the House sit as a Court of Appeal in a case like this? Hon. Members would recollect that last year it was suggested in that House that Commander Heron had been convicted on the evidence of tainted witnesses unsupported by any corroborative evidence, and that the question whether there had been any corroborative evidence had not been before considered, and that there was a strong presumption that he had been improperly convicted. That was the case put before the House last year, and the Prime Minister then said he would lay the matter before the Attorney General and himself (the Solicitor General), in order that they might examine the evidence taken before the court martial, and say whether there was anything in that evidence which would justify any Constitutional interference in the case, or justify any other course being taken. Accordingly, his hon. and learned Friend and he devoted themselves to the task, which was no light one, for they had to read over many hundred pages of evidence given before the court martial, and they determined to exercise a perfectly impartial judgment on it. They entered upon their task with an inclination rigidly to scrutinize everything that had occurred before the court martial, and with every disposition of sympathy for his hon. and gallant Friend who had brought the matter before the House; they read the whole of the evidence independently, and by agreement they exchanged their views by letter, so that each might record his views without knowing the conclusion at which the other had arrived. Having done so, the conclusion arrived at was that the evidence laid before the court martial was such as to justify the finding of that court martial; that there was ample evidence without the tainted evidence to justify the decision at which they had arrived; and he did not think that the court martial could have come to any other conclusion. How, then, could that House deal with the question? Unless they were prepared to go through the whole of the evidence given, how could they sit in judgment on the conclusion at which the court martial had arrived? He had read through the whole of the evidence, and he could not help saying that he had never perused the proceedings of a Court of Justice which showed more scrupulous propriety than the proceedings before this court martial; and he was bound to say that it reflected the highest credit upon the person whose duty it was to advise the Court. Throughout the whole case not a single question was put that there was any doubt about; every question objected to in any way was withdrawn and another course adopted; in short, he had never known in any Court of Justice a case tried with more care. Of course, he did not want to enter on the circumstances brought before the court martial—it would be unnecessary to do so—but he must demur to the statement of the right hon. and gallant Gentleman opposite that they were trivial matters. They were serious matters proved by evidence beyond all possibility of question, and with regard to which it would have been impossible to arrive at any other conclusion than that at which the court martial had arrived. With regard to what had been said in palliation of Commander Heron's conduct, he knew that the officers who tried him gave every consideration to his good character and distinguished services; yet they were bound to act also with regard to the evidence, and it was impossible for them to allow any feeling of sympathy for the individual or his past services to cause them to arrive at a conclusion not warranted by the facts of the case. He said that, so far as his hon. and learned Friend and himself had been able to judge, no injustice had been done in this case; and when his hon. and gallant Friend spoke of the case as having been exceptionally dealt with, he could assure him that it had been dealt with with the sole object of finding out the truth. Now, with reference to the constitution of the court martial, his right hon. and gallant Friend opposite had raised what was purely a technical question. His words were to the effect that he was satisfied with the honour, ability, and integrity of the officers who constituted the court martial.

SIR JOHN HAY: I said that the Commander of the *Clyde* was satisfied with that.

THE SOLICITOR GENERAL (Sir FARRER HERSCHELL): Then, the Commander of the *Clyde* was satisfied that these officers were men by whom he was willing to be tried. That being so, the judgment they arrived at could not be complained of, even if, as the right hon. and gallant Admiral said, the tribunal ought to have included two captains more. [Sir JOHN HAY: Hear, hear!] That, he said, was a purely technical question. There could be no doubt that, in former times, there were occasions in connection with which questions were raised, subsequently, as to the constitution of courts martial, where persons who had been summoned did not attend; but in order to prevent invalid proceedings by court martial, on this ground, the Legislature had intervened and passed an enactment, which he would shortly refer to. He admitted that the Statute provided that all officers within call should be present on board the flagship; but he was not prepared to admit that this applied to an officer who had obtained leave of absence, which was running at the time when the court martial was summoned, or that he was bound to attend, without it was necessary to summon him to do so. There was nothing in the Statute which, according to his judgment, bound an officer so placed to attend. That, he thought, disposed of the case of the captain of the *Vernon*. The other case was that of Captain Codrington. That officer was conducting some important experiments at a distance from the port. There was nothing more to say with regard to his case; and he was not prepared to admit that, these two officers being absent for the reasons stated, the court martial was, upon that ground, improperly constituted. But the Enactment of 1866 disposed of the technical point altogether, for it distinctly laid down that any objection to the constitution of a court martial must be raised before the trial, and not afterwards. That provision was passed by the Legislature to prevent technical objections being afterwards taken to the proceedings of courts martial. If a particular officer happened to have friends in that House who were interested in his case, and could rely upon it being re-opened by them on every occasion, it was obviously impossible that any decision could be arrived at by a court martial which would be final; and, therefore, he met the technical objection of the right hon. and gallant Admiral by saying that objection to the constitution of the court must be taken before, and not after, the trial. The right hon. and gallant Gentleman asked them to say that in this particular case, in the face of the evidence given, the finding of the court martial should be set aside. But would it be right, would it be Constitutional or fit, upon the grounds stated by the right hon. and gallant Admiral, that that should be done? He was sure that nothing would be more properly made the subject of adverse comment than such a course of action. Of course, they could sympathize with the relatives of a man who had sustained a great misfortune; but their sympathy ought not to allow them to deal with this question in the exceptional and dangerous manner suggested by the hon. and gallant Gentleman (Captain Maxwell-Heron). It was impossible they could set a precedent in this case; indeed, it would be a precedent of very evil omen if they were to deal exceptionally with this case, simply because the officer affected happened to have friends who could bring his case foward in the House of Commons.

CAPTAIN MAXWELL-HERON said, it was, no doubt, laid down that the constitution of the court should not be afterwards impeached; but that did not mean by anybody but by the prisoner. Certainly, the prisoner was the person referred to in that clause of the Act; but how could the prisoner in this case possibly know that the court was not properly constituted? The prisoner knew that the names of the two officers referred to were read over, and that it was stated that the officers were absent on leave. If they were both absent on leave, he (Captain Maxwell-Heron) had nothing more to say; but they were not absent on leave. One was on duty on board the tender, and the tender of the ship must have left the harbour that morning. There could be no doubt of that. The second officer had applied to have his leave cancelled. ["No, no!"] He (Captain Maxwell-Heron) understood, from an Admiralty Minute, that the officer had applied to have his leave cancelled. He saw it in writing, and it came from the Admiralty. The fact, however, remained that Captain Gordon was on board his ship, and, if that were so, he could not leave on leave; he could not be absent on leave and be present on his ship, and that was an argument he (Captain Maxwell-Heron) had used all along. He had said that the Commander of the *Clyde* could not challenge the constitution of the court—it was so laid down by law—but he submitted that any Member of Parliament could do so if he thought the constitution of the court was illegal. He thought this would have been a fair opportunity for the Admiralty to have given this officer of 32 years' standing, with five medals and the Order of the Mejidie, mentioned in the despatches from the Black Sea, a chance, at all events, for he was quite certain that if the case were tried over again by the light of the evidence they had now, there might be a very different result arrived at. He admitted now, as he did last year, that they were very unfortunate in the defence that they could bring up. The counsel for the defence, a very able man, told him, after the evidence was given—and one of the witnesses distinctly perjured himself, for he was convicted of the very thing he swore he did not do—that it was his belief that had the case been tried before a Judge and jury the verdict would have been very different. He (Captain Maxwell-Heron) agreed with the Solicitor General (Sir Farrer Herschell) that the prisoner could not impeach the constitution of the court after the decision; but that law only applied to the prisoner, and not to anybody else. The Act of Parliament did not lay down that he (Captain Maxwell-Heron), or any other Member of Parliament, should not do it. He maintained that it was impossible for the Commander of the *Clyde* to know that the two officers, Gordon and Codrington, ought to have been in the court, because he was then a prisoner on board the *Duke of Wellington*, and had been so for some days.

Mr. WARTON said, all those who had any recollection of the debate which took place last year on this subject must remember how deeply impressed the House was with the very able and feeling manner in which the hon. and gallant Gentleman (Captain Maxwell-Heron) brought forward his case. Nothing could exceed the good taste and judgment displayed by the hon. and gallant Gentleman in the impressive remarks he, on that occasion, addressed to the House. For a long time the House was put off with the usual cold-blooded official answer, and the sneer that if the gallant officer had not relatives in the House his case would not have been brought before Parliament. It was not until the Prime Minister came in and, gathering up what had taken place, found that the cold-blooded officialism would not do, that anything like a satisfactory solution was arrived at. The Prime Minister, who was wonderfully smart in gauging the sense and feeling of the House, saw in a moment that the matter must be treated in a conciliatory spirit. As there was, according to the present miserable system, no Court of Appeal to which parties might take a decision of a court martial, the Prime Minister, with his high sense of justice and honour, promised that all the points which had been raised by the hon. and gallant Gentleman (Captain Maxwell-Heron) should be referred to the Law Officers of the Crown. It appeared to him (Mr. Warton), however, after listening with care and attention to the able statement of the Solicitor General, that all the points had not been so referred.

The SOLICITOR GENERAL (Sir Farrer Herschell) begged the hon. and learned Gentleman's pardon. He was present during the whole of the debate last year; he read the whole of evidence, and every point which was then raised had been considered by the Law Officers.

Mr. WARTON said, the point to which he particularly referred was the constitution of the court. Although the hon. and learned Solicitor General argued the case with regard to the impeachment of the constitution of a court martial, he did not say in so many words that the point was referred to the Law Officers of the Crown. He (Mr. Warton) was justified, therefore, in saying that the pledge given by the Prime Minister had not been kept, and that instead of all the points raised by the hon. and gallant Gentleman (Captain Maxwell-Heron) being referred to the Law Officers, only one point was so referred, and that was the question of the sufficiency of evidence given before the court martial.

THE SOLICITOR GENERAL (Sir FARRER HERSCHELL) said, he was bound to correct the hon. and learned Gentleman the Member for Bridport (Mr. Warton). In the first instance, it was not understood that the question of the constitution of the court was to be referred to the Law Officers; but as the right hon. and gallant Admiral the Member for Wigton (Sir John Hay) considered that that point ought to have been referred, the Admiralty brought the point before the Law Officers.

MR. WARTON said, he was perfectly right so far that, in the first place, the pledge given by the Prime Minister was not kept. Until the Solicitor General rose for the last and third time that night, nothing had been said to show that the question of the constitution of the court had been referred to the Law Officers, and it was only when they were about to divide, that they were told that something took place between the right hon. and gallant Gentleman (Sir John Hay) and the Admiralty, and that then the point was referred to the Law Officers. He thought that what the Prime Minister meant was, that there should be a reference of all the questions raised; and, therefore, he was a little surprised that the Law Officers should have stood upon any technicality of the Act of 1866. Whatever was the intention of the right hon. Gentleman, the Law Officers of the Crown had very wide liberty given to them, so that they were hardly justified in standing by technicalities. It was rather hard for this unfortunate officer, about whose services they had heard so much—who seemed to have been so worthy an officer—that the House did not come to a decision last year in respect to these wretched charges about paint pots and other trivial things. It was only by means of the promise given by the Prime Minister that a decision was averted last year; and he hoped now, that more light had been thrown on the case, it would be found, as suggested by the hon. and gallant Gentleman (Captain Maxwell-Heron), that much of the corroborative evidence was supplied by tainted witnesses, and that no reliance was to be placed upon it. He (Mr. Warton) did not pretend to have read all the evidence; but the impression made on his mind by the debate last year was that the Commander of the *Clyde* was very unjustly treated, and that the witnesses brought against him were tainted. Though the Law Officers of the Crown were of opinion that there was corroborative evidence, it was quite possible, when all the ramifications of the conspiracy had been discovered, that a new inquiry would be granted. He hoped that, under all the circumstances, the Government would take a larger and broader view of the case than they had hitherto done; and that, considering the long service of the officer, the trivial nature of the charges preferred against him, and the tainted character of the evidence, they would have no more of the cold-blooded officialism which had been displayed, or of the sneers at the fact that the gallant officer had relatives in the House.

SIR JOHN HAY asked if the Committee were to understand that, for the future, a court martial in a Fleet, or elsewhere where there were nine officers, would be legally constituted if the admiral, or other persons summoning the court, chose to constitute the court of five or seven, or any smaller number than nine? He had certainly understood the Solicitor General (Sir Farrer Herschell) to say that it was competent for the court to be composed of any smaller number than nine. Although the Act of Parliament said that nine officers should constitute the court, and although the Admiralty themselves understood that that was so, because in the Bill of last year, which they failed to pass, there was a clause altering the present law on the subject, was the Navy to understand that for the future an admiral or any other officer holding a court martial, might, if he pleased, select a number of officers inferior to nine? It had always been understood that the officers to compose a court martial should be appointed according to their seniority. It was, therefore, important to know whether it was possible that a court martial could be packed; that the members of the court need not be the nine senior officers present in the Fleet or on the Station? He hoped they would hear from the Solicitor General whether the Admiral or the officer authorized to summon a court martial might select a number inferior to the number which was intended by the Act of Parliament, and might choose them without reference to their seniority, as was done in the case under consideration?

THE SOLICITOR GENERAL (Sir FARRER HERSCHELL) said, he had not suggested anything of the kind. The Act provided that a court martial should not consist of less than five, or more than nine.

SIR JOHN HAY begged the hon. and learned Gentleman's pardon. The words "if they be present" were significant.

THE SOLICITOR GENERAL (Sir FARRER HERSCHELL) said, that was another point; the right hon. and gallant Gentleman was referring to another provision. The number of officers who were to compose the court martial was not definitely fixed; the Act merely provided there should not be more than nine, or less than five.

SIR JOHN HAY said, he was sorry to have to pledg his opinion against that of the hon. and learned Gentleman; but every naval officer's reading of the Act was that, if there were nine officers present, the court martial should consist of nine. It was understood that the admiral had no power to make the number smaller.

THE SOLICITOR GENERAL (Sir FARRER HERSCHELL) said, he did not want to disagree with the right hon. and gallant Admiral; but it was competent for the President of the court to give leave of absence to an officer who had been summoned, and there was nothing in the Act providing that the court should consist of nine officers.

Question put.

The Committee *divided*:—Ayes 21; Noes 51: Majority 30.—(Div. List, No. 190.)

Original Question again proposed.

MR. HEALY asked the Secretary to the Admiralty (Mr. Campbell-Bannerman) if he could give the Committee a guarantee that there would be any sum taken on which the question of the assistance given by the Navy to Mr. Tuke could be raised?

MR. CAMPBELL-BANNERMAN stated that emigration had nothing to do with Martial Law. The Vote for Pay was the one on which the question referred to by the hon. Gentleman could be raised.

MR. KENNY said, he should like to ascertain from the Secretary to the Admiralty whether, assuming the Vote were to be passed now, there would be an opportunity on some future day to raise the question of the manner in which some of Her Majesty's ships had been utilized for the purpose of assisting the enterprize of certain supposed humanitarians? As many as four of Her Majesty's ships had been used for the purpose of carrying away emigrants, mostly pauper emigrants, from Connaught. If they consented to this Vote, would they lose their opportunity of discussing that question? So far as he could see it was competent for them to raise the question on almost any Vote.

MR. CAMPBELL-BANNERMAN said, the Votes for Ships and Men had been passed in Committee and on Report, so there would be no further opportunity that he could see on these Estimates of raising the question the hon. Gentleman desired to raise. But, of course, it was rather for the Chairman of the Committee to say what was in Order and what was not.

MR. HEALY said, the Committee could not accept the ruling of the hon. Gentleman (Mr. Campbell-Bannerman). If the Vote now under consideration was passed, he (Mr. Healy) could see no objection to raising the question on Vote 14, because in that Vote there was an item for piloting and towing Her Majesty's ships.

Original Question put, and *agreed to.*

(14.) Motion made, and Question proposed,

"That a sum, not exceeding £116,900, be granted to Her Majesty, to defray the Expense of various Miscellaneous Services, which will come in course of payment during the year ending on the 31st day of March 1885."

MR. HEALY said, this appeared a very proper Vote on which to raise the question of the assistance given to Mr. Tuke. He observed there was a sum of £8,000 asked for for piloting and towing

Her Majesty's ships, and he wanted to know upon what principle the Government piloted and towed the famine ships in Black Sod Bay for the purpose of clearing some 40,000 or 50,000 unfortunate Irish people off to Canada? He wished to know, in the first place, why Her Majesty's officers undertook the duty of assisting Mr. Tuke in importing these poor unfortunate people from their homes? A number of gentlemen, who knew nothing whatever about Ireland, went about making promises to the people of the West, many of whom did not understand a word of English—making them promises of remarkable situations and great benefits if they would emigrate to Canada or elsewhere; and Her Majesty's Government helped these gentlemen, at whose head was Mr. Tuke, in their nefarious business, to the tune of £46,000. In addition to that grant, they lent Mr. Tuke's Committee Her Majesty's ships, in which the emigrants were taken from the shore to the emigrant ships, from which, in due course, the emigrants were shot, like so much rubbish, on the Canadian shore. On whose authority were the ships lent to Mr. Tuke; and would a guarantee be given that Her Majesty's ships would not be again used for the same purpose? Unfortunately, Mr. Tuke had done his work, and, therefore, there was not much probability of the Government doing any more mischief by lending their ships to carry away Irish emigrants.

MR. CAMPBELL-BANNERMAN said, that, as a matter of fact, he should think it was extremely unlikely that anything was paid for piloting and towing Her Majesty's ships on the West Coast of Ireland.

MR. HEALY: Then, how did the ships get into Black Sod Bay?

MR. CAMPBELL-BANNERMAN, continuing, said, that with regard to the general question, he was not prepared to enter into the merits of Mr. Tuke's enterprize, because he was not officially advised. The Admiralty were pressed to give this small assistance, and they did so; but from what he could understand, it was not intended to make a further request to the Admiralty.

MR. KENNY said, he did not know whether the question arose here; but there was a sum down for wars against pirates?

THE CHAIRMAN: There is no item for war, and the question is, in my opinion, altogether out of Order. I did not stop the hon. Member for Monaghan, because it seemed to me that he was putting a simple question, requiring only a simple answer. It is clearly out of Order to raise such a question as emigration on a Vote for Pilotage. That refers to pilotage in the Suez Canal, and clearly has no reference to Mr. Tuke's scheme.

MR. HEALY asked if he could raise the question on Vote 14?

THE CHAIRMAN: Yes.

MR. HEALY pointed out that this was a Vote for the pilotage of Her Majesty's ships on Foreign and Home stations, and said Black Sod Bay was a Home station into which vessels could not get without pilotage. He challenged the Secretary to the Admiralty to say that iron-clads could get into that bay without pilotage. That being so, he failed to see why Black Sod Bay did not come in under this Vote for Pilotage; and he, therefore, submitted that he was entitled to raise this point.

THE CHAIRMAN: I must adhere to my opinion that it would be out of Order to raise a question like emigration upon a Vote for the Pilotage of Her Majesty's ships, and for towing them through the Suez Canal. Such a discussion would be altogether out of Order.

MR. KENNY rose to a point of Order, and observing that as he understood these ships had been engaged on special service, said, there was item of £300, under Sub-head D, for gratuities for special services.

THE CHAIRMAN: No part of this item is devoted to that purpose.

MR. KENNY said, the Committee were not aware of that, and he should move to reduce the Vote by £300, this mysterious sum for gratuities for special services. That Motion, he apprehended, would raise the question of the allocation of this Fund.

THE CHAIRMAN: I have no desire to stop any discussion that is at all regular; but I could not allow such a question as gratuities for special service to be discussed, after the statement of the Minister in charge that no portion of this money would be applied to Mr. Tuke's emigration scheme.

MR. KENNY thought it would then be desirable to take time to examine the

Appropriation Account, and see how this sum would be expended. He would recommend the Government to postpone this Vote, in order that Members might satisfy themselves upon this matter, and he would move that Progress be reported.

Motion made, and Question, "That the Chairman do report Progress, and ask leave to sit again,"—(*Mr. Kenny*,) —put, and *negatived*.

Original Question again proposed.

MR. HEALY mentioned that there was an item of £4,500 for allowances for lodging and subsistence for officers and crews of Her Majesty's ships detained by stress of weather when on temporary or special services, and he asked the Secretary to the Admiralty to state what those special services were, if they were not connected with this emigration scheme? These crews were a long time occupied upon this emigration scheme, and he wished to know what were the special services that entitled them to this £4,500, or what the total cost of this emigration was?

MR. CAMPBELL-BANNERMAN replied, that he was not aware that there were any special services whatever. The cruisers employed were on their natural Station on the West Coast of Ireland, and that the allowances for officers and men went on all the same, whether they were engaged in assisting Mr. Tuke's Society, or on the ordinary duties of their Station. He did not believe there was any special expense incurred.

MR. HARRINGTON said, that, in any case, it seemed to him that this was a particularly large item. Had the hon. Gentleman no information to give upon this matter? How did it happen that a number of officers and men went on shore, and were detained on shore so long? Sailors were rather fond of going on shore whenever they could get an opportunity, and they remained as long as they could; but that was quite a different thing, and he apprehended that this item only meant charges for occasions when they had been detained on shore for special services. Were the casualties in the Service so numerous that this large item was required? He hoped the hon. Gentleman would give such general lines of detail as would indicate the special services upon which it would be likely that so many men as this sum would pay would be engaged.

MR. KENNY asked whether any portion of this £4,500 had been devoted to the maintenance of Marines in Dublin?

MR. CAMPBELL-BANNERMAN replied in the negative, and said, this was not a very large sum, when they considered that the ships were employed in all quarters of the globe on different services, and on various Stations. This item was based upon the experience of many years past. The same sum was taken last year, and he thought that would go to show that there was nothing in this item connected with Mr. Tuke's or any other Fund.

MR. HARRINGTON said, he was not speaking of Mr. Tuke's Fund, and this item had not been justified by the hon. Gentleman's observations. When expeditions were sent from ships abroad, they were supplied with provisions from the ships for a three, or four, or seven days' journey, and, as a matter of course, they always provided themselves for emergencies. Therefore, the number of casualties must be very large indeed if, after they had been fitted out from the ships, they were still detained so long beyond the time provided for that this large item should be required to defray the incidental expenses.

MR. CAMPBELL - BANNERMAN said, he could give no further information, beyond the fact that this item was based on the experience of past years. It was found that for the ordinary contingencies of the Service an amount of this kind was required, and, therefore, this sum was again asked for.

MR. HEALY asked how much of this was for the Marines?

MR. CAMPBELL - BANNERMAN replied, that he could not tell.

MR. HEALY said, he would assume that something was paid in regard to the Marines in Dublin last year, and he asked how many Marines were detained in Dublin last year?

MR. CAMPBELL - BANNERMAN said, they were not included in this sum. This was for special subsistence allowances for officers and crews detained on shore, or by stress of weather, or temporary or special services.

MR. HEALY asked if the Marines were not temporarily landed in Dublin?

SIR WALTER B. BARTTELOT asked whether this Vote included any of the

Marines landed for the expedition to Tokar?

MR. HARRINGTON said, it seemed to him that this Vote included nothing they wanted to know anything about. It was a remarkable thing that they could find out nothing about any Vote they came to. This was the usual excuse of the Government; but he did not suppose the Chairman would accept such excuses for the purpose of bowling Irish Members over. He must ask how many Marines were detained in Dublin?

MR. CAMPBELL-BANNERMAN said, these were Estimates from the 1st of April last year, and he was not aware that since the 1st of April this year any Marines had been detained in Dublin. None of this sum was for the Marines landed at Tokar.

MR. KENNY asked whether the special Supplementary Estimate of £28,000 for special services in Egypt came under this head?

MR. CAMPBELL-BANNERMAN replied that it did not.

MR. HEALY said, he thought the statement of the hon. Gentleman extremely unsatisfactory. They could get no information, and he respectfully submitted that it was needless to detain the Committee by making these little explanations, and obliging Members to go through this system of cross-examination. If the Government were frank, they would get their Estimates much more rapidly. As Representatives of the people, they were entitled to more information. At that late hour they did not intend to worry the Government about these matters; they were in an extremely amiable mood, and if the Government would give some information they would get their Estimates more rapidly. He hoped the hon. Gentleman would state how many Marines there were in Dublin, and would promise that such a thing should not occur again. A more ill-bred and ill-conditioned set of men were never detained for special service.

MR. PULESTON said, that, according to his experience, in whatever part of the world they had been, the Marines had gained the greatest praise for the performance of their duty; and even the Colleagues of the hon. Member had spoken of the Marines, while they were in Ireland, in a way very different from that of the hon. Member. Gentlemen representing Ireland, who might not altogether like the duty upon which the Marines were employed in that country, had more than once volunteered statements to him respecting the Marines which were in the highest degree creditable to that Force; and he hoped that, whatever differences of opinion there might be in that House, that excellent body of men, standing, as they did, very high in the estimation of all parties in this country, would not be disparaged.

MR. HARRINGTON quite believed that the Marines were a valuable body of men in their own way when employed for proper purposes; but he thought that preserving the peace in Dublin was not a duty originally intended for those men, and that in performing that duty they were very much out of place. There was another item in this Vote about which he wished to ask a question. He found a sum put down for contributions in aid of religious and charitable institutions, and he wished to know what were the religious institutions to which these charitable contributions were given? It seemed to him that it was not the intention of that House, when voting Supplies of this kind, that contributions should be given to any particular religious institutions; but the point he wished to raise was this. The Navy was a very mixed Service, containing men of all religions, and largely composed of his fellow-countrymen and co-religionists; and he wished to know to what institutions this money was given, and whether any Roman Catholic institutions received any contributions? There was a very large number of Catholics and Irishmen in the Navy, and he wished to know whether any part of this money went to their benefit? If not, he should not agree to the Vote.

MR. CAMPBELL-BANNERMAN said, he was quite certain that no charitable or public institution was refused assistance because of its religion. The Admiralty did a good deal to meet the wants of the men in the Navy, whether they were of the Catholic religion or not. For the last two or three months he had himself been engaged in arranging one or two points which, he thought, were not properly provided for in reference to Roman Catholic and other religious wants. These contributions were made chiefly to Sailors' Homes and similar institutions. He had not a list of all the contributions with him; but they were, as a rule, only small sums.

MR. KENNY said, he should not have felt disposed to press this matter to a Division but for the speech of the hon. Member for Devonport (Mr. Puleston) and the speech of the Secretary to the Admiralty. He felt very strongly with regard to the matter of the Marines in Dublin, and he very much objected to their having been sent there, as they were to tyrannize over the people——

THE CHAIRMAN: The hon. Member is not in Order. There is no question before the Committee respecting Marines in Dublin.

MR. KENNY said, he would move the reduction of this Vote. The question of the Marines in Dublin was not raised last year, and he was not aware that hon. Members were strictly confined, upon a Vote which was practically devoted to the payment of these men, to a discussion of matters which could technically only be brought forward. He should not have referred to this matter of the Marines in Dublin but for the observations of the hon. Member for Devonport. He held quite a contrary view to that of the hon. Member as to these Marines, and he greatly regretted that the Chairman would not allow him to give his reasons. All he could do, therefore, was to move the reduction of the Vote by £4,500.

Motion made, and Question proposed,

"That a sum, not exceeding £112,400, be granted to Her Majesty, to defray the Expense of various Miscellaneous Services, which will come in course of payment during the year ending on the 31st day of March 1885."—(*Mr. Kenny.*)

MR. DEASY wished to ask one question. He had received a communication stating that the usual grant to the Cork Sailors' Home had been reduced from £100 to £25; and he should like to know what the explanation of that reduction was?

SIR THOMAS BRASSEY explained that there had simply been a transfer of the grant from Cork to Queenstown, on the ground that Her Majesty's ships very seldom visited Cork, whereas they were constantly at Queenstown. Therefore, the institution at Queenstown had greater claims on the Admiralty than that at Cork.

MR. DEASY asked whether the hon. Gentleman would be willing to receive a deputation on the subject from the Committee of the Cork Sailors' Home?

SIR THOMAS BRASSEY replied, that he would be happy to receive any representation on the subject.

MR. KENNY said, he would withdraw his Amendment, in consequence of the somewhat conciliatory answer of the hon. Gentleman.

Motion, by leave, *withdrawn.*

Original Question put, and *agreed to.*

(15.) £853,900, Half-Pay, Reserved Half-Pay, and Retired Pay to Officers of the Navy and Marines.

MR. PULESTON desired to say a few words on this Vote with reference to the Paymasters. A long time ago the allowance to these men was settled at 2*s.* 6*d.* a-day, which was at that time above the ordinary pay; but now, he understood, the pay of the Paymasters had risen to something like 12*s.*, and this 2*s.* 6*d*, a-day was still called half-pay. This was perhaps, a small matter, but it was very unjust, and he wondered whether it was possible to remove the injustice? A case had been brought under his notice in which an Assistant Paymaster was invalided from foreign service on account of injuries he had received, and which had entirely unfitted him for active service. He was put on half-pay for nine months at 2*s.* 6*d.* per day, and it seemed very hard that the allowance should be so small. This allowance was little enough when men were ill and unable to do duty, but it was particularly hard that they should receive so little when they had been disabled by injuries received in war. This might be a small matter, but he felt sure the Secretary to the Admiralty would see that it was hard upon the men.

MR. CAMPBELL - BANNERMAN promised that if the hon. Member would let him know the facts of the case, he would look into it.

MR. PULESTON said he had merely mentioned this case as an illustration; but there were similar cases constantly occurring.

Vote *agreed to.*

(16.) £889,600, Military Pensions and Allowances.

(17.) £328,400, Civil Pensions and Allowances.

(18.) £130,900, Extra Estimate for Services not Naval.—Freight, &c. on Account of the Army Department.

(19.) £156,007, Greenwich Hospital and School.

Resolutions to be reported *To-morrow.*

Committee to sit again *To-morrow.*

MAGISTRATES (IRELAND) SALARIES BILL.—[Bill 292.]

(*Mr. Courtney, Mr. Trevelyan.*)

SECOND READING.

Order for the Second Reading read.

Motion made, and Question proposed, "That the Bill be now read a second time."—(*Mr. Courtney.*)

Mr. COURTNEY said, that on a former occasion he had sufficiently indicated the nature of this Bill, therefore he did not propose to delay the House by going into detail upon it on the Order for the Second Reading.

Mr. HEALY said, he was extremely surprised at the very curt manner in which the Secretary to the Treasury submitted the second reading of this Bill at that hour of the morning (1.45). A short statement was not surprising, indeed, it would have been much more satisfactory to Irish Members if the hon. Gentleman had postponed the Bill and given them some further opportunity of considering it; but under any circumstances they had a right to expect that something in support of the Bill should be offered by the Government. When the right hon. Gentleman the Prime Minister had decided, in consequence of the action of the House of Lords, to shorten the Session, he had given a pledge that contentious legislation would not be taken. That pledge had been completely broken. Notwithstanding the Prime Minister's undertaking, they had this Bill brought in by the Government with the knowledge that it must inevitably prolong the Session. The Government wished them to get away on Saturday week; but how could they possibly do it if this Bill was to be passed? How could they expect, without tremendous consumption of time, to pass a Bill, the object of which was to set up Mr. Clifford Lloyd and other such disgraceful officials permanently in the country? Surely the Government knew the feeling of the Irish people with regard to Mr. Clifford Lloyd and similar individuals. And what were the facts as to this Bill? It was an extremely short measure, but as they knew from the Home Secretary the other night, a short Bill might sometimes take a long time to pass, and he was surprised that had not occurred to the hon. Gentleman the Secretary to the Treasury (Mr. Courtney) when he undertook to introduce the Bill to the House. The measure was a reversal of the position taken up by the Government. He (Mr. Healy) did not know whether hon. Members recollected what had taken place during that famous Saturday Sitting. What occurred was this. The Irish Members pointed out that the Government were asking the taxpayers for a larger sum than the Act of Parliament—that was to say, the 37 & 38 *Vict.* c. 33—entitled them to ask. But they had the learned argument of the English Attorney-General — who had conveniently left them in the lurch on this occasion that he might not be confronted with the echoes of his own statement that night—to the effect that it was needless to have an extra charge on the Estimates. The Irish Members had pointed out that the sum was charged in the Estimates on account of that Act of Parliament, and that it was largely exceeded in consequence of the bloated salaries given to Mr. Clifford Lloyd and other officials. The Government had said—"That does not matter, because this sum is included in the Appropriation Bill at the end of the Session, and becomes an Act under the Appropriation Act." The Government now found out their mistake; and what became of the argument by which they had snatched a Division on that famous Sunday morning? [Mr. Courtney dissented.] The Secretary to the Treasury shook his head. He (Mr. Healy) would ask the hon. Gentleman how was it that he had given no explanation whatever of the change of front that had taken place between now and April last?

Notice taken, that 40 Members were not present; House counted, and 40 Members being found present,

Mr. HEALY said, it must be extremely gratifying to the Government to be able to carry their Bills by a bare majority. They found that there were just 44 Members in the House, and that appeared to him to be legislating by the skin of their teeth with a vengeance. He had hoped that the Chief Secretary would have been summoned to his place by the "count" so opportunely moved by the hon. Member for Ennis (Mr. Kenny); but the right hon. Gentleman had not on that occasion seen fit to enter the House, and he (Mr. Healy) extremely regretted that they should have to discuss this measure, which had so much in it about the welfare of Ireland, without the presence of the chief Irish Official. He had said the English Attorney General on a previous occasion had given them an extremely learned argument to show that the measure was absolutely needless. The date of that discussion was the 15th of March. He believed it had been said by the hon. and learned Gentleman that it was not competent for the Committee to vote a salary of £1,000 a-year; but it was competent for them to vote a specific sum of money. The hon. and learned Gentleman continually dwelt on that question of a specific sum. He had said that that was the first time he had ever risen to answer a legal question at 4 o'clock in the morning. Well, it was now only 2 o'clock in the morning, and it was to be hoped that the hon. and learned Gentleman would find his legal faculties much better now than they had been on the last occasion at a later hour. If the Attorney General's argument was worth anything, why introduce this Bill? If the Government was entitled to keep them out of their beds during the whole of Saturday and part of Sunday because of the strength of their desire to pay these unprecedented salaries, why were they now, at the end of July and near the end of the Session, to be asked to prolong the Session for the purpose of passing such a measure as this? The Attorney General's argument was that, so long as this extra sum was sanctioned by the Appropriation Act, there was no need to have recourse to a Bill. What had become of that position of the Government? That the Secretary to the Treasury should move the second reading of this Bill, without a single word of explanation of the right-about wheel which had characterized the policy of the Government, seemed to him (Mr. Healy) about the most extraordinary feature in the action of the present volatile Government that they had ever had to deal with. But, apart from this technical question, the Irish Members, on other grounds, had a strong objection to the Bill. Its object was really to enable the Irish Government, with the consent of the Treasury, to give certain Resident Magistrates increased salaries not exceeding the sum of £1,000 a-year, and to enable the Lord Lieutenant to order that such increased salaries might be paid from the 1st of April before the passing of this Act. The measure was retrospective in spite of what had fallen from the Attorney General for England. The hon. and learned Gentleman had succeeded in obtaining the votes of Englishmen who followed the Government Whip. These Gentlemen marched through the Lobby on the strength of the Attorney General's statement, and now, at the end of July, the Government found it necessary to endeavour to amend their hand by obtaining credit from the 1st of April last. The Irish Members had pointed out the illegality of the Act. [MR. COURTNEY: No, no.] The hon. Gentleman interrupted him, but why had he not explained the Bill? He had not done so, and the Irish Members were therefore entitled to explain it for themselves. They had not been told who the five gentlemen were who were to be affected by the Bill. He should like to know the names of those five champions of Christendom. Why should they not know the meritorious gentlemen who were to have these positions? Was one of them Mr. Clifford Lloyd; and, if so, why had they not had a statement to that effect?

MR. COURTNEY said, there had been a perfect understanding come to on that point.

MR. HEALY said, he had asked the Prime Minister on a former occasion whether an opportunity would be allowed to the Irish Members to discuss the return of Mr. Clifford Lloyd to Ireland before the end of the Session, and the right hon. Gentleman had said there would be. In spite, however, of that, this Bill was brought in, and the Irish Members were not told whether Mr. Clifford Lloyd would return to the office he had vacated in Ireland or not. Would the Secretary to the Treasury answer that question in the negative? No; the hon. Gentleman declined to shake his head now. His declining to answer in the negative was a tolerably good indication that Mr. Clifford Lloyd was to return to Ireland. If it were not the intention of the Government to send him back, what was to prevent them from putting a clause in the Bill to that effect? For his own part, he believed that such a clause as that would have a very salutary effect. It would prevent the Government from bringing Mr. Clifford Lloyd back in spite of a pledge which might be obtained from them; but, as he (Mr. Healy) intended to move a clause to that effect, he would abstain from going further into the question now. He would content himself with merely informing the Secretary to the Treasury that it was the intention of the Irish Members to seriously propose a clause to that effect when the Bill got into Committee. When a measure of this kind was proposed, a measure for the purpose of increasing the salaries of Resident Magistrates, he would ask the House to remember that these five gentlemen were to have these increased and added salaries at a time when the peace of the country, as the Government had to admit, left nothing to be desired. They had, in Ireland, passed through three or four years of most remarkable excitement, and there had been a considerable amount of crime; but yet the Government had managed without a Bill of this kind. Now, when the country was quieting down and the crime was expiring, the Government proposed to add fuel to the flame by the giving of these increased salaries to Resident Magistrates. What construction was to be put upon that? Why, these gentlemen affected would put this construction upon it—that in order to earn these increased salaries they would have to keep up a requisite modicum of crime. If the Government paid these men these extraordinary amounts they must expect value for it. Even the Treasury, generous as it was to officials in the Irish Criminal Department, would, after a year or two, come forward and declare that the money was absolutely thrown away on these gentlemen if they did not get any crime for it. The Government, to justify themselves for passing Acts of this kind to increase the salaries of magistrates so extensively, must have a certain number of men hanged every year, and a certain number of men sent to penal servitude. At the present time the number of hangings was considerably reduced, and the number of men they were enabled to send to penal servitude for agrarian crime had almost sunk to zero; therefore, he (Mr. Healy) failed to see what value they were to get for these increased salaries. The magistrates would say—"If crime stood at the vanishing point there is no reason for our existence;" and, therefore, they would continue to get up false reports, which hitherto had succeeded in deluding the people of England. It was a very serious thing when they had a number of people preying on the country whose salaries depended on the amount of crime which existed in the community. The Government might be anxious to see crime diminish in Ireland, but they would never see any substantial diminution while men were paid high salaries on account of that crime. Crimes were invented, or, if they were not invented, bogus reports were sent in to the Government, and the country was blackened by stories of what was likely to occur. The Government, he thought, should proceed on the system which prevailed in China with regard to doctors. When the Emperor was well they got their salaries; but directly he was taken ill they were paid nothing. He would suggest that so long as crime existed in Ireland these highly- aid magistrates should get no salariep whatever; but that when crime was extinguished and the efficiency of these gentlemen became apparent, they should get substantial remuneration. Probably that principle would recommend itself to the economic mind of the Secretary to the Treasury. It was right for the hon. Gentleman to increase the salaries of those Civil servants who deserved substantial payment; but the Irish Members did not see the force of paying salaries for firebrands—of paying increased salaries to bring about a state of things such as that which existed under the *régime* of Mr. Clifford Lloyd. Statements would have to be made in Committee as to the lives and adventures of the various gentlemen connected with the Government of Ireland. He supposed it would not be out of Order for Irish Members to discuss the conduct of Mr. Clifford Lloyd in Egypt, as bearing on what would likely to be his conduct in Ireland if he came back. Those would be questions which it would not be desirable to go into in the month of August, or at the end of July; but if the Irish Members were bound to go into them the fault would lay not with them, but with the Government. He should like to know from the Government whether there was any prospect whatever of the five gentlemen to be appointed being drawn from any other class than that of the miserable half-pay officers, who had hitherto been the ruin of the paid Magisterial Service of Ireland—officers who had been scraped up from Bombay, Burmah, and North America? Hitherto they had had these officers forced upon them for no reason that they could make out other than that they happened to be the relatives of someone in high position in Ireland. They had had Mr. Blake, whom the Duke of St. Alban's had now managed to get off as the Governor of the Bahamas. They should like very much to know how Mr. Blake had managed to make that bound? Then they had had Mr. Clifford Lloyd sent to them from British Burmah, and he also had made a jump from Ireland to Egypt. This gentleman, after having imprisoned thousands of men in Ireland, went and wept salt tears over the imprisonment of the Egyptains, administering the courbash at the same time in a manner which the Irish Members would have occasion to refer to later on. Where it was possible, a clause would be inserted in some Bill to put a stop to the use of such an instrument as that by such officials as Mr. Clifford Lloyd.

MR. COURTNEY said, that, perhaps, with the permission of the House, he might be allowed to say a few words on the Bill, although it would only be to repeat what had been succinctly said in introducing it. He had referred on the previous occasion to what took place on the Civil Service Estimates. A discussion had occurred with regard to this class of magistrates, and he had stated that it was proposed to pay them a higher rate of salary than was mentioned in the Act of Parliament. The legality of that course was questioned by the hon. Member for Queen's County (Mr. A. O'Connor), and it was then explained that after notice had been given and the question discussed, and a Vote for the purpose subsequently incorporated in the Appropriation Bill, the payment would be thoroughly legal. That was the statement which had been made, and to which be now adhered. He had stated that a departure, under these circumstances, from the statutory limit, was perfectly legitimate, and that a note would be put into the Estimates calling the attention of the Committee to the fact that this was a variation from the normal salaries. Hon. Gentlemen opposite did not seem to recognize the force of the argument; this measure, therefore, would substitute for the Estimate, which exceeded, year after year, the statutory limit, another statutory limit of £1,000. There was no contradiction whatever between the present proposal and the last. The hon. Member had touched upon a great variety of topics, some of which, perhaps, might with propriety be discussed in Committee. He asked questions about Mr. Clifford Lloyd, whether that gentleman would return to Ireland? Whether he would do so or not was a question upon which he (Mr. Courtney) could say nothing; but he could say that that gentleman would not be one of the five gentlemen to whom these salaries of £1,000 would be paid, and so would not come within the operation of the Bill. Then the hon. Member referred to the present condition of Ireland, and he was glad to agree that it was one of quiet and order. But, at the end of his speech, the hon. Member introduced an illustration, which, if worth anything as an argument, told in favour of the Bill; for if, as he said, these salaries should be paid only when the state of things was quiet and orderly, then there was a good argument for the payment of the salaries, the position to which the hon. Member referred being realized.

COLONEL NOLAN said, the whole statement of the Secretary to the Treasury amounted to this—that he did not like the course of the Estimates to be interfered with by the necessity of voting a sum for these salaries year after year. As a general rule, Irish Members had been rather anxious to simplify the Estimates, and to do all they could to put them clearly and distinctly before the Committee, so, if they now resisted the Bill, it was not from any wish to cause any inconvenience to the discussion of the Estimates. The statement of the hon. Gentleman was altogether beside the real facts of the case. Irish Members looked at the Bill as a step in the direction of the French system, dividing the country into five great Police Departments, sub-dividing these again among other Resident Magistrates. Whether this was desirable, or whether it was more desirable to leave things as they were in Ireland, certainly it was no trivial matter. The position so long as the Special Magistrates depended upon special Votes in the Estimates was one of truce; but if once the Bill were allowed to pass, it would be the starting point for that system of division and sub-division to which he had referred. So, the principle of the Bill was of sufficient importance to be thoroughly discussed on its merits. He did not think they had had the history of the Bill. He had referred to the Library, and he could give the House the result of a Commission on the subject, after an inquiry, presided over by a well-known man, to which he would direct the attention of the House. What happened to the Bill last year? This Bill, or one like it, was then introduced——

MR. COURTNEY: No; a much larger Bill.

COLONEL NOLAN: Then it was a much larger Bill. It was manifest there was a considerable difference of opinion in reference to it. The Government found that they might or might not have the Conservatives with them, while they would have all the Irish Members against them, and there was a prospect of a troublous end of the Session, much to be deplored. He did not think they should separate with a feeling of division from English Members, the latter overruling the general opinion of Irish Members; that was a deplorable condition of things, much to be deprecated. And now came the Bill of last year in disguise. A good deal had been eliminated, they were told, by the Chief Secretary; but the essential money part was that there were to be five Resident Magistrates with salaries higher than those of other Resident Magistrates, and, if there was any meaning in the Bill, these five would be placed over the heads of the others. Last year it was found that the state of Business was such that it would be greatly facilitated by the withdrawal of a Bill so extremely objectionable to Irish Members; but now the Government appeared to take a different view, and there were two faults to be found with them for it. He considered it a violation of the promise of the Prime Minister that no contentious matter should be taken in the course of winding up the Business of the Session—his hon. Friend had touched upon that—and the other point was the unreasonableness of proceeding with such a Bill at 2 o'clock in the morning. To expect the Irish Members, then, after a long Sitting, to give all the reasons, financial and otherwise, against the Bill, was treating those Members extremely unfairly. There were enough English Members present to outvote the Irish Members; but, before they did so, it was right they should have a little information in regard to the subject. The proposition was to give salaries of £1,000 each to five Special Magistrates. Now, in reference to that, he would point out that a Commission which sat in 1872 drew a great distinction between consolidated salaries and salaries with allowances. The allowances were considerable for two horses for an ordinary Resident Magistrate, an orderly and a clerk, and stationery; but this last was a small item not worth taking into account. Now, he should like to ask whether the Secretary to the Treasury intended this to be a consolidated salary to include all expenses of horses, orderly, and clerk, or were they to understand that these allowances were to be in addition to the salary of £1,000 a-year? This was important; the Secretary to the Treasury should be aware of the difference. The Report of the Commission of December, 1872—a small Commission in numbers, but a strong one—Lord Monk, extremely well qualified to preside; Major Miles O'Reilly, well acquainted with Irish affairs; and Mr. S. A. Blackwood—these gentlemen made a Report in reference to the Irish Resident Magistracy, and it had relation to the subject of the Bill, and the question of the division of Ireland into Departments. But he would be glad if the Secretary to the Treasury would hold out some hope that this might be entered upon in the daytime, for it was extremely troublesome to ask the attention of the House to it at such a time.

Notice taken, that 40 Members were not present; House counted, and 40 Members being found present,

COLONEL NOLAN continued. It was an ungrateful task to enter upon figures at such a late hour, and he was sure Members would be glad to have the matter postponed to a more reasonable hour, say before midnight; but it was useful, as bearing upon the Bill, to touch upon the Report of the Commission he had mentioned. In 1872, when the Commission reported, they found that the Resident Magistracy of Ireland were divided into three classes—first, those with £500 a-year; secondly, those with £400 a-year; and, thirdly, the class with £300 a-year. £400 was the normal figure; but a certain small number received an extra £100. And then they came to the important question of allowances. If these were insignificant he would not trouble the House with them; but, as the Commission pointed out, they were considerable—two horses, £73; orderly, £42; clerk, £36; stationery, £8; a total of £159 a-year. Now, he asked the Secretary to the Treasury a few minutes since, did the £1,000 mean a consolidated salary, or was it exclusive of allowances? and he had been informed it was exclusive of allowances. So, then, the Bill would give £1,200 a-year, for he supposed the scale would be somewhat higher than that allowed for ordinary magistrates. Under some circumstances he might not object to providing this salary; but coupling with this the fact that the Bill was brought in between 2 and 3 o'clock in the morning, that there was going to be a revolution in the Civil procedure in Ireland, and that the Government would have, besides officials, only one Irish Member to support them, surely they might be allowed the benefit of speaking at a time when their words could find attention. However, as that was not allowed, he must go on, and he would point out that the Commission of 1872 did not recommend anything like this rise of salary of £1,000 a-year. They proposed an increase of £100, and the same scale as that of the Royal Irish Constabulary. In spite of this Report, the Government now wished not to make an increase of £100; but they wished to introduce a new class of magistrates, not raising salaries to £500 or £600, but to £1,000, *plus* allowances —an extraordinary increase of £400 or £500 over what was recommended by a Royal Commission composed of men thoroughly trusted by the Government, and who were at the time fair exponents of Irish feeling. Now, the Government were completely overruling their own Commission. Not only so, but there was no assurance that these would be inclusive salaries, as the Commission recommended; so very likely the increase would be £600 instead of the £100 recommended—an extraordinary increase in these days, when economy, though not practised, was advocated by every speaker with a view to the General Election; and it must bring considerable discredit to the Government. Not only was this extravagant sum to be paid, but the proposition was brought on at a time when protests against it on the part of Irish or English Members on behalf of the taxpayers could not be made known through the usual channels of information. As to the point of objection, other Members could treat it much better than he could. Why should Ireland be made the subject of this very extraordinary experiment in Civil administration? When he said extraordinary, he meant according to English ideas; he was aware that France was divided and sub-divided for Civil and Military purposes, all jurisdiction centralizing to one Department. Up to two years ago there was nothing of the kind in Ireland. So far as he understood from general knowledge, each Resident Magistrate reported directly to the Government, each Resident Magistrate in his own district was totally independent of others, though, no doubt, when a senior magistrate was at hand, his advice was availed of; but, in reference to his administration, the magistrate communicated with the Government direct, and this independent position was valuable to him in his position of Judge. But now all this was to be changed at 3 o'clock in the morning, without the country having an opportunity of hearing all about it or expressing an opinion; and, accompanied with an extravagant waste of money, it was proposed to put a group of from 10 to 20 magistrates under a Head Magistrate, with power of reporting upon and checking their action. Consequently, instead of dealing with a Central Authority, composed of men of position like the Chief Secretary, men who might fairly be supposed to represent English feeling and the power of England, instead of that magistrates would be put under gentlemen chosen from the Police, to whom they would be entirely subordinate, and who would have the power of reporting upon their conduct. So far as they acted as a Police Force in their administrative capacity, he found no fault; but part of the functions of a Resident Magistrate in Ireland was to act as a minor Judge. The Resident Magistrate held very much the same position as a Police Magistrate in England; and if in England four or five of these gentlemen were subordinated to a superior, it was not in human nature to suppose that they would not desire to please their immediate superior by the decisions they might be called upon to give. A great amount of injustice would result, not, perhaps, for the first 10 or 20 years, because English justice was founded very much on precedent; but there would eventually be a great amount of injustice, and certainly a want of respect for English law thus administered. This was what the Bill sought to do in Ireland. Not having their own Parliament and Ministry, Irish public opinion would not have the slightest influence on these magistrates, who would, of course, look to their immediate superior, and unless they were something more than men their judgment would be influenced by the wish to conciliate their superior. He thought he had made out a very fair case against passing the Bill now. He had not much faith in the efficacy of arguments delivered between 2 and 3 o'clock in the morning; but if resistance was hopeless, it was better than no resistance at all, and it was his duty to point out the injustice sought to be enforced against the wish of Irish Members. The Government were going to give an extravagant sum to a new class of Irish magistrates, and to make a complete change in the administration of Ireland—they were going to put one set of magistrates under another set raised from their own ranks. Magistrate after magistrate had spoken and written to him of the great pecuniary losses they had suffered a couple of years ago when there was the reorganization. A whole lot of magistrates had been placed on pension, and this was a state of things the Bill would perpetuate. A magistrate had written to him saying how he had kept his district perfectly quiet; he was then transferred to another district where a serious crime had been committed; he did all he could to pacify the people, and did so; but he was put out of the service—he was reorganized. Formerly magistrates had some influence with the Government; but now they were under the Special Magistrate and liable to be put on pension, not always getting the full-time pension. Thus Mr. Percival, who would have had one scale of pension at 15 years' service, and a higher scale at 20 years, was superseded at the end of 19 years' service. He said that the duties of the magistrates, who sometimes acted as Judges, and at other times acted largely as a sort of superior police, should be clearly defined if a Bill of this kind must be brought in; but he warned the Government that they were taking a dangerous step with regard to Ireland. He was of opinion that in their judicial functions the magistrates should be placed under the Judges; let them, at any rate, be placed under men of high professional position and of high character, and then the Irish people would have some guarantee of a fair result. But the Government were going to put them under five gentlemen, of whom the people knew little or nothing, who were not men of high professional or social position, who could not be looked up to as guides, and who he feared, moreover, would wish to make all their decisions uniform. They would, of course, say amongst themselves that they did not want one decision given in Kerry and another given in Cork quite different to it. They would say—"We want uniformity of decisions;" and in that case he thought the course of justice was likely to be somewhat interfered with. The system which the Government proposed to pursue must necessarily bring about that vicious state of things; and, therefore, he hoped that some Member of the Government would rise, either then or later on, and give them some assurance that these five magistrates were not to be placed over the heads of all the other magistrates in Ireland. The Bill had much more importance than the Secretary to the Treasury had attributed to it; and he thought the hon. Gentleman would be well advised either to withdraw it altogether for that Session, or, at any rate, put it off until it could be properly discussed.

Mr. WARTON pointed out that the Bill was against the spirit of the Act of 37 & 38 *Vict.*, which provided that the Resident Magistrates in Ireland should be in certain classes—not more than 20 in Class 1, and not more than 32 in Class 2, and a certain number in Class 3, the salaries being for each class more than for the class below it. He contended that this Bill, which dealt with so small a matter, ought not to have been decorated with the title of "Money Bill," which had led many Members interested in the question to go away under the impression that it was blocked.

MR. HARRINGTON said, he thought the hon. Gentleman the Secretary to the Treasury could not have communicated with the Chief Secretary to the Lord Lieutenant of Ireland, because the views he had expressed in its justification were not embodied in the Bill before the House. He asked the hon. Gentleman how he could justify the insertion in the Bill of such a clause as that which began—

"Provided that no more than five of such magistrates shall at any time be entitled to receive by way of salary &c.?"

It seemed to him that if the statement of the right hon. Gentleman was true, and if, as was alleged, the argument of the hon. Member for Monaghan (Mr. Healy) was not justified by facts, this was an idle provision to insert in the Bill. It also seemed to him that if they were to allow the Act to pass in its present form the Government would have an opportunity under the Estimates of further increasing the salaries of the magistrates in Ireland. He looked particularly to this question of salaries; and he considered that the action of the Government in introducing this Bill at a late period of the Session, and at a time when the public mind in Ireland had, to a great extent, settled down, as nothing short of a deliberate attempt to stir up strife in Ireland. No matter what might be the end and aim of the right hon. Gentleman the Chief Secretary to the Lord Lieutenant of Ireland, it could not fail to stir up feeling, because the Bill was known to be an effort to reward men who had been established as a Directory in Ireland during the last few years, simply because they had done their duty towards their friends. Then, who were the men whose salaries were to be increased? Would the right hon. Gentleman give an assurance that Mr. Clifford Lloyd was not one of them? Again, he had to ask whether Captain Plunkett was included in the number? Mr. Clifford Lloyd, in the worst days, had never been so brutal or reckless of the feelings of the people of Ireland as Captain Plunkett had been; and, by this Bill, the Government were simply opening up again questions with regard to the conduct of this man which had already been discussed. He was astonished that hon. Members opposite should remain out of their beds to enable the Irish Executive to perpetrate a job for the administration of Ireland. If these men were entitled to reward there might be more reasons for the Bill. But when it was known that they were simply men of one or two years' standing, that they were not men of local position or experience, it was quite clear that it was only because they were the relatives of Lords and of certain gentlemen who could put the machinery of the Government in motion in Ireland that a Bill was brought in to increase their salaries. The hon. and gallant Member for Galway (Colonel Nolan) had drawn attention to the enormous salaries which these officials already received; and he had shown that, over and above their fixed salary, they received allowances for horses and orderlies, and that if they did not employ the police they received £20 or £30 a-year for orderlies to carry their messages. The right hon. Gentleman need not be at all incredulous on this matter; he had very little practical knowledge of Irish questions, and Irish Members had been brought into more intimate connection with the magistrates of Ireland than the right hon. Gentleman, and they could speak more correctly as to their duties and the manner in which they discharged them. One of the first debates of the present Session arose with regard to these extraordinary magistrates, and day by day Questions were asked in that House concerning their conduct. They had recently a statement read by the hon. Member for the City of Cork (Mr. Parnell), signed by the members of the Corporation of Limerick, to the effect that their city had been kept in a state of turmoil from the moment Mr. Clifford Lloyd went there to the moment when he left, at which time every kind of disturbance disappeared. These magistrates did not belong to the people—they belonged to the landlord class, and they used their position to serve the class interested in oppressing the people; and, so long as the Government endowed them with enormous salaries, the Government might be assured there would be the element of continued disturbance in Ireland, and a source of trouble to the Government whenever Irish Members had an opportunity of addressing that House on the question? He thought that the Irish Government should have learned by experience in past years, by disturbances occurring in the country, and, above all, by the abominable actions recently brought to light, not to endow the magistrates with the enormous salaries proposed. By this Bill the Government proposed, in the first place, to divide the country into sections, and to put it under the charge of a certain number of magistrates. Now, that was entirely opposed to the feelings of the people, and was a system which the Government would not for one moment think of introducing into this country. How, then, did they justify its introduction into Ireland? It was certainly not for the purpose of keeping peace in that country; the object of the Bill could not be to further the interests of peace and order. Its effect would be directly opposite to that; and it was never in the interest of peace that such a proposal occurred to the minds of whatever Ministers were responsible for the Bill. It was simply to order a certain number of officials to be rewarded for their deliberate lying and slandering the people, and for the manner in which they had kept them in a state of excitement during the last few years. The persons he had mentioned had reduced the names of the magistracy and Government to a scandal. He thought it his duty to protest in the strongest manner against the action of the Government in introducing the Bill at that period of the Session. There was no necessity for the Bill; the people of Ireland did not want it, and the persons to be served by it were the small landlord class only. They were not men of experience, nor men of intelligence; nor were they men whose impartial dealing had commended them to the confidence of the people; on the contrary, the men who were to receive the advantage of the Act were the disturbers of the peace, men who would use their position to serve the class to which they belonged, and who were likely to be a continual source of strife and disorder.

MR. KENNY said, it appeared that, owing to the "unfortunate conscientiousness" with which the Estimates were prepared, hon. Members had sometimes an opportunity of discovering very extraordinary breaches of the Orders of the House with regard to the Vote for the Irish Magistracy. So far back as last March a discussion took place in that House upon a Vote asked for by the Secretary to the Treasury. That Vote was one which was illegal in respect of its being in excess of the amount allowed by the State; but at the time it was argued skilfully by the Secretary to the Treasury, and also by the Attorney General for England, that the matter would be set right by the fact that the Votes had to be legalized by the Appropriation Act, and that the passing of that Act was sufficient in itself to legalize any Vote of money passed in that House. That was the opinion which the Secretary to the Treasury put forward in very definite language. He would quote from *Hansard*, because the expression made use of on that occasion by the Secretary to the Treasury, in replying to the hon. Member for Queen's County (Mr. A. O'Connor), seemed to him of importance. The hon. Member said that what he stated was that the terms of the Act would be superseded by the terms of the Appropriation Act. Now, he (Mr. Kenny) wanted to know, if the terms of the Act of Parliament were to be superseded by the Appropriation Act, what was the use of introducing, at that hour of the morning, a Bill which must be entirely unnecessary? It seemed to him that every argument advanced at the time by the Secretary to the Treasury tended to show that the House of Commons was now being asked to go through a mockery, and to waste the public time. He should now like to ask what were the functions of the five gentlemen whom it was proposed to pay under this Act?

Notice taken, that 40 Members were not present; House counted, and 40 Members being found present,

MR. KENNY, continuing, said, he was, when he was interrupted by the counting of the House, asking what were the special functions of the gentlemen whom it was proposed to appoint and to pay enormous salaries under this Act? As well as he could understand, the functions of those gentlemen were to supervise the actions of the various Stipendiary Magistrates within their district, and to represent to Dublin Castle occasionally the result of their experience; but, beyond that, to take no active part in discharging any duties which were usually discharged by magistrates, or to serve any useful purpose whatever in Ireland. Now, it was proposed to pay these men £1,000 a-year, and it was proposed, in addition, to allow them a sum of £100 for expenses; in other words, they were each to receive £1,100 a-year. The right hon. Gentleman the Chief Secretary made, at one time, a great deal of the proposed saving on the allowances. The ordinary magistrates in Ireland succeeded in obtaining from the Treasury something like £460 for allowances, and these gentlemen were only to receive an allowance of £100 each per annum. The difference was very easily accounted for, because the men who were stationed in different districts had, practically, little or no work to do; whereas the ordinary Resident Magistrates had to travel from place to place for the purpose of proceeding to Petty Sessions Courts. He should like to hear from some responsible Irish official—the Solicitor General (Mr. Walker) was the only responsible official now in his place—and he (Mr. Kenny) should like to know from him what particular advantage there was in appointing a man like Mr. Reed to preside in the County Galway? How would that gentleman know what took place in a remote district of Connemara? The proposed appointments seemed to be entirely superfluous. He was not much in favour of centralization; but the species of centralization which was now proposed seemed to him to be the worst of all, because it delegated to minor officials the powers which at the present time were discharged by men in a more responsible position, and who had a check placed over them which the new magistrates would be entirely free from. He should also like to know what assurance the Government would be prepared to give that the men who were appointed would not be equally as objectionable to the people as Mr. Clifford Lloyd was? The Secretary to the Treasury made a great deal, at the beginning of the Session, of the statement that Mr. Clifford Lloyd was not duly appointed; but the Irish people had no guarantee that Mr. Clifford Lloyd would not be re-appointed at some future date. Anyhow, they were perfectly aware that one of the officials proposed to be made under this Act was Captain Plunkett, who, if it were possible, was even more obnoxious than Mr. Clifford Lloyd. Of the four Special Magistrates receiving these allowances, three of them were Protestants, and only one, Captain Plunkett, was nominally a Catholic, or he pretended to be something of the sort. They would like to know whether it was proposed to continue to appoint to these important positions men who were of the Protestant religion, men who were Freemasons, and who were probably appointed to these responsible positions because they were Freemasons? He did not think the Secretary to the Treasury was at all well advised in introducing a Bill of that kind at that period of the Session. It was perfectly clear that the Bill had very little or no chance of passing; and upon his (Mr. Courtney's) own showing, at an earlier period of the Session, and on the showing of the hon. and learned Gentleman the Solicitor General for Ireland (Mr. Walker), the Bill was entirely unnecessary and frivolous. He (Mr. Kenny) hoped that if the Bill was intended to proceed further, many very sweeping alterations would be made in it during its passage through Committee. He noticed in the ill a great many points that required remedying; and he found that his Colleagues objected to many of the details of the Bill, short as it was. He supposed he and his hon. Friends could not very well prevent the Bill being read a second time at that Sitting; but there was one thing certain, and that was that, even at the risk of prolonging the Session for an indefinite period, they must demand that in Committee the Bill should receive full and ample consideration.

MR. GRAY said, that if the Secretary to the Treasury was determined to take the second reading of the Bill that night, as he evidently was, he (Mr. Gray) took it that it would have to be by the exercise of those physical powers which the hon. Gentleman used to display with so much advantage when he sat upon the Opposition side of the House. He (Mr. Gray) remembered that at that time the hon. Gentleman thought nothing of sitting up till 5 or 6 o'clock in the morning when he wanted to elucidate the condition of the Zulus, or the South African problem; indeed, it was only about 5 or 6 in the morning that the hon. Gentleman used to get lively. This Bill was from every conceivable point most objectionable, and the manner in which it was being pressed forward that night was only characteristic of it as a whole. He could scarcely imagine what the House would think of a measure of this kind if it referred to any other portion of the United Kingdom, and it was being dealt with in the manner in which the Government was dealing with this Bill. In the first place, they had an exceedingly important measure introduced without any kind of explanation, and in the absence of the responsible Minister who ought to have charge of it, and who ought to be prepared to explain and defend it. In the second place, they had the vast majority of the Members representing that portion of the Kingdom with which the Bill dealt strongly opposed to it, and they had present a bare quorum of the House composed of English and Scotch Members, most of whom, happily for themselves, had been enjoying that repose here which they ought to have been enjoying, and which they would have been enjoying, more comfortably elsewhere, but for the action of the hon. Gentleman the Secretary to the Treasury, and who were only remaining to force their opinions, or the opinions of the Secretary to the Treasury, upon the Irish people. Well, if such a procedure were applied to Scotland, the Scotch Members would resist it very determinedly, and probably very much more acrimoniously than the Irish Members were resisting this Bill. But the Government would never dream for a moment of attempting at 4 o'clock, or half-past 3 o'clock in the morning, of forcing a Scotch Bill through the House in spite of the determined opposition of the Scotch Representatives who happened to be in attendance; they would never dream of doing such a thing with reference to the smallest detail of English legislation. Of course, this Bill merely referred to Ireland, and as it was merely the Representatives of Ireland who objected to it, it was a good subject for a joke on the part of the Government. He had no doubt the Government would succeed that night in doing what they desired. Whether it would serve good government in Ireland, or serve the rapid advance of Governmental Business during the remainder of the Session, was yet to be seen. Now, what was the justification which the right hon. Gentleman the Chief Secretary endeavoured to make out for the somewhat changed views of the Government with reference to this measure? The Secretary to the Treasury had denied that there had been any change of front at all, and that the introduction of a note in the Estimates was sufficient in itself to sanction the payment of these increased salaries, and that the legality would be quite covered by embodying the practical repeal of a former Act of Parliament in the Appropriation Bill. Now, for the sake of omitting a note in the Estimates, the hon. Gentleman did not hesitate, as the Representative of the Government that night, to contend with the entire body of Irish Members. The hon. Gentleman had not got one single Irish Member that night to say one solitary word in support of his Bill, and he evidently did not care whether he did or not. For the sake of omitting a note in the Estimates, the hon. Gentleman would keep the Irish Members there until their right of speech was exhausted, until their energies, which could not compete with those of the hon. Member himself—until they were exhausted, and until he had forced the Bill through a second reading. The Bill contained a vitally important principle; but if the contention of the Secretary to the Treasury were correct—namely, that the payment of these Resident Magistrates would be legally covered by an Estimate embodied in the Appropriation Bill, the position was very different indeed, if that method were adopted, than it would be if the method which they now proposed were acceded to—namely, the embodiment of the Estimate in a separate Bill. What was the case? The condition of Ireland for the last few years had been exceedingly exceptional. As had been pointed out by former speakers, in consequence of the distress and excitement and agitation which had prevailed, crime had existed in the country. Under similar circumstances there would be an unusual amount of crime in any country. The Government, however, found the necessity of taking extraordinary measures to deal with the state of affairs. One of the extraordinary measures they took—wisely or unwisely, he did not propose to discuss now—was the appointment of a number of gentlemen whom they were pleased to call

Special Resident Magistrates, and whom they endowed with exceptional powers. They wanted to pay these gentlemen, and they did pay them, special remuneration for their services, and up to this they had embodied the payments in the Estimates. From the explanation of the Secretary to the Treasury—he (Mr. Gray) had not looked at the Estimates himself, for he was not present when the subject was discussed some time ago—the Treasury put a sub-note to the Estimates calling attention to the fact that special remuneration was meted out to the Special Resident Magistrates in question. Now, if that procedure was followed in the future this fact would be clearly marked out—that this was an exceptional transaction which the Irish people might hope some day or other to see an end of, and it would be a legitimate subject for discussion on the Estimates whenever the Irish Members thought fit to raise it, until the time had come when an arrangement of a permanent character was made and the note for the exceptional demand disappeared. That would be proper and perfectly legitimate; but the Secretary to the Treasury wanted to get rid of the opportunity of discussion—he wanted to shelve this question once for all, and he wanted to obtain, not a Vote to reward five men for exceptional services rendered in exceptional times, but the power, in perpetuity, of selecting from the Irish Resident Magistracy five men to be specially rewarded for special political services. If there was one principle more dear to the average Englishman than another, and which was treated as absolutely a portion of the Constitution, it was that the Judges of the land, and the Judges in an inferior position to those in the Superior Courts, should be, in the first place, unapproachable, and should, in the second place, be placed above political temptation by having their position fixed, and should not be subject to have their judgments or actions warped by political rewards which might be held out to them. But that was all very fine and admirable for England; but for Ireland it was a mere subject of jest between the Attorney General (Sir Henry James) and the Secretary to the Treasury (Mr. Courtney), who could not even conceal their laughter at the notion that principles which were sacred in England were at all applicable to Ireland. It was now proposed to leave the position of the ordinary body of Resident Magistrates in Ireland absolutely unchanged, and to pay those magistrates salaries varying from a minimum of £300 to a maximum of £500 a-year. But it was proposed to take power by this Bill to select, at the discretion of the Executive of the day, five of these magistrates to be rewarded with twice the maximum salary. He had looked over the evidence given before the Commission to which reference had been made, and he found that the first witness examined was the gentleman who signed the Memorial to the Lord Lieutenant, on which Memorial the Commission was issued. Mr. Edward Fitzgerald Ryan was examined, and said his salary was £500 a-year, and that he had held the post of Resident Magistrate since February, 1846—that was to say, that at the time he was examined he had held the office for nearly 40 years. This man had served the Queen faithfully for nearly 40 years, and he and such as he had done their duty to the satisfaction of the Crown, and the Executive, and probably also to the satisfaction of the people for 35 or 40 years; he and such as he were to be left at a salary of £500 a-year, while Mr. Clifford Lloyd, Mr. Blake, and Captain Plunkett, who only came over two or three years ago, who had made themselves extremely obnoxious, who had been the cause of great disturbances, of quartering extra police on many districts, and the effects of whose mischievous system would long be felt in the country, were to be picked out and rewarded with double salary of the men who had really done their duty faithfully. The Secretary to the Treasury proposed that they should give to the Executive, in perpetuity, the power thus to corrupt the entire Magistracy of Ireland, because the evil effects of the proposed system would not be confined to the five men who would be appointed in the first place. The Executive would have an improper and corruptive influence over the Resident Magistrates in the country; the Resident Magistrates would have constantly dangling before their eyes a reward of a double salary, if only they made themselves sufficiently obnoxious to the people. And that was the little Bill which the Secretary to the Treasury said was a mere formality. That was what the hon. Gentleman gave them to understand was the effect of the Bill, the second reading of which he proposed in the absence of the responsible Minister the Chief Secretary in a two sentence speech; and were he (Mr. Gray) and his Friends to be considered unreasonable or obstructive because they opposed such a Bill as that by all the Forms of the House? He did not hesitate to say that if the same principle were to be applied to the portions of the country represented by other hon. Members, those hon. Members would do precisely the same as the Irish Members were now doing, and it did poor credit to the good sense of English or Scotch Members to remain there at the dictation of the Government Whips for the purpose of crushing the Irish Members. Of course, the speeches that were made were of no interest to English and Scotch Members. Naturally enough they were not affected by the Bill, their constituencies would not be harassed or overtaxed by the action of the men it was proposed to create a special class by this Bill; but the people of Ireland knew by experience the mischief that such men had caused in Ireland. The Irish people knew perfectly well that if they gave power to override the ordinary law, and to hold out to Judges the prospect of exceptional and enormous rewards for what the Government called special services, but what the Irish people called special injuries, the effect upon the country would be most disastrous. What was the excuse for this proposal? A few years ago a Memorial signed on the part of all the Resident Magistrates of Ireland, complaining that their pay was fixed in the year 1836 at a figure which was altogether inadequate now-a-days, in view of the increased cost of living, was presented to the Lord Lieutenant. The Government, at the request of the Memorialists, appointed a Royal Commission to inquire into the grievances of the Resident Magistrates, and in the Treasury Minute appointing the Commission it was stated that they had written to Mr. Ryan to the following effect:—That his Memorial of the 17th instant, representing the insufficiency of the salaries received by the Resident Magistrates, had been brought under the notice of Her Majesty's Government, and that the subject would be included in the scope of the inquiries about to be made by the Commission into the salaries of the Civil servants of Ireland, and it was added that—

"The present system of allowances to Resident Magistrates is considered to be open to objection, and that the attention of the Commissioners will be directed, not only to the amount of salaries received by magistrates, but also to placing their emoluments under more satisfactory regulation."

Was that done in this Bill? Why, there was not a single word to that effect. The whole body of magistrates applied to have a reasonable increase made to their salaries, which varied from a minimum of £300 to a maximum of £500 a-year. A Commission was appointed, evidence was received, and the Commission recommended various increases. The Government did not attach any importance to those recommendations, or, if they did, they did not act upon any single one of them. Instead of that they introduced an extraordinary Bill giving power to double the maximum salaries of five individual magistrates, and leave the condition of the Resident Magistrates in Ireland unchanged. The Government did not think it necessary to say one single word in justification of this measure, not even one word of explanation until it was wrung reluctantly from the Secretary to the Treasury by the opposition of Irish Members, though they did think they were quite justified in keeping a House until that hour (3.40) to compel the Representatives of Ireland to pass the second reading of the Bill. The Irish Members did not pretend to have the marvellous powers which enabled the Secretary to the Treasury to resist so long and so successfully on some previous occasions large majorities in the House of Commons when that hon. Gentleman found himself in Opposition. They were not able to speak for two or three hours at a stretch in the face of a majority who would not listen to one word they said, a feat he remembered the hon. Gentleman performing in speaking upon the question of Woman Suffrage. ["Oh, oh!"] Well, perhaps the hon. Gentleman only spoke an hour or an hour and a-half; but he seemed to speak two or three hours. If the Irish Members did not succeed in counting out the House on this occasion, the Government would exhaust them and succeed in carrying the second reading; but they would probably prolong thereby the debates in Supply for two or three days. The action the Government were now taking had caused the greatest discontent in Ireland, and it would still further demoralize the whole body of Resident Magistrates in the country; it would make the Resident Magistrates discontented; it would give to the officials of Dublin Castle further means of corruption, which undoubtedly they would use, as they always had used them, in opposition to the interests of the country; it would increase the difficulties of governing Ireland, and, personally, he failed to see what conceivable good object could be served by it.

MR. SMALL said, that as he listened to the progress of the debate he was reminded of one that took place in the House during the last Session, a short time after he had the honour to be elected a Member of the House. The debate appeared to be very similar to the one which took place upon the Bill for the reconstitution of the Constabulary Force in Ireland. As if it were to make the parallel more remarkable, the Irish Constabulary Bill also singled out five officers for special rewards. That Bill came to a more untimely end than its promoters wished, and he had little doubt that would be the fate of the Bill now under consideration. He listened most attentively to the speech which the hon. Gentleman the Secretary to the Treasury made in introducing the measure, and from that speech he gathered that the principal reason for the introduction of the Bill was that the Treasury might be spared the trouble of putting some foot-note in the Estimates in future years. That argument he failed to understand; because if the payments which had been made in former years were legal, what earthly necessity was there for a special Bill providing for those payments? If the payments, however, were not legal, did the Government mean to say that it was coming to the House to ask for a Bill of Indemnity? He had taken the trouble to look into the accounts which had hitherto regulated the salaries of Resident Magistrates in Ireland, and he had observed with some surprise there had been a regular and constant rise in the salaries of those officials. Why that should be so greatly puzzled him, and it had puzzled him all the more because the population of Ireland had not increased during the last 30 or 40 years. As a matter of fact, the number of people in Ireland, over whom the Resident Magistrates had exercised jurisdiction, had very much decreased instead of increasing; and, therefore, he could not see why the pet officials of the English Government in Ireland should receive larger salaries with a smaller number of people to deal with and with similar duties to perform. In the year 1836 an Act was passed declaring that every magistrate appointed should receive a salary not exceeding £400 a-year; but the House must bear in mind that the Act did not declare that every magistrate should receive that amount, but that that should be the maximum, and a magistrate might have received only a nominal salary. In 1853 another Act was passed, by which the Lord Lieutenant was empowered to increase the salaries of not more than 20 magistrates to a sum not exceeding £500 per annum, and there, again, £500 was the maximum that any magistrate could receive. Since that time the salaries of these magistrates had been increased at different periods, until at last, by an Act 37 & 38 *Vict.*, they were divided into three classes. The third class were, under that Act, to receive salaries of £300, or not exceeding £425; the second class were to receive salaries of £400, or not exceeding £550; the first class were to receive salaries of £500, or not exceeding £675. From that it would appear that the largest sum to be paid to any one magistrate was only two-thirds of the amount now proposed to be given to five Resident Magistrates in Ireland. Probably the hon. Gentleman in charge of this Bill was not so well acquainted with the *personnel* of the Resident Magistrates as Members on the Irish Benches were. He had had an intimate acquaintance with them. They were as ignorant as daws, and had no sympathy with the people. The hon. Member for Monaghan (Mr. Healy) had referred to the class from which these Resident Magistrates were chiefly drawn—namely, from half-pay military officers. They were very objectionable in many cases; they knew nothing about law, but were martinets, familiar with martial law, and were therefore not suitable for Civil positions. But these military magistrates were not the most objectionable, for the Constabulary officers, who were also found in considerable numbers among these Resident Magistrates, were ten times more objectionable. They were ignorant of all law except police law; once policemen they were always policemen. Their principle was to get a conviction and reverse the old Constitutional maxim, and they took a policeman's word before anyone else's. He believed that when once a gentleman received an official position in England he remained in that position for the rest of his life; and promotion from one office to another in England was very rare; but in Ireland that Constitutional maxim seemed to be altogether inapplicable. The rule, and not the exception, was that every official should have inducements held out to him to be subservient to the Castle at Dublin. That was the case in the Supreme Court, and he had seen Judge after Judge promoted from Puisne Judgeships to seats in the Supreme Court, and to seats as Lords of Appeal here in the House of Lords. Consequently, it was no wonder that officials in Ireland were the tools of Dublin Castle. It was not enough that the ordinary officials should be corrupt, but corruption must be extended to the Resident Magistrates and to the County Courts. He had heard many reports that the Law Courts in Ireland were instruments of tyranny; but his experience was that no Courts were more really instruments of tyranny than the Magistrates' Courts. In some parts of Ireland there were no special laws in operation which were governed by the old Statute Law, and in some parts of the country he had seen how they could be turned into instruments of tyranny; and if that was so in those parts, what must be the tyranny exercised in those parts of the country where exceptional laws were in operation and exceptional powers were conferred on the magistrates? Members from Ireland had known for years what the Resident Magistrates were. They were bad enough; but the idea on the Treasury Bench seemed to be that they were not bad enough, but ought to be worse—that there were not sufficient inducements to them to remember that they were not intended to be judicial officers, but administrative officers. Ireland was a poor country, and yet it was proposed by this Bill to give an additional sum of £325 a-year to five magistrates. That might not seem a very large sum to Gentlemen on the Treasury Bench; but it would be a good deal to an Irish county magistrate. Now, he thought the House would understand that the Irish Members were perfectly justified in their opposition to this Bill, and he hoped the Bill would never pass into law. He was satisfied it never would; and it seemed an extraordinary thing that, after the solemn announcement of the Prime Minister that no more legislation or concessions for Ireland could be got from that House, this important Bill should have been introduced.

Notice taken, that 40 Members were not present; House counted, and 40 Members being found present,

MR SMALL said, he also observed that in every little matter of detail this Bill was made as objectionable as possible. It might not be so objectionable if it declared that the five magistrates should be the five who were senior in office or in years; but what did it say?—

"It shall be lawful for the Lord Lieutenant, with the consent of the Commissioners of the Treasury," &c.

As a rule, the Treasury were averse to granting Ireland money; but, no doubt, in this case they would be quite willing. The Lord Lieutenant was to have absolute discretion as to who the magistrates should be, and he had some suspicion as to the mode in which they would be selected. He would, no doubt, select those who had been most obnoxious in the districts in which there had been most crime, and they would be the favourites of the Castle, and would receive these increased salaries. Taking the Bill in its entirety, and in all its details, he did not think it could be made more objectionable than it was; and he thought that perhaps the reason why the Bill was made so long, and was brought forward at this end of the Session, was that the Secretary to the Treasury thought that would enable it to slip quietly through. It seemed to him rather strange that this debate had not been favoured by the presence of a single Member of the Cabinet. He saw several hon. Gentlemen on the Treasury Bench, but not one Member of the Cabinet, and that was a circumstance that should be complained of. There ought to have been some more responsible Member of the Government present to defend the Bill; but not a single Member of the Government had risen to say a single word upon it, except the hon. Gentleman who moved the second reading. He had made two speeches, but not another Member of the Government had spoken upon it in answer to the speeches of his hon. Friends. He thought that was scarcely fair treatment, and he should therefore move the adjournment of the debate.

Motion made, and Question put, "That the Debate be now adjourned."—(*Mr. Small.*)

The House *divided*:—Ayes 11; Noes 38: Majority 27.—(Div. List, No. 191.)

Question again proposed, "That the Bill be now read a second time."

MR. MOLLOY said, he rose to oppose this Bill, which was introduced by the Secretary to the Treasury, as far as he could ascertain, without any explanation, without any reason, and without any justification, but simply in that spirit of obstinacy of which the Secretary to the Treasury had already given some indications. It would be in the recollection of the House that only the other day, in the discussion which took place on the subject of Mr. Bolton's salary, some Irish Members had asked the Secretary to the Treasury whether, under the circumstances, he would consent to the adjournment of the debate; but the hon. Gentleman seemed determined to carry out the scheme he had placed before himself with that obstinacy of which he had already spoken, and which appeared to be a growing characteristic of the hon. Gentleman. The House would also remember that on that occasion, after the debate had proceeded for some time, the Prime Minister came in, and as soon as he had obtained a clear and accurate knowledge of what had taken place, and of the course pursued by the Secretary to the Treasury, indicated, with that generosity which distinguished him, his sincere regret at that course, and in the gentlest manner went on to blame the Secretary to the Treasury for having opposed his single will to the will of the country, and of a large number of Members who were specially interested in the subject. On the present occasion, the hon. Gentleman, desirous, no doubt, of scoring a little victory at the end of the Session, had brought forward the second reading of this Bill actuated by exactly the same feeling of obstinacy as that which distinguished him on the previous occasion. On the former occasion, the Financial Secretary could not be said to have scored any great victory, nor did he think the hon. Gentleman would score any victory on the present occasion. Few as were the Irish Members now presen , the hon. Gentleman would, perhaps, at 9 or half-past 9 in the morning, succeed in obtaining the second reading of this Bill; but what would be the effect of that upon the course of Business? The Estimates were not yet finished; but the Secretary to the Treasury had that night thrown down the glove to Irish Members by introducing a Bill for which there was not the slightest necessity. He had endeavoured to envelop the subject in a veil of mystery in order not to show any reason for introducing the Bill, and those who heard his speech would admit that he gave no information whatever to the House as to the subject-matter of the Bill. He did not know that any information was particularly sought for by some Members of the House, for when sound and argumentative reasons were being given against the Bill he looked round the House, and on the Treasury Bench, and found three Members of the Government asleep on the Government Bench, seven Members below the Gangway asleep, and one distinguished Member of the Government asleep in a dark corner of the House. Those were the conditions under which this Bill had been brought forward that night. He, for one, took exception to any legislation introduced under such circumstances, and he took still stronger exception to any legislation for Ireland under those most extraordinary and exceptional conditions. The Members of the Government had not all spoken. They had heard the speeches made from those Benches, and although the Secretary to the Treasury was precluded from making any further observations, still there was the Attorney General, who was most capable of giving the soundest reasons and information upon any legal Bill affecting either Ireland or England; but the hon. and learned Gentleman made no sign of doing so. There were other Members of the Government present who might answer some of the speeches that had been made against this Bill. The hon. and learned Gentleman the Solicitor General for Ireland (Mr. Walker) had a great store of legal knowledge, and he might give the House his opinion of the Bill now under consideration; but he (Mr. Molloy) supposed it was contrary to the tactics of the Government that the hon. and learned Gentleman should afford hon. Members from Ireland any satisfaction. The hon. Gentleman the Secretary to the Treasury (Mr. Courtney) declined, in introducing the Bill, to give them any explanation, because, in point of fact, the foot-note argument, which on so many occasions had been the stock-in-trade of the Government, had come to grief. The Secretary to the Treasury introduced the Bill, and the hon. Members who, to the number of 41, consented to remain during the long hours of the night, did not care for any explanation; indeed, at one period of the debate more than one-half of the hon. Gentlemen who had rallied to the standard of the Secretary to the Treasury were asleep. Last year a Bill was introduced in the House by the right hon. Gentleman the Chief Secretary (Mr. Trevelyan) which dealt with the Royal Irish Constabulary, and with the Irish Resident Magistrates. On the occasion of the introduction of that Bill, he (Mr. Molloy) produced to the House a Report which had been made to the Lord Lieutenant of Ireland and to the Chief Secretary upon the subject of the Bill. That Report was made by Mr. Jenkinson and three other Resident Magistrates. He (Mr. Molloy) only alluded to the Irish Constabulary Bill because this Bill was the outcome of that Bill. Mr. Jenkinson and the three other Magistrates wished to be considered disinterested persons, and they made a Report to the Lord Lieutenant and the Chief Secretary. They had previously resolved themselves into a Secret Committee, and Mr. Jenkinson officiated as Chairman. On behalf of this Committee, Mr. Jenkinson reported to the Lord Lieutenant that, in their own opinion, their salaries required to be increased. He (Mr. Molloy) stated these facts with absolute confidence, because he mentioned them last year, and the Chief Secretary admitted their correctness. He (Mr. Molloy) challenged the right hon. Gentleman to deny the facts as stated; but the Chief Secretary was silent. Mr. Jenkinson reported to the Lord Lieutenant that in future his own salary should be £2,000 a-year, with £400 a-year as forage allowance, and that, of course, in addition to his small pension of £1,000 a-year; and that the salary of each of the other magistrates who sat in secret with him should be, as well as he (Mr. Molloy) remembered, £1,500 a-year, with £200 a-year for forage. Now, that clearly showed whence the Bill which the Secretary to the Treasury had introduced that night came. The hon. Gentleman entered into no explanation, for the simple fact that he knew nothing about the Bill, or the circumstances connected with it. The Bill had been put into the hon. Gentleman's hand, he brought it forward, and there ended his task. But the Bill was born in the imagination of Mr. Jenkinson, and the three magistrates who were to benefit by the Bill. He should like to ask the Radical Members of the House, who were supposed to be friends of economy and liberty, what they would think if, instead of the words Ireland and Irish magistrates, the words England and English magistrates were used in the Bill? He saw one hon. Gentleman opposite who had often given the Irish Members considerable help in their endeavours to obtain in the House what they claimed to be justice; and he would like to ask his hon. Friend what he would think if such a state of affairs as that which existed in Ireland were presented to his mind in connection with his own country? What would his hon. Friend think, if the words were changed in the manner he had stated, and he (Mr. Molloy) and other Irish Members were, at the beck and call of the Whips of a Party, and knowing little or nothing of the circumstances, to sit there through the long hours of the night to support such a Bill—a Bill in which they did not believe, or had the slightest interest in? His hon. and learned Friend (Mr. Warton), who was the sole Representative of Her Majesty's Opposition now present, had also taken considerable interest in matters relating to Ireland. If the hon. and learned Gentleman could put himself in the position of an Irish Member, would he, having heard what it was proposed to do by this Bill, be prepared to rise in his place and support the Bill? If the Bill were one simply for the purpose of paying the magistrates who had done their work, and were doing it at the present moment, well, he (Mr. Molloy) would certainly not be found waiting there through the small hours of the morning to oppose it. But this was a Bill born in the mind of Mr. Jenkinson for the purpose of recompensing himself—for he (Mr. Molloy) would be able to show that Mr. Jenkinson was going back to Ireland—and others, and for establishing not only extensive payment under exceptional circumstances and peculiar conditions, but for establishing for all time these inordinate salaries for men who in Ireland were little better than superior policemen. The old Resident Magistrates in Ireland, who were men of position, men who had served in the Army or in the law, were satisfied with a salary of £500, which he thought was not too great a salary; but the importations from Burmah and other distant parts of the world, where civilization was certainly at a discount, thought they were entitled to much larger salaries than those which had hitherto been held to be sufficient for the ordinary Resident Magistrates. It was because the new and higher salaries were to be made permanent that he objected to them as he did that night. Now, one might look with some curiosity at the future course of the Bill. He supposed the Bill would go into Committee. They were all anxious to get away for their holidays and to prepare for the coming Autumn Session; but the introduction of this Bill would prolong the Session for at least two days, and he should be glad if his statement reached the ears of the superior Members of the Government; it might prolong the Session considerably longer, but that it would prolong the Session at least two days he was fully persuaded. [Mr. HEALY: Oh, a week.] The introduction of the Bill had created an irritation which would be felt in every debate which took place during the remainder of the Session; not that Irish Members would act in any childish or revengeful spirit, but simply in a spirit of fair and honest retaliation. Personally, he had no hesitation in saying that he entirely approved of such a spirit influencing his hon. Friends, and he should join them in whatever course they chose to adopt in the pursuance of such a spirit. Now, one was in the habit of making appeals in the House of Commons, and he might, of course, occupy the time of the House, if to occupy time were the only object he had in view, by making an appeal to the better sense of the Secretary to the Treasury to let the Bill now drop. But he did not make any such appeal, because the hon. Gentleman had set his heart upon the passing of this Bill, a Bill of which, as he (Mr. Molloy) had already said, the hon. Gentleman knew nothing. He could not help thinking that by his action the hon. Gentleman was very discourteous—of course, he meant politically discourteous—and it was for this reason he thoroughly endorsed the feeling of retaliation which he was sure would prompt the action of his hon. Friends during the remainder of the Session. He assured the hon. Gentleman the Secretary to the Treasury that by the introduction of this Bill he had not facilitated the Business of the House; he had done no good to the Government of which he was a Member; he had done no good to anybody; but he wished to make himself and his Government the subservient slaves of Mr. Jenkinson, and those who, like Mr. Jenkinson, looked upon the positions they held in Ireland from the point of view of their own selfish interest, and not from the point of view of the good of the country. He did not like to make such a statement without giving some proof of it, and he would give proof. The year before last, when the Special Resident Magistrates were appointed, a friend of his came to him and asked him to recommend him as a Resident Magistrate. He (Mr. Molloy) said to his friend he had no sympathy with the system; but, even if he did recommend him, he would be sure not to get it. He added—"Personally, I wish you every success; but what in the world do you know about the duties of a Resident Magistrate? You have been in the Army; you are still in the Army; you have spent most of your time in India, and now you seek the position of an Irish Resident Magistrate. Whatever has put it into your head to apply for the post of Resident Magistrate?" His friend replied to him that Mr. So-and-so, mentioning one of the principal Resident Magistrates by name, had written to him and to two or three others in the same regiment, telling them now was their time, if they would come over to Ireland he would get them in. He (Mr. Molloy) need hardly assure the House that these were facts within his own knowledge. He asked Members of the House to put aside the ill-feeling usually engendered by these little competitions of strength on the part of Parties in the House, and to put this question seriously to themselves—Was this a system under which those onerous and responsible positions were given away, in the manner he had just described, one which they were there that night to uphold and support? He asked hon. Members if they thought that, by following the beck and call of the Whips of the Liberal Party, of which they themselves were Members, and in voting for a Bill of which they knew nothing, they were acting wisely? Did they not think that they would be acting more honourably in walking out of the House than in stopping there to vote for a system which was, on the very best authority, alleged to be pernicious in the last degree, and contrary in every way to the principles of the Party to which they belonged?

MR. DAWSON said, he was surprised to find on this Constitutional question Radical Members, and Members who had sworn——

MR. SPEAKER: Am I right in supposing that the hon. Gentleman seconded the Motion for Adjournment?

MR. DAWSON: I only raised my hat.

MR. SPEAKER: I thought I was right in supposing that the hon. Gentleman seconded the Motion for Adjournment; in that case, the hon. Gentleman has exhausted his right to speak.

MR. HEALY: May I ask, Mr. Speaker, whether it is not a fact that the hon. and learned Member for Brighton (Mr. Marriott), who was then sitting on the opposite side of the House, not merely spoke, but moved the adjournment of the House during the course of the debate on Egypt, and that you allowed him to speak subsequently?

MR. SPEAKER: That is not the question now before the House. The question is whether the hon. Member for Carlow (Mr. Dawson) seconded the Motion for the Adjournment of the House. The hon. Gentleman says he did do so; and I, therefore, rule that he cannot now speak upon this subject.

MR. HEALY: May I ask whether an hon. Member can move the adjournment, and then speak subsequently; or does your ruling only apply to a case of an hon. Member who seconds the Motion for Adjournment?

MR. SPEAKER: In neither case is the hon. Member entitled to speak again.

MR. HEALY: The hon. and learned Member for Brighton, on the occasion I refer to, did speak again.

MR. DEASY said, he was sorry that his hon. Friend the Member for Carlow (Mr. Dawson) had not an opportunity of addressing the House on this subject; because, on account of the position the hon. Member occupied for a very considerable time as the Chief Magistrate of the first City in Ireland, he would have been able to throw considerably more light on the question now under discussion than any Gentleman who had spoken up to this. But he (Mr. Deasy) however, ventured to say that before half-an-hour was over his hon. Friend would have an ample opportunity of discussing this Bill, and that the House generally would have an opportunity of hearing the Members of the Government who had not condescended, so far, to reply to the many speeches which had been delivered from the Irish Benches during the last few hours. He was not connected with any branch of the Legal Profession, and, therefore, he was particularly anxious to hear the opinion of the Law Officers of the Crown sitting upon the Treasury Bench as to the merits of the Bill now under consideration. He was sorry that the right hon. Gentleman (Mr. Trevelyan), who would be mostly concerned in the administration of this Bill if it became law, had not put in an appearance that night. The right hon. Gentleman had not shown himself in the House since this Bill was introduced, and he (Mr. Deasy) did not suppose they would see him during the remainder of the debate. He was sorry for the Solicitor General for Ireland (Mr. Walker), who, together with other hon. Members, would have to attend an important Committee that day at 12 o'clock, for it was evident that the Committee to which he alluded could not, after so late a Sitting as this, carry on its inquiry in a manner which would at all be satisfactory. But, however that might be, he had no wish to dwell upon the matter any longer. He was bound to say he was considerably surprised when he found the hon. Gentleman the Secretary to the Treasury rise in his place and propose the second reading of this Bill, because he understood the Prime Minister distinctly to lay down some few days ago that no Bill of this character would be introduced during the remainder of the Session; that no Bill of a contentious character would be proceeded with; and it was just by the merest chance that he (Mr. Deasy), and many of his hon. Friends, had not already left for Ireland. No matter in what way the pledge of the right hon. Gentleman the Prime Minister was intended, it certainly, in the opinion of the Irish Members, had not been kept. Now, the Bill amounted to a most serious innovation, and it was a Bill which, if it became law, would not conduce at all to the peace or contentment of Ireland. Already a very strong feeling existed against the police of Ireland, and a still stronger feeling existed against the police magistrates who had recently been appointed, and he could not conceive anything which would be likely to make the people more dissatisfied than the permanent appointment of these five Pashas. They knew in the South of Ireland, from personal experience, in what manner the five Special Resident Magistrates to be appointed under the Bill would be likely to administer the law. He knew how Captain Plunkett had been conducting himself as Resident Magistrate of Cork, and he supposed Captain Plunkett would be one of the gentlemen who would be appointed under the Bill. One of his (Mr. Deasy's) liveliest recollections of the scenes which had taken place in the House since he had been a Member of Parliament was that of the scene connected with the discussion which took place as to the conduct of Captain Plunkett, with regard to the way he treated people in public meeting in County Cork. The proceedings of that night reminded him very strongly of what took place upon the occasion referred to, because they then remained sitting until, he believed, 6 o'clock on the Sunday morning. They were now approaching the hour of 6, and he thought it was very probable that their deliberations on this occasion would extend beyond that hour. As to the manner in which Captain Plunkett was likely to conduct himself in the future, he (Mr. Deasy) could only judge by the past. During the whole of last winter Captain Plunkett, who was not responsible to the Irish Government, or responsible, in fact, to any Government at all, took upon himself the authority of the Executive Government of the country, and would not permit a single meeting to be held throughout the County of Cork. Not only that, but when this Captain Plunkett became a Special Resident Magistrate, the county was at once flooded with a large number of extra police. Those extra police still remained quartered upon the people, and had formed the subject of discussion several times in the House of Commons, and would form the subject of discussion many more times before the House adjourned previous to the Autumn Recess. At the present time Captain Plunkett's personal staff numbered 22 men. These men have nothing to do but to drive about the whole of the South of Ireland, and were a constant source of annoyance and of heavy expense to the people. He (Mr. Deasy) had hoped that in discussing a matter of this kind, and in bringing under the notice of the House the unconstitutional conduct of men of the character of Captain Plunkett, the Irish Members would have had the support of those Gentlemen opposite, who so often professed to be the advocates of freedom of speech, and, indeed, of freedom in all things. He was sorry to say that since he was returned to the House, he and the Party to which he belonged had not experienced very much sympathy from those Gentlemen. He assured the Radical Members that their conduct on the present occasion might have the effect of causing the Irish Members to withdraw their support from the agitation which the Radicals were now carrying on against the Upper House. As to that agitation he would not say more than that he did not believe it was sincere.

MR. SPEAKER: The hon. Member is not now speaking to the particular subject before the House—he is not speaking with any relevancy to the subject now in hand.

MR. DEASY said, he would endeavour in the remainder of his remarks to address himself to the subject. He would not say anything further concerning the hon. Gentlemen below the Gangway opposite, of whom he had entertained opinions which he did not think they themselves would be very glad to hear. He thought the House had a right to demand from the Attorney General for England (Sir Henry James) some explanation of his extraordinary conduct on this occasion. On the 16th of March a Supplementary Estimate for the salaries of Resident Magistrates in Ireland was brought in, and the hon. and learned Gentleman pointed out to the House that it was perfectly regular to introduce a foot note in the Estimate, explaining any increase which had been made in a salary. He was glad the hon. and learned Gentleman was now in his place, because the Irish Members would like to hear his opinion on the subject. The hon. and learned Gentleman defended, on the 16th of March, that mode of increasing the salaries of the magistrates in Ireland; but now the Secretary to the Treasury (Mr. Courtney) said that the plan hitherto adopted was a very inconvenient, if not irregular, way of increasing the salaries of magistrates. The Attorney General (Sir Henry James), however, did not now get up and explain the position he had taken up on the subject. Now, a most important Report bearing on this subject was read by the hon. and gallant Gentleman the Member for County Galway (Colonel Nolan), than whom none was more fitted to deal with the question, because he had taken part in the investigations into the Irish Constabulary system. The hon. and gallant Gentleman had pointed out that the recommendations of the Committee of which he was a Member were greatly exceeded by this Bill; that it was proposed by the Committee that the salaries given to the magistrates of the special class should not exceed £600. Without any reason being assigned, the House was now asked to sanction an increase of salary amounting to £400 a-year each to five magistrates. Nothing had given greater dissatisfaction to the people of Ireland than the appointment of divisional magistrates. As he had already pointed out, they had considerable experience of one of such magistrates in the South of Ireland; but it was a well-known fact that whenever one of these magistrates had been appointed, the greatest irritation amongst the people had resulted from his action. Let him (Mr. Deasy) call attention to the debate which took place a few nights ago with regard to the quartering of an extra police force in Limerick. It was clearly proved that the extra police were only drafted into that city when Mr. Clifford Lloyd was appointed Special Magistrate. They had got a sort of understanding that Mr. Clifford Lloyd would not be brought back; but there were other men quite as bad as he. He did not see any difference between Mr. Clifford Lloyd and Captain Plunkett—in fact, he thought Captain Plunkett would make a far more objectionable and more severe magistrate than even Mr. Clifford Lloyd was. These men had the control of the police, all their sympathies were with the police, and it would be utterly impossible for any person brought before such magistrates to get his case dismissed, or to get a verdict against a policeman. That was always the way with the police magistrates. The word of a policeman was taken to the exclusion of the oaths of 20 respectable civilians, and it would be impossible for people to have any respect for the law, if these men had the administration of it. The police and these magistrates would have a direct interest in manufacturing crime, and getting all the convictions they possibly could against men charged with the commission of misdeeds. He had very little confidence in their consciences. He did not for a moment believe they would run the risk of sacrificing their incomes of £500 per annum, if that depended on the misfortune, or even the lives, of men. Whatever confidence he might have had in them was now quite shaken. They were quite as bad as those employed in Ireland by English Governments, who, in times past, were in the habit of gibbeting and pitch-capping men; and the present Government would countenance the same mode of dealing with political opponents in that country, but that public opinion was too strong for them. After all the speeches that had been made, he hoped they would now obtain some legal information from the Treasury Bench. They were fairly entitled to that information, and in order to give the Government a full and fair opportunity of replying to the many speeches they had heard, he should move, as an Amendment, that at that period of the Session the House was not prepared to proceed with a Bill of such importance involving grave considerations of Irish policy. He would say nothing on the Amendment, except that he moved it in order to hear the observations of hon.

Members on the Treasury Bench, because he was really at a loss to understand the position in which he and his hon. Friends stood with regard to this measure. He hoped, therefore, that they would at last hear the Attorney General (Sir Henry James), who took up a very different position three or four months ago.

THE O'GORMAN MAHON seconded the Amendment.

Amendment proposed,

To leave out from the word "That" to the end of the Question, in order to add the words "at this period of the Session this House is not prepared to proceed with a Bill of such importance involving grave considerations of Irish policy,"—(*Mr. Deasy,*)

—instead thereof.

Question proposed, "That the words proposed to be left out stand part of the Question."

MR. HEALY said, he hoped they would now have some observations from the Treasury Bench. They had no more to gain than the Government, and the Prime Minister had given a distinct pledge that they should not be kept sitting there, as they would have to come again for an Autumn Session. As the President of the Local Government Board (Sir Charles W. Dilke) was now present, he would ask him if the Prime Minister had not given that distinct pledge; and whether that pledge was now being kept in the spirit in which it had been interpreted when given? This matter was raised in March last; but the Government had waited until now to bring in this Bill. Four months had passed, and the Government had withdrawn the rest of their Bills; and surely this was not the right way in which to treat hon. Members. They had been told that the Session would wind up on Saturday week, and now they were required to go on with this Bill, which was certainly more contentious than many of those that had been dropped, simply because the Half-past 12 Rule did not apply to it. If there was to be any alteration in the Rules of the House, Money Bills ought to be brought within this Rule, except Exchequer Bills, making a distinct charge on the taxpayers. He appealed to the right hon. Baronet (Sir Charles W. Dilke) not to keep the House sitting longer. There were still a number of Votes to be taken, many of them being Irish, and would the Government get them the more easil by having this Bill? What excuse was there for having delayed this Bill, if it was of so much importance? Surely, since March there had been ample time to bring in the Bill, instead of waiting till the fag-end of the Session? If the Government simply wished to save their honour, Irish Members would have no objection to that, if they said they would then withdraw the Bill; but if they persisted with it, they would only prolong the Session. The Government had given a distinct pledge not to keep the House sitting longer than Saturday week; the Irish Members were not disposed to delay Supply; but they had some questions to raise on Irish Votes; and it would greatly help the House to close the Session if only they could get some distinct statement upon this measure from a responsible Member of the Government.

MR. DILLWYN said, he had supported the Government in this contention so far; but he must confess that he should like to see some explanation given of this matter. The statement, in the first instance, was not as ample as it might have been; there was a good deal in the appeal of hon. Members opposite; and he should support them in asking whether the hon. Gentleman really thought it worth while to continue this contention any further at the present time? He thought the Government would hardly gain much by doing so.

MR. COURTNEY said, the Government would certainly do their best to promote the early closing of the Session; but hon. Members knew very well that the Government had no desire to remain there to that hour in the morning. When this matter was raised in March last on the Supplementary Estimates, they were urged to bring in a Bill with respect to this subject, instead of proceeding by way of extra Votes, and the Chancellor of the Exchequer then distinctly stated that it would be dealt with by a Bill. It was, no doubt, true that the Bill had been brought in at a late period of the Session; but the subject had not been lost sight of, and it was only because of the pressure of other Business that this Bill was not introduced earlier. They had now sat to a late hour, in the hope of obtaining the second reading; but, under the circumstances, he would move that the debate be adjourned.

Motion, by leave, *withdrawn*.

Motion made, and Question proposed, "That the Debate be now adjourned." —(*Mr Courtney*.)

Motion *agreed to*.

Debate *adjourned* till *To-morrow*.

EXPIRING LAWS CONTINUANCE BILL.—[BILL 306.]

(*Mr. Herbert Gladstone, Mr. Courtney*.)

SECOND READING.

Order for Second Reading read.

Motion made, and Question proposed, "That the Bill be now read a second time."

MR. HEALY said, he noticed that, for the first time, the Corrupt Practices Act was included in this Bill. Of course, that was the usual practice, and he did not wish to offer any opposition to it; but he should like to know whether it was the intention of the Government to put that measure annually into this Bill; and whether, if hon. Members desired to raise any points after the General Election, there would be any chance of revising the Act?

SIR CHARLES W. DILKE said, he thought that the fact of this measure being put in the Continuance Bill would not prevent Members from raising questions as to its amendment on a future occasion—for instance, after a General Election. Although the Ballot Act was continued annually by the Continuance Bill, Amendments had been made in that Act, and in the same way all the corrupt practices that had been passed had been included in this Bill, so that he did not think there would be any difficulty in proposing Amendments.

Motion *agreed to*.

Bill read a second time, and *committed* for *To-morrow*.

METROPOLITAN ASYLUMS BOARD (BORROWING POWERS) BILL.—[BILL 310.]

(*Sir Charles W. Dilke, Mr. George Russell*.)

SECOND READING.

Order for Second Reading read.

Motion made, and Question proposed, "That the Bill be now read a second time."—(*Sir Charles W. Dilke*.)

Mr. Courtney

MR. WARTON asked whether this Bill was similar to the Further Powers Bill?

SIR CHARLES W. DILKE replied that it was not. It was a Bill to enable the Metropolitan Asylums Board to borrow under their Act of last Session.

Motion *agreed to*.

Bill read a second time, and *committed* for *To-morrow*.

ULSTER CANAL AND TYRONE NAVIGATION BILL.

Viscount CRICHTON, Mr. ARTHUR O'CONNOR, and Mr. COURTNEY, nominated Members of the Select Committee.

AGRICULTURAL LABOURERS (IRELAND)

Ordered, That Sir HERVEY BRUCE be discharged from further attendance on the Select Committee on Agricultural Labourers (Ireland):—Mr. CORRY added to the Committee.—(*Mr. Solicitor General for Ireland*.)

House adjourned at a quarter after Five o'clock in the morning.

HOUSE OF LORDS,

Tuesday, 29th July, 1884.

MINUTES.]—PUBLIC BILLS—*First Reading*—Public Works Loans * (221); Metropolitan Board of Works (Money) * (222).
Committee—Report—Contagious Diseases (Animals) Act, 1878 (Districts) * (205); Naval and Greenwich Hospital Pensions * (203); Teachers' Residences (Ireland) * (214).
Report—Yorkshire Registries * (219).
Third Reading—Strensall Common * (195), and *passed*.

PRIVATE BILLS—AMENDMENTS TO STANDING ORDERS.

RESOLUTIONS.

THE EARL OF REDESDALE (CHAIRMAN of COMMITTEES) moved that the Standing Orders relating to Private Bills be amended—(1.) All Bills (not being Estate Bills) seeking power, with reference to certain subjects (which are set out at length), are in their Orders termed Local Bills, and are divided into two classes, according to the subjects to which they respectively relate. (2.) Notices in reference to Street Tramways Bills; Subway Bills; diversions of water — deposit of maps, plans, and diagrams; deposit of Bills precedent to applications; estimates; proofs of consents; restrictions as to mortgage [and other particulars].

THE EARL OF CAMPERDOWN was understood to say that under the Standing Orders it was sometimes doubtful whether a Bill should be introduced as a private one or a public one.

THE LORD CHANCELLOR said, that on two occasions this Session the question had been raised—once when the Archbishop of Canterbury brought in a Bill to prevent the creation of charges on ecclesiastical lands, under any Land Improvement Act, without the consent of the Patron and Ordinary —there being a Company in the West of England in whose Private Act there were no such safeguards—when it was said that certain notices were necessary, though the Bill did not affect the vested right of any person, but would apply generally. It was said that it was a Private or Hybrid Bill; but he (the Lord Chancellor) objected to that view of the matter. The other instance was when his noble Friend (the Earl of Camperdown) brought in a Bill enabling all persons to know what charges of Water Companies they had to meet. That Bill took away no right whatsoever, and it did not come within the Standing Orders. It was to all intents and purposes a Public Bill, and not a private one; but it was objected to as being a Private Bill, and was not proceeded with. He hoped that next year his noble Friend would persevere in his efforts, and he would give him all the support in his power.

THE MARQUESS OF SALISBURY pointed out that if any question arose in the House of Commons as to whether a Bill was a private or public one, it was decided by the Speaker, and in their Lordships' House by a vote. If there were any doubt as to the character of the Bill, the question should be decided by a vote of the House.

Motion *agreed to*.

Moved, "That the Standing Orders in relation to Labouring Class Dwellings be amended, and New Orders added."—(*The Marquess of Salisbury.*)

Motion *agreed to*.

The said Orders to be *printed*, as amended. (No. 224.)

EGYPT—THE CONFERENCE.

QUESTION.

THE MARQUESS OF SALISBURY: I beg to ask the noble Earl the Foreign Secretary, Whether he has any information to give the House with respect to the Conference?

EARL GRANVILLE: I have to inform the noble Marquess that the Plenipotentiaries met to-day; but they had not received an answer to the representations which they made to their different Courts, and, at present, I have nothing to add to what I stated yesterday.

LITERATURE, SCIENCE, AND ART— NATIONAL PORTRAIT GALLERY.

QUESTION. OBSERVATIONS.

LORD FORBES asked, Whether there were any funds available for the purchase of pictures for the National Portrait Gallery; and also when the catalogue was likely to be re-issued? He declared that it would be much to be regretted if the nation lost the chance of acquiring from the Blenheim Collection Raphael's "Madonna" and Vandyke's equestrian picture of Charles I. The latter certainly should be purchased for the Portrait Gallery—one of the most interesting collections of pictures in the country. But, notwithstanding its valuable and interesting character, it was miserably housed, and almost unprotected against fire.

LORD LAMINGTON said, he quite agreed with the noble Lord as to the great value of the collection; but thought that the building in which the pictures were placed was unworthy of them. He also concurred in thinking that something ought to be done to guard these pictures against the extreme danger they were exposed to from fire. The Gallery was a most valuable one, and largely consisted of donations from various families; and yet the Government were content to see it liable to be burnt down at any moment.

LORD THURLOW said, that he was afraid he must confine his answer to the Questions on the Paper. It appeared that the funds at the disposal of the National Portrait Gallery Trustees were very limited, and consisted only of an annual Vote in the House of Commons of £750. As regarded this year, he might state that £500 of that amount had been anticipated by the Trustees in the purchase of important pictures in the recent Hamilton sale. Therefore, there remained available of this year's Vote only £250, and that had all been spent. The National Portrait Gallery Trustees would not be in a position to make any further addition to the collection until after March next, when they would come into the receipt of the usual Vote of £750. A new catalogue, he was informed, was in the hands of the printers, and would be available almost immediately. There would be also a supplementary pamphlet, which was in course of preparation, and that would be obtainable by the public for *6d.* A brief list, for the price of *2d.*, would likewise be issued by the Trustees of all the more recent interesting acquisitions which had been made by them.

LORD FORBES again inquired whether the valuable Vandyke could not be secured for the collection?

[No reply.]

THE SUEZ CANAL.

OBSERVATIONS.

LORD LAMINGTON, in calling the attention of Her Majesty's Government to the condition of the Suez Canal, said, he had received terrible accounts of the foul condition of that Canal; and when they reflected that 79 per cent of the vessels passing through it were British, their Lordships would see that the question was one of importance. The [illegible] Earl (Earl Granville) stated, [illegible] noble [illegible] in answer to a Question recently put [illegible] to him, that it was the duty of the [illegible] Company to see to the condition of [illegible] the Canal; but who controlled [illegible] the Canal; but who [illegible] the Company in case they neglected their duty? The presence of the cholera in France made this matter all the more serious. This was the foulest cesspool that ever existed; there was no current through it at all, and unless some steps were taken by Her Majesty's Government, who in all these matters were virtually supreme, no remedy would be found against so dangerous a state of things.

EARL GRANVILLE: I am afraid I have not much to add to what I stated the other day. The noble Lord informs us that he has received the information he has stated to the House; but Her Majesty's Government have received no complaints, the Suez Canal Company have received no complaints, and the Commanders of Her Majesty's ships passing through the Canal have made no complaints. At the same time, I think it extremely likely that that narrow piece of water may not be free from some of the charges the noble Lord has brought against it. But the waterways in this country are not altogether free from these charges. The noble Lord has described the condition of things in Egypt, and I need not go into that. I would remind him that there is no doubt whatever of the position of the Government and of Parliament as to the waterways in this country, and yet I believe the state of the River Thames is not so perfect as we could desire. What I stated the other day was, that the Canal Company is responsible for the waterway; and I may add that the Egyptian Government is responsible for the towns on the shores of the Canal. The noble Lord knows that it is a very thinly-populated country, and that the only town there, except Port Said and Suez, is the small town of Ismailia, situated in the recess of a very considerable lake, and that the real difficulty we have to deal with arises from the small dimensions of the Canal. The noble Lord is aware that a Technical Commission is employed in considering a plan for the deepening or very much enlarging the Canal, and I hope the result of their labours will be known at the end of the year or the beginning of the next year.

House adjourned at Five o'clock, to Thursday next, a quarter past Ten o'clock.

HOUSE OF COMMONS,

Tuesday, 29th July, 1884.

MINUTES.]—SELECT COMMITTEE—*Report*—Charitable Trusts Acts [No. 306].

SUPPLY—*considered in Committee*—CIVIL SERVICE ESTIMATES—CLASS III.—LAW AND JUSTICE.

Resolutions [July 28] *reported.*

PRIVATE BILL (*by Order*)—*Second Reading*—Bristol Corporation (Docks Purchase).

PUBLIC BILLS—*Second Reading*—Public Health (Ireland) (Districts) [311].

Committee—Burgh Police and Health (Scotland) (*re-comm.*) [296] — R.P.; Revenue, &c.

[300]—R.P.; Supreme Court of Judicature Amendment [307]—R.P.
Committee — Report — Metropolitan Asylums Board (Borrowing Powers) * [310]; Superannuation * [146]; Expiring Laws Continuance * [306].
Committee—Report—Third Reading—Chartered Companies [304], and *passed.*
Considered as amended—Infants [308].
Considered as amended—Third Reading—Prosecution of Offences * [287], and *passed.*
Third Reading—Military Pensions and Yeomanry Pay * [302], and *passed.*
Withdrawn — Magistrates (Ireland) Salaries * [292]; Shannon Navigation * [201].

PRIVATE BUSINESS.

BRISTOL CORPORATION (DOCKS PURCHASE) BILL [*Lords*] (*by Order*).

SECOND READING.

Order for Second Reading read.

Motion made, and Question proposed, "That the Bill be now read a second time."

MR. WARTON, in moving to leave out from the word "That" to the end of the Question, in order to add the words—

"This House declines to sanction a Bill which involves the principle of trading by a Corporation, which provides for the sale of Docks to the Corporation of Bristol at an excessive price, which is opposed to the interests of the ratepayers of that city, which is obnoxious to a large number, if not the majority, of those ratepayers, and on which those ratepayers have not had a fair opportunity of expressing their views,"

said, he felt it his duty, in consequence of representations made to him on behalf of a very large number of owners of property and ratepayers in Bristol—a very large number indeed—to try and get the passage of this Bill delayed, in order that the interests of some thousands of persons might be fairly considered. The persons he represented had not yet had an opportunity of having their case considered. Their agent and representative was Mr. Henry Brown, of Bristol, who was the owner of some 20 houses in that city, and ground landlord of 24 more; and Mr. Brown was prepared to show, from his own case, how the rates would be increased by the Bill. It was rather a difficult and complicated matter to deal with. If it had been the practice of the House to present Petitions before proceeding with Private Bill Business, he should have had an opportunity of presenting the very largely signed Petition he held in his hand, bearing the names of more than 15,000 owners of property and ratepayers in Bristol; but by the Rules of the House he could only refer to it in this indirect manner. He believed it was not competent for him to present the Petition then; but if it had been the practice to present Petitions before the time of Private Business, he should have been able to lay this upon the Table, and have it read by the Clerk. The Petitioners were apprehensive that their interests would be very much injured by the provisions of the present Bill. The number of signatures would have been very largely increased, as a great number of ratepayers were anxious to sign the Petition; but, owing to the accident of Mr. Brown now living at Eastbourne, a considerable number of the signatures had been sent there, and were not included in the Petition. Whatever the number of signatures to the Petition was, it should be remembered that the Petition itself followed a much larger one signed by 5,000 or 6,000 of the ratepayers of Bristol, which had been lodged in the Private Bill Office on the 19th of the present month. His objections to the Bill were of a two-fold character. He objected to it first on general principles, upon which point, however, he would not say much, as it was not necessary to do more than simply indicate his belief that it was a very unsound principle for a Corporation to buy up a number of Docks and become a private trading Company. Such action on their part must necessarily amount to undue interference with private enterprize, and certainly was not an economical way of carrying on a trade. He found that in London all the great Dock undertakings were in the hands of private individuals, and even in that wonderful Bill for the government of London, introduced by the Home Secretary, only to be withdrawn, there was no proposition to give power to the Corporation of London to take over the Dock undertakings of the Metropolis. Again, at Liverpool the same principle obtained, and the large Dock interests were kept quite clear and distinct from the business and functions of the Corporation. He knew that, owing to a serious accident, there had been no opportunity yet for the thousands of ratepayers of Bristol who were opposed to the Bill to be heard before in Committee. There was an attempt made by Mr. Brown to obtain a hearing before the House of Lords; but that hearing failed, because it was held that he had no *locus standi*, and that he was really represented by the Corporation, who were the promoters of the Bill. Now, it was quite evident, from what had recently taken place in that House, that it was the tendency of the feeling and wish of the House to give a fuller opportunity to all classes of persons who believed they were injured by a Private Bill to have a *locus standi* before Committees. Onl a week or two ago, the House carried by a small majority, but still by a majority, a Resolution affirming the principle that such Bodies as a Chamber of Commerce or a Chamber of Agriculture should be entitled to be heard before Railway Bill Committees in reference to a projected railway. Now, whatever value a Chamber of Commerce or a Chamber of Agriculture possessed, it could not be said to be of the same importance or to have the same interests as thousands of ratepayers in a large city like Bristol. Without wearying the House with details which might be somewhat difficult to follow, he would simply say that the present Bill was introduced for the purpose of sanctioning the purchase of no less than four different Dock properties—namely, the Avonmouth Company, the Avonmouth Warehouse Company, the Portishead Company, and the Portishead Warehouse Company. The confusion was made worse confounded by the proposals contained in the Bill for payment by instalments. Nothing appeared to be made quite clear until they came to the amounts that had to be paid. What was it that had to be paid? If they turned to the ninth and tenth pages of the Bill, they would find particulars of the enormous sum that was to be paid by the unfortunate ratepayers of Bristol in order to carry out the designs of the Corporation. Adding up the amounts to be paid to the different Companies by separate instalments, it would be found that they came to the total of £800,000. He altogether objected to these terms, quite apart from the general principle to which he had referred, on the ground that the price was excessive, because these Docks were an utter failure. Hitherto they had not been carried on at a profit; and, so far as the Corporation of Bristol was concerned, he contended that the ratepayers would be required to complete a purchase which would involve a considerable amount of loss. More than that, the people who advocated the buying of these Docks were also the sellers of the property, being holders of shares, and the consent of the Town Council to the purchase had been accorded in a manner that was highly improper. It was quite true that the statutory meeting was held; but the Mayor at that meeting induced the Town Council to leave the matter in his hands. He said, in effect—"Leave it all to me. There are certain difficult matters connected with the business which you will never understand; I can manage the whole matter myself." When the Mayor condescended to give an explanation to a few private friends, they ingenuously confessed that they were no wiser than they were before. The Mayor himself was deeply interested in the transfer, and probably that was the reason why all his proceedings had been shrouded in mystery. He (Mr. Warton) saw both of the hon. Members for Bristol present, and he thought they would not deny that they were also interested, the one to a large extent, and the other to a lesser degree. In fact, many of the would-be purchasers were vendors at the same time; and, therefore, there was no wonder that the matter was pressed before the House as the transfer of the Docks to the Corporation was the only way of saving the undertaking from financial ruin. According to the most common rules of equity, no man ought to be the buyer and the seller at the same time. Regardless of the interests of the ratepayers, the Mayor induced the Council to believe that he alone understood this complicated matter, and the Council acquiesced, although it was true they were given to understand that the annual cost to which the ratepayers would be subjected would only be £900 a-year. But at a subsequent meeting, last Tuesday, the Mayor admitted to the Council that there had been a miscalculation in estimating the expense, and that it would be £8,000 a-year. A meeting was held in May last of the inhabitants; but the agents and servants of the Mayor were able to overpower them by the admission of

Avonmouth roughs, who played their part somewhat in the same way as the hired men in the Hyde Park Demonstration last week. Thus the free views of the ratepayers was not heard. In order to show what might be expected if that free view could be heard, he might mention that in reference to the intention of the Corporation to carry out another scheme, having, however, no connection with the present Bill—and he merely gave it as an illustration to show that the Corporation had not the confidence of the ratepayers—the proposal of the Mayor and Corporation was defeated on a poll by 15,000 to 6,000. This afforded ample proof that the Mayor and Corporation did not possess the confidence of the great majority of the ratepayers of Bristol. All he claimed now was that there should be afforded ample opportunity for inquiry. In his opinion, it was eminently a case for inquiry. They were now getting near the end of the Session; time was precious, and the Bill was being pushed forward in a way which prevented it from receiving full consideration. It certainly seemed rather hard that the ratepayers of Bristol should be required to come forward and find out all that was being done within the week. He was satisfied that if the House would allow a full inquiry, and would give the ratepayers an opportunity, in some way, of acquiring a *locus standi* before the Committee, in order to ventilate the matter free from the hands of the Avonmouth roughs, the House would not consent in the end to pass the Bill. A Petition, largely signed, had already been presented; and he was assured that a very considerable number of ratepayers, who had not yet signed the Petition, were ready to do so. The manner in which the negotiations had been conducted by the Mayor certainly justified the suspicion that things were not altogether as they ought to be, and that, at all events, a considerable body of ratepayers who would be burdened with increased taxation ought to have their case heard. In regard to the price to be paid, he had already stated that these Docks were not worth buying at all; but if the House would analyze the provisions of the Bill they would find that no less a sum than £800,000 was to be paid for them. He contended that such a price was excessive. For the Portishead Dock £230,000 was to be given, added to which was £100,000 recited in the Bill as having been already advanced in some mysterious way by the Corporation, making £350,000 altogether, when, so far as the Portishead Company was concerned, their undertaking might have been purchased for £300,000. It was evident, therefore, that £50,000 were entirely thrown away by the Corporation of Bristol, and that the interests of the ratepayers, which they ought to have protected, had been altogether neglected. He strongly deprecated the manner in which the negotiations had been conducted. It was exceedingly improper for the Mayor to manage everything by himself; no attempt was made to obtain the views of the Town Council before the business was completed. Under such circumstances, it was most objectionable to hurry the Bill through the House, and it was in the interest of thousands of the ratepayers, who were anxious to obtain a *locus standi* in opposition to the Bill before the Committee, that he submitted this Resolution.

COLONEL KING-HARMAN seconded the Resolution.

Amendment proposed,

To leave out from the word "That" to the end of the Question, in order to add the words "this House declines to sanction a Bill which involves the principle of trading by a Corporation, which provides for the sale of Docks to the Corporation of Bristol at an excessive price, which is opposed to the interests of the ratepayers of that city, which is obnoxious to a large number if not the majority of those ratepayers, and on which those ratepayers have not had a fair opportunity of expressing their views,"—(*Mr. Warton,*)

—instead thereof.

Question propose , "That the words proposed to be left out stand part of the Question."

MR. SAMUEL MORLEY said, he had utterly failed in his attempt to discover the ground upon which the hon. and learned Member for Bridport (Mr. Warton) was opposed to this Bill. He was there to express his opinion that a more straightforward transaction had never been submitted to the House of Commons. He represented a city which he ventured to say, without any boast, contained about the usual average of men engaged in trade and commerce to be found in any large town; and as to the reflection cast upon the Mayor, in reference to his conduct in this transaction, it was utterly undeserved. The Mayor occupied that distinguished position for the fourth time, having been re-elected without opposition, with a view to carrying out the very scheme with respect to which the sanction of the House was now asked. In 1848, under the provisions of an Act of Parliament, the Corporation purchased the City Docks; and since that period there had been established two large Docks, and there had been carried on for some years a very foolish and a very ruinous competition, by which the trade of Bristol had been seriously affected. Owing to the bitterness of the controversies which it caused in reference to these Docks, it was thought most advantageous that the Docks should be secured under one management. The usual course was followed of calling a public meeting of the ratepayers. He might say that the Council of the Corporation, numbering 64, had, with perfect unanimity, without a division, sanctioned, on two or three occasions, the motions which had been laid before them for the carrying out of this scheme. A meeting of owners and ratepayers had also been called, at which the terms of the purchase were made known, the matter discussed, and the Bill passed in the ordinary way. Any owner or ratepayer could at the meeting have demanded a poll, and a poll was, in fact, demanded by one ratepayer, who was really the Petitioner on this occasion, and who was connected, as he understood, with the Liberty of Property Defence League. [Mr. WARTON: No.] He had had a paper placed in his hands yesterday which was headed "The Liberty of Property Defence League," and it had reference to a Petition to which, no doubt, a number of names had been attached. The Corporation had learnt that the signatures had been obtained to this Petition by canvassers who got so much a hundred for the names attached. It was said that the negotiations which had been carried on by the Mayor were in secret. It was perfectly well known that the individuals engaged in carrying on original negotiations in a matter of this kind must have confidence reposed in them; and he ventured to say there was no man in the City of Bristol in whom confidence had been more largely extended than in the gentleman who occupied the distinguished position of Mayor of Bristol. The meeting at Bristol was almost unanimous upon the question; and the only Petition which had been lodged against the Bill was one bearing a few hundred names, many of which were alleged to be fictitious, in a city of more than 200,000 inhabitants. He sincerely trusted that the House would give the Bill a second reading.

Question put, and *agreed to.*

Main Question put.

Bill read a second time, and *committed.*

EARL OF DEVON'S ESTATES BILL.

[*Lords.*]

RESOLUTION.

Motion made, and Question proposed,

"That, in the case of the Earl of Devon's Estates Bill [*Lords*], Standing Order 235 be suspended, and that the Bill be read a second time."—(*Sir Charles Forster.*)

MR. PULESTON said, he rose to a point of Order; but he did not know whether, if opposition were raised to a Bill, it would be right to discuss the question then?

MR. SPEAKER: If the hon. Gentleman objects to the proposal, the Bill must stand over until to-morrow.

MR. PULESTON said, he had no objection to discuss the Bill now.

LORD RANDOLPH CHURCHILL said, that as the Motion had been made, and the hon. Member was desirous of discussing it, it must, as a matter of course, stand over.

MR. SPEAKER: That is what I intended to convey to the hon. Member.

Question again proposed.

MR. SPEAKER said, the Standing Order directed that when Notice of opposition was given a Private Bill must stand over until the following day.

LORD RANDOLPH CHURCHILL asked if it was understood that the Bill would not come on to-morrow?

COLONEL GERARD SMITH said, that in the case of the Hull and Barnsley Bill, where a similar Notice was given, it was put down for the next day.

LORD RANDOLPH CHURCHILL said, he apprehended that it would be competent to move that the Order stand over until Thursday.

MR. SPEAKER: The time for making that Motion will be to-morrow, until which day, under the Standing Order, the Bill must now stand over.

Ordered, That, in the case of the Earl of Devon's Estates Bill [*Lords*], Standing Order 235 be suspended, and that the Bill be read a second time To-morrow.

GREAT WESTERN RAILWAY AND BRISTOL AND PORTISHEAD PIER AND RAILWAY COMPANIES BILL. [*Lords.*]

RESOLUTION.

Motion made, and Question proposed,

"That, in the case of the Great Western Railway and Bristol and Portishead Pier and Railway Companies Bill [*Lords*], Standing Orders 211, 236, and 237 be suspended, and that the Committee on the Bill have leave to sit and proceed upon Thursday next."—(*Sir Charles Forster.*)

MR. WARTON said, he thought that a longer time ought to be given for the consideration of the Bill. It was all very well for the hon. Member for Bristol (Mr. S. Morley) to say that it was satisfactory to the Body which he represented. The hon. Member, in regard to a previous Bill, made a comparison between the population of Bristol, which was over 220,000, and the 5,000 or 7,000 ratepayers who petitioned against it. The comparison, however, was scarcely fair, because the inhabitants of the city included women and children; and it was a well known fact that when a poll was taken upon a recent occasion 15,000 ratepayers were on one side, and 6,000 on the other. It was, therefore, only fair to assume that the persons who occupied the position of ratepayers in the City of Bristol did not exceed 21,000 or 22,000, and out of that number 6,000 to 7,000 had already shown that they were in opposition to the Bill. Therefore, to say that the question they were dealing with affected 220,000 persons, and that the number who wished to be heard in opposition was consequently very insignificant, was hardly a fair comparison; and, in order to afford further time for the consideration of the matter, he would move that the Committee upon the Bill be not proceeded with until Monday next. He strongly objected to the wholesale suspension of Standing Orders in order that a Bill should be proceeded with which proposed to effect a purchase contrary to the interests of the ratepayers.

Amendment proposed, to leave out the word "Thursday," in order to insert the word "Monday,"—(*Mr. Warton,*)—instead thereof.

Question proposed, "That the word 'Thursday' stand part of the Question."

MR. SAMUEL MORLEY wished to make an appeal to the House. It would be fatal to the measure if this postponement were to take place; and he must, therefore, resist the Amendment of the hon. and learned Member.

COLONEL GERARD SMITH thought that the rule which had been followed in the Hull and Barnsley case ought to be followed in this instance. This was a case of emergency; and, as the Bill was opposed, the further hearing ought to be deferred until to-morrow.

Question put, and *agreed to.*

Main Question put.

Ordered, That, in the case of the Great Western Railway and Bristol and Portishead Pier and Railway Companies Bill [*Lords*], Standing Orders 211, 236, and 237 be suspended, and that the Committee on the Bill have leave to sit and proceed upon Thursday next.

QUESTIONS.

THE CONGO RIVER—THE INTERNATIONAL ASSOCIATION.

MR. JACOB BRIGHT asked the Under Secretary of State for Foreign Affairs, What progress has been made in regard to the proposed International Commission for the Lower Congo; and, whether, with regard to the Upper Congo, Her Majesty's Government is prepared to recognize the International Association under the presidency of the King of the Belgians?

LORD EDMOND FITZMAURICE: Some further communications of a confidential character have passed in regard to the proposed International Commission. Her Majesty's Government have not decided to take any step to recognize the International Association.

SIR HERBERT MAXWELL: Would the noble Lord inform the House whether it is true, as has been stated, that the right of pre-emption of the territory under the control of the Association was offered to Her Majesty's Government in preference to France?

LORD EDMOND FITZMAURICE: I think any Question in regard to the pre-emption in regard to France had better be put on the Paper. If the hon. Baronet puts it down for Thursday, I shall endeavour to answer.

said on a former occasion. Before the original Report was submitted to me, the Head Constable of the district had made personal inquiries at the houses of both John Cobain and William Hunter, and had learned from the wife of the former that no permission had been asked to erect the arch; and from the latter, that, when asked, he had refused permission for its erection. It is now alleged that it was his wife who had refused the permission. With regard to the suggestion that the house of the parish priest was not concerned in the matter, the facts are that the arch was attached on one side to a pipe which runs down between the houses of the parish priest and John Cobain, and was stretched across the street at an angle in front of the priest's windows, being fastened on the opposite side to a pipe on Hunter's house. I was correctly informed that a disturbance occurred in connection with an arch erected in this place on a former occasion. The circumstance took place in 1878, and a repetition of it on this occasion was apprehended.

MR. SEXTON asked whether the arch was not within two feet of the parish priest's window?

MR. TREVELYAN said, he thought that extremely probable.

POOR LAW (IRELAND)—ELECTION OF GUARDIANS—INQUIRY AT COOTEHILL, CO. TYRONE.

MR. HEALY asked the Chief Secretary to the Lord Lieutenant of Ireland, Is it the fact that, at the Cootehill inquiry, it transpired that Vaughan Montgomery, Esq. J.P., Crilly, Aughnacluy, county Tyrone, lodged a claim to vote as lessor of Patrick McCabe, Mountain Lodge, on a valuation of £19 10*s*., and that, by the sworn evidence of Mr. P. McCabe, his lease, and rent receipts, it was proved that Mr. Montgomery had no interest, directly or indirectly, in this holding; and, will he ask this magistrate for an explanation of the filing of this claim?

MR. TREVELYAN: I have already more than once answered the Question as it stands on the Paper; but I presume that what the hon. Member desires to know is what view is taken of Mr. Montgomery's explanati[illegible] Attorney General advised n[illegible] th[illegible] it is not satisfactory, a[illegible] give such directions as he may think proper for the enforcement of the law. I have, however, this day received, through the hon. Member for the County of Tyrone, a further statement from Mr. Montgomery on the subject, which I shall forward at once to the Attorney General. Whether or not it will modify his view of the case I cannot at present undertake to say.

MR. HEALY: In addition to that, will the facts be laid before the Lord Chancellor?

MR. TREVELYAN: I think the best way to ascertain the facts is to try them in a Court of Law.

WAYS AND MEANS—INLAND REVENUE DEPARTMENT — LIGHT SOVEREIGNS AND HALF-SOVEREIGNS.

SIR EARDLEY WILMOT asked the Secretary to the Treasury, If, for the convenience of the public, he will direct written notices to be affixed in various parts of the Inland Revenue Department at Somerset House, informing persons who come there to make payments in gold, that they will be mulcted for any deficiency of weight in the sovereign and half-sovereign?

MR. COURTNEY: I am told that a printed notice to the effect suggested by the hon. Baronet is already affixed to every desk in Somerset House at which money is received.

SIR EARDLEY WILMOT: Was it done yesterday?

MR. COURTNEY: No; they have been there some time.

PUBLIC HEALTH—VACCINATION—THE DEWSBURY GUARDIANS.

MR. HOPWOOD asked the President of the Local Government Board, Whether the stipulation proposed by the Dewsbury Guardians on the appointment of a public vaccinator, that he should "guarantee children from any injury from vaccination, and accept the responsibility of any injuries that might arise from his vaccination of any person," will be sanctioned by the Department?

MR. GEORGE RUSSELL: As regards the function of a public vaccinator, he is bound to obey rules which are sufficient to prevent any but a very minute risk of injury to any vaccinated [illegible]; and the Local Government [illegible]onsider that such an official

trary to the advice of their chairman, Mr. Foley, up to the 8th July, he remaining at lodgings; did the Lay Commissioners go back to Lord Rossmore's hotel on the 15th July, although their chairman returned to the former lodgings; did the latter inform them there was accommodation for all, and, in spite of his request that they should leave, did the Lay Commissioners refuse to do so; did the Commissioners adjudicate on a large number of cases on Colonel Lloyd's, the Westenra, and Lord Rossmore's estates, after they went to sojourn in Lord Rossmore's hotel; is the Government aware that their decisions are most unsatisfactory to the tenants; and, are any of these gentlemen to be re-appointed after the 31st of August?

MR. TREVELYAN: I fear I have no means of ascertaining the facts as to all the details which the hon. Member asks for in the earlier paragraphs of this Question. The Chairman of the Sub-Commission reports as follows with regard to them:—

"The communications which passed between me and my colleagues on the matter of their sojourning at Lord Rossmore's hotel were purely of a private nature, and I will not answer any inquiries in reference to them. Mr. Healy inquires whether, during the sojourn at that hotel, the Sub-Commissioners adjudicated on a large number of cases on Colonel Lloyd's, the Westenra, and Lord Rossmore's estates. On referring to the printed list, I find the numbers are—on Colonel Lloyd's estate, one; on Lord Rossmore's eight; and on the Westenra, about 41. Whether the decisions were satisfactory or the reverse the Commissioners have not heard."

In reply to the last paragraph of the hon. Member's Question, I may say that the list of gentlemen which I read to the House a few days ago as having been selected for re-appointment did not include the names of any of the gentlemen who constituted No. 8 Sub-Commission.

CRIME AND OUTRAGE (IRELAND)—ORANGEMEN AND ROMAN CATHOLICS—FIRING INTO A TRAIN.

LORD ARTHUR HILL asked the Chief Secretary to the Lord Lieutenant of Ireland, Whether he is aware that a train, conveying members of the Loyal Orange Institution, on the 12th instant, from Newry to Ballyroney, was fired into whilst passing through a Roman Catholic district, known as Tullyorien, near Banbridge; and, whether any, and, if so, what steps have been taken by the police with a view to discovering the perpetrator of the above outrage?

MR. TREVELYAN: I am informed that the facts are that several shots were fired from a considerable distance at a special train leaving Banbridge for Ballyroney after the sham fight at Scarva, on the evening of the 14th July. One bullet entered a carriage; but, fortunately, no one was in the compartment. A number of Orangemen were in the train. The locality is a Roman Catholic one. The police have made very minute inquiries; but they have not succeeded in getting any information which would enable them to take action. Shots had been fired by Orangemen from a train in this locality on the 12th, and the shots on the 14th are supposed to have been fired in retaliation. It is right to add that it is not known that the shots fired from the train on the 12th contained bullets.

IRELAND — ORANGE PROCESSIONS — THE 12TH OF JULY CELEBRATIONS — ORANGE ARCH, GLENARM, CO. ANTRIM.

LORD ARTHUR HILL asked the Chief Secretary to the Lord Lieutenant of Ireland, Whether his attention has been drawn to a letter which appeared in *The Belfast News Letter* on the 23rd instant—

"The Arch at Glenarm.—Sir, We, the owners and occupiers of the two houses from which the Orange arch was suspended on 12th July last, are very much surprised at the reply given by the Chief Secretary to Lord Arthur Hill in the House of Commons last night.

"We beg to give the statements therein made the fullest and most emphatic contradiction. No arch was ever erected there against our will, nor was there ever any disturbance in Glenarm in connection with an arch.

"We are prepared to make affidavits to this effect.

"In to-day's issue of *Morning News* we see that Mr. Sexton insinuated that the arch was attached to the house of the parish priest. All we can say in reply to this is that neither of us is a parish priest.

"(Signed) JOHN COHAIN,
"WILLIAM HUNTER;"

and, whether he still adheres to the statement which he made on the 22nd instant, or whether he proposes to modify it in any manner?

MR. TREVELYAN: The further inquiries made in this matter do not necessitate any material alteration in what I said on a former occasion. Before the original Report was submitted to me, the Head Constable of the district had made personal inquiries at the houses of both John Cobain and William Hunter, and had learned from the wife of the former that no permission had been asked to erect the arch; and from the latter, that, when asked, he had refused permission for its erection. It is now alleged that it was his wife who had refused the permission. With regard to the suggestion that the house of the parish priest was not concerned in the matter, the facts are that the arch was attached on one side to a pipe which runs down between the houses of the parish priest and John Cobain, and was stretched across the street at an angle in front of the priest's windows, being fastened on the opposite side to a pipe on Hunter's house. I was correctly informed that a disturbance occurred in connection with an arch erected in this place on a former occasion. The circumstance took place in 1878, and a repetition of it on this occasion was apprehended.

MR. SEXTON asked whether the arch was not within two feet of the parish priest's window?

MR. TREVELYAN said, he thought that extremely probable.

POOR LAW (IRELAND)—ELECTION OF GUARDIANS—INQUIRY AT COOTEHILL, CO. TYRONE.

MR. HEALY asked the Chief Secretary to the Lord Lieutenant of Ireland, Is it the fact that, at the Cootehill inquiry, it transpired that Vaughan Montgomery, Esq. J.P., Crilly, Aughnacluy, county Tyrone, lodged a claim to vote as lessor of Patrick McCabe, Mountain Lodge, on a valuation of £19 10*s*., and that, by the sworn evidence of Mr. P. McCabe, his lease, and rent receipts, it was proved that Mr. Montgomery had no interest, directly or indirectly, in this holding; and, will he ask this magistrate for an explanation of the filing of this claim?

MR. TREVELYAN: I have already more than once answered the Question as it stands on the Paper; but I presume that what the hon. Member desires to know is what view is taken of Mr. Montgomery's explanation. The Attorney General advised me yesterday that it is not satisfactory, and that he would give such directions as he may think proper for the enforcement of the law. I have, however, this day received, through the hon. Member for the County of Tyrone, a further statement from Mr. Montgomery on the subject, which I shall forward at once to the Attorney General. Whether or not it will modify his view of the case I cannot at present undertake to say.

MR. HEALY: In addition to that, will the facts be laid before the Lord Chancellor?

MR. TREVELYAN: I think the best way to ascertain the facts is to try them in a Court of Law.

WAYS AND MEANS—INLAND REVENUE DEPARTMENT — LIGHT SOVEREIGNS AND HALF-SOVEREIGNS.

SIR EARDLEY WILMOT asked the Secretary to the Treasury, If, for the convenience of the public, he will direct written notices to be affixed in various parts of the Inland Revenue Department at Somerset House, informing persons who come there to make payments in gold, that they will be mulcted for any deficiency of weight in the sovereign and half-sovereign?

MR. COURTNEY: I am told that a printed notice to the effect suggested by the hon. Baronet is already affixed to every desk in Somerset House at which money is received.

SIR EARDLEY WILMOT: Was it done yesterday?

MR. COURTNEY: No; they have been there some time.

PUBLIC HEALTH—VACCINATION—THE DEWSBURY GUARDIANS.

MR. HOPWOOD asked the President of the Local Government Board, Whether the stipulation proposed by the Dewsbury Guardians on the appointment of a public vaccinator, that he should "guarantee children from any injury from vaccination, and accept the responsibility of any injuries that might arise from his vaccination of any person," will be sanctioned by the Department?

MR. GEORGE RUSSELL: As regards the function of a public vaccinator, he is bound to obey rules which are sufficient to prevent any but a very minute risk of injury to any vaccinated person; and the Local Government Board consider that such an official ought not to be called on for more than a due observance of those rules.

MR. HOPWOOD: I understand, then, that the public vaccinator cannot guarantee children from any injury, and cannot accept responsibility for injuries.

[No reply.]

INDUSTRIAL SCHOOLS (IRELAND)—TIPPERARY GRAND JURY, SOUTH RIDING.

COLONEL COLTHURST asked the Chief Secretary to the Lord Lieutenant of Ireland, Whether he is aware that the Tipperary Grand Jury, South Riding, have persistently declined to contribute towards the support of children from that county in industrial schools?

MR. TREVELYAN: The Inspector of Reformatory and Industrial Schools informs me that the Grand Jury of the South Riding of Tipperary have never, so far as he is aware, contributed to industrial schools. It has been recommended by the Royal Commission that such contributions from local rates should be made compulsory; but this would, of course, require legislation.

LITERATURE, SCIENCE, AND ART—THE ROYAL ACADEMY.

SIR ROBERT PEEL asked the First Commissioner of Works, Whether it is a fact that the annual value of the premises occupied by the Royal Academy, at the public expense, at Burlington House, may be estimated at £7,000 a-year, or what is the estimated annual value of the said premises?

MR. SHAW LEFEVRE, in reply, said, that the value of the land and buildings handed over to the Royal Academy in 1866 was £84,000. They were transferred for a term of 999 years at a nominal rent. Since then the Academy had made large additions to the buildings, by adding a storey and a gallery, at their own cost.

ARMY—MILITARY PENSIONERS—COMPETITION FOR THE CIVIL SERVICE.

MR. GREER asked the Secretary of State for War, Whether it is a fact that Military pensioners are not permitted to compete with civilians for an appointment in connection with the War Office Department; and, if so, whether he will consider the advisability of altering the Warrant, so as to enable pensioners to compete for such appointments?

THE MARQUESS OF HARTINGTON: Not only are pensioners not excluded from competition for offices in the Civil Service, but they are protected from exclusion under the limits of age by being allowed to deduct from their actual age at the time of competition the period they have passed in the Military Service.

STRAITS SETTLEMENTS—THE RAJAH OF TENOM—CREW OF THE "NISERO."

MR. STOREY asked the Under Secretary of State for Foreign Affairs, Whether the Dutch Government continues to make it one of the conditions of its joint action, that the Rajah shall give in his submission to Holland as his lawful suzerain, thereby using the affair of the *Nisero* as a lever for securing what it has vainly sought for years to gain by force of arms; and, whether it is the case that the Government are prepared to embark in joint Military action with the Dutch, in face of the view of the Governor of Singapore that only a compromise between the Dutch and Acheenese can save the loss of the crew of the *Nisero*, and without obtaining the opinion of our competent officers on the spot as to the wisdom and sufficiency of the contemplated action?

LORD EDMOND FITZMAURICE: The Rajah some years ago signed a formal submission to the Netherlands Authorities; and, as may be seen from Mr. Maxwell's Report (page 8, Netherlands, No. 1), the Netherlands Government have now made it one of the conditions of their re-opening the ports to trade, and thereby putting an end to the state of things which has been the cause of the seizure of the crew of the *Nisero*, that the Rajah should cease from his rebellion. The blockade, as I have already explained, was a belligerent measure adopted by the Dutch; and unless Her Majesty's Government were prepared either to have had recourse to naval action so as to put an end to it, and thereby enforce their own views, or to have violated Dutch territory by sending an armed expedition into the interior without the consent of the Netherlands Government, no other course was open to them but that now adopted, which is the most likely to succeed—namely, to act in concert with the Netherlands Government on terms mutually agreed upon. The projected action is taken on the full responsibility of the Home Authorities. The projected arrangement is in the character of a compromise, as the Dutch undertake, in the event of the surrender of the crew and the submission of the Rajah, to open the ports, and keep them open, and also to pay the Rajah a sum of money. I trust that, all the principal points for which the Rajah has been contending having now been practically conceded to him, the prisoners will be released, and Her Majesty's Government will be spared the necessity of having recourse to the only alternative which will then be left to them—namely, a joint armed expedition to effect their release by force, and punish the Rajah.

ABYSSINIA—CONCESSION UNDER THE TREATY OF ADOWA.

BARON HENRY DE WORMS asked the Under Secretary of State for Foreign Affairs, Whether, by Articles II. and III. of the Treaty of Adowa of 3rd June 1884, concluded between Admiral Hewett, on behalf of Great Britain and Egypt, and King Johannis of Abyssinia, Kassala, Amedib, and Sanhit are, after the 1st of September of this year, to be ceded to King Johannis; whether Kassala, Amedib, and Sanhit did not become the property of Turkey after their conquest by Mehemet Ali and the subsequent Treaty of 1840; and, whether the Porte was consulted by Her Majesty's Government prior to the conclusion of the present Treaty, and consented to relinquish its rights over the above-named places in favour of King Johannis?

SIR WILFRID LAWSON asked the Under Secretary of State for Foreign Affairs, Whether Article III. of the Abyssinian Treaty, by which the King of Abyssinia engages to facilitate the withdrawal of the Khedive's troops from the Soudan, means that he is to allow these troops to pass through his territory, or whether it contemplates his sending an army into the Soudan?

LORD EDMOND FITZMAURICE: Neither Kassala nor Amedib has been ceded under the Treaty. On and after the 1st of September the disputed territory called the Bogos country, in which Sanhit is situated, is to be restored to Abyssinia. The respective claims of Egypt and Abyssinia to the Bogos country have been a matter of dispute between Egypt and Abyssinia for many years, and there is nothing to show that it ever formed part of the territories comprised in any of the Firmans; and it was, therefore, not necessary to consult the Porte. My hon. Friend the Member for Carlisle (Sir Wilfrid Lawson) will see by the text of the Treaty that the Third Article only contemplates facilities being afforded for the passage of the Egyptian troops through the territory of King John; but if he will refer to Abyssinia, No. 1, 1884, page 6, he will find that Sir William Hewett believes the King to intend to take possession of Kassala and Amedib upon the retirement of the Egyptian garrisons.

POST OFFICE (SCOTLAND)—POSTAL FACILITIES IN LEWIS.

MR. MACFARLANE asked the Postmaster General, If his attention has been called to the want of postal facilities in the district between Loch Erisart and Loch Shell in Lewis, where, with a population of over 1,500, there is no postal communication of any kind; and, if he will consider the possibility of opening a Post Office at some convenient point?

MR. FAWCETT: My attention has not been previously called to the postal deficiency referred to; but I will make inquiries and communicate with the hon. Member.

CHURCH OF ENGLAND—THE ENGLISH CHURCH AT VIENNA.

MR. LABOUCHERE asked the Under Secretary of State for Foreign Affairs, By what right the Foreign Office appropriated a church in Vienna, which was paid for by the British residents in that city, and whether he will see that it be handed back to its real owners; and, whether he is aware that this church is at present closed, as the Chaplain of the Embassy has left Vienna on a holiday without making any provision for the services of the church to be conducted during his absence?

LORD EDMOND FITZMAURICE: The Foreign Office has not appropriated a British church at Vienna. The funds for building the church referred to were raised by public subscription. The property is not vested in er Majesty's Government, but in the Bishop of London and his successors, with the consent of the British residents at Vienna who were subscribers to the church fund. The building was placed under the control and jurisdiction of the British Ambassador in 1875, in order to remove difficulties caused by the fact that the Church of England form of worship not being one of those recognized by Austrian law the services would have been illegal. It is presumed that the Chaplain, if he is absent, has proceeded on leave of absence; but Her Majesty's Ambassador at Vienna has not reported his departure or the closing of the church.

MR. CAUSTON: I would like to ask the noble Lord if the Chaplain referred to is the same as the Chaplain at Vienna, to whom we vote every year £300 in the Estimates?

LORD EDMOND FITZMAURICE: That is quite correct. That Chaplain has an annual holiday, and he is taking that holiday now.

FOREIGN OFFICE—FRONTIER REGULATIONS ON THE CONTINENT.

MR. LABOUCHERE asked the Under Secretary of State for Foreign Affairs, Whether, for the benefit of those travelling or about to travel on the Continent, he will direct Her Majesty's Diplomatic and Consular Agents abroad to keep the Foreign Office informed of all regulations affecting passengers, which are temporarily ordered by Foreign Governments at the Frontiers of their respective States, and make public the same through the medium of the Press?

LORD EDMOND FITZMAURICE: The regulations referred to by the hon. Member are supplied regularly by Her Majesty's Diplomatic and Consular Agents abroad, and are at once published by the Board of Trade in *The London Gazette*.

LAW AND POLICE (IRELAND)—THE ARREST OF MR. CHANCE.

MR. HEALY asked the Chief Secretary to the Lord Lieutenant of Ireland, What course he intends to take with the policeman who arrested Mr. Chance, solicitor?

MR. TREVELYAN: The Commissioner of Police reports as follows:—

"Owing to threats by letter and otherwise Alice Carroll has been under police protection since the Phœnix Park trials. Yesterday, between 2 and 3 o'clock, Constable 79 D saw two men, strangers to him, go into the house of Alice Carroll. The girl's father said they were strangers, and remarked to the constable that they might not be after any good. Mrs. Carroll then came out of the house, and told the constable he need not be uneasy as the two men inside were police-constables of the F Division, and they were joking Alice about Constable Fanners, of that division, who had formerly been a sweetheart of hers. The constable remained outside the door, and in a few minutes Mrs. Carroll again came out and appeared frightened, saying that the two men were questioning Alice in the room alone with them, and that the questions were about Mr. Bolton. Mrs. Carroll then called Alice to come out of the room, and on her coming out Alice spoke to the constable. She said she was afraid the two men were not up to any good, that at first they had told her they were sent by Mr. Mallon to make inquiries, but that they now denied it; also that they had been asking her about Mr. Bolton, and that she knew nothing about Mr. Bolton. Jane Carroll, sister to Alice, then also came out, and said the men were not there with any good intention. 149 D came up, and he accompanied 79 D into the house. On going into the room in which the two men were, the man who was afterwards identified as Mr. Chance said, 'What do you want?' The constable replied that he wanted to know his (Chance's) business there, as the family were afraid of him. Mr. Chance said they need not be afraid, as he was making inquiries. The constable asked his name, and Chance gave his name as well as that of Meiklejohn. The constable said they must come to the station-house until inquiries would be made as to their identity. Mr. Chance replied he could not go unless he was arrested. The constable said he must bring him to the station, and did so. On coming to Mountjoy Station Mr. Chance gave his name, and being recognized by a sergeant was at once released. Mr. Chance asked to have a charge preferred against him, but the constable replied that as the name and address given were correct he had no charge against him. On coming into the Carroll's house Mr. Chance and Meiklejohn distinctly stated that they got the address from Mallon, and that he had sent them; but afterwards, on Alice Carroll's saying she would go and see Mr. Mallon herself, Mr. Chance told her not to imagine that they had come from Mr. Mallon, that their names were Chance and Meiklejohn, and that they were making inquiries about Mr. Bolton. They did not get the length of asking many questions about Mr. Bolton before the constables came in. The entire circumstances under which this inquiry was attempted to be carried out by Mr. Chance were so extraordinary, and so unusual in a professional way, that it was not very surprising to find the suspicions of the constable aroused."

MR. HEALY: Is this your own?

MR. TREVELYAN: No; it is all part of the Report. [Resumes reading.]

"I think the constable's action was justifiable under all the circumstances."

This Report is signed by Mr. Harrel, Chief Commissioner of Police.

Mr. HEALY: My Question was not addressed to Mr. Harrel, but to the right hon. Gentleman himself. I wished to know from the right hon. Gentleman what course he himself intends to take?

Mr. TREVELYAN: In the case of a person who is under police protection, and who, with her family, are in great danger of annoyance and intimidation, I must say that, when two persons go in and represent themselves—I am now making the case given by the police—when two men represent themselves as detectives and sent by the head of the Detective Force, and then afterwards allow that they were not sent, I think a person in that position has a perfect right to appeal for protection to the police, and I think the police should afford that protection. [*Ministerial cheers.*]

Mr. HEALY: As the right hon. Gentleman has secured the applause of the House by that statement, I would ask him whether it does not rest solely upon the testimony of two policemen incriminated in this matter? I would ask him whether any application has been made to Mr. Chance and Mr. Meiklejohn for their version; and whether he is now content to leave the matter of this arrest of two persons carrying out an investigation against a Government official simply upon the statement of two policemen who have committed the crime of false imprisonment?

Mr. TREVELYAN: As I stated before, what passed in Mrs. Carroll's house is not in question. The question is what the Carrolls told the policemen which induced the policemen to go in for the purpose of taking measures to protect them.

Mr. HEALY: If I am to understand from the Government that they will take no steps whatever—[*Cries of* "Order!"]—I am quite in Order in this matter—I will call attention to the subject on the Vote for the Dublin Metropolitan Police.

Mr. GRAY: Have any policemen in Ireland a right to take into custody any individual, and then refuse to enter a charge against him? [*Cries of* "Answer!"] Did the right hon. Gentleman give any authority to policemen to take any person into custody, and then to refuse to enter a charge against him?

Mr. TREVELYAN: That is a Question of which I would prefer Notice. If there are suspicious circumstances against a man who is stated to have given a false name to a person who demands protection, and he is arrested, when he gives his true name he should be released.

Mr. HEALY: Will the right hon. Gentleman read the Report again, and say where—["Oh, oh!"]—well, the right hon. Gentleman has insinuated that Mr. Chance gave a false name. According to the statement read by the right hon. Gentleman, Mr. Chance, when asked his name, gave it on two occasions. I wish to ask is that the fact?

Mr. TREVELYAN: Mr. Chance gave his name.

Mr. HEALY: Then, what is the insinuation about a false name? [*Cries of* "Order!"]

Mr. TREVELYAN: Perhaps the hon. Gentleman will treat me with the courtesy I always show him. I made no insinuation about a false name; but the statement certainly of Alice Carroll and her sister, which was conveyed to the policeman, was that these men had stated they were detectives sent by Mr. Mallon. "False name" would not be a correct expression to use; but they began by saying they were detectives sent by Mr. Mallon. Afterwards they gave their real names. When they had given different accounts of themselves it was only natural the police should arrest them.

IRISH LAND COMMISSION (SUB-COMMISSIONERS)—GLEBE LANDS OF DRUMCREE, CO. ARMAGH.

Colonel KING-HARMAN asked the Chief Secretary to the Lord Lieutenant of Ireland, Whether it is the fact that the Land Commissioners have, in the case of the Glebe Lands of Drumcree, county Armagh, reduced, by 18 per cent., rents proved to have been unchanged since 1827, and, subject to which, tenants were proved to have, even so lately as 1880, given 12 10*s.* per acre for the tenant-right; whether said lands were purchased from the Church Commissioners by the present owner, Mr. Law; whether the rental furnished by them showed the old rents; and whether the valuation made by the Commissioners' valuator, Mr. M. O'Brien, to give the tenants the benefit of the clause in the Church Act in their favour, placed nearly twenty-four years' purchase on said rents, and thus represented them as moderate rents; and, whether the Government are prepared, out of the Irish Church surplus, which got the benefit of the price produced by the Commissioners' representations, to refund Mr. Law the proportion of the purchase-money so obtained from him by such representations?

MR. TREVELYAN: This Question is on the Paper without Notice, and it cannot be answered without reference to the Sub-Commission sitting in the county of Armagh.

CONTAGIOUS DISEASES (ANIMALS) ACTS—CATTLE IMPORTATION FROM IRELAND.

COLONEL KING-HARMAN: I beg to ask the Chancellor of the Duchy of Lancaster, Whether it is true that, at the reception of a deputation which waited upon the President of the Council and himself on Friday, and which was composed of gentlemen interested in the importation of cattle from Wyoming, it was stated by Lord Wenlock that the English graziers ran constant risk by the importation of diseased cattle from Ireland; whether this statement was allowed to pass without contradiction; whether he was aware of a Parliamentary Return recently issued, in which it is shown that in 1879 only 64 cases of foot-and-mouth disease existed in Ireland; that in 1880, 1881, and 1882 the country was free from disease, and that in 1883 the number of cases amounted to 114,502; and, whether, having regard to the fact that for three years Ireland has had clean bill of health, and that in 1883 it was well known that foot and mouth disease were introduced into the island by a bull imported from England, and bearing in mind that that outbreak was speedily stamped out, and that there has not been for some months a case of foot and mouth disease in Ireland, he will take steps to remove the impression that English farmers have reason to fear the importation of Irish cattle, which his silence with regard to Lord Wenlock's statement might foster?

MR. ARTHUR ARNOLD: I rise, Sir, to a point of Order. The hon. and gallant Member states in his Question that the deputation which waited upon the President of the Council and the Chancellor of the Duchy of Lancaster, on Friday, was composed of gentlemen interested in the importation of cattle from Wyoming. Now, that deputation, as I have reason to know, consisted mainly of Members of this House. I wish, therefore, to ask you, Sir, whether the hon. and gallant Member is not called upon to take steps in order to remove an erroneous impression?

MR. SPEAKER: I understand the hon. Gentleman to object to the recital in the Question on the ground that it seems to imply that the deputation had a direct interest in the matter?

MR. ARTHUR ARNOLD: Yes.

MR. SPEAKER: I have no doubt that the hon. and gallant Member will amend the recital in that respect.

COLONEL KING-HARMAN: I have no wish to convey an impression that the deputation had any direct personal interest in the matter.

MR. DODSON: I do not know the precise words used by Lord Wenlock; but the question under discussion was the risk of the introduction of pleuro-pneumonia into this country if cattle were admitted from Wyoming. It is, of course, possible that in referring to the risk of importation of disease from Ireland, the noble Lord may have had foot-and-mouth disease in his mind as well as pleuro-pneumonia. It is obvious that the risk of the introduction of disease from one part of the United Kingdom to another is greater than from a foreign country, because animals from abroad are inspected at the port of landing, and if one be found diseased the whole cargo is slaughtered. I believe that Ireland was free from foot-and-mouth disease in 1880, 1881, and 1882, and that in 1883 it unfortunately prevailed to a considerable extent, as mentioned in the Question. Ireland was officially declared free from it in April last, and since the end of that month no case of it was brought to our knowledge till a few days before the deputation. I regret to say that on the 18th instant, an outbreak took place in the county of Meath, two animals being affected out of a herd of 11. The whole number were, however, slaughtered by order of the Local Authority, and I hope that no further cases will occur.

EGYPT—THE ARMY OF OCCUPATION (REINFORCEMENTS).

MR. ASHMEAD-BARTLETT asked the Secretary of State for War, Whether a second regiment has been despatched to Assouan; and, whether fresh troops have been ordered to Egypt?

THE MARQUESS OF HARTINGTON: I have not been informed by General Stephenson that another battalion has been despatched to Assouan. No other troops have been ordered to Egypt since I gave an answer on the 17th of the month.

MR. ASHMEAD-BARTLETT inquired whether the noble Marquess was aware that half a battalion had been ordered from Cyprus to Egypt within the last 10 days, and whether the 56th Regiment was under orders to proceed from Cairo to Assouan to-morrow?

THE MARQUESS OF HARTINGTON: I am aware that there is a transfer of troops from Cyprus to Egyptian and other stations, but I cannot give details. It is not an absolute increase of the Force in Egypt. As I stated, I have not been informed by the General Officer Commanding in Egypt whether he has ordered another battalion to Assouan.

EGYPT—(EVENTS IN THE SOUDAN)—GENERAL GORDON.

MR. ASHMEAD-BARTLETT asked the Under Secretary of State for Foreign Affairs, Whether General Gordon, in the message alleged to have been received through the Mudir of Dongola, stated that he would on no account desert those whom he went out to rescue?

LORD EDMOND FITZMAURICE: The message, as far as Mr. Egerton has communicated it, contains no statement of the kind.

MR. ARTHUR O'CONNOR asked whether Her Majesty's Government had considered the advisability of sending out a General Officer of superior rank to General Gordon to bring him home?

[No reply.]

NAVY—DOCKYARD FACTORY DEPARTMENT—COMPULSORY RETIREMENT.

MR. PULESTON asked the Secretary to the Admiralty, Whether he has now considered the Petition of the hired men of the Factory Department, praying for extension of time for compulsory retirement?

SIR THOMAS BRASSEY: The present rule is that all classes of workmen in the Dockyards should be retired at the age of 60. This rule is only relaxed in exceptional cases. It has not yet been decided whether any further relaxation of the rule is desirable.

INDUSTRIAL SCHOOLS (IRELAND)—NUMBER OF CHILDREN CHARGEABLE TO CORPORATION OF CORK.

MR. DEASY asked the Chief Secretary to the Lord Lieutenant of Ireland, If he can state how many children, male and female, distinguishing Catholics from Protestants, in industrial schools in Ireland, are partially chargeable to the Corporation of Cork; and, whether he is prepared to alter the certificate of the Greenmount School, so as to enable the managers to accommodate 50 additional boys?

MR. TREVELYAN: Sir John Lentaigne informs me that, according to the latest Returns, dated June 30, there were on that date 444 children in industrial schools who had been committed from Cork Police Court. Of these, 132 boys and 200 girls were Roman Catholics, and 67 boys and 45 girls were Protestants. The Government cannot hold out any hope at present of enlarging the certificates of industrial schools.

POST OFFICE—THE TELEPHONE.

MR. GRAY asked the First Lord of Treasury, Whether he is aware that the late Government, by Clause 3 of the Telegraph Bill, 1878, as brought from the Lords, sought to obtain control over the telephone by an extended definition of the word telegraph, within the meaning of the original Telegraph Act; whether he is aware that the Journals of this House show that, on the 12th of August, the Commons "disagreed to the said Clause;" whether the Government have, ever since, invited the House to reverse or reconsider that expression of opinion; whether he is aware that, although the House had thus refused to give to the Post Office control over the telephones, the Department obtained a legal decision on a technical point, to the effect that a telephonic message was a telegraphic message within the meaning of the Act of 1869, although at the time the Act was passed the telephone was not in existence; and, whether he is aware that since that date the Post Office has levied a tax upon the use of the telephone, and has imposed constantly increasing restrictions, eventually amounting to practical prohibition of its use for exchange purposes?

MR. GLADSTONE: This Question refers more to a Treasury matter, and would be more correctly addressed to my right hon. Friend the Chancellor of the Exchequer. I have made inquiry on the subject, and I find that it is true that a certain clause in the Telegraph Bill of the late Government was disagreed to by the House of Commons. Objection has been taken to the sufficiency of the present law. The hon. Gentleman asks me whether a legal decision was not obtained by the Department on a technical point? According to the advice which the Government have received, the judgment was by no means on a technical point, but upon a substantial matter, and it was to the effect that the Crown was in possession of a certain right by the existing law. That being so, it was the absolute duty of the Department to assert that right. But with regard to the last paragraph of the Question, whether—

"Since that date the Post Office has levied a tax upon the use of the telephone, and has imposed constantly increasing restrictions, eventually amounting to practical prohibition of its use for exchange purposes?"

I am not prepared to say what the proper decision to arrive at may be; but the Postmaster General is seriously engaged in considering whether he can, in justice to the Crown and the country, introduce relaxations into the rules now in force.

THE SUEZ CANAL.

SIR ROBERT PEEL asked the First Lord of the Treasury, What results have been arrived at in the matter of the Suez Canal negotiations, with the view of providing the requisite increased accommodation for British trade to the East through the Isthmus of Suez; and, whether the widespread dissatisfaction at the overcharges and general mismanagement, expressed last year at a meeting representing upwards of three million tons of British shipping, against M. De Lesseps and his agents, and brought under the notice of the Government, has induced the Government to take any steps in furtherance of the interests of British trade and commerce in respect of the waterway of the Canal?

MR. GLADSTONE: I am under the impression, from seeing this Question, that my right hon. Friend is not aware of what has taken place in this House upon the subject. This Question repeats, in the main, the substance of a Question put to me on the 23rd of June by the hon. Member for Bedford (Mr. Magniac), and then answered. But, briefly stated, the answer is this. In pursuance of the Articles of Agreement entered into between M. de Lesseps and the representatives of the shipowners, a Commission was appointed, consisting of engineers, naval men, and shipowners, to examine and report on the best method to be adopted to carry out the objects in view. That Commission appointed a Sub Commission which was to visit—and, I believe, has visited—the Isthmus, and it will prepare a Report on the subject for the consideration of the Commissioners. With respect to the latter part of the Question, the Agreement between the Suez Canal Company and the shipowners provides for a large reduction of the dues levied in the Canal, besides securing ultimate advantages of great importance to the interests of British trade and shipping.

THE ROYAL IRISH CONSTABULARY (NUMBERS).

MR. PARNELL asked the Chief Secretary to the Lord Lieutenant of Ireland, If he will state to the House what is the number of officers and men in the Constabulary Force in Ireland permitted to be wholly chargeable to the Consolidated Fund, under the Acts regulating the same; what is the number of officers and men wholly paid for out of moneys to be provided by Parliament for the year ending the 31st March 1885; what is the number of extra officers and men, the moiety of whose cost is charged upon the ratepayers for the same year; and, the number of additional officers and men whose cost, or a portion thereof, is charged upon the ratepayers for the same year, under the provisions of the Crimes Act?

MR. TREVELYAN: The total number in the Constabulary Force in Ireland which may be charged to Votes of Parliament, if the Lord Lieutenant so fixes, in the quinquennial redistribution, is 280 officers, 350 head constables, and 10,006 sergeants and constables. This maximum limit, it is to be observed, is permissive, and not a right. The total number of officers and men wholly paid for out of moneys to be provided by Parliament in the current financial year, is 269 officers, 268 head constables, and 9,469 men, exclusive of Revenue force and reserve, and these, I suppose, are some 500 men. The extra force, the moiety of which will be charged for portion of the year, is under Section 12 of the Act 6 & 7 *Will.* IV., under Section 13, 2,383, under Section 12, 561. There is also an extra force in Belfast and Derry of 365. The number charged under the Crimes Act is 195. The numbers under Section 13 of the Act of 6 *Will.* IV. and under the Crimes Act, have been greatly reduced since this estimate was framed. They now stand at about 1,870 and 30 respectively.

LITERATURE, SCIENCE, AND ART—THE ROYAL ACADEMY.

SIR ROBERT PEEL asked the First Lord of the Treasury, with reference to his recent statement that he was awaiting a communication from the Royal Academy, Whether he is now in a position to state when the promised Returns will be laid upon the Table? He should like to say in explanation that, although this Question had been repeatedly on the Paper, it really appeared that the Academy were shirking from giving the information which he had asked for in continuation of the Returns which had been already laid on the Table.

MR. GLADSTONE: I am bound to say that, in my opinion, the view which my right hon. Friend has expressed is wholly without foundation. The Academy is, to a certain extent, and, I think, justly, jealous of that degree of independence which has been established for it by its history and its relations with the Crown; and I do not believe that the House of Commons has the slightest inclination to interfere with that qualified independence, or to substitute a different description of relations, or to place a great Institution, which stands now apart, under Parliament, as if it were an ordinary Department. With regard to the communication which I am waiting from the Royal Academy, the matter stands thus. I believe it would have been possible to have secured the completion of the communication in time to be laid before Parliament during the present Session if the current year had been excluded from the Return; but the President communicated to me that he thought it would be very unsatisfactory to Parliament to have this year excluded, and, consequently, it will not be possible to make the statement complete during the present Session. Therefore, it cannot be laid on the Table before the Prorogation. The communication when made will contain all the particulars which have been given in any former Return or communication.

PARLIAMENT—THE HOUSE OF LORDS AND THE REPRESENTATION OF THE PEOPLE BILL.

MR. LABOUCHERE asked the First Lord of the Treasury, Whether, in view of the frequent statements throughout the Country of the Conservative Leaders, that the House of Lords has not thrown out the Franchise Bill, the Government will again move the Second Reading of the Bill in the Upper House, and give to their Lordships another opportunity to vote on that measure before the end of the Session?

MR. GLADSTONE: I believe that my hon. Friend is correct in his reference to statements to the effect that the Franchise Bill has not been thrown out by the House of Lords, although I find that in a speech ascribed to Lord Salisbury—I rather think in the papers of to-day—there is the following passage:—

> "The House of Lords has a right to say, 'We do not approve of the measure which you bring forward. If you like to accept its rejection, well and good; if you object to its rejection, your remedy is to go to the people.'"

That I take to imply that the Bill has been rejected. However, I am under the impression that the Bill has not been strictly rejected as regards the Forms of the House of Lords; but it has been laid on the shelf by two Motions—one made after the other, and carried by not inconsiderable majorities, although the second majority was somewhat less than the first. I have communicated with the Leader of the House of Lords, and I find that the Representatives of the Government in that House have no intention of making any further Motion on the Bill as at present advised; and their reason is, that without insuring any important public advantage, it would give trouble to the House of Lords, which ought not to have any trouble of that kind put upon it, and would only result in the production of some third bye-Motion. If we could have some direct issue taken on the Bill itself, I think that would be very desirable; but I do not think it would be in our power to procure it.

LUNACY LAWS—"WELDON *v.* SEMPLE."

MR. MOLLOY asked the First Lord of the Treasury, If his attention has been drawn to the case of Weldon v. Semple, the evidence given in the case in connection with the granting of certificates, and the summing up of the learned Judge; if he will undertake, as a Government measure, to introduce a Bill for the alteration of the Lunacy Laws in respect to the granting of certificates of insanity, and for the abolition of private lunatic asylums; and, whether the Government propose to take any action in the matter of Weldon v. Semple?

MR. GLADSTONE: This is a matter with respect to which interesting evidence has been given to the country; but the Government has no special information with reference to it, and the hon. Member will not be surprised when I say that I am not able to make any communication upon the subject to the House. At the same time, I quite recognize that it is a subject of very great delicacy and importance, and due attention will be given to it.

MR. MOLLOY asked whether he was to understand that the right hon. Gentleman required more time in which to consider the case?

MR. GLADSTONE: The matter is not one for my especial consideration. It is a matter of great delicacy and importance, and, perhaps, no more difficult subject can be proposed in connection with law. Therefore, I need not make any apology to the House for not making a detailed statement. What I say is that attention will be given to the subject.

EGYPT—THE CONFERENCE.

SIR STAFFORD NORTHCOTE: With reference to the statement made by the Prime Minister yesterday, in regard to the proceedings of the Conference, I wish to ask whether the members of that Conference have received the answers to the communications which the right hon. Gentleman said that they would have to make to their respective Governments, and we should like to know what is the general position of the Conference?

MR. GLADSTONE: The Conference met to-day, in pursuance of the arrangement of yesterday; but the answers to which I referred had not been received.

SIR STAFFORD NORTHCOTE: Not any of them?

MR. GLADSTONE: I understand that none have been received. At the request of the Members of the Conference, Lord Granville agreed to postpone the next meeting until Thursday instead of until to-morrow; but I have no reason to withdraw the statement I made, that I believe the Members of the Conference are exceedingly anxious to bring it to a prompt conclusion.

PARLIAMENT—BUSINESS OF THE HOUSE—PROGRESS OF PUBLIC BUSINESS.

LORD RANDOLPH CHURCHILL: Will the right hon. Gentleman state when the Diplomatic Vote will be taken, and whether it will be taken first in the evening?

MR. GLADSTONE: Business is not sufficiently advanced to allow me to make a statement on that point.

MAGISTRATES (IRELAND) SALARIES BILL.

MR. PARNELL asked at what hour the Government proposed to take the Magistrates (Ireland) Salaries Bill?

THE CHANCELLOR OF THE EXCHEQUER (Mr. CHILDERS) said, that he was not present during the discussion which had taken place last night; but he had been made aware of what had passed on a former occasion earlier in the year. The question arose on the Supplementary Estimates in respect to the salaries of certain magistrates in Ireland. On that occasion the matter was discussed until a very early hour on Sunday morning. The strong impression then seemed to be that the increased salaries should be fixed by Statute, and not made from year to year greater than the present Statute named by Vote in Supply, and in a Bill brought in early that Session a clause to that effect was introduced. That Bill had been, with a number of other important measures, dropped; but another Bill of a single clause effecting this had been introduced and discussed on the previous night. Considering the number of hours which the Bill was under discussion, they did not propose, so far as the present Session was concerned, to advance it further; but the increased salaries would be discussed in a Supply Vote that night.

MR. PARNELL: In reference to the statement of the Chancellor of the Exchequer last night as to the position of the Irish Members regarding these salaries, I beg to say that their opinion remains the same, and that they entirely object to have these salaries increased.

THE CHANCELLOR OF THE EXCHEQUER (Mr. CHILDERS): I was not in the House last night; but I heard from others that they were not unwilling that the discussion on these Votes should take place in Supply.

MR. GIBSON: I would ask the right hon. Gentleman whether, having brought in this Bill, in deference to the wishes of the hon. Member for the City of Cork (Mr. Parnell), and having now dropped it under a misconception, in apparent deference to the wishes of the hon. Member for the City of Cork, he would state what the Government propose to do?

THE CHANCELLOR OF THE EXCHEQUER (Mr. CHILDERS): I entirely dispute the premises of the right hon. and learned Gentleman. As to the future, we propose to take these increases in Supply.

MR. GIBSON: Is that a conclusion without a premise?

THE CHANCELLOR OF THE EXCHEQUER (Mr. CHILDERS): That is the correct conclusion.

SIR JOSEPH M'KENNA: Have the Government determined who are the fortunate individuals who are to receive this additional pay?

MR. TREVELYAN: The gentlemen who will receive it are the four gentlemen at present holding the posts of Divisional Magistrates, and the fifth, if a fifth should be appointed. It is the clear intention of the Government that any Divisional Magistrate appointed from this time forward shall be an officer serving in the Police Force.

ORDERS OF THE DAY.

—o—

SUPPLY.—CIVIL SERVICE ESTIMATES.

SUPPLY—*considered* in Committee.

(In the Committee.)

CLASS III.—LAW AND JUSTICE.

MR. COURTNEY said, he proposed to make a statement to the Committee in reference to these Estimates.

The Chancellor of the Exchequer

LORD RANDOLPH CHURCHILL rose to Order. He wished to know if it was competent for the hon. Gentleman to make a statement when there was no Question before the Committee?

THE CHAIRMAN: I understood that the hon. Gentleman was about to move a Vote.

LORD RANDOLPH CHURCHILL remarked, that the hon. Gentleman had himself said that he desired to make a statement.

MR. COURTNEY said, that, in the ordinary course, the Committee would begin where they left off; but he proposed that the Votes for Law Charges and Prosecutions in Ireland, and for the Court of Bankruptcy in Ireland, which would be taken first, in the ordinary course, should be postponed. He, therefore, intended to move the third Vote in Order—namely, that to complete the sum of £18,670 for the Registry of Deeds.

Motion made, and Question proposed,

"That a sum, not exceeding £12,670, be granted to Her Majesty, to complete the sum necessary to defray the Charge which will come in course of payment during the year ending on the 31st day of March 1886, for the Salaries and Expenses of the Office for the Registration of Deeds in Ireland."

MR. HEALY wished to ask the Chairman, upon the point of Order, in what way the manner in which the Secretary to the Treasury was acting at the present moment could be challenged? But before the Chairman gave his decision, he should like to point out the important points that were involved in the course now proposed to be taken. They were promised yesterday that the Votes should be taken *seriatim*, and they had come down to the House that day with the intention of so discussing them. It was notorious that the reason why it was proposed that these two Votes should be postponed, although the Secretary to the Treasury had not said so, was because they included the salary of Mr. George Bolton. The idea in the mind of the Secretary to the Treasury, therefore, was that he would wait until the trial in Belfast, in which Mr. George Bolton was concerned, was over, and then, if the verdict was given for Bolton, he would be able to come down to the House triumphantly, and move the Vote. The contention of the Irish Members, however, was that, no matter what the verdict might be in

Belfast, Bolton ought to be dismissed from the offices he now occupied. The verdict in Belfast could have nothing to do with Bolton's position. The point to be decided at Belfast was whether this man had been libelled in having been charged with committing a certain offence; but the charge made against Bolton in the House of Commons had nothing to do with that. He was charged here with being a bankrupt, a fraudulent trustee, a gentleman who had acted dishonestly in regard to his own wife; and there were various other charges against him which need not be gone into. It was a monstrous thing, therefore, for the Secretary to the Treasury to attempt by a side-wind, in defiance of a pledge which had been given to the House, to place a crown of glory on Bolton's head, after the verdict at Belfast had been given. How long were these Votes to be postponed? Would they postpone the Bankruptcy Vote until they had an opportunity of hearing the decision of Judge Walsh upon Bolton's Petition in Bankruptcy? Judge Walsh, the Judge of the Court of Bankruptcy, had already postponed Bolton's case in that Court for 10 days, and they would arrive at the 9th of August before they could possibly get the decision of that Judge. He wished to know whether the Secretary to the Treasury intended to postpone the Bankruptcy Vote until a decision had been given in that case also; or whether these Votes were to be postponed simply in view of the trial which was to take place in Belfast that day? If he did so intend to postpone the Vote for the bankruptcy proceedings, he (Mr. Healy) must say that a more uncalled for, or a more unheard of, proceeding had never taken place in that House. What he wished to ask was—whether the postponement asked for was merely in consequence of the proceedings in Belfast, which had nothing to do with the Vote, or whether everything relating to Bolton was to be put off until after the decision of the Court of Bankruptcy; and whether the House was to be kept sitting until there was a final decision as to whether George Bolton was a bankrupt or not?

LORD RANDOLPH CHURCHILL, as a point of Order, wished to say that the Secretary to the Treasury had moved the postponement of three Votes. ["No!"] He had distinctly heard the hon. Gentleman say that he intended to move the postponement of three Votes. He wanted to know whether that could be done—whether, if the Votes were not moved in their proper order, the Votes left out were not withdrawn from the Estimates by that course of action?

THE CHAIRMAN: There is no obligation to take the Votes in the order in which they stand in the Estimates. The hon. Gentleman can propose any Vote in the Civil Service Estimates which is upon the Paper for consideration to-day. He is not obliged to proceed with the Estimates in the order in which they stand here in the Book of Estimates.

MR. JOSEPH COWEN remarked, that if the Secretary to the Treasury were not absolutely bound to take the Votes in the order in which they stood, he ought to give some explanation of the course he proposed to take. Some time ago, a Question was directly put to the hon. Gentleman as to the order in which the Estimates would be taken, and he had then stated that they would be taken in their regular order. It was distinctly within his (Mr. Cowen's) own knowledge that that answer was given, and yet now, without any explanation whatever, the hon. Gentleman asked the Committee to deviate from that arrangement. He thought the hon. Gentleman might fairly be asked if there was any reason for that course?

MR. COURTNEY said, he had not the slightest hesitation in giving his reason for postponing these Votes. He had thought that, in making the proposal, he was really consulting the wishes of hon. Members opposite, for it was only on Tuesday or Wednesday last that they had proposed the postponement of the Valuation Vote while the trial of Mr. Bolton's action was pending. On that occasion hon. Members urged the withdrawal of the Vote, or its postponement until the trial was over. As the same questions could be raised on the Votes for Criminal Prosecutions and the Court of Bankruptcy, he had thought that he would be consulting the convenience of the Irish Members by not taking those two Votes now, while the trial was proceeding. That was his simple reason for asking for a postponement. He certainly thought that the House would be in a better position to discuss those Votes on Thursday than they were then. [MR. HEALY: No.] As he had said, that was the real reason why he asked the Committee to put aside this Vote for the present. He had no interest in the matter, either one way or the other.

MR. SEXTON said, that upon the last occasion on which the Votes came on a number of Irish Votes were allowed to pass without question, on the understanding that the Estimates would be proceeded with *seriatim*. Whatever recommendation the course now proposed might have in the mind of the hon. Gentleman, it certainly amounted to a breach of faith with the Committee. If the hon. Gentleman wished to get through Supply for Ireland, without the case of Mr. George Bolton being discussed, he would have very considerably to disorganize the order of the Votes, as Mr. Bolton took a salary under most of them. The claims of George Bolton upon the Crown were comprised in various Votes. It was quite true that he took a salary under the Criminal Prosecutions Vote, and his character and antecedents would come under the purview of the Committee when the Vote for the Court of Bankruptcy was reached. Upon Votes 29 and 30 the Irish Members would also be entitled to call Bolton to account in relation to his visits to certain Irish prisons in connection with the Constabulary. Upon Votes 7 and 8, in Class III., an opportunity would also be afforded for discussing George Bolton's affairs. Therefore, there must be an extreme disorganization of the Business of Supply, if everything upon which Mr. Bolton's conduct could be discussed was to be postponed. He would only point out, further, that the present proposal involved a reversal of the Constitutional theory that Supply was the proper occasion for calling attention to grievances. He presumed that it was because grievances existed in the case of George Bolton that the facts relating to his salary and employment were not brought before the House on the last occasion the Vote for Bolton's salary was brought on. In that case, there was no previous Notice; but on this occasion, the Vote was brought on after a Notice, to a certain extent, had been given, and the Irish Members had come down for the express purpose of discussing Bolton's career. It was, therefore, highly objectionable that the Secretary to the Treasury should now suddenly seek to withdraw the Vote from the consideration of the Committee, in order that he might plunge into others, to which the Committee had no opportunity of devoting their attention.

LORD RANDOLPH CHURCHILL said, he hoped the Government would not press this course of procedure, because it was not only an abandonment of the pledge the Secretary to the Treasury had himself given to the Irish Members, but it was a total departure from the pledge given by the Prime Minister to the House at large, that the Votes would be discussed *seriatim*. Only yesterday, an attempt was made to persuade the Prime Minister to take them a little out of their turn; but the right hon. Gentleman distinctly told the House he was not able to do so, because he had promised to take them *seriatim*. All this jumping about from Vote to Vote was extremely inconvenient for those who wished to discuss a particular Vote —such, for instance, as the Diplomatic Vote—and had been calculating when it would be reached. If any hon. Member was inclined to go to a Division against the proposal of the Secretary to the Treasury, he (Lord Randolph Churchill) would certainly support him, as a protest against this alteration of the original arrangement of the Government. He could only regard the proposal as an attempt to evade a Constitutional discussion in that House, and as far as the plea went that they were not to consider certain Votes in Supply, because an action brought by a private individual was pending, was, to say the least of it, a remarkably singular one. What had the House of Commons to do with the proceedings in the Law Courts; and what had the proceedings in the Law Courts to do with the Votes in Supply in the House of Commons? The proceedings of the Committee of Supply had nothing to do with actions pending in the Law Courts, and it was altogether unconstitutional for the Secretary to the Treasury to put forward such a plea as a ground for delaying the Vote.

MR. TREVELYAN said, the point which had been raised was a very narrow one. He had come down there fully prepared to discuss the Vote for Law Charges and Criminal Prosecutions; but his hon. Friend the Secretary to the Treasury, who had been attending more recently to the debates on the matter, had led him to imagine that it would be more convenient to the Committee if this Vote were postponed. He was absolutely certain that his hon. Friend had no other motive in the course he had suggested; but he had gathered that that was the wish of the House, from the debate which took place on Wednesday last. It was pretty plain, however, from the discussion which had just taken place, that such was not the wish of the Committee, and he was anxious, therefore, with the shortest possible expenditure of time, to revert to the original order of the Estimates. He would remind the noble Lord that it was not always the Government who wished to postpone particular Estimates, or to take them out of their proper order. Hitherto, on three or four occasions, the Irish Estimates had been taken out of their proper course at the suggestion, and with the full concurrence, of the Irish Members. It was always a proceeding the Government were unwilling to resort to, and they were quite ready to withdraw the Vote, and proceed with the Vote for Law Charges.

MR. HEALY: The Government will withdraw the Vote?

MR. TREVELYAN: Yes.

Motion, by leave, *withdrawn*.

Motion made, and Question proposed,

"That a sum, not exceeding £49,031, be granted to Her Majesty, to complete the sum necessary to defray the Charge which will come in course of payment during the year ending on the 31st day of March 1885, of Criminal Prosecutions and other Law Charges in Ireland, including certain Allowances under the Act 15 & 16 Vic. c. 83."

MR. SEXTON said, it appeared to him that the Irish Members had a right, upon this Vote, to demand from the Government very full and particular explanations. He confessed that he regarded it as an Estimate of a very suspicious character, and he did not think that it was the Irish Members only who had the right, or the inclination, to demand from the Government explanations in regard to it; but every Member of the House, whether he came from Ireland or not, who had a regard for the interests of public economy and the purity of the Public Service, would be startled, if not disgusted, by the extravagant amount of the Estimate now before the Committee. The first fact upon which he desired to fasten the attention of the Committee was the extraordinary one that the amount of the Vote had, during the past year, undergone no material diminution. The amount last year was slightly over £100,000. The amount now was only £1,000 less, because the Committee were asked to vote £99,031 for this year's cost of the Law Charges and Criminal Prosecutions in Ireland. He would not quarrel with the undiminished amount of the Vote, if it could be contended, or if it could be alleged, that crime had not greatly fallen off, and that tranquillity had not greatly increased in Ireland. He would remind the right hon. Gentleman the Chief Secretary to the Lord Lieutenant that he had inaugurated his part of the Business of the Session by a remarkable speech which still lingered in the memory of most hon. Members—a speech in which the right hon. Gentleman congratulated the House and the country on the great improvement which had taken place in the state of crime in Ireland. The right hon. Gentleman had told the House, still more recently, that the diminution and falling off of crime was still going on, and that tranquillity was generally on the increase throughout the length and breadth of the country. Indeed, he had gone so far as to say that but for some isolated efforts on the part of the Orange Brotherhood in the Province of Ulster, they would have enjoyed last year a very quiet winter in Ireland. He might also refer to the great change which was visible to anyone who glanced over the criminal calendar, or who studied the speeches of the County Chairmen, and contrasted them with a similar calendar of crime and speeches a year or two ago, they would be aware that the outrages, which were then counted by the hundred, were now counted by the unit. The Returns of special outrages were for the most part blank. The Judges of Assize, instead of painting in vivid colours the growth of crime and the disorganization of society, were now vieing with each other in congratulating the Grand Juries of the various counties on the disappearance of crime. They had heard of the presentation of white gloves this year in many cities of Ireland, and they had also heard, what it would be difficult to rival either in England or Scotland, that the Judges of Assize had themselves been the recipients of white gloves. For a long time grave crimes had almost entirely disappeared, and every kind of crime was becoming rare. That being so, he called upon the Government to account for the inflated condition of this Estimate for Law Charges and Criminal Prosecutions. Crime was the material from which prosecutions largely sprung. The Government of Ireland, however, appeared to be able to make bricks without straw, and to carry on prosecutions although crime had practically ceased. That was an anomaly which he called upon the Government to explain. He found on Page 273 of the present Estimates certain items which seemed to him to go far towards explaining this extraordinary condition of affairs. The salary of the Attorney General for Ireland was £1,159 a-year; and he was entitled also, in the shape of an allowance in lieu of fees now abolished, to the sum of £1,420, making the total emoluments, in the way of salary received by the Irish Attorney General for the year, £2,579. The salary of the Solicitor General was £974, and he was entitled, by way of an allowance in lieu of fees abolished, to a further sum of £800, making the salary of the Solicitor General £1,774; and, with the £2,579 paid to the Attorney General, making the salaries of the two Law Officers £4,353 a-year. He asked the Committee to turn now to an item in the Estimates under the head of Fees to the Law Officers in the course of the year for which the Estimate was framed—fees to the Attorney General for conducting criminal prosecutions and other contentious business, and also similar fees to the Solicitor General, amounting to—what did the Committee think?—to the sum of £8,000. The salaries paid to these two Officers amounted to £4,000, and their fees for directing prosecutions to £8,000. Now, he contended that if the salaries of the Attorney General and the Solicitor General for Ireland were too small, they ought to be increased. So far as the Solicitor General was concerned, he knew him to be a most careful and painstaking Officer; and if his remuneration was insufficient, he was satisfied there would be no objection to make a reasonable increase. But he did object to the system on which these Law Officers were paid—namely, one-third by salaries, and two-thirds by fees. The Law Officers of the Crown shared the heritage which was the common lot of human nature; and it was not fair to them, nor considerate to the public, to put the bulk of their income on a system which obliged them to direct prosecutions in order that they might get fees. He would much prefer that the salaries of these Law Officers should be fixed at £8,000, because, if the learned Solicitor General, in addition to the £1,700 he received in the shape of salary, was to receive £2,000 or £3,000 more, in accordance with the number of prosecutions he directed, it was evident that a direct premium was held out in favour of prosecutions. He should be sorry to say that the hon. and learned Gentleman would direct a prosecution unless he found ample cause for doing so; but what he contended was, that they were subjecting the hon. and learned Gentleman to a temptation which he ought not to be placed under. He entirely condemned the system of fees, and he was of opinion that both the Solicitor General and the Attorney General ought to be paid for the services they performed by salary, and that the temptation and inducement ought not to be held out to them to direct prosecutions in order that they might receive the fees. Then, again, it would be seen from the Estimate that the fees of Counsel, other than the Attorney General and Solicitor General, for conducting Crown prosecutions, which amounted last year to £18,500, had amounted this year to £17,000. In the name of reason, and in the name of common sense, he asked the learned Solicitor General and the Chief Secretary to the Lord Lieutenant to make it apparent and intelligible how it was that the amount of fees to Counsel in Ireland remained practically the same as last year, in face of the notorious fact that the gaols were empty, that agrarian crime had disappeared, that crime of any kind was of rare occurrence, and that the Judges had nothing to offer to the Grand Juries but congratulations on the peace, order, and tranquillity which prevailed throughout the country. Then, again, there was this year, as there was last year, an item of Miscellaneous Charges, under which would probably be found the special expenses of persons like George Bolton, who went to the West of Ireland in order to visit a prisoner, and succeeded in driving him to a state of desperation, and then to the commission of suicide. The Miscellaneous

Charges last year were £5,679, and this year they amounted to £6,740. It was quite evident that the trade of prosecution in Ireland was a merry trade, if the salaries and amounts derived from it were so very large. There was, however, another sub-head of which he asked for an explanation from the Government. He referred to the expenses of prosecutions and witnesses previous to the 1st of April. According to the Estimate, they amounted to £26,000 last year; this year they had reached the same total of £26,000. What was the explanation of that? He was afraid it was a sad and sorry explanation. It was one of the most disgraceful and scandalous items in the Estimates, the money being spent, in reality, in maintaining a brood of social vipers—informers and spies—men who were easily engendered by unscrupulous employers with plenty of mono in their hands, and willing to spendy it lavishly; but although easily engendered, they were not so easily got rid of. When the Executive Government once took into the public pay a body of creatures, whose trade was perjury—when once they showed them that the necessity for hard work on their part was over, and that they could live for the rest of their lives in ease and plenty by merely betraying the liberties and swearing away the lives of men—they established a lucrative business that was very apt to thrive on their hands, and not likely to cease when they simply desired it. He said that this £26,000 a-year, which was a scandal and a disgrace to the Public Estimates, was being spent in the nurture and sustenance of this brood of social vipers. He was entitled to be heard; and he asserted that the time had come when, according to the Government's own figures and Returns, and the statements of their own Judges, there was nothing in the criminal or social condition of the country to justify the continuance of this charge, and that they ought to feel called upon to discontinue it, and to send these informers and spies about their business. He could not wonder at the inflation of the Estimates when he considered the fact that he had himself been compelled to complain not long ago in that House of the course which the Law Officers of the Crown were pursuing. He had found that 11 of his own constituents had been arrested on the gravest of all possible charges except that of murder. They were taken away from their business, removed from their families, and thrown into prison four months ago—men occupying a respectable position, against whose character, until the voice of the informer was listened to, nothing had been alleged; and he had found these men remanded week after week, dealt with by private inquiries only, and the evidence against them doled out by instalments. After four months' imprisonment, when the Assizes came round, the Crown, on the flimsiest of pretences, declined to put these men upon their trial. He was afraid that the country would have to go on paying these enormous sums every year unless Parliament compelled the Irish Government to refrain from arresting at random men against whom there was no evidence, and whom they kept in prison, postponing their trial from time to time, in the hope that some informer would turn up against them. By these means, and by these inflated Estimates, the purity and independence of the Bar itself were injured, if not destroyed, and the members of it were converted into *employés* of the Castle, because the gentlemen of the Irish Bar received refreshers during the prolonged course of every one of these investigations. What he called upon the Government to do was to return to the ordinary paths of the Constitution. There was nothing in the condition of Ireland to justify the Committee in agreeing to this Vote. So long as conspiracies existed and crime was committed, or so long as there was anything dangerous or threatening in the social condition of Ireland, no one would object to such expenses as these; but in the present condition of Ireland the claim to the disallowance of this expenditure was irresistible and unanswerable. He would say to the English Members, that, whatever their desire might be to economize the expenditure of public money, that expenditure would continue to go on year after year until the Government refrained from arresting men without evidence, and, having arrested them, abstained from bringing them to trial. They were holding them in prison year after year, hoping that some informer more base than another might turn up with evidence, instead of bringing every man who was arrested to trial at once, with a view to his conviction if guilty. If there was anything unreasonable in what he had stated, he desired the Government to point it out. He had made a series of plain assertions, and he held them to apply to the figures contained in the official Returns. If any of his allegations could be denied, let him have the denial. This assertion, at any rate, could not be denied, because it rested upon undeniable facts—namely, that the claim he had urged was a claim which neither in the spirit of good government, nor in the pursuance of a wise policy, ought to be questioned. He would leave it to his hon. Friends near him to consider what reduction of the Vote they would move in respect of the whole of this horrible system of prolonged examinations and telescopic trials in Ireland; but there was one subject upon which he felt bound himself to move a reduction. He had no doubt that the Government and the Chief Secretary would anticipate what he was about to say. He felt himself again obliged, by a sense of public duty, to mention the name of George Bolton; and so long as that man continued in the Public Service, and he (Mr. Sexton) remained a Member of that House, he would never suffer 1*d*. of public money to be voted for Mr. Bolton's emoluments without giving to the proposition the utmost resistance he was able to give with the assistance of his Friends. The position of George Bolton had been made a little more plain since his case had been discussed last week. There was some doubt last week whether Bolton had himself lodged a Petition before the Court of Bankruptcy in Dublin. He had now before him a copy of the Petition, and it showed beyond doubt that Bolton himself had applied to the Court of Bankru tcy for an arrangement. On the last day when the case was under discussion, it was said that if an English Civil servant of any grade had placed himself in a similar position, there was no Department in England in regard to which the House, and even the Department itself, would not have demanded his suspension. He contended that the moment George Bolton brought his affairs into the Court of Bankruptcy he ought to have been suspended. The question whether he should afterwards resume his post, or be allowed to retain it, might very well be left to await the result of the Petition; but as the first and preliminary dstep, the Crown should have suspen ed Bolton from his public offices the moment he applied to the Court of Bankruptcy to effect an arrangement between his creditors and himself. This gentleman owed, not, as had been said before, £90,000, but £100,000; and he appeared to derive from the public an income of about £2,000 a-year. He had given Notice a few days ago to the hon. and learned Solicitor General that he would ask him upon this Vote what was the amount of emolument derived by George Bolton. It was well known that he had £400 a-year as Solicitor to the Valuation and Boundary Office; that he had £400 a-year as Crown Solicitor for the County of Tipperary; and he (Mr. Sexton) would now call attention to a statement made in the Irish Court of Bankruptcy on Friday last. The learned gentleman who appeared for the executors under the will of the late Sophia Bolton—the wife of this official—asked for a return of Bolton's salaries, and pointed out that, even taking the account which had been mentioned last year, it amounted to at least £1,900 a-year. Yet this man, who was receiving from public employments £1,900 or £2,000 a-year, owed between £90,000 and £100,000; so that if he devoted the whole of his income to the payment of his creditors, he would arrive at a complete settlement of his affairs somewhere about the middle of the 20th century. And what was the offer which this gentleman made to his creditors? He had offered—hon. Members would hardly believe the audacity that was developed in the bosom of an Irish official—George Bolton had offered to allot £200 a-year to the benefit of his creditors; and when pressed by their representative, he consented to increase the sum to £300, but would not go beyond that amount. From that date there had been no advance upon £300 a-year. He held that the position taken by Mr. Bolton was scandalous and disgraceful; and he wanted to know, now the facts had been made known, whether the Government meant to tolerate his continued employment? Was it not an audacious trifling with the principles of justice for a man owing £90,000, and receiving £2,000 a-year from the public purse, to appear in Court and say that he was only willing to allow £300 for the settlement of the claims of his creditors? They had been told that it was not desirable to discuss this Vote that day, because the trial, in which George Bolton was plaintiff and Mr. O'Brien—the Member for Mallow—was defendant, was proceeding at Belfast. Now, what had happened at Belfast that day? Mr. Bolton went to Belfast to defend his character, and the Government were so anxious that he should be allowed a full opportunity to patch up his somewhat damaged character, that they were unwilling that a word should be said in the House in the discussion of his salary until the trial was determined. Mr. Bolton saw himself described from week to week and month to month in *United Ireland* as a person who was guilty of fraud and forgery, and who had introduced the arts of a swindler into his own house, and defrauded the wife who trusted him. So long as those charges were made against him he was silent; and it was only on a question of the construction of the heading of a paragraph, which he looked upon as imputing to him an unnatural offence, that Mr. Bolton went into Court to clear his character. How had he proceeded to clear his character? He (Mr. Sexton) was informed that in the Court at Belfast that day Mr. Bolton had been called upon to go into the witness-box, and that he had refused to do so. Did the Government regard that as fulfilling their hope as to the manner in which a public official should defend his character? Was that the way to meet accusations of the kind which had been levelled against Mr. Bolton? If the reports which reached him from Belfast were true, and no one could doubt them, he maintained that the case against Mr. O'Brien had already closed, and by the refusal of Mr. Bolton to go into the witness-box to offer himself for examination, and to throw open his life before the jury and the Court—by his refusal to go through that ordeal—the case against the hon. Member for Mallow (Mr. O'Brien) had gone by default, and George Bolton was already practically found guilty. He (Mr. Sexton) begged to move the reduction of the Vote by £1,600, which, so far as he was able to estimate, was that portion of the Vote which would otherwise go to George Bolton for salaries and expenses; and in making that Motion he would conclude by saying that he awaited with curiosity to learn what action was left for the Crown, in the new condition of things revealed at Belfast that day, in carrying further their obstinate and unwise defence of this disgraceful official.

Motion made, and Question proposed,

"That a sum, not exceeding £47,431, be granted to Her Majesty, to complete the sum necessary to defray the Charge which will come in course of payment during the year ending on the 31st day of March 1885, of Criminal Prosecutions and other Law Charges in Ireland, including certain Allowances under the Act 15 and 16 Vic. c. 83."—(*Mr. Sexton.*)

MR. TREVELYAN said, the hon. Member for Sligo (Mr. Sexton), in approaching this Estimate in the character of an economist, regretted that the amount had undergone no material diminution since last year. He thought the hon. Member would, indeed, have good reason to regret it if such was in any sense the case. Undoubtedly the Estimate this year was, on the face of it, very much the same as last year; but the hon. Member had omitted a most important consideration. The Estimate for 1883-4 was £100,000; the Estimate for 1884-5 was £99,000. The hon. Member, however, could not have forgotten that in the course of the many debates in which they had been engaged this year, and especially early in the Session, the Government had found it necessary to bring forward a Supplementary Estimate of something over £15,000; so that the actual Estimate for last year amounted, not to £100,000, but to £115,000; and, therefore, the reduction between this Estimate and the actual Estimate of last year amounted to £16,000. The hon. Member connected the amount of the Estimate with the state of crime in Ireland. In that respect it would be interesting to the economists of the House to watch the gradual growth, and he was glad to add the gradual reduction, of the Estimate now under consideration, and to observe how closely it followed the course, not so much of crime as the detection and punishment of crime in Ireland. In the year 1878-9 the actual expenditure on this Estimate stood at £82,000. It was noticeable that this was the amount, roughly speaking, of the actual expenditure of the Estimate for a great number of years past. There had been only one exceptional year since 1870, and that was the year 1873-4. In that case there had been a Supplementary Estimate of £22,000, which brought up the expenditure upon the Law Charges to £100,000. That was the year in which the riot cases in the Phœnix Park were tried, and the Estimate was swelled by a considerable amount of expenditure on what might be termed the public litigation which took place before the period on which he was about to enter. In 1878 the actual expenditure was £82,000. In 1879-80 the actual expenditure was £80,244; but in the last months of 1879 and in the earlier months of 1880—with increasing velocity throughout 1880—that state of crime began which they had all deplored, and the first signs of it were shown in the Estimates of 1880-1, which rose to £87,000. In 1881-2, as crime grew worse, the Estimate rose to £105,000.

Mr. SEXTON: The Estimate or the expenditure?

Mr. TREVELYAN: The expenditure. In 1881-2 the expenditure rose to £105,000. In 1882-3, which he took to have been a sort of culminating point when the state of crime was worse and its detection had begun, the Estimate rose to £118,000. In 1883-4 the actual expenditure, as shown by the bills already got in up to the present time, amounted to £110,633.

Mr. SEXTON: £10,000 over the Estimate.

Mr. TREVELYAN: £10,000 over the Estimate, and £7,000 under the combined Estimate and Supplementary Estimate together. That was to say, that while the expenditure for the detection and suppression of crime had risen gradually from £82,000 to £118,000, in 1882-3 the actual expenditure fell off by about £8,000, as far as he had been able to ascertain. Being anxious not to have a Supplementary Estimate, they had estimated the expenditure in November and December at £99,000, thus showing another steady falling off. He had every reason to hope that next year, by which time not only would crime have very much diminished from what it was at its worst, but its detection would have begun to be much less material in its operation, and, therefore, much less active, they would be able, judging from the actual expenditure of 1884-5, to make a very sensible reduction in the Estimates of 1885-6. To show how completely this was the case, and how far this expenditure was due, not to salaries, but to the actual operation of the punishment and detection of crime both present and old, he had taken out the fees to the Law Officers, the fees to counsel, the general law expenses in regard to prosecutions, and the witnesses' expenses, as items which spoke of the actual work done; and he found that in 1878-9 they amounted to £48,000; in 1880-1 to £55,000; 1881-2, £74,000; 1882-3, £83,000; 1883-4, 75,000; and the present Estimate was £69,000, which brought the expenses upon these items down to £14,000 below the actual expenditure of 1882-3. The hon. Member for Sligo (Mr. Sexton) thought this was not a sufficient reduction to represent the actual diminution of crime; but it was, nevertheless, a large reduction, and a steady reduction. Crime had fallen off, and so had the expenditure; and he was bound to say that a great part of the tranquillity which Ireland now enjoyed was due to the manner in which the crimes in the past had been dragged to light, and the manner in which they were followed up—an operation still going on, and which had certainly not yet come to an end. [Mr. Parnell: Hear, hear!] He hoped that all hon. Gentlemen would cheer that sentiment. The detection of past crime was one of the most important functions of the Government. It must be remembered, however, that they must not talk even of a diminution of crime with too much triumph. It was quite true that a beneficial change had taken place up to that moment. The outrages reported in some months of the year had fallen very much in number below what were recorded in the most peaceful years in Ireland. But the country was still, in some districts especially, in a state where justice must still keep a tight hand upon crime and disorder; and although the expenditure upon justice must be most closely watched, and reductions made, he maintained that reductions had been made in such a manner as to afford sufficient scope for the operations of justice, while, at the same time, gratifying the economists of that House. He by no means wished to boast; but he still desired to impress upon the Committee that, taking the actual Estimates of last year, and the actual Estimates of this, there was an actual reduction of about £19,000.

MR. H. H. FOWLER asked if his right hon. Friend could give the actual number of cases represented in the prosecutions last year?

MR. TREVELYAN said, he was not able to say that.

MR. MOLLOY asked if the right hon. Gentleman could give any indication within 30 or 50?

MR. TREVELYAN said, he did not know that he was even able to give that information; nor was he aware that the Returns even in the case of England gave judicial statistics in that respect. He was under the impression, so far as Ireland was concerned, that the judicial statistics were not drawn on the principle of giving a Return of that kind. The hon. Member for Sligo (Mr. Sexton) objected to the system on which the Irish Law Officers were paid. Although he admitted that their salaries were small in proportion to those of the English Law Officers, the hon. Gentleman said the salaries ought to bear a larger proportion to the expenditure which was incurred in the shape of fees. The hon. Member objected to the payment of fees as holding out an inducement to the Law Officers to promote prosecutions, although, at the same time, he added that he did not think the Solicitor General was influenced by that fact. The hon. Gentleman must remember that prosecutions were not always bad things. He (Mr. Trevelyan) had heard from the Benches on which the hon. Member sat a very warm protest against the Government abstaining from prosecutions in certain cases. Hon. Members opposite were constantly referring to cases in which they thought there ought to be prosecutions. Only that day he had informed an hon. Gentleman who sat near the hon. Member that a person who had falsified voting papers would probably be prosecuted, and that information appeared to give the hon. Gentleman some satisfaction. But he himself reminded the hon. Member for Sligo (Mr. Sexton) that, as far as the payment by fees appertained, it appertained in preventing prosecutions which ought not to be undertaken from being set on foot. An uncalled-for prosecution was disgraceful, and the injury done to the reputation of the Law Officers who set it on foot, if it could be shown that it was set on foot from any such motive, would be infinitely greater than any compensation that could be obtained from the fees. The hon. Member had referred to the imprisonment without trial of a number of persons in a district where his own political opinions had great influence.

MR. SEXTON said, that since he last spoke he had received a telegram from the Tubbercurry prisoners, who wished to have it pressed upon the House that their trial should take place on the 5th of August, and intimating their willingness to waive all right to notice—such as that which was required to be given in a change of venue.

MR. TREVELYAN said, it was unfortunate that those telegrams came during the debate, and thus acquired additional interest from so coming, because it was absolutely impossible that they could receive the attention which properly ought to be given to them. He would certainly prefer that his hon. and learned Friend the Solicitor General should consider the bearing of this request, as he certainly could not answer off-hand what would be the proper course to take. He could only say, in regard to the complaints of the hon. Member of the arrests of men on insufficient evidence, that in the heat and hurry of the early days of the suppression of the state of crime which had existed in Ireland, it was possible, as it was in the case of a terrible war, for things to have been done hastily in the way of arrests, and from the want of proper communications having been kept up between the Law Officers and others who were Law Officers no longer, and the responsible magistrates and police. He did not know much about the facts of this particular case; but nothing had engaged his attention more than this—namely, the propriety of impressing upon all those who were concerned in the detection of crime that they were not to make arrests, except in serious cases, until the case had been laid in full before the Law Officers. That ought not to be done except in the most exceptional cases, where the suspected person was likely to leave the country, or where there was imminent danger of a crime being about to be committed. Exceptional circumstances only would warrant a sudden arrest being made, because a sudden and ill-considered arrest was frequently productive of fatal results. He had been glad to hear the hon. Member for Sligo (Mr. Sexton) lay particular emphasis upon this particular case, because it made him think the hon. Member realized the fact that there were not many unfortuuate men still left in the position of being remanded over and over again. He believed that resulted from the caution now displayed by persons in authority, who saw that arrests were not made without very great deliberation, and on a full case being established. He thought he had now gone through everything the hon. Member had alleged, with the exception of his remarks in reference to Mr. Bolton. He must say that he deprecated any conclusion being drawn—such as the hon. Member had drawn from the telegram he had read to the House. He knew nothing about the facts of the case; but he could very well conceive that when a very grave charge had been made, and the person who made it was being prosecuted as a libeller—he could well conceive that before going into the box to be examined as to the whole of his life, on any question which might be put to him, the plaintiff might insist that some *primâ facie* case should be made out against him. He might give an instance in illustration of what he meant. If a man was charged with having stolen a watch, he might bring an action for libel, but refuse to go into the box to be examined as to whether, at a contested election, he had given a man 5*s*. to buy some ale. He might insist that a *primâ facie* case of his having stolen the watch should be made out, in the first instance, and that the libel should be properly established before he was called upon to refute it. But he did not think that this was a case to be argued in Parliament while it was pending in a Court of Law, and he had no wish to argue it. But if the hon. Member thought it right to prejudice the case against Mr. Bolton during the progress of the trial by commenting upon a single fact which had come to his knowledge, and which might bear a very different complexion from that which the telegram put upon it, he thought it right to say, on the other side, that there might be a possible explanation of everything stated in the telegram. He did not think, however, that the House of Commons ought at present to concern itself with the general character of Mr. Bolton. He thought that the character of that gentleman was at that moment sacred; and hon. Members must have an opinion whether the course pursued was not calculated to prejudice the case in the public mind. While litigation was proceeding with regard to the attempt of Mr. Bolton to vindicate his character, and while Mr. Bolton was in the position of a litigant vindicating his character, that character ought to be sacred, and ought not to be discussed in that House. From that point of view, he altogether deprecated any remark upon Mr. Bolton's general character. As to the question of Mr. Bolton's bankruptcy, he was aware how grave a matter the question of bankruptcy in regard to a public officer was. He was perfectly aware what the practice was in the case of English Civil servants, and he considered that practice, in the essence of it, to be a righteous one, and that no man whose private affairs were brought under the notice of the Government, by bankruptcy, or by proceedings equivalent to bankruptcy, should be continued in his position, unless, on examination, it turned out that his difficulties were not occasioned by fraud, or by culpable extravagance, or by culpable improvidence.

Mr. SEXTON asked if the right hon. Gentleman meant that the Government was to form its opinion upon these matters by the examination which took place in the Bankruptcy Court?

Mr. TREVELYAN said, that, of course, the materials upon which the Government would be required to form a conclusion would be what came before the Court of Bankruptcy. What he maintained was, that the Government would have to satisfy themselves on these points by what was brought under their notice by the proceedings in bankruptcy, or proceedings equivalent to bankruptcy. That was the principle adopted in regard to the English Civil servants, and it was the principle on which the Irish Government intended to act in regard to Mr. Bolton, and in the case of any Civil servant who received a salary under the Crown. He thought that was a plain and simple statement on the part of the Government, so far as Mr. Bolton was concerned. In regard to any other question relating to Mr. Bolton, they could not enter into it while the trial was pending.

MR. ARTHUR ARNOLD said, he had never heard anything more convincing than the speech delivered by the Prime Minister last Wednesday against the postponement of the Vote. He agreed with what the right hon. Gentleman then said, that the proceedings now going on at Belfast had nothing whatever to do with the Vote before the House; and if he had any influence with hon. Members opposite, he would certainly ask them to avoid in this discussion any reference to the trial now going on, which could have nothing whatever to do with the present Vote. There was not a Member in that House who did not think that very great extravagance was apparent in regard to the Irish Law Charges, and he knew that in the whole of Europe there was not a similar case in which the salaries of the judicial officers of the country bore such an extravagant proportion to the Revenues of the country in which they lived. He had risen, however, for the purpose of making one or two remarks directly in reference to Mr. Bolton. His right hon. Friend the Chief Secretary had given a definition of what he considered ought to be the policy of Her Majesty's Government in reference to Civil servants. He was sorry to differ from so great and respectable an authority as his right hon. Friend, but he did differ entirely from him in regard to this matter. When the discussion took place the other day, the right hon. and learned Gentleman the Member for the University of Dublin (Mr. Gibson) said that Mr. Bolton had not presented a Petition in Bankruptcy. The right hon. Gentleman did not pretend to make that statement to-day. It was now admitted by the learned Solicitor General for Ireland, and it was perfectly well known in all quarters of the House, that Mr. Bolton had presented a Petition in Bankruptcy. That being so, he held that there ought to be an inviolable rule that when a public servant presented a Petition in Bankruptcy he should be immediately suspended. He differed entirely from the Chief Secretary in thinking that Her Majesty's Government ought to suspend their judgment until there had been an adjudication in reference to that Petition in Bankruptcy. What had happened in this particular case was this. Only two days ago it came to light in the proceedings connected with Mr. George Bolton's bankruptcy, which were fully and accurately reported in *The Times* newspaper, that Mr. Bolton had made an offer to his creditors of £300 from his annual official salaries. The Judge of the Court was advised to make Mr. Bolton a bankrupt; but he declined to do so, because that course would probably involve the loss of the official salaries. What was now happening was only what would happen in any case of default. Bolton, farmed by his creditors, might go on for years, and it might happen that the money voted by the House of Commons might, under the existing conditions of the case, be made available by a person who had presented a Petition in Bankruptcy for meeting the demands of his creditors, and preventing an adjudication in bankruptcy from taking place. The debtor had in this case an interest in continuing in the receipt of his salary in order that it might be farmed—although the debtor was an officer in Her Majesty's Service—by his creditors. Now, he held most strongly that no officer of the Crown ought to be in that position—that he ought not to be in a position in which he could be farmed by any one of Her Majesty's subjects. Holding that view, he should support the Motion for reducing the Vote by the amount of Mr. Bolton's salary.

MR. T. P. O'CONNOR said, they had had a speech from the right hon. Gentleman the Chief Secretary for Ireland of a kind which had unfortunately become too common in connection with this case. The right hon. Gentleman, a man of brilliant abilities, well able to hold his own in debate with almost all 'comers, had been struggling almost incoherently, for half-an-hour, in a lame and halting speech, to screen Mr. Bolton. In fact, he did not think there had ever been a more remarkable instance in that House of an official palpably and obviously discharging a duty which was odious and loathsome to him than that which the right hon. Gentleman had afforded that evening. As to the excessive amount of the Estimates now under the consideration of the Committee, he would leave the case where it had been put by his hon. Friend the Member for Sligo (Mr. Sexton), and the hon. Gentleman who had just now spoken. The conviction was firm and fixed, and no amount of rambling speeches by the Chief Secretary would remove it from the mind of the Committee and from the public of this country, as well as of Ireland that the Law Charges in connection with Ireland were beyond all reason and beyond all decency. That was a fact which had passed out of the sphere of disputable or disputed proposals, and was well established in every rational and unofficial mind. He would now refer to the Tubbercurry prisoners. The right hon. Gentleman commented on the fact that the case had been brought forward so frequently by his hon. Friend, and he had drawn the extraordinary inference that it was the only case of the kind in Ireland. As a matter of fact, the explanation of the interest taken by his hon. Friend in the case was that the prisoners were his own constituents, whose grievances he was specially required to bring under the notice of the House. That there were other cases in which similar hardships were experienced he had not the slightest doubt; but in all probability the persons who had been so treated had not the good fortune to possess a Representative in that House as energetic and as influential as his hon. Friend. With regard to the Tubbercurry prisoners, they had been in gaol since the 2nd of April, and now on the 29th of July they were still untried, and had not been admitted to bail. The right hon. Gentleman had himself deprecated the principle of making fishing arrests in Ireland; but the circumstances of this case, in which men had been kept in prison from the 2nd of April until the 29th of July without being brought to trial, afforded convincing proof that the arrest was a fishing arrest. The mere statement of the facts must bring conviction home to the mind of every hon. Member that when the Government arrested these men they had no evidence against them; but that they took up the case experimentally, in the hope of being able to get evidence by-and-bye. When at last, in obedience to the strong pressure put upon the Government by his hon. Friend, these men were brought to the Assizes for trial, the Government again suggested the postponement on the miserable and flimsy pretence that subscriptions were being got up by their neighbours to assist them in their defence. In this country, even in the case of the most odious criminal, if the public had an idea that he was in danger of being unfairly tried for the want of legal advice, an appeal would at once be made for support, in order to produce evidence and see that the case was adequately conducted. It was within his own recollection that many criminals of the worst type had been helped in this way to defend themselves lest the sacredness of trial by jury should be violated, and they should not receive proper treatment. The Tubbercurry prisoners, through their solicitor, had addressed a telegram to his hon. Friend, asking that they should be tried on the 5th of August; and he should like to hear from the Solicitor General for Ireland any ground why this reasonable request on their part should not be complied with. They were perfectly convinced of being able to establish their innocence. All that they asked was that they should be tried on the first opportunity, and not kept languishing in prison week after week and month after month because no opportunity was afforded to them of establishing their innocence. The re-appearance of the right hon. Gentleman the Chief Secretary on the present occasion suggested some strange inquiries. Why was the right hon. Gentleman not in his place when the case of George Bolton was under discussion last week? There was a general impression last Wednesday that the absence of the right hon. Gentleman from the House was due to the fatigue he had undergone for several days in defending his Department from the attacks which had been made upon it in that House. No doubt the amount of labour the right hon. Gentleman was obliged to go through owing to the responsibilities which attached to his Office were extremely onerous; but he wanted to ask the right hon. Gentleman this question. It was a categorical question, and he hoped that a categorical answer would be given. Was the right hon. Gentleman wilfully absent from the House on Wednesday last when the Vote for Mr. Bolton's salary was under discussion? Was his absence deliberate and intentional, or the result of accident and the consequence of fatigue? All he (Mr. T. P. O'Connor) could say was that the Irish Members had seen the reappearance of the right hon. Gentleman upon the Treasury Bench in order to defend these Votes with a certain amount of curiosity and interest, especially after his absence on Wednesday. He must say that the position of the right hon. Gentleman was one which entitled him to sympathy. What evil fate had condemned him to stand up in the defence of such men as George Bolton; and if his conscience did not justify him, what evil fate compelled him to swallow the odious dose? The right hon. Gentleman ought not to stop a moment longer in Office if he found that he could not discharge the duties of it with the full consent of his heart and conscience. He would recall to the memory of the right hon. Gentleman a remarkable incident which occurred in the last Parliament, and in which the right hon. Gentleman himself took a prominent part. A noble Lord sitting on the Bench which the right hon. Gentleman now occupied was a Member of the Administration of Lord Beaconsfield. There was a financial trial going on in the City of London at the time, and in the course of the evidence at the trial certain transactions with which the noble Lord had been concerned were brought to light. They were supposed to have been of a somewhat questionable nature. Who was the man who then stood up in that House and compelled the resignation of the noble Lord? It was the right hon. Gentleman the Chief Secretary for Ireland, who was now the advocate and exponent of George Bolton. Although the noble Lord might have committed a certain amount of indiscretion, there was sufficient proof in the exposure which took place that there was nothing criminal in the transaction. His conduct might have been foolish, thoughtless, and unworthy of a man occupying his high position; but his (Mr. T. P. O'Connor's) sympathies were with the noble Lord, rather than with the right hon. Gentleman, who had taken a malignant course in matters which he himself—a man of large fortune—might have treated with indulgence. Yet this rigid economist, this relentless purist, was the man who got up now night after night to defend as bad a class of criminals as any who ever had the misfortune to be connected with the Civil Service of any country in the world. He wished to correct one misconception on the part of the right hon. Gentleman. The right hon. Gentleman, speaking on the attitude of the Irish Members towards George Bolton, admitted that the result of the trial at Belfast would have a material influence upon the action of the Government. Now, the position of the Irish Members in reference to George Bolton was that he ought to have been dismissed long ago. He asked any English Member to rise in his place and declare that any man with the antecedents and character of George Bolton ought to have been retained for a single week in the Civil Service of this country? That was a fair challenge. Would any Member who was not a Member of the Government—indeed, would any Member of the Government except the Chief Secretary and the Solicitor General for Ireland get up and declare that a man with the antecedents and character and position of George Bolton ought to be kept for a single hour in the service of this country? He awaited with some curiosity to see the manner in which that challenge would be taken up by the Government. The real secret of all these matters was that the Government of Ireland were determined to stand by their tools, no matter what dirty instruments they might be. There was not a single man whose dismissal had been agreed to by the Government during the last two or three years who had been dismissed voluntarily, or who would have been dismissed at all but for the constant pressure of public opinion, and after wearisome discussions in that House. Every official who had been prosecuted had been proceeded against at the eleventh hour, and after the Government had exhausted every means of evading a prosecution. He maintained that that was a shameful and pitiable position for the right hon. Gentleman to occupy. For the right hon. Gentleman himself he had great respect and sympathy; but he must say that his official conduct in these matters had brought about all the trouble in which he found himself involved.

MR. LABOUCHERE said, the question was not precisely whether Mr. Bolton ought to be dismissed for his past misconduct, because all that had been condoned. The real question was whether he ought to be suspended at present. Now, it appeared to him that in suggesting his suspension hon. Members only treated Mr. Bolton precisely in the same way as every other public servant was treated, and as they were treated themselves if any one of them filed a Petition in Bankruptcy. If an hon. Member presented a Petition in Bankruptcy he was suspended from all legislative functions until that Petition was disposed of; and he thought they had a right to ask that the same rule which was applied to Members of Parliament, and which was applied to all public servants in England, should also be applied to those who were employed in Ireland. They had been told that one reason why this course had not been taken in regard to Mr. Bolton, and why Mr. Bolton had not been suspended, was that he was proposing to enter into some bargain with his creditors, by which he was to hand over to them some portion of his official emoluments. He had always understood that the salary given to an official was in order that he might maintain a certain position in society; and it would be very strange to have a man occupying an official position, with the greater part of his salary in the hands of his creditors. What could be more objectionable than that a man, holding the position of Crown Solicitor in Ireland, and exercising legal functions, and obliged to conduct the prosecution of prisoners, should be, to all intents and purposes, in the hands of his creditors? He knew nothing about Mr. Bolton, except what he had read and heard in that House; but, speaking generally, he thought the facts which were admitted by the Treasury Bench rendered it only jus and proper that Mr. Bolton should be at once suspended.

Mr. GREGORY said, it was not his province to defend Her Majesty's Government, nor did he know anything about this case beyond what had been said in that House; but he did think that there ought to be some right understanding as to the course which should be adopted. What was now before the Committee was the proposal that Mr. Bolton's salary should be omitted from the present Vote; that he should, in fact, be deprived of his professional remuneration, and dismissed as a solicitor from public employment. He did not think that sufficient reasons had been assigned for taking such a course. He had very little respect for the antecedents of Mr. Bolton, and he was not there to defend that gentleman; but if he had been a fraudulent trustee there were remedies in Ireland, as well as in England, which could be put in force against him, and he might have been prosecuted in that capacity. If he had committed an unprofessional act, he presumed that there might have been an application to strike him off the rolls in Ireland, as in England; but he could not find that either one step or the other had been taken against Mr. Bolton. All that was left was the Petition in Bankruptcy, and the proceedings which were now pending in the Court at Belfast. It was admitted that that House ought not to be influenced by those proceedings. Reference had been made to the fact that Mr. Bolton had not appeared when he was called upon to appear as a witness in Court in the case now pending at Belfast. He thought the right hon. Gentleman the Chief Secretary had put that matter very fairly. He might, of course, have been examined from one end of his life to another; and until some case was made out by the other side to justify the libel it was not for Mr. Bolton to go into the box at the call of the otherside. ["Oh!" *from Irish Members.*] He hoped that hon. Members would hear him out. If a plaintiff was required by the defendant to appear in the witness-box, the defendant had the means in his own hands of putting him there. He might summon him by subpœna, and ask him pretty well what questions he liked, treating him even as a hostile witness. Therefore, he did not think much importance attached to the refusal of Mr. Bolton to go into the witness-box in this instance. In all probability the telegram which had been referred to was founded upon some observation in Court — such as "Where is Mr. Bolton?" or something of that kind. Nor did it follow that Mr. Bolton would not present himself as a witness at the proper time. Then it was said that Mr. Bolton had presented a Petition in Bankruptcy. Now, as he understood, the bankruptcy was brought about in consequence of some unfortunate purchases which Mr. Bolton had made in the Landed Estates Court of Ireland. Mr. Bolton had fancied the purchases he made to be of very much larger value than they turned out to be. Many other gentlemen had made mistakes in the purchase of land, and had lost something in consequence. The Committee had a right to assume that, being pressed by his creditors, Mr. Bolton had presented a Petition in the Court of Bankruptcy for the proper administration of his estate, in order to secure that it should be duly administered among his creditors generally. It would appear from the investigation, when it took place, whether the circumstances attending the bankruptcy were discreditable to Mr. Bolton or not; and, therefore, he did not see that there was sufficient ground for taking steps against Mr. Bolton until the circumstances of the bankruptcy were disclosed. Until those proceedings were fully heard, he did not think it would be right to suspend Mr. Bolton during the pendency of the bankruptcy proceedings he had invited. Of course, if it turned out that the circumstances of the bankruptcy were discreditable to him, or that there had been anything fraudulent in his transactions, the case would be different, or even if it should turn out that the bankruptcy had been brought about by undue means, such as extravagance, or wanton expenditure, it would be another question, and the Government would have it in their power to deal with him; but until that fact was ascertained, he did not think there was any ground for the refusal of his salary. If it were purely a bankruptcy of misfortune, not attributable to the fault of the bankrupt, it would be a harsh thing that he should at once lose his appointment.

MR. ILLINGWORTH said, he thought the point raised by the hon. Member for Salford (Mr. Arnold) was really the one which the Committee were called upon to consider. As to the trial at Belfast, it seemed to him that the Government were wise in not throwing the weight of a feather in either scale. The simple question was, what was the ordinary rule of the Service in the case of the bankruptcy of a public servant? If it was the rule in other Departments to suspend a public servant in the event of bankruptcy where the bankruptcy was the act of the servant or of his creditors, there ought to be no difference made in Mr. Bolton's case. He knew the case of a young officer in the Army who had undertaken to pay his father's debts by instalments, and, having failed to do so, bankruptcy proceedings were brought against him; and he (Mr. Illingworth) was told that, in spite of all the interest brought to bear to save this young officer, he had been compelled by the Commander-in-Chief to resign his position. What he held, and what every right-minded man would hold, was that if the rule ordinarily observed was suspension there ought to be no exception made in the case of Mr. Bolton. Of course, if any of the charges now made against Mr. Bolton were substantiated, then it was clear that suspension would not be sufficient, but that it must be followed by absolute dismissal with disgrace. All he said was that the Government would not be justified in this case in deviating from the clear and well-understood rule in all other cases when a man was overtaken by embarrassment in regard to his pecuniary circumstances, and matters had proceeded so far as to involve a Petition in Bankruptcy. It seemed that the proper course which ought to be taken in this case was to suspend Mr. Bolton.

MR. GIBSON said, he had understood on the last occasion this question was before the House that it was stated from the Treasury Bench that there was no certain rule laid down as to bankruptcy or arrangement with creditors. Of course, there were bankruptcies and bankruptcies; and, therefore, it was absolutely impossible to lay down an absolutely rigid rule. Last Wednesday the statement made was that the presentation of a Petition for arrangement, or even adjudication, in bankruptcy would not, *ipso facto*, necessarily cause dismissal from the Public Service, and it was pointed out that every case must be considered on its own merits, and on the circumstances which brought the bankruptcy about. As an illustration to show the reasonableness of this rule, the case was given of a person who had been trustee of moneys invested in shares in the City of Glasgow Bank. The failure of that bank had brought about the ruin of such trustee, whose own affairs were put into the Bankruptcy Court, with the result that the trustee was adjudicated a bankrupt. Now, it was obvious that such a bankruptcy was perfectly consistent with the entire innocence of the man who was made bankrupt, and it would be an extreme hardship to subject a man under such circumstances, who ought to have the sympathy of all persons, to a dismissal which would deprive him of the only means he had of effecting a settlement with his creditors. He did not assert that that was the case here, and he did not pretend to have any special knowledge of the rules enforced either in the Army or in the Public Service. But the statement from the Treasury Bench on Wednesday last was not challenged or contradicted in any part of the House; and he was bound to say that it seemed to him to be a rule which, if applied with discretion, would recommend itself to the common sense of everyone.

MR. JOSEPH COWEN said, it was quite possible that a man might become bankrupt by accident or misfortune, and many bankrupts were neither fraudulent or disreputable persons. In his part of the country he was satisfied that many persons whose estates were administered under the Bankruptcy Act, and who were held to be bankrupt, had become so by misfortune; but in this case it was evident that Mr. Bolton was a man of questionable character, and while legal proceedings were pending against him in the Courts of this country the Government, having full knowledge of the proceedings, not only took no steps against him, but actually promoted him. In this case, instead of suspending him or instituting a full inquiry into the charges against him, his superiors acted as his protectors. He (Mr. Joseph Cowen) maintained that the Government were fully aware of Mr. Bolton's antecedents, and therefore he should support the Amendment.

MR. T. D. SULLIVAN said, he also intended to support the Amendment for the reduction of the Vote, and he agreed with the Mover of the Motion in the opinion he had expressed that the Law Charges in Ireland were altogether swollen beyond the necessities and requirements of the case. His hon. Friend the Member for Sligo (Mr. Sexton) had shown the Committee that there had been very little diminution in these charges, notwithstanding the fact that there had been a very considerable diminution in the crime of the country, and not only in the crime of the country, but in many other respects. The one thing which would not diminish, so long as it was possible to keep it up to high water mark, was the Law Charges, the fees paid to lawyers and policemen, the reward of spies, informers, Crown Prosecutors, and all the rest of them. Those charges were kept up at the highest level, notwithstanding the fact that crime and outrage were decreasing, and the population and wealth of the country were also decreasing. No doubt there had been a high old time for the lawyers, who had an interest in keeping up the Law Charges as long as they could. This class of people had been rolling in wealth and wallowing in the public money for years past; and, of course, it was very desirable on their part to continue the same game as long as possible. As regarded George Bolton, he had been the pet of Dublin Castle—the pet of the Executive, and the Public Service of that country. He had not one salary only, but many; and yet, out of those many salaries, he could not afford to pay his creditors. He enjoyed an income from the Government of £2,000 a-year. He contracted debts to the amount of £100,000, and he found that the Government and the House of Commons did their best to shield and shelter him. He (Mr. Sullivan) had seen the evidence of what had occurred recently in Dublin, when the Judge of the Bankruptcy Court kindly consented to postpone the hearing of Bolton's case in order that Mr. Bolton might have an opportunity of obtaining damages at Belfast. That was the sort of support he got from men in high office in Ireland. When they came into that House—the highest Court of Justice—they found an endeavour to post: one the Votes lest the fair fame of Mr. George Bolton should suffer. They found Ministers of the Crown standing up and defending him when there was a clear case against him. Using the word "Crown" put him in mind that in Ireland Mr. George Bolton was "the Crown;" that admirable gentleman, in conducting prosecutions in Ireland called himself "the Crown," and the Judges and Magistrates referred to the excellent and famous George Bolton as "the Crown." Ought not the Government to be ashamed at such a name being applied to such a man, and that such a man should be retained in the Public Service? He said it was a public scandal that these things should be; it was one of the many scandals connected with the Government Departments in Ireland, and the Government had good reason that night to be ashamed of it.

MR. TREVELYAN said, he was not quite sure whether the Treasury Minute of November, 1868, had been read to the House; but it had been very often cited, and it might be well to read the exact words, which were as follows:—

"In the event of any civil servant being arrested, or being adjudicated a bankrupt, or entering into a composition with his creditors under the Bankruptcy Act, he will, on the fact being known, be suspended from duty and from salary, and he will not be reinstated unless, after examination of the facts and of the schedule prepared for the Court, it shall appear that his difficulties have been occasioned by misfortune, and not by extravagance or culpable improvidence, or unless the case shall be characterized by previous circumstances of extenuation."

That was the measure which the Irish Government were anxious to apply to Irish Civil servants; they included Mr. Bolton in that category, and that measure, and no other, they proposed to apply to him. The question obviously was, whether he had hitherto come under any one of the first three heads—being arrested, or being adjudicated a bankrupt, or entering into a composition with his creditors. What was the meaning of "adjudicated a bankrupt?" That was the point, and he was not willing to state the opinion of someone on the Treasury Bench on so purely legal a question; but they proposed to lay the case before the Law Officers, and likewise to apply to the proper authority, whom he would not then name, to ascertain what was the practice in the English Civil Service; and exactly that practice, so far as it could be ascertained, would be followed in this case. This was a clear statement of the course which the Government proposed to take, and he earnestly hoped it would be satisfactory to the Committee.

LORD RANDOLPH CHURCHILL said, he thought the Committee were in a position of some difficulty, because they had not had much light from the Chief Secretary to the Lord Lieutenant of Ireland, or from the right hon. and learned Gentleman the Member for the University of Dublin (Mr. Gibson), who contented himself with the oracular remark that there were bankruptcies and bankruptcies, and then sat down and left the Committee where they were before. The Committee wanted to know the rule that was in force in the Service from official sources, and that had been clearly stated by the right hon. Gentleman who read the Treasury Minute. And they wanted to ascertain clearly the course which the Government intended to pursue, and they learned that it was one which differed widely from the course they had taken in other cases, because it appeared by the Minute that where a man was arrested or adjudicated a bankrupt, or made a composition with his creditors, he was to be at once suspended from the Public Service. He understood that, under the new Bankruptcy Act, the first step to be taken in order to make a composition with creditors was to file a Petition; and though he did not state it as a question of law, he was informed that a composition could not be made without first filing a Petition in Bankruptcy. At any rate, the fact remained that, on the 24th of June last, Mr. Bolton filed a Petition in Bankruptcy, with a view to compounding with his creditors; and, without sympathizing with hon. Members behind him in their attack on Mr. Bolton, he did not see why a rule should be laid down for him different from that applied to others. Nor did he see why the fact that Mr. Bolton was attacked by a certain party and defended by others should give him a privileged position. They had Mr. Bolton applying to the Bankruptcy Court on the 24th of June last, with a view to compounding with his creditors. Why, then, did not the Treasury Rule come into operation? Not only did the Rule not come into operation when Mr. Bolton filed a Petition in Bankruptcy, but he doubted whether it would have come into operation at all but for the question having been raised by hon. Members behind him. If Members of that House and of the House of Peers became, during the time of bankruptcy, incapable of discharging public duties, he would ask the Prime Minister whether he thought that exceptional treatment should be adopted in the case of a legal official in the Public Service, and whether he thought it advantageous with regard to Ireland that an official who had come very prominently before the public, and who occupied a position which exposed men to much adverse criticism—namely, that of Crown Prosecutor—that such an individual should be singled out above all other officials for exceptional treatment? He thought, if it were necessary, as a general rule, to exercise care in administration, that extreme care should be exercised when the Irish Government was concerned, because, unfortunately, the Irish Government did not enjoy the respect of the great majority of the people of Ireland; and he could conceive nothing more likely to stimulate the unpopularity of that Government than that the House of Commons should be led to understand that an official of the Government was to be exempt from the operation of one of the ordinary Rules of the Public Service.

MR. GLADSTONE said, he could venture to assure the noble Lord that nothing was further from the intention of the Government than to apply an exceptional mode of treatment to the case of Mr. Bolton. The whole question was this. What was the rule of the Public Service, and what was the just application of that rule? The question put by his hon. Friend the Member for Bradford (Mr. Illingworth) a few minutes ago had been answered by what had been read by the Chief Secretary to the Lord Lieutenant of Ireland from the Treasury Minute of November, 1868. When the noble Lord spoke to him he had no recollection in the matter which was very serviceable; but his recollection was, that the administration of the Minute had generally been in conformity with what had been said by the right hon. and learned Gentleman the Member for the University of Dublin (Mr. Gibson)—that there were bankruptcies and bankruptcies—that was to say, that everything depended upon the character of the bankruptcy. It might be said that this was with regard to the ultimate steps to be taken, and that suspension was not inevitable in any case; but suspension was not invariably insisted upon, and there was the case of a person in the Education Department, whom it would not be necessary to name, holding an important situation, who was actually adjudicated a bankrupt, but who was not suspended for an hour, so far was the nature of the case known to be in his favour. That, however, he admitted, was not a case in the same sense. It appeared to him that there was no room left for doubt. The Minute of November, 1868, was clearly in the nature of a penal law, and, being so, it was the duty of the Treasury to administer it strictly; and, whatever might be the amount of feeling in that House, it was their duty to ascertain its legal construction—not stretch its application—and that his right hon. Friend said was being done by the best means in his power. The Secretary to the Treasury was said to have been defending Mr. Bolton; but the extent of that defence was to see that strict justice was administered to him. He had one addition to make to what had been stated by his right hon. Friend, which, he thought, would satisfy the Committee. His right hon. Friend had promised that he would obtain the best legal judgment he could of the meaning and construction of this Rule; and to that he might add, as it was fair matter for discussion, that if this Vote were now allowed to pass, the Government proposed that the Report of the Vote should not be taken until his right hon. Friend had obtained the judgment he sought. He hoped the Committee, under the circumstances, would see that, if the Vote were passed, this question could be raised at a time when the Government would be in a position to state decisively their course.

MR. SEXTON said, they were entitled to demand from the Government to take immediately a step which they were clearly not disposed to take. He failed to discover any reason in the statements of Members of the Government why this should not be done. The right hon. Gentleman the Chief Secretary to the Lord Lieutenant of Ireland had read a Treasury Minute to the Committee, the existence of which was quite as well known to the Government on Wednesday last as it was that night. Now, that Minute provided that if a Civil servant became bankrupt, or entered into a composition with his creditors, he should be suspended in consequence. What was the position of Mr. Bolton? He had filed affidavits in the Court of Bankruptcy; one of them, dated the 2nd of July, was headed "In the Bankruptcy Court, Ireland, in the matter of George Bolton. Petition for arrangement." He (Mr. Sexton) said then that Mr. Bolton had entered into a composition with his creditors, so far as it was possible for him to do so. He had done all in his power to make a composition with his creditors; and he maintained that, applying the rule of the English Civil Service, the Government were bound to suspend him. They were told that action would be taken when the construction of the Minute was ascertained; but he said that Mr. Bolton ought to be suspended now. No doubt, as it was said, there were bankruptcies and bankruptcies—so much the worse for Mr. Bolton, for a bankruptcy like his had not been seen for a long time. Judge Walsh had declared his conduct towards his own relatives and family to have been of a fearful character, and yet the Prime Minister contended that there were reasons for still further delay. He would not go so far as to say that if the Government agreed to take the Report of the Vote at a reasonable hour, and undertook before that to ascertain the law, they might not change the character of their present opposition to the Vote.

MR. GLADSTONE said, the term "reasonable hour" was a relative one. As Mr. Speaker had stated the other day from the Chair, it did not mean exactly the same thing in August as it did in the month of May. With that reservation he was prepared to assent to the proposal of the hon. Member.

MR. HEALY said, he supposed the Government meant by a "reasonable hour" 9 or 10 o'clock. [Mr. GLADSTONE dissented.] No doubt, then, they considered 1 or 2 o'clock in the morning a reasonable hour. They had just had an instance of that, for the House had been discussing the Irish Magistrates Bill until 5 o'clock that morning. But there was one point about which he should like to have some information at the present moment. Mr. Bolton had committed flat perjury on Thursday last. What notice had been taken of that by the Government? He swore before Judge Walsh, in order to procure a postponement, that he required an adjournment on the ground that he was a material and necessary witness. His words were—

"I say I am a material and necessary witness, and I believe a material witness for myself on the trial of both actions."

That affidavit was sworn in the Bankruptcy Court on Thursday last. But what had occurred to-day in Belfast? After swearing in the Bankruptcy Court the other day that he was a necessary and material witness for himself for the purpose of procuring a postponement, Mr. Bolton declined to go into the witness box at Belfast. Now, he asked, what notice were the Government going to take of that affidavit? Here was a man charged with a series of crimes by the hon. Member for Mallow (Mr. O'Brien) in *United Ireland;* he had been called by that hon. Member everything but one thing; and, notwithstanding the affidavit he had made, his case had to-day been closed without his daring to go into the witness box. They asked the postponement of the Vote; but he must say it was not merely as a bankrupt that he impeached Mr. Bolton. He regarded him as a fraudulent, perjured swindler, all along the line. He cared nothing whether he was a bankrupt or not. However his bankruptcy might go, or whatever might be the verdict, he said it was a disgrace and a scandal for the Government to keep the case over the Belfast Assize. Then they were told that it was a question whether Mr. Bolton's bankruptcy was of a character which ought to carry with it the penal action prescribed by the Treasury Minute. He would ask, who were the people seeking to make Mr. Bolton a bankrupt? Why, it was his wife's trustees, who claimed to the extent of £26,000; and it was with regard to that money that Judge Walsh declared that Mr. Bolton had acted in a fearful manner towards his wife. Bolton had been let off by the late Lord Chancellor Law in this way—he produced a letter from his wife stating that if she got this £26,000, she was willing that her husband should continue in the Public Service—she did not want, so to speak, to take the bread out of his mouth. Having entrapped Lord Chancellor Law into continuing him in his position, what did he do? So far from paying the £26,000, he had pocketed the money which he got by a fraudulent deed; he had acted as a fraudulent trustee, and in a way contrary to the rules of the Profession, and in such a way that the Judge declared that he ought to be struck off the Rolls. And now it was his wife's trustees who were seeking to make him bankrupt in Dublin. Such was the man whom the Government retained in the Public Service. The declaration of the Judge alone, with regard to his conduct, he should have thought would have been sufficient to induce the Government to come to a speedy issue in this matter. Whether the Rule of 1868 applied or not, George Bolton was not the man whom it was desirable should conduct prosecutions in Ireland. Hon. Members on those Benches had pointed out his acts in that House; they had shown exactly the position in which he stood to English Gentlemen, not once but many times.

MR. DAWSON said, the right hon. and learned Gentleman the Member for the University of Dublin (Mr. Gibson) had used the expression with regard to this case that there were "bankruptcies and bankruptcies;" and the Prime Minister also appeared to convey that the nature of the bankruptcy should be considered; but one of the most extraordinary excuses for Mr. Bolton was that which had been put forward by the right hon. Gentleman the Chief Secretary to the Lord Lieutenant of Ireland. Mr. Bolton, it appeared, had bought a lot of land; he had raised the rents, and when he was wringing out of his unfortunate tenants sufficient to pay his debts, that laudable object was defeated by the operation of the Land Act. He (Mr. Dawson) asked whether that would be considered an extenuating circumstance when Mr. Bolton's bankruptcy was considered? Would any man, who had acted as Mr. Bolton had acted, be allowed to remain member of a London Club, an institution which, of course, had no responsibility, as the Government had, towards the people of Ireland. He wished to say a few words on a subject referred to in connection with this Estimate before the Prime Minister entered the House. There were remarks made upon the payments by fees instead of by salary, in the case of the legal officials in Ireland. That practice, payment by results, pervaded the whole system of Government in Ireland. It was the cause of the delay in the administration of the law, because every delay was money to the Law Officers; it was profit in the hands of those who denied justice; and the people of Ireland in consequence did not get that justice which, as the Attorney General for England said, the English people so much respected. The right hon. Gentleman the Chief Secretary pointed out that the hon. Member for Sligo had forgotten to refer to the £15,000 in the Supplementary Estimate, which he should have taken into his calculation. But how, he asked, were hon. Members to have information which was not put into their hands until it was too late to be considered? The right hon. Gentleman the Prime Minister had disestablished the English Church in Ireland; the right hon. Gentleman must also disestablish that hierarchy of people in Ireland, who held their position on the pernicious system of payment by results, if he would complete the improvement of the condition of the Irish people. It had been shown by evidence given before the Committee sitting to inquire into the prisons' system that there were Assizes in Ireland without crimes to try, and prisons without prisoners; and, therefore, that there was no need for the expensive arrangements with which the country was saddled, and no reason for this enormous expenditure on prosecutions and law establishments. They had no Assize business of any moment; and, therefore, it came to this—that if the men who were receiving the enormous salaries complained of were to give some value for the money they received, crime must be directly promoted, so that there would be some justification for the great Law Charges in Ireland. He agreed with the hon. Member for Sligo (Mr. Sexton) that the Solicitor General for Ireland (Mr. Walker) was very badly paid. He (Mr. Dawson) had a very high opinion of the conspicuous professional ability of the hon. and learned Gentleman, and he should certainly be disposed to give him a salary commensurate with his abilities; but to give a salary of £5,000 a-year, and fees to the amount of £8,000 a-year, pointed the moral of the tale which the Irish Members were anxious to lay before the Committee. He trusted that at no distant date public officials in Ireland would be paid by some fixed salary.

MR. HARRINGTON said, there was just one point he wished to direct attention to with regard to Mr. George Bolton. He was perfectly satisfied with the assurance given to his hon. Friend by the right hon. Gentleman the Prime Minister, and he believed that that the inquiry which the right hon. Gentleman had promised to make could result in nothing but that which he (Mr. Harrington) and his hon. Friends had for some time been fighting for. He wished, however, to point out to the Government what the position of Mr. George Bolton was at the present time before the Court of Bankruptcy. As a matter of fact, Mr. George Bolton pledged the Government and the character of the Government and the Treasury in trust to his creditors. Now, that was a position which the Government ought immediately to take steps to disassociate themselves from. The chief objection to the position Mr. Bolton had assumed was that he pledged himself to give out of his salary a sum of £300 a-year to his creditors as a portion of his arrangement. Now, he thought it should be made clear at the earliest possible moment to Mr. Bolton and his creditors that while the Government was considering the question of the character of the bankruptcy—that was to say, considering whether Bolton had been brought into Court by his own misconduct or by the course of circumstances over which he had no control—the Government should take steps to secure that his promise to pledge them and their credit should not be a portion of any arrangement which he proposed to make with his creditors. He (Mr. Harrington) was sure the right hon. Gentleman the Prime Minister would see the justice of that suggestion. In the first place, what he suggested was only just to the country. It was not that a public servant, whose conduct was to be made the subject of an official inquiry, should be able to pledge the credit of the Government as one of the means he intended to employ in order to escape from the position he had been reduced to. Then, again, it was not just to the creditors that Bolton should be able to state to them that he would allocate the sum of £300 a-year out of his salary. The creditors knew the man's position in the Government of Ireland, they knew the character of the man, they were aware of the influence he had with the Executive, and they would naturally imagine that it was only by an arrangement with Her Majesty's Government that he was able to make the offer in question. It was, therefore, of the utmost importance that, at the earliest possible moment, it should be clearly stated that Bolton was not in a position to offer £300 a-year out of his salary until Her Majesty's Government had considered whether his bankruptcy had been brought about by his own misconduct, or by the course of circumstances over which he had no control. That was the only point to which he (Mr. Harrington) wished to direct attention. The right hon. Gentleman the Prime Minister had taken a very judicious and proper course in promising to inquire into this case. No doubt, Mr. George Bolton had for a long time been in the service of the Crown in Ireland; but if the right hon. Gentleman knew the character of Mr. Bolton's services—if he knew the estimation in which those services were held by the vast majority of the people of Ireland—a majority composed of people who differed very widely as to political opinions and religious convictions—he would have no hesitation in saying that the length of Bolton's services to the Crown in Ireland should be no element in the consideration of whether justice ought to be done; whether a man who had misused his position, and who had been a source of vital contention between the Government and the people of Ireland for years, should not be removed from office.

MR. D. GRANT said, he could not fail to admire the Irish Members for the clearness and power with which they had put their case before the Committee. As they always did, they had on the present occasion put their case in the very best aspect before the Committee; but it was impossible to disguise from one's mind the fact that for a considerable time the Committee had been subjected to a repetition of the same arguments, the same phrases, and the same expressions, all of which led to the same conclusion. He put it to hon. Members opposite whether, when they had once stated their case with great fulness, and with the skill and power which was characteristic of their race, it was not fair to the Committee generally that they should be allowed to proceed with the work in hand? Was it not particularly reasonable that hon. Gentlemen should allow Business to be done on the present occasion, inasmuch as they had extracted from the right hon. Gentleman the Chief Secretary for Ireland a pledge, as distinct and clear as it was possible to be, that before the matter proceeded one step further, it should be fully considered in all its bearings? Furthermore, the pledge had been given that Mr. George Bolton should be placed on exactly the same footing as that on which any English Civil servant stood. What more could be asked? If the pledges of the Government were accepted, why discuss the subject further? If they rejected the pledges of the Government, of course, the question assumed an altogether new phase. He hoped the Irish Members would now be content with the assurances of the Government, and allow the Vote to be taken.

MR. GLADSTONE said, that, inasmuch as the assurance had been given that the subject should be discussed on Report, it would be rather hard on the Committee and on the Government, if hon. Gentlemen insisted on debating it now. It was generally admitted that the offer of the Government was a fair one; and, therefore, he thought he would not be asking too much if he asked that the Committee should now be allowed to proceed with its Business.

MR. PARNELL said, the right hon. Gentleman the Prime Minister had made an offer which, under all the circumstances of the cases, was a fair one, and one which the hon. Gentleman the Member for Sligo (Mr. Sexton), before he left the House, commissioned him to accept in his name. But before doing so, he wished to direct the attention of the Committee to two points with reference to this matter. First of all, they might fairly ask that the decision of the Government with regard to the suspension of Mr. Bolton should be taken without any unnecessary delay. They were entitled to ask that, because it was two months since this matter was first brought to the attention of the Chief Secretary to the Lord Lieutenant, and he (Mr. Parnell) was certainly entitled to say that so far there had been very unreasonable delay on the part of the right hon. Gentleman. It was only now, after the lapse of two months since the differences in the customs regulating the English and Irish Civil Services was first brought before the notice of the House, that the Irish Members were told that the Irish Executive would inquire how far the suspension of Mr. Bolton would be necessitated by following out the custom of the English Civil service. Under the circumstances, he thought he was entitled to ask, firstly, that there should be no unnecessary delay in coming to the decision with regard to Mr. Bolton's suspension; and, secondly, that the Report of this Vote should be brought on at a not unreasonable hour—say, after 11 or half-past 11 o'clock at night. He had now to ask, in the name of his hon. Friend the Member for Sligo (Mr. Sexton), for leave to withdraw the Amendment.

Motion, by leave, *withdrawn*.

Original Question again proposed.

MR. KENNY said, he did not rise for the purpose of continuing the discussion with regard to the case of Mr. Bolton; but there were one or two points on this Vote which he should like to bring under the notice of the Committee. He should like, in the first place, to say, in passing, that if Irish Members were sometimes forced to repeat arguments, it was owing to the stolid indifference with which their arguments were received by the Members of the Treasury Bench. One of the points to which he wished to direct attention concerned the Law Adviser to the Crown. It seemed, from a foot-note, that the salary attached to this Office had ceased; and what he desired to know was, whether it was proposed to discontinue it altogether? The second point to which he had to refer was that some time ago he called attention to the conviction of two persons at the Cork Winter Assizes of last year. The name of the persons convicted was Delahunty, and the significant point in the case was that one of the witnesses examined had since died; but immediately before his death he made a declaration to the effect that a policeman had induced him to swear against the prisoners, although, as a matter of fact, he knew nothing at all against them. That dying declaration was of so unusual a character that the Chief Secretary decided to submit it to the Judge who tried the case—Mr. Justice Barry—and to ask the learned Judge's opinion as to its bearing upon the conviction. Seeing that that dying declaration was submitted to Mr. Justice Barry six weeks or two months ago, and seeing that the Delahuntys were still in penal servitude, and knowing, as he (Mr. Kenny) did, they had been convicted on the most trivial evidence, a portion of which, according to the dying declaration of a witness, was suborned, it would be of great interest to the people of the district in Ireland to which the prisoners belonged, and also of great interest to many Members of the House, to know what the opinion of the learned Judge was in the matter. He (Mr. Kenny) gave Notice last night of his intention to ask further questions of the Chief Secretary on the subject next Friday, in order that, perhaps, the right hon. Gentleman might, when the Vote was taken—he (Mr. Kenny) was not aware it would be taken to-night—be in a position to make some explanation regarding the case of the unfortunate men in question.

MR. TREVELYAN said, he should prefer to say nothing upon the question that night. His impression was that the papers were still with Mr. Justice Barry. He would attend to the matter at once, and he had no doubt that by Friday he would be in a position to answer the question of the hon. Gentleman the Member for Ennis (Mr. Kenny). He had no difficulty, however, in answering the question with regard to the Vote for the Law Adviser. It was absolutely necessary that the Government in Dublin —at any rate, it had been thought necessary during the last four or five years —should have someone who could fill the part of Law Adviser. That position was filled at present by the Attorney General for Ireland (Mr. Naish). If the time should ever come when the Attorney General for Ireland and the Solicitor General for Ireland (Mr. Walker) both found seats in the House of Commons, it would become necessary to consider whether a Law Adviser should be appointed. He assured the hon. Gentleman that the Office would not be revived unless the services of a Law Adviser would warrant the payment of his salary. That contingency had not occurred, and he conceived it would not occur for some little time to come. He trusted the hon. Gentleman would be satisfied with his assurance as to the case of the Delahuntys.

MR. KENNY said, of late it had been very difficult to get opinions on legal subjects from Dublin Castle. He did not know whether that arose from the lapse of the Office of Law Adviser; but he hoped that in future it would not take three or four months to get an opinion from the Law Officers with respect to a very simple point of law. There were two other items in the Vote which struck him as very remarkable. One was the increase in the Estimate for the support of Crown witnesses. He presumed that the Estimate was for the year beginning on the 1st of April, 1884, and ending on the 31st of March, 1885, so that the £1,000 which was put down for the support of Crown witnesses was pure guess work. But the charge was £250 in excess of the amount which was required last year. Now, they all knew that criminal prosecutions in Ireland, especially prosecutions of that character in which it was necessary for the Government to get under their control, and to keep under their control, for a considerable period persons who were required to swear against others charged with serious crimes and offences had greatly diminished; and, therefore, he was anxious to receive some explanation of the extra amount which was asked for. The other item he had to bring under notice was the defence of prisoners in case of murder. Now, the fees which were paid by the Crown under the Prevention of Crime Act to counsel who were engaged to defend prisoners were notoriously small; indeed, they were so small that it frequently happened—it happened in the case of the Phœnix Park murders—that the prisoners were deprived of the most efficient legal advice which was obtainable, and which, if it had been obtained, might have seriously altered the aspect of affairs. The item for the defence of prisoners was increased by the sum of £85. In view of the diminution of cases of murder, it was very surprising that the expenses in connection with them should have increased in so striking a manner.

THE SOLICITOR GENERAL FOR IRELAND (Mr. WALKER) pointed out that the item for defence of prisoners charged with the crime of murder had no reference to the cases of murder which came under the Prevention of Crime Act.

MR. PARNELL said, that some time ago his hon. Friend the Member for Sligo (Mr. Sexton) asked the Chief Secretary to the Lord Lieutenant a Question with regard to the case of the Tubbercurry prisoners, and the right hon. Gentleman read a telegram which had been received from the prisoners' solicitor, asking that those of them whom the Government intended to bring to trial should be brought to trial at once before the Dublin Commission, and waiving, on their behalf, the usual notice of trial which prisoners were entitled to receive. He (Mr. Parnell) would be glad to know whether the matter had received the attention of the right hon.

Gentleman in the interval which had occurred, and whether he had any announcement to make?

THE SOLICITOR GENERAL FOR IRELAND (Mr. WALKER) said, the Government would be very glad to bring these prisoners to trial at the earliest possible moment; but, as the hon. Gentleman must see, it would be impossible to dispense with the usual notice, because the result would be a mistrial.

MR. PARNELL: What are you going to do?

THE SOLICITOR GENERAL FOR IRELAND (Mr. WALKER) said, the prisoners could not be tried at the coming Commission. It was impossible. [Mr. PARNELL: Why?] Because there was not sufficient time to serve the notice of trial; the earliest day the men could be tried would be some day in October.

MR. PARNELL said, he thought that the statement of the hon. and learned Gentleman was monstrous. It was now some weeks since the postponement of the trial of these prisoners was obtained from the Judge at the Sligo Assize, on the ground that the trial could not fairly take place in Sligo. [The SOLICITOR GENERAL for IRELAND (Mr. Walker): Not very long ago.] It was more than 10 days ago; that was to say the Crown had ample time, and more than ample time, to serve the requisite notice with regard to the trial of these prisoners at the August Assize. Did he understand the hon. and learned Gentleman adhered to that statement as a matter of fact? [The SOLICITOR GENERAL for IRELAND (Mr. Walker): I do.] He should like to know why it was, if the only motive of the Government, with regard to the case of Mr. Fitzgerald and the other Tubbercurry prisoners, was to secure a change of venue, in order to obtain a fair and impartial trial, they did not proceed to take steps for a trial elsewhere immediately after they obtained the postponement of the trial? What were the Irish Members and the Irish people to infer from the conduct of the Government in this matter? Was it the opinion of the Government that it was undesirable to keep untried prisoners in Ireland awaiting trial for lengthened terms; and if it be not the opinion of the Government that it was so undesirable, then all he could say was that all the understandings, and protests, and accusations upon which the Government obtained the powers conferred upon them by the Act of 1882 for changing venues would be utterly thrown on one side by their conduct with reference to this case. Having regard to the whole course of the Crown prosecution with reference to the Tubbercurry prisoners, it was monstrous that a Liberal Government, having resorted to the policy of delay from the very commencement of these proceedings, after having obtained repeated adjournments of the proceedings before the magistrates, after having postponed the trial before the Sligo Assize upon flimsy pretexts that the act of another person in connection with the prisoners had prejudiced the chance of the Crown obtaining a conviction—he said it was monstrous they should not have immediately proceeded, with all the machinery at their command, to put the men upon their trial in a Dublin Court. What had the Attorney General for Ireland (Mr. Naish), with his swollen salary and his enormous fees, which the Committee were asked to pay him, to do but to attend to matters of this kind? He (Mr. Parnell) asserted it was monstrous that the Government should lose a single minute in taking the necessary steps to bring these Tubbercurry prisoners to trial. On a former occasion his hon. Friend (Mr. Sexton) read a telegram, which he had received from the solicitors to the parties, offering to waive the customary notice; but the hon. and learned Gentleman the Solicitor General for Ireland now said that the waiver would be of no use, and that it was impossible to bring the prisoners to trial on the 5th of August, as 10 days' notice of trial must by law be served on the prisoners, and that it was not in the power of prisoners in criminal cases to waive that duty on the part of the Crown. But this matter was under discussion four or five days ago in Committee, and the demand was specifically made that the Government should bring these men to trial at once. A telegram was sent from the prisoners claiming to be placed on their trial at the forthcoming Dublin Sessions; and the Chief Secretary replied, in the usual stereotyped fashion, that there was no unnecessary time being lost. He had another telegram from one of these long-suffering men from Sligo Gaol—

"Please press the Chief Secretary to put us on trial at the Commission which opens early next month in Dublin."

In the face of the repeated delays and subterfuges resorted to by the Government, if these men could not be placed on their trial next month, the only other honest and straightforward course open to the Government was to release them all on bail. How could they trust the declarations of the Government that they would bring these men to speedy trial, when this was the way in which a number of prisoners were bandied about, and kept in prison for seven months, as they would have been next October, which, according to the Solicitor General for Ireland, was the next earliest time when they could be put on their trial? The truth of the matter was that, from the first moment of their arrest, the Government had no case against them, and they knew it. They were fishing for evidence, and were attempting to work on the fears of the prisoners, and in that illegal manner to induce them to turn Queen's evidence against each other. They had a wretched informer, a man whose character was so bad that the Government were obliged to apply for a change of venue, because they could not produce this wretched character in the box as their sole reliance, in a district where his character and history were so well known. What evidence had they against Mr. Fitzgerald, one of his constituents in Cork? He was a gentleman whom he had known for years, and was as incapable of any dishonourable act as the Chief Secretary himself; and he would say that, although Mr. Fitzgerald had opposed him more than once in political matters. He was arrested in the streets of London opposite Scotland Yard five months ago, and the English newspapers were at once instructed to insert paragraphs about his arrest, saying that it signalized the arrival in London to show what a great man he was, and how speedily he could unravel the designs of the rebels against the Queen. He was arrested without a warrant. They had heard the other day of the unwillingness of the police to arrest persons accused of the most horrible offences without warrant; but there was no such unwillingness in the case of Mr. Fitzgerald. He was arrested without a warrant, and the English papers were at once instructed to say that the chief of the dynamiters had been discovered. He was then hurried over to Ireland and put in prison in Dublin; he was then sent to the prison in Sligo, and a rumour was sent round by the Crown officers that he had turned Queen's evidence against the persons who had been previously arrested. Every attempt was made to prejudice his case and excite public opinion in this country against him. Then he was charged with treason-felony; then with conspiracy to murder; next the charge of conspiracy to murder was withdrawn, and the charge of treason-felony only was proceeded with. In 1882, when the Prevention of Crime Act was being passed, the Prime Minister and the Home Secretary gave an assurance that these charges of treason-felony should not be raked up against men under the provisions of that Act, and he now claimed the fulfilment of that pledge. In view of the fact that the Government had taken the necessary steps to bring these prisoners to trial at the Special Commission in Dublin and not at Sligo, and that there had been abundant time to serve the notices on the Judges in Dublin for a change of venue, there was now no course open to the Government but to release these men on the solid and substantial bail they were prepared to give. They would all come up for trial when the time arrived. It was abominable and infamous that the wives and families of these men should be left in starvation owing to the illegal conduct of the Government towards these prisoners. He could not see what difference there was between the state of affairs in Ireland now and last year under the Prevention of Crime Act of the present Chief Secretary and under the Coercion Act of the former Chief Secretary (Mr. W. E. Forster). The right hon. Member for Bradford kept a vast number of men in prison for a long time without trial under the ordinary laws; and it was not right, or just, or Constitutional, or in accordance with the traditions of the Liberal Party, that this course of conduct should be persisted in, and he demanded from the Government the release of these men on that solid and substantial bail they were prepared to offer, or else that they should be at once put upon their trial.

MR. HARRINGTON said, the Chief Secretary would do well to listen to the advice of the hon. Member for the City of Cork (Mr. Parnell). It was evident that the Government had been doing all in their power to delay bringing these men to trial; and although, no doubt, the Solicitor General for Ireland was technically accurate when he said there would be no opportunity of accepting the offer of the prisoners to bring them to trial before October next, yet he wished to draw attention to this fact—that a true bill had been found against these men at the Sligo Assizes. It was not necessary that they should be put on trial at the opening of the Commission in Dublin. A true bill having been found against them by the Grand Jury in Sligo, it was not necessary to have their case submitted to the Grand Jury in Dublin. If the Commission was to last several days in Dublin, was there not still time to serve the 10 days' notice of bringing these men to trial before the end of the Commission? If not, then he would ask the Government to recognize the fact that the delay in this case had been all their own. From the commencement these men had been most anxious to be brought to trial, and they had challenged the Government to bring them into Court and try the charge made against them. A postponement was obtained at the recent Sligo Assizes, on the ground that a document had been circulated throughout the country asking for evidence for the defence of these men, and that that had been circulated in order to prejudice their trial. If that was so, the document was certainly circulated a month or two before the day of trial; and if the document was circulated so early as that, the Government had cognizance of it. Why, then, did they not change the venue in time to bring the men to trial on the 5th of August? Whatever might be the interpretation Ministers in London put on the action of officials in Ireland, the people in Ireland would only take one view, and that was that this was only a part of the Government policy in that country for years past. They had taken innocent men and put them in prison, and then worked upon their fears to get some of them to give information against others, and so get convictions against them. If that was not the intention of the Government what was their objection to admit these men to bail? They might, at least, admit some of them to bail. They had said the evidence was not so strong against some as against others; but they had no right to set themselves up as judges of these men. The delays were not the fault of the men, but of the Government, and it was quite time that the Government stated they would not oppose the release of these men on bail. Bad as was the administration of the right hon. Member for Bradford when he was in Ireland; infamous as was the system practised under his *régime*, the policy of keeping men in prison month after month and year after year without trial was far more infamous and disgraceful than anything practised by the right hon. Member for Bradford. There were now in prison in Ireland men who had been kept there for 18 or 19 months; and some men who had recently been put upon their trial at Sligo had been kept in prison waiting for trial 18 months. When the man who was charged with and convicted of the murder of a policeman in Galway was put upon his trial he had been kept waiting for 18 months in prison, and whatever means he had of defending himself having been exhausted in that time, when he met his accusers in Court he was unable to meet the charge against him. When this man was convicted a further postponement was obtained of the trial of the other men who had been kept in prison 18 months. He himself had seen them brought to the prison office day after day, and there, without the presence of any of their friends, or of the Press, or any protection such as men in their unfortunate position ought to have had, an informal inquiry was made, and the remand was granted. On no less than nine occasions they were removed, and what was the object? Was it to get additional evidence? No; the evidence obtained at first was not altered in the least, and the evidence upon which they were committed on the last day was the evidence sworn to on the first day. What, then, was the object of the Crown in these repeated applications for delay? Simply to allow the Assizes then being held to slip over, so that the Crown would then not have to make application to the Assizes for an adjournment; and that enabled the Government to get over one Assizes. The March Assizes came on shortly afterwards, and then they claimed an adjournment on the strange ground that they were searching for witnesses, and because they were searching in America for evidence these men were kept in prison six months longer. At the end of those six months there was another opportunity of bringing them to trial; but another application was made by the Crown for an adjournment, and on the very same ground that they were searching for a witness in America. A more monstrous proceeding could not take place in any part of the world—on the flimsy pretext that they were searching for a material witness in America! That material witness in America had not yet turned up, and the Crown could not possibly make an application for another adjournment on that flimsy pretext; but this time they had applied for an adjournment at Sligo, and another remand had been granted. They had no faith in the intention of the Crown to try these men. They believed that their policy with regard to these men was precisely the policy they had been pursuing and intended to pursue with regard to Mr. Fitzgerald and the other prisoners in Sligo Gaol. What had occurred with regard to the man who had been convicted of the murder of a policeman? He had been offered a free pardon if he would give evidence against other men. The Government might say they had not offered that; but so long as they engaged such a man as Bolton they knew what the system was. If the Government wished to free themselves from the character of keeping men in prison in order to give information against others, and to swear away the lives of other men—a character which they held in Ireland, and very well deserved—there was only one course to adopt, and that was to at once consent to the release of these men on bail. He would ask the right hon. Gentleman the Chief Secretary to look at this question in something like a fair spirit. Here was the case of Fitzgerald, 200 miles away from his home and friends. He was first arrested in London, and most infamous rumours were circulated about him by the police officers who arrested him, to the effect that he intended to become an informer, and had offered to do so. That unfortunate man was taken not to Cork, his native place, where he could have communicated with his family and his friends, but to Sligo; and although his material witnesses were in Cork, and all the expense of bringing them to Sligo would fall upon him until his innocence or his guilt was established, yet the Government would not admit him to bail on the substantial securities he was able to give them. What was it the Government wanted? They wanted, he supposed, to put these men on trial. Well, the largest possible security necessary they were willing to give to come up for trial and to meet their accusers and establish their innocence; and if they offered the most solvent security, what was the pretext upon which the right hon. Gentleman defended the action of the Crown in refusing to admit these men to bail? If he wanted to rid himself of the character of keeping men in prison in order to make them become informers and swear away each other's lives, he would no longer justify their continued imprisonment.

MR. SEXTON said, this Tubbercurry case was a very painful one, and he had no choice but to denounce the course pursued by the Government, as announced by the Solicitor General for Ireland, as a scandalous outrage upon justice. Four months had passed away since these men were arrested. There was no pretence for saying that their conduct in life or their personal character was open to the slightest suspicion. Their lives had been honourable; their position was respectable. They were suddenly seized on the 2nd of April, upon the whisper of an informer, and were taken from their farms in the district of Tubbercurry, and from their shops in the town, and thrown into the gaol at Sligo. The whole course of the Government in regard to these men had been furtive and stealthy. It was the course of men who, conscious that they had no case aginst the prisoners, deprived them of their liberty on one pretext or another in the hope that some man might come and patch up a case against them. The first step taken by the Government was significant of the course they intended to take against these men. It was to refuse the admission of their relatives and their solicitor to the gaol. It had been said, when he had repeatedly called attention to this case, that such cases were few in Ireland. If he had been obliged repeatedly to call attention to this case, it was because at every step he had found the Government, and the agents of the Government in England, determined to pursue these men by mean and cowardly tactics. Why were they refused the right of the admission of their relatives? Why was their solicitor forbidden to see them? Why was it necessary for him to take advantage of the Rules of that House before the ordinary right of prisoners under such conditions to see their friends and their legal adviser was granted? After their arrest, what was the next step? A system of "Star Chamber" inquiry—secret examination. There was an absurd pretence of a judicial inquiry by the Resident Magistrate, who went to Sligo Gaol every eight days, and went through a formal examination of these men. What was there in that proceeding in the nature of a proper examination? No witnesses were examined. The paid agent of the Government went every eight days, and sat down at a desk and received some formal police evidence, and then went through the insulting and outrageous form of further remanding these men, although the principle of the Constitution was that no man should be imprisoned unless there was cause shown. Several weeks had passed away, several remands had taken place, without anything like a proper examination. At last he had succeeded in putting an end to that system; but what happened then? He found, as he had found at every stage of this disgraceful case, that the Government pursued oblique and cowardly tactics such as the right hon. Member for Bradford (Mr. W. E. Forster) was never mean enough to pursue, and while "giving a promise to the ear broke it to the hope." After they had undertaken to abandon this system of secret remand, he had surely reason to expect that they would proceed in a proper way to prove their case in Court, or confess that they could not do so. They had already exhausted all the tactics of their unscrupulous police agents and spies. They had circulated from day to day general rumours with regard to Fitzgerald and the other men. He would invite hon. Members to allow their minds to travel to the prison cells where these men were lying without association with other men; and to consider the state of mind of a man in such a position when a George Bolton or some other agent crept into the cell and told him the abominable lie that some of his friends had informed against him. No matter how innocent that man might be, no one could tell what suspicions might enter his mind, and he might say it was better to save his own name and liberty, at the cost even of perjury, than to allow others to do so at his expense. This was how perjury was promoted. During the weeks following the arrest of these men, society in Sligo was saturated with such rumours by the agency of the police. The police went to every one of these men and told him if he wanted to save his own life and liberty, and to have a fortune by-and-bye, he had better be the first to give information, lest he should be too late. At the same time, they were scouring the county of Sligo day and night for evidence. They established in Tubbercurry an inquisition far more terrible than that of the Star Chamber, and so ruthlessly was that conducted that the aged mother of two of these men was taken by the police to Sligo Gaol, and there subjected to a secret examination. And now, he asked if, after four whole months of constant endeavour to convict these men by resorting to these shameful tactics, it was not time to do either one thing or the other with regard to them? If it had taken so many months to make out a case against them, was there not a strong presumption of their innocence? There had been secret inquiries conducted by a magistrate who had raised himself from a humble position in connection with the Constabulary; but all the skill of Mr. Horne and of the police had not been sufficient to enable them to send the men for trial with a confidence that they would be convicted. Under such circumstances, had not the time come when the prisoners should be set free, or allowed to go out on bail; or, failing these alternatives, to be put upon their trial at once? When did the Government mean to have them tried? When was this private inquiry system to end? When they professed to bring it to an end they only "kept the promise to the ear and broke it to the hope." They distributed the evidence of informers as if it was precious manna—they gave it only in small fragments; it was evidently too rich a thing to be wasted. They would not allow it to be published all at once; and it was only at intervals of eight days that the Gospel, according to the Informer Moran, was doled out. Some months had been wasted in this way, and when he had renewed his appeals for justice, he had found himself fooled and humbugged over and over again. It was impossible for any public man to place any reliance nowadays upon the words of a Minister. If a Member of Parliament chose to believe the statements that were made to him, he would find that he would gain nothing by his credulity, but that he would be regarded by the constituents he represented as little short of an idiot. In this way the Irish Executive exhausted a few more weeks, and in the meanwhile the minor Fouches of Ireland were roaming all over the county of Sligo, holding private inquiries, although nothing came of them in the end. On his third appeal upon the floor of that House he obtained a promise that the Crown would give them the last fragment of their precious manna, by either bringing the men to trial, or by setting them at liberty. All this time the families of these men were left without care or guidance, and their businesses, both in town and country, were without supervision, so that the men themselves had been driven by the efforts of the Crown to secure what they called justice to that pitch of bankruptcy which seemed now to be so fashionable among the pet Crown agents in Ireland. On the 16th of June, when the Crown made up its mind to commit these men for trial, an appeal was made for funds to help the prisoners and to assist them in obtaining a fair trial. That appeal was circulated throughout the county of Sligo, and the learned Solicitor General claimed that it was framed in terms that were calculated to intimidate the jury and prevent a fair trial in that county. If that were so, why did the Government delay to take action in reference to that appeal until the Sligo Assizes were over. The Attorney General went down to Sligo to conduct the trial—at least, so it was said. Let who would believe it, he (Mr. Sexton) refused to do so. The Attorney General knew on the day he went down to Sligo, as well as upon the day he left it, that this appeal had been in print and had been circulated. The hon. and learned Gentleman went down for the purpose of other trials, and not for this. He would be aware at the earliest possible moment what the terms and substance of the appeal were; and he would, therefore, know whether it was calculated to warp the judgment of any jury who might be selected in the county of Sligo. What did the Attorney General for Ireland do? He allowed a week or a fortnight to pass; and it was only when the Assizes were coming to a conclusion, and when it was too late for the unfortunate prisoners to secure that any action should be taken in their own behalf, that the Attorney General for Ireland, at the last moment, came forward, possessed of full knowledge of the evidence on which he claimed a conviction from a jury, and having all the facts in the dark recesses of his mind; but instead of avowing them, and allowing the prisoners out on bail, he came down at the last moment and pitifully put forward the fact of this appeal, published eight weeks before, as a reason why the trial was to be postponed. And now as to the question of bail. These 11 prisoners were almost all of them in the same boat. Two informers—one, a branded soldier dismissed from the Army; and another, possessing a treble qualification in consequence of having first committed a cowardly highway robbery upon a poor woman, next an attempt to murder a Judge, and charged, lastly, with being mixed up with the murder of Lord Frederick Cavendish and Mr. Burke—it was upon the evidence of such a man as that that these unfortunate prisoners were kept month after month without their liberty. The whole of the evidence against them was that of this branded soldier and this monstrous criminal. What happened? When the question of bail arose, the Solicitor General for Ireland spoke to him (Mr. Sexton) as if he ought to be thankful because the Crown allowed three of the accused persons to be admitted to bail, and also because the bail was small. Now, if the Crown seriously believed that such an offence as treason-felony, and such a combination of offences as treason-felony and conspiracy to murder, could be proved against these three men, or that there was a shadow of hope of securing their conviction, did the Solicitor General mean to say that the Crown would have liberated them on bail for the paltry sum of £25? The admission of a man to bail upon such terms would appear to show that it was not of the least importance whether he ever turned up again or not. It was perfectly evident that if the Crown had a case against these men, they would never have admitted them to bail upon such terms as would be hardly likely to secure their appearance in the event of their being wanted again. Further, there was no difference whatever in the case of any one of these men as contrasted with that of the rest; and he could only conclude that the Crown believed that no jury would—he would not say hang a dog, but even consent to put a dog to momentary discomfort, upon the evidence of this wretched brace of informers. He had received two telegrams that evening, which his hon. Friend the Member for the City of Cork (Mr. Parnell) had already read to the Committee. In the first of these he was desired to impress upon the Government and the Committee the necessity of putting these men upon their trial at once. In the second telegram the prisoners implored that they might be brought to trial, and declared their readiness to waive their right in respect of any change of venue. The Solicitor General for Ireland was a lawyer, and he told them that this waiver of right by the prisoners would not save the Crown. When he (Mr. Sexton) stated the other night that the motion of the Attorney General for Ireland at Sligo for the postponement of the trial was interpreted by some persons as indicating the intention of postponing the trial to the next Assizes, the hon. and learned Gentleman told him that the Crown had no such intention at all. Then why, when the postponement of the trial was moved for, had not due notice been given in regard to when and where it was to take place? It had been said that the appeal which had been made to the public would have the effect of preventing a fair trial in the county of Sligo; but the Attorney General for Ireland had not conveyed, in any way, an opinion that the circulation of that appeal would prevent a fair trial in any other county of Ireland. The 5th of August, when the Commission was to meet, was still seven days distant, and there had been between a fortnight and three weeks for the Attorney General for Ireland to give the necessary 10 days' notice. What he now pressed for was a trial in some other part of Ireland than the county of Sligo, and he could not understand why the Attorney General for Ireland, on making the application to postpone the trial, had not served the prisoners with the necessary 10 days notice of his intention to move the High Court of Justice in Dublin to change the venue and proceed with the trial elsewhere. He contended that the Government had broken faith with him, and that there was not a shadow of pretence for any further delay. There was no evidence which they did not possess now which they would get hereafter. He therefore called upon them, and he hoped his hon. Friends would support him and persist in the demand, to take the necessary steps for bringing forward the trial at once. The course they were at present pursuing simply conveyed to the public mind a sense of the unfairness of the treatment to which these men were subjected. After four months of imprisonment, and after having exhausted all the tactics of prosecutors, informers, and spies, it was their duty either to bring the men to trial at once, or to liberate them. He could not say where they were to be tried, and the prisoners themselves cared not; they were ready for trial anywhere. If the Crown declined to put them upon trial, let them then take the only legal alternative, and accept bail for their appearance, setting them at liberty until they were prepared to put them upon their trial.

Notice taken, that 40 Members were not present; Committee counted, and 40 Members being found present,

THE SOLICITOR GENERAL FOR IRELAND (Mr. WALKER) said, the hon. Member for Sligo (Mr. Sexton) had called attention at some length to the case of the Tubbercurry prisoners. He desired, therefore, to state to the Committee the position in which the matter stood. The crime of which these men were accused occurred some years ago. There were in all 12 men charged, and the charge brought against them was for one of the most grievous offences which could be imagined—namely, conspiracy to murder a Government official connected with the workhouse in that town, who, beyond all doubt, was fired at by some person. The other charge against these 12 men was one of treason-felony, which was also in itself a grave and serious crime. As he had said, these crimes occurred some time ago—as a matter of fact, two years ago—and he thought it would occur to the common sense of all in the House that when crimes of that nature had occurred a couple of years ago, and the number of men accused was 12, that it would require a much greater time to complete and to inquire into the evidence than if the charges were against one man, or if the crime had been of recent date. Some time in April last, these prisoners having been arrested, evidence was taken in the usual and authorized way, according to the Act of Parliament, under the powers vested in the Executive by the Prevention of Crime Act. It was the duty of the Executive to enforce the law, and they would be very much to blame if they did not do so. In pursuance of the power the law vested in them for the suppression of crime, inquiries were held from time to time under the provisions of the Act of Parliament, and also when the men were arraigned. It was perfectly true that there had been a considerable number of remands in the course of the inquiries, and it was inevitable from the nature of the case that these remands should take place. There were a considerable number of prisoners, and a very large number of witnesses, and they had to make out a case not only against each, but against everyone of them. It was, therefore, impossible to bring the case to a complete issue until a considerable time had elapsed, and it was for the benefit of the prisoners themselves, and in the interests of justice, that in every case a complete case should be made out before they were committed for trial, so that they might not find fresh charges launched against them on the trial. The evidence given upon the committal was the property of the prisoners. They were able to use it, and sift it thoroughly between the date of the committal and the period fixed for the trial. Therefore, it was in the interests of the prisoners themselves, and in the interests of justice, that a complete case should be made out, as far as possible, in every instance before prisoners were committed for trial. The hon. Member for Sligo (Mr. Sexton) had commented upon the refusal to allow the prisoners to see their solicitor. What occurred was this. There were 12 men accused, and the 12 men had one solicitor in common, and the Prison Rules did not allow the 12 men to be brought into one room for the purpose of consulting him. The Attorney General for Ireland, however, as soon as the difficulty was communicated to the Government, in the exercise of his discretion, gave orders that the prisoners should be allowed to see their solicitor together, subject to the Prison Regulations, and that was done. The inquiries had proceeded, and necessarily they had occupied considerable time. They went on *diem in diem* for a number of days. The evidence of Moran, the informer, took up a considerable time. He told a long and a succinct story; but his cross-examination occupied a considerable time. It was said that a rumour had been circulated throughout the prison that information had been given by A. and by B., and Mr. Bolton's name was mentioned as appearing on the scene, and endeavouring to poison the mind of this or that person in obtaining evidence for the Crown. That was altogether a gratuitous assertion as far as Mr. Bolton was concerned. He had neither acted nor appeared in any shape in this prosecution, which had been conducted entirely by the Solicitor for the county—Mr. Anderson. It was stated by the hon. Member for Sligo (Mr. Sexton), that after the prisoners were committed for trial, the Attorney General for Ireland did not go down to conduct the prosecution. He would not notice the imputation which had been made against his right hon. and learned Friend in regard to the motives upon which he had acted. It was asserted that his right hon. and learned Friend went down there as a sham, and that he had no intention when he went down to Sligo of conducting this trial at all. Now, what was it that occurred? His right hon. and learned Friend went down to Sligo. The hon. Member for Sligo (Mr. Sexton) had taken the opportunity, in the course of his speech, of going through the evidence, from his own point of view, and of commenting upon the evidence of the informer, Moran. He had not only commented upon that evidence, but all the other evidence, and with all the eloquence he was master of he had condemned the case for the Crown. He (the Solicitor General for Ireland) proposed to leave the evidence against the prisoners exactly where it was, remembering that these men were still to be tried, and because he did not think it his duty for one moment to answer the hon. Member. All he could say was that there was a strong *primâ facie* case against the prisoners; but it would be improper for any person holding the position he did, now that a trial was pending, to go into the evidence and endeavour to establish a case in answer to the statements of the hon. Member. Then, what was it that occurred? In the local newspapers there was circulated a document, dated the 16th of April, appealing to the public throughout the county for what was called a fair trial for these men. This appeal was made before the trial was to have taken place; and in consequence of the influence which such appeals were likely to have upon the minds of the jurors, the document having been circulated throughout the county not two months before the trial, but immediately preceding it—in consequence of that, a conclusion was arrived at that the trial ought to be postponed. The learned Judge who presided at the Assizes, in the exercise of his discretion, came to the conclusion that a fair trial could not be had in the county of Sligo, and he, therefore, postponed the case. It was proved, to the satisfaction of the Judge, that these documents had been circulated, and circulated in order to influence the minds of the jury, and to produce such an amount of terrorism as might affect their verdict. It was upon that ground, and upon that ground alone, that the learned Judge, who was otherwise quite prepared to try the case, came to the conclusion that the trial ought to be postponed. He was not there to say that the learned Judge did not exercise a proper discretion, having the documents before him; it certainly was a wise and prudent discretion. He had gone down solely for the purpose of hearing the Tubbercurry trial. The Judge had come to the conclusion that a fair trial could not be had in Sligo. Was it, then, the fault of the Public Prosecutor that the venue had been changed? The prisoners could not be altogether dissociated from those who were their false friends. The letters of these false friends it was which led the Judge to the conclusion that a fair trial could not be had on the spot. The Attorney General for Ireland, therefore, was coerced to the conclusion that a fair trial could not be had in Sligo, and the case was postponed until the next Assizes. What, then, did he start with? In the first place, with the authority of the Judge that a fair trial could not be had in Sligo. He was told that the Crown was responsible for the delay—abuse was poured on the Crown officials unstintingly because of the postponement; but through whose act was the postponement? Why, through the act of the prisoners themselves, or those for whom they were responsible.

MR. MOLLOY: Who made the affidavit on which the Judge acted?

THE SOLICITOR GENERAL FOR IRELAND (Mr. WALKER): The District Inspector of Tubbercurry himself, who was thoroughly acquainted with the circumstances of the case. [*"Oh!" and a laugh.*] Hon. Members opposite sneered—did they wish to imply that a District Inspector was not to be believed in Ireland?

MR. WILLIAM REDMOND: Not as a rule.

THE SOLICITOR GENERAL FOR IRELAND (Mr. WALKER) said, he should let that observation have all the weight it was entitled to. He should pass from it.

MR. WILLIAM REDMOND: District Inspectors are entitled to no more credence than any other officials in Ireland.

THE CHAIRMAN: If the hon. Member for Wexford continues these interruptions after I now call him to Order, I shall have to call attention to his conduct.

THE SOLICITOR GENERAL FOR IRELAND (Mr. WALKER) said, the Judge had considered the evidence impartially, and, acting on his discretion, had come to the conclusion that the trial should be postponed. It was the Judge who had come to that conclusion, and no one else. When this matter was considered in the House on Friday last, the complaint was that the prisoners were not going to be tried in Dublin at all. The hon. Member for Sligo (Mr. Sexton) had brought it forward in Committee of Supply, and he (the Solicitor General for Ireland) had said a few words in answer to him. He had stated then, as he stated now, that the men were to be tried in October, the earliest time at which they could be tried. No complaint was made then about the postponement, the only grievance being that the venue was to be changed, and that the prisoners had not been let out on bail. The complaint now seemed to be that, at the time the order was made to postpone the trial, the Judge should have seen that such postponement was unnecessary, and that the venue should have been changed then, if it was necessary to change it at all. But at that time it was doubtful whether it was necessary to change the venue. The Attorney General for Ireland had to exercise his discretion in the matter. Within a few days the Attorney General for Ireland came to the conclusion that the proper course for him to follow, in the exercise of his discretion, was to change the venue; and before this subject was discussed on Friday last, July 25th, the Attorney General for Ireland had come to the conclusion that the proper course for him to adopt was to change the venue, and change it to Dublin. It was said now—telegrams were produced by the hon. Member for the City of Cork (Mr. Parnell) and the hon. Member for Sligo (Mr. Sexton) from the legal adviser of the prisoners — that the prisoners were willing to waive the 10 days' notice to which they were entitled under the Prevention of Crime Act. That was an idle and empty offer. Coming from a lawyer it was an idle and empty argument, because every lawyer knew that prisoners could not waive their right. No man accused of a crime could give any consent of the kind on which the Crown could act. The Government were in the position in which they were on Friday last, when they stated openly in the House that the case was to be tried in October, the earliest time at which it could be tried. No objection was made on Friday, the objection then taken being against the trial being held in Dublin at all, instead of the locality in which the offence was committed, which would have led to the case being postponed until March. So far as the interests of justice would permit, and even stretching a point—considering the observations which had been made about a delay of two months—the Attorney General for Ireland would, he was sure, carefully consider the case of every one of the prisoners, in order to see how far he could add to the number who had been let out on bail—namely, three; and, speaking for himself, he might say he should be glad to see the Attorney General for Ireland exercise his discretion as largely as possible with that object.

MR. HARRINGTON: Is it not possible to serve the 10 days' notice and take the prisoners to trial at a later date?

THE SOLICITOR GENERAL FOR IRELAND (Mr. WALKER): No.

MR. HARRINGTON: A true bill has been found. It is not necessary for the case to go before the Grand Jury at all.

MR. WILLIAM REDMOND said, he did not rise for the purpose of unnecessarily prolonging the discussion; but he was bound to say, having listened very carefully to the speech of the hon. and learned Gentleman who had just sat down, that the only impression that speech had conveyed to his mind was this—that the hon. and learned Gentleman evidently was aware that he had a very bad case indeed to defend, and had endeavoured to make that case appear less bad by making a long and rambling speech such as they had just listened to. He (Mr. W. Redmond) ventured to think that the case now under discussion was absolutely without parallel. It was a case which affected the liberty—he might almost say the lives—of 11 respectable men in Ireland, and the people who were dependent on them for a livelihood. It was a case which he really believed would recommend itself to the consideration of the people of England, if it could be fairly stated to them. It would, if properly presented, create such an impression in this country as would compel Her Majesty's Government to take that action which it appeared they would not take upon the mere representation of the Irish Members of the House. Complaints were made from time to time against matters of this kind being discussed in that Assembly. Well, that Assembly was commonly called the High Court of Justice of this Kingdom. And what did they find when they came to this High Court to discuss a case of this kind? [*Laughter.*] It was all very well for two right hon. Gentlemen on the Treasury Bench to laugh when the case of 11 men who might be about to lose their liberty, even their lives, was mentioned; but he did not complain of it, for that was not the first time they had had experience of the great disposition on the part of right hon. Gentlemen on the Treasury Bench to be unnaturally hilarious when serious matters affecting the welfare of Irishmen were under discussion. He had been going to observe, when interrupted by the somewhat boisterous laughter of Members on the Treasury Bench, that it was a discouraging thing for Members from Ireland to come there and state calmly and fairly the affairs of certain men in Ireland who were about to be brought to trial, and to find that not more than a couple of dozen English and Scotch Members attended to hear the matter discussed. It was frequently said the Irish Members had no right to complain, because Ireland was fairly represented in the House. What representation had she? Why, whenever a case of this kind cropped up—a case which interested a large majority of the Irish Members—little or no attention was paid to it by the bulk of the Members of the House. They found it as much as they could do to get a quorum of Members to come in, from time to time, moving a "count." It was an extremely discouraging thing, and a thing which should be impressed on the people of Ireland, that when their Representatives discussed a case of this kind they did so to absolutely empty Benches, no English or Scotch Members considering it worth their while to come down to listen to the claims the Irish Members were bringing forward. However, the Irish Members would not be deterred, by the absence of English and Scotch Members, from discussing the grievances and claims of their country. What was the case of these men in Sligo Gaol? Why, some four months ago 11 men were arrested without any specific charge being brought against them at all. They had been four months in gaol, cut off from their occupations and their families. They had been remanded time after time, with no evidence against them. If that was considered by the Government a proceeding consistent with justice, he did not think there were many people in the country who would agree with them. If these men were arrested on specific charges, why had they not been placed in the dock, why had not evidence been brought against them, and why had they not been made to stand their trial before their fellow-countrymen? Why, they had not been tried because there was no case against them. They had been arrested, it was believed, in order to satisfy the ambition of certain police officials who were craving distinction in this particular way. They were arrested upon what with even a jury of Englishmen and Protestants would fail to obtain a conviction, and they were kept in gaol while the police and officials were scouring the country for informers to give evidence against them. The Solicitor General for Ireland, who spoke just now, and had precipitately retreated after his speech, as though ashamed of the part he had had to take, had said it was impossible, from the nature of the case, to avoid frequent remands. It was all very well to say that there was something in the case which made these remands necessary; but in order to prove their justice it was desirable that the circumstances which had led to them should be plainly stated, and not hinted at, as the hon. and learned Gentleman had hinted at them in his speech. The hon. and learned Gentleman in the course of his observations complained that until that evening no dissatisfaction was expressed by the Irish Members at the trial having been postponed until October. Well, it was true no dissatisfaction had hitherto been expressed; but the reason was that it was only that evening that Members on the Irish Benches absolutely realized or even heard that such a monstrous outrage was going to be perpetrated by the Government as the postponement of the trial of these men for two months longer, and the consequent detention of the accused for another two months longer without a tittle of evidence being brought against them. It was not at all the duty of Irish Members of Parliament to see that men who were arrested by the Government were brought to trial at once. It was not a part of their legitimate duty; it was owing to the distorted state of affairs in Ireland that Irish Members of Parliament were obliged to occupy the attention and time of the House of Commons in pressing claims of this kind upon the attention of Englishmen and Scotchmen. He could perfectly realize that it was with considerable indifference that Gentlemen representing English and Scotch constituencies listened to a case such as that now under discussion; but it was absolutely necessary that if justice was not meted out to the people of Ireland by the authorized officers of the Crown in that country, the Irish Members should bring the action of those officers before Parliament, and, if possible, try to create such a state of public opinion as would serve to cause these unfortunate men to be brought to trial at the earliest possible moment. Supposing these men when brought to trial were acquitted—as very probably they would be—what would be their position? They would have been six months in prison, cut off from their occupations, from their friends and from their families, and then even an acquittal would give them little satisfaction. The way the men were being treated was absolutely outrageous. He did not believe that any where else in the world, even under the most despotic Government in existence, could men be arrested in the light of day, could be thrown into prison, and remanded day after day, week after week, and month after month, without a single iota of evidence being brought against them. This kind of thing could not go on much longer in Ireland. The Irish Members had thrashed the case out very fully in the House of Commons. They had shown the injustice of arresting men and keeping them in prison without bringing evidence against them—they had shown the system to be inhuman, unconstitutional, and distinctly despotic. He (Mr. W. Redmond) would say, from his position as an Irish Representative, that he believed in his soul that if cases like these multiplied in Ireland, and if the Government persisted in arresting men and sending them to prison for long terms without bringing evidence against them, there would be a feeling aroused in that country against English rule far more extensive than any which had ever yet been aroused. If the Government did not take steps to put an end to the present mode of government—the present Liberal mode of government—they would find at the next General Election and in the House that the Irish people and their Representatives knew how to treat an Administration which called itself Liberal, but which was before the world the most despotic in existence.

MR. JUSTIN M'CARTHY said, this was a very serious case, and one which appeared to him to be made much more serious by the kind of defence set up by the hon. and learned Gentleman the Solicitor General for Ireland. He (Mr. M'Carthy) had not known much about the facts until he heard that night the powerful appeal of the hon. Member for Sligo (Mr. Sexton), and the singularly confused and confusing answer of the Solicitor General for Ireland. Out of all the brambles and brushwood of law, with which the hon. and learned Gentleman encumbered his speech, they got two or three facts for the understanding of men who were not lawyers. They got the fact that some four or five months ago some men were arrested on some charge or other, that from that time to this they had been kept in gaol without trial, and that the earliest date at which they could be brought to trial was two months off. They got the fact that though the men were seemingly charged with a grave and serious crime, three of them had been since set at liberty, on a bail of £25 each. He would ask the Committee to say whether there could be anything serious in the charge, or whether they believed there was evidence of any kind to be brought against any of these men, seeing that some of them were allowed to be at large on bail of £25? What reasons did the hon. and learned Gentleman give for keeping these men in prison? Why, first of all, he said that the 11 men were charged with the one offence, and that it took a much longer time to bring charges of guilt home against 11 men than against one man. If that was so, it was, he supposed, owing to his having an unlegal and unenlightened sort of understanding that he was unable to comprehend it. If these 11 men were all accused of the same crime, the same evidence which would convict one would convict all of them, or, at least, so he should suppose. If they committed one crime, it must have been committed together, or in some kind of combination; and he altogether failed to understand why a longer time should be required to get together evidence to convict 11 than would be required to get together evidence to convict one. He did not know why, in a case of murder, it should take longer to prove that a person was killed by three men, by five men, or b a dozen men, than that he was killed by one. He could not see what reason there could be for postponing the trial month after month in a case where the Crown must soon have exhausted the evidence. The hon. and learned Gentleman had given them another reason. He had told them what one official thought and what he did not think, and then he declared that the trial had to be put off because someone had said or done or published something rather indiscreet, which made the learned Judge think that there should be a postponement. If this was a principle of law, they placed accused persons not only at the mercy of indiscreet friends, but also at the mercy of enemies who chose to publish statements apparently on their behalf. The hon. and learned Gentleman had said the fault was the prisoners' own. How could that be? How could he hold persons in prison responsible for statements published by other persons outside? What reason was there for saying the prisoners had authorized the publication? Were they to understand it as a point of their law, that when a man was charged with an offence, and some friend or enemy of his did an indiscreet thing, the man so charged was to be punished, as a sort of vengeance on his head, by having his case postponed? He did not think such a principle would be listened to for a moment, unless in the case of a charge brought against some Irishman. If the hon. and learned Gentleman's contention was correct, he (Mr. M'Carthy) saw no reason why these men should ever be released or tried. At any moment, as the time of trial drew near, some indiscreet friend or some malignant enemy might publish or say something which would make the Judge say justice could not be done whilst the echo of it lived in the minds of the people. If the hon. and learned Gentleman's statement were the defence of the Government, all he could say was, that the speech of the hon. Member for Sligo (Mr. Sexton), eloquent as it had been, was made ten times more eloquent in its defence of public justice by the hon. and learned Gentleman's attempt to reply to it.

MR. JUSTIN HUNTLY M'CARTHY said, the hon. and learned Gentleman the Solicitor General for Ireland had now left the House; but his place had been taken by the right hon. Gentleman the Chief Secretary to the Lord Lieutenant. These two Gentlemen reminded him of a toy which combined instruction with amusement—a toy in which there were two figures, one of which came out in fair weather and the other in foul; the only difference being that, in the case of the two Gentlemen, they both represented foul weather. With regard to the case under discussion, if it had occurred in the Dominions of the Czar, they would have had Englishmen speaking in the House and writing in the newspapers about the tyranny of the Russian officials; they would have had presented to them highly-coloured pictures of miserable men confined in dungeons for months without trial — for months of wretched days and melancholy nights — and they would have heard a great deal about the blessings of English rule and the happiness of living in Great Britain. The history of the case was in many ways an instructive one. It was now many months since Mr. Fitzgerald was arrested. He was arrested, as he (Mr. M'Carthy) believed, without warrant, and hurried over to Ireland without being allowed to see anyone. He had been imprisoned and kept for many months without any attempt at a trial, although, on the 24th of April, the Irish Members were informed that he would be brought to trial as soon as possible. The hon. Gentleman the Member for Mallow (Mr. O'Brien) at that time was censured in the House for speaking of the inquiry as it was then being conducted, as a "hugger-mugger inquiry." It was difficult to say what the words "hugger-mugger" precisely meant; but if they were at all applicable to this case at the time they were used, they were certainly much more applicable now, when the "hugger-mugger" inquiry was becoming more "hugger-mugger" than ever. These unfortunate prisoners, no doubt, had a fair appreciation of the position in which they had been placed by Her Majesty's Government when they spoke of being "robbed" by the Government. They were robbed of their worldly goods by being kept in prison, and deprived of the means of earning their livelihood; but, more than that, they were robbed of their liberty, and of that sense of truth and justice which every citizen had at heart; while, seemingly, the only hope the Government had of obtaining a verdict was by some "Star Chamber" inquisition. The hon. Member for Sligo (Mr. Sexton) had been informed, months ago, that Mr. Fitzgerald was to be tried on charges of treason-felony and conspiracy to murder; but when it was pointed out that the two offences could not be included in the one indictment, the right hon. Gentleman the Chief Secretary promptly shifted his ground, and declared that the time for drawing up the indictment had not yet arrived. It seemed that the time for framing the indictment was never going to arrive. The prisoners were in a worse position than the historical *Flying Dutchman*—they were never going to be set free at all. On the 23rd of April, the right hon. Gentleman the Chief Secretary again informed the Irish Members that it was the desire of the Executive to close the case at the next hearing, and that there was no intention whatever to postpone the trial over the summer. Now they learnt that the trial was to be postponed over the summer. It would probably be postponed over the autumn, and then over the spring. Next summer might come and go and find these men still in prison. It was almost useless to make an appeal to the Government in these cases; so he would only ask them whether in this matter they thought their conduct just and reasonable—whether they did not think it passed into the region of the absurd?

MR. T. D. SULLIVAN said, he had listened to the speech of the hon. Member for Sligo (Mr. Sexton), and also to the reply delivered by the Solicitor General for Ireland. A lawyer was a trained disputant, and it would be a very bad case indeed in which the Solicitor General for Ireland could not bring some arguments to bear in support of the position he was defending. The hon. and learned Gentleman could not, however, be congratulated on the strength of his arguments that night. The hon. and learned Gentleman had assumed the whole case as he went along. Again and again he had repeated the statement that every delay which occurred was owing to the fault of the prisoners; but never once did he offer an atom of proof. He had said it was owing to the fault of the prisoners. What fault? If the hon. and learned Gentleman were present, he (Mr. Sullivan) should press for an answer to that question. The hon. and learned Gentleman ought to be present whilst this subject was under discussion; why was he not? Could he not be summoned—he was within the precincts of the House? What fault had he to allege against the prisoners as having caused the delay of the trial? The hon. and learned Gentleman had never stated that; but he had gone on triumphantly assuming to the end that it was the prisoners' own fault. That style of debate ought not to pass muster in the House of Commons, or elsewhere. Then, apologizing for the fact that these prisoners were not allowed freely to see their solicitor, he had said that they all had the one legal adviser, and that it was not desirable that they should all see him at one time. Why was it undesirable? The hon. and learned Gentleman had said these men were charged individually and collectively. It came to this, then—that the men were to be charged collectively, and might be hanged in a batch; but they were not to see their solicitor collectively, so as to prepare a common defence? Was that fair play? Was it fair that the Crown should be able to make a collective charge against them, whilst they were not allowed to make a collective defence? Would that be considered fair play by any other assembly of Englishmen or Scotchmen in the world? Another great point of the hon. and learned Gentleman was that the learned Judge, acting on his discretion, decided that because certain documents had been published in the locality it was not desirable that the case should there and then be brought to trial. The hon. and learned Gentleman said—"The Judge so decided." Did he suppose that amongst Irishmen in Ireland that statement would carry any weight whatever? They knew how Judges decided cases in Ireland—they knew that as soon as the Judges found how the wind blew from Dublin Castle they trimmed their sails according to the breeze. The Judges knew what was required of them by Dublin Castle, and acted accordingly. It amounted to nothing to say the Judge, acting on documents submitted to him by the Crown, took a certain view of the case. But a more startling doctrine still, propounded by the Solicitor General for Ireland, was this—that the prisoners were responsible for the acts of their indiscreet friends. "It was impossible," said the hon. and learned Gentleman, "to dissociate these individuals from the action of their indiscreet friends." He (Mr. Sullivan) denied that doctrine altogether. It was simply monstrous. There could be no safety for prisoners in Ireland if they were to be held accountable while safe behind prison bars for the action of their friends. That House was becoming accustomed to extraordinary and unconstitutional doctrines, and he thought there should be some revolt against them, not only from those Benches, but from all parts of the House. The doctrine the hon. and learned Gentleman had laid down that night was monstrous and unconstitutional, and a case which rested in any way on such a device as that was flimsy and rotten. It was said that when things were done in a hurry, doubtless, mistakes were made—it was said there had been no deliberation exercised in connection with these matters. He said that the defence offered by the Solicitor General for Ireland, instead of meeting this case, had made it worse. The case was one which called for speedy action, and he asked the Committee to consider it in order that justice might be done.

MR. GREGORY said, this case had been laid before the Committee by the hon. Member below the Gangway (Mr. T. D. Sullivan) as one calling for the interference of the Committee. If it were true that these men, having been arrested in Ireland, had been subject to constant remands without evidence; if their trial had been adjourned by the Judge without any proper justification; if they had been put on their trial without any evidence, or without any indictment being preferred against them —why, then, the case was monstrous. But, as an old practitioner, he ventured to doubt whether such things could happen; he doubted whether men could be remanded from time to time without any evidence being brought against them. In England, he knew they could not. Nor would men be put on trial in England without any indictment being prepared against them. He took the case as stated by the Solicitor General for Ireland. The hon. and learned Gentleman had very truly remarked that it took considerably more time to complete a case against a number of persons than would be required to complete the case against one individual, because the prosecution had, with regard to the commission of a certain act, to connect them with it and with each other—to bring them together, so to speak, and to ascertain their motives in connection with each other. All that, as a matter of fact, occupied a great deal of time, which everyone would know who was practically acquainted with business of the kind. Again, he presumed that evidence was from time to time brought before the magistrates previously to the remands of the prisoners; and he was satisfied that the magistrates would not have remanded them without evidence sufficient to justify that course, nor would they have committed them for trial without sufficient presumption. Then he came to the postponement of the trial. It was alleged by the Solicitor General for Ireland that when the trial was about to take place in Ireland, a large number of publications appeared, which would necessarily influence the jury, and which, in the opinion of the Judge, was calculated to prejudice the minds of the jury in respect of the trial of the prisoners. Now, that was a matter on which the Judge was strictly correct in exercising his discretion; if the Judge on that occasion thought that a fair trial could not be had, it was quite right that the trial should be postponed. With regard to the place of trial, he did not know why the case was not tried in Dublin. He freely admitted that the 10 days' notice was an objection as to the time; but yet it seemed to him that the trial might have taken place at Dublin. It appeared to him that, in all other respects, the statement of the hon. and learned Gentleman was a sufficient answer on the Crown case—that time was necessary to get the case up, and that remands were necessary from time to time, and he was satisfied that evidence was produced to justify those remands. He also believed that evidence was produced before the magistrates to justify the committal of the prisoners for trial; and, further, that an indictment was preferred against them; and, finally, having regard to the circumstances of the time, bearing in mind the effect which the publications to which the Solicitor General for Ireland had referred were likely to have on the minds of the jury, he ventured to think that the Judge was fully justified in changing the venue.

MR. HARRINGTON said, the Committee had to deal, not with the presumptions of the hon. Member for East Sussex (Mr. Gregory), but with the facts of the case, and those facts had been stated by hon. Members on those Benches, and were known to everyone in the House. They by no means accorded with the extraordinary and fanciful presumption on which the hon. Gentleman who had just sat down took up his position. The hon. Gentleman assumed, of course, that everything had been done in a perfectly regular manner. Hon. Members in that House invariably did presume that everything was regularly done in such matters in Ireland, and it was only the force of circumstances that in time compelled them to admit that things did not go on quite so happily there as they had been led to believe. It was not at all strange that the hon. and learned Solicitor General for Ireland, who represented at that moment the Irish Government in that House, had not made use of any of those extraordinary presumptions which the hon. Member for East Sussex had indulged in. He had referred, in the earlier part of the discussion, to a case within his own cognizance in Ireland in which there were no less than nine remands, extending over a period of nine weeks, and in which the evidence adduced at the final remand was precisely the same as that brought forward on the first day. The Solicitor General for Ireland knew the case he was referring to, and he could give him the names of the prisoners. He challenged the hon. and learned Gentleman to deny the statement he had made—that the evidence on the ninth day was precisely the same as that brought forward on the first. The Crown had recourse to those remands in order to tide the trial over the period of the Assizes; to keep the prisoners in their cells for months, in order, if possible, to pry into their thoughts, and to hold the thumbscrew over them with the object of making them give evidence against their companions. One of those prisoners was offered a free pardon if he consented to give evidence against his companions, He asked the Members of that House to look at the actual facts, and to contemplate the position of the unfortunate man in gaol without friends, as that unfortunate policeman was; let them consider what a risk was run in asking him to give evidence to save his life. The hon. and learned Gentleman could not blot out from the minds of the people of Ireland the belief that fearful misdeeds were worked by a system like this, and no amount of persuasion on the part of the hon. and learned Gentleman could get rid of the fact that everything of this kind was possible under the system of legal chicanery which was bringing the English Government in Ireland into disrepute. He should be sorry to accuse the hon. and learned Gentleman of making a statement which was calculated to injure men in the position of these unfortunate prisoners, or of intending to do them an injury; but, undoubtedly, one portion of his speech was as unfair and ill borne out by facts as if he had the deliberate intention of injuring the prisoners. He alluded to the statement that the cause of the delay which had taken place in regard to the trial of the prisoners was due to the conduct of the prisoners themselves. The statement was that the prisoners in gaol were connected with the circulation of the appeals which were made in their behalf for a fair trial; and with reference to that he challenged the hon. and learned Gentleman to produce one tittle of evidence in support of his statement. The Chief Secretary to the Lord Lieutenant of Ireland, in the last debate on this subject, admitted that there was no opportunity of establishing any connection between the prisoners in gaol and the documents circulated throughout the country; and everyone who knew anything of the gaol practice in Ireland, and the rigid gaol supervision exercised towards prisoners, would know perfectly well that the statement about their being able to publish documents outside was absolutely absurd. Again, the Solicitor General for Ireland had not at all addressed himself to the case to which he (Mr. Harrington) had drawn his attention—that was to say, to the case of the Galway prisoners who were remanded nine times. He mentioned the case, because in it the Crown had, in his opinion, acted in a manner precisely similar to that in which they had acted towards the men now in prison in Sligo. In the Galway case, it was then two years since the unfortunate men were taken away from their homes; and, in spite of all the means at their disposal under the Prevention of Crime Act for packing juries and for bringing them to speedy trial, the Crown still kept them in prison without trial. Irish Members knew what the Crown had done in the case of the Galway prisoners, and they felt that, were it not for the advocacy of the hon. Member for Sligo (Mr. Sexton), the Crown would act towards the Tubbercurry prisoners in the same manner —that was to say, keep them in gaol for two years without trial, working on their fears, and tempting them with bribes, in the hope of inducing them to give information which would save their own lives, by taking the lives of others perfectly innocent. He thought that the Solicitor General for Ireland would find it necessary to supplement by another statement his observations made with the endeavour of connecting these unfortunate men with the documents circulated in their behalf. There had been no evidence brought forward at any time that these men shut up in prison had any opportunity of communicating with persons outside. Besides, he contended that the document, although, perhaps, strongly worded, was perfectly fair, and a perfectly lawful document, and that, although it might have created some sympathy amongst the people, it could not at the trial have had the slightest effect on the jury, because the Crown took care that they should pack into the jury boxes in Ireland not men standing impartially between Crown and prisoner—men who were sworn to look impartially at the facts of the case—but men from whom they were secure of a verdict.

COLONEL KING-HARMAN said, the sympathies of hon. Members below the Gangway throughout the discussion was all on one side. There did not seem to be any sympathy for the unfortunate persons who had been foully murdered during the Reign of Terror in Ireland, or for their families. The hon. Gentleman the Member for Westmeath (Mr. Harrington) had said a good deal about presumptions. He (Colonel King-Harman) was inclined to think that it was a fair presumption that these men were the perpetrators of some of the deeds which had disgraced Ireland, and that they should be kept in gaol as long as there was a fair opportunity of getting evidence against them. And then the hon. Gentleman spoke of the merciless grasp of the law. He would like to know what mercy had been shown to the unfortunate men whose lives had been taken? Why did the assassins now plead for mercy; or why did the advocates of assassins plead for mercy in their behalf?

MR. HARRINGTON rose to Order. He asked whether the hon. and gallant Member was entitled to charge Members of that House with being the advocates of assassins and murderers in Ireland?

THE CHAIRMAN: I did not understand the hon. and gallant Gentleman to apply the term to hon. Members.

COLONEL KING-HARMAN said, he had not done so. If any charge of making false accusations could be brought against any Member of that House, it would not be brought against him, but against hon. Members below the Gangway, who charged the Government with keeping these men in gaol in order to get information from them which would enable them to bring innocent men to the gallows. It was they who charged the Government with being the defenders of assassins. [*Laughter.*] They might think this a matter for laughter; but they knew there had been a Reign of Terror in Ireland for the last four years, and they knew that it was only by the determination of the Government in Ireland, and by the determination of the Judges and jurors, that crime had been put down there, and that honest men had now a little chance of living in security. When murder was going on throughout the length and breath of the land, hon. Members below the Gangway took care not to denounce it; and now, whenever there was a reasonable case against the murderers, they vilified the Government for trying to bring them to justice. If these men had not committed the crimes imputed to them, they would have the security of being tried by a jury of their countrymen; and it was perfectly ridiculous to tell the House about jury-packing under the present law. If the men were guilty, they would be convicted; and if they were not, they would be acquitted. And hon. Members had no more right to step between them and the jury, and try to prejudice the House in their favour, than he should have were he to declare that they were guilty, and try to prejudice the House against them. But there was this to be said. He knew the neighbourhood where the crime was committed, and he had lived in the county in spite of combination and intimidation, and had refused to be driven out of it. There was a foul conspiracy there to commit outrage, and murder was committed there. If hon. Gentlemen chose to defend men accused of murder, the condition of their minds must be such as he did not envy, and their conduct was but a simple waste of the time of the House, for they had not adduced a single fact that was not already known. And as to the persons for trial, he did not think they would be benefited by it.

MR. SEXTON said, the hon. and gallant Gentleman had gone through a very chivalrous performance; he was for some time Member of Parliament for the county in which these unfortunate men resided, and he said that he lived in the county, and was obliged to leave it. That might be true in a certain sense; but in a political sense he had been driven out of it when he became recreant to the principles of his life, and he (Mr. Sexton) could assure him that the sentiments of the people in Sligo towards him were such that the Orders of Debate would not allow him to discuss them. The hon. and gallant Member, either by the profession of arms, or from some other source, was entitled to be called "gallant" in that House; and it was a great thing for him to stand up there, and with a voice which, although loud, was but the exponent of a puny intellect, to declaim against an appeal on behalf of these unfortunate men for the right to which they were entitled. He had cast insinuations on hon. Gentlemen below the Gangway, and when those insinuations were found out he had retired behind those insinuations; and when called to Order, refused to accept the obvious meaning of his own language—the only meaning of which that language was susceptible —and withdrew.

COLONEL KING-HARMAN: I never withdrew a single expression.

MR. SEXTON said, the hon. and gallant Gentleman had spoken of murder, and the advocates of murder. He (Mr. Sexton) knew as much of Ireland as the hon. and gallant Gentleman, and he preserved quite as vivid a recollection of the scenes which had taken place there during the last four years. He knew that Irish Members did denounce murder, and not murder alone, but they denounced the smaller forms of outrage and illegality; and he knew, too, that men who denounced murder and outrage were thrown into prison; and, further, he knew that when the right hon. and learned Gentleman the Secretary of State for the Home Department announced, in reply to a Question, that Mr. Davitt had been thrown into a cell at Portland, the House shook with the cheers of hon. Gentlemen.

COLONEL KING-HARMAN: I was not a Member of the House at the time.

MR. SEXTON said, he supposed the hon. and gallant Gentleman would accept the cheers of the Tory Party on that occasion. There was, probably, no one more glad than he was to hear of the arrest of Michael Davitt. It required a strong conscience to denounce illegality when the landlords did nothing to help their starving tenants, and when the Government rewarded those who did denounce it with a convict cell. Would the hon. and gallant Gentleman say that the landlords helped the people?

COLONEL KING-HARMAN: I say that they helped the people enormously.

MR. SEXTON: I say that when the peasants were shivering in the cold, the hon. and gallant Gentleman cut off the supply of turf.

COLONEL KING-HARMAN: I rise to make a personal explanation. There is not the slightest foundation for that statement.

THE CHAIRMAN: The hon. and gallant Gentleman will have an opportunity of replying.

MR. SEXTON said, the hon. and gallant Gentleman came down that evening and raised his voice against the undeniable right of these men to be brought before a jury even of Orangemen in Sligo. Did they say a single word in palliation of murder or outrage? What was their contention? Simply, that these men who were in prison were respectable men, and had been so throughout their lives; that they were honourable men, and that they should have the same right of having their case brought before a jury which was given to the commonest foot-pad, and which would be granted to those criminals, nurtured in Dublin Castle, whose atrocities were now the horror of the civilized world. They asked nothing but what was right; and he trusted that no Member of that House would be led away by the hon. and gallant Member, who had made an attempt, which he would not characterize in the language it deserved, to interpose between these unfortunate men and the House of Commons in their appeal for justice.

COLONEL KING-HARMAN said, he wished to reply to one portion of the attack made upon himself by the hon. Member for Sligo (Mr. Sexton), and from that point he would ask the Committee to judge of the rest of the hon. Member's statements. The statement was that in the winter of 1880-1, when fuel was scarce, he took the opportunity of cutting off the supply of turf from his tenants. Upon his honour—as he stood before God—during all that winter he strained every nerve to supply his tenants with fuel; he never charged them a single 6*d.*; he put down every farthing he could afford to raise fuel for them. He had had timber cut down, and the tenants were allowed to take away every root and branch and everything else they could take, and there was hardly a man on the whole property who suffered from a want of fuel. And he did not think there was one of them who at the end of the winter had not thanked him for what he had done. He had done his best, and the charge brought against him by the hon. Member was entirely unfounded.

Mr. T. D. SULLIVAN said, the hon. and gallant Gentleman's contradiction turned on a question of time; but there was a period when the turbary was taken away.

Mr. SEXTON wished to add a word or two in reference to a certain matter that was notorious in Roscommon and all over Ireland—namely, the correspondence which was published in *The Freeman's Journal*, in which it was shown that those who previously owned this property never charged the tenants for turbary; but the hon. and gallant Member avenged himself for the Land Act by putting a charge on the turbary. This was exposed in *The Freeman's Journal* by the hon. Member for Mallow (Mr. O'Brien), who had never made an accusation against any man, whether an official or not, without proving it.

Colonel KING-HARMAN said, this statement was made in *The Freeman's Journal*, but he had proved it to be absolutely false, and he was willing to appeal from the hon. Members to his own tenants as to what he had done.

Mr. HARRINGTON said, there was a matter which had not been touched upon by any of the previous speakers, and that was the item for the expenses of Crown Solicitors in connection with crimes in Ireland. He wished to point out to the Committee that one of the greatest injustices inflicted on men in Ireland who were waiting for trial was this changing of the venue, which threw upon them the onus of bringing their witnesses down and keeping them for many days during the Assizes at enormous cost. At the Winter Assizes many of the prisoners were removed from the different counties within the Circuit to the one town appointed for the Province. He would take the case of the prisoners awaiting their trial in Kerry. When their cases came on they were removed to Cork, where the Winter Assizes were generally held, and the rule at the Assizes as to prisoners was the same as with regard to Special Commissions and generally with regard to cases in which the venue had been changed. There was a case in the past year in which a number of prisoners who had been arrested in Mayo were taken for trial in Cork. That was practically disabling those unfortunate men, whatever might be the charge against them, or whatever might be the evidence by which the Crown was able to sustain the charge, from meeting the charge. It reduced them to this position—that to get anything like a fair trial they would have to incur enormous expense, which men of their position were not able to bear. That inflicted upon them great hardships, and even the risk of losing their liberty, because they were unable to bear these expenses. He believed that it was provided by Statute that when prisoners had been removed by a change of venue it should be competent to the Crown to pay the expenses of witnesses for the prisoners. That was all very well, but when did the Crown pay these expenses? Not before the witnesses left home to attend the trial; not when they reached the Assize town where the trial was to be held, but after the trial was over. Then the Crown would pay the expenses of any witnesses whom the Crown Solicitor had considered necessary for the defence of the prisoner, but that was not a practice in accordance with justice. It did not meet the justice of the case to pay the expenses of a prisoner's witnesses after the issue had been tried, and after the onus had first been thrown upon the prisoner of maintaining those witnesses, whether few or many, for many weeks in some cases, in the Assize town. Hardship of the gravest nature was inflicted in that way;

and he knew of cases in which prisoners had been absolutely unable to bring up the witnesses necessary for their defence. Numerous cases of this kind had occurred—cases in which prisoners had witnesses who would have been able to prove an *alibi*, and completely rebut the evidence of the Crown. The Crown officials, of course, looked after their own witnesses, brought them up at the public expense, provided their travelling expenses, and everything else; but what was the case with regard to the witnesses whom the unfortunate prisoner might find necessary? They might come up if they desired to come; there was no compelling them to do so; and, taken as they were from a humble rank in life, and having such slender means as they generally had, it was impossible for the prisoner to have adequate justice done him by having the necessary witnesses present, except by the aid of some influential friends such as, unfortunately, rarely assisted them. What he contended was that the Crown, where it undertook to pay the expenses of a prisoner's witnesses, should do precisely what it did in the case of the witnesses for the Crown. The Solicitor for the Crown should obtain from the prisoner's solicitor a list of the witnesses whom he considered necessary for the defence of the prisoner, and that the expenses of those witnesses, or, at least, a reasonable portion of the expenses, should be given to them before they were required to leave their homes to go long distances and remain for long periods at the Assize town. Suppose a prisoner required a dozen witnesses; he must have them up at the opening of the Assizes. He had known cases in which the Assizes lasted three weeks. In Cork they had more than once extended over three weeks. A prisoner must assume that his trial would come on upon the opening day; and he must, therefore, have his witnesses up on that day. They must now come up at his expense, if they were not sufficiently devoted to him and to the interests of justice to come up at their own expense. The *onus* of bringing them up was thrown upon the prisoner; the Assizes might last three weeks, and he might have to keep them there all that time at his own expense, or get his solicitor to maintain them on his behalf. That provision for paying the expenses of a prisoner's witnesses was absolutely useless and worthless; because, owing to the money not being paid until after the trial, the witnesses for the defence could not be brought up at the time when they were necessary. He was not speaking of abstract matters at all, but of cases within his own knowledge. He knew that cases had occurred in Sligo County, in which prisoners had been taken from Galway to Sligo, and kept waiting some weeks for their trial, and their witnesses were knocking about the streets begging, in the endeavour to maintain themselves until the trial at which they were to give evidence should come on. And he had known of cases in which witnesses had been unable, through this cause, to remain in the Assize town long enough to give their evidence in defence of unfortunate prisoners. If the Crown wished to meet the justice of the case they must make provision for giving to the witnesses for a prisoner the same facilities for travelling and maintenance as they gave to Crown witnesses. They took great care of the witnesses for the Crown, giving them travelling expenses and maintaining them in the Assize town; but they told the prisoner that if he was rich enough to bring up his witnesses for his defence and keep them as long as they were wanted, then, when the case was over and he had been consigned to a cell or had regained his freedom, the Crown would consider whether they would pay for those witnesses. If such a case occurred in the county in which the prisoner was arrested, the grievance would not be so great, because the witnesses would not have to travel very long distances, and it would be easier to maintain them; but it was unfair, unjust, and contrary to every principle of equity that the *onus* should be thrown upon a prisoner of bringing witnesses perhaps 200 miles away from home, and of maintaining them for weeks in the town to give evidence for him, when he should have been tried in the county in which he was arrested. He hoped they would have some statement from the Solicitor General for Ireland upon this point. The hon. and learned Gentleman's connection with these cases had not been a very long one yet; but he could assure the hon. and learned Gentleman that he could quote many cases in Ireland in which witnesses had returned home from the Assize town before a trial had come on, and left the prisoner to his fate, simply because they were unable to maintain themselves, and the prisoner, owing to his position in life and having no friends to assist him, could not maintain them.

THE SOLICITOR GENERAL FOR IRELAND (Mr. WALKER) said, the point to which the hon. Member had called attention was one which might produce hardship; but the hon. Member surely did not contend that in every case under the Prevention of Crime Act the expenses of witnesses for a prisoner had not been paid until after the trial was over. In his own knowledge that was not the case; and the course adopted by the Crown in regard to prisoners' witnesses was the same as with regard to Crown witnesses.

MR. HARRINGTON said, he had known of several cases in which applications for the expenses of prisoners' witnesses before a trial had been refused. The hon. and learned Gentleman said the course adopted was the same in regard to Crown and prisoners' witnesses. Undoubtedly the expenses were paid in the end; but Crown witnesses were taken in hand at once by a policeman who paid their railway fares, took them to lodgings, and paid all that was necessary until they were paid by the Crown on the close of the trial. But the opposite to this was the practice with regard to the witnesses for the defence. No care was taken of them unless the prisoner had sufficient means to maintain them.

THE SOLICITOR GENERAL FOR IRELAND (Mr. WALKER) replied that he had no doubt that if, in such a case as the hon. Member had mentioned, application was made to the Attorney General for Ireland or the Solicitor General for Ireland, he would take care that the expenses were provided.

MR. ARTHUR O'CONNOR said, he had expected that the hon. and learned Gentleman would intimate that the Government would reconsider their position in regard to this matter; but he had been disappointed, for the hon. and learned Gentleman had confined himself to observations on the minor point raised by the hon. Member for Westmeath (Mr. Harrington). The hon. and gallant Member for Dublin County (Colonel King-Harman) sympathized very warmly with the persons who had been murdered in Ireland in recent years; but why the hon. and gallant Member reserved all his sympathy for those persons he did not know. He and his hon. Friends sympathized with men who were still suffering from injustice and oppression. The men whom the hon. and gallant Member for Dublin County had denounced were men who, in the theory of the law, were at that moment innocent men, because they had not yet been proved guilty. They believed those men could not be proved guilty, because they were innocent. The speech of the hon. Member for East Sussex (Mr. Gregory) was to an Irish Member perfectly disheartening. That hon. Member presumed that everybody employed under the Government was acting honestly, conscientiously, and consistently; that whatever the Crown might do was done on good grounds; that there was ample evidence to justify constant remands of these men, and that there was good ground for supposing that a conviction was likely to follow. That sort of view was calculated to drive Irish Members to despair. English Members would always assume that whatever was done by the Crown in Ireland was beyond challenge. They assumed that French was an immaculate person, although Irish Members had denounced him until it was impossible at last for the Government to pretend that they had any faith in him. They had denounced Cornwall in the same way, and now he was abandoned. They had denounced Bolton, and now Bolton had been dealt with in the same way. Now, when they complained of the treatment by the Crown of these unfortunate prisoners, there was the same presumption, always readily springing up in the mind of English Members, that their complaints were utterly groundless, and that the Crown was beyond rebuke in regard to its action in Ireland. They must, therefore, go on, as they had in the past, and endeavour by constant iteration to drive into the minds of English Members, who were not particularly quick to comprehend anything from Ireland, that there was a grievous cause of complaint; and however long it might be, and however hard it might be, they would not shrink from doing their duty in that House. The Committee was about to proceed to the discussion of a Scotch measure. That might be of great importance to Scotchmen; but they must excuse Irish Members if, in the discharge of what they conceived to be their duty, they stood some time longer in the way of the Scotch Bill being brought before the House. The Solicitor General for Ireland had not, in his opinion, given a satisfactory declaration, or manifested that readiness to be considerate in his dealings with these prisoners, which a fair-minded and considerate man ought to have manifested. Englishmen ought to understand that the Irish Members were fighting now the same fight that was fought by Hampden and his friends in England. They were contending now for those principles which the learned Selden did so much to engraft upon the recognized law of this country, and they were maintaining for these 11 unfortunate men at Sligo that right which was established beyond question in this country under an Act of *Geo.* III., which provided that, after a man had been committed, he should have an absolute right to be tried at the next ensuing Term, or Session, or Assize. That right was withheld from these men; but it was a right which was admitted and recognized in this country, and they claimed for these Irishmen who were now committed that same right which was unquestionably the birthright of Englishmen. They had not yet got that, and it was necessary to keep on hammering away as best they could by the instrumentality of these Estimates, first of all upon Parliament, and then indirectly on the public mind of England. However long it might take them, they must pursue that course, and as a first step he begged to move the reduction of this Vote by the first item—namely, the pay of the Attorney General for Ireland and his allowances, and the pay and allowances of the Solicitor General for Ireland, £4,353.

Motion made, and Question proposed,

"That a sum, not exceeding £44,678, be granted to Her Majesty, to complete the sum necessary to defray the Charge which will come in course of payment during the year ending on the 31st day of March 1885, of Criminal Prosecutions and other Law Charges in Ireland, including certain Allowances under the Act 15 and 16 Vic. c. 83."—(*Mr. Arthur O'Connor.*)

MR. DEASY said, he was glad his hon. Friend had moved to reduce the Vote by the salaries of the Attorney General and Solicitor General for Ireland, because he wished to make some remarks with regard to their conduct in forcing the trial of prisoners from different parts of the South of Ireland on the jurors of the City of Cork. Last March he had brought under the notice of the House the manner in which the County and City of Cork were treated under the Prevention of Crime Act; and he was sorry to have to say, with regard to the undertaking which he then understood the Solicitor General for Ireland to give—namely, that no further jury-packing should take place—that that practice still prevailed as much as ever. It had again been put in force in the City of Cork, and jurors who had served in the last three or four Assizes under the Prevention of Crime Act had again been summoned to attend the present Assizes. He need not point out to those who knew Ireland the serious inconvenience and loss to which these men were subjected by being drawn from their business day after day, though they were scarcely ever permitted to act on a jury. Under the old system the penalty for non-attendance was only £2; but under the Prevention of Crime Act it was £20, and although these men were invariably told to stand aside by the Sheriff, yet they were not released from duty, and if they failed even on one occasion to answer to their names the Judge inflicted the full penalty of £20. He protested against that practice, and against the way in which prisoners who had been brought to Cork for trial under the Prevention of Crime Act were treated. It was impossible for them to get a fair trial under the system now pursued. He did not say that juries empannelled in these cases went into the box with a determination to bring in verdicts of "guilty;" but they were so prejudiced by passion that they could not take an impartial view of any case of an agrarian character. In a few days these jurors would again be called upon to try prisoners; and he appealed to the Solicitor General for Ireland to do all in his power to prevent these juries from being packed, and to prevent Roman Catholic jurors in Cork from being insulted when called upon to act as jurymen. There was another item in this Vote to which he wished to call attention, and that was the item for the expenses in connection with actions taken against Resident Magistrates, Divisional and other Justices, and the Constabulary, for acts

done in the execution of their duty. How much of this, he wished to know, had been spent in conducting the case of Constable Griffin at Cork Assizes, for the balance of 2*s.* 7½*d.* blood tax? The circumstances were as follows:—A gentleman, named Hallissey, in Cork, had had to leave the country some time ago, because he was "Boycotted;" but before he left a large force of police were quartered in the district where he lived, and the cost of these policemen levied on that district. The farmers refused to pay it, and one of them living near Mallow had a mule taken for the debt .This mule was put up for auction by Constable Griffin and bought by the hon. Member for Westmeath (Mr. Harrington) for 2½*d.* This left a balance due of 2*s.* 7½*d.*, which Constable Griffin sought to recover before the Judge of Assize, but failed, the jury having given a verdict for the defendant. He (Mr. Deasy) should like to know how much of the expenses under this head had been devoted to paying counsel in the case? It would be interesting to know how much this 2*s.* 7½*d.* had cost the Government. There was another matter under Sub-head D to which he wished to draw attention. Some months ago, a case was brought before the Riverstown, near Cork, Petty Session, in which an Emergency man was charged with having fired at a farmer with intent to kill him. The Crown Prosecutor refused to prosecute the Emergency man; and the result was that the magistrates, who, from their Orange leanings, were on the side of the landlord, did not send the case for trial. He was in favour of reducing the Vote on account of the case he had cited; and when the Division had been taken upon the Motion of his hon. Friend the Member for Queen's County (Mr. A. O'Connor) he (Mr. Deasy) should consider the propriety of asking the Committee to reduce it by £300, which he believed was the salary of the Crown Prosecutor in that part of the county of Cork in which the case to which he had referred occurred. As to the case which the Committee had been considering all that evening, he did not wish to say much; but he had personal knowledge of the fact that on the arrest of Mr. Fitzgerald that gentleman's solicitor's agent was not permitted to see him in Sligo Gaol. His hon. Friend the Member for Mallow (Mr. O'Brien) asked a Question on the subject in the House, and the answer given by the Chief Secretary (Mr. Trevelyan) was that the police made all possible inquiries as to whether the agent was authorized by the prisoner's solicitor to interview him in Sligo Gaol; and they were unable in the course of 24 hours to ascertain whether the man was really a solicitor's clerk or not. He (Mr. Deasy) met the clerk on his way from Sligo, and he gave a different account altogether of what took place. The clerk stated that the policemen knew him well; but told him that they were instructed by the authorities not to permit anyone, even the solicitor himself, to see Mr. Fitzgerald. He (Mr. Deasy) hoped the discussion which had taken place would have the effect of bringing about either the release of the prisoners or their speedy trial. There would be no difficulty at all in trying the prisoners in the City of Cork; and hitherto the Government had not objected to bringing prisoners from all parts of Ireland to Cork to be tried. The case of the Tubbercurry prisoners was an exceptional one; and there was not one on the Irish Benches who would object to have the prisoners tried even by an Orange jury in that city, if the alternative was indefinite imprisonment without trial; but he supposed the Government would keep the men in confinement a little longer, in the hope that they might get such evidence against them as would lead a jury to convict them, it being quite clear that no such evidence was then in the possession of the Crown. If the men were not brought to trial immediately, surely it was not unreasonable to ask that they should be liberated on bail. If Mr. Fitzgerald were liberated on bail, or gave his word that he would not leave the country, he would be as sure to appear when called upon as he would now that he was shut up in Sligo Gaol. Although he (Mr. Deasy) had no personal knowledge of the other prisoners, he believed the same could be said of them. Why was it, therefore, that, perhaps in a week or so, only two out of 11 might be released? It had been said, in palliation of the action of the Government in the case, that three of the prisoners were already on bail in the nominal sum of £25 each. He did not regard the admission of the three men to bail as any great concession on the part of the Government. The people of Ireland could not be expected to have confidence in the administration of the law if these unfortunate men were kept, month after month, and perhaps year after year, in prison, so that the Government might be able to trump up a case against them. He hoped that before the debate closed, and he did not propose that it should close for some time, the Committee would receive some more satisfactory assurance from the Government than they had done up to the present. He believed that if the right hon. Gentleman the Chief Secretary could, even at the eleventh hour, give them the assurance that the Tubbercurry prisoners would be treated justly and fairly much would be done to bring about the early Prorogation of the Session. It could not be expected that the Irish Members would go back to Ireland without being able to show that they had done everything in their power to see that justice was meted out to the men who had been so long and unjustly confined within the walls of Sligo Gaol.

Question put.

The Committee *divided*:—Ayes 29; Noes 126: Majority 97.—(Div. List, No. 192.)

Original Question again proposed.

MR. SMALL said, he thought all Members were agreed that some explanation ought to be afforded of the item of £5,650, which represented the office expenses of the Crown Solicitors. To admit of an explanation being afforded by the Solicitor General for Ireland he moved to reduce the Vote by £4,000.

Motion made, and Question proposed,

"That a sum, not exceeding £45,031, be granted to Her Majesty, to complete the sum necessary to defray the Charge which will come in course of payment during the year ending on the 31st day of March 1885, of Criminal Prosecutions and other Law Charges in Ireland, including certain Allowances under the Act 15 and 16 Vic. c. 83."—(*Mr. Small.*)

COLONEL NOLAN said, that perhaps he might trespass upon the time of the Committee before the Solicitor General for Ireland replied to his hon. Friend, as he wished to call attention to a point he had on previous occasions brought before the House. He noticed that there was a great deal of money put down for Law Officers; but only a small sum was charged for jurors. Now, he had always contended that jurors should be paid as well as counsel. Counsel were paid large sums of money; and why should the jurors who had to assist in trials be absolutely out of pocket in consequence of their attendance in Court? In his county jurors were summoned in large numbers to attend the Court in the town of Galway. Many of them had to travel so far as 16 statute miles, and they had to pay their expenses the whole way. He did not propose exactly that the jurors should be paid money in pocket; but he thought that at least the Crown should pay them their travelling expenses, and so much to cover their hotel bills. Jurors were fully entitled to the payment he suggested, because they had to give up their time, which at this time of the year—harvest time—especially was very valuable; and if farmers gave up their time they had done a great deal for the country. As he had said, the jurors in Ireland were summoned in large numbers, and a great many of them were objected to. They had, however, to remain in Court. Under such circumstances, it would be far better not to bring them in, because they would then be saved considerable trouble and expense. If the Crown were obliged to pay jurors their travelling expenses and so much a day, he was convinced that too many would not be summoned. It was really high time that the Executive Government in Ireland should pay some attention to this matter. He had no doubt it would be said that jurors were not paid in England, and why should they be paid in Ireland? He was not sure they should not be paid in England; but, anyhow, the case of Ireland was very different. In England, jurors were, as a rule, men in good positions; and, besides, the Circuits were very conveniently arranged. Yorkshire, for instance, was divided into three Ridings, and the railway facilities were very great. In Ireland, however, the jurors were required to travel very long distances, and very frequently they had to do so by road. He submitted to the Irish Law Officers, and also to the Prime Minister, whom he was glad to see in his place, that some arrangement should at least be made by which Irish jurors could be paid their travelling expenses and hotel bills, because it was not defended for a minute that jurors should have to pay hard cash out of pocket for their attendance in Court. There was another reason why jurors in Ireland ought to be paid. Unfortunately, the weight of the Irish jury system fell, in almost all cases, on the farming class. Somehow or other the landlords escaped the duty of serving on juries; and they either lived out of Ireland, or they had certain occupations which exempted them from serving; and most of the professional men were exempted also. The consequence was that a great deal too much jury-work was thrown on the farmers, upon whom, as long as they were obliged to pay their own expenses, the duty was a very heavy tax. He hoped the Law Officers would take this great practical grievance into their serious consideration.

SIR JOHN HAY rose (at 20 minutes to 12 o'clock) to move to report Progress. He pointed out that at the commencement of the Sitting an arrangement was made that at half-past 11 Progress should be reported, in order that the Burgh Police and Health (Scotland) Bill should be taken into consideration. He understood that the discussion upon this Vote was likely to last some considerable time longer; and if that were so, it would be extremely inconvenient to Scotch, and other Members, that they should be kept in attendance until the small hours of the morning, in order to consider the merits of such an important measure as that he had mentioned. He was sorry to interfere with the Business of the Committee; but, under the circumstances, he felt bound to move to report Progress.

Motion made, and Question proposed, "That the Chairman do report Progress, and ask leave to sit again."—(*Sir John Hay.*)

MR. GLADSTONE said, the right hon. and gallant Gentleman knew very well that such engagements as to which he had alluded were made in perfect good faith, but that some latitude must be allowed. The Government would not ask very much latitude; but it must be borne in mind that they had not yet taken the Vote. Under the circumstances, and having disposed, as the Committee had done, of several important Amendments to the Vote, he hoped that more time would be allowed tonight in which it might be possible to take the Vote. The Government would not trespass upon the patience of hon. Members too much.

SIR JOHN HAY asked leave to withdraw his Motion.

Motion, by leave, *withdrawn*.

Question again proposed,

"That a sum, not exceeding £46,031, be granted to Her Majesty, to complete the sum necessary to defray the Charge which will come in course of payment during the year ending on the 31st day of March 1885, of Criminal Prosecutions and other Law Charges in Ireland, including certain Allowances under the Act 16 and 16 Vic. c. 83."—(*Mr. Small.*)

THE SOLICITOR GENERAL FOR IRELAND (Mr. WALKER) said, that in reply to the hon. Gentleman (Mr. Small), he had simply to say that the Crown Solicitors undertook certain duties, and they were paid fixed salaries. The question which was raised by the hon. and gallant Gentleman the Member for County Galway (Colonel Nolan) was a very large one. It was, indeed, a question of general policy, and therefore did not lie within the province of any Law Officers; it could not be dealt with by any administrative official.

MR. SMALL said, the item he referred to was the allowance for office expenses of Crown Solicitors. He wished to know what those expenses were?

THE SOLICITOR GENERAL FOR IRELAND (Mr. WALKER) said, the item represented the salaries of the clerks which Crown Solicitors were obliged to keep, in order that they could discharge their duties properly.

MR. HARRINGTON said, there was one other case to which he wished to direct the attention of the Chief Secretary (Mr. Trevelyan) and the Solicitor General for Ireland (Mr. Walker). From time to time he had drawn attention to the case—namely, that of the failure of justice in the prosecution instituted by the Government against Colonel Digby, a landlord in the county of Westmeath. The case curiously illustrated the manner in which the law operated with regard to the different classes in Ireland. If a poor person had been involved, no difficulty would have been experienced; but it was simply because the man concerned was a landlord and a Justice of the Peace that the Crown had found themselves wholly unable to bring him to justice. As early as the commencement of the

Session his attention was drawn to a case where this gentleman made a deliberate attempt to obtain arrears by fraud—by lodging an affidavit, and getting a certain number of tenants to join him in it, alleging, falsely, that rent was due to him. Some time after that, attention was called to another case by the hon. Member for Monaghan (Mr. Healy); and Colonel Digby then saw the danger of the course he was entering upon, and wrote to the Land Commissioners, after they had certified him that the Court was prepared to fix the arrears, to say that he had made a mistake in the case. This was when attention was drawn to the case of John Burke, the Surveyor General in Dublin. It was strange that the Solicitor to the Land Commissioners acceded to the application of Colonel Digby to have the case withdrawn. The Commissioners had before them the affidavits sworn by the landlord and by the tenants; and though he had made his formal application, the Land Commissioners, having before them the clearest evidence of an attempt to commit a fraud, allowed the withdrawal of the application, and never took the slightest step to bring the offender to justice for an attempt at fraud. This was in itself a very extraordinary case, and it showed how the whole system of officials and official life in Ireland worked for the benefit of one class of people as against the benefit of another class, and how, with perfect impunity, a certain class of men occupying high social positions in Ireland did what they liked to trample on the laws, and to commit injustice and attempt embezzlement. When the facts were brought under his notice, as the Representative of the county, he had drawn the attention of the Land Commissioners to them. He had pointed out the early period at which the affidavit had been made by the landlord and the tenants, and had laid before the Land Commissioners two depositions sworn to by tenants, in which they stated that Colonel Digby had entered into a treaty with them to endeavour to defraud the Court; that he had told them they were fools, and that he could get money for them from the Court. The tenants also, in these depositions, stated that, in order to satisfy the very pointed demands of this gentleman for his rent, they had borrowed the money to pay him; and that, therefore, they themselves believed, the money having been borrowed, that they had acted in *bona fides*. How about the position of the landlord? Here was a Grand Juror of Westmeath swearing falsely that arrears of rent were due, and getting these men also to swear an affidavit in the matter. The attention of the Land Commissioners had been specifically drawn to the case. At first they decided it as an application to discharge the case from Court, and they made no effort to bring the offender to justice. Several months afterwards, when he brought it again under the attention of the Commissioners, drawing their attention to that section of the Act which invested them with the power, where an attempt had been made to commit a fraud on the Court, to proceed against the person so attempting to commit a fraud. Not alone did the Act empower the Commissioners to take action where a person had committed a fraud, but where he had attempted to do so. The Commissioners did not move themselves, and when he brought the facts clearly before their notice through a solicitor in Dublin, in whose charge he gave the case, the Commissioners refused to move one step in the matter. It would be a long time before the impression was removed from the minds of the people of Ireland that these Commissioners, to whom they had given the power of settling rents in Ireland, if they made themselves the friends of the landlords by refusing to punish them for fraud, would equally make themselves the friends of the landlords when appeals were lodged against decisions in favour of tenants. He (Mr. Harrington) had felt it necessary, when the Land Commission refused to take up the case, to send all the documents to the Attorney General for Ireland. It was complained in another case that evidence had not been given; but the right hon. and learned Gentleman could not raise such a plea in this matter, because all the evidence, including depositions sworn before the magistrates, and the rent receipts, clearly establishing the fraud, had been submitted to him. Well, after some time, the Attorney General for Ireland did move in the business, and sent down the Crown Solicitor for Westmeath to examine into the circumstances of the case, with the result that a prosecution was instituted against Colonel Digby for attempting fraudulently to obtain arrears from the Land Commissioners in respect of two tenants. What happened? Why, at the Petty Sessions where the case was tried, the Resident Magistrate attended, and with him two local Justices, one of whom put in an appearance for the first time for two years. Mark this fact. For a period of two years this dispenser of justice, this officer of the law in Ireland, had not put in an appearance in that local Petty Sessions Court; but he came down on this occasion, when one of his friends was in a little trouble, to shield him from that justice which he was supposed to be there to administer. The second of the two local magistrates, he was informed, had not, until the occasion in question, attended at the Petty Sessions for a period of nine months. He was a very irregular attendant at the Court—he very rarely turned up. At the conclusion of the hearing of the case, the trial having proceeded upon only one of the attempts at fraud, one of the tenants was examined, and the rent receipts were produced in Court; and because Colonel Digby had written this letter to the Land Court, withdrawing his application, or endeavouring to save himself from the consequences of his action, the two local Justices founded their decision upon that fact, and refused to return him for trial at the Assizes, though the Resident Magistrate expressed an opinion the other way, and was strongly in favour of committing the man for trial. Justice, therefore, was not done in the case. He (Mr. Harrington) believed it was competent for the Resident Magistrate to have committed Colonel Digby for trial, in spite of the local magistrates; and, if that were so, it was surprising that he had not done it. He did not know whether he was right in his statement of the law; but he believed it was competent for the Resident Magistrate, even where the local magistrates did not concur, to have received the informations and have returned the case for trial at the Assizes. He (Mr. Harrington) had put a Question to the Government in the House on this case. He had asked whether they intended to prosecute, and a further step had been taken. The Grand Jury of Westmeath had been asked to present a bill; but they had decided in favour of Colonel Digby, and had saved him from the consequences of the heinous crime of endeavouring to embezzle a sum from the Treasury. The Grand Jury threw out the bill. It was competent for the Crown to move to change the venue from the County of Westmeath; but they had done nothing at all of the kind. They had not changed the venue, and up to the present time they had taken no step whatever to endeavour to bring this gentleman to justice. A stronger case had since come to light, and stronger facts had been gathered. Immediately after the bill had been thrown out by the Grand Jury, he (Mr. Harrington) had received information directing his attention to a case where not alone was an effort made by this gentleman to abstract money from the Land Court, but where he succeeded in getting it. The right hon. Gentleman the Chief Secretary to the Lord Lieutenant had admitted the facts so far as this—that, in the instance pointed out, application was made for arrears of rent which were alleged to be due, and that at the time the application was made this man had actually disposed of his interest in the holding—that when he had made the application, he had sold the holding to a tenant who had promised to pay him the amount of the rent due. Now, this was a case where there could be no question at all as to intention. The question raised before, in the other case, was as to the intent to defraud. Here, however, where the man received the money and pocketed it, there could be no question of the intention. He (Mr. Harrington) contended that a most unfortunate impression would be produced in the minds of the people of Ireland if the Government showed they were unable to bring men to justice when they attempted a fraud and admitted — as they seemed inclined to do in this case—that they were wholly unable to bring to justice men of high social position who attempted to swindle the Government. Would the Crown attempt to bring this man to justice — would they, as they had done in the case of so many agrarian crimes in Ireland, change the venue and bring the man to trial outside his own county, where he would not be on the Grand Jury and have brother jurors to protect him?

MR. TREVELYAN: This is a case which, so far as it relates to Members of the Government and officers whose salaries are being considered, can be dealt with in one sentence. The charge is against Justices of the Peace, who are unpaid, and against members of the Grand Jury, who are unpaid likewise. The main charge is, that this gentleman attempted to take money corruptly from the Exchequer — attempted first, and then obtained it afterwards. What was the action of the Government? Why, in the first instance, they applied for information from the Bench of Magistrates. The magistrates refused to give it, and there, in the ordinary course of events, the case would have stopped. But the Government, thinking the case important, went further. They sent the case up to the Grand Jury without obtaining information from the magistrates, and the Grand Jury threw the bill out. The Government may, therefore, be said to have exhausted all the means at their disposal for obtaining a conviction.

MR. HARRINGTON: Why did you not change the venue?

MR. TREVELYAN: That would have been improper at a time when there was no reason to suspect favouritism. The Government made full use of all the documents placed in their hands on the previous occasion. The Crown Solicitor—who is the only person concerned whose salary we are now considering—was not to be blamed. The Government are still considering the matter—they are obtaining information and explanations. If they are satisfactory, the case will stand as at present; if they are not, the Attorney General for Ireland will adopt the best means for bringing about a prosecution. Until he has the full case before him, it is impossible to say what may be done.

SIR HERBERT MAXWELL said, he rose to move that the Chairman do report Progress, and ask leave to sit again. He should be very much surprised indeed if the Scotch Members were satisfied with the attempt the Prime Minister had made to release himself from the engagement he had deliberately entered into in the hearing of every Member of the House with reference to the Burgh Police and Health (Scotland) Bill. What reason had the right hon. Gentleman given for it? Why, that the Government had not obtained any money. Why had they not obtained money? Because of their determined defence of a position for three hours—their defence of a position which, in the end, they had abandoned—surrendered to hon. Gentlemen sitting behind them. The Scotch Members were not responsible for that. He believed the Scotch Members would join with him in refusing to have their Business postponed to such a late hour. The Burgh Police and Health (Scotland) Bill was a considerable Bill, consisting of 529 clauses. It was opposed, and could not be taken after half-past 12—that was to say, in another 20 minutes it could not come on. It was opposed, not by Members representing Scotch constituencies, but by an hon. Member representing an English borough.

THE CHAIRMAN: The hon. Member cannot discuss the position of the Bill on the Question that I report Progress.

SIR HERBERT MAXWELL: I want to point out that the Bill, being blocked, cannot be brought on after half-past 12. I move to report Progress.

Motion made, and Question proposed, "That the Chairman do report Progress, and ask leave to sit again."—*(Sir Herbert Maxwell.)*

MR. GLADSTONE: I think the speech we have just heard might very well have been spared, coming from a Scotch Member who desires to save time, and to prevent this Bill, being blocked. I will not reply to his kind compliment to me, that I have endeavoured to escape from my engagement. I think there are very few in this House who will agree with him in that charge. I do not think I am capable of endeavouring to escape from an engagement.

SIR HERBERT MAXWELL: The right hon. Gen—[*Cries of* "Order!"]

MR. GLADSTONE: The hon. Baronet has had his say. The right hon. and gallant Gentleman opposite (Sir John Hay) kindly and courteously admitted the force of what I said; and I have actually suggested to my right hon. Friend the Chief Secretary to the Lord Lieutenant that it was time for us to say we might now report Progress and bring on the Bill. I shall say no more. Progress will be reported.

Question put, and *agreed to.*

Committee report Progress; to sit again *To-morrow.*

REVENUE, &c. (LICENCE, &c.)

Considered in Committee.

(In the Committee.)

1. *Resolved*, That it is expedient to authorise the imposition of an Excise Duty of five shillings and three pence for the sale of Tobacco in Railway Carriages.

2. *Resolved*, That it is expedient to authorise the Commissioners of Her Majesty's Treasury to direct to be written off, the claim of the Exchequer for any sum due in account from the Post Office, in respect of the excess of the expenses of granting and managing Government Annuities over and above the fees received.

Resolutions to be reported *To-morrow*.

BURGH POLICE AND HEALTH (SCOTLAND) (*re-committed*) BILL.—[BILL 296.]

(*The Lord Advocate, Mr. Solicitor General for Scotland.*)

COMMITTEE.

Order for Committee read.

Motion made, and Question proposed, "That Mr. Speaker do now leave the Chair."

MR. M'LAREN said, that though he had given Notice of opposition to this stage, he had no desire to oppose it in any disagreeable spirit, as he understood it was the wish of the majority of the Scotch Members that the Bill should be proceeded with as far as possible at that late period of the Session. But he thought it right to call the attention of the House to the very great importance of this measure, as well as to its enormous length. It was a Bill of over 500 clauses, which dealt in the most drastic and severe fashion with every phase of life in urban districts in Scotland; and such a Bill seemed to him to deserve a greater degree of attention in that House than it had received or was likely to receive. It interfered with the liberty of every citizen in Scotland in his domestic and public relations; and it was singular that the discussion of the Bill had not taken place in any public shape. Hon. Members who had received the Report of the Select Committee to which the Bill was committed would observe that the first Division in Committee was on the question whether reporters should be admitted, and he was surprised to see that the Committee decided to deal with the Bill with closed doors. He believed it was a fact that during all these days the Bill had been under discussion, not one single day's proceedings had been reported in any of the Scotch newspapers. The Committee was so appointed as to supply the place of the Grand Committee. Well, the proceedings of the Grand Committees were reported, their business being conducted with open doors; but not so in the case of this Bill. In 1882, a large number of Private Bills were introduced by the authorities of English and Scotch boroughs, going over much the same ground as the present Bill; and, thanks to the energy of the hon. and learned Member for Stockport (Mr. Hopwood), those Private Bills were referred to a Select Committee, presided over by the right hon. Gentleman the Member for North Hampshire (Mr. Sclater-Booth). As a Member of that Committee, he (Mr. M'Laren) was bound to say that the attention given to those Bills, of far less relative importance than the present measure, was far greater than the attention given to this Bill. He did not wish to disparage the Select Committee on the Police Bill; but the Police and Sanitary Committee of 1882 took evidence in regard to the clauses which were now to be passed without the slightest discussion in this measure. The Local Government Board had supplied memoranda with regard to all parts of the Bills. Gentlemen attended from the Local Government Board, and gave their opinion as to the effect of these clauses. They cross-examined these gentlemen with considerable minuteness, and also numerous Medical Officers, Officers of Health, Aldermen, Town Councillors, and all who came up in support of the Bills, the result being that a vast number of clauses were struck out which now appeared in this larger measure. He admitted there was a difference between the Bills of 1882 and the present measure. The Bills in 1882 were Private Bills, and the Committee had proceeded on the principle that it was not right to discuss in Private Bills matters affecting popular liberty, and which ought to be dealt with by the Whole House. He admitted this was a Public Bill, and that it was perfectly right to deal with all these questions in it; but he did appeal to English as well as to Scotch Members—was it possible for a Bill of 500 clauses, at that period of the Session, to meet with the attention it deserved? He did not wish to occupy the time of the House in debating the clauses of the Bill, therefore, he would say nothing whatever about them. When the Speaker left the Chair —as he would shortly—he should not hesitate to press the Amendments of which he had given Notice; and he trusted his hon. Friends and other Scotch Members who had given Notice of Amendments would do the same. He felt sure that his right hon. and learned Friend the Lord Advocate would, under the peculiar circumstances of the case, be disposed to make such concessions as he could in these particular clauses. If that were not done, he (Mr. M'Laren) was confident in the wisdom of "another place," and he had very little doubt that the Bill would receive very severe treatment if ever it left the door of this House. He should not press the Amendment of which he had given Notice.

MR. HOPWOOD said, the hon. Gentleman opposite (Sir Herbert Maxwell) seemed to think that he (Mr. Hopwood) owed an apology to the House for interfering in this matter, because he was an English Member who had undertaken to call attention to this Bill, which proposed to deal with Scotland alone. But he supposed the hon. Member had no objection to Englishmen travelling in or residing in Scotland; and it did seem necessary that English Members of Parliament should take under their care the laws which greeted them when they arrived in Scotland. Nobody disputed the fact that Scotch Members had a perfect right to interfere in, and to endeavour to improve, English legislation. With this short apology, he would just say a word or two on the action he had ventured to take in this matter. His hon. and learned Friend who had just sat down had described what was done by a former Committee. His hon. and learned Friend had rendered excellent service on that Committee, and so also did his hon. Friend the Member for Wolverhampton (Mr. H. H. Fowler); and the same Gentlemen, with other Members of the House, rendered great service in going through a number of Bills. They had spent 30 days in going through those Bills relating to England. The Scotch Members who sat on the Committee upon the Scotch Bills devoted a number of days to the work, no doubt; but they had not sought to bring the measure into harmony with English law, which was what he wanted to see done, as much as possible, in these matters, and the result was that there would be different laws for the two countries. He quite admitted that it was impossible for that House to effect this in Committee; but it was possible for him to make some protest upon the subject; and he thought it was right that he should do so, because, with all respect for the hon. Members who supported this measure, there was in Scotland a notion among the higher orders of men — the baillies, magistrates, Commissioners, and such like—that arbitrary powers were to be placed in their hands and in the hands of the police to guide and govern everybody in minute relations of life. He would avoid going into details generally; but he wished in several respects to invite the attention of the House to the condition of things. Most of the provisions of this measure were, he believed, founded upon the various Improvement Bills which had been passed into law for various burghs in Scotland, and some of these Improvement Bills had been of the most arbitrary description. He was aware that the Lord Advocate had considerably modified some of these provisions—provisions of such a character that they strongly attracted attention in the case of several Scotch towns, and provisions which were far more arbitrary than those sought to be brought in by the Municipal Authorities of English towns. It was this which brought about that reference to the Select Committee on which his hon. Friend (Mr. H. H. Fowler) did such excellent service. A short review of what was intended to be done by some of these provisions would certainly prove interesting. There were police regulations as to lighting and cleansing on the staircases of "common dwellings," and so on. That was a specimen of the minuteness with which they condescended to such small matters in Scotland—nothing was to be done without the police, and the public authority insisted on the carrying out of the details of the private relations of people under the terror of penalties. Then there were orders for licensing porters and news-vendors. There was no such thing as free trade—everybody was to be dependent on the goodwill of a couple of magistrates, as would be found on reference to Clause 360. That was the sort of thing that was to find its way into an Act for the whole of Scotland. It was thought necessary to provide power to break into a house in case of fire—that was how they legislated for Scotland—though he should have thought that the very necessity of the matter provided law and excuse enough. Then he absolutely found that if a swimmer passed certain boundary posts, when he came back he would find himself in the hands of the police, and would be fined 40*s*.! That was the sort of thing which ran through the Bill throughout. He should abstain from going into details, though they would make his case very much stronger. There were a series of bye-laws for controlling old clothes dealers, and he protested against any burgh being allowed to frame such a series of bye-laws, even though the high sanction of the Sheriff was required to be given to them before they were to have the force of law. He found that the only check upon all this was that it was to be not repugnant to the law of Scotland. But he supposed that every fresh enactment was in a sense repugnant to the existing law, because it was a new law; and if these burghs were to be permitted to control all these various matters, and others which he did not specify, because other Members might call attention to them bye and bye, the situation would be intolerable. Then there was authority to repeal, to alter, and to re-enact these bye-laws, so that there might be a perpetually shifting body of law. It was true that most of these provisions had reference to humble trades and occupations, where, perhaps, the poverty of the people, or their lowness in the social scale, might render them powerless to object; and he protested on behalf of poor Scotchmen, just as he would on behalf of poor Englishmen, against their being made subject to shifting bye-laws and to various penalties to be altered at the will of the Commissioners when sanctioned by the Sheriff. Then he came to the sanitary provisions, and he would commend them to the attention of any hon. Member as a perfect curiosity. He believed these sanitary provisions were not considered stiff enough for one or two towns which already had more severe ones of their own; but they presented a remarkable curiosity in legislation, as anyone might see, by looking at the clauses following the 321st. He did not intend to go through them in succession; but he thought he might pronounce them to be exceedingly arbitrary. He found that, having named certain infectious diseases, for the notification of which provision was made, there was power given to the Commissioners, with the approval of the Board of Supervision—which was something like the Local Government Board in this country—to add any other infectious disease to the number of those specifically mentioned. Then there were powers to remove persons, to prevent the spread of infectious diseases; and all that had to be done was to get a certificate, signed by a medical officer, for the removal from a house of all the residents therein who were not suffering from the disease. The whole thing depended upon the discretion of a medical officer. He would ask hon. Members how they would like to inflict such a law upon their own friends and families—to apply it to their own houses? Here was a single medical officer, who might be a first class man, or who might, on the other hand, be a very inferior man; and, at all events, as a rule, he would be a man who had his spurs to win, for the best medical men were not likely to take these appointments—and upon the certificate of that man a whole family might be removed at his will and pleasure. Of course, it was argued that this sort of thing could only be done on the production of a certificate signed by a medical officer; but, on the production of such a certificate, any magistrate might make the order. Then there were powers as to the disinfection of premises, and so on. Of course, all these provisions were perfectly futile and useless in the case of persons who had good houses of their own, and who might be as daring and as reckless as they pleased; but those who happened to be rather poor, and who had not a house to themselves, but dwelt with others, could not call their house their own, or be free from the Inspector or the medical officer, who might harass them in any way he pleased. He would give another specimen. It was provided that no one must deposit in any midden anything that might communicate any infectious disease. He would abstain from reading the clause, for decency would not allow it; but it was Clause 328. Many of the powers given were such as could be much better carried out, not by legislative enactment, but by coaxing, and by moral authority; and to give to a magistrate power to tear away from a family those who were most dear to it, whether living or dead, and all at the will of a medical officer—these were things which he must most strongly protest against. He believed that the sanitary regulation of the burghs of Scotland could be much better provided for without all these terrors and penalties, or the placing of such extensive powers in the hands of the police. One of these sanitary regulations he should like to draw attention to for a moment. It provided that any person who took in washing, and whose house contained anyone supposed to be suffering from an infectious disease, was liable to a penalty for allowing the linen to go back from her house. That affected the poor laundress; and here he wished to point out how little the other side of the case was thought of, for he did not find any prohibition against those who employed the laundress. A man who had a house of his own, and who was rich enough to order the linen to be sent out, might have a child laid up with measles or scarlet fever, and might recklessly send the whole of the linen used by that child to the laundress, and infect her family with the disease; but if the laundress did it she was liable to a penalty. That was Clause 230. What he complained of was that nothing was left to personal prudence. Then he came to the offences, beginning at Clause 392, and they really formed a curiosity of legal study. He could hear an hon. Friend rather boasting, as if these were patterns to be followed; but he could only say that if such enactments were to be applied to England, he hoped that all the old women of the streets would stand up in revolution against them. He would mention one provision as a matter of curiosity. If anyone used in any way whatever any sham bank note, whether it was done in sport or not, he would be liable to be charged as for an offence in Scotland. Then, in the street regulations, great care was taken in pointing out on which side of the street—whether on the right or the left—a man should be permitted to drive a cart; and, by Sub-section 9 of Clause 393, a penalty was provided for the man who was driving a cart slowly, and who would not get out of the way quickly enough for a swift carriage, perhaps driven by some imperious fellow. It was also provided that prostitutes and street-walkers should be liable to penalties, if they loitered about or importuned passengers; and that anybody who habitually or persistently importuned or solicited women or children should be liable to penalties. This was the first time that such a provision had ever been put into a Bill; and it did seem to be carrying the law to a point that had never been reached before. At the same time, he was rather glad to see that men who habitually or persistently importuned were to be put on a more equal footing with the other sex for breaking the laws of morality. He did not see why the law should not be a little levelled down, to put men and women more on an equality in this matter. Then he found it was an offence to place a flower pot in an upper window without a sufficient guard to it to prevent accidents, or for anyone to throw from a roof any slate or brick. Surely, these things might be left to the natural protection afforded by the fact that the man who did this sort of thing was liable to damages for any accident that might happen, and that fact generally induced people to act with sufficient caution. If an injury was caused, then let the conduct of the offending person be an offence. He did not wish to waste the time of the House, and he thought he had justified, to some extent, what he undertook to do. He found it was provided that no one under the age of 14 years should drive anything, or be in charge of any vehicle, or, he supposed, should even hold a horse for a horseman. Then he turned to disorderly houses. He did not wish to dwell on that subject; but he maintained that the whole policy pursued in that matter was to put things into the hands of the police, and everybody knew the difficulty and danger that ensued from that. When the police were employed for these matters very great risks were run. The proper business of the police was to preserve order and to detect crime; and when they were provided with inducements to watch these houses and control them they became a source of manifest danger to the country, for, possessing the power of laying informations, or informing their superiors of the existence of these places, it was not to be expected that men who were being paid 25*s*. a-week would be able to resist the temptations which the keepers of disorderly houses would be sure to place in their way. It was very possible that any policeman might, under such circumstances, be corrupted; and when a policeman was corrupted it was easy to imagine what would be the result. The consequence of too great severity in the laws was well enough known. Where a policeman had power to bring a man before the magistrates for an offence, the first penalty for which was £20, with accumulating penalties for every subsequent offence, the natural result was to make their cities whited sepulchres, looking well enough outside, but no one knowing what abominations were going on inside, or, possibly, just outside their boundaries, where all the immorality might be congregated together. Then there was the question of the suppression of vagrants. It was very desirable to suppress vagrants; but it might be done too cruelly, with too great severity—and he believed that many people who read the clauses of the Bill, from Clause 423 onwards, would look upon them as exceeding the real requirements of the case. He did not think he had wasted the time of the House; but he could not pursue this particular point any further. He came now to brokers and pawnbrokers, and he found that they were treated with uncommon severity. He found that it was not possible for a broker to carry on his trade without having his books, and the nature of his entries therein, prescribed for him. Such provisions did not repress the dishonest man, who would have his books in order with sham entries; but the honest trader was harassed in every way in carrying on his business. He had now done all that he could in pointing out these matters, though he felt that he could, perhaps, interest the House by continuing the catalogue. Hon. Gentlemen who were enamoured of this despotic kind of legislation did not like to hear all these things; and, no doubt, it would be much easier and more comfortable to pass the Bill and go home to bed than to stop there to discuss it. But here were 500 clauses to be passed in this way long after midnight, and he suggested that this was not the way in which legislation should be carried on. He did not undervalue the services of those of his hon. Friends who sat on the Committee, and his personal inclination to gratify them would incline him at once to withdraw from any further opposition, but for the fact that duty was a matter far beyond any personal gratification of that kind. However, he felt that the House had now given him a sufficient hearing, and he could assure hon. Gentlemen that his statement of the case had much suffered from his anxious desire to bring his remarks within as small a compass as possible. He begged to move that the House do go into Committee on the Bill on that day three months.

MR. WARTON, in seconding the Amendment, desired to say that while he had every disposition to believe in the good sense of Scotland, he could see very little common sense in this Bill, which was one of a most extraordinary nature, abounding in petty tyrannies, and containing so many absurdities and tomfooleries that he thought the good sense of those Scotchmen who approved of it had utterly vanished. The hon. and learned Member for Stockport (Mr. Hopwood) had not at all exaggerated the absurdities of the Bill. In this country it had been found necessary to check the almost insane tendency of little petty persons dressed in a little brief authority to make tyrannical laws in the most Puritanical spirit. If there had been collected all the most ridiculous specimens of regulations that could be found, and they had all been concentrated into one single focus of absurdity, there could not have been made a worse Bill than this. He saw sitting on the Treasury Bench opposite the parent of the phrase "grandmotherly legislation;" and he must say that he hoped the right hon. Gentleman would do something to rescue his Colleagues from the shame that would be cast upon them if this Bill were allowed to pass. If such a Bill were to pass at all, it should have been brought in at an earlier period of the Session, when it could have been properly discussed and amended. At 5 o'clock that morning the Government gave way in the case of another measure, because the Irish Members had the sense to see that the Bill was absurd; but Scotland, it seemed, was to be treated differently, and a Bill was to be passed to prohibit children under 10 years of age from selling newspapers in the streets. Some of the extraordinary provisions of the Bill dealt with swine, and the places in which they were to be kept. It almost seemed to give colour to the view that their Scotch fellow-citizens were descendants of the lost tribes, for they seemed to have the Jewish antipathy to swine. Then the curfew was actually to be re-established. The old Saxons, who did not like to be played with, almost thought that the most cruel and bitter thing which their conquerors did was to extinguish their fires at 8 o'clock; but the curfew was actually to be re-established in the 19th century in civilized Scotland, or semi-civilized Scotland, as it ought now to be called. Times were to be fixed for lighting and extinguishing the lights in common-stairs, passages, and private coverts, and the order was to be fixed in which the occupiers of flats were to be responsible for extinguishing the lights. The Norman Conqueror cruelly fixed a time for putting out the lights; but these modern people not only said when the lights were to go out, but how it was to be done, and fixed the order of rotation. Then there were regulations as to when the stairs were to be swept. The people must not sweep their stairs when they liked—it was to be a matter of regulation and law. Then there were regulations as to the numerous receptacles for every kind of filth, mentioned with elaboration and scant decency, in the Bill. Without entering into anything uncommonly nasty—though the Bill was full of such material—he might mention that one bye-law forbade foul water from percolating from one house or building to another; and then there were to be depôts established—a grand word for receptacles for bones, carrion, and rags. These ridiculous and paltry little matters were to be dealt with by a fine of 10*s*. for every day the offence was committed. It was difficult to express one's opinion of this without indignation. Then they were weak enough to think that they could make everyone moral by petty restrictions; but the days of Puritanism had gone by. It might be a sad thing that women should traverse the streets; but this wretched piece of legislation decreed that they must move at a certain regulated pace, according to the bye-laws. The poor wretch must not loiter. Again, the boy who threw a snowball, which was an act contrary to the bye-laws—what Member of that House had not thrown a snowball?—was liable to severe punishment, and, worse than that, the poor boy who flew a kite was also liable to be punished. Wherever this Act was not extremely tyrannical it was supremely ridiculous. Here was another instance. If they were building a house and were having any lime ground up with the plaster, and the wind blew it about, that was another crime, because they ought to have put down water to prevent its being blown about. And then there was a moral injunction against shaking and beating any carpets or rugs, because it was contrary to the bye-laws. If one happened to crush up against a person in the streets of a town in Scotland, that was a crime; and if a person stood on the sill of a window for the purpose of cleaning the panes, even if the sill were only two feet from the ground, he was to be punished. Then there was another provision about pieces of orange peel being thrown upon the pavements, which was also an offence under this Act. Hon. Members must know that a great number of offences set forth in the Bill were punishable at Common Law; but that was not sufficient for the framers of this Bill; they must deal with acts of juvenility in the way he had described. In Clause 334 they found an extraordinary provision, which he did not think would be sanctioned by Parliament. In that clause they were told that no public procession should take place without the consent of the magistrates. He rather commended that clause to the consideration of Liberal Members who might want to get up demonstrations; and he would ask them whether it was, or was not, a violation of the freedom of the subject? Was it, or was it not, the right of all persons to walk in an orderly way through the streets in procession? As a Tory, he was in favour of the liberty of the subject; but he found that tyranny was always inflicted by the Liberals. He asked them whether it was really intended that no public procession, not even that of a Sunday School with its teachers, should be allowed to walk along the streets, however small the procession, five, six, or seven, as the case might be, without the consent of the magistrates? If the Bill were a sensible one, he should have no objection to its being read a second time; but, under the circumstances, he should feel it his duty to support the Motion of the hon. and learned Member for Stockport; and unless Scotch Members wished to cover themselves with ridicule he thought they would do well in following his example.

Amendment proposed,

To leave out from the word "That" to the end of the Question, in order to add the words "this House will, upon this day three months, resolve itself into the said Committee,"—(*Mr. Hopwood*,)

—instead thereof.

Question proposed, "That the words proposed to be left out stand part of the Question."

MR. WEBSTER said, without at all adopting the views of the hon. and learned Member for Bridport (Mr. Warton), he felt bound to express the strong feeling which prevailed in Scotland, that sufficient time and opportunity had not been allowed for the full consideration of this measure. He was in favour of the codification of the law, and also, in the main, in favour of the Bill itself. He had been a Member of the Committee, which had devoted the greatest attention to this Bill in discussing the clauses *seriatim* for very many days; but he could inform the House that the prevailing feeling in Scotland was one of regret with regard to the shortness of time at their disposal for the consideration of the measure. He held in his hand a letter from the Town Clerk of the Town Council of Aberdeen which had passed a Resolution to this effect—

"That the Town Council are of opinion that sufficient time has not been allowed for the consideration in Scotland of this Bill, as amended, and they strongly recommend that it be not passed by Parliament during the present Session."

The Bill was of enormous length, and it embraced the whole field of the duties and functions of administration in burghs with regard to police, public health, and the details of sanitary matters generally. The Bill had, no doubt, been carefully considered by the Select Committee; but there were very many clauses struck out altogether, and many materially altered; and he was sorry to find that the Town Council of Aberdeen, at least, did not consider that in many cases any improvement had been effected thereby. There had been, besides, many clauses added, and other large changes made, and the Bill, as amended, was formally ordered by the House to be reprinted so recently as the 18th of the present month; and, therefore, he was bound to admit that there was some solid ground for the contention of the public Bodies that they had not been allowed sufficient opportunity to consider a measure which travelled over so wide a field, and which was of such immense importance. It must be considered also that the present Bill overrode and superseded the existing Police Acts, which had been framed with very great care, and which, in many of their clauses, were, perhaps, actually better than the corresponding clauses in this Bill. He felt bound to say, in conclusion, that the feeling prevailing in the burgh which he had the honour to represent (Aberdeen) appeared to him to be very greatly in favour of the postponement of the Bill.

SIR HERBERT MAXWELL said, that in the remarks which he made at an earlier part of the discussion he intended no reference whatever to the hon. and learned Member for Stockport (Mr. Hopwood) with regard to the course he had taken in this matter. As a matter of fact, he thought that the hon. and learned Member was fully justified in opposing this Bill. It was not reasonable to ask the House to consider a Bill containing 529 clauses on the 30th of July at 1 o'clock in the morning, especially when they remembered that the House was still sitting at 5 o'clock yesterday morning. He rose, however, for the purpose of offering some observations on the course adopted by the hon. and learned Member for Stafford (Mr. M'Laren). The hon. and learned Member had stated that he would not persist in his objection to the Bill; he said he was not reconciled to the measure; but he expressed himself perfectly satisfied that the Bill would be effectively and finally dealt with in "another place." Now, he did not think that that was a course either creditable to the hon. and learned Member or that House. They had to decide with regard to the Bill upon its merits; and he thought it likely that when the hon. and learned Member went into the country he would have something to say more or less complimentary of the other House. And one of his complaints would probably be that the time spent by hon. Members in the House of Commons in the consideration of Bills such as this was utterly lost in consequence of the action taken by the House of Peers. He thought he had replied to the observations which fell from the hon. and learned Member as to whether the Bill should be allowed to go into Committee or not. They would probably hear the right hon. and learned Gentleman the Lord Advocate on that question, as it was that on which would probably depend all his hopes of carrying the Bill through. In his opinion, it would be most regretable, if, in consequence of the mode in which Her Majesty's Government had dealt with the time at their disposal, the labours of the Select Committee should be entirely lost. Had Her Majesty's Government seen fit to introduce this Bill at a reasonable period of the Session, which he thought was quite within their power, it would have received the amount of consideration given it by the Select Committee; and there would have been, besides, ample time for it to have been discussed and fully considered in that House. Believing that the Bill, as a whole, was desirable, if the Lord Advocate persevered in his determination to carry it through the Committee stage, he should very cordially support him.

MR. BUCHANAN said, the Bill was of a very detailed character, and such as only men of great experience in municipal affairs could adequately criticize; but it had been very carefully considered by the Select Committee. It had issued from them within the last two weeks, and the earliest day on which his constituents could have got a copy of the amended Bill was last Wednesday morning. They proceeded immediately they received the Bill to take it into consideration, and in order to make the position plain he would relate to the House what took place before the Bill was received. The Bill was sent to a Select Committee; according to the Rules of the House that Committee sat with closed doors; but it was moved in the Committee that the public should be admitted in order that the various Amendments proposed might be reported and the progress of the Bill known out-of-doors. But that Amendment was defeated, and the result was that the municipal authorities in Scotland had been unable to follow the discussions which had taken place, or the Amendments made in the Committee, and that the Bill came down to the House practically a new measure. He would put it to the Government, in view of what had taken place, whether it was reasonable, at that period of the Session—within, as they hoped, a week of the Prorogation, to endeavour to urge through the House a Bill of these enormous dimensions, which, on account of its great elaboration of detail, could not possibly be discussed as it ought to be. Not only did the Corporation of Edinburgh strongly disapprove the Bill being hurried through Parliament without adequate discussion, but every day that the Bill was before the Select Committee he received numbers of letters asking if such or such a clause was retained in the Bill, what was the meaning of this alteration, was there any possibility of having the Bill restored its original form, and what opportunity there would be of submitting to the House the Amendments thought necessary? The Bill had been very carefully considered in the Committee; but in the case of an enormous measure like this, when a great number of Amendments were suggested, it was almost impossible, with even the utmost care, to avoid inserting Amendments in one part that were contradictory of other portions, and to avoid the insertion of clauses which were absolutely incongruous with others. The right hon. and learned Gentleman the Lord Advocate must be aware that the Bill was full of errors and contradictions, and he would ask him what line he proposed to take with the view of amending those defects? Of course, he did not consider it the duty of a private Member of the House to attempt to cope with the matter; and, for his own part, he had only to propose one or two Amendments on behalf of his constituents. He trusted there would be a general expression of opinion on both sides of the House, and he was certain that the opinion of all the large burghs in Scotland was against the further progress of the Bill that Session. Finally, he put it to Her Majesty's Government whether it was fair, at that late period of the Session, to proceed with a Bill of such enormous detail, and which could not fail to put in endless confusion the whole burgh administration of the country?

MR. ANDERSON said, he felt bound to support the view taken by the hon.

Member for Edinburgh (Mr. Buchanan) with regard to this Bill. Ever since the Bill had passed from the Select Committee, he had been receiving the strongest remonstrances from the authorities in Glasgow against its being allowed to go any further that Session. They complained that the Sittings of the Select Committee were held *in camerâ*, and that they knew nothing of what was going on, and that they knew nothing of the form of the Bill until they saw the reprint of it. He had that morning received a telegram requesting him to replace all the Amendments which they had on the Paper, many of which had been rejected. They complained that the Bill had been made worse rather than better by the Amendments which had been introduced into it. He had also received a letter from Dr. Russell, a man of great authority in Glasgow in sanitary matters, who had been so successful in stamping out small-pox there, and whose opinion was deserving of the greatest attention. That gentleman wrote to say that the Bill, as it stood, was in his opinion unworkable, and that he would not like to undertake to work it in its present form; and, further, that it would upset many private local Acts which had been passed. He had represented the matter to the Lord Advocate, who had given his assurance that these things would be put right in one way or another, and he (Mr. Anderson) had agreed to stop in his opposition to the Bill going forward. But he was now bound to say that if the Bill went forward he should be obliged to vote against it. His constituents in one point considered the Bill a very dangerous one, and that was in respect of the clause enabling burghs to amalgamate; but they had offered to withdraw their opposition to that clause if the right hon. and learned Gentleman the Secretary of State for the Home Department would agree to a Royal Commission to deal with the boundaries of the great burghs in Scotland. That the right hon. and learned Gentleman had refused to do, and the Bill therefore found no favour in Glasgow; and consequently he was satisfied that he should be doing his duty to his constituents in voting against the Bill going into Committee.

SIR JOHN HAY said, he should regret it as much as anyone, if the Bill did not pass into law; and he confessed that he should be astonished if the Lord Advocate were to drop the measure without making an attempt to get it into Committee. Such a course would be simply trifling with the people of Scotland, who were most anxious about the Bill, and also with regard to the Bill for creating a Secretary of State for Scotland. He ventured to say that those two measures were of far more value and consequence to Scotland than the Representation of the People Bill, because they knew that either this year or next the franchise would be extended. He was in a position to know what was desired in the matter of legislation in Scotland, and he could assure the House that the people of Scotland were most anxious about this measure. He had had the honour of being a Member of the Committee upstairs, and he was bound to say that nothing could exceed the courtesy of their Chairman, the Lord Advocate, in all matters relating to the Bill. The Bill, he believed, was in a shape which provided better law than at present existed in Scotland. It might be improved, no doubt; but he considered it better to pass it now as it was, than wait another year for this legislation.

THE LORD ADVOCATE (Mr. J. B. BALFOUR): I believe this measure is very generally desired throughout Scotland, except in the case of four or five of the largest towns which have Acts of their own open to grave question; and but for these large towns there would be no opposition to the Bill at all. In 1862 a very important measure was passed, generally known as the Police Act, for Scotland. That Act has been of infinite benefit to the populous places of that country. We have had 22 years' experience of it, and in the course of that time it has been found that in several particulars it required amendment. The consequence was that many boroughs and populous places, which desired to obtain the benefit of municipal institutions, made a representation to the Government that it would be extremely desirable to amend the measure and extend its benefits. As a result, the first edition of this Bill was prepared two years ago. I may say it originated very much with the Convention of Royal Burghs. It has been before the country for two years, and has been the subject of a great deal of adjustment, and I am not guilty of inaccuracy when I say that I do not believe there has been any Bill placed before this House to which there has been so large a contribution of assistance and of suggestion from the various towns and populous places throughout the country. No doubt, we should have been very glad if it had been in our power to have had the measure brought forward at an earlier period of the Session; but after the Bill had been before the country for two years it was referred to a Select Committee, consisting of 27 Members, of whom 22 were Scotch. We had some nine or ten meetings, and the Bill was gone through with very great care, with the benefit of multitudes of suggestions from all the classes interested, and what is now before the House is the result. I do think it would be a great misfortune if the result of so much labour, and, I believe, beneficial labour, were lost. The number of Amendments on the Paper for this evening is very small, and I do not think that when we get to them their discussion will last any length of time. It is only right that the House should be aware that the opposition, at least so far as we believe, and has been indicated by the speaking to-night, has come almost entirely, if not entirely, from those places which have Acts which are open to the very gravest criticism. I am not going to follow what has been said by some of my hon. Friends; but I may just say that, in framing the measure, we had before us the result of the labours of the Committee presided over by the right hon. Gentleman opposite (Mr. Sclater-Booth) two years ago. We had their Report before us, and one of the advantages of that Report was that it put an end to legislation by separate Private Bills, which very often contained provisions that, if brought before the House distinctly in important measures, never could become law. The fact of the Committee having reported and recommended against that separate legislation in these Bills made it all the more imperative that such a measure as the present should be brought forward. I do not desire to delay the House by going into arguments as to the different provisions of the Bill. I gather that there is a great majority of Scotch opinion in favour of it. We have been very much pressed to carry it through, and, under the circumstances, believing that the Bill is a good Bill—I do not know that there is any measure which could not be made more perfect if the ordinary conditions of time and place were to be disregarded —and taking into consideration all that has conduced to make the Bill what it is now, I think it would be a great misfortune if we did not go into Committee.

MR. HENDERSON said, he rose for the purpose of corroborating what had fallen from his hon. Friends the Members for Aberdeen (Mr. Webster), Edinburgh (Mr. Buchanan), and Glasgow (Mr. Anderson). He could assure the House that it was with great reluctance that he rose to offer any objection to the Bill. He knew very well there was a very strong feeling in Scotland, especially amongst the small boroughs, that some such measure as this was necessary, and that they had waited patiently for the Bills which had been brought before the House during last year and this year. He could quite corroborate what the right hon. and learned Gentleman the Lord Advocate had said as to the strong desire which existed in Scotland for the measure; but, at the same time, for years he had taken an active interest in local administration, and, having some knowledge of this kind of legislation, he was bound to say that he was afraid that this Bill, as presented to the House, would not fulfil the expectations of those who had been so long desiring legislation. He made that statement with great reluctance, because, as he said, he believed the Bill contained many very valuable provisions. Looking at its full sense, at the manner in which it was drafted in the first instance —or, he might say, at the manner in which it was constructed—and considering that it had passed through Committee, and that great care and attention had been devoted to it, he was very reluctant to offer opposition to it; but, in passing through the Select Committee, it had been so altered that many of the large boroughs had not had time to consider what its present effect would be. He could not describe himself as adverse to the measure; but, from representations which had been made to him by authorities in his own burgh—particularly by the police clerk, who was one of the most experienced police clerks in Scotland—it seemed there was a very strong feeling that it would be well to allow the Bill to be thought over by the country for another year before being pressed. These representations, he was bound to say, corresponded with his own opinion. From his own experience in matters of this kind, he was afraid that the measure would disappoint those who looked forward with so much pleasure and satisfaction to its passing. Altogether, therefore, if the hon. and learned Member for Stockport (Mr. Hopwood) pressed his Resolution, he (Mr. Henderson) should have to support it, although from very different reasons to those which prompted the hon. and learned Gentleman in bringing it forward. He, in fact, took this opportunity of protesting against the line the hon. and learned Gentleman took with reference to these Bills promoted by Scotch burghs. The hon. and learned Gentleman seemed to look at these matters from a purely political point of view, and—as he understood from his remarks, and as he could show if necessary—knew nothing whatever of local administration. If he had known anything about it, he would never have uttered the sentiments he had uttered in that House. The hon. and learned Gentleman had taken the strongest objection to the Bill proposed in 1882 by his (Mr. Henderson's) own burgh (Dundee), and also to the Bill of the hon. Member for Kilmarnock (Mr. Dick-Peddie), who had fallen into the same mistake of bringing the Bill in as a small private measure. The great objection taken to the Dundee Bill, which was a Consolidating Bill, relating to clauses which had been in operation for 11 years, with the sanction of the House, to the great benefit of the community, was that it was proposed to re-enact these clauses in it with the full consent of the inhabitants. The sanitary provisions of the present measure, instead of being too stringent, were, in his opinion, too lax, and that was one of the reasons why Dundee objected to the Bill. The Lord Advocate had stated that legislation in respect of these matters had fallen back since 1862, and that the large boroughs had been obliged to promote local Acts of their own to remedy the existing evils. Well, the fault he (Mr. Henderson) found with the Bill was that, instead of bringing up the general law of Scotland to the advanced position reached by the burghs which had secured their own local Police Acts, it proposed to level down these particular burghs to the condition of the whole country. It would level down, instead of bringing the whole country up to the position which the burghs he referred to had arrived by long experience of the defects of the existing law. In the present Bill a retrograde reactionary step was taken. He felt very strongly on this point, and in Committee he should have to bring forward many Amendments. Some Amendments he had put on the Paper; but there were many more which he should have to move which he had been unable to bring forward up to this time; and he believed there were other hon. Members in the same position as himself. Though the Motion for going into Committee were passed, there would still be a great deal to do. The Amendments on the Paper did not by any means represent the number which would be put down if they got into Committee. He made these remarks, as he had said, with the greatest reluctance. He should have been much better pleased if he could have found himself able to support the Lord Advocate in pushing forward the measure. He should have supported it if it had not been for the conviction that if it were passed it would, instead of reflecting credit on the legislation of this year, so far as Scotland was concerned, tend to the reverse state of things, and prove provocative of opposition and objection.

Mr. SCLATER-BOOTH said, there were many things in the Bill of which he did not approve, and which he should be glad to see altered; but, for the most part, these clauses referring to them were of a re-enacting and consolidating character. They had heard quite enough from hon. Members representing important towns in Scotland—and they had also heard the mild and mitigated protest of the Lord Advocate—to show the extravagance of the Acts in force in some towns in Scotland. These Acts did not always meet with the concurrence and approval of the Local Authorities; and he (Mr. Sclater-Booth) had come to the conclusion that it would be better to go forward with this Bill, and get a reasonable measure passed for the whole of Scotland, than to allow these eccentric Acts in force in some Scotch towns longer to prevail. For his own part, he was entirely in favour of the policy which guided the Committee of 1882, to which reference had been made, and which guided the Committee which had been sitting this year. He trusted the hon. and learned Member for Stockport (Mr. Hopwood) would see that this measure was a step in the right direction. The Lord Advocate had been of great service in 1882, when the Scotch Improvement Bills were under consideration, in getting some extravagant provisions cut out of them. The right hon. and learned Lord had been very much struck by the views which prevailed on that Committee; and it had, evidently, been his intention and desire in framing the Bill to have regard to those views. He (Mr. Sclater-Booth) would be very sorry indeed if they were not to go into Committee on the Bill.

MR. DICK-PEDDIE wished to point out that the Scotch Members who had spoken against proceeding with the Bill were, without exception, Representatives of the large burghs, which had already Acts of their own. It might be of no great consequence to these large burghs that a general measure, such as that before the House, should pass; but it was of very great importance to the small burghs, which had not the benefit of special Acts, that there should be a consolidation of the various imperfect general Acts, under which their police and sanitary affairs were regulated. At the same time, it was most desirable that the large burghs should be freed from the tyrannical provisions which were found in their special Acts. His hon. Friend the Member for Edinburgh (Mr. Buchanan) spoke of Edinburgh as "enjoying" its Acts. He (Mr. Dick-Peddie) had been a citizen of Edinburgh for a much longer time than his hon. Friend; and he could testify that, by many of his fellow-citizens, the provisions of the local Acts were regarded as most oppressive. The Acts would have been found intolerable, had it not been that the authorities did not venture to enforce many of the powers conferred on them by these Acts. He sympathized generally with much that had fallen from his hon. and learned Friend the Member for Stockport (Mr. Hopwood) regarding the undue interference with personal liberty, authorized by some of the local Acts, and the inquisitorial nature of many of their provisions; but he thought that some of the criticisms of the measure now before the House, which had fallen from his hon. Friend, would not have been made had he been more familiar with Scotland than he was. While the Bill before the House contained clauses which might be objected to, it went far in the direction of modifying the stringency of many provisions found in existing local Acts; and, therefore, he trusted the House would agree to proceed with it. The small burghs wished to have a consolidation of the various Acts regulating their police and sanitary affairs. Though hon. Members said that Edinburgh enjoyed its Act, and had done so for many years, those who had resided in the Scotch capital for a long period—longer than those hon. Members—knew that it did not enjoy the advantages which were supposed to have been conferred upon it. If similar Acts were in force in England, it would not be long before there would be a revolution in the country. Seeing that the present was a modified Act, he trusted that the House would take it into consideration.

MR. J. W. BARCLAY said, he quite agreed with his hon. Friend (Mr. Dick-Peddie) when he said that the small burghs desired to have a consolidation of their various Acts, and that an Act should be passed which would be generally applicable to the small burghs. He must say, however, as representing two small burghs, that he understood they were opposed to the Bill. As a matter of fact, he had presented a Petition from one of them, the other day, against the passing of the Bill. Speaking from his own experience—and he must claim to have had some experience of local administration—he thought the measure, in many of its parts, was very unworkable, and required a great deal more adjustment, consideration, and amendment than it had, apparently, received. He sympathized with the views of the hon. and learned Member for Stockport (Mr. Hopwood) to a great extent. Many of the clauses of the Bill gave extreme powers—utterly despotic powers—to the police. He had made some attempt to modify them; but was bound to say he had met with little support on the Committee. A great many people thought that these powers could only be applied against evilly-disposed persons. If that were so, there would not be much to object to; but it must be remembered that the application of the clauses in the Bill lay, in the first place, in the hands of the policemen who exercised the powers they had in many cases in an arbitrary manner. The chief power would be exercised by the magistrates or baillies, as they were called in Scotland—very excellent gentlemen, no doubt, but gentlemen who knew very little about the law. They were very respectable townspeople; but, however respectable townspeople might be, it could not be expected of them that they should know much about the Laws of Evidence, or even enough to be able to say what was evidence, and what was not. He was, therefore, very reluctant to give such powers as some of those contained in the Bill to ordinary citizens. The Lord Advocate said that many of the Police Bills, under which many large towns were governed, would not be able to withstand the scrutiny of the House. Well, he (Mr. Barclay) would say that many of the clauses of this Bill would not be able to withstand the scrutiny of the House. They were very stringent—seriously affecting the liberty of the subject—and he did not think that if they were brought under the scrutiny of the House there would be the smallest chance of their becoming law. He had another objection to the Bill. The Lord Advocate said that one of its objects was to prevent burghs, for the future, coming to Parliament for separate enactments. Now, he did not think this measure would be applicable to the case of small burghs growing into large ones. From his own experience, he knew how, when a burgh grew, and new streets and pavements and municipal arrangements became necessary, how necessary it was to come to the House for a special Act dealing with these improvements. The clauses embodied in this Bill were very much the same as the law already existing in the burghs, but which was from time to time found to be insufficient. He was, therefore, of opinion that in these respects, at all events, the Bill was open to very considerable amendment, so as to make it workable and applicable to the cases of all the burghs, whether small or large—particularly to small burghs, to enable them to grow from time to time without a special Act. For the reasons he had given, speaking on behalf of two small burghs at least within his own constituency, he thought it would be much better for the consideration of the Bill to be deferred till another Session. To make it a workable Bill and insure the purpose intended, a good deal more consideration than it had yet received should be given to the Bill. No doubt the Select Committee—of which he had had the honour to be a Member—had devoted a considerable amount of attention to the measure; but he did not think sufficient attention had been given to it to make it what it ought to be. The Session had not provided sufficient time to make the Bill such as deserved to receive general support. He should support the Motion of his hon. and learned Friend (Mr. Hopwood).

MR. A. GRANT said, he must express the great regret he felt at the opposition which had developed itself against this Bill on the part of some of the Representatives of the large burghs in Scotland. The burgh he had the honour to represent (Leith) was, perhaps, the largest in Scotland which had not a Police Act of its own. It was at present under the General Police Act of 1862; and he could assure the House—after having been very lately in conversation with some of the members of the Corporation of Leith—that that burgh most cordially approved of the Bill, and earnestly hoped it might pass into law that Session. He was sure the opinion the Corporation of Leith entertained was the opinion of all other Corporations under the General Police Act. The Bill made provision for a great many new wants which had sprung up in connection with municipal government since the passing of the Act of 1862; and it embodied all that was really useful, and all that was defensible, and all that was reasonable in the Act of 1862, as well as all that was defensible in the different Private Acts which had been obtained by the various burghs since the Act of 1862 was passed. The measure—as had been already stated—after having passed its second reading, was referred to a large representative Select Committee, by whom it was carefully scrutinized, and gone over at the expense of much time and labour. He might say, further, that the Bill had the cordial approval of the Convention of Royal and Parliamentary Burghs; and he thought he might say, with the exception of one or two of the largest towns, had the cordial approval of public opinion throughout Scotland. Furthermore, he might say that the Bill was framed in such a way as to deal most leniently with the large towns which were now opposed to it. Out of seven parts of the Bill there were only two made obligatory, and those two were concerned with police offences, and penalties, and sanitary regulations. He appealed to the House whether it was not desirable that all the burghs in the country should be placed under one uniform law as to police offences and penalties? Whence came the opposition to the Bill which had developed itself that night? It had come partly from hon. Members who had no connection with Scotland at all; but that was not where the real opposition had come from. The real opposition lay amongst certain Municipal Corporations of Scotland, and it had been expressed by their Representatives, not as the individual opinions of these gentlemen themselves, but as the opinions furnished to them by the Local Authorities of burghs which had their own Acts—Local Authorities who were really the authors of those Acts. It was natural that the authors of those Acts should be in love with them, and should think they were the perfection of municipal government. He frankly admitted that in many aspects the clauses of these Local Acts were most useful for local purposes. Some of the clauses referring to police offences were useful, no doubt; but there were other clauses in the Private Acts of a different character. Many of them were most indefensible encroachments upon private rights, and upon the liberty of the subject under the Common Law; and it was only last year—as had already been noticed that night—that the House had found that the practice of putting these indefensible stipulations into Private Bills had reached to such a height that it was compelled to interfere and prevent the practice from going further. He would only give the House one instance of the way in which these clauses in the private measures acted to the detriment of the people living in neighbouring towns. The Burgh of Edinburgh had obtained a very strict and stringent private Police Act in 1875. In that Act there were clauses referring to the regulation of improper houses. Those clauses were of such a nature that raids were made on the houses, and the inmates were driven out of the Burgh of Edinburgh. The burgh which he represented (Leith) lay contiguous to Edinburgh, the division line being often only a formal one running down the centre of a street; and what was the consequence to Leith of this exceptional clause, which had been slipped into the Edinburgh Act merely because there was no one present to prevent it, the Bill being passed as a private measure? In fact, with regard to that Private Bill the Earl of Redesdale in "another place" declared that if anyone lifted his little finger against it, he would prevent the Bill being passed, saying also—"If Edinburgh is unanimous in demanding such a Bill I must give it to them; but God forbid that I should ever find myself in Edinburgh after this Bill has been passed!" To such an extent had this exceptional legislation on the part of Edinburgh acted to the detriment of Leith that the state of things had become intolerable. A Memorial had been presented by the inhabitants of the districts in Leith which these people had invaded, stating the condition of things brought about by these persons in the neighbourhood. This district was immediately adjoining Edinburgh, and the Memorialists complained that since the Act came into operation in 1875 they had been sorely afflicted by these people, and that there were now in the district 59 brothels, containing 177 prostitutes, conducted in the most shameless manner, and exercising a most injurious influence, the behaviour of the inmates, even in the broad daylight in Leith Walk and other places, being most indecent. They added that the effect had been to lower the value of property in the neighbourhood, to drive respectable people away, and alter entirely the character of the locality. Now, he would not say for a moment that it was in the power of that House to put down immorality; but he did say that Parliament was bound to interfere to compel each different locality to bear its own burden of the mischief, and to prevent its neighbours from being inundated by its moral sewage. The proposal in this Bill to make the keeping of an improper house an offence, and to make the penalties uniform throughout the country, would have that effect; and he trusted the Lord Advocate would not be turned aside by any selfish representations on the part of large towns, such as Edinburgh, from using every effort to pass the Bill into law in the present Session.

MR. H. H. FOWLER said, that having sat on the Committee of 1882, and for 30 days this Session on a similar Committee, he should like to say a few words on the facts of the question. The Scotch Bill which came before the Committee of 1882 was, without any exception, the worst of them all, and the most grotesque; and he should be within the mark if he said that the Committee struck out 100 clauses from that Bill. They were very much assisted in that by the Lord Advocate. He agreed in the necessity for some general legislation with reference to sanitary matters, and the Report of the Committee strongly urged that with reference to England and Wales. This was an attempt, and a very praiseworthy attempt, on the part of the Lord Advocate to secure general legislation for Scotland; but he wanted to ask the Government how they were going to deal with this as a practical matter of business when winding up the affairs of the Session? This was not, as he understood it, exceptional legislation, but a general enactment of what the House thought should be the law which ought to prevail in Scotland; and no doubt it would be argued that if it was good for Scotland it was good for England and Wales. The Bill had been sent to a Select Committee, which he thought most unfortunately sat with closed doors. The Committee only sat for nine or ten days; and, therefore, it must be assumed that there was a vast mass of matter still demanding consideration, if they were to pass any general legislation which would be quoted as a precedent. Several of the clauses which had been read that night had been struck out unanimously by the Committee of which he was a Member, for they would not allow them to apply to England, considering them improper and oppressive. The Members of that Committee could not sit still and be parties to passing for Scotland enactments which they had reported ought not to be applied to England. There were 429 clauses in this Bill; it was now 2 o'clock on the 30th of July; when the Government had got their last Vote in Supply they would bring in the Appropriation Bill and close the Session with a view to the Autumn Session; and, valuable as this Bill might be, was there any reasonable prospect of its receiving that consideration which it deserved and ought to have? He did not think Scotland would suffer by the Bill standing over for six months for consideration. That interval would enable Local Authorities to give it careful consideration and suggest Amendments next Session, and the Bill next year would have that moral support which it had not at the present time, and would be the more likely to secure the general approbation of the House. He hoped the Government would say whether they thought that on the 30th of July, when they were intending to wind up the Session within a few days, they could pass a contentious Bill containing between 400 and 500 clauses; and whether they could expect the House to give time and attention to a portion of the Bill, and then turn round and say it was useless to attempt to proceed with it. He thought they had a right to ask the Government to say either that they would go on with the Bill to the bitter end, even to the end of August, or that they would abandon it now.

MR. J. A. CAMPBELL agreed with many hon. Members that some Bill of this kind was required in Scotland; but he also agreed that this Bill was of too voluminous a character, and dealt with subjects too complicated, to be properly considered at that period of the Session. It must also be considered that the Bill was not known in Scotland in its present form, for it had been considerably altered by the Committee, and Scotch Members were receiving letters from Scotland every day with regard to it, showing that there was a good deal of dissatisfaction with many of the alterations made by the Committee. It would, he thought, be a misfortune if a measure of this kind was rushed through Parliament at the end of the Session; and it would, therefore, be better to postpone legislation upon this subject until the country had had a fuller opportunity of considering the Bill in its altered form. He hoped the Lord Advocate would reconsider his decision, and agree to postpone this measure until another Session,

MR. JACOB BRIGHT said, he thoroughly agreed with every word of the appeal of the hon. Member for Wolverhampton (Mr. H. H. Fowler). It should be remembered that a considerable majority of Members were against this Bill, and had announced that they would vote against it. Four or five of the Members who had spoken that night had deprecated proceeding with it further. Some Members from Scotland surrounding him had said a good deal in favour of the Bill; but they would vote with the hon. and learned Member for Stockport (Mr. Hopwood); and, therefore, under all the circumstances, it would, he thought, be unreasonable to go on with it now.

MR. GRAY observed, that it was commonly said to require a surgical operation to get a joke into the head of a Scotchman; but after looking at this Bill he thought there was no truth in that saying. The Bill contained some of the most comical provisions. Clause 329 provided a penalty against "any person who attempts to commit a falsehood." He supposed the Bill only applied to Scotchmen, as Scotchmen in Scotland, and within a special district.

THE LORD ADVOCATE (Mr. J. B. BALFOUR) said, the hon. Member had been misled by the punctuation. "Falsehood and fraud" was the name in Scotland for the well-known crime of swindling.

MR. GRAY said, he presumed that the penalty would only apply to a certain district. Then the police regulations in Part VII. were of the most extraordinary character. A boy who dropped a piece of orange peel, or laid hold of the end of a cart without the express permission of the owner, and so on, was to be punished by a fine of 40*s*. Really, to ask the House of Commons at the end of the Session to discuss all those details was something too preposterous. There was a provision against cruelty to animals, and another providing a penalty for anyone who drove a bull through the streets unless the bull had a ring through its nose, which, of course, was not at all cruelty to the beast. If these provisions were intended to be enforced they were really of a most tyrannical character. For instance, a medical man must not send out circulars even enclosed in envelopes, without being liable to penalties. He did not wish to detain the House; but there was a provision that any person who hung from the back of any cart or carriage was to be punished; and, again—

"If any persons shall stand together in the street so as to annoy foot passengers"—

not so as to obstruct them, but only so as to annoy them—they were to be liable to punishment; and—

"If any person loiters, sits, or lies, on the footway to the annoyance of the foot passengers,"

he should be fined. In fac , under this Bill people might be fined for anything. The only excuse for these provisions was, he supposed, that the Bill was not intended to be carried out. No person might have a bagatelle or a billiard-table. With regard to the regulations for disorderly houses, no doubt the special constituency which the hon. Baronet (Sir Herbert Maxwell) represented would desire to have some regulations of that kind after the history he had given; but after the statistics that had been given he thought no one else would desire to impose such ridiculous regulations as these. It could not be seriously intended to enforce the provisions of the Bill. Any person finding any goods and not giving them up was to be subject to a penalty. He did not think it could be seriously intended to enforce that.

MR. ILLINGWORTH asked for some authoritative statement as to the prospect before the House. It would be objectionable for English Members to interfere with Scotch Business, and he did not mean to do so, except to say that it would be a most extraordinary thing if a Bill of this magnitude should be passed through Parliament without any proper public discussion; without even a discussion on the second reading, and after a few Sittings of a Committee upstairs, and without any Reports of their proceedings having been published. If the Bill was a valuable one it must not be pushed through at the tail end of the Session, but must be deliberately entered upon. His object in speaking was to ask what the Government intended to do with regard to general Business. To go on with this Bill seemed to him a breach of the understanding generally arrived at. It was understood that contentious Business was not to be proceeded with, and that the Government were strongly opposed to any such Business being entered upon. He would like to know why the Home Secretary had withdrawn his London Government Bill if that was not the case. If they were to enter upon any Bill of length and importance, that Bill, having advanced so far, was entitled to be taken up. He was satisfied that nothing would be lost by taking the winter for a fair and careful consideration of this measure, and that it could be entered upon early next Session, and passed with greater satisfaction than was now possible.

Mr. DILLWYN said, he thought the House had a right to a categorical answer to the question of the hon. Member for Wolverhampton (Mr. H. H. Fowler)—namely, whether the Government did or did not intend to carry this Bill to its conclusion? If they did, the House must prepare to sit until September. If they did not, they were wasting time, and it was not fair to ask Members to make a House for them to take up Bills which they did not intend to push to a legitimate end. He hoped that before the House went into Committee the Government would give some answer to that question.

Sir WILLIAM HARCOURT: Of course, the Government are in the hands of the House, and more particularly of the Scotch Members, upon a measure of this kind. Certainly, the Government had very strong reason to believe with reference to this Bill that there was—I will not say a unanimous, but—a predominant agreement on the part of Scotch Members in favour of this Bill; but when the Division is taken we shall see what the opinion of the Scotch Members is, and, of course, the Government will be guided very much by the result of the Division. Everybody knows that a Bill of this kind affords opportunities for opposition; but certainly this Bill having been through a Select Committee, we supposed that, with the exception of several large towns in Scotland which had Bills of their own, and did not want any general Bill, the greater part of Scotland was in favour of this Bill, and wanted it. The Government were prepared to go as far as they could to try to pass this Bill into law this Session; but this question must be decided very much by the Division about to be taken.

Question put.

The House *divided*:—Ayes 58; Noes 32: Majority 26.—(Div. List, No. 193.)

Main Question, "That Mr. Speaker do now leave the Chair," put, and *agreed to.*

Mr. Illingworth

Bill *considered* in Committee.

(In the Committee.)

Mr. M'LAREN: I beg to move that the Chairman do now report Progress.

Motion made and Question proposed, "That the Chairman do report Progress, and ask leave to sit again.—(*Mr. M'Laren.*)

The LORD ADVOCATE (Mr. J. B. Balfour): We will agree to reporting Progress after the 1st clause is disposed of.

Clause 1 *agreed to.*

Mr. GRAY: It is moved that the Chairman do report Progress.

Question put, and *agreed to.*

Committee report Progress; to sit again upon *Thursday.*

CHARTERED COMPANIES BILL.

(*Mr. Attorney General, Mr. Chancellor of the Exchequer, Mr. Solicitor General.*)

[Bill 304.] COMMITTEE.

Bill *considered* in Committee, and *reported*, without Amendment.

The ATTORNEY GENERAL (Sir Henry James): I would appeal to the House to allow the Bill to be read a third time—looking at the period of the Session, and at the fact that the measure is only a small one.

Bill read the third time, and *passed.*

PUBLIC HEALTH (IRELAND) (DISTRICTS) BILL.—[Bill 311.]

(*Mr. Solicitor General for Ireland.*)

SECOND READING.

Order for Second Reading read.

Motion made, and Question proposed, "That the Bill be now read a second time."—(*Mr. Solicitor General for Ireland.*)

Colonel NOLAN said, he did not think there was much harm in the Bill. It seemed to him to afford a great opportunity to the Executive for removing a blot in the Public Health Act by which Town Commissioners were precluded from borrowing money to build Town Halls unless they were sanitary authorities. That was a most absurd state of things. It was a mistake in the legislation of the past, and the Government ought to pass a Bill and rectify the error as soon as possible.

Motion *agreed to.*

Bill read a second time, and *committed* for *To-morrow.*

SUPREME COURT OF JUDICATURE AMENDMENT BILL [*Lords*].

(*Mr. Attorney General.*)

[BILL 307.] COMMITTEE.

Order for Committee read.

THE ATTORNEY GENERAL (Sir HENRY JAMES): I understand there is no opposition to the House going into Committee on this Bill; but the hon. Member for Wolverhampton (Mr. H. H. Fowler), I believe, desires to move an Amendment in Committee. I shall, therefore, propose to take the Committee stage *pro formâ*—moving at once, when in Committee, to report Progress.

Bill *considered* in Committee.

(In the Committee.)

Committee report Progress; to sit again upon *Thursday.*

SUMMARY JURISDICTION (REPEAL, &c.) BILL.—[BILL 254.]

(*Mr. Hibbert, Secretary Sir William Harcourt.*)

CONSIDERATION OF LORDS' AMENDMENTS.

MR. HIBBERT said, there were three Amendments, two being meant to amplify and explain an Amendment in the 4th clause of the Bill by the hon. and learned Gentleman the Member for Bridport (Mr. Warton), the others being merely explanatory as to auditors.

MR. WARTON said, he merely wished to complain that no means were adopted to bring before the notice of the House what the Lords' Amendments were—not only in the case of this Bill, but in the case of all other Bills. There were no Amendments on the Paper to-day, and no one, but, he supposed, those in charge of the Bill, had any opportunity of knowing what the Amendments were. He must acknowledge the courtesy with which the hon. Gentleman the Under Secretary of State for the Home Department (Mr. Hibbert) had met him; but he must insist that the House should be afforded some better opportunity than at present existed of knowing what was going on between the one House and the other. It was very doubtful whether anyone but himself and the hon. Member (Mr. Hibbert) knew what, in the present instance, the Lords' Amendments were. To his mind it was a serious defect in the procedure of the House that there was no way of informing hon. Members, as they ought to be informed, of what was going on, and what Amendments were being considered.

Lords' Amendments *agreed to.*

INFANTS' BILL.—[BILL 308.]

(*Mr. Bryce, Mr. Horace Davey, Mr. Anderson, Mr. Staveley Hill.*)

CONSIDERATION.

Order for Consideration, as amended, read.

MR. BRYCE: I move that this Bill, as amended, be now considered.

Motion made, and Question proposed, "That the Bill, as amended, be now considered."—(*Mr. Bryce.*)

MR. WARTON: I rise to Order——

MR. SPEAKER: The hon. and learned Member (Mr. Bryce) is in charge of the Bill; he has a right to make the Motion.

MR. WARTON: I have a right to be heard. I have given Notice of a Motion to re-commit the Bill.

MR. SPEAKER: The hon. and learned Member (Mr. Bryce) is in Order.

MR. WARTON: I have a right to be heard.

MR. SPEAKER: That is not the case; the hon. and learned Gentleman is disorderly.

Question put, and *agreed to.*

MR. BRYCE: I beg to move that this Bill be re-committed with respect to a new Clause.

Motion made, and Question proposed, "That the Bill be re-committed in respect of a new Clause (Court may make orders as to custody)."—(*Mr. Bryce.*)

MR. WARTON: With the utmost deference, Mr. Speaker, I beg to call your attention to the fact that, under Standing Order 375, I was entitled to move my Motion. The words of the Standing Order are very distinct indeed, as it appears to me; and I now put it to you whether the fact of the hon. and learned Gentleman in charge of the Bill having put down one Amendment has not precluded him from the right to re-commit the Bill generally?

MR. SPEAKER: The hon. and learned Member for Bridport is entitled to raise this question. He can move to leave out the words "in respect of a new Clause;" and, if the Motion is carried, he can move the general re-commitment of the Bill.

MR. TOMLINSON said, he did not know what the form of the Motion before the House was, as it was not on the Paper; but he desired to move that the Bill be re-committed as a whole, or to strike out the words "in respect of a new Clause." He wished to call attention to the manner in which the Bill was carried through the Committee last week. It was considered two days—first on Tuesday, and the Committee was then ordered for Thursday; but, by subsequent arrangement, the day was altered to Friday, and the consequence of that, to his (Mr. Tomlinson's) knowledge, was that several hon. Members who had intended to take part in the discussion in Committee were not present. It was probably owing to that circumstance that the Bill came before them in its present form, a form which all must confess a very awkward one. Clause 3, it seemed to him, was in a shape which was quite nonsensical. The hon. and learned Member in charge of the Bill had given Notice of two new Clauses on Report, and there were a large number of Amendments, some of which, he submitted, were necessary to make the measure a workable one. If the Bill was to pass at all, it was very unfortunate that they should have all these Amendments on Report.

Amendment proposed, to leave out the words "in respect of a new Clause."—(*Mr. Tomlinson.*)

Question proposed, "That the words proposed to be left out stand part of the Question."

MR. WARTON said, he was very sorry that he should have appeared disorderly in trying to press a point on Mr. Speaker when Mr. Speaker did not think he was right in so doing. He (Mr. Warton) had given Notice of his Motion; he did not wish to argue the point; but desired to apologize if he had been disorderly in putting to Mr. Speaker what he thought he was entitled to put. He was within the hearing of Members who were present late on Friday night, when the Solicitor General took a lively interest in the Bill. The hon. and learned Gentleman, it would be remembered, was opposed to reporting Progress, a Motion for which was made because there was an extraordinary clause in the Bill, a clause which had not met with the approval of the House. There had been a dispute as to whether the clause should be withdrawn or Progress should be reported. Ultimately the clause was withdrawn, on the understanding that it should be brought forward again in a modified form. He found to-day that very slight alteration had been made in accordance with the Amendment proposed by himself to the proposal of the hon. and learned Member for the Tower Hamlets (Mr. Bryce). The obnoxious provision had only been slightly altered. But, irrespective of that, it was obviously the feeling of the Committee with regard to the Bill—which was an important one, affecting the relations existing between husband and wife, between father and mother and child, and bringing up a great number of important questions—that it should not be gone on with this Session. The 2nd clause had been cut out, and was to be very materially altered; and, seeing that it was such an important measure, interfering so seriously with domestic relations, it should not be proceeded with at so late an hour in the morning; but, under any circumstances, it was important that it should go back to Committee, for the reason that, on Report, Members could only speak once on each Amendment. They could have fairer, fuller, and freer discussion in Committee, and could lay their heads together and see what could be done to improve the Bill. The Solicitor General was very fair and candid in the matter on Friday; and he (Mr. Warton) would put it to him whether the Bill should not be now re-committed?

COLONEL NOLAN said, he wished to make an observation on a point of procedure and Order. He believed that all the objection the last time the Bill was before them was to a particular clause now withdrawn. It had been omitted by the hon. and learned Member in charge of the measure, and another was to be substituted for it. What he wanted to know was, where they were to see this new clause? It was not on the Paper.

MR. BRYCE: It is on the Paper.

COLONEL NOLAN: The clause moved last time?

MR. BRYCE: No; the substituted clause.

COLONEL NOLAN: That, then, is satisfactory.

Question put.

The House *divided*:—Ayes 44; Noes 5: Majority 39.—(Div. List, No. 194.)

Main Question put.

Bill *re-committed.*

(In the Committee.)

MR. BRYCE said, he had to move the new Clause—"Court may make orders as to custody." It provided that the Court might, on application, make order for the custody of the infant. He had omitted all reference to the question of religion and education, to which objection was taken at the last Sitting, and he hoped the Committee would see no objection now to accepting it.

New Clause:—

(Court may make orders as to custody.)

"The court may, upon the application of the mother of any infant (who may apply without next friend), make such order as it may think fit regarding the custody of such infant, having regard to the welfare of the infant, and to the conduct of the parents, and to the wishes as well of the mother as of the father, and may alter, vary, or discharge such order on the application of either parent, or, after the death of either parent, of any guardian under this Act,"

—*brought up*, and read the first time.

Clause read a second time, and *added* to the Bill.

Bill *reported*, as amended.

Bill, as amended, *considered.*

MR. BRYCE said, the clause of which he had given Notice he moved in consequence of a suggestion of the Solicitor General. It had reference to the removal of proceedings and to appeals, giving either party to a case power to make application for the removal of the case from the County Court, or in Scotland from the Sheriff's Court, to the Superior Court—namely, the High Court of Justice in England or Ireland, or to the Court of Session in Scotland. Precedents in regard to the removal of cases had been followed in either case. There was also a provision for an appeal from the County Court or Sheriff's Court decisions to the Superior Court in England, Ireland, or Scotland.

New Clause:—

(As to removing proceedings and appeals.)

"(In England and Ireland when any application has been made under this Act to a county court the High Court of Justice may, at the instance of any party to such application, order such application to be removed to the High Court of Justice and there proceeded with before a judge of the Chancery Division, on such terms as to costs or otherwise as it may think proper.

"In England and Ireland an appeal shall lie to the High Court of Justice from any order made by a county court under this Act; and, subject to any Rules of Court made after the passing of this Act, any such appeal shall be heard by a judge of the Chancery Division of the High Court of Justice at Chambers or in Court, as he shall direct.

"In Scotland any application made under this Act to a sheriff court may be removed to the court of session, at the instance of any party, in the manner provided by and subject to the conditions prescribed by the ninth section of 'The Sheriff Court (Scotland) Act, 1877.'

"In Scotland an appeal shall lie to either division of the court of session from any order made by a sheriff court under this Act.)"—(*Mr. Bryce*,)

—*brought up*, and read the first time.

Motion made, and Question proposed, "That the Clause be read a second time."

MR. WARTON said, his objection was in regard to the jurisdiction of the County Court under this Act. It was rather an awkward manner of discussing the point on this Amendment. He was sure the hon. and learned Member did not wish to get the consent of the House beforehand, so that they would come to the consideration of the point with hands tied. It was obvious they could not give it the same consideration they could in Committee. But he had a great objection to any jurisdiction of the County Court whatever—it would be better in such cases to go at once to the High Court. In so far as this clause involved the County Court, he thought this clause was unnecessary; and he submitted to the hon. and learned Member that the fairer way to decide the point would be to withdraw the clause now, and to introduce it as a sub-section at the end of the 6th section; because those who attacked the clause altogether could raise the question fairly there, for though this was a new clause, logically it would come after the 6th clause, and should not be introduced on a previous Amendment. If the House did not pass the clause now, he should, in one sense, be sorry; for if the House adhered to the retention of the County Court jurisdiction which the Committee adopted in Clause 6, of course there would be no objection to this clause; as a part of and necessary pendant to Clause 6, it would be a very proper provision indeed. But the objection now was it committed the House in advance, and tied them down to the 6th section. For his own part, he might say it was his intention to strike out County Courts, for he was quite sure it was an improper tribunal to be intrusted with jurisdiction over such delicate points as these. He did not know what view the Solicitor General might take; he should like to have it, for it would very much guide his (Mr. Warton's) opinion. What he submitted now was that if the House assented to this clause they committed themselves to Clause 6, whereas if it were withdrawn now it could very well be introduced at the end of Clause 6.

THE SOLICITOR GENERAL (Sir FARRER HERSCHELL) said, the course he proposed to take was to propose certain Amendments to the clause to make it clear—which he did not feel it was at present—that any party to the application should have the right to remove the case to the Superior Court. At present the clause stood—"the High Court of Justice may, at the instance of any party, &c."; he would have it made clear that parties were entitled to have it removed. Safe-guarded in that way they might leave the County Court with jurisdiction safely where no party objected.

MR. HORACE DAVEY said, he regretted the Solicitor General had proposed this Amendment.

THE SOLICITOR GENERAL (Sir FARRER HERSCHELL) explained he had not done so yet.

MR. INCE said, he thought the question would be better considered after Clause 6. He thought the hon. and learned Member had not improved his Bill by putting in the reference to County Courts. In cases of dispute between husband and wife it was as well there should be a little difficulty and some expense before the parties could rush into Court. He should be prepared to strike out the words "or County Court of the district," his object being not in the slightest way to cast a doubt upon the County Court, but simply because, if disputes arose, there should be a little difficulty in the way before the parties could make those disputes public by rushing into Court, giving a little time for reflection and for the bitterness to pass away. The practitioners in County Courts were not of the highest class, and he thought it was very undesirable that second or third-rate attorneys should be brought into actions of this kind. The more a little difficulty, and even a little expense, could be introduced, the better for all parties it would be in the long run. He would ask the hon. and learned Member for the Tower Hamlets (Mr. Bryce) to defer further consideration of the clause, to postpone it to the 6th clause, in order that the House might not be fettered when they approached the consideration of that.

MR. TOMLINSON said, an appeal had been made to the hon. and learned Member for the Tower Hamlets to take the clause after Clause 6; he would like to ask the Speaker's ruling, could not the House accede to that? His desire was to put the Bill in the best form possible.

MR. SPEAKER: That cannot be done.

Motion *agreed to.*

Clause read a second time.

THE SOLICITOR GENERAL (Sir FARRER HERSCHELL) said, he proposed to amend the clause in the second line by leaving out the words "the High Court of Justice may, at the instance of;" and then, in the next line, after "application," to leave out "order such application to," and insert, "shall be entitled to an order of the High Court of Justice that such application shall." So the clause would run thus—

> "In England and Ireland, when any application has been made under this Act to a County Court, any party to such application shall be entitled to an order of the High Court of Justice that such application shall be removed to the High Court of Justice,"

and so on. That would make it clear it was a matter of right. And then, in the next line but one, he would propose to leave out the words after "division." He did not think there should be any other power but the absolute right of removal from the County Court to the High Court.

Amendment proposed, in line 2 of new Clause, to leave out the words "the High Court of Justice may, at the instance of."—(*Mr. Solicitor General.*)

Question proposed, "That the words proposed to be left out stand part of the new Clause."

MR. HORACE DAVEY said, he regretted the Solicitor General had proposed this Amendment. He quite recognized the desire that there should be a line drawn beyond which applications should be to the High Court, and, of course, there was no line that could be defined by value; but, at the same time, those who were interested in this Bill felt that it was a Bill for the benefit of the poor as well as the rich—perhaps mainly for the benefit of the poor. Though it might be quite true, as the hon. and learned Member for Hastings (Mr. Ince) said, that County Court jurisdiction might not always be administered with that nicety and precision which characterized the High Court, still people did appreciate the County Courts whose purses were not long enough to go to the High Court. He regretted that the Solicitor General made it compulsory for the Court to make an order, for the effect would be in some cases to deprive those persons whose purses were not long of the benefit of the Act. An applicant to a County Court, perhaps, might not have the means of applying to the Higher Court; and the other side might then, having larger means, by the transfer to the High Court, deprive the applicant of justice. But they were at the mercy of the Government in respect of the Bill. His hon. and learned Friend (Mr. Bryce) would have an opportunity of speaking; perhaps, in the interest of the Bill, he would accept the Amendment; but if his hon. and learned Friend divided against it he should support him. As a matter of drafting, he would suggest to the Solicitor General that, with less alteration of the clause, his object would be accomplished by substituting the word "shall" for the word "may."

MR. HEALY said, speaking with some knowledge of the County Courts of Ireland, and their manner of administering justice, he strongly endorsed what the Solicitor General had said.

MR. HOPWOOD said, he agreed the Amendment would result in a denial to many of the benefit of the Act. In cases of a struggle between man and wife, it was ten to one the husband had the heaviest purse, and the wife small means of asserting her right. In going to a County Court, the result would very likely be the parties would be satisfied with the fair decision of the County Court Judge, and he should have hoped this was the case in Ireland as well as England; if they were not satisfied, there was still an appeal open. But now, instead of that, there would be the means in the hands of the party who wished to delay the matter to say—"No, it shall be removed to the High Court in the Metropolis or in Dublin." He extremely regretted the Amendment had been moved.

MR. BRYCE regretted the line the Solicitor General had taken, and he thought it would considerably impair the value of the Bill; but at that hour of the night and time of the Session it would be useless to oppose the suggestion from the Government Bench, and he should not oppose the Amendment.

THE SOLICITOR GENERAL (Sir FARRER HERSCHELL) said, it must be remembered this proposal in respect to the County Court having jurisdiction was only an afterthought; it was not in the original Bill.

MR. INCE said, he had some doubt if the Amendment really carried out the Solicitor General's intention. There would be always a dispute whether the case should be heard in a Superior Court or not, interlarding another dispute to the one in existence. Would it not be better to introduce after "shall" the words "as a matter of course," or "as a matter of right?" That would carry out the intention which, as he understood it, was that, as a matter of course, it should be carried to the Superior Court. If the words were left as they stood, there would always be a preliminary dispute as to whether it was a case to be taken to the Superior Court or not.

THE SOLICITOR GENERAL (Sir FARRER HERSCHELL) said, perhaps the simpler way would be to substitute "shall" for "may." It was sometimes objected that to make it peremptory and say "the High Court shall," was not respectful to the High Court; but he did not see much in the objection himself. He would, with the leave of the House, withdraw his Amendment.

Amendment, by leave, *withdrawn.*

Amendment proposed, in line 2 of the new Clause, to leave out the word "may," and insert the word "shall."—(*Mr. Solicitor General.*)

Amendment *agreed to.*

Amendment proposed, in line 5 of new Clause, to leave out the words "or otherwise."

Amendment *agreed to.*

MR. TOMLINSON said, he did not quite know whether his Amendment would now come in; it was to add, after the word "Division," the words—

"Or, in the case of any application within the County Palatine of Lancaster, to the Court of Chancery of the County of Lancaster."

He wished to introduce this, for it was a Court that for many centuries had had jurisdiction over infants, and was perfectly competent to have that jurisdiction; and it had the advantage that it lay at the door ready of access to parties.

MR. SPEAKER: The hon. Member cannot move the Amendment as he proposes; the House has passed the point at which he wishes to insert his Amendment, and has omitted subsequent words.

MR. TOMLINSON said, then he would move the Amendment at the end of the sixth line after the word "Justice." The Amendment would then apply to appeals; and he urged it for the reasons he had given.

Amendment proposed,

In line 6, after the word "Justice," to insert the words, "or, in the case of any application within the County Palatine of Lancaster, to the Court of Chancery of the County of Lancaster."—(*Mr. Tomlinson.*)

Question, "That those words be there inserted," put, and *negatived.*

Clause, as amended, *added* to the Bill.

MR. TOMLINSON said, he should now move the insertion of the new clause, of which he had given Notice, after Clause 3. The House was well aware by this time that the Bill effected very great changes in the law relating to infants; and he thought that parties entering into the state of matrimony would have before them the state of things applicable to their own case; and, under the circumstances, it was only fair and right that persons should have the power of determining, by ante-nuptial settlement, the relations they wished to exist in the event of premature death, which might happen shortly after marriage. He thought it essential, in view of the change in the law, that parties should have the power of making such provision as they thought proper.

New Clause:—

(Power to appoint guardians by ante-nuptial settlement.)

"It shall be competent for all persons in contemplation of marriage, by ante-nuptial settlement or agreement for settlement, to make provision for the guardianship of the infant children of the marriage; and in such cases sections two and three of this Act, so far as they are inconsistent with such provisions, shall not apply,"—(*Mr. Tomlinson,*)

—*brought up,* and read the first time.

Motion made, and Question proposed, "That the Clause be read a second time."

MR. BRYCE said, he hoped the House would not agree to the second reading of this clause, which was quite contrary to the principle of the Bill.

Question put, and *negatived.*

MR. WARTON said, the next new clause standing in his name was intended to provide for the religious education of children by deed or marriage settlement executed before marriage. If a father promised to bring up his children in a certain religion, and afterwards broke that promise, he could avail himself of the Common Law right. It seemed to him that the clause was very necessary, because without it there would be no means of carrying out the wishes of the parents with regard to the religion of their children. The effect of the clause would be to prevent hasty promises being made, and afterwards broken. The clause of which he begged to move the second reading was as follows:—

(Effect of marriage settlement.)

"Any contract made, or covenant entered into, by means of any deed or marriage settlement executed before, and in contemplation of, marriage, touching the religion, education, or guardianship of any child or children to be born of such marriage, shall prevail over the provisions of this Act."

MR. ANDERSON rose to Order. He asked whether this clause, if not in the same words, was not substantially the same as the clause which had just been negatived?

MR. SPEAKER: I do not see any difference between the two clauses. The Motion of the hon. and learned Member cannot be put.

Amendment proposed, in page 1, line 8, to leave out the words "and shall come into operation on its passing."—(*Mr. Warton.*)

Amendment *negatived.*

MR. TOMLINSON said, it was now by Statute a rule of construction that the masculine included the feminine, but the neuter included neither the feminine nor the masculine. In line 10 of Clause 2, the word "its" occurred, and as it was not customary except in the case of very young children to speak of infants as of the neuter gender, he should move that the word "his" be substituted for "its."

Amendment proposed, in page 1, line 10, to leave out the word "its," and insert the word "his."—(*Mr. Tomlinson.*)

Question, "That the word 'its' stand part of the Bill," put, and *agreed to.*

MR. WARTON said, he had to propose an Amendment to Clause 3, which did not make it at all clear that it was to apply when the parents of the infants were living together. However repugnant the idea of divorce might be, yet divorce was the law of the land. It was quite clear that marriages were dissolved in two ways by law—sometimes by divorce, and sometimes by judicial separation. He wanted to know whether the hon. and learned Gentleman who brought in this Bill had considered for a moment the positions of parties who, although married, were separated by the law? He did not speak of those who separated themselves, but of those who were judicially separated—that was to say, persons separated by order of the law; because it was the duty of those otherwise separated to come together. Had the hon. and learned Gentleman considered whether a person divorced on the ground of cruelty or adultery was to have the same rights as a person only judicially separated, or did he consider that the words were sufficiently wide to cover this case? If not, he hoped the hon. and learned Solicitor General would interpose the weight of his authority in favour of his Amendment.

Amendment proposed,

In page 1, line 12, before the word "each," to insert the words "while the marriage is subsisting, and before any decree or order for divorce or judicial separation has been made."—(*Mr. Warton.*)

Question proposed, "That those words be there inserted."

MR. BRYCE said, the point raised by the Amendment of the hon. and learned Member was, no doubt, important; but he and his hon. Friend had considered it, and come to the conclusion that that case was met by the 35th section of the existing Act, and they were, therefore, unwilling to disturb the wording of the clause.

MR. TOMLINSON said, he felt bound to state that the explanation of the hon. and learned Gentleman did not satisfy him. The Act referred to related to a state of things which would cease when the present Bill became law. They must remember that this Bill was introduced for the purpose of changing the law with regard to infants, and he did not understand how it could be said that under the previous Act the Court had power to deal with the cases contemplated by the Amendment of his hon. and learned Friend.

Question put.

The House *divided*:—Ayes 2; Noes 32: Majority 30.—(Div. List, No. 195.)

Notice taken, that 40 Members had not voted,

House accordingly adjourned at twenty-five minutes before Four o'clock.

HOUSE OF COMMONS,

Wednesday, 30th July, 1884.

MINUTES.]—SELECT COMMITTEE — *Report*— Ventilation of the House [No. 309].

SUPPLY—*considered in Committee*—CIVIL SERVICE ESTIMATES—CLASS V.—FOREIGN AND COLONIAL SERVICES—Vote 7.

PRIVATE BILL (*by Order*)—*Second Reading*—Earl of Devon's Estates.*

PUBLIC BILLS—*Ordered*—*First Reading*—Corrupt Practices (Suspension of Elections)* [314].

Second Reading — Cholera, &c. Protection* [303].

Committee—Report — Public Health (Ireland) (Districts)* [311].

Considered as amended—Third Reading—Superannuation* [146], and *passed.*

Third Reading—Metropolitan Asylums Board (Borrowing Powers)* [310]; Expiring Laws Continuance* [306], and *passed.*

Withdrawn — Waterworks Rating* [158]; Waterworks Rating (Scotland)* [197]; Municipal Corporations (Borough Funds)* [112]; Public Health Acts Amendment* [113]; High Court of Justice (Provincial Sittings)* [121].

PRIVATE BUSINESS.

—o—

HULL, BARNSLEY, AND WEST RIDING JUNCTION RAILWAY AND DOCK (MONEY) BILL.

CONSIDERATION. THIRD READING.

Motion made, and Question proposed,

"That, in the case of the Hull, Barnsley, and West Riding Junction Railway and Dock (Money) Bill, Standing Orders 84, 207, 214, 216, and 239 be suspended, and that the Bill be now taken into consideration, provided amended prints shall have been previously deposited."—(*Colonel Gerard Smith.*)

MR. PULESTON said, he had no desire to occupy the time of the House, nor did he wish unnecessarily to divide the House upon this Bill, and he was perfectly prepared to state his views in opposition to the measure yesterday. He might say that he had no personal interest whatever in the Bill, nor was he acquainted with anyone who was directly or indirectly concerned in it. His opposition to it was based entirely upon a question of procedure, and he would venture to suggest that the hon. and gallant Member for Wycombe (Colonel Gerard Smith) should give some reason why he proposed that all the Standing Orders of the House should be suspended by wholesale for the purpose of passing, in this way, a Bill of very great importance, the provisions of which were at variance with all the Forms of the House and with Parliamentary usage. It also ignored some very important principles laid down by the Standing Orders for the conduct of Private Business. The promoters of the Bill applied to Parliament for power to create Debenture Stock to the extent of £1,500,000, and hitherto the rule upon which Debenture Stock was granted had been rigidly enforced by Parliament—namely, that a proportionate amount of share capital should also be issued. As he understood, this Company had already passed a Bill which sanctioned the issue of this £1,500,000; but they had failed to issue it under the name of Preference Stock. They, therefore, came to the House for power to call it Debenture Stock. Now, he thought it was only reasonable that there should be very strong reasons assigned before the House consented, in a hurried manner, at a late period of the Session, to accede to a request to suspend by wholesale every Standing Order of the House in such an important case as this. The Standing Orders required that a Bill should have been printed three clear days before the House was asked to consider it; and, further, that the third reading and the consideration of it should not be taken on the same day. There were one or two other Standing Orders which also involved important principles, but which were proposed to be set aside exceptionally in this case. He thought it was necessary, before the House consented to the Resolution proposed by the hon. and gallant Member, that they should have a statement of the main provisions of the Bill, and know why this extraordinary course was proposed to be taken. He certainly must protest against such an attempt to promote Private Bill Legislation, and to occupy the time of the House by stretching its Rules to a point never previously proposed. He might further state, for the information of the House, that the Company promoting the Bill had already had, during the Session, two Bills before the House, one of which only obtained the Royal Assent last month, and it was certainly competent for the Company to have included in that Bill the provisions now asked for, instead of leaving an important matter of this kind to the last days of the Session, and then rushing the Bill through the House at railroad speed, in violation of every Rule and Standing Order of the House, and in violation of the fixed principle he had referred to—that a proportionate amount of shares should accompany the issue of Debenture Stock. The Bill, utterly regardless of the interests either of shareholders, or debenture-holders, or of the time of the House, involved an innovation in the legislation of Parliament which ought not to be sanctioned. Having said so much, he would add that he had no desire whatever, in opposition to the opinion of the House, to call for a Division; and he thought a Division might be avoided if the hon. and gallant Member who had charge of the Bill would assign any adequate reason for departing from the usual course of Business in that House.

MR. THOROLD ROGERS said, he thought it was desirable that he, as one of the Members of the Committee appointed to deal with the Bill, should make an early statement as to what the facts were. It appeared to him that the opposition of the hon. Member opposite (Mr. Puleston) ought to have been directed against the suspension of the Standing Orders on the second reading of the Bill. The House, however, had determined that they would take the Bill into consideration. They had appointed a Committee to consider it, and had instructed that Committee to inquire into its provisions. The Committee sat for two days, and did not dispose of the Bill in any hurried manner whatever. Four hours each day they devoted to a consideration of the Bill, and they listened to the bondholders' view of the subject, because the bondholders were represented before them by counsel. He could only say that the Committee were unanimous in passing the Preamble of the Bill. The fact was, as far as the Committee were able to make things out, that the original promoters of the undertaking had miscalculated the cost which was involved in the construction of the works. It was also mentioned that they had suffered indirectly from losses which no prudence or foresight could have guarded against, and which no precaution, as far as he could see, would have prevented. Under those circumstances, the Committee unanimously decided that the Preamble of the Bill was proved. They took pains, however, to insert clauses in the Bill, by means of which the interests of the bondholders were protected in the fullest way; and they also took precautions to provide that the money to be raised under the Bill should be devoted entirely to the completion of the original projected line from Barnsley to Hull. As he had said, they devoted two days to the consideration of the measure, and they were not responsible for the suspension of the usual Forms of the House. Whatever injury was done to the Forms of the House, the House itself had done with its eyes open. He would add, however, that a vast amount of injury would be done if, after the Committee had arrived at the conclusion they had, solely upon the merits of the case, the House were now to reject the Bill. If the House decided that the Standing Orders ought not to be suspended, the labours of the Committee would have been entirely thrown away.

MR. PULESTON said, he begged his hon. Friend's pardon. The Committee had nothing whatever to do with the suspension or non-suspension of the Standing Orders.

MR. THOROLD ROGERS said, the House had decided to suspend the Standing Orders, and had referred the Bill to a Committee; and that Committee now, in accordance with the reference to them, suggested that the Standing Orders might be further suspended, in order that the Bill might pass through its financial stages.

MR. PULESTON said, he maintained that the Committee had nothing to do with the proposal for suspending the Standing Orders of the House.

MR. THOROLD ROGERS said, he would admit that the suspension of the Standing Orders was a very grave proceeding; but this was a very peculiar emergency, and one in which the House might easily concede the request now made, without inflicting any great amount of injury upon the regularity and safety of their proceedings. All he would say was that he was under the impression—and he believed it was the impression of the entire body of the Committee—that it was fair and right to give this important undertaking the chance of going on. The Committee had been assured, on unquestionable evidence, that the expenditure of the sum now asked for would be sufficient to complete the railway and convert it into a going concern, turning that which was at the present moment an unprofitable and unsuccessful undertaking into one of profit and success. At any rate, that was the view taken by the Committee. He hoped, therefore, that the House would agree to suspend the Standing Orders, and allow the Bill to proceed. The difficulties which had been stated in regard to the conduct of this Bill were very considerable. A large amount of money had been laid out, and the suspension of the works upon the railway would necessitate, if not the final abandonment of the scheme, a considerable deterioration of property. The non-construction of the railway would be most injurious to the district which it was intended to serve. It was well known that the railway was greatly desired by a large body of persons who were connected with the locality; and, beyond that, he thought, although he made no charge against anybody, for he had no right to do so, that it was the business of the House to do all it possibly could to assist this struggling railway in competing with larger and more powerful Companies. One of the greatest dangers this country ran was in the monopoly of the great Railway Companies, and in a combination among a few Companies to get the traffic in their own hands. They did not always succeed, even where they had obtained a monopoly, in getting all the gain for themselves, for one of the leading gentlemen connected with a great Railway Company remarked to him the other day that he believed Railway Companies occupied much more of their time in spending £5, in order to prevent competition, than in earning an honest sovereign for themselves. He thought it was the duty of Parliament to assist in the creation of independent lines, as far as possible, and not to throw an obstacle in the way of their being carried out. It was true that there had been a great miscalculation in the case of this line, and that was the reason why the scheme had proved a failure; but, for all that, it was most desirable, in the general interests of the public, that the project should be carried into effect.

SIR WALTER B. BARTTELOT said, he wished to say a very few words on this very important Bill. He quite agreed that, under ordinary circumstances, the suspension of the Standing Orders of the House ought not to be permitted. But the Committee which sat upon this Bill was a Hybrid Committee, and he presumed that fact was due to the very peculiar character of the Bill, it having been considered by the House that the question involved in the measure deserved more serious consideration than Bills which were originally sent to a Private Bill Committee. But he, for one, was not prepared to blink the great question involved in the Bill, because it had been proved to the Committee, even by the leading counsel who promoted the Bill. He would not say that there had been gross extravagance; but there had been very great extravagance in the construction of the line. It was a highly responsible matter for a body of Directors, like those of the Hull and Barnsley Line, having already called up capital to the amount of £4,000,000 of money, not to take every means in their power to see that the works they had undertaken to perform for a certain amount of money were carried out. He was not going to say there might not have been some excuse, but hardly for the great miscalculations they had made; nor did he think, under the circumstances, they deserved any great amount of sympathy. He believed the line might have been constructed at a far less cost, and he only mentioned the matter because he thought it was right that the House and the public should know the real state of the facts, and especially that the shareholders, who had subscribed their money in good faith, on the understanding that the capital was fairly, judiciously, and properly expended, should know what the position of affairs was. That, however, was not a matter with which the Committee had anything to do. What they had to deal with was a line which was very nearly completed. When the main line was laid down, a very important communication would be established between one great centre of industry and another, and he presumed that Parliament had originally granted the undertaking on the ground that it was to be independent of other lines. That was the point of view from which the Committee had to look at the matter, and they had also to consider the interests of the shareholders themselves, who, if this money was not raised, would, in many instances, be absolutely ruined. The Committee took into their consideration whether it was right that the money should be raised, and, if so, under what conditions it should be raised? They did not agree to the Preamble of the Bill, until they had framed in their own minds what should be done, and they insisted upon certain clauses being inserted in the Bill, by means of which important conditions were laid down. First of all, they provided that the present debenture-holders should have their money repaid in full, with all insterest, before any other dividends were paid; and they further provided that the new shares to be raised on Debentures should rank after and behind the £1,000,000 of Debentures created by the original scheme. That was the first condition the Committee imposed, and he was of opinion that their intentions were very well carried out by the provisions of the Bill as they now stood. The second condition was that no extension to Huddersfield and Halifax should be carried out until the line between Barnsley and Hull was absolutely completed. The third condition was that the money the Company were authorized to raise should be expended in completing that portion of the line, so that the Company should be able to earn something towards paying the interest on the cost of the construction of one portion of the undertaking. At any rate, until that was done, it was provided that no extra expense should be incurred. They had the assurance of Mr. Forbes that no extra expense should be incurred. ["Oh, oh!"] He heard murmurs; but surely they would all admit that Mr. Forbes knew how to make a pound go as far as any man. He believed the only interest Mr. Forbes had in becoming a Director of the line was to see that it should be put into working order, which was one of the conditions which the Committee had imposed upon the Company. Having seen that these three proposals were embodied in the Bill, the Committee thought it right to pass the Preamble, and to ask the House to accept the Bill. He was not surprised at the remarks which had been made. He had made some strong remarks himself, but it was an exceptional case. He hoped they would never have another case of the kind; and he trusted the House would agree to the recommendation of the Committee, which they themselves—a perfectly independent Committee, who had nothing whatever to do with the line—had agreed to, and that they would allow the Bill to pass through its remaining stages that day.

MR. CROPPER said, that although in some degree he agreed with the remarks which had fallen from the hon. and gallant Baronet opposite (Sir Walter B. Barttelot), he felt bound to support the the views of the hon. Member for Devonport (Mr. Puleston). He thought the Committee had given powers to this Company which enabled them to break the ordinary laws and rules which had been long established in regard to railway undertakings, and, especially, that when Debenture Stock was issued it should represent a certain amount of the ordinary and preference shares which had gone before it. If Parliament consented to interfere with those rules, what would be the result? They would inevitably reduce the value of Debenture Stock, and prevent it from having the value it had hitherto invariably possessed with the public of the country. They were calling this Stock by the name of Debenture Stock, whereas it possessed a totally different value from ordinary Debenture Stock. They called it Debenture Stock; but, in reality, it was simply a substitution for Preference stock. He would be one of the last Members of that House to interfere with the decision of a Committee; but he maintained that this question was not intrusted to the Committee, and that they had nothing whatever to do with the suspension of the Standing Orders. He entirely agreed with the hon. Member for Devonport, that they ought to require the promoters to give very strong reasons indeed before they consented to such extraordinary deviations from the rules which were applied to the construction of railways generally. He had not the smallest interest in this railway, or in any railway remotely connected or concerned in the matter. He looked merely upon the question as one of public policy, and he believed the interests of the public would be best served by protecting them, he would not say from fraud, or fraudulent pretences, but from the issue of Stock under a misleading name, lest it should be accepted by persons too thoughtless to go thoroughly into the matter, but who would find ultimately that what were called Debentures, were only ordinary Preference Stock after all.

SIR ROBERT PEEL said, he agreed that the matter was one of considerable importance, and that it was one in which the House should not only take interest, but should proceed to legislate upon with caution. He put it to the House whether, in asking the House to deal with hundreds of thousands of pounds, it would not have been only fair and right for the hon. and gallant Member for Wycombe (Colonel Gerard Smith) himself to have explained to the House what the circumstances were under which he came to Parliament for this large sum of money? The hon. and gallant Member was Chairman of the Company. He (Sir Robert Peel) thought it very irregular for the Chairman of a Company to submit the case of the Company to the House. But, in addition to being Chairman of the Company, the hon. and gallant Member was the banker of the Company. Being both Chairman and banker of the Company, he came there in the interests of a particular railway, proposing to deal with hundreds of thousands of pounds, and to ask the House to suspend its Standing Orders, in order that he—independent, of course, and in no way concerned as Chairman and banker—should, at the tail end of the Session, pass this Bill. The hon. Member for Southwark (Mr. Thorold Rogers), who spoke from the other side of the House, said that the Committee were unanimous in passing the Preamble of the Bill; but it would not be altogether an unprecedented thing for the House of Commons to reject the unanimous decision of one of their own Committees. There was nothing unusual in such a matter whatever. He recollected himself, many years ago, upsetting the third reading of a Bill which had passed unanimously through Committee, and which had cost £30,000 to the persons promoting the Bill. The hon. Member for Southwark said that the Company, in their original prospectus, had greatly miscalculated the cost of the line. Now, what was the original prospectus? The Hull and Barnsley Railway and Docks Company originally proposed to make a line 50 miles in length. [Colonel GERARD SMITH: 66 miles.] Well, 66 miles. That almost made the case worse. They had not, he believed, completed 55 miles; and the original sum asked for as capital, and which had all been expended, was £4,000,000—£3,000,000 of Stock, and £1,000,000 of Debentures. Now, he did not say there had been any fraud in the matter; but he did say that there had been an attempt to deceive the public, and to induce them to invest in a concern which appeared to him to be rotten at the very core of it. He was speaking from information which had been placed in his hands, and which he had been requested to submit to the House, having no interest himself in the matter. He was told that, in the original prospectus, the capital was fixed at £4,000,000; but that the Company let the works for the construction of 66 miles of line for something like £2,700,000. For that sum, both the railway and the docks were to be completed. It was not intended that the equipment of the line was to be completed for that sum; but £2,700,000 was the amount at which the works were let, and for which they were to be completed. [Colonel GERARD SMITH said, the right hon. Baronet was altogether in error.] He should like to be informed in what way he was in error? There had been no statement from the Chairman and banker of the Company; and, instead of getting up and saying that he (Sir Robert Peel) was completely in error, it would be better for the hon. and gallant Member to rise in his place and state what all the circumstances were. He had seen the original prospectus, and he would defy the hon. and gallant Member to say that the sum of £2,700,000 was not the amount at which the works were let, and for which they were to be completed, except in regard to their equipment. [Colonel GERARD SMITH said, he would only repeat that the right hon. Baronet was in error.] If he was in error on that point, he was not in error in what he was about to say—namely, that this railway never had been completed. It was not completed in January in this year. This same Company tried to raise £3,000,000 at 4 per cent. ostensibly for making a line from Halifax to Huddersfield, but, in reality, as he was informed by those who had invested their money in the Company, to complete the original line and docks. The Company, however, of which the hon. and gallant Member was Chairman and banker, were not to be put aside by one failure. Of course, the banker and Chairman of the Company knew better than that; and, therefore, immediately afterwards the same Company tried to issue Preference Stock to the extent of £1,300,000 at 4 per cent. The shareholders at once said—"That will not do at all;" and, consequently, that scheme of the Chairman and banker was withdrawn. Therefore, there had been two failures in the course of the present year to raise money. But that was not all. In the month of June in this year a third attempt was made by the Company, of which the hon. and gallant Member was Chairman and banker, to raise £1,800,000 at 5 per cent—at £85. That also failed; and those three attempts to raise money in the present year had been entirely unsuccessful. What would the House suppose was the actual amount subscribed? There was only £75,000 applied for; and in June last the Company issued an announcement that it would require £2,016,000 to complete the original railway of 66 miles between Hull and Barnsley, together with the docks, and yet there was an attempt now to induce the House of Commons to believe that, by the present proposal, £1,500,000 of Debenture Stock would be sufficient to complete and equip the line. At any rate, that was the statement of the hon. Member for Southwark (Mr. Thorold Rogers). The hon. Member said that £1,500,000 would be sufficient to complete the railway and docks, and all he (Sir Robert Peel) could say was, that in the announcement made in June last it was clearly stated that £2,016,000 were required to complete it. Of course, he did not say in that House that there was anything underhand, or suspicious, or dishonest in this transaction; but all he would say in the interests of the public—and he had nobody else to consider in the matter—was, that where they were dealing with hundreds of thousands of pounds, where they were asking the public to subscribe to a concern which he maintained, without fear of contradiction, would not bear the light of day, the hon. and gallant Gentleman, who was Chairman and banker of the Company, was bound to get up and state to the House what were the grounds for the extraordinary proceeding he was desirous of inducing the House of Commons to take for the purpose of passing a Bill in which he was himself so directly and primarily interested.

COLONEL GERARD SMITH said, he rose to answer the appeal which had been made to him by the hon. Member for Devonport (Mr. Puleston) and the right hon. Baronet opposite (Sir Robert Peel). The hon. Member for Devonport (Mr. Puleston) said he thought that he (Colonel Gerard Smith) ought to have given some reason why the Motion had been placed on the Paper. As far as concerned the general course of procedure adopted in regard to the Bill now before the House, he could only say that the promoters of the Bill had, in the first instance, as a matter of course, communicated with the Chairman of Ways and Means. No Motion for the suspension of the Standing Orders could be made without the consent of the right hon. Gentleman. Now, the Chairman of Ways and Means had already given to the House what he (Colonel Gerard Smith) thought were excellent reasons why the Standing Orders should be suspended and facilities given for the introduction and passing of this Bill. The most prominent ground given by the Chairman of Ways and Means was that the state of affairs had become such that, at present, from 5,000 to 6,000 men, either had been, or were about to be, discharged and turned out of employment, thereby creating a considerable amount of distress. The same reasons held good at the present moment. The men had, as a matter of fact, been discharged, and he regretted to say that, unless they could be re-employed, there was every prospect that a considerable amount of distress would be brought about in the locality. He trusted that it would not be of long continuance; but, nevertheless, the fact remained that a very large number of labouring men had actually been discharged. The hon. Member for Devonport asked why the provisions now asked for were not incorporated in the omnibus Bill which the Company had introduced into Parliament at an earlier period of the Session? The reason why they were not so incorporated was that at the time the former Bill was introduced into Parliament and the plans deposited—namely, in the month of November last—the Company were busily engaged in endeavouring to raise money, in the belief that the powers they then possessed were sufficient to enable them to obtain adequate capital for the completion of the works. Under those circumstances, he certainly would not have been a party to putting the provisions, now sought to be obtained, in the omnibus Bill to which reference had been made, because it was perfectly obvious that the Com-

come after the 6th clause, and should not be introduced on a previous Amendment. If the House did not pass the clause now, he should, in one sense, be sorry; for if the House adhered to the retention of the County Court jurisdiction which the Committee adopted in Clause 6, of course there would be no objection to this clause; as a part of and necessary pendant to Clause 6, it would be a very proper provision indeed. But the objection now was it committed the House in advance, and tied them down to the 6th section. For his own part, he might say it was his intention to strike out County Courts, for he was quite sure it was an improper tribunal to be intrusted with jurisdiction over such delicate points as these. He did not know what view the Solicitor General might take; he should like to have it, for it would very much guide his (Mr. Warton's) opinion. What he submitted now was that if the House assented to this clause they committed themselves to Clause 6, whereas if it were withdrawn now it could very well be introduced at the end of Clause 6.

THE SOLICITOR GENERAL (Sir FARRER HERSCHELL) said, the course he proposed to take was to propose certain Amendments to the clause to make it clear—which he did not feel it was at present—that any party to the application should have the right to remove the case to the Superior Court. At present the clause stood—"the High Court of Justice may, at the instance of any party, &c."; he would have it made clear that parties were entitled to have it removed. Safe-guarded in that way they might leave the County Court with jurisdiction safely where no party objected.

MR. HORACE DAVEY said, he regretted the Solicitor General had proposed this Amendment.

THE SOLICITOR GENERAL (Sir FARRER HERSCHELL) explained he had not done so yet.

MR. INCE said, he thought the question would be better considered after Clause 6. He thought the hon. and learned Member had not improved his Bill by putting in the reference to County Courts. In cases of dispute between husband and wife it was as well there should be a little difficulty and some expense before the parties could rush into Court. He should be prepared to strike out the words "or County Court of the district," his object being not in the slightest way to cast a doubt upon the County Court, but simply because, if disputes arose, there should be a little difficulty in the way before the parties could make those disputes public by rushing into Court, giving a little time for reflection and for the bitterness to pass away. The practitioners in County Courts were not of the highest class, and he thought it was very undesirable that second or third-rate attorneys should be brought into actions of this kind. The more a little difficulty, and even a little expense, could be introduced, the better for all parties it would be in the long run. He would ask the hon. and learned Member for the Tower Hamlets (Mr. Bryce) to defer further consideration of the clause, to postpone it to the 6th clause, in order that the House might not be fettered when they approached the consideration of that.

MR. TOMLINSON said, an appeal had been made to the hon. and learned Member for the Tower Hamlets to take the clause after Clause 6; he would like to ask the Speaker's ruling, could not the House accede to that? His desire was to put the Bill in the best form possible.

MR. SPEAKER: That cannot be done.

Motion *agreed to.*

Clause read a second time.

THE SOLICITOR GENERAL (Sir FARRER HERSCHELL) said, he proposed to amend the clause in the second line by leaving out the words "the High Court of Justice may, at the instance of;" and then, in the next line, after "application," to leave out "order such application to," and insert, "shall be entitled to an order of the High Court of Justice that such application shall." So the clause would run thus—

"In England and Ireland, when any application has been made under this Act to a County Court, any party to such application shall be entitled to an order of the High Court of Justice that such application shall be removed to the High Court of Justice,"

and so on. That would make it clear it was a matter of right. And then, in the next line but one, he would propose to leave out the words after "division." He did not think there should be any other power but the absolute right of removal from the County Court to the High Court.

Amendment proposed, in line 2 of new Clause, to leave out the words "the High Court of Justice may, at the instance of."—(*Mr. Solicitor General.*)

Question proposed, "That the words proposed to be left out stand part of the new Clause."

MR. HORACE DAVEY said, he regretted the Solicitor General had proposed this Amendment. He quite recognized the desire that there should be a line drawn beyond which applications should be to the High Court, and, of course, there was no line that could be defined by value; but, at the same time, those who were interested in this Bill felt that it was a Bill for the benefit of the poor as well as the rich—perhaps mainly for the benefit of the poor. Though it might be quite true, as the hon. and learned Member for Hastings (Mr. Ince) said, that County Court jurisdiction might not always be administered with that nicety and precision which characterized the High Court, still people did appreciate the County Courts whose purses were not long enough to go o the High Court. He regretted that the Solicitor General made it compulsory for the Court to make an order, for the effect would be in some cases to deprive those persons whose purses were not long of the benefit of the Act. An applicant to a County Court, perhaps, might not have the means of applying to the Higher Court; and the other side might then, having larger means, by the transfer to the High Court, deprive the applicant of justice. But they were at the mercy of the Government in respect of the Bill. His hon. and learned Friend (Mr. Bryce) would have an opportunity of speaking; perhaps, in the interest of the Bill, he would accept the Amendment; but if his hon. and learned Friend divided against it he should support him. As a matter of drafting, he would suggest to the Solicitor General that, with less alteration of the clause, his object would be accomplished by substituting the word "shall" for the word "may."

MR. HEALY said, speaking with some knowledge of the County Courts of Ireland, and their manner of administering justice, he strongly endorsed what the Solicitor General had said.

MR. HOPWOOD said, he agreed the Amendment would result in a denial to many of the benefit of the Act. In cases of a struggle between man and wife, it was ten to one the husband had the heaviest purse, and the wife small means of asserting her right. In going to a County Court, the result would very likely be the parties would be satisfied with the fair decision of the County Court Judge, and he should have hoped this was the case in Ireland as well as England; if they were not satisfied, there was still an appeal open. But now, instead of that, there would be the means in the hands of the party who wished to delay the matter to say—"No, it shall be removed to the High Court in the Metropolis or in Dublin." He extremely regretted the Amendment had been moved.

MR. BRYCE regretted the line the Solicitor General had taken, and he thought it would considerably impair the value of the Bill; but at that hour of the night and time of the Session it would be useless to oppose the suggestion from the Government Bench, and he should not oppose the Amendment.

THE SOLICITOR GENERAL (Sir FARRER HERSCHELL) said, it must be remembered this proposal in respect to the County Court having jurisdiction was only an afterthought; it was not in the original Bill.

MR. INCE said, he had some doubt if the Amendment really carried out the Solicitor General's intention. There would be always a dispute whether the case should be heard in a Superior Court or not, interlarding another dispute to the one in existence. Would it not be better to introduce after "shall" the words "as a matter of course," or "as a matter of right?" That would carry out the intention which, as he understood it, was that, as a matter of course, it should be carried to the Superior Court. If the words were left as they stood, there would always be a preliminary dispute as to whether it was a case to be taken to the Superior Court or not.

THE SOLICITOR GENERAL (Sir FARRER HERSCHELL) said, perhaps the simpler way would be to substitute "shall" for "may." It was sometimes objected that to make it peremptory and say "the High Court shall," was

dation of the Committee, and the suspension of the Standing Orders.

Mr. MACFARLANE said, that as one of the Members of the Committee which had investigated the facts of the case, he wished to put before the House the issue which was raised before the Committee. It was, whether the existing undertaking should be practically extinguished by the exhaustion of the money already expended, and the amount of objection referred to by the right hon. Gentleman the President of the Board of Trade, consisting of five shareholders who represented £30,000, out of a capital of £3,000,000? The Committee felt that that was a very small minority of the shareholders; and they were, moreover, acquainted with the fact that the objecting persons did not attend the meeting of the Company called for the purpose of approving the Bill, because they knew that they would be swamped. That was a very candid admission that they did not represent the opinion of the shareholders of the Company generally. As to the question of the miscalculation in the original estimates, the right hon. Gentleman had told the House that probably no Directors were ever free from it. The right hon. Gentleman might have added that no private individual was free from it also, for he (Mr. Macfarlane) was quite sure that most people who had ever had anything to do with estimates for building or other purposes, had invariably found that they were wrong to the extent of 50 per cent. Therefore, that argument would have no weight. The issue was a very simple one—namely, whether the House would suspend its Standing Orders? And he maintained that that question was decided when it was agreed to refer the Bill to a Select Committee, and the Select Committee themselves were unanimous in the decision they had arrived at. But the issue really was, whether this undertaking should be sacrificed? It came out incidentally in the inquiry before the Committee, that the real motive of the opposition was that the undertaking might be strangled, and thus be thrown into the arms of one of the large Companies. He had himself put that question distinctly to one of the witnesses, and had pointed out that unless something of that kind were contemplated, the whole of the money expended so far would be lost. He had no interest whatever in these works; but he was told by this particular witness, that the money expended would not be altogether wasted, because the Midland Railway Company were quite willing to take over the property. That admission let the cat out of the bag. It was an attempt to strangle this small concern—very small as compared with the great lines; and, in the interests of the public, he thought it was desirable that those who were promoting the undertaking should be protected. The country was suffering at this moment from the process of railway strangulation adopted by two or three of the great lines, who thought that the sooner they were allowed to absorb all the smaller ones, the better. He hoped the House would not be induced, on any technical ground whatever in reference to these Standing Orders, to set aside the decision of the Committee, unanimously adopted only a few days ago.

Sir WALTER B. BARTTELOT said, that he had mentioned in his remarks the name of Mr. Forbes; and he wished to say that that gentleman had only just joined the Board, and that he had had no connection with the line until two or three months ago.

Mr. TOMLINSON said, that he had no personal interest in the matter; but his attention having been called to the character of the Bill, he had examined it carefully. The point to which he wished to call the attention of the House was this. It appeared to him that not only the Committee who sat upon the Bill, but also the right hon. Gentleman the President of the Board of Trade, had missed the real point which ought to be brought under the notice of the House—namely, whether they ought to allow to this Company borrowing powers to the extent now asked for; that was, whether they ought to allow the Company to raise money by borrowing in excess of the powers which Parliament ordinarily allowed? He understood the President of the Board of Trade to say that a similar case had occurred somewhere or other; but, be that as it might, he thought they ought to be most reluctant to allow the borrowing powers of any Railway Company to exceed the due proportion of their share capital. The President of the Board of Trade had described the stock proposed to be issued as Preference Stock. It was nothing of the kind. It was not Preference Stock at all. It was Debenture Stock, constituting part of the loan capital of the Company, and carrying with it the right on the part of the holders to put in a Receiver, if the Company failed to meet the interest as it fell due. He mentioned that to show that it was not in any sense part of the share capital. It was a mortgage on the concern, to a limited extent—namely, for securing the interest on the money raised. The importance of the matter was, that by relaxing the Rules laid down by Parliament in reference to borrowing powers, they were really weakening the value of securities which were open to trustees to invest in, as the noble Lord the Member for Woodstock (Lord Randolph Churchill) had pointed out. He thought Parliament ought to be most cautious before it did anything to diminish the value of such security in the market, and for that reason he should oppose the Motion.

Question put.

The House *divided*:—Ayes 82; Noes 31: Majority 51.—(Div. List, No. 196.)

Bill *considered*.

Ordered, That Standing Orders 207, 223, and 243 be suspended, and that the Bill be now read the third time.

Bill read the third time, and *passed*.

QUESTION.

PEACE PRESERVATION (IRELAND) ACT, 1881—POLICE HUT AT RATHGORMAC.

MR. LEAMY asked the Chief Secretary to the Lord Lieutenant of Ireland, Whether a police hut was erected in the parish of Rathgormac, county of Waterford, over three years ago, in a district in which not a single outrage was committed during the whole of the agitation, and which is a most peaceable district; and, if he will state why the hut was erected, why it has been kept up for three years at the expense of the ratepayers, and when will it be removed?

MR. TREVELYAN: A police station was established at Rathgormac a little over two years ago. The men are included in the county force, and are not charged to the district. It was necessary to establish a station in that locality, as there was a large tract of country without a police barrack. I am informed that it is not correct to say that the district was free from outrage, and that a good deal of intimidation was carried on. The formation of this station enabled the Government to do away with two protection posts which it had been necessary to establish in the neighbourhood for the protection of caretakers on evicted farms.

ORDER OF THE DAY.

SUPPLY—CIVIL SERVICE ESTIMATES.

SUPPLY—*considered* in Committee.

(In the Committee.)

CLASS V.—FOREIGN AND COLONIAL SERVICES.

Motion made, and Question proposed,

"That a sum, not exceeding £38,867 (including a Supplementary sum of £30,000), be granted to Her Majesty, to complete the sum necessary to defray the Charge which will come in course of payment during the year ending on the 31st day of March 1885, for certain Charges connected with the Orange River Territory, the Transvaal, Zululand, the Island of St. Helena, and the High Commissioner for South Africa."

MR. GUY DAWNAY said, that, in rising to move the reduction of the Vote, he must explain that he had no wish to deprive Sir Henry Bulwer of secretarial assistance with regard to his duties in Zululand, if only the Government would give the Committee some assurance that they would take the necessary steps to make that Office something more than the pretence and sham which their policy had made it become during many months past. He moved the reduction of the Vote in order that he might have an opportunity of calling attention to the terrible and disgraceful state of Zululand by the only means in his power—short of availing himself of the Forms of the House, to which hon. Gentlemen on those Benches were always reluctant to have recourse. He thought it had been most unfortunate that, for two successive years, the House had not had an opportunity of expressing its opinion on this question by a Division; and he was anxious that the Committee should not lose this opportunity of recording against the Government, the censure which every impartial Member who had paid the slightest attention to the subject must acknowledge they had most fully and richly deserved. Having obtained an opportunity at last of criticizing the policy of the Government in South Africa, he wished to trespass, as briefly as possible, on the attention of the Committee, and the reason which would induce him to curtail his remarks was not because he failed to realize the immense importance of the subject, but because it seemed to him that the case was so clear, and that the mismanagement of the Government in Zululand so acknowledged, that it would be mere waste of time for him to further prove such well-known facts, or to enter into the details of a story which for months past had been writing itself but too clearly and too plainly in such vivid characters of blood. It was curious that the same policy which had anarchized the Soudan, if he might use the expression, had been tried in South Africa with a precisely similar effect. All the skeletons which were at that moment whitening the sands of Northern Africa, had their counterpart in the Southern hemisphere, in the Golgotha into which Zululand had been converted under the "No Responsibility" policy of Her Majesty's Government. He had no doubt that the Government would find words to defend, if they could not find arguments to justify, that policy, and that they would attempt to do so on religious, moral, and philanthropic grounds. But could they also attempt to defend it as successful—as successful in this, that it had done anything to lessen the sufferings of humanity in Zululand? Could they deny that, from every point of view, the welfare of the Zulus, the security of Natal, the maintenance of the honour of the English name among the Natives of South Africa—from each and every such point of view, the policy of the Government had failed in as complete and ghastly a manner as ever discredited a Government? He must express a hope that, in the interest of honesty and fairplay in politics, no hon. Member would on that occasion, as last year, rise in his place and throw the blame of the present state of anarchy in Zululand on the late Government and the Zulu War. That had been done last year; but he was sure that no hon. Gentleman on the Treasury Bench could feel it consistent with his own self-respect to again rake up that past history as in the smallest degree offering any justification for another 12 months' continued and even more hopeless anarchy, and for an amount of unceasing inter-tribal slaughter which surpassed anything that Zululand had known since the Zulus first won the dignity of a nation. Last year, that ludicrously inadequate excuse was given, but only because the Government could find no other words to excuse the effects of their policy of restoring Cetewayo. They could not deny that they were warned of the results which would follow that restoration, that they had neglected those warnings, or that those warnings had turned out to be true. He had urged as strongly as he could last year, however little weight his words might carry, that in view of the fatal *fiasco* in which the restoration policy of the Government had then terminated, the Government should no longer lend an ear to the mistaken voice of unpractical humanitarians in that House or in the country, but that they should rather listen to those whose experience in South Africa, either as English officials or as Native-born dwellers in that land, entitled their opinions to be treated with consideration and their advice to be listened to with respect. He had urged, as earnestly as he could, that, as the only possible solution of the question, the Government should extend the principle of Reserved Territory up to the Black Umvolosi; he pointed out that such a policy would entail no expense upon the country; and he had overwhelming evidence to show that such a plan would have been gladly received and willingly adopted by the majority of the people in Zululand, and that it would have put an end to that anarchy and bloodshed which now for 18 months had disgraced our connection with the land. Sir Henry Bulwer had expressed the opinion that that course was one which ought to be followed as the one most hopeful for the welfare of the Zulus of any course, excluding our actual assumption of the rule of that country. He did not think they could justify their disregard of that advice on the ground of the success of their own policy, and still less could they justify that disregard on humanitarian grounds. Nor did he think that any hon. Members who last year warmly opposed this plan, could now, in the light of the history of the past 12 months, congratulate themselves on the success of that policy of leaving the Zulus to manage their own affairs, which they then advocated, and under which system, as the Bishop of Zululand had pointed out in a letter in *The Times* at the beginning of the year, "mutual extermination became the only possibility." If it had been the deliberate, the diabolical design of the Government to settle the question on the "Kilkenny cat" principle, they could not have gone to work in a surer manner to effect that end. The country was settling down under the old Settlement of Lord Wolseley; and whether or not that settlement might have been the best possible settlement, still, had that policy been faithfully followed, it would have preserved order there. Hon. Members who differed from him might again talk of the Sitimela fight. What had happened in that case bore out his statement, and was the best proof of the propriety of that policy. That was the case of one Zulu, who, with a considerable following, revolted against his Chief; the Chief called in the help of a neighbouring Chief, and the revolt was put down with one fight. That was the exact reason why Lord Wolseley divided Zululand amongst a number of Chiefs—that if there was a revolt in the territory of one Chief, a majority of the other Chiefs would support the loyal subjects of the Chief. It was, however, absurd to talk now about the Sitimela fighting, or to make much of the Native bloodshed which then took place. Why, all the fighting that took place during the three years after Cetewayo's deposition did not result in as many deaths as took place in one half-hour of one morning within six weeks of his restoration. All the bloodshed during those years were but as a single drop as compared with the ocean of blood which had deluged that land since that unhappy morning when Cetewayo was once more restored to his Chieftainship at Ulundi. The Government first encouraged the agitation of a few malcontents, who pretended to be anxious for Cetewayo's restoration; and having done that, they insisted on forcing back Cetewayo on an alarmed and reluctant people. And in order to do that they broke the solemn engagements made four years ago with the Chieftains. Now, that was a deliberate breach of faith with the Chieftains which he had last year challenged Her Majesty's Government to justify, to defend, or to deny—he challenged them, quoting the Prime Minister's own words spoken in that House in support of the charge he brought against them, and they were dumb. He knew that that engagement was made by the Representative of a Power which boasted that on its Dominions the sun never set, with a party of uneducated and naked Zulus in a Kaffir kraal; but he said that it was as solemn and sacred, and the breach of it as shameful and wrong, as if it had been made with the Representatives of a European Power and signed in a Royal Palace. Her Majesty's Government had set this solemn engagement aside, and had restored Cetewayo; and the firebrand having done its natural work in producing a general conflagration throughout the land—

> "The torch being lighted, and the flame being spread,
> And carnage smiling on her daily dead"—

the Government had then announced their intention of standing calmly by and waiting till the fire had burnt itself out, only watching to see that the flames did not come into too dangerous proximity with their own immediate Possessions. This was the general result, this was the magnificent outcome of our philanthropy, our humanity, our Christianity, and our statesmanship in the 19th century, under a Liberal Government—

> "To make a solitude and call it peace"—

or, rather, to encourage the Zulus to make the solitude, and then, on the hustings, to point to it as peace. He did not know of any instance, and he believed no instance existed, of a Government behaving at the same time in worse faith, with more consummate folly and shortsightedness, and with more conspicuous and disastrous unsuccess. With the permission of the Committee, he would read the following extract from a Natal newspaper, which gave an excellent account of the state of Zululand—

> "It looks as bad now as can be in all the country between Umhlatusi and the Umvolosi. The people are leaving their kraals, and they who are there sleep outside, because they are afraid. A great number of Zulus are wavering and afraid, fearing both sides. The people are surprised at the English Government doing nothing; they cannot understand it. They could when a King was alive, because it was a difficult question what to do with him. But now

that is taken away, a lot of Chiefs have refused to pay taxes. The Resident went back to his residence the day after the women disturbed him, and the next day he set out to take the taxes, but heard there would be trouble up country, so turned back. He might easily have settled affairs in the Reserve; but I suppose his hands are tied and he can do nothing. The Zulus are thoroughly demoralized, and they have lost all respect for the English. This is annoying when one thinks how easily the English might have managed the country after they conquered it. The Zulus now say, 'We trusted in you, and you do nothing.' They say further that the English only know how to write letters."

The next extract which I will read, is a short one from a letter received a few weeks ago from John Dunn himself. He said—

"Affairs here are in a pretty muddle. The Boers have got possession of the central part of Zululand, and in the Reserve the Resident has been attacked by Dabulamanzi at night, but fortunately he was warned and prepared, and beat them off. I have all my men under arms ready, and this is the only part of Zululand up to this where there has been no fighting or bloodshed."

And in one of the letters contained in the last Blue Book which had been issued with reference to Zululand, they had this account sent by Sir Henry Bulwer from Mr. Osborn with regard to the state of things in the Reserve Territory itself—

"The attitude of the Usutus, Mr. Osborn states, is causing great alarm to the loyal people for many miles round the Inkandhla, who are repeatedly insulted and threatened by individuals of the Usutu party, so much so that they and their families dare not sleep at their kraals for fear of being attacked at night, and after dark retire to the hills and donzas; and this is the case even with some of the people residing a long distance from the Inkandhla. The loyal Chiefs and people cannot understand why the lawless and defiant proceedings of the Usutus should be tolerated in the Reserve. They consider they are in danger from the Usutus, and unless he (Mr. Osborn) takes steps to deal with Ictuka, they will take the matter into their own hands."

And now, as a corollary to that, they heard that at the date of a letter received three weeks ago, our Representative in Zululand, Mr. Osborn, had actually been attacked by 10,000 Usutus, under Dabulmanzi, the same Chief to whom the Government had been deferring, and coaxing, and patting on the back for two years; the result being that about 200 people had been killed. They found that a large proportion of the Zulu people, not only in the Central and Northern parts, but also in the Reserve Territory, were hiding and starving in the bush; and, finally, they heard that Usibepu, the one gallant, plucky, and loyal Chief, had been routed, not by the Usutus, for he had already defeated them, but by some 500 of those infamous marauding Boers, who were the outcome of another portion of the policy of Her Majesty's Government in South Africa. The Government refused to rule, or to take any part in the ruling, of Zululand, and the result was that carnage, starvation, and desolation reigned triumphant in that country. He congratulated the right hon. Gentleman opposite (Mr. Gladstone) and the Colonial Office, on the brilliant success which had followed from the diplomatic wisdom and the timely courage which they had manifested throughout in dealing with the Zulu question. Now, answerable as they were for this state of things in Zululand, as they must confess they now were, he asked them what they intended to do, or, rather, whether they intended to still pursue the shameful—he might say murderous—policy of doing nothing—that policy of "writing letters," as the Zulus had so graphically described it? Did they still intend to disregard the advice of Sir Henry Bulwer, and every competent authority, recognizing, as they must, that on every previous occasion on which they had disregarded it they had been utterly and fatally wrong? Just to show how consistently wrong they had been, and how persistently they had neglected advice, he would read a telegram from Sir Henry Bulwer, dated the 5th of May last, which ran thus—

"It is reported that the Boers have proclaimed Dinuzulu King of Zululand, and have declared an independent Republic. The report requires confirmation; but there is good information to the effect that a large number from the Transvaal and Pretoria Free State have agreed to the conquest of Zululand for Cetewayo's son in return for territorial cession. It is said that they will join in the united attack on Usibepu. Usibepu is well able to hold his own against the Usutu party, but not against the unjustifiable combination, and he will be destroyed; and Zululand, except the Reserve, will fall under Boer domination, unless we interfere."

Then, 10 days later, he said—

"The action of the Boers is an interference with a Chief made independent of us. It introduces a new element in the Zulu question, and entirely revolutionizes it, destroys balance of

Mr. Guy Dawnay

power existing in Usibepu, encourages the Usutu party, and intimidates the Natives of the Reserve, who, fearful of the establishment of the Usutu party, powerful under Boer protection and not sure of us, will think how to save themselves. The question of the Boers, therefore, presses for decision. In the meantime, the Reserve is seriously endangered by the Usutu party being able to concentrate against it, and already people are taking refuge in Natal."

On the same page there was another letter, if anything, stronger; but he would not trouble the Committee by reading it. He would only ask if they were to stand still while they saw a new Stellaland arising in South Africa? Were they to remain passive while they saw these rascally filibustering Boers taking possession of the country, and carving it out into farms for themselves? It was curious, and he thought worthy of notice, that the Boers were, with regard to Zululand, occupying very much the same position as the Abyssinians now were to occupy towards the Soudan; and as their civilization was in about the same rudimentary condition, and as their Christianity was in about the same fossilized state, they were equally valuable allies to the Government in carrying out a policy which in both countries appeared to aim at the utter extermination of those Native races, whose struggles for freedom and whose patriotic valour they were once bidden to admire and respect. Was that, he asked, their policy? It was, at least, an intelligiblo policy, because the extermination of the Zulus would relieve the Government of any further responsibility or troubles in regard to Zululand. [MR. WARTON: Just what they want.] And while the Government would reap all the advantages of that extermination, all the dirty work—all the direct bloodshed—would be done by the Boers, and the Government would be able to relieve their conscience by a combined Scribe and Pharisee policy of writing letters and publishing Blue Books, deprecating bloodshed and addressing remonstrances to the officials of the South African Republic. He would not, however, seriously charge Her Majesty's Government, or any Member of Her Majesty's Government, with a policy so ineffably mean; but it was a possible policy, and a policy to which there were only two alternatives—one that a Commissioner should be appointed to reside on the frontier to prevent aggression by the Boers, and to allow the Zulus to exterminate themselves without any White man's assistance; the other, that policy which he had already advocated in that House, and which he now again advocated, as warmly as he could—namely, the extension of the Reserve Territory to the Black Umvolosi. It was of no use going again into details; but let it be understood that such extension and its proclamation would mean at once the cessation of bloodshed in Zululand, the future civilization of that country, and the saving from extermination of the finest race of savages which South Africa had produced. Let the Committee understand that, from the midst of the misery and desolation of their land, the cry of the Zulus themselves was for such a settlement of the question, and for such a deliverance for themselves. Now, he said that, at least, if the Government would not consent to extend the Reserve Territory, it was their duty to give some reason for such refusal. What was their reason? Did it rest on the ground of expense? They might almost believe that, for Lord Derby, some few months ago, telegraphed to Sir Henry Bulwer, asking him what would be the expense of extending the Reserve Territory, and the latter replied that, for the first year, it would be about £6,000, and after that there would be no further expense at all. Since that time they had heard nothing more on the subject of the extension. £6,000 for putting an end to all this savagery and bloodshed! Why, it would probably save the country a hundred times the amount in future. £6,000—only three times greater than the amount of expense entailed upon the country by the determination of our æsthetic Government to banish the statue of the Great Duke from Hyde Park Corner to its place of exile at Aldershot. It was true that, at the same time, they got rid of a somewhat unpleasant subject of reflection and comparison. The cost of moving round troops from Cape Town to Natal alone, on account of these disturbances, went far to reach this total of £6,000, which it was said this extension would cost; and Sir Henry Bulwer pointed out in that letter which he had referred to, but not read, that the expense would be just as great, whether the troops were employed to extend the

Reserve to protect the Reserve, or to ultimately protect the borders of our own Colonies from the victorious Usutus. In conclusion, he would point out—and it was a lesson which the Government should by this time have learnt by heart—that the longer they delayed, in the folly of their misplaced economy, to take that one step, which sooner or later they would be forced to take, the heavier would be the expense which this "penny-wise and pound-foolish" policy would lay on the British taxpayer, the more prolonged and cruel would be the bloodshed which they would entail on the Zulu people, and the darker and more inexcusable would be the guiltiness for that blood which would lie at the door of the Government, and of the Party which supported them in their misused or wasted power. He begged to move the reduction of the Vote by £300.

Sir HENRY HOLLAND said, he rose to second the Motion for the reduction of the Vote; but in doing so he wished to explain, as his hon. Friend the Mover of the reduction (Mr. Guy Dawnay) had done, that he did not, of course, desire the reduction itself; but that was the only way left to them to protest against the policy of the Government in Zululand. He would have been glad if the question could have been discussed on the Resolution which he had placed on the Paper, but which he had now been compelled to withdraw, as it would have been discussed in the House, and not in Committee, and would have afforded a larger basis for argument. That Resolution contained the view which he now desired to bring under the consideration of the Committee—namely, that, looking to the policy of Her Majesty's Government, and the responsibilities which the country had incurred, owing to that policy, the Government and the country could not get rid of, or properly meet, those responsibilities by merely maintaining, as by the telegram of May 16, 1884, they had decided to do, "the integrity and peace of the Reserve." He desired to get the Committee practically to affirm that the Government were bound to endeavour to restore some kind of peace and order in the part of Zululand beyond the Reserved Territory. In that way the hands of the Government would be strengthened in any forward action they might take to restore peace in that unfortunate country, to which our interference had been so fatal. It was not necessary for him to go back to the original Zulu War. He would content himself with saying that he had always considered that war to have been unnecessary, and therefore unjust—so unnecessary and so unjust, that he had felt himself compelled both to speak and vote against the late Government, because, though they disapproved of the war, they had not, in his opinion, sufficiently condemned the policy of Sir Bartle Frere. He could not mention the name of Sir Bartle Frere without expressing, however imperfectly, his sense of the loss this country had sustained by the death of so zealous a servant of the Crown. We could never forget his able administration in India; we could never forget the splendid service he rendered in the time of the great Mutiny, in denuding of troops, at considerable personal risk to himself, the Province over which he presided, in order to assist the efforts of Sir John Lawrence. And with regard to his policy in South Africa, those who, like himself (Sir Henry Holland) differed entirely from it, had never doubted but that it was adopted from most conscientious motives, and in the belief that it was necessary to save Natal from a great and impending danger. The argument which he desired to lay before the Committee, and which he would afterwards support by proof, was briefly as follows:—That after the termination of the war, Zululand, its Chiefs, and people, were at our mercy; and that it was our duty, more especially if the war was an unjust one, to endeavour to restore peace and order in that country; that the Settlement of 1879 made by Lord Wolseley, by which the country was divided and placed under 13 appointed Chiefs, was the best that could then have been made; that it was effectual in fairly securing peace and order; not absolute peace and order, for that could not have been secured in a country so lately devastated by war, and with Natives whose feelings had been embittered by the contest, and who were hostile to us, but a fair amount of peace and order; that it was certainly beneficial to the Zulu people, and appreciated by them; that certain defects in the working and administration of that Settlement could have been remedied, he would not say without difficulty, but with the exercise of a little tact and judgment, and by our willingness to take upon ourselves a little more direct and guiding authority; that this could have been done without the employment of British soldiers, and without the expenditure of British money; that the unfortunate and ill-judged restoration of Cetewayo destroyed this Settlement of 1879; and that as that policy proceeded entirely from this country, and was against the wishes of the majority of the Chiefs and Zulu people, as he would prove later on, we were bound morally to protect the Zulu people against any evil consequences resulting from the failure of that policy; that the scheme failed, mainly owing to the conduct of Cetewayo himself; and that, therefore, our responsibility attached, and we were bound to endeavour to restore to the Zulus such peace and order as they enjoyed under the Settlement of 1879, and which they would probably have enjoyed to a still greater extent, if the Settlement, instead of being destroyed, had been confirmed and strengthened in the manner which he had already indicated. He must add, further, that the settlement of the Boers in Zululand, while greatly complicating the case, made it still more necessary for the Government to take some action beyond the Reserved Territory in order to protect the Zulus against the Boers. That was the argument he desired to press upon the Committee, and he would now endeavour to support it, by reference to the evidence contained in the Papers presented to Parliament. For that purpose he had read and re-read those Papers with care; and if he had arrived at a wrong conclusion, he could conscientiously state that it was not from want of study of them. But a difficulty arose from there being so great a mass of Correspondence, and the necessity of dealing with it as a whole, because many stories of misconduct of Chiefs, and acts of cruelty and hardship, and cases of disturbance which were relied upon in the earlier stages of the Correspondence, and which were brought forward as proof against the working of the Settlement of 1879, were contradicted, or explained away, or materially weakened, in a later stage; and he would give an instance of that later on, in connection with complaints brought against Chiefs. His first point was that the Settlement of 1879 was the best that could have been then made; that, on the whole, it had worked well; and that it was beneficial to the Zulus, and appreciated by them. It was the best that could then have been made, because Her Majesty's Government, rightly as he ventured to think, had decided not to annex Zululand, and govern it as a Crown Colony. They had determined, and wisely determined, that the country should be governed by Native Chiefs, under Native laws; but the defect in the scheme was that it did not retain any direct and guiding authority. That it worked well, upon the whole, was shown by the following facts:—In August, 1880—that was something like a year after the making of the Settlement—we find Sir Pomeroy Colley reporting that—

"The conditions are sufficient to shield the people from serious injustice and abuse of power on the part of the Chiefs;"

and Mr. Brown, the Resident, reports that "order and quiet prevail." Indeed, as stated by Sir Evelyn Wood, in his address to the Legislative Council of Natal, in October, 1881, peace prevailed in Zululand till July, 1881. The Sitimela outbreak then occurred; but, as shown by his hon. Friend (Mr. Guy Dawnay), Sitimela was an impostor, and he was soon put down—and to this fact he would call the special attention of the Committee, as bearing upon another point in the case—by John Dunn and Native levies. In truth, as Sir Henry Bulwer says, this case of Sitimela "can scarcely be said to bear upon the Settlement." It was true that, in April, 1881, cases of oppression against two out of the 13 appointed Chiefs were brought forward. But they were brought forward by the ex-Prime Minister of Cetewayo, and by two brothers of Cetewayo, and not sustained by the decision of Sir Evelyn Wood, to whom all the parties agreed to refer their differences. He would venture to call the attention of the Committee to this fact, as showing the readiness of the Chiefs to submit their differences to the decision of the British Governor of Natal. Order was certainly restored before December, 1881, for Mr. Osborn then reports that "the country is at present perfectly quiet in every part." The Settlement of 1879 worked then, upon the whole, peacefully up to and well into the year 1882. But then came the rumours of Cetewayo's intended visit to England; and thence arose agitation and doubts in the minds of the Natives as to the continuance and permanency of the Settlement. These rumours also afforded a ground to the discontented members of Cetewayo's family to agitate for his restoration. But what he (Sir Henry Holland) wished to impress upon the Committee was, that all this agitation, excitement, and disturbance arose, not from any internal defect in the working of the Settlement, but from causes outside that Settlement; and, indeed, it might be said outside the country itself. That the Settlement worked beneficially for the Zulu people, and was appreciated by them, could hardly be doubted. He would give one very conclusive proof. In the latter years of Cetewayo's reign, hundreds of families fled from Zululand into Natal; fugitives from a cruel despotism, under which no man's life was safe; but, in 1881, permission was given to no less than 1,630 Natives, men, women, and children, to return from Natal into Zululand. Surely this fact showed conclusively two things; first, that Cetewayo's rule was feared; and, secondly, that the change from his rule was acceptable, and that the working of the Settlement was appreciated by the Natives. But there was further proof of this feeling, for Sir Evelyn Wood reports in April, 1881—

"There can be no doubt that the bulk of the nation already appreciate its improved condition;"

and, again, in September, 1881, after he had traversed a large part of the country, he reports—

"Every Zulu whom I met alone in my ride through Zululand told me, in the course of conversation, that the Zulus would not willingly go back to the old system which obtained under Cetewayo, preferring the present system."

No doubt, there were stories of Chiefs "eating up" and ill-treating their people, and those had been relied on; but, as he had already pointed out, many of these were afterwards proved to be much exaggerated, or without foundation. Some were clearly disposed of by Sir Henry Bulwer, in his Report of August 25, 1882, with which, of course, he would not trouble the Committee; but he would venture to read a few words, in which Sir Henry Bulwer sums up the case. He said—

"I, at least, must do them justice, and acquit them of the great crime, so wrongfully and unjustly charged against them;"

and, finally, in his Report of February, 1883, in which he reviewed, after full consideration, the state of Zululand, he wrote—

"The Settlement of 1879 had conferred great benefits upon the Zulu people, benefits which every true friend of the Native races ought to rejoice at."

He (Sir Henry Holland) could have added to those proofs, had there been time; but he trusted that he had established the first point of his argument. Now, as to the second point; he had admitted that during the working of the Settlement certain defects became manifest, and he had indicated the nature of the chief defect—namely, the want of a more direct and guiding authority on the part of the British Government. That defect had early been pointed out by Sir Henry Bulwer and Mr. Osborn; but Her Majesty's Government had declined to exercise it, on the ground that the exercise of it, if it did not amount to annexation, would, of a certainty, lead to annexation. He thought that the Government were wrong in this view, and in their fears. They were exercising this authority through their Resident in Bechuanaland, but they had not annexed that land, nor would they have to do so; they were exercising that authority in the Reserved Territory, and, as yet, they had not had to annex it; and if they had to do so, it would be on account of the Boers, and not on account of any authority exercised over the Natives in that territory. It was very desirable that immediate rule should be carried on by the Native Chiefs over their people, and it would have been unwise to have deprived them of that power; but a direct and guiding authority was necessary to maintain that power to them; to prevent these Chiefs from quarrelling among themselves; and to check in the bud intertribal disputes, before they had attained to such a size as to render it difficult to repress them without bloodshed and expense. There could be no doubt that the Zulu people themselves expected the exercise of such a paramount authority. It was characteristic of all Natives to expect that the victors in a contest would not retreat, but would continue to hold and exercise the power they had won in battle. This authority, he contended, might then have been secured and exercised without fear of annexation, and without the employment of British troops, or British money, by the appointment of Residents and Sub-Residents, exercising certain judicial and *quasi*-political powers. There was a remarkable consensus of opinion in favour of the appointment of Residents by men most competent to form an opinion. He would cite the names of Sir Henry Bulwer, Sir Theophilus Shepstone, Mr. Osborn, Bishop Douglas, Mr. Robertson, and John Dunn, men of very different views, of very different characters, looking at the question from very different sides, and yet all agreeing upon this point. That the Zulu Chiefs would have been ready to yield to such authority was shown by their readiness to refer their disputes upon the occasion to which he had already alluded. That no British troops would have been required was the opinion of Sir Henry Bulwer in his Report of February 15, 1883; and they could probably have engaged all the Chiefs to assist in putting down quarrels at the request of the British authority. Upon that point he would refer to the telegram of Sir Evelyn Wood of September 2, 1881—

> "All Chiefs agree to combine for the repression of rebellion, if advised to do so by the Resident;"

and to the fact, before alluded to by him, that Sitimela was put down by Dunn and Native levies. The Chiefs would have been ready to recognize that the primary obligations of maintenance of territory and maintenance of peace rested upon them and their people, acting in concert with the Residents. Upon that point also, he would add that a Hut Tax, or some other tax or contribution of a like kind, would have covered the expenses. If these steps had been taken in this direction, he believed that the Settlement of 1879 might have been strengthened and continued, and the good effects of its working would have been largely increased. It might be said that this was, after all, a matter of speculation and conjecture; but the view was supported, as he had shown, by the actual working of the Settlement till 1882, and by the opinions of men best acquainted with the state of affairs, and with the wishes and views of the Zulu Chiefs and people. But if this were matter of speculation, there could be no doubt at all as to the absolute failure of the alternative plan adopted by Her Majesty's Government—namely, the restoration of Cetewayo. From that plan he entirely dissented; it put an end to the Settlement; it was a violation of our pledges to the Chiefs and people; and it was, he believed, against the wishes of the great majority of the people themselves. The first unfortunate step was the visit of Cetewayo to England. The announcement of the proposed visit had given rise in Zululand, as he had already pointed out, to agitation, and uncertainty and doubts as to the continuance of the Settlement of 1879, and all the disturbances in 1882 were traceable to this cause. It was clear that Cetewayo himself looked upon this visit as the first step towards his restoration; and no less clear that the Zulus took a like view. And it was to him most extraordinary that Her Majesty's Government did not seem to have foreseen, or suspected, that agitation would arise in Zululand when the reports of the proposed visit reached that country. They seemed to have been taken by surprise when they had temporarily to postpone the visit upon receiving a strongly worded Report from Sir Henry Bulwer in May, 1882, that the intended visit had—

> "Led to the report of his restoration, and had been the cause of the recent demonstration of the ex-King's brothers, and was producing uneasiness in Zululand, and interfering with the settlement of that country."

He (Sir Henry Holland) was justified in assuming that Her Majesty's Government were thus wanting in foresight, because no steps were taken in Zululand to explain the state of the case to the Chiefs, and to prevent any uneasiness and agitation, nor were any instructions to that effect given to Sir Henry Bulwer. Well, the restoration was decided upon; it was decided upon against the strongly expressed opinions of hon. Members on that (the Opposition) side of the House, and, if he remembered rightly, on the other side also. He himself had ventured to point out the almost certainty of the failure of such a scheme. It was decided upon against the views of Lord Wolseley, who protested against it on the ground of danger to Natal; of causing serious trouble and bloodshed in Zululand; and as being in direct contravention of the guarantee given to the 13 Chiefs that, under no circumstances, should Cetewayo be allowed to settle again in the territory. It was against the views of Sir Theophilus Shepstone, who thought it would "be certain to produce the most disastrous consequences." It was against the views of Sir Henry Bulwer, who strongly opposed the scheme, and only yielded when he was informed that Her Majesty's Government had decided upon it, and when he was instructed to take the necessary steps to prepare the country for the return of the ex-King. It was against the views of the Colonists of Natal, if we might judge from a protest of the Legislative Council of that Colony, and from resolutions passed at such important places as Durban, Pietermaritzburg, and Newcastle. And, lastly, it was against the wishes of the majority of the 13 appointed Chiefs, and of the bulk of the Zulu people. As regarded the Zulu people, he had shown how entirely satisfied they were with the working of the Settlement of 1879, and there was no reason to suppose that the bulk of the people had altered their views. No doubt a certain number of the people, who had been most intimately connected with Cetewayo and his family, were interested and excited by the prospect of his restoration; but, even when he came back, their number was so limited that he was almost alarmed at the want of enthusiasm. It was true that no direct protest was made by the people against the return; but, at all events, there was no Petition in favour of it; and whatever advances in civilization the Zulus had made it might be admitted that they had not advanced so far as they had in this country in the art of getting up and presenting Petitions. And it must not be forgotten that Natives very readily fell in with the decision of higher Powers, when once made, however much they might dislike it, from fear of opposing it. And when they were considering the feeling of the people, they could not but treat the protests of the Chiefs and Headmen as representing, to a considerable extent, the views and wishes of their followers. Now, how did the case stand as regards the 13 appointed Chiefs? In October, 1882, five only were disposed to acquiesce in the restoration, while eight were opposed to it; and even after the decision was announced, 7 out of 13 expressed dissent. It was to him somewhat surprising that after the determination of Her Majesty's Government was made known, so many Chiefs were bold enough to protest, because the Chiefs might naturally have feared that further opposition would draw down on them the hostility and vengeance of Cetewayo when he returned to Zululand, backed up by the power of the British Government. And, again, as late as January, 1883, they would find 30 Chiefs and Headmen protesting; and the tone of their complaints was so simple and touching that he would venture to read it to the Committee. They said—

"Is it true that you White people now find that Cetewayo has done no wrong? What wrong have *we* done that we are to be driven from our homes? We cannot live under Cetewayo again. We look to the Government to protect us, and to allow us to occupy the country to which we belong, and which we must leave if Cetewayo is put over us."

Sir Theophilus Shepstone also reports that—

"All complain bitterly of the changes now made without in any way consulting their feelings."

The restoration was made, as he thought he had shown, against the wishes of the majority of the Chiefs, and, therefore, against the pledges given to them in 1879. It had been urged that, in partial redemption of those pledges, the Reserved Territory had been set aside for such Chiefs as did not wish to serve under Cetewayo. But when one came to look at it, this offer was little better than a mockery. There would be a very natural reluctance on the part of the people to leave their property, and homes, and settle down in a new territory; and, unless the people would move, it was hopeless to suppose that the Chiefs would separate themselves from their people, and power, and property. He believed that, in fact, not a single Chief had up to this time availed himself of the offer, with the exception of Usibepu, who, after his total defeat by Boers and Usutus, had no other place of refuge. The result of the restoration was, as predicted, disastrous. The scheme failed, and mainly owing to the conduct of Cetewayo himself. He returned to his country dissatisfied with the conditions imposed upon him; sore that so large a portion of the country had been separated from his rule; and especially sore that the Chief Usibepu, his "dog," as he called that Chief, had been allowed to retain his separate power and territory. He began at once to assume power over the Chiefs and Natives in the Reserved Territory, in spite of repeated warnings from Sir Henry Bulwer and Mr. Fynn; he soon commenced hostilities against Usibepu—an attack utterly unprovoked, and characterized by Sir Henry Bulwer as "another direct and most serious violation of the conditions." Cetewayo was defeated, and died, and the scheme of the restoration failed, after destroying the Settlement of 1879. He (Sir Henry Holland) believed that he had so far proved his argument that this country had incurred a responsibility to the Zulu people that they should not suffer—he would not put it higher—from the failure of a scheme which they did not desire, and which was forced upon them by the policy of Her Majesty's Government. They should be restored, as far as possible, to the state in which they were under the Settlement, and which they would still have been in had not that Settlement been destroyed. Her Majesty's Government had, however, declared that they would not extend British authority or protection over Zululand, but would only undertake to preserve the peace and integrity of the Reserved Territory. He quite admitted that it was absolutely essential to protect this territory. It was essential in the interest of the Colony of Natal, and it was essential not only in the interest of the Natives within that territory, and who proposed to remain there, but for the interest of those without the territory. The pledge that was given originally, that this territory should be reserved as a place of refuge for those who did not desire to remain under Cetewayo's power, must certainly be held to continue in full force for those who desired to fly from the fighting and bloodshed which had followed upon the failure of the scheme of restoration. It was not easy to know exactly what was going on in the Reserve, and what danger there was of an attack upon it; but as British troops were employed there, he could not conceive that there would be any substantial difficulty in maintaining it. The difficulty—and a very grave and serious difficulty it was—with which we had to deal, arose from the state of things outside the Reserve. Here, again, it was not easy to ascertain what was the exact state of things, as the conditions were constantly changing. We knew that the Chiefs had been fighting amongst themselves; we knew that Usibepu had been attacked and defeated by a united force of Boers and Usutus; but the state of things had been undoubtedly complicated, and the difficulties greatly increased, by the introduction of the Boer element. The Boers were like stormy petrels. They scented storms from afar, and were always to be found East or West of the Transvaal, wherever Native quarrels arose. They combined also the rapacity of vultures, for they always got good pickings from the battlefields where Native quarrels were fought out. Their mode of proceeding was simple enough. They began by settling down in small numbers on the land which they desired to have. They created or fostered tribal disputes, and they took one side or the other in consideration of concession of land; and then, when the time was ripe, and the Natives were sufficiently weakened by fighting each other, they threw off all disguise and annexed the land. That plan had been pursued with great advantage to themselves on the West of the Transvaal, and that plan they were pursuing on the East of the Transvaal; and they would succeed unless we interfered, which, apparently, we were not going to do. We found them negotiating with the Usutus in 1882, and we learnt in 1884 that a large number, from 400 to 800, armed Boers had entered the territory, and had made Dinizulu King, in return for territorial concessions. He would venture to read to the House Sir Henry Bulwer's remarks upon this Boer invasion or settlement, as they seemed to him to carry great weight. Sir Henry Bulwer said—

"The situation is very grave. If we allow the Boers to interfere and make Dinizulu King, it will be a most serious blow to British power in South Africa. They will also become masters of Zululand, to the permanent loss of the Zulu people, and to the great injury of Natal, to which will resort refugees, for whom there is no room and no future outlet. The Native question will be thereby gravely complicated. In the Reserve, also, we should probably have immediate Usutu contests."

Those fears were probably well founded. What, then, had been the result of the policy of the Government in Zululand? They had destroyed the power of the Zulu people, and now it was proposed to leave them in the hands of their most hated enemies, whom, in Cetewayo's time, they could easily have conquered, and would have conquered but for our remonstrances with Cetewayo. What policy had been suggested to meet the difficulty of the case? Sir Henry Bulwer had suggested an extension of the Reserved Territory; but this suggestion was made before Usibepu was defeated, and if any extension were now to be made it would have to include all Zululand. He did not know whether Sir Henry Bulwer would recommend such an extension; but Her Majesty's Government had, at all events, declined to be parties to any extension beyond the Reserved Territory, and he was not prepared to find fault with that decision. It was not for hon. Members on that side of the House to state what policy the Government should pursue. They had not the Papers and the confidential information which the Government had, and were not in a position to advise. But he ventured, with very great diffidence, to submit to the Government a course of policy which he thought was worthy of consideration, which was quite distinct from annexation, but which, if practicable and acted upon, might even now restore peace and order in this unfortunate country, and relieve us of much of the danger and difficulty surrounding the present position. He would endeavour to treat the country again as we treated it in 1879; in other words, he would endeavour to revert to the lines of the Settlement of 1879, and to govern the people by Native Chiefs; but, at the same time, to strengthen the authority of those Chiefs by the retention and exercise of a direct and guiding authority through Residents who should have judicial and political powers. It might be asked, how could this plan now be put in operation? He would suggest that Sir Hercules Robinson, or Sir Henry Bulwer, or someone in whom the Chiefs had confidence, should be deputed to summon the Chiefs to meet at some point outside the Reserve Territory. The Chiefs should be asked to appoint, or to allow the British Government to appoint, some single Chief, or as many Chiefs as they desired, under whom they would serve. The Chiefs should be required to agree, as Sir Evelyn Wood suggested, to combine to put down any fighting or disturbance at the request of the British authority. Residents should be appointed with judicial and political powers. An appeal should lie to the Lieutenant Governor of Natal in all intertribal disputes; and provision should be made against the sale of land to White men. Of course, he did not conceal from himself the difficulty arising from the Boers. A firm hand would have to be kept on the Boers who had settled down in Zululand. They must be called upon either to assent to the authority of the Chiefs and the British authority—and they might be induced to do that if their titles to the lands which they now held were confirmed to them—or to retire. Some might be disposed to take the latter course, if their hopes of further gain, and of establishing a Boer Republic, were thus taken from them; and he would not be disinclined to give them some compensation for the land they gave up. Compensation, he knew, was an ugly word; but he believed any amount of compensation would be well spent if, by giving it, we could once get the Boers out of Zululand, and thus free the Zulus. Then, as regarded the prevention of further encroachments, he did not believe we should have much difficulty if the Government would have the courage to act firmly with the Transvaal Government—a quality in which they had been deficient up to this time. The Government should call upon the Transvaal Government to act upon the Second Article of the recent Convention. By that Article it was provided that—

"The Government of the South African Republic will strictly adhere to the boundaries defined in the First Article of this Convention, and will do its utmost to prevent any of its inhabitants from making any encroachments upon lands beyond the said boundaries. The Government of the South African Republic will appoint Commissioners upon the Eastern and Western borders, whose duty it will be strictly to guard against irregularities and trespassing over the boundaries. Her Majesty's Government will, if necessary, appoint Commissioners in the Native territories outside the Eastern and Western borders of the South African Republic to maintain order and prevent encroachments."

He had read this Article in full to the Committee, because, a short time ago, in answer to a Question, the hon. Gentleman the Under Secretary of State for the Colonies (Mr. Evelyn Ashley) said that they could not well call upon the South African Republic to appoint a Commissioner until Her Majesty's Government had appointed one themselves, which they had not determined to do; but it was clear from the terms of Article II. that, while the Boers were bound to appoint Commissioners, the British Government were only required to do so if necessary. [Mr. EVELYN ASHLEY: The Convention has not been ratified.] That was true; but he (Sir Henry Holland) thought that if this Article could not be legally enforced, a compliance with it might be pressed upon the Boers, or that the Boers might be required to take such a step under the former Convention. We were bound to settle this Boer question; and so important was it to prevent any further trespassing that he would be ready to make further concessions to the Transvaal Government—as, for example, the abandonment of the large debt now due to this country—if he could thereby obtain an honest and *bonâ fide* security that the Republic would prevent any further encroachments. He had ventured to suggest some policy of this kind for the consideration of Her Majesty's Government; but he did not ask the Committee to affirm this or any other special course of action, but only to affirm that, under all the circumstances of the case, this country had incurred obligations and responsibilities to the Zulu people outside as well as inside the Reserved Territory; and that the Government ought to endeavour faithfully to meet those obligations and responsibilities, and to secure some kind of peace and order in this unhappy Zululand. He must apologize to the Committee for havin detained them so long, and for having gone so far back into the history and details of this case. His excuse was that he had to contend with the very natural reluctance of this country to engage in further expeditions and further expenditure in Zululand; he had to contend with the still more natural reluctance to engage ourselves in further complications with the Boers; and he had to contend with the desire to limit our responsibilities, instead of extending them, and to content ourselves with maintaining peace in our own Colonies. He had been compelled, therefore, to make it clear that we had, by our policy, incurred duties and responsibilities towards the Zulu people. If he had convinced the Committee that that was the case, he could not doubt that this country, however unpalatable the task might be, or however expensive and difficult, would support the Government if they firmly, manfully, and honestly endeavoured to perform those duties and responsibilities.

Motion made, and Question proposed,

"That a sum, not exceeding £38,567 (including a Supplementary sum of £30,000), be granted to Her Majesty, to complete the sum necessary to defray the Charge which will come in course of payment during the year ending on the 31st day of March 1885, for certain Charges connected with the Orange River Territory, the Transvaal, Zululand, the Island of St. Helena, and the High Commissioner for South Africa."—(*Mr. Guy Dawnay.*)

MR. WODEHOUSE said, he did not propose to follow the hon. Baronet (Sir Henry Holland) in his vindication of the Wolseley Settlement, nor in his observations adverse to the restoration of Cetewayo. He would confine himself exclusively to the present state of affairs in Zululand. He never heard the hon. Gentleman the Member for the North Riding of Yorkshire (Mr. Guy Dawnay) speak of the affairs of these distant territories, which he knew so well, and on which he was so well entitled to speak, without regretting that the weight and authority which would naturally attach to his words were marred by that exuberant animosity against Her Majesty's Government which seemed to inflame all he uttered. But he fully shared the hon. Member's (Mr. Guy Dawnay's) sense of the gravity of the situation in Zululand, and of the need of prompt and decided action there. It was time for a more direct and determined exercise of authority on the part of Her Majesty's Government. We could not, without discredit, ignore our obligations to the entire Zulu people, whether they were in the Reserve or beyond it. The hon. Member for the North Riding for bade them, if he (Mr. Wodehouse) might say so, to allude to the Zulu War. But they must allude to it, because that war was the origin of our responsibility for the present distracted condition of Zululand. Until that war the Zulus were a strong and compact Native race, more than able to hold their own against the Boers. We shattered their strong cohesion, and left them a prey to the greed of the Boers. He must remind the Committee that when Her Majesty's Government were negotiating the Pretoria Convention, through their Commissioners on the spot, they proposed to sever from the Transvaal a strip of territory on its Eastern border; but the Boers objected, and Her Majesty's Government gave way to them on this point. From this decision, however, one of the Commissioners, Sir Evelyn Wood, dissented, on the ground that the separation of the Transvaal from Zululand was essential for the prevention of intrigues which would be fatal to the peace of Zululand, and might even menace the safety of Natal; and certainly the sequel of events had tended to prove rather than disprove the accuracy of Sir Evelyn Wood's foresight. We must anticipate sustained aggression on the part of the Transvaal Boers, in whatever directions they were free to advance. Some check had been put on their encroachments on the Western side of the Transvaal by the appointment of Mr. Mackenzie as Commissioner in Bechuanaland; and he wished that some similar action were taken to check their advance on the Eastern border. It was vain to suppose that the Transvaal Boers would observe any boundaries fixed by Treaty or Convention. They would violate without scruple the most solemn assurances and the most formal engagements; and they were more than ever likely to do so now. He would tell the Committee why. When the Transvaal deputation were over in this country negotiating the recently-made Convention, their ostensible organ and advocate in the London Press was *The Times;* and *The Times* argued throughout that, as we had no intention of undertaking military operations against the Boers in any case, we had better accept at once whatever terms they might be graciously pleased to offer. Now, if the Transvaal deputation had carried back to their countrymen the information that, do what they would, England would never fight them again, why should they observe inconvenient engagements? But that was not all. The Transvaal deputation made a tour on the Continent, and visited some of the principal capitals of Europe. In Paris and Berlin, every newspaper that wished to be spiteful to this country flattered them about their military prowess, which had thrice defeated British arms. In Berlin they were received with effusive honours by the German Emperor and his Chancellor; and they were further gratified by the Imperial patronage of the German settlement at Angra Pequena. Now the reports of all these things had gone out to South Africa, and were circulating through every Dutch farmhouse, inflaming the vanity and self-assertion of the Boers, and giving a fresh impulse to their restless aggression. Again, there was another circumstance which pointed in the same direction. There had recently been a change of Ministry in the Cape Colony, and the new Ministry could not stand without support from the extreme Dutch Party. Moreover, these new Ministers were the very men who forced the Basutos into rebellion by their disarmament policy, and who would have confiscated Basuto territory, if Her Majesty's Government had not intervened. And what was the first declaration of policy made by them after taking Office? Why, that they intended to keep a firmer hand on the Natives than their Predecessors had done. Every Native in South Africa would understand the meaning of that declaration. All these circumstances pointed to the likelihood of self-assertion and increased aggression on the part of the Dutch farmers, and a corresponding increase of alarm and uneasiness on the part of the Natives. Now, whether we had to deal with trouble in Zululand, or Swaziland, or Basutoland, or Bechuanaland, one dominant consideration always lay at the root of the question; and that was, did England intend, or not, to be, in fact, as in name, the paramount controlling and guiding Power throughout South Africa? The Transvaal deputation made no secret of their views as to the proper position of England in South Africa; they would leave to England neither place, nor power, nor duty there, except the single duty of guarding those territories from transmarine invasion. Happily, these pretensions met with no countenance from Her Majesty's Government. They had rescued the trade route through Bechuanaland from the Transvaal Boers; and they had got rid of the Sand River Convention. That Convention being gone, we were free, if we thought proper, to enter into friendly relations, by Treaty or otherwise, with Native Tribes all round the Transvaal, and free also, if ever we found it expedient, to supply the Natives with arms and ammunition. Moreover, Her Majesty's Government had reserved to themselves the right of veto upon all Treaties concluded by the Boers with Foreign States. They had put a British Commissioner in Bechuanaland, and had also resumed Imperial administration in Basutoland. All these acts were clear recognitions of Imperial duties and responsibilities in South Africa. If, then, these duties and responsibilities were recognized—if this line of policy was deliberately chosen, he hoped that whatever was done might not be marred by procrastination and half-heartedness. Whatever we meant to do let us do it quickly, because every hour of delay raised fresh obstacles in our path. We ought to do our work well, or else we had better leave it alone altogether. He made these observations because he gathered from the language of the Secretary of State for the Colonies (the Earl of Derby) that he regarded the resumption of Imperial rule in Basutoland, and the appointment of Mr. Mackenzie in Bechuanaland, as measures of a tentative and experimental character. He (Mr. Wodehouse) strongly deprecated such language. It carried misgiving and uncertainty to the minds of all friends of English policy in South Africa, and was a direct incentive to its enemies to plot and intrigue to make the policy a failure. If these qualifying phrases were intended to diminish Imperial responsibility, or to provide paths of escape from future embarrassments, they were futile; they would not lighten the burden of our responsibility by the weight of a single grain, nor shorten its duration by a single hour. This was not a time to temporize and minimize in South Africa. Things would not settle down, if left to themselves; but they would go from bad to worse. In addition to the aggression of the Transvaal Boers, we had to reckon with the fact that, owing to the discovery of the Diamond Fields, and all the recent wars there had been, South Africa swarmed with adventurers of the worst kinds, who fostered all intertribal quarrels and family feuds of Native Chiefs for their own sordid advantage. He therefore hoped that Her Majesty's Government would grasp the situation in Zululand and elsewhere with vigour and decision, and that they would not shrink from appointing Representatives of Her Majesty, wherever the peace of South Africa demanded the presence of such officers. It would be better for us to make an abrupt and complete repudiation of all our obligations to the Natives, and extricate ourselves by a sudden wrench from every quarter of South Africa, except Simon's Bay and Cape Town, rather than linger on the scene while we suffered the name of the Queen, which had been to the Natives in the past a symbol of fidelity to Imperial obligations and the pledge of national honour, to fade into a mere delusive phantom, and be known to them only as a broken reed to lean on.

MR. R. N. FOWLER (LORD MAYOR) said, he had listened with great interest to the speech of the hon. Gentleman who had just sat down (Mr. Wodehouse). The hon. Gentleman had given them a very graphic description of the position of things with respect to the Boers at the present moment. With all the remarks of the hon. Member he cordially agreed. He had had an opportunity of speaking on this subject during the present Session, and he did not propose to trouble the Committee at any length. They had listened to a very remarkable speech from his hon. Friend the Member for Midhurst (Sir Henry Holland), and they knew that everything the hon. Baronet said in that House was always worthy of the utmost attention, and on this question particularly everything which fell from the hon. Baronet deserved the greatest consideration. He (Mr. R. N. Fowler) approached the matter, however, from a different point of view to his hon. Friend. The hon. Baronet was a consistent opponent of the restoration of Cetewayo; but, so far as an humble Member like himself could, he (Mr. R. N. Fowler) took the responsibility of having recommended that restoration. His hon. Friend seemed to think that, in 1881, under the Settlement of 1879, the condition of Zululand was as nearly that of a paradise as it could well be. His (Mr. R. N. Fowler's) recollection of the condition of Zululand, so far as he could gather from what he heard when he made a personal visit to the Cape and Natal in November, 1881, was that Zululand was not in the very peaceful, and happy, and Elysian state described by his hon. Friend. At that time many people were recommending that John Dunn should be made King of the Zulus, *vice* Cetewayo deposed. John Dunn himself was certainly going about recommending that there should be a Paramount Chief, and suggesting that he was the man who would best promote the peace of the country by assuming that position. He rather thought that his hon. Friend the Member for the North Riding (Mr. Guy Dawnay), judging from his speeches at the time, was an advocate of that course; at all events, the hon. Gentleman was not very much opposed to it. Well, therefore, they had the evidence of that well-known character, John Dunn, that the state of Zululand at that period was not as peaceable as his hon. Friend the Member for Midhurst (Sir Henry Holland) had represented. Her Majesty's Government thought it proper to restore Cetewayo. Those of them who recommended that course might be twitted for having given such advice, inasmuch as it had failed; but, in the first place, he ought to say the course the Government took was not altogether the course he and others recommended. The restoration of Cetewayo was done in a half-hearted manner. Cetewayo was only restored to a portion of his Kingdom. Though, no doubt, Her Majesty's Government thought he ought to be very grateful for what they had done, Cetewayo and others thought he had not received full justice; and, therefore, there was a misunderstanding in that respect. Again, although Her Majesty's Government sent back Cetewayo in accordance with their own policy, that policy was very strongly disapproved of by the Government of Natal. The Government of Natal, as a matter of fact, took a very different view to that taken by Her Majesty's Government; and he asked anyone what was the chance of the policy being successful, when it was carried out by an agent who utterly disapproved of the views of his superiors? What chance was there of the success of the policy, when Sir Henry Bulwer, who was the agent appointed to carry it out, disapproved of it? He did not mean to say that that distinguished man would not do his best to carry out the orders of the Government; but still they knew that when a man had to carry out a policy which he considered was foredoomed to failure, that policy was sure to be carried out in a half-hearted sort of way; all sorts of difficulties were sure to be raised; and it seemed to him (Mr. R. N. Fowler) that, under such circumstances, the policy of Her Majesty's Government, which was urged upon them by Members on both sides of the House, never had a chance of success. If the Government wished their policy to succeed, they had only one course to pursue, and that was to promote Sir Henry Bulwer to some other Colony, and place in Natal a Governor who was prepared to carry out their views. He would remind the Committee that the position of things at Natal had altered very considerably of late; there was a great alteration in the condition of things at Natal in the beginning of 1882. Her Majesty's Government at that time proposed to revert to the old system, by which Natal was administered by a Lieutenant Governor, subordinate to the Governor at the Cape. When Lord Kimberley had appointed a gentleman to take the place of Lieutenant Governor, under Sir Hercules Robinson, Natal raised considerable opposition. Her Majesty's Government altered their plans, and appointed Sir Henry Bulwer as full Governor. Whether that proceeding had answered was open to question. A point had been made about the disturbance before Cetewayo's return, and it had also been said that Cetewayo promoted disturbances amongst the other tribes. The Bishop of Natal (the late Dr. Colenso), however, in a letter, had said—

"At the present moment there is no evidence that Cetewayo has had anything to do with these disturbances; they seem to be the outcome of Sir Henry Bulwer's Settlement."

He quoted this extract to show that it was just possible that Cetewayo was not open to the charges brought against him by the hon. Baronet (Sir Henry Holland). He did not quite understand what his hon. Friend's (Mr. Guy Dawnay's) view was as to the Motion he submitted to the Committee. He thought it was as well they should have a discussion on this very important question, and for that reason he was glad his hon. Friend had initiated the debate; but, at the same time, he did not quite understand what was the exact question they were to decide by a division. As he had already said, the policy of Her Majesty's Government had failed; and he (Mr. R. N. Fowler) was as much responsible as a private Member could be for the adoption of that policy. If his hon. Friend meant, by proposing to reduce the Vote, to censure the Government for the restoration of Cetewayo, he (Mr. R. N. Fowler) certainly could not support him; but would be obliged to go into the Lobby against him. He did not well see what could be the use of dividing on a question of this kind; certainly, if his hon. Friend did go to a division, he ought to tell the Committee more clearly than he had yet done what his object was.

MR. RYLANDS said, he did not propose to follow the Lord Mayor (Mr. R. N. Fowler) into the question of the restoration of Cetewayo, because he thought, in the short space of time they had at their disposal, they ought to direct their attention specially to the future; he did not think they need go at all into the past. If he were to venture upon a discussion of what had taken place, he certainly should condemn the late Government; and he was not quite sure also that he would not have something condemnatory to say about the present Government. But that was not the point. They were placed in circumstances of great difficulty, occasioning great anxiety; and the real question was, what was to be our policy. The hon. Gentleman the Member for Bath (Mr. Wodehouse) had made a speech, in which he advocated what might be called the Imperial spread-eagle policy. The hon. Gentleman had said that we must have a substantial and real Suzerain power over the whole of South Africa. What did he mean? Did he consider that two-thirds of the White inhabitants of South Africa were Dutch, and that the remaining population, for the most part, consisted of various African tribes? Did he remember that British Imperialism was represented by a comparatively small number of Colonists, and by the red coats of the British Army; and did he wish the Committee to understand that the policy he was prepared to recommend to Her Majesty's Government was that that small handful of British Colonists should be backed up by all the force of the British Army, in order to compel the Natives to submit to the Imperial Suzerainty of England? Did the hon. Member propose that? because, if so, he was only proposing what had been tried again and again, and the consequence of which had been that we had caused bloodshed and misery over many parts of Africa. We had entailed upon the British taxpayer large burdens, that had gone on increasing from year to year, and for which they had actually nothing to show. He recollected reading, some years ago, a book by Anthony Trollope, in which the writer commented upon the fact that, when he was in Natal, he saw very few Whites who did not wear red coats. It struck Mr. Anthony Trollope that these red coats were doing the work of the Natal Colonists, but were not paid by the Natal Colonists, but by the British taxpayer at home; and he said he could not help fancying that he saw each of these red coats being carried on the back of the struggling operatives of Lancashire. And so it was with these Colonies. He (Mr. Rylands) knew precisely what the motive of the hon. Gentleman the Member for the North Riding (Mr. Guy Dawnay) and his hon. Friends was. What they wanted was that we should take an active part in Zululand; that we should stand all the burden; and that the Natal Government should have any advantage that might arise from our endeavours and exertions. Were the Natal Government prepared to pay for any operations that might be undertaken? No; they would not pay the miserable amount that was now owing to us, and we had a number of soldiers in Natal, for whom they did not pay anything at all. Why should we protect these Colonies if they would not do anything to protect themselves? Hon. Gentlemen argued that it was important we should take care that all the tribes who were fighting with one another should be bound over to keep the peace. How bound over to keep the peace? Were we to occupy that enormous territory by our soldiery; were we to decide between the tribes; and were we to use our power to crush any portion of the Natives we thought were doing wrong? We had done all that before; and he ventured to say that, whenever we had intervened amongst the Natives — no doubt we had done so with the best motives—we had produced evils that had been absolutely greater than those we sought to suppress. Hon. Gentlemen who had been accustomed to read South African Blue Books, as he had for several years, could not fail to have noticed the sameness in the story. They might take up a Blue Book published 10 years ago, and, while probably they would not be familiar with the names of the Chiefs and, it might be, the districts of South Africa there mentioned, they would find that the course of events was so similar, one time with another, that they might say that the whole history of South Africa ran upon the same line. There were constantly men, on the verge of civilization, who oppressed the Blacks. These men were all of the same character; they had few scruples; they were men, perhaps, of enormous energy, and of little fear; they pressed upon the Blacks, and by-and-bye there was a larger range of the disputes; certain Chiefs took one side, and some the other; the White men allied themselves to some or other of the Chiefs; and so gradually the White men were involved in the conflict. The Chiefs were sometimes loyal, and sometimes not; they were barbarians, and were influenced at the moment by what they thought would promote their special interest. Such was the course of South African events. But of all the schemes he had heard of for the settlement of South African affairs, the scheme of the hon. Baronet the Member for Midhurst (Sir Henry Holland) was the most untenable. What was the hon. Baronet's scheme? Why, that we should take possession of Zululand to that extent that we must become actually the Suzerain Power, and get rid of the Boers. But how were we to get rid of the Boers? By buying them off! Now, he thought that was about the most unwise suggestion that could possibly be made. His hon. Friend (Sir Henry Holland) actually said that the British Government were to go to the Boers, who had invaded a certain portion of Zululand, and out of the taxes of this country buy them off. He (Mr. Rylands) thought that that would not only be an unwise policy, but that it would be a policy which would altogether fail. His hon. Friend also suggested that we should go to the Boer Government, and say to them—"We will give up our charge against you—that is, the debt you owe to us—on condition that you pledge yourselves to leave the country." Why, if we did do that, and the Boers consented to those terms, in five years' time there would be a new race of Boers ready to enter the district. It was really no use attempting impossibilities, whether it was from the Imperial sentiments of the hon. Gentleman the Member for Bath, or the Natal sentiments of the hon. Gentleman the Member for the North Riding of Yorkshire, or the philanthropic sentiments of some of his (Mr. Rylands's) Friends; it would be useless to adopt the suggestions which had been made. He feared that hon. Gentlemen would drag us into a policy that past history had proved to be a bloody and wicked policy. It was impossible to interfere in these things from a philanthropic point of view. We could not interfere in these affairs with any good effect; and he would recommend to the Government that they should, as far as possible, narrow their obligations with regard to South Africa. The hon. Gentleman the Member for Bath had admitted that the new Ministers at Cape Colony were obliged to rest for a certain amount of support upon the Dutch element. It was an undoubted fact that the Government of the Cape Colony must always rest upon the Dutch element to a great extent. He (Mr. Rylands) well recollected that at the time the question between the Transvaal and ourselves was to the fore, he was told by a very high authority from the Cape whom he happened to meet—it was the Speaker of the House of Assembly of the Cape of Good Hope—that if the Government pressed on their views with regard to the Transvaal, that which appeared so simple a thing in the beginning would develop into a very large and difficult question, and he feared that the Free State would be dragged in in the first place, and that subsequently there would be dragged in the sympathy of the entire Dutch population of the Cape, who would feel it was their duty to prevent any action of the British Government as against their brethren in the Transvaal. He (Mr. Rylands) considered that if the Government of the Cape, representing, as it did, a large Dutch element, chose in any way to sympathize with the action upon its borders, we had no right to step in with our Imperial authority, in order to put a stop to that action. We ought not to allow the Natal Government to drag us, at our own cost, into their quarrels; if we did, the only effect would be that more mischief than good would be done, and many lives sacrificed.

MR. EVELYN ASHLEY said, it was refreshing, in discussing the very thorny and difficult question of South Africa, to encounter a speech like that of his hon. Friend the Member for the North Riding of Yorkshire (Mr. Guy Dawnay), couched, as it was, in such eloquent terms, and showing that there was, at least, one hon. Gentleman with no doubt or hesitation as to what was the right course to pursue. He (Mr. Evelyn Ashley) must confess he was not in the happy position of the hon. Gentleman, and he was consoled to see that his hon. Friend the Member for Midhurst (Sir Henry Holland), tempered as he was by official experience, was more moderate and more hesitating than the Mover of the Amendment. He fully appreciated the earnestness of the hon. Gentleman the Member for the North Riding; but he was bound to say the hon. Gentleman failed to make any practical suggestion for the solution of the difficulty. The hon. Gentleman certainly suggested that we should annex Zululand; but this the present and also the late Government had persistently refused to do. Anybody who took up the map of Zululand would see that if the proposal of the hon. Gentleman were adopted, there would be nothing left of Zululand proper, except a very small strip of territory. Briefly, he would say to the hon. Member that the annexation of Zululand was what Her Majesty's Government had declined, and what they still declined to do. In their opinion, the proposal of the hon. Gentleman would be tantamount to the annexation of Zululand. Let him come to the more detailed, and, he might say, the more plausible suggestion of the hon. Baronet the Member for Midhurst (Sir Henry Holland); and he must ask the Committee to allow him, very shortly, to follow the hon. Baronet in what he had said. It was necessary to do so, although he respectfully protested against the question being again raised in the House as to the rights or the wrongs of the restoration of Cetewayo. He ventured to submit that that belonged to ancient history, although it was legitimate in the course of argument for the hon. Baronet to point out that that restoration had caused this or that evil, and had involved this or that responsibility. The hon. Baronet had done more than that, for he had discussed at length the advisability or the non-advisability, under the circumstances then existing, of the restoration of Cetewayo. He (Mr. Evelyn Ashley) was not prepared to follow the hon. Baronet into the details of that question, inasmuch as he did not expect that the question would be started to-day; furthermore, he was not prepared to follow the hon. Baronet in detail as to his statement that, at the time of Cetewayo's restoration, Zululand was in a state of tranquillity and quiet. He could have armed himself with passages from the Blue Books to prove the contrary if he had expected that the hon. Baronet would have raised the point.

SIR HENRY HOLLAND said, he was sure the hon. Gentleman did not wish to misrepresent what he had said. He did not say that Zululand was in a state of tranquillity and quiet at the time of Cetewayo's restoration; but that it was in a fairly peaceful condition until it was rumoured in the country that there was a probability of Cetewayo being restored.

MR. EVELYN ASHLEY said, he thoroughly understood the hon. Baronet to mean that the rumours of Cetewayo's restoration, which were subsequently fulfilled, were the cause of the disturbances that existed in Zululand. As he had said, he was not prepared to answer the hon. Baronet's allegations in detail, although he was sure he could have brought sufficient evidence to show that his assertions were not correct, had he known that the question would be raised. The right hon. Gentleman the Lord Mayor of London (Mr. R. N. Fowler), who took considerable interest in the restoration of Cetewayo at the time, had told them that, in his opinion, Zululand was in a very unsatisfactory state at the time the King was restored; and the hon. Baronet himself delivered a speech in the House in April, 1882, in which he said—

> "He would admit it to be probable that the arrangement made at the conclusion of the war had not worked in an altogether satisfactory manner, and that acts of bloodshed and cruelty had been perpetrated."—(3 *Hansard*, [268] 778.)

He quite agreed with the hon. Baronet, who, in the passage quoted, acknowledged that Zululand was not in a satisfactory condition at that time. It was not in open revolt, because of the very uncertainty as to whether Cetewayo would return or not; but if it had become certain that Cetewayo would not be restored, it was very probable that the people would have broken out very much in the same way as they had done at present. Her Majesty's Government finding it was universally acknowledged that the Settlement was an unsatisfactory one, there were only two alternatives before them; and if the hon. Baronet would look at the Papers, and the information laid before the House at the time, he would easily see what those alternatives were. One alternative was the restoration of Cetewayo; and the other alternative was annexation. The hon. Baronet said just now, very accurately, that the fault of Sir Garnet Wolseley's Settlement was the want of a paramount authority. He (Mr. Evelyn Ashley) quite agreed with the hon. Baronet; but how was that paramount authority to be supplied? It could only be supplied by the restoration of Cetewayo, or by the substitution of the paramount authority of this country. The hon. Baronet, speaking in the House of Commons in 1882, said—

"If the state of things described continued, it would undoubtedly be the duty of Her Majesty's Government to interfere and put an end to it—by deposing those Chiefs who behaved in this outrageous manner; by strengthening the hands of the British Resident; and by appointing, if necessary, more Residents and Magistrates."—(*Ibid.*)

But to appoint more Residents and magistrates was virtually to annex the country; and he (Mr. Evelyn Ashley) would, in a short time, when they approached the question as to the present condition of the Reserve, show that we were, in spite of ourselves, approaching very rapidly the condition where its annexation might become necessary. Well, then, as he had said before, the Government had before them, by universal consent, only two alternatives, and they chose the alternative which he believed the nation thought the wiser—namely, that of restoring Cetewayo, and creating a permanent Native power, in preference to annexing Zululand and making British rule permanent. It was said that the restoration of Cetewayo was a mistake, and he did not deny that it had failed to restore peace and order to Zululand; but he confessed, at the same time, that it was a far happier solution of the question that Cetewayo should have returned to his own country and fallen, as he had done, a victim to his own impetuosity, than that he should have died a captive in our hands. We had, at all events, escaped the obloquy that would have attached to his dying in captivity. But had the Settlement failed by any fault of the English Government, or was it a Settlement manifestly foredoomed to failure, and a Settlement that no set of reasonably wise men would have proposed? He maintained that it was not a Settlement that had failed owing to the action of the British Government, and that it was not an experiment absolutely foredoomed to fail. The hon. Baronet the Member for Midhurst told them that he condemned the Zulu War, and always had done so; and in his speech on the 17th of April he said that Cetewayo never broke his pledges, but constantly sought the assistance and advice of the Lieutenant Governor of Natal and of Sir Theophilus Shepstone, and almost always acted upon the advice they gave. [Sir HENRY HOLLAND: That was before he was deposed.] Yes; but they should judge of a man's character by his antecedents. Such was the character given Cetewayo by the hon. Baronet himself. It was naturally supposed that his captivity, instead of destroying those good qualities, would have strengthened them. It was the belief of the Government that Cetewayo was capable of taking the good advice offered to him; and he (Mr. Evelyn Ashley) asserted that Cetewayo would have succeeded after his restoration, if it was not that he took the advice of people who pretended to be his friends, but who were not so far-seeing as they ought to have been. He spoke of people whom he would not name, both in this country and in Natal, who seemed, in the case of Cetewayo, to have raked up the old doctrine of the divine right of Kings, and who thought that Cetewayo had a right to rule over Zululand, the whole of Zululand, and nothing but Zululand. They told Cetewayo that he ought to be restored to the whole of his territory, that its reduction was wrong, that the establishment of the Reserve was unjust, and that if he only exerted himself sufficiently many friends in this country and elsewhere would assist him in regaining the whole of his old Kingdom. He (Mr. Evelyn Ashley) maintained that it was this advice which led Cetewayo

had not been for these

Cetewayo mistook for the voices of many.

important people, he would have been content with the territory over which he was placed. But while he said that the Government had no reason to suppose that the experiment they were going to make was foredoomed to failure, he owned it did fail; it failed entirely by the spontaneous action of Cetewayo himself. Usibebu was left in the North-Eastern corner of Zululand, for a very good and practical reason, and people dealing with public affairs must take a practical view of them. The practical reason in this case was, that Usibebu had so esconced himself in his position, that he could not be removed without the use of considerable force. The Government, therefore, recognized Usibebu. But the fact was, that Cetewayo was not only misled by officious friends and others; the savage nature of the Zulus also came to the fore, and the people were bent upon revenge. It was a most singular thing that not one of the speakers that day, who had dealt with the question of the invasion of the freebooters, had pointed out what was the turning point of the matter, when it was considered from the Government's point of view. The turning point really was that the Boers had come there at the pressing invitation of the inhabitants of Zululand themselves. It was not an invasion, in the strict sense of the term, although he very much believed that the Zulu people would suffer just as much as if it had been an invasion. The Boers received a deliberate invitation, and the majority of the Zulu people living in the centre of Zululand distinctly made up their minds that revenge was sweeter than land, and that they would part with their land, in order to buy the assistance of those who would revenge them on their enemy Usibebu. That was the secret of the whole matter. It was perfectly true that a Government like that of the Transvaal was responsible, to a great extent, for what happened on its frontier; but let him remind hon. Members what were the qualities of the people who engaged in these feuds. We talked about the frontier, but there was no frontier to them; they were a floating population, and were on one side of the frontier on one day, and on the other side the next day, ready to fight wherever profit led the way. What he wanted to point out to hon. Gentleman was, that though we had called on the Transvaal Government to use their authority to prevent the violation of their frontier, and the Transvaal Government had acknowledged their duty in that respect, and had put out proclamations strongly forbidding any violation of the frontier, it must be remembered that the freebooters were not a class of men over whom a Government like the Transvaal Government, which was not well established, and had no abundant means of repressing disorder, could exercise any great control. Well, then, he maintained that the Zulus had, by reason of their own spontaneous action, caused the incursion of Boers. We were, therefore, to a very great extent, absolved from protecting them in any way from the evils which they had so deliberately brought upon themselves. It had been said by some hon. Members to-night that when the death of Cetewayo occurred, we ought to have put the Natives in the position in which Cetewayo's restoration found them—that was to say, that upon the death of Cetewayo, we ought to have endeavoured to re-establish the Settlement of Sir Garnet Wolseley. Whether we ought to have done so or not he would not delay the Committee by arguing; but he would point out that the Government had very little time allowed them by the Zulus to exercise any moral influence, or any guidance, or give any advice, or send any messenger or Commissioner, if they had been disposed to do so. The moment the breath was out of Cetewayo's body, preparations were made to declare his successor. While these preparations were going on, the Usutus proceeded to perform certain rites of burial over Cetewayo, and then proceeded to attack Usibebu without any delay, calling on the Boers to assist them in their attack. There was an account given by Mr. Grant, who was the spokesman of the Usutu Party, which, if he could only lay his hands on it, he should be very glad to read to the Committee, because, on many occasions, the matter had been dealt with as a case in which this country was coercing the Usutus, in consequence of their presence in the Reserve, and most abominably injuring a lamb-like and civilized race. Mr. Grant was himself an advocate of the Usutu Party. He (Mr. Evelyn Ashley) could not lay his hand on Mr. Grant's statement; but he could recollect what it was. It would be included in the Papers which would be laid on the Table of the House in the course of a few days. Mr. Grant described the funeral rites of the Zulus, and said it was their habit, directly their King was buried, to go and "wash their spears," as a religious rite, in the blood, usually, of some neighbouring and defenceless tribe; but, as there was no defenceless tribe in this case, they performed the right by attacking Usibebu. So that the attack by the Usutus was a part of the burial ceremonial of Cetewayo. He did not wish to delay the Committee by going at any greater length into this matter. He had brought the case down to this point—that Cetewayo having died, Her Majesty's Government were allowed no time to exercise any moral influence, or give any advice for the settlement of Zulu affairs, for the reason that the Usutus, who were the majority of the Zulu race, at once, contemporaneously with the death of Cetewayo, plunged into an attack upon Usibebu, and called upon the Boers to assist them. This was all very deplorable, and he regretted it in the extreme; and he should like to ask hon. Gentlemen opposite to say at what point they would have had the British Government interfere? Did they mean to say that the British Government should have sent a body of troops to take the side of Usibebu? He admitted that his sympathies were on the side of Usibebu, who had shown himself a good tactician and a gallant man, and had proved himself the friend of England; but why were they to send troops to attack him, and to take part in a civil war taking place in Zululand? He could not follow that; and, short of annexation, he did not see that the Government could have done anything to prevent the state of things brought about by the ferocious spirit and general lack of civilization of the Zulu people, coupled with what the defects in the character of Cetewayo had brought into existence. The question now was, what were the Government to do in the future; and, what had the Government announced as their policy? Well, they had, first of all, declared that the Reserve Territory should be defended and maintained in good order; and he might tell the Committee that there was at that moment a very considerable body of British troops in the Reserve, ready to guard it against attacks from outside. In the Papers which would be laid on the Table of the House in the course of a few days, hon. Members would find recorded the attacks which had been made by the Usutu Party upon certain loyal Chiefs in the Reserve. They would see the means taken by the British Resident to put a stop to these attacks and violations of peace; and they would see that at present, owing to the energetic steps which had been taken, matters wore a much more peaceful and orderly aspect than they had some time ago. The hon. Member who had opened the discussion had made some reference to the defeat of Mr. Osborn, the British Resident. [Mr. GUY DAWNAY: No; to the attack on him.] He thought the hon. Member had implied that Mr. Osborn had been defeated; but, at any rate, the matter was not very important. He did not know what were the arguments which the hon. Member drew from the attack, except that the Reserve was not maintained in that state of order in which it ought to be. He could only say that the attack was made upon Mr. Osborn most unexpectedly, and was the first sign of the real activity of the rebellious element in the Reserve. When Mr. Osborn knew that this rebellious spirit existed he retired some distance, and communicated with the Governor of Natal and the Officer in command of the Forces, who took such steps as succeeded in absolutely coercing and overcoming the disturbing elements in the Reserve. The hon. Member, therefore, might take it for granted that when the House had these things brought before it, it would see that nothing had been wanting on the part of the Government to vindicate the position and authority of England within the Reserve. That policy would be continued in the future. But he would point out to those hon. Members who talked about extending the Reserve, that the question would become one of incorporating surrounding land. We had a considerable body of troops in the Reserve, and very likely they would have to be retained for some time; and he demurred entirely to the statement of the hon. Member for Midhurst, that if the principle of the Reserve had been extended over a very large part of Zululand, they could have acted without any large body of troops.

SIR HENRY HOLLAND said, he had not advocated the extension of the Reserve, but a development of the system of Residents, as advocated by Sir Henry Bulwer—the substitution of the guiding authority of Residents for the present system.

MR. EVELYN ASHLEY said, that would have involved much larger measures, both civil and military, than the Government had thought it expedient to adopt. The Papers which would be laid on the Table of the House very shortly would, he believed, show that as far as the Reserve was concerned the Government had done what they ought to do. As to the Transvaal Border, the Government were still considering whether, under the provisions of the Convention, they should appoint a Resident on the Border or not. Of course, the matter was more difficult and complicated now than it was a short time ago, owing to the action of the Zulus. ["Oh, oh!"] No less an authority than Sir Hercules Robinson had told them that, in the present state of things, the matter was much more difficult to deal with than it was a short time ago. With regard to what was said a little earlier as to calling on the Transvaal Government to appoint a Resident, what he had stated the other day was, that it would be premature to do that at the present moment, for the reason that the Convention had not been ratified by the Volksraad. It would be better to wait to see if the Convention was ratified. When he said that things were now more complicated than they were a short time ago, some hon. Gentlemen opposite had chuckled. His point was, that what had complicated matters during the last three or four months was the action of the Zulus themselves. The Zulus would have followed the same line of conduct, whether a Resident had been on the Transvaal Border or not. They would have sacrificed everything to their desire for revenge against Usibebu. He wished, before concluding, to allude to the speech of his hon. Friend the Member for Bath (Mr. Wodehouse). That hon. Member, in very eloquent language and largely-extended views, had told them that they must everywhere, and at once, assert the Suzerainty of England in South Africa, if they wanted to maintain the supremacy of this country in that quarter of the globe. He would only say one word on the point, and that was, that the future of British rule and influence in South Africa depended a great deal more, in his humble opinion, upon the action of the Anglo-Saxons, as individuals and communities, than on the action of the Imperial Government. They must remember the very curious circumstances of the South African Colonies. They could not have it repeated too often—because it was the key to the whole of our difficulties in that part of the world—that though, in common language, these Colonies were called "British," yet the British-speaking and British-educated Colonists were in a distinct minority. Not only at the Cape, but in Natal itself, at least half, or more, were Dutch. But he would point out something still more peculiar—namely, that this distinction of race and language was coincident with the distinct condition and pursuits, and, therefore, with the aims and aspirations, of the Colonists, because the British-speaking part of the population would be found almost entirely in the towns, carrying on trades; whilst the Dutch and Africander races would be found in the country districts, carrying on the pursuit of farming. All the crucial, perpetual difficulties in South Africa were owing to the coming together of these different races, holding diametrically opposite views, not only from their habits, but also from their interests. They had, on the one hand, the British element, desiring to see the Native races prosper, and increase, and live in safety, in order that they might carry on trade with them; and, on the other hand, they had the Dutch element, the land seekers and landowners, desiring to see the Native races more or less swept out of the way, in order that they might enter into possession of their land. They had these two elements constantly at variance. Which of the two was to succeed in the long run? He ventured to say that the future of that country must depend upon the British people, quite apart from the Imperial Government. He confessed he deprecated any rivalry of races; but the facts were there, and were not to be got rid of by simply ignoring them. If the emigration from these shores to the shores of South Africa was large, and if the enterprize and perseverance of the Anglo-Saxon race continued to be what it was, then the future was with us; and, in that case, he ventured to prophesy that the Mother Country, whatever Government might be in power, would not be backward in protecting and maintaining the elements of British influence there. But if emigration from the Mother Country was small, if enterprise fell off, and if the Colonists in South Africa were disposed to look too much—as they were very often—not to their own exertions for the prosperity of the Colony, but to the expenditure of Imperial money, to deliver them from the stagnation of trade; if the men of the Africander and Dutch races increased in numbers and power, while the others remained stationary or declining, it would only be a mistake on the part of the Imperial Government to try to bolster up what would be a dying interest. He was only speaking his own opinion in these matters; but it seemed to him that to engage in such expeditions as had often been advocated by hon. Members of the House into countries which had not yet been occupied by a civilized race, which were far removed from the centres of population—partly abandoning countries not yet peopled for the purpose—expeditions, whether over the Zulu border, the Zwasi border, or the Amatonga border, would entail unfortunate and useless responsibilities, and would not really and truly tend to what hon. Members desired, and what he himself certainly desired—namely, the extension and maintenance of the British name in South Africa. No; let them consolidate what they had got. Let them consider every question put before them which required the acceptance of new responsibilities in South Africa as forming a part of a whole question, and not as new and separate questions. He had no doubt it was perfectly easy to prove that if Zululand were the only place in which we had responsibilities, actual or accruing, it would be an infinitely better thing for Zululand, for Natal, and for this country, that Zululand should be annexed. But that was not the fact. It was necessary to convince men who were responsible for the whole of the Empire, and who had the same call coming from a thousand different places—from New Guinea, Basutoland, Walfisch Bay, Bechuanaland, and elsewhere—that the responsibility ought to be assumed. He ventured to submit that Her Majesty's Government were, no doubt, as successors of a former Government, responsible for the disturbed state of Zululand; and, before he sat down, he would just answer what had fallen from the hon. Member who made the Motion they were discussing with regard to their saying nothing more as to the heritage of the Zulu War. He could only answer the hon. Member as he had answered a Conservative Friend of his, who had said—"I am sick of hearing you all talk of the heritage left by the late Government." He had replied—"My dear Sir, you are not half so sick of hearing of it as I am of dealing with it." That was the feeling of the Colonial Office on this matter. There was a responsibility imposed on Her Majesty's Government by the heritage of the Zulu War, and the affairs of Cetewayo and the Zulu people; and, he imagined, they had done the best they could, short of taking the step they had declined to take in the past, and must still decline to take in the future—namely, the annexation of Zululand to the Empire.

Lord RANDOLPH CHURCHILL: We have been told, from authoritative sources, that the policy of the Tory Party, at the present moment, is to force an appeal to the people. Certainly, no stronger argument in favour of such an appeal could have been well adduced than the appearance of the House of Commons ever since half-past 12 this afternoon; because, although this is a matter of first-class Imperial importance, as everyone will admit, and although it is a question in which the Liberal Party are supposed, as a whole, to be animated by the strongest and most ardent views — they, in particular, posing as the champions of aboriginal races, and as the friends of nationality — there has not, to my knowledge, since the debate began, been an attendance of 20 Liberal Members in the House. I think if that is the state of the House, at a period of the Session not too far advanced for an important discussion on a matter of Imperial concern—if you cannot get 20 Liberal Members to give the Government the assistance of their counsels—it is not a bad argument in favour of the construction of a new House of Commons, and an appeal to the people. The hon. Gentleman the Under Secretary for the Colonies (Mr. Evelyn Ashley) has made a speech of some length and immense pretensions. He appeared to sug-

to imagine that he was, for the moment, filling the place of the Prime Minister, and to be making as good an imitation as he could of the manner, the great eloquence, and the variety of expression which that right hon. Gentleman usually exhibits. The object of the hon. Gentleman was excellent, but the performance fell very short of the object. His whole tone appeared to be extremely didactic, but the substance of the speech was extremely feeble. The hon. Gentleman seemed to me to have been studying recently some child's "Guide to South Africa," and to have detailed from it some elementary information about the geography of that country to the House of Commons. There were one or two points in his address which deserve brief notice. In the first place, he freely admitted the total failure of the policy of the Government with regard to Cetewayo. Well, Sir, I do not know what state of mind other hon. Members may be in, but, for my own part, I am getting extremely tired of these confessions of total failure. We have never yet discussed the question of South Africa without the Government admitting that their policy has been "a total failure." Their policy with respect to the Transvaal, Bechuanaland, Basutoland, and now Zululand, has been admitted by the right hon. Gentleman the President of the Board of Trade and the Under Secretary of State for the Colonies to be a total failure. Five or six times in succession—as regularly as these subjects come before us—it is notified by the Under Secretary of State for the Colonies or by the President of the Board of Trade, at the Table, that the policy of the Government has totally failed. But it is not only on these subjects that the House has had to listen to these confessions of failure. The House has listened to the confession of the total failure of the Government's Irish land legislation, and of their Egyptian policy, before now. For the sake of variety, to say nothing of the credit of the Government, if only once in a way, I could wish they had been able to announce some slight success. The Under Secretary of State for the Colonies was extremely frank, and said—"I admit that our policy with regard to the restoration of Cetewayo was a total failure; but it was not a failure which was foredoomed, or which any reasonable man could anticipate. The failure was entirely owing to the Liberal Party, and," he said, "especially the advanced wing of the Liberal Party." ["No, no!"] Yes; those were his words, and that was the only interpretation any man of sense could place upon his observations. The hon. Gentleman said the restoration of Cetewayo would have been gloriously successful, and that Cetewayo would have been at this moment King of Zululand, if it had not been for the bad advice given to him by the Liberal Party, especially the advanced wing of the Liberal Party. So far, indeed, is this a cause of failure, that it seems to me to be one—to use a French expression—which "jumps to the eye." You might be certain that the advice given from such a quarter to the King of a historic race would be one that would necessarily lead him to his ruin. The hon. Gentleman used the words—"The policy of restoring Cetewayo was, in the opinion of Her Majesty's Government, inaugurating a reign of peace;" but, a little farther on, he proceeded to say—"I do not deny that the present condition of Zululand is wretched in the extreme." Now, when we have Ministers getting up at the Table and making statements of that kind, what are we to conclude, except that the whole Colonial policy of Her Majesty's Government is defective, from beginning to end? The restoration of Cetewayo was the subject of a debate in this House some two years ago, and, fortunately, by the kindness of some unknown friend, I have come across an article on Zululand in a highly respectable journal—a journal whose views, I think, on ecclesiastical doctrines, will recommend themselves to the Prime Minister—I mean *The Guardian*. In this article an expression used by the Prime Minister was quoted—an expression of immense value at this moment. When the policy of Her Majesty's Government in restoring Cetewayo was under consideration, it was said—

"The subject was brought forward two years ago, and the Prime Minister was kind enough to express sympathy with the Monarch in his adversity; but he said that it must be remembered that the peace and welfare of the country ought to be the dominant consideration; and he went on to remark that Cetewayo's release, unless desired by the great body of the Zulu people, would be a new cause of political disturbance and of the extensive shedding of blood. And he said, further, that a restoration bereft of such result would be no relief to the responsibility we had already incurred; on the contrary, he thought there would be a very serious addition to that responsibility."

Well, Sir, the Prime Minister, having stated that Cetewayo's release would be likely to produce extensive shedding of blood, shortly after consented to that restoration, and we are now told by the Under Secretary of State for the Colonies that that was a policy which no reasonable man could see was foredoomed to fail. Then the Prime Minister states that the restoration of Cetewayo, if effected, would greatly increase the responsibility of Her Majesty's Government. [Mr. GLADSTONE: Unless desired.] The article says—

"And he said, further, that a restoration bereft of such result would be no relief to the responsibility we had already incurred; on the contrary, he thought there would be very serious addition to that responsibility."

How do they meet that responsibility? The condition of Zululand is wretched in the extreme, and the Under Secretary of State for the Colonies gets up and states that the policy of Her Majesty's Government will never, under any circumstances and conditions, be a policy which can lead to any extension of British authority in Zululand. I submit to the House that there is a total, obvious, and complete contradiction between what the Prime Minister said two years ago, and what the Under Secretary of State for the Colonies has said to-night. I do not think it at all possible to acquit Her Majesty's Government of carelessness in respect to the carrying out of their policy, because how was Cetewayo restored? He was restored to a small and most barren and unproductive portion of his territory. The British Government took away from him an enormous slice of Zululand, which they called "the Reserve," and gave another slice to Usibebu, and then they expected that this Monarch, who had been dethroned, and had lost his prestige beforehand by being defeated by the British Forces, would be able to assert himself as King of Zululand. They expected this of him, although they had sent him back in that degraded and humiliated and diminished way. I venture to say that if the restoration had been carried out in a larger and broader manner, there is no reason to suppose it would have failed; but the means the Government took to carry out their policy were the means that foredoomed it to fail.

Before I leave the speech of the Under Secretary of State for the Colonies I should like to notice one more argument. He said, in the lengthy peroration with which he concluded his remarks, that he regretted to say there were some hon. Members on his own side who were anxious that British Sovereignty should be asserted in South Africa. We know that there are opinions of that kind—heretical, sadly heretical opinions—amongst some Members of the Liberal Party. Only yesterday, some Members of the Liberal Party, under the presidency of the right hon. Gentleman the Member for Bradford (Mr. W. E. Forster), met for the purpose of advocating a very large extension of British Sovereignty and Imperial rule, and I imagine the Under Secretary of State must have had that meeting in his mind when he spoke so bitterly of people who wished British Sovereignty to be asserted in South Africa. But what was the reason he gave against British Sovereignty being asserted in South Africa? Why, it was that the British Colonists were in a minority. That was the convincing reason why British Sovereignty, instead of being asserted, should rather be withdrawn. Apply that argument to India. How would your British Sovereignty succeed in India if, because you are in a minority, it must not be asserted? Apply the argument, again, to Ireland. How many "British-speaking" and "British-educated" subjects are there in Ireland who are in favour of British Sovereignty? They are in a minority; and I think, therefore, that the great theory of Colonial and Imperial policy, which the Under Secretary of State has laid down, though it may be accepted in his own Department, is one which it will be very useful and advantageous for us, his political opponents, to develop before the enlightened constituencies of the country. I venture to think that in all these matters there are two things which Her Majesty's Government ought to consider, and one thing that they ought not to consider; and the one thing they ought not to consider they have considered, while the two things they ought to have considered they have not given a thought to. In the first place, they ought to consider the interests of the Colony of Natal; and, secondly—and only secondary to that—they ought to consider the interests of

Zululand. What they need not consider —the parties whose interests they need not consider are the Boers. Those who have absolutely no claim or title for one moment to their consideration are the Boers and the Boer Republic, for whom they have, up to now, sacrificed almost every shred of their dignity. The whole of our difficulties in South Africa—our modern difficulties, for I decline altogether to go back to what occurred under the late Government, that being, if you like, ancient history—the whole of the difficulties which the Committee is considering, spring from the surrender to the Transvaal Boers which took place in 1881—that utterly disgraceful and cowardly surrender of a British Army, nearly 10,000 strong, admirably equipped, with one of our best Generals at its head, before a parcel of undrilled, plundering, freebooting Boers, whom they could easily have swept from off the face of the earth. That is the origin of all these difficulties. All along the Government has been frightened of these Transvaal Boers. I took down the expression of the Under Secretary of State—"Under the last Convention the Government have a right to appoint a Commissioner-Resident upon the frontier of Zululand and Boerland. But," says the hon. Gentleman, "we cannot appoint a Resident now, because the Zulus" —he ought to have said the Usutus— "have invited the Boers into Zululand; and, that being the case, we can no longer proceed—in fact, we dare not proceed—to put in force an important Article of the Convention just concluded." Therefore, I am right in my statement that, in all these matters, the Government are actuated by fear of the Boers. It seems ridiculous to say it; but you can hardly doubt the truth of it when Her Majesty's Government, with a great Army in the field which could, by no possibility, have been checked, first of all begged for a Convention, and concluded one which was repudiated and broken in every Article by the Boers, then begged for another, and concluded that also—the Boers sending over Ambassadors to negociate it—and when you find the Under Secretary of State now getting up and saying—"We dare not, under the circumstances, appoint a Resident to carry out the Article of the Convention." What is the state of things existing in Zululand? Why the same state of things which existed in Bechuanaland. You have the freebooting Boers there, and you know that the result of their operations in Bechuanaland was that a large part of the country was cut off and handed to them, and that there existed there any amount of slaughter, disturbance, and disorder, and plundering, cruelty, and misery of every kind. The same condition of things is coming about in Zululand, under the eyes of the House of Commons. The Boers, in spite of their Treaty with you, invade the country. How can it be expected that the quibble, the colourable statement, by the Under Secretary of State, that they were invited there, will satisfy the House of Commons? *The Guardian* says—

"By the help of some hundreds of these Boers the loyal Chief Usibebu, made independent by us, has been attacked with great slaughter and driven from his territory."

And it goes on to say that hundreds of thousands of acres have been taken, and are in process of being taken away, from the Native races who are ruined. I do not think that is a bit too strong. What I want to point out to the House of Commons is this—that the same state of things, which the House of Commons felt so deeply about Bechuanaland last year—and which, but for their great respect for the Prime Minister and the great hold he, personally, had upon them, his own Party would have censured—is coming about in Zululand. It is absolutely impossible that the statement of the Under Secretary of State for the Colonies can satisfy this House. You said you would not undertake the protection of Basutoland. You have been obliged to protect it. You said you would not undertake the protection of Bechuanaland; but that is now under the protection of the British Crown; and so it will be with Zululand. At least, if Her Majesty's Government will not recognize their responsibilities in South Africa, the country will place other persons in their place who will do so.

MR. W. E. FORSTER: I will only detain the Committee a short time; and I should not rise at all to take part in the debate, if I did not feel that the speeches we have heard to-day have regard quite as much to the principle on which the action of Her Majesty's Government should be based as to the actual measures which have been proposed, and that some remarks have been made which I could hardly hear without rising to pro est against. My hon. Friend the Member for Bath (Mr. Wodehouse) made a speech, which I was very sorry there were not more hon. Members present to hear—a speech evidently of great thought, and, as it seemed to me, of remarkable ability, as well as power. He was followed by my hon. Friend the Member for Burnley (Mr. Rylands), who attributed to him and his speech views which he entirely disowned. The hon. Gentleman attributed to the hon. Member for Bath the advocacy of spread-eagle Imperialism. I cannot accept that definition of my hon. Friend's speech; for what I understood my hon. Friend to be advocating was, that where we incurred responsibilities, we should fulfil them; and if we were not prepared to take that line, I understood him to say we had better creep out of the country as soon as possible; and I think he is quite right. My hon. Friend the Member for Burnley evidently thinks it due to the taxpayers of this country, that matters in Zululand should be left alone, and left to take care of themselves, and that we should see that no money is spent on the place, and that no troops, under any circumstances, are sent out there. Well, the whole meaning of that policy is, that we should withdraw from South Africa altogether. If we are to remain in Zululand at all, we must bear in mind the responsibilities we have undertaken. It is said that it is a mere question of pounds, shillings, and pence. If that is the case, we may meet our difficulties there at the present moment by a comparatively small expenditure; whereas, if we wait until these difficulties have increased, we shall have to incur a great and an unknown expenditure. Let us keep to the particular matter before us. I am not going to say a word about past history, or, as my hon. Friend the Under Secretary of State for the Colonies (Mr. Evelyn Ashley) calls it, the ancient history of the subject, except in so far as it bears upon our actual position in Zululand at the present moment, and upon the responsibilities which we have undertaken there. I, like many others, was opposed to the original Zulu War, but it was undertaken. The Zulus were defeated, and the King of Zululand was deposed. We did not feel at that time that, in destroying the only recognized Government of that country, we had divested ourselves of all responsibility for the future of the country; and certainly the English Government did not then attempt to take that line, and, had they done so, the people of England would have protested against their action. Whether wisely or unwisely, an arrangement was then entered into with 12 or 13 of the Native Chiefs. The arrangement was open to a great deal of objection. There were grave doubts as to how far peace and order could be maintained; but the arrangement, upon the whole, worked quite as well as could have been expected, and, perhaps, rather better. Then came the restoration of Cetewayo, and that was a matter upon which I do not agree with many of my hon. Friends with whom I generally act in these matters. I agreed with what fell upon the subject from the Prime Minister—as quoted by the noble Lord—"that we had to consider the peace and welfare of the country." I had grave doubts whether any Chief—above all, any savage Chief—who had been deposed, could be sent back to rule the country with any great chance of peace, especially after the English Government had entered into an arrangement with these 13 Kinglets, under which they had parcelled out the country among them, but which was set aside on the restoration of Cetewayo. It was impossible for Cetewayo to be restored, without infringing on this arrangement. Therefore, I think the arrangement was foredoomed to great difficulty, though, perhaps, not necessarily to failure. It could not be expected that these 13 Kinglets, or any number of them, would willingly subject themselves to the rule of this man whom we sent out. What has been the result of such a policy? I do not want to throw blame upon either the present or the past Government. The Zulu question is difficult and complicated beyond measure, and I think anyone would be most unreasonable who complained of the present or even the past Government, and did not sympathize with their difficulties. What are the actual circumstances of the case? We have to deal with this country, which is in a state of disturbance and disorder owing to our action—a state of disorder for which we are responsible. In consequence of our having set aside our own arrangement, the country is in a state of warfare and bloodshed, and for that state of things we are in some measure, certainly, responsible. It has been remarked that the Zulus have dreadful customs, such as washing their spears in each other's blood. So they have, undoubtedly; but they appear to have washed their spears in rather a more bloody manner within the last two or three years than they did before. How can we regard such a state of things, which has been brought about by our own action, and say, with any degree of self-respect or without shame, that, having got the Zulus into this state, we will leave them to kill one another off in order to save ourselves from further trouble? I do not think that we can safely leave matters there. When the hon. Member spoke about the future of Zululand, I confess, if he will allow me, good-naturedly, to say so, what he told us about the future was very little indeed. His plan for the future appeared to be limited to the protection of the Reserve Territory—which is absolutely necessary. No one would think for a moment about not protecting it. His plan, however, appears to be limited to the protection of the Reserve, and the production of some fresh Papers. I do not think he gives us an idea as to how we are to deal with these difficult circumstances. Difficult, however, as they are, the Government will have to deal with them, and to feel that they have some responsibility for the warfare that is going on in Zululand, and that it is their duty to try and see how it can be stopped. I believe it will be found, in the long run, that duty and expediency go together, and that the fulfilment of our responsibilities is, after all, the most economical course. As regards the actual matter, what is likely to happen? In consequence of having left this country entirely to itself, after having, by our arms and by our arrangements, utterly disorganized it, freebooting adventurers are coming over from both borders—not only from the Transvaal, but also from Natal—and fermenting disorders, and the opinion of those in South Africa best fitted to judge is that the danger will not be confined to Zululand, but will spread to Natal itself. The instant that danger is realised, economy will be no longer considered, and we shall send over a Force which will probably cost 10 or 100 times the sum for which Lord Derby is informed the whole difficulty can now be settled. I must acknowledge that I am not sufficiently acquainted with the subject to take upon myself to recommend to Her Majesty's Government the adoption of any particular course; but I am convinced of this, that, whatever be the difficulties, the Government cannot rest contented with merely protecting the Reserve Territory, but must feel that it is their duty to try and restore that peace and order which we, by our arms first, and then by our diplomacy, and next, and lastly, by our change in that diplomacy, disturbed.

MR. CHAMBERLAIN: I think the right hon. Gentleman (Mr. W. E. Forster), in the speech that he has just made, and to which we have attentively listened, has merely emphasized the difficulties which have been brought into view in the course of this debate; and his observations go to show that there are only two alternative policies which can be adopted by this country in reference to Zululand. In the first place, there is the policy which has been adopted and defended by Her Majesty's Government—that of interfering as little as possible with the internal affairs of Zululand. We have come to the decision to abstain from all such interferences, and to accept the policy of our Predecessors, so far as to refuse any proposal in any shape or form for the annexation of the country. That policy has been condemned as strongly as possible by the hon. Member for the North Riding of Yorkshire (Mr. Guy Dawnay). The hon. Member made us a very eloquent and very interesting speech at the commencement of this discussion, and the only criticism that I shall make upon it is to say that it was too emphatic, and rather too full of superlatives. The hon. Member described our policy as "ghastly," "vile," "infamous," "consummate folly," "murderous," and as "dictated by fear of the scoundrelly and infamous Boers." I admire very much his command of invective and adjectives; but I followed with still greater interest his subsequent remarks, in which he proposed an alternative policy for our acceptance. I find that the hon. Member was in favour of what is called "expansion of the Empire." He was in favour of a policy which practically would amount to the annexation of the whole of Zululand—of a policy which would have entailed the annexation of the Transvaal. If I were to imitate the style of the hon. Member, I should be entitled to say that that would be a blundering policy, a plundering policy, a policy of pick-pockets, filibusters, and brigands. At all events, without developing the argument any further in the style of the hon. Member, I would say that, while I am prepared to accept the statement just made by my right hon. Friend (Mr. W. E. Forster), that this country is bound to fulfil the responsibilities which it has undertaken, I am also of opinion that it is bound to look all round to see whether it has not responsibilities at home as well as in these distant places, and to inquire whether it would be wise and judicious to undertake new responsibilities from which so little advantage can possibly be expected to result to anyone. Well, Sir, I think the House listened with some amusement to the rather extraordinary speech of the noble Lord the Member for Woodstock (Lord Randolph Churchill). The noble Lord commenced his observations by referring to the state of the House when he was addressing it, as a proof of the lack of interest taken in the question. I do not think there is any lack of interest in it, either on the Liberal or Conservative side; but I think, perhaps, it is rather natural, at this late period of the Session, and when the House has been sitting until 3, 4, or 5 o'clock in the morning on previous nights, that no very large attendance should be brought down on a Wednesday afternoon to listen to a discussion that is understood to be somewhat hollow in its character, and, above all, to listen to the noble Lord the Member for Woodstock, when—to use an expression of his own—"careering" about a subject with which he has the smallest possible amount of practical acquaintance. The noble Lord says that I and my hon. Friend (Mr. Evelyn Ashley) on this and on previous occasions have admitted the failure of their policy. I confess I do not plead guilty to ever having made any such admission, and I certainly have not heard such admission made by the Under Secretary of State for the Colonies. What my hon. Friend really did say was, that the state of Zululand was not, at the present time, entirely satisfactory. It would hardly be expected that the policy of the Government, or of anyone else, could secure a perfectly satisfactory state of Zululand in the course of a few months. The state of Zululand is now very much what it has been ever since the country was disturbed by the policy of the late Government, and by the policy of the Zulu War. From that time down to the present day, the state of Zululand has been unsatisfactory. All that can be said of us is, that our policy of non-intervention has not resulted in a satisfactory state of things. The noble Lord went on to say that the condition of affairs in Zululand was owing to Cetewayo having been left with a miserably small portion of territory when he was restored. The noble Lord is perfectly aware that two-thirds of the whole territory ruled over by Cetewayo was restored to him. [Lord RANDOLPH CHURCHILL: No, no!] That is perfectly true, as the noble Lord will see if he will study the map on a large scale. The fact is, that if the whole of the country was not restored to him, it was because we took the view which has been put before the Committee by the right hon. Member for Bradford, that having come under obligations to the Kinglets, by reason of Sir Garnet Wolseley's Settlement, we did not think it right to hand them over, against their will, to the restored Chief. My right hon. Friend the Member for Bradford made a statement, in which he followed, I think, the hon. Baronet the Member for Midhurst (Sir Henry Holland). He said that, after all, the arrangement with Sir Garnet Wolseley for setting up these Chieftians was working satisfactorily, when the restoration of Cetewayo was contemplated by the Government. Nothing could be further from the truth than that statement. In this House, on the occasion of the last debate, there was not a single Member who did not admit that the state of the country was wholly unsatisfactory; that the Settlement made by the late Government, or by Sir Garnet Wolseley, under their instructions, had absolutely and entirely failed. In order to be quite certain about this, let me ask the Committee to listen to two quotations giving an account of the state of the country before the restoration of Cetewayo. The first, which I take from the Blue Books, is this—

"The relations between Ohamu and his too powerful subject Umnyamana, which were, from the first, unfriendly, became this year strained almost to the point of war. Ohamu was also defied by the tribe of the Amaquilisi, living in the north of his territory, who, no doubt, acted under the influence of Umnyamana. The authority of Usibebu, another of our 13 nominees, was persistently resisted by Undabuku and Usiwetu, two of Cetewayo's brothers. Umlandela, another of our nominees, was driven out of his territory by Sitimela, a grandson of Dingewayo, Chaka's Predecessor; and Sitimela, who perhaps aspired to reunite Zululand under his own rule, was joined by Somkeli, himself one of the nominated Chiefs. Three other selected Chiefs, Chingwayo, Seketwayo, and Unfanawenahlela, reported at different times that they were being opposed by their people, whom they could not control—the reason being apparently in some cases that they had been imitating the tyrannies which popular belief ascribes to Cetewayo."

In fact, according to this statement, and to other statements which will be found in the Blue Books, there was hardly a single portion of the territory that was not, at the time of the restoration of Cetewayo, the scene of tumult, disorder, and massacre. In April, 1882, speaking in the debate on Zululand in this House, the hon. and learned Member for Chatham (Mr. Gorst), I think, quoted a passage from a letter dated October 27th, written by the Rev. R. Robertson, in Zululand. The hon. Member for the North Riding of Yorkshire (Mr. Guy Dawnay) has told us that the policy of Her Majesty's Government had led to inter-tribal slaughter, which exceeded anything ever known since Zululand was annexed. I beg to call attention to this statement by Mr. Robertson, who is one of the missionaries in Zululand—

"You have heard, no doubt, of the recent slaughter of the Abagulusi. I am told it was greater than that of Isandlana. I fear there will be more yet. In fact, I am expecting every day to hear that the Usutu (Cetewayo's own tribe) have broken out. Their patience has been severely tried, and it needs just a little more provocation to bring about another crash. Maduna is strong enough to make mincemeat of Hamu and Zibebu any day. What he will end in doing, I know not."—(3 *Hansard*, [268] 766.)

MR. GUY DAWNAY: What is the date of the letter?

MR. CHAMBERLAIN: October 27th, 1881.

MR. GUY DAWNAY: What I said was, that the greatest slaughter ever known in Zululand had been during the last 18 months.

MR. CHAMBERLAIN: My object is absolutely to deny the statement of the hon. Member. I say that the disturbances previous to the restoration of Cetewayo were quite as serious as any that have since occurred. And let me say that, although Sir Henry Bulwer has been referred to several times as being opposed to the restoration of Cetewayo, his opposition was based, as his despatches show, entirely on the fear that, if Cetewayo was restored, the military power of the Zulus would be recreated, and great danger would arise in consequence to Natal. He admitted that the state of Zululand could not continue as it was previous to the restoration of Cetewayo, and he put before the Government in effect two alternatives. He said—

"Either you must consent to exercise paramount authority over the thirteen Chiefs, or you must endeavour to carry out the policy you prefer and restore some kind of Native authority."

Her Majesty's Government declined, without due consideration, to accept the suggestion of Sir Henry Bulwer to assume paramount British authority in Zululand, because they were convinced by all past experience—and subsequent experience has shown that they were right—that the creation of this British authority in Zululand would necessarily result in the practical annexation of the country. But having decided against that policy, then I think it was impossible to avoid the conclusion that, at all events, the restoration of Cetewayo was an experiment that ought to be tried. If the Zulu War was, as is admitted by the hon. Baronet opposite (Sir Henry Holland), so unjust and so unnecessary, then common justice required that Cetewayo should be restored, as far, at least, as was consistent with the engagements into which we had entered with the other Chiefs. But there is another reason—the reason of policy. Cetewayo's name, was, at all events, the most powerful name in Zululand, and the probabilities were more in favour of a peaceful settlement of the country under his leadership, than under the leadership of any other single Chief; and I entirely agree in what has been said by my hon. Friend the Under Secretary of State for the Colonies (Mr. Evelyn Ashley), that if he had been well advised, in all probability that Settlement might have been a lasting and satisfactory one. The proposals now made to us vary very much. The proposal of the hon. Member for the North Riding of Yorkshire is that we should extend the Reserve Territory to the Black Umvolosi. That would practically be to assume absolute control over two-thirds of Zululand. The proposal of the hon. Baronet the Member for Midhurst, although a little more specious, comes to practically the same result—that is, that we should exercise paramount authority over the country by means of British Residents and Magistrates. But who is to enforce that authority? It is absurd to tell us that the Zulu people would welcome these gentlemen among them. We know, from all past experience, that friction would inevitably arise, and then we should be called upon to defend the authority of the servants of the Crown by a British Army, and when we heard of bloodshed, we should be told that we were responsible for it. But suppose we adopted the plan of establishing authority on the Black Umvolosi, or extended the Reserve up to that line, there would still be Natives beyond that frontier, and Boers outside it. There would still be freebooters, and all the difficulties we have had we should be called upon to encounter still further away. What we have done has been to reserve the least possible amount of territory under our control which, in our opinion, was consistent with our obligations to those Chiefs who were unwilling to accept the rule of Cetewayo. We have reserved the territory of John Dunn, and have allowed fugitives from other parts of the country to come in and find security within that Reserve. The formation of this Reserve border is a protection to Natal. Either the noble Lord the Member for Woodstock (Lord Randolph Churchill) or the right hon. Gentleman the Member for Bradford (Mr. W. E. Forster) declared that the result of the Government policy had been to create danger to the Colony of Natal; but, as a matter of fact, on the contrary, a band of neutral and protected territory has been interposed been Natal and the country of the Zulus. Then there only remains the question of what responsibility falls upon this Bench with reference to the territory which is beyond the Reserve—the territory inhabited by the Basutos. The position there is truly and entirely due to those from whom we have inherited it. I agree with the opinion expressed by Sir Hercules Robinson, the High Commissioner. He is the best authority on such a subject; and while, as he says, he is reluctant to offer advice upon a matter which is not within his High Commissionership, he gives this opinion—

"I think it right to say that, in my opinion, we shall be spared future complications and questions if we define without further delay the precise limits of our obligations in relation to the Reserve Territory. Nothing short of a Protectorate over the whole of Zululand, supported by force, can prevent the eventual occupation by the Boers of a large portion North of the Reserve. I confess I do not see that we are bound to incur grave trouble and expense to save those outside the Reserve from the consequences of their own folly and misconduct."

Now, that is exactly the state of the case. The condition of affairs North of the Reserve is due to the folly and misconduct of the Chiefs in that part of the country. The noble Lord opposite (Lord Randolph Churchill) says it was a rotten pretext to pretend that an invitation was sent by the Basutos to the Boers; but there is most distinct evidence of invitations addressed to the Boers, probably by both parties, and certainly by the Basuto Party, and there is no doubt that portions of land have been awarded to these fortune-hunters. That is the commonest thing in South Africa. There is never a tribal conflict in which the Chiefs do not get the Whites in their neighbourhood on their side. Usibebu himself, who is now suffering from the interference of the Whites, had previously received assistance from the Whites against Cetewayo. Under these circumstances, it would be monstrous that we should involve the English taxpayer and the English people in responsibilities in order to prevent a state of things brought about by no fault of our own, and for which we are not in the slightest degree responsible. I will go further, and say that I am certain that we could not bring about a state of things which would offer a better chance of the settlement of this matter than the present system. Disturbances there must be, after such a war as that which destroyed and broke the power of the Zulu Chiefs; but it is absolutely untrue to say, as the hon. Member for the North Riding of Yorkshire said, that the rule of the

Boers over the Natives has been brutal and tyrannical. The proof is, that the Native population in the Transvaal has increased enormously and multiplied many-fold by the voluntary migration of the Natives into the Transvaal.

MR. GUY DAWNAY: I never said anything of the sort.

MR. CHAMBERLAIN: I should be sorry to misrepresent the hon. Member; but when he comes to read the report of his speech, he will find it was one of his contentions that we ought not to leave the country to the incursions of the Boer freebooters, because they were people of a low and barbarous civilization who had brutally ill-treated the Natives.

MR. GUY DAWNAY; I entirely agree in that; but I never said it to-day. The right hon. Gentleman is putting into my mouth words which I never used.

MR. CHAMBERLAIN: I am sorry to misrepresent the hon. Member. Will he state what he did say?

MR. GUY DAWNAY: The only expressions I used in reference to the Boers were applied to the Boer freebooters; those I called "infamous" and "scandalous." I never said a word about their ill-treating the Natives in the Transvaal.

MR. CHAMBERLAIN: I can assure the hon. Member that he does injustice to his own graces of oratory. He used, I think, many words equally abusive, and I am certain he will find that he did accuse the Boers of having ill-treated the population under their rule. But it is not necessary that I should say more about that, because I understand that the hon. Member admits that, if he did not say that to-day, he did say it on a previous occasion. Whenever he did say that, he was entirely mistaken as to the facts of the case. So far from the rule of the Boers being brutal and barbarous towards the Natives, it must be a very much better rule than the Natives have been accustomed to; otherwise, they would not have migrated in these enormous numbers into the Transvaal Territory. Although I do not pretend to say that the government of the Transvaal State is to be compared with the European civilization, I have no doubt it is an immense improvement on anything to which the Natives have been accustomed; and even if the result of this should be that the Boers acquire some footing in Zululand, I am not certain that that will constitute any disadvantage to the Natives, and certainly it will not cause any danger to British rule in South Africa. At any rate, it is a problem much too doubtful for us to undertake the responsibility urged upon us by the hon. Member; and, under no circumstances at present, can we indefinitely extend British rule in this part of South Africa, for such an extension would involve enormous additional responsibilities, and entail very serious fresh demands on the treasure and resources of this country.

SIR STAFFORD NORTHCOTE: Sir, I do not feel myself competent to decide the question between the right hon. Gentleman who has just sat down (Mr. Chamberlain) and my hon. Friend the Member for the North Riding of Yorkshire (Mr. Guy Dawnay). Although I heard a considerable part of my hon. Friend's very spirited speech, I did not happen to hear the portion which has given rise to so much controversy. It is quite clear, at all events, that between the opinion which my hon. Friend entertains of the Boers, and that which Her Majesty's Government, as represented by the right hon. Gentleman the President of the Board of Trade, hold, there is a very considerable difference, and a large amount of latitude. I am not going to trouble the Committee with a discussion of the question as to the precise mode in which the Boers have been in the habit of treating the Natives of this country. If they really deserve all the commendations which have been bestowed upon them by the right hon. Gentleman, I must say our position is very much more simple, and much less difficult, than I supposed; but I fear the general impression under which we have laboured for a long time is very different from that rather rose-coloured view which the right hon. Gentleman has taken. What I wish to call attention to is the barrenness and meagreness of the statements on the part of the Government with regard to the policy they have pursued. Whatever may be said about the past history of the Zulu question, and whatever charges may be made on the one side or the other with regard to particular events, there is no doubt that the matter has now come to that position in which we are, as a nation, deeply responsible for the condition of that country; and it is important that we should really have some assurance on the part of the Government that they are pursuing a policy which is likely to be for the benefit and safety both of our own Colony of Natal and of the Zulu people, in whom we have, or ought to have, great interest, and for whom we ought to entertain a sense of responsibility to a great extent. As far as I can gather, the policy of Her Majesty's Government was summed up by the right hon. Gentleman when he said it was their intention to interfere as little as possible with the internal affairs of the country. Accepting those words literally, I agree with the right hon. Gentleman that we ought to interfere as little as possible with the internal affairs of Zululand; but we have to take into consideration, and in connection with those affairs, the admission of the hon. Gentleman the Under Secretary of State for the Colonies (Mr. Evelyn Ashley) that we have responsibilities which we cannot get rid of, and that it is our duty, and part of the policy of the Government, to protect the Reserve Territory. If you have to protect the Reserve Territory, then you have to consider in what manner that it is to be done. It is all very well to say, as the hon. Member for Burnley (Mr. Rylands) said, that these are matters which will involve great questions and very great responsibilities on the part of this country. If you are to accept the view of the right hon. Gentleman the President of the Board of Trade in regard to the character of the Boers, and if you are to carry out the views of the hon. Member for Burnley, I suppose we might solve the whole question by retiring from the country and leaving everything to take its chance. But if we are not to leave things to take their chance, if we are to recognize certain responsibilities, and if we are to make ourselves responsible for the protection of the Reserve Territory, then it becomes a serious question whether we have such a policy as will reduce this responsibility to a minimum, and enable us to discharge the duties which devolve upon us in a manner which shall be the simplest, the easiest, and the best; and, therefore, it is a question, not whether we ought to interfere, but on what lines we ought to fulfil the duties which we acknowledge. My hon. Friend the Member for Midhurst (Sir Henry Holland), in the very temperate and able speech which he made this afternoon, and which I am sorry there were so few Members present to hear, laid down on broad lines, and, of course, avoiding questions of detail, what he considered to be the right policy to pursue—and that was to the effect that we ought to fall back on the lines of the Settlement of 1879; that we ought to take that for our main guidance, but in connection with that we ought to establish a Resident and Sub-Residents who should have certain powers with regard to the affairs of the Transvaal. But my hon. Friend said he would not interfere with the details of local government, and that his view was that we should hold a meeting of Chiefs; that those Chiefs should be in communication with us, and should establish the lines of a home policy which they would pursue, and to them should be left the administration of the country which belongs to them. It was not my hon. Friend's proposal—it was, as far as possible, from his intention—that we should accept or claim for ourselves anything approaching to annexation or a Protectorate. His object was that we should insure and guarantee to those Chiefs the right to administer their own affairs, and that we should maintain ourselves in a position which would give us authority, and enable us to settle questions that might arise. These questions are of two classes—questions which will arise among the Zulus themselves—quarrels among themselves, and disputes between the tribes; and then you have the difficulties that may arise between the tribes of the Zulus as a whole, and the Boers, their neighbours. Now, with respect to both the one and the other of these classes, I do not venture so much as to give my own opinion; I am rather speaking of what I understand to be the opinion of my hon. Friend, who is so well qualified to speak on these matters; and his opinion is, that you would prevent a great deal of difficulty from arising—which difficulty, if you do not prevent it, will arise sooner or later, and put you to much greater expense than you would otherwise incur—by being wise and firm in time. That is really the whole of the contention between, I will not say the two sides of the House, because there are several hon. Gentlemen on that—the opposite—side of the House, who take the same view, and who have expressed it extremely well, such as the hon. Member for Bath (Mr. Wodehouse) and the right hon. Member for Bradford (Mr. W. E. Forster), who have indicated that these are their opinions. Those are the two views of the subject, and I venture to think the experience we have had so far is decidedly in favour of that general policy advocated by my hon. Friend behind me (Sir Henry Holland), rather than that which is now indicated by Her Majesty's Government; and when we talk about these questions of the restoration of Cetewayo and other matters, we talk about them in order to show that, in the policy which Her Majesty's Government have carried out since they have had charge of this business, they have not been successful. The right hon. Gentleman the President of the Board of Trade was very angry with my noble Friend (Lord Randolph Churchill) for saying that their policy had failed, or that they had admitted that it had failed. The right hon. Gentleman said he had never said that it had failed; only that it had not succeeded. That, of course, is a distinction, and, no doubt, it is one satisfactory to the mind of the right hon. Gentleman; but what we want to point out is, that this policy which has not succeeded was a policy which was not very likely to succeed. At all events, it was undertaken only, as the right hon. Gentleman had said, as an experiment. It was an experiment which the Government may have been justified in trying; but it was an experiment which, when they tried it, certainly ended with a considerable amount of non-success; and it is to be remembered that when that policy was under the consideration of the Government, and before it was adopted, the Prime Minister himself pointed out to the House, as a reason for being slow in adopting such a suggestion, that if we did so, and the policy was not successful, the Government and the country would have incurred a large addition to their responsibilities. That is so. They adopted that policy, and they have incurred that additional responsibility, I will not say through any blameable motives, they were doing that which they considered was, on the whole, the best thing to do; but, undoubtedly; they did incur that additional responsibility; they did disturb and destroy the system which had been established but a very short time before, and which there was every prospect they might have maintained and improved. ["No, no!"] We say that this is the view we take, and my hon. Friend the Member for Midhurst brings forward the evidence upon which he supports his contention. I am not saying that everything before was perfect, or that when you began to talk of the restoration of Cetewayo, and of unsettling all that had been settled before, that then disturbances would arise; but I am speaking of a time when it was thought that that Settlement was to be maintained; and I think the evidence which my hon. Friend brings forward, as to the numbers of people returning to the country which they had left, seems to me to show very strongly that you were disturbing that which had considerable elements of hope in it, and that you were disturbing that new state of things, the result of which must have been felt to be very doubtful. That was the result at the time; but now we have very clear before us that the result was bad, and no longer doubtful. The result was the introduction of more troubles, more quarrels, and more bloodshed; and all that must be borne in mind in the presence of a further element in the question—namely, the settlement of the question with the Boers. It was not only the question of inter-tribal disturbances in Zululand; it was the encouragement given thereby to the Boer population in the neighbourhood to advance themselves into that country, to disturb the position of the inhabitants, and no doubt to cause a great deal of mischief which we, in our position, had no longer the means to stop or nip in the bud. My hon. Friend (Sir Henry Holland) sees the weakness of the position, as it stood under Sir Garnet Wolseley's Settlement. He sees that something more was required, and he suggested that that something might have been supplied in a manner which would not have involved annexation or a Protectorate, but would have put us in a position which would have enabled us to deal quickly and firmly with the domestic inter-tribal difficulties, and at the same time give us a position in which we could check the incursions and the depredations of the Boers. That is, I take it, the position of the case, and this discussion has been raised for the purpose of expressing dissatisfaction on the part of my hon. Friend (Sir Henry Holland) and others, with the course which matters have taken under the recent administration of the Government—of expressing our dissatisfaction and our uneasiness at the position of affairs there, and to endeavour to obtain, what I am afraid we have not yet obtained from the Government—namely, some more satisfactory statement of the policy which it is their intention to pursue than we have yet been favoured with.

MR. GLADSTONE: Sir, I do not feel in all respects dissatisfied with the speech of the right hon. Gentleman who has just sat down (Sir Stafford Northcote). I own myself to have been very considerably alarmed by the high-sounding doctrines of the noble Lord the Member for Woodstock (Lord Randolph Churchill); but nothing could be more remarkable, and nothing could offer a more glaring contrast, than the difference between his opinions on this subject, and those of the right hon. Baronet opposite who has just spoken. The whole sense of the noble Lord's speech was annexation and more annexation.

LORD RANDOLPH CHURCHILL: No; I beg pardon, it was not.

MR. GLADSTONE: The noble Lord says "No." Very well; then I will go a little further into detail. I am not speaking of the noble Lord's words; but I am putting my own construction upon his speech, and as he questions my construction, I want to know what he meant when he said that the restoration of Cetewayo would have succeeded if it had been undertaken on a larger basis, and in a bolder manner?

LORD RANDOLPH CHURCHILL: I meant if you had given back the whole of the country.

MR. GLADSTONE: Exactly so; so much for the basis; and now what is the bolder manner? To support Cetewayo by force, no doubt. To give him back the whole country—that is the cool recommendation of the noble Lord; but what had happened? We had made a Settlement in 1879. We had set up 13 Kinglets in Zululand. None of those men, so far as I recollect, had been guilty of any breach of faith to us. We had established them, and put authority into their hands. A large number of the people were I think, as was clearly shown to our satisfaction at the time, desirous of the return of Cetewayo; but a portion of them were determinedly opposed to the restoration; and these were the Kinglets whom we had set up, and who had committed no fault against us. The noble Lord says we ought to have deposed them, putting back Cetewayo in their place. That is the manner in which the noble Lord thinks a peaceable restoration might have taken place. That would have been a most gross breach of faith, which it was impossible for us to entertain for a moment, on the part of the Government. The noble Lord adopts a method of proceeding which really involves an assumption by us of authority over Zululand, and, if I understand him rightly, of authority over South Africa in general. That is what I understand the noble Lord to intend.

LORD RANDOLPH CHURCHILL: I did not say so.

MR. GLADSTONE: I am aware of that, and I am not using the noble Lord's own words; I am simply using every effort to construe what the noble Lord said; and, as I understood his high-sounding words as to the extension of British authority, I understood him to mean that the extension of British authority ought to be exercised over the Orange Free State and the Transvaal, in one form or another. *It is in that* view that I say the noble Lord is in glaring contrast to the right hon. Baronet. Now, I wish to come to the closing remarks of the right hon. Baronet. He says this debate has been raised for a certain purpose; and I agree with him that it has been raised for a very proper purpose. It was quite right that, in a matter of this kind, an opportunity should be taken before the close of the Session to discuss the difficulties of our position in Zululand; but the right hon. Gentleman says that the Settlement which was set up in 1879 was working in a tolerable manner; that there was something to be desired which ought to be supplied; but that, on the whole, the Settlement was not unsatisfactory, and our fault was that we did not endeavour to improve it. Now, the right hon. Gentleman, I conclude, was not present in this House on April 17th, 1882, when that subject was discussed for a whole evening; for if he had been present, or if he had read that debate, he would have been struck of that which is evidently at present totally unknown to him—namely, that while we debated that subject through an entire evening, while the hon. and learned Member for Chatham (Mr. Gorst) made a very able speech, exhibiting the deplorable condition of, and the almost prevalence of bloodshed and anarchy in Zululand, not only did the Government find themselves obliged to concur substantially with his statements, but there was not a single speaker that evening—I believe I am correct in saying that—who rose while the subject was fully discussed, from all quarters of the House, to maintain that the Settlement of 1879 was in any degree tolerable. That was the state of things in 1882; and permit me to say that when the subject has been debated in that way, as it was in this House—not as a Party question, but with great ability and impartiality from all quarters of the House—it is idle in 1884 to overlook and ignore entirely what was then admitted and demonstrated, and to speak of that state of things as a state of things upon which we ought to have fallen back. I am not prepared to agree to that. The right hon. Gentleman thinks matters are worse now than they were then. That is not my opinion, for what have we to consider? We have to consider two things—first of all, the anarchy and bloodshed in Zululand; and, secondly, the question of danger to the Colony of Natal. With regard to the latter point, I am prepared to contend that that danger has been wholly removed, because a neutral fringe of territory has been interposed between Natal and the disturbed parts of Zululand, where British authority is effectively maintained, where peace prevails, and which serves to hold off Natal from the different parts of Zululand. Therefore, as to that important part of the case, and as to the fact that a large piece of Zululand—about one-fourth or one-third, I believe—is in a peaceful condition, much has been attained, though certainly with an increase—I do not deny it—of British responsibility, an increase which it was absolutely necessary for us in honour to agree to, because we could not for a moment think of the restoration of Cetewayo to the prejudice of those Chiefs who objected to the restoration, and for whom we were bound to find a refuge in what is now known as the Reserve Territory. We adopted the restoration of Cetewayo, not as a measure that was certain to succeed, but as a measure the most hopeful of any before us. In the state of things then existing, it was absolutely necessary for us to find a remedy; and that was the remedy which appeared to offer the least amount of responsibility with the greatest amount of compromise. I am not prepared to admit that a great addition of responsibility has fallen upon us in consequence of the failure of that plan as a remedy. What we said in 1882 was, that if we restored Cetewayo without obtaining, in the first place, competent and sufficient evidence that his return was desired by a large proportion of the masses of the people, then, indeed, we should incur a great responsibility; but that evidence we did obtain; and I have no reason to believe that even now there was an untrue impression of the state of things then conveyed to our minds. I will not now go back to that part of the matter, because the important part of the question is that which is before us. My right hon. Friend the Member for Bradford (Mr. W. E. Forster) has, with great prudence, stated that he holds that we ought to discharge all the responsibilities we have undertaken, and that no benefit is to be gained by shrinking from that duty. I entirely agree with the right hon. Gentleman in that view; but our responsibilities, although they should be acknowledged, ought not to be exaggerated, and, above all things, new responsibilities ought not to be assumed in a hurry, and without sufficient consideration. What, then, is the question before us, as defined by the right hon. Baronet? He says there are two plans. I say there are three, because, unquestionably, a large and distinct portion of the debate has tended in the direction of annexation of territory not now ours; but that is put aside so far as the right hon. Gentleman is concerned. He condemns that policy, as we did; but he says that the hon. Baronet behind him (Sir Henry Holland) has recommended a return to the system of 1879; but the system of 1879, if I remember rightly, was a system under which no authority was assumed over the Chiefs. They were entirely independent; whereasyas I understand the recommendation of the right hon. Baronet it is that some authority should be assumed over the Chiefs in the Settlement which he recommends. My hon. Friend the Member for Burnley (Mr. Rylands) has contended—and we contend—that if you assume partial authority over these Chiefs, that can only end in becoming a complete authority, and, consequently, in amounting to an equivalent of the annexation which has been recommended as the measure to be at once adopted. At any rate, that is not a return to the system of 1879. There is in that no recommendation of a return to the system of 1879. The system of 1879 was essentially different, inasmuch as it fully recognized the independence of the Chiefs, and only offered them any friendly aid, in the way of good offices, that our Resident might be able to give them.

SIR HENRY HOLLAND: I did not suggest that. I suggested, very diffidently, a return to the system of 1879—that is to say, the government of the Natives by the Native Chiefs, under Native laws; but that the system of 1879 should be so extended that we should exercise a more direct and guiding authority by Residents and Deputy Residents.

MR. GLADSTONE: The hon. Baronet spoke in subdued tones; but how that is to be done is a most important part of the plan. The hon. Baronet says he made the suggestion diffidently. I have no doubt—nay, I am sure he did, because he is a man of sense and experience; and all those who know South Africa will be apt to make recommendations with considerable diffidence; but one point is this. We do not see how the assertion of authority by us over these Chiefs can possibly end in anything except the establishment of a virtual supremacy. You were very liberal in your system. I do not question that. I am sure that was the intention of the hon. Baronet; but we are not prepared to establish in these portions of Zululand beyond the Reserve a British supremacy, which we feel must amount virtually to that annexation which is disclaimed by us, disclaimed by the late Government, and disclaimed by the hon. Baronet in his speech to-day. I do not, on the other hand, say we wash our hands of all duty whatever with regard to Zululand beyond the Reserve. A friendly interest we should, in any case, feel towards it. The circumstances—the unhappy circumstances—under which it was broken up at a former time undoubtedly leave us in a condition in which it is impossible to say we look upon that land as if it were a mere portion of Central Africa; but, at the same time, we are not in a position in which we have any other duty towards that country than this—of doing so far as we can what is best for that country. Now, we are not prepared to say that it is best for that country, or best for South Africa generally, that we should assume authority over it. If the time comes—and it may come—when we can be useful in promoting its peaceful settlement, I think it will be our duty to avail ourselves of such an opportunity; but what we disclaim, under all the circumstances now before us, or which we can anticipate, is the desire to establish British supremacy over that country. The noble Lord used, I think, strong language in his description of the inhabitants of the Transvaal; and the hon. Member for the North Riding of Yorkshire (Mr. Guy Dawnay) does not disclaim having used language which I think would have been exceedingly strong, even if applied to some country with which we were at war, and which I must take the liberty of saying was a great deal too strong for the present occasion. It was described by the right hon. Baronet as interesting; but, in my opinion, it was too strong, especially having regard to the fact that it was applied to people with whom we profess to be on friendly terms; and it is also unjust, in face of the fact that enormous multitudes of the Natives are living under the dominion and auspices of the Transvaal; and in face of the fact that we were content to go to the Cape of Good Hope, where these people had prior possession, and make it so uncomfortable for them that they migrated in large numbers. In face of the fact that we have had indisputable evidence that the Natives have migrated into the Transvaal, on account of the peace and good government they can enjoy there, I must say it is imprudent, impolitic, and hardly consistent with those terms of comity and decency which ought to prevail between people of one State and another, to describe these people in the superlative language used by the hon. Member for the North Riding. I feel that the time is exhausted, and that it would be wrong in me to enter into the details of the question, which have been so fully stated by my right hon. Friend (Mr. Chamberlain), and my hon. Friend the Under Secretary of State for the Colonies (Mr. Evelyn Ashley). With their statements I am perfectly content. I am further contented and satisfied with the limited and cau ious terms in which the right hon.t Baronet opposite (Sir Stafford Northcote) has expressed himself. I may point out to him that our object has been gained by the establishment of the Reserve; and as to the maintenance of British authority, he must be aware that it will be maintained there by the same means as those adopted in other places in case of need, and that there are, I believe, a force of nearly 1,000 men in the Reserve for that purpose. With regard to what is beyond it, I by no means say that that is a country which does not excite our interest; but we see no reason for violent interference in that country. In fact, the people themselves have chosen to invite Natives into the Transvaal to settle there in a peaceful manner, totally different from the proceedings of Bechuanaland; and we decline to be bound by a scheme of policy which we believe to be dangerous, impolitic, and not in conformity with any sound principle, even of morality, by extending British authority over that country.

MR. GUY DAWNAY said, the Prime Minister had rebuked him for having used strong terms with regard to people with whom we were on friendly terms. He denied that we were on friendly terms with these filibustering Boers; and it was to these filibustering Boers, and not to the inhabitants of the Transvaal, that he had referred. He had compared the action of the Boers in Zululand with the action which, so far as he could understand, the Government were allowing the Abyssinians to take with regard to the Soudan, and had said that their civilization was in the same rudimentary condition, and their Christianity in the same fossilized state. He denied that he had advocated a policy of annexation—unless the Government considered—which they said they did not—that the Reserve had been annexed—for he only desired an extension of the principle which applied to the Reserve to other parts of Zululand. The right hon. Gentleman the President of the Board of Trade (Mr. Chamberlain) had declared that a policy of annexation was, to use the term borrowed from his (Mr. Guy Dawnay's) vocabulary, a policy of filibusters, brigands, and pickpockets; but if he (Mr. Guy Dawnay) had wished to brand such policy in the strongest term, he should not have employed any such feeble words from his own vocabulary, but should have denounced it instead in the right hon. Gentleman's own language as a policy of shipowners. He should ask the Committee to divide, and to express their opinion that the responsibility which the House and the country had incurred owing to the reversal of the policy of the late Government, and owing to the Convention with the Boers, especially with regard to the Articles in relation to the Border Tribes, would not be fulfilled merely by protecting the Zulus in the Reserved Territory in the future, after failing to do so in the past.

Question put.

The Committee *divided:*—Ayes 99; Noes 155: Majority 56.—(Div. List, No. 197.)

Original Question put, and *agreed to.*

Resolution to be reported *To-morrow.*

Committee to sit again *To-morrow.*

MOTION.

CORRUPT PRACTICES (SUSPENSION OF ELECTIONS) BILL.

On Motion of Mr. ATTORNEY GENERAL, Bill to suspend, on account of corrupt practices, the issue, during the Prorogation of Parliament, of writs for the holding of Elections of Members to serve in the present Parliament for certain cities and boroughs, *ordered* to be brought in by Mr. ATTORNEY GENERAL and Mr. SOLICITOR GENERAL.

Bill *presented,* and read the first time. [Bill 314.]

House adjourned at Six o'clock.

HOUSE OF LORDS,

Thursday, 31*st July,* 1884.

MINUTES.]—PUBLIC BILLS—*First Reading*—Chartered Companies * (231); Military Pensions and Yeomanry Pay * (232); Prosecution of Offences (233); Metropolitan Asylums Board (Borrowing Powers) * (234); Superannuation * (235); Expiring Laws Continuance * (236).

Second Reading—Prisons * (213); Smoke Nuisance Abatement (Metropolis) (109); Turnpike Acts Continuance * (206); Public Works Loans * (221); Metropolitan Board of Works (Money) * (222); Municipal Elections (Corrupt and Illegal Practices) (212).

Committee—Canal Boats Act (1877) Amendment (198-228); Cholera Hospitals (Ireland) (204-229); Trusts (Scotland) * (209).

Third Reading—Tramways (Ireland) Provisional Order (211); Tramways (Ireland) Provisional Order (No. 2) * (144); Yorkshire Registries * (219-230); Naval and Greenwich Hospital Pensions * (203); Teachers' Residences (Ireland) * (214), and *passed.*

REPRESENTATION OF THE PEOPLE BILL—THE MARQUESS OF SALISBURY AND MR. GLADSTONE.

PERSONAL EXPLANATION.

THE MARQUESS OF SALISBURY: I wish, before the Business of the House commences, to refer to a statement the Prime Minister made in "another place" with respect to some observations of mine. The Prime Minister was pleased to quote, and, as I think, misconceived the meaning of some observations which I made at the Cannon Street Hotel on Monday. The Prime Minister is reported to have said this—

"I find that in a speech ascribed to Lord Salisbury—I rather think in the papers of to-day—there is the following passage:—'The House of Lords has a right to say—"We do not approve of the measure you bring forward. If you like to accept its rejection, well and good; if you object to its rejection, your remedy is to go to the people."' That I take to imply that the Bill has been rejected."

That seems to be a very captious criticism; and although I do not ordinarily take any notice of misconstruction of things that I say, I think that, if the Prime Minister condescends to misunderstand you, you are bound, as a matter of respect, to correct him. What I wish to point out is that I was speaking when I used those words—as anyone who will consult the speech will see—of the general Constitutional rule affecting the action of the House of Lords upon the question of Dissolution, and it was impossible for me to state it in more limited terms than I did. As a general rule, it is perfectly true that the House of Lords has a right to say—"We do not approve the measure you bring forward; if you like to accept its rejection, well and good; if you object to its rejection, your remedy is to go to the people." But in saying that I did not mean, nor does it necessarily follow, that in every particular case coming under that general rule the statement would require to be in equally large terms. The general rule is necessarily larger than the particular instance. What happened in this particular instance was, that we did not reject the measure, but that we rejected a Motion in respect of that measure, which rejection had for its effect that the Bill could not pass until certain necessary and supplementary legislation had been added to it. But what I wish to point out is that I was discussing the general rule, and that I did not in any way impugn the fact that our rejection of the Motion in respect to the measure had not involved the rejection of the measure, if Her Majesty's Government had been pleased to take the steps which we thought necessary to its passing. The matter is only of importance, as I say, because the Prime Minister is pleased to misunderstand me. He himself is perfectly aware of what really took place, for he goes on to say that, in strictness, the measure had not been rejected as regards the Forms of the House of Lords. But he goes on to make one further observation, which, I think, in the interest of this House, I ought to notice. He says that the noble Earl opposite (Earl Granville)—

"Has no intention of making any further Motion on the Bill as at present advised; and our reason is, that, without insuring any important public advantage, it would give trouble to the House of Lords, which ought not to have any trouble of that kind put upon it, and would only result in the production of some third by-Motion. If we could have some direct issue taken on the Bill itself, I think that it would be very desirable; but I do not think it would be in our power to procure it."

Now, when a man offers me wine and water and leaves out the wine, it seems to me that I am taking a very direct issue with him in declining to drink the water by itself.

EGYPT—THE CONFERENCE.

QUESTION.

THE MARQUESS OF SALISBURY: I wish to ask the noble Earl opposite (Earl Granville), Whether he can now give the House any information with respect to the progress of the Conference?

EARL GRANVILLE: My Lords, I am afraid my answer will appear somewhat unsatisfactory, and, indeed, monotonous; but it will not surprise the noble Marquess, who has had the experience of more than one Conference. He is aware how unavoidable delays are at meetings of the Representatives of all Europe, who have to refer to their respective Governments. The Conference met this morning, when the French Ambassador expressed his regret that he had not yet sufficient instructions to answer questions which had been raised. He requested—and was supported by other Plenipotentiaries in the request—that we should meet again on Saturday morning.

SMOKE NUISANCE ABATEMENT (METROPOLIS) BILL.

(*The Lord Stratheden and Campbell.*)

(NO. 109.) SECOND READING.

Order of the Day for the Second Reading, read.

LORD STRATHEDEN AND CAMPBELL: My Lords, I rise to move the second reading of the Bill on Smoke Abatement, although, during this Session, I do not wish it to go further than the stage in question. If it is once read a second time, the subject will be ripe for Governments to deal with. If it does not reach that point, much toil of many persons will be wasted. Since it was presented at the end of May, it has been supported by a public meeting under the Lord Mayor in the City; by the Westminster District Board of Works; by the Parish of St. Martin's; by the Hampstead Vestry; by the Council for the Institute of Architects; by the Association under the noble Duke the Master of the Horse (the Duke of Westminster); while it has also had a favourable echo in the Provinces. At the same time, I do not ask your Lordships to accede to it, even to the qualified extent I have described, unless a proper case can be submitted in its favour. Instead of going through all the clauses in detail, which anyone can look at, I will explain at once, if it should become law, the course of operation to be anticipated from it. A number of Local Bodies would find themselves invested with a discretionary power of restraining smoke in houses, under bye-laws which must have the previous sanction of the Home Office. The City would be, probably, at first, the only Local Body to apply it, in consequence of the greater public spirit which prevails there, of the municipal authority which is strong enough to urge it into action; of the desire to vindicate itself against powers which are hostile to it; of the readiness to lead the way which becomes an ancient Corporation; and of the superior facility for restraining smoke in offices and warehouses, which make up that part of London far more than domiciles and residences. The last advantage is a most important one belonging to the City, and should not be forgotten by your Lordships. If the result was good, other Local Bodies would exert themselves, and the whole of London would be gradually purified, at least of the carbonic matter which oppresses it. If the result was bad, nothing more would follow, except a better heating apparatus in new buildings, which the Bill provides for. More I should scarcely add to justify my limited demand upon the House, if it were not that the Vestry of St. James's, under great misapprehension, as I shall soon point out, have petitioned against the measure being adopted. The Vestry of St. James's, whose Petition I have carefully examined, quite forget that, as regards themselves, there is nothing compulsory or threatening. If they do not like the power, they need not exercise it. The force will only be a latent one. It cannot injure or embarrass them. Indeed, their modesty is singular. It is a proclamation of unfitness to be invested with a right to act in a given manner, which, as they think, may lead to inconvenience. But if it leads to inconvenience in their eyes, of course it cannot be exerted. They cannot mean that the temptation will be so great that, against their better judgment, they will use it. They can hardly urge either that, because they are not prepared to exercise the right, no other Local Body should possess it. Although they represent a celebrated parish, are they the only Local Body to whom prudence has been granted? The Petition is not so much unfounded as irrelevant. If the inhabitants of St. James's united to petition against imparting a new power to the Vestry, which might be dangerously resorted to, their language would be perfectly intelligible. But nothing of the kind has happened. The inhabitants regard the Vestry with confidence, which has not been diminished, but which the Vestry blushes to enjoy, awakened to a sudden consciousness of dangerous fallibility. It is true the Vestry urge that science has not gone far enough to make the object of the Bill attainable. That point might be insisted on in their proceedings, as a reason for not exercising the new authority conferred; but it is not a reason for withholding it. It might be shown, with ease, that a Bill of this kind is certain to advance the science of mechanical invention, which they think defective, if enacted. But on the question of mechanical invention being inadequate I join issue with the Vestry altogether. I am prepared to show that great facilities exist for averting smoke in houses at this moment. It may be prudent to remark at first that I have for years attended to this point, in concert with a scientific engineer, whose mind has been directed to all the intricacies of the problem. We have made various experiments together. We recently inspected all the fireplaces the Health Exhibition furnishes, and he is thoroughly conversant with everything which appeared before in the same line at the South Kensington Museum. These are the leading methods by which smoke may be prevented. You might attempt the Russian system of central furnaces in houses, by which hot air or hot water is distributed to rooms in flues or pipes respectively. You might make that central furnace smokeless, on the principle by which Lord Palmerston's enactments are carried out, wherever they are operative. Such a change would be too violent, although the merit of the system in diffusing equal warmth is undeniable. In this way, St. Petersburg becomes almost a winter quarter. To pass on to another, a mechanical inventor came to me the other day, and explained his mode of introducing orifices at the top of chimneys, by which the draught is so augmented that it becomes easy to burn coke or anthracite in ordinary fireplaces. They may be burnt in ordinary fireplaces if there is sufficient draught, and they are smokeless. Next, I may touch upon the principle of Arnott, by which coals are constantly moved upwards, instead of added to the surface, and thus ignition forwarded while smoke is overcome, since, when ignition is complete, smoke naturally vanishes. Some years ago, a gentleman in Stratford Place, who is not living now, resorted to this method over nearly all his house, which I have visited, and deemed it thoroughly successful. Asbestos is a good expedient, and, lighted up by gas, presents a cheap and unobjectionable fuel. Gas stoves may be employed, and are now much more attractive than they used to be. Oil stoves may be substituted where gas is not laid on; but, unless of excellent construction, do not recommend themselves. The best invention we have reached as yet, if I am not deceived, is that of the late Sir William Siemens. It consists in the union of coke and gas, so that heat is thrown out, combustion is promoted, and flame is never wanting. The outlay would be soon recovered in the economy of chimney sweeping. In answer to the Vestry of St. James's, I have now enumerated seven modes among which the householder would choose, as soon as the Local Body of his district brought the law to bear upon him. Leaving behind these technical researches, there is a wide consideration which might recommend the second reading to your Lordships. This Bill is the best security against too rapidly erecting a vast and central Body for the government of London. A vast and central Body of that kind is incompetent to deal with smoke, because it must bring its restrictive effort to bear upon the whole circumference or none of it. It has no *locus standi* for a partial operation. It could not fix upon one district; it could not venture to control the aggregate of districts. It would be disabled as the Legislature is disabled—except through intermediate agency—by the necessity of acting on too large a surface of resistance. To conquer smoke, you must uphold a distribution of municipal authority. But it by no means follows that the existing Vestries ought to be perpetuated. Under this Bill, they may appear still more inadequate than they are felt to be already. A Bill of this kind points rather to the control of London by a group of Corporations, with a well-poised authority to lead them—such as the late Sir George Cornewall Lewis, such as the late John Stuart Mill, such as the lamented politician, Mr. Buxton, recommended; such as every inquiry has proposed; such as the experience of the present

Session powerfully urges. Her Majesty's Government ought not to be alienated from the present Bill by the expressions I have hazarded, and that when the noble Duke the Master of the Horse is known to be in favour of it. It really offers them a good retreat from an untenable position. But those who are resolved at any hazard to form a large and central power for directing the Metropolis are bound to legislate effectually against smoke before they plunge into that system. It might uphold restraints upon the evil; it cannot possibly initiate them. My Lords, if I detain the House, it is only to secure the Bill, as I am bound, against any dangerous opposition. It is well known that many noble Lords have leagued themselves into the defence of liberty and property, and that, intent upon that aim, they view all legislation with considerable jealousy. If, however, they oppose every project which involves restraint with undistinguishing severity, their cause will suffer, their end will be defeated, and they will come to be regarded as the blind and zealous scourges of improvement. If you condemn all interference, you condemn all sanitary benefits. I share the doctrine of these noble Lords; but it ought not to be exaggerated. In fact, it is a question of degree. They ought in every case to ask, is the object great, and is the interference moderate and limited? The object in the present case is to retain London as a capital, elevate its architecture, purify its atmosphere, correct its fogs, and check the inconveniences, the depression, the disorders, the mortality they generate. The interference is most guarded. It depends upon a Local Body which the householder can influence. No course of action is dictated to him; no right is overthrown. On general and abstract grounds the householder is no more entitled to pour smoke out of a chimney than on such grounds he is entitled to fling sewage from a garret. It may be said that long custom has sheltered one of these proceedings in our capital. No doubt it is so. But I have often been informed that in the old town of Edinburgh long custom authorized the other. When it was first restrained the friends of liberty and property may have been exceedingly dissatisfied. But, if I understand the noble Lords who form this League, they are not indifferent to architectural improvement. They would willingly raise London to a higher level than it has yet attained in everything which relates to beauty, order, and magnificence. The Council of Architecture have furnished me with the best authority for the position that, until smoke is overcome, these ends will be frustrated. It is that of the late Mr. Street, in his Presidential Address of 1881. In substance, he affirmed that new modes of heating were essential; that there could be no excellence in his (Mr. Street's) vocation, however just the plan, however accurate the workmanship, if, in a short time, the colours and materials employed were certain to degenerate. I have heard from a considerable quarter, well entitled to attention, that the restraint of smoke is inexpedient; that it is not without an hygienic influence; that it dries the air, and ought, for some complaints, to be perpetuated. A theory of this kind was once advanced by Horace Walpole. But there is a fallacy involved in the opinion. The atmosphere is dried not by smoke, but by ignition. It is quite true that, if you put out all the fires of London, more humidity would follow; but, by removing the carbonic particles, an opposite result is forwarded. These carbonic particles attract and fix the moisture, which would otherwise be volatile, which would otherwise ascend, and thus they render London damper than it would be. As it enters the domain of science, I have brought this point under the notice of a medical authority. Of all the grounds which recommend the Bill, those which relate to atmospheric influence appear to me the strongest. At present, in November and December the most important public questions are resolved by Cabinets in London, under conditions which must often depress the mind beneath its normal level, whether of invention, enterprize, or firmness. But I will not pursue so large a topic at this moment, or one which noble Lords on either side are so well qualified for judging. My Lords, although, even if the Bill was negatived to-day, I should feel no doubt of legislation on its principle eventually arriving, the result would be in a high degree unfavourable to its object. It would discourage unexpectedly and harshly the current of mechanical invention which exists, and which is still desirable to give perfection to the various contrivances I have referred to. It would be taken as an indication that your Lordships are not disposed at any time to go beyond the statutes of Lord Palmerston. It would prevent those statutes from being more rigorously executed. It would proclaim distrust of Local Bodies with the City at the head of them. It would furnish Governments, whoever may compose, whoever may direct them, with a pretext for avoiding or abandoning the subject as a hopeless one. There is a further consequence to mention. At a time when the name of this House is about, or has begun already, to be driven to and fro between the battledores of faction, it would be said that no social measure can be originated in it with any prospect of succeeding. If, on the contrary, the second reading is accepted, there will be a guarantee that the House is not indifferent to the welfare of the capital, however slow to try political experiments. If the second reading is accepted there will be a guarantee that the House has taken for its motto words of which I cannot find an adequate translation, or else I would not mention them in the original—

> "Non fumum ex fulgore, sed ex fumo dare lucem cogitat,"

in order that new triumphs may occur in architectural as well as sanitary progress. I move that the Bill be read a second time.

Moved, "That the Bill be now read 2ª."—(*The Lord Stratheden and Campbell.*)

THE EARL OF DALHOUSIE said, that the Government could not accede to the second reading of the Bill, because it was still their intention, at some time or another, to pass a Bill for the Municipal Government of London; and in spite of what his noble Friend (Lord Stratheden and Campbell) had said, this was a subject which must be dealt with by a Municipal Council of the whole Metropolis. Moreover, there was no chance of the Bill passing into law at that period of the Session. He desired, however, to give emphasis to the first reason, as the principal one, why the Government abstained from supporting this measure. He must also add that there did not appear to be any strong feeling in its favour on the part of those most concerned in it.

THE MARQUESS OF SALISBURY said, he did not wish to challenge the decision of the Government, since it was obvious that if the Bill were to go any further the House would have to deal with it at an earlier period of the Session. He wished, however, to protest against the remark of the noble Earl opposite (the Earl of Dalhousie), that they must wait for legislation in regard to the government of London before any of those questions affecting the Metropolis were taken in hand. He thought that that was a practical arrest of all legislation of that kind for a considerable time to come.

EARL GRANVILLE said, he thought that this was a matter in which they might exercise some individual influence. Many of their Lordships were influential members of the committees of clubs, who were, in his opinion, among the greatest offenders in this respect. They were, no doubt, most hospitable institutions; but every day they poured forth immense volumes of smoke, to the great detriment of the surrounding atmosphere. Another new offender he had noticed was the great hotel in Trafalgar Square, where, no doubt, without any idea of the consequences, a huge volume of smoke was now poured out. All this showed that this was a question by which they might with advantage use their individual exertions.

THE EARL OF HARROWBY said, he thought that the noble Lord opposite (Lord Stratheden and Campbell) deserved very great credit for this attempt to deal with a great evil; and he should be sorry if the Bill was dealt with by their Lordships in a manner which showed a want of sympathy in the subject. There was nothing more depressing to the poor of the Metropolis than the dark canopy of smoke which enveloped the town, and the dust and soot which covered everything in their houses, and amidst which they lived. He could only hope that when the House came to deal with the matter, they would do so in a manner which showed that they were conscious of the magnitude of the evil.

LORD MOUNT-TEMPLE said, he considered that the question was too large to be dealt with by a private Member, though, in common with the noble Earl opposite (the Earl of Harrowby), he must acknowledge the obligations under which they lay to his noble Friend (Lord Stratheden and Campbell) for having called attention to the subject. While he (Lord Mount-Temple) was in favour of some general measure to apply to the whole Metropolis, it should be kept in mind that the Local Authorities had the best chance of knowing the exact desires of the district which they administered. It would be useful, therefore, if they were allowed powers of adapting a general measure to the particular wants of their district.

THE EARL OF REDESDALE (CHAIRMAN of COMMITTEES) said, that he would look with very great jealousy upon the granting of these powers to the Local Authorities. The matter was one which required very great attention to details. If powers were given to Local Authorities, and if two neighbouring parishes were to differ, it would lead to considerable difficulties. Not only that, but it would be objectionable to have a set of bye-laws adopted by one Vestry on the subject, while no similar restrictions were in force under adjacent Vestries. He thought it would be necessary to have some general scheme, and not leave too much to the Local Bodies. He, therefore, hoped the matter would be taken up by the Government.

EARL FORTESCUE said, he deeply regretted that the Government had wished to deprive them of the opportunity of recording their opinion on the principle of the Bill, with which he cordially sympathized; and that they must, so to speak, hold their admiration of the principle in reserve until the passing of some gigantic scheme for subjecting all the 4,000,000 of people in London to one centralized authority.

LORD TRURO said, he thought it was due to the noble Lord who had moved the second reading of the Bill (Lord Stratheden and Campbell) to acknowledge the good intentions evinced in the effort he was making to deal with this subject; but, in his (Lord Truro's) view, it was just one of those questions which must be dealt with rather by the Government than by a private Member. He considered, however, that it would be extremely difficult, owing to the varying structure of houses in London and other circumstances, to carry out legislation on that subject with any degree of uniformity.

LORD STRATHEDEN AND CAMPBELL: My Lords, I am compelled to make a few remarks before this question is disposed of. It seems to me the House can hardly be directed by Her Majesty's Government on this occasion, as they have heard one speech against the Bill from the Treasury Bench, and another in its favour. The speech against it from the noble Earl who followed me (the Earl of Dalhousie) was based a good deal on an extraordinary statement that the Bill had gained no countenance in London. I feel entitled to protest against that statement, having already mentioned that, on the 10th of July, it won the sanction of a public meeting in the City under its first magistrate, and I also enumerated other quarters where it is approved. The noble Marquess opposite (the Marquess of Salisbury) has not attempted, nor do I believe he wished, to overthrow a single proposition by which it was maintained, that the second reading ought to be adopted. Whatever falls from the noble Earl the Chairman of Committees deserves and gains consideration from your Lordships. But there is no ground for apprehending in the Local Bodies too much impatience to exert the discretionary power when they have it. In St. James's it is clear that they are not at all disposed to use it. As it is only proposed to read the Bill a second time this Session, it is not necessary to defend it as if it was on the border of the Statute Book. The noble Earl beneath (Earl Fortescue), and the noble Lord upon the left (Lord Mount-Temple), have given it support so perfectly unanswered, that I am bound to ask your Lordships to divide upon it. I am bound still more by my own language, in the sense that the defeat of such a Bill at such a time would add something to the elements of obloquy accumulating out-of-doors against the House and its decisions. I may incur defeat; but it is better than the discredit which would justly fall upon me, if, without a plea of any kind, I withdrew a Bill, on which even Her Majesty's Government are free to vote according to their judgment. I ask the House at once to go to a division.

On Question? Their Lordships *divided*:—Contents 31; Not-Contents 17: Majority 14.

Resolved in the *affirmative*.

Bill read 2ª accordingly.

CANAL BOATS ACT (1877) AMENDMENT BILL.—No. (198.)

(*The Lord Carrington.*)

COMMITTEE.

Order of the Day for the House to be put into Committee, read.

Moved, "That this House do now resolve itself into Committee on the said Bill."—(*The Lord Carrington.*)

THE EARL OF WEMYSS said, he wished to say a few words in reference to this Bill, which he looked upon, to a great extent, as a piece of superfluous legislation. The Canal Boats Act of 1877 provided that boats which were inhabited during the day or night were to be reckoned as dwellings, and treated accordingly. They had to be registered by the registration authorities—namely, the Sanitary Authorities having districts abutting on the canal where the boats plied. A registration fee had to be paid, and the Local Government Board had the power to regulate those fees, and for the lettering, marking, and numbering of the boats, &c. The Local Government Board had also the power, under the existing Act, to fix the number, age, and sex of the persons to be allowed to dwell in a canal boat, the power to regulate the cubic space of air and ventilation, the separation of the sexes, the general healthiness and convenience of accommodation, and the removal of persons affected with infectious disease, and might detain the boats for the purposes of disinfection. It was also provided that officials of registration or Sanitary Authorities might enter a canal boat by day for purposes of inspection, and that a fine of £2 would be incurred for obstructing the officials in their examination. Children on registered canal boats were brought under the Elementary Education Acts, and provision was made for the continuous instruction of a child in the several school districts through which the boat to which he belonged successively passed. Their Lordships, he thought, would see that these provisions were already very stringent, stronger and more stringent provisions by far than any which were applied to houses in any towns on shore, or in ships afloat. He contended that the Report of the Registrar General did not bear out altogether the statements of Mr. George Smith, of Coalville, to whose efforts this legislation was due; and he ventured to think that if any attempt were made to apply to working men's houses in the Metropolis, or in any other of our large towns, the powers given under the Act of 1877 as regarded canal boats, it would not be listened to for a moment, and would not be sanctioned by the other House of Parliament. It appeared to him, therefore, that it was not desirable to extend this kind of legislation. He desired to point out that the present Bill sought to draw tighter the restrictions placed upon the inhabitants of the canal boats by the Act of 1877. The main provision of the measure was one to which he wished to draw their Lordships' particular attention. It was to the effect that the Local Government Board had to appoint a special staff of Inspectors for the purpose of inspecting the work of the Inspectors of the local registration or Sanitary Authorities. He might say—he thought with justice—that the Inspector in this country was becoming a public nuisance. Here, for example, it was provided that Inspectors were to be appointed to inspect—for what purpose?—Inspectors. There were already Inspectors, sanitary and educational, working under the Local Government Board; and because Mr. George Smith, of Coalville, was not satisfied, it was asked that more should be appointed. Speaking on this question of Inspectors last year, he had said that an Englishman, instead of having no shadow like Peter Schlemil, would soon have two—his own shadow and the shadow of the Government Inspector; but if this Bill passed he would have three—his own shadow, the Inspector's shadow, and the shadow of the Inspector's Inspector. He thought this was a superfluous measure, and in it philanthropists showed that their zeal outran their discretion. In the case of a philanthropist like Mr. George Smith, it was well that their Lordships should know what was before them in the matter of legislation on social lines. Mr. Smith was not only anxious for legislation dealing with canal boats, but for travelling vans throughout the country. He was also anxious that the gipsies should become settled members of society; but how did he propose to convert them into such? In a Memorandum which

Mr. Smith handed in to the Select Committee last year, he showed how he would deal with the gipsies, and mentioned his plans for putting them under State inspection in the same way as the canal population. He said—

"I would grant to each (gipsy) family of man, wife, and two children four acres. . . . The Government should grant small sums of money to the tenants by way of loan, at a small interest, to enable them to erect a hut, and to provide food for the first year. I should think £100 for each family would be amply sufficient to tide them over the first year, and to be spent as follows:—£30 for the hut, £40 for one year's keep, £17 for a little Welsh cow, £3 for a pig and fowls, and £10 for tools and implements."

This was the sort of legislation they were threatened with from philanthropists in these Socialistic days; and he could not help thinking that, in the case of all Bills of this kind, it would be well to call them in future "little Welsh cows."

LORD CARRINGTON said, he did not complain of the speech of the noble Earl opposite (the Earl of Wemyss); but he must take exception to one remark which he had made. That remark was to the effect that this Bill was superfluous. He (Lord Carrington) maintained that it was not superfluous. If the Act of 1877 had been beneficial in its effect, it had also been found to have some defects as well. Those defects were remedied in the Bill now before their Lordships, which consisted of additions and explanations. He believed it was Clause 4, dealing with the Inspectors, which the noble Earl opposite proposed to cut out of the Bill; he hoped to be able to show, when they went into Committee, that it would be inadvisable to do so. He also hoped their Lordships would support him.

Motion *agreed to;* House in Committee accordingly.

Clauses 1 to 3, inclusive, *agreed to.*

Clause 4 (Inquiries and report by Local Government Board).

THE EARL OF WEMYSS, in moving the omission of the clause, said, it proposed to appoint additional Inspectors. He thought they were quite unnecessary, and should, therefore, move its rejection.

Moved, "That the Clause be omitted from the Bill."—(*The Earl of Wemyss.*)

LORD CARRINGTON, in supporting the retention of the clause, said, that the duty of enforcing the Act remained with the Local Authorities, many of whom had acted uncommonly well. There were instances, however, in which it could not be denied that they had rather failed in their duty; and the object was that the Inspector, by visiting the canal boats in the different districts, should ascertain how the Local Authorities were doing their work.

THE EARL OF KIMBERLEY said, that, in his opinion, the provisions of the Bill were in exact accordance with the policy which had been usually pursued by Parliament in legislation of this kind. It was the ordinary practice, and a necessary one, when they gave such powers to Local Authorities, for the Central Authority to appoint Inspectors to see that they did their duty efficiently.

EARL FORTESCUE, in supporting the Amendment, said, he considered so many Inspectors superfluous. They did not require the agency of a steam-engine to draw a cork.

On Question, "That the Clause stand part of the Bill?"

There being no Second Teller for the Not-Contents,

Amendment *disagreed to.*

Remaining Clauses *agreed to,* with Amendments.

On the Motion of The Lord CARRINGTON, the following new Clause *inserted* after Clause 5:—

"The Education Department shall every year report to Parliament as to the manner in which the Elementary Education Acts, 1870 and 1873, 1876 and 1880, are enforced with respect to children in canal boats, and shall for that purpose direct Her Majesty's Inspector of Schools to communicate with the School Boards and School Attendance Committees in their district."

The Report of the Amendments to be received on *Tuesday* next; and Bill to be *printed* as amended. (No. 228.)

CHOLERA HOSPITALS (IRELAND) BILL.—(No. 204.)

(*The Lord Keane.*)

COMMITTEE.

Order of the Day for the House to be put into Committee, read.

Moved, "That the House do now resolve itself into Committee upon the said Bill."—(*The Lord Keane.*)

The Earl of MILLTOWN said, he thought their Lordships were entitled to some explanation in regard to the provisions of the Bill, and the source whence it came. It was hardly respectful to their Lordships to propose to go into Committee upon the Bill without some such explanation. He had looked at the Bill, and he found that it was a measure of very considerable stringency and scope, giving Sanitary Authorities in Ireland power to take possession of land for the purpose of erecting cholera hospitals, and also providing for the infliction of very severe penalties on persons interfering with the officers of the Sanitary Authorities, or persons deputed by them to carry out the provisions of the Act. One of the provisions was, that any person so interfering might be summarily convicted by two Justices, or one stipendiary magistrate, and sentenced to a term of imprisonment not exceeding six months, apparently without the alternative of a fine. The Bill might be a necessary one; but he thought they were entitled to some light as to where it came from. He knew, of course, that it came from the House of Commons; but he was not aware who had charge of it there. They were all the more entitled to hear something about it, inasmuch as the wording of the Bill was very remarkable. Clause 2 provided that certain notices should be posted on the "walls of the Union." What did the drafter of the Bill think a "Union" was? Did he imagine it to be a room, or a park? Then, the last clause was one the meaning of which utterly puzzled him; for it said that "when the Sanitary Authorities of any Maritime Union" — what on earth was a Maritime Union?—

"That when the Sanitary Authorities of a Maritime Union had been directed by order of the Local Government Board to exercise jurisdiction for the prevention or suppression of cholera over any port which included portions of any other Union or Unions, then the words 'sanitary district' in this Act shall be construed to include such portions of the lands comprised within the limits of the said port as lie within one mile of high-water mark."

He fairly failed to comprehend what this meant.

After a pause,

The Marquess of SALISBURY asked whether Her Majesty's Government had any information to give the House respecting the Bill? Had they taken charge, or in any way made themselves responsible for it?

Earl GRANVILLE: Certainly not. The noble Lord opposite (Lord Keane) is in charge of the Bill.

The Marquess of WATERFORD said, that, while agreeing that some explanation was certainly required respecting the Bill, he thought it would be a great pity if it were lost. Cholera was too evidently approaching our shores, and although some Amendments were required, the Bill was very useful. He thought the House ought to go into Committee, and consider the clauses.

After a further pause,

The Marquess of SALISBURY said, he was surprised that Her Majesty's Government had expressed no opinion with reference to the measure. The matter was one in regard to which they were entitled to ask for their advice. He, also, should be sorry if it were lost, and once more invited the opinion of the Government upon it.

Earl GRANVILLE said, that as his noble Friend the Lord President of the Council (Lord Carlingford) was unavoidably absent, and as he (Earl Granville) was not present when the Bill was introduced, it would, perhaps, be better to go into Committee, and then, if thought desirable, report Progress upon the Bill, in order to afford noble Lords on both sides of the House an opportunity for forming a judgment with regard to the measure.

Lord FITZGERALD said, that he had carefully considered the Bill, and had given Notice of several Amendments in it with the view of making it safe, and of preventing it from being abused. If those Amendments were inserted, he believed they would carry out that purpose. The Bill provided for a passing emergency, being intended to be in operation only till May 1, 1885; and it was almost identical with one that had been passed last year for a temporary purpose. In point of fact, it was simply a renewal of that measure. It would enable the inhabitants of a district, on the certificate of the medical officers of the Union of the existence of Indian cholera in the district, to take immediate steps for the erection of a cholera hospital in the district. He recommended the House to go into Committee upon the Bill.

THE EARL OF MILLTOWN said, that, in view of the announcement of the noble and learned Lord opposite (Lord Fitzgerald), he would not persist in his opposition to the Bill. He must, however, at the same time, protest against Her Majesty's Government taking no part in the decision of the question.

Motion *agreed to;* House in Committee accordingly.

THE EARL OF MILLTOWN said, that the author of the Bill in the other House might have supplied a translation of the phrases used.

Amendments made: The Report thereof to be received on *Monday* next; and Bill to be *printed* as amended. (No. 229.)

MUNICIPAL ELECTIONS (CORRUPT AND ILLEGAL PRACTICES) BILL.

(*The Earl of Northbrook.*)

(NO. 212.) SECOND READING.

Order of the Day for the Second Reading, read.

THE EARL OF NORTHBROOK, in moving that the Bill be now read a second time, said, that its object was to extend, in the main, the principle of the Act passed last year dealing with corrupt practices at Parliamentary elections, not only to municipal elections proper, but elections for Boards of Guardians, Local Government Boards, Town Improvement Commissioners, and School Boards. It was a purely English measure, applying to neither Scotland nor Ireland. It was to provide against illegal practices and illegal payments. The Bill had been before the Standing Committee on Law in the other House, and had passed through that House with very general assent, and it was hoped that it would prevent corrupt practices at elections. He moved the second reading.

Moved, "That the Bill be now read 2ª."—(*The Earl of Northbrook.*)

THE EARL OF MILLTOWN said, he felt great regret and surprise that Ireland had been omitted from the Bill. Why that had been done perhaps the noble Earl, or some of his Colleagues, would explain, as Ireland was included in the Bill up to the last moment, and, indeed, passed through the Standing Committee with "Ireland" in it. He did not know that there were any corrupt practices at Irish elections; but there certainly was terrorism, and that might be the reason why some Members in the other House objected to the application of the Bill to Ireland. He asked, why had Ireland been omitted? Unless a satisfactory reason were given for it, he should move to re-insert the word "Ireland."

THE EARL OF NORTHBROOK said, his answer to the question was a very simple one. It was, that great objection was taken by Irish Members to the Bill being applied to Ireland, and that the objection was of such a nature that, if Ireland had not been excepted, the Bill would probably not have been passed this Session, and it was thought better to retain it so far as it related to England.

THE MARQUESS OF SALISBURY said, he wished to point out that the limitation of expense as fixed in the Bill was placed at a very low figure, and he had heard complaints that it would be impossible to work the scheme. Although it might suffice in some places, it would be found, on inquiry, utterly insufficient in others. He thought that was a point which ought to be carefully considered, more especially as the figures now in the Bill were not those which were in it when it first appeared. He desired also to suggest the Bill should be made uniform as to duration with the Act of last year. That Act was limited to a certain period, whereas this Bill was permanent.

THE EARL OF LONGFORD agreed with the noble Earl (the Earl of Milltown) that the Bill might properly be applied to Ireland. Practices amounting to terrorism were resorted to there, to deter intending candidates from coming forward, so that apparently there were few contests.

Motion *agreed to;* Bill read 2ª accordingly, and *committed* to a Committee of the Whole House on *Monday* next.

TRADE AND COMMERCE—COMMERCIAL AGREEMENTS WITH FOREIGN COUNTRIES.

QUESTION. OBSERVATIONS.

THE EARL OF HARROWBY, in rising to ask the Secretary of State for Foreign

Affairs, What is the present position of the negotiations with Spain, Turkey, and Japan for fresh commercial agreements, which were mentioned in Her Majesty's Most Gracious Speech from the Throne? said, he should not have thought of raising this question at a time when his noble Friend must be overwhelmed with a very important work, but for the urgent necessity of the case. He hoped his noble Friend, if not then, would, at all events, soon be able to give them the information he asked for. It was grievously needed by many persons of influence and consideration in the country. He would only say that, from his long connection with these matters in the House of Commons, he watched them with great interest and anxiety, and also any announcements with respect to commercial affairs. Unfortunately, as he had heard from all quarters, the state of their commerce was such as to cause the greatest anxiety among men of the greatest experience; and he thought they were bound to take every opportunity of impressing on Her Majesty's Government the great desirability of doing everything that was possible to push on whatever negotiations they might be engaged in with foreign countries in regard to new tariffs and other similar matters, to open up fresh outlets for commerce. During his absence abroad for the benefit of his health, he saw with the greatest possible satisfaction that the Government had announced in the Queen's Speech that they were proceeding to take steps with regard to Spain, Turkey, and Japan, with the object of securing enlarged commercial intercourse with those countries. From his connection with Liverpool and other circumstances, he knew that commercial circles were largely interested in the countries mentioned in the question, especially with Spain. In trade matters, Turkey had always been more liberal in her treatment than almost any other country in Europe; and he hoped the noble Earl would be able to assure them that, if they did not get better treatment, they should, at all events, fare as well in the future as they had done in the past. As to Japan, he would point out that the tendency of the whole people was for larger and more extended commercial intercourse with Europe. Before sitting down, he could not help remarking that the prolonged depression of trade in this country had not, up to the present, shown any satisfactory signs of righting itself; and to whatever commercial authority they addressed themselves they would find that they all spoke with great alarm of the want of elasticity and the want of power of recovery which almost every trade in the country showed. Formerly periods of depression were succeeded by periods of prosperity; but the outlook now was as depressing as ever. When they spoke of commercial depression, they sometimes forgot what a terrible meaning those words had for the working population. They saw something to-day in the Bankruptcy Returns and something in the number of unused houses; they also saw a diminishing demand among the population for fresh meat. This, again, re-acted on the price of stock, butchers being unable to dispose of so much as they used. He had recently visited a leading county town, and, on asking how the farmers in the district were getting on, he had been told that they were doing very badly, because there was no active demand for stock. One butcher in the town, who had formerly killed 14 sheep a-week, now killed only 10; and he (the Earl of Harrowby) thought that was a proof that working people could not afford to buy so much butcher's meat as formerly on account of the depression of trade. He trusted the noble Earl would be able to supply a satisfactory answer to his Question, and to assure them that these Treaties, which promised to give increased openings to our commerce, were, if not concluded, at any rate in a fair way of being concluded.

EARL GRANVILLE: My Lords, I am aware that my noble Friend and Relative (the Earl of Harrowby) has, for many years, taken a great interest in all commercial questions; and, therefore, I am not surprised that he has put this Question to me, which relates to three very important points. With regard to Japan, our new Minister has been for some time there, and he has been constantly in communication with the Japanese Government on commercial matters; but this simply illustrates what I mentioned before—that the revision of the Treaties have not been begun yet in consequence of some of the European Representatives not having received their instructions. With regard to Spain, Her Majesty's Government attach the greatest importance to the Protocol signed by the Spanish Minister and the English Representative in December of last year. The reasons why we deferred that Protocol are stated in a Parliamentary Paper which has been presented to the House. They are shortly these—It was found, in April last, that in consequence of the then coming elections the Sitting of the Cortes would be so short that it would be impossible for the Spanish Government to press upon the Cortes the consideration of a question of that sort; and it was, therefore, quite necessary to defer to the December Session both the question of the English Protocol and the question of the Treaties and Conventions which had been signed by the Spanish Government and by other European Powers. That being the case, it was impossible for Her Majesty's Government to make a corresponding proposal to Parliament in regard to that Protocol, and it was necessary to postpone it till next Session. It can only then be done if the Cortes approve of the Protocol. Our Minister in Spain is still in communication with the Spanish Government on the subject, and he is under instructions to press it on most urgently. With regard to Turkey, the position is somewhat different. Delegates have been appointed, and they are at this moment considering the new Tariff; but they have not yet arrived at a conclusion which will enable me to state anything to the House. I do not wish to say one word on the general subject of depression which the noble Earl has introduced, or as to the character, the causes, or even the extent of it; but what I feel perfectly certain about is that, both with regard to agricultural depression and as to the question of prices as they affect our industrial population, we are certainly not in a worse, and I believe we are in a better, position than any other country in the world.

THE EARL OF WEMYSS said, the expectations which had been raised by the Liberal Party, prior to their coming into power in 1880, with respect to a return of commercial prosperity, had not been realized. At the last General Election, he remembered having seen a placard at Oxford with these words—"Vote for Harcourt, Chitty, and Prosperity."

EARL GRANVILLE: I cannot answer for all the election placards put up in different boroughs by respective candidates.

BURGH POLICE AND HEALTH (SCOTLAND) BILL.—QUESTION.

In reply to the Marquess of LOTHIAN,

THE EARL OF DALHOUSIE said, there was no chance of the Bill reaching their Lordships' House. In fact, he believed its withdrawal had been announced "elsewhere."

House adjourned at a quarter before Seven o'clock, till To-morrow, a quarter past Ten o'clock.

HOUSE OF COMMONS,

Thursday, 31st July, 1884.

MINUTES.]—SELECT COMMITTEE — *Report*— Education, Science, and Art Administration [No. 312].

SUPPLY—*considered in Committee*—CIVIL SERVICE ESTIMATES—CLASS III.—LAW AND JUSTICE—Votes 20, 22, 24, 26, and 28.

Resolutions [July 30] *reported.*

PUBLIC BILLS—*Second Reading*—East Indian Unclaimed Stocks [269].

Report of Select Committee—Ulster Canal and Tyrone Navigation.*

Committee — *Report* — Revenue, &c. [300]; Cholera, &c. Protection [303].

Considered as amended—Third Reading—Public Health (Ireland) (Districts)* [311]; Criminal Lunatics [295]; Infants [308], and *passed.*

Withdrawn—Crown Lands* [99]; Royal Courts of Justice* [139]; Burgh Police and Health (Scotland) (*re-comm*) * [296].

QUESTIONS.

ROYAL IRISH CONSTABULARY—SERGEANT CORBETT.

MR. BIGGAR asked the Chief Secretary to the Lord Lieutenant of Ireland, If it is true that Sergeant Corbett, of Stradbally, is in the habit of firing shots out of the barrack door and on the barrack premises, killing birds and crows, the barrack being beside the public street, or if it is a breach of the regulations to have a gun other than the one served out to him; and, whether the sergeant has an excise licence?

MR. TREVELYAN: The District Inspector reports that Sergeant Corbett is not in the habit of firing shots as stated. But on the morning of the 3rd of July he fired two shots with a borrowed fowling piece, at the back of the barrack premises, for the purpose of frightening away birds which were injuring crops in the garden. He was more than 60 feet from the public street at the time. The sergeant has not an Excise licence, nor was one required, as he had the gun within the curtilage of the barrack.

INDIA (MADRAS)—THE LAND QUESTION IN MALABAR.

MR. BIGGAR asked the Under Secretary of State for India, Whether he will cause inquiry to be made into the complaints of certain tenants in the district of Malabar that they are being evicted from their holdings for giving evidence before the Special Commissioner, Mr. Logan, against their landlords; and, whether affairs in that province are not in a most critical state?

MR. J. K. CROSS: The Government of Madras deputed, in 1881, a Special Commissioner to inquire into the Land Question in Malabar, which, from the complexity of the tenures, the density of the population, and the keen competition for land, is a difficult one. They are now considering Mr. Logan's Report; and, pending a decision, they have appealed to the loyalty and good sense of all classes to disturb as little as possible the existing state of the relations between all parties interested in the soil.

INDIA (MADRAS)—FOREST LEGISLATION—ACT 5, 1882.

MR. BIGGAR asked the Under Secretary of State for India, Whether attention will be paid to the increasing number of complaints of ryots at the vexatious nature of the recent legislation in Madras, Act 5, of 1882, Forests; and, whether it is true that section 56 declares that all wood timber, produce, &c., &c., shall be presumed to be Government's, and that, in consequence, such enormous powers are placed in the hands of low paid officials, that most serious discontent is spreading over the Madras Presidency?

MR. J. K. CROSS: Act 5 of 1882 did not come into force until the 1st of January, 1883, and no Report on its working has yet reached this country. Neither have any complaints been received, so far as is known, of the vexatious nature of its clauses. Section 56 provides that when a question arises under the Act whether forest produce is the property of Government, such produce shall be presumed to be the property of the Government till the contrary is proved. The powers reserved to the District Forest Officers are, in many instances, not capable of being delegated to subordinates; and, in any case, there is no reason to suppose that "enormous powers are placed in the hands of low-paid officials," or that serious discontent has arisen therefrom.

POOR LAW (IRELAND)—ELECTION OF GUARDIANS, CARLOW UNION.

MR. GRAY asked the Chief Secretary to the Lord Lieutenant of Ireland, If he is aware that there were twelve contested divisions at the late election of Poor Law Guardians for the Carlow Union; were the Nationalist Guardians defeated in eight of them; were the elections of three of these eight set aside, on the ground that the returning officer (Mr. E. L. Jameson), who is also clerk of the Union and sub-sheriff of the county, received informal claims to vote, and allowed votes thereon to the Conservative candidates; is it a fact that in the other five divisions investigations have been made and numerous similar informal and improper claims discovered as having been received by the same returning officer, and votes improperly allowed by him on said claims for the Conservative candidates; if these matters were brought before the Local Government Board by resolutions and statements of the Carlow Board of Guardians, and by petitions of the defeated candidates several weeks ago, and has any answer since been given by the Board, and what is the cause of the delay; will the defective claims be permitted to be amended before the new elections; if the said Local Government Board, in the case of the Rathanna Division of the above Union, received two resolutions of the Guardians calling for a sworn investigation on numerous grounds; did the Board disallow eight votes recorded for the Conservative candidate (his majority being nine), but refuse to grant the sworn investigation, although the Guardians by resolutions objected to over

20 more votes that were counted for the successful candidate; did the Guardians of the Carlow Union, by resolution of the 26th of June, call on the Local Government Board to discontinue Mr. Jameson as such returning officer, as they had no confidence in him; did the people of the county of Carlow (in public meeting assembled) protest against the conduct of Mr. Jameson, and have copies of such resolutions been sent to the Local Government Board, and has the Board taken any, and what, steps in the matter; and, will the Board continue Mr. Jameson as clerk of the Carlow Union, he being sub-sheriff of the county?

MR. TREVELYAN: The Local Government Board inform me that 12 elections were contested in the Carlow Union; but they have no record of the politics of the candidates. The returns in three districts were set aside, on the ground that the persons returned did not obtain a majority of valid votes—some votes having been allowed in respect of informal claims. Statements of objections to the validity of elections have also been received with regard to several other districts; and the Local Government Board, having obtained the explanation of the Returning Officer, have communicated with the Guardians, and await any further observations they may wish to offer. It is competent to have the defective statements of claim amended, so that they will contain all the particulars required, and thus be available at subsequent elections. In the Rathanna Division, which is named in the Question, the Board disallowed eight votes which were given on invalid claims; but the disallowance of these votes does not affect the result of the election. The Local Government Board have communicated to the Guardians their views respecting each of the other cases to which objection was raised, and have stated that from the information then before them they were not prepared to accede to the request for a sworn inquiry. The Board have received applications for the discontinuance of Mr. Jameson as Returning Officer; and have informed the applicants that they do not feel called upon to comply with that proposal. There is nothing to show partiality towards any particular candidate on the part of the Returning Officer; and the errors he committed were made apparently in ignorance of the law. They have been pointed out to him, and he has been warned that he will be held strictly responsible for the proper discharge of his duties.

MR. ARTHUR O'CONNOR: May I ask if that is the first occasion on which there was a complaint against this Returning Officer?

MR. TREVELYAN: I am not ready to state at this moment.

FISHERY PIERS AND HARBOURS (IRELAND)—TEELIN PIER, CO. DONEGAL.

MR. HEALY asked the Secretary to the Treasury, Whether the so-called "soft" foundation, for 20 feet in front of Teelin Pier, county Donegal, is not the same or nearly the same nature as that upon which the pier has been built; whether the 20 feet which has been cut off from the most important part of the pier-head was not part of the work contracted for with the contractor, and paid for as if same had been duly executed; whether the nature of the foundations, upon which the Board of Works were going to erect so important and expensive a structure, were correctly ascertained in the first instance, and not when too late; whether a strong representation has been forwarded to the Lord Lieutenant by or on behalf of the Grand Jury of the County of Donegal, at this Assizes, protesting against the mismanagement and waste, by the Board of Works, upon numerous fishery piers around that county, and complaining of the ruinous state of some of the very newest piers on the Coast, and calling for an investigation; and, whether the supervision of these important works at Teelin was left to a young and inexperienced man, son of a clerk in the office of the Board of Works, and whether his name and previous qualifications will be given?

MR. COURTNEY: It is not the fact that the completed part of Teelin Pier rests on a soft foundation, nearly the same as that which had to be abandoned, as the former is built on rock or other hard material. The 20 feet length cut off was originally contracted for; but as it appeared that the contractor was entitled to extra payment for unforeseen work, no deduction was made from the total amount paid him. No doubt, it was unfortunate that the existence of this soft bed was not discovered at first; but it should be remembered that the arrangements for this pier were not made by the Board of Works, but by the special Relief Committee of 1880, and so were probably more hurried than they would otherwise have been. The county surveyor of Donegal has complained of the condition of four piers in that county, though nothing has yet reached the Lord Lieutenant on the subject, and a special inquiry will be made into the matter; but I must observe that it is the duty of the Grand Jury to maintain these piers, and the Board of Works have nothing to do with it. The Clerk of the Works at Teelin was named Latimer; he is a regularly trained engineer and member of the Irish Institute of Civil Engineers, besides which he had three years' practical experience before he was employed by the Board. I am told he is the son of a clerk in the Board of Works.

General Sir GEORGE BALFOUR suggested that the Treasury should order an altogether independent inquiry into the matter.

Mr. HEALY said, that he could not catch what the hon. Gentleman the Secretary to the Treasury (Mr. Courtney) had just said; but he would ask if the Government would kindly send some gentlemen from England who would be competent to find out whether the Board of Works had done the work satisfactorily or not?

Mr. COURTNEY said, he was not prepared to take that step; but he would take care that a full inquiry was made.

Mr. HEALY said, he would renew this subject on the Vote.

POST OFFICE (SCOTLAND) — IRREGULARITIES IN SOUTH UIST.

Mr. DICK-PEDDIE (for Mr. Fraser-Mackintosh) asked the Postmaster General, Whether, in reference to the grave irregularities in certain Post Offices in South Uist, recently brought to his notice, and made the subject of Question in this House, it is the fact that William Mearns, Sub-Postmaster of Loch Boisdale Pier, one of the persons implicated, was formerly a domestic in the service of the proprietors of South Uist; and, whether, in view of the Report (page 65) of the Crofters' Commissioners—

> "In the remoter parts of the Highlands and Islands it is considered specially desirable that, in the nomination of Postmasters and telegraphic officials, persons be selected who are altogether independent of local or political authority or influence,"

he will take care, in future appointments in these localities, that discrimination be exercised on the lines indicated in the Report?

Mr. FAWCETT, in reply, said, he was not aware whether the Sub-Postmaster to whom his hon. Friend referred was formerly in the service of the proprietors of South Uist. He was appointed on the recommendation of the surveyor that he was the most suitable person in the locality. He thought there would be great difficulty in carrying out the suggestion of the Crofters' Commission; because if no one in the locality could be appointed to these offices, it would be necessary largely to increase the salary of the offices, in order to induce persons to come from a distance to hold them. Moreover, he thought it would hardly be just to act on the principle that no one in the locality was fit to be trusted with the charge of a Post Office. He might add that in *The Post Office Circular* of that week a special notice had been issued to Postmasters and Sub-Postmasters in Scotland which would, he hoped, prevent any further irregularities of the kind alluded to.

IRISH LAND COMMISSION — LAND VALUATION—COUNTIES CAVAN AND LEITRIM.

Mr. BIGGAR asked the Chief Secretary to the Lord Lieutenant of Ireland, Whether it is a fact that Mr. Bell, the Court Valuer to the County Court Judge for Cavan and Leitrim, gave a report as to the value of land in Nedd, near Killeshandra, county Cavan, also in Annagh, Curraghaboy, Corglass, and Dumbrick townlands, parish of Carrigallen, county Leitrim, without having gone on the farms; and, if so, will he appoint a more careful valuer?

Mr. TREVELYAN: Mr. Bell emphatically denies that he gave reports of such valuations without visiting the lands.

CRIME AND OUTRAGE (IRELAND)—MAIMING HORSES—CARRICKMACROSS PRESENTMENT SESSIONS.

MR. HEALY asked the Chief Secretary to the Lord Lieutenant of Ireland, Whether his attention has been called to the action of the Monaglen Grand Jury in granting £50 compensation to Messrs. Tenison and Porter for alleged malicious injury to horses, although the presentment had been rejected as bogus by the cesspayers, and the police, according to *The Belfast Morning News* of 10th instant, made the following depositions, showing that the injuries had been deliberately inflicted on the animals by the Emergency men, Nelson and Weir, paid by the landlords to take care of them:—

"Sergeant M'Donnell stated that he was stationed at Carrickmacross, and no complaint had been made to him by either Nelson or Weir up to the 7th January. He had gone to every person who could throw any light on the subject, and, up to the present time, he had never met a man who could corroborate the statements made by Nelson and Weir. He had deposed, at the Presentment Sessions at Carrickmacross, that he believed this outrage had been committed by the wife of Nelson, and he still held that opinion. Mrs. Nelson seemed to be the prime mover in the whole matter:

"Constable Farrell corroborated, and added that he believed the statements of Nelson and Weir to be a fabrication, and their statements were conflicting. He was further of opinion that there was collusion between Nelson and Weir with regard to the stabbing of these horses:

"Sergeant Timothy Kerry corroborated;"

will the Government assist the ratepayers to get the presentment traversed before the Assize Judge; and, can he hold out any hope that the Law will be so amended as to place the taxes of the people beyond the control of irresponsible magistrates?

MR. TREVELYAN: This outrage was not considered by the police to be of an agrarian character, and it was not recorded as such; but that circumstance did not preclude the owners of the horses from a right to seek compensation for the injury to the horses, which there can be no doubt was inflicted, whether by the person in charge of them or not. The opinion of the police as to their suspicions on that point is accurately quoted in the Question; but no conclusive evidence could be obtained. It is true that the claim for compensation was thrown out by the Presentment Sessions; but the Grand Jury, after a long inquiry, found that the injury was malicious, and made a Presentment for compensation. This has already been traversed at the Assizes; but the Judge stated that the ratepayers who opposed "had no case, as malice was clearly proved," and he fiated the presentment.

CROWN MINING LEASES—THE COMMISSIONERS OF WOODS AND FORESTS.

MR. ROLLS asked the Secretary to the Treasury, Whether holders of mineral leases under the Commissioners of Woods and Forests, more especially in the counties of Cardigan and Merioneth, are required to pay higher rents and royalties than those asked by the adjoining landowners; whether clauses are inserted in the leases from the Commissioners of Woods and Forests not known of in any private mineral leases; whether, in some cases, the lessees have been threatened with forfeiture of their leases for not working the mines, although their doing so, in the face of the present price of minerals, would entail a serious loss, and although all rents have been paid up; whether he would grant. as an unopposed Return, a statement of the number of acres belonging to the Crown in the counties of Cardigan and Merioneth, and how many acres of the same are at present let under mineral leases; and, whether he is aware that the conditions imposed by the Commissioners of Woods and Forests in these two counties are such as to practically prohibit searches for minerals therein?

MR. COURTNEY: I have no reason to think that Crown mining leases are more onerous in respect of royalty or other conditions than those given by other Welsh landowners. The only special provision in the former, known as "the one-fourth clause," is now no longer inserted. In no recent case has forfeiture been threatened because the mines were not worked. I will obtain for the hon. Member the acreages for which he asks; but I do not think there would be any use in laying them before Parliament. I have seen no evidence to show that the terms required by the Crown injure mining enterprize; on the contrary, the Commissioners of Woods are especially anxious to develop their mining properties in every proper manner.

LAW AND POLICE—THE DYNAMITE EXPLOSIONS AT WESTMINSTER —COMPENSATION.

MR. W. H. SMITH asked the Secretary of State for the Home Department, If application has been made to the Government on behalf of inhabitants of Westminster who have suffered by the explosions caused by the criminal acts of persons known to the police, but who have not yet been apprehended; and, if it is the intention of Her Majesty's Government to make any compensation for the losses and sufferings resulting from those acts?

SIR WILLIAM HARCOURT: I have received various applications on this subject, and I need not say that Her Majesty's Government have the greatest possible sympathy with the persons who have suffered by the explosions; but it is necessary to consider on what principle compensation could be awarded to them. Many people, unfortunately, suffer every day from crimes of violence, such as burglary, highway robbery, and arson, in which property of value is destroyed and injured; and the State never makes any compensation in these cases, nor would it be expedient or safe to do so. I have not been able to discover any distinction between these ordinary crimes and the crimes referred to in the Question; and, therefore, I have not felt myself justified in applying to the Treasury on the subject.

LITERATURE, SCIENCE, AND ART—THE RELIQUARY OF ST. LACHTEEN.

MR. DAWSON asked Mr. Chancellor of the Exchequer, Whether, in view of the willingness of the Science and Art Department to hand over the reliquary of St. Lachteen to the Royal Irish Academy, where similar objects of interest are collected, he would be willing to recoup the Science and Art Department in Dublin the sum of £450 paid for the reliquary out of their annual grant?

THE CHANCELLOR OF THE EXCHEQUER (Mr. CHILDERS): No, Sir; the reliquary will go to the Royal Irish Academy, and a Vote will be asked for.

RAILWAYS (INDIA)—THE RAJPOOTANA RAILWAY.

SIR GEORGE CAMPBELL asked the Under Secretary of State for India, Whet er it is the case that the working of the Rajpootana State Line of Railway is about to be made over to the Bombay and Baroda Railway; and, if so, whether, in addition to other precautions for the benefit of the public, the Government have reserved a complete control over the rates charged, and have not, as in the case of the East Indian Line, handed the Railway over to a private Company, with certain prescribed maximum rates, which the Government has no power to vary or decrease from time to time in the interest of the public without the consent of the Company?

MR. J. K. CROSS: The working of the Rajpootana Railway is about to be made over to the Bombay and Baroda Company; and the Government has reserved the power of fixing and varying from time to time both maximum and minimum rates.

LAW AND JUSTICE—CIRCUIT EXPENSES OF JUDGES.

MR. RYLANDS asked Mr. Chancellor of the Exchequer, Whether the Treasury Minute of 16th June, as to the payment of the Circuit expenses of the Judges and their suites, is to be treated as temporary only, so that, if the Order in Council is amended and the Chancery Judges and the Admiralty Judge are hereafter required to go on Circuit, it will be competent for the Crown to require them to do so without increase of salary?

MR. LABOUCHERE said, he wished to add the further Question, whether the Judges had the right to roam about the country abusing Her Majesty's Government?

THE CHANCELLOR OF THE EXCHEQUER (Mr. CHILDERS): I cannot answer the second Question. The Treasury Minute provides that, if the ordinary Circuit business of the country is performed by the Judges of the Queen's Bench Division, the Judges who go on Circuit will be allowed £7 10*s*. a-day during their absence from London, and *per contra* one of their two clerks will, as vacancies occur, be discontinued. This is part of, and dependont upon, the arrangements as to Circuit business which have been agreed to by the Judges generally; and if these arrangements should fail in their object of relieving, as far as possible, the Court of Appeal, and the

Probate and Admiralty and Chancery Divisions, they would be open to reconsideration. While stating this as a matter of right, I must not be understood as having arrived at any conclusion with respect to the best arrangements for the discharge of Circuit business.

In reply to Mr. HEALY,

THE CHANCELLOR OF THE EXCHEQUER (Mr. CHILDERS) said, that the salaries of the Judges were fixed by the law, and the expenses did not form any part of their salaries; therefore, their expenses must be submitted as Votes in Supply.

ARMY—DIRECT COMMISSIONS IN THE ROYAL ARTILLERY.

MR. GIBSON asked the Secretary of State for War, How many officers obtained direct commissions in the Royal Artillery between 1852 and 1857; how many of those officers are still in the service; was the average age of those officers three or four years higher than that of officers who did not obtain direct commissions; had some of those officers been recently superseded by a large number of Indian Majors, gazetted in May last to the Royal Artillery; and, is it intended to now compulsorily retire some of those officers who so entered the service at the aforesaid age, and thus deprive them of the advantages which were within their contemplation when they entered the service at the invitation of the Government?

THE MARQUESS OF HARTINGTON: Direct commissions in the Royal Artillery were obtained between 1852 and 1857 by 46 officers, of whom 14 are still serving in the Corps. Their average age exceeded the average age of those otherwise appointed to the Corps during the same period by three-and-a-quarter years. In May last, in consequence of vacancies among the lieutenant-colonels of the Indian cadres, Indian majors junior not only to some of these direct commission majors, but also to those commissioned at the same time from the Royal Military Academy, were promoted to be lieutenant-colonels in their own cadres. It is expected that three majors who entered by direct competition will be compulsorily retired during the next three months on attaining the age of 50 years. The promotion of the majors in the Indian cadres has had no bearing on the compulsory retirement of the other officers referred to in the Question.

THE ROYAL UNIVERSITY (IRELAND)—THE SUSTENTATION FUND.

MR. HEALY asked the Chief Secretary to the Lord Lieutenant of Ireland, What proportion of the funds voted for the Royal University is spent, first, on rewards for the Students; second, for the payment of Fellows and Examiners; third, on the Sustentation Fund of the Senators; do the Senators of the Royal University, in addition to their travelling expenses, usually allowed to members of public Boards, also get Sustentation money; is this a usual practice; on what scale is the Sustentation allowance to the Senators calculated; do they send in their hotel bills to the secretaries of the Royal University; is the benefit of the Sustentation Fund extended to the families of the Senators; do the Senators draw any Sustentation money when under no expense; and, will he consent to grant a Return of the names of the Senators who have availed of the Sustentation Fund, with the amount drawn in each instance?

MR. TREVELYAN, in reply, said, the accounts of the Royal University, which were annually certified by the Auditor General and presented to Parliament, would afford the hon. Member the first portion of the information he required. It was in Paper No. 289. The expenses and allowances to Senators comprised their actual travelling expenses, together with one guinea for each night necessarily spent away from home on the business of the University. No payment whatever was made to members who could attend without travelling for the purpose. All members of the Senate necessarily away from home were entitled to the subsistence allowance, although they did not all claim it. They were not required to send their hotel bills to the secretary. There was no ground for suggesting that any expenses or allowances were paid for in respect of any member's or Senator's families. He was not prepared to consent to such a Return as the hon. Member suggested. It would be regarded as invidious and of an inquisitorial character, and it might imply that those Senators who asked to be paid the allowance did so improperly. Similar

Returns in regard to the Commissioners of National Education were recently objected to on the same ground.

EDUCATION DEPARTMENT (IRELAND) —CASE OF MRS. CRAIG — SLIGO MODEL SCHOOLS.

Mr. WARTON (for Colonel King-Harman) asked the Chief Secretary to the Lord Lieutenant of Ireland, Whether it is true that Mrs. Craig, who was head teacher of the Sligo Model Schools, was obliged to resign her situation, owing to ill-health, after fourteen years' meritorious service, and was granted by the Commissioners of Education the sum of £78, to which she was entitled; whether Mrs. Craig died before the cheque was drawn, and if it is true that the authorities have refused to give the money, or any portion of it, to her aged mother; and, whether he will consider whether the whole or, at any rate, a portion of the money fairly earned by Mrs. Craig may not be given to the mother, who nursed her in her illness, and who is in straitened circumstances?

Mr. TREVELYAN: Mrs. Craig held the appointment stated, and resigned on the ground of ill-health. She signed a claim for gratuity on the 1st of December, and after the usual investigations the Treasury approved the award; but it subsequently transpired that in the meantime Mrs. Craig had died, and no payment under the award could legally be made to her representatives.

Mr. HARRINGTON asked, whether, having regard to the repeated delays in these matters on the part of the Treasury, the right hon. Gentleman would make such representations as would expedite the grants?

Mr. TREVELYAN said, he would get a list of cases and see how long the delays were. This class of applications ought to be dealt with promptly.

ARMY—THE GARRISON OF DUBLIN.

Mr. TOTTENHAM asked the Secretary of State for War, Whether there are now six battalions of Infantry, forming the Dublin Garrison, having a paper effective strength of 3,859 of all ranks, according to the latest Returns, and whether this is not in excess of the usual number; if he will state what number of this total are available for garrison duty; and, why it has been found necessary to supplement this large force by additional detachments of other Regiments from the Curragh to assist in furnishing the duties?

The Marquess of HARTINGTON: The garrison of Dublin consists nominally of about 3,600 of all ranks, which is not in excess of the usual number; but about 450 are on detachment duty. It is the practice at this time of the year to detach two companies per battalion for musketry and special drill; and after deducting these, the necessary duty men, and the sick, there scarcely remains enough privates, considering the heavy garrison duties, to allow the men four nights in bed. When, from time to time, the strength has fallen too low for this purpose, detachments from the Curragh have been made available.

EGYPT (RE-ORGANIZATION)—AUTONOMOUS INSTITUTIONS.

Sir GEORGE CAMPBELL asked the Under Secretary of State for Foreign Affairs, Whether, considering the great stress laid by Her Majesty's Government on the experiment of autonomous institutions in Egypt formally instituted last year, he is yet able to lay upon the Table any Reports on their working, and to explain the circumstances of the difference between Mr. Clifford Lloyd and the Legislative Council in connection with the proposed Municipality Bill; if he will state generally whether the provisions of the Decree of 1st May 1883 have been complied with; whether the Legislative Council have met on the dates appointed by Article 26; whether they have been consulted regarding every Law and every Decree regulating the public administrations, as required by Article 18; whether, in accordance with the same Article, the reasons have been communicated to them for any decisions contrary to their advice; whether the Budget has been submitted to and discussed by them in accordance with Article 22; and, whether, in accordance with Article 35, the General Assembly has been consulted regarding all loans raised, and will be consulted on any fresh loans which may be raised?

Lord EDMOND FITZMAURICE: As I have already informed the House, Sir Evelyn Baring, on his return to Egypt, will forward to Her Majesty's Government a Report on the working of the autonomous institutions, which will be laid before Parliament. I am not aware of any differences between Mr. Clifford Lloyd and the Legislative Council on the subject of the Municipality Bill. The provisions of the Decree of May 1, 1883, appear to have been complied with. I am unable to say whether the Legislative Council have always met on the days appointed. I understand that they have been consulted respecting Administrative Laws and Decrees; but I cannot say whether, in case of dissent from their views, the reasons have been communicated to them. Owing to the uncertainty of the finances, the Budget has not as yet been submitted, and Decrees have from time to time been issued postponing the date of its presentation. One of these Decrees is given at page 57 of "Egypt," No. 12, 1884. No loan having been raised, it has not been necessary to consult the Assembly.

SIR GEORGE CAMPBELL: May I ask if the noble Lord can tell us if the Legislative Council is still in existence; and whether it will meet to-morrow, the 1st of August, under Article 26?

LORD EDMOND FITZMAURICE: The Legislative Council is still in existence; and if my hon. Friend will refer to a very interesting letter by Mr. Sheldon Amos in *The Times* of to-day, he will find some information in regard to it.

LUNACY LAWS OF FOREIGN COUNTRIES.

SIR HENRY HOLLAND asked the Under Secretary of State for Foreign Affairs, Whether he will call for Reports from the Secretaries of the different Embassies as to the working of the Lunacy Laws on the Continent, and in the United States, and especially as to the following points:—Whether there are private as well as public asylums; what are the checks against improper admission or detention of persons in an asylum; what supervision and inspection, if any, is exercised by any public and recognized authority; and, the nature and powers of such authority; and, whether he will present such Reports to Parliament?

LORD EDMOND FITZMAURICE: I think my hon. Friend will find most of the information he asks for in a collected form in a work privately printed in Philadelphia by Dr. Harrison, *Legislation on Insanity*, which I shall be happy to show him; but any further information he may require will be at once procured.

SIR HENRY HOLLAND said, what he wished to do was to get the information placed in the hands of Members of the House before the Session of next year.

EDUCATION DEPARTMENT—ELEMENTARY EDUCATION.

MR. DAWSON asked the Vice President of the Committee of Council, Whether it is a fact that, owing to the very easy compliance with the Fourth Standard, the number of children under fourteen years, who never return to school, is largely increasing; whether he will make any change in the Code to insure longer attendance and more extended knowledge; whether, in view of this extremely early abandonment of ordinary schools, he will take any steps to provide night schools for the classes affected; and, whether the Education Department will purchase, for the use of industrial exhibitions in the United Kingdom, the exhibits of technical teaching and its results in Foreign Countries, and now on view at the International Health Exhibition?

MR. MUNDELLA: It is true that children pass the Fourth Standard at an earlier age than heretofore, owing to better attendance and better teaching. The Standard of exemption, however, cannot be raised by the Code, which merely deals with the curriculum, and has nothing whatever to do with the Standard prescribed by the bye-laws, the raising of which without the consent of the Local Authorities can only be effected by legislation. Very considerable changes have been made in the new Code with a view to the encouragement of night schools. The purchase of some of the most desirable exhibits is at present under the consideration of the Science and Art Department.

THE MAGISTRACY (IRELAND)—CO. WATERFORD.

MR. LEAMY asked the Chief Secretary to the Lord Lieutenant of Ireland, Whether it is the fact that, while three Catholic magistrates of the district of Kilmacthomas, county Waterford, have died within the last seven or eight years, only one gentleman, a non-Catholic and a land agent, has been appointed to the magistracy in that district during that time; whether it is the fact that there is not at present a single justice resident in Kilmacthomas Petty Sessions district; whether the Kilmacthomas Board of Guardians, in April last, forwarded a Memorial to the Lord Chancellor, setting forth these facts, and asking him to appoint Dr. Walsh, of Kilmacthomas, and Mr. Brian Finn, of Carigmorna; whether a similar Memorial was forwarded by the priests of the parish; and, whether the Lord Chancellor has received these Memorials; and, if so, whether he intends to act upon them?

MR. TREVELYAN: The Lord Chancellor informs me that, in consequence of a want of magistrates in the Kilmacthomas district, he appointed two gentlemen to the Commission of the Peace last month, on the recommendation of the Lord Lieutenant of the county. One of them is a Roman Catholic and a farmer; the other is believed to be a Dissenting Protestant—neither of them is a land agent. They will be immediately available for the Kilmacthomas Bench. The Memorials on behalf of the two gentlemen named in the Question have been received; and the Lord Chancellor is at present in correspondence with the Lord Lieutenant of the county on the subject.

MR. LEAMY: Can the right hon. Gentleman give the names of the two magistrates who have been appointed?

MR. TREVELYAN: No, Sir. The names are not given in the Minute of the Lord Chancellor.

PALACE OF WESTMINSTER—WESTMINSTER HALL (WEST FRONT).

MR. DICK-PEDDIE asked the First Commissioner of Works, Whether, having regard to the important effects which the proposed works on the west side of Westminster Hall will have on the architectural character of the group of buildings of which the Hall forms part, and to the insufficiency of the opportunities which have been given for consideration of the designs, he will postpone till next Session submitting an estimate for the works, and will agree to the appointment of a Select Committee to consider the question of the best mode of dealing with the west side of the Hall?

MR. SHAW LEFEVRE: When I laid Mr. Pearson's plans before the House, about three weeks ago, I stated that if I found that there was likely to be serious opposition to them on behalf of Members, I would refer the subject to a Select Committee. Since then I have been in communication with a large number of Members in all parts of the House, and I find that there is a general concurrence of opinion favourable to these plans. There are some few exceptions, but that must be expected to any scheme; the general verdict, however, is certainly favourable. Under these circumstances, I do not think it necessary to refer the question to a Committee, and I shall ask for a Vote during the present Session to commence the work during the Autumn. This is the more necessary, as the walls of the Hall were much injured during the past Winter, and I am unwilling to expose them to the injury of another Winter. There is, however, one part of the work which cannot be commenced at present—namely, the raising of the towers at the north end of the Hall. The Vote I shall ask for will not include any money for this purpose. This part of the work will stand over, and hon. Members who object to it will have an opportunity of raising the question next year.

MR. DICK-PEDDIE asked the right hon. Gentleman whether he was aware that all the architectural journals had written strongly in disapproval of the designs; and whether he had not received from the Society for the Protection of Ancient Buildings a very urgent request to postpone the matter until next year, in order that the public, as well as the Members of the House, might have an opportunity of considering it?

MR. SHAW LEFEVRE said, he was aware that two of the architectural papers had commented unfavourably on the designs; but he had observed that they commented unfavourably upon anything he proposed. So far as he had observed, papers of that kind were nothing if they were not critical. The Society for the Protection of Ancient Buildings had pressed him to postpone the question; but he did not understand that they were unfavourable to the scheme; they only criticized some of the points. He should consult the architect as to details, and later on he should be able to tell the House whether any modifications were thought desirable.

MERCHANT SHIPPING—THE "CONSOLATION."

SIR HENRY HOLLAND (for Lord CLAUD HAMILTON) asked the President of the Board of Trade, Whether, in face of the statement of facts relative to the case of the *Consolation* contained in the letter of the Directors of the Clyde Steam and Sailing Shipowners' Association, dated July 26, and addressed to him, he still adheres to his declaration publicly made that—

"The case of the *Consolation* was one in which no lives were lost; that the vessel was insured for £17,000; that her original cost was £17,000; that she was ten years old, and valued at £11,500?"

MR. CHAMBERLAIN: I have not seen the statement in the letter referred to in the noble Lord's Question; but I have been in correspondence with the owners of the *Consolation*, and I very readily accepted the statement from them to the effect that the sum I stated as the original cost of the vessel was considerably understated. This, however, does not affect the other statements in my speech upon which my argument was founded. It is the fact that that vessel was insured for £17,000, and she was valued by my orders by those independent valuers. The highest of these valuations was the sum I quoted—namely, £11,000, and I have since applied to the valuers, Messrs. Bayley and Ridley, and they adhere to their original valuation. I ought to add, although I do not think this is a matter of complaint against me, that when I referred to this case I was under the impression that no lives had been lost in connection with this ship, and I thought it fair to the owners to state that; but I have since learnt that, unfortunately, two sailors were drowned when the ship was lost.

MR. WHITLEY: Had the valuers seen the vessel?

MR. CHAMBERLAIN: No; they could not, as she was lost. They valued it, after it was lost, in the usual way in which such valuations are made.

BANKRUPTCY ACT, 1883—CIVIL SERVICE ESTIMATES.

MR. WAUGH asked the President of the Board of Trade, Whether, as compared with the charge of £34,677 for Bankruptcy last year, the following represents the total charge this year, viz.:—

	£
Inspector General, &c.	78,377
Transferred to Supreme Court, &c.	16,360
	£94,737

whether any other sums are charged in the Estimates in respect of Bankruptcy for the year 1884-5; why are the particulars of the gross sum of £23,514 charged in Class 6, for abolishing officers and compensation in the Court of Bankruptcy, not given in this year as usual; and, whether such sum has been added to by further abolitions under the Act of 1883, or whether the charge has been diminished by the appointment out of officers on the abolished list to new offices under the Act of 1883; and, if not, why have none of such persons been appointed?

MR. CHAMBERLAIN: The charge of £34,677 in the Estimates for 1883-4 was the charge for bankruptcy in the Supreme Court only. In addition, the sum of £40,000 was charged for Registrars in Bankruptcy in County Courts, making a total of £74,677. The charge for bankruptcy in the Estimates for 1884-5 consists not only of the sum of £78,000 on the Board of Trade Vote, but also of the sum of £14,000 for Registrars, &c., in the Supreme Court; £36,000 for Registrars in County Courts, and minor charges for rents, furniture, &c., amounting to about £5,000. This gives a total of £133,000. The additional income is estimated by the Board of Trade at £76,300. As to the third Question, I must refer my hon. Friend to the Treasury. With regard to the last Question, I may say there are very few abolitions under the new Act of 1883; and at present the greater part of the increased work has been performed by old officers. All the changes made will be fully detailed in the next Report on Bankruptcy.

MR. W. H. SMITH: Is the increased charge in consequence of the expenses of the Act?

MR. CHAMBERLAIN: I do not anticipate any increased charge at all.

ARMY (INDIA)—THE NORTH-WEST FRONTIER—QUETTA.

MR. SLAGG asked the Under Secretary of State for India, Whether it is the case that certain regiments of Cavalry have been added to the Indian Forces in connection with the frontier exploits in the district of Quetta?

MR. J. K. CROSS: I do not understand what my hon. Friend means when he speaks of frontier exploits in the district of Quetta; but there has been no increase in the Indian Cavalry.

CIVIL SERVANTS OF THE CROWN—SIR WILLIAM GURDON.

MR. TOMLINSON asked Mr. Chancellor of the Exchequer, Whether Sir William Brampton Gurdon, K.C.B., who is an accepted candidate for the representation of West Norfolk, is still a first-class clerk in the Treasury, in receipt of a salary of £1,000 a-year?

THE CHANCELLOR OF THE EXCHEQUER (Mr. CHILDERS): I have to say that Sir William Brampton Gurdon is a principal clerk in the Treasury, receiving £1,000 a-year. I have received from him no intimation that he intends to become a candidate for a seat in Parliament.

PARLIAMENT—DISTRIBUTION OF THE STATUTES TO MEMBERS.

MR. TOMLINSON asked the Secretary to the Treasury, Whether he is aware that, notwithstanding his promise to direct that the Acts passed this Session shall be issued as they are passed to those Members who require them, no orders to that effect have been given at the Vote Office; and, whether he will at once inquire into the cause of the failure to carry out his promise?

MR. COURTNEY: I have no control over this matter, which rests with the authorities of the House. But, on inquiry at the Vote Office, I learn that no application for loose copies of the statutes has been made there. They will, however, be supplied to any hon. Members who require them and give Notice to that effect.

POST OFFICE (IRELAND)—THE MAIL SERVICE BETWEEN DUBLIN AND CORK.

MR. LEAMY asked the Postmaster General, If the mail train under the new service from Dublin to Cork could not, without slackening speed, slip a carriage containing passengers and mails for Waterford at Maryborough; and, if so, whether, considering the desire of the people of Kilkenny and Waterford that this should be done, and the willingness of the Waterford and Central Ireland Railway Company to send a special train to meet the mail at Maryborough, he will, in the contract about to be entered into between the Post Office and the Great Western Railway Company, make an arrangement for the slipping of a carriage at Maryborough?

MR. FAWCETT: So far as I have been able to ascertain, no postal advantage would be likely to result from sending the Kilkenny and Waterford mails by way of Maryborough. If the Great Southern and Western Company wish to slip a carriage at Maryborough for the convenience of passengers, I certainly should offer no opposition, provided the mail train was not delayed.

MR. LEAMY: No; but will the right hon. Gentleman, in the interest of the public, require it to be done by the contract he is about entering into with the Company?

MR. FAWCETT: If there are no postal advantages, I do not think I could. I do not know what my legal powers are; but if, for the convenience of passengers, the Company would like to do it, I would not offer opposition, unless it would interfere with the Postal Service.

PARLIAMENT—"REMINGTON PERFECTED TYPE-WRITERS."

MR. LABOUCHERE asked the First Commissioner of Works, Whether he would have any objection to place in one of the rooms of the Library of the House of Commons, or in some other room set apart for the purpose, a small number of "Remington Perfected Type-Writers," for the convenience of the Members of the House?

MR. SHAW LEFEVRE said, he could not recommend what the hon. Member proposed.

PUBLIC HEALTH (IRELAND)—MULLINGAR GUARDIANS.

MR. HARRINGTON asked the Chief Secretary to the Lord Lieutenant of Ireland, Whether the Guardians of the Mullingar Union agreed to delegate their duties, as a Sanitary Authority of that town, to the Town Commissioners as a Sub-Committee; whether the Local Government Board refused to agree to this arrangement; and, whether, having regard to the necessity for prompt action on the part of the Sanitary Authorities, owing to the danger of a spread of cholera, the Local Government Board will reconsider their decision?

Mr. TREVELYAN, in reply, said, it was the case that the Guardians of the Mullingar Union, being the Rural Sanitary Authority, desired to appoint a Sanitary Committee for Mullingar; and the Local Government Board were obliged to point out to them that they could not legally carry out such an arrangement, as the power to appoint Committees under the 5th section of the Public Health Act was limited to Urban Sanitary Authorities. The danger of a spread of cholera would not enable the Local Government Board to authorize the appointment of such a Committee by the Board of Guardians.

POST OFFICE—SORTERS AND LETTER CARRIERS—THE PARCEL POST.

Mr. HARRINGTON asked the Postmaster General, Whether any step has yet been taken to remedy the complaints of sorters in connection with mail trains, or to give additional remuneration to letter carriers in connection with the increased duty under the parcel post?

Mr. FAWCETT: In reply to a Question put to me a few months ago by the hon. Member for Mallow, I stated that in the matter of Sunday duty arrangements were being made to place the Irish mail sorters, as far as possible, on an equality with those employed in England. Assuming that to be the matter to which the hon. Member refers in the first part of his Question, I beg to state that to those arrangements effect is now being given. In reply to the second part of the Question, there is no intention of entering upon another general revision of letter-carriers' wages, which was completed only two years ago; but where information reaches me of the need of revision in any particular case, the circumstances are carefully considered.

POST OFFICE (IRELAND) — LETTER CARRIERS—THE PORTUMNA LETTER CARRIER.

Mr. T. P. O'CONNOR asked the Postmaster General, Whether it is a fact that the rural postman has to carry the mails between Portumna and Power's Cross, county Galway, a distance of twelve Irish miles, for six days of the week; whether, in order to accomplish this task, the postman has to leave at six in the morning; and, whether the remuneration given for this work is eight shillings per week?

Mr. FAWCETT: The facts appear to be substantially as stated in the Question of the hon. Member, the distance mentioned being, of course, understood to be the total distance travelled by the postman there and back. The postman does not hold a regular appointment, but is one employed by the local Postmaster, who receives an allowance to provide for the performance of the duty. I will, however, make further inquiry, with a view to revising the allowance if necessary.

THE IRISH LAND COMMISSION—FAIR RENTS—GLEBE LANDS OF DRUMCREE, CO. ARMAGH.

Mr. WARTON (for Colonel King-Harman) asked the Chief Secretary to the Lord Lieutenant of Ireland, Whether it is the fact that the Land Commissioners have, in the case of the Glebe Lands of Drumcree, county Armagh, reduced, by 18 per cent., rents proved to have been unchanged since 1827, and, subject to which, tenants were proved to have, even so lately as 1880, given £12 10s. per acre for the tenant-right; whether said lands were purchased from the Church Commissioners by the present owner, Mr. Law; whether the rental furnished by them showed the old rents; and whether the valuation made by the Commissioners' valuator, Mr. M. O'Brien, to give the tenants the benefit of the clause in the Church Act in their favour, placed nearly twenty-four years' purchase on said rents, and thus represented them as moderate rents; and, whether the Government are prepared, out of the Irish Church surplus, which got the benefit of the price produced by the Commissioners' representations, to refund Mr. Law the proportion of the purchase money so obtained from him by such representations?

Mr. TREVELYAN, in reply, said, that the Land Commission reported that in the case referred to the rents were reduced, on the whole, by a little more than 18 per cent. Evidence was given that the rents were not changed since 1837; that in some cases a considerable sum was paid for tenant-right; and that

Mr. Law paid 30 years' purchase for the land at the old rents, that being the just value, according to Mr. O'Brien's valuation. No evidence as to value was given by the landlord at the re-hearing of the appeal, and the Commissioners came to a conclusion on the whole evidence laid before them. He could not hold out any hope that he would make the representations to the Treasury suggested in the last paragraph of the Question.

SWITZERLAND—THE "SALVATIONISTS."

SIR ROBERT PEEL asked the Under Secretary of State for Foreign Affairs, Whether any more Papers, in continuation of "Switzerland, No. 1, 1884," manifestly incomplete, will be laid upon the Table; and, what information he can supply respecting the recent renewal of outrages, and of religious persecutions on British subjects and others, of a most serious description in the town of Bienne, on which occasion a house occupied by British subjects was attacked with the utmost violence and completely gutted; the local police being overpowered by the mob, so that it was deemed necessary by the Cantonal authorities, at the instance of the Federal Government, to call out the Military?

LORD EDMOND FITZMAURICE: Further Papers will be prepared and laid. The Cantonal authorities of Neuchatel, Vaud, and Berne recently agreed that private meetings of Salvationists were to be allowed in those Cantons under certain conditions. The Salvationists commenced to hold private meetings in a building at Bienne, which they had hired for the purpose; a mob attacked the building, and serious disorder ensued. The Council of State of the Canton of Berne have, in consequence, and in order to keep the peace and preserve public order, prohibited the holding of Salvationist meetings in Bienne and its neighbourhood.

AFRICA (WEST COAST)—THE CONGO RIVER.

SIR HERBERT MAXWELL asked the Under Secretary of State for Foreign Affairs, Whether the right of pre-emption of certain territory on the Congo, occupied by the International Association, has been obtained by the French Government; and, whether this right had been previously offered to Her Majesty's Government?

LORD EDMOND FITZMAURICE: From an agreement between the French Prime Minister and the President of the Belgian Association, which has appeared in the public Press, it would appear that the right of pre-emption, to which the hon. Baronet refers, has been obtained by the French Government; but Her Majesty's Government have no official cognizance of this agreement. This right had not previously been offered to Her Majesty's Government.

THE WEST INDIA ISLANDS—CONDUCT OF A COLONIAL OFFICIAL.

MR. O'DONNELL asked the Under Secretary of State for the Colonies, Whether he has received any information as to the conduct of a high Colonial official, in consequence of which he was placed in irons on board the Royal Mail Steamer *Don*, which left Barbadoes on the 30th of May of the present year; and, whether any steps will be taken in consequence?

MR. EVELYN ASHLEY: We have received a newspaper containing an anonymous statement of that sort; but we have given no credence to it. We do not think it necessary to take any steps at present.

MR. O'DONNELL: Is the hon. Gentleman aware that what he calls an anonymous statement is a leading article in the newspaper which charges this official with crime? Will the Under Secretary make any inquiries from the authorities of the steamship *Don*, on board which such crimes are said to have taken place? If the Under Secretary cannot answer now I will postpone the Question.

MR. EVELYN ASHLEY: I can answer now. We believe the charges to have no foundation; and until we have something more substantial to go upon we cannot make any inquiries.

MR. O'DONNELL: Will the Government require this official to bring an action for libel against the newspaper which charges him with crime?

MR. EVELYN ASHLEY: I cannot answer that Question without Notice.

IRISH LAND COMMISSION—SALE OF GLEBE LANDS, CO. KERRY.

MR. HARRINGTON asked the Secretary to the Treasury, Whether his attention has been called to the following letter addressed to tenants in Kerry who have purchased Glebelands:—

"Irish Land Commission,
"Church Property Department.

"You are hereby informed that, unless the amount claimed in the inclosed receivable form is paid within the time specified therein, the Commissioners will direct their solicitors to take legal proceedings to recover the amount due without any further notice.

"By Order,
" ———, Secretary."

Whether this notice only allowed a month after date for the payment of the instalment, though in every other year since the purchase of their farms they were not called upon until the end of September to pay the instalment falling due on July 1st; and, whether it is true that, in the lands adjoining these farms in Kerry, the Sub-Commissioners have fixed judicial rents at 25 per cent under the amount of such annual instalment?

MR. TREVELYAN (who replied to the Question) said: I find, on inquiry from the Land Commissioners, that the receivable orders, issued to persons owing one instalment, due on 1st of July, allow in all cases three months (to the 30th of September) for payment. If two or more instalments are due one month only is given, and in such cases the notice referred to in the Question accompanies the receivable order. These regulations have been in force for 14 years, and legal proceedings are not taken unless it is found impossible to recover the instalments in any other way. With regard to the last paragraph of the Question, it appeared that there are about 38 persons scattered throughout different parts of the county of Kerry whose holdings were purchased from the Church Temporalities Commissioners — the purchase moneys being still outstanding on mortgage; and, unless further particulars be given, it is impossible to say what reductions, if any, have been made in the rents of tenants whose farms adjoin the properties of these persons.

POST OFFICE—THE GALWAY MAILS.

MR. T. P. O'CONNOR asked the Postmaster General, Whether he will consider the necessity of accelerating the arrival of the English and other mails in Galway; whether such an acceleration could not be carried out by the starting at eight o'clock from the Broadstone Terminus of the train that now leaves at nine, by the reduction of the number of stoppages, and by the increase of the speed from 24 to 34 miles an hour; and, whether the Chairman of the Midland Great Western Railway Company has not declared his readiness to supply an accelerated mail service in the case the Post Office offer sufficiently remunerative terms?

MR. FAWCETT: In reply to the hon. Member, I beg to say that an acceleration of the mails to Galway (such as that suggested in the Question) is quite feasible, but would involve the running of an additional train, and is, largely, a question of expense. I am in correspondence with the Midland Great Western Railway, and will come to a decision on the subject as quickly as possible.

MR. T. P. O'CONNOR: Am I right in saying that for mail services, while the Great Southern and Western Railway Company receives £70 a-mile, and the Great Northern £90, the Midland Company receives only £40 a-mile?

MR. FAWCETT: It is impossible to draw any comparison between the mail service to Cork, which carries all the American mails, and the mail service to Galway and Sligo, which is comparatively light. The Companies are also paid in proportion to the pace of the trains.

MR. SEXTON: Is there any essential difference between the Great Northern Railway Company in this matter and the Midland Company; and has the right hon. Gentleman, in his communications with the Midland Company, offered them any improvement whatever on the present terms?

MR. FAWCETT: The Great Northern Company is going to start from Dublin at an earlier hour, and will arrive at Belfast earlier than now. The whole subject of the acceleration of the mails throughout Ireland generally is now being considered. It is a very complicated subject; but I am pushing it on as quickly as possible.

MR. SEXTON: Has the right hon. Gentleman offered any improvement in the terms to the Midland Company?

MR. FAWCETT: I find it rather difficult to answer that Question without notice. I have so many offers made to carry them in mind; but if the hon. Member will write to me I shall be happy to give him information.

LAW AND JUSTICE (ENGLAND AND WALES)—CASE OF FRANK STOCKWELL—SENTENCE ON A CHILD.

MR. GRANTHAM asked the Secretary of State for the Home Department, If he will state the reason for remitting any portion of the sentence on a boy named Frank Stockwell, sentenced by Baron Pollock, at Reading, to a month's imprisonment, without hard labour, for setting fire to hay ricks?

SIR WILLIAM HARCOURT: As soon as I was aware that a child of seven years old had been imprisoned for a month, I wrote to the learned Judge, a most humane man, on the subject, and he said, in reply—"I shall feel very much pleased if you can do better for him than I could." Subsequently, I wrote to the Governor and the Chaplain of the prison to report to me specially upon the case. The Chaplain's Report has been received. He says—

"According to the Prison Rules, the boy was allowed one hour's school with other juveniles, if any; but there were none in the prison when Stockwell arrived. Subsequently, a boy of 14 years of age was sentenced to a month's imprisonment, so that the present class of juveniles consisted of two. But for the one hour's instruction the child has the rest of 24 hours in solitary confinement, except for most casual interruption. I am very decidedly of opinion that this is not morally healthy for the child. I gather from my own observation, and from the schoolmaster, that Stockwell is not sharp, but rather idle, and without any show of application, and, if anything, dull, and even apparently sullen, which, I take it, means that he feels strange in a strange place. He is not quick of speech, and also seems as if he knew what it was to be in fear of a scolding. I find nothing artful or vicious about him, I have studied him much, owing to the bad opinion held of him by the Vicar of the parish. I have talked to him quietly, and he has admitted he was sorry for what he did, and that he would be a better boy. I am quite sure the boy lighted the hay-rick to see how it would burn, but never dreamt of the probable consequence, and ran away frightened. I have a very strong opinion of the unsuitability of the prison for such a child, and I should greatly rejoice if it were thought better to give the boy a second birching and discharge him. Such a case as this is for home treatment."

Before this communication was received the child had been in prison—practically in solitary confinement—for nearly three weeks; and I do not think that anybody in this House will condemn my conduct when I decided that the best thing to do was to discharge the child. I wish those who pass sentences of this kind would remember what solitary confinement is as applied to a child of tender years. It is a most terrible—I think improper—punishment. I have known a case in which a child suffered so dreadfully from solitary confinement that the warder took him into his own house—a breach of prison discipline—which I had not the heart to condemn.

POOR LAW (METROPOLIS)—POLAND STREET WORKHOUSE—MR. BLISS.

LORD ALGERNON PERCY asked the President of the Local Government Board, Whether the Guardians of the Poland Street Workhouse of the Westminster Union have unanmously decided to suspend Mr. W. J. D. Bliss from the office of master of that workhouse; whether the Local Government Board have confirmed, or propose to confirm, that suspension; and, how soon their decision will be made known?

MR. GEORGE RUSSELL: It is true that the Guardians of the Westminster Union unanimously suspended Mr. Bliss from the office of Master of the Poland Street Workhouse. We have since communicated with Mr. Bliss and the Guardians on the subject; and on the 26th of this month we received from the Guardians their reply to the explanation which had been furnished by Mr. Bliss. That letter is now under our consideration, and we will very shortly inform the Guardians of our decision.

INLAND REVENUE—THE INCOME TAX—ASSESSMENTS UNDER SCHEDULE D.

MR. LEAHY asked the Secretary to the Treasury, If he is aware that it is the practice of Mr. Turner, surveyor of taxes at Tralee, and other surveyors in Ireland, to increase, year after year, the assessment for income tax on traders under Schedule D, without assigning any reason for so doing until appealed against, at very considerable trouble and expense to the trader; and, whether, when the assessment is once fixed, it can be so arbitrarily increased by those officers?

MR. COURTNEY: This Question only appeared on the Paper to-day. Assessments under Schedule D are only fixed for one year, and it is the duty of the surveyors to increase them if they appear to be insufficient, ample opportunity of appeal against such increase being given by law. If the hon. Member will communicate to me the particulars of any case of apparently arbitrary assessment at Tralee it shall be at once inquired into.

IRELAND—THE MUSEUM OF SCIENCE AND ART, DUBLIN.

MR. MAURICE BROOKS asked the Secretary to the Treasury, Whether he can say if some one of the architectural plans for the Science and Art Museum, Dublin, will be adopted before the Prorogation of Parliament?

MR. COURTNEY: I hope it may be possible to decide this matter before the House rises; but I can give no promise, as the decision depends, in part at least, on the result of certain valuations now being made.

MR. DAWSON: Seeing the great delay there is in getting a building up in Dublin, and seeing the promptness with which the First Commissioner of Works is going to proceed with the works at Westminster Hall, I would ask him whether he would not take the Irish Museum into his hands also?

EGYPT—THE MUDIR HUSSEIN WASIF.

MR. LABOUCHERE asked the Under Secretary of State for Foreign Affairs, Whether he has noticed the following statement, in a Despatch from Mr. Clifford Lloyd to Mr. Egerton, dated 11th May 1884:—

"In the early days of September 1883 a serious robbery had been committed in the Province of Garbieh. The mudir accordingly arrested about seventy persons of the locality, including many sheiks and other respectable persons. They were all put in prison, and tortured in the most barbarous manner. They were thumbscrewed, tied up to beams by their feet and by their fingers, and were kourbashed to such an extent that two unfortunate men were said to have died under the operation. It was with great difficulty that I succeeded in getting an English Officer, attached to the Ministry of the Interior, sent down to assist the mudir in the inquiry he was making. The result of this inquiry proved that there was no evidence of any description against any of the accused, but that many of them had been forced, under torture by the mudir's subordinates, to sign prepared confessions, implicating themselves and other prisoners in the robbery. I have but to add that it was only by calling for the support of our Government that I was able to obtain the removal of this mudir, who was immediately promoted to be Governor General of Eastern Soudan;"

whether, in the original Despatch, the name of this mudir was suppressed; and, if not, why it is in the published Document; and, whether he can give the House some assurance that this official is no longer employed by the Egyptian Government either as a governor or as a mudir, or in any other capacity?

MR. HEALY, before this Question was answered, said, he would like to ask the noble Lord whether he was aware that there was no essential difference between the conduct of the Mudir and Mr. Clifford Lloyd's own conduct in Ireland?

MR. SPEAKER: Order, order! That is not a proper Question to be asked.

LORD EDMOND FITZMAURICE: The name of the Mudir referred to is not given in the original despatch; but the evidence shows him to have been Hussein Wasif Pasha, who, as I have already informed the House, is no longer in the employment of the Egyptian Government.

LAW AND JUSTICE (IRELAND)—ARREST OF MR. CHANCE.

MR. HEALY asked the Chief Secretary to the Lord Lieutenant of Ireland, Is he aware that Mr. Chance wholly denies the allegations of the policeman who arrested him, and declared that, on seeing Alice Carroll, he at once told her he was solicitor for Mr. O'Brien, M.P., and that he wanted her evidence about Bolton, and that he denies the statement about being sent by Mallon; and, will the Government grant an inquiry, sworn or otherwise, into the arrest, or rely solely on the policeman's version of the matter?

MR. TREVELYAN: This Question, the hon. Member knows, only appeared this morning; but I think I have an adequate answer to it. There are two ways in which a person in the position of a constable acting wrongly may be dealt with. He may be dealt with criminally, if the case comes within the law; or he may be dealt with by the Head of the Department by way of punishment or dismissal. In the present case, I am advised that the constable cannot be proceeded against criminally, and the other branch of the case is to be dealt with by the Chief Commissioner. Assuming that the constable was told by the Carrolls what he says he was told, I see no reason for holding that he acted otherwise than he ought. He had a most responsible duty to discharge, and I think he acted as he was in duty bound to act. If the arrest was unwarranted, and if Mr. Chance feels aggrieved, as I hear he does, he may take an action against the constable for unwarranted arrest, and so elicit the facts on oath.

MR. HEALY: If he takes such an action, will the Government defend him and pay his damages?

[No reply.]

ITALY—CONFISCATION OF THE PROPAGANDA PROPERTY.

MR. O'DONNELL asked the First Lord of the Treasury, Whether he has been informed of the resolutions of the Irish Catholic Hierarchy, against the confiscation of the Propaganda property in Italy; and, whether any communications, in reference to the Propaganda property, have been addressed by the British Government to the Government of Italy since questions on the subject were asked in this House three months ago?

MR. GLADSTONE: I have not any particular cognizance of the resolutions to which the hon. Member refers; but I am aware that the Roman Catholic Hierarchy consider themselves and their Church materially aggrieved. That is the substantial part of the Question. With respect to the latter part of it, I have to say that the British Ambassador in Rome was directed, some time back, to make any representations to the Government of Italy which he could make with propriety and which might appear to be useful. He was also instructed to have some regard to what was done by the Representatives of the other Powers. The Ambassador has not seen any such opportunity; and I am informed that no Power has been in a position to make representations to the Italian Government on the subject.

MR. HEALY: May I ask whether the United States Congress did not pass Resolutions on the subject, and has not the Ambassador of the United States taken action, if no other Power has?

MR. GLADSTONE: I am really not aware what Resolutions the United States Congress passed; but if they did pass such a Resolution, it would not in any degree modify the statement I have made, which was with regard to representations of the Powers to the Italian Government.

MR. SEXTON: I beg to give Notice that on the Diplomatic Vote the hon. Member for the City of Cork (Mr. Parnell) will call further attention to this subject.

EGYPT—THE CONFERENCE.

MR. ASHMEAD-BARTLETT asked the First Lord of the Treasury, Whether he will now state to the House the nature of the financial proposals made by Her Majesty's Ministers to the Conference in order to pay the costs of the bombardment of Alexandria and the evacuation of the Soudan, and restore equilibrium to the Egyptian Budget?

MR. GLADSTONE: The hon. Member has on this occasion done what he has done on some other occasions—he compels me to repeat an answer which I have given him formerly, and in regard to which I have no option. It would be a breach of understanding and a breach of faith with the Conference, independently of anything else, if any communication with regard to the proceedings within it were made during the time that Conference has its sitting. But I may take the opportunity which the Question of the hon. Gentleman affords me to say with much regret, and to my own disappointment and to that of the House, that the Conference which met to-day was informed by the French Ambassador that he was not in possession of sufficient instructions, and that he had to request a further adjournment until Saturday. To that request, under the circumstances, there could be but one answer; and perhaps I may say this —though I have no doubt it is a disappointment to the House to receive the intelligence—yet those who have paid attention to what has been passing in France within the last few days will be prepared for it—it will be seen that the French Cabinet has been placed in a peculiar position with regard to domestic concerns.

SIR STAFFORD NORTHCOTE: In consequence of that answer I am obliged to ask the right hon. Gentleman what course he proposes to take with a view of giving the House an opportunity, before the Prorogation, of pronouncing an opinion on the proceedings of the Conference?

MR. GLADSTONE: I am afraid, Sir, it would be premature if I were to endeavour to explain precisely the course of the proceedings we should adopt until the Conference shall arrive at a decision. We shall lose no moment after that; but I am in the confident hope that the House will not be put to any practical inconvenience. We shall not lose a moment in telling the House both what the Conference has done, and likewise what we intend to do with a view to redeeming the pledge which I gave the right hon. Gentleman.

SIR STAFFORD NORTHCOTE: Is the right hon. Gentleman in a position to say whether it is probable that he will have to submit a proposal to the House upon which its judgment will have to be taken?

MR. GLADSTONE: No, Sir; I think it would not be advantageous to state what is probable or what is improbable, for [illegible]

MR. ASHMEAD-BARTLETT: With regard to [illegible]

[illegible]

that they have not been brought before the Conference, because the Conference is limited to the object which was described in the invitation.

MR. BOURKE: I should like to know whether any Papers will be laid on the Table of the House when the right hon. Gentleman makes his Statement, because it would be perfectly impossible for the House to gain even a slight notion of the case from the statements of the right hon. Gentleman, however clear they may be. The right hon. Gentleman said the other day that by far the most important part of these negotiations had taken place in the Commission, and I think the right hon. Gentleman used the expression—"The chief labour with respect to this business has been performed by the Commission." [illegible] Papers with respect to [illegible] already. At any rate, they ought to be presented in a few days [illegible] and I hope, therefore, the Foreign Office will be prepared with them at a very early [illegible]

MR. SCLATER-BOOTH: Can the [illegible]

MR. GLADSTONE: [illegible]

[illegible]

stable was told by the Carrolls what he says he was told, I see no reason for holding that he acted otherwise than he ought. He had a most responsible duty to discharge, and I think he acted as he was in duty bound to act. If the arrest was unwarranted, and if Mr. Chance feels aggrieved, as I hear he does, he may take an action against the constable for unwarranted arrest, and so elicit the facts on oath.

MR. HEALY: If he takes such an action, will the Government defend him and pay his damages?

[No reply.]

ITALY—CONFISCATION OF THE PROPAGANDA PROPERTY.

MR. O'DONNELL asked the First Lord of the Treasury, Whether he has been informed of the resolutions of the Irish Catholic Hierarchy, against the confiscation of the Propaganda property in Italy; and, whether any communications, in reference to the Propaganda property, have been addressed by the British Government to the Government of Italy since questions on the subject were asked in this House three months a o?

gMR. GLADSTONE: I have not any particular cognizance of the resolutions to which the hon. Member refers; but I am aware that the Roman Catholic Hierarchy consider themselves and their Church materially aggrieved. That is the substantial part of the Question. With respect to the latter part of it, I have to say that the British Ambassador in Rome was directed, some time back, to make any representations to the Government of Italy which he could make with propriety and which might appear to be useful. He was also instructed to have some regard to what was done by the Representatives of the other Powers. The Ambassador has not seen any such opportunity; and I am informed that no Power has been in a position to make representations to the Italian Government on the subject.

MR. HEALY: May I ask whether the United States Congress did not pass Resolutions on the subject, and has not the Ambassador of the United States taken action, if no other Power has?

MR. GLADSTONE: I am really not aware what Resolutions the United States Congress passed; but if they did pass such a Resolution, it would not in any degree modify the statement I have made, which was with regard to representations of the Powers to the Italian Government.

MR. SEXTON: I beg to give Notice that on the Diplomatic Vote the hon. Member for the City of Cork (Mr. Parnell) will call further attention to this subject.

EGYPT—THE CONFERENCE.

MR. ASHMEAD-BARTLETT asked the First Lord of the Treasury, Whether he will now state to the House the nature of the financial proposals made by Her Majesty's Ministers to the Conference in order to pay the costs of the bombardment of Alexandria and the evacuation of the Soudan, and restore equilibrium to the Egyptian Budget?

MR. GLADSTONE: The hon. Member has on this occasion done what he has done on some other occasions—he compels me to repeat an answer which I have given him formerly, and in regard to which I have no option. It would be a breach of understanding and a breach of faith with the Conference, independently of anything else, if any communication with regard to the proceedings within it were made during the time that Conference has its sitting. But I may take the opportunity which the Question of the hon. Gentleman affords me to say with much regret, and to my own disappointment and to that of the House, that the Conference which met to-day was informed by the French Ambassador that he was not in possession of sufficient instructions, and that he had to request a further adjournment until Saturday. To that request, under the circumstances, there coul be but one answer; and perhaps I may say this—though I have no doubt it is a disappointment to the House to receive the intelligence—yet those who have paid attention to what has been passing in France within the last few days will be prepared for it—it will be seen that the French Cabinet has been placed in a peculiar position with regard to domestic concerns.

SIR STAFFORD NORTHCOTE: In consequence of that answer I am obliged to ask the right hon. Gentleman what course he proposes to take with a view of giving the House an opportunity, before the Prorogation, of pronouncing an opinion on the proceedings of the Conference?

MR. GLADSTONE: I am afraid, Sir, it would be premature if I were to endeavour to explain precisely the course of the proceedings we should adopt until the Conference shall arrive at a decision. We shall not lose a moment after that; but I am in the confident hope that the House will not be put to any practical inconvenience. We shall not lose a moment in telling the House both what the Conference has done, and likewise what we intend to do, with a view to redeeming the pledge which I gave the right hon. Gentleman.

SIR STAFFORD NORTHCOTE: Is the right hon. Gentleman in a position to say whether it is probable that he will have to submit a proposal to the House upon which its judgment will have to be taken?

MR. GLADSTONE: No, Sir; I think it would not be advantageous to state what is probable or what is improbable, for it would probably be the cause of further disappointment.

MR. ASHMEAD-BARTLETT: With regard to the statement of the right hon. Gentleman, that the reason for declining to answer my Question as to the financial proposals was that it would be a breach of faith with the Conference, I beg to ask him whether it is not the fact that out of the four main heads of the proposals now before the Powers, three—namely, that with regard to the evacuation by the British troops; that of the extra powers proposed to be given to the Debt Commissioners; and that with regard to the neutralization of Egypt and the Canal—have already been before this House; and whether he will explain what reasons exist for considering that the communication of the financial proposals to the House would be a greater breach of faith than the communication of the other proposals?

MR. GLADSTONE: The other proposals are not before the Conference. The financial proposals are.

MR. ASHMEAD-BARTLETT: I would ask the Prime Minister whether the House is to understand that the statement made by him, I think on the 23rd of June, that the proposals of the Government would be laid before the Powers, has not been carried out?

MR. GLADSTONE: Certainly they have been communicated to the Powers; but they have not been brought before the Conference, because the Conference is limited to the object which was described in the invitation.

MR. BOURKE: I should like to know whether any Papers will be laid on the Table at the same time as the right hon. Gentleman makes his Statement; because it would be perfectly impossible for the House to gain even a slight notion of the case from the statements of the right hon. Gentleman, however clear they may be. The right hon. Gentleman said the other day that by far the most important part of these negotiations had taken place in the Commission; and I think the right hon. Gentleman used the expression—"The chief labour with respect to this business has been performed by the Commission." Of course, the Papers with respect to the Commission are now ready. At any rate, they might be presented at a few days' notice; and I hope, therefore, the Foreign Office will be prepared with them at a very short Notice.

MR. SCLATER-BOOTH: Can the right hon. Gentleman say that after the meeting on Saturday—that is to say, on Monday—he will be in a position to make a statement?

MR. GLADSTONE: All I can say is, that I hope it, and I expect it. I cannot go beyond that. With reference to what I said of the Commission, I did not say that the most important part of the labours was performed by the Commission—I think I said it was the most laborious, requiring time, and a great deal of hard work. I quite agree with the right hon. Gentleman that any statement would be inadequate to the object in view that did not deal with the operations of the Commission. I cannot undertake to say what Papers will be presented; but, undoubtedly, Papers giving what Her Majesty's Government may think a full view of the case will be in readiness, and will be presented at once.

LAW AND POLICE (METROPOLIS)—MR. W. H. SMITH'S WATCH.

MR. LABOUCHERE: Sir, I do not see the Home Secretary in his place; but, as I see the hon. Gentleman the Under Secretary of State for the Home Department, perhaps he will be able to answer my Question. It is, Whether he has observed in the public Press to-day that the right hon. Gentleman the Member for Westminster lost his watch at a Conservative meeting last night; and, whether the Home Secretary will do his best to induce the police to take measures to prevent such an occurrence taking place again?

MR. W. H. SMITH: I did not suppose the hon. Gentleman the Member for Northampton would have thought it necessary to bring any question affecting myself personally before the House. If I had had any complaint to make against the police, or any application to make to the Government, I should have made it myself. But I wish to say that the circumstance to which the hon. Gentleman alludes did not occur at the meeting, but outside the meeting, where the hon. Gentleman's friends objected to my entering the meeting.

THE MAGISTRACY (IRELAND)—MR. CLIFFORD LLOYD.

MR. HEALY asked the First Lord of the Treasury, If the Government have come to any decision as to the future employment of Mr. Clifford Lloyd?

MR. GLADSTONE: I must appeal to the hon. Member to postpone this Question until Monday. I have only seen it this morning, and Lord Spencer is not in town.

PARLIAMENT — BUSINESS OF THE HOUSE—COMMITTEE OF SUPPLY—STANDING ORDER 425A.

MR. GLADSTONE, in whose name the following Notice of Motion stood on the Paper:—

"That, for the remainder of the Session, the Standing Order of the 27th November, 1882, relating to Notices on going into Committee of Supply on Monday and Thursday, be extended to Friday and Saturday,"

said: I wish to postpone my Motion until to-morrow, in order that we may acquaint ourselves more fully with the desire of the House upon the subject.

LORD RANDOLPH CHURCHILL: I wish to ask the right hon. Gentleman whether he can say when the Diplomatic Vote will be taken; and, whether he will undertake that when it is taken it will be with Notice? It would be an immense convenience to a number of hon. Members if he could do so.

MR. GLADSTONE: I am afraid that until I am able to make the communication to the House about the Conference, on which the course of Business will somewhat depend, it would be idle to give any undertaking about the date of taking the Diplomatic Vote.

LORD RANDOLPH CHURCHILL: I cannot see what connection there is between the Conference and the Diplomatic Vote.

MR. GLADSTONE: The Conference may lead to a statement, and a statement to a debate; for a Notice of Motion might be given asking the Government for the redemption of the pledge they have already made, and that might render it necessary to interrupt the course of Business.

LORD RANDOLPH CHURCHILL: The Prime Minister will not take the Diplomatic Vote without Notice?

MR. GLADSTONE: No, Sir.

PARLIAMENT—HOUSE OF COMMONS—VENTILATION OF THE HOUSE.

MR. BORLASE: I wish to ask the President of the Local Government Board, Whether his attention has been called to the horrible smells in the "Aye" Lobby of this House to-day, and to the danger that must accrue to the Party therefrom?

SIR CHARLES W. DILKE: The matter has nothing whatever to do with me. I understood, however, that the First Commissioner of Works had appointed a Committee to inquire into the subject, and I have not yet seen the Report of that Committee.

MR. W. H. SMITH: Perhaps I may be allowed to say, as Chairman of that Committee, that the Committee sat on two occasions and took evidence; but were not able to trace the cause of the nuisance. They have, however, requested further assistance to be given them in the Recess in order to trace the origin of these smells.

SIR CHARLES W. DILKE: I may say that, although I have not seen the Report of the Committee, I have already instructed the Local Government Board to place Inspectors at the service of the Committee.

PARLIAMENT—BUSINESS OF THE HOUSE—BURGH POLICE AND HEALTH (SCOTLAND) BILL.

GENERAL SIR GEORGE BALFOUR: In the absence of the hon. and learned Member for Stafford (Mr. M'Laren), I beg to ask the Lord Advocate, Whether he intends to proceed further this Session with the Burgh Police and Health (Scotland) Bill?

THE LORD ADVOCATE (Mr. J. B. BALFOUR): Having regard to what passed in the discussion on Tuesday night, we could not hope, in the short period of this Session which remains, to pass this Bill through both Houses of Parliament; and, therefore, we are reluctantly obliged to abandon the intention of proceeding further with it now. [Mr. WARTON: Hear, hear!]

EGYPT (EVENTS IN THE SOUDAN)—MAJOR KITCHENER.

MR. ASHMEAD-BARTLETT asked the Under Secretary of State for Foreign Affairs, Whether it is true that the friendly tribes near Agig on the Red Sea have been massacred by Osman Digna's followers; and, whether Major Kitchener has gone to Dongola?

LORD EDMOND FITZMAURICE: No, Sir; it is not true that the friendly tribes have been massacred. Major Kitchener has gone to Dongola in order to open communications with the Kababish Arabs. If the hon. Member will refer to "Egypt, No. 25, 1884," page 113, he will find Papers on the subject.

INDIA—REVENUE SETTLEMENT DEPARTMENT—NATIVE APPOINTMENTS.

MR. THOROLD ROGERS asked the Under Secretary of State for India, Whether he can inform the House what the answer was which was given to a Memorial or Letter forwarded by Mr. Rungiah Naider Garu in reference to the appointment of Messrs. Tarrant and Thornhill to offices in the Revenue Settlement Department, which offices the writer of the Memorial is said to contend are by the terms of the Royal Proclamation confined to Indian Natives; and, whether it is the case that the noble Lord, the former Secretary of State for India, desired that such infractions of the Proclamation should be pointed out to him?

MR. J. K. CROSS: On the 9th of June I informed the hon. Member for Cavan County (Mr. Biggar) that Mr. Garu's letter had been returned to him for submission through the Government of Madras, in accordance with fixed rules. The Secretary of State in Council has disallowed the appointments of Messrs. Tarrant and Thornhill, which were made by the Madras Government, subject to the sanction of the Secretary of State. Natives of India have no exclusive right to such appointments in the Revenue Settlement Department, nor is there any Royal Proclamation to that effect.

ORDERS OF THE DAY.

—o—

SUPPLY—CIVIL SERVICE ESTIMATES.

SUPPLY—*considered* in Committee.

(In the Committee.)

CLASS III.—LAW AND JUSTICE.

(1.) Motion made, and Question proposed,

"That a sum, not exceeding £49,031, be granted to Her Majesty, to complete the sum necessary to defray the Charge which will come in course of payment during the year ending on the 31st day of March 1885, of Criminal Prosecutions and other Law Charges in Ireland, including certain allowances under the Act 15 & 16 Vict. c. 83."

Whereupon Motion made, and Question proposed,

"That a sum, not exceeding £45,031, be granted to Her Majesty, to complete the sum necessary to defray the Charge which will come in course of payment during the year ending on the 31st day of March 1885, of Criminal Prosecutions and other Law Charges in Ireland, including certain Allowances under the Act 15 & 16 Vict. c. 83."—(*Mr. Small.*)

MR. SEXTON said, he wished, in a few words, to direct the attention of the right hon. Gentleman the Chief Secretary to a case which had been under the notice of the Irish Executive Government for the last six mouths, but in regard to which it had been found impossible to extract from them, up to the present moment, any other than a formal answer. He referred to the case of a man called Brian Kilmartin, who was now undergoing penal servitude for life at Chatham. The facts of the case were these. On the 5th of April, 1882, a land bailiff, named Kernaghan, was shot at, at 10 o'clock at night, on the Island of Arran, in the county of Galway. The year previously the same bailiff had been shot at, and a man named Varney was accused of the crime, and put on his trial; but, although the bailiff Kernaghan positively swore that Varney committed the offence, the jury acquitted him. On the 5th of April, 1882, this bailiff was shot at a second time, and, on his information, Brian Kilmartin was arrested, and lodged in gaol. He had been placed upon his trial in the month of December at the Winter Assizes at Sligo, and, on the unsupported evidence of Kernaghan, he was found guilty, and sentenced to penal servitude for life. He must go back now to what happened in the month of May, 1882. A young man named Thomas Gauly, between whom and Kilmartin there was a strong personal resemblance, and who resided on the Island of Arran with his mother, was evicted by Kernaghan. He suddenly fled from the Island and went to America, without telling his friends anything of his intention. He lived at Boston for a year, at the end of which time he died. On his death-bed he sent for a Roman Catholic clergyman, the Rev. Father Curran; and a little before his death, under the tremendous sanction of the last Sacrament, he confessed that he was the man who shot the bailiff Kernaghan, and that he was the man who had committed the crime for which Brian Kilmartin was now undergoing his sentence of penal servitude for life. Father Curran reported the matter to his ecclesiastical Chief, the Archbishop of Boston, at whose recommendation Father Curran lodged an affidavit, embodying the facts, with the British Vice Consul. The Committee had, therefore, these three facts—first, the statement of the doctor who attended the young man Gauly; secondly, a certificate of his death and burial; and, thirdly, the affidavit from the Rev. Father Curran that a man, in confession, had made a statement that he was the person who had fired the shot. There was also a certificate from the Archbishop of Boston that Father Curran was duly ordained, and that any statement he made was worthy of complete belief. These documents fully established the guilt of Gauly, and the innocence of Kilmartin. Several months ago he (Mr. Sexton) had called attention to the case at the instance of the Rev. Father O'Donoghue, the parish priest of the Island of Arran, who was thoroughly convinced that Gauly was the man who fired the shot; that the man now undergoing penal servitude had nothing to do with the matter; but that it was a clear case of mistaken identity. He had frequently applied to the right hon. Gentleman the Chief Secretary to know what was to be done; but, up to the present, he had failed to receive anything beyond a formal answer. He thought that was a favourable opportunity for extracting from the Government a statement of their intentions; and he would impress upon the Committee that there were two points which went a long way towards establishing Kilmartin's innocence. In the first place, the bailiff Kernaghan must have been a person with a very defective power of identification; because, having been fired at on a previous occasion, he fully identified a particular person as the man who fired at him; but the man was unanimously acquitted by the jury. The time at which the shot was fired was 10 o'clock on a very dark night, when the identification of the assailant must have been a matter of difficulty, if not of impossibility. There was a further fact, that the man Gauly fled from the Island soon after the arrest of Kilmartin; that he was a man who, in his personal appearance, strongly resembled Kilmartin; and that he, together with his wife and mother, had been evicted from their farm by this very bailiff. Further, there was conclusive evidence that he had confessed his guilt to the Roman Catholic clergyman who attended him, and who administered to him the last rites of the Church. He (Mr. Sexton) had never heard a more conclusive case; and he asked the right hon. Gentleman to inform the Committee what he proposed to do with regard to it.

Mr. TREVELYAN: The hon. Member for Sligo (Mr. Sexton) has given an account of the additional documents with perfect accuracy, so far as Gauly's confession, which was made some little time before his death, is concerned; and I am also ready to admit that the hon. Member has not spoken too highly of the character of the Rev. Father Curran, who is a gentleman beyond all suspicion; but I am, nevertheless, obliged to give an unfavourable answer to the appeal which has been made to me. The case has been very carefully gone through, as is necessary when the only fresh element in the matter is a declaration of guilt, unsupported by other circumstances on the part of a person who has not been tried. It must be quite clear to hon. Members that the mere fact of the confession is not sufficient to absolve a person who has had a regular trial, because it is a very common thing for persons to charge themselves with crime. [Mr. SEXTON: On their death bed?] Such a thing is not unknown at all. Persons have been known to charge themselves with crimes even upon their death bed, especially in cases where it is possible that the person who made the declaration may not have regarded the act as highly criminal, and where his feeling for the person who had been condemned on account of such act was a feeling of genuine sympathy and pity, and not impossibly of admiration. That being so, it was necessary to go into the case very carefully, and to see what bearing this declaration of Gauly's had on the evidence. The case was carefully gone into by the Judge who tried it. All the papers were sent to the Chief Secretary, whose sole function it is to represent the mercy of the Crown, and the power which the Crown has of re-trying the case. [Mr. SEXTON: Who was the Judge who tried it?] Judge Lawson. [*Cries of* "Oh!" *from the Irish Members.*] Yes; Judge Lawson, than whom, I must say, there is no abler nor juster Judge. The Lord Lieutenant went carefully into the case himself; and as an application had been made to me in this House, and as it was not improbable that the question would come before the House upon the Estimates, His Excellency submitted the papers to me, and I studied them with great care. I may say that I entirely concur with the judgment of His Excellency and of Judge Lawson that the case stands quite complete, and separate from the confession of Gauly, and that that confession does not shake the case as it stands in the very least particular. I regret very much that this decision has been come to; but we have felt ourselves bound to arrive at it; and I do not consider that the House of Commons is a place where cases can be tried over again. I cannot, in the least, concur in the opinion of the hon. Member that the evidence of the bailiff was unsupported. I think it was supported by very material testimony indeed. I repeat that I am sorry His Excellency had to arrive at this decision; but I believe he could arrive at no other.

MR. SEXTON was bound to say that the statement of the right hon. Gentleman was very different from that which he had a right to expect. It was extremely disappointing in its result, and very extraordinary in its substance; and if the right hon. Gentleman had given such careful and exhaustive study to the case, he might have spoken for five minutes longer at the Table for the purpose of informing the Committee what the points were which had induced the Government to arrive at that decision. The right hon. Gentleman said that the identification of this unfortunate man by Kernaghan, the bailiff, was not unsupported; but he had not told the Committee how it was supported. His (Mr. Sexton's) opinion was that in the essential facts of the identification the evidence of the bailiff, Kernaghan, stood alone. On a previous occasion, the same man, having been shot at, fully identified a man named Varney as his assailant; but the identification was so weak, and so little worthy of credence, that, although the bailiff swore positively, and the jury had both men before them, one in the dock and the other in the witness-box, they unanimously gave a verdict of acquittal. How did the right hon. Gentleman explain that fact? There was another fact; this youth Gauly, who died in Boston, had been evicted from his farm, together with his mother, a few months before the bailiff was fired at, and evicted, too, at the hands of this very individual. There they had evidence of motive in regard to the man who confessed his guilt. It was not asserted that Kilmartin, or any member of his family, ever suffered any wrong at the hands of Kernaghan; whereas, on the other hand, the man Gauly had sustained a grievous wrong at the hands of the bailiff. How did the right hon. Gentleman deal with the sudden flight of Gauly? There was no doubt that Gauly had suddenly fled from the country, without informing his family or his friends where he was going. Then, again, was it denied that there was a strong physical resemblance between the youth Gauly, who fled to America, and the man Kilmartin, now lying in Chatham Gaol? Was it denied that the attack took place at 10 o'clock on a dark night, when even the sharpest man might very well have been mistaken? The right hon. Gentleman had said that it was common for persons, who were ill or dying, from motives of sympathy, or admiration for prisoners who were found guilty of crime, to make statements which were untrue. He thought that such a case would be heard of very rarely indeed; and would anybody who was acquainted with the Catholic religion, who knew that a man on the point of death, confessing to his priest under the sacred seal of the Sacrament, the most solemn and awful ceremony known to persons who professed the Roman Catholic faith—would anybody tell him that a man, under such circumstances, would be prepared to enter eternity, and appear before his Maker with a falsehood upon his lips, or that he would accuse himself of a crime which he had not committed, necessarily believing that such an accusation would condemn him to eternal damnation? Any man who was acquainted with the forms of the Catholic religion must be of opinion that the confession made to Father Curran was a sincere and honest confession of guilt, and must be driven to the conclusion that the youth Gauly, who died in Boston, was the man who fired the shot, and not the unfortunate man who was now undergoing penal servitude for life. On considering the whole of the evidence, documentary and otherwise, only one conclusion could be arrived at.

Mr. JACOB BRIGHT confessed that he had heard the reply of his right hon. Friend the Chief Secretary with regret. The right hon. Gentleman did not seem to imply that there could be any doubt as to the facts. This was the first he had heard of the case; but, from the statements which had been made, it certainly appeared to him far more probable that the man Kilmartin was not guilty of the crime. The probability was extremely strong that a confession made upon a death-bed was a true confession; and he therefore hoped that the case might not be ended in that House, but that there might yet be some fresh inquiry. It was not very long ago that in England a man imprisoned for murder was released from imprisonment upon the confession of a man named Peace, who was himself of notoriously bad character and a convicted murderer. The case was inquired into, and Peace's confession was accepted. In this case the doubt was in favour of the prisoner; and if there were to be an error at all, it was far better that it should not be on the side of keeping an innocent man in prison.

Sir JOSEPH M'KENNA said, he hoped that the Government would take up the matter seriously. He had no doubt in his own mind that the man now in prison under a sentence of penal servitude for life was as innocent of firing at, and attempting to murder the bailiff, as the right hon. Gentleman the Chief Secretary himself. He had not the slightest hesitation in saying that all the circumstances, apart from any case of proof accepted at the trial, showed that the man who had since then accused himself must probably have been guilty of the crime which he confessed; whereas there was no evidence whatever, except the identification by the bailiff, to criminate the man who had been convicted. There was *primâ facie* evidence that the man who made the confession was guilty, and not the man who was in gaol. He had had a good deal of experience from time to time in regard to this class of confession—statements made to priests and others by persons on the point of death. He knew perfectly well that the greatest solemnity prevailed on such occasions, and it was absurd to present to him the idea that a Catholic would have confessed to his priest that he had been guilty of an attempt to murder an individual, for which another person was suffering at the time, if he was altogether innocent, or that he would have died leaving his spiritual adviser under that impression. The impression conveyed to his mind was that it was much more likely the jury and Judge Lawson were wrong. To ask him to believe that a true case had been put forward on the trial of Kilmartin, or that the verdict of the jury was right, when upon his death-bed, or immediately before it, the man Gauly had confessed to his priest and spiritual adviser, under the seal of the Sacrament, that he was the guilty person, was perfectly absurd. He ventured to say that there was no place outside the House of Commons where a confession, under such circumstances, would not be received as the truth. He hoped the matter would not be lost sight of for a moment by Her Majesty's Government. He was not in the habit of mixing in disputes of this kind, or even of speaking in the House on subjects upon which he had no strong feeling; but he was prepared to say deliberately—although, of course, his assertion might be taken for what it was worth—that having had great experience in cases of this kind, he was as convinced as he was of his own existence that the individual now under sentence of penal servitude for life was a perfectly innocent man, and that the man who had accused himself was the only guilty man in the matter.

MR. NEWDEGATE wished to express all possible respect for the religious feelings of hon. Members who professed the Roman Catholic faith. It was well known that he was opposed to the policy of the Church of Rome; but no man ever heard him express any disrespect for the religious feelings of hon. Members belonging to that Church. But, as an English Member—the hon. Member for Manchester (Mr. Jacob Bright)—had taken the same view as hon. Members from Ireland who had spoken, he (Mr. Newdegate) wished, as an English Member, to express his sincere hope that the House would not attempt to arrogate to itself the privilege of pardon which was vested in the Crown. Let the Minister of the Crown exercise that privilege, and be responsible to the country for the exercise of it; but he deprecated most sincerely the idea of the House arrogating to itself functions superior to those of a Court of Law. He had himself, under the Act of 1866, been subjected to pecuniary penalties for prosecuting a person who arrogated to himself the right to sit in that House until he had gone through the forms prescribed by law. He lamented that circumstance, and, perhaps, it had no bearing upon the present case. This was a case in which the Crown had exercised an undoubted discretion vested in itself, and in its immediate advisers; and that which he deprecated was that the House should attempt to constitute itself a superior tribunal, not only to the Courts of Law, but superior to the Crown, so far as the privileges of the Crown were concerned. He maintained that if the House of Commons was to lend itself to either of those courses it would be distinctly violating the fundamental terms of the Constitution, and it was upon that ground, and because he held that the Minister of the Crown was sufficiently responsible, that he could see no reason why the House should incur the danger of a just imputation of transgressing and invading the functions and the duties of another Estate of the Realm.

MR. T. P. O'CONNOR wished to call the attention of the Committee to the fact that the position taken by the hon. Member for North Warwickshire (Mr. Newdegate) was not that which was taken up by the Chief Secretary. On the contrary, the right hon. Gentleman went into the merits of the case. He would further remind the hon. Member that the Irish Members were not attempting to interfere with the exercise of the mercy of the Crown. They had no power to do so, even if they felt inclined, and they were only calling upon the Crown to exercise that mercy. With regard to the general principle, it was one of the platitudes of Parliament that Parliament was not a Court of Appeal. It was a platitude which had no meaning except in the mind of the hon. Member. It was one of the highest functions of that House to represent every grievance of every subject of Her Majesty throughout the Realm, and it was the right of every Member to ventilate those grievances and see them redressed. If any hon. Member was conscious of any injustice done by a Court of Law, it was his duty to bring it before Parliament as a high Court of Appeal. The platitudes of the hon. Member for North Warwickshire had now been as often repeated as the celebrated illustration of King Charles's head by Mr. Dick, which was so familiar to everybody. Parliament was the highest Court of Appeal in the Realm, and every Member had a right to bring any case of grievance into that Court of Appeal. He had been much surprised at the answer of the Chief Secretary, and his surprise was not unmixed with indignation, although the answer of the right hon. Gentleman was characteristic of the whole attitude of the Government with regard to the administration of justice in Ireland. It was a mistake to substitute the blind fury of revenge for the calm strength of men who were anxious to govern in accordance with justice. The Chief Secretary, as a literary man, and accustomed to write about various matters, might be supposed to have something of a sympathetic nature; but he had noticed that whenever the Chief Secretary spoke about the religious feelings of the Irish people he invariably introduced something that was absurdly and grotesquely wrong. There was not a man who had any knowledge of the feeling of the Irish people who did not know that a man on the brink of the grave, receiving the last Sacrament, and being on the point of death, would not be prepared to perjure himself. He maintained that such an assertion was so grotesque as to be almost beyond the bounds of imagination. He trusted that the right hon. Gentleman would pay attention to these remarks. [Mr. TREVELYAN: I am doing so.] The right hon. Gentleman must be even an abler man than he gave him credit for if he was able to pay attention to the debate and carry on a conversation at the same time. What he (Mr. T. P. O'Connor) asserted was, that anybody who had any acquaintance with the feelings of the Irish Catholics would be prepared to say that it was not within the bounds of reason and probability that a man who was receiving the last Sacrament would be guilty of an atrocious lie, and perjure himself by confessing a crime of which he was innocent. He challenged the hon. and learned Solicitor General, now seated beside the right hon. Gentleman, who, although not a Catholic, knew something about Ireland and Irish Catholics—he challenged the hon. and learned Gentleman to get up and say he agreed with the Chief Secretary that it was at all probable an Irish Catholic, receiving the last Sacrament, and within a few hours of his death, would pledge himself to what he knew to be a wilful lie. That was a deliberate challenge. Such an assumption could only show the grotesque ignorance of the man who made it in regard to the feelings of the Irish people. If the right hon. Gentleman were speaking of the religious feelings or sentiments of the Hindoos or Mahomedans of India, among whom he had spent some years of his life, he would not have been guilty of so great a misrepresentation. He saw another right hon. Gentleman upon the Front Opposition Bench, who was in Ireland once as Chief Secretary (Sir Robert Peel). He appealed to the right hon. Gentleman to get up and say whether he agreed with the Chief Secretary that an Irish Catholic, within a few minutes of his death, would receive the Sacrament of penance and forgiveness for all his sins, and then would add to his soul the sin of a lie on his death bed? Would the hon. and learned Solicitor General,, or the right hon. Member for Huntingdon (Sir Robert Peel), deny that they had in this case, besides a confession made under solemn and convincing surroundings, a motive on the part of the man who confessed the crime. In the second place, there was the case of the man, which went to prove the truth of his story as well as his own confession. He had absconded from the Island almost immediately after the crime was committed, and there was evidence that before doing so he made no communication with his relatives or friends. In the third place, there was the fact that, in addition to the confession, the man who was convicted bore a strong resemblance to the man who confessed, and the fact that Gauly ran away in the interval between the arrest of Kilmartin and the trial was a strong additional testimony of the consciousness in his mind that he was guilty. They had the fact that the men resembled each other, the further fact that the crime was committed in a dark hour of the night, that the identification was confined to one witness, and that he was a witness so weak on the question of identification that on a previous occasion his evidence against the person whom he accused of a similar crime was disbelieved by the jury. He would venture to say that there was not a single Member of that House who had listened to the case who did not consider that the Chief Secretary's attitude in this matter was shameful to the Administration of which he was a Member. He knew that a great deal of crime had been committed in Ireland between the years 1882 and 1883. He deplored the fever of crime which had taken place; but it ought to be remembered that, as had happened in France, the red terror had been succeeded by a white terror equally terrible, so in Ireland the red terror had been succeeded by a white terror, and there was not a man who did not believe that Her Majesty's Government were now retaining in penal servitude a man who was wholly innocent of the crime imputed to him.

SIR WILLIAM HARCOURT: In dealing with a matter of this kind, it certainly requires the calmest exercise of judicial faculties, and I hope that it will not be approached in the spirit of the speech to which we have just listened. We are, however, used to the violent and abusive language in which the hon. Member for Galway (Mr. T. P. O'Connor) has indulged.

MR. HEALY: Sir Arthur Otway, I rise to Order. I wish to know whether the expression which the right hon. and learned Gentleman has used is in Order? The right hon. and learned Gentleman has spoken of the violent and abusive language of my hon. Friend.

THE CHAIRMAN: I cannot say that the words used by the right hon. and learned Gentleman are out of Order. I have often heard language to the same effect used in this House.

SIR WILLIAM HARCOURT: I should like to know what hon. Members opposite would say if I applied the epithet "shameful" to them, as the hon. Member has applied to the conduct of my right hon. Friend? He has distinctly charged my right hon. Friend and the Government of Ireland with exercising a white terror. Probably the hon. Member does not consider that violent and abusive language. I do; and I say that habitually the language used by the hon. Member, and by hon. Members sitting by him, towards my right hon. Friend is violent, abusive, and most unjustifiable. [*Cries of* "Oh!" *from the Irish Members.*] Well, that is my opinion. I dare say that hon. Members opposite do not share it. I am quite as much against white terror as hon. Members opposite; and I am glad to hear, for the first time, that they do not approve of red terror. At the same time, I must say that I have heard very little from those hon. Gentlemen in denouncing red terror since I have been in Office. I can only say that this is not the spirit in which a question of this kind is to be approached. It is a very serious thing to reconsider, in a matter of this description, the deliberate decision of a Judicial Tribunal. I say, in spite of what has been affirmed by hon. Gentlemen opposite, whether it be the Irish Government, or whether it be the English Government, there is no duty they undertake with a graver sense of responsibility than that of revising or inquiring into the sentences passed by the Judges. Although, of course, I do not deny for a moment the right of any Member of Parliament to bring forward a matter of this kind, still I assert that it is most inconvenient, and almost impossible, for this House, upon *ex parte* statements, or even upon an argument upon the case, to arrive at any proper decision upon the matter. Now, I have every day to deal with such matters, and I can assure hon. Gentlemen that if they were to attempt to discuss the questions I have every day to deal with, days would not suffice for discussing and arguing, in a public Assembly, the various points which are raised in a string of questions of this kind. What is the present case? As I understand it, a man has been convicted upon evidence which, apart from this confession, has never been challenged. Nobody says that the evidence given at the trial was not such as might well have satisfied the jury; and if it satisfied the jury, then the sentence was justified.

MR. SEXTON: We impeach the evidence of the bailiff, which was the sole evidence in the case, on the ground that his previously sworn evidence, in identification of a man alleged to have committed a similar crime, was not believed by the jury, and the prisoner was acquitted.

SIR WILLIAM HARCOURT: The hon. Member may impeach the evidence; but surely, in such a case, the evidence of the man who was shot at was very strong evidence. What is now wanted is to get in the confession of another person, who says that he committed the crime. It is supposed, apparently, that the confession of this man is an unexampled and conclusive case. Now, instances of confessions of this character, entirely unfounded, are very numerous.

MR. SEXTON: No.

SIR WILLIAM HARCOURT: The hon. Member chooses to say "No." I, who have to deal with these matters, say "Yes."

MR. T. D. SULLIVAN: Were they dying declarations?

SIR WILLIAM HARCOURT: On the whole, I should say that dying declarations are a great deal more suspicious than other confessions. ["Oh!"] Really, if hon. Members opposite will only be calm and patient, and hear what I have to say, they will have ample opportunity by-and-bye of replying to me. The man who is dying has nothing to suffer in this world, at all events. ["Oh!"] If hon. Members opposite wish the matter to be discussed, they are pursuing a very improper method of disposing of a question of this kind. I am only endeavouring to say what my experience of cases of this kind—cases in which there has been no question of Party sentiment, or religious prejudice—has been. It would, however, be entirely ridiculous to discuss the question on the basis on which the hon. Gentleman has put it—that the declarations of Irish Catholics are to be treated otherwise than those of English Protestants. I regard the one with neither more nor less favour than the other; but we are bound to pay respect to all the circumstances which surround it. In the first place, the confession of a man that he has committed a crime, for which another man has been convicted and punished, is a very serious matter indeed. No doubt, such a confession throws a grave *primâ facie* doubt upon the conviction. But it is not, and ought not to be, regarded as conclusive. It is nothing of the kind There are great temptations, under certain circumstances, to make a confession of that character. I have known several cases of confessions made by men under such circumstances.

MR. SEXTON: Dying confessions?

SIR WILLIAM HARCOURT: I have answered the word "dying" already. I say that dying confessions are not to be regarded differently from a confession made by a man who is not dying, because the man who is dying has nothing to fear, so far, at least, as this world is concerned. Dying confessions are most of all suspicious on occasions of this kind. I have known how confessions have sometimes been made. It may have been that the man who confessed had already received penal servitude for life, and he would know that he had no more favour to expect; but he thinks that he can benefit a friend by making a confession of this kind. Such declarations have been made from time to time, and I have had to examine them, and I have found them totally unfounded. Hon. Members would be astonished if they knew, as well as I do, the circumstances under which confessions of this kind have been made. The motive is not difficult to conjecture. The man knows that he has nothing to suffer in making such a confession. He is already beyond the reach of justice; and if under a sentence, for instance, of death, he knows that he has nothing more to fear. He wants no protection against the consequence of making a false confession. Therefore, I say, having had a considerable amount of experience in matters of this kind, that they must all of them be carefully examined. No doubt a confession arouses a strong presumption, in the first instance, against the sentence. It, therefore, becomes necessary to inquire into the whole facts of the case, and see whether the circumstances of the case itself corroborate the confession. I have had to consider cases in which the surrounding circumstances have corroborated the confession, and the man who has been innocently convicted has been pardoned. But there have been cases of true confession, and cases of false confession; and it has required the most careful judgment and the most anxious exercise of the judicial faculty to determine to which of the two classes of cases the confession belongs. It can only be done by a very careful and impartial examination, and by considering the confession together with all the facts which led to the conviction. If it were once assumed that those charged with the duty did not bring to the performance of the task those qualities which are necessary to its performance, the assumption would condemn the system of administering the prerogative of mercy. It has been found that the administration of the prerogative of mercy can only be effectually discharged by leaving it in a very few hands. We cannot dispose of matters of this kind by a debate—even if it be most calmly and carefully conducted—in a popular Assembly. We could not hope to arrive at a fair and just conclusion upon it without a most laborious comparison of particulars in each individual case. I believe Earl Spencer will not deliberately refuse to give weight to the important circumstances of a confession of this character. Indeed, if it were believed that Earl Spencer would not examine into the surrounding circumstances of the case, there would be no use in arguing the matter further. If, on the other hand, hon. Members opposite are disposed, as I believe the majority of this House will be disposed, to entrust the Executive Government with the discharge of this duty, and to leave the matter within their responsibility, then I believe the House will be of opinion that, however right it may have been to call attention to such a case, the ultimate judgment must rest with those who alone are capable of forming a judgment upon it.

SIR ROBERT PEEL said, that as the hon. Member for Galway (Mr. T. P. O'Connor) had referred to him he should like to say a word upon the subject. The Home Secretary had commenced his remarks by saying that it was necessary to approach the subject in a calm and judicial spirit, and then he proceeded to point out that his experience upon the subject gave him a vast superiority over any other man in the House. From that point the right hon. and learned Gentleman, instead of approaching the question in the calm and judicial spirit he had suggested, proceeded to use language towards the Irish Members, which, if it had been used against the Lord Lieutenant and the Irish Government, would have been received with a torrent of disapprobation. Now, any hon. Member who had sat in the House during the last three months must have heard cases submitted to the House which had certainly startled English Members. He did not shrink from that declaration. The hon. Gentleman had talked about white terror. There could be no doubt whatever that the system of Government in Ireland at this moment, and during the last three years, had been most repugnant to English feeling; and what must it be to the Irish people? [*A laugh.*] The right hon. and learned Gentleman the Home Secretary sneered and laughed at his remark; he was in the habit of doing so; but it would not have the least effect upon him (Sir Robert Peel), nor would it prevent him from saying what he was entitled to say in that House. He would only take this one case which had been brought under the attention of the House of Commons. He knew the difficulties which his right hon. Friend the Chief Secretary had to contend against. No doubt he had to deal with difficult cases day by day, and he admired the admirable way in which the right hon. Gentleman had dealt with them, and the tact and temper which he had displayed. He had told the right hon. Gentleman so himself on more than one occasion; but here was a case where the hon. Member for Sligo (Mr. Sexton) told them that a person whom he believed to have been really guilty, on escaping to America and dying abroad, confessed that he was guilty of the commission of a particular crime. Upon his death bed, in the presence of a Roman Catholic priest, this man declared that he was the person who committed the crime, and that it was not the person who had been convicted in Ireland. His right hon. Friend, nevertheless, said that he attached no weight or trust to such a death-bed confession. The right hon. and learned Gentleman the Home Secretary said that in regard to death-bed confessions he would have attached just as much weight to that of a Protestant as that of a Catholic. Now, he (Sir Robert Peel) had had some experience of Ireland and the Irish people many years ago; and he was bound to say that in his humble judgment, if a Roman Catholic upon his death bed, and in the presence of his priest, were to make a declaration that he himself had unhappily committed a crime for which another had been convicted, he (Sir Robert Peel) would be far more inclined—and he said it as a Protestant—to place weight and confidence in the statement of that man, than he would be in a similar declaration made by a Protestant. He had lived for years in Catholic countries, and he firmly believed, if this man Gauly made the statement in question to a priest in the hope of receiving absolution after having escaped from Ireland in consequence of an attempt to commit murder, that his right hon. Friend the Chief Secretary, and the hon. and learned Solicitor General for Ireland, would do well to consider whether it might not be necessary, not, as his hon. Friend the Member for North Warwickshire (Mr. Newdegate) said, to refrain from interference, but for the House of Commons to take the matter into their own hands. They did not seek to take from the Government the exercise of the prerogative of mercy, nor the faculty which rested in the Crown of granting pardon. This was the case of a man sentenced to penal servitude for life, and he thought the House of Commons might well express an opinion upon the subject. He hoped the hon. and learned Solicitor General would address the Committee in a very different spirit from that in which the Home Secretary, who always had his sneers and his flouts whenever anybody differed from him, had addressed it, and that he would address himself to the point which had been submitted from the Irish Benches—namely, that the Government should exercise the power they had of inducing the Sovereign of the country to consider a question which in the Irish mind was entitled to consideration, and grant to this unhappy man a pardon.

SIR EDWARD WATKIN said, that a case had occurred not long ago in Manchester in which an Irishman was convicted and sentenced to penal servitude for life on a charge of murder—namely, shooting a policeman. Afterwards, a man named Peace was tried for another murder, condemned, and subsequently hung for it; and that man confessed that he had committed the murder for which the Irishman had been sentenced to penal servitude. Upon that confession, of which there was no corroboration or anything else, the Government pardoned the man under sentence of penal servitude, and even compensated him for the sufferings he had undergone. Surely this was a similar case, if it was anything at all, of mistaken identity. Did anybody in that House mean to say for a moment that the identification by the bailiff who had sworn to the man was so undoubted that it might not be a case of mistaken identity? It was not a case of political dispute, but something more—namely, of human life; because the case of a human being kept during the whole period of his life in slavery—for penal servitude was slavery—was surely worthy of something more than an answer stating that there had been a comparison of papers by lawyers, and a balance of probability without any evidence whatever. Would it be too much for a rich country like this to send over to the priest at Boston, to the doctor who attended Gauly, and to the others who were acquainted with the facts of the case? It would be remembered that for the murder of a policeman in the attack on a police van at Manchester, several persons were convicted, including a man named Maguire, who was found guilty and sentenced to be hung. It happened that he (Sir Edward Watkin) was on intimate terms with one of the Judges who tried the case, and he saw that Judge off from the Manchester railway station on his way to London. He remarked to the learned Judge, having heard the evidence in Court, that he did not believe the man Maguire was guilty. The Judge—it was Sir John Mellor—said that he himself had the gravest doubt upon the subject, and that he would require more conclusive evidence than had yet been given to convince him that Maguire was one of the persons who had murdered the policeman. The learned Judge further said that he intended to write to the Home Secretary upon the subject. By following up all the circumstances, it was afterwards proved to absolute demonstration that it was impossible for the man Maguire to have been in the Manchester Road on the day the policeman was murdered; and on the Report of the Judge that he had grave doubts in his own mind, and on the new evidence obtained, the man was ultimately pardoned, and through the kindness of the right hon. Gentleman the Chancellor of the Exchequer, who was then Secretary to the Admiralty, was reinstated in the ranks of the Marines, to which he had formerly belonged, and, he believed, had been compensated for the sufferings he had undergone. He mentioned that as a case which had occurred within his own knowledge; and he would ask, in the present case, was it too much for this country, instead of balancing probabilities on documentary evidence, to send to the priest and the doctor in Boston in justice to a man who would otherwise be doomed to a life of slavery?

MR. TREVELYAN: I think the very few observations which I made early in the debate have been quite justified by what has occurred since. The discussion has shown how inconvenient it is to try a case of this kind over again in the House of Commons; for the hon. Member who has just spoken practically tried this case over again, not from any new evidence he has brought forward in regard to the case itself, but upon an argument in connection with a case that occurred in Manchester some years ago, in which it was shown that there had been a case of mistaken identity. He, therefore, contends that there may have been a similar case of mistaken identity here. That only shows how extremely inconvenient it is to argue a case of this sort in a popular Assembly, and, above all, to argue it without Notice of the intention to discuss it. In a matter of this extreme importance, it certainly would have been well if the hon. Member for Sligo (Mr. Sexton), being determined to take a course which I must say I deprecate, had given Notice of his intention.

Mr. SEXTON: The case has only just been brought before me; but I may remind the right hon. Gentleman that he has had six months to give an answer to the representations made to him.

Mr. TREVELYAN: I do not know what the date was when the case was first brought to my notice; and as a matter of fact, in answering the appeal of the hon. Member for Sligo, I purposely abstained from entering into the facts of the case, because I think we should, as far as possible, recognize the principle that the question of dispensing the mercy of the Crown should not become a matter of debate in this House. But this debate has now gone on for some time, and statements have been made by hon. Members opposite, on the full faith that they are correct, which have been accepted by other hon. Members chiefly sitting on this side of the House, and by the right hon. Baronet opposite the Member for Huntingdon (Sir Robert Peel). Those statements have been accepted as premisses from which to argue the case; and, therefore, I may say that when I remarked that this bald statement on the part of the poor man Gauly that he had committed the crime—a statement made without any circumstances whatsoever, that had any bearing on the trial, I spoke with a full knowledge of what the circumstances of the trial were. Now, the hon. Member for Sligo says that the case rests upon the unsupported evidence of the bailiff who identified Kilmartin as the man who fired at him. In the first place, the identification of a person who has attempted to commit a murder, or has committed a murder, is not in itself necessary. Frequently a man has been punished for committing a murder who has not been actually seen in the act of committing it. But here you have, at any rate, the man who was fired at stating that he did identify his assailant. Nor is it the case, as the hon. Member for Sligo has been informed, that Kilmartin is a man who might easily be confused with Gauly. Kilmartin, judging from the evidence in the papers, and I am not going to put forward any point which I have not absolutely ascertained—Kilmartin was a very remarkable looking man indeed, and that fact strongly weighed upon the mind of Judge Lawson in coming to his decision, and also upon Earl Spencer in accepting Judge Lawson's decision. In the next place, besides the direct identification, there was a considerable amount of strong corroborative evidence. A perfectly reliable witness had seen Kilmartin in what he called his stocking feet or "pouchetts," which meant that he had no boots on. Now, the marks of stockinged feet answering to those which would have been made by Kilmartin were traced from the scene of the murder to Kilmartin's house. That is a piece of evidence of which I have a clear recollection, although there is a great deal more, of an important nature, which I do not remember. Then, again, Kilmartin's house was searched, and some extremely suspicious things were found there, or on the immediate premises. I remember that, among other things, a cartridge and a mask were found. Recollect that I am not trying the case; but I am merely giving a few of the strong points which remain in my mind to show that there was a great deal of corroborative testimony. Against this evidence there is the single statement of the man Gauly that he committed the murder, and nothing else.

Mr. SEXTON: It was not a murder, only an attempted murder.

Mr. TREVELYAN: I mean the attempted murder. The only corroboration of that statement is that Gauly had fled from the country, and might have had a motive for committing the crime. It is very difficult to unravel these crimes; but to say the least it was possible, when we remember what the machinery of crime has been in Ireland, that there may have been men who have been selected as the instruments of crime, and it may have been the case, in this as in other crimes in Ireland, that a man had been selected who may have had no special quarrel with the person sought to be injured. With regard to the declaration made by Gauly, I must say that I do not think it showed any ignorance of Ireland on my part to have said, or now to repeat the observation, that there are men there, perhaps many men, who would regard a person who committed a crime that would be called a political crime, as, indeed, I have heard crimes called in this House—who would regard a person of that sort with sympathy, with pity, and even with admiration, and would feel that he was doing a justifiable act in accusing himself in order to get that person off. I hope hon. Members will not jump at the conclusion that I am saying anything offensive. I state it as a matter of fact, quite apart from the religious question. Putting the religious question aside, I believe that a man who, like Gauly, is said by hon. Members opposite to be a murderer in intention would be capable, from motives of sympathy and admiration for a man accused of a crime of this description, of making a false statement that he had committed the crime. The Irish Government, by the light thrown upon the evidence by the confession of Gauly, on considering Gauly's declaration, have come to the conclusion that it does not in the least degree shake the evidence that whatever knowledge Gauly might have had of the crime, Kilmartin committed it, or took part in it. I may say, however, if it will be satisfactory to hon. Members opposite, that the Government have no objection to send an adept to the spot in order to make special inquiries about Gauly; but I am satisfied that anyone who is accustomed to investigate criminal charges upon similar evidence to that on which Kilmartin was convicted, and who afterwards saw Gauly's confession, would come to the conclusion that Gauly's confession has not in one whit shaken the strength of the evidence which convicted Kilmartin. I purposely abstain from answering further the observations of the hon. Member for Galway (Mr. T. P. O'Connor).

Lord RANDOLPH CHURCHILL said, the suggestion which the Chief Secretary had thrown out was a most remarkable one. The right hon. Gentleman had suggested that a man, on his death bed, just before going into the presence of his Maker, at the moment of accomplishing the most solemn act of the Roman Catholic religion — more solemn, perhaps, than a Protestant could realize—had, for what might be called the sake of glorification, accused himself of a crime of which he was entirely guiltless.

Mr. TREVELYAN: I did not say it was for the purpose of glorification; but I said that perhaps the confession was made out of sympathy or admiration for another person whom he was anxious to save from a terrible fate.

Lord RANDOLPH CHURCHILL said, the explanation of the Chief Secretary did not, in his mind, alter the case at all. That a man under such circumstances, just before his death, in the presence of his priest, should deliberately accuse himself of a fearful crime of which he was guiltless, knowing that his name would be handed down with infamy to his family and in the locality in which he had lived as that of a man who had committed a fearful crime, was a proposition which he ventured to say might be submitted to the right hon. Gentleman himself, from Dublin Castle, for the purposes of Irish justice, but would not convince one single independent person in the House of Commons. He did not wish to say a word against the Home Secretary, for it would be difficult for any impartial person to find fault with the present administration of the Home Office. The right hon. and learned Gentleman had on more than one occasion proved that he possessed a generous and merciful disposition, and he was always desirous to lean to the side of mercy, and give a convicted person the benefit of a doubt. But in reply to the evidence given at the trial, which the Chief Secretary had just quoted, as to the remark about the appearance of Kilmartin, the absence of his boots, and other details, the Home Secretary must know perfectly well that cases were constantly arising where there was apparently the most crushing circumstantial evidence, and yet that evidence was absolutely compatible with the complete innocence of the prisoner. A case occurred the other day which he wished to call to the mind of the right hon. Gentleman—the recent case of a man named Siddell, which occurred somewhere in the North, at Newcastle or Durham. He was a man who was charged with being concerned in a murder with another man, and against him the evidence was perfectly crushing. The jury found him guilty, the Judge sentenced him to death, and, as far as he (Lord Randolph Churchill) remembered, the Judge concurred in the verdict; and yet, within a very few days after that trial, the Home Secretary accidentally discovered that Siddell was absolutely innocent, and in the interests of justice he was given a free pardon, the pardoned man having only a few days before been convicted of wilful murder and sentenced to be hanged. When an astonishing case of that kind could occur, it showed the importance of thoroughly investigating such cases, and ought to put them on their guard as to the nature of some of the verdicts that might be found. Although there might be strong corroborative testimony in Kilmartin's case, he fairly thought the confession of the man Gauly ought to be investigated with special care by the Home Office. No doubt, there were death-bed confessions of persons who were about to undergo a capital sentence to which it would be almost impossible for the Executive Government to attach any value. It was not, however, necessary to go into that point—namely, that when a man was convicted, and about to be executed, he might make a statement of the innocence of someone else in the nature of a death-bed confession which it would be impossible for the Government to act upon. But this declaration was not a death-bed confession of that character; it was one of a person who had escaped from all the consequences of his act, who could not be got hold of by the police, and who had not been suspected of committing the crime; and, moreover, it was made when the man was lying upon his death bed from natural causes. It was made in the presence of a Roman Catholic priest, whose respectability was vouched for, not only by the Archbishop of the Diocese, but by the British Vice Consul. He dared say that the Roman Catholic priest, Father Curran, had never heard of this man before; but he had published the story told by Gauly because he felt it to be true. He maintained, therefore, that when they had a deliberate statement of that kind made in the presence of a priest, and without fear of arrest, it threw the gravest doubt upon the corroborative evidence on the other side; and he thought the Government were bound to investigate the matter thoroughly, especially when a man had been condemned to the awful penalty of penal servitude for life. Even if it were necessary to send out a special Commission to Boston to make a further investigation he was certain the House would not grudge the expense. The Chief Secretary, to a certain extent, had acceded to the demand, because he had stated that he was going to send down an adept to the locality where the attempted murder was committed to inquire into the facts of the case; but he was sure the House of Commons on both sides would support the right hon. Gentleman in sanctioning an extension of the inquiry if there was any possibility of relieving a man who had been unjustly condemned to a most fearful punishment.

MR. NEWDEGATE said, the right hon. Gentleman the Member for Huntingdon (Sir Robert Peel) and the noble Lord who had just addressed the Committee had quoted the fact of the confession having been made before a priest, as if it added to the importance of the man's declaration. In the name of religious equality he asked the Committee to discard that fact from their minds in any decision at which they might arrive. He claimed, in the name of religious equality, that the case should be judged by Her Majesty's Government as if the man were a Protestant, and that no weight whatever should be attached to the fact of his having been a Roman Catholic, or having confessed to a priest. He would make no observation upon the possible conduct of a Roman Catholic priest; he would not enter into that subject. But this he did claim—that in the name of religious equality there should be no favour shown in this case on account of a confession having been made to a priest; and he trusted that the right hon. Baronet the Member for Huntingdon (Sir Robert Peel) and the noble Lord the Member for Woodstock (Lord Randolph Churchill) would not be deaf to that appeal. Both of their speeches attached to this confession a peculiar gravity, because it was made before a Roman Catholic priest. That was distinctly inviting the Committee to depart from the principle of religious equality, because if a confession was to have an extraneous weight given to it from the fact that it was made to a priest, there would at once be established a violation of the principle of religious equality as between a Roman Catholic and a Protestant. Hon. Members, no doubt, knew that. [MR. SEXTON: Hear, hear!] Would not a Protestant who had not confessed to a priest have been under a disadvantage under similar circumstances? [Mr. SEXTON: No.] If the hon. Member denied that, he clearly attached no weight to the fact of the confession having been made before a priest. Two speeches, however, had been made by English Members, in which peculiar emphasis was given to the confession of a Catholic as distinguished from the confession of a Protestant, and because it was made before a priest. Therefore, he claimed that the fact of this confession having been made to a priest should be discarded from the mind of Her Majesty's Ministers, and from the mind of the Committee, or otherwise they would attach to a Roman Catholic confession a peculiar virtue which would not be coincident to the confession of a Protestant. He thought he had made that position perfectly clear, and he further maintained that since the Long Parliament no House of Commons without evidence had ever entered into questions which had been decided by the Courts of Law, in minute detail. Perhaps the Long Parliament might have appointed a Committee to try this case over again; and what he deprecated was, either the notion that the Committee should follow the precedent of the Long Parliament, or, without a tribunal, should presume to decide upon the case.

MR. GLADSTONE: It appears to be the general feeling of the Committee that this is a case which could only be properly discussed in the House upon exceptional grounds—the grounds of necessity. The discussion, however, ought not to take place on the grounds of necessity. A very strong feeling has been manifested with regard to the possibility of an error, which is inherent in all human affairs, having occurred; but I wish to remind the Committee that my right hon. Friend has, in deference to that feeling, undertaken to adopt a step which is not usual, and which is of great importance. We all admit that in a case of this kind, where a doubt is raised as to a question of identity, there ought to be an exhaustive inquiry, and that nothing which applies to the case ought to be left uninvestigated. On that ground my right hon. Friend has stated that he will undertake to send a competent and suitable person to the spot where Gauly lived, to institute an examination into all the circumstances relating to Gauly which may have any bearing on the commission of the crime. It was quite a mistake—an unintentional mistake I am sure—on the part of my right hon. Friend the Member for Huntingdon (Sir Robert Peel), when he said that the Home Secretary had treated the matter as one of minor importance.

SIR ROBERT PEEL: The right hon. and learned Gentleman spoke of Gauly's confession as a bald statement.

MR. GLADSTONE: It was a bald statement of course. It was a statement put forward without corroboration or collateral evidence. What my right hon. and learned Friend said, was that a statement of that kind did not constitute a strong presumption, or provide strong *primâ facie* evidence, and, therefore, that it ought not to be absolutely received; but it ought to be made the subject of careful examination. What I wish to point out to the Committee is that the pledge which has been given by my right hon. Friend the Chief Secretary will embrace that careful examination. The noble Lord says that my right hon. Friend ought not to grudge even the expense of sending a person to Boston if that would tend to elucidate the truth. I quite agree with that, and if it should be found that the sending of a person to Boston would tend to elucidate the truth, it shall be done. But my right hon. Friend has pointed out that the measure which is evidently the best measure to be taken, and he has engaged that the matter shall be fully inquired into, and that, so far as human means can go, there shall not be left an element of uncertainty in the case; because, on the one hand, there is this *primâ facie* presumption which the Home Secretary frankly admits, and, on the other hand, there is a great mass of corroborative evidence which, in the view of my right hon. Friend the Chief Secretary and the Lord Lieutenant, and the Judge who tried the case, has not been met by the examination they have made. A thorough examination will be made, whether it involves sending to one place or another. What I hope is that under these circumstances, and with that admission, it will be felt that no advantage would arise from pursuing the subject further, for the Committee may confidently rely on the engagement of my right hon. Friend.

MR. SEXTON said, he thought the speech of the right hon. Gentleman the Prime Minister had considerably altered the complexion of affairs. With regard to the pledge given by the right hon. Gentleman, both as to the nature of its details and its extent, it was very different from anything they could extract from the doubtful language of the Chief Secretary. He hailed the pledge with satisfaction, and he would express a hope that, in sending an expert to the spot, the Government would select some person of known and unimpeachable character. He was himself proceeding to Boston shortly; he would see Father Curran and the Archbishop, and he should be happy to do what he could to have all the facts placed at the service of the gentleman who might be sent by the Government to make the inquiry.

COLONEL NOLAN said, he was obliged to his hon. Friend the Member for Sligo (Mr. Sexton) for having brought the matter under the notice of the Committee. His hon. Friend had not done so until all other means had been exhausted. He had himself forwarded a Memorial to the Chief Secretary some months ago, and he did not think that the Irish Members could, for a moment, be accused of a desire to try the case in the House of Commons until they had exhausted every other means. There was one circumstance connected with the case which he had been told not to bring forward unless it was absolutely necessary; but he thought it was absolutely necessary, after some of the remarks which had been made by the Home Secretary and the Chief Secretary. The circumstance in question had reference to the manner in which this confession came to the knowledge of the near relatives of Gauly, who had accused himself on his death-bed of having committed this crime. His relatives were in a highly respectable position, and the papers were forwarded to them—if necessary, he would give the Government the name; but naturally they had no desire to be mixed up with the case. It was painful for them that such a thing should have occurred; but they had thought it their duty, and a matter of conscience, to forward the papers to their parish priest, who had since taken great interest in the case. He really believed that when the Government fairly inquired into the matter, they would arrive at the conclusion that the confession was an honest and sincere one. It was the very last thing the family of Gauly would desire, that his name should be connected with a crime of this kind; but, however painful it was to them personally to stir up the matter, they had considered that they had no alternative but to place the papers in the hands of their parish priest in Ireland. He must say that the Irish Members were under many obligations to the noble Lord the Member for Woodstock (Lord Randolph Churchill) and the right hon. Gentleman the Member for Huntingdon (Sir Robert Peel) for the great assistance they had afforded in the matter. That assistance was of the utmost importance to the Irish people, because there was a general impression in that country that justice to Ireland was not generally conceded in that House.

Question put, and *negatived*.

Original Question put, and *agreed to*.

(2.) £7,561, to complete the sum for the Court of Bankruptcy, Ireland.

MR. HEALY said, he thought the time had now arrived when the Committee should hear some statement from the Government in regard to the course they proposed to take with reference to Mr. George Bolton. That gentleman had just obtained a verdict against his hon. Friend the Member for Mallow (Mr. O'Brien) from an Orange jury at Belfast for certain alleged charges of libel. That, however, did not in the slightest degree change the position Mr. Bolton occupied in that House. Neither the charges made against Bolton at Belfast, nor the verdict of the Orange jury of that town, had in the slightest degree altered the position of Bolton so far as Her Majesty's Government were concerned. Two days had now elapsed since the verdict, and, of course, Her Majesty's Government had had ample time to communicate with their Legal Advisers, all of whom were Members of that House with the exception of Mr. Naish. He would, therefore, ask them if they would state what course was proposed to be taken in reference to Mr. Bolton?

MR. TREVELYAN: I suppose that the affairs of any person who is in the Bankruptcy Court may be said to come under this Vote. I will only, therefore, remind the hon. Member of one or two facts in order to show him that he is premature in his application. Wednesday was the first day on which my right hon. and learned Friend (Mr. Naish) and myself could take action in this matter. The debate upon Mr. Bolton's affairs lasted until long after post time on the Tuesday, and I remember distinctly stating that the comparative leisure which Wednesday would give us would enable us to approach the question. That letter, written on Wednesday, would obviously only reach Dublin on Thursday for the consideration of the Attorney General, who, of course, would approach the matter from a legal point of view, and the Under Secretary, who would approach it from an administrative point of view. The matter has been discussed both by letter and by telegram, and it is maturing towards a decision. But it would be wrong altogether to hurry it on. Undoubtedly, and above all, it would be extremely wrong to come to a decision until the views of the Irish Government have been ascertained in the matter. We fully agree that it is a matter in which the views of the Government should be clearly ascertained with the utmost expedition, because the decision to be adopted is one of the premises which are already before us. At all events, before the Report is taken of the last Vote, the right hon. Gentleman at the head of the Government has promised that the decision of the Irish Government on the question of Mr. Bolton's suspension shall be announced. The statement of the Prime Minister appeared to be received with satisfaction by hon. Members opposite, and it may be regarded as a binding bargain on both sides. From that bargain I do not suppose that any hon. Member would for a moment insult the Prime Minister, by saying that he had any intention of receding.

Mr. Healy rose.

The CHAIRMAN: I do not wish to interrupt the hon. Gentleman; but I wish to point out to him that the person in reference to whom he has made this inquiry is not an officer of the Bankruptcy Court, and it would be necessary, in discussing the Vote, to connect the discussion with some member of the Bankruptcy Court. The hon. Member has now asked a question; the right hon. Gentleman the Chief Secretary has replied to it, and it will not be in Order to continue the discussion in reference to the affairs of this gentleman upon this Vote. The fact that a person has presented a Petition in Bankruptcy does not give a right to any hon. Member to discuss the question of that bankruptcy in connection with the present Vote.

Mr. HEALY said he did not intend to continue the discussion; but he would submit that the conduct of Judge Walsh would regularly come under the Vote. Time after time Judge Walsh had made statements in regard to Bolton, and, therefore, it would be in Order to call attention to the conduct of Judge Walsh. He had risen, however, merely to express a hope that after the statement of the Chief Secretary, no further postponement by Judge Walsh would be allowed to affect the decision of the Government. It must be borne in mind that Judge Walsh, who had already granted two postponements of 10 days in succession, might be prepared to propose another.

Vote *agreed to.*

(3.) Motion made, and Question proposed,

"That a sum, not exceeding £12,670, be granted to Her Majesty, to complete the sum necessary to defray the Charge which will come in course of payment during the year ending on the 31st day of March 1885, for the Salaries and Expenses of the Office for the Registration of Deeds in Ireland."

Mr. FINDLATER said, he desired on this Vote, to call attention to the case of a very hard-working, intelligent, and deserving class of men—the clerks in the Registry of Deeds Office in Ireland. They complained that in regard to their position they were not well treated as compared with that of other public servants in Ireland. Their principal and most pressing complaint had reference to classification. They had minor grievances as to the maximum salaries of the first class clerks, and the annual increment being less than in other Offices; but he would pass those minor grievances by. In 1874 a reorganization of several Public Offices in Ireland took place, including the Registry of Deeds. As regarded other Offices, this reorganization was not final. Subsequently, a further change was made in their favour by the abolition of the third class of clerks, and the limitation of classes to two. It was not necessary to point out to the Committee how very beneficial this reduction of classification was to the men in whose favour the change was made. By it promotion was stimulated, and a man of merit saw his way within a reasonable number of years to attain to the first class. He did not know for what reason the Registry of Deeds clerks were omitted from the reorganization. In this Department the three classes still existed; and the result was, that while in the other Offices a salary of £300 was attainable in 16 years, in the Registry of Deeds it would take some of the second, and all of the third class, from 31 to 38 years to attain it—more than double the service in other Departments. On this point he begged to refer to the evidence of the Registrar given before the Royal Commission in 1878, of which he had had the honour to be a Member. The Committee consisted of eminent legal authorities, and, among others, of Vice Chancellor Chatterton, who, in examining Mr. M. F. Dwyer, asked—

"According to the present system it would appear that it would take a man 22 years in the Department, as I make it out, before he reaches the maximum of £300 a-year. Supposing there was no distinction between the second and third classes, and that they were to go on up to the maximum of the second class, that is, to £300 a-year by £10 annual increments from £90, before he could attain the maximum of £300 a-year, I think he would be 21 or 22 years in the Department? Answer: I think you are correct in that.—1413. And that is, supposing he went on without any stop? Yes.—1414. Would it be an unreasonable thing to say that a man at the end of 21 or 22 years' service should be entitled to a salary of £300 a-year? I do not think it would.—1415. Considering the duties to be discharged by these men? I do not think it would, and it is very painful to me to see a number of meritorious officers at the small salary of £200 a-year doing first class duties without even any approximate prospect of improvement in their position."

Now, as the Office was at present constituted, there was a very slender prospect of promotion for many members of the third, even to the second class, and none to the first class. In one group there were several clerks of nearly the same age, whose service did not vary to the extent of five years. Of this group the senior reached the second class after a service of 10½ years; the 11th in number, and the last promoted, reached it after 20 years and 10 months. At that rate, it would require a service of 28 years to enable the last of the group to reach the second class. He had already a service of over 17½ years. On referring to the Report of the Royal Commission, he found this passage—

"It is a Department which requires to be officered by a superior class of clerks who should have every fair inducement to make it their permanent employment, and to look to promotion in it as their only reward for long and efficient service. The entire landed property of Ireland is dependent upon this Department for the security of its titles, and the services to be performed in this respect are of high importance to all who have any dealings with land. It takes many years of training to fit a clerk to discharge the higher duties of the Office. We have had statements from the different classes of clerks employed in the Office laid before us, and have also examined representatives of these classes, selected by themselves. They all complain of the slowness of promotion in this Office in comparison with other Departments of the Civil Service, and they attribute this slowness to the division of the clerks into three classes, and to the small number of first class clerks. We have inquired into the necessity for the present classification, and find that there is no distinction in the nature of the business performed by these different classes. The only use, then, of the division into three classes is that it may afford a check upon the advancement of persons not entitled to promotion, and may enable promotion to be awarded to men of special merit. We do not attach much weight to these reasons as regards the division between the second and third classes; and we think that they are more than counterbalanced by the delay it causes in the increase of the pay of deserving officers and the discontent thereby produced. We, therefore, recommend that the present second and third classes be united as a second class, the salaries to commence, as at present, at £90, and to advance by yearly increments of £10 to £300, the present maximum of the second class."

Would the Committee believe that that Report was issued in 1880, and that, notwithstanding repeated applications, not one single step had been taken to improve the position of these gentlemen occupying posts of responsibility and discharging these very onerous duties? There could be no doubt that an Office of this importance, through which the whole land of Ireland might be said to pass, required the fullest consideration on the part of Her Majesty's Government, and he could not conceive why its claims should remain in abeyance, while the claims of other Departments of the Civil Service, which certainly discharged duties by no means so responsible nor fraught with such consequences, were attended to. For his own part, he considered that the Office demanded the fullest attention on the part of Her Majesty's Government. He might mention that the search given in the Registry of Deeds negatived the existence of any encumbrance not appearing on its returns. And then with regard to the accuracy of the work, purchasers and lenders had the security of a £10,000 bond given by the Registrar, and two bonds of £2,000 each given by the two Assistant Registrars, while the personal monetary responsibility of the clerks was secured by Statute 2 & 3 *Will.* IV. c. 87, s. 8. There was no other Office with such responsibility. The importance and magnitude of the work done in the Registry of Deeds Office might be judged of from the fact that in 1880 there were registered 18,414 deeds, representing the consideration of £15,000,000 sterling. In 1881 there had been a diminution of the amount of work, but it had since then increased. Again, had the Purchase Clauses of the Irish Land Act of 1881 been in operation the work would still farther have been increased, because it would have been necessary to register two documents in each of the 600,000 tenures. As a further illustration of the magnitude of the transactions of this Department, he could inform the Committee that property had passed on the security of its searches and certificates to the extent of many hundreds of millions sterling in value. Now, he wished to point out to the Committee and to Her Majesty's Government that the relief sought in this case would cost but little to the country; and at this point he would ask permission to refer to the second Report of the Royal Commission, page 24, which stated that the entire income would be sufficient to counterbalance the expenditure. The words of the Report were these—

"But the entire revenue of the Office derived from duty stamps, seals, and fee stamps, appears from the evidence before us to have been at all times sufficient to counterbalance the expenditure; and inasmuch as we are of opinion that the revenue derived from duty stamps, seals, and fee stamps should be expended exclusively on the maintenance of the Office, we do not consider that the deficiency of revenue from 1864 to the present time, made out by taking fee stamps alone into consideration, could be relied upon by the Treasury as affording any answer to the claim of the Office against the surplus fees realized before 1864."

Now, in addition to these there was the sum of £40,000 from fees earned, and now in the Consolidated Fund, by Statute 2 & 3 *Will.* IV. c. 87, s. 35, expressly permitted to be expended in maintenance and improvement. This money was ordered to be invested in the name of the Office, which it would be perceived stood in an entirely different position from other Offices seeking improvement, inasmuch it was able to pay its way, and had funds available to meet the expenditure necessary. Those funds were invested in Government securities. From what he had said he thought it was clearly established that the character of the Office entitled it to improvement; and as he had shown that it required improvement, and that its financial position permitted the carrying out of such improvement without expense to the State, he hoped the Secretary to the Treasury would consider the case of these gentlemen. He had himself very large and constant dealings with the Office, and he was bound to say that in the whole course of his practice he had never met with a more efficient, intelligent, and hard-working class of men. They devoted the whole of their time to the duties of the Office, they were always at their post, and he never heard against them a single charge of neglect, which, he thought, could hardly be said of any other Public Office.

MR. PATRICK MARTIN said, he was very glad his hon. Friend the Member for Monaghan (Mr. Findlater) had called attention to what had been for years justly the subject of complaint on the part of the clerks in the Registry of Deeds Office, Dublin. He desired to supplement what had been stated in respect to the unfair scale of remuneration given in the Registry of Deeds Office, and the gross act of injustice on the part of the Treasury in withholding and applying, in contravention of statutory provisions, the surplus of £42,000, of which they had obtained possession. It should be borne in mind that so far back as 1880 a Royal Commission had investigated these complaints, and suggested that the Treasury should grant the trifling addition of pay which was asked for by the copyists and other clerks in the Office. He used the word "copyists" advisedly, because the hon. Member for Monaghan, in calling attention to the case, did not dwell on the grievances of a body of clerks in the Office, who were specially pointed out in the Report of the Commission. These unfortunate men were mere copyists, receiving 1½*d.* per folio of 72 words transcribed. They were paid no salary, like the copyists of the Courts of Justice; they received no compensation for the other work they might do in the Office; but, in addition to that, the Treasury required them to transcribe the heads of Memorials, which often amounted to two folios, and for that they were not paid a single farthing. Again, these transcribers had, as the Committee would be aware, to do their work on parchment which they had to prepare at a considerable expenditure of time, and for that preparation they were not allowed any payment whatever. Now, the Commissioners had alluded to this matter most forcibly in their Report; they pointed out that it was not fitting that men should do work for which they were not paid, and that the grievance was one which demanded early consideration. That Report had been sent into the Treasury as far back as the year 1881; but nothing whatever had been done to remedy the existing state of things, and the copyists were left at the miserable pay of 1½*d.* per folio. The Commissioners also suggested the mode in which the management of the Office might be improved, and the unnecessary loss of time and money to which those transacting business at the Office had been and were still subjected, might be saved. Yet nothing had been done. The Committee ought not to pass this Vote until they had a clear and satisfactory explanation of this culpable neglect. It would not do for the Secretary of the Treasury to say there were no available funds. The sum of £42,000, with its accumulations, thus wrongfully received by the Treasury, was, as a matter of right, specially intended to be applied in aid of the suggested improvements. Let him remind the Committee that, under the 2 & 3 *Will.* IV. c. 87, s. 35, it was provided that no greater sum should be charged in fees than would amount annually to a sum of money sufficient for the current expenses of the Establishment. But there had been an excess over the expenditure of the Office, and the Treasury had taken that excess, and, instead of applying it to the bettering of the arrangements of the Office, and for the use of the Office, they had put it into their own pockets, so to speak, and applied it to their own purposes, contrary to the statutory provisions. He asked what was the meaning and object of appointing Royal Commissions, if their recommendations when printed were to remain on the shelves of the Treasury covered with dust and without the slightest attention being paid to them by Her Majesty's Government? He trusted that some satisfactory answer would now at last be forthcoming from the hon. Gentleman the Secretary to the Treasury in respect of this matter, which, as he had said already, vitally concerned every person having dealings with land in Ireland. Registration was a matter made compulsory in that country to give validity. It never was intended, indeed it was expressly provided, that the duties levied in respect of this compulsory registration from the public should not be applied otherwise than in the proper maintenance of the Registry Office, or for the benefit of those dealing with land in Ireland. The conduct of the Treasury in the matter might, if a private individual had so acted, been fairly characterized as a fraudulent breach of trust.

MR. GRAY said it appeared to him that the claim of the clerks in the Registry of Deeds Office was almost, if not absolutely, irresistible; it appeared to him that the charge against the Treasury in relation to these matters was two-fold. First, it was that they did not fairly remunerate the officials of the Office, whereas the recommendation of the Commissioners was that the remuneration of the officials in the various Departments in Ireland should be made to correspond as far as possible. The second charge appeared to be that while they underpaid the officials they overcharged the public in respect of fees. It appeared that the Treasury had accumulated a sum of more than £40,000, which they had put into the Consolidated Fund, and which they had used for Imperial purposes, contrary to the intention of the Act of Parliament, and that while doing so the officials of the Department were left in a position very much inferior to that of the officials of other Irish Offices—that was to say, the officials of the Local Government Board, the Board of Works, the Paymaster's General's Office, the National Education Office, and others. Now, the Commission which sat in 1880 recommended that the third class clerks in the Office should be merged with the clerks in the second class, and thus afford relief to the inferior clerks. But there were three classes of clerks in the Deeds Office, the result of which was that promotion was very much retarded, and he understood that some of the clerks had worked for 20 years without getting anything like adequate pay. If the hon. Gentleman the Secretary to the Treasury could plead that the revenues of the Office were insufficient, if he could plead that the cost of increasing the salaries of the clerks in this Office would constitute an additional public burden, why, then, he might have the sympathy of the Committee. But he could scarcely say anything of that kind in this case, because the question would then be asked, "Where is this £40,000?" If the Treasury did not intend to give any part of that sum for the equalization of the salaries of the clerks in the Deeds Office with the salaries of the clerks in other Departments in Ireland—why, then, if they insisted on paying the money into the Exchequer, and not acting up to the spirit of the Statute, Irish Members were perfectly justified in the charge they made. The revenue from the registration of deeds was sufficient for the maintenance of the Office. No one would contend that the Treasury ought to make a profit out of this transaction, and therefore he hoped that the hon. Member for Monaghan (Mr. Findlater) would follow up his observations by a Motion, and that he would have the courage to carry it to a Division, because it was of no use raising questions of this kind unless the opinion of the Committee was taken, and unless something was done. But when the hon. Gentleman the Secretary to the Treasury rose to speak on this Vote, he should be glad if he would give the Committee some information as to the mechanical improvement some time since proposed to be introduced into the Office. He understood that an instrument was being introduced for the purpose of mechanically registering all the deeds in the Office, and doing away with the services of clerks altogether. That, as far as he could remember, was the object of the patent. Perhaps the hon. Gentleman had himself investigated this marvellous mechanical contrivance, and could state to the Committee whether the public were to have the advantage of it? He would be glad to know whether the Treasury had completely abandoned this scheme, or whether they were still considering it? He trusted the hon. Gentleman would consider the appeal which had been made to him on behalf of the clerks in the Office in a favourable spirit, and that he would carry out the recommendation of the Commission, which, as he understood it, was that the clerks in the Registry of Deeds Office should be placed on an equality with the clerks in the other Departments.

MR. COURTNEY said, he had not heard lately much about the ingenious invention to which the hon. Member for Carlow (Mr. Gray) had referred. His impression was that, although the ingenuity of the plan was well recognized and admired, it was practically unworkable, and would not be introduced. With regard to the clerks in this Office, the change would be analogous to that adopted in all the other branches of the Civil Service—namely, there would be a large introduction of the lower division of clerks. He would point out that the figures before the Committee showed that the expenses of this Office, having regard only to the effective charge, was something between £18,000 and £19,000 a-year, and that there was a non-effective charge of between £2,000 and £3,000 a-year, so that the whole charge of the Office was £21,000 a-year. Against that charge of £21,000 a-year, the receipts for fees for the last year amounted to £12,000, so that there was absolutely an excess of expenditure over revenue of something like £9,000. He admitted that last year was a bad year as regarded the Revenue. It was true that the hon. Member for Monaghan (Mr. Findlater) attempted to bring in aid of the deficiency the duties charged; but they were no part of the fees of the Office any more than the stamps in Chancery would be part of the fees of that Office. The duties were part of the general Revenue of the country. The fees for work done were those which strictly related to the Office. The duties had to be paid when the deeds were registered; but they formed no part of the income of the Office, and if the Office were abolished to-morrow, the duties on Memorials would still have to go to the Revenue. With respect to the £40,000, that was a very old story, and dated as far back as 1864, and with regard to which he might say that the Treasury had acted perfectly within their rights. With regard to the complaints that had been made respecting the position of the clerks, he had to say that the Government would wish to remove the obstacles which existed in the way of their receiving some advance and promotion; but that could not be done without removing some of the superior clerks, and the superior clerks resisted their removal as much as the lower clerks desired it. Many of those clerks had served for a considerable number of years, and he, at one time, believed it quite possible that some of them might be willing to retire on superannuation terms, and communications were accordingly made to the Office with that object. But it was found that the proposal could not be carried out; that the clerks had no desire to retire; and, consequently, the Treasury were not justified, at all events for the present, in compelling them to do so. They were efficient servants of the public; they were doing their duty well; and, therefore, for the time, they would be left in their present position. He thought, however, that something might be done hereafter in the direction indicated. With regard to the position of the transcribing clerks, it was, no doubt, extremely deplorable that persons of education and trustworthiness should labour at the low rate of 10*d.* an hour; but all he could say was that whenever a vacancy occurred there were always two or three applications for it. There was, in fact, a full supply of such men ready to work on those terms both in England and Ireland. It was natural that copyists who entered the Service on these conditions should, after a few years, ask for an improvement of their position; but the fact was that the work of transcribing was purely a mechanical operation, and however much the Government desired to see persons of this respectable and intelligent class adequately remunerated for their work, they were quite unable to add to their pay in the interests of the public.

Mr. PATRICK MARTIN feared the Secretary to the Treasury (Mr. Courtney) had not yet even glanced at the Report of the Royal Commission. If he had, he would have found a full and detailed answer to those arguments on which he rested his defence. What answer did he give to the complaint of the copyists? Their case was that they were obliged to write that for which they were not paid. In point of fact, under the Treasury Regulations, there were deducted from the folios written by the clerks the headings to the Memorials, which formed a considerable portion of the clerks' work. The Irish transcribers, who were, according to the Secretary to the Treasury, gentlemen of charater and position, were, under the Treasury Regulations, forced to do work at the rate of 94 words to the folio. He (Mr. P. Martin) denied that that was the case in England. In England, the transcribing clerks were paid at the rate of 1½*d.* for 72 words, and the headings of the Memorials were not deducted. He certainly was astonished to hear the hon. Gentleman the Secretary to the Treasury gravely stating that the duties and fees specially paid for registration formed no part of the fees of the Office, but were a portion of Imperial Revenue. Forsooth, said he, if this Office was abolished the fees would remain. Evidently, the Chief Secretary did not understand on and in respect of what those duties and fees were levied and paid. He appeared to consider them as ordinary stamp duties. A deed was stamped according to its value in both countries, under the same Act of Parliament; but in Ireland, in addition to that, it was insisted that there should be a Memorial of a deed prepared, and on that Memorial another duty stamp should be affixed; it was not a stamp duty on the deed, but a stamp duty on the Memorial. In addition to all this, in Ireland, the poorer country, a duty must be paid on the demand for a search. There were also fees on affidavits charged. If these special fees and duties were accounted for, this Office, instead of showing a deficiency, would really show a surplus. He was rather surprised at the Secretary to the Treasury falling into these extraordinary and confusing blunders, because, if the hon. Gentleman had paid the slightest attention to the Report which he received from the Royal Commissioners, he would have found the matter very plainly set forth. As he (Mr. P. Martin) endeavoured to point out a moment ago, the hon. Gentleman would have found, if he had carefully studied the Report in question, that the charges imposed on the public in respect of the Registry Office consisted of two classes—firstly, the fees taken in the Office; and, secondly, the stamp duties payable to the Crown in respect of Memorials such as he had described, and in respect of register searches. They did not appear in the account; if they did, so far from the balance being against the Registry Office, the balance would be in its favour. He maintained that the Treasury at the present moment were wrongfully withholding from the Irish public £42,000, of which mention had been made. It was a most singular thing that the Treasury officials, in withholding money of this description from the public, should have had recourse to a statement such as the Committee had listened to, because, in the very Report to which reference had been made, it was held that the fees and duties received ought to go towards the maintenance of the Office. The Royal Commissioners said that—

"It is plain from the language of the deputation that the Office fees of the Registry of Deeds were never intended to form a source of Imperial revenue, but were intended to be applied for the benefit of persons dealing with lands in Ireland, and the proper maintenance of the Office; but, notwithstanding the provisions of the section, we have evidence that sums amounting to upwards of £42,000 have been received by the Treasury on account of these excess of fees."

Under these circumstances, he contended that it was trifling with the common sense and judgment of the Committee for the Secretary to the Treasury to tell them that the expenditure of the Office had been in excess of the receipts. Up to 1881, £42,000 received in emoluments was invested and applied to Imperial sources; and he asked the Secretary to the Treasury to give the Committee the accounts since 1881. He believed, that if those accounts were given, they would show that, even in the recent bad years, there had been an excess of receipts over the expenditure in the Office in question; and he certainly trusted that his hon. Friend the Member for Monaghan (Mr. Findlater) would move to reduce the Vote.

MR. GRAY said, the Secretary to the Treasury had argued that certain fees could not be taken into account or placed to the credit of the revenue of the Office; and he had said that, if the Office were abolished to-morrow, the duties payable to the Crown would remain the same. Was that the fact? If the Office were abolished to-morrow, the stamp duties would, no doubt, remain the same; but what would become of the duties now charged upon Memorials? As he understood it, no such thing as a Memorial existed in England, except in connection with particular legal arrangements for the registry of deeds in Yorkshire and Middlesex. [MR. COURTNEY: There are many Memorials.] He was not talking of the deeds registered in the Court of Chancery; but he was talking of the register kept in Dublin of all transactions in relation to land. What he wanted to fix the attention of the Secretary to the Treasury upon was this particular point. If the Office were abolished, would these payments still come to the Crown? If they would not, was it not manifest that they should be credited to the Office, and not to the general Imperial Revenue? He asked the hon. Gentleman to explain the positive statement he made that, if the Office were abolished, these fees—by these fees he meant the Office fees payable on Memorials, and payable for searches in the Office—would still be payable to the Crown. What right would the Crown have to receive the fees if the Office were abolished? If they were only fees payable in connection with the Office, and not general fees chargeable and payable for Imperial purposes, how could the Secretary to the Treasury contend that they ought not to be paid to the Office? If the hon. Gentleman's contention be wrong, a grave question of principle was involved in the withholding of the sum of £42,000. Of course, if there was a deficit, the public would have to meet it; but if, on the contrary, there was a surplus, the Office ought to be credited with it. He imagined that the Secretary to the Treasury would admit that if his (Mr. Gray's) contention were right, and the stamp duties on Memorials and the fees of 21*s.* for searches were put down to the Office, the revenue of the Office would show a surplus, and not a deficit. If it be the fact that, if these sums were credited to the Office, there would be a surplus, that surplus should, according to the whole argument of the hon. Gentleman, be devoted to the Office. He (Mr. Gray) imagined that the hon. Gentleman would not consent to that; therefore, it became a matter of extreme importance to decide the question whether these particular sums should or should not be credited to the local Office, and not to Imperial purposes. He contended that the fees should be credited to the Office; and he wanted the Secretary to the Treasury to tell him whether he would have any objection to give the House a Return showing the revenue in connection with the fees—that was to say, the amounts which he acknowledged should be credited to the Office, and the amounts payable in stamp duties on Memorials, and for searches which some people thought ought to be credited to the Office, so that they would know exactly how this Office account stood, and whether they had good ground to make good their contention that the Treasury ought to refund the £42,000, and whatever other accumulations might have taken place since 1881? If, after crediting the fees to the Office, the account still showed a deficit, his (Mr. Gray's) argument, of course, went by the board. [Mr. COURTNEY: I have no objection.] Then he would move for the Return. He did not think the hon. Gentleman had sufficiently recognized the difference between the stamp duty on a deed, which, of course, went to the Consolidated Fund, and the stamp duty in connection with a particular local Office procedure. Where they had a local Office exacting stamp duties which were not generally charged elsewhere, it was manifest that those charges ought to be credited to the Office.

MR. WARTON said, the hon. Member for Carlow (Mr. Gra) had said so well a good deal of whatyhe was about to say that it was not necessary he should occupy the Committee at any great length. He would not accuse the Secretary to the Treasury of deliberately trying to confuse their minds; but the hon. Gentleman certainly appeared to wish to confuse their minds by stating that the stamp duties on conveyances would not, of course, be paid to the Office. They were all agreed about the stamp duties on conveyances; but, apart from that altogether, it seemed to him that the stamp duty on Memorials could not exist unless Memorials were registered. It seemed to him that no payment for a search could be made unless there was a registry in which that search could take place; therefore, they ought to have a complete and honest statement—not a vague statement about £12,000 or £14,000—of what was received in every kind of way. They would then know what was the income of this Registry Office, and be able to make up their minds as to the future arrangement that ought to be made. The Secretary to the Treasury never shrank from what he said, and the objection he had taken to the proposal which had been made by hon. Members was, that if all the payments made in the Office were credited to the Office, there would still be a deficit. If there would be a deficit, how was it there was a surplus of £42,000; how had that money been accumulated? He (Mr. Warton) thought there might also be given an account of what had become of the £42,000. He supposed it was absorbed in the general Revenue of the country. Well, now, a point with regard to the remuneration of clerks had been raised. There was no doubt that whenever a post was vacant there was always a large number of applications for it, and he thought it would be throwing away the money of the country if they were to make extravagant payments for very humble services; but it was one of the elementary evils of the social condition of the present day that there were so many hundreds of thousands of persons who wished to be writers and clerks. The fact was, that there was a sort of contempt thrown on the handycraftsman, and therefore it was that so many people were found to refuse to work with their hands. Discontent came, and that discontent did not fail to find expression. He sympathized with the argument of the Secretary to the Treasury as regarded the remuneration of clerks, subject, however, to one exception. The Secretary to the Treasury compared the payment of 1½d. a folio with the payment of 10d. an hour. He (Mr. Warton) was not going to say how many folios a scribe could write in an hour; but there was this difference between the two systems of payment—that a man who was paid 10d. an hour, wrote accordingly; but if they told a man that he was to be paid at the rate of 1½d. per folio, and then gave him a number of words to write for which he was not paid, that was a distinct breach of faith. It would be well to remedy such a little matter, because, when men received such very small salaries, every penny or half-penny was of importance to them, and if any emoluments were deducted, the *employés* became dissatisfied. It was not fair that, if men were paid 1½*d.* for every folio, that they should write a single word that did not form part of the total. If men were paid upon the piece system, they ought to receive payment for every bit of work they did. It was only natural if, upon the piece system, a man ought to receive 1*s.*, but as a matter of fact only received 4*d.*, that he should become discontented. Honesty was the better policy, as far as the Government were concerned, and it was far better that they should say that 1½*d.* a folio would not be paid when they really did not give it. A little justice in that respect would be a good thing, and the Secretary to the Treasury ought to take good care that men in the service of the Crown were not defrauded out of anything which was their due.

MR. SMALL confessed that he heard with great surprise and dissatisfaction the statement of the hon. Gentleman the Secretary to the Treasury, especially that portion of it which related to the clerks of the Registry Office. The hon. Gentleman had said that the clerks were not men of very superior intelligence. That was quite true; but, at the same time, there was no Public Department in Ireland which was so satisfactorily worked as the Registry of Deeds. He (Mr. Small) had been acquainted with the working of the Office for many years, and he was hardly aware of any mistake made by the clerks. The hon. Gentleman (Mr. Courtney) had not as yet explained to the Committee why it was that in almost every other Public Office in Ireland — the Local Government Board Office, the Office of the Board of Works, the Paymaster General's Office, the National Education Office—there were first and second class clerks, while there were only third class clerks in the Office of the Registry of Deeds. He certainly did not think that the clerks in the other Offices required any greater intelligence than those in the Office of the Registry of Deeds. As a matter of fact, the Office of the Board of Works was unsatisfactory and inefficient, whereas the Registry of Deeds Office did its work very satisfactorily. The Local Government Board was distinguished for doing nothing that they could possibly avoid doing. The Paymaster General's Office and the National Education Office were Offices with which he was not well acquainted. The hon. Gentleman the Secretary to the Treasury said that in a very short time he thought the Office of the Registry of Deeds could be worked by one or two Registrars who would supervize a number of clerks of the same standing as those now employed. [Mr. COURTNEY: No.] He understood the hon. Gentleman to say that one or two Registrars and an Assistant Registrar with a number of clerks, would be sufficient to do the work of the Office; but perhaps the hon. Gentleman would kindly state what he did say?

MR. COURTNEY said, he would be glad to do so. The hon. Gentleman (Mr. Small) asked him why it was that third class clerks were employed in the Registry of Deeds Office, whilst first and second class clerks were employed in other Public Offices in Ireland? He had previously stated that the Government wished to remove the obstacles that existed in the way of the clerks receiving some advance; but they could not do anything without taking steps at the same time for the removal of the superior clerks. Great responsibility was thrown upon the Registrar, and it was thought that if an Assistant Registrar and a limited number of first and second class clerks were appointed, the work of the Office might be performed very satisfactorily.

MR. SMALL said, he could not see very much difference between what the hon. Gentleman had now said, and the observations he (Mr. Small) thought he had made originally. The hon. Gentleman spoke of a limited number of first and second class clerks, together with an Assistant Registrar, being drafted into the Office; but why should not the superior clerks in the Office be made first class clerks, and the clerks of an inferior grade be made second class clerks? He failed to understand whether the mode of admission to the Office of the Registry of Deeds was different to the mode of admission in any other Office he had mentioned. He was aware that the admission into the Registry of Deeds Office was by a very open system of competition; but he was not aware whether that was so with regard to any other Office. If there was not the same open competition in the Board of Works and the Local Government Board Offices, and so on, he could easily understand how it was there were so many third class clerks in the Registry of Deeds Office, and none in the other Offices. The Registry of Deeds Office, as a matter of fact, was a popular Office, and that, no doubt, was the reason why the clerks discharged their duties so extremely well.

MR. FINDLATER said, he thought that the stamp duties would at all times be sufficient to counterbalance the expenditure of the Office; indeed, the Royal Commissioners were of opinion that they would, if all the Duty and Office fees went towards the expenses of the Office. He admitted the courtesy of the Secretary to the Treasury; but he could not allow that the hon. Gentleman had at all satisfactorily answered the different points which had been raised. He, therefore, moved to reduce the Vote by £1,000, in order to test the feeling of the Committee by a Division.

Motion made, and Question proposed,

"That a sum, not exceeding £11,670, be granted to Her Majesty, to complete the sum necessary to defray the Charge which will come in course of payment during the year ending on the 31st day of March 1885, for the Salaries and Expenses of the Office for the Registration of Deeds in Ireland."—(*Mr. Findlater.*)

MR. DICK-PEDDIE said, he was surprised to find that Irish Members should expect, after what took place with regard to the Register House, Edinburgh, that the Secretary to the Treasury would listen to their case. He entirely sympathized with the case put forward on behalf of the clerks in Dublin; but their case was very much less strong than the case of the clerks in Edinburgh. The third class clerks in Dublin began at £90 a-year, rising by £10 a-year to £200; but the unfortunate third class clerks in Edinburgh, though beginning at £90, only rose by £5 a-year to £160. At the same time, the latter did more important work than the clerks in Dublin, not only doing all the work the clerks in Dublin did, but also preparing all the minutes of the deeds sent in for registration, which was not done by the clerks in Dublin, but by solicitors who charged largely for the work. The clerks in Edinburgh received a less income and a less yearly increment than the Dublin clerks, and they could not expect promotion in less than 25 or 30 years. Still, he did not think that because the Edinburgh clerks were badly treated it would be right to treat the Dublin clerks badly, and, therefore, he should support the Motion for reducing the Vote. He thought the Irish case was one which the Secretary to the Treasury should carefully consider; and he hoped that by helping to vindicate the case of the Dublin clerks, he might do something to induce the hon. Gentleman next year to look with a more favourable eye on the claims of those unhappy clerks who did the national work in Edinburgh, and were worse paid than they would be in any private office in the country.

MR. HEALY observed, that the hon. Member (Mr. Dick-Peddie) had several times taunted the Irish Members upon their action with regard to Scotch Votes; but he would remind the hon. Member that the Irish Members had all voted with him, except the hon. Member for Cavan (Mr. Biggar), who was well-known to be a rigid teetotaller in respect to financial matters. They had voted in favour of the Scotch clerks; but he did not at all agree with the hon. Member, on the merits of the case, that the Dublin case was not so strong as that of Edinburgh, because the clerks in the Registry of Deeds Office in Dublin performed duties to which there was no parallel in England or Scotland. The Office in Dublin was recognized as one of the most important and most valuable Offices in the country, in which no mistakes were made, and in which the clerks performed duties of a most laborious and important character, but were worse treated than the clerks in any other Office. A Bill had been passed some time ago, to give them some additional remuneration, on the representation of his hon. Colleague (Mr. Findlater); and the very fact that a Bill had to be passed showed how these clerks had been treated. If this was an Office of the Board of Works, or some other routine Office, there would be no difficulty whatever in giving the clerks what they wanted. The Board of Works did nothing; it was hated by everybody, and got everything it wanted; while a body like the clerks of the Registry of Deeds Office, who were admitted to be efficient, against whom he had never heard a breath of complaint, and with regard to whom, on the contrary, solicitors and suitors were loud in eulogium, were refused b the Government what they had asked for with great moderation. He did not wish to disparage the Scotch clerks. He had voted in their favour; but, at the same time, he certainly thought the clerks in the Dublin Office occupied a peculiar position, and ought to be treated with regard to that fact. In comparison with the duties they discharged they had not been fairly treated by the Government, and if they looked at the onerous and responsible duties cast upon them, he certainly thought there was no body of men in the country who more deserved the consideration of the House and the Treasury.

MR. COURTNEY pointed out that the Bill to which the hon. Member had referred was necessary because of an Act of Parliament. These clerks were paid according to commercial principles, having regard to what they would receive for similar duties in a private office, and the question was, whether that plan should be adhered to, or whether an appeal should be made to Parliament for a special and a compassionate allowance? The receipts of the Registry of Deeds in Dublin did not at present pay the expenses of the Office; but there were accumulations from the time when the Office was remunerative. With regard to what the hon. and learned Member for Bridport (Mr. Warton) had said, the rate of pay was 1½*d*. a folio, and the clerks had accepted their position with a full knowledge of what the remuneration would be.

MR. WARTON agreed with the hon. Gentleman as to the proper principle of paying these clerks, though he did not much like the commercial principle. He considered 1½*d*. a folio a low rate of pay. The Attorney General charged for bills of costs at the rate of 4*d*. a folio, and, of course, he got a good profit.

MR. FINDLATER asked whether the Secretary to the Treasury would produce a Return, if moved for, showing a statement of the revenue derived from duty stamps, seals, and fee stamps on all the documents, so that they might test the question whether they were applicable to the expenses of the Office?

MR. COURTNEY said, he would be willing to give these particulars, without prejudice.

MR. GRAY said, the issue was not, as the Secretary to the Treasury supposed, whether these clerks should be paid on commercial principles or not. That was only a very small portion of the total issue. The issue, as it appeared to him, was whether, considering the nature of their duties, these clerks should be given advantages equal to those given to clerks in other Departments. That was a very different thing from whether they should be paid only upon commercial principles, or receive a compassionate allowance. He was not at all in favour of that course; but he was in favour of paying what was fair, judging by the current rate of pay. The question at issue was whether these clerks should be paid adequately, and he contended that they should be, but were not. An important point was whether the revenues of this Office were dealt with in consonance with the spirit of the express words of the Act of Parliament. The Secretary to the Treasury had not explained how he maintained his assertion that the special duties charged in this Office in connection with the services of the Office should not be credited to the Office, and that if the Office did not exist the fees would still have to be paid. That was what the hon. Gentleman had specifically stated. Then as to the commercial principle, that was, no doubt, a very admirable sentiment, and came very well from the hon. Gentleman. Was the hon. Gentleman ready to abide by that principle generally, or did he only apply it to these poor scriveners—these animated machines? How about the Head of the Office? Who was the Head of the Office, and was he appointed by the late Government on commercial principles? He was a broken-down editor, and he was appointed solely because he had for years and years constituted his paper the tool and organ of the Whig official class in Dublin. When, in consequence of public opinion deserting him, his paper was reduced to a worthless condition, and practically to bankruptcy, the Government rewarded this gentleman, on commercial principles, of course, by giving him the Headship of an Office of which he knew nothing at all, and a salary of £1,000 or £1,200 a-year. He was certain that when that gentleman entered the Office he had not the most remote notion of how a deed was registered, and his sole claim to the office was that he had been the proprietor of a paper in Dublin which he had made the tool of the Government, and which became no longer useful for that purpose, because the people would have nothing more to do with it. In saying that he was not animated by any personal feeling, for the paper had disappeared for 10 or 15 years, deserted by the people. He held that the commercial principle should be applied to the entire Office, if applied at all, and he contended that any man who had served for a long time in any Public Department should be allowed an opportunity of becoming a permanent official and of rising to other posts when they became vacant. It was most discouraging and demoralizing to such men to find persons from outside put over their heads, not on commercial, but on political principles.

Question put.

The Committee *divided*:—Ayes 28; Noes 45: Majority 17. — (Div. List, No. 198.)

Original Question put, and *agreed to*.

(4.) Motion made, and Question proposed,

"That a sum, not exceeding £83,430 (including a Supplementary sum of £25,340), be granted to Her Majesty, to complete the sum necessary to defray the Charge which will come in course of payment during the year ending on the 31st day of March 1885, for the Salaries and Expenses of the Office of the Irish Land Commission."

MR. HEALY said, that it was an unfortunate thing to have to rise to speak on this matter, when there was no one connected with the Irish Office on the Treasury Bench; but he wished to draw attention to two or three matters in connection with this Vote, in regard to which he had already given Notice to the House. He observed, in the first place, that there was a very large decrease in the Vote this year of nearly £70,000, the amount last year having been £157,381, while this year it was £88,090. That decrease was, of course, due in a large degree to the fact that the fair rent cases appeared, judging from the statistics, to be in a fair way to being all settled. He noticed that, according to a Return dated June 30th, of 114,544 cases, the Land Commission claimed to have disposed of 105,058 cases, leaving about 9,000 cases still to be disposed of. In reality, of course, they had only disposed of about 74,000 cases, as over 30,000 had been either withdrawn or dismissed. His complaint that night was that the Committee were asked to discuss this Vote without having any information as to the character of the Sub-Commissioners, except a simple statement by the Chief Secretary, that certain gentlemen would no longer continue Sub-Commissioners. There was no printed document to which they could refer, giving the names of the gentlemen who were to continue and those who were not to remain. That was not a proper way in which to discuss this Vote, and he must complain of those who were responsible in this matter for not having provided the House of Commons with information of a precise and adequate character respecting the gentlemen who were charged with the responsible duties of fixing fair rents. It was true the Chief Secretary had stated that certain gentlemen were to be dismissed; but they were left to work out piecemeal and by subtraction those who were to remain.

MR. TREVELYAN said, he had given the names of the gentlemen who were not to be continued; but there was no occasion to give those who were to remain.

MR. HEALY said, his impression was the other way; but, at all events, his point was, that merely giving a statement in the House which no one could carry away in his head was no way in which to deal with this matter. The Government were at no loss for funds, and to print a small slip or document giving the names of those who were remaining or leaving could not have been too much even for the intelligence of the Irish Office. He had been at some pains to find out which gentlemen were to be continued—without reference that was to the seven years' men—and he must say that anything more calculated to infuse distrust into the minds of the Irish tenants he had never imagined. With regard to the Commissioners, it was most extraordinary that the Government had dismissed everyone whose term would elapse on the 31st of August, who was trusted by the tenants, and had kept on everybody who had been the subject of complaint on the part of the tenants. All whom the Tory Members had assailed had gone down before the landlords' advocates; whereas men like Mr. Grey, Mr. Meek, Mr. Davidson, and others of that stamp, who had given satisfaction, to a large extent, to the Irish tenants, had gone "where the woodbine twineth." Everyone attacked by the right hon. and learned Member for the University of Dublin (Mr. Gibson) and the hon. and gallant Member for the County of Dublin (Colonel King-Harman) had gone, while those Commissioners, whom he (Mr. Healy) and his Friends had assailed, remained in office. Who had been left at that moment. Let them consider the residuum. He proposed to give a biographical account of the gentlemen who were to be retained. There was, first of all, Mr. Burke, a Protestant gentleman, son of an Inspector of the Local Government Board—that in itself being, of course, a recommendation for him to be appointed to fix rents—a Conservative and a strong landlord partizan. The very fact that he was the son of a Local Government Board Inspector made him almost a man sent from Heaven with a stamp of extra fitness to discharge the duties of the office. Mr. Burke was a barrister. Hon. Members would not be able to discover that fact from having seen his name in the papers, because he (Mr. Healy) could not find that he ever held a brief, but they would discover it if they put themselves to the trouble of looking over *The Law List*. Well, Mr. Burke was, of course, a Conservative in politics—a strong Tory partizan—and what could be a higher qualification for any man to fix rents in Ireland? Well, Mr. Burke was No. 1. Then he came to the name of Mr. M'Devitt. Now, if there was any person in Ireland in whom the people of that country had no confidence, it was Mr. M'Devitt. He was the son of a tenant farmer; but he had discarded that position in life, and he was now imbibed with the worst prejudices of the class in whose ranks he aspired to enter, and whose favour, to a certain extent, he appeared to have obtained. At any rate, he had the confidence of Her Majesty's Government, and they had continued him in the service of the Crown as a fit and proper person to fix rents. He had already described Mr. M'Devitt's visit to Ulster; and when he considered the letters that had been written to the newspapers, and the hue and cry raised in the country about Mr. M'Devitt, he was certainly amazed to find that Earl Spencer should fly in the teeth of the opinion of the people of Ireland by continuing this man in office. Of course, Mr. M'Devitt had a conscience, but it was a landlord's conscience, and whenever the interests of the tenant had to be balanced against those of the landlord, Mr. M'Devitt's qualms of conscience always weighed him down upon the landlord's side. While they dismissed men like Wild, Meek, Davidson, and Grey, they continued to employ men like M'Devitt. If they desired to employ certain officials, who were notorious landlords' men, why did they not mix up half-a-dozen of them with half-a-dozen tenants' men, so as to do the thing with some appearance of fairness and decency? Mr. M'Devitt, like Mr. Burke, had been called to the Bar; but he was a barrister under false pretences. He had made a representation to the Benchers that he had no intention of practising in Ireland; but as soon as he had succeeded in getting called to the Bar by the Benchers, Mr. M'Devitt practised at the Bar like any other Irish gentleman. The North-West Bar, which Mr. M'Devitt had joined, had marked their disapproval of his breach of faith by having "blackbeaned" him, and therefore he had been appointed a Sub-Commissioner. Those were his credentials; but he believed that Mr. M'Devitt had a further claim in the assistance he had given at a recent Tyrone election on behalf of the Liberal candidate. His claims to the confidence of the tenants were absolutely *nil*, although he professed to have worked in their behalf prior to the passing of the Prevention of Crime Act of 1881. At the outset of his career, no doubt, Mr. M'Devitt declared himself the friend of the tenant; but at the moment it became necessary to obtain a position as a friend of the landlords, Mr. M'Devitt was not ashamed to wheel entirely round. He passed on now to the next gentleman, also a barrister, Mr. Reardon. Mr. Reardon, like Mr. Burke and Mr. M'Devitt, never had any practice at the Bar, and, of course, as the Government were at great straits to get gentlemen to act as Legal Commissioners, they had been obliged to fall back on the brigade of briefless barristers who hung about Dublin, and to shove them anyhow into the position of Legal Commissioners. Mr. Reardon's principal claim to office was that, on several occasions, as representing the Commission on which he had served, he had been burnt in effigy by the tenants. Mr. Reardon had, accordingly, been appointed a Sub-Commissioner. Now, a gentleman who had been burnt in effigy should, undoubtedly, enjoy the confidence of Her Majesty's Ministers. Certainly the fact ought to increase his credit with Earl Spencer at Dublin Castle, because that noble Earl had over and over again been burnt in effigy; and it ought to require no other credentials whatever to entitle a man to an appointment as Legal Commissioner. Then he came to the next gentleman, Mr. Doyle. Mr. Doyle happened to belong to the county, the borough of which he (Mr. Healy) had represented for some time—namely, Wexford. Mr. Doyle was also a Legal Commissioner, and he was a Legal Commissioner because he had never had a brief in his life. That fact, of course, gave him unquestionable claim upon Her Majesty's Government. The mere fact that a man was required for the office of Legal Commissioner, and that persons could be found who never held a brief, undoubtedly constituted at once a very strong reason why Earl Spencer should employ them. Mr. Doyle further had the influence of his Conservative friends who were very powerful in Dublin Castle, and Mr. Doyle had very little difficulty in retaining his position. Mr. Doyle's legal light was, in the first instance, not recognized, and his original appointment was that of Agricultural Commissioner; but having gained experience as a fixer of rents, from a landlord's point of view, Mr. Doyle suddenly blossomed out as a Legal Comsioner, and was now continued in that capacity. He now came to the gentlemen who were appointed to act as Lay Commissioners. First, there was Mr. Walpole. Of Mr. Walpole he would only say that if the voice of his own tenants could penetrate into that House, Mr. Walpole would never have been heard of as a Sub-Commissioner. He was a Tory in politics, and a notoriously bad landlord, distrusted by every man who had been brought in contact with him. His decisions were appealed against and dismissed. But it would be found that Mr. Walpole possessed everything that ought to constitute a Landlord Commissioner. Then came Mr. Barry. Mr. Barry was a Catholic gentleman; but it was remarkable in Ireland how the Government picked out all the "Shanneen" Catholics they could find if they desired to appoint any man to any office of profit. Mr. Barry was a Catholic landlord, and he had shown himself, throughout his judgments, one of the greatest and bitterest enemies of the tenant farmer. It seemed as though the Government, having exhausted all the bigoted Protestants they could find, fell back upon the rotten Catholics; and he must say that this system of governing a people by men whom the people themselves detested and despised was a remarkable feature of the Government of Ireland. Her Majesty's Ministers appeared to have employed a microscope in order to discover and drag out their agents by that means from utter obscurity. As long as there was an objectionable man left in Ireland, Earl Spencer would get hold of him and utilize him in building up the foundation of peace and order and security in Ireland, at any rate, for the next 15 years. The next man was Mr. Bamford. Mr. Bamford was a land agent, and a detested land agent, and, therefore, as a matter of course, he had been appointed by Her Majesty's Government; and Mr. Bamford had been sent round upon estates, in which he was himself personally interested, in order to fix rents upon his own relatives. The manner in which he had fixed those rents upon tenants, who were his own relatives, had already been brought under the notice of the House. Of course, a man of such a character was bound to be employed as a Sub-Commissioner. Mr. Mowbray, another Sub-Commissioner, was, as far as he recollected, a Scotchman. Of course, in dealing with Irish rents, they must naturally have a Scotchman. The first thing to do in Ireland was to subject the Irish people to the judicial influences of a Scotchman; that appeared to be one of the great principles of Her Majesty's Government. Even the Chief Secretary represented a Scotch borough; but whether he was a Scotchman himself, he (Mr. Healy) was unable to say. Of course, that fact might have had nothing to do with the appointment of Mr. Mowbray. Mr. Mowbray's first claim to the appointment was that he was a Scotchman; secondly, that he was a Tory; and, thirdly, that he was Secretary to the Agricultural Society of Ireland, which was a Landlords' Association. Mr. Mowbray's conduct on the Bench had been of such a character that the tenants regarded him as their worst enemy; and, therefore, Mr. Mowbray had been continued in his position as Commissioner, while such men as Meek, Davison, Crane, and Grey had been got rid of. There was still another—namely, Mr. Lynch—who, strange to say, although a barrister, had not been appointed a Legal Commissioner. He could not understand why Mr. Lynch had been appointed a Lay Commissioner, because Mr. Lynch, like all the other gentlemen to whom he had referred, had never held a brief. He, therefore, failed to see why he should not have been appointed a Legal Commissioner. By some strange freak the Government had only appointed Mr. Lynch a Lay Commissioner. He (Mr. Healy) thought it was a great mistake. He did not know whether Legal Commissioners drew higher salaries than the rest; but the fact that Mr. Lynch had never held a brief had not been sufficient to insure his promotion. He certainly saw no reason in the world why Mr. Lynch should be allowed to remain among the common herd of Lay Commissioners. What Mr. Lynch did not know about land would fill a library. Mr. Lynch, being an extremely young man, had had no real agricultural experience whatever, and, having had none, he was considered fit to adorn the position of Lay Commissioner. He had now gone through the list of the gentlemen Her Majesty's Government proposed to continue in the office of Sub-Commissioner; but he would ask why, in the name of common sense, gentlemen of this kind had been continued, and why other gentlemen had been dismissed? The inference was plain. Why had Mr. Meek been dismissed? Why had Mr. Wild gone? Why should they never hear again of Mr. Davidson, of Mr. Grey, of Mr. Crane, and others? It was because the Government had found it inconvenient, in view of the Tory attacks upon them, and especially of the attacks in "another place," to continue them; and the Commissioners who were dismissed were those who had acted with the greatest fairness towards the tenants. The conduct of the House of Lords in this matter had been the curse of the Land Act. In the House of Commons the friends of the tenants had never been able to bring forward their grievances, because the Rules of the House, and the time which was at the disposal of private Members, were such that even with constant attempts it was impossible to bring the grievances of the people before the House. But noble Lords, who were themselves interested in land in Ireland, when they found the Land Commissioners acting improperly, from a landlord's point of view, had only to put down a Motion on the Books in order to bring on a discussion. Everybody who knew him knew that he had never had, nor was ever likely to have, an acre of land in his life. He had, therefore, no more interest in this matter, from a personal point of view, than the first man they might meet in the street; but Members of the House of Commons could not bring their grievances fairly forward, and speak on behalf of those they represented, while noble Lords in "another place," the moment they found that things were going in a way they considered improper, as landlords, had only to put down a Motion on the Books of the House, and in a jiffy apologetic speeches came from Lord Carlingford and other noble Lords who represented the Government, but who were totally unfitted to speak on Irish subjects. The consequence was that the attacks on the Commissioners conducted in the House of Lords had been sufficient to intimidate the Sub-Commissioners who had been endeavouring to do their duty. Their decisions had been distinctly attacked in that House. Motions had been put down which enabled certain noble Lords to bring the question forward; and the result was that every Sub-Commissioner who had acted with any approach to fairness had been dismissed. They might call it dismissal, discontinuance, or suspension, or anything else they liked in the vocabulary of official phrases; but he called it dismissal, and dismissal because they were attacked in "another place" by noble Lords who belonged to the Tory Party. In the House of Commons, the only facility they had for attacking the Commission or the agents of the Government was once a-year, when the Vote for the Land Commission was brought forward. He ventured to assert that if the Government had been willing to pay attention to the complaints and demands of the Irish people, instead of pinning their faith on the complaints of noble Lords, that very few of the gentlemen who had been continued in office would have been acting now as Sub-Commissioners. This was the state of affairs. They had created a gangrene in the minds of the tenants of Ireland. They thought they were settling the Land Question. Aye, they were settling it with sticking-plaister—underneath the old sore was running; and, although it might be that by their Prevention of Crime Act, for a time, they might be keeping down the real public sentiment upon the abortive work of the last few years, these sticking-plaister remedies would yet be found to be utterly futile. They could not keep the country in its present position, straight-waistcoated as it was. He would like to call the attention of the Committee to what happened the other day at the Limerick Convention. At that Convention the question of the rents fixed by the Sub-Commissioners was considered by a representative body in the most calm and moderate manner. It was an expression of opinion by tenant farmers; and what was the opinion expressed by the delegates? The County of Limerick was one of the most prosperous and comfortable in the whole of Ireland, enjoying as rich a soil as any county in the country. But at that Convention the delegates expressed their opinion by resolution that sooner or later a strike would come against the judicial rents imposed upon them by the Sub-Commissioners. Of course, having passed that resolution, no notice was taken of it. The Government might treat the matter lightly, because anyone could govern in a state of siege; but they would find in the end that it was deserving of their serious consideration. Nobody admired more than he did the straight up-and-down way in which the Chief Secretary endeavoured to address himself to his duties. He had never attempted to depreciate his uniform courtesy to the Irish Members; they were treated by him at all times with fairness, as far as fairness could be exhibited by the partizan of one side towards the partizan of another; but, at the same time, while he admired the speeches of the right hon. Gentleman, and believed that he endeavoured to discharge his work with official conscientiousness, as far as his mind would enable him to address himself to the work, from every practical point of view the right hon. Gentleman was just about as fit for the position he occupied as he (Mr. Healy) would be to govern the entire world. There was a total want of sympathy on his part with the Irish people; a failure to appreciate and to understand what it was they wanted. As a matter of fact, the right hon. Gentleman was altogether in the hands of a few first-class clerks in Ireland, and if he wanted to carry on any new idea, he dared not initiate it or take it in hand. It was impossible for the right hon. Gentleman to say—"I will have this or that done." He was immediately put off by some first-class clerk in Dublin, with a salary of £750 a-year, who said—"You cannot do that; that would be altogether against the rules. You must continue Mr. M'Devitt, but we cannot have Mr. Meek or Mr. Grey; because in Dublin Castle we understand all these things, and you do not. You may understand something about India and a little about Devonshire, or the Border Burghs; but you do not know anything about Ireland." The result was that the right hon. Gentleman followed humbly in the track into which he was directed. Now, he (Mr. Healy) wished to know whether this was a Land Act passed for the people or not, or were the Government prepared to depend upon the Land Act when they had got the Prevention of Crime Act no longer in operation? That was the point to which hon. Gentlemen opposite and the Radicals of England must address themselves. They could not coerce the people of Ireland for ever, and sooner or later they must give up their coercive *régime*. Next year they would have the Representation of the People Bill to consider, and they knew, from the Prime Minister, that it was impossible to pass a Redistribution Bill in the same year; but surely it would be harder to pass a Prevention of Crime Act. Already hon. Members were beginning to appeal to their constituents. The hon. and learned Member opposite the Member for Chelsea (Mr. Firth), who had voted steadily all through for the Prevention of Crime Act——

MR. FIRTH said, he was sorry to interrupt the hon. Member; but it was quite a mistake to represent him as having steadily voted all through for the Prevention of Crime Act.

MR. HEALY said, he accepted the statement of the hon. and learned Member; but, nevertheless, he had the impression that the hon. and learned Gentleman, and a good many of his Friends, had voted steadily for the Prevention of Crime Act. They now found that it was necessary to go to their constituents, and it was wonderful how they were beginning to appreciate the statistics of Ireland in regard to the decrease of crime. As their only reliance must be the Irish Land Act, why on earth could not they see that it was necessary to have it carried out honestly and fairly? He had never been an advocate of the justice of fixing rents; he believed they could not do it. He had never voted for the Land Act, because he believed that it was an impossible settlement of the Land Question; but he had endeavoured to improve the Act as much as possible. But the fact that it was an impossible settlement of the Land Question was no reason why its administration should be given into the hands of landlord partizans. If there were to be partizans of the landlords, let them act in a straight up-and-down manner, and have partizans appointed on the side of the tenants. If they were to have 40 partizans of the landlords, let them have 40 partizans of the tenants. He ventured to think that out of the 70 or 80 men the Government had appointed, they had not appointed more than a dozen who represented the tenants' side of the question; and the moment any one of them gave a decision against the landlord, he was instantly dismissed at the instance of some noble Lord in "another place." The landlords did not know what a deep debt of gratitude they owed to the right hon. and learned Gentleman the Member for the University of Dublin (Mr. Gibson). He ventured to think that by the action of the right hon. and learned Gentleman on the Land Act alone he had saved the landlords, at least, £1,000,000 a-year, and by his constant and untiring efforts on their behalf he had saved them hundreds and thousands of pounds in the shape of an adequate reduction of rents. The landlords did not realize the service of their best friends; but the unwearied patience of the right hon. and learned Gentleman on their behalf had simply astonished him (Mr. Healy). The tenants had arrayed against them the Whigs and the Tories combined, and, with the exception of a dozen or a score of the people's advocates in that House, there was no one to present their cause to the country. With the House of Lords closed against them; with all the entire hierarchy opposed to them; with Earl Spencer a landlord, Mr. Vernon a landlord, and Mr. Justice O'Hagan an invertebrate Whig, the entire body of the Land Court were in favour of the landlord and against the tenant. He believed the Government had never made a greater mistake than they had in their conduct in regard to this Commission. He ventured to think that, before many years were over, the whole of this business would have to be done over again. At the end of 15 years the rents fixed for the first general term would come to a close; but he was of opinion that long before 15 years there would be a revision of rents, and, if that were so, the landlords would only have themselves to thank for it. They had appointed a set of gentlemen upon the Land Commission, in whom nobody had confidence except the landlords. Every man who had evinced a disposition to befriend the tenants had been chassed, while every man who was necessarily a friend of the landlords had been continued in his post. At the present moment they had 17,000 appeals lodged for hearing, and out of them only 6,000 had been disposed of. When they had only been able to dispose of 6,000 appeals in the course of three years, and when they had 11,000 left, he left it to the calculations of any statistician in that House to say what would be likely to be the state of things. Out of the decisions which as yet had been taken to the Court of Appeal, how many had been confirmed before Mr. Justice O'Hagan or Mr. Vernon? About one in 20. How many were altered? All the other 19. And how were they altered? By the rents being raised in almost every single instance. Landlord appeals had been increased by the system of rent-raising initiated by Mr. Justice O'Hagan. When an appeal was made, in almost every case the old rent had been imposed. The real rent reducers, the real Sub-Commissioners, were the gentlemen who signed the "No Rent" Manifesto. The tenants were buoyed up with the false hope of their rent being reduced 10, 15, or 18 per cent; but by the present system of rent-raising the old rent, or very nearly so, was reverted to in the Appeal Court. The Prime Minister had admitted that he would run the Land Act against the Land League, and so the right hon. Gentleman ran the Act against the Land League. The bayonet, false alarms, the gibbet, the cell, and exile reduced the Land League to comparative quiescence, and from that moment the rent regulation fell from 28 to 24 per cent, until at last in the Appeal Court they were left at 15 and 10, and even 5 per cent. In certain instances, as he had noticed the other day, they had stood higher than they had ever been before. Landlords like the Marquess of Waterford and Mr. Blennerhassett, the Member for Kerry, had sent in applications to have their rents raised. He should like to have seen them send in such applications when the "No Rent" Manifesto was in force. These things would not have been done "in the brave days of old." The Government Sub-Commissioners would have looked twice at these petty little mountain grazing plots before they attempted to raise the rents of the noble Marquess (the Marquess of Waterford). What was the conclusion drawn from all this experience? It was this. As long as the tenants of Ireland depended on the sense of justice of the British Government, so long would they be baffled, beaten, and defeated; but whenever they attempted to raise an agitation, whenever they showed themselves desperate and determined, then, and then only, would their claims receive attention.

COLONEL O'BEIRNE said, the Land Commission arrangement was a sham from beginning to end, the supposed valuation of land which was going on being a pure pretence. It could not be anything else, looking at the work the Commissioners had to do, therefore this Vote was a pure waste of money. Only the other day he saw a statement in a newspaper to the effect that 197 Irish estates had been, in one place, valued in four hours, the Commissioners having had a drive of six miles out and six miles back again for the purpose. How was it possible that such an extent of land could be valued in so short a time and under such circumstances? It was simply impossible. He had heard, also, that as much as 600 acres of grazing land in Tipperary had been valued in a space of two or three hours—nearly a square mile. How was such a thing possible? It was not to be done—the whole thing was the merest farce. Seeing what the Judge of the Appellate Court had been able to say before the House of Lords Committee, he (Colonel O'Beirne) could not think that this was a Court which valued land as carefully as it should. When the Prime Minister was introducing his Bill, he stated that the Court which was to fix the rents was to be a Judicial Court; but that statement had not been verified. They knew what had happened since 1881. A number of Commissioners had been appointed for political reasons—it was quite true, as the hon. Member for Monaghan (Mr. Healy) had stated, that this was much more of a Political Court than a Land Court, and that "Political Court" ought to be its proper name. He protested most emphatically against this waste of money; and, if anyone would support him in moving a reduction of the Vote by £5,000, he should only be too happy to propose it. There was one observation made by the hon. Member for Monaghan with regard to the Appellate Court, which had struck him (Colonel O'Beirne) as unfair. The hon. Member had said the Court was more an institution for raising rents than anything else; but the fact was that by far the larger proportion of the rents submitted to the Court had been confirmed or lowered. That was the case in the Province of Connaught, at any rate, whatever it might be in the rest of Ireland. He had it from persons connected with the land in that Province. He did not wish to say more on the subject than that—he was satisfied with entering a protest against what appeared to him to be nothing more or less than a sham.

MR. LEA said, he did not how far it was desirable to raise a discussion as to the working of the Land Commission on this Vote; but his object in rising was to take exception to some observations which had fallen from the hon. Member for Monaghan (Mr. Healy) with regard to one of the Sub-Commissioners, Mr. M'Devitt. He did not know much about the working of the Commission; but he was sure that Mr. M'Devitt was an honest, conscientious man, who might be depended upon to do his best as between landlord and tenant. The hon. Member for Monaghan had also said that the House of Lords had been averse to the Land Act. To a certain extent he (Mr. Lea) was bound to agree with the hon. Member, because, no doubt, whilst the Act was passing through the House of Lords it was altered to an appreciable extent; and, further, there could be no question that the discussions which had taken place in that Chamber from time to time had had the effect of intimidating the Land Commission. He had been sorry to see discussions taking place in this House regarding the operations of the Commissioners. Mr. Grey—to whose conduct reference had several times been made by Questions in the House—had been dismissed in consequence of his working of the Act in Donegal; and the result was that nothing would ever drive out of the minds of the tenants that Mr. Grey was in favour of them, and that he had been sent away because his decisions had been favourable to them. They would never be able to wean the tenants from the belief that Mr. Grey was dismissed, not because he was less capable than the other Commissioners, but because he was supposed to be just in his dealings with the peasantry. This gentleman had been engaged in deciding cases in the West of Donegal, one of the poorest districts in the whole of Ireland. Since his removal another Commissioner had heard cases there, and had given valuations of a very similar kind; and, strange to say, a second Commissioner had given decisions there of a somewhat different character. The public had been made acquainted with this difference. He did not know under what procedure it had taken place; but, of course, it had given rise to the opinion that the Chief Commissioners had been influenced not to permit gentlemen of Mr. Grey's views to try the cases of the tenants. He (Mr. Lea) could not believe that the Chief Secretary was responsible; but probably the right hon. Gentleman dealt too much with the head Commission, in Dublin, who saw the Questions put to him in the House from time to time, and were, to a certain extent, intimidated. He believed the system of intimidation had done very much to prejudice the fair working of the Land Act.

MR. DAWSON wished to ask the right hon. Gentleman the Chief Secretary to the Lord Lieutenant whether it was convenient that acting land agents like Mr. James Green Barry—the land agent of Lord Emly—paid as servants by landowners, should have to do with the consideration of tenants' applications? Was it possible that men receiving salaries could properly sit as Land Commissioners to adjudicate between landlords and tenants? He must press for an answer to that, because, if the facts were as he stated, it must be apparent to the Committee that no system of Land Commission carried on in such a way could have the confidence of the country. The right hon. Gentleman might tell him that Mr. Barry did not sit to adjudicate rents in the district in which Lord Emly owned land; but, in whatever part of Ireland he sat, unless he (Mr. Dawson) was misinformed, he was the agent, and the paid agent, of Lord Emly and other landlords; and it was utterly impossible that a man who was receiving a portion of his daily bread—a large portion of his daily bread—from landlords who derived their livelihood from largely-increased rents, could do justice when he came to adjudicate on these matters. When a man was made a Land Commissioner, he ought to give up other occupations—certainly those connected with land. If a man took an ordinary public office, he was obliged to give up other occupations. An ordinary official could not even receive a salary from the Government, and come here and perform the duties of a legislator. The two things were incompatible; how, then, could a man receive a salary from a landlord, and then go and adjudicate, as a servant of the Government, between landlords and tenants? He could not do it; the position of such a man was absolutely untenable. If he were as snow or ice, he could not escape calumny. And yet the hon. Member for Monaghan (Mr. Healy) had shown that several of the Commissioners were circumstanced in this way. Mr. Vernon himself was agent to Lord Pembroke—the richly-paid agent of the largest landlord, and bound to him by more or greater monetary ties than he was to the Land Commission. How could a man like this adjudicate fairly between landlord and tenant, when his first duty, his first love, was to the landlords who paid him? Would the right hon. Gentleman answer this simple question—was it possible that paid land agents could adjudicate fairly between landlords and tenants?

MR. TREVELYAN: Sir, the hon. Member for Monaghan (Mr. Healy) has made a speech to which I listened with interest and considerable admiration of the great fertility of criticism which it displayed in regard to gentlemen who had been retained as Sub-Commissioners in Ireland. But I do not propose to follow the hon. Member into the details of his criticisms, in the first place, because I consider it would be extremely unfortunate that we should discuss—at any rate, that I should discuss—in this House the fairness or unfairness of people who hold a judicial position. It was another matter when there were 70 or 80 gentlemen who had to be taken out of the ranks of private persons in Ireland, and taken on very short notice —— [MR. HEALY: Hear, hear!] Obviously, on very short notice. How could it be otherwise when 70 or 80 men had to be appointed as Judges who had never been Judges before? It was very possible that out of this number —nay, it was almost certain—that there must be many who would not possess a judicial temperament. But it was a very different matter when, after two or three years' experience, three gentlemen of the very considerable qualities of the Land Commissioners in Ireland, having watched the proceedings of these gentlemen, have picked out from among them, for recommendation to the Lord Lieutenant, those whom they consider to possess judicial faculties. The hon. Member uses the word "dismissed" in connection with the Sub-Commissioners, and says that it will be impossible to invent any words which will veil the fact that the 50 or so gentlemen whose appointments had been discontinued were practically dismissed and discredited because of the decisions they had given. Sir, the position of the Irish Government was this—the work which this large number of Sub-Commissioners was appointed to perform had been nearly accomplished. It was absolutely necessary, in the interests of public economy, that the Commission should be largely reduced in numbers—should, in fact, be reduced to less than half its size—and, under these circumstances, it was absolutely impossible that the whole number of the Sub-Commissioners could be retained. It was absolutely necessary to select from the total number about a third. That is the state of the case, and I think that, under these circumstances, I have been quite justified in deprecating the use of the word "dismissal." The Chief Commissioners inform me, in view of this debate, that what has most struck them, in the enormous majority of the decisions that have been given by the Sub-Commissioners, is the absence of any trace of partizanship; and they are very anxious that from this Bench, at any rate, there should not be said one disparaging word of the gentlemen whose appointments have not been continued. It was necessary that out of a large number a few should be selected; and the Lord Lieutenant, who was charged with the function of making the selection, made it after most careful consultation with the Commissioners, and, for the main part, I may say pretty well entirely on their advice. Now, perhaps the most eloquent —certainly the most pointed—sentence of the hon. Member's speech was that in which he described the Land Commission. His description is still in the memory of the Committee, or of such part of the Committee as heard it; and I must say that I think that, pointed as it was, the hon. Member did not convince the Committee that such men as Mr. Litton, Mr. Vernon, and Mr. Justice O'Hagan can be called a Board who are in the interest of the landlords as against the tenants. I believe these three gentlemen may be thoroughly trusted to make suggestions which can be relied upon by the Irish Government; and, carefully as I listened to the criticism of the hon. Gentleman, I cannot say that my confidence in their recommendations was at all shaken. I will take, for instance, the case of Mr. M'Devitt, who was referred to as a man whom the tenants could not trust. Now, Mr. M'Devitt was a gentleman who was thoroughly conversant with the Land Act to begin with. He wrote an exposition of it in the early part of the history of this question which, in a very short time, ran through four editions.

He was recommended by the Bishop of Raphoe.

Mr. HEALY: He is the Bishop's brother.

Mr. TREVELYAN: No.

Mr. HEALY: Then he is a Bishop's brother.

Mr. TREVELYAN: That is no disqualification for the Land Commission. The Bishop said that, in addition to his legal qualification, he had an intimate knowledge of the land tenure of Ulster, and possesses one quality that is sure to win the confidence of all——

Mr. HEALY: Why do not you send him to Ulster, then?

Mr. TREVELYAN: Really, I must ask to be permitted to go through my task without interruption. The Bishop said—

> "He possesses one quality that is sure to win the confidence of all—that is, scrupulous honesty of purpose. From what I know of him, I believe it would be difficult to find anyone who would take greater pains to discharge conscientiously any duty entrusted to him."

The hon. Member for Carlow (Mr. Dawson) objected to the re-appointment of Mr. Barry, and described him as a pure landlord's man, who could not be trusted to do justice between landlord and tenant.

Mr. DAWSON: I beg pardon. I mentioned his as a typical case, describing him as an agent. He is a personal friend of mine, and I certainly was not objecting to him as an individual. What I desired to point out was, that a land agent, whoever he may be, is hardly the person calculated to be a disinterested adjuster of rents.

Mr. TREVELYAN: The hon. Member states it as a fact that Mr. Barry holds an appointment as land agent. I should be sorry to say, in the face of that, that Mr. Barry has given up his agency; but I certainly understood that he had.

Mr. DAWSON: I am under correction—I may be wrong.

Mr. TREVELYAN: I do not say that this gentleman is not an agent. The subject is one on which I should like to inform myself before making a statement; but my impression is certainly not the same as that of the hon. Member. I should be very glad to abandon my opinion if it turns out that the hon. Member is right and I am wrong. It is difficult to imagine a person who has a more intimate knowledge of matters affecting Irish land than Mr. Barry. So far back as 1869 he was an advocate of the reform of the system of land tenure as it then existed; and I am told that when he was acting as land agent the property under his management was one that was singularly, if not entirely, free from eviction. When I consider these things, and when I look at the Gentlemen who recommended him—whether they are Members of Parliament or Members of the House of Lords—and when I remember also that the Archbishop of Cashel, Dr. Croke, recommended him, I must say that the retention of Mr. Barry as a Sub-Commissioner can in no sense imply that the Land Commissioners, in their recommendation, or the Lord Lieutenant in his acceptance of that recommendation, has done anything which ought to induce the tenants to look with suspicion on the Sub-Commissioners. Then, as to Mr. Vernon himself, whom the hon. Member describes as a land agent, it is very true that he is still an agent, but he is the agent of Lord Pembroke, and the property with which he has to do is in the nature of ground rents. I do not know that it would be too much to say that Lord Pembroke had no agricultural tenants on the property over which Mr. Vernon is agent; but, as a broad assertion, it may be stated that Mr. Vernon, when appointed as Land Commissioner, gave up the agricultural agency of the Marquess of Bath, and, I believe, several other agencies. The hon. Member for Monaghan (Mr. Healy) remarked that the noble Lords have very great advantages for starting questions connected with the Land Commission. Now, with that part of his speech I must own I have sympathy. I do not quite know what one may say about what passes in "another place." Remarks are made in "another place" as to what passes here with very great freedom; but we, I suppose, are bound by much stricter Rules than prevail there. In so far as advantage has been taken of facilities afforded for debate in "another place" for throwing discredit upon the Sub-Commissioners, who are, as I think, doing their duty in Ireland, it has been excessive and very unfortunate. Noble Lords have taken advantage of their privileges much too frequently, and I have no doubt that their conduct in that respect has had a disturbing influence, so far as it has gone, upon the minds of the Sub-Commissioners. It is because I do not wish to lay myself open to similar charges that I do not propose to speak in detail of the Sub-Commissioners who have been re-appointed. I conceive that the effect of a hot discussion on the proclivities of any given Judge has always a tendency—human nature being the same on the Bench as off it—to disturb the balance of that Judge's mind. But the hon. Member says that those Sub-Commissioners who have been attacked in the House of Lords have been removed. Well, Sir, on that point, again, I do not wish to enter; but this I will say—that if all the Sub-Commissioners who have been attacked in this House and in the House of Lords, from one side or the other, had been removed, we should have had no Sub-Commissioners at all. [Mr. HEALY: Oh, oh!] Yes; I think that is hardly too broad an assertion to make. During the past year, no doubt, owing to my earnest expostulations, there has been a happy suspension of those attacks on the Sub-Commissioners, which used to be made from more than one quarter in this House at Question time. Months and months may be said to have passed with scarcely a complaint of the conduct of the Sub-Commissioners; but it was not so in the early days of the Commission. Then, scarcely a day passed without some remonstrance as to the course taken by these officials. The hon. Member made some remarks, which, I must say, did not meet with the general approbation of the Committee, as to the Appeal Court. I do not refer to his remarks as to the number of appeals. That is a matter of statistics, and has attracted the observation of everyone interested in Ireland. The number is to be regretted, and it would have gratified the Government very much if they had been able to establish two Courts to get on with the appeals more quickly than they have been doing. But, when you pass on to the procedure of the Court and the character of its decisions, I do not think the hon. Member at all carried with him the unanimous adhesion of the Committee. He described the Appeal Court as a "rent-raising" Court. He stated that in one case out of 20 the rent remained as it was, and that in 19 cases out of 20 they were altered. Well, on that point I have not by me accurate statistics; but, as it is a question of assertion against assertion, I would venture to say that he has been misled, and greatly misled, by the feelings with which he regards the decisions of the Appeal Court. As a matter of fact, the Court is far from being a rent-raising Court. The amount to which it has raised rents is quite as likely to be counted by hundreds as by tens of thousands. Taking Ireland through, I think that, so far from 19 rents out of 20 having been altered, it will be found that decidedly those which have been confirmed are a large proportion of the total number of cases. On that point, however, I speak more from general observation than from statistics. I will try and ascertain exactly how the case stands; but I do not hesitate to say that the sweeping condemnation the hon. Member passed on the Appeal Court was one which did not meet with the adhesion of the Committee. The hon. Member speaks of the real effective Land Commission being the body which issued the "No Rent" Manifesto. He says that Manifesto had great influence; that soon after its issue large reductions were made, and that the reductions have now come down to a very small figure. Sir, it is quite true that during the very first months the reductions were distinctly larger than they have been at any other period; but I believe the reason of that was a very simple one—namely, that the worst cases, to a very large extent, came into Court first. There was a fall very soon, but that fall, after the very first period, has been extremely slow; and I have no reason to think that at this moment there is any fall at all. I believe that at present the reductions of rent are on an average of 18 or 19 per cent, and that is very little below the figure at which they have stood during almost all the period the Sub-Commissioners have been sitting, with the exception of the very first months. The hon. Member says that certain noblemen and gentlemen have lately contrived to get their rents raised. Well, I must say that considering the enormous number of cases that have been brought into Court, and considering that on some estates in Ireland the tenants were very lightly rented, that it would be a very serious imputation against the Sub-Commissioners if the rents were not occasionally raised. I think that to make a general observation to the effect that rents have been raised, and that, therefore, the decisions have been unjust, is to make a charge against a Judicial Body which should not be made. The hon. Member says that in these matters I am in the hands of first class clerks who are paid £750 a-year. In this case, at any rate, it is not so. I do not deny that I am in the hands of certain gentlemen who understand these matters better than I do; but they are not first class clerks with salaries of £750 a-year —they are the Land Commissioners who are paid £3,000 a-year. I trust to these gentlemen, and if it be possible to get three persons who represent the average opinion and the average judgment of Ireland as between landlord and tenant, they are the persons, and it is upon their recommendation that the appointments have been made. There is not one appointment with regard to which our hands have been forced. The original recommendations may have been modified—no doubt they have been modified by discussion—but the 10 or 15 gentlemen who have been selected out of the entire body of Sub-Commissioners are those who have acquired the confidence of the three Land Commissioners. The hon. Member says that the Act of 1881 was passed in order to pacify Ireland, and he asks me whether I think that it has done so. I do not know, but at any rate I should be right in saying this—that the work which has been done by the Land Commission is a gigantic work. It has been probably in amount in excess of that which was expected even by those who took a favourable view of the operations that might be anticipated from the Land Commission. In the course of two years no less than 105,000 cases of fair rents have been disposed of. Some 74,000 have been actually fixed, and 70,000 agreements have been arrived at under the auspices of the Court —that was to say, that in 144,000 cases a lease of 15 years and a judicial rent has been given to the tenants, with a reduction on the previous rents of £540,000 a-year. That represents only the direct work of the Commissioners. The indirect work is recorded nowhere except in the rent books of the various estates where arrangements have been made between landlord and tenant under the knowledge that, if arrangements are not made in an amicable manner, they must be made under litigation. The Land Act has proved so far a real land settlement for Ireland. If that be so—and I believe it is—the effect which it must have on the country will be a pacifying effect. I do not know what result it may have upon the political movement in which the hon. Member and his friends take so much interest; but I know that the Irish tenant farmers now entertain a sense of security such as they have ardently wished to enjoy, and such as they have never enjoyed before, and that, at the same time, even on the very worst estates in Ireland, they have been able to obtain that reduction of rent which the English and Scotch tenants have obtained by economical causes. These are propositions which can hardly be denied. As I have before stated, I am unwilling to enter into any discussion on the personal merits of the gentlemen who have been selected for appointment; but I believe they represent the result of the most careful observation on the part of the Land Commissioners during the last two years, and I am certain that the Commissioners themselves, who have been the advisers of the Government in this matter, have been actuated alone by the love of justice towards Ireland.

Mr. GIBSON said, that this Motion was one of such extreme importance that he did not like to allow the opportunity to pass without making a few brief observations upon it. The Land Act was now the law of the land, and the position which he had always taken up in reference to it had been uniform and consistent—namely, that since it had been placed on the Statute Book it was entitled to be regarded fairly and reasonably by all members of the community, and that it was bound to be administered by those who were responsible for its administration impartially, temperately, and fairly, not in the interest of one class, but in the legitimate interests of all parties concerned. He had never swerved from that attitude towards the Land Act since it became law, and it was not his intention to do so now. But he thought it should not be open to objection if he were to point out where the administration of the Act had failed to substantiate the statements of its authors. When it was passing through Parliament, they were told it would only apply to exceptional, few, and rare cases in Ireland; that was stated in speech after speech by right hon. Gentlemen on the Treasury Bench; but, as a matter of fact, they found that the Act had been applied to almost all classes of estates in Ireland; that no class of property and no class of rent had been in the slightest degree exempt from the operation of the Act. They had been told over and over again by the Prime Minister and others that the old properties were safe, and that it was only the new proprietors who had abused their rights who would be called into question under this Act. But that was not their experience of its administration. Some old proprietors had been brought into the Land Court, and they could undoubtedly point to substantial reductions made in their rentals. It would appear, without going into details, that those who had been rack-renters got off best, and that the man who had not raised his rents at all, inasmuch as it was thought wise and politic to have reductions, had his rent reduced; and if a man had raised his rent to a rack-renting level, his rents were, of course, reduced too, but rarely had he been reduced below the level from which he had succeeded in raising them for himself. The hon. Member for Donegal (Mr. Lea) had mentioned what was at that moment a rather prevalent theory on the other side of the House. The hon. Member had had a fling at the action of the House of Lords. He did so most temperately, as if he were not standing upon strong ground; he alluded to the changes made in the Act when it was passing through the other House of Parliament. He need not go into the details of those changes; but he presumed that the hon. Member had some belief in Earl Granville and in Lord Carlingford. Now, those eminent statesmen had pointed out that when the Land Bill was emerging from the House of Lords, it was emerging with distinct improvements effected by the changes made in it by the other House. That was the statement made by responsible Members of the Government with reference to the few and limited alterations to which the House of Lords had subjected the measure. If the Prime Minister, in the progress of the discussion on the Land Act, with his boundless resources of language and his absolutely illimitable ingenuity, had foreshadowed what would be its actual working, as they now knew it by experience, he had a strong suspicion that the right hon. Gentleman would have had considerable difficulty in making a statement which would be acceptable to the House. With respect to the gentlemen who had been appointed as Sub-Commissioners—a very important and serious appointment—he was bound to say that the system of having temporary Judges without stability in their appointments, and without any guarantee whatever for their independence, appeared to him to be radically unsound. It was, in his opinion, quite absurd to have men, invested with the most tremendous judicial discretion, hanging upon the breath of the Government for the bread they ate day by day and month by month; and it was a perfect miracle to him that the administration of the Act had not utterly broken down under the logic of facts. He declined to go in detail into the very disagreeable task of canvassing the particular merits of the Sub-Commissioners. He presumed that the Government had proceeded upon some system of selection, and that they had acted, as had been stated by the right hon. Gentleman opposite (Mr. Trevelyan), on the recommendation of the Land Commissioners. If that were so, he supposed they had tried to discharge this most difficult and delicate function in the best way they could. He did not mean to say that if other people had had the selection of these gentlemen, that the very same names would have been found on the list. But he declined to go into that question. He had now come to that point of experience with regard to the Land Act that he preferred not to indulge in prophecy, but to wait for further experience of its operation. He found that some of those Sub-Commissioners, whom he believed would turn out fairly good, had not come up to that very moderate expectation, and that those from whom he expected nothing had not proved to be quite so deficient. No one could say that he was using the language of exaggeration. He had not used words of great eulogy on the one side or severe condemnation on the other—he simply said he had been somewhat disappointed in the expectations he had formed. He did not like to ask any questions on one subject of the right hon. Gentleman the Chief Secretary to the Lord Lieutenant of Ireland. It seemed to him, however, that Lord Monck occupied a very curious position; and he inferred from the fact that a Bill was to be introduced that he was within the last days of his judicial career. He did not know the position in reference to the new Bill for the appointment of a new Land Commissioner; but he supposed that some information on that subject would one day be forthcoming. He did not like to go beyond negatives on that occasion; but he supposed they would be told in due time who was the remarkable person pointed at. He should be glad to know when they might look for a reduction of the enormous expense of the administration of the Land Commission. He had always understood that there would, in a year or two, be a considerable reduction of expense, and that at the end of seven years there would be a still further reduction, and that it might be assumed that then the matter would settle down to something like a normal state. There was one figure quoted by the right hon. Gentleman which ought not to be forgotten. It was stated that the Land Act had done very little; but it had had one tremendous effect—namely, that of reducing the rents by over £500,000 a-year. That was a great fact which should not be forgotten in considering this question. The right hon. Gentleman had mentioned —he did not know whether he intended to make any charge against the Irish landlords—that the English tenants had gained their reduction of rents by the operation of economic laws; and he seemed to point out that the Irish tenants were gaining a similar reduction by the operation of the Land Act. But he (Mr. Gibson) would make this remark—that the English tenants had gained a reduction of rent by the application of economic laws which could not be resisted or controlled, while the Irish landlords had had to submit to a reduction by putting aside economic laws. There had been in England nothing like the demand for land which existed in Ireland; the Irish landlords, therefore, were compelled to submit to the reduction of their rents in the face of that demand, whereas the question of rent in England had been simply settled by the operation of the law of supply and demand. At that period of the Session he did not propose to discuss the Rent Purchase Clauses, which were, of course, a very tempting subject; but he was bound to say that the Bill dealing with those clauses might, as to several of its clauses at least, very well have been kept alive. Upon that subject there was no considerable difference of opinion; and while he believed that the Guarantee Clause had not many friends in any part of the House, he thought there was a substantial agreement of opinion upon other parts of the Bill. He thought it was a matter for regret that some efforts had not been made to get rid of the controversial matter, and to adhere to those parts of the measure in regard to which but little controversy was likely to arise. If the Guarantee Clause had been dropped, no doubt many other things might have gone with it; but there were other portions of the Bill which might have done something substantial to remove friction in the working of the Purchase Clauses of the Land Act, and which might have tended to modify the present deadlock in the land market. Even at that late period of the Session he should be glad to welcome any effort that could be made, or any suggestion that could be offered, for the removal, or the modification at all events, of the present dead-lock in the Irish land market, which everyone must deplore, and the modification or removal of which would be well worth a substantial expenditure of Imperial funds.

Mr. SYNAN said, there were some observations in the speech of the right hon. and learned Gentleman who had just sat down to which he desired to reply briefly. The right hon. and learned Gentleman had told them that the Prime Minister, when he introduced the Bill, had held out a promise which induced the House to pass that measure, and that that promise had never been fulfilled. But there was nothing very extraordinary in that. It was the business of everyone who introduced a Bill to the House of Commons to hold out hopes that the Bill would not be so bad as certain persons thought it would be; and the Prime Minister had, in order to tempt the Irish landlord to swallow the pill, to make certain promises which had not been realized, and which could not be realized. The right hon. and learned Gentleman had told the Committee that the reduction of rents, brought about as between England and Ireland, had been effected by different means. The argument of the right hon. and learned Gentleman was that the demand for land in Ireland was so much greater than in England. But that was the argument on which the Land Act of 1870 was founded, and on which the Act of 1881 was also founded; it was that the demand for land had raised the rent above its ordinary price and produced rack-rentals. The consequence was that the Irish landlords had had to yield to Acts of Parliament when they would not yield to the force of economic laws. Then the right hon. and learned Gentleman had gone into the question of property, and had concluded his remarks upon that subject by saying that he would not prophesy; he had, in fact, adopted the maxim—"Do not prophesy before you know." That was the principle upon which the right hon. and learned Gentleman acted, and he had very prudently done so on the present occasion. Then he said that £500,000 a-year of reduction in Irish rents had been made; but he did not tell the Committee what proportion that amount bore to the amount of the reduction of rents in England, and whether that proportion was more or less than the proportion which the right hon. Gentleman the Chief Secretary to the Lord Lieutenant of Ireland stated had been brought about by economic laws in England; so that he thought the right hon. and learned Gentleman had left that part of the case in the same position in which he found it. The right hon. and learned Gentleman had addressed himself to the Motion before the House in a general sense; and he did not think he had produced the case of any landlord to show that the landlords had been greatly injured. But he had not said one word as to whether the tenants had been injured, or whether they were satisfied with the working of the Act. Now, that brought him to the statement—perhaps the cardinal statement made that evening by the Chief Secretary to the Lord Lieutenant of Ireland—that the Land Commission was a representative body of the tenants of Ireland, as well as of the landlords of Ireland. But where, he asked, did the right hon. Gentleman discover that? Would he give the Committee the name of one Land Commissioner who was the representative of the tenants of Ireland? There was the first Commissioner, whom he knew to be a distinguished man in every sense, as a lawyer, a man of letters, and, as the hon. Member for Monaghan (Mr. Healy) had called him, a poet. He did not wish to say one word deregatory of that gentleman; but he himself had stated that he did not know much about the value of land in Ireland, and that he was simply the administrator of the law; he knew nothing as to whether rents ought to be raised or reduced; all he had to do was to consider the evidence laid before him. But he was bound to express the opinion in his behalf that his sympathies were as much for the tenants as for the landlords; and that when he (Mr. Synan) was personally acquainted with him, that, perhaps, they were more with the tenants than with the landlords. But how could anyone in the position which he now occupied be said to be a representative of the tenants? Surely that could not be maintained, because he was a Judge to administer the law, and he would perform his office without sympathy either for one class or the other, simply carrying out the law upon the evidence before him. The second Commissioner was a lawyer, a mediocre lawyer, bearing no proportion in respect of abilities or attainments to those exhibited by the Chief Commissioner. Could the right hon. Gentleman the Chief Secretary to the Lord Lieutenant of Ireland tell the Committee that he was a representative of the tenants of Ireland? This gentleman sprung from the landlords. He did not know whether his sympathies were with the landlords or with the tenants; but he had spent a few months in that House, and certainly had shown himself to be conversant with the Act of 1881. But what evidence had he given in that House, or what evidence had he given since his appointment, of his being the representative of the tenants of Ireland? Surely, then, it was absurd to say that either the first or second Commissioners were representatives of the Irish tenants. Now with regard to the third Commissioner. He had been an agent for the collection of ground rents; there was a good deal of agricultural land in his district; but, surely, from his whole life and associations, Mr. Vernon must be rather a representative of the landlords than of the tenants of Ireland.

Indeed, when there was a difference of opinion between the Commissioners, he had almost always sided with the landlords as against the tenants, and he had succeeded to this extent—that he always managed to get the Court of Appeal to decide in his favour. Now, he had gone through the qualifications of the Commissioners one by one, and he trusted that he should never hear again that they constituted a Body representative of the tenants of Ireland. What was the opinion of the tenants themselves? Did they think that the Land Commission was representative of their interests? He was not going into any cases; but he could say that the Irish tenants certainly did not regard the Land Commission in that light. And now he came to the question of appeal, on which subject he could not go to the same length as his hon. Friend the Member for Monaghan (Mr. Healy) had gone. He said that the rents in one case out of 20 had been left the same as before they came into Court. Now, so far as his (Mr. Synan's) experience and knowledge of the matters published to Members of the House, and which he had seen in the newspapers, went, the Commission, unless where overruled by the third Member of the Commission, who was a landlord Commissioner, generally adopted the decision of the Sub-Commissioners; but that did not prove that the Sub-Commissioners were right. He had a word or two to say to the Committee as to what the tenants of Ireland thought upon this question. Let him allude to what had been stated by the right hon. and learned Gentleman the Member for the University of Dublin (Mr. Gibson). The right hon. and learned Gentleman had stated—and he (Mr. Synan) was astonished to hear him—that the House of Lords improved the Bill of 1881. He (Mr. Synan) thought he knew something about the Bill, and also about the Bill of 1870. Who destroyed the Improvement Clause of the hon. Gentleman the Member for Monaghan (Mr. Healy), the very thing that the tenants of Ireland complained about, the very thing that constituted the grievance of the tenants? Who destroyed the effect of the clause suggested by his hon. Friend but the House of Lords? That was certainly an improvement of the Bill in a wrong direction; and if the right hon. and learned Gentleman meant that, he (Mr. Synan) agreed with him; but if he meant to say that they improved the Bill in the tenants' direction, surely the proof was palpable that the tenants of Ireland had lost all confidence in the Bill and the administration of the Bill since the decision of the Court of Appeal in the case of "Adams *v.* Dunseath," upon the Improvement Clause of the Act of 1881, which Improvement Clause was the act of "another place." Well, now he came to the general question as to the action of the Sub-Commissions. He did not propose to go into the individual merits of the Members of the Sub-Commissions; beyond the legal Members of the Sub-Commissions he knew nothing about the Commissions. He, however, knew this—that he recommended that it was his duty to recommend several men in his own county whom he thought ought to be on the Sub-Commission. The men he proposed were large working farmers; but every recommendation of his was rejected, and they were, he thought, rejected on the ground that the sympathies of the men were with the tenants, and not with the landlords. He did not mean to say that their sympathies were not with the tenants, but they certainly had no prejudices against the landlords; but every man who was known to have sympathy with the tenants, and who was a working farmer himself, was, to his (Mr. Synan's) knowledge, rejected. He did not complain of that; he did not blame the Irish Government; he did not mean to say that the Lord Lieutenant knew anything about these men; His Excellency took the recommendations submitted to him by Members of Parliament, by landlords, and by others. He (Mr. Synan) understood that the Members for Ulster had the nomination of the whole of the Sub-Commissioners, so far as the North of Ireland was concerned. He did not deny that the Lord Lieutenant made the appointments faithfully and honestly; but then what was the body that appointed; to whom did the Lord Lieutenant refer the appointments? *Viris custodes custodiet?* What did the two lawyers of the Land Commission know about the merits of the men who were submitted to them so far as the valuation of land was concerned? Nothing whatever; how was it possible they could know anything about it?

Mr. Vernon might know the merits of the men with whom he was personally acquainted; but he could not know anything about the others who were recommended, and what he (Mr. Synan) had said about the third Member of the Commission, both in and outside that House, he was quite prepared to repeat. Mr. Vernon's sympathies were decidedly with the landlords; and if he was to be the person who was to have the nomination of the Sub-Commissioners, what was the meaning of telling him (Mr. Synan) that the Sub-Commissioners were really men who sympathized with the tenants? He did not want to say there were not excellent men on the Sub-Commissions, numbering 24. The Commissions, however, had now been reduced to 10; and what was the character of the 10? He would not say anything about it himself; but his hon. Friend the Member for Monaghan (Mr. Healy) had expressed his opinion. The hon. Member had told them that the Sub-Commissioners, who were to be dismissed on the 18th of August, had sympathies and leanings with the tenants, and the hon. Gentleman had stated that to the Committee as a grievance. The hon. Gentleman (Mr. Healy) considered the statement he had made well founded; and surely he ought to be a good judge, inasmuch as he had taken great interest in the Land Act, and knew the opinions of the tenant farmers in Ireland as well as any man. He (Mr. Synan) had a great knowledge of the tenant farmers himself, he had mixed with them all his life; but his hon. Friend (Mr. Healy) had the unanimous sympathy of the tenant farmers of Ireland wherever he went, and he told the Committee that every man on the Sub-Commission who sympathized with the tenants had been dismissed, while only those were being retained who had landlord leanings and proclivities. Now, he (Mr. Synan) came to another point of a general character, and he mentioned it because it had been forced upon him; he mentioned it because the Chief Secretary (Mr. Trevelyan) had said that the Land Commission was a representative Body of the tenants of Ireland; but it was nothing of the kind. When did the Committee think that the 10 Commissions would have disposed of the cases of the 600,000 tenants of Ireland? If they deducted the 100,000 leaseholders there would still be left 500,000 tenants. The 24 Commissions which had been sitting up to this had decided only 100,000 cases, while 70,000 cases had been decided out of Court. If, therefore, 24 Commissions could only decide 100,000 cases in three years, how long would the 10 Commissions be occupied in deciding the remaining cases? The right hon. Gentleman could work the matter out for himself. What was the goal at which they were aiming, and at which the right hon. Gentleman endeavoured to aim by the Bill he introduced a short time ago, but which he dropped so very hastily? Was it peasant proprietory? If so, how could they have peasant proprietory until they had fixed the judicial rents of the tenants of Ireland? Would any man of the 400,000 or 500,000 who had not gone into Court come to any arrangement with his landlord as to number of years' purchase that he was to give for a rack rent? Why, the most remarkable instance had occurred in his own county. The Earl of Devon had his land for sale, and he was willing to take less even than the 20 years' purchase which the right hon. Gentleman the Chief Secretary, by his Bill, fixed as the value of Irish land. Why, some of the tenants refused to make an offer; some of them would give 10, some of them would give 12; but he did not know that any of them went as far as to offer 16 years' purchase. This was only a single instance of the impossibility of arriving at a settlement of the question upon the present system. He did not mean to say that some of the tenants were not as unreasonable as some landlords; but was it unreasonable for any man to ask how a tenant and landlord could come together to fix the number of years' purchase which should be paid for a holding when the judicial rent of that holding had not been fixed? And by the scheme the Government had just framed they were postponing the settlement of the question until the remote future. He had given the Committee a rule-of-three sum, and if they worked it out they would find that the 10 Commissions would be 15 years in deciding the remaining applications for the fixing of judicial rents. It was impossible to obtain a peasant proprietary in Ireland until the judicial rent of the different holdings had been fixed; and yet the Government would stop, by the very thing they were now doing, the progress of their Bill of 1881. The Government were, by their own action, defeating the object of their own Bill. His hon. Friend the Member for Monaghan (Mr. Healy) had said that the judicial rents which were now being fixed were rack rents, and that an amendment of the law was necessary. He did not go as far as his hon. Friend; but he did go the length of saying that some of the judicial rents were rack rents, and he would give a proof of his assertion. In his own county there were two estates lying side by side, on one of which the judicial rents had been settled. In the one case the tenants went into Court and came out with a reduction of about 5 per cent, the land there being very good. Upon the adjoining estate, however, the landlord had settled with his tenants. The land was of the very same character as that in the first case, and yet the landlord had granted reductions of rent of 10 per cent. Did they mean to tell him that under such circumstances the tenants would go into the Land Courts; but even if the tenants were disposed to go into the Courts, the Government had so limited the number that many cases could not be decided for years to come. He was sorry to say that tenants would not go into the Courts. He knew many leaseholders who had refused to go into Court, even where the landlord had given his consent; they would sooner deal with the landlord outside the Court than go to the Court and come out with what they considered rack rents. What had produced this feeling on the part of the tenants? A want of confidence in the Sub-Commissions. He did not say that the Sub-Commissions were not useful. Where there was a rack-renting landlord the Sub-Commissions were most valuable, because the tenants had some chance at all events of having a fair rent fixed. Unless, however, the tenants had confidence in the Sub-Commissions they would not resort to the Land Courts, but would prefer to arrange with their landlords. He believed in the indirect benefit of the Land Act rather than in its direct benefit. The Act had induced landlords to make arrangements with their tenants; but by what they were now doing, and by alleging that the Land Commission and Sub-Commissions represented the tenants as well as the landlords of Ireland, the Government were making the greatest mistake they ever made. They were destroying the benefit of their Act. They were postponing its operation to the remote future, and doing much to prevent the establishment of that peasant proprietary which they were all anxious to see. He was afraid that unless the administration of the Act was vastly improved there would be another land agitation as violent as that which had just closed.

Colonel COLTHURST said, he should confine the few remarks he had to make to one portion of the subject. It would be in the recollection of the Committee that by Clause 19 of the Land Act an attempt was made to encourage the building of labourers' cottages on the farms of Ireland. He noticed that in their Report this year the Land Commissioners stated that the 19th section of the Act had not been operative to any large extent. The number of orders made by the Sub-Commissioners under this section, during the year ending August, 1883, was 260, and in the preceding year 226—that was to say that in round numbers, up to August of last year, about 500 orders were made by the Sub-Commissioners for the erection or repair of labourers' cottages; and, supposing the progress to be about the same up to August in this year, about 700 orders had been made. Now they came to the subject of how these orders had been carried out. His hon. Friend the Member for Waterford (Mr. Leamy) succeeded in passing an Act making and putting a heavy penalty upon the occupier who, having obtained a reduction of rent himself, and having been ordered to provide for his labourer, failed to do so. But he added a condition which, unfortunately, was not accepted by the Treasury. He suggested that the Land Commissioners should have the power of appointing Inspectors to see that their orders were carried out. The Treasury objected, and obliged the hon. Member to withdraw that provision from his Bill, and a very unfortunate interference it was on the part of the Treasury.

When the Labourers' Act was passed last year a clause was introduced seeking to remedy that evil by making the Sanitary Authority—that was to say the Boards of Guardians—responsible for the carrying out of the orders of the Sub-Commissioners, and the Land Commissioners stated in their Report that they had in every instance communicated the order to the Union concerned. He hoped that by a Return that would shortly be furnished to the House the Committee would be able to form a correct opinion as to how many of the orders had been carried out. He was perfectly certain that it would turn out that not half of the 600 or 700 orders had been complied with; because, although the Act said that the Sanitary Authority should do so and so, there was no one to see that any given Board of Guardians put the Act in force in its Union, unless the labourer himself came forward. Now, they knew that the labourer was generally in a very dependent position, and that, therefore, he was not likely himself to come forward and complain of the inadequacy of his dwelling. It was very much to be regretted that the action of the Treasury had marred the effect of that clause, and the question now was what legislative enactment could be passed to remedy the defect. He thought his right hon. Friend (Mr. Trevelyan), in his capacity as President of the Local Government Board, might do something; he might have the attention of Boards of Guardians called to the necessity of putting the clause into operation, and of employing the relieving officers, who were also sanitary officers, for the purpose of seeing that the orders made under the section were carried out. He thought, also, something might be done by hon. Members opposite, because there was no doubt that if there had existed any public opinion on this subject many cottages would have been built before now. Boards of Guardians in Ireland represented to a very great extent public opinion. The hon. Member for Sligo (Mr. Sexton) on a recent occasion attacked very warmly the Board of Works, because they did no carry out in a proper spirit Acts whicht had been passed for the benefit of the Irish people. Now, here was an Act involving no expense upon the Treasury, no responsibility upon the Boards of Guardians, except that of seeing that an occupier who had obtained a reduction of rent should share that reduction, in a sense, with his labourers. Hon. Members opposite had possession of the platform and of the Press to a great extent in Ireland; and, therefore, they could do a great deal—and he hoped they would—to secure the operation of the clauses affecting labourers' dwellings. He was sorry to see the other day in Coutny Limerick an advocate of the labourers complaining that the Labourers' Act was not put in force in a certain Union, the farmers in which Union were opposing the operation of the Act. He hoped the Chief Secretary would see that the 19th clause of the Land Act was made operative.

MR. T. D. SULLIVAN said, he thought that from the action of the Sub-Commissions in Ireland lately, and from the manner in which the most popular of those Commissions were about to be dealt with by the Government, there was a plain moral to be drawn which the Irish people would not be slow to draw; and that was that it was an evil day for popular interests in Ireland when political agitation in that country declined. The Government professed to be very anxious for a return of peace and quietude, and of what they called law and order in that country; and from time to time they quoted, with great pleasure, statistics tending to show that that was the course which events were now taking. But what did the Irish people see concurrently with all this? They could see that as crime declined, and as peace and order were restored in Ireland, in the same proportion the reduction of rents which the Sub-Commissions had been making declined. When Ireland was alive, when the people were determined, and when there was a serious agitation for popular rights and common justice and relief from oppression, the rack rents came down pretty fast; but now that a period of comparative quietude had come it was remarked that the reductions of rent had dwindled down from 25 per cent to 18 and 15 per cent. He had no doubt whatever that as the condition of Ireland improved, the reduction of rack rents or unfair rents would become smaller and smaller until they did not amount to more than 10 or 5 per cent. Now, they were told by the Chief Secretary (Mr. Trevelyan) that the difference in the amount of reductions made by the Sub-Commissions was owing to the fact that there was a rush into the Land Courts in the earlier stages of the business, and that the worst cases were the first to be dealt with. How did the right hon. Gentleman make that out? Undoubtedly there was a great accumulation of cases when the Land Courts commenced their sittings, but how did the Chief Secretary make out the allegation that the worst cases were the first to be dealt with? He (Mr. Sullivan) maintained that the cases taken first were average cases and that the cases were taken in the order in which they came. There was no selection made of the worst cases, none whatever, and he challenged the right hon. Gentleman the Chief Secretary to make good his allegation. But if it were true that the reductions of 25 per cent made by the Land Commissions in the early stages of their inquiries were the consequence of the rush that was made into Court the Government stood convicted. The Government were convicted of preventing the Irish National Land League submitting test cases. It was declared by the Leader of the Irish people, and by the Leaders of the Irish National Land League, that they intended to submit to the Irish Land Commission a set of test cases on the very opening of the Commission's business, and for so saying and doing the Leader of the Irish people was thrown into prison. That was one of the counts of the indictment against him—namely, that instead of allowing the rush into Court he intended to have submitted to those Courts a series of test cases. It was for recommending the Irish people to await the result of the test cases that the hon. Gentleman the Member for the City of Cork (Mr. Parnell), and others who acted with him, were thrown into the cells of Richmond and Kilmainham Gaols. Therefore, he (Mr. Sullivan) thought that the explanation on the part of the Government lay very badly indeed in their mouths. Now, with reference to some of the Sub-Commissions which were about to be discontinued, the right hon. Gentleman the Chief Secretary did not like the word "dismissed." It was a very remarkable fact—and nothing the right hon. Gentleman could say would explain it away to the satisfaction of the Irish people—it was a very remarkable fact that the Sub-Commissions in which the tenantry of Ireland had the most confidence were those which were to be discontinued. They did their business in the most impartial and most proper manner; but it happened, nevertheless, that the services of the gentlemen in whose decisions the people of Ireland had the greatest confidence were to be dispensed with, while the pets and favourites of the landlords, and of the Irish Tories and Orangemen, were to be continued in office. The Chief Secretary was very fond of the dismissed gentlemen, no doubt; but they might apply to him, with singular appropriateness, the old saying:—

> "Perhaps it was right to dissemble your love;
> But why did you kick me downstairs?"

Taking the case of M'Devitt, the right hon. Gentleman said he was highly recommended—highly spoken of and written of by, amongst others, eminent and respected Catholic Bishops in Ireland. He (Mr. Sullivan) did not see anything very astonishing in that. It was not with what had been said about these gentlemen before their appointment that they had to deal, but with what was to be said of them now that the Irish people had had some experience of their way of thinking and way of acting. It was within the recollection of all that gentlemen of very excellent reputations indeed had been appointed to various public offices in Ireland, and had very soon changed. That was their experience in his country. It was a well-known fact that men soon changed their colours and their minds, or, at least, their mode of action, after commencing to put Government pay into their pockets. Therefore, the question was not "What sort of a character had Mr. M'Devitt before he became a Government placeman?" but "What character has he earned for himself since he has been in the Government service?" His (Mr. Sullivan's) contention was that this gentleman's conduct had not been such as to cause the Irish people to prefer him to any of the Sub-Commissioners who had been dismissed by the Irish Government. The Committee heard a great deal about the Chief Commissioners. They, too, were all excellent and able men; but he recollected very well that the very moment the names of these three gentlemen were first mentioned to the House, it was said by Irishmen who knew them all that one man was, in reality, the whole Commission, and that man was the representative of the landlords—Mr. Vernon. It was said and believed at the very first, and experience from that day to this had confirmed the judgment, that that one man would rule the Commission. Mr. Litton—whom he (Mr. Sullivan) had had the pleasure of knowing in the House—was a very excellent gentleman, a fair-minded, just man; but he was no match, in a contest of this kind, for Mr. Vernon—a representative of the landlord party—a very extensive land agent. So with regard to Mr. O'Hagan. He was a very estimable man, no doubt; at one time a man of patriotic and national proclivities—a man who wrote some beautiful poetry, full of national sentiment, which would live long after the character of its author, as a patriot, had departed, which would live in Irish literature long after the man himself had been gathered to his fathers. But the man who, in his youth, or in his manhood, as the case might be, had written national poems, or national letters, or national articles, was about the last man he (Mr. Sullivan) would trust after he had become a placeman in the pay of the British Government; because the memory of his former reputation would be always before him, and he would be always trying to convince his colleagues, wherever he might be, that he was no longer a Nationalist, no longer a patriot, and that he could be relied on as much as any other man to do the work that the British Government had appointed him to do. So it was with the Sub-Commissioners, and so it was with the Chief Commissioners. And now they came to this—that Ireland, being again forced down in one way or another—the stress of public agitation in that country having somewhat abated—had to submit to constantly-decreasing reductions of rent in the Land Court. The reward of the Irish people for this so-called return to peace, law, and order was this coming down of the Land Commissioners—this falling-off in their mode of dealing with unfair rents. What was the lesson the Irish people had to derive therefrom? The people read these things broadly and roughly; but they read them, he thought, rightly on the whole. The moral they would draw from the whole set of circumstances was this—that if they wished justice to be done to them, as justice did yet remain to be done, they must keep up agitating, and make their enemies, as they had made them before, afraid of them. He was old enough to remember in Irish history periods in which there was no political life. He remembered the time of depression which followed the Famines of 1848 and 1849, and the traitorism of the Keogh and Sadleir party, who betrayed the interests of the Irish people on the floor of that House. He remembered the hush of misery and despair that came over the country; and this also he remembered—that during the whole of that time nothing was done for Ireland. Nothing was done until the people took heart again, and rose to a certain sense of their position in their own country. They had won something, and he was glad of it—proud of it. He had never denied it—he had stated on Irish platforms, as he stated here, that the Land Act had been a great Act of Emancipation for the Irish tenantry, and for the whole Irish nation, not merely because of the reduction of rents that it had brought about, but because of the lifting up of the hearts of the Irish people, who found that, after all, notwithstanding the mighty forces arrayed against them, they could yet conquer as they had conquered in the past. The Irish people, up to this, however, had only conquered half justice, and he counselled them not to subside and suspend their efforts, but to go on with open and fearless agitation for their rights. If they did, in time they would win the other half measure of justice which was their due. That was the moral he drew from existing circumstances, and that was the moral he trusted the Irish people would draw from them. It was not well, he maintained, for the Government to teach that moral to the Irish people—to teach that, in proportion as they subsided and held their peace, and were not organized, so did the desire of the British Parliament to do them justice decline, and that it was only as they rose in agitation, and almost set the country aflame, that that House, and those who ruled it, would listen to their demands, however just and reasonable they might be. He had heard that night that about £500,000 per annum had been saved to the tenantry by the action of the Irish Land Act. He did not doubt it—he was glad of it—but every penny of this money was their own. They had got nothing from anybody—nothing which did not belong to them. He had heard the taking of this money from those who lately had been receiving it stigmatized as "robbery." Aye, there was robbery in the case, but the robbers were those who had been taking the £500,000 out of the pockets of the Irish peasantry, with no justice for it except the permission of the law of the land. That there was that permission he granted. But what was this law of the land? It was law made by landlords to enable them to plunder the peasantry. He had heard hon. and right hon. Gentlemen in that House speak of the Irish servant girls in America, England, and elsewhere, sending over money to Ireland to sustain their poor relatives. The fault found with these servant girls was that they no longer sent this money over to go into the pockets of these hon. and right hon. Gentleman. Where had these earnings gone hitherto? Why, into the pockets of the Irish landlords. Such was the old system—of so cruel and infamous a character was it that it extracted not only from the poor people at home, working and living on the soil, the fruits of their toil, but it put under contribution their sons and daughters who had fled to other lands to sustain themselves, and to escape the misery and poverty that they had experience of at home. It was a fact that in years gone by the rack rents in Ireland were paid, to a large extent, out of the earnings of the young men and young women in England, America, and Australia. Thank God that that system, if not quite ended, at all events had been broken down; and, he asked, with what face could these rack-renters—whose names appeared in the Blue Books as such, whose names were on record and would stand in these official volumes, in everything but the strict legal sense, as those of convicted thieves—with what face could these people stand upon the Benches of that House, or anywhere else, and censure the Irish people at home and abroad for their efforts to mitigate this oppression and end this cruel law? If he had unduly detained the Committee, it was because he had wished to put before it this plain fact—that he felt himself, and believed that others felt also, that the cause of this proportionate diminution in the reduction of rents was the peace and quietness and absence of excitement in Ireland, and he hoped there would be an end to that. Not that he counselled disorder, not that he counselled criminal acts; but he did counsel organization and legitimate public action, and did tell the Irish people that failing in that they would fail in everything, and that maintaining that as they ought to maintain it they would obtain from this House of Commons or from any House of Commons, and from this Government or from any Government which might follow it—they would ultimately obtain, in spite of all the powers arrayed against them, the full measure of the rights they were so justly entitled to, and for which they had so long and so patiently struggled.

Colonel KING-HARMAN: It is not my intention to trespass for long on the time of the Committee; but when an hon. Member below the Gangway, without your interfering at all, Sir, speaks of a party in this country as a party of "convicted thieves," and with his finger deliberately points to hon. Gentlemen sitting on these Benches, emphasizing the expression, I think it is only right that I should rise, not to say much as to what has fallen from the hon. Member, but to say that I do not much care about his opinion; that I do not think we are "convicted thieves;" but that I, and those who believe with me, are strongly of opinion that there are convicted thieves in Ireland, and murderers and associates of murderers, and that they are sitting, not where I am sitting, but not very far off——

Mr. JOHN REDMOND: I rise to Order. I wish to ask you, Sir, whether the hon. and gallant Member is in Order in saying that he believes there are not only convicted thieves, but murderers and associates of murderers, sitting, not where he sits, but not far from him?

The CHAIRMAN: I think the expressions used by the hon. and gallant Member highly improper, and I must call upon him to withdraw them.

Mr. T. D. SULLIVAN: Who minds? [*Cries of* "Withdraw!"]

The CHAIRMAN: The hon. and gallant Member will withdraw the observation, if he applied it to any hon. Member in this House.

COLONEL KING-HARMAN: Sir, I wish—[*Loud cries of* "Withdraw!"]—I trust I may be allowed to say what I have to say. I wish to remark that, as the words "convicted thieves" were applied to the Bench on which I sit, I did think I might be allowed to use some strong expression in reply. I acknowledge that I used a strong expression—a stronger one than that used below the Gangway. The words "murderers" and "associates of murderers" were stronger than "convicted thieves," and, therefore, I beg to withdraw and to apologize for having used the expression.

THE CHAIRMAN: I must say I listened very carefully to the remarks of the hon. Member for Westmeath (Mr. Sullivan), and did not understand him to apply the observation to which the hon. and gallant Member takes exception to anyone in this House. If I had, I certainly should have called him to Order.

COLONEL KING-HARMAN said, he was sure the Chairman would allow him to use 15 seconds in the remarks he was about to make. He could assure him that not only were the words to which he had called attention used, but the words were accompanied with a gesture —the hon. Member had pointed to the place where he (Colonel King-Harman) sat. It was because of that that he had taken it that the expression was applied to that part of the House where he sat. If it were not so, he apologized most distinctly and decidedly for what he had said. If, however, he was right in his suspicion that the observation was applied to where he sat, he was sure the Chairman would support him in saying that, while he withdrew the expressions he had used, and apologized for using them, there had been, at the same time, some excuse for his indignation and for using the words he did. It was not his intention to go into the question as to whether or not the Land Commissioners in Ireland had done their duty; it was far too late in the Session to venture upon such a subject. He had very strong opinions on the subject, and he believed those opinions were tolerably well known, at any rate, to the right hon. Gentlemen who represented the Irish Government. He believed the working of the Land Act had been contrary to the declaration which the right hon. Gentleman the Prime Minister made when he brought in the Bill and when he put it to the House. The Prime Minister had said that no damage would be done to the landlord interest, and he was supported in that statement by a noble Lord in the House of Lords, who said that the landlord interest would be rather improved by the measure than otherwise. But they knew perfectly well what had happened. They knew perfectly well that the landlord interest had been reduced by from 25 to 30 per cent all over Ireland. They knew perfectly well that it had not been a question of whether rents were high or rents were low, but that the Sub-Commissioners, wherever they had gone, had obeyed an unwritten, although a perfectly understood, law, which was that the landlords' rents were to be reduced whether they were high or whether they were low. It was perfectly well known that in Ireland where there had been two landlords side by side, one a rack renter and the other a fair and considerate man—one having raised his rents during the bad times 20 per cent, and the other never having raised his rents at all—the man who had raised his rents had had them reduced 20 per cent, while the same, if not a greater, reduction had been made in the case of the man who had never raised his rents. It was a well known fact—hon. Members below the Gangway knew it as well as he did, and hon. Members sitting by the side of the right hon. Gentleman the Chief Secretary to the Lord Lieutenant knew it as well as he did—that the good landlords, so called, had suffered far more than the bad landlords. It was perfectly well known that the operation of the Land Act had been this—that the man who had bought his estates under the Landed Estates Court, or when it was established, or had acceded to them at that time, and had raised his rents to an exorbitant extent, rendering the introduction of some Land Act or other imperative, was the man sitting in his saddle rejoicing; whilst the man who had always worked with his tenantry and had done the best he could for them, not asking rents which were too heavy, not raising them when he could do so, was the man who was now suffering poverty because of the action, he would not say of the Government, but of the Sub-Commissioners appointed by the Government. He would not say more about that. The Government brought in the Land Act, and appointed three Commissioners, whose names commanded, to a great extent, the respect of Irishmen of all classes. The Land Act had been accepted by them in the belief that the three Commissioners to whom he referred were a true and legitimate sample of the Officers who were to be appointed under it. After that, a number of Sub-Commissioners were appointed such as the Irish people never could, and such as he did not believe the House of Commons ever could, have expected. It had been shown that the appointment of these men was wrong, and that the men were not fit to go through the evidence they had had to go through, and to deal with the extraordinary perjury and malversation they had had to deal with during the past two or three years; yet these men, being men of honour, though, perhaps, prejudiced in one way or another, had come round, and had not gone on reducing rents in the way in which they had done when they were inclined to accept the sworn testimony of those from whom, at first, they had to take evidence. He did not mean to go on on this particular subject, but merely made these observations in commencement of what he had to say. In the Vote for the Land Commission they had to take an item for the chief agent for the land sales, and he said that, while they could not go back, and while he did not seek to go back—he wished they could, of course; but he knew that what was done could not be undone—in the matter of the appointment of the Commissioners and Sub-Commissioners, he did want to go back on the question of the Commission for the Sale of Land. He was glad to see the First Lord of the Treasury in his place, for he was sure the right hon. Gentleman would agree that he (Colonel King-Harman) had a right to speak on that question, as he had had the honour of speaking to the right hon. Gentleman not long ago upon it in Committee. It was said, when the Land Act was passing through, that the Irish landlords would not be prejudiced by it—that their rights would not be disturbed, and that the land would, if anything, be made of greater value than it was before. Now, what was the fact? They knew perfectly well—they saw it from the Returns he held in his hand bearing on the value of land—that if a landlord wished to sell his estate he could not get more than 10, 12, or 14 years' purchase for it, whereas, before the Land Act was passed, he could get 22, 24, or 25 years' purchase. How was that? He was not going to inflict a long speech on the Committee, and he did not believe in long speeches. He believed in making a few short statements, and one short statement he would make was this—that a very few years before the Land Act was passed, there was a certain gentleman of the name of Murrough O'Brien appointed a Commissioner by the Church Commission to regulate the sale of lands to tenants who held under the Church Body. Mr. Murrough O'Brien used to go down and value these lands, and he valued them, generally speaking, at from 24 to 25 years' purchase. He (Colonel King-Harman) was putting this at the very lowest average he could possibly adopt. After the Land Act was passed, Mr. Murrough O'Brien went down on behalf of the Land Purchase Commission, and wherever he went the tenants, after listening to him, considered that from 10 to 12 years' purchase was as much as they were entitled to offer for the land. They were told to believe that the establishment of a peasant proprietary was the only means of pacifying Ireland; but could it be believed that Irish landlords would be disposed to part with their lands at 10 or 12 years' purchase, when their tenants, four or five years ago, were forced by the same man who now valued the estates at 10 or 12 years' purchase to give 24 or 26? He (Colonel King-Harman) was at a loss to know how these things could be reconciled. The facts were certainly as he stated, and he did not think the right hon. Gentleman the Prime Minister could put them in any other way. If this question were deferred to a time when there was a possibility of more thoroughly considering it, he would be able to mention several cases in support of his statement. He would be able to show the extraordinary way in which the Purchase Clauses of the Land Act had been administered. He had been from the first, even before the Land Act was passed, an advocate of the extension of peasant proprietary in Ireland. When sitting some years ago, immediately behind where the Prime Minister was now sitting, speaking in support of a Motion for a Select Committee by the right hon. Gentleman the present First Commissioner of Works (Mr. Shaw Lefevre)—then an unknown Member of the House—he had made the suggestion that a certain sum of money should be applied each year towards the solution of the problem of peasant proprietary. He believed he had proposed that for 10 years £1,000,000 a-year should be applied to the purpose. At the end of that time they would see whether the plan succeeded. £10,000,000 would not have been much to have spent, even if the plan was a failure, whereas, if the experiment had turned out a good one, the gain would have been very great. But the House of Commons in its wisdom would not listen to that system. What was now going on in Ireland made a peasant proprietary impossible. They might wish for it; but the right hon. Gentleman the Prime Minister could not expect, not only in the interest of the landlords in Ireland—who had been forgotten and forsaken, and, he might say, trampled upon by the Government—but in the interest of the mortgagees, and those who had embarked their money in land securities, that 9 or 10 years' purchase would be accepted. All the landowners wanted was to have a fair and proper mode of sale. He did not say they wanted to force sales, for he did not think it would be right to do that; but he did think the majority of them would be glad to sell and get out of the country as fast as they could. Whether that would be good for the country he did not know—and he would not tell hon. Members below the Gangway whether he was leaving or not—but he would tell the Prime Minister this, that if he really wished to carry out the Purchase Clauses of the Act—if he really wished to benefit the people of Ireland by these clauses, if he really wished to act in a fair and legitimate manner to those who were interested in this subject, he should look into the matter. If he would look into it, he would see that the Purchase Department of the Land Commission was not carried on properly by those gentlemen who were associated with it. He assured the right hon. Gentleman that, personally, he had not a single word to say against the gentlemen who had to do with the Purchase Department of the Land Commission. He did not know them—he had only seen one of them, Mr. O'Brien, once. He had, however, watched the matter very carefully, and had thought over it, and he was perfectly certain that the idea of these gentlemen was that it was their business to induce the tenants to give as little as possible for the land, to grind down the landlords in such a way that they would accept, under duress, the smallest sum of money to turn out. In support of his statement, he would mention one case—that of a gentleman who he knew could be trusted, and who was an honourable man. He had known him for many years; but he had not been in communication with him upon this matter, and he had the facts from that gentleman's solicitors. Mr. Arthur Costello, a member of one of the oldest families in Mayo, held some property in a wild district where the Land League had considerable authority, and during two or three years he had received no rent. Driven into a corner, his mortgagees pressing him hard, he asked the tenants if they would purchase their holdings, and after some negotiation they said they would give him 16 years' purchase. Would any hon. Member say that 16 years' purchase was a fair sum to give for land which was not over-rented?—and no one accused Mr. Costello of having over-rented. The tenants were prepared to give that, and they applied to the Land Commission for the two-thirds of the money required which they were entitled to have under the Land Act, they being prepared to provide the other one-third. In the cases where they were not prepared to put down the money themselves, the local bank was ready to provide it. Could there be a better proof that the security was good enough for the Government to advance two-thirds, when the local bank—which was only a branch of a larger bank—was prepared to advance the remaining one-third? The Land Commission sent down Mr. Murrough O'Brien, and the result was that the Land Commission told the landlord that they did not consider the land worth 16 years' purchase, but only 12 years' purchase. Were Irish landlords to be beaten down in that way to 12 years' purchase? Did the noble

Marquess (the Marquess of Hartington) suppose that his property, or the property of his father, would be sold at 12 years' purchase? If he carried this matter to a Division, no doubt the noble Marquess would vote against him; but he should like to know whether the Duke of Devonshire's property would be sold on those terms? In Heaven's name, were Irish landlords to be crushed down in that way? If the Government were going to carry out their Land Purchase scheme, they must put fair and honest men on the Land Commission. Having mentioned Mr. Murrough O'Brien's name, he should move to move to reduce this Vote by the sum of £750, the amount of that gentleman's salary. He was not going to impute anything dishonest to Mr. O'Brien, for he believed him to be as honest a man as could possibly be; but he was a man of the strongest possible political opinions, and believed that landlords ought to be brought to their knees and driven out of Ireland. He was, therefore, not the proper person to hold the position he was now in.

Mr. T. A. DICKSON said, Mr. Murrough O'Brien was a gentleman whom he did not know by sight. With regard to the valuations of land in 1874-5-6, he must say that during those years the price of land reached a very high point in Ireland. Mr. O'Brien valued the Church land; but he did not calculate the tenants' rights, although he did estimate the tenants' improvements. Since he did that, the Church Lands Act had been passed, and that provided that tenants' improvements should be excluded, so that his valuations in 1874-5-6, of 24 and 26 years' purchase, included not only the fee simple of the land, but the entire improvements. He regretted deeply that tenants should have had to pay such enormous prices for land. In his own county they had had to pay 28 and even 30 years' purchase, and they were still suffering extreme poverty. But in connection with the remarks upon Mr. O'Brien, they must take into consideration the entirely altered circumstances between 1874 and 1883, when he valued under the Land Act. With reference to Mr. M'Devitt, the hon. Member for Monaghan (Mr. Healy) had stated that one reason why that gentleman was maintained on the Land Commission was owing to speeches he had made in connection with the contest in Tyrone; but he was not aware that that gentleman had made any speech in connection with that contest. With regard to Mr. Wyllie, he believed the Land Commission could not have an abler lawyer or a more upright man than Mr. Wyllie in connection with the work of the Commission; and he regretted that some other men were to be removed from the Commission. He had inquired as to their removal, and the explanation was that they were of recent appointment, but were to be displaced. There were 85 in all; but 55 must go, and he deeply regretted that men like these, and Mr. Maguire and others, had been removed. With respect to the Appeal Court, he had looked carefully into their decisions, and he would undertake to say that the variations in the rents fixed by the Commissioners, and confirmed by the Appeal Court, would not amount to £1,000 all round. The hon. and gallant Member for Dublin County (Colonel King-Harman) had referred to the Purchase Clauses for small improvements. No one regretted more than he did that the Government had allowed the Purchase Clauses Bill to fall through. That was a great loss to Ireland; and he thought that, no matter what might have been the difficulties of the Session, the Government ought to have passed, at least, some of the clauses of that Bill. That would have given great relief to the state of affairs in Ireland, and he only hoped that one of the first things the Government would do next Session would be to reintroduce that Bill.

Colonel KING-HARMAN said, he believed that hon. Members on both sides were in favour of promoting the efficacy of the scheme for purchasing land in Ireland; but he considered the Bill as it stood inefficacious. He did not wish to cast any reflection on Mr. Murrough O'Brien; and what he wanted to imply by his Motion was that the Purchase Clauses ought to be most carefully considered during the Recess, so that a really useful measure might be brought in, and not a Party measure.

Motion made, and Question proposed,

"That a sum, not exceeding £82,680 (including a Supplementary sum of £26,340), be granted to Her Majesty, to complete the sum necessary to defray the Charge which will come in course of payment during the year ending on the 31st day of March 1885, for the Salaries and

Expenses of the Office of the Irish Land Commission."—(*Colonel King-Harman.*)

MR. KENNY said, he thought the hon. and gallant Member for Cork County (Colonel Colthurst) had done well in pointing out that the average of Mr. O'Brien's valuations for the Church Commission was 22½ years' purchase. Those might be taken as representing the landlords' interest; but since then there had been agricultural depression, and that had brought down the value of land considerably, and also the landlords' interest in the land. He, for one, entirely disagreed with the Motion to reduce the Vote by Mr. O'Brien's salary, believing that when that gentleman fixed the landlords' interest in the land in Ireland at only 10 or 12 years, or, at the outside, 14 years' purchase, he fixed a fair level. He wished now to call attention to the present position of the Commissioners. The hon. and gallant Member for the County of Dublin (Colonel King-Harman) had said the original appointments of the Sub-Commissioners were not to be found fault with; but that subsequent appointments were extremely bad. It was a remarkable thing that a Gentleman sitting on the landlords' Benches should not have made himself acquainted with the practice in regard to these appointments; and it so happened that the reductions made by the original Sub-Commissioners were considerably greater than those made by the subsequent Sub-Commissioners. He was, therefore, surprised to hear that the subsequent Sub-Commissioners were not so satisfactory as the original Sub-Commissioners. It had been stated that the Sub-Commissioners who were not to remain, had been discontinued because their appointment was of more recent date; but whoever had informed the hon. and gallant Gentleman, he could not agree that these Sub-Commissioners were discontinued simply because their appointments were of more recent date than the appointments of those who were to be continued. He had a list of the dates of the appointments of those who were to be continued, and also of those who were to be discontinued; and he found that one of the gentlemen, Mr. Davidson, who was discontinued, was appointed in November, 1881, and the fact that he was one of the first who received an appointment, showed that the date of his appointment had nothing whatever to do with his discontinuance. He was well known to be a fair man and a friend of the tenants, and that, perhaps, had more to do with his dismissal than the mere date of his appointment. Then he found that of six Sub-Commissioners who were appointed in December, 1881, four had been retained, Mr. Wyllie being one of the number appointed at that time. He would like to know why that gentleman had been discontinued? Again, while the Legal Commissioners appointed since then had been continued, none of the Legal Commissioners appointed in April, 1882, were now on the Commission. Of the non-Legal Commissioners appointed in 1881, three had been dismissed, and six continued; and it was a singular thing that all those gentlemen who were appointed in 1881, and had been now continued, were all gentlemen who notoriously sympathized with the landlords.

COLONEL KING-HARMAN rose to Order, and asked whether it was right for an hon. Gentleman to say that Judges appointed by the Government—although they were not sworn Judges—were notoriously in favour of the landlords, and sympathized with any one class?

THE CHAIRMAN: The observation of the hon. Gentleman did not reach my ear. If the hon. Gentleman spoke in any way disrespectfully of the Judges, that would be very improper.

COLONEL KING-HARMAN said, he would quote the words of the hon. Member. He said "the Judges who were reappointed to the Land Commission were notoriously sympathizers with the landlords," implying that they were corrupt.

MR. KENNY challenged the accuracy of the hon. and gallant Gentleman's statement. He had not implied that these gentlemen who had been reappointed were corrupt.

COLONEL KING-HARMAN said, he was speaking of the gentlemen who had not been reappointed.

MR. KENNY said, the hon. and gallant Gentleman had entirely mistaken him, because his contention was not that the gentlemen who had been reappointed were gentlemen who acted unfairly, but simply that they were sympathizers with the landlords. He was endeavouring to show the Committee that a number of gentlemen had been continued on the Commission as Sub-

Commissioners not because, as had been stated by the hon. Member for Tyrone (Mr. T. A. Dickson), of the date of their original appointment, but simply because their reappointment or non-reappointment had fallen into the hands of the Chief Commissioners, they being gentlemen who sympathized with the landlords, and who recommended gentlemen for appointment who were of their own way of thinking.

COLONEL KING-HARMAN again rose to Order, and said the hon. Gentleman was repeating what he had previously stated, and asked whether the hon. Member was in Order?

THE CHAIRMAN: I think it will be better for the hon. and gallant Gentleman to reply to these observations, and explain his views, when the hon. Member for Ennis has concluded

MR. KENNY, resuming, asked for the protection of the Chairman against the interruptions of the hon. and gallant Gentleman. The hon. and gallant Member had grown suddenly very fastidious as to the use of Parliamentary language, and a few minutes after accusing Gentlemen of being "murderers," it was strange that he should carp at his language. With regard to the Land Commissioners, the Lay Commissioners were not entitled to associate with the Legal Commissioners in the decision of legal points; but he thought that if the law was fairly interpreted, they were entitled to associate with the Legal Commissioners in the decisions of such points. Under the Land Act, he believed, it might fairly be assumed that the Lay Commissioners, instead of being virtually merely valuers, as they now were, and entitled only to consult with the Legal Commissioners on questions purely as to the value of land, were as much entitled to consult with them on other points which arose as the Legal Commissioners to consult with the Chief Commissioner, Mr. Justice O'Hagan. The present composition of the Land Court and the Sub-Commissioners' Courts was very different now from what it was at first, the plan of attaching mere valuers to each Court having been found to work badly, and having, therefore, to be discontinued. But he feared that, under the present arrangements, the non-Legal Commissioners were little better than the official Valuers originally appointed in 1882, and he thought that if they were deprived of the right to consult with the Legal Commissioners, the same state of things would come about, and the same state of dissatisfaction which arose before would recur, and, in like manner, the non-Legal Commissioners would have to be discontinued. The hon. and gallant Member for Cork County (Colonel Colthurst) had called attention to the manner in which orders for the erection of labourers' cottages, made out by the Sub-Commissioners, had been disregarded. An Order had been made for a Return showing the number of such orders, and he wished to ask whether the Solicitor General for Ireland would be able to include anything like an accurate estimate of the orders that had been complied with? If all the orders of the Sub-Commissioners for the erection of labourers' cottages had been complied with, the necessity for a sham Labourers' Act would have been obviated. The number of orders that had been made by the Sub-Commissioners was also, he thought, below the number that ought to have been made; and that was so apparent to the Chief Commissioners that, he believed, twice, if not three times, new orders had been issued for the direction of the Sub-Commissioners who had drawn attention to the matter. He hoped the recommendations made by the Chief Commissioners upon this matter would not be lost sight of. But there was another point in relation to this Vote to which he would, in a few words, call the attention of the Committee, and that was with regard to the effects of the operation of the Act in respect to the leaseholders. This was a question of particular importance; and although he did not propose to discuss it at length, he could not but express his great regret that when the Land Bill of 1881 was introduced in two successive Sessions in that House it had been rejected by enormous majorities, and that Her Majesty's Government, although some of their Irish Legal Advisers had a contrary opinion, should have gone in the face of the almost unanimous desire of the Irish Members, and concurred in the rejection of that salutary proposal to amend the law. He sincerely trusted that when the question of the admission of the labourers to the benefits of the Land Act was again brought forward in that House, another and a better state of feeling would have arisen, and that those who might be in power at the time would see their way to the acceptance of the recommendations of the Commissioners of the Irish Land Act. There was another point to which he would also call attention, and that was to the enormous increase that had taken place in the number of appeals from the Sub-Commissioners' decisions. The appeals in the Chief Commissioners' Court numbered altogether something like 17,000, and the number remaining was about 11,000. At this rate of progress, it was quite evident that the number of appeals to the Chief Commissioners, unless some additional machinery were brought into play, would not be disposed of for a great many years to come, and that, in point of fact, the statutory term under the Land Act would almost have expired before that result could be achieved. The hon. Member for Monaghan (Mr. Healy) had called attention to the manner in which these decisions were given. He had stated that in about 19 out of every 20 appeals the rent had been raised. He might say, with all deference to his hon. Friend, that this estimate was accurate to this extent—that in 19 out of 20 appeals which had originated with the landlords the rents had been raised. If, in connection with this point, the number of appeals by the tenants were taken into consideration, he was disposed to think that the estimate of his hon. Friend was by no means inaccurate. He had noticed that, in a great many instances, the amount to which the rents fixed by the Sub-Commissioners had been raised had been extremely ridiculous. He knew instances in which something like an increase of 5*s*. on a rental of £20 had been made. In looking over the opinions that had been from time to time expressed before the decision of the House of Lords by some of the Chief Commissioners, he found that it had been laid down by them that changes should not be made on the granting of leases by Sub-Commissioners, unless the Court should be of opinion that the rent fixed by the Sub-Commissioners was substantially wrong. But, instead of this principle having been adhered to, they found that the Chief Commissioners had gone down into the country and made changes in the rent that were of so trifling a character as to be merely vexatious. What object, he asked, could the Chief Commissioners have in making these trivial alterations? It was always an invidious thing to attribute motives; but one thing was quite certain, and that was that, whatever the motive of the Chief Commissioners might have been, the effect of these alterations on their part had been to stimulate the number of appeals, and to encourage the landlords throughout the country to rush into the Appeal Court, in the hope that their rents would be, at least, slightly raised, they being well aware that the tenants, in a great number of instances, were too poor to be able to appear with advantage in the Court of Appeal. There was another point, and it was one of the few that had been advanced by the hon. and gallant Gentleman the Member for the County of Dublin (Colonel King-Harman) in which he agreed, and that was that, in a large number of instances, the greater the rack-renter, the better off was the landlord likely to be when he came into Court. He had known instances in which the rent charged had been six times the valuation put upon the holding, and in which it had been reduced to three times the valuation, and he ventured to think that if, in the first instance, it had only been three times the valuation, it would have been reduced to the actual valuation, or to something very near it. This was the state of things which practically prevailed all over the country, and it was notoriously true in the case of those who had only in very recent times become the owners of land which had been chiefly purchased through the medium of the Landed Estates Courts, and who had raised the rents so as to give themselves a dividend of 5 or 10 per cent on the outlay they had made, purely from selfish motives, and who ought to have those rents reduced proportionably to the merits of the case. There were a few points in the Vote which were more in the shape of mere matters of figures, to which he desired briefly to direct the attention of the Secretary to the Treasury. He found on Page 289, which gave the details of the summary of the Vote, that there was one accountant who had a salary of £610 per annum. He wished to point out that the minimum figure was £600, and that the annual increment of the income was £25; consequently, he was unable to see how it was possible that the salary could be £610, unless the person in receipt of it had commenced at that figure? There was also a number of other inaccuracies noticeable throughout the details of the Estimate. For instance, there was a sum of £333 put down as the salary of an agency clerk. Now, in that case, the minimum salary was £300, and the annual increment £15. That being so, he failed to see how it was possible for the figure of £333 to be reached. Then there was an item under the head of Deputy Superintendent of Church Property, and his salary was stated at £255. The minimum, according to the Table given, was £350. There were other and similar instances running through the page, and he hoped the hon. Gentleman the Secretary to the Treasury would be able to state how it was that these inaccuracies occurred?

MR. COURTNEY said, he could at once explain the apparent discrepancies pointed out by the hon. Gentleman. The accountant referred to was appointed on some date such as the 1st of January, and his salary would be £600 for the year ending on the 1st of January following. The Estimate, however, gave the salary for the official year from the 1st of April to the 1st of April following, and the salary of the officer from the 1st of April to the 1st of January—or whatever the date might be—would be at the rate of £600 per annum, and would then begin to run at the rate of £625 per annum, so that the sum payable from April to April would be £610, as stated in the Estimates. The other differences referred to were to be accounted for in the same way.

MR. ARTHUR O'CONNOR said, he did not wish to detain the Committee more than a few minutes longer. There was, however, one point with regard to the action of the Land Commission in his own constitency which he desired to mention. He referred to the action of Mr. Thomas Walpole, one of the Assistant Commissioners. In the district in which that individual was best known the idea of retaining him upon the Commission was regarded with anything but favour. He was a man who, in the opinion of the people of that district, was utterly unfit for the post he held. His relations to his own tenants had been of the most unsatisfactory description. He was a man who, some five or six years ago, had foisted on one of those tenants, a man named Higgins—an ignorant man—an agreement for a lease, which, however, had never been executed, the terms of that agreement being of an exceptionally hard and aggressive character. The yearly rent was £15, and the value of the holding was only £8 per annum. The first clause of the agreement was against burning anything but bog, and the penalty was £25 per acre. The next was against disposing of turf, and the next against cutting timber, the penalty being £1 per acre. In consideration of liberty to reclaim the bog, which was very much to the benefit of the landlord, the tenant was required to forfeit all right to compensation under the Land Act of 1870, or any other Act which might be passed. The other clauses of the lease were also particularly hard; but that which was to exclude the tenant from the benefit of the Act of 1870, which had been passed, and any other Act which might be passed for the relief of the tenant, showed the kind of man the landlord was. The tenant refused to execute the lease or any other with such covenants. But Mr. Walpole handed the man a draft agreement, and gave him to understand that those were the terms on which he was to hold, and no other. A short time afterwards, the land of the tenant being practically at the mercy of the landlord, he added some acre and a-half to the holding, and at once raised the total valuation to £10, and, at the same time, raised the rent by £4, making the total £19. When the tenant applied to the Assistant Land Commissioners, he was met by the alleged agreement, and although he repudiated it and had never signed it, and although the draft agreement was never dated, the case was decided against him on the assertion of the Assistant Commissioner landlord. The tenant took the case to the Land Commissioners themselves, and they in turn refused him any relief. This was only one illustration of the treatment Mr. Walpole's tenants had received at his hands, and it was not to be wondered at that, under these circumstances, the tenants generally throughout Ireland should regard him as a man from whom they were not likely to meet with even-handed justice. So much with regard to Mr. Assistant Commissioner Walpole. The next matter to which he desired to call the attention of the Chief Secretary was one with regard to which he thought he should be able, at least, to excite the surprise of the right hon. Gentleman. In order not to make the story too long, he would confine himself to the reading of a short statement which he had received from the tenant whose interests were affected. The tenant was a Mr. George Hetherington, and he said—

"I served an originating notice in time for the first sitting of the Land Court under the Act of 1881, and my case was listed for hearing at Maryborough in July, 1882, when the Court dismissed the case owing to Mrs. Dix"—who was the landlord—"being a middle landlord, and having only a profit rent of about £7 per year."

Some years ago, there was a very celebrated series of letters written by a gentleman who was now a County Court Judge in Ireland, and who acted as Special Commissioner for *The Times*, in regard to the Land Question in Ireland. That gentleman devoted a considerable portion of those letters to the task of showing that the great curse of Ireland at that time was the middleman landlord. What he then said about the middleman landlord was perfectly true. Well, Mrs. Dix was in the position of a middleman landlord, and she drew only £7 profit out of the particular holding referred to. Mr. Hetherington went on to say that—

"The Sub-Commissioners refused to come out and inspect my farm, although I am paying a rent of £155 per year for 63 Irish acres, the Poor Law valuation of which is £80 per annum, £20 of this being for buildings, leaving the Government valuation of the land only £60. My valuator, Mr. William Grange, auctioneer and land valuator of Portarlington, valued the farm at £81 odd, to which valuation he swore at Maryborough. I lodged an appeal against the decision of the Sub-Commissioners, which was heard before the Head Commissioners in Dublin on the 19th of June last, after two years' waiting, and then they decided it in the same way as the Sub-Commissioners in Maryborough in July, 1882. The Sub and Head Commissioners all admitted that my rent was too high; but, owing to the small profit, they said they could not think of reducing the rent. I was under the impression the Act was passed to give redress to tenants who paid exorbitant rents, irrespective of how their landlords held their holdings or what head rent they paid; and if such is not the case, I hope you will bring this defect in the Act under the notice of the Legislature with the view of having it redressed. Here am I, an unfortunate tenant, paying a rent of nearly 100 per cent. over the Government valuation, and what my own practical valutor swore it was worth, and because my landlady holds as a middle one, I must continue to be rack-rented without redress."

This was the statement of Mr. George Hetherington; but he had had confirmation of the story from quarters altogether independent of the tenant. He thought the Committee would agree with him that anything more monstrous than what had happened in this case could hardly be imagined. Here was a Tribunal that had been established for the purpose of fixing, when necessary, what was a fair rent. The Sub-Commissioners admitted that the rent demanded was not a fair rent; but they found that if they reduced it the middleman would hold the land at a loss, and, therefore, they who were appointed to look after the interests of the tenant, refused to make any reduction, but left the tenant to pay a rental which they themselves acknowledged to be exorbitantly high. This finding of the Assistant Commissioners was upheld by the Chief Commissioners of the Land Court. Under these circumstances, he should be disposed to support a Motion for the reduction of the Vote; but, of course, he could not think of giving his support to that which had been moved by the hon. and gallant Member for the County of Dublin (Colonel King-Harman) in his interesting and singularly sober statement, which was calculated to attract the attention of all who heard it, and which had led him (Mr. A. O'Connor) to look into the record of the Land Commission, which he held in hand, to see how the hon. and gallant Gentleman had himself fared at the hands of the Land Tribunal against his own tenants in support of appeals; but as the hon. and gallant Member was no longer in his place, he would not further refer to that matter. He must say, however, that he could not understand the ground on which the hon. and gallant Gentleman had moved to reduce the Vote, except it was that he objected to Mr. Murrough O'Brien, because he had not thought the land was worth as many years' purchase as the hon. and gallant Gentleman had estimated it to be worth. He (Mr. A. O'Connor) trusted that some Official on the Treasury Bench would give the Committee an undertaking that the statement he had read, as having been written by Mr. George Hetherington, of Ballintougher House, Monasterevan, would receive some consideration at the hands of Her Majesty's Government.

Mr. TREVELYAN said, if the hon. Member for Queen's County would put his request in reference to the Land Commission in the form of a Question, it would be much better, because, when applications for opinions on particular cases had to be taken from the Parliamentary Reports taken in that House, the result was not always so satisfactory as hon. Members might wish. With regard to the remarks the hon. Member had made in reference to Mr. Walpole, he (Mr. Trevelyan) had been informed that the rent at which the tenant alluded to sat was actually £5 less than the rent Mr. Walpole paid the head landlord.

Mr. ARTHUR O'CONNOR: What has that to do with it?

Mr. TREVELYAN said, it had this to do with it, that when Mr. Walpole proposed an agreement to a tenant holding under him, giving him a farm at a rental of £5 less than he himself was paying to the head landlord, it was not unnatural that he should ask for and expect some concession on the part of the tenant. This, therefore, was a matter that had to be taken into consideration when the Committee were asked to criticize the terms of an agreement Mr. Walpole had made with one of his tenants. When the agreement in question was referred to the Sub-Commission, the Sub-Commissioners decided that it should stand, and after that it was confirmed by the Court. The observations he should have made in answer to the speech of the hon. and gallant Gentleman the Member for the County of Dublin (Colonel King-Harman) he did not now think there was any occasion for him to make; but he believed he should have been able, had it been necessary, to have put a very different face on the case from that which had been put upon it by the hon. and gallant Member. He was bound, however, to say, in justice to Mr. Murrough O'Brien, that he had found in the case referred to that where that gentleman had sanctioned the sale to the tenant, the purchase was at the rate of 20 years' purchase. The real difficulty in those cases was that the tenant was unwilling to give the 20 years' purchase which the hon. and gallant Member had put as the standard. Mr. Murrough O'Brien had been considered as rather an enthusiast in favour of the peasant proprietor, and not one who would be likely to throw any difficulty in his way. With regard to what had been said by the hon. and gallant Member for Cork (Colonel Colthurst), he (Mr. Trevelyan) thought it a very good suggestion that the Local Government Board should call the attention of the Boards of Guardians to the powers given under the Labourers' Act.

Mr. GRAY said, the speech just made by the right hon. Gentleman the Chief Secretary certainly seemed to him a marvellous piece of logic. The argument of the right hon. Gentleman seemed to point to this—that if the tenant paid a rack rent it was right that he should continue to pay it, however exorbitant it might be, if it so happened that, in consequence of any reduction in that rental, the intermediate holder as between the landlord and the tenant in occupation would be compelled to pay more than he was himself receiving. This, putting it shortly, was the argument which the right hon. Gentleman was putting before the Committee as applicable to all cases where it was said that the tenant was paying £5, or any other sum, less than the middle landlord was paying. When the right hon. Gentleman was interrupted by the hon. Member for Queen's County (Mr. A. O'Connor), who had very pertinently asked, "What has that to do with it?" he (Mr. Trevelyan) had emphasized his argument by saying he thought it had a great deal to do with it; so that, according to the right hon. Gentleman's view, the immediate occupier ought not to be relieved of the rack rent in any case in which the giving of such relief would injuriously affect the interests of the middle landlord. If the Chief Secretary wished to initiate the very extraordinary principle that the payment of a fair rent was not to apply fully if it were found to be injurious to the middleman, he would be going entirely outside the principle of the Land Act, and leaving untouched an evil which the Land Act was intended to remedy. The statement just made by the Chief Secretary was a very serious one, and he ought either to make his meaning quite clear, or else to qualify what he had been saying. There was one point which he (Mr. Gray) wished to put to the hon. Gentleman the Secretary to the Treasury. A case was recently tried before Chief Justice Morris. It was a case in which one of the parties, named Bromfield, was a tenant of Lord Congleton. The point was this—whether the holder of a lease could not claim the full benefit of the Land Act, except where the entire land was in the hands of the immediate lessee. The case of the tenant Bromfield was as follows:—He got a lease in the year 1880 from Lord Congleton, and was middleman as regarded the entire property, which was all occupied by sub-tenants. A good deal of the land fell out of the hands of the sub-tenants at that time, owing to death and other causes, and came into the hands of Bromfield's father and Bromfield himself. But, when his lease was almost expired, he had to consider whether he would evict all the sub-tenants or leave them alone. He adopted the plan of leaving them alone. The sub-tenants claimed to have a fair rent fixed, and were now statutory tenants. For the portion of the land in his own possession, Bromfield also claimed a similar right; but the Court ruled that he had no *locus standi*, but that he would have had if he had evicted all the tenants and got all the land into his own possession. He (Mr. Gray) wished to ask, whether this was really the law?

CAPTAIN AYLMER said, the right hon. Gentleman the Chief Secretary to the Lord Lieutenant had just stated, in reference to the arguments used by the hon. and gallant Member for the County of Dublin (Colonel King-Harman), that he need do no more than make a cursory reference to what had been urged. But hon. Members on that side of the Committee were anxious to hear some more explicit answer to the points that had been raised, especially with regard to what had been stated in reference to Mr. Murrough O'Brien. That was a matter on which the right hon. Gentleman had not given a satisfactory reply. The Committee had not been told why it was that when the tenants had agreed with the landlord for what must be considered not an unfair price for the land, and had applied for the money under the Purchase Clauses of the Land Act, that gentleman had recommended the Commissioners not to allow the money, because he did not approve of the price. The price was 16 years' purchase, and Mr. Murrough O'Brien had said it was not worth more than 11 or 12 years' purchase, the result being that the sale had not been carried out. If this was the course that was to be pursued in these cases, he was afraid it would not be of much use to try to sell land under the Purchase Clauses of the Land Act. He would like the Committee to be informed what was the reason of this remarkable change? Mr. O'Brien was for some time an agent under the Church Commissioners for valuing land, and for naming the price which the tenants were to pay for it; and in that capacity he had valued it, in some cases, as high as 26 years' purchase. But now that he represented the Land Commissioners, he was valuing it at 11 or 12 years' purchase. Now, it must be evident that the real value of the land could not have changed to that extent in so short a time. One hon. Member had endeavoured to explain the difference by saying that the tenants' interest in the land had reduced its value—that was to say, that the tenants' interest must be taken out of the valuation; in other words, the hon. Member allowed that the Land Act accounted for a diminution in value of 50 per cent.

MR. GRAY said, the hon. and gallant Gentleman who had just spoken had not carried his argument far enough. He should have gone a step farther, and shown that in this case the property was the same which, at one time, had been valued by Mr. O'Brien at 26 years' purchase, and, at another time, at 11 or 12 years' purchase. The hon. and gallant Gentleman clearly did not understand the position, which was simply this. The land valued by Mr. O'Brien at 26 years' purchase might have been the property of a Corporation, such as the Church Commission, who might have allowed the tenants to acquire a very considerable interest in their property; and, again, the land might have been tolerably good. Church lands generally were good; and 26 years' purchase of such land, held upon liberal conditions, and at a low or moderate rental, from a Corporation not accustomed to disturb its tenants, might have been a very proper valuation; whereas 12 or 14 years' purchase of land of low quality, and rack-rented, might be a very high value. There was no comparison between the two cases.

CAPTAIN AYLMER: I spoke of a fair rent.

MR. GRAY said, that could not be applied as a basis of valuation. One lot of land might be had for 12 years' purchase, if it were fully rack-rented, and of poor quality; another lot of good land, which yielded a profit on the rent, and was moderately rented, might be had for 26 years' purchase. It was entirely a matter of business, and the land valued at 26 years' purchase might be a better investment than that valued at 14 years' purchase. What the hon. and gallant Gentleman should do, in order to establish a bias in the action of Mr. O'Brien, would be to show that the tenants paid the same rent, had the same interest, and that the quality of the land was equal in both cases. Until the hon. and gallant Member could show that, he did not think he was justified in bringing against Mr. O'Brien the charge that he was acting *malâ fide*. If Mr. O'Brien did not exercise some discretion as to the money to be advanced, he would not be fit for his office at all, and landlords and tenants would have nothing more to do than to arrange a value between themselves, and get the money from the Treasury; all they had to do was to place upon the land a value so high that three-fourths of the amount would pay the landlord. The Treasury was, of course, right in securing itself against transactions of that kind; and Mr. O'Brien had not to consider whether the rent of the property was fair, but whether the property constituted a full security to the Treasury for the amount which they were called upon to pay.

MR. SMALL said, he thought the Committee were entitled to some information as to why some of the Sub-Commissioners had been reappointed, and others dismissed. He should like to know on what principle the Land Commissioners or the Lord Lieutenant of Ireland had acted in this matter?

MR. TREVELYAN said, he could not afford the hon. Member any more information on this point than that the Land Commissioners watched, with the greatest care, the action of the different Sub-Commissioners. When cases came up on appeal, they were able to form a correct estimate of the fitness of the Sub-Commissioners, and would be guided thereby in their recommendations. With regard to the case referred to by the hon. Member for Carlow (Mr. Gray), he had not laid down in his observations any doctrine of law; he had simply explained the decision of the Land Court in the case, and defended the gentleman in question from what he imagined to be the effect of the very imperfect account of the case given by the hon. Member.

THE SOLICITOR GENERAL FOR IRELAND (Mr. WALKER) said, he could express no opinion on the case, which he understood was before the Law Courts.

MR. T. D. SULLIVAN said, before the discussion on this Vote came to an end, he desired to make a personal explanation. He had learned that it was the opinion of the Chairman that the expression "convicted thieves," used by him (Mr. Sullivan) some time since, was un-Parliamentary when applied to Members of that House. In that case, he begged to say he most unhesitatingly withdrew it, because he never desired in any way to contravene the Rules of the House. Further, he begged to say that in using that phrase he had no intention whatever to apply it to any Member of the House.

THE CHAIRMAN said, he was glad the hon. Member had withdrawn the phrase; and, as he had done so, it did not appear to him necessary to say anything more on the subject further than that it would have been not only un-Parliamentary, but highly improper, if the hon. Member had applied it to any hon. Member of the House. Had he supposed the hon. Member meant so to apply it, he should at once have called upon him to withdraw it.

Question put, and *negatived*.

Original Question put, and *agreed to*.

(5.) Motion made, and Question proposed,

"That a sum, not exceeding £86,094, be granted to Her Majesty, to complete the sum necessary to defray the Charge which will come in course of payment during the year ending on the 31st day of March 1885, for the Salaries and Expenses of the Commissioners of Police, the Police Courts, and the Metropolitan Police Establishment of Dublin."

MR. HEALY asked why the Vote for the County Courts, Ireland, was not taken next in its regular order?

MR. COURTNEY said, it would be better to go on with this Vote next. His object was to save time, and he did not think the discussion of the Vote would occupy more than an hour or an hour and a-half.

COLONEL KING-HARMAN said, he was not quite sure that the hon. Gentleman the Secretary to the Treasury was right in his estimate of the time that would be occupied in discussing this Vote. The Vote might open up some large questions, in the discussion of which many hon. Members would wish to take part. The subject was in itself a difficult one, and ought not, in his opinion, to be considered at 1 o'clock in the morning. His own opinion was that the discussion on the Vote should not be taken then.

MR. HEALY said, the question he desired to raise on this Vote had reference to the conduct of the police in the matter of the arrest of Mr. Chance. The complaint which he and his hon. Friends had to make was, that two individuals, one of them at least a gentleman, had been arrested by policemen in the service of the Government on a charge of entering a house for an unlawful purpose, and that these persons on being arrested were taken to the police station, and then instantly discharged. Now, the right hon. Gentleman the Chief Secretary to the Lord Lieutenant of Ireland had stated that if the persons interested in this matter were not satisfied, they could bring their action for damages; that the Government would simply stand aside and take no steps in the matter. But they had had from the Government no real explanation of the conduct of the police in this affair. He would ask the right hon. Gentleman to be good enough to say whether, if an action for false imprisonment were brought against the police, the Government would or would not defend it and pay the damages, if the verdict went against the police? He had yet to learn that the Government would not do this in Ireland. They were informed that the Lord Lieutenant had no control over the local police; but the right hon. Gentleman had given them no satisfaction whatever. The question was whether the police in Ireland had power to take up whomsoever they chose on flimsy charges, and march them with ignominy through the streets to the police station without giving them any satisfaction. He put the case to the English Members, whether British liberty was held at so cheap a price that any policeman might arrest a man on a totally false charge, drive him to the station-house and then, instead of bringing him before the magistrates, having ascertained who he was, turn him loose into the streets? He had put that case to the right hon. Gentleman the Chief Secretary the Lord Lieutenant of Ireland, and he said that any respectable lawyer would take the case up. But the question was, would the police be defended by the Government if an action were brought? The police, however, had a bogus story to tell in this matter, and the Government, of course, defended them. He had often observed the right hon. Gentleman's receptivity of mind with respect to the statements of the police; a policeman had only to make a statement and the right hon. Gentleman swallowed it at once. He asked whether he was prepared, in this instance, to accept the policemen's statement as against that of persons equally credible? Policemen in Ireland were regarded as very superior persons, no doubt; but he had yet to learn that a policeman was necessarily a man of high character, and that his account of his own conduct in the streets was to be received without question. Now, the statement of Mr. Chance bore the stamp of truth on the face of it. He went to a woman to get evidence against Mr. George Bolton in connection with the trial at Belfast. Was it likely that anyone wanting to get evidence against Mr. Bolton would say that he came from Inspector Malone? But the Government had accepted that statement on the part of the police, and the right hon. Gentleman the Chief Secretary was willing to allow the matter to rest solely upon that statement. This was not the way in which matters were usually conducted in this world; if people could get off on their own statements alone, every thief and burglar would escape punishment. But the Government took the statement of the incriminated parties in this case, and had no regard whatever for anything said on the other side. His case was dual—Did the Government approve the arrest; and, secondly, if the action were brought would the Government defend the action and pay the damages, if damages were awarded? In order to give the right hon. Gentleman an opportunity of replying.

he would move the reduction of the Vote by the sum of £1,000.

Motion made, and Question proposed,

"That a sum, not exceeding £85,094, be granted to Her Majesty, to complete the sum necessary to defray the Charge which will come in course of payment during the year ending on the 31st day of March 1885, for the Salaries and Expenses of the Commissioners of Police, the Police Courts, and the Metropolitan Police Establishment of Dublin."—(*Mr. Healy.*)

MR. TREVELYAN said, he believed that what had passed on this subject in the House up to the present time was that the hon. Member for Monaghan had, four or five days ago, read out a telegram giving, he supposed, Mr. Chance's view of what had passed. He (Mr. Trevelyan) had since read a longer telegram giving the official account, in which the essential point was that the police were under the very decided impression that the Carroll family had been frightened by people whose identity turned out to be different from that which they supposed it to be. He thought then, and he thought now, that under those circumstances, with that information before them, the police were in the right to interfere. He should compare the case to that of a man who was arrested in the act of getting into his own house through the balcony; it would be a parallel case if, under those circumstances, the policeman pulled him down, and took him off to the station-house, and then discovered that having lost his latch-key he was merely getting into his own house. He was informed that under such circumstances, if a complaint were made by a person so arrested, an official inquiry would be held. He understood that Mr. Chance maintained that he had not been properly treated, and that his story was not the same as that represented to the police by the Carroll family. However, he would consult with the Solicitor General for Ireland as to whether an inquiry should be advised. He was informed that an action for unwarrantable arrest would lie; but he hoped the matter would not go as far as that.

MR. DAWSON said, he trusted he should be in Order in drawing attention to the question of the continued postponement by the Government of any action with regard to the recommendation of the Royal Commission appointed by the late Government to inquire into the extension of the boundaries of the city of Dublin. The people of Dublin were situated in this way with regard to the police reserve—they had to pay a contribution towards the police maintenance of 8*d.* in the pound, while the Metropolitan Police were scattered over a vast area. Now, that was one of the hundred disabilities the city laid under from the want of an extension of the boundaries, and an increase of the area of taxation. A Commission was issued some time ago, and the Corporation was represented by the present Solicitor General for Ireland (Mr. Walker), and, therefore, very well represented. The net recommendation of that Commission was that the city boundary, for the purposes of police and other things, should be extended, and that the outlying townships should be brought within the city area. From that day to this, not a single thing had been done, and if a case was wanted to show the sort of legislation there was in regard to Ireland it was this—Whatever was just, whatever was reasonable, and whatever was equitable was put off from day to day, and from year to year, while the most obnoxious things and regulations, totally opposed to the interests and wishes of the people, were immediately put in force. He would like to know if there was any chance whatever of this Liberal Government giving any effect to the recommendations of the Royal Commission of the late Government? He had nothing to say against the police in Dublin, indeed, in his official capacity of Lord Mayor of Dublin, he did what he could in a time of great disturbance to bring about a *rapprochment* between the city authorities and the police; he did everything he possibly could in order to preserve the order of the city, and to try and bring about a unity of purpose, by saying a kind word between the police and the authorities. But he had this, nevertheless, to complain of, that there was no sympathy between the police and the people. He saw the other day that magnificent demonstration in London conducted with marvellous regularity and order, simply because of the conduct of the police towards the people. Why, if there had been a similar concourse of people in Dublin, and if the police had been called upon to preserve order, there would not have been the same results. He would mention a case to illustrate the way in which the Dublin police failed to discharge their duty. On the occasion of any popular demonstration the police of Dublin afforded no facility whatever for keeping order. Recently a banquet was given to the Parliamentary Party; but the utmost confusion arose in the streets, in consequence of the complete absence of the police. If His Excellency the Lord Lieutenant, however, had been going to the Mansion House, policemen would have been stationed at different parts of the route taken to preserve order. On the occasion to which he referred, thousands of people collected around the Hall; but the police did not turn up until the confusion had almost become appalling. On another occasion there was a reception in Dublin of a distinguished actor, Mr. Barry Sullivan. On that occasion, though the railway authorities applied for the services of the police to keep order, the police were conspicuous by their absence. While the police were always prompt to strain their duty in matters that were obnoxious, they were never present to give assistance to the Civil authorities whenever it ought to be given. In conclusion, he asked the Chief Secretary (Mr. Trevelyan) if he could hold out any hope of an extension of the boundaries of Dublin according to the expressed wish and recommendation of a Royal Commission which had held a long and arduous inquiry?

MR. GRAY said, he had a question to ask the right hon. Gentleman the Chief Secretary, with regard to a question which had already been raised by the hon. Member for Monaghan (Mr. Healy). It was a very important question, involving official sanction to the new practice about to be introduced of arresting men and bringing them to the station, and then refusing to prefer a charge against them. The right hon. Gentleman quoted, in justification of a proceeding of that kind, the case of a man who, being found under suspicious circumstances, might be arrested and brought to the police station, and then set at liberty. He (Mr. Gray) thought it was very dangerous for the police to act in such a manner; and he would like to ask the right hon. Gentleman, or possibly some official connected with the English Administration could tell him, whether, if a man arrested under suspicious circumstances demanded to be charged, or asked the Inspector at the station to prefer the charge against him, the Inspector could refuse to enter a charge? That was the point at issue in the case of Mr. Chance. If a man be arrested through some mistake of a constable, and was content then to suffer inconvenience and annoyance, and be set at liberty, there was little to be said. He could quite understand a policeman in ignorance arresting a man and then setting him at liberty, although he believed that to be against the Rules of the Force. He had always been under the impression that there was a regular Rule, both in England and Ireland—certainly in Ireland—that when a policeman set hands on a man and took him into custody, he had no discretion to liberate him; and manifestly such a Rule was very necessary, if for no other purpose than to guard the police against terrible temptations. A policeman might be open to a bribe, and money might be offered to him to liberate a man. He had always understood that when once a policeman took a man into custody and laid hands upon him, that he was bound to bring him to the police station, and that, having done that, he was bound to make some charge against him. In such a case as that instanced by the right hon. Gentleman the Chief Secretary in justification of the arrest of Mr. Chance—the case of a man arrested on his own premises because he was found under suspicious circumstances, and the police thought he was a burglar, he wanted to know, and perhaps the Home Secretary would tell him, would a subordinate police officer dismiss that man and refuse to enter a charge against him if the man claimed to have a charge entered against him, in order that, in a summary manner before the magistrate next morning, he should have an opportunity of clearing his character? It was one thing for a man to be dismissed with his own consent, in fact condoning the offence of his arrest; but this was not such a case. Mr. Chance, when he was arrested and brought to the station-house, asked the Inspector to enter a charge against him, in order that, on the following morning, he should have an opportunity of clearing himself before the magistrate. The Inspector, however, refused to enter the charge, and insisted upon Mr. Chance going away and taking his own remedy by law. Would such a practice be allowed in England? He hoped the Home Secretary would tell them whether he would permit a policeman to arrest any man, and then, if that man wanted to have a charge entered against him, he would permit a subordinate officer to refuse to enter a charge, but to turn the man out? He thought that such a practice, if allowed, was manifestly fraught with the greatest danger; it was fraught with the greatest possible temptation to the police, who were open to temptation like other human beings. By such a practice they would open the door for very grave abuse; and he could scarcely believe that such a practice, which had been followed in the case of Mr. Chance, would be permitted in England.

The SOLICITOR GENERAL (Sir Farrer Herschell) said, he knew from experience in Courts of Justice that it was by no means uncommon in England for an Inspector to refuse to take a charge against a person brought to the station—not at all an uncommon thing. If a mistake had been made and the Inspector refused to take the charge, the man would be set at liberty. The hon. Gentleman the Member for Carlow (Mr. Gray) had asked if an Inspector would not be obliged to enter a charge if the man arrested insisted upon it? He (the Solicitor General) would certainly say the Inspector would not be bound to enter a charge if it was clear a mistake had been made. An Inspector who believed a mistake had been made would not keep a man in custody a whole night, because the only effect of that would be to aggravate the wrong and increase any possible damages that might be given. It sometimes happened that when a person insisted upon a charge being entered the Inspector made a note of the fact that the man was brought in, but he had refused to enter the charge. If it was perfectly clear that no offence had been committed, the Inspector certainly would not enter a charge.

Mr. HEALY said, the point was this. If a man was taken to the station on some serious offence—loitering for an unlawful purpose, or for burglary, or for assault of some kind, or perhaps for murder—was it in the power of the constable who arrested the man to refuse to make the charge, but to turn him loose? If a policeman saw him (Mr. Healy) in Palace Yard, and, thinking he was loitering about Westminster Palace for an unlawful purpose, arrrested him and took him to the nearest police station, would the constable be at liberty, on his own motion, to turn him out in the street on finding who he was? Who was it who was supposed to have discretion in such matters?

Sir WILLIAM HARCOURT said, that if a policeman saw a man getting over the area railings, he would think possibly that it was intended to make a felonious entry of the premises, and he would arrest the man. The man might be the owner of the house, who had lost his latchkey, and took this method of getting into the premises. The policeman, however, would be perfectly right in arresting him and taking him to the station. If the man satisfied the Inspector that he was the proprietor of the house, and that though he was entering in an unusual manner he was not there for an unlawful purpose, it was quite plain that he would be immediately discharged. It would be a monstrous absurdity to insist that the proprietor of the house should be charged with burglary. The Inspector, by discharging the man, would show his common sense. If the man said, "I will be charged with burglary," it would not be a reasonable request. If, of course, the policeman acted in any improper manner—if there had been no reasonable grounds for doing what he did, he would be punished by the Police Authorities; and if he was not sufficiently punished, an action for unlawful arrest would lie. Of course, these were not details with which he (Sir William Harcourt) was every day conversant; but, so far as he knew, the practice in England was the same as that elsewhere.

Mr. HEALY said the right hon. and learned Gentleman (Sir William Harcourt) had put a case of an extreme character; and, of course, if a man was seen, at 2 o'clock in the morning, climbing over area railings, everyone would say a policeman was justified in arresting him. It was another question altogether whether it was a suspicious circumstance for a solicitor and an attendant to be pursuing certain investigations in broad daylight. He accepted for the moment the statement of the right hon. Gentleman the Chief Secretary (Mr. Trevelyan) that he would grant an inquiry; but what he wanted to know was, whether the Government—if the inquiry was against Mr. Mallon, the Head of the Police, and if Mr. Chance was not satisfied—would assume the position of judicial bottle holder as regarded damages, if in an action brought against the policeman damages were given? That question had not been touched upon that night. If such a case as that described by the Home Secretary occurred in London—that of the arrest of a man found climbing over the area railings under suspicious circumstances — everyone would say it was quite right to defend the policeman who made the arrest, in the event of an action for false arrest being brought. But the question involved in the arrest of Mr. Chance was totally different. This was a matter occurring in broad daylight, and a solicitor was not a man who was likely to act in an illegal manner. Mr. Chance and Mr. Meiklejohn entered Carroll's house to make inquiries from her respecting the case in which Bolton and the Crown were mixed up, and a policeman stepped in and arrested them for, so far as he (Mr. Healy) could see, no earthly reason at all. The question he had now to put was, whether the English practice was or was not to be followed in this case, and whether the Government would, in case an action was brought against the constable, defend him, and pay his damages if any were given?

MR. TREVELYAN said, the answer to the question of the hon. Member practically depended on the result of the inquiry. It was quite certain that if it was stated that hereafter the Government in all cases would defend any action that might e brought against its servants the effect would be to give to those servants too much latitude and induce them to act rashly at critical times. On the other hand, to say positively that the Government would not back up its servants would cause their servants to act timidly on occasions when they ought to act boldly. Every case must be judged by itself. In this case an inquiry would be held, and the whole thing depended upon the inquiry.

MR. HEALY: Will the inquiry be public?

MR. TREVELYAN said, that as to the nature of the inquiry he would consult with his right hon. and learned Friend the Home Secretary, so as to see what would be done in England under similar circumstances. The object of granting the inquiry was to give full satisfaction to all concerned, and to give them the assurance that the case had been treated fairly. He would take good care that the inquiry should be in every respect fair.

MR. HEALY asked leave to withdraw his Motion. He supposed, however, the Government would tell them before Report what the nature of the inquiry would be?

MR. GRAY agreed with his hon. Friend (Mr. Healy) that it was only fair the Government should undertake to tell them what the nature of the inquiry would be before the Report stage.

MR. COURTNEY remarked that the inquiry might not possibly be held before next month.

MR. HEALY said, he and his hon. Friends only wanted to know what the nature of the inquiry would be. Personally he had no desire to delay the Vote that night, and he would be satisfied if the Government gave them an answer to-morrow.

MR. DAWSON asked the right hon. Gentleman the Chief Secretary to say something about the Dublin Commission?

MR. TREVELYAN said, it was impossible to bring forward, at that period of the Session, a Bill dealing with the Dublin boundaries in the manner recommended by the Commission to which the hon. Gentleman referred. Answering a question put to him a few days ago by the hon. Gentleman the Member for the County of Carlow (Mr. Gray), he stated that at the beginning of next Session—the Session which would commence in the usual course in February next—he should be prepared to bring forward a Borough Funds Bill, to bring about the very limited result of enabling the Dublin Corporation to spend Corporation money in the interests of the Corporation. He did not think he could go further than that.

MR. DAWSON said, there was not so much contention in this matter as the right hon. Gentleman seemed to suppose. The Royal Commission which inquired into the question of the extension of the Dublin Municipal Boundaries sat for some weeks, and their recommendation was perfectly clear and lucid, and it was very improbable that its carrying out would create any contentious agitation.

MR. GRAY said, he did not wish to discuss the question of the boundaries at that moment; but he wished, in the mildest possible manner, to convey to the right hon. and learned Gentleman the Home Secretary, who possibly did not take any profound interest in the question of the boundaries of Dublin City, and who had on previous occasions taken care to inform the House that he never read Irish newspapers, that the Irish Parliamentary Party had resolved, that so far as it in their power laid, no Bill for the reform of London should pass unless the Government would give a pledge to endeavour to carry a Bill embodying similar principles in regard to the Metropolis of Ireland. Now, he could not allow this Metropolitan Police Vote to pass without a word of protest against the whole Dublin police system. He had very little concern with the amount of money which the Government might think fit to vote for the maintenance of the expenses of the Force called the Dublin Metropolitan Police Force; but it so happened that this Force was maintained not merely out of Imperial funds, but to a large extent out of local funds. Dublin City and the Dublin Metropolitan District, which extended beyond the City, was taxed to the nominal amount of 8*d.* in the £ for the maintenance of this Force; but not only had the people to pay that direct tax, but they also had to pay indirect taxes, which he calculated brought the rate which they had to pay for the maintenance of the Dublin Metropolitan Police up to a sum equal to about 1*s.* 2*d.* in the £. A cruelly unjust and oppressive tax was maintained in Dublin simply because the proceeds of it went towards the maintenance of the police—he alluded to the £100 licence paid by every pawnbroker in the City of Dublin. He need not explain to the Committee that pawnbrokers did not pay that tax out of their own pockets; they must levy it on the poor whose goods they took in pawn. The tax had been condemned as a thing which could not be justified by a Royal Commission or by a Committee—he was not sure which—he believed it was a special Committee of the House of Commons which investigated the whole question of the Pawnbroking Laws. The tax was only paid in Dublin, and there was no excuse for its maintenance there except that the £100 a-year paid by the pawnbroker was added to the local contributions towards the maintenance of the police. The Government did not care to re-open the question of the local contributions towards the Police Force, because they knew perfectly well that an overwhelming case would be made out against the present system. To levy so cruel a tax as this upon the poorest of the poor was exceedingly unjustifiable; and he thought the Chief Secretary ought to consider whether he could not modify the system in some way. It was patent to everyone that the Force was not kept up to prevent crime, or to maintain order, but purely as a Governmental *gendarmerie.* He contended that there was no reason why Dublin should not be placed in the same position in regard to its police as every other City in the United Kingdom, except London, which, of course, was governed in a very exceptional manner in every respect. All the great cities which corresponded with Dublin—Manchester, Edinburgh, Glasgow, and Liverpool—had their police under the control of the Local Authorities, and they were maintained exclusively from local rates. Now, he wanted to know whether the Government intended to maintain in Dublin this exceptional system in perpetuity? The police in English towns were liked by all the people, except the professional criminal classes. The great body of the population looked to the policeman as a friend, they went to him for information and for assistance in various ways, and his experience of the police in London and in the great English towns was that they were extremely civil and attentive, and desirous to make themselves agreeable to those with whom they came in contact. The Dublin Metropolitan Police, however, were trained in a totally different school; they were trained to regard not only the criminal classes, but the whole body of the population, as the natural enemies of the police. They treated the people with a brutality that was unnatural to them; but it was taught them; and one of the main causes why they struck last year was the amount of drill they were subjected to by their late Chief Commissioner (Mr. Talbot), who was a pure martinet, and quite unable to govern them or any other force, and whom the Government were obliged to dismiss with an annuity. What reason was there for training the police as military men? There was no reason. It made them neglect their ordinary police duties, and they were not of very much use as detectives. They simply regarded themselves as a species of Governmental body guard; they were not a municipal or local force. He had pointed out before that if the local officials wanted anything done they could not control the police; but in English towns, the entire body of police being the servants of the Local Authorities, they were governed by that Body for all local purposes, including sanitary purposes. The Lord Provost of Edinburgh, two years ago, asked him if the Dublin Municipal Authorities had control over their police, and, on his replying that they had not, the Lord Provost said that until they had they could not hope to keep the City in a good sanitary condition, adding that it was because the Edinburgh authorities had control over the police that they had a good sanitary system. The result of the system in Ireland was demoralizing. It caused the people to dislike the police, and it imposed a grievous burden on the people; and, at the same time, it was said the Exchequer gave them large contributions, for which they ought to be grateful. But the Government gave money only for their own police, and taxed the people for the remainder. The Municipal Authorities could maintain a better local police force at less cost than they were now compelled to bear for this inferior force. They had to provide this money, and impose a heavy tax on the poor to provide it. They had to pay duty for every carriage in the police district, and the Government took all the fees, while the Local Authorities had to bear the rates and pay for the wear and tear of the hackney carriages of the Government. The Government took the sum paid for carriages, and then put it in the Consolidated Fund as part of the contribution to the local expenses. The time would, he believed, come when the Government would have to apply to the Dublin police the same principles as those which were applied and were satisfactory in every other town in the United Kingdom. When were they going to do that? The police themselves were dissatisfied, and they had struck and brought the Government to their knees, and would do so again as soon as it suited them. He found a Vote put down for "extra pay;" but he thought that ought to be put down as "strike money," £7,500. The police would say they did not see why they should not have another £7,500, and the Government would be absolutely helpless, and would have to swear in Emergency men and special constables. The only duty the police who did not strike had to do was to arrest special constables and take them off to gaol. He himself happened to be in gaol at the time, thanks to the attention of the Judges, for a so-called misdemeanour—though he did not acknowledge that he was a misdemeanant at all—and he remembered being very much amused by seeing bodies of special constables brought in every evening and locked up, having been sworn in in the morning only. If the Chief Secretary had not caved in to the police, Richmond Gaol would have been full of special constables. The whole thing was, in itself, perfectly ridiculous; but it was not a ridiculous matter to the people of Dublin. He thought the right hon. Gentleman should give some hope of a better system, and that the whole system would be reconsidered and placed on a more reasonable basis. With regard to the subject of boundaries, he wished to point out that while a reform was being considered Dublin was suffering. It was surrounded by a ring of towns to which all the wealthy people were migrating, and the result was that Dublin itself was suffering every year from a heavier burden of taxation, from which the wealthier inhabitants escaped by going outside, although they had a share in all the benefits of the City, and thrived by them. Every man who went outside the City threw an additional burden on those who remained, and he could assure the Committee that a terrible amount of injury was being done to the City by this being allowed to continue. The authorities were naturally disinclined to incur any extra expense while the Commission was sitting, and unless the Government stepped in and gave some assistance nothing could possibly be done. That was a state of things created by the Government, and not by any default on the part of the Local Authorities. The remedy of the right hon. Gentleman was this—he said they had the power which English authorities had, to promote a Bill; but that was simply a power enabling various Local Authorities interested to enter upon a Parliamentary contest which would probably cost Dublin something like £25,000; and, no matter who the victor might be, that would probably leave the state of affairs somewhat worse than it was already. It would largely benefit Parliamentary agents on this side of the Channel, but that would be all at the expense of the Irish people; and if the Government felt themselves called upon to introduce a Bill for the reform of the Government of London, the case was at least as strong for Governmental intervention in Dublin. There was a precedent in 1859 which could not be quoted in regard to London, and it would materially increase the difficulties of passing the London Government Bill if the Government convinced Irish Members that the best way to obtain redress for Irish grievances was to block the London Government Bill.

Mr. TREVELYAN said, he did not propose to deal at length with the remarks of the hon. Member for Carlow (Mr. Gray); but it was quite impossible, having regard to the public safety, that the control of the police in Ireland should be in any hands but those of the Chief Executive Authorities, and the time had not yet come when a change could be made in that respect. As Chief Secretary he could not enter into the question of taxation in Ireland; that was a matter for the Chancellor of Exchequer, and not for an Executive Officer; but as to the other subject, his opinion and that of the Government at large was that they could not entertain any proposition at that moment for making over the police or Constabulary in Ireland to any other management.

Mr. HEALY said, he thought £50,000 a-year was a pretty penny to pay for the police; and if they were not to have the control of the police they had better have that money back. It was all very well to put the matter off by avoiding any statement; but the people of Dublin would take the matter into their own hands. The English people would never see anything in any argument from Ireland, and he thought the best plan for the people of Dublin to adopt would be to refuse to pay this money. Were the Government prepared to remit this £50,000 a-year to the Corporation of Dublin? If the Corporation of Dublin had the control of the police in their own hands they could do the work with a small number of men and at a less cost. The Government gave police protection to some of their own people, and he thought every Nationalist in Dublin ought to claim police protection. If every man in Dublin claimed police protection the Government would require 400,000 policemen, and what would be the position of the Government then? This was really a very serious grievance, and the time would come, before very long, when the citizens of Dublin would refuse to have these police, and refuse to pay this money.

Mr. GRAY said, he did not wish to persist in his opposition; but he was satisfied the time would come when Dublin would no longer submit to this burden. They regarded this as a most injurious and most unjust system, and they would probably adopt the course of declining to pay this tax until they had the control of the police in their own hands.

Motion, by leave, *withdrawn.*

Original Question again proposed.

Motion made, and Question put,

"That a sum, not exceeding £35,094, be granted to Her Majesty, to complete the sum necessary to defray the Charge which will come in course of payment during the year ending on the 31st day of March 1885, for the Salaries and Expenses of the Commissioners of Police, the Police Courts, and the Metropolitan Police Establishment of Dublin."

The Committee *divided*:—Ayes 19; Noes 73: Majority 54.—(Div. List, No. 199.)

Original Question put, and *agreed to.*

Resolutions to be reported.

Mr. COURTNEY said, this left four Votes—the County Court Officers, the Constabulary, the Prisons, and the Reformatory and Industrial Schools. If they were to take the Reformatory and

Industrial Schools that would leave three to stand over till to-morrow. Of course, at that late hour (2.15 A.M.) he would not press another Vote if there was any strong objection to it. Hon. Members, however, must consider the period of the Session. Formally he would move the Reformatory Vote.

Motion made, and Question proposed,

"That a sum, not exceeding £51,944, be granted to Her Majesty, to complete the sum necessary to defray the Charge which will come in course of payment during the year ending on the 31st day of March 1885, for the Expenses of Reformatory and Industrial Schools in Ireland."

MR. ARTHUR O'CONNOR said, he really must ask the Government not to press the Vote at that hour of the night, for the reason that there was no question which was more interesting than the position of these industrial establishments in Ireland. All the elementary industrial schools required to be looked after and fostered in Ireland. Ireland, far more than other countries, required the development of its industrial schools, and the subject was one which deserved a very different sort of discussion from what they could expect to have at that hour of the night. He would, therefore, ask the Government to allow the Chairman to report Progress, and ask leave to sit again.

Resolutions to be reported *To-morrow.*

Committee also report Progress; to sit again *To-morrow.*

REVENUE, &c. BILL—[BILL 300.]

(*Mr. Courtney, Mr. Herbert Gladstone.*)

COMMITTEE.

Bill *considered* in Committee.

(In the Committee.)

Clauses 1 to 11, inclusive, *agreed to.*

Clause 12 (Licences for the sale of tobacco in railway carriages).

MR. WARTON said, that, in this clause, he saw something which struck him as requiring some explanation. The clause referred to tobacco and snuff, and the words he could not understand had reference to sale. They were "personal, mechanical, or otherwise." He could comprehend a "personal" sale; but what other means of selling could there be? How could there be a "mechanical" sale, and of what use could the words "or otherwise" be?

MR. COURTNEY confessed the words the hon. and learned Member had called attention to had rather puzzled him when the clauses were submitted to him by the Commissioners of Inland Revenue, who were responsible for them. The words referred to certain methods by which cigars or cigarettes might be sold—ingenious arrangements that persons could adopt in the belief that they were not personally selling these things. A penny was dropped into a box, and out came a cigar or cigarette.

MR. WARTON said, he must move that the words "or otherwise" be omitted, as they were sheer nonsense. He should have thought that every mode of selling cigars or cigarettes must be "personal;" at any rate, he was certain they must be either "personal" or "mechanical," therefore it was absurd to retain the words "or otherwise."

Amendment proposed, in page 6, line 34, to leave out the words "or otherwise."—(*Mr. Warton.*)

Question proposed, "That the words proposed to be left out stand part of the Clause."

THE SOLICITOR GENERAL (Sir FARRER HERSCHELL): The method may be electrical.

MR. WARTON: That is a sufficient answer. I shall not divide the Committee.

Amendment *negatived.*

Clause 13 (Payment of sum due to Exchequer from Post Office in respect of expenses for grant of Government annuities. 16 and 17 Vic. c. 45. 27 and 28 Vic. c. 43. 36 and 37 Vic. cc. 44, 67.)

MR. WARTON said, that in this clause it was cited that the fees were paid into the Exchequer. As a matter of fact, they were not paid into the Exchequer, notwithstanding that the Post Office made a profit of many millions every year.

MR. COURTNEY said, the question was merely one of the presenting of accounts between the two Departments—the Exchequer and the Post Office.

Clause *agreed to.*

Remaining clause *agreed to.*

Bill *reported,* without Amendment; to be read the third time *To-morrow.*

CRIMINAL LUNATICS BILL.—[Bill 295.]

(*Mr. Hibbert, Secretary Sir William Harcourt.*)

CONSIDERATION.

Bill, as amended, *considered.*

Mr. HIBBERT: It is desirable to send this Bill up to the House of Lords without delay. I would, therefore, propose that it be now read a third time.

Bill read the third time, and *passed.*

EAST INDIAN UNCLAIMED STOCKS BILL.—[Bill 269.]

(*Mr. J. K. Cross, Mr. Courtney.*)

SECOND READING.

Order for Second Reading read.

Motion made, and Question proposed, "That the Bill be now read a second time."—(*Mr. J. K. Cross.*)

Mr. WARTON wished to say just one word on this Bill. He had the other night ventured to ask a Question of the Government with regard to the measure in the absence of the hon. Gentleman in charge of it. It was understood, though it could not be stated by any Minister in the hon. Member's absence, that everything in reference to the East India Company was to be withdrawn from the measure?

Mr. J. K. CROSS: Yes; I said so the other night.

Motion *agreed to.*

Bill read a second time, and *committed* for *To-morrow.*

CHOLERA, &c. PROTECTION BILL.—[Bill 303.]

(*Mr. Gray, Mr. Dawson.*)

COMMITTEE.

Bill *considered* in Committee.

(In the Committee.)

Mr. GRAY: The Amendments in my name are simply for the purpose of improving some clauses—to which the hon. and learned Member for Stockport (Mr. Hopwood) objected—for applying the Act to Ireland. I hope the Government will not object.

Mr. COURTNEY: No.

Bill *reported;* as amended, to be considered *To-morrow.*

INFANTS BILL.—[Bill 308.]

(*Mr. Bryce, Mr. Horace Davey, Mr. Anderson, Mr. Staveley Hill.*)

CONSIDERATION.

Further proceeding on Consideration, as amended, *resumed.*

Question proposed,

"That the words 'while the marriage is subsisting, and before any decree or order for divorce or judicial separation has been made,'—(*Mr. Warton,*)—be inserted before the word 'each,' in page 1, line 12."

Mr. WARTON said, the first Amendment was in his name to page 1, line 12. He was glad that, through a fortunate accident the other evening, he was now enabled to move the Amendment with an argument which, he thought, would prevail with the hon. and learned Gentleman the Member for the Tower Hamlets (Mr. Bryce), who had taken a very strong objection to the Amendment, and one which he (Mr. Warton) felt the full force of at the time——

Mr. SPEAKER: Does the hon. and learned Member rise to move the Amendment on the Paper?

Mr. WARTON: Yes.

Mr. SPEAKER: Then the hon. and learned Member has lost his right to speak. A division took place on it on the last occasion.

Mr. WARTON: I should be glad to make an explanation, as the point is an important one.

Mr. SPEAKER: I am afraid the hon. and learned Member would be out of Order.

Mr. TOMLINSON said, he wished to say a few words in support of the Amendment——

Mr. BRYCE rose to Order. The hon. Member had already spoken.

Mr. SPEAKER: The hon. Member, having already spoken to the Amendment, will not be in Order in speaking again.

Question put.

The House *divided:*—Ayes 2; Noes 61: Majority 59.—(Div. List, No. 200.)

Mr. WARTON said, in his next Amendment of the clause he proposed to leave out the words "or persons," and he submitted it was rather important that this should be adopted, considering that in the 2nd clause the reference was to "guardian," in the singular; and he thought that to agree with the word "guardian," the word in this clause should be "person," not "persons." There might be too many "guardians," as each of the parents would have the rig of appointment of guardians by deed or will, and it would be better to have one guardian on behalf of each parent. On looking back to that part already passed, it would be observed that the survivor of the guardians might alone or jointly appoint a guardian—it did not say "guardians;" if it did, then in this place they should read "persons." He presumed there was some meaning in putting "guardian" in the singular, and supposed it was to have one guardian, while the other guardian would be the surviving parent. But, then, when the "hereinafter provided" was arrived at, it was found that any number of guardians might be appointed—there was no limit whatever. He really thought that to prevent too man guardians being appointed, persons who might quarrel about the training, the religion, or the estate of the infant, it would be far better to strike out "persons" and make the clause agree with the 2nd clause.

Amendment proposed, in page 1, line 13, to leave out the words "or persons."—(*Mr. Warton.*)

Question proposed, "That the words 'or persons' stand part of the Bill."

MR. BRYCE said, in Clause 2 any guardian included any possible guardian; and in this clause it was necessary to keep to the wording, because if only one guardian were appointed and he died there would be no guardian at all.

Question put, and *agreed to.*

MR. TOMLINSON said, since he had put down the first of the next two Amendments he had looked into the matter, and found it was possible that a male infant, if it became married, might become exempt from the control of its guardian. He, therefore, begged to move the Amendment standing next, and, perhaps, the shortest and simplest way to explain it would be to read the clause as it would stand with the Amendments put in—

"Each of the parents of any infant may by deed or will appoint any person or persons to be guardian or guardians of such infant after the death of the survivor of such parents; and where guardians are so appointed by both parents they shall act jointly, &c."

In line 15, he proposed to insert "where," instead of "the guardian or." It was necessary to make such an alteration in order to make sense of the clause, for if the clause remained as it stood each parent might appoint a guardian; and what was meant was that these guardians should act jointly with each other, and not with any other guardians.

Amendment proposed, in page 1, line 15, to leave out the words "the guardian or," and insert the word "where." —(*Mr. Tomlinson.*)

Question proposed, "That the words 'the guardian or' stand part of the Bill."

MR. BRYCE said, he was willing to agree to this Amendment.

Amendment *agreed to.*

Amendment proposed, in page 1, line 15, after the word "guardians," to insert the word "are."—(*Mr. Tomlinson.*)

Amendment *agreed to.*

Amendment proposed, in page 1, line 16, after the word "appointed," to insert the words "by both parents they." —(*Mr. Tomlinson.*)

Amendment *agreed to.*

Amendment proposed, in page 1, line 16, to leave out from "with" to end of sub-section."—(*Mr. Tomlinson.*)

Amendment *agreed to.*

MR. BRYCE said, the next Amendment was merely a matter of drafting. He had omitted to mention an old Irish Act.

Amendment proposed, in page 2, line 9, after the word "has," to insert the words "in England."—(*Mr. Bryce.*)

MR. WARTON said, he was not acquainted with this old Act of the Irish Parliament; but he would ask the hon. and learned Member if there was any section corresponding to that in the Act of Charles II. for England?

MR. BRYCE said, the Acts were just the same.

Amendment *agreed to.*

MR. BRYCE said, the next Amendments were consequential on that just accepted.

Amendment proposed,

In page 2, line 10, after the words "twenty-four," to insert the words "or in Ireland under the Act of the Irish Parliament, fourteen and fifteen, Charles the Second, chapter nineteen."—(*Mr. Bryce.*)

MR. WARTON said, he presumed that the Section 6 mentioned was the same as Section 8 of the English Act.

MR. BRYCE assented.

Amendment *agreed to.*

Amendment proposed,

In Schedule, page 3, line 8, insert—"14 and 15 Charles 2, c. 19.—An Act for taking away the Court of Wards and Liveries and Tenures in Capite, and by Knights' Service. Section six."

Amendment *agreed to.*

MR. BRYCE said, he hoped the House would be kind enough to allow him to take the third reading now.

MR. WARTON rose to Order. He wished to know, in reference to the request made, whether the expression generally used, "the permission of the House," meant in such a case the unanimous wish of the House, or whether the Question could be put if any Member or Members objected?

MR. SPEAKER: It does not mean the unanimity of the House, but the general pleasure of the House.

Bill read the third time, and *passed.*

MOTIONS.

——o——

VAGRANTS.

Return *ordered*, "of the number of Vagrants relieved in each Union in England and Wales, the Unions being arranged in order of Union Counties, on the first Wednesday in each of the first six months of the year 1884, with the totals for the period of six months in the year for each Union and each Union County, together with totals in respect of each Union County, and of England and Wales for each day included in the Return (in continuation of Parliamentary Paper, No. 86, of the present Session)."—(*Mr. R. H. Paget.*)

HOUSE OF COMMONS (COUNTS-OUT).

Return *ordered*, "of the number of times the House has been counted out during each Session of the present Parliament, specifying the day and the hour at which it was counted out, and whether after a Morning Sitting or not."—(*Mr. Monk.*)

RATING OF THE METROPOLIS.

Return *ordered*, "with respect to each parish in the Metropolis, of the Population in 1881; the number of Inhabited Houses in 1881; the rateable value according to the Valuation Lists in force on the 6th day of April 1883; the several Rates made by the Rating Authority during the year ending on the 25th day of March 1884, &c. (in continuation of Parliamentary Paper, No. 87, of the present Session)."—(*Mr. Sydney Buxton.*)

IRISH LAND ACT (ORDERS).

Return *ordered*, "of the number of Orders received by each Union in Ireland under Clause 19 of the Land Act of 1881, and the action taken in each case up to the 30th day of June 1884, as under:—Name of Union; number of Orders received; number of houses built or repaired voluntarily; number of proceedings taken in case of default; number of Orders made by magistrates."—(*Colonel Colthurst.*)

CHANCERY EXAMINERS' OFFICE.

Committee to consider of the payment, out of moneys provided by Parliament, of any compensation that may be granted, under any Act of the present Session of Parliament, to persons holding the office of sworn clerk to the late Chancery Examiners on the abolition of that office (Queen's *Recommendation* signified), *To-morrow.*

NAVY AND ARMY EXPENDITURE, 1882-3.

Considered in Committee.

(In the Committee.)

1. *Resolved*, That it appears by the Navy Appropriation Account for the year ended the 31st March 1883, as follows, viz.:—

(a.) That the sums expended for certain Navy Services exceeded the Grants for those Services, and that the deficits on such Grants amounted together to £1,427,161 4*s.* 0*d.*, as shown in column (a) of the Schedule hereto appended;

(b.) That the sums received in respect of Appropriations in Aid of the Grants for certain Services fell short of the sums estimated, and that such deficiencies amounted together to £1,264 17*s.* 4*d.* as shown in column (b) of the said appended Schedule;

(c.) That the sums received in respect of Appropriations in Aid of the Grants for certain Services exceeded the amounts estimated by the total sum of £48,481 6*s.* 8*d.* as shown in column (c) of the said appended Schedule;

(d.) That surpluses arose on the Grants for certain Services, and that such surpluses amounted together to £150,636 0*s.* 6*d.* as shown in column (d) of the said appended Schedule.

2. *Resolved,* That to provide in part for the first two above-mentioned sums (a) and (b), amounting together to £1,428,426 1*s.* 4*d.* the Commissioners of Her Majesty's Treasury have temporarily authorised the application of the fourth above-mentioned sum (d) of £150,636 0*s.* 6*d.* and of £1,264 17*s.* 4*d.* out of the third above-mentioned sum (c) of £48,481 6*s.* 8*d.*

3. *Resolved,* That the application of such sums be sanctioned.

SCHEDULE.

No.	Navy Services, 1882-3, Votes.	(a) Deficits on Votes.			(b) Deficiencies of Appropriations in Aid.			(c) Excess of Appropriations in Aid.			(d) Surpluses on Vote.		
		£	s.	d.	£	s.	d.	£	s.	d.	£	s.	d.
1 ..	Wages, &c. to Seamen and Marines ..	..			..			1,508	12	1	19,969	15	3
2 ..	Victuals and Clothing for ditto	57,340	11	4	..			16,484	15	3			
3 ..	Admiralty Office ..	..			666	11	8	..			2,175	7	0
4 ..	Coast Guard Service and Naval Reserve ..	..			..			13	0	10	3,100	11	10
5 ..	Scientific Branch ..	..			..			1,607	17	0	8,097	16	2
6 ..	Dockyards and Naval Yards, &c.	121,174	5	2	..			160	16	5			
7 ..	Victualling Yards, &c...	413	6	0	568	12	2						
8 ..	Medical Establishments, &c.	1,401	3	9	12	6	10						
9 ..	Marine Divisions ..	..			17	6	8	..			1,168	7	[illegible]
10 Sec. 1 ..	Naval Stores	91,394	4	5	..			160	16	6			
10 Sec. 2 ..	Machinery, Ships built by Contract, &c. ..	..			..			6	14	0	76,197	11	9
11 ..	New Works, Buildings, and Repairs ..	..			..			17,581	11	9	31,395	13	4
12 ..	Medicines and Medical Stores	..			..			355	19	0	2,663	10	7
13 ..	Martial Law, &c. ..	764	6	0	..			9	16	7			
14 ..	Miscellaneous Services..	23,998	16	2	..			444	4	3			
15 ..	Half Pay, &c. ..	..			..			96	4	4	4,988	0	5
16 Sec. 1 ..	Military Pensions and Allowances.. ..	..			..			10	13	5	879	6	2
16 Sec. 2 ..	Civil Pensions and Allowances	463	5	6	..			28	6	11			
17 ..	Army Department—Conveyance of Troops ..	1,126,338	3	9	..			10,011	18	4			
	Amount written off as irrecoverable ..	3,873	1	11									
		1,427,161	4	0	1,264	17	4	48,481	6	8	150,636	0	6
		£1,428,426	1	4									
	Amount authorised to be applied towards making good deficiencies ..	151,900	17	10									
	Deficit chargeable to the Vote of Credit Forces in the Mediterranean	£1,276,525	3	6									

4. *Resolved*, That it appears by the Army Appropriation Account for the year ended 31st March 1883, as follows, viz:—

(a.) That the sums expended for certain Army Services exceeded the Grants for those Services, and that the deficits on such Grants amounted together to £934,418 5*s.* 7*d.* as shown in column (a) of the Schedule hereto appended;

(b.) That the sums received in respect of Appropriations in Aid of the Grants for certain Services fell short of the sums estimated, and that such deficiencies amounted together to £36,885 0*s.* 2*d.* as shown in column (b) of the said appended Schedule;

(c.) That the sums received in respect of Appropriations in Aid of the Grants for certain other Services exceeded the amounts estimated by the total sum of £55,182 9*s.* 1*d.* as shown in column (c) of the said appended Schedule;

(d.) That surpluses arose on the Grants for certain Services, and that such surpluses amounted together to £81,094 8*s.* 3*d.* as shown in column (d) of the said appended Schedule.

5. *Resolved*, That to provide in part for the first two above-mentioned sums (a) and (b), amounting together to £971,303 5*s.* 9*d.* the Commissioners of Her Majesty's Treasury have temporarily authorised the application of the fourth above-mentioned sum (d) of £81,094 8*s.* 3*d.* and of £36,885 0*s.* 2*d.* out of the third above-mentioned sums of £55,182 9*s.* 1*d.*

6. *Resolved*, That the application of such sums be sanctioned.

SCHEDULE.

Votes.	Army Services, 1882 - 3, Votes.	(a) Deficits on Votes.			(b) Deficiency of Rects. below Estimate.			(c.) Surplus of Receipts above Estimate.			(d.) Surpluses on Votes.		
		£	s.	d.	£	s.	d.	£	s.	d.	£	s.	d.
1	Pay of the General Staff, Regimental Pay and Allowances, and other Charges	164,975	17	2	..			1,380	0	9			
2	Divine Service	3,637	9	8	11	0	8						
3	Administration of Military Law..	..			..			291	11	4	1,351	0	11
4	Medical Establishment and Services	14,720	1	11	..			318	10	4			
5	Militia Pay and Allowances	..			..			5,044	13	7	7,858	10	3
6	Yeomanry Cavalry ..	..			..			..			2,381	19	10
7	Volunteer Corps ..	..			..			4	10	5	17,252	17	9
8	Army Reserve Force (including Enrolled Pensioners)	..			..			491	2	9	1,980	4	2
9	Commissariat, Transport, and Ordnance Store Establishments, Wages, &c.	63,745	7	11	..			417	13	10			
10	Provisions, Forage, Fuel and Light, Transport, &c.	283,672	10	10	..			27,165	4	10			
11	Clothing Establishments, Services, and Supplies..	211,346	14	9	..			2,759	16	6			
12	Supply, Manufacture, and Repair of Warlike and other Stores for Land and Sea Service ..	116,953	12	3	25,241	0	8						
13	Superintending Establishments of and Expenditure for Works, Buildings, and Repairs at Home and Abroad ..	..			..			16,358	1	10	16,618	0	1
14	Establishments for Military Education	..			6,949	13	7	..			10,876	3	1
15	Miscellaneous Effective Services	7,522	16	10	875	18	7						
	Carried forward ..	869,574	11	4	33,077	13	6	54,231	6	2	58,318	15	11

SCHEDULE—*continued.*

Votes.	Army Services, 1882-3, Votes.	(a) Deficits on Votes.			(b) Deficiency of Recta. below Estimate.			(c) Surplus of Receipts above Estimate.			(d) Surpluses on Votes.		
		£	*s.*	*d.*	£	*s.*	*d.*	£	*s.*	*d.*	£	*s.*	*d.*
	Brought forward ..	869,574	11	4	33,077	13	6	54,231	6	2	58,318	16	1
16	War Office	3,593	10	1	..			49	9	0			
17	Rewards for Distinguished Services, &c.	..			..			288	16	10	3,247	1	6
18	Half Pay	..			..			7	10	0	14,188	3	2
19	Retired Full Pay, Retired Pay, Pensions and Gratuities, &c. including Payments allowed by Army Purchase Commissioners..	22,540	14	6	3,807	6	8						
20	Widows' Pensions ..	1,311	3	1									
21	Pensions for Wounds ..	1,656	7	8									
22	Chelsea and Kilmainham Hospitals	..			..			47	11	0	667	16	3
23	Out-Pensions	30,796	7	3	..			385	15	8			
24	Superannuation Allowances	..			..			172	0	5	2,231	12	4
25	Militia, Yeomanry Cavalry, and Volunteer Forces, Retired Pay	..			..			..			2,440	18	11
	Amount written off as irrecoverable	4,945	11	8									
		934,418	5	7	36,885	0	2	55,182	9	1	81,094	8	3

	£	*s.*	*d.*
	£971,303	5	9
Amount authorised to be applied towards making good deficiencies ..	117,979	8	5
Deficit chargeable to the Vote of Credit Forces in the Mediterranean ..	£853,323	17	4

Resolutions to be reported *To-morrow.*

House adjourned at five minutes after Three o'clock.

HOUSE OF LORDS,

Friday, 1*st August*, 1884.

MINUTES.]—PUBLIC BILLS—*First Reading*—Infants* (237); Public Health (Ireland) (Districts) * (238); Criminal Lunatics * (239).

Second Reading—Expiring Laws Continuance * (236); Metropolitan Asylums Board (Borrowing Powers)* (234).

Committee—Report—Prisons* (213); Turnpike Acts Continuance* (206); Public Works Loans* (221); Metropolitan Board of Works (Money) * (222).

Report—Trusts (Scotland)* (209).

Third Reading—Contagious Diseases (Animals) Act, 1878 (Districts)* (205), and *passed.*

COLONIAL NAVAL DEFENCE ACT, 1865 —COLONIAL WAR VESSELS.

QUESTION.

THE EARL OF ASHBURNHAM asked the First Lord of the Admiralty, Whether an Order in Council under Section 6. of the Colonial Naval Defence Act, 1865, giving to the Victorian vessels of war *Victoria*, *Albert*, and *Childers* the status of ships of the Royal Navy, was issued by Her Majesty under his advice, and on conditions specified by him; whether the Law Officers of the Crown have advised the Admiralty that such vessels, on being placed at Her Majesty's disposal, are to be deemed to all intents vessels of war of the Royal Navy, and would be entitled to fly the white ensign; whether the Government of Victoria, through its Agent General, did not place the vessels in question at Her Majesty's disposal on the 15th of last January; whether the naval officer in command at Gibraltar was instructed by the Admiralty to order the commandant of these vessels to haul down the white ensign when he arrived there on his way to the Red Sea, on the ground that its assumption was premature; whether, after the Council held on the 4th of March, the Lords of the Admiralty requested the Secretary of State for the Colonies to move the Agent General for Victoria to communicate with the commandant by telegraph, instructing him to proceed without delay to Suakin, and place the Colonial Squadron at Admiral Hewett's disposal; whether, this having been done, and the vessels having arrived at Suakin, after the battle of the 13th of March, Admiral Hewett informed the commandant that they would not now be required and might proceed to Melbourne, at the same time expressing his thanks for their presence at Suakin; whether the Admiralty have since declared that they never in any way accepted the services of the vessels, that the Order in Council has conferred no status upon them as ships of the Royal Navy, and have refused to instruct the naval officers in command at Ceylon and on the Australian station to authorize them to resume the white ensign; and if, in view of the obviously inoperative character of an Act intended to encourage the Colonies to establish local squadrons to co-operate with the Royal Navy, he will lay the correspondence with the Agent General for Victoria and the Colonial Office on the Table, with a view to its amendment? In putting the Question as he had, he thought he had sufficient reason to think that, in their conduct in this matter, the Government seemed to show an indifference to the interests of the Empire, which contrasted in a strange manner with their devotion to Party politics. They desired a great deal more to advance those politics than to do anything that might increase the well-being of the Colonies as regarded their relations with the Mother Country.

THE EARL OF NORTHBROOK, in reply, said, he should not attempt to follow the last observation of the noble Earl opposite (the Earl of Ashburnham), but would confine himself to the Question put to him; and, in the first place, he begged to assure the noble Earl and their Lordships generally that it was entirely a misapprehension to suppose that the Board of Admiralty, or any naval officer in any part of the world, for a single moment intended to act with any discourtesy to the Colonial Government of Victoria, or in any way to discourage them in their most admirable efforts to supply themselves with ships of war. Ever since they took up this question of providing naval forces, there was nothing that the Board of Admiralty could do that they had not done to assist them in every way; and they had lent them some of their best officers. He thought he had better give the facts of the case in his own way, without reference to the form in which the Question was put. Last year the Victorian Government built in this country three vessels—*Victoria*, a gun vessel; *Albert*, a gunboat; *Childers*, a torpedo vessel. These vessels were intended to be vessels of war. In dealing with vessels of this kind, the Board of Admiralty could only act according to law, and it was quite out of the power of the Admiralty to create Colonial vessels of war. The law on the point was contained in the Colonial Naval Defence Act, 1865, which, in the 3rd section gave power to a Colony to establish, maintain, and use a vessel or vessels of war, subject to such conditions as Her Majesty in Council might from time to time approve. Their Lordships would see that to constitute a vessel built by a Colony a ship of war it was indispensable that there should be an Order in Council. As respected the ensign borne by these vessels, that was determined by the Queen's Regulations and Admiralty Instructions which were issued in 1879, which laid it down that Colonial vessels of war should wear a blue ensign and pendant. In January last the Agent General of Victoria applied to the Board of Admiralty for an Order in Council to place these vessels under another section of the Act—the 6th section. That section authorized the Admiralty to accept any offer made by a Colony to place at their disposal any vessels of war, and such vessels would be deemed vessels of the Royal Navy. When this application was made the Admiralty considered the matter, and they thought it desirable to consult the Law Officers of the Crown, and they advised that the 6th section only authorized the Crown to accept, for Imperial purposes, vessels already legally existing as Colonial ships of war. It was clear, therefore, that a *status* must first be obtained under Section 3 before the vessels could come under Section 6, and that there must be an Order in Council before the Admiralty could accept their services. The Colonial Government had not applied for this Order in Council under Section 3, and, therefore, the services of the vessels could not be accepted under Section 6. In the meantime, the vessels had gone to sea, and, by some misapprehension, they flew the white ensign and pendant as ships of war in Her Majesty's Service. It therefore became necessary for the officer at Gibraltar to ask by what authority that was done, and he asked that by orders from home. There was nothing approaching an insult, and everything was done in the most courteous manner. The Instructions laid down the ensign to be borne by Colonial vessels of war. Nothing could be more courteous than the way in which the communication was made. As soon as the defect in the position of these vessels was communicated to the Victorian Government, application was made for an Order in Council to constitute these vessels vessels of war, and application was, at the same time, made by Her Majesty for the authority necessary, under the 6th section, to enable the Admiralty to accept the services of these ships. Both Governments, therefore, took immediate steps to remedy the defect and to allow these vessels, if necessary, to be employed as Her Majesty's vessels. This Order was passed on the 4th of March; but, by that time, the vessels had left the country, and, in the meantime, the Agent General for Victoria offered their services in the Red Sea. It was then the time when operations were going on in the Suez Canal; and the Colonial Government was desirous, if their services were required, that they should be offered. An answer was at once given to the Agent General, requesting him to instruct the officer commanding the vessels to communicate with Sir William Hewett on their arrival, so that, if it was found they were in want of vessels in the Red Sea, he might accept the services of those vessels. They arrived in the Red Sea, and when they arrived there happened to be plenty of Her Majesty's ships there for all purposes necessary, for the House would, of course, recollect that Osman Digna had no ships, and, therefore, there were absolutely no naval services to perform, so they proceeded on their voyage to Australia. After that, the Agent General of Victoria made a communication to the Government, and inquired if the vessels might fly the white ensign and pendant. The Government were absolutely bound by law in the matter. The proper ensign and pendant of these vessels was blue, with the badge of the Colony. He might add, that this distinctive flag for Colonial vessels of war had been communicated to all foreign nations. He could not understand that there could be any misapprehension in this matter as soon as the somewhat complicated legal questions were explained. He could assure the noble Earl opposite that there had not been, from the first, the very slightest idea of casting any slur of any kind or sort upon the Victorian ships; the Admiralty had simply followed the Act of Parliament. There was nothing they felt a greater interest in, or greater concern for, than to encourage the Colonies of Australia to proceed in the patriotic and laudable course they were following now of providing themselves with an efficient Navy.

Lord BRABOURNE said, that he never imagined that any slur was intended to be cast upon the Victorian Government; but, in matters of such delicacy and importance, the greatest care ought to be taken to avoid even the slightest misunderstanding arising in the minds of the Colonists. He was, therefore, glad the question had been at once brought before Parliament by his noble Friend (the Earl of Ashburnham), so that it had not had time to fester into a grievance painful to both sides. Without going into the legal authorities of the question, the explanation was satisfactory. In future, it would be desirable, in order to prevent any misunderstanding, pains should be taken to ascertain what the Order in Council provided for.

After some remarks from the Earl of Wemyss,

The Earl of ASHBURNHAM said, that he was very well satisfied, and he had no doubt that the Colonial Government would be equally satisfied, with the discussion that had taken place. He would, however, point out to the noble Earl opposite (the Earl of Northbrook) that he had omitted to answer the concluding paragraph of the Question.

THE EARL OF NORTHBROOK said, it would not be well to lay the Correspondence upon the Table, as it contained reference to other matters.

THE NEW PUBLIC OFFICES — THE DESIGNS FOR NEW ADMIRALTY AND WAR OFFICE.

QUESTION. OBSERVATIONS.

THE EARL OF WEMYSS asked Her Majesty's Government, If they will cause a model of the selected design for the War Office and Admiralty to be made and publicly exhibited? He asked for this because the only way of judging of the effect of a building was from a model. Drawings, as anyone conversant with such matters well knew, were very deceptive. Further, in this case, it was necessary that the new building should harmonize with the Horse Guards and its surroundings; and this could only properly be judged of by having the whole of the buildings, old as well as new, shown upon the model. Now, he must again ask his noble Friend what had become of the large model that, in Sir Henry Layard's time, had been made of all that part of London where our public buildings and offices were situated, with a view to showing upon it any new building or alteration it was proposed to erect or make? His noble Friend had informed him, on two previous occasions, that this model, which was as large as the Table in the centre of their Lordships' House, could not be found; but he hoped further search for it had proved successful, and that they might hope to see it utilized on this occasion. As a matter of fact, the designs for the new Admiralty and War Office were being exhibited in Spring Gardens to Members of both Houses of Parliament; but he thought they should be exhibited in some public place, in order that all those persons who took an interest in the matter might inspect them, and be able to offer their criticisms.

VISCOUNT BARRINGTON asked, with reference to Mr. Pearson's plans for the restoration of Westminster Hall, whether the flying buttresses would be obscured? They were of great interest; and, as shown in the plans now being exhibited, he was afraid they would be almost entirely concealed. He therefore wished to know whether those plans had been definitely adopted?

LORD SUDELEY, in reply, said, that his right hon. Friend the First Commissioner of Works was, at present, considering the advisability of having a model made to represent the plans of the new public buildings, which had been selected by the judges. It was a question how far that model should be made on the present scale of drawings; but the First Commissioner hoped to be able to construct a model during the autumn. The old model plan, showing both buildings and sites, that had been made many years ago, when Mr. Layard was in Office, when the new Public Offices were being considered, and which had the Horse Guards and many other public buildings shown upon it, was on a very small scale, although it covered a large area. If the proposal made by the noble Earl opposite (the Earl of Wemyss) was adopted, and a model constructed of the new buildings, to place upon it, in lieu of the old designs, it would undoubtedly show its position as respected the Horse Guards, but only on a very small scale. That would necessitate reducing considerably the scale of the present drawings, and it was a question whether, if the expense was to be incurred, it would not be better expended on a large scale model, without reference to the old ground plan model. That old model, which had been made some years ago, and which was supposed to have been lost, had only been mislaid, having been discovered at South Kensington, where it still remained. It would be preserved, and would be placed in some convenient room; and if the noble Earl would meet the First Commissioner when it was ready, he would be very happy to consider with him how his suggestion could best be carried out. As to the point to which the noble Earl had alluded, as to the drawings being thrown open for public inspection, he belived that next week there would be no difficulty in people seeing them; but this week it had been limited to Members of both Houses, and the various societies. In reply to the noble Viscount opposite (Viscount Barrington), he had only to say that the First Commissioner of Works had already stated, in "another place," that the general plan of Mr. Pearson for restoring the West front of Westminster Hall had been definitely decided on, and a small Vote had been submitted, so that the work might be commenced this autumn. It was most desirable that the old Norman wall should not be exposed to another winter. There were some minor points still left open, and among these the question of raising the towers at the North end, and whether the corridor along the West front should be an open one or not. Mr. Pearson attached much importance to its being open, and used for carriages; but it was possible that it might be adviseable to use it as a gallery for rooms. No money would be, however, asked for the purpose this year. The flying buttresses would not be hid. The proposed gallery and cloister would be inside the buttresses, which would stand out six feet, and also be visible above the gallery.

THE EARL OF WEMYSS said, he was greatly obliged to the noble Lord and the First Commissioner of Works for their consideration.

REPRESENTATION OF THE PEOPLE BILL.

NOTICE OF QUESTION.

THE EARL OF REDESDALE (CHAIRMAN of COMMITTEES): My Lords, I beg to give Notice that on Tuesday I shall ask, Whether it is the intention of the Government, in accordance with the strongly expressed wish of this House, and the precedents of other Reform Bills, to introduce proper provisions for redistribution in the Representation of the People Bill in the next Session of Parliament?

House adjourned at half past Five o'clock, to Monday next, a quarter before Eleven o'clock.

HOUSE OF COMMONS,

Friday, 1st August, 1884.

MINUTES.]—SELECT COMMITTEE—*Report*—Agricultural Labourers (Ireland) [No. 317].

SUPPLY—*considered in Committee*—CIVIL SERVICE ESTIMATES—CLASS III.—LAW AND JUSTICE—Votes 27, 30, and 31—CLASS IV.—EDUCATION, SCIENCE, AND ART—Votes 4 to 7.

Resolutions [July 31] *reported.*

PUBLIC BILLS—*Committee—Report* — Supreme Court of Judicature Amendment [307].

Third Reading — Revenue, &c.* [300], and *passed.*

Withdrawn—East Indian Unclaimed Stocks* [269.]

PRIVATE BUSINESS.

PARLIAMENT—STANDING ORDERS—AMENDMENTS.

MR. HOLMS said, he proposed, at the request of the hon. Gentleman the Chairman of Ways and Means (Sir Arthur Otway), to move a series of alterations in reference to the Standing Orders applicable to Private Bills. He would propose, in the first instance, to move, in Standing Order No. 1, 2nd Class, after "Street," to insert—"Subway, to be used for the conveyance of passengers, animals, or goods, in carriages, or trucks, drawn or propelled on rails." The alterations were merely formal.

Standing Order, No. 1, 2nd Class, read.

Amendment proposed to the said Standing Order, by inserting, after the word "street," the words—

"Subway, to be used for the conveyance of passengers, animals, or goods, in carriages, or trucks, drawn or propelled on rails."—(*Mr. Holms.*)

Question proposed, "That those words be there inserted."

SIR EDWARD WATKIN said, he would make an appeal to the hon. Gentleman (Mr. Holms) to allow a little more time for the consideration of the proposed Amendment of the Standing Orders. It was altogether impossible for hon. Members who were in attendance in their places until 3 or 4 o'clock in the morning to appear in the House again at half-past 3 in the afternoon to consider a series of proposals which, for aught they knew, might effect an entire revolution in the existing Standing Orders relating to Private Business. He hoped the hon. Gentleman would not object to a postponement of the discussion, which, under the circumstances, was a most reasonable request.

MR. WARTON said, he supported the appeal of the hon. Baronet the Member for Hythe (Sir Edward Watkin). He

(Mr. Warton) was altogether opposed to undue haste in legislation. He was quite willing to accept the statement of the hon. Gentleman (Mr. Holms) that these alterations were only of a formal character; but even formal things were sometimes improper. He scarcely thought it was proper to lay before the House proposals for the wholesale alteration of the Standing Orders without even allowing as much as a day for considering their effect. If the hon. Member for Hythe would divide the House against the consideration of these Amendments now, he (Mr. Warton) would support him.

SIR EDWARD WATKIN said, he wished to know whether, as the further proceeding with the proposals of the hon. Member for Hackney (Mr. Holms) was objected to, it must not, as a matter of necessity, stand over?

MR. SPEAKER: These proposals do not come under the Standing Orders which apply to opposed Private Bills.

SIR EDWARD WATKIN said, that, under those circumstances, he would join the hon. and learned Member for Bridport (Mr. Warton) in going to a Division if necessary. He hoped, however, that the hon. Member for Hackney (Mr. Holms) would not force the House to take such a course.

SIR CHARLES W. DILKE said, that one part of the proposed alterations stood in his name; and it had reference to artizans' and labourers' dwellings. The object was simply to render operative certain Rules which had been passed by the House of Lords on the Motion of Lord Salisbury.

MR. WARTON rose to Order. He desired to know whether the right hon. Baronet was in Order in referring to a Motion which he had down upon the Paper, which related to another subject, and did not apply at all to the Motion they were now discussing?

MR. SPEAKER: I apprehend that all the new Standing Orders hang one upon another in such connection that it would be for the convenience of the House if the right hon. Gentleman were to state his view of the matter.

SIR CHARLES W. DILKE said, he had been about to state that the Motion relating to the Standing Orders, which appeared in his name upon the Paper, especially those which applied to artizans' and labourers' dwellings, were suggested, after a great deal of evidence had been given on the subject, by the senior Member for Oldham (Mr. Hibbert). They were put in shape, in the first place, by his hon. Friend; but they had been a good deal amended, in accordance with suggestions made by Lord Salisbury. The agents for Private Bills had been seen by Lord Salisbury on the subject, and these proposals had already been assented to by the House of Lords without a Division.

SIR EDWARD WATKIN said, he wished to say one word by way of explanation. The Standing Orders the right hon. Gentleman (Sir Charles W. Dilke) had spoken of—those relating to workmen's dwellings—were very good Standing Orders, and he was quite prepared to support them. But that was not the point. The point was whether it was really business to lay upon the Table of the House, at half-past 3 in the afternoon, something which had not been seen by any one of the various interests affected, and to force it to a decision? These Standing Orders affected many hundreds of millions of money vested in tramways and railways, and all he asked for was delay, so that the public might have an opportunity of knowing what the nature of the proposals was.

LORD RANDOLPH CHURCHILL said, he trusted the House would not listen to the remarks of the hon. Baronet the Member for Hythe (Sir Edward Watkin). These Standing Orders had now been before the public for a considerable time, and an ample opportunity had been afforded to the railway interest, which the hon. Member represented, to the prejudice of the public, for considering what effect they would be likely to have. They had already been before the House of Lords, and might have been opposed there, if necessary. It was perfectly clear that if the railway interest was likely to be affected in any way by these Standing Orders, they would have had a lively opposition from the hon. Baronet the Member for Hythe; but the House had never shown any disposition, in matters of this kind, to be in the smallest degree affected by the opinions which might be entertained by the hon. Baronet. He (Lord Randolph Churchill), therefore, hoped the House would not listen to the insidious proposal of the hon. Baronet to obstruct and delay the formal carrying of these proposals, which would have a most beneficial effect upon the interests of the working classes.

Sir EDWARD WATKIN said, he wished to explain that he had not opposed the proposals of the hon. Member for Hackney (Mr. Holms) in any way.

Lord RANDOLPH CHURCHILL said, he did not know that the hon. Baronet was entitled to address the House twice.

Mr. SPEAKER: The hon. Baronet, having already spoken, has forfeited his right to speak again.

Mr. HOLMS said, the matter had been very fully considered by the House of Lords. During the present Session certain Bills had been passed, which permitted subways to be used as railways; and the only object of these Standing Orders was to explain clearly to the public that that was intended. He did not think there was much necessity for any protracted deliberation.

Question put, and *agreed to;* words *inserted* accordingly.

Standing Order No. 6 read.

Amendment proposed, to add at the end thereof, the words—

"The Notices shall also state what power it is intended to employ for moving carriages or trucks upon the Tramway."—(*Mr. Holms.*)

Question proposed, "That those words be there added."

Mr. WARTON said, that as there was now another question before the House, the noble Lord the Member for Woodstock (Lord Randolph Churchill) would not be entitled to object to him, on the ground that he was speaking twice on the same question. He had no personal interest in the matter. His only interest was in seeing the Business of the House duly conducted; and he thought that fairytime should be afforded for the consideration of any proposal, so that the House might really know what they were about. Hon. Members who had not got the Standing Orders before them would not have the slightest idea what the effect of these alterations might be. He did not say a word against the proposals; they might all of them be very excellent; they might do things that were probably for the good of the general public; but he did not think that was enough to justify the House in passing these wholesale Amendments without having first been afforded adequate time for considering their effect.

Sir EDWARD WATKIN said, he wished to say a word, as there was now another Motion before the House. It was altogether inaccurate to say that every hon. Member must know the nature and effect of the alteration now proposed. The Amendment now under consideration was one which had as yet been before nobody, and hitherto there had been no discussion upon it. Of course, the Standing Orders in relation to artizans and labourers' dwellings had been before the public, and its effect was obvious and well known to everybody. This Standing Order was not in the same position, and it was only a reasonable request that its consideration should be postponed. In making that request, he was certainly not disposed to be intimidated by the would-be Leader and *enfant terrible* of the Conservative Party.

Mr. HOLMS said, he would only say in support of the Motion that its only object was to make the Standing Order perfectly clear.

Sir R. ASSHETON CROSS said, he thought it would have been better to postpone the consideration of these proposals until Monday.

Question put, and *agreed to;* words *added* accordingly.

Remaining Amendments *agreed to.*

Ordered, That the said Orders be Standing Orders of this House.

QUESTIONS.

IRELAND — THE QUEEN'S COLLEGE, GALWAY—MR. CHARLES GEISSLER, PROFESSOR OF MODERN LANGUAGES.

Mr. HEALY asked the Chief Secretary to the Lord Lieutenant of Ireland, What academic degree did Mr. Charles Geissler hold when he was appointed to the Chair of Modern Languages, in Queen's College, Galway; what steps did the authorities of Queen's College, Galway, and those responsible for the appointments in the Queen's Colleges, take to ascertain whether Mr. Charles Geissler was properly qualified to fulfil the duties of a Professor in Modern

Languages, and whether the academic degree assumed by Mr. Charles Geissler was a bona fide degree; in what University did Mr. Charles Geissler graduate and take the degree of Doctor in Philology; and were any documents submitted to the President of Queen's College, Galway, showing that Mr. Charles Geissler was not a bona fide Doctor in Philology?

MR. TREVELYAN: Mr. Geissler, when appointed to the Chair of Modern Languages, held the degree of Doctor of Philology in the University of Gottingen. He was appointed to the Professorship at Galway in November, 1868, by the then Government, after consultation with the late President of the College, and presumably after full consideration of his testimonials. The present President, Dr. Moffatt, informs me that he is aware that his Predecessor instituted most careful inquiries as to Dr. Geissler's abilities and character, and that he was assured by some of the highest authorities in Ireland, among whom were the late Rev. Dr. Todd, S.F.T.C.D., the late Dr. Lottner, and Professor Meisner, of Queen's College, Belfast, and others, that he was eminently qualified for the Chair of Modern Languages, the testimony of these gentlemen in his favour being exceptionally strong. Many years ago a letter was brought under the notice of the late President and the Council of the College, which stated that Professor Geissler had not obtained the degree he claimed. This allegation was carefully investigated at the time by the late President, who subsequently stated that the Professor had submitted documents to him which proved that he had taken the degree.

MR. HEALY asked whether inquiries had been made at Gottingen?

MR. TREVELYAN said, he was not aware. Professor Geissler was at present abroad.

THE MAGISTRACY (IRELAND)—THE KING'S CO. AND CO. TIPPERARY.

MR. KENNY asked the Chief Secretary to the Lord Lieutenant of Ireland, Whether the names of several gentlemen resident in Roscrea and its vicinity were recommended by the priests and people of the district to the Lord Chancellor as suitable for the Commission of the Peace; and, if any action has yet been taken with regard to their appointment thereto?

MR. TREVELYAN: The Lord Chancellor informs me that such representations have been received, and that he has been in correspondence thereon with the Lieutenants of the King's County and the county of Tipperary with respect to them; but they have not as yet been finally disposed of.

THE MAGISTRACY (IRELAND)—MR. KELLY, Q.C., COUNTY COURT JUDGE FOR CLARE.

MR. KENNY asked the Chief Secretary to the Lord Lieutenant of Ireland, What explanation Mr. Kelly, Q.C., County Court Judge for Clare, has given the Lords Justices for his conduct towards a juror in his Court?

MR. TREVELYAN: Sir, the County Court Judge states that, in his opinion, the juror referred to improperly interfered with the prosecution at a time and in a manner which was not warranted. This was a matter entirely for the County Court Judge to determine, and he was bound to stop such interference if it was improper as he asserts it was. The Lords Justices have accepted Mr. Kelly's explanation as satisfactory.

LAW AND JUSTICE (IRELAND)—DYING DECLARATIONS—CASE OF THE BROTHERS DELAHUNTY.

MR. KENNY asked the Chief Secretary to the Lord Lieutenant of Ireland, If the opinion of the learned Judge who tried the case has been given with regard to the importance of a dying declaration made relative to the conviction of the brothers Delahunty at Cork Winter Assizes 1882?

MR. TREVELYAN: The learned Judge has not yet expressed an opinion on the case, which is still before him. He telegraphs to-day that he will send the Papers at the earliest possible moment. When they arrive they will be carefully considered.

LAW AND JUSTICE (IRELAND)—THE DUBLIN SCANDALS—MR. BOYLE, J.P.

MR. HEALY asked the Chief Secretary to the Lord Lieutenant of Ireland, Whether a warrant has been issued against Mr. R. Boyle, J.P., stockbroker, in connection with the Dublin scandals; has he fled from justice; and, is he to be allowed to remain in the Commission of the Peace?

MR. TREVELYAN: I am informed that a warrant in this case has been issued; but that it has not been executed, as Mr. Boyle has left the country.

MR. HEALY: The Government are, of course, aware that Mr. Boyle holds a stockbroker's warrant?

MR. TREVELYAN: Yes. The whole of the circumstances are before the Lord Chancellor.

CRIME AND OUTRAGE (IRELAND)—ATTACK ON THE SALVATION ARMY AT COOTEHILL, CO. CAVAN.

MR. BERESFORD asked the Chief Secretary to the Lord Lieutenant of Ireland, Whether his attention has been called to an attack made by a riotous mob on a number of members of the Salvation Army in the town of Cootehill, county Cavan, Ireland, on 22nd May, 1884, in the presence of the head constable and other constables of the local force of the Royal Irish Constabulary; whether, on the following Sunday, several hundred persons again assembled with the intention of attacking the Salvation Army, but were prevented doing so by Captain Mansfield, R.M. and a large force of police; and, whether the Government intend to prosecute the ringleaders of the mob, who are well known to the police?

MR. TREVELYAN: The matter has not previously been specially under my notice; but I have a Report now, from which I find that the circumstances of the disturbances which occurred on the 22nd of May were fully before my hon. and learned Friend the Attorney General for Ireland, who decided not to direct any prosecutions. It is true that on occasions subsequent to the 22nd of May further disturbance was apprehended, and police arrangements were made accordingly. My hon. and learned Friend acted on the well-advised opinion of the Sessional Crown Solicitor.

LAND LAW (IRELAND) ACT, 1881—CLAUSE 19 — LOANS FOR LABOURERS' COTTAGES.

COLONEL COLTHURST asked the Chief Secretary to the Lord Lieutenant of Ireland, Whether he will suggest to the Land Commissioners to include in their Report of Proceedings (furnished monthly) the number of orders made under Clause 19, Land Act, 1881, for the building or repair of labourers' cottages?

MR. TREVELYAN: The Land Commissioners have drawn my attention to the fact that information on this subject is given in their monthly Returns of judicial rents. They do not think it would be desirable to attempt to include this detail in their monthly Return of proceedings—the issue of which would be greatly delayed thereby.

PEACE PRESERVATION (IRELAND) ACT, 1881 — POLICE HUT AT RATHGORMACK, CO. WATERFORD.

MR. LEAMY asked the Chief Secretary to the Lord Lieutenant of Ireland, Whether a police hut was erected in the parish of Rathgormack, county of Waterford, over three years ago, in a district in which not a single outrage was committed during the whole of the agitation, and which is a most peaceable district; and, if he will state why the hut was erected, why it has been kept up for three years at the expense of the ratepayers, and when will it be removed?

MR. TREVELYAN: The police station was established at Rathgormack a little over two years ago. The men are included in the county force, and are not charged to the district. It would be necessary to establish a station in that locality, because a large tract of country there was without police. It is not correct to say, I am informed, that the district is free from outrage. A good deal of intimidation is being carried on. The forming of this station enabled the Government to do away with two protection posts, which were necessarily established for the protection of persons in charge of evicted farms.

In reply to a further Question from Mr. LEAMY,

MR. TREVELYAN said, that he was not informed whether, numerically, the two protection posts or the police station included the more men. He should imagine, from the information given him, that there was no extra charge on the county in consequence of the police station, which enabled the protection posts to be dispensed with.

MR. LEAMY: Will this be kept up?

MR. TREVELYAN: It will certainly not be kept up, if it is not necessary; but I am informed it is still necessary.

VACCINATION ACTS—CASE OF THE REV. W. KEAY, GREAT YARMOUTH.

MR. HOPWOOD asked the President of the Local Government Board, Whether his attention has been called to the case of the Rev. W. Keay, curate of Great Yarmouth, who has been twice prosecuted and fined the maximum penalty and exceptionally heavy costs for refusing to submit his child to vaccination, and is now served with notice of further proceedings; and, whether he will call the attention of guardians to the "Evesham" letter?

MR. GEORGE RUSSELL (for Sir CHARLES W. DILKE), in reply, said, the Board had received letters from this gentleman, copies of which had been forwarded to the Board of Guardians, together with a copy of the "Evesham" letter referred to in the Question.

MADAGASCAR — NAVAL OPERATIONS OF FRANCE—PROTECTION TO BRITISH COMMERCE.

MR. ALEXANDER M'ARTHUR asked the Under Secretary of State for Foreign Affairs, Whether the Government have received any authentic information from the French Government as to their intentions in Madagascar; and, whether, having regard to the great injury inflicted upon British commerce by the French Naval operations on the Malagasy coast, Her Majesty's Government will take such steps as may be necessary to protect the interests of this Country in the island, and to promote the restoration of peace?

LORD EDMOND FITZMAURICE: No, Sir; no such information has been received. I have already stated, in reply to the hon. Member for Eye (Mr. Ashmead-Bartlett), that a British man-of-war has proceeded to the station, and that the Consular Staff has been strengthened in order to afford to British subjects the protection to which they were entitled. Her Majesty's Government have also received assurances from the French Government that the Naval Commanders have had instructions sent to them to carry on their operations in such a manner as to injure as little as possible neutral subjects and their property.

ROYAL IRISH CONSTABULARY—SECRET SOCIETIES — NUMBER OF FREEMASONS.

MR. SMALL asked the Chief Secretary to the Lord Lieutenant of Ireland, Whether he can state the number of Freemasons in each grade of the Constabulary Force in Ireland, distinguishing them also by their religious denominations?

MR. TREVELYAN: No, Sir; the Government have no information on the subject which would enable them to prepare the Return.

MR. HEALY asked, if his information was correct, that every policeman on joining had to take the Oath of Allegiance to Her Majesty, and that while the members of the force were not permitted to belong to any other secret society, they were allowed to become Members of the Freemason secret society?

MR. TREVELYAN: Yes, Sir; that is the case.

INDIA (MADRAS)—PERSONAL STAFF OF THE GOVERNOR—POSTAL FACILITIES.

MR. JUSTIN M'CARTHY asked the Under Secretary of State for India, Whether he will inform the House from what year the practice dates of allowing Officers, Civil and Military, on the personal Staff of the Governor of Madras, to send letters home for two pence the half ounce, against five pence the usual rate; under what circumstances this new arrangement was made; and, why these Staff Officers, who draw high rates of pay and allowances, should enjoy an advantage denied to poorly paid Regimental Officers?

MR. J. K. CROSS: Sir, the practice described by the hon. Member does not exist. Letters inclosed in the Governor's bag are carried free, as I informed the hon. Gentleman on Monday.

EGYPT—THE CONFERENCE.

BARON HENRY DE WORMS asked the Under Secretary of State for Foreign Affairs, Whether it is a fact, as stated by *The Cologne Gazette* and *The London Observer*, that Her Majesty's Government has urged Germany to employ her influence to modify the hostile attitude taken up by France towards England in the Conference on the finances of Egypt, and that Germany has declined to interfere?

LORD EDMOND FITZMAURICE: Sir, as stated yesterday by the First Lord of the Treasury, it is impossible, until a full statement is made in regard to the Conference, to make incomplete communications in the House in regard to particular points; but I must ask that, meanwhile, no inferences should be drawn, either positive or negative, from my refusal to make such communications.

AUSTRALIAN COLONIES—IMPORTATION OF FRENCH RECIDIVISTS.

MR. ERRINGTON asked the Under Secretary of State for Foreign Affairs, Whether he can give the House any information as to the results of the remonstrances which, in the interests of our Australasian Colonies, Her Majesty's Government has been making to the Government of France against the proposed wholesale deportation of French criminal classes to New Caledonia, and against the serious injuries which, even with their present limited development, the French penal settlements entail on our fellow-subjects?

LORD EDMOND FITZMAURICE: Sir, Her Majesty's Government have not yet received a reply to the representation which Her Majesty's Ambassador at Paris addressed to the French Government on the 23rd of May last; but it is probable that, before replying, they have awaited the Report of the Committee of the French Senate upon the Bill relating to this matter. This Report was only laid before the Senate on the 29th ultimo, and then ordered to be printed. This question continues to engage the serious attention of Her Majesty's Government.

EDUCATION DEPARTMENT—SCHOOL ACCOMMODATION.

MR. J. G. TALBOT asked the Vice President of the Committee of Council, Whether the Law Officers of the Crown have given their opinion as to the necessity laid upon the School Boards to supply school accommodation; and, whether he can communicate the result of their opinion to the House?

MR. MUNDELLA: We have received the opinion of the Law Officers of the Crown; and the result is that the action of the Department since the passing of the Act of 1870 is fully sustained. In their view, the necessity is laid upon School Boards to supply school accommodation. They are, further, of opinion that when a School Board is established to supply the deficiency of accommodation, it is bound to supply such deficiency by School Board schools, and the Department has not the discretion to accept a voluntary supply in substitution for the accommodation to be provided by the School Board.

ARMY (AUXILIARY FORCES)—MILITIA QUARTERMASTERS—RETIRED PAY.

DR. LYONS asked the Financial Secretary to the War Office, What rate of Army retired pay are Militia Quartermasters, who received Army commissions in 1874, 1875, and 1876, and who had previously served in the non-commissioned rank of the Regular Army for 21 years, entitled to for a service under five years with a Brigade Depôt if they are willing to surrender their claim to Chelsea Pension?

SIR ARTHUR HAYTER: The quartermasters referred to, if compulsorily retired at the age of 55, are entitled to 4*s.* 6*d.* a-day as retired pay. If, on the 31st of March, 1877, they were in receipt of Chelsea pension, they can draw such pension concurrently with retired pay; but the surrender of their Chelsea pension would not give a title to higher retired pay.

ARMY—QUARTERMASTERS—PROMOTION.

MR. BIGGAR asked the Financial Secretary to the War Office, What prospect a Quartermaster in the Army has of further promotion; and if he could state why this class of soldier is ineligible for promotion to the position of Paymaster in consequence of the present regulations?

SIR ARTHUR HAYTER: In answer to the first part of the hon. Member's Question, I have to say that a quartermaster in the Army may be recommended for promotion to the rank of lieutenant in either Cavalry or Infantry by Article VI. of the Revised Pay Warrant, provided he shall not exceed the age of 32 years. When promoted to be a lieutenant, he is eligible for promotion to the rank of captain after two years' service, either upon half-pay or in a regiment; and, in the latter case, he becomes eligible for a regimental majority up to 40 years of age, and afterwards to promotion to the higher grades. If he remains a quartermaster, he obtains by Article VIII. the honorary and relative rank of captain after 10 years' commissioned service as quartermaster on full pay, which carries with it an increase of allowances and widow's pension. In answer to the second part of the Question, I have to say that the quartermaster is a commissioned officer as defined by the Army Act, and not "a soldier," as stated in the Question; while the present Regulations for admission to the Pay Department do not render him ineligible, but rather facilitate his entry into the Department by reducing the qualifying service from ten to seven years in the combatant ranks for first appointments as paymasters.

EDUCATION DEPARTMENT—OVER-PRESSURE IN BOARD SCHOOLS.

MR. J. G. TALBOT asked the Vice President of the Committee of Council, Whether he will consider, during the recess, the practicability of making inquiries, in the case of Elementary Schools in which over-pressure is alleged to exist, by persons unconnected with the management of those schools?

MR. MUNDELLA: We are satisfied that the provisions of the New Code and the Instructions to Her Majesty's Inspectors will do all that can be done by the Education Department to prevent the alleged over-pressure. Until it is shown by experience that these precautions are insufficient, any inquiry which would prejudice the action of managers and Local Authorities would appear to be objectionable and unnecessary.

MR. J. G. TALBOT: Perhaps I may be allowed to explain. We have had many complaints of the kind; and I must say the right hon. Gentleman has given them his best attention. But what I want to know is, will an inquiry be made in each case by an Inspector independent of the Department, in the same way as the Home Office, in case of accident, inspects mines?

MR. MUNDELLA: That would be hardly fair. The School Boards in the country are most anxious to prevent over-pressure, and I wish that some of the voluntary schools would do now what the board schools are doing. The London School Board, I am informed, have put their pupil teachers on half time. It would be very unfair to institute an independent inquiry, when the School Boards are doing the best they can.

MR. DAWSON asked whether the attention of the right hon. Gentleman had been called to the fact that the introduction of a system of manual or industrial employment during a portion of the day would be a great relief from over-pressure?

MR. MUNDELLA: Yes, Sir; my attention has been brought to the subject.

ARMY—PURCHASE OFFICERS—COMPULSORY RETIREMENT.

SIR JOHN HAY asked the Secretary of State for War, Whether his attention has been directed to the case of the hardship inflicted on some officers who, having purchased their Subaltern's commissions, have been compulsorily retired from the rank of Major at the age of 48; and, whether, in order to abate this hardship, he will consider if it be possible to extend the age in this case to the age of 50, as has been done in the case of those who had purchased their captain's commission?

THE MARQUESS OF HARTINGTON: If the right hon. and gallant Baronet will refer to the Report of the Royal Commission of 1874 on Army Promotion, he will find that one of the general principles adopted in dealing with the purchase officers was that—

> "Officers who had been promoted to a higher regimental rank since the abolition of Purchase cannot claim exemption from any new rules affecting that higher rank."

In reply to the right hon. and gallant Baronet, my Predecessor stated, in 1881, that he would not be justified in disturbing the settlement of 1877 as to these officers, and I can only concur in that decision.

IRELAND—THE ROYAL COLLEGE OF SCIENCE, DUBLIN.

MR. DAWSON asked the Chief Secretary to the Lord Lieutenant of Ireland, What facilities are afforded by the Royal College of Science in Dublin for the practical teaching of the artizan classes; what lectures there are on industrial subjects; and, whether there are evening classes for the benefit of persons employed at labour by day; and, if so, how many artizans are in attendance?

Mr. MUNDELLA: Full information as to the courses of instruction in the College of Science are given in the directory of that institution, which is published annually. The only special facilities offered to the artizan classes are the Royal Exhibitions, national scholarships, and free admissions, annually open to competition. The College was intended to afford advanced scientific instruction, the general scheme of which was laid down by a Commission presided over by Lord Rosse in 1866. Their Report will be found in Parliamentary Paper No. 219 of 1867. The Professors are not required to give evening lectures by that scheme, or by the terms of their appointment, such evening lectures for the working classes being provided for by the general system of Aid-to-Science and Art Classes; but they have voluntarily given courses at different times. The courses given in the Session 1882-3 will be found at page 307 of the last annual Report of the Department. No evening lectures were given during the Session just terminated, because those during the previous Session were not sufficiently well attended to induce the Professors to continue them. I trust I may be allowed to supplement my answer to the hon. Gentleman the Member for the University of Oxford (Mr. J. G. Talbot), and add that in cases of over-pressure in board schools inquiry is always made by an Inspector of the Education Department, independently of the School Board concerned.

Mr. DAWSON: Might I ask if there is any scientific or other institution in Dublin, a city of 300,000 inhabitants, to give instruction to artizans?

Mr. MUNDELLA: There are the same facilities in Dublin as in London, and in every other city and town in the United Kingdom. We make just the same grants to students in Ireland as to students in England and Scotland, and the same scholarships are open.

EAST INDIAN UNCLAIMED STOCKS BILL.

Mr. BOURKE asked the Under Secretary of State for India, Whether Her Majesty's Government propose to proceed with the East Indian Unclaimed Stocks Bill this Session; or, if not, whether the discharge of the Order will be moved this evening?

Mr. J. K. CROSS: Yes, Sir.

CENTRAL ASIA—DELIMITATION OF THE AFGHAN FRONTIER.

Mr. BOURKE asked the Under Secretary of State for India, Whether the Russian escort which is to accompany the Commission for delimiting the frontier of Afghanistan is to consist of a battery of artillery, a regiment of cavalry, and a regiment of infantry?

Lord EDMOND FITZMAURICE: No information of that character has been received by Her Majesty's Government.

Mr. BOURKE: Then I will ask—I hardly know whom—but will Her Majesty's Government take steps to ascertain, before the Commission starts from India, what the nature of the Russian escort is to be; and whether, if this Commission is to go on, they will make arrangements for having a suitable escort for the British Commissioners?

Lord EDMOND FITZMAURICE: I think the Question regarding the escort to the British Commissioners would be more properly asked of the Under Secretary of State for India; but I can certainly say that the question is receiving attention, and I have no doubt that, in regard to the Russian escort, Her Majesty's Ambassador at St. Petersburg will keep the Government fully informed.

Mr. BOURKE: Has the noble Lord noticed a statement in *The Bombay Gazette* with regard to the Russian escort? If not, I shall be very happy to supply him with it.

Lord EDMOND FITZMAURICE: I have seen a notice in one of the newspapers; it is probably that the right hon. Gentleman refers to.

Mr. JOSEPH COWEN: In the event of this Frontier being settled, I wish to ask the noble Lord if the Government are prepared to state what means they are going to take to maintain it afterwards?

Lord EDMOND FITZMAURICE: No, Sir. I stated the other day that, while these negotiations were going on, it was quite impossible to make a statement in regard to the subject.

MINES REGULATION ACT, 1872—INSPECTORS OF MINES.

Mr. BROADHURST asked the Secretary of State for the Home Department, Whether he can now inform the House as to the decision of the Government regarding the necessity for increasing the number of inspectors of mines?

Sir WILLIAM HARCOURT, in reply, said, he had been in communication with the Treasury on the subject; and, having received the sanction of that Department, he hoped soon to make arrangements for appointing additional Inspectors, in accordance with what he thought was the general view of the House expressed during the recent debate on the question.

INLAND NAVIGATION AND DRAINAGE (IRELAND)—THE RIVER SHANNON.

Mr. T. A. DICKSON asked the Financial Secretary to the Treasury, If the outlay of £58,757, expended in sluicing the weirs to regulate the Shannon floods, has been defrayed entirely by the Treasury?

Mr. COURTNEY: Yes, Sir; the navigation over the whole of the Shannon is managed by the State, which collects the receipts, and applies them towards the necessary expenditure. The improvement of the weirs was commenced in the distressed period of 1880, and, being a work intimately connected with the navigation, had to be paid for entirely by the public, although local proprietors have, no doubt, partly benefited by it.

NAVY—NAVAL COURTS MARTIAL.

Mr. STEWART MACLIVER asked the Secretary to the Admiralty, Whether it is contemplated to take steps to secure for Naval Courts Martial such a degree of legal revision as is given to Army Courts Martial?

Mr. CAMPBELL-BANNERMAN: Yes, Sir; it has appeared to the Board of Admiralty to be desirable that the proceedings and findings of courts martial should be submitted to the Judge Advocate of the Fleet, with reference to any points of law that might arise concerning them, and some time ago orders were given accordingly.

REFORMATORY AND INDUSTRIAL SCHOOLS (IRELAND) — INDUSTRIAL SCHOOLS, LIMERICK—SURCHARGES.

Mr. BERESFORD asked the Chief Secretary to the Lord Lieutenant of Ireland, Whether it is the fact that Sir John Lentaigne, C.B., surcharged some of the male and female managers of industrial schools situated in Limerick a considerable sum of money for inaccuracy in their reports, and representing to him that a number of children were in the schools when they were inmates of the Limerick Union Workhouse; whether the managers were paid a sum of money, from several counties, for the same children, who were supported at the expense of the ratepayers; and, whether he will state to the House the several amounts which have been thus paid to these managers?

Mr. TREVELYAN: Sir, it is a fact that Sir John Lentaigne, when auditing the accounts of the Government grant in aid, surcharged the managers of three Limerick schools, in respect of certain children, who were paid for at a time when they were in Limerick Workhouse Hospital. The amounts were—St. Vincent's Industrial School, £109; Limerick Male School, £29; St. Joseph's Reformatory School, £1. It is also a fact that the Government have received an explanation from the managers, which has enabled them to decide to remit the surcharge—the explanation being shortly that there were always in the schools a larger number of children than the Government grant was paid for, and that when it was necessary to send some of the children to the workhouse hospital, in consequence of their suffering from infectious disease, the managers omitted to send forward to the Industrial Schools Department the names of the children to be substituted in respect of the claim for the rate in aid. This is probably the circumstance to which the hon. Member refers, as Sir John Lentaigne does not audit the county grants. They are audited by the Local Government Board auditor. He is at present on leave of absence, and I have not been able to communicate with him.

PREVENTION OF CRIME (IRELAND) ACT, 1882—EXTRA POLICE.

Mr. PARNELL asked the Chief Secretary to the Lord Lieutenant of Ireland, Whether he can state the number of extra police, including officers and men, quartered in each county and city in Ireland; also the dates respectively of the several proclamations of the Lord Lieutenant, under which they are so quartered; also the counties and cities in which the recent reduction of extra men has been made; and the amount of such reduction in each county or city?

Mr. TREVELYAN: The information asked for could not be conveniently given in answer to a Question; but I shall be happy to hand to the hon. Member, at once, a table showing the number of extra police in each county on the 31st of December last and the 30th of June respectively, under Section 13 of the old Act, and under the Prevention of Crime Act, and the reductions made in the six months intervening. I could not give the dates of the several proclamations under the Prevention of Crime Act without a reference to Dublin, which time does not permit of, no notice of the Question having been received. But the Papers will contain the dates of the proclamations under Section 13 of the Act of William IV.

Mr. PARNELL said, that the information referred to would be sufficient for his purpose.

EGYPT (EVENTS IN THE SOUDAN)—RAILWAY AT SUAKIN.

Mr. JUSTIN HUNTLY M'CARTHY asked the Secretary of State for War, If it is a fact that different kinds of "plant," with which it is impossible to construct a Railway, have been sent for that purpose to Suakin; and, if the Government authorize this pretended construction of a Railway, and for what purpose?

The Marquess of HARTINGTON: Sir, in view of the possibility of a railway being constructed in the Soudan, a light contractor's tramway of 18-inch gauge, which was in store, has been sent out to facilitate operations at the landing stages, piers, and depôts at Suakin. A small quantity of the mètre gauge has also been sent out, which will be the gauge adopted, if the railway is made. The contractor's railway which was sent out was not for the purpose of the construction of a line of any considerable length; but only for putting the place in a state of preparation if a railway were to be constructed.

NAVY—H.M.S. "GARNET"—THE INQUIRY INTO CHARGES AGAINST OFFICERS.

Mr. DEASY asked the Secretary to the Admiralty, What has been the result of the investigation into the charges made by Mr. Donovan, editor of *The Granada People* newspaper, against certain officers of H.M.S. *Garnet*?

Mr. CAMPBELL-BANNERMAN: We still await the Report on this subject which was called for from the Commander-in-Chief of the Station. As there has been considerable delay, we have renewed our request for a reply.

EGYPT (ARMY OF OCCUPATION)—RAMLEH BARRACKS.

Mr. A. ROSS asked the Secretary of State for War, Whether any Report was made on the sanitary condition of the barracks at Ramleh, in Egypt, before their occupation by British troops; and, whether there is an unusual amount of sickness, especially enteric fever, prevalent among the battalion quartered there?

The Marquess of HARTINGTON: Sir, I am aware of the painful circumstances which has induced the hon. Gentleman to call attention to this matter—the death of a near relative, his gallant son. I hope the hon. Gentleman will permit me to express my sympathy with his family. I, however, may say that in September, 1882, owing to the prevalence of fever among the Force at Alexandria, and especially among that portion of it encamped in and about Ramleh, it became necessary to find barrack accommodation for the troops, and all available buildings were then inspected and a Report furnished. The Ramleh barracks were stated to be large and good barracks, occupying an admirable site exposed to the sea, with a bathing stage available; they required to be cleansed, ventilated, and provided with proper sanitary arrangements. In the Sanitary Report for 1883 it is stated that a large amount of sanitary work has been carried out in these barracks, and that all the sewers and pits are now in a good sanitary state. The present sick rate at Ramleh is high; by the last Return there were 16 cases of enteric fever under treatment, and a total of 185 sick from all causes in a strength of 1,303. An increase of febrile disease is to be expected at this season in Egypt, and the principal medical officer in Egypt (now at home) states that it would be impossible to attribute all the enteric fever to the insanitary state of these barracks after the extensive sanitary work that has been carried out in them. There were 25 cases of enteric fever under treatment at Cairo.

POST OFFICE PROTECTION BILL.

Baron HENRY DE WORMS asked the First Lord of the Treasury, Whether, having regard to the importance to the public interests of the provisions in the Post Office Protection Bill, relating to the forgery and disclosure of telegrams, the mischievous destruction of letters in pillar boxes, and the manufacture of fictitious stamps, and seeing that the Bill has passed the House of Lords, he will give an early opportunity for the discussion of the measure, so that it might pass into Law this Session?

Mr. GLADSTONE, in reply, said, the Government were very desirous of passing the Bill. They could not stop Supply for the purpose; but, as the Bill had been through the Lords, he had very good hope that they should find an opportunity of passing it this Session.

PARLIAMENT—WESTMINSTER HALL (WEST FRONT)—SITE OF THE OLD LAW COURTS.

Sir GEORGE CAMPBELL asked the Prime Minister, Whether he will use his influence to provide, on the ground lately occupied by the Law Courts, to the West of Westminster Hall, accommodation for the Grand Committees?

Mr. GLADSTONE, in reply, said, that he must first have an opportunity of consulting the First Commissioner of Works before he expressed any opinion on the subject.

MOTION.

——o——

PARLIAMENT — BUSINESS OF THE HOUSE—COMMITTEE OF SUPPLY—STANDING ORDER 425A.

RESOLUTION.

Mr. GLADSTONE, in rising to move—

"That, for the remainder of the Session, the Standing Order of the 27th of November, 1882, relating to Notices on going into Committee of Supply on Monday and Thursday, be extended to Saturday,"

said, it would be evident to the House that if he were to move the Motion which stood in his name on the Paper yesterday, to include Friday as well as Saturday, that a great deal of time would be lost, as such a Motion would lead to the expression of great difference of opinion. It might be, perhaps, of interest to the House, and they would see that the Government had some justification for the proposal, when he told them that for the whole of Supply last year there were 26 Sittings, and that they had already spent 30 Sittings in Supply this Session, and had some more in prospect. Therefore, he hoped the House would be generally favourable to the Motion, and support it. With regard to the Sitting to-morrow, it would be for Supply, and Supply alone. The Government should not think it right, as far as they were concerned, of promoting any other Business, either of their own or of private Members. He moved the Resolution of which Notice had been given.

Motion made, and Question proposed,

"That, for the remainder of the Session, the Standing Order of the 27th of November, 1882, relating to Notices on going into Committee of Supply on Monday and Thursday, be extended to Saturday."—(*Mr. Gladstone.*)

Mr. NEWDEGATE said, it could not be a matter for surprise that the Prime Minister was adopting the best means he could to bring the Session to an end. He (Mr. Newdegate) could not help asking with Martial—

"When men begin with so much pomp and show,
Why is the end so little and so low?"

The product of all this labour was small. Now, independent Members were asked to give up the remainder of their opportunities. He was no advocate of Obstruction—he had made proposals to prevent it on November 21st, 1882, which the Prime Minister had described as too severe; and he had not, until the last opportunity, called attention to one of the gravest subjects, the defensive power of the Royal Navy. ["Oh, oh!"]

Mr. SPEAKER said, he was sorry to interrupt the hon. Member, whom he would remind of the Question before the House.

Mr. NEWDEGATE said, if he had trespassed, he apologized; but when hon. Members were asked to resign privileges, it was only natural they should discuss opportunities of usefulness resigned in contrast to the object to be gained. He was not aware until he saw the letter from the Admiral of the Fleet——

MR. SPEAKER: The hon. Gentleman is entirely out of Order in pursuing this subject; his remarks have no reference whatever to the Motion before the House.

MR. NEWDEGATE said, he respectfully asked whether, on the Appropriation Bill, or on what other occasion during the remainder of the Session, it would be competent to bring this grave subject before the House, if the Resolution proposed by the Prime Minister were adopted? His apology for not having intervened sooner was because it was not until the 21st of last month that the letter of the Admiral of the Fleet was written. [*Cries of* "Order!" *and* "Name!"]

MR. SPEAKER: I have already ruled this subject to be irrelevant to the Motion before the House; therefore, I must again ask the hon. Gentleman to abstain from that line of observation, and apply himself to the Motion before the House.

MR. NEWDEGATE said, he begged again to apologize. He would sit down again, putting to Mr. Speaker this question—If the Resolution of the right hon. Gentleman passed, when would there be an opportunity of bringing the subject to which he referred before the House?

SIR R. ASSHETON CROSS said, he did not rise to oppose the Motion, which, at that time of the Session, he thought a very reasonable one, provided the Saturday's Sitting was restricted to the Business of Supply. But he hoped, first, that the House would not be asked to sit to an unreasonable hour on Saturday; and, next, that when they had got the Supply they wanted, the Government would themselves move the Adjournment of the House, and do all in their power to carry the Motion. [Mr. GLADSTONE nodded assent.]

MR. CAVENDISH BENTINCK said, that on a former occasion, not long ago, when the Government gave an assurance that nothing but Supply would be taken, the hon. Member for Glasgow (Mr. Anderson) combined his forces with those of hon. Members below the Gangway, defeated the Government, and brought forward and passed through Committee a measure which was not expected, and in which they were interested. Bearing that in mind, he would ask the right hon. Gentleman to give an assurance to the House that if they agreed to the Motion they would not find themselves in the same position as that to which he had referred.

MR. LABOUCHERE said, he gathered from hon. Gentlemen opposite that they had a good deal to say on the Irish Votes. Besides those Votes, there was the Diplomatic Vote, and there were Supplementary Estimates. The House ought to have an understanding that, if the Irish Votes took a considerable time, neither the Supplementary Estimates nor the Diplomatic Vote should be brought on.

MR. GLADSTONE said, that the Government would do all in their power to confine the Business to Supply. They had no intention of taking either the Diplomatic or the Supplementary Votes to-morrow. If the House adopted his Motion, then he thought he should have sufficient confidence about Supply to be able to engage to take the Diplomatic Vote as the first Vote on Monday. With respect to the observations of the right hon. and learned Gentleman opposite (Mr. Cavendish Bentinck), the incident he referred to was the misfortune and not the fault of the Government. They were bound by every means in their power to secure the adjournment of the House when they moved it at a reasonable hour.

MR. ANDERSON said, with reference to what the right hon. and learned Gentleman opposite (Mr. Cavendish Bentinck) said about him, he wished to point out that nothing irregular whatever was done on the occasion referred referred to. It had always been the practice of the House to allow whatever Members of the House were present at the time the Order of the Day was called to decide when that Order was to be taken; and if there was a Saturday Sitting, and the Member in charge of the Bill wished to put it down for Saturday, it rested with the Members of the House present at the time to say whether it should be put down for that day or not. Further, when the Order was reached on the Saturday, it rested with the House to say whether it should then be proceeded with or not. He merely rose, however, to vindicate the right of private Members to deal with their Bills in that way in the future as they had done in the past. It was in no way tyrannizing over the House, or taking an undue latitude, because it rested with the House to say what should be done.

Mr. GRAY said, that he had for some time on the Paper a Motion in which several hon. Members, irrespective of politics, took an interest. It was a Motion with respect to the policy of the Post Office in regard to the telephones. He was anxious to test the opinion of the House by a formal vote on the question. He did not expect to have that opportunity now. In view of these facts, the hon. Gentleman the Secretary to the Treasury (Mr. Courtney) ought to see that the Postal Vote should be taken at such an hour as would give facilities for discussing the question.

Mr. WARTON said, he hoped the Government would resist the putting down by private Members of Orders for to-morrow.

Mr. BOURKE said, he supposed the House might conclude, notwithstanding anything that had just passed, that the Prime Minister would be able to carry out to-morrow the conditional promise he made yesterday—that he would make a statement in reference to the Conference.

Mr. GLADSTONE: On Monday.

Mr. HEALY said, he would ask that a time should be fixed at which Progress should be reported to-morrow, so that they should not be kept until an unreasonable hour. To try to get all the Irish Votes passed on Saturday would only lead to wrangling. There was a strong desire on the part of Irish Members to get the Irish Votes passed and go away home; and, therefore, there was not any likelihood of their unduly prolonging the debates. He would wish that they should have an understanding with the Government that the adjournment should take place at 6 or 7 o'clock. On such Sittings the Government counted on their fingers how many Irish Members were present, and they brought down a number of hard-headed men, who would not be influenced by argument, to outvote them, and put them down. When the Constabulary Vote was taken to-morrow, he hoped the Government would not press on the Vote for the Queen's Colleges. He would like to have a specific statement of the Votes to be taken on Saturday; and, also, whether the proceedings at that Sitting would exclude the Report of Supply.

Mr. COURTNEY said, that both the hon. Member for Monaghan (Mr. Healy) and the hon. Member for Carlow (Mr. Gray) knew that it was not in the power of the Government to entirely arrange how the Votes should be taken. He thought he could suggest a plan by which matters could be arranged, so as to appropriate the time remaining at the disposal of the House in a fair and equal way. It would, however, be impossible to carry it out unless there was some concurrence on the part of the hon. Member and his Friends, and unless there was some economy of time and economy of speech. He trusted it was not too much to expect that the Motion with regard to the National School Teachers in Ireland might be disposed of upon the Irish Education Vote, and then they might be able to get through the remaining Votes in Class III. that evening.

Mr. HEALY: Including the Constabulary Vote?

Mr. COURTNEY said, that Vote was in Class III., and he hoped it might be disposed of that night, though they might have to sit to a late hour. Saturday might then be confined exclusively to Class IV., which might be got through by a reasonable hour in the evening. Then on Monday Class V. might be taken, beginning with the Diplomatic Vote; and they might hope, at an early hour on Tuesday, to take the Revenue Votes, when the question could be raised in which the hon. Member for Carlow (Mr. Gray) and others were interested. In that way, Supply might be got through in four Sittings.

Lord RANDOLPH CHURCHILL said, he thought the hon. Gentleman the Secretary to the Treasury (Mr. Courtney) had distinctly overstepped the limits of his functions. He (Lord Randolph Churchill) had never understood it to be a part of the hon. Gentleman's duty to dictate to the House the manner in which it should proceed with its Business, or the order in which the Votes should be taken. ["Oh, oh!"] He was perfectly certain that if such a statement had come from the Prime Minister, it would have been listened to with attention, and, perhaps, followed up. He had risen, however, for the purpose of communicating to the House and the Prime Minister an idea which had come across him. The Secretary to the Treasury had not noticed the only remark of the hon. Member for Monaghan (Mr. Healy) which he might have answered with advantage, and that was whether Report of Supply could be taken on Saturday. But matters turned upon that, for if the Prime Minister could take the Report on Saturday, and on the Report would communicate to the House the result of the sittings of the Conference, he thought some advantage would be gained. They were very much pressed for time, and great inconvenience arose from the uncertainty of the time that might be set apart for a discussion on Egypt, and it might be necessary for hon. Members to consider what line of action they would take on the question. It would be very inconvenient to postpone the statement until Monday at 4 o'clock.

MR. JUSTIN M'CARTHY said, it was almost useless to hope to get through the Constabulary Vote that night, and he would therefore propose that it should be postponed until Saturday. It was desired by hon. Members who sat near him to discuss the Vote fully and fairly, but without undue expenditure of time.

MR. ASHMEAD-BARTLETT said, he would ask whether the Government could not make a definite statement as to what Votes would be taken on Monday? If the discussion on the Irish Votes were prolonged beyond the period the Government anticipated, the Diplomatic Vote might be postponed to Tuesday. He thought that if the Diplomatic Vote could not be taken for certain on Monday, it would be better to fix it for certain on Tuesday.

MR. GREGORY said, he thought the programme of the hon. Gentleman the Secretary to the Treasury (Mr. Courtney) somewhat over-sanguine. He (Mr. Gregory) wished to express a hope that Bills would not be proceeded with, as they had been lately, at 4 or 5 o'clock in the morning after Progress had been reported on Supply.

THE CHANCELLOR OF THE EXCHEQUER (Mr. CHILDERS) said, it was practically impossible, as suggested by the hon. Member for Longford (Mr. Justin M'Carthy), to take the Constabulary Vote as well as Class IV. on Saturday. They must, therefore, finish the Constabulary Vote that night, if Class IV. was to be taken on Saturday. As to the question of the hon. Member for Eye (Mr. Ashmead-Bartlett), the Diplomatic Vote would, under any circumstances, be the first Order on Monday. The noble Lord the Member for Woodstock (Lord Randolph Churchill) had attacked the hon. Gentleman the Secretary to the Treasury (Mr. Courtney) in a very unfair way, for having done his best to explain the probable course of Supply. The noble Lord forgot that the Prime Minister had already spoken, and could not speak again. Besides, his hon. Friend was more conversant with this subject than any other Member of the Government, and it was only natural that he should point out what he considered to be the best course to adopt. As to the suggestion of the noble Lord, he (the Chancellor of the Exchequer) thought it was evident that it would be extremely hard on the Government to undertake to make a communication on the Conference to-morrow, assuming that the Conference arrived at a decision the same day. He was not aware of any Vote upon the Report of Supply upon which any reference to the question of the Conference could be made; and it would be irregular to make an important statement about foreign affairs upon a Vote which had nothing to do with them.

SIR JOSEPH M'KENNA: I beg to ask you, Mr. Speaker, whether it is not the case that the Prime Minister may, with the leave of the House, make a statement at any time?

MR. SPEAKER: Yes; that would be so.

MR. ARTHUR O'CONNOR said, he thought it was unfair on the part of the Government to try and force all the remaining Irish Votes through on Saturday. He protested against that manner of burking Irish questions.

MR. A. J. BALFOUR asked whether the Speaker had ruled that it would be in Order, at 6 o'clock to-morrow, by leave of the House, for the Prime Minister to make a statement as to what had passed in the Conference?

MR. SPEAKER: It will be clearly competent.

MR. A. J. BALFOUR said, that he would then make an appeal to the Prime

Minister to make some statement on the Egyptian Question to-morrow, more particularly when they remembered what had been the course pursued by the Government in connection with the Conference. It had been such as to give rise to grave suspicion, in some quarters, that the Government desired to burke discussion. [" Oh, oh!" *and* "Shame!"] He made no accusation of that kind himself; nevertheless, the accusation had been made, and had been believed in; and he would, therefore, in their own interests, recommend the Government to take every opportunity of allowing the House to discuss the question. He could not but think that it would be for their own interests that they should tell the House to-morrow, if it was in their power, what had happened in the Conference, so that hon. Members might have Sunday and Monday to consider the position, and determine what was to be done. He ventured to make an earnest appeal to the Government on the subject.

BARON HENRY DE WORMS said, he concurred in the appeal made by his hon. Friend (Mr. A. J. Balfour) to the Government to make such a statement to the House as they might be in a position to make. The right hon. Gentleman the Chancellor of the Exchequer thought that such a proceeding would be out of Order; but they had now the authority of the Speaker for saying that it would not be. The Prime Minister, moreover, had given a pledge that the House should be made acquainted with the result of the Conference; and it was only reasonable, in view of the great interests concerned, that the Government should make a statement at the earliest possible moment.

MR. GLADSTONE said, that the fact was that the time of hon. Members was valuable. On the other hand—he had to take this view—that there was some inconvenience in a conditional pledge; and a conditional pledge was the only pledge that the Government could give. It would be impossible to say to-day how long the Conference would sit to-morrow, or what deliberation on the part of the Cabinet as to the conclusions arrived at by the Conference might be required. But, subject to that uncertainty, they should desire to accommodate hon. Gentlemen in any request if it was reasonable. Consequently, if they were so happy as to have it in their power to do so, they would make that statement to-morrow.

MR. JOHN REDMOND said, he was anxious that some definite understanding should be come to between the Irish Members and the Government. It was utterly impossible to cram into to-night and to-morrow a full discussion of the remaining Irish Votes; and he told the Government plainly that, if they forced the Irish Members, by a policy of fatigue, to pass these Votes before they were amply discussed, it would be the duty of himself and his Irish Colleagues to discuss them again on the Appropriation Bill. He asked the Government not to take the Constabulary Vote that night.

COLONEL KING-HARMAN said, that, seeing the House would be infallibly occupied with other Irish questions, he would also urge the Government to postpone the consideration of the Constabulary Vote until to-morrow.

Question put.

The House *divided*:—Ayes 123; Noes 23: Majority 100.—(Div. List, No. 201.)

MR. NEWDEGATE said, he hoped the House would allow him to express great regret at his having appeared to differ from the Speaker's ruling. He wished to give Notice that he would, to-morrow, ask the Speaker this Question—What opportunity, after the adoption of the Resolution now passed, would be available to hon. Members who might desire to bring forward the question of the sufficiency of our Naval preparations to meet any combination that might be brought against us?

MR. SPEAKER: It would not be in Order for the hon. Gentleman to give such a Notice to the Chair. It is not for me to state what opportunities may be open to the hon. Gentleman; but, if he asks me, I may point out that the various stages of the Appropriation Bill afford a wide scope, and perhaps he may find an opportunity on one of those occasions.

ORDERS OF THE DAY.

—o—

SUPPLY.—COMMITTEE.

Order for Committee read.

Motion made, and Question proposed, "That Mr. Speaker do now leave the Chair."

NATIONAL SCHOOL TEACHERS (IRELAND).—RESOLUTION.

MR. JUSTIN HUNTLY M'CARTHY, in rising to call attention to the grievances of National School teachers in Ireland; and to move—

"That this House views with deep regret the impossibility of at present introducing the Education Bill for Ireland promised last year by the Chief Secretary, and that, seeing the hardships which the Irish National Teachers are undoubtedly subjected to, and the necessity which exists of rendering so important a body of public servants contented with their work, this House is of opinion that provision should be made forthwith to improve their incomes temporarily, and that a Bill removing their several grievances should be introduced early in the next Session,"

said: Sir, the grievances of the Irish National School teachers, of which I have the honour to be the mouthpiece to-day, are three-fold. In the first place, the teachers complain of insufficient salaries; in the second place, they complain of the want of fit and proper dwelling-places; in the third place, they complain of the want of proper provisions for retiring pensions, when they have worn out their lives and their usefulness in the Public Service. Now, all these grievances are very great grievances, and no apology whatever is needed, on the part of the teachers who make them, or of any hon. Members of this House who support them, in pressing them upon the attention of the Government. There is no duty more incumbent upon a State than the proper education of its citizens, and that duty presses with especial gravity upon a State in its dealings with citizens who bear their citizenship not by choice, but by compulsion. The English Government have insisted upon taking into their own hands the care of Ireland and of the Irish people; they have adopted Ireland, according to that Oriental principle which gives to adoption all the rights and privileges of veritable parentage. Yet, in the Eastern method of adoption, there are generally two parties to the transaction. But though we are by no means a willing party to this process of adoption, though we absolutely refuse to regard England as our mother among the nations, we have the right to insist, and we do insist, that, so long as this principle of adoption holds good, England shall properly fulfil all the duties she has thereby incurred, and of all those duties the duty of properly educating the Irish people takes a foremost place. In no part of this Empire is education more important than in Ireland. Thanks to the fostering care which this country has exercised for so long over our destinies, we have not those large manufactures which, in the happier condition of England and Scotland, afford employment to their peoples. By education, and by education alone, can the vast bulk of the Irish people hope to rise to influence, to affluence, or to ease. Now, you cannot have fitting education without fitting teachers, and you cannot have fitting teachers, except under certain conditions. One of the greatest authorities on education, the great German author Jean Paul Richter, in the exquisite treatise on education which is called *Levana*, likens teachers and taught to the Gods and the first men. Teachers, he says, physical and spiritual giants to children, descend to these little ones, and form them to be great or small, and he declares that it is a touching and a mighty thought that the teacher has the great spirits and teachers of our immediate posterity under his influence, and that he leads future suns like little wandering stars in his leading strings. The mission of the educator of youth is, indeed, one of the most important that a man can be intrusted with; but it is impossible for any man to attend to that important mission with the necessary wholeheartedness, if his mind is incessantly harassed by cares both now and in the future, and his mind must always be thus harassed so long as the wage he receives is so cruelly insufficient for his daily wants as it is at present. Now, what is the wage which is deemed sufficient for Irish National School teachers, every one of whom, be it remembered, has in his hands the education and, in consequence, the future destiny of a large number of Irish citizens? The average income of an Irish National School teacher, by the Parliamentary Return of June, 1881, is under £60. This sum, most unfairly insufficient in itself, appears yet more insufficient and unfair when we remember that it is rather less than one-half of the average income of teachers in England and in Scotland. The highest salary an Irish National School teacher ever gets is poor enough; the lowest is miserable in the extreme. Attempts have been made from time to time to better this condition of things by systems of results fees; but the attempts have so far wholly failed to materially improve the position of the Irish National School teacher. It is only one other example of the unconquerable patience of the Irish race, that, in defiance of the privations that so unjust a scale of wage brings with it, the Irish National School teachers have so far been able to hold their own well, as far as results go, with their better-paid brethren of England and Scotland. But, when we take into consideration the terribly unequal conditions of the competition, this successful rivalry of results cannot be expected to continue. There is—it is really not surprising—there is a dearth of candidates for the posts of National School teachers in Ireland. You cannot lure men into the acceptance of posts of grave res onsibility and arduous labour by the ptemptations of starvation wages, miserable habitations, and no prospect of a provision for their helpless old age. Does the House think that Irish teachers can live on the air, promise-crammed? Does it consider less than £60 a-year a tempting salary for human beings in the responsible position of teachers of the rising generation? At least, the Irish people do not think so. From all parts of Ireland come official Reports, recording the difficulty of finding teachers. District after district announces—

"A great dearth of candidates. We are told by competent authorities that the Service is only the last resort of those despairing of more coveted posts."

Melancholy stories are told of teachers who—

"Would be sore pinched if their incomes were not augmented by the profits of their little shops."

And so the dismal record runs on, instance after instance, for page after page. Some of the Irish National School teachers, sorely pressed by need, have endeavoured to combine their duties as the instructors of youth with the pursuit of farming on their own account. This is greatly to be deplored, if it is not greatly to be wondered at. We learn that these half-teachers, half-farmers—

"Never apply themselves to their studies with a view to improving their classification, but spend the greater part of their time, outside school hours, in working upon their farms;"

that they make neither good teachers nor good farmers; we learn that, in their manner, dress, and conversation, they have a greater resemblance to agricultural labourers than to school teachers. Such a combination of rural pursuits with the duties of the education of others might have been possible in a simpler age than ours, when the shepherds of Theocritus tended their flocks upon the Sicilian slopes and Virgilian shepherds hived their bees on the Roman Campagna. There was no reason why Comatas should not teach Lacon how to pipe and sing in the intervals between pressing his wine and shearing his sheep. Melibœus might easily snatch leisure from his thatching or digging to instruct Tityrus in the movements of the stars and the change of the seasons, or the fortunes of the Trojan War. But we have passed away from those pastoral days. Modern education requires something more from its professors than Comatas and Melibœus could offer to their pupils, and "modern education does not look with a very favourable eye upon the attempt to combine the quiet pleasures and cares of a farmer's life with the task of giving instruction to the young. At the same time, the teachers who thus become farmers are not to be too severely blamed. What reward have they? What hope have they? It is scarcely strange that they endeavour to glean from the cultivation of the fruitful earth some better means of keeping body and soul together than is afforded to them by the cultivation of the human mind. Nor is it strange that these teachers turned farmers should, in the end, become more of the farmer than of the teacher. The farmer's is the more profitable occupation of the two. It is the State that is to blame for the niggard spirit which tries to cheat the human understanding by underpaying its teachers. It is the State that is to blame for doling out, with parsimonious fingers, the pitiful sums that it now offers to the ministrants of education in Ireland, sums so pitiful that, if they are persevered in, the State will soon have no teachers at all, or only teachers that are worth no more than the beggarly *denier* they are bought for. But the lack of salary is not the Irish teachers' only want. The want of a proper dwelling too often presses just as heavily upon him as the scarcity of salary. The cases in which provision is directly made for the teacher's abode are few. Even by the most recent figures, some 80 per cent of the teachers were unprovided with residences connected with their schools. It is not very long since London was stimulated to unexpected pity by ghastly, yet, I have no doubt, perfectly accurate pictures of the miserable way in which the London poor were housed. It became quite fashionable to go "slumming." I wish it could become, for a few weeks, the fashion for some of the sympathetic spirits in London to cross the Irish Sea, and learn how, not the poor alone, but the teachers of the poor—those whose task it is to make men forget or conquer their poverty—are housed. The dwellings in which many of the teachers have to live would not be chosen by a charitably-minded manager of a menagerie as hutches for hyenas. The teachers are often pent up in narrow limits, badly lighted, badly drained, badly ventilated, except indeed when, as frequently happens, the roof blows off or falls in, and allows of too much ventilation. Even these wretched dwellings, which defy alike the laws of health and the custom of decency, are miles and miles away from the schools in which the teachers have to teach. Now, Sir, I come to my third point—pensions. In all vocations of life, men look forward to a time when they may rest from their labours and wait with folded hands for the hour of their death; in many vocations men hoard for themselves the small sum which will allow them to end their days of toil in an evening of peace. But the vast majority of the Irish National School teachers cannot possibly do this. Their meed is barely sufficient to keep them alive; it allows them no margin for laying anything by. They are amongst the most valuable servants of the State and they deserve a pension Well, the Government has made some provision at last for this, but what provision? The Government seems to have acted on the principle of the survival of the fittest, and to have retarded its pensions as long as possible, in the hope, apparently, that very few Irish teachers may live long enough to profit by its delusive munificence. For example, a first class teacher, on entering the Profession at 18, would receive at 65, after 47 years' service, a pension of £88. The third class teachers, who are, of course, the most numerous, would only receive £35 for the same life's labour. Yet, if the same teacher retired at the age of 58, after 40 years' toil, he would only receive a pension of half the amount he would receive if he held on for seven years longer. Thus, the Government apparently regards the last seven years of a man's work as of exactly the same value as the whole 40 years preceding. In fact, the Government pension is really a reward for physical endurance—the survival of the fittest. The education of the Irish people has always been accomplished in the face of difficulties that would have driven a less-determined people to despair. Through darkened generations, the Irish people strove with all their strength to be educated, and the English people strove with all their strength to prevent them from being educated. The Irish priests, as heroic as the disciples of Patrick who carried Christianity to the Highlands of Scotland, the pine forests of Germany and the Islands of the Northern Seas, fought once again a fight with barbarism, and once again prevailed against it. When no Catholic might open a school, the priests established what were known as "hedge schools." The new defenders of the Faith gave to a hungry people that intellectual food which the harsh law denied them. In the end, the hedge school and the hedge scholars triumphed, and England had to learn that she could not withhold education from the subject people. But she has not learnt the lesson thoroughly yet. The State provides the means of education, but the means are not sufficient. The Government has accepted the responsibility, and it must face that responsibility in a proper spirit. I trust the Government will see their way to do something at once, and to promise more for the future, for the Irish National School teachers. I beg, Sir, to move the Resolution that stands in my name.

Colonel NOLAN, in seconding the Motion, said, that it was hard that the National School teachers in Ireland were not remunerated on the same scale as their brethen in England and Scotland. While the salaries of these teachers were £127 in England, and £138 in Scotland, in Ireland they averaged only a little over £60, or less than one-half. At the same time, the cost of living was in no instance less, and in some greater, in Ireland than in those countries. The consequence was that the Irish teacher, who could not be expected to dress like a labouring man, was, in reality, worse off than the peasant; and he could inform the House that many of the Irish School teachers were obliged to walk about in peasant dress on account of their poverty. The Government were always going to do something "next Session," but the Irish Members never got such a promise as would bind gentlemen of honour to bring in a Bill. It was said that on account of the amount of money received from England and Scotland by taxation, that all the more should be expended in these countries. What he (Colonel Nolan) contended was that the Education Estimates for England and Scotland had advanced by leaps and bounds, while those for Ireland had remained stationary. The statistics on the question went to show that the cost of the Government per head for education in Ireland was practically the same as the cost per head in Great Britain, as during the last 12 years the grant to Ireland had been becoming proportionately less. The difficulties of educating people who were spread over a wide area, as they were in the case of Ireland, were greater than those involved in educating the people of towns, and even the population of Scotland was, on the whole, more concentrated than that of Ireland. Yet the Government did not give Ireland a little more on this account, and it left the teachers in a wretched condition. It had been said that they ought to look to the localities for some help; but the fact was, that whereas in England the cost of education was largely contributed to by various wealthy classes, and by the application of endowments, of which both that country and Scotland had a great many, in Ireland there were very few endowments remaining, what there originally were having been confiscated, and the only rich class in the latter country who, in the event of their decease, were likely to bequeath money for the purpose of endowments for educational purposes, were out of sympathy with the people as regarded religion, and were to a large extent absentees. Neither was it of any use to expect assistance from the Poor Law Guardians, who, though not indifferent to education, thought it ought not to be maintained out of the poor rates, and therefore some other resource must be looked to. A very heavy responsibility rested upon the Government in regard to the subject, and he thought the Government ought to provide about £100,000, which would suffice to meet the case for some time to come.

Amendment proposed,

To leave out from the word "That," to the end of the Question, in order to add the words "this House views with deep regret the impossibility of at present introducing the Education Bill for Ireland promised last year by the Chief Secretary, and that, seeing the hardships which the Irish National Teachers are undoubtedly subjected to, and the necessity which exists of rendering so important a body of public servants contented with their work, this House is of opinion that provision should be made forthwith to improve their incomes temporarily, and that a Bill removing their several grievances should be introduced early in the next Session,"—(*Mr. Justin Huntly M'Carthy*,)

—instead thereof.

Question proposed, "That the words proposed to be left out stand part of the Question."

COLONEL COLTHURST, in supporting the Motion, said, he should be sorry to think that the success or partial success of the teachers' claim should depend upon whether the Government were appreciably to increase the grant for education. Even if it were not increased a great deal might be done to remedy the great grievances of the Irish teachers. When the Unions were made contributory, a large number at first availed themselves of the power of contributing, and they did not find their contributions burdensome to the rates. The Cork Union contributed up to the present time, and did not find it burdensome to do so. But one Union after another dropped off; the example became contagious, and now the number contributing was reduced to four. Whether or not a National rate for Poor Law purposes would be justifiable he did not say; but there could be no question it would be justified in the case of education; and he believed still if the right hon. Gentleman the Chief Secretary for Ireland brought in a Bill next year, authorizing a National rate of 1*d*. in the pound, it would amply provide the Irish National School teachers with an adequate addition to their salaries.

There should be a minimum below which the salaries of the [illegible] teacher [illegible] salary would be provided. With regard to pensions [illegible] It was also nearly impossible [illegible] owing to the want of sympathy [illegible] between the rich and poor classes in Ireland; and since the passing of the Land Act there was the greatest disinclination on the part of [illegible] to part with a bit of land upon any terms whatever; and if teachers were to be properly housed [illegible] powers should be given to [illegible] which [illegible] residences. He [illegible] Mr. Justin Huntly McCarthy [illegible] good service in bringing [illegible] before the House, and he hoped that the Chief Secretary for Ireland would give precedence next Session over all other [illegible] to the Irish Sunday Closing Bill [illegible] Parliamentary [illegible] grievances [illegible] redressed [illegible] the National School teachers of Ireland.

Mr. DAWSON said, he had great [illegible] in congratulating the hon. [illegible] Member for Athlone (Mr. Justin Huntly McCarthy) on his [illegible] congratulate the [illegible] Member who had [illegible] the Irish National School [illegible] grievances. [illegible] in Ireland were [illegible] that [illegible] trusted by the Government, while, in Ireland they were scarcely officially recognized. [illegible] salaries formerly [illegible] National schoolmasters [illegible] maximum salaries, [illegible] their value. [illegible] things had been [illegible] of the [illegible] Member for Kildare (Mr. M[illegible]) [illegible] remuneration was [illegible] commensurate with [illegible] devotion to work. [illegible] which existed between [illegible] English and Scotch [illegible] were almost inexplicable [illegible] to see any reason why [illegible] of an English teacher [illegible] better than that of an Irish teacher, or why in this country [illegible] should be 100 per cent. [illegible] than they were in Ireland. He hoped the Government in the future would give the same protection to Irish teachers [illegible] had afforded in the past to teachers in England. The teachers in Ireland were paid by results, but there was no compulsory education in the country as in England, so that the teachers were not given the materials for producing results. With regard to pensions, teachers [illegible] If they retired at [illegible] after [illegible] years' service, they got £[illegible] a year pension; if they retired at 48, after [illegible] years' service they got £18; if at [illegible] after [illegible] years' service they got £2[illegible], and if at [illegible] after 45 years' service they got half their salary. An Inspector [illegible] on the other hand, retired at 60 after 27 years' service got a pension equal to his full pay of £200 a year. [illegible] the teacher was obliged to pay [illegible] in order to add to his pension. [illegible] back, but if after [illegible] years of labour he died before getting it back, the money was confiscated instead of going to his family [illegible] of its greatest need. [illegible] that they had obtained some advantages, the Government having at [illegible] given them a small [illegible], but since then [illegible] and in the main, [illegible] promises which had been made [illegible]. They got [illegible] as their [illegible] was [illegible] perfectly [illegible] which [illegible] the teachers were still [illegible] (Colonel NOLAN:

no instance less, and in some greater, in Ireland than in those countries. The consequence was that the Irish teacher, who could not be expected to dress like a labouring man, was, in reality, worse off than the peasant; and he could inform the House that many of the Irish School teachers were obliged to walk about in peasant dress on account of their poverty. The Government were always goin to do something "next Session," but the Irish Members never got such a promise as would bind gentlemen of honour to bring in a Bill. It was said that on account of the amount of money received from England and Scotland by taxation, that all the more should be expended in these countries. What he (Colonel Nolan) contended was that the Education Estimates for England and Scotland had advanced by leaps and bounds, while those for Ireland had remained stationary. The statistics on the question went to show that the cost of the Government per head for education in Ireland was practically the same as the cost per head in Great Britain, as during the last 12 years the grant to Ireland had been becoming proportionately less. The difficulties of educating people who were spread over a wide area, as they were in the case of Ireland, were greater than those involved in educating the people of towns, and even the population of Scotland was, on the whole, more concentrated than that of Ireland. Yet the Government did not give Ireland a little more on this account, and it left the teachers in a wretched condition. It had been said that they ought to look to the localities for some help; but the fact was, that whereas in England the cost of education was largely contributed to by various wealthy classes, and by the application of endowments, of which both that country and Scotland had a great many, in Ireland there were very few endowments remaining, what there originally were having been confiscated, and the only rich class in the latter country who, in the event of their decease, were likely to bequeath money for the purpose of endowments for educational purposes, were out of sympathy with the people as regarded religion, and were to a large extent absentees. Neither was it of any use to expect assistance from the Poor Law Guardians, who, though not indifferent to education, thought it ought not to be maintained out of the poor rates, and therefore some other resource must be looked to. A very heavy responsibility rested upon the Government in regard to the subject, and he thought the Government ought to provide about £100,000, which would suffice to meet the case for some time to come.

Amendment proposed,

To leave out from the word "That," to the end of the Question, in order to add the words "this House views with deep regret the impossibility of at present introducing the Education Bill for Ireland promised last year by the Chief Secretary, and that, seeing the hardships which the Irish National Teachers are undoubtedly subjected to, and the necessity which exists of rendering so important a body of public servants contented with their work, this House is of opinion that provision should be made forthwith to improve their incomes temporarily, and that a Bill removing their several grievances should be introduced early in the next Session,"—(*Mr. Justin Huntly M'Carthy,*)

—instead thereof.

Question proposed, "That the words proposed to be left out stand part of the Question."

COLONEL COLTHURST, in supporting the Motion, said, he should be sorry to think that the success or partial success of the teachers' claim should depend upon whether the Government were appreciably to increase the grant for education. Even if it were not increased a great deal might be done to remedy the great grievances of the Irish teachers. When the Unions were made contributory, a large number at first availed themselves of the power of contributing, and they did not find their contributions burdensome to the rates. The Cork Union contributed up to the present time, and did not find it burdensome to do so. But one Union after another dropped off; the example became contagious, and now the number contributing was reduced to four. Whether or not a National rate for Poor Law purposes would be justifiable he did not say; but there could be no question it would be justified in the case of education; and he believed still if the right hon. Gentleman the Chief Secretary for Ireland brought in a Bill next year, authorizing a National rate of 1*d.* in the pound, it would amply provide the Irish National School teachers with an adequate addition to their salaries.

There should be a minimum below which the salaries of no well-classed teacher should fall, and if such a rate as he had suggested were adopted, the minimum salary would be provided. With regard to pensions, he was of opinion that the demands of the teachers were fair. He thought 35 years' service should entitle a teacher to a pension, irrespective of age. The Teachers' Residences Act was no doubt a very liberal and praiseworthy measure, as it offered to any locality in which it was desired to build a teacher's house, a sum of £200. It was possible for a teacher in a good district to take advantage of that Act; but a teacher with a poor salary, and with managers who would not assist him, could not. It was also nearly impossible to obtain suitable sites for teachers' dwellings, owing to the want of sympathy that existed between the rich and poor classes in Ireland; and since the passing of the Land Act, there was the greatest disinclination on the part of occupiers of land to part with a bit of land upon any terms whatever, and if teachers were to be properly housed, compulsory power should be given to acquire sites on which to build residences. He thought his hon. Friend (Mr. Justin Huntly M'Carthy) had done good service in bringing this matter before the House, and he hoped that the Chief Secretary for Ireland would give precedence next Session over all other measures, including the Irish Sunday Closing Bill, to a well-considered Parliamentary scheme for redressing the many grievances which harassed and embarrassed the action of the National School teachers of Ireland.

MR. DAWSON said, he had great pleasure in congratulating his hon. Friend the Member for Athlone (Mr. Justin Huntly M'Carthy) on his admirable speech in introducing the subject; but he could not congratulate the hon. and gallant Member who had just sat down (Colonel Colthurst) on the remedy of hope deferred, which he had proposed as a solution of the Irish National School teachers' grievance. Educators of the people in Ireland were shamefully neglected. The teachers in England and in foreign countries were treated with the deepest respect; but in Ireland the reverse of that was the case. This was, he contended, due to the fact that, in the latter, the teachers were protected by the Govenment; while, in Ireland, they were scarcely officially recognized. The minimum salaries formerly offered to National schoolmasters—namely, £15, were such as a cook would not accept; and the maximum salaries, £45, they would not offer to their valet. No doubt, that state of things had been improved through the exertions of the hon. and learned Member for Kildare (Mr. Meldon); but still their remuneration was entirely incommensurate with their abilities and devotion to work. The disproportion which existed between their salaries and those of English and Scotch teachers were almost inexplicable, and he failed to see any reason why the social position of an English teacher should be better than that of an Irish teacher, or why, in this country, teachers' salaries should be 100 per cent more than they were in Ireland. He hoped the Government in the future would give the same protection to Irish teachers as they had afforded in the past to teachers in England. The teachers in Ireland were paid by results; but there was no compulsory education in the country as in England, so that the teachers were not given the materials for producing results. With regard to pensions, teachers usually entered the Profession at 17 or 18. If they retired at 38, after 20 years' service, they got £6 a-year pension; if they retired at 48, after 30 years' service, they got £18; if at 53, after 35 years' service, they got £25; and if at 65, after 47 years' service, they got half their salary. An Inspector of Police who, on the other hand, retired at 49, after 27 years' service, got a pension equal to his full pay of £200 a-year. Again, the teacher was obliged to pay something in order to add to his pension. If he lived he got it back; but if, after years of labour, he died before getting it back, the money was confiscated, instead of coming to his family in the hour of its greatest need. He did not deny that they had obtained some advantages, the Government having, at one time, given them a small taste of their bounty; but since then they had withdrawn it, and, in the main, all the promises which had been made to them had proved illusory. They got the promise of residences; but as their erection was made perfectly optional with the managers, the teachers were still without residences. [Colonel NOLAN:

The managers could not get sites.] Then, they were to get grants from the Unions; but that promise had also proved illusory. The contributions from the Poor Law Unions were practically nothing; and, looking at the unpopular and unpatriotic character of the administration of the Commissioners of National Education, he must confess he did not blame the Guardians for not contributing to a system with which they had no sympathy. Soon after the passing of the Act, the teachers got £27,000 from 65 Unions, but, in 1882, they only got £9,000. These things might be amended by a Bill which he was told the right hon. Gentleman had in his pigeon-holes. But the question was, what would the Government do to relieve the teachers to-day? He would suggest that the right hon. Gentleman the Chief Secretary for Ireland, with the aid of the Prime Minister, should introduce a Supplementary (*ad interim*) Vote to help those unfortunate people.

Mr. TREVELYAN said, that the hon. Member for Athlone (Mr. Justin Huntly M'Carthy) had introduced the subject in a speech which showed, at any rate, that he sympathized with everything which concerned education. It was an extremely cultivated speech, and one which, as a veteran of the House, he might be allowed to say gave very good hope as to the contributions which, in after years, the hon. Member might make to the debates of that House. The hon. Member had stated the case of the Irish teachers with a view to an immediate solution, which was put in a more definite and pointed form in the peroration of the hon. Member who had just sat down (Mr. Dawson). The proposal of the hon. Members was that a Supplementary Grant should be made out of the general Exchequer; but before the Government acceded to such a proposal, they would have to examine the premisses upon which it was asked; and, in examining those premisses, he had come to a conclusion very different from those of the hon. and gallant Member for Galway and the hon. Member for Carlow. It had been said by the hon. Member for Athlone that unsuccessful attempts had been made to better the position of the teachers, and that their position was now as bad as for many years back. Upon that point, he at once joined issue with the hon. Member. The position of Irish teachers had improved to a wonderful degree of late years. Since 1871 their position had been improved in one way and another, the most definite and remarkable of which was the introduction of the system of result fees. In the year 1872 the salaries of masters in the way of class ranged from £52 to £24, whereas they now ranged from £70 to £35; while the class salaries of mistresses, which, in 1872, ranged from £20 to £42, now ranged from £27 to £58. The payment per pupil had risen from 13*s.* 11*d.* in 1871, to £1 3*s.* 8*d.* in 1882, and the collective figures proved still more that an immense improvement had been made in the course of the last 10 years. Again, in the year 1871 the grant to Ireland from the Exchequer was £381,000, and in 1883-4 it was £726,000. Of those amounts, £262,000 was paid to the teachers in 1870-1; and in 1883-4 the amount was £580,000. That was an immense rise, and absolved the Government, as he thought, from the charge that they had done little or nothing in the matter for many years past. Comparisons which, though sufficiently striking, were, he thought, considerably exaggerated, had been made between the position of the teachers in Ireland and those in England and Scotland. It had been asserted that teachers in England and Scotland were paid twice as much as those in Ireland. The fact was that the average teacher in Ireland got as much as £80 a-year; while the average certificated master in England received £120. That was, no doubt, a very considerable difference; but it was not twice as much. [Mr. Dawson: What about the female teachers?] The average annual salary of the female teachers in Ireland would certainly amount to £60 from all sources; while in England it would amount to £72. He had not taken the general average. The difference would be represented very much more accurately by half as much again than by twice as much. When a demand was made for money from the Exchequer—that was, for money paid by the taxpayers of the whole Kingdom—it was necessary to look not only at the actual position of the people it was to benefit, but also at what the taxpayer had done for them already. Respecting it, he had to take a great deal of exception to what had been said by hon. Members. He would not enter into the general causes which had been referred to to explain the very different average which local aid occupied in Ireland and in England; but there could be no doubt it was very great indeed. In England, the population at the last Census was 26,000,000, and the Parliamentary Grant was £2,400,000. The number of pupils was 3,000,000, and the payment for each pupil from the Exchequer was 15*s.* 10½*d.* The payment for each pupil in Scotland was 17*s.* 8½*d.*, and in Ireland £1 11*s.* 1½*d.* Now, he was sure no Englishman or Scotchman, neither would he himself, grudge that favourable proportion to Ireland; but it was a serious matter to ask the taxpayers of the Kingdom to increase that amount. If £100,000 were granted to these teachers, it must be recollected that of that amount Ireland would only pay £10,000, Scotland £11,000, and England about £79,000. The hon. and gallant Member for Galway (Colonel Nolan), who was a clever statistician, had somehow made out that Scotland received more than Ireland in the matter of education; but the calculation he (Mr. Trevelyan) had made was that it did not receive as much as Ireland, though the proportion of population was as 4 to 5. In Scotland at the last Census there were 3,735,000 people, and 421,000 pupils on the rolls. As he had said, in England there were 26,000,000 of people, and £2,400,000 was paid by the Exchequer. That was something less than 2*s.* a-head for the population. In Ireland there were 5,160,000 people, and £730,000 paid by the Exchequer, or nearly 3*s.* a-head for the population. In Scotland there were 3,700,000 people, and only £372,000 paid for popular education, or about 2*s.* a-head for the population; so that, instead of Scotland having more or as much paid to her for education as Ireland, she had only a little more than half as much. That being so, he thought the House should be very slow indeed to improve the condition of Irish teachers any further by direct money payments out of the Exchequer. He was sure, however, that there was no Englishman or Scotchman who would not improve the position of the Irish teachers, if it was done by the same process as in England and Scotland, and that was by securing a better attendance of the pupils, and, consequently, better results. One great cause of the poorness of the condition of the Irish teacher as compared to those of England and Scotland, was the deficiency in the result fees, owing to the number of children who went to school being so very much less for each teacher; and, therefore, the one method of improving the position of the Irish teachers, which, more than anything else, would, he thought, be approved of by hon. Members in every part of the House, was the introduction into Ireland of a system of compulsory education. He did not wish to press too far the argument which had been alluded to by anticipation by almost every speaker on this subject that night; but the real cause why Irish teachers were so badly paid was the absence of local aid. What the cause of that absence of local aid might be, he would not discuss at the present moment. The absence of that aid, however, was more striking than hon. Members opposite were aware. The hon. Members opposite had referred to the want of endowments in Ireland, and to the absence of the rich class; but there was one source of local aid which did not depend upon the presence of the rich, except indirectly, and that was the school pence. In England, with 3,000,000 of children, the school pence amounted to £1,500,000—that was to say, each child contributed 10*s.* a-year. In Ireland, with 469,000 children, the school pence amounted to £93,000, or about 4*s.* a-head. Then he came to the voluntary subscriptions; and here he must express his entire sympathy with those hon. Members who lamented the very small sum which was contributed voluntarily towards the support of the Irish schools. There was not in Ireland the same class as in England, who were inclined to subscribe voluntarily towards the support of the schools, or, at all events, its benevolence and public spirit did not run in that direction; and by far the most striking grievance of Ireland was the existence of Irish landlords in the South who did not do their duty, nor a tithe of their duty, towards the education of the people. [MR. KENNY: Or anything else.] He would confine himself to the matter of education at present. In England the sum raised by voluntary contributions for educational purposes was £724,000, in Scotland it was £30,000, and in Ireland it was £40,000. The deficiency this caused, which he thought was a serious evil, had to be met, and he thought it was made up by very much larger contributions from the Exchequer to Ireland in proportion than to England. Then he came to the income derived from rates, and this was a most significant fact, because the rates were, after all, the contributions not only of the few rich men, but they were exactly in proportion to the wealth and poverty of the members of the entire community. In England the sum derived from the rates was £808,000; in Scotland, £191,000; and in Ireland, £11,904. The main reason for this difference in figures was that in Scotland, the rates were entirely compulsory; in England, they were to a large extent compulsory; while in Ireland, they were voluntary. He could not concur on this point in the observation of the hon. Member for Carlow (Mr. Dawson), who said that the English Government had just let the teachers taste of their bounty, and had then withdrawn it. That observation should have referred not to the English Government, but to the Boards of Guardians. The latter had the power of contributing in exactly the same way as all the Boards of Guardians in Scotland did, and as a considerable number in England did. Under the circumstances, however, it was not his business to blame the Irish Boards of Guardians for their action in this matter—in fact, he did not think that they were to blame in reference to it, because people would not, in the long run, bear their share of a voluntary rate, for the purpose of giving a man a larger salary than he was willing to work for. By subscribing this money they would not get more children educated; they only gave the teachers a better salary, and considering how formidable the increase of rates was, he did not wonder that so few Boards subscribed, or that the people declined to take fresh dues voluntarily upon themselves. But if the ratepayers of Ireland would not do in this matter as the ratepayers of England and Scotland did, the responsibility no longer rested upon the English Government, but upon the people of Ireland, speaking through their Representatives, who objected to the rates in aid being made compulsorily. In the very poorest parishes in Scotland, the school rate was paid cheerfully, and sometimes eagerly. With regard to the residences of the school teachers, he entirely sympathized with the Bill dealing with the subject, which had been introduced by the hon. and gallant Member for Cork County (Colonel Colthurst). There, however, again, Parliament was not to blame. Money might be borrowed for their construction, maintenance, and improvement, repayable in 35 years, at 3½ per cent interest, which were far more reasonable terms than England could obtain, and it was hardly fair to reproach the Government, when those facilities were not taken advantage of. With reference to sites for these residences, however, there was a difficulty, and no Bill would be introduced by the Government which did not remove that grievance thoroughly and completely. The hon. Member for Athlone had referred to the question of pensions, and had remarked that the reason why there was better provision for teachers' salaries in England and Scotland than in Ireland was the superior educational endowments in those countries. In England and in Scotland the teacher had not got a pension. In Ireland, although the conditions were not so favourable as could be wished, the teacher had a pension, and the fact was that there was greater provision in Ireland for paying teachers' pensions out of endowments than in England. A sum of £1,300,000 out of the Irish Church Funds was set aside for teachers' pensions, which was as much an endowment fund as anything could be; and, further, owing to the ancient endowments which had now been diverted to another purpose, the Irish teachers had an advantage which they appreciated, and which was not possessed by England and Scotland. As to the methods by which these pensions were distributed, the fair comparison was not with the Irish Police, but with the teachers of England and Scotland, and the fair question to ask was—whether the £1,300,000 allotted for pensions was distributed so as to be of the greatest advantage to Ireland. The allowances for long and meritorious services were calculated by actuaries on the quinquennial scale, the mean period being 35 years. Five years was the very least period at which a system of pensions ought to be revised, and as to the system it was necessary to adopt age in preference to time of service, so as not to exclude the great number of Irish teachers who had not originally been Government teachers; and until, at any rate, these men and women had passed off the scene, the Government could not alter this arrangement. The quinquennial distribution would come next year. He had reason to believe that there was a surplus, and it would be disbursed so as to be of the greatest advantage to the main body of the teachers. [Mr. Arthur O'Connor: How is the scheme received by the teachers?] Hon. Members seemed to doubt whether the teachers valued the system. The best evidence of that was that out of 10,621 teachers in the Service, 9,343, or 88 per cent, had joined in it, though it involved a payment from their own resources. Beyond that, he thought the vast majority of them would be found supporting it when it became known that the membership was voluntary, not compulsory. There was no way of improving the teachers' incomes except they obtained a higher classification, and one reason they were unable to obtain a high classification was the deficient and anomalous system of training in Ireland. Still, he thought when hon. Members made speeches condemning the shortcomings of the Government, they ought to say something about what the Government had done. They ought to remember that for a Minister who had left a former Government on the question of undenominational education, it was not an easy matter for him to go back on his antecedents and persuade successfully a House, which was largely leavened with strong undenominational sentiments, to do in Ireland that which alone could enable the Irish teachers to take advantage of the system of training. They must not expect too much in the first year of a new system; but this year they proposed to divide a sum of £10,000 between three Training Colleges of the sort to which Irish teachers were willing to resort, and to which Irishmen in general were glad to contribute. But that was not all; for the Government had viewed with favour, and very practical favour, the proposal that public money should be lent for the building of Training Colleges. His general reply, he was afraid, would disappoint many hon. Members. The Government would not bring in an Education Bill for Ireland which did not deal drastically with the question of sites, and that did not establish a system of compulsory education of a nature which the Leaders of the Irish people would generally accept; the Government would not bring in a Bill which would give the Irish Members an opportunity of saying that they would call upon the ratepayers of Ireland to do what the ratepayers of Scotland had done, though he could well understand that the Government would not make that a point on which the other provisions of the Bill must stand or fall. But when it came to a question of paying more money out of the Exchequer, except in the shape of improved result fees and kindred matters, there he must stop and say that he could not advise the Treasury to assent. He could not accept the Resolution of the hon. Member for Athlone, except on a condition which the hon. Member would hardly accept—namely, to leave out all the words from "opinion" down to "that Bill." Unless he accepted that offer, he was afraid he could not do anything in the matter.

Mr. ARTHUR O'CONNOR: Would the right hon. Gentleman tell the House what is the present position of the Training Colleges?

Mr. TREVELYAN said, the system of grants to these Colleges was exactly the same as in England and Scotland; £10,000 had been taken this year, of which £3,319 was to go to the College in Bagot Street; £5,273 to St. Patrick's Training College, in Drumcondra; and £1,440 was to be expended on the new College of the Church of Ireland, to be opened in Kildare Street in September.

Mr. ARTHUR O'CONNOR: Are there only three denominational Training Colleges in Ireland?

Mr. TREVELYAN: Yes.

Mr. HEALY said, he was sorry to say he was sure the statement of the right hon. Gentleman (Mr. Trevelyan) would be received with intense disappointment, not only by teachers in Ireland, but by the entire country. The right hon. Gentleman had told the teachers they had nothing to expect from the Government. There was no hope whatever of the Bill suggested being accepted in Ireland, and he was amazed, and thought it extraordinary, that when a Gentleman distinguished for candour, as the Chief Secretary to the Lord Lieutenant was, was making his stinging contrast between the contribution from the local rates in England and Scotland and those made in Ireland, that he overlooked the important point that the Irish people, unlike the English and Scotch, had no more to say to the class of education they received than the people of Lapland. Compulsorily educational contributions from local rates would be fought tooth and nail by the Irish Members, unless the Boards of Guardians were previously altered upon the lines of the Poor Law Guardians Bill, and unless there was a complete reform of the so-called Board of National Education, whose leading characteristics he (Mr. Healy) declared were anti-national. That Board included the Judges, Mr. Chief Justice Morris, Mr. Justice Lawson, together with other successful patriots, and likewise four Protestant clergymen and one Protestant Archbishop; but it had not upon it any Catholic Bishop or priest. They must have that Board made representative and thoroughly national. In fact, there was no hope of their ever obtaining a thoroughly efficient system, until they swept away, root and branch, the whole of what was called the National Board, or, at any rate, they must swamp them, before they would have the confidence of the Irish people. With respect to the new denominational Training Schools, he was anxious to know how they were to be maintained? Were Roman Catholics to support their Training College, the Presbyterians theirs, and the Protestant Episcopalians theirs, or were they to be supported out of a common fund? If that were so, he would ask the House to look at the injustice of the proposal. The majority of the ratepayers in Ireland were Catholics, they constituted four-fifths of the population, and were they to be made to find the largest share of the money, and pay rates for the benefit of other denominations, with whose schools and teachings they had no sympathy? They must have a stringent guarantee, before they would consent to compulsory rating, that they should have proper representation, and that the money of the Catholic and Protestant and Presbyterian people would go to Catholics and Protestants and Presbyterians respectively. He would now ask the House to consider the position and prospects of the Irish teachers as compared with those of the Irish Constabulary. Why, there were more policemen than there were teachers in Ireland, showing that it was the policy of the Government to coerce the people, and at the same time keep them plunged in ignorance. So, too, the Vote for Education was £732,627, while that for the Police was £1,440,095, or nearly double. The constables were far better paid and received far better pensions than the Irish National School teachers. It took a teacher 47 years to gain a pension of £35 a-year; while a constable, after 20 years' service, received £30 a-year, a teacher receiving the magnificent sum of £6 a-year for the same period. If the Constabulary did not get the pay they wanted, as had lately been seen in Dublin and in Limerick, they instantly struck, and they received what they wanted. In fact, the Government had not so much power over them as, in ancient times, the Romans had over the Prætorian Guards. The reason of that was that the British Government knew that, without the aid of their bayonets, they could never keep up English rule in the country. But if the teachers were to try to follow their example, the Secretary to the Treasury would be quite tranquil, for the Government would be only too pleased to save the cost of the education of the children, whom they would prefer to see grow up in ignorance. Then the right hon. Gentleman had told them that he would bring in a Bill for compulsory education in Ireland. So far as he (Mr. Healy) was aware, there was no feeling in the country adverse to compulsory education, and he thought that, with proper safeguards, the system would be received with satisfaction by the country at large. The real cause of the non-attendance of children was, in his opinion, due to the extreme poverty of the people, whose children had such wretched clothing that they were not able to go to school and associate with children who were better dressed. On the other hand, if those who did not attend for that reason did attend, children of a better class would not care to mix with them, and would probably be withdrawn. The right hon. Gentleman had, no doubt, come down again to the House prepared to rebut the case he (Mr. Healy) was endeavouring to present to the House on behalf of these poor people; but the statements on which he was going to rebut them had been prepared by officials in Dublin, with salaries of £1,000, or £1,500 a-year, who were clad in broadcloth, whose stomachs were not empty, and who lived in grand houses. Those were the people who were trying to prevent any improvement being effected in the condition of a wretched class of persons with an income of £55. The expenses of the Office which supplied the right hon. Gentleman with his facts amounted to £732,000. Then, £26,000 was paid for agents, £40,000 for Inspectors, £33,000 for model schools, which were not wanted, and £10,000 for normal establishments. Those services, paid for on that scale, left only a total of £570,000 for Irish National School teachers. They were told that the teachers' positions must be improved out of the rates; but they would not find the Irish people disposed to vote a penny out of the rates in addition so long as the working of the system was controlled by a Board full of Protestants and Presbyterians. As to the teachers themselves, taking into consideration the amount received by those in England and Scotland, it could hardly be expected that they could get the best class of men for the post for £57 a-year. The comparative treatment of the Constabulary and the teachers was a disgrace. There was far more inducement to become a policeman in Ireland than a teacher; not only were the former better paid, for a sub-constable on joining the Force got, on an average, £4 a-year more than a well-paid National School teacher, but, in addition, they also got both clothing and lodging free, besides magnificent pensions. There was no question about sites for police barracks; but there was for schoolhouses. Indeed, police barracks and workhouses were the most ornamental objects in Irish landscapes. He ventured to think there was not so disgraceful a story to tell of Russian government in Poland, as the one he had read with shame and humiliation—namely, the treatment of the teachers in connection with their annual dinner which had taken place in Dublin. Because, after drinking the health of the Queen, they had not drunk that of Earl Spencer, who was simply a Member of Mr. Gladstone's Cabinet, an explanation was demanded, and every teacher would have been dismissed had they not made an abject apology. The circulars had been signed by a Mr. Sheridan; and he (Mr. Healy) should be happy, at the proper time, to move the reduction of the Vote by the amount of his salary. Where was this absurdity to end? The meanness and the odious and contemptible character of such tyranny were atrocious, yet the right hon. Gentleman the Chief Secretary for Ireland winked at it. He (Mr. Healy) never heard him utter a word in extenuation of a system which in Ireland excited only indignation and disgust. He supposed that, after drinking the health of the Lord Lieutenant and of the Lady Lieutenant, it would henceforth be necessary to drink that of His Royal Highness the Prince of Wales, and that of Her Royal Highness the Princess of Wales, and then that of the little Princes of Wales, and the little Princesses of Wales, and so on, until they came down to policemen. That was the absurdity to which they had come. He hoped that, on the Estimates, they would have some explanation of that state of things, failing which, it would afford him great satisfaction to move a few Resolutions. He had to say, finally, that the few miserable grants that were made were doled out in the most wretched way imaginable to the teachers and their relatives. He charged the Government with, in some instances, keeping the money from the sick and dying men. To a man who was sick a grant of £30 or £40 was of great consequence. It could, at all events, procure him a great many necessaries which were essential to the alleviation of his suffering, and it might, at least, be sufficient to cover the expenses of burial when the man was dead. But the Government, or those well-paid persons in Dublin who were charged with its administration, carped at these trifles in the spirit of Shylock, and denied the amounts to the persons who were entitled to them or to their relatives. That state of things, he thought, could not be defended by the Government. He regretted the action which had been taken by the Government with respect to the Motion, and in declining to yield to the demands of the teachers. The right hon. Gentleman had not shown the least sympathy, or the least intention of yielding anything for the poor people for whom he was pleading; but he could tell the right hon. Gentleman that those 11,000 or 12,000 persons would remember how they had been treated.

MR. TREVELYAN said, he wished to explain, with reference to the averages given by the hon. and gallant Member for Galway (Colonel Nolan), that the comparison which he made was between the certificated masters in London and the principal masters and mistresses in England, and the principal masters and mistresses in Ireland. Although the comparison of the hon. and gallant Member was not an unfair one, yet, on reflection, he saw that the hon. and gallant Member included the assistant teachers in his comparison. He (Mr. Trevelyan) had not made out the comparison between the principal and assistant teachers combined with the certificated and uncertificated masters.

MR. PATRICK MARTIN said, it appeared to him that the present was not a fitting or opportune occasion to enter on the discussion of, or to express his individual opinion on, questions of such importance as the establishment of a system of compulsory education in Ireland or the constitution of the Board of Commissioners for National Education. What, then, the friends of the National School teachers desired was to hear a statement made, showing that the Government had given some real consideration to the demands made, and were prepared to apply a speedy and efficacious remedy for the principal grievances which had been admitted to affect this important and deserving body of public servants. He had been much disappointed at the tone of the reply of the right hon. Gentleman the Chief Secretary for Ireland. He proposed no feasible solution for the difficulties incident to the failure of the Act of 1875. Vague statements were made that at some distant date, and contingent on a general change in the system of education, the funds required were to be provided from local sources. The late Chief Secretary (Sir Michael Hicks-Beach) stated that the teachers were to participate in the full benefits contemplated by the Act.

Notice taken, that 40 Members were not present; House counted, and 40 Members being found present,

MR. PATRICK MARTIN, continuing, said, he recollected that the late Chief Secretary, when the Act of 1875 was under discussion, and he had been warned in the House that the Act was destined to be a total failure, stated that it would be tried only as an experiment, and if it failed, means should be devised by the Government to obtain funds to pay result fees in full to the teachers. Subsequently, in 1876, when it became clear the Act would not work, he proposed to make the provisions in the Act compulsory; but, on inquiry, he found that to pass an Act by which the Boards of Guardians should be compelled to contribute to the result fee was impossible, and that such a measure would receive the opposition of the great bulk of the Irish Members. The very figures of the Permissive Act showed, in the clearest manner, that the ratepayers in Ireland would never consent to the passing of a Compulsory Act. For what did they find? That the number of contributory Unions, which began under the Act at 70, had, since it had been made manifest that the Government did not intend to bring in a Bill by which the grievances of the teachers could be remedied, successively decreased, until it had reached the present number of four. Under these circumstances, he thought the House had a right to feel disappointed with the reply of the Chief Secretary for Ireland. It was but a repetition, in its main statements, of the promises made and expectations held forth in 1876. It was high time the Government should make up their mind on this question. If, as was plain, the Government were determined, in the present state of things in Ireland, to retain the entire control of education in the hands of Commissioners appointed by, and responsible alone, to the Government, it was just they should provide the funds required. It was absurd to expect the Guardians to contribute, unless they had also a voice in the management, and there was a popular element in the management and control of the educational system. Was the right hon. Gentleman prepared to say that national education should be controlled by the popular vote? If not, then it would have been better to have said that the Government had no intention of doing anything, than to have made the speech he did. It would have been better not to have raised expectations that would only lead to disappointment. The right hon.

Baronet the late Chief Secretary for Ireland, backed by a strong Government, could not bring in a Bill to make the contributions of Boards of Guardians compulsory. Was it not, then, most unreasonable that the Chief Secretary, after the promises he had made and the answers he had given to the teachers' deputations, should now suggest that after he had consulted with and ascertained the views of the Irish Members he would consider the propriety of bringing in a Bill of this character? The majority of Irish Members had more than once stated that any measure framed on those lines would have their opposition to encounter. As to the privations suffered by the teachers from want of suitable residences, he thought the House had a right to complain of the conduct of the Government. The Government had opposed the Bill of the hon. and gallant Member for Galway (Colonel Nolan) to make provisions for teachers' residences. Nothing was done. Not the slightest effort was made by legislation to provide a remedy for the difficulties incident to the procuring of sites from landlords either legally unable or unwillin to give them. The Treasury, too, had, as was pointed out by their Minutes, in fact, frustrated the intentions of Parliament. Yet even in this respect, as well as in respect to the pensions question, where remedies might be at once provided by an alteration in the Treasury Minutes and Regulations, no satisfactory assurance had been given. He trusted the Secretary to the Treasury would now at last rise and promise that his Department would recede from the position they had taken up in these matters. It was conceded by the Chief Secretary that many of the complaints of the teachers were well-founded, and that their conduct as a body entitled them to favourable consideration. The fact that they were not as highly trained as the English and Scotch teachers was the fault of the Government; and if their English and Scotch brethren were better educated, they were in receipt of double their salary. Nothing was more calculated to create discontent than the admission that grievances existed without any earnest attempt to remedy them. He, therefore, trusted that the Government would reconsider the position they had taken up, and that, instead of opposing, they would accept the terms of the Resolution, which were only fair and reasonable.

Mr. O'DONNELL said, he thought that the treatment of the question under discussion during the evening had been characteristic of the manner in which Irish questions were generally treated by the House of Commons. Nearly all the 500 and odd English and Scotch Gentleman who undertook to govern Ireland had been mainly conspicuous by their absence during the discussion of this important subject. At all events, those Gentlemen who were absent had been spared the mortification of hearing the set of utterly callous platitudes with which the Scotch Secretary for Ireland replied to the complaints of the Irish Party. The speech of the right hon. Gentleman was mainly composed of direct or indirect compliments to the independence of the Scotch people; but he seemed to have no sympathy whatever with the people whose affairs he was sent to administer. There was no indication in it of a promise to do anything for the Irish teachers. He (Mr. O'Donnell) came down to give his warmest support to the Resolution; but it was no disappointment to him to hear the speech of the Chief Secretary for Ireland, because he full well knew that there would be no substantial reform hinted at by the Government. They were told that the Government were not unwilling to bring in a Bill for compulsory education. With proper guarantees, such a Bill would be welcomed by all who were interested in the education of the Irish people; but, apart from that, some prompt and efficient measure for remedying the grievances of the teachers ought to be introduced. The Irish National School teachers were obliged to eke out their miserable pittance by burdening themselves with the obligation of cultivating plots of land. They laboured under this disability—that they were a peaceful and a law-abiding body of men, who brought up their pupils on peaceful and law-abiding principles, and, consequently, Her Majesty's Government felt they could despise their complaints and disregard their feelings. If there were any danger whatever that a refusal to redress their grievances would be followed by a healthy development of what would be called in this country "Constitutional sedition" among this large body of public servants, a great deal more attention would be paid by the Government to their complaints than was now given to the utterances of their Parliamentary Representatives. The course now taken by Her Majesty's Government was a distinct violation of the pledge made by their Predecessors in 1875, when the right hon. Baronet the late Chief Secretary for Ireland (Sir Michael Hicks-Beach), in proposing a measure for the relief of the teachers, said—

"If it succeeds, well and good; the teachers will be reasonably remunerated. If not, the Government will take such steps that the remuneration now intended shall be paid to them."

That intended remuneration had not been paid to them, and the speech of the Chief Secretary for Ireland showed that the present Government had no intention of fulfilling the pledge so clearly and emphatically given by their Predecessors in Office.

SIR PATRICK O'BRIEN said, that he deprecated the language that had been applied to the right hon. Gentleman the Chief Secretary for Ireland. Notwithstanding his "platitudes," as the hon. Member for Dungarvan (Mr. O'Donnell) had termed them, he (Sir Patrick O'Brien) was of opinion that, so far as policy was concerned, a more honest Chief Secretary than the present holder of the Office had never sat upon the Treasury Bench. But if the Poor Law Guardians did not do their duty in the matter of education, it was for the Government to compel them to do it; and the statement of the right hon. Gentleman showed that no other course was open. What did the hon. Member for Monaghan mean when he said that the Poor Law Guardians could not be expected to assist the teachers when they had not the control of education? Did he mean that they should be a distinguished Philosophical Society to draw up the curriculum? [Mr. HEALY: No.] Was it that they had not the arrangement of the money matters? He was in a difficulty with the hon. Gentleman; but, with all his astuteness, if he accepted either alternative, he (Sir Patrick O'Brien) would impale him on the horns of a dilemma. He agreed with the hon. Member who said that the case was harassing and painful, and required immediate attention; and as the Chief Secretary for Ireland had not seen fit, or rather had not been empowered, to put down on the Estimates a sum to meet the present difficulty, he should vote for the Motion of the hon. Member for Athlone (Mr. Justin Huntly M'Carthy), if he went to a Division. He should do so, however, without using the grievances of the teachers as a political stalking horse, by claiming local control of finances, or curriculum. The remedy was to be found in compelling the Guardians to pay their contributions, instead of leaving it optional with them; and he hoped the right hon. Gentleman, in the Bill he proposed to bring in, would tax the nation in the interests of the nation—namely the education of the people.

MR. MARUM said, that the people of Ireland were greatly alarmed at the growth of local taxation, and, while there was every disposition on the part of Boards of Guardians to act fairly by the National School teachers, they would object to an increase of the burden of local taxation, which had increased since 1866 by £1,000,000 sterling. It already amounted to 35 per cent of the rental of Ireland, and if this taxation went on increasing, the ratepayers would soon be swamped by it. Apart from that pressure, there was no indisposition on the part of the Guardians to spend rates for educational purposes; but they felt that to put the entire burden upon the land was unfair, owing to the relations which existed between Ireland and England. He thought the parallel drawn by the Chief Secretary for Ireland, between Ireland and England in this regard, was altogether unfair, seeing that, in Ireland, they had practically no manufactures or commerce as they had in England, and that the entire population was thrown upon the land. The incidence of local taxation and the Imperial burdens placed upon it required as much consideration in Ireland as in England, and the hardship was greater in Ireland, because of the absence of commercial wealth, which was kept out by continued misgovernment.

MR. FINDLATER said, he decidedly deprecated the introduction into the debate on that question of any violent Party politics. He did not think any such controversy was in the interest of the Irish teachers. He should say he did not think that the teachers were treated fairly by the Government, and he would cordially support the vote for the Resolution.

MR. JOHN REDMOND said, he quite agreed with the hon. Member (Mr. Findlater) as to the undesirability of mixing up Party politics with a question of this kind. All classes in Ireland were actuated with the one desire to see the admitted grievances of the Irish teachers remedied. They were told that it would be necessary to make the rate in aid compulsory. That might or might not be necessary. At the first blush, he was not disposed in its favour; but until that was done—if it were to be done—were the grievances of the teachers to remain unredressed? What they claimed that night was that the Government should endeavour at once to remove the injustice under which the National School teachers of Ireland now suffered. There was no Party in Ireland—National, Liberal, or Tory—which did not admit the grievances of the Irish teachers, and yet these most deserving men were left without the means of a decent livelihood. He believed the people of Ireland would be quite ready to contribute freely to the expenses of education, if they had the control of it in their own hands. That night the teachers' case entered on a new phase. He heartily congratulated them on the fact that their case was no longer in the hands of a Gentleman representing an Irish constituency, who, at the same time, no doubt, showed some zeal in the interests of his clients, but who appeared now to consider much more keenly the interests and the convenience of the Government than the interests of the teachers. It was now in the hands of the Irish Parliamentary Party, and on behalf of himself and his Colleagues he would say night or day henceforward they would not cease their active exertions until the justice so long delayed was done to this deserving body of men.

MR. KENNY, in supporting the Resolution, said, that Irish National School teachers had been compelled to live in houses which were entirely unsuited to persons in their station in life. Therefore, the time, he thought, had come when proper dwellings should be provided for them. At the close of the year 1880 there were 7,429 teachers in charge of the Irish National Schools, and the number of residences supplied rent free was 1,515. Out of that number, 235 had been built under the provisions of the Residences Act since 1875, and the remaining 1,280 had been provided without aid from the State. In England 47 per cent of the teachers, and in Scotland 57 per cent, were provided with residences; but in Ireland only about 15 per cent were so provided, and in many cases their residences were very miserable. The Chief Secretary for Ireland had said that, with regard to pensions, the Irish teachers were better off than their brethren in England and Scotland, who had no such provision made for them. That difference, however, arose from the merest fortunate accident. When the Church in Ireland had been disestablished and disendowed, a sum of £1,300,000 was set apart, the interest of which was to furnish three-fourths of the pensions, while the teachers themselves contributed one-fourth, which was withheld from their salaries. But as no male teacher was entitled to a pension until he was 65, and no female teacher until she was 60, it might be concluded that there were very few National teachers in Ireland who were pensioners. The Chief Secretary for Ireland had also stated that, while in England the children contributed 10*s.* per head of the school fees, in Ireland they contributed only 4*s.* per head. That was a very creditable contribution from the Irish children, considering that the comparative wealth of the two countries was as 13 or 14 to 1. The hon. Gentleman the present economical Financial Secretary to the Treasury was, he was sorry to say, one whose policy was not such as would lead them to believe that there was much likelihood that the demands of the teachers would be granted. He quite agreed in the observations of the preceding speakers as to the inadequate salaries which the teachers were paid for the services which they rendered the country.

MR. T. D. SULLIVAN said, he considered the case of the National School teachers embodied a distinct breach of faith against Her Majesty's Government. The Bill they had introduced completely broke down, the ratepayers having declined to support the experiment which the right hon. Gentleman the late Chief Secretary for Ireland (Sir Michael Hicks-Beach) promised would adequately deal with the grievances, under which it was admitted a most deserving body of men suffered. They had been told that, within some definite number of years, the position of these men had been very considerably improved. To a certain degree, no doubt, it had; but only from the point of starvation and disgrace. It had been improved, but had not as yet reached the level of justice. It was the old story, for, like all English legislation, the grievances were not redressed, but were dealt with in the usual peddling, piecemeal fashion, which satisfied nobody. The system which had been adopted by the Government of that country, in dealing with Irish affairs, had been always of that piecemeal character, which satisfied nobody. It was a little patch here and a little patch there, wasting the time of Parliament and breaking the hearts of the unfortunate people who had been kept all this time waiting for justice. He had heard their condition contrasted with that of the Police, both with regard to salaries and pensions, and he felt compelled to say that the case afforded a true indication of the whole system of British rule in Ireland. The position might be summed up with these words—they petted the policemen and they starved the teachers. The Government had had their reward for all this. The men whom they had trained to bludgeon their fellow-countrymen had been rewarded; whilst those who were intrusted with the enlightening, educating, and moral training of the children, had been despised and neglected. One of the chief features of the case was that these teachers were not paid on a similar scale to the teachers in England and Scotland. Liberals thought nothing of giving £30,000 to an Admiral who had performed the noble feat of bombarding an almost defenceless town; but they begrudged the Irish teachers the moderate grants they justly claimed. If they had Home Rule in Ireland, this meritorious class of men would be treated in a very different manner. Why should the Irish teachers, who produced good results, be underpaid at least 50 per cent to the amount given to English and Scotch teachers? It was of no use to say that some of the emolument of the teachers in England and Scotland was derived from sources other than the Exchequer; they were wealthy countries. It was a matter of proof that the Irish teachers did their business as well as the Englishmen and the Scotchmen, and it was also a fact that the cost of living in Ireland was quite as high as in England and Scotland. What encouragement was it to education in Ireland to use the teachers in such a way? He protested against the system of delay, deceit, and disappointment that had been practised, by those who sat on the Treasury Bench and received large salaries, towards this poor and deserving class who had worthily performed their duties. Many of these unhappy men and women had to walk miles through the wet and the snow to reach their schoolhouses. The whole subject was a disgrace to the Government, who were bound in honour to do something at once to alleviate the condition of these deserving people.

MR. BIGGAR said, the lower *employés* of the Post Office and these National School teachers were the worst treated officials in Ireland, and their condition contrasted very unfavourably with the emoluments received by other officers. The Government ought to introduce a measure upon a liberal basis which should put an end once for all to that discussion.

MR. ARTHUR O'CONNOR said, he cordially joined with his hon. Colleagues in the advocacy of the claims of a class of men whose claims had been recognized by successive Governments, and whose grievances had not been remedied by any. He must say he had been very much disappointed with the statement of the Chief Secretary for Ireland, and the Irish teachers, who had been very moderate in their demands, would also be disappointed with the tone the right hon. Gentleman had adopted. He thought the anomalous position of the assistant teachers was well worthy the attention of the Chief Secretary for Ireland. He also thought the right hon. Gentleman's figures were entirely wrong, as he had included in them the normal establishments, the Metropolitan model schools, and the training establishments. As it was, the pay of the Irish teacher was only half of that of the English teacher. He thanked the right hon. Gentleman for the establishment of denominational Training Colleges, which had done much to meet the wishes of the vast mass of the Catholic people of Ireland, and he believed valuable results would follow the taking that step. He complained of the niggardly system under which the Irish Teachers' Pension Fund was administered, under which the fund had been increased some £59,000, by unexpended interest, while the teachers themselves were obliged to contribute largely to the fund out of their scanty incomes. Another point was, that was a great grievance on the school teachers that they had to provide the school materials for their pupils out of their own funds, and wait to be recouped for their outlay by the desultory payment for them by the parents. They applied to have the usual trade allowance of 10 per cent made to them, to cover any loss they might sustain; but their application was passed by with contempt. There were several other matters which rankled in the minds of the teachers, showing them they had nothing to expect from this Administration, and it was impossible that their feelings towards the Government which treated them in such an illiberal manner should not be reflected in the teaching of their pupils. That was perhaps the best feature in the whole matter, as it was an earnest of the next generation being imbued with a strong national feeling.

MR. EUGENE COLLINS said, he thought that it had been admitted on all sides that the condition of the National School teachers in Ireland was an unsatisfactory one as regarded their remuneration, their residences, and their pensions, and that they should not be allowed to remain so any longer than was possible. He dissented, however, from the mode in which the right hon. Gentleman the Chief Secretary for Ireland had brought forward his own views before the House. The right hon. Gentleman had argued the subject ably and moderately, but from a point of view that did not apply to the condition of Ireland. In his (Mr. Collins's) view, there should be such a reform of the Educational Department in that country instituted as would make it a representative Body, and bring it into unison with the views of the people. The right hon. Gentleman had quoted statistics showing how much pupils paid in this country as compared with Ireland, while the real business before them was to see how far it was possible to improve the condition of the teachers. In his opinion, a compulsory rate for the payment of the teachers was a necessity. On the valuation of Ireland a rate of 1*d.* in the pound would produce £70,000, which would increase the salaries of the teachers by about £7 per head. But a compulsory rate could not be levied in Ireland so as to give satisfaction, unless a board were constituted that would represent the views of the people. If, in addition, the Government could be induced to supplement that £70,000 by an equivalent sum, the pay of each teacher would be increased by £14. Whether the rate he proposed should be a national, a county, or a Union rate, was a matter which could be discussed afterwards. He would advise the Government to agree to the general proposition of the Motion, but without committing themselves to immediate action.

MR. PARNELL said, he was afraid the right hon. Gentleman the Chief Secretary for Ireland, when he came to consider this question after he came into Office, adopted an attitude which he must now see upon reflection would result in leaving the question unsettled, and the admittedly just claims of the poor people unadjusted for a number of years to come. It must be very evident to the right hon. Gentleman, upon the whole course and tone of this debate, that it was hopeless to expect that the suggestion which he had made for the settlement of this question—namely, that the Irish Members should agree to a compulsory rate in aid of the salaries of the National School teachers being levied upon the Irish Unions—that it was quite hopeless to expect that such a proposition as that would ever be acceded to. Unless, therefore, the right hon. Gentleman was likely to find himself in a position to force a Bill, providing this settlement of the question, through the House in the teeth of the opposition he would meet from the Irish Benches, there were only two other courses open to him—either the just and universally admitted claims of the National School teachers with regard to increased salaries, improved residences, and a better system of pensions would have to remain unsettled, or else some rate in aid would have to be provided out of the Imperial Treasury. So long as they allowed them no local representative institutions in Ireland it was perfectly impossible for the Irish Members to agree that compulsory rates should be levied upon the Irish ratepayers to supply the admitted deficiencies in the salaries of these teachers. On the other hand, he could very well imagine that if a system of local government were adopted in the Irish counties, some plan or arrangement might be devised by which this difficulty with regard to local contributions might be got over; but in the present aspect of affairs, with the Board of Guardians as the only Body in the slightest degree approaching a representative capacity in the Irish counties and cities, it was impossible for them to consent to the proposition of the right hon. Gentleman. What he wanted to ask the right hon. Gentleman was this—whether, in the meanwhile, until these local representative institutions were introduced in Ireland, which they were so long expecting, and which they might hope to obtain in the ordinary course of things after a few years —what he wanted to ask the right hon. Gentleman was, whether they were really to take it as finally and definitely stated that nothing was to be done for these unfortunate men in Ireland? Meanwhile, a large body of teachers whose claims were admittedly just were neglected, and their salaries were, upon an average, much lower than either the English or Scotch teachers. They were now living on an average salary of only £57 a-year; and he would further ask whether the right hon. Gentleman considered that it was right that a large proportion of the National School teachers in Ireland should continue to exist on a salary of less than 30*s*. a-week? The increasing paucity of candidates for teacherships showed how serious the matter was becoming. Had this been a question of increasing the pay of the Constabulary, the Chief Secretary for Ireland would have found no difficulty in applying for an extra grant from the Imperial Exchequer; but he refused to do so in this case, although there could be no question that a greater back debt existed in respect of education than with regard to any other matter. There was nothing in the past dealings of the English Government with Ireland which did them more discredit. They had deliberately in past times, by penal laws and coercive legislation, prevented the Irish youth from obtaining the advantages of legislation, and that should be taken into account by the right hon. Gentleman, who had inherited, to some

extent, the odium which attached in this matter to the English Government and the people of England. He believed it was quite impossible for the right hon. Gentleman to maintain the position which he had taken up that evening, and that before many months, in consequence of that debate and others that would follow, the right hon. Gentleman would be obliged to make some other proposition than that made that evening.

Question put.

The House *divided*:—Ayes 63; Noes 61: Majority 2.—(Div. List, No. 202.)

Main Question, "That Mr. Speaker do now leave the Chair," again proposed.

PARLIAMENT—PUBLIC BILLS—UNPRINTED BILLS—

OBSERVATIONS.

MR. WARTON, on rising to call attention to the possibility of Bills being read a second time in this House before they were printed, said, that he was precluded, by the Rules of the House, from moving the Resolution which he had placed upon the Paper, and which was to the effect—

"That, in the opinion of this House, no Bill should be read a second time unless it has been printed, excepting a Bill brought in by a Minister of the Crown, and then only if and after such Minister shall have stated in this House that such Bill relates to a matter of urgent public importance."

In justification of the action he had taken he would refer to the case of a Bill which was introduced this Session by an hon. Member below the Gangway, and which was actually read a second time before it was drafted, and he observed that other instances of a similar kind had fallen under his notice. The present Speaker, and also his Predecessor in the Chair, had ruled that there was nothing to prevent such a proceeding. He would not occupy the time of the House any longer, as he hoped the Government would do what they could to prevent the repetition of what he considered a scandal by giving effect to the terms of his Resolution.

MR. DODSON said, he must commence by thanking the hon. and learned Member opposite (Mr. Warton) for the courteous manner in which he had brought this matter forward. He had brought forward a case of more force than anticipated, for he (Mr. Dodson) had only been aware of one Bill having been read a second time without being printed. The hon. and learned Member had, however, drawn attention to other cases; and, of course, they were all violations of the unwritten, and of what was generally supposed to be the invariable practice of the House. A proceeding of that kind amounted, in fact, to a breach of the received custom of the House, although there was no express Rule prohibiting it. All Bills were printed; but there were some—Ways and Means Bills, for instance—which were not circulated for obvious reasons. It was quite possible, under circumstances of pressure—although he did not know of a case—that a Ways and Means Bill might have been read a second time before it was printed. A case of that kind, however, would come under the exception for which the hon. and learned Member had provided in his Resolution, for the reason that such a measure must necessarily be in the charge of a Minister of the Crown. The proposition of the hon. and learned Member would require careful consideration before it could be adopted, because it would really tend to relax the practice of the House rather than to maintain it. If the hon. and learned Member made out any objection to the existing practice in the case of the Ways and Means Bills, no doubt his hon. Friends at the Treasury would be glad to consider the matter. With this assurance he trusted the hon. and learned Member would be satisfied.

Colonel KING-HARMAN said, that, in his short experience of the House, he had known three cases in which Bills had been read a second time without having been printed. He could give the names of these Bills, but he preferred not to.

Main Question put, and *agreed to.*

SUPPLY—CIVIL SERVICE ESTIMATES.

Supply—*considered* in Committee.

(In the Committee.)

Class III.—Law and Justice.

(1.) £66,837, to complete the sum for County Court Officers, &c., Ireland.

Mr. HEALY said, that on this Vote the Prime Minister would be able to answer a question which he (Mr. Healy) had put concerning the possible future employment of Mr. Clifford Lloyd.

Mr. GLADSTONE said, he had written to Lord Spencer on the subject, but had not yet received a reply; and, consequently, was not yet able to deal with the matter. It was understood, he thought, that the Question was to be answered on Monday.

Vote *agreed to.*

(2.) £99,980, to complete the sum for Prisons, Ireland.

Mr. HEALY said, that on this Vote a pledge had been given by the Chief Secretary for Ireland last year which did not appear to have been carried out. The Government, during the Phœnix Park trials, made some rules as to prison discipline which were much more strict than those obtaining in England; and the right hon. Gentleman had promised that the rules, particularly those regulating visits to prisoners, should be considered with a view to their revision. The matter seemed to be left entirely in the hands of the Governors of the gaols.

Mr. TREVELYAN said, he regretted he could not say whether the Report of the Prisons Commission, which had just been unanimously agreed to, referred to this subject or not.

Mr. HEALY said, that what had occurred was this. In the month of May, in the period to which he had referred, the Government made Rules, and laid them on the Table of the House, 30 days being required to elapse after that before they came into force. Previously, every prisoner had been entitled to receive certain periodical visits; but under these Rules such visits were only to take place at the discretion of the Governor of the gaol.

Mr. TREVELYAN said, that unless something had been done by the Prison Commissioners during the present Session, he could not say that any step had been taken in the matter. It certainly appeared to him unsatisfactory that the question should be left to the Governors of gaols. It ought to be in the hands of the Lord Lieutenant.

Mr. HEALY said, he regarded the right hon. Gentleman's statement as very satisfactory. When he was in prison, he had found the Governor of the gaol a very excellent and obliging person; but he did not think that, generally speaking, it was safe to entrust these powers to such officials, and some alteration ought to be made in the Rules.

MR. DEASY said, he wished to know whether it was intended to accede to the request of the Corporation of the City of Cork to permit them to appoint one or two justices to visit the male prison of that city, in order to hear any complaints the prisoners might have to make as to their treatment? The request was a very reasonable one, and should be granted, in view of the fact that serious complaints had been made regarding the prison, and unpleasant facts had been revealed in connection with it.

THE SOLICITOR GENERAL FOR IRELAND (Mr. WALKER) said, he was sensible of the evil the hon. Gentleman referred to, and it had occupied, and was still occupying, the attention of Her Majesty's Government. At present the law did not permit the visitation the hon. Member desired to see instituted—it could not be done under the 24th section of the Prisons Act—but, in a Bill recently brought in, power was given to the Lord Lieutenant to alter the rule regarding the visiting justices of prisons.

Vote *agreed to.*

(3.) Motion made, and Question proposed,

"That a sum, not exceeding £51,944, be granted to Her Majesty, to complete the sum necessary to defray the Charge which will come in course of payment during the year ending on the 31st day of March 1885, for the Expenses of Reformatory and Industrial Schools in Ireland."

MR. MOORE said, he was sorry to be obliged to stand for a few moments between the Committee and this Vote; but he felt bound to call attention to the fact that there had been of late a good deal of unpleasant feeling existing in regard to the action of the Government in connection with industrial schools in Ireland. There could be no doubt that within the past 12 months, at least, the Government had obstructed the development of Irish industrial schools in every way in their power. A comparison between the English and Irish industrial schools would show that the latter were not at all liberally treated. Ever since the beginning of this year—indeed, even further back than that—every attempt to extend the industrial school system in Ireland had been met by a determined and resolute resistance on the part of Her Majesty's Government. Almost every application made to the Government by those interested in the matter, however reasonable, was met in a most arbitrary spirit, and one of the most arbitrary refusals had been that in the Ballinasloe case. The managers of the school there had been most anxious to have it turned into an Industrial Institution, and had made application to the Government with that object; but—certainly up to three or four weeks ago—no answer had been received. No more proper application could be made than was made in this Ballinasloe case, and that the matter was deserving of attention was evident from the fact that there was not a single industrial school in the Province of Connaught. At Letterfrack, a large sum of money had been subscribed for the purpose of forming an industrial school, and yet nothing had been done, although he could not say that the Government had absolutely refused the application in this case. The case of Tipperary, also, had been neglected. In that case, a large sum of money had been subscribed for the extension of the existing building, so as to provide for the accommodation of a larger number of children, and the Government had only sanctioned the maintenance of 64 children, whereas the building was capable of maintaining double that number. In such cases as these, he thought the Government should only be too ready to recognize and encourage local effort. A great and important work, substantial in its effects, was being carried on by these schools, and he hoped the Government would do all they possibly could to support them.

COLONEL COLTHURST said, he wished to be quite fair on the subject, and to admit that the limitation was not imposed without some reason, because there could be no doubt that there was a much larger percentage of children in proportion to the industrial school accommodation in Ireland than there was in England. That fact was to be accounted for in this way. In Ireland they were not, as in England, any Poor Law schools where children were brought up and educated. In Scotland, where the people had always made good use of their opportunities, they did not want

Poor Law schools—they had all their poorer children in industrial schools. But this limitation was especially hard in the case of Ireland, because it was not placed upon the schools according to their merits; it was, he believed, fixed on a certain day, in 1879, when the number of children in every school was taken without any reference whatever to the size of the school, the amount of school accommodation, or the place where the school was situate. The consequence was that this anomaly was created—that in some places they were over-supplied with schools for girls; which in other places were absolutely deficient, just as his hon. Friend had pointed out with regard to board schools. That matter had been brought very forcibly before the Commission on which he sat as a Member. That Commission, of which he was a Member, made recommendations which they believed would meet the case, at the same time insuring due caution in the administration in order to prevent the admission of children to the schools who ought not to be admitted. They also recommended that there should be no limitation beyond the size and accommodation of the school subject to the control of a Secretary of State. His hon. Friend (Mr. Moore) would, however, find that question treated in detail in the Report of the Commission. There was another hindrance to the working of the system in Ireland—namely the uncertainty of contributions. In England, contributions were voluntary as in Ireland. In England, he did not suppose there was a Town Council which did not contribute a fair sum towards industrial schools; but in Ireland it was entirely different. As the Committee would be aware, it was the Grand Juries and Corporations which contributed in Ireland, and these only to the extent of a 1*s.* or 1*s.* 6*d.* a-week, per head, of the children; while the Grand Juries of the South Riding of Tipperary and of Queen's County refused to give a single 6*d.* towards the expense of industrial schools. The managers, as his hon. Friend had pointed out, had not, in consequence, sufficient income to carry on the work. Thus the only school in his county was that in the City of Cork, in which he was personally interested, which the Committee would perceive was a totally inadequate provision for a population of 500,000 Catholics. He believed that all Catholic opposition would disappear, if only the limitation complained of were taken away, and the other recommendations of the Commission were carried out. Further, he thought, although some persons had a great objection to compulsory contribution, that the contributions should be made constant, without which he believed that the requirements of the industrial system could not be carried out in Ireland. Finally, he hoped his right hon. Friend the Chief Secretary for Ireland would take the recommendations of the Commission into his careful consideration, and, if legislation was to follow, as he understood it would in the case of England, that it would follow speedily.

MR. MARUM said he should like to supplement the statement of the hon. and gallant Gentleman who had just spoken (Colonel Colthurst), whose statement with regard to the Grand Juries was perfectly true. He himself had committed two children to an industrial school, objecting to sending them to a reformatory, where they would be treated as prisoners and convicts. The managers declined to receive the children. He employed counsel, and the matter was contested; but such was the law that the Grand Jury of the Queen's County refused to give any capitation grant for the juveniles committed to an industrial school. The Grand Jury of that county consisted of 22 Protestant and one Catholic gentlemen. Now the result of this was that when the children were released they were unable to get any employment, and were consequently thrown upon society; those who were interested in them could not get them admission into any situation. The mere statement of this case ought to be sufficient to teach the Government that a reform of the existing system was urgently required. The natural solution of the question was, in his opinion, that power should be given to magistrates to compel the managers to admit juveniles committed to industrial schools, and that the Grand Juries should be compelled to pay for them.

MR. TREVELYAN said that any change that the administration might require—that would restore the industrial schools in Ireland to their proper use of receiving children committed by the magistrates—must meet with the hearty concurrence of Her Majesty's

Government. He did not think the hon. Member for Clonmel (Mr. Moore) had brought forward any argument to show that there was any great laxity of administration; but, at all events, there was a very different idea in the minds of those connected with industrial schools in Ireland from that with regard to the schools in England. In Ireland, every child sent to an industrial school was paid for by the Government at the rate of 5*s.* a-week; whereas in England a majority of children were paid for at rates varying between 2*s.* 6*d.* and 3*s.* 6*d.* a-week, 6*s.* a-week being paid for boys sent to training ships. The fact of the matter was that the ideas which prevailed in Ireland with regard to industrial schools were so very different from those in England that it was necessary to have some limit, and the question was as to what that limit should be. Ought it to be an arbitrary limit of number, such as had been laid down; or a limit on the freedom of committal by the magistrates? He very much preferred the latter, if it could be carried out; and if there was legislation on this subject next year, as he hoped there would be, he would certainly help his hon. and gallant Friend (Colonel Colthurst) in trying to get Ireland included, and in trying also to get the recommendation in Section 24 of the Report of the Commission, of which his hon. and gallant Friend was a Member, applied to that country. He thought the schools in question should be, as far as possible, kept to their proper and legitimate object—namely, that of providing the children for whom they were intended with some place in which they could be properly brought up. He spoke of orphans, destitute children, and beggars, wandering about without a home, and likely to follow the footsteps of the habitual criminal. If it were possible to confine the committals of children to these schools to that class, he should certainly be glad to make the limit one of limitation of committals and not of number. If children committed could be confined to the classes specified in the Acts, there would be less reason for restriction; but other classes were sent into the schools, and, without giving the name either of the school or the manager, he might mention to the Committee that a case had been brought before his notice in which a manager wanted to change a school which provided for children of one sex into a school for the other sex. He wrote to the manager, and he replied that he found the children were improper objects, and he had sent them all home to their parents. Hon. Members would, he thought, allow that the case had given him a considerable amount of work. He should be glad if this vexed question could be settled by legislation in the course of next year.

MR. WARTON asked for an explanation of the decrease with regard to the estimated extra receipts from parents of children sent to reformatory and industrial schools; the amount received last year being £1,350, and this year only £1,150. He thought the comparatively speaking large difference of £200 ought to be explained.

MR. ARTHUR O'CONNOR said, before the right hon. Gentleman answered the question of the hon. and learned Member for Bridport (Mr. Warton), he (Mr. Arthur O'Connor) should like to urge on the attention of the Government a point which had been impressed upon it by the Inspector of Reformatory Schools for some years past in his annual Report. It was a matter of the greatest consequence to the unfortunate children that they should receive some protection when they left the schools. The period of their discharge was, of course, most important in view of their future welfare. When they were discharged from the reformatory, they were particularly liable to all sorts of temptations and dangers, and to fall into the hands of the criminal class. He complained that the money which was given in England towards meeting the cost incurred in connection with children after their liberation was not also given in the case of Ireland. It was not necessary to emphasize the importance of this point, because it was perfectly clear that an allowance of this kind would enable boys to escape from those dangers at the outset of their industrial career which certainly brought down a great number of them to the ranks of crime. There was no reason why Irish reformatories and industrial schools should be treated differently from similar institutions in England. Now, that the question had been raised in the House, perhaps the right hon. Gentleman the Chief Secretary (Mr. Trevelyan) would give it the attention it deserved.

MR. COURTNEY said, the point raised was one of great importance; but it was one which must be considered with the whole question of reformatory and industrial schools by the Royal Commission. As to extra receipts, he had only to say that, unfortunately, experience had shown them that the estimate of extra receipts made last year was too liberal. The present estimate corresponded more exactly with what might be expected to be realized now. He could not help thinking that the hon. Member for Clonmel (Mr. Moore) was under a misapprehension with regard to the scale of payment of Inspectors in England and Ireland. Sir John Lentaigne received a salary of £400.

MR. HASTINGS said, that, as a Member of the Royal Commission on Reformatory and Industrial Schools, he should be sorry to let it be supposed that the feeling with regard to the want of subsidization for Irish industrial schools was confined to Irish Members. English Members felt the want quite as strongly as Irish Members; and he hoped that, at no distant time, the Irish Government would find it in their power to make some greater provision for the Irish schools. The Commission were very much struck with what many of the schools were doing, and they would be very glad if the schools were extended. While he thought there was room for improvement in English industrial schools, much more was needed to be done in the industrial schools of Ireland.

MR. MOORE said, he hoped the hon. Gentleman the Secretary to the Treasury (Mr. Courtney) would allow him to correct him. Sir John Lentaigne's salary as Inspector of Schools was only £300 a-year; the additional £100 a-year was granted him by the Duke of Marlborough on his retirement from the Prison Board, and was strictly personal to himself. He (Mr. Moore) was sorry the right hon. Gentleman the Chief Secretary for Ireland (Mr. Trevelyan) alluded again to the comparison between England and Ireland. It was very easy to go into comparisons. Perhaps Ireland had been generously treated in respect to her industrial schools, and it was perhaps true that the Irish industrial schools were much ahead of similar institutions in England. But if the right hon. Gentleman had made a little comparison of the expenditure in other Departments he would not have found the advantage on the side of Ireland. In the matter of the training of teachers, for instance, Ireland did not receive her fair proportion of grant from the State. He did not understand the policy of the Irish Government in respect of industrial schools, which had been a source of great benefit to the poorer classes. He moved to reduce the Vote by £1.

THE CHAIRMAN: Is the hon. Member serious?

MR. MOORE: If it would be more convenient, I will move to reduce the Vote by £100.

Motion made, and Question put,

"That a sum, not exceeding £51,844, be granted to Her Majesty, to complete the sum necessary to defray the Charge which will come in course of payment during the year ending on the 31st day of March 1885, for the Expenses of Reformatories and Industrial Schools in Ireland."—(*Mr. Moore.*)

The Committee *divided*:—Ayes 20; Noes 66: Majority 46.—(Div. List, No. 203.)

Original Question put, and *agreed to.*

MR. COURTNEY said, the hour (12.45) was still early; and, therefore, he proposed to take a few of the non-contentious Votes. They had to meet again at 12 o'clock, and, in consequence, he would not take anything that would occupy much time. He proposed, in the first place, to take the Votes for the National Gallery, and a few other Votes in Class IV.

CLASS IV.—EDUCATION, SCIENCE, AND ART.

(4.) Motion made, and Question proposed,

"That a sum, not exceeding £13,143, be granted to Her Majesty, to complete the sum necessary to defray the Charge which will come in course of payment during the year ending on the 31st day of March 1885, for the Salaries and Expenses of the National Gallery."

SIR ROBERT PEEL said, he wished to ask the First Commissioner of Works (Mr. Shaw Lefevre) if he could give the Committee any explanation with regard to an erection that had been put up outside the National Gallery? To what purpose was the building to be devoted; if the cost of the building was intended to be defrayed by Parliament; and for what length of time that most unsightly erection was to remain to disfigure what was very properly considered the finest site in Europe?

MR. SHAW LEFEVRE, in reply, said, the building had been placed there by the desire of the Trustees of the National Gallery, in order that photographs might be taken of certain pictures in the Gallery. It had been found that the light in the Gallery itself was not sufficiently good to admit of proper photographs being taken. The building would be removed at the end of two months. He did not think the public would raise any serious objection to the building under the circumstances.

SIR ROBERT PEEL: What will be the expense?

MR. SHAW LEFEVRE: I believe the whole thing is a private enterprize.

MR. WARTON said, he protested against the manner in which the Estimates were now being taken. He was sure that the hon. Member for Middlesex (Mr. Coope), who entertained a strong feeling with regard to the opening of the National Gallery in the evening, would have been present had he had the slightest idea that the Vote would be taken that night. He (Mr. Warton) was of opinion that there should always be a clear understanding what Votes would be taken at a particular Sitting, in which case time would not be wasted in considering which Votes should be taken, and which should not. Upon this particular Vote he had to complain; and he was sorry he had to do so in the absence of the only person who could give him an answer on the subject—namely, the hon. Member for East Cumberland (Mr. G. J. Howard), that there was no accommodation of a certain kind in the National Gallery. In the Louvre in Paris, and in other great picture galleries, proper accommodation was provided. He had himself been inconvenienced by the absence of accommodation of the nature he referred to in the National Gallery. It was perfectly disgraceful that in this country there should be a Puritanical objection to recognizing the necessity of what vitally affected life.

MR. COURTNEY said, he knew the hon. Gentleman the Member for Middlesex (Mr. Coope) took a great interest in lengthening the time during which the National Gallery was open to the public. The question was not an unimportant one; but it belonged strictly to Class I., where the buildings for the National Gallery were provided for, and not to this class, which dealt solely with pictures.

MR. TOMLINSON said, there was another matter which ought not to be passed over in silence, and that was the small amount of room there was to see the pictures.

THE CHAIRMAN: That is not a matter which can be dealt with under this Vote.

SIR ROBERT PEEL said, the Prime Minister gave a distinct pledge the other day that the Votes should be taken *seriatim*. Of course, if the Committee decided to jump over several Votes, and take a particular Vote, it was all very well; but he thought that, in view of the pledge of the Prime Minister, they ought to take the Votes in their order. The Committee ought to be very careful what they did; because, if it did not now, it might on a future occasion, lead to great inconvenience to take Votes out of their regular order. It was not fair, at 1 o'clock in the morning, to jump over Votes, in opposition to the assurance of the Prime Minister.

MR. COURTNEY said, he quite concurred with the right hon. Baronet that the Votes ought not to be taken out of their order unless the Committee was so agreed.

SIR ROBERT PEEL: We have not been asked.

MR. COURTNEY said, the question was before the Committee. [MR. WARTON: Progress!] He really thought that, at that time of the year, they were consulting the convenience and interests of the Committee in taking now those Votes which did not involve matters of dispute, deferring to another Sitting the contentious Votes.

MR. KENNY asked why, if the Votes were non-contentious, they should not be taken a couple of days hence? It was highly inconvenient to take the Votes out of the regular order. No one had the slighest idea that this Vote would be taken that night. It was extremely desirable that some system should be devised, by which the Votes which had been taken should be enumerated for the guidance of Members, say, in the Paper showing the Orders of the Day. Only that night an hon. Member asked if a certain Vote had been taken, or was to be taken; but no one could tell him. It was subsequently ascertained that the Vote had been taken out of its proper order, the result of which was that the hon. Gentleman was prevented from raising a point in which he was interested. Nothing would be gained by endeavouring to take this Vote to-night; indeed, it was evident time would be saved if the hon. Gentleman the Secretary to the Treasury (Mr. Courtney) put the Vote down for to-morrow. It was very inconvenient that hon. Members should be kept there late that night, because they were required to assemble again at 12 o'clock, with the possibility of their sitting into Sunday morning.

Mr. BIGGAR said, he would move to report Progress. He considered that the Government, which represented the majority of the House, were bound by the pledge given by the Prime Minister. He (Mr. Biggar) had known many a squabble to arise upon the endeavour to pass a few non-contentious Votes at a late hour of the night. When such an endeavour was made, it generally happened that there was a lot of talk about the desirability of reporting Progress, and the result was that very little progress was really made. If the Votes had been put down for the next day, in all probability they would have been taken with a run. To come back, however, to the primary point, he really could not see on what ground the Government advised the Committee to act in contradiction of the pledge given by the Prime Minister. It was quite possible that not one of the Votes which were called contentious would be so. He did not wish time to be occupied unnecessarily; indeed, he should like the House to adjourn for the holidays at the earliest possible moment. At the same time, some hon. Members interested in this Vote might have stayed away in consequence of the pledge of the Prime Minister; and, therefore, he moved to report Progress.

Motion made, and Question put, "That the Chairman do report Progress, and ask leave to sit again."—(*Mr. Biggar.*)

The Committee *divided*:—Ayes 18; Noes 56: Majority 38.—(Div. List, No. 204.)

Original Question again proposed.

Mr. GRAY said, he must move that the Chairman do leave the Chair; but he merely wished to make a suggestion. A considerable number of Votes had been passed; but the Return in the hands of hon. Members did not show what Votes remained to be passed; and he hoped that next Session the Government would improve that Return, so that it should show each week the Votes that had been passed, and the Votes that remained to be passed. The Return would then be of real use to Members, and he did not think it would involve any real additional expense or trouble. For the convenience of the Committee he made this suggestion, which, if adopted, would, he believed, prevent a good deal of difficulty. He begged to move, formally, that the Chairman leave the Chair.

Motion made, and Question proposed, "That the Chairman do now leave the Chair."—(*Mr. Gray.*)

Mr. ARTHUR O'CONNOR said, he thought it would probably prevent misunderstanding if the hon. Gentleman the Secretary to the Treasury (Mr. Courtney) would state in what order he intended—without making an absolute promise—to take the Votes to-morrow?

Mr. COURTNEY, in reply, said, that he proposed to take the Constabulary Vote first, and then proceed with the remaining Votes in Class IV. As to the point raised by the hon. Member for Carlow (Mr. Gray), the Return was not prepared under his authority; but he would see what could be done.

Motion, by leave, *withdrawn*.

Original Question again proposed.

Captain AYLMER asked, whether any arrangement had been come to respecting the Duke of Marlborough's pictures?

Mr. TOMLINSON said, he wished to point out that there was nothing in this Vote to show what was the cost of producing the catalogues in the National Gallery. He would ask whether there was any means of ascertaining the cost?

Mr. COURTNEY said, he did not think the sale of the catalogues paid the cost of their production; but they would come under the Stationery Vote. No arrangement had been come to respecting the Marlborough pictures.

Mr. WARTON complained of the contemptuous treatment of the hon. and gallant Member for Maidstone (Captain

Aylmer) by the Secretary to the Treasury, and said it would be a national loss if these pictures were allowed to go from the country. There was no other country in Europe that would not pay any price for them; and probably some American millionaire would buy what ought to belong to the nation. It would probably be a long time before another such opportunity as this would be presented, and considering the action of the Government a disgrace he should move that Progress be reported.

Motion made, and Question proposed, "That the Chairman do report Progress, and ask leave to sit again."—(*Mr. Warton.*)

MR. T. P. O'CONNOR said, he would recommend the Secretary to the Treasury not to proceed with this Vote, considering that the House would meet again in a few hours for a Saturday Sitting. By persevering, the hon. Gentleman was only inflicting prolonged agony on those Members who would have to be here again when the House met.

SIR ROBERT PEEL said, he wished to make an appeal to the noble Marquess opposite (the Marquess of Hartington). He understood the hon. Gentleman the Secretary to the Treasury to say, in reply to the noble Lord the Member for Woodstock (Lord Randolph Churchill), that Class III. would be taken on Friday, Class IV. on Saturday, Class V. on Monday, and Class VI. on Monday. That was the statement of the hon. Gentleman; and he (Sir Robert Peel) wished to ask the noble Marquess if he did not see the expediency and justice, after the statement of the Prime Minister, of taking the Votes *seriatim*, and that with Class III. the Estimates should cease for to-night, Friday?

THE MARQUESS OF HARTINGTON said, the right hon. Baronet's recollection was not very accurate. His hon. Friend the Secretary to the Treasury (Mr. Courtney) had given no distinct pledge, but had only made suggestions as to the order in which the Votes should be taken. The Government had hoped that the Irish Constabulary Vote would be concluded that night, and they were endeavouring to carry out the indication given as to the Votes. With respect to the observations of the hon. and learned Member for Bridport (Mr. Warton), his impression was that the Chancellor of the Exchequer, or the Prime Minister—one of them, certainly—had made a statement respecting these pictures, and had said all that could be said on the subject. More than had been said could not be stated. He hoped the Motion to report Progress would not be pressed.

MR. J. G. TALBOT said, he would join in the appeal of the noble Marquess (the Marquess of Hartington) to the hon. and learned Member (Mr. Warton) not to press his Motion; although he thought some little ground had been given for the Motion by the way in which the hon. Gentleman the Secretary to the Treasury had treated the question of the hon. and gallant Member for Maidstone (Captain Aylmer) respecting the Marlborough pictures.

MR. COURTNEY said, there was nothing further to be stated on the subject.

MR. J. G. TALBOT said, he was aware that that was the state of the case; but he wanted to point out that these pictures had created a great deal of interest, not only inside, but outside this House; and he thought that if the Government would give an assurance that this matter was under careful consideration, and that they would do their best to secure some of the pictures, that would give great relief and satisfaction. Some of these pictures, it was acknowledged by all acquainted with the subject, were of the highest value, and could not be rivalled; and although those who took great interest in such matters did not occupy so much time as Irish Members did when they had a grievance, that was no reason why they should not receive courtesy from the Government. If some such assurance were given as he had suggested, he thought the Committee might allow the Vote to be taken.

MR. GRAY said, he was dissatisfied with the reply of the hon. Gentleman the Secretary to the Treasury.

Question put, and *negatived.*

Original Question put, and *agreed to.*

(5.) Motion made, and Question proposed,

"That a sum, not exceeding £1,607, be granted to Her Majesty, to complete the sum necessary to defray the Charge which will come in course of payment during the year ending on the 31st day of March 1885, for the Salaries and Expenses of the National Portrait Gallery."

Mr. WARTON said, that, as several hon. Members had left the House, on the understanding that the Votes in Class IV. would be taken to-morrow, he felt it his duty to move that Progress be reported. He believed that the Gentlemen he referred to had much to say upon this particular Vote.

Motion made and Question proposed, "That the Chairman do report Progress, and ask leave to sit again."—(*Mr. Warton.*)

Mr. COURTNEY said, he had selected these Votes on account of their non-contentious character; he therefore trusted the hon. and learned Gentleman would not press his Motion, but allow the Vote to be taken, as also the Votes for Learned Societies and the London University.

Mr. WARTON said, he would ask leave to withdraw his Motion to report Progress, on condition that the Vote for the London University was not taken in the absence of the hon. Baronet the President of the University.

The SOLICITOR GENERAL (Sir Farrer Herschell) said, the hon. Baronet (Sir John Lubbock) was not President of the University; he was a Member of the Senate; and, as he (Sir Farrer Herschell) was likewise one of that Body, he thought he should be able to answer any questions which might arise on the Vote.

Motion, by leave, *withdrawn.*

Captain AYLMER said, he would point out that the building in which the National portraits were deposited was by no means safe. It appeared to him that the pictures were exposed to danger both from the weather and from fire; and he would be glad to learn whether something could not be done to protect them.

Mr. COURTNEY said, the question raised by the hon. and gallant Gentleman opposite (Captain Aylmer) had been over and over again under consideration. The Government looked upon the building as temporary only; and he (Mr. Courtney) would be glad to see the pictures removed to a place of greater safety.

Captain AYLMER said, it had been his intention to move a reduction of this Vote, unless the Government gave an assurance that the pictures would be removed to a place of safety; but after the intention expressed by the hon. Gentleman the Secretary to the Treasury (Mr. Courtney) that they would be so removed, if possible, he would not do so.

Mr. TOMLINSON said, he would point out that the danger of fire to the pictures arose not only from the nature of the building in which they were deposited, but from its proximity to the buildings of the Health Exhibition—that was to say, the temporary buildings that had been put up. He would ask whether extra precautions were taken in consequence of that proximity; and, if so, whether the cost incurred thereby would fall upon the Health Exhibition, or the National Portrait Gallery?

Mr. COURTNEY said, he believed that all necessary precautions were taken. The real danger to which the building was exposed arose from the fact that there was a spirit warehouse in its immediate vicinity.

Captain AYLMER said, that there had been a fire close by the building not many days ago.

Original Question put, and *agreed to.*

(6.) £16,400, to complete the sum for Learned Societies and Scientific Investigation.

Mr. BUCHANAN said, there was one point in relation to this Vote that he desired to bring before the Committee. He referred to the question of meteorological observations. The Committee would recollect that a good deal of discussion had taken place a few years ago with reference to the Meteorological Council. As he understood the position of that Body, at the present time, it was established for five years, at the termination of which period its members would have to be re-appointed. A great deal of dissatisfaction had prevailed in many quarters as to the manner in which this Body distributed the money granted by Parliament; and it appeared that the Treasury instituted an inquiry into the subject, which had been fully discussed. But the dissatisfaction had come up again, particularly with regard to the smallness of the sums devoted to meteorological work in Scotland. An important meteorological observatory had recently been established by private effort on Ben Nevis. And yet only £100 was allocated to it out of the £15,000 voted. Even this sum it was possible might be withdrawn, owing to a petty quarrel between the English and Scottish authorities. The Scottish Meteorological Society, which did more work than any other meteorological body, had no representative on the Council, which was simply a Committee of the Royal Society of London. He would like to receive from the hon. Gentleman the Secretary to the Treasury (Mr. Courtney) an assurance that this matter would be looked into, in order that, after all that had been done, the best meteorological work done in the country lately should not be put aside and ignored by those who had the disposal of the funds voted by Parliament for the purpose.

MR. COURTNEY said, he would point out that the action of the Government towards the Meteorological Council had been the same as that with regard to all learned societies—that was to say, they did not interfere with the manner in which they distributed the funds placed at their disposal. They could not, therefore, intervene in the question between the Royal Society of Edinburgh, and the Meteorological Council.

MR. BUCHANAN said, it had been recommended by the Treasury Departmental Commission that the Council, in its annual Report presented to Parliament, should specify the way in which the money at their disposal was expended. He thought that the House, having voted the funds, ought to see whether the money was properly spent.

CAPTAIN AYLMER said, he objected to the grant of £500 for the Royal Geographical Society, which produced very small results.

MR. TOMLINSON said, that in this case he dissented entirely from the view taken by his hon. and gallant Friend who had just sat down (Captain Aylmer). He believed that no money was better spent than the £500 voted for the Royal Geographical Society, and that, considering the value of the work done by the Society, the amount of the grant was very small.

Vote *agreed to.*

(7.) £8,346, to complete the sum for the London University.

House *resumed.*

Resolutions to be reported *To-morrow.*

Committee sit again *To-morrow.*

Mr. Buchanan

SUPREME COURT OF JUDICATURE AMENDMENT BILL [*Lords.*]—[BILL 307.]

(*Mr. Attorney General.*)

COMMITTEE. [*Progress 29th July.*]

Bill *considered* in Committee.

(In the Committee.)

Clauses 1 to 6, inclusive, *agreed to.*

Clause 7 (Appeals in matters under £200).

THE ATTORNEY GENERAL (Sir HENRY JAMES) said, that he had been in communication with the hon. and learned Gentleman the Member for Launceston (Sir Hardinge Giffard), in relation to this clause and Clauses 8 and 9, the Appeal Clauses of the Bill, and in deference to what he thought was the wish of the Committee he would consent to those clauses being struck out.

Clause, with Clauses 8 and 9, severally *struck out* of the Bill accordingly.

Clause 10 (Appeals from referees).

THE ATTORNEY GENERAL (Sir HENRY JAMES) said, he had great doubt whether it was intended by his hon. and learned Friend (Sir Hardinge Giffard) that this clause should also be struck out. It was not of the same class as the other clauses which had been struck out; but if it was desired to omit the clause the omission could be effected on Report.

MR. WARTON said, he had had some communication with his hon. and learned Friend (Sir Hardinge Giffard) in regard to the Bill, and he was able to say that this was not one of the clauses the hon. and learned Gentleman desired to see struck out.

Clause *agreed to.*

Clause 11 (Judge may order trial by an official referee in certain cases).

MR. WHITLEY said, this was a very objectionable clause, and he should have liked to see it struck out. If, however, he could not get some assistance from the Committee he should not put hon. Gentlemen to the trouble of dividing.

THE SOLICITOR GENERAL (Sir FARRER HERSCHELL) said, he was quite aware that, in many quarters, there was some apprehension that if the clause remained in its present shape its operation would be very objectionable; but it must be seen that there was full power given to refer issues to referees. At the same time, in order to confine the clause to cases where all parties consented, he proposed to amend it by omitting all the words from "and," in line 31, to the word "officers," in line 36, inclusive.

Amendment proposed, in page 1, to omit the words from "and," in line 31, to "officers," in line 36, inclusive.—(*Mr. Solicitor General.*)

Question proposed, "That the words proposed to be left out stand part of the Clause."

MR. TOMLINSON said, he was not sure that the omission of these words would cure all the mischief of the clause. Perhaps the Law Officers would say whether, in their opinion, the Amendment would cover a case in which any of the parties were under disability.

THE SOLICITOR GENERAL (Sir FARRER HERSCHELL) said, there would be very rare cases—he hardly knew of any—in which parties to an action, who were under disabilities, would not consent. If there were, however, persons under disabilities whose consent could not be got, that would be a reason for a Judge to consider whether he should refer it.

MR. WHITLEY said, he was quite content with the Amendment suggested by the hon. and learned Gentleman.

Question put, and *negatived*; words *struck out* accordingly.

Clause, as amended, *agreed to.*

Clauses 12 to 23, inclusive, *agreed to.*

New Clauses.

MR. COURTNEY moved the insertion of the following Clause:—

(Officers not to be employed without good service certificates—42 & 43 Vic. c. 78.)

"The provisions of section twenty of 'The Supreme Court of Judicature (Offices) Act, 1879, with respect to pensions under that Act shall, as regards appointments made after the commencement of this Act, extend to salaries under that Act."

Clause (Officers not to be employed without good service certificates—42 & 43 Vic. c. 78,)—(*Mr. Courtney,*)—*brought up*, and read the first time.

Question, "That the Clause be read a second time," put, and *agreed to.*

Clause *added* to the Bill.

MR. WHITLEY proposed the addition of the following clause after Clause 12:—

(Trial of actions in district registries.)

"Nothing in this Act shall prevent the right of parties to try actions in district registries, and to refer same to the district registrars when the parties so desire."

Clause (Trial of actions in district registries,)—(*Mr. Whitley,*)—*brought up*, and read the first time.

Question proposed, "That the Clause be read a second time."

THE SOLICITOR GENERAL (Sir FARRER HERSCHELL) said, he had no objection to offer to the clause.

Question put, and *agreed to.*

Clause *added* to the Bill.

MR. HASTINGS proposed the addition of the following Clause:—

(Judges of county courts to have the same qualification as Queen's Counsel.)

"Judges of county courts shall have every qualification conferred on Her Majesty's Counsel learned in the Law by the Act of the thirteenth and fourteenth Victoria, chapter twenty-five."

The hon. Member said, the object of the clause was to enable Judges of County Courts, whether Queen's Counsel or not, to be placed on the Commissions of Assize for the purpose of assisting, if called upon, Judges in the performance of their civil and criminal duties.

Clause (Judges of County Courts to have the same qualifications as Queen's Counsel)—(*Mr. Hastings,*)—*brought up*, and read the first time.

Question proposed, "That the Clause be read a second time."

MR. WARTON said, this was an extraordinary and grave proposal. By his clause, the hon. Gentleman (Mr. Hastings) suggested that County Court Judges, many of whom were not even Queen's Counsel, should rank as Judges. He (Mr. Warton) felt it his duty to say that, judging from his own personal experience, four out of every five County Court Judges were totally unfit to try Assize cases. He should like to know on whose suggestion the hon. Gentleman proposed the clause.

THE SOLICITOR GENERAL (Sir FARRER HERSCHELL) said, that he, on the contrary, thought that some of the County Court Judges were well fitted to try Assize cases. Some inconvenience had been found under the present rule, which provided that only Queen's Counsel should be deputed to assist a Judge in the trial of Assize cases, and it was suggested that, in some cases, it would be a public convenience if County Court Judges could be put in the Assize Commission. He trusted the clause would be adopted.

MR. HASTINGS said, he proposed the clause upon his own responsibility, knowing, as he did, many County Court Judges who were well qualified to try Assize cases.

MR. TOMLINSON said, he would ask if the clause of the hon. Gentleman (Mr. Hastings) had really anything to do with the Bill under consideration? The Bill was one to amend the Supreme Court of Judicature Act; but this clause related to County Court Judges.

THE SOLICITOR GENERAL (Sir FARRER HERSCHELL) said, he thought this was a clause which distinctly came within the purview of the Bill, because the Bill dealt with Assizes, and regulated those who were to be put in the Commission of Assize.

Question put, and *agreed to.*

Clause *added* to the Bill.

THE CHAIRMAN said, he must rule that the next two new clauses, standing in the name of the hon. Member for East Worcestershire (Mr. Hastings)—namely,

("No writ of mandamus or prohibition to issue to Judge or officer of county court, but persons aggrieved to have right of appeal as under the 'County Courts Act, 1875.'")

and

("The court or judge hearing such appeal may make order to do complete justice between parties, and direct as to costs.")

could not be proposed, as they were not relevant to the Bill.

MR. WARTON said, he had received a letter from the hon. Gentleman the Member for Wolverhampton (Mr. H. H. Fowler), urging him (Mr. Warton) to move the new clause which stood in the hon. Gentleman's name. He therefore begged to move the insertion of the following Clause:—

(Vacations may be regulated by Order in Council.)

"Her Majesty in Council may from time to time make, revoke, or modify orders regulating the vacations to be observed by the High Court of Justice and the High Court of Appeal, and in the offices of the said Courts respectively.

"The provisions of section twenty-five of 'The Supreme Court of Judicature Act, 1875,' shall apply to every Order in Council made under this Act."

Clause—(Vacations may be regulated by Order in Council)—(*Mr. Warton,*)—*brought up*, and read the first time.

Question proposed, "That the Clause be read a second time."

THE ATTORNEY GENERAL (Sir HENRY JAMES) said, he sympathized a great deal with his hon. Friend (Mr. H. H. Fowler) in his desire to regulate the Vacations for the public convenience; but he could not assent to this clause. The adoption of the clause would show a total want of confidence in those who now regulated the Vacations.

Question put, and *negatived.*

Preamble *agreed to.*

Bill *reported;* as amended, to be considered upon *Monday* next.

SUPREME COURT OF JUDICATURE (CHANCERY EXAMINERS' OFFICE) [COMPENSATION].

Considered in Committee.

(In the Committee.)

Resolved, That it is expedient to authorise the payment, out of moneys to be provided by Parliament, of compensation to persons holding the office of sworn clerk to the late Chancery Examiners, on the abolition of that office, under the provisions of any Act of the present Session for amending the Supreme Court of Judicature Acts.

Resolution to be reported upon *Monday* next.

House adjourned at a quarter after Two o'clock.

HOUSE OF COMMONS,

Saturday, 2nd August, 1884.

The House met at Twelve of the clock.

MINUTES.]—SUPPLY—*considered in Committee*—CIVIL SERVICE ESTIMATES—CLASS III.—LAW AND JUSTICE, Vote 29.

Resolutions [August 1] *reported.*

QUESTION.

EGYPT—THE CONFERENCE.

Sir STAFFORD NORTHCOTE: I wish to ask what is to be the course of procedure to-day? I understand there was a conversation yesterday in the House from which it was inferred that the Prime Minister might be able, upon the Report of Supply, to make some statement with regard to the issue of the Conference. I shall be very much obliged if any Member of the Government—perhaps the Home Secretary—could tell us whether it is probable that such a statement will be made; and, if so, at what time it is probable that the progress of the Civil Service Estimates will be interrupted, and the Report of Supply taken?

Sir WILLIAM HARCOURT: I believe the Conference is at this moment sitting, and it would be the desire of the Prime Minister to make an announcement as to its decision at the earliest possible time, in order to give the necessary information to the House; but, at the present moment, it is impossible for me to state at what time that information will be given.

Sir STAFFORD NORTHCOTE: At what time will Progress be reported on the Civil Service Estimates?

Sir WILLIAM HARCOURT: I am afraid it would not be very judicious to make that statement; we had better reserve it. I think, from what the Prime Minister said the other day, there is no intention to carry on the proceedings to an unreasonable hour.

Sir GEORGE CAMPBELL asked whether the Votes to be taken to-day would be confined to Class IV.; and whether Supplementary Estimates would not be taken?

Mr. COURTNEY replied that the Votes for to-day would be the Constabulary Vote and the Votes in Class IV., including the Supplementary Estimates in that Class.

ORDER OF THE DAY.

SUPPLY—CIVIL SERVICE ESTIMATES.

Supply—*considered* in Committee.

(In the Committee.)

Class III.—Law and Justice.

Motion made, and Question proposed,

"That a sum, not exceeding £940,095, be granted to Her Majesty, to complete the sum necessary to defray the Charge which will come in course of payment during the year ending on the 31st day of March 1885, for the Constabulary Force in Ireland."

Mr. O'SULLIVAN said, he wished to call the attention of the Committee to the course which the Government had pursued in reference to the imposition of a force of extra police upon the County of Limerick. He found that during the year 1882 the county had been charged the enormous sum of £6,966 for extra police. He did not object to extra police being sent into the county if there were reason to suspect disorder or outrages upon life and property; but the County of Limerick was able to challenge comparison with the most peaceful county in England in regard to crime and outrage. Notwithstanding that fact, a tax was imposed upon it in one year of £6,966 for extra police. These extra police were distributed broadcast all over the county, not for the sake of preserving peace and order, but to assist the landlords in collecting their rents. Their services were entirely unnecessary so far as the protection of life and property was concerned, and their time was occupied in driving cattle, and in enabling the landlords to extort rack rents. There was no more quiet or peaceable county in Ireland until, in an evil hour, Mr. Clifford Lloyd made it his headquarters. In the town of Kilmallock, in which he (Mr. O'Sullivan) resided, and which he was consequently thoroughly acquainted with, the peace and order of the place were maintained by 10 or 11 constables up to that time; but immediately after Mr. Clifford Lloyd arrived at Kilmallock 50 or 60 extra police were drafted into the town, notwithstanding the fact that it was altogether free from anything in the shape of crime and outrage. From that moment the inhabitants saw every morning scores of police going out with the military, not for the purpose of putting down crime and outrage, but to collect the rents of the rack-renting landlords. The majority of the landlords in the county were good men; but, unfortunately, there were among them some black sheep. Perhaps there was not throughout the whole of Ireland a worse landlord than a gentleman in that county named Coote. It was almost entirely owing to the action of this gentleman with regard to his tenants that the force of extra police had been imposed upon that part of the county. He had been known to serve writs upon his tenants for a single half-year's rent. His land was more highly rented than any other in the county. He obtained for it £3 or £4 an acre, and yet, notwithstanding that fact, the moment a tenant got six months in arrear he was served with a writ. Three of Mr. Coote's tenants had been evicted who had held their farms for years. Because, owing to the depression which occurred in regard to agricultural operations in 1878, 1879, and 1880, these unfortunate persons found themselves unable to pay the rack rents imposed on them they were summarily evicted from their farms, no terms whatever being offered to them. Mr. Coote was perfectly aware that these three tenants had offered on several occasions even within the last three months to settle the rent at whatever sum the Land Commission might fix as a fair rent. They wrote to Mr. Coote making that offer, but it was contemptuously refused. Indeed, the landlord did not condescend to return an answer to their communication. Nevertheless, this was a man for whose protection Her Majesty's Government had put up a police hut and kept six extra police on his farm. He thought it would afford to the Committee a good illustration of the way in which the tax for additional police operated. As he had said, there were six police stationed upon Mr. Coote's farm. Yet it was a place in which there had been no crime or outrage, and their sole duty appeared to be to mind the farms from which the tenants had been evicted, notwithstanding the fact that they had offered to pay up all arrears and to pay any rent which the Land Court was prepared to fix. It was the conduct of this class of unscrupulous landlords which gave rise to the land agitation of 1879-80, and was the cause of the Land Bill being brought in by the Government and passed by Parliament. If Mr. Coote's tenants' rents were not paid by the 1st of May, he sent them notice that it must be ready on the 14th, and those who were unable to pay it on that day were served with an attorney's letter on the 16th. Certain tenants who went on the 20th to pay the rents were told that it would be refused unless they were prepared to pay 10*s.* 6*d.* in addition in the shape of costs. He had known one of these unfortunate tenants go to the solicitor's office, six miles off, on the 21st of May, in order to pay half a-year's rent due on the 1st of the same month, with 10*s.* 6*d.* to the solicitor for writing a letter. Was that a gentleman who was likely to bring peace, contentment, and happiness to the Irish people, or make his tenants satisfied with their lot, even under the provisions of the Land Bill? This was the same gentleman for whom the Government continued to provide a hut and police protection, for no other purpose than to watch the farms of his evicted tenants. Surely the course pursued with regard to him encouraged him in the style of action he adopted towards his tenants. He had received a letter from one of this gentleman's tenants—a tenant whom he (Mr. O'Sullivan) knew intimately, and one of those who had been evicted by Mr. Coote. He was able to say, without fear of contradiction, that the person to whom he referred was one of the most honest and industrious tenants in the County of Limerick; but he had found it impossible to pay the rack rent demanded of him when the seasons turned against him. He would only trouble the Committee with a short extract from the letter written by this tenant, in order that hon. Members might be able to comprehend what it was the Government were upholding by keeping an extra police force in the County of Limerick. He wrote—

"I have been evicted by my landlord, Mr. Coote, for one half-year's rent. My rent was £103 15*s.* per year, but my poor rates on the entire farm and outhouses were only assessed upon £49 15*s.*, or less than one-half of the rent. I offered, shortly after my eviction, when I had raised some money from my friends, to pay the half-year's rent and costs, which offer my landlord refused, unless I would pay the full rent of the land during the time it was lying idle, although Mr. Coote had possession himself of it during that time."

Mr. Coote had the land in his possession, or in the possession of his bailiff, because no other person would take possession of it. So anxious, however, was this poor man to regain possession of the land, that he said in his letter—

"I further offered to give £150 if I could get my farm again on the same terms as the Land Commissioners had fixed in the case of two farmers on the two next farms to mine, but this offer was also refused."

He (Mr. O'Sullivan) did not wish to go any further into this case; but it was regarded, in the county of Limerick, as a great hardship that this poor man should have been served with a writ and evicted for the non-payment of a single half-year's rent, the rent itself being double that at which the farm was assessed by the poor rate valuation. Yet this landlord, who refused those fair offers to pay rent and arrears, was the gentleman for whose protection the Government imposed upon the county a heavy police tax. He was sorry to say that there were other cases of the same kind in the county of Limerick; but he had selected this one, because he was personally acquainted with the circumstances, residing as he did within two miles of the farm to which he had directed attention. He had stated that the extra police tax amounted in the year 1882 to the sum of £6,966. That extra force was sent into the county, not in consequence of any disturbance, or in order to prevent crime and outrage, but solely because evictions were being carried out broadcast, and the evicting landlords were in dread that either themselves or their property would be injured. He appealed to the justice of Her Majesty's Government to say whether this state of things ought to be continued, and whether this heavy additional tax should still be imposed upon a county which would bear a favourable comparison for peace and order and absence of crime and outrage with any county in England? Would they persevere in this imposition? He contended that it would be disgraceful if they did, especially when their sole object—at any rate in the case of the landlord to whom he had referred—was to uphold a man who refused to make any terms whatever with his tenants, who evicted them when simply half-a-year in arrear, who refused every fair and reasonable offer made to him, and who wrung from his unfortunate victims the highest rack rents it was possible to impose. Could it be supposed that while landlords were permitted to follow a course like this, it would be possible, even with the aid of extra police, to sow the seeds of peace and contentment in the neighbourhood? It was too bad that the county should be kept in a fever of excitement and compelled to pay what amounted to a heavy fine on account of the oppressive action of one man. He knew that the Government had no control over the action of this individual; but, at any rate, they could withdraw the police, who were now employed in assisting to evict tenants, notwithstanding their willingness to come to a settlement on fair and reasonable terms, and who were told off to protect the deserted property from which the tenants had been removed.

MR. MARUM said, he had stated at the time this extra police tax was imposed upon the county of Limerick that it was entirely unnecessary, and that it would produce the discontent and ill-feeling which it was intended to prevent. If it had ever been necessary to place 50 additional police in the county the times had very much changed since, and at the last Assizes the matter was brought under the attention of the Grand Jury by a Presentment. It was said, however, that that was not the time for taking action in the matter, and that they were assuming to themselves the functions of the Executive. It was pointed out to them that it was a matter with which they had nothing to do, but that the extra police were sent into the county by the Executive Government; that the cost of it was, under the Prevention of Crime Act, to be charged upon the locality in which it was employed; and that, as a matter of fact, the same course had been pursued in other districts where it was feared that serious outrages might be committed. But in most cases the extra police had been withdrawn when tranquillity was restored, and the local expenditure incurred had not been very large. Moreover, he found that in this very county, at the Lent Assizes, Mr. Justice Barry had congratulated the county upon its peaceful and orderly condition, and upon the absence of crime and outrage. Nevertheless, the Government still declined to withdraw the extra police, and the result had been to create great dissatisfaction throughout the county. A more peaceful and law-abiding county than the county of Limerick it was impossible to find, and yet this enormous local taxation was still imposed without the slightest necessity. The Grand Jury declined to take any action in the matter, and threw the entire responsibility upon the Executive. He believed that one main ground of the present condition of affairs was the defective distribution of the regular Police Force. At one time the population of his own county of Kilkenny was more than 150,000; it was now only 90,000, but the police force was maintained at the same strength as when the population numbered 60,000 more. In Limerick the same result had been brought about; and he would appeal to the Chief Secretary and the hon. and learned Solicitor General for Ireland, whether such a condition of affairs afforded any pretence whatever for continuing the imposition of an additional force of police? If there was any disturbance in any part of the county, the Lord Lieutenant had the power of drafting into it an extra force, and to call upon the locality to pay the expense. In the county which he represented the greatest dissatisfaction was expressed at the action of the Executive. Only the other day there was a large meeting of the ratepayers, who had appealed to him to take some steps in the matter. All he asked the Government was that if 50 additional police, or any number of extra police, were required in the county, and their employment were justified by the state of crime and outrage, then let their services be continued, but if not let them be removed. At that moment the extra police were costing the ratepayers of the county of Kilkenny a sum of £2,400 a-year, without the slightest necessity for their employment, and, in addition to that heavy tax, the farmers were suffering from the continued depression of agriculture, and the competition to which they were subjected from abroad. As a matter of fact, the local taxation was becoming enormous and unbearable. Everything was thrown upon it, and every fresh Bill introduced into Parliament added to the local burdens. A great deal of the necessity for having the local Constabulary was owing to the want of perfect confidence on the part of the people in the administration of justice. If the people had perfect confidence in the local Courts, they would not take the law into their own hands; but if they had not that confidence, of course they fought it out. He could not express too strongly the general dissatisfaction there was in the county with this enormous taxation, which the people believed to be unnecessary; the question was not whether this system was more secure, but whether it was necessary, and he challenged the Chief Secretary to say that it was necessary.

MR. DAWSON said, there never had been a better instance than this in which the people ought to take the advice of Lord Macaulay to "tell those who call for obnoxious taxes to call again," because there had never been so unjust and so unnecessary an impost as this. He would like to know what Englishmen would say if they saw ladies dragged through English streets, as they had been in Limerick, because they sympathized with those who, for their patriotism, had been put in prison? One of the right hon. Gentleman's reasons for these extra police was that when the people saw others being degraded in this way they lost their temper. They were naturally indignant. What could the right hon. Gentleman say to a state of facts which he could not deny? If Limerick was in such a state of tumult; if these occurrences were of such a dangerous character as to render these extra police necessary, why were the rioters not brought before the Judges? The County Court Judges, every Judge of Assize, and every Chairman of Quarter Sessions, had said they had nothing to try; but if there was this disorder, why were not the rioters brought before those Judges? He challenged the right hon. Gentleman to deny that during the presence of the police the County Court Judges had nothing to try. Could there be anything more grievous than that? When did a policeman ever lose his life in Limerick? Did Mr. Clifford Lloyd even lose a hair of his precious head, which had been the cause of so much trouble and tumult wherever he went? Had there been any case to bring before the Judges of Assize? They had gone to Limerick again and again, and had declared that their appearance there was almost unnecessary. In one breath the right hon. Gentleman declared Limerick to be in such a state of crime and danger that he must deluge it with police at every corner, irritating the people with their menaces; while, on the other hand, the Judges declared that there was no crime. Whenever the Judges were attacked a great deal was heard from the Government Benches about the inviolability of the Bench and the purity of the law; but now it seemed that the Judges had been lax, and the law had not been applied, for the Judges had done nothing in the state of things in Limerick which the right hon. Gentleman had described. How would the right hon. Gentleman's statement as to the state of Limerick tally with the fact that the Judges did nothing? He should be glad to hear the answer to that; and, meanwhile, he must again refer to the extraordinary contrast between the salaries of the police who were to repress crime and the salaries and incomes of the teachers whose duty was to teach the young. Last night he and his hon. Friends had pointed out that while there were only 11,000 teachers in Ireland, there were 13,773 policemen. The Government provided fewer people to prevent crime than police to put it down. They paid constables £59, £69, and £79 a-year; but they only paid National School teachers, whose labours would tend to render the police unnecessary if they were properly paid, only £57 a-year. The Chief Secretary must also be aware that the Constabulary in the counties and towns were beyond the control of the Municipal Authorities, while the contrary was the case in England; and yet the right hon. Gentleman was continually drawing comparisons between the two cases. If he would give the Irish Local Authorities a share in the control of the police, they would be quite willing to bear the burden in proportion to their means. The right hon. Gentleman seemed to have forgotten what that proportion should be, and to think they should pay the same proportion from their local resources as the people in England; but he thought the proportion should be only as one to seven. Ireland had grown poorer; her means of wealth had been dammed and dried up by a hostile and inauspicious Government, and she was now less able than she was at one time to pay a large proportion; and yet they were constantly told by this country, which was really the cause of the poverty of Ireland, that they ought always to pay similar sums to the amounts paid in England. Why did the Government think it so necessary to protect Mr. Clifford Lloyd when he went to a town with a population of 40,000, like Limerick? And how many men did they think were required for that purpose? An army of police he supposed. This potentate could not go out without a large body of police, not to protect him, but to intimidate the people; and they had heard how he had been guarded even when going to garden parties by a *posse* of police. Therefore, upon this Vote Irish Members must take the opportunity of calling attention to these things. If more money was spent upon those who would teach the people to refrain from crime, there would be little need for the maintenance of this enormous army of police. If this God-given Government would take away their police and their soldiers, and leave him and his Colleagues and the hon. and gallant Member for the County of Dublin (Colonel King-Harman) to manage their own affairs, there would soon be an end to this difficulty. It was said that they would quarrel; but what did Shylock say?—

> "If you prick us, do we not bleed? if you tickle us, do we not laugh? if you poison us, do we not die? and, if you wrong us, shall we not revenge?"

He was sure that if the people of England could once grasp the true state of things in Ireland they would rise up as defenders of justice to Ireland. Last night they had heard a great deal of the abolition of Slavery, which occurred 50 golden years ago; but the people of Ireland were still in a state of slavery under these English Pashas, and the slaves of Jamaica and America never suffered more keenly. But there was no Royal Highness, and there were no great Lords, or a great people to take as much interest in the wrongs of Ireland now as they did in the abolition of Slavery half-a-century ago. When speaking of the abolition of Slavery, these people did not forget to pay a tribute to the great Irishman, Daniel O'Connell, who helped to free the slave by his great advocacy. In conclusion, he would ask the right hon. Gentleman to tell him, as a Limerick man, who had filled the office of High Sheriff, who had lived there all his life, and had been there when all these police were there, and saw that there were no cases to be tried, how he could go back to Limerick and tell the citizens to keep quiet under this iniquitous tax? If he could get no answer from the right hon. Gentleman, his advice to the people within the law about these police and the extra tax would be to use that pithy sentence, "call again." He hoped the right hon. Gentleman would return to the *rôle* of an historian and an English statesman, and give up the *rôle* of a statesman not inspired by Englishmen, but by Dublin Castle. He had faith in Englishmen, and believed that if they were well-informed upon these matters they would not pursue their present course in regard to Ireland. What a contrast there was between Ministers who were free from the fetters of Dublin Castle, and those who were in its fetters! He hoped the Chief Secretary would forget that he was Chief Secretary for Ireland, and would only remember that he was the biographer of Lord Macaulay, and would not drive the people of Ireland to the necessity of putting into practice the advice to "call again."

MR. DEASY said, he would confine his observations to the extra police in the County and City of Cork. He believed that Captain Plunkett, the District Resident Magistrate, meeting the Mayor of Cork in the street, said that if the Corporation would express the opinion by resolution that 170 police were sufficient to maintain the peace, 20 men would be added to the free force of 150, and the remainder of the extra force would be removed. But when the Corporation passed such a resolution, the Chief Secretary said he could not at present increase the force to 170, and that the Corporation would have to wait three years for that to be done. Captain Plunkett must have known what the state of the law was, and he was not satisfied that he had not, in this instance, made that statement in order to lead the Corporation into a trap, and give an excuse for continuing the force in the City. The extra police quartered in Cork for the last 17 years had cost the people £15,000, though no reason was assigned for continuing those men in the City. Year after year the Judges had declared the City to be in a most peaceable condition, and there had been a great absence of crime. In fact, he was sure no community in England could show such an absence of crime as Cork had in the last 17 years; but he believed the reason for maintaining the police there was that Captain Plunkett saw that the country was returning to its normal state of peace and quietude, and he was determined to show that there was some necessity for his presence in the South of Ireland. If he did not keep up this force he would not retain his present office, for which he got £2,000 or £3,000 a-year. That, he believed, was the reason for his action; but he was satisfied that if the Chief Secretary had been allowed to exercise his own judgment, these complaints would not now have to be made. A kind of promise had been given that this extra force, which now numbered 39 men, should be reduced by 19, and that would still leave 20; but, owing to some change introduced by the Divisional Resident Magistrate, he believed the police of the borough were paraded frequently in some central place, thereby throwing such an unnecessary amount of work on their shoulders, that even 170 men were scarcely able to discharge the ordinary police duties. If the police had been left in the hands of the ordinary magistrates there would have been no difficulty, because the people had more confidence in them than in the magistrates who had lately been appointed. If the Government would listen to the advise of the people, who really understood this matter, they would remove these police. The only duty the extra policemen had to perform was to dance attendance on the Special Resident Magistrate. He had 20 detectives on his own staff. What they did no one knew, and yet the people were charged with their cost. Another cause of complaint was that eight of the regular men were absent from the City, which the citizens did not get credit for, and that, in consequence of that, Captain Plunkett pretended that he had to keep a larger force than would otherwise be necessary to preserve the peace. But, strange to say, with all this force in Cork, the only crimes of any consequence which had been committed there for a number of years had remained undetected, and there was a strong suspicion that one of these crimes—a case of manslaughter—was committed by three detectives. The way in which the charge against those three detectives had been investigated had met with the universal disapproval of the people of Cork; the belief being that the officers of these men had deliberately shielded them from justice, and that if the investigation had been properly conducted these men would have been brought to justice. However that might be, as the incident was now eight months old, he would not further refer to it; but he would ask the Chief Secretary whether any information had been received from Captain Plunkett or from the police authorities of Cork as to the perpetrators of the outrage which he had already several times brought under his notice—namely, the wrecking of the Lough Chapel? The Corporation, Magistrates, High Sheriff, and other gentlemen of position had several times petitioned the Government to withdraw the extra police from Cork, on the ground that 150 men would be sufficient to maintain the peace; and, in 1882, the then Chief Secretary (Mr. W. E. Forster) promised that when the time arrived for a redistribution of the police, the Lord Lieutenant would consider the desirability of removing the extra police. He would like to ask what steps the Lord Lieutenant took in 1882 to ascertain whether it was necessary to keep these extra police in Cork? He was inclined to think that, as the Corporation did not then refuse to pay the extra tax, the Lord Lieutenant did not take any steps to ascertain whether these men were necessary. He hoped these questions would be fully discussed that day, and that the matter would be carefully considered. The whole question of extra police in Ireland would be raised by the senior Member for the City of Cork (Mr. Parnell), and would have to be discussed, and it was for that reason that he had now mainly confined himself to that portion of the force in Cork County and City. Looking over the interesting Returns presented last year, he found that the cost to the ratepayers in 1882, on account of the extra police quartered in the county, was £10,000; and, as far as he could see from the Return supplied to the senior Member for Cork (Mr. Parnell) last night, no important reduction had since taken place in the number of men in Cork County. But the Judges had declared at the Assizes in the last two years that the county of Cork was in a very peaceable state indeed, and the number of outrages was very small. Even when the late agitations had been at their highest point, the county of Cork was in its normal condition. Why, then, was this cost of £10,000 to be put upon the ratepayers? He could not understand it, unless it was that the Government wished to take every opportunity they could get for annoying the people and punishing them for endeavouring to wring justice from Parliament. The way in which these police conducted themselves in the country was another matter upon which he had to find fault. He would only refer to one case, about which he had asked a Question in the House a week or two ago. That was a case in which the Head Constable went to the keeper of an hotel, a widow with six or seven children, in Ballydehob, and threatened her that if she permitted meetings of the National League to be held in an outhouse attached to her hotel, he would oppose her application for a fresh licence at the Licensing Sessions, and persuade the magistrates not to grant it. She at once, of course, communicated with the Secretary of the National League, and he (Mr. Deasy) was then furnished with the Question which he had put to the Chief Secretary. The right hon. Gentleman expressed a very strong opinion as to the conduct of the Head Constable, and promised that he would not permit such a wanton interference with the rights of the people. He was perfec ly satisfied with the right hon. Gentleman's promise, and he did not think it necessary to prolong his observations now, because, as he had said, the whole question would have to be dealt with in a much more extensive manner. The Government, however, had not the excuse for quartering these extra police on the county of Cork, which they gave with regard to the extra police in Limerick. They could not point even to a single case of a boy throwing stones, and, in fact, he thought that if they looked through the calendar of crime in Cork they would find that it compared very favourably with any county or city in the United Kingdom. There was one other matter to which he wished to draw attention, and that was the course taken by the police in the City of Cork four months ago, after the election in that City. Several meetings of Queen's College students were held at a place belonging to a Benefit Society. Two or three evenings after these young gentlemen had held a meeting, and passed a resolution in favour of one of the candidates and condemning the system of the Queen's Colleges, two policemen visited the room, and endeavoured to frighten the old woman who was in charge of it into giving the names of all who had been present at the meeting. He had put a Question to the Chief Secretary upon that matter, and the right hon. Gentleman gave a very evasive answer indeed. So strongly was that answer condemned in Cork that he had received several letters from people altogether unconnected with the Society or with the Queen's College, asking him to press for further information. He believed the cause of this visit was that a few weeks before the election another meeting was held at the same place, at which a strong resolution was passed condemning the way in which Captain Plunkett had acted in the South of Ireland, and particularly his action with regard to the public meetings of the National League in the county of Cork. He did not know whether the right hon. Gentleman could give him any answer as to the visit of the police to the rooms of the Society in question; but he hoped he would give an assurance that meetings of the National League would not be suppressed during the Recess. There would, he was sure, be great danger to the peace in the county of Cork, if, during the Prorogation, Captain Plunkett was allowed to act as he had acted last winter in suppressing National League meetings throughout the county. These meetings had been most orderly, and he hoped the right hon. Gentleman would give this assurance with regard to meetings which the League proposed to hold during the Recess. A series of meetings had already been held, and he would appeal to the Chief Secretary to give an undertaking that they would not be interfered with so long as the people were orderly and kept the peace.

MR. M'MAHON said, there had been thousands of people parading the streets of Cork on one night, without any disturbance taking place; but these police, when under the control of men of the stamp of Captain Plunkett, were a constant source of irritation to the people.

COLONEL NOLAN contended that there was no necessity for these extra police, and complained that those who paid for them had not the control of them. The county was in a most peaceable condition, and there was no wish on the part of even the most desperate character to commit any outrage. If at one time these extra police might have been necessary, the necessity had ceased two or three years ago. There were a number of police barracks in the county which served no useful purpose, and in the same way a large number of people received police protection, which, in a great many cases, was quite unnecessary, but for which the county had to pay. At the same time, he acknowledged that the responsibility of deciding whether people needed police protection or not was one of a serious nature; but unless it was very clear that people wanted protection, it should not be paid for by the county, but by the country generally. The Government was bound to protect the lives and property of the public; and unless there was a flagrant case in which a man had been threatened, such protection came within the ordinary circumstances of the general security of life and property which any civilized Government undertook at the expense of the country at large. It was a matter of opinion whether a particular locality or a particular person should be protected. The Chief Secretary might give this protection if he liked; but he certainly ought not to charge it upon the people. The increase of taxation had become enormous, and was most injurious to the people. As an instance of the vicious way in which this system worked, he would mention one barony. It was on the sea shore; the people did not want any rates, and they refused to pay the county cess, which was very heavy. Then they were charged for extra police and for several other things which came under the county cess. The Chief Secretary ought to look into such a case as this, and see that in a poor locality in a mountainous district the taxes were not so heavy as to be oppressive and to drive the people into a state of passive resistance. Then there was another district which was absolutely free from crime, but which, nevertheless, had to pay for the extra police in the county. That tax they regarded as simply vindictive punishment; and he did not think the Government took sufficient trouble with regard to these cases. The Chief Secretary, of course, could not visit all these places, and he had to take the advice of the magistrates, and unpaid magistrates were generally prejudiced. Others were unprejudiced; but the unprejudiced did not take the trouble to write to Dublin Castle. It was to the interest of the police to pretend that a locality was in a dangerous state, in order to show how efficient they were in keeping the peace, and how necessary they were, and how advisable it was, in the interest of the State, to increase their emoluments and promotion; but the Chief Secretary should be kept on his guard against the Reports of people of this kind. He did not pay the slightest attention to the representations of those who were elected by the people. Questions on these matters had been repeatedly put by hon. Members who generally voted with the Government on foreign and other questions; but, as a general rule, the Government did not pay the slightest attention to the elected Representatives of the country. In his view, the Chief Secretary ought to take care to obtain—he knew that was hard—unprejudiced Reports as to the state of the country; and if there was no absolute necessity for these extra police, or a doubt as to whether they were necessary, then he should say he would not put the burden on the people. A second reason why he did not think the people should pay this tax was this—English Members were not always aware of the manner in which the money was allotted in Ireland for police. The Government found a certain number of police which were not charged on the county; and if there were any extra police, then they called upon the county to pay for a certain number of men over their ordinary strength. In England the county would decide for itself whether it should apply for additional police, and then the county would have to pay. It was important to insure that the police were not withdrawn from their ordinary duties; but that frequently occurred. He was perfectly certain, speaking with regard to Galway, that the authorities at the depôt in Dublin found it extremely convenient to keep back 50 or 60 men who ought to be in Galway, so that they could send out three orderlies, instead of only one, for an officer, and in order that they might be able to keep the recruits a little longer under instruction. He had not the least objection to their doing that, so long as it was at the expense of the Government; but he thought that when they charged the county for an extra 100 men, and then only sent 40, in order that the depôt in Dublin might have a few more men for other purposes, they inflicted gross injustice on the ratepayers of Galway. His remedy for this was very simple, and was one which the Chief Secretary ought to have adopted long ago. There should be someone to inspect the Reports, so as to see what men were away, and whether their places were filled up; and the Reports ought to be open to Members of Parliament and others concerned in Dublin. The only person who could be intrusted with the inspection of the Returns would be someone representing the cesspayers. The Government might say there were the Grand Juries to represent the cesspayers; but they did not altogether represent the cesspayers, and it would be useless to hand over this duty to a Grand Jury unless there was some special man to look to it, who would not be influenced by the general body of the Grand Jury. This plan would not cost much money or trouble, and ought, he thought, to be adopted by the Government. For the last three years the people had been paying money which ought to have come from the pockets of the Government on their own showing. He had brought forward this idea of public Returns as to the state of the police last year, and the Solicitor General for Ireland then said he would look into the matter. He would like now to know what had been done, and whether he, or any other Member, could go and inspect Returns showing where men were, and why they were charged upon districts when they were not in those districts? This might be considered a matter of detail; but it was more than that to Irish Members, and he must press the Government to take steps to enable them to see these Returns. As to another point, the character of the police seemed to vary a great deal. In his own county (Galway), they did their duty quietly and efficiently. During the last three or four months there had been no complaints; but before that, especially in the Southern part of the county, they had been anxious to pick quarrels, and had been enforcing the regulations with very bad temper. It was most essential that, if there was any excitement, the police should act with good temper and moderation; but, instead of that, their action had, in many cases, tended to provoke quarrels and disturbances. They had been very irritating at Loughrea towards the people, and one of the officers had encouraged them in that foolish practice. He saw an instance of it himself. He attended a meeting, which was very quiet and orderly, and nobody who was there wished to interfere in the slightest degree with the police constable who was in attendance, if he would only remain quiet. The constable, however, acted most ostentatiously; indeed, it was evident his instructions were to make as much fuss and as much of a demonstration as possible. The chairman of the meeting was very efficient, and, fortunately, everything passed off quietly. If the police were anxious to interfere with the people, it was not to be wondered at if conflicts occasionally occurred. All he asked was that the authorities should send to the town of Loughrea efficient and good-tempered constables, and not encourage the officers to get in conflict with the inhabitants. It appeared to him that, in many instances, the police, instead of setting an example of moderation and good sense, went out of their way, as they certainly did in Loughrea, to arouse the indignation of the people, and cause petty fights. Complaints to this effect were constantly reaching him from different parts of Ireland, and he could not help thinking they were well-founded.

MR. JUSTIN M'CARTHY said, there were two or three points to which he wished to call the attention of the right hon. Gentleman the Chief Secretary. One point to which he would particularly direct the attention of the right hon. Gentleman was the wholesome monotony in the expressions of the Judges of Assize with regard to the present condition of Ireland. The Charges of the Judges of Assize showed that from Antrim to Cork and from Galway to Drogheda there was a remarkable and unprecedented absence of serious crime. Only that morning he took up an Irish paper in which he saw the statement that at the recent Assizes there was no case of general interest to the public. As a matter of fact, crime and popular excitement appeared to exist to a greater extent in those places where extra police were quartered than in any other. He supposed the right hon. Gentleman the Chief Secretary would say that special police were only sent to districts where there was crime; but the Chief Secretary would see, if he examined the matter carefully, that some of the places in which disturbance and crime prevailed were particularly quiet before the extra police were sent there. He trusted that the right hon. Gentleman would take the recent statements of the Judges of Assize into account in any future police arrangements for the country. Another point he wished to direct the attention of the Chief Secretary to was that in almost every case, if not in every case, where the Resident Magistrate asked for extra police, the request was made without any consultation with the ordinary Bench of Magistrates. He did not think that ought to be the case; the Resident Magistrate ought in such matters to take the advice of his colleagues on the Bench. Another thing to which he would direct the attention of the Chief Secretary was that in the majority of cases the extra police were not stationed under the Prevention of Crime Act, but under previous legislation. He held that if extra police were required, they ought to form part of the permanent force of the country, and ought to be paid for by the Government, and not be an extra charge on the country. Then, he should like to say a word or two upon the question which his hon. Friend (Mr. Deasy) referred to—namely, that of the extraordinary treatment of the Cork Collegians upon the occasion of a recent meeting of theirs. He felt a personal interest in the City of Cork. He was born there, and at one time belonged to the same class as the young men now attending the Cork College. He could hardly imagine anything more wantonly oppressive than to send the police to watch the proceedings of these young students on the occasion of their meeting to pass a resolution in favour of the candidature of the hon. Gentleman (Mr. Deasy). The right hon. Gentleman the Chief Secretary knew perfectly well that in the times of the Wars of Napoleon, the patriotic spirit, extinguished in almost every other class in Germany, was kept alive by the young men of the Colleges; and it was the spark from their patriotic feeling which lit up the whole country. He hoped, therefore, that in future the right hon. Gentleman would be as careful as possible not to allow his policemen to interfere with the demonstrations of the students of Ireland, unless there was the gravest and most pressing cause. Furthermore, he thought the Executive Government should, as far as possible, discontinue the employment of members of the Police Force as shorthand writers to take down the speeches of National and popular speakers. He did not know whether the Chief Secretary knew anything about shorthand writing; but he (Mr. Justin M'Carthy) knew that it was a very difficult art to acquire with anything like facility. He remembered Lord Palmerston once saying in the House of Commons that he had given some study to shorthand, and he found he could write it well enough, but when he had written the notes he could not read a word of them. That he (Mr. Justin M'Carthy) fancied was very often what happened with the gentlemen of the Irish Police Force. It was, undoubtedly, more difficult to learn shorthand than some foreign languages, and he could not believe that Irish police officers could be efficient shorthand writers. He might give an illustration of the way in which police shorthand writers took notes. He once made a speech in his own county, and the shorthand notes taken of his remarks by a policeman were produced in the State Trials. He did not know whether the right hon. Gentleman the Chief Secretary thought he (Mr. Justin M'Carthy) ever talked sedition; but, if he did, he would perhaps admit that the sedition would probably be couched in decent English. He could assure the right hon. Gentleman, however, that in the report of his speech there was neither sense, nor meaning, nor construction, nor grammar. That was of no consequence, because he was not charged with any seditious offence; but it might have been in the case of some younger man carried away by the excitement of the moment; it might easily have been made to appear that a speaker said the very opposite to what he did say. Again, he happened to be in the county of Waterford, and it was announced he would deliver a lecture to a purely Literary Association upon a purely literary subject. He was favoured with the presence of a couple of shorthand writers, although he had nothing to say that might not have been delivered to a Church Congress. He now asked the Chief Secretary whether he would not direct that, as far as possible, public men who were going to make speeches, especially on purely literary topics, should not be honoured by the presence of any of these unprofessional shorthand writers, who were supposed to be sent as guardians of law and order? These were two or three points he pressed on the attention of the Chief Secretary, and he thought that the right hon. Gentleman by attending to them would do a good deal more to secure contentment and good order in Ireland than he could by any extra police he quartered on the country.

Mr. T. D. SULLIVAN said, he thought the system of charging extra police in Ireland upon particular localities was a barbarous device, and one that worked very unfairly and inequitably. No doubt, there were historical precedents for it. The Norman tyrants of old inflicted such injuries upon the Saxons; but the system certainly could not be considered applicable to the present day. Extra police might sometimes be required in some parts of the country; but a reasonable thing to do in that case was to let the charge for those police fall upon the general fund, because, see how the matter, as it now stood, worked. It was well known that the men who met together and concocted outrages and atrocities, took every possible care that their secret should only be known to a very narrow circle. That was notoriously the state of the case, and yet it was found that the punishment for whatever offence was committed was levied upon a wide district of the country, and people who had not been privy to the outrages, and who did not even sympathize with them or approve of them, people who often were very badly able to pay this unjust taxation, were called upon to pay these iniquitous taxes. There had been very striking instances of the unfair working of the system. A gentleman in the county of Westmeath, whose sister-in-law was killed by a shot intended, it was generally believed, for the gentleman himself—at all events, for whomsoever it was intended it certainly was not intended for the lady—and the district was taxed and fined in order to pay compensation to the relatives; a portion of the compensation actually was to be paid by the brother-in-law of the lady who was in the carriage with her and at whom, it was believed, the shot was fired. That was a specimen of the working of that splendid machinery for repression of crime in Ireland. This gentleman, the brother-in-law of the lady who lost her life, wounded in heart and bleeding internally from the cruelty he witnessed and the loss he sustained, was asked by this British Government to pay a tax as if he were associated, or as if he sympathized, with the crime that had been committed; he was asked to pay a portion of the compensation which was to be awarded to the relatives of the deceased lady. There was another instance of this hateful system in another part of Ireland. The nuns residing within the peaceful walls of their convent, spending their days and nights in prayer and good works, were served with notice that they had to pay a share of taxation for the compensation for some outrages committed. Could anything be more unjust or unfair? If outrages occurred, and if extra police were required in some localities, surely it was the business of the whole community; it was the business of the British Government to send the necessary force for the preservation of order and to pay for them themselves. There was also this additional argument in the case. Was the British Government free from responsibility for the disorders in Ireland? Could the British Government hold its head up and say—"We are innocent in this matter, we have nothing to do with the promotion of disturbance or the cause of discontent in Ireland?" Why, the British Government—he did not allude to any particular Administration — was itself the chief offender; the mal-administration of the British Government in Ireland was to blame for whatever disorder and disturbance and discontent arose in that country, and therefore no one had a better right to pay for the extra police quartered on the country than the British taxpayer. Now, he believed that in the county of Westmeath there were about 86 extra police—the Chief Secretary, of course, was in a better position to give the correct figures than he (Mr. Sullivan) was—there were, he believed about 86 extra police in the county, and he supposed that the cost of that extra force would be something like £8,000 per annum. On the average it was a little less than £100 a-year per man. That was a large amount to be levied upon a particular locality.

MR. TREVELYAN pointed out that only a moiety of the sum was paid by the county; he believed that, as a matter of fact, it was about £2,600.

MR. T. D. SULLIVAN thanked the right hon. Gentleman for the correction; but the charge of £2,600 was quite sufficient for his argument. If the tax were levied upon the whole county it would fall pretty lightly upon individuals; but levied as it was upon a small area, it became a very oppressive tax. And it must be borne in mind, too, that the tax, levied as it was upon limited areas, was, strictly speaking, paid by people who were innocent of any participation in the crime and who entirely disapproved of it. This taxation was no cure for the evil complained of. The few men who made up their minds, for one reason or another, to perpetrate these outrages, would never be deterred by the consideration that a tax would be levied upon any particular district. They were desperate men, and forgot the terrible consequences that might accrue to themselves from their action; and was it to be supposed they were going to be deterred from their evil practices by the consideration that a tax of 1*s.* in the pound, or 10*d.*, or 2*s.*, as the case *might* be, would be levied upon a certain part of the country if the crime they contemplated were committed? He claimed from these considerations that this system of taxation was unjust, that it worked no good, but that, on the contrary, it worked great harm. Let the Committee see what means the Government took to discourage crime and outrage in particular localities, to produce contentment, and to preserve peace. A man from the county of Westmeath, who confessed to having been a participator in criminal matters, and to having been a conspirator for the perpetration of murder and outrage, turned an informer some time ago against his fellow-conspirators. What did the Government do with this odious man, upon whose information his accomplices were prosecuted to conviction? Did they send him out of the country; did they send him to some place where his previous career would have been unknown, where his bad character would not have been notorious, and where, consequently, his presence would be no incentive to disturbance and disorder? No; the Government allowed this man to return to the very part of the country from which he came; they allowed him to resume his ordinary mode of living in the place where he was naturally and inevitably hated and detested by everybody, especially by those whose relatives, connections, and friends he had sent to penal servitude, or to the gallows. The Government let that man come to the very spot where they knew his presence must be hated, and especially by one class. And what more did they do? They sent a police force there to protect him. That, certainly, was not the way in which to promote quietude, contentment, and good order in that part of the country, or, indeed, in any other part of the country. As he had said, they sent a police force with the man, and planted a hut there for their accommodation. Just a word with regard to informers. He knew it was said that informers assisted in bringing criminals to justice, and that on that account there was something to be said for them; but it must be recollected that it did not follow at all that informers did, in very many cases, aid in doing justice; they aided in doing injustice, inasmuch as they had been the cause of innocent men being brought to the prison or to the gallows. They had a direct incentive so to do, in the fact that by prosecuting a man to conviction, whether innocent or guilty, they saved their own necks. He had the firm belief that many of the informers in Ireland had, for the sake of saving their own necks, or saving themselves from penal servitude, given testimony on oath that was very acceptable to the Government, but which was decidedly untrue. He maintained that the course pursued by the Government in the case of the informer to whom he had referred was unbecoming, unwise, and improper; it was remonstrated against by the clergy of the locality. They knew the danger of having this odious man reinstated in the part of the country to which he formerly belonged, and they sent a Memorial on the subject to His Excellency the Lord Lieutenant. In that Memorial they said—

"We have heard that it is intended to allow Crowe, the informer in the recent conspiracy trials, to return to his former place of abode; we believe that his presence would seriously endanger the public peace."

Such was the representation made to His Excellency in the interest of peace, order, and quietness, and surely it was worthy attention. It received, as a matter of fact, very little attention—at all events, no practical action was taken upon it by the Lord Lieutenant. The Memorialists went on to say—

"Therefore, we humbly pray Your Excellency will make it a condition of his pardon that he shall reside elsewhere."

The Memorial was signed by the Catholic clergymen of the locality, men who were anxious for the peace and good order of the district; but it was disregarded by the Lord Lieutenant, who chose to send Crowe, who, upon his own confession, stood convicted of outrage and crime, to the place from whence he came, and amongst the people whose hearts and feelings were excited and exasperated by his conduct. Such were some of the beauties of British government and British rule in Ireland. He maintained that in many cases the protection police were not necessary at all, and that they were got from the Government by representations made by Resident Magistrates and others. But who convinced the Resident Magistrates of the necessity of such police? About a month ago he asked, in the House, the Chief Secretary a Question concerning a lady in the county of Kerry named Miss Lucy Thompson. Miss Lucy had a force of six policemen to take charge of her, and she was very proud of her escort, and the men themselves seemed to be very pleased with their employment. The belief of all well-informed people was that Miss Lucy was in no more danger of attack or outrage than any Member of the House; but a friend of her's—some Pasha in the shape of a Resident Magistrate—recommended that the force should be sent down for her protection. He asked the Chief Secretary, the other day, if the policemen were tenants of Miss Lucy Thompson, and whether she, consequently, had any pecuniary interest in the retention of the force? And the right hon. Gentleman was good enough to say that such matters well deserved looking into. He believed the right hon. Gentleman intimated that he would have inquiries made on the subject; and, therefore, if it was within the memory of the Chief Secretary, he (Mr. Sullivan) would be glad to learn, before the debate closed, whether the protecting force were tenants of the lady? The belief in the locality certainly was that the force was not needed; therefore, their retention was a great outrage upon the people. Now, there was another lady of even more warlike and dashing deportment than Miss Lucy Thompson. He referred to Miss Gardner, who lived in the West of Ireland. He did not know how many policemen she had for her protection; but her house was a little arsenal, and she herself went about heavily armed like a trooper. There was, of course, a ridiculous aspect in the matter; but it was very annoying and provoking to the people of the locality to see this heroine flourishing about, armed and equipped in that fashion. He had often wondered, considering this lady's great military capacity, why the Government had not thought it right to employ her in the Soudan; he certainly thought she would have given as good an account of herself against the Mahdi as scores of the warriors the Government had sent out against him. The presence of these extra policemen was nothing more nor less than an encouragement to bad landlords and bad landladies all over the country; they felt that they were superior to public opinion, and that they could defy the common feelings of the people; that they could do just as they liked within the limits of the law; and there was no compulsion upon them to soften their hearts and do justice to the people round them. The readiness of the Government to send out an extra police force was an encouragement to landlords and landladies to continue in a state of hostility to their neighbours. He should like the Chief Secretary to inform them what earthly need there was for 86 extra policemen to be quartered upon Westmeath? He granted that some outrages had been committed in some particular localities; but he could not grant that the localities were in any way responsible for them. Agrarian outrages were committed, as a rule, by small parties of men who laid their plans in private, and carried them out with all possible secrecy. The localities, as he had said, could not be held responsible for them, and, therefore, to put a heavy tax upon the people, mostly struggling tenant farmers who were totally unable to bear the infliction, was as gross an injustice as it was possible to conceive. He hoped the right hon. Gentleman the Chief Secretary would consider whether the enormous extra force of 86 men in Westmeath ought not to be greatly reduced, and whether the whole system of charging extra police upon localities was not one that should be discontinued.

MR. JUSTIN HUNTLY M'CARTHY said, that, unfortunately, the very objectionable dynasty of Resident Magistrates was by no means extinct in Ireland. For example, Cork was cursed with the presence of a particularly objectionable specimen of this dominant race. The Government seemed to have an almost marvellous instinct for finding out the kind of men who were most likely to be distasteful to the Irish people, and making them captains over them. Captain Plunkett had succeeded in making himself exceedingly objectionable and unpopular in Cork in quite a variety of ingenious ways. One of the devices this magistrate had adopted was the frequent shifting of members of the police force. A large number of the police force in Cork were comparatively popular with their fellow-townsmen; that was to say, they were of the same faith, and in many ways were in sympathy with the people. Captain Plunkett, however, had adopted the ingenious method of transplanting such constables to the North of Ireland, and bringing down from the North a large number of young and inexperienced policemen, unsympathetic in feeling and almost diametrically opposed in faith and race. By that process he contrived to make the citizens of Cork, not only personally uncomfortable, but to have little trust in the administration of the law. Moreover, Captain Plunkett had deprived many of the ordinary magistrates—who were not conspicuously or remarkably unpopular magistrates—of almost any power whatever. The extra police in Cork had been very largely increased since Captain Plunkett came there; indeed, it was a curious fact that wherever members of this particular school of Resident Magistrates arrrived the extra police were almost invariably increased. It was so when Mr. Clifford Lloyd came to Limerick. The presence in that historic city of Mr. Clifford Lloyd was almost immediately followed by an increase of the police. The question of the extra police was a serious one for the Irish people, and very naturally they strongly objected to the way in which half of this obnoxious tax was to be paid by the occupier. If any proper portion of the tax were paid by landlords, the Government, no doubt, would have long since abolished this wholly indefensible tax.

MR. KENNY said, that Irish Members had up to this attacked this Vote, on the ground of the extraordinary and entirely unjustifiable manner in which extra police were drafted into almost every county in the South of Ireland. Extra police were quartered upon particular counties under two Statutes. The first of these Statutes was that of *Will.* IV., under which the Treasury paid half the cost of the force, and the county cess was levied for half. The majority of the extra police drafted into the Irish counties were so drafted under the Act of *Will.* IV.; but there were a great number of extra police drafted into the counties under the Prevention of Crime Act, and when police were drafted into a district under that Act the district became liable for the cost of the force; and it not unfrequently happened that policemen were quartered in out-of-the-way districts, so that the tax for their maintenance proved very burdensome to the people. There were cases in which certain localities had been taxed to the extent of 12*s.* or 14*s.* in the pound for the staff of extra police. He complained that, in the majority of instances, the presence of extra police was entirely and absolutely unnecessary. The fact was, there were too many policemen in Ireland. Three or four years ago, a great effort was made to recruit the Police Force in Ireland. The original number of the Force was something like 10,000; he should think the present number was 15,000. The Government did not know what to do with their policemen, and the result was that, partly with the object of getting rid of them, they sent them down to places where their presence was absolutely unrequired, and taxed the county with the moiety of their expense. He entirely objected to the adoption of such a principle. His hon. Friend the Member for the City of Cork (Mr. Parnell) asked the Chief Secretary yesterday whether he would give a Return, or state in reply, the number of extra police drafted into the different counties in Ireland? The Chief Secretary stated that it would be inconvenient to reply to the Question within the usual limits of an answer; but he would be glad to place the hon. Gentleman in possession of the facts. It would be of interest to the Committee to hear from the Chief Secretary, in his speech upon this question later on, a statement as to the number of extra police quartered in the various counties of Ireland, not only under the Prevention of Crime Act, but under the Act of *Will.* IV. He (Mr. Kenny) had frequently noticed that, when he had asked the Chief Secretary under what Act certain extra police were quartered in a given district, the right hon. Gentleman invariably succeeded in getting out of the responsibility of answering the Question by stating that he was not informed, or something to that effect, or else that the immediate district was not taxed for the maintenance of the force. That was a disingenuous method of avoiding questions upon the subject. As a matter of fact, the localities were taxed, and taxed very heavily. If extra police were drafted into a district under the Act of *Will.* IV., a moiety of the expense would, of course, be defrayed out of the Consolidated Fund; but if a hut was erected for the men's accommodation, the entire expense of the building would be thrown on the district, so that in one way or another it was contrived to seriously tax every district in which the extra police were brought. He would come later on to a few special instances in which the drafting of extra police into a district was entirely unnecessary. But, previous to doing so, he would ask the right hon. Gentleman the Chief Secretary to state, in his reply, what was the present position of Mr. Jenkinson? To the general public in Ireland the position of Mr. Jenkinson was a complete mystery. He desired to know whether Mr. Jenkinson was to be paid under this Vote, or, if not, under what Vote he was to be paid? If Mr. Jenkinson's pay had ceased in Ireland, perhaps the right hon. Gentleman would tell the Committee when it did so. Was it proposed to reappoint him in Ireland? If so, what position was he to hold in the future? They also wanted to have a clear understanding with regard to Mr. Clifford Lloyd. The other evening, when the Magistrates' (Ireland) Salaries Bill was brought forward, the

Secretary to the Treasury (Mr. Courtney) ventured the statement that Mr. Clifford Lloyd would not be one of the magistrates appointed under that Bill. He (Mr. Kenny) desired to know whether the fortunes of that Bill had in any way affected the fortunes of Mr. Jenkinson? Mr. Jenkinson was now a pensioner under the Crown, and received something like £1,000 a-year for services he had rendered in the past. It was somewhat too bad to have him foisted on the people of Ireland, as he believed it was proposed, because, when it was found inconvenient to continue the gentleman in the position of Director of Criminal Prosecutions, the Government went to the trouble of introducing a Bill in the House to make provision for his further maintenance. There was an item in the Vote, under the head of "Good Service Pay," for five County Inspectors. He believed that four of those Inspectors were Captain Reed, Captain Plunkett, Mr. Butler, and Mr. Slagg. He should like to know whether County Inspector Smith, the gentleman who issued the famous Circular to the police, instructing them to shoot down any person they saw looking in a menacing manner towards Mr. Clifford Lloyd, was one of the gentlemen who was to receive good service pay? It looked very like a matter in which the Irish Government desired to patronize the persons who offended most violently against popular feeling in Ireland, if County Inspector Smith was to be one of the five gentlemen rewarded. There was an enormous difference between this year and last, in the allowances which were made to the Constabulary. The difference consisted in an increase of £22,000. He should like to know how the extraordinary change from £55,000 to £77,000 had been brought about? Furthermore, in the ordinary pay of the police, there was an increase of £20,000 making altogether an increase in those two items on this Vote of over £42,000. These were increases which required explanation. They were very grave and serious items, and it was too bad to have the expense of the Constabulary increasing year by year in Ireland, especially now, when the services of the police were more than ever unnecessary. Wherever they went in Ireland they found the country swarming with policemen. If they drove along a road they found a police hut at every corner; policemen were to be seen at every turn, and in the most out-of-the-way places, and for this state of things the country was to be severely taxed. It was a well-known fact that the policemen in Ireland did nothing towards the discharge of the functions which policemen performed in this and other countries. The Irish police were a military force; they prowled about the country armed with rifles and bayonets, and they looked with disdain upon any such menial function as attending to sanitary arrangements, or other properly organized police duties. There must be a complete and radical change in the Irish Constabulary system; but until the firearms and other military accoutrements were taken from the men, it was impossible to expect that the duties of the Constabulary in Ireland would be efficiently and properly discharged. Now, he begged to bring under the notice of the right hon. Gentleman the Chief Secretary a case to which he had already directed the attention of the House by way of Question, and that was the extraordinary claim that was made for compensation under the Prevention of Crime Act by a certain police constable in the county of Clare. The police constable in question claimed £405 compensation for money and a watch which he alleged were destroyed by fire—maliciously destroyed, as he represented, by fire in a wild and out-of-the-way district in Ireland, where he was on police duty; £395 of the total amount had been, according to the statement of the constable, in the bank. He represented that he had had that amount in his possession for a number of years, and he produced, in support of his statement, a pass book, or what he represented to be a pass book, which was supposed to prove everything. Now, that pass book was all written at the same time, and was offered by the constable for the purpose of proving his case. He represented that he had lost, or in some way mislaid, the original book in which the accounts were entered, and consequently he improvised this new book in order to prove the amount of money in his possession. He stated in his evidence that at a certain date a fire took place, and he had in his possession a sum of £196; but when the items in the improvised account book were examined, it was found that he had only the sum of £110. Furthermore, he represented in his evidence before the Chairman of Bounty Sessions, that a sea captain in Galway had cashed a cheque for him of the amount of £196. Now, sea captains were not in the habit of cashing cheques for £196, and policemen were not in the habit of having such cheques in their possession. The constable further stated that the sea captain sold him a watch, and that he presented the cheque for that enormous sum in payment and received the balance. He (Mr. Kenny) considered that, upon the face of it, the statement was a lie; it must be perfectly plain to any person who knew anything of sea captains and policemen, that sea captains were not in the habit of placing so much confidence in ordinary policemen as to change cheques for them. The evidence called to prove the case of the constable was extremely weak indeed. The wife of the man was called, and she swore she had never seen such an amount of money in the possession of her husband. In reply to his (Mr. Kenny's) Question, the right hon. Gentleman the Chief Secretary stated that £100 of the total sum came from the constable's father-in-law and £100 from some other relative of his. In evidence before the Grand Jury, he stated distinctly that he only got £35 from his father-in-law and £48 from another relative; altogether the amount he received from extraneous sources did not reach £100. The Chairman of Bounty Sessions, at which the claim was in the first place decided, stated that, in his opinion, there was no evidence whatever that Sub-Constable Carlow lost his money; but that, on the other hand, his witnesses contradicted themselves in a variety of essential particulars; in fact, in the opinion of the Chairman of Bounty Sessions, the claim was utterly groundless. The Chief Secretary had stated that it had been known that a sub-constable of police in Ireland had had in his possession £1,500. It appeared to him (Mr. Kenny) that if police officers in Ireland could, out of their earnings, amass such a large amount of money as £1,500, or even as £395, as Sub-Constable Carlow represented he had in a hut, which he was in the habit of leaving unguarded for days together, there was very small ground indeed for the proposal which the Chief Secretary made last year to increase the pay and pensions of the members of the Irish Constabulary Force. There was, however, such a habit to champion the Constabulary in the House of Commons, that he was not at all surprised the right hon. Gentleman should get up and defend them. Of course, the Chief Secretary would base his defence of Sub-Constable Carlow upon the action of the Grand Jury. But hon. Gentlemen knew what Irish Grand Juries were. They knew that Grand Juries were not representative bodies. They were directly nominated by the Sheriff of the county, and indirectly by the Lord Lieutenant. They knew that Grand Juries were essentially a class of men who were not concerned by the taxation they levied, that they were men who took good care to levy taxes upon small districts, and possibly to increase a rate of 5*s*. in the pound to 10*s*. in the pound. Of course, it was a very convenient method for policemen who wanted to make a little money, to come forward and swear that they had had bank notes, the numbers of which they did not remember, maliciously destroyed. It was a convenient way of making money, and as policemen in Ireland could not make money so easily as by committing perjury, they were great fools if they did not commit perjury. ["Oh, oh!"] Yes; hon. Members knew that the chief qualification of a man for the office of policeman in Ireland was that he had no regard for the truth. The experience of many hon. Gentlemen was, that Irish policemen never told the truth when it was not convenient for them to do so; and his opinion was that policemen would be perfectly certain to take the advantage of the prejudice of a Grand Jury and make money at the expense of the ratepayers, if they found it necessary. Furthermore, his opinion was that those ratepayers who were taxed by an irresponsible body, such as a Grand Jury, were fools if they paid the taxes levied upon them. He recommended the people who were taxed unjustly to precipitate reform by refusing to pay iniquitous taxation. He could cite many cases in which the police tax in Ireland was unjustly levied. He did not propose to go into them at any length; in fact, he would only cite one. There was at Lisdoonvarna a person named

Gardner, who had a police hut and five policemen to guard him. Notwithstanding the fact that there were seven or eight constables, and a sergeant-constable, in Lisdoonvarna, the sergeant-constable had thought fit to recommend that five constables should be told off for the special protection of Mr. Gardner. To judge by recent circumstances, Mr. Gardner was quite able to take care of himself, the last instance of which occurred a short time ago, when he assaulted a peaceful individual, and was sentenced to a fine or seven days' imprisonment. Besides, Mr. Gardner had told the police that he did not require their services; and it appeared to him that it was only a piece of false generosity on the part of the Irish Government to insist on forcing that assistance on persons who were not anxious to have it. It simply bore out the argument used in the beginning of his remarks, that there was an excess of police throughout the country, and that for their employment the Government had to adopt an extraordinary and unjust course towards the various districts. As long as the Government retained in their service in Ireland a number of policemen largely in excess of the number required, it was certain that those districts would be mulcted by the Government in order the more conveniently to dispose of the extraditing, and so long would the country be forced to suffer the imposition of unjust taxation, which was at that time creating feelings of dissatisfaction and political rancour, which would not very easily be allayed.

Mr. O'SHEA said, he would ask the right hon. Gentleman the Secretary to the Lord Lieutenant of Ireland, before he replied, whether, in connection with the case mentioned in debate, he intended to give any instructions with regard to police constables keeping large sums of money in their barracks, or huts, with the object of discouraging them from asking for compensation should those barracks, or huts, be burnt down? He would also ask the right hon. Gentleman whether, in consideration of the absolute peace which reigned throughout County Clare, a large number of police were to be removed, or had been removed; and, if so, whether he would cause inquiry to be made with regard to those who remained, with the view of removing them also?

Mr. LEAMY regretted that the right hon. Gentleman the Chief Secretary was not in his place, because he wished to ask him for some explanation with regard to the extra police force in the county of Waterford. He had put a Question to the right hon. Gentleman a few days ago on this subject, and the right hon. Gentleman stated, in reply, that the number of the police force in Waterford County was 219. He (Mr. Leamy) submitted, that if these figures were correct, it was most extraordinary that so large a force should be kept there, chargeable upon the ratepayers, especially as the county had been distinguished for its quietness for some years past. If the right hon. Gentleman thought it necessary to have this extraordinary force in the county, it would be perfectly easy for him to apply to Parliament for the powers necessary for the purpose; but he contended that it was manifestly unjust to send this large force into the county and charge them upon the ratepayers, at a time when they were already burdened with taxation. If the Lord Lieutenant of Ireland had to pay for the extra police out of his own pocket, he would, no doubt, think a very much smaller force sufficient. He would ask on whose recommendation these men were sent into the county? The right hon. Gentleman, when he answered his former Question, said that the county was not the most peaceful place in Ireland, and that there had been many cases of intimidation there; but it was extraordinary that the Prevention of Crime Act should be put in force there under the actual circumstances, and a very large number of extra police sent there. Such a state of things would not be permitted in an English county for 24 hours. The whole proceeding was most unconstitutional; and to charge people who had no voice in the control of the police force with a large sum of money for its maintenance, was an act of which no honest man would be guilty. It was all very well for the right hon. Gentleman to get up and make statements about the disturbed state of the district; but, of course, he must know that no one had any means of ascertaining whether those statements were correct; but there was no doubt that in making them he was dependent upon others for his information—that was to say, upon the Resident

Magistrates—who could show their gratitude in no better way than by saying that the districts were disturbed. Perhaps an additional force of 20 or 30 men might have been required; but to send down the enormous number complained of was out of the question. Was it Captain Stack that recommended the men to be sent? He trusted the right hon. Gentleman would be able to give some information to the Committee on this point. The right hon. Gentleman said they were not extra police at all; but how could he (Mr. Leamy) know whether they were extra or ordinary police? It was perfectly absurd to tell him, under the circumstances, that they were not extra police. Were they to be told that they were not extra police because they had been withdrawn from the ordinary force, their place being filled up by others? It was not the custom in England, when crime was committed in a county, for the Home Secretary to send down an extra police force; he hoped, therefore, that this extravagant expenditure for police in Ireland would be at once abolished.

MR. PARNELL: Sir, upon two occasions during this Session it came to my lot to call attention to part of the question of the extra police in certain districts of Ireland with regard to the quartering of extra police in the cities of Cork and Limerick. We had discussions in this House upon this limited branch of the question, and we received very little satisfaction from the right hon. Gentleman the Chief Secretary to the Lord Lieutenant of Ireland. We made out an overwhelming case against the necessity of extra police in those two cities; but we were put off in the usual way. Although there was considerable correspondence between the Local Authorities in Cork and the right hon. Gentleman the Chief Secretary and the Resident Magistrate, Captain Plunkett, the result has been, practically speaking, to leave the people of Cork pretty much as they were before, to pay for the extra police until the time when the right hon. Gentleman promises that the subject of the amount of the police force to be allowed for that city shall receive the attention and reconsideration of the Lord Lieutenant of Ireland. But the question to which I have to direct the attention of the Committee is of a very much wider scope, extending, in fact, to the quartering of extra police throughout the whole of Ireland—throughout, I may say, almost ever county and city of Ireland; and I think I shall be able to show that there exists no longer any practical necessity for this extra force of men—in fact, that the necessity never existed at all, or, at any rate, that it cannot be said to have existed during the last two years as regards a considerable proportion of Ireland. I shall, I think, be able also to show that although the right hon. Gentleman the Chief Secretary may have recently, within the last three months, turned his attention to the advisability of reducing the extra police force in some of the Irish counties, yet that he commenced to do so very much too late; that the steps he has taken in that direction are entirely inadequate; and that we have a fair claim to urge upon him a very much larger and more immediate reduction with regard to a very considerable proportion of these extra forces in many Irish districts and counties. Speaking generally, the Irish Executive is entitled, under the Act regulating the matter, to have a free force of 10,636 men and officers, besides a reserve force of, I believe, 400 men and officers, and the revenue force, the number of which I do not exactly know, but which may be somewhere between 150 and 200. Exclusive, then, of revenue and reserve men, the total free force for which the authorities are entitled to charge extra when they are sent out of the county, and for whose payment the Executive was entitled to ask Parliament to grant a Vote, is 10,636. The actual free force distributed under this power by the Lord Lieutenant of Ireland at the last quinquennial period in 1882—in July, I believe—amounted to 10,030, or 630 men short of the actual full free force which might have been legally raised for service in Ireland. Now, Sir, at the very threshold of our case I think we are entitled to make a very serious complaint with regard to the action of the Lord Lieutenant of Ireland in this matter. I believe that the free force in Ireland was distributed in 1882 by Earl Spencer, after the period of Office of the present Chief Secretary to the Lord Lieutenant had commenced—at a time when the Government had applied to Parliament for their coercive powers, and were representing to Parliament and the country that the state of Ireland was very serious indeed. Well, Sir, at that time, and under such circumstances, the Lord Lieutenant and the Irish Executive deliberately refrained from raising a free force in Ireland to the extent of the number of men which the Act of Parliament authorized. They kept it 630 men short. I suppose I am not allowed to impute intention or motive to such an impersonal body as the Irish Executive; but if I were allowed to do so, I can only say that it would appear that their intention must have been to obtain further means of fining and levying imposts upon the districts and counties concerned—further means than those supplied to them by the Act of *Will.* IV. and other Acts by which they are entitled to send extra men into the different districts. Well, as I have shown, the Irish Government deliberately kept the free force at the last quinquennial period of redistribution 530 men under the number authorized by Parliament; on the other hand, they sent into various Irish counties the enormous extra force of 3,426. As I have just explained, there are various enactments under which the Executive Government can levy and send extra forces, and quarter them on the inhabitants. Under the 13th section of the Act of *Will.* IV., which gives power to the Lord Lieutenant to proclaim a district, they levied and quartered on the districts 2,221 men. Under Section 12, which gives the magistrates power to call for an extra force, and which requires a representation from the magistrates before it can be sent, 859 men were sent, and I think the Committee might with profit note the smallness of the number of men who were considered by the local magistrates to be necessary as compared with the number that the Lord Lieutenant sent without their advice or request: 859 men were quartered on the 31st of December last, and on the 30th of June of the present year they had been reduced to 844. The authorities have also sent from the reserve force 91 extra men; and under the Prevention of Crime Act, which permits all the force to be levied upon the district, no matter how small, upon the 31st of December, 1883, there were 195, making a grand total of 3,421 extra men quartered on the 31st of December, in the greater portion upon the ratepayers, and with respect to 195 wholly so quartered. I wish to call the attention of the Committee to the section of the Act of *Will.* IV., under which these quarterings have been made. Section 12, under which 859 were quartered, provides that in any case in which seven or more magistrates of any county, at any Petty Session, being a majority of magistrates present, shall certify to the Lord Lieutenant that the number of chief or other constables and sub-constables so appointed for any such county is inadequate for the due execution of the law, it shall be lawful for the Lord Lieutenant to appoint such further number of constables to such county as may be so certified to be necessary, and to remove such chief, or other constables and sub-constables, from time to time. There are some points in regard to the application of this section which we have no information upon, and I should be glad if it could be supplied to us in the course of the debate by the right hon. Gentleman the Chief Secretary. In the first place, I am anxious to know the dates of the applications by magistrates for the extra forces in the different counties, whether they are of recent date or of late date, and what the practice of the Irish Executive has been in reference to the removal of such extra forces. There is no provision, and it appears to me to be a serious omission in the section, for the removal of this force which has been quartered on the application of the magistrates. It is left optional to the Lord Lieutenant to remove them as he thinks fit. It is very possible that the applications in some cases for these 950 men may have been of ancient date, and that they have been allowed to remain, possibly against the wishes of the local magistrates themselves. Then I come to the 13th section, under which the great bulk of the extra police in Ireland have been, and are still quartered, a moiety of the maintenance being levied on the ratepayers. This section provides that the Lord Lieutenant, by the advice of the Privy Council of Ireland, may declare by Proclamation—and I wish distinctly to direct the attention of the Committee to these words—that any county, city, or town, or barony, or half barony, or county at large, or any district that is, or are, in a state of disturbance and require an additional establishment of police, and thereupon the Lord Lieutenant may appoint such extra police as he may think proper, not exceeding so many in each district so declared to be in a state of disturbance. Well, Sir, it appears to me that the true meaning of this section is that there shall be an actual state of disturbance within the district to entitle the Lord Lieutenant to issue this Proclamation; but I doubt very much whether in respect of any of those counties where it has been made the issue of the Proclamation was originally justified; but if, in any case, this were so, that justification no longer exists. It is quite impossible for the right hon. Gentleman to say that any county or district in Ireland is at present in a state of disturbance, and consequently the original justification for the Proclamation has entirely ceased, and we are entitled to ask upon what ground this large force of extra Constabulary is still kept quartered upon the ratepayers throughout the country. Since the 31st of December there has been some slight reduction of the number of extra police. The figures on the 30th of June, 1884, as supplied to me by the right hon. Gentleman the Chief Secretary to the Lord Lieutenant of Ireland, give for the extra men under the 13th section of the Act of *Will.* IV. 877, and for the extra men under Section 12—namely, those originally requested by the local magistrates, 849; for the extra men from the reserve, 86; and for extra men under the Prevention of Crime Act, 30. This last head is the only one which shows any material reduction—namely, from 195 to 30, leaving the total number of extra men quartered in the different districts under the enactments which I have explained, on the 30th of June, 1884, at the enormous figure of 2,827, or a reduction of 599 extra men in six months; a reduction which amounts to something like one man in every six. Now, I wish to refer to the cost of these extra men in the counties, and I find the total given in the Estimate as the cost of the extra men is £110,800. Under the Prevention of Crime Act there is £18,000, making the enormous sum of £128,800, which is levied violently, unconstitutionally, and, as we contend, illegally, and without the slightest local control, upon the Irish ratepayers. Now, Sir, it has been very much the custom with English Ministers, and particularly with the right hon. Gentleman the Chief Secretary to the Lord Lieutenant of Ireland, to allude to this amount of reduction which has been obtained by the tenants under the Irish Land Act; but I find that the reductions given by the Land Courts during the three years' working of that Act amount to £270,000. The Irish ratepayers consequently have to pay back to the Government for extra police half of the money which they have received in reductions. The Government having decided to despoil the landlords to the extent of £270,000 a-year under the working of the Land Courts for three years, in order to make themselves still more beloved in Ireland, they proceed to despoil the ratepayers by compelling them to pay a sum equal to half that sum for the cost of extra police. I stated a short time ago that I wanted to prove that there was nothing in the state of Ireland which required this extra force of police. Now, the fact is that the Government, having deliberately neglected at the last quinquennial period to raise the number of free men to the amount they were entitled to do by the Act, and having also raised a large number of extra men—having thus raised the total number of men authorized by Parliament from 10,636 to 13,456—now do not know what to do with them. They have no power under the law to distribute these 3,000 extra men as a free force, and they therefore distribute them as extra men, part of the cost of whom is to be paid by the localities. In view of the peaceable state of Ireland, which has now continued for two years, and in view of the Charges of the Judges, I maintain that if the Government still desire to keep up t is swollen police establishment in Ireland they should apply to Parliament either for a Supplementary Estimate, or for an amending Act enabling them to make this charge upon the taxpayers. It is monstrous that it should be charged upon the districts. This matter affects nearly every county in Ireland. The county of Clare does not seem to have participated in the reductions made in some of the other counties between December, 1883, and June, 1884; indeed, it heads the list for the large number of extra men which, on the 30th of June, were still quartered in that county. I find that at a former period in 1883 there were 235 extra men quartered there under the Proclamation of the Lord Lieutenant under the 13th section of the Act of *Will.* IV. There were in June last still 235 extra men, involving a charge on the ratepayers of that impoverished county of between £8,000 and £9,000. I find that at the first period in 1883 there were 33 additional Constabulary under the Prevention of Crime Act, and that the only reduction which was made in the county of Clare between the end of March last and the middle of this year has been in respect to these 33 men, the cost of the large force of 235 extra men being still left to be borne by the taxpayers of the county. I do not know whether any recent reduction has been made; I am now speaking from the most recent information I have received on the subject, some of which has been furnished to me by the right hon. Gentleman the Chief Secretary to the Lord Lieutenant of Ireland this morning. The free force to which that county is entitled is 328 men under the last distribution of the Lord Lieutenant. Therefore, there are very nearly as many extra men placed in this county as there are free policemen—that is to say, that the police force of the county Clare is nearly double the normal number. Let us turn to the state of the county, as disclosed by the Parliamentary Returns for the last quarter. I find that for the whole of county Clare—a very large county, containing a very considerable population of small farmers who have derived little benefit from the Land Act—in the whole of the county the number of outrages, exclusive of threatening letters, which I do not notice in matters of this kind, amounted to four. I will ask the right hon. Gentleman what justification there is for keeping up this swollen police force in that county in view of the Returns in reference to crime during the last 12 months? Well, now, another county which is very much imposed on is the county of Cork. In the East Riding of the county of Cork, on the 31st of December, 1883, there were altogether 185 extra men—11 extra men sent from the reserve force, and 174 men sent under the Lord Lieutenant's Proclamation. In this Riding of Cork there has been no reduction whatever made in the six months between December, 1883, and June, 1884. The same number of extra men that were quartered there on the 30th of June last are now quartered on the ratepayers at an annual cost to them of £7,500 for the half county. Well, now, Sir, in the East Riding of county Cork there were only three agrarian offences committed in the last quarter. This Riding is entitled to a free force of 422 men, so that the number of extra men is over one-third of the total of the free force. Going on to the West Riding I find that on the 31st of December, 1883, there were 143 extra men quartered, all under the 13th section, or Proclamation Section, of the Act of *Will.* IV. During the period of six months, up to the 30th of June, 44 of these extra men were removed, still, however, leaving the enormous and entirely unnecessary extra force of 99 men for this Riding, in which only six agrarian offences were committed during the quarter. I should also like to direct the attention of the Committee to Judge O'Brien's Charge to the Grand Jury at the recent Assizes in county Cork with reference to the state of the county. He says—

"So far as I can collect from the sources which are open to me, I am happy to state that the condition of this great county is one that very nearly justifies the description of entire and absolute quiet and security."

He refers to a temporary small increase of crime since the last Assizes in the East Riding; but he goes on to say—

"I find that that small increase is more than balanced by a very large diminution of offences in the West Riding of this county, in the proportion of 68 reported offences."

Of course, Judge O'Brien is speaking of all offences, agrarian and otherwise, which came before him—

"In the present year, as against 114 in the past year for the same period, and I find that this great decrease appears to be almost entirely in offences that tend to indicate by their diminution a restoration of social peace and tranquillity, and the absence of agrarian outrage in both Divisions of this county."

He goes on to say—

"I observe as a most important feature of the change that has taken place the subsidence of almost all forms of intimidation, and an absence of all restraint on personal conduct,"

and so on. Well, now, Sir, I ask the right hon. Gentleman if he does not intend to show his appreciation of this state of affairs in the county of Cork? Perhaps I had better not weary the Committee by going over the whole list of Irish counties; but, speaking generally, I may say that the list shows that there are extra men quartered in almost every county and city in Ireland. In county Donegal the number of extra men was not so large as it was in some other counties. In that county there were 100 extra men at the end of 1883, and they were quartered there at a cost to the ratepayers of over £2,000 a-year. Seventy of these extra men have been taken away in the six months which have elapsed since December, 1883, leaving 30 men still as an extra charge upon the district at a cost of nearly, according to the information in my possession, £1,000. In the East Riding of Galway there were 183 extra men on the 31st of December, 1883, there were now 145 extra men in that Riding, and during the last quarter there were only two agrarian offences, exclusive of threatening letters. The total cost of the extra men in this Riding during the year ending the 30th of June last was £5,800. In the West Riding of Galway there were on the 31st of December, 1883, 270 extra men, and on the 30th of June, 1884, there were 200 extra men quartered there under the Act of *Will.* IV. On the 31st of December last there were in the same Riding 22 extra men under the 12th section of the Act of *Will.* IV.—that is under the magistrates, requisitions, and there were eight extra men on the same date sent from the reserve force. There were 70 extra men under the Prevention of Crime Act, making altogether an extra force in this one Riding of 300 men, or 12 men in excess of the free force establishment to which the Riding was entitled. Well, now, Sir, in the county of Kerry there were on the 31st of December, 1883, 11 extra men from the reserve force, and on the same date there were, under the 13th section of *Will.* IV., 196 extra men, and these numbers remain now practically unchanged, for the total number of extra men quartered in this county on the 31st of December was 207, and the total number of extra men now quartered there was 203, or a diminution of only four men. These men involved a cost to the county of over £8,000 a-year. In his Charge to the Grand Jury of the county of Kerry on the 16th of July, Mr. Justice O'Brien said—

"The present condition of the county compares favourably with the past."

The county of Limerick was another very oppressed county in this respect. On the 31st of December, 1883, there were 235 extra men quartered, and that number has not been diminished in the six months ending the 30th of June, 1884; 235 extra men still remained in county Limerick, this county being entitled to a free force of 281 men. There were only six agrarian offences, all of them of a very trivial character, committed in the county of Limerick for the last quarter of which we have any Return. Judge Fitzgibbon, in addressing the Grand Jury of the county of Limerick on the 11th of July, said—

"There are altogether eight cases to go before you. There is one of manslaughter, but there does not appear to be any great difficulty in dealing with it. The other seven cases are simply for assaults. Having regard to the large population of your county, and the circumstances of your district, there is nothing on the face of the list requiring any observations from me."

The question of the extra police force of the City of Limerick has already been debated fully in this House, and I will not refer to it further. The county of Mayo on the 31st of December, 1883, had 50 extra men under the 12th section of the Act of *Will.* IV.—that is to say, requisitioned by the magistrates. On the same date, there were in the county 125 extra men under the Lord Lieutenant's Proclamation. Mayo does not appear to have had any men quartered upon it under the section of the Prevention of Crime Act. There were altogether at this date a total extra force in Mayo of 178 men. That force has been reduced in the period of six months to 112 men, involving a cost to the ratepayers for the year of nearly £4,500. For the last quarter in which we have any Returns, the number of agrarian offences in the county of Mayo only amounted to three—that is to say, the ratepayers of the county have been charged £1,500 for each agrarian offence committed during the quarter. The county of Sligo, on the 31st of December, 1883, had 50 extra men under the magistrates' requisition section. They had 45 extra men under the Lord Lieutenant's Proclamation, making altogether 95 extra men in this county—a force which was not reduced up to the 30th of June, 1884. The list of agrarian offences discloses only the small number of two for the last quarter, and the cost to the ratepayers of the county of Sligo for the extra men will amount to something like £4,000, or about £2,000 for each agrarian offence committed during the last quarter. In the North Riding of the county of Tipperary on the 31st of December, 1883, there were 114 extra men quartered under the Lord Lieutenant's Proclamation. That number was reduced on the 30th of last June to 94, involving an annual cost to the ratepayers of £3,760. In that Division of the county of Tipperary there were no agrarian offences during the last quarter. In the South Riding of the county of Tipperary there were 80 extra men quartered under the magistrates' requisition section of the Act of *Will.* IV. On the 31st of last December there was one extra man from the reserve, and there were 100 extra men quartered on the Riding under the 13th section of the Act of *Will.* IV.—that is to say, under the Lord Lieutenant's Proclamation, making altogether 181 extra men in the South Riding of Tipperary on this date. That number on the 30th of June was reduced to the number of 155. The 100 men under the Lord Lieutenant's Proclamation have been reduced to 75, and the extra man from the reserve has been taken away. The number of agrarian offences in the South Riding of Tipperary during the last quarter only amounted to four, while the cost to the ratepayers of the extra force amounted to something like £6,000 a-year, or, on the average, £1,500 for each agrarian offence. The offences, I notice, were of a very trivial character. Now I should like to direct the attention of the Committee also to the Charge delivered to the Grand Jury by the Judge who presided at the Tipperary Assizes. On the 8th of July the Lord Chief Justice, addressing a Grand Jury, congratulated them on the smallness of the Calendar, the disposal of which, he said, would not detain them very long. Westmeath is the next county on my list. I find on the 31st of last December there were 23 extra men quartered on this county upon the requisition of the magistrates. There were 63 extra men quartered there under the Lord Lieutenant's Proclamation, and one man was quartered upon the county under the Prevention of Crime Act. During the six months which elapsed from December last to June, the one man had been removed, so that the extra force of Westmeath still stood at 86 men. Now, I wish to direct the attention of the Committee to the case of some other counties which have always been regarded as quiet counties, and in the case of which there seems to be still less justification for the maintenance of extra police forces. Take the case of Meath. In December, 1883, there were 72 extra men quartered there under the 12th section of the Act of *Will.* IV., and three under the Prevention of Crime Act. There are now 52 extra men quartered in this county under the Act of *Will.* IV., at a cost to the county of something like £2,000. I should like to know if the right hon. Gentleman the Chief Secretary could give me any information as to the date of the representations made by the magistrates with regard to those counties on the list where extra police are quartered under the 12th section of the Act of *Will.* IV.? I refer to the West Riding of Galway; to the county of Kilkenny, where 55 men are quartered under this section, and none under the Proclamation of the Lord Lieutenant; King's County, where 15 men are quartered under the provisions of the 12th section, and only 12 under the Proclamation of the Lord Lieutenant; Queen's County, where 15 men are quartered under the 12th section, and none under the Proclamation of the Lord Lieutenant; the county of Longford, where 34 extra men are quartered under this section, and only 22 under the Proclamation of the Lord Lieutenant; County Mayo, where 50 men are quartered under this section, and 60 under the Proclamation of the Lord Lieutenant; County Meath, where 52 extra men are now quartered under this section, and none under the Proclamation of the Lord Lieutenant; the county of Kildare, where 18 men are still quartered from the reserve force by the Lord Lieutenant, but none under his Proclamation; the county of Louth, where 15 men are quartered under the 12th section, but none under the Lord Lieutenant's Proclamation; the county of Sligo, where 50 men are quartered under the 12th section, and 45 under the Lord Lieutenant's Proclamation; the South Riding of the county of Tipperary, where 80 men are quartered under the 12th section, and 75 under the Lord Lieutenant's Proclamation; the county of Waterford, where 16 extra men are quartered under the 12th section, and 50 under the Lord Lieutenant's Proclamation; the county of Westmeath, where 23 extra men are quartered under the 12th section, and 63 under the Lord Lieutenant's Proclamation; Belfast, where 320 extra men are quartered under the 12th section by the desire of the magistrates or the Corporation, and none under the Lord Lieutenant's Proclamation; the county of Dublin, where 10 extra men are quartered under the 12th section, and none under the Lord Lieutenant's Proclamation; the county of Fermanagh, where 10 extra men are quartered under the 12th section, and none under the Lord Lieutenant's Proclamation; the county of Monaghan, where 12 extra men are quartered under the 12th section, and none under the Lord Lieutenant's Proclamation; and the city or county of Londonderry, where 45 extra men are quartered under the 12th section, and none under the Lord Lieutenant's Proclamation. Now, Sir, I could go on indefinitely referring to the statistics on this subject; but I think I have proved enough to show that in almost every Irish county there is an extra force of police; that in every Irish county there is a very low Calendar of crime; that at all the Assizes the Judges were unanimous in their testimony to the peaceable condition of the different counties. The police force throughout Ireland generally is enormously swollen by the number of 2,800 extra men over and above the free force authorized by Act of Parliament. I think we are entitled to ask the right hon. Gentleman for his justification of this state of things. I do not see how the Government can expect us calmly to pass this Estimate upon the Returns with which we have been presented—Returns showing that the condition of Ireland is absolutely normal as respects its tranquillity and freedom from crime. All the contentions upon which successive Chief Secretaries have justified the retention of extra police forces are entirely absent. In the present case it is impossible for us to allow this Estimate to pass without very strenuous protest and opposition, unless we hear something far more satisfactory than we have yet heard from the Government. The reduction of 500 and odd men which has taken place during the last few months out of the total force is entirely inadequate. There are several of the counties to which I have alluded which are amongst the most impoverished throughout Ireland. The county of Clare contains a very large population of very small tenant farmers. The county of Cork is also in a similar position; the county of Galway, where the police tax is also most crushing, is in a very impoverished state; the county of Kerry is notorious as being one of the most poverty-stricken counties in Ireland; the county of Limerick, the only rich county on the list where the force is very high, is remarkable for having been absolutely free from crime of any kind during the last two years; the county of Sligo is another impoverished county; and the county of Tipperary is at present, and has been for a considerable time, exceedingly quiet. I might go over the whole list and show, in the same way as I have abundantly done with respect to those counties, that there is not the slightest justification, even from the point of view of the Government, for the maintenance of this cruel tax resulting from the quartering of large extra forces of police upon the people. Three years ago the Predecessor (Mr. W. E. Forster) of the right hon. Gentleman the Chief Secretary (Mr. Trevelyan) informed the Committee, during one of the discussions which took place on this Vote, that in a short time he hoped to be able to hand over the police force to elective authorities in Ireland. The lapse of time which has taken place since then do not justify the prediction and hope of the right hon. Gentleman (Mr. W. E. Forster). Instead of the force being reduced, we have had it enormously increased. Apart from the hardship to thé localities, and to the ratepayers who have to pay these crushing inflictions, the force in its character is absolutely unconstitutional. Eminent Constitutional lawyers, like the late Mr. Butt, have given it as their opinion that the maintenance of this police force in Ireland, an absolutely military force in its character, is a breach of the annual Army Discipline Act. Certainly, the right hon. Gentleman the Chief Secretary should tell us to-day that he proposes to diminish this extra force by at least one-half during the next six months, and that he hopes within the subsequent period of six months to dispense with it altogether.

If we do not receive some assurance of that kind, the action which will have to be taken by the people of Ireland and by their Representatives is a matter which will have to be very carefully considered. The rates for extra police are now levied by the Grand Juries, bodies absolutely without any particle whatever of a representative character. If in any district the Grand Jury refuse to levy the rate, there is the Judge's *fiat* to compel them to do so; and if they then refuse to levy the rate, there is the further order of the Queen's Bench; in fact, the whole levying of the extra police is beset with a series of cast-iron enactments which might do credit to an age of barbarism and a rule of despotism, but which are certainly out of place on the Statute Book at the present time. For our part, we shall not cease to protest against these enactments; and, as I have just said, in the absence of any satisfactory assurance from the right hon. Gentleman the Chief Secretary to the Lord Lieutenant, it will become a matter for serious consideration whether the collection of this oppressive tax cannot be prevented by the organized action of the people of Ireland. We have from the glowing pen of the right hon. Gentleman (Mr. Trevelyan) himself some very significant and good advice upon the subject. The taxes, the refusal to pay which was referred to by the right hon. Gentleman in terms of approval, were taxes levied upon the people by the Representatives of the people in Parliament, so far as the people were then represented; but these taxes are not levied upon our people by Parliament; they are levied by an irresponsible clique in Dublin Castle, some of whose iniquities have recently been brought to light by the exertions of my hon. Friend the Member for Mallow (Mr. O'Brien). I have no doubt that the distribution of these extra police amongst the unhappy counties I have referred to depended very much upon the Reports of the notorious person whose conduct is now the subject of examination by the Dublin Police Court sitting *in camerâ*. I have no doubt that if the system could be further examined into, and I trust that a long time will not elapse before an opportunity may be found of examining into the system which obtains in Dublin Castle—I have no doubt that if the system were further investigated and examined into, we should find that the action of the Irish Executive was directed and depended upon the advice of men very little better in character and position than that of the Government officials, whose conduct so recently became the subject of criminal investigation. So long as you rule Ireland by a centralized system of Government at the dictation of a group of permanent officials in Dublin Castle the possessors of swollen and enormous salaries, whose existence necessarily depends on keeping up a state of alarm in the minds of the English people and Parliament with regard to the condition of Ireland, so long you will find it is impossible for you to rule her justly, and that it will continue impossible for you to escape the complaints and the criticisms which we have been compelled to direct against you and against your system of administration during the present Session, and so long will the administration of Ireland by England and by the ring in Dublin, who have got possession of that administration, be a subject of reproach amongst the peoples of the civilized world. I beg to move the reduction of this Vote by the sum of £100,000.

Motion made, and Question proposed,

"That a sum, not exceeding £848,096, be granted to Her Majesty, to complete the sum necessary to defray the Charge which will come in course of payment during the year ending on the 31st day of March 1885, for the Constabulary Force in Ireland."—(*Mr. Parnell.*)

Mr. TREVELYAN: Sir, I propose, in replying to the considerable number of Gentlemen who have spoken upon a subject of such interest to Ireland, to go through their speeches consecutively, and to come last to the speech of the hon. Member for the City of Cork (Mr. Parnell), who spoke with an amount of statistical preparation that deserves special notice. While, however, the last words he spoke are still ringing in our ears, I cannot but enter my protest against them. The hon. Member said that he considered that it was very likely that if some leading officials in Dublin Castle had their conduct examined, their characters would stand little higher, I think he said, than the characters of the two people connected with different parts of the government of Ireland, one of them not connected with Dublin Castle at all, who have been accused of very great crimes indeed. Sir, it is quite plain that if the hon. Member has evidence of that fact, he ought to produce it. I must call the greatest attention to this, because it is a very serious matter. Everybody knows very well who the Lord Lieutenant and myself are advised by in high matters of criminal and police administration. If the hon. Member has evidence against any of the persons who are well known to advise us, that evidence ought to be produced in a Court of Law.

MR. PARNELL: Will the right hon. Gentleman give me a Select Committee of the House of Commons to inquire into the whole system of criminal investigation in Ireland?

MR. TREVELYAN: This is not a question of the criminal system of Dublin Castle; it is a question whether a singularly odious imputation, which I am inclined to think the hon. Member does not feel the full gravity of, ought to be made without evidence against any people, whether they are members of the Irish Administration or whether they are private individuals. The first hon. Gentleman who addressed the Committee was the hon. Member for Limerick (Mr. O'Sullivan), and the particular point to which he referred in connection with this question was the protection of a certain landlord, a Mr. Coote. The hon. Gentleman said Mr. Coote was an extremely unpopular landlord, and he asks if we uphold him and the system he adopts towards his tenants. We neither uphold Mr. Coote nor the system of his dealings with his tenants; his dealings are not, as a matter of fact, a subject for consideration by the Executive Government. What we did was to give him such protection as his safety required. It is certainly a very unfortunate thing that these relations between landlords and tenants should have existed in Ireland, and that so much evil should have come out of them; but if one consequence of them is that the life or the limb of any individual, be he landlord or tenant, is in danger, it is plainly the business of the Executive to afford them protection. I may say with regard to the question of the hon. Member for Limerick (Mr. O'Sullivan), respecting the police of Limerick, there is some prospect that at no distant date there may be a reduction of the extra police quartered in the county.

MR. PARNELL: To what extent?

MR. TREVELYAN: To the extent that safety will allow. I hope hon. Members will think I do my best to reduce the number of extra police whenever I can. I now come to the review of the remarks of the hon. Gentleman the Member for Kilkenny (Mr. Marum). Kilkenny is a county in which the Lord Lieutenant has had no direct concern with the police. In Kilkenny there are extra police, because they were asked for originally by the magistrates. The hon. Member (Mr. Marum) says the number of police ought to be reduced on account of the suffering of agriculture and the overburdened rates of the county. Well, Sir, I do not think that on that account alone Kilkenny has any special right to a reduction of its local burdens, which reduction would mean throwing the expenses on the general taxpayer. There has very recently been a reduction of 15 extra police in Kilkenny. The extra police in that county are now 55 in number, so that that county, a rich county, and a prosperous county agriculturally, compared with a great number of the English counties which have to join in paying the taxes out of which these police would be paid for if they were not paid for by the county of Kilkenny—that county is only burdened to the extent of about £2,200 or £2,300 a-year. If the hon. Member for Kilkenny (Mr. Marum) would take an English agricultural county of the same rating as Kilkenny, a county in which the agricultural industry is the same as in Kilkenny, he will find that that county would be glad, and glad many times over, if its contribution to the police of the county only amounted to £2,300. I am bound to say there is no county in England which stands in the same position pecuniarily as Kilkenny, which has not to pay at least twice as much for its police; and, therefore, I think it would be extremely hard if the English counties were to be called upon to pay for the extra police required in Kilkenny. The hon. Member may say that these 55 extra police are not required. It was not the Lord Lieutenant who placed them there of his own accord; he placed them there on the application of the magistrates. The hon. Member for the City of Cork (Mr. Parnell) asks on what date these applications of the magistrates were made? On that point I am quite ready to call for a Return; they are, for the most part, of considerable standing, because the present number of the police, generally speaking, represent what the magistrates, who are responsible for the quiet and peace of the country, consider ought to be the nominal force of the country. In the case of Kilkenny, however, the application was made in 1882. I have only made a general observation, because, whether they are of long or short standing, the magistrates, I feel sure, would listen to the general opinion of the country; and, at any rate, whatever their own opinion might be, the Government most certainly would listen very attentively to the opinions of the magistrates upon a subject of this kind. The hon. Member for Carlow (Mr. Dawson) began his speech by referring to the City of Limerick, and he said we had increased the police force there in 1882 on account of the riotous state of the town, and yet we had obtained no convictions; we had not brought any prisoners either before the Petty Sessions magistrates, or before the Assize Judges. Well, Sir, that is not the case. I say that in the case of almost every riotous disturbance that is recorded in Limerick there was some conviction more or less important. But that in itself is not all, because the main cause of the bringing extra police into Limerick in 1882 was the general riotous state of the streets, and the danger in which policemen would be who were either patrolling singly, or patrolling at too great a distance from their nearest comrade. The hon. Member for Carlow (Mr. Dawson) says that the state of things in Ireland is so oppressive that he almost expects, or at any rate hopes, that the English people themselves will rise up and put an end to it. Sir, I am not quite certain whether it is altogether judicious to call the attention of the English people to the question of police in Ireland. I have got the figures here which are taken from the last published Criminal and Judicial Statistics—namely, those published in 1883 for the year 1882.

Mr. HEALY: The English people control their police.

Mr. TREVELYAN: I am aware of the main arguments of hon. Members from Ireland upon this question; but I was speaking about the financial state of Ireland, to which the hon. Member for Carlow (Mr. Dawson) referred. I find that in England the total cost of the police was £3,264,000; of that the proportion paid by the localities is £1,985,000—that is, 1*s.* 6*d.* per head is paid by the population of England towards the maintenance of their police. In Scotland the cost of the police is £331,000, and £197,000—that is to say, 1*s.* 1*d.* per head of the population is paid for the maintenance of the police by the localities. In Ireland the total cost of the police in 1882 was £1,452,000. The part paid by the people was £124,000 —that is to say, 6*d.* per head of the population. Since then the total cost of the police in Ireland has somewhat risen; and I take it that the part paid by the community has risen to such an extent that probably it comes to 7*d.* per head. I cannot see that that represents a state of things which would excite the overwhelming indignation of the people of England if it were brought before them. Well, now, the hon. Member for Monaghan (Mr. Healy) has just suggested one argument bearing upon this question; but there is another which, of course, every hon. Member on those Benches feels the force of, and that is that though Ireland pays extremely little for the cost of her police the cost is very unequally distributed. If it were 7*d.* per head for the whole of Ireland that was paid towards the cost of the police, the tax would not be so severely felt, and I allow that 7*d.* per head grows to be considerably more in the counties which are specially taxed; but in only one case does the police tax amount to anything like what it does in English counties; in no part of Ireland, except in the City of Dublin, is the payment at all equal to that of an ordinary English county or an ordinary English town; still, undoubtedly, in many places it is considerably more than 7*d.* per head. The hon. Gentleman the junior Member for Cork (Mr. Deasy) referred for a time to the police for the City of Cork. He stated that Captain Plunkett had 20 detectives on his staff. Well, Sir, he has not 20 detectives on his staff; he has nine; and these detectives are not paid for by the City. I explained the other day that the hon. Member labours under a misapprehension with regard to the police question in the City of Cork; no exception is made and no more of the police force are charged for than those on duty.

MR. DEASY: Is the right hon. Gentleman aware that Captain Plunkett stated before a Committee of the Cork Corporation, a few weeks back, that he had 22 detectives on his staff?

MR. TREVELYAN: I am not aware of it. Captain Plunkett has nine detectives quartered at Cork, and those are not paid for by the City. If there are any other detectives besides, they would be used for purely local purposes, and they would be as much local policemen as any other of the local staff. The nine detectives who are there, are there for the purpose of providing for the general safety of the Kingdom by preventing the importation of dynamite, and checking the arrival of dangerous men from America; but, as I have said, they are not charged to the City. The hon. Member (Mr. Deasy) asked me for an assurance that meetings would not be interfered with this year. On that point I can speak very positively to this effect, that our interference or non-interference depends upon those who call the meetings together. If meetings are called together in places where there are "Boycotted" farms in any number, and places where outrages directed against special persons are really apprehended, and places where special persons would be put, for some reason, in fear of their lives, the Irish Government would have to act up to its now somewhat long-established principle of action. It is impossible to allow meetings to be so announced, so placarded, and so conducted as to interfere with the civil rights of individuals by putting them in terror of life or limb. Those parts of the country in which that is likely to be the case are now few, I am glad to say; and most certainly, so far as ordinary political excitement is concerned, the Government is of opinion that such excitement is rather healthy than unhealthy. ["Oh, oh!"] Yes, that is my opinion; and I think it is borne out by my speeches. The hon. Member for Limerick (Mr. O'Sullivan) explained to us that during his election, which he said was an election exciting a good deal of interest in the town, no outrage or rioting took place. Our general experience in Ireland, as elsewhere, is that well-contested elections, whether they are for municipal or Parliamentary purposes, are times when the worst passions of the people are merged in the great flood of healthy and legitimate excitement in which the population are involved. So far as that is the case with elections, it is the case with meetings which are held for purposes of getting up political feeling, and not for the purpose for which some meetings have been held in certain parts of Ireland, of putting pressure upon the minds of particular individuals. The hon. and gallant Member for Galway (Colonel Nolan) said he considered the number of the free force was too many, and he asked for Returns from the different counties. I will see whether the Return for which the hon. and gallant Member asks can be given. I have got a little Return here which shows that the difference between the regular normal force and the real force is about 5 per cent. The hon. and gallant Member thinks that Galway is badly used in this particular. Well, Sir, that is not the case. The free force in each of the Divisions of Galway is in one case 288, and in the other 289 men, while the normal strength is 266 and 268 men; so that Galway preserves, as nearly as possible, the actual average. I am glad to inform him that Galway is a county in which there have been pretty considerable recent reductions of the extra force. The force has recently been reduced in the East Riding from 173 to 145, and in the West Riding it has recently been reduced from 220 to 200. There are still a certain number of people under protection in the West Riding; but the Riding is becoming steadily more peaceable, and further reductions may be hoped for at no very distant period. The hon. Member for Longford (Mr. Justin M'Carthy) asked a question about the attendance of shorthand writers with the police at meetings—a matter which shall receive my almost immediate attention. I should be very glad if the police authorities could be induced to see that, at large open meetings attended by Members of Parliament, shorthand writers could be dispensed with, for this appears to me one of the relics of a more turbulent state of things which we may hope has passed away. The hon. Member for Westmeath (Mr. Sullivan) has spoken with some severity of the Government, because they allowed a witness to come back to the country where he had been living, and then sent a police force to protect him. The hon. Member applied to that person very strong, though possibly not undeserved, language, though I must say I think he should have applied it to those persons who were convicted by that man's testimony. He described him as a pet of the Government, and as a very valuable individual. Now, Sir, I must say that I think it would have been a most arbitrary stretch of power for the Government to say where a man should or should not live; and if he lives where he chooses to live, I must say that I think he has as much right to our protection as every other citizen. The hon. Member has asked me whether a particular lady—a Miss Thompson—profits by the protection of the police. I have been asked that question before, and it shall not go without an answer. I regret to say that I have known some other instances where a person does profit owing to the attendance of the police. As to the presence of extra police being an encouragement to bad landlords, that would carry the hon. Member very much further than he probably meant to go. In the first place, the relations between landlord and tenant have now been placed upon such a footing that, except in comparatively rare cases, a man can hardly show himself a bad landlord.

Mr. HEALY: There are 100,000 leaseholders.

Mr. TREVELYAN: I said in the majority of cases. In the next place, it is an extremely dangerous principle to lay down that you are not to keep the number of police—the force which the law requires—in order to enforce the law, because certain individuals may strain the law. I cannot imagine any doctrine which would lead to a more perfect state of lawlessness, upheld by the moral sanction of the people. Whether a man strains it or not, the law is still the law; and you cannot accuse the police, who are required to enforce the law, because it is put by some people to a use which you would not wish it to be put to. The hon. Member for Ennis (Mr. Kenny) has asked for the number of extra police under all heads; but I think that in some respects the hon. Member for the City of Cork (Mr. Parnell) has relieved me from that task. At the same time, I shall be glad to provide the hon. Member for Ennis with any papers or particulars that he may wish for. They lie in a narrow compass, and half-an-hour's reading will put him in possession of the facts. The hon. Gentleman has asked what is the present position of Mr. Jenkinson, and whether he is paid out of this Vote. During the last few months Mr. Jenkinson has been much in London, guarding the public from the attacks which have been made upon them. The very serious case which was brought to an end yesterday proves that these attacks are not imaginary. Now that the case is over, I may say that it is impossible for anyone to read the scientific evidence as to the effect produced by these bombshells without feeling sure that they were meant for murder, and that they could not be used for any other purpose, and murder of the most terrible sort. Anyone who reads this evidence cannot fail to see that the men who use these weapons are terrible enemies, and Mr. Jenkinson's duty in London has been to enable the Government to meet these enemies with success. But Mr. Jenkinson is paid out of the Civil Service Vote, and not out of the Vote now before the Committee.

Mr. KENNY: Will he for the future be paid out of the Irish Establishment, or will he be paid out of the English Votes? Will he be sent back to Ireland?

Mr. TREVELYAN: He is, of course, on the Irish Establishment at present; but his ultimate position will have to be arranged between the Irish Government and the Home Office. The hon. Member has asked about Mr. Clifford Lloyd—whether Mr. Clifford Lloyd's position, as defined by the Secretary to the Treasury, is to be modified by the withdrawal of the Magistrates (Ireland) Salaries Bill? Sir, what was stated by the Secretary to the Treasury was stated, if I may use the expression, baldly, without any other circumstance being mentioned. The fact of the matter is this—it is the intention of the Irish Government that all appointments to these Divisional Magistracies shall henceforth be made from the ranks of the officers of the police, and Mr. Clifford Lloyd does not belong to that Force. The hon. Member for Ennis asks me to explain the cause of the increase of the Estimate; but I must say that I am almost afraid to say anything to meet his wishes, because on one occasion, when I made a speech explaining an increase in the Estimate in the case of the Vote for Law Charges, the hon. Member for the City of Galway (Mr. T. P. O'Connor), in a very bright speech of his own, charged me with having made a discursive and rambling speech, although I kept very closely indeed to the Estimate. The principal cause of the increase in pay arises out of the Act 46 & 47 *Vict.*, which was passed by Parliament last year, and is caused by the lodging and bait allowances, which were granted pursuant to the recommendation of a Committee of Inquiry, and which formed part of the elaborate financial statement which I made to the House on a previous occasion. The principal decreases are in extra pay and in travelling expenses, owing to the country being in a more settled condition. A great deal, however, occurs on the item of rent of barracks. Actually the amount paid has risen by £400; but I apprehend that the very great decrease in the rent arises simply from the fact that the police have now ceased to pay the 1*s.* a-week which they did pay by way of rent for their quarters. The hon. Gentleman referred to the case of Sub-Constable Carroll, which was certainly a very singular and curious case; but a case in which the Grand Jury, so far as I can gather, are absolutely responsible. It is not a case for the Executive Government at all, except so far as we might adopt the recommendation of the hon. Member for Clare (Mr. O'Shea), and issue a Circular to inform police constables that they must not keep large sums of money about them in the expectation of being compensated by the Grand Jury. Whether there is sufficient likelihood of such cases recurring to make such a Circular necessary I do not know; but if such a case did recur, and no such Circular was issued, I should feel a little guilty towards the locality that had to pay. I now pass on to the hon. Member for Clare, who asks me whether there is any chance of the number of protection huts in Clare being diminished. I am glad to be able to inform the hon. Member that there has been a very substantial reduction recently in Clare. As to the instances in reference to which the hon. Member for the City of Cork (Mr. Parnell) has provided statistics, I may say that those statistics are not up to the very latest date, and I take all blame to myself for that; but within the last few days the number of extra police has been reduced from 235 to 200.

MR. KENNY: Is the right hon. Gentleman aware that the sum paid for them was over £9,000?

MR. TREVELYAN: I said at the beginning that this was a very important point, and that I believed there were counties in Ireland where considerable reductions might be made. If the force in Clare is still somewhat in excess—and I take the hon. Member's word for that—I cannot hold out the same hopes of further reduction as in other counties, because there have been rather serious outrages in Clare within the last month, and the state of the district is very decidedly disturbed. The hon. Member for Waterford (Mr. Leamy) inquires as to the extra police at Waterford, and he is evidently under the impression that they are still at the number at which they were recently put. But the police have been reduced to about 66 from all sources—16 from one source and 20 from another. He asks me on what information they were originally sent down there. It was upon the information of the Special Resident Magistrate that they were sent, and they have been reduced upon the recommendation of the same gentleman, who is now a Divisional Magistrate. The hon. Member for the City of Cork (Mr. Parnell) began with an allusion to the grievance of that City. Sir, I stated that I was very anxious to take into consideration the opinion of the Corporation of Cork. Their view was that the City requires 170 police. Some hon. Gentleman—I do not remember who—said that, in his opinion, that was in consequence of some misstatement, or some misrepresentation; but their statement is that their City requires 170 men, and we should have to weigh their opinion most carefully. If they think it requires 170 men to do the duty, then I must say that a great community like Cork does not labour under a great pecuniary grievance, whatever may be their grievance in not having the control of the police, in having to pay for 10 extra police—a moiety of 20—at a cost of between £800 and £1,000 a-year. The hon. Member, speaking of the Proclamation under which the police were sent down, states that he doubts whether any Proclamation was justifiable. But it must be remembered that these

Proclamations were made, for the most part, in the years 1881 and 1882, when the country was in a state of very great and dangerous excitement, and when there was a very great amount of crime. During the period of the late Government and of the Government before it the Police Force of Ireland was 9,800 men or thereabouts, and the outrages were very few; but when the outrages grew up to the enormous numbers of 1881, 1882, and 1883, the additional police were all required—they were necessary to preserve the peace of the country. The hon. Member for the City of Cork has compared the amount gained in the reduction of rents with the amount paid for extra police; but the hon. Member, when dealing with the reduction of rents, only gave us the figures of the reductions obtained by the fixture of fair rents. I always claim to have added to them the reductions made under agreements, and these two come together to considerably over £500,000; and I am inclined to think that at least as much more—hon. Members opposite would say very much more than that—is due to the indirect operation of the Land Act, and if we make the comparison in that way, I should say that at the very least the Land Act has put 10 times as much into the pockets of the farmers, in the shape of reduced rents, as has been taken out to pay for extra police.

Mr. PARNELL: It was not the Land Act that did that.

Mr. TREVELYAN: The hon. Member has so completely confined himself to the operations of the Land Act, that I naturally gave the Land Act credit for it. Now, the hon. Member, in his appeal to the Committee, has entirely left out of sight one most important question, with regard to which I have not heard a single word said to-day, and that is the question of the police pensions. It must be remembered with regard to these pensions—of which we heard a good deal yesterday, when they supplied an argument or a comparison with the pensions of the National School teachers—that, while in England the State contributes nothing at all of any sort or kind, in Ireland it contributes everything.

Mr. HEALY: Shame! Give them nothing.

Mr. TREVELYAN: I am stating a financial fact. I am not quite sure to which country that expression applies; but, as I have already stated, this matter has not been mentioned before to-day, although it greatly reduces any grievance which Ireland may have against the payment of the extra police. The moment the extra policeman is taken off, the county pays nothing for him—it gets rid of him entirely—but, in England, a moiety of every policeman is paid for by the locality, and his pension is paid for by the locality alone. The hon. Member for the City of Cork (Mr. Parnell) has asked what we are going to do with the reduction of the police? The hon. Member for Ennis (Mr. Kenny) did the same, and both hon. Members gave vent to something approaching to a serious menace in the shape of a sort of appeal to the Irish people not to pay police tax. But I think that even those hon. Members will confess that if you reduce the police too suddenly and too entirely in all the counties in Ireland, you would give rise to a state of things which would compel an increase of the police tax. I would never for a moment consent to the immediate total reduction of the extra police in such counties as Kerry or Clare. I should consider it most wicked to do so, both for the sake of those counties immediately, and for the sake of the peace of Ireland in the future. But the Government have been, and are, anxious to take advantage of the improved state of the country, and to reduce the police in a fair proportion. The hon. Member has stated, with perfect accuracy and fairness, the amount of the reduction that has been made in the last six months. The net reduction in the number of the police during that period has been about 475, counting those in Clare, of which the hon. Member was not aware. The extra police have been reduced at the rate of about 80 a month—I wish I could say that during the last month the outrages had fallen off quite in the same proportion. Well, Sir, at such frequent intervals do I consider it my duty to write around to the Resident Magistrates and ascertain what reductions can be made, that even since these figures, from which I was enabled to provide this Return, came in, I have been told of four counties where there are hopes of reduction, and all round Ireland the authorities are constantly looking about to see what reductions can be made. At this moment it is hoped that almost directly we may reduce all the extra police in Donegal, all the extra police in King's County, and make a substantial reduction of 25 in Sligo, and of 20 in Tipperary. If the police can be reduced in this way—not doing it for dramatic purposes; not for political purposes; not in such a manner as to spare six or eight hours' debate upon the Estimates, and a disagreeable Division at the end of it; but doing it conscientiously and practically, and with reference to the state of each given locality where the reduction is made—I can see that at the end of the next six months there would be a very substantial relief to the ratepayers of Ireland. I can say for myself that I will spare no exertion to see that these reductions are kept up to the very maximum which we can induce the local police authorities to agree to. Further than that I certainly cannot go; for, in the first place, I am of opinion that to run the risk of burdening again the taxpayers of the country by any renewal of the state of agitation and lawlessness which before existed in Ireland would be extremely wrong; and, in the next place, I am very much struck by the small price which the Irish people are called on to bear for the police of the country as a whole.

Mr. HEALY: Cannot the right hon. Gentleman give us the relative figures for England, Ireland, and Scotland?

Mr. TREVELYAN: I will directly. I am very anxious, I repeat, to reduce the police; but I cannot do it at the risk of any renewed agitation or disturbance. Another motive which governs me is that I conceive it would be a most terrible confession, both for rulers and ruled, if the alienation between the two countries should be so complete that we could not hope to return to the same state of law, order, and goodwill that existed before the occurrence of the outrages and crimes of 1881 and 1882. Sir, the figures which have been given to me are taken from the Criminal and Judicial Statistics for the year 1882, when the total cost of police in England and Wales was £3,264,000, of which £1,985,000 was paid by the localities—that is to say, about 1*s*. 6*d*. per head. In Scotland the total cost was £331,000, of which £197,000 was paid by the localities; and in Ireland the cost was £1,452,000.

Mr. PARNELL: What is the sum this year?

Mr. TREVELYAN: I have not got the figures; but it will be more than that. A sum of £94,000 was paid for extra police in the country, and £50,000 in Dublin. I should think that £144,000 would be about the amount.

Mr. PARNELL: The statement in the Estimates does not refer to the Dublin police?

Mr. TREVELYAN: No.

Mr. PARNELL: What is the amount for Dublin?

Mr. TREVELYAN: About £51,000; and my impression is that it is about £94,000 for the counties.

Mr. HEALY: What we want to get at is this—is the county and City of Dublin included in this?

Mr. TREVELYAN: They are not.

Mr. PARNELL: Then you add these?

Mr. TREVELYAN: By adding the three items together it would come to £180,000.

Colonel KING-HARMAN said, there was one point that the Chief Secretary did not touch upon in that part of his speech in which he expressed his desire to lower the tax now levied upon the ratepayers, and that was the number of men short upon the Establishment. He (Colonel King-Harman) had called the attention of the House to this subject at various times by Questions and in other ways; but he had never been able to get a satisfactory reply from the Government. Not only he, but others had also called attention to this question without getting any satisfactory answer. He understood that in December 1882, the free force, so called, was 630 men short, and the extra force for which the country had to pay was 3,426. That number had now been reduced to 2,827; but he had not been told what state the free force was in. If it was 600 men short at the present moment, as he believed it was, why was not the country—why were not the ratepayers—credited with those 600 men; why did not the Government give the country their full free force, and reduce the extra men by 600? That was to say, why did not the Government reduce the extra police by about one-fourth? To him it seemed they were entitled to have a free force of 10,000 men; but instead of having that number they only got 9,000, and yet the Government charged them for the full 3,000 extra men. He thought they ought to have their full free force before they were charged for an extra force.

MR. HEALY said, he was sure the Irish Members below the Gangway were extremely glad to receive the support the hon. and gallant Gentleman the Member for the County of Dublin (Colonel King-Harman) had given them. He thought that when Gentlemen in the position and holding the politics of the hon. and gallant Gentleman supported them, it was time for the Government to consider whether this grievance was not one that should be seriously looked into, especially when it was evident from the remarks of the hon. and gallant Gentleman that there was no privilege at stake. They were told that it required a certain number of police to keep down crime and outrage; and although they were entitled to a certain number under the Act of Parliament, they did not get them, and he was sure that the Irish people would be as satisfied with coercion by a free force as being coerced by a force for which they had to pay extra. That was a contention that every Conservative could support as well as every Nationalist, and it was astonishing that the Government should act in the way they were doing. He trusted that the speech of the hon. and gallant Gentleman the Member for the County of Dublin (Colonel King-Harman) would be read by the narrow-minded landlords throughout the country, for it really proved that it was not in the interest of the landlords to go on maintaining a force that ought to be paid for out of the British Exchequer. The right hon. Gentleman opposite used a very remarkable sentence when he said he would make a maximum reduction if he could induce the local police authorities to agree. But what did that mean? It meant that they were altogether in the hands of the local landlords; the local landlords would "Boycott" them and their wives and families unless they did as they were required. The Police Inspector would not be asked to the landlords' dinner, and the magistrates' wives and daughters would not be able to stretch their legs under the landlords' mahogany. Now they had had the sensible and clear speech of the hon. and gallant Gentleman he was sure the stupid landlords would begin to see they had no particular interest in allowing the country to be swindled on the present system, and would cease to "Boycott" the local magistrates and local Inspectors of police if they made the recommendations that the Government said they would appeal for. This was entirely a matter which was dependent on the local feelings of the landlords. If the landlords would now be induced to see, from the speech of the hon. and gallant Gentleman, that the free force was quite sufficient to get them their rents, they would at once have recommendations from all the little landlords throughout the country, recommendations coming up from them that the free force might be relied on, so that expense should be saved, and they would thus have very valuable results from the speech of the hon. and gallant Gentleman. But if that was not the case, he would put this point to the Government. If the Government still persisted in keeping up the paid free force he would put this case. At present the expense of the force was thrown entirely upon the county cess, as there was much more likelihood that people would strike against the poor rates than the county cess. The poor rates involved a vote, and the people had always been recommended to pay their poor rates in order that they might have a vote. In his opinion, however, this charge ought to fall on the poor rates and not on the county cess, more especially as the landlord paid half the poor rate. The landlord was the person who wanted these extra police, and it was therefore monstrous that the people should have to pay that out of the county cess. If it was thrown upon the poor rates, and the landlords having to pay half the rate, and not now being able to raise the rents as they used to do, the landlords would be much more careful in asking for these extra police when they knew they would have to pay half the cost. He would ask the Government to consider, if there were not to be a stand against this extra police tax, and in view of the unfair amount that the people had to pay, whether they would not change the incidence of the tax to the poor rate, which the people had a clear incitement to pay in view of obtaining the vote, and which was an incitement to the landlords not to call for extra police because they would have to pay some trifle of the money themselves? It was very remarkable that the Government should rely solely on the demands of the magistrates in these instances. The hon. Member for the County of Kilkenny (Mr. Marum) referred to that, and stated that the Government would be willing to listen to what the magistrates had got to say. Of course, seeing that the right hon. Gentleman just admitted it was on the demand of the magistrates the extra police force was given, of course on the demand of the magistrates that force would be reduced. It had been said that the landlords were out of the country, but he believed that if every one of them were out of the country there would be more peace and order than there was at present. The landlords in the country were the chief cause of the crime, disorder, and outrage that prevailed; the magistrates, therefore, being the sole fount of opinion the Government had to go to, the Government could only expect the one reply, so long as it cost them not one single penny to saddle the people with this extra police force. Let them get some other advice in Ireland besides these interested parties. Where were the people to come in in this matter? There were 5,000,000 of people in the country and about 100,000 officials; the 5,000,000 counted for nothing, and the 100,000 officials counted for everything. Had not the time come, therefore, when the people should have some assurance on this matter? As had been said by the right hon. Gentleman, he hoped they should come back to the time when there might be pleasant relations between England and Ireland, but how could they have those pleasant relations when the people were entirely unconsulted on these matters? Take, for instance, the way in which Captain M'Kernaghan was treated after Francis Hines was hanged. He was removed from the County Fermanagh because he gave decisions against the Orange interest. He was "Boycotted," and he was now scarcely received by a single magistrate in the country. Such things exercised an enormous pressure upon the minds of these people. These local officials were obliged to go in accordance with the opinion of the local hierarchy, the landlords; therefore, when the Government asked for the opinions of the officials they were only getting the opinion of the magistrates themselves, not the opinions of the people of the country. The Government to-day had also drawn attention to the extraordinary generosity of the Government towards the police in the matter of pensions. There was also a Police Bill before the House to give pensions to the police of Scotland. But did the Irish Members wish to pension the Irish police? Not a bit of it. Cut the pensions off to-morrow and ask for their support, and they would be most joyfully gambolling to the Lobby to support the Government. They spoke of the high amount they paid per head to what they paid in Ireland. Was that the Irish Party's fault? If the Government increased the wages and the pensions, the Irish Members did not ask them to do it. No, it was because the police struck, and would have turned their bayonets against the Government. It was a condition of things brought about entirely by the Government. They paid the Irish police extravagant sums and gave them pensions, and then said that in England they only paid 8*d.* or 10*d.* in the pound, whilst in Ireland it was 3*s.* 6*d.* in the pound. He was surprised that the Government should resort to that kind of logic. If they wished to make a proper comparison between England and Ireland, they must put in force the system that prevailed in England. He thought a great deal of weight would be attached in Ireland to the remarks of the hon. Member for the City of Cork (Mr. Parnell) with regard to this free force. The fact that the country was paying £180,000 per annum for police they did not want and could not control, would be taken into serious consideration by the people of Ireland. The grievances of the people of Ireland were so cunningly glossed over by the Administration of the country, that it was hard to get at them. They had to peg away in that House for weeks and weeks, and months and months; and it was only now that they had succeeded in getting the facts of this free force out of the Government. Now that the people would know that in the City of Dublin alone they paid £50,000 a-year, and outside £130,000, he ventured to think that the Irish people would take this matter seriously to heart, and before long they would have such an outcry that the Government would be compelled to change the system.

LORD RANDOLPH CHURCHILL said, he wanted to draw the attention of the Committee for a few minutes to the cost of the Liberal Government in Ireland, as the right hon. Gentleman the Chief Secretary to the Lord Lieutenant had made some remarks as to what happened, and endeavoured to show that the state of Ireland was never better than it was now. The Chief Secretary to the Lord Lieutenant was asking the Committee for a very large sum of money; he was asking for £1,440,000 for the Constabulary of Ireland, and had just had £146,000 for the Dublin Metropolitan Police. He (Lord Randolph Churchill) thought the right hon. Gentleman should have followed the example of his Predecessor, the right hon. Gentleman the Member for Bradford (Mr. W. E. Forster), and should have given the Committee some information as to the state of Ireland. The right hon. Gentleman gave absolutely no information as to the state of Ireland, and not a single Member of the Committee would be able to say whether the condition of the country was more favourable or less favourable than last year or the year before. Considering this sum was very large, considering it was an increase on last year, and considering that it had been, as far as he could recollect, the invariable practice of former Chief Secretaries always to give some information as to the social condition of Ireland, he certainly trusted that the Committee would not sanction this Vote without getting further information from the Government as to those points, because it appeared to him the design of the Government was perfectly obvious. They wished to go down to the country, to their constituents and followers in England, and point to the greatly improved condition of Ireland, to the almost total absence of crime, and then attribute that improvement to the ground of their remedial legislation. But what did they find from the speech of the hon. Member of the City of Cork (Mr. Parnell)? They found there was an extraordinary diminution of agrarian outrage, having sunk, as they saw from the list of the last quarter, from four to nothing. The outrages during the last quarter were 130, of which 93 were threatening letters; and, of course, threatening letters were excluded from the calculation in considering Irish crime; so that the state of Ireland, so far as agrarian crime was concerned, was really nought. Without agrarian crime, there was hardly any sort of crime in the country. The hon. Member for the City of Cork pointed out that, although the state of Ireland, so far as agrarian crime was concerned, was normal, or less than normal, the extra police who were being maintained in Ireland by the ratepayers, over this Vote for which the Committee was now being asked, amounted in number to 3,000 practically, and cost in money £180,000 over the Vote. That was what the hon. Member for the City of Cork had stated; but he should like to add an illustration for the advantage of the Committee, or anyone outside who might care to read it. The cost of the administration, in addition to the £50,000 for Dublin, and in addition to the £180,000 for extra police, should be put down at another £100,000, or nearly £100,000 for the expenses of their land legislation. That was the cost of the Liberal government of Ireland. That being so, he had the curiosity to get the Estimates for the last two years the late Government were in Office, and they were really worth the attention of the Committee. He would take the year 1878, at the same time asking the Committee to bear in mind what the Chief Secretary insinuated as to the condition of Ireland at that time. The Vote the Chief Secretary was now asking for was £1,500,000. The Vote which the late Government asked for was, in round numbers, £1,000,000. That was in 1878; so that there was now an increase over 1878 of £500,000. But the cost of the extra police in 1878 amounted to only £27,500, and the extra police in proclaimed districts was only £332. £27,000 in 1878 against £180,000 in 1884, after four years of Liberal Government. But the year 1879 was a still more favourable one. In 1879 he found —and this was the last year of Office of the late Government—the cost of the Constabulary in Ireland was again, roundly speaking, £1,000,000, no increase to speak of; and the extra police cost to the Irish people was less than the year before, being only £25,000, and the extra police in proclaimed districts was only £350. That was in 1878 and 1879, when, he ventured to state, the statistics of Irish crime, such as they had been favoured with to-day, were, if possible, higher than at the present moment. That was what the people of this country and the people of Ireland had to pay for the luxury of Liberal Government; an increase of £500,000 alone in the Constabulary Vote, and an increase of £160,000 in the cost of extra police; and yet, in the face of those figures, the Chief Secretary did not trouble to give to the Committee the slightest authentic information as to what were the Government's views of the state of Ireland; notwithstanding the extraordinary crisis Ireland went through two or three years ago, the right hon. Gentleman did not trouble to give the Committee the slightest information as to the state of Ireland from the records of Dublin Castle, or as to the policy the Government meant to pursue. The Chief Secretary did say that, so far as the reduction of the extra police was concerned, he had been looking it over calmly, and, perhaps, in four counties there might be some hope of a reduction.

MR. TREVELYAN: I said that for the last six months we had been reducing the number of extra men by 80 a month; that I could not name the reduction that would take place; but I named those counties in which the force had been reduced, and I have every hope of going on reducing the number for some time to come.

LORD RANDOLPH CHURCHILL said, he apologized to the Chief Secretary if he did not hear him correctly, for there were some Liberal Members below the Gangway who carried on so loud a conversation that he had the greatest difficulty in following what the right hon. Gentleman did say. But he wished to put this to the Chief Secretary and the Committee. Seeing that the Session had nearly terminated, and that statistics were now before the House; considering that was the last opportunity they would have of ascertaining the state of Ireland before the Autumn Session, he should like the Chief Secretary, if he would so far trouble himself, to state to the Committee more comprehensively and more lucidly what was the exact state of Ireland with respect to crime, and what were the prospects of Ireland returning before long to a more Constitutional and more normal Government. The right hon. Gentleman who represented the borough of Huntingdon (Sir Robert Peel) said that the state of Ireland was repugnant to the English mind. So it was, and he (Lord Randolph Churchill) believed there was not a man on either side of the House who did not admit that the form of Government which they applied to Ireland was repugnant. Therefore, viewing the fact that the form of Government was entirely different from that of this country; viewing the utterances that the Liberal Ministry were continually using with respect to Ireland and the success of the present Administration; viewing all these things, and seeing the enormous contrast between the sums of money asked for by the late and the present Governments, he invited the Chief Secretary to give them some further information as to the state of Ireland.

COLONEL NOLAN said, that as the Chief Secretary did not rise immediately, he would like to draw attention to one point in connection with this extra police force—namely, that the taxation for extra police should only be put in force when the free force, to which the country was entitled, stood at its full complement. In the year ending March 31, 1883, they had voted £11,632,000 for the cost of the Constabulary in Ireland. Of that no less than £92,000 had been saved; but the saving was to some extent balanced by £33,000 of extra cost. The saving was, to a large extent, made out of pay and extra pay, the country being so quiet that there was no necessity to spend all the money that had been voted. But, in regard to extra money, fuel and light were stated as having cost nearly £5,000. The Committee ought to know how this large sum came to be required, the exact sum put down as being spent for these purposes was £4,894. Then, again, there was a large sum, £3,840, for arms and ammunition for the Constabulary; a great deal of the extra charge of £33,000 consisting of money put down for these purposes. It might be asked, why was it that when they had effected so large a saving on the previous year that the Government should charge the country anything in the shape of extra rates? As it was, the Government charge to the country, by way of extra rates, was £84,000. This question of over-estimating the cost of the police and charging the counties with extra rates was an important one, and he thought the system most unfair;

and he should like to ask the Chief Secretary to the Lord Lieutenant if there was any expectation that there would be a saving out of the £150,000, such as there had been last year. This over-drawing of accounts should be avoided as much as possible, because it was sure to lead to waste. The right hon. Gentleman the Chancellor of the Exchequer (Mr. Childers) should look after that matter very closely. The ordinary Estimate for arms and ammunition was £1,900, and yet the sum that had been expended in these things was £3,840. That could not have been needed by anything that had occurred in the country, and, to his mind, there had been extravagance and waste simply because Parliament had voted so much money. The House of Commons ought not to encourage this sort of thing by voting any larger sum than was likely to be actually needed.

Colonel COLTHURST said, he, for one, should be sorry to interfere with the charge made for extra police in any district where outrages were shown to have occurred; but he desired to point out how unfairly the existing system worked. In the county of Cork, in a district with which he was acquainted, the police force had been reduced below the necessary level, and the number of men at the station was the smallest number that could supply patrols, the strength being reduced to some two men, the rest being sent to some other county instead of the necessary number of extra men being sent from Dublin to such counties where the numbers might be short of the full establishment, or of what might be specially needed. Under a system by which men were taken from this or that county station to supply deficiencies elsewhere, the consequence was that patrolling ceased and outrages commenced, so that, in a little time, it might be necessary to send extra police, which would be charged on the district in which outrages might occur, owing to the number of police having been thus reduced. He thought the whole system of extra police, as had been well pointed out by the hon. and gallant Member for the County of Dublin (Colonel King-Harman), required to be revised; and he certainly should support any proposal to reduce this Vote, for this reason and no other—that he did not object to making the districts pay for extra police where they were rendered necessary by outrages; but he did object to the rules being increased through the necessity of sending extra men to districts in which the stations had been denuded of their ordinary complement of men.

Mr. T. P. O'CONNOR said, he was sorry to intervene between the Government and the statement they were about to make to the Committee, which he was sure was at the present moment in a state of nervous anxiety, that had been created by the reference made to another subject, to be discussed bye-and-bye. He felt assured that Her Majesty's Government would kindly pardon him for preventing them, by this interposition, from fulfilling the expectation of the last triumph they had prepared for themselves in the statement on that other matter they were desirous of submitting to the House. But, in spite of the anxiety of the Government to announce their victory, he must take leave to detain the Committee by a few remarks on an important question that had been brought before it by various Members for Irish constituencies. He could not think that this discussion had been particularly satisfactory to Her Majesty's Government. It had been characterized by what had been the main features of all the discussions they had had throughout the week on this question of the Irish Constabulary—namely, that all the facts and arguments were on one side, and all the miserable and shallow pretences on the other. There was, on the one hand, this remarkable fact, that they had had the Representatives of all sections of Irish opinion denouncing Her Majesty's Government, and they had had the Representatives of every constituency that was practically affected by the police tax rising up, and, in the names of their constituents, condemning that tax. They had had that tax denounced with equal fervour by the hon. and gallant Gentleman the Member for Cork (Colonel Colthurst), who was ordinarily one of the loyal supporters of the Government; and they had also had it reprobated by hon. Gentlemen on those (the Irish) Benches, who could scarcely be regarded as persistently loyal in the confidence they gave to Her Majesty's Government. Even the hon. and gallant Member for the County of Dublin (Colonel King-Harman), who almost invariably disagreed—and hotly disagreed—with the opinions expressed on those (the Irish) Benches, had concurred with them on that occasion, in bringing against Her Majesty's Government the charge that they had not deferred in any way to the wishes of the Irish people. The statement of the hon. and gallant Gentleman the Member for the County of Dublin agreed with that of the hon. and gallant Gentleman the Member for Cork (Colonel Colthurst), that the Government ought to be compelled to pay for the large extra force with which they sought to charge the Irish people. He would now turn to another point — namely, that upon which the right hon. Gentleman the Chief Secretary to the Lord Lieutenant, in dealing with the large amount the Irish people had to pay for the police, had indulged in one of his favourite answers to the arguments employed by the Irish Members. The right hon. Gentleman had entered on what he (Mr. T. P. O'Connor) could not but term a mischievous and foolish comparison between the respective payments of the English and Irish taxpayers. Did the right hon. Gentleman think that the conditions of the taxpayers in the two countries supplied a fair basis of comparison? The right hon. Gentleman was positively eloquent on the small amount per head paid by the people of Ireland as compared with those of this country. Let them take, for example, the case of the county of Galway. Let them just look at the large amount the people of the county of Galway had to pay—namely, £14,960. There were several other counties that had to pay equally large sums; and yet it was a fact that the Province of Connaught, which was called upon for such vast sums as compared with its actual resources, was a Province in which the people were in such a condition that they could not afford to pay so heavy a charge, many of them having to live in houses which had been frequently discribed as hardly fit for beasts. In that part of Ireland, in which the tenant farmers were scarcely above the position of labourers, they were, nevertheless, compelled to pay these exorbitant charges for the maintenance of the police employed by the Government. The right hon. Gentleman, in reply to the interruptions which had come from those (the Irish) Benches, had asked what was the difference between the amount of crime that had to be dealt with under the late Conservative Government and that which had to be met by the present Liberal Administration? The question was, he (Mr. T. P. O'Connor) thought, sheer nonsense. The right hon. Gentleman said there was three times the amount of crime during some of the years in which the late Conservative Administration held Office.

MR. TREVELYAN said, he had not made that statement.

MR. T. P. O'CONNOR said, at any rate, the right hon. Gentleman had said there was under the late Government sometimes as much crime as there was at the present moment in Ireland. Now, how did that statement agree with the very remarkable figures that had been brought before the Committee by the noble Lord the Member for Woodstock (Lord Randolph Churchill)? The fact was that crime was three times less than it was during the last months of the late Administration; and yet, notwithstanding the decrease of crime there was the enormous increase of £500,000 in the amount charged for its repression. Let the Committee realize this—three times as little crime, and £500,000 more to pay in the shape of police taxation! He could not but think that the Government must be utterly unable to reconcile these two sets of figures. The noble Lord would be justified, when he went down to his constituents, in drawing attention to these bloated charges which a Liberal Administration were calling on the Irish people to pay. He would ask the Committee to recall the remarkable scenes they had lately witnessed in that House when the arguments of the Irish Members on the different questions they had brought forward had found acceptance in all parts of the House. These things showed that the exposures made by the Irish Members of what had been going on in Ireland were beginning to tell, and that the secret of Irish Government was ceasing to be a secret, but was rapidly becoming one of the common places of politics, the discussion of which must immediately precede a drastic reform. They had discussed, last night, the question of National Education in Ireland; and a great many English Members must have been astonished to find that there was such a system in Ireland as had then been disclosed. He remembered the famous boast that was said to have been made by the Minister of Education under Louis Napoleon. He said that when the clock struck a certain hour exactly the same lessons were being repeated in every school in France; and, in the same way, the so-called Board of Education in Ireland, consisting of men alien in every sense of the word to the Irish people, could say that, in spite of all the wishes and aspirations of the Irish population, at a certain hour of the day in every school in Ireland a particular system of education was being enforced. In regard to the police, the right hon. Gentleman the Chief Secretary to the Lord Lieutenant had had the courage to enter into a comparison between the treatment of the police, in the matter of pensions, in the two countries—England and Ireland. In doing that, he had left out of the question the great central fact that in England the Local Authorities had the control of the police, while in Ireland, as had been stated over and over again, they were simply and mainly a military garrison, neither controlled by the Local Authorities, nor wanted by the people. They were not required to keep the peace; they were not needed to preserve order; but were maintained as the only sanction to British rule—the sanction of subsidized bayonets.

MR. GLADSTONE: I have now to ask the Committee that as the discussion has lasted several hours, this Vote may be agreed to, and any further remarks upon it postponed until the Report, inasmuch as the House is in expectation of a statement upon an important matter as to which delay would be highly inconvenient.

MR. O'DONNELL said, he did not intend to stand for any length of time between the Committee and the statement about to be made by the Prime Minister; but he would remind the Committee that since 12 o'clock that day and down to within a very few minutes ago, hon. Members on the Irish Benches had been obliged to retail the grievances of their country in connection with the Constabulary Vote to almost empty Benches; but now the House had began to fill they were asked to put aside these Irish questions, in order that the Prime Minister might announce the collapse of the Conference to an anxious and expectant audience. Not a Cabinet Minister had been present during the whole of the discussion on the Irish Constabulary Vote. During most of the time occupied by the exhaustive address by the hon. Member for the City of Cork (Mr. Parnell), the strength of the Liberal Party had varied between six and four Members, including the Representatives of Her Majesty's Government. That was the sort of attention the Imperial Parliament had been in the habit of giving to the statement of Irish grievances in that House; and now, after six hours of discussion carried on before empty Benches, when there was at length an opportunity of having something like a full House to listen to a debate on Irish affairs, the Premier suddenly and confidently came in and asked that the Irish question might be put off until the Report or some other period, in order that he might have the joy and satisfaction of telling his faithful henchmen that he had managed to wriggle out of the Conference. He asserted that the proceeding of the Government that day in interrupting the discussion of an important matter, under such circumstances, was a scandal which, however, was entirely in keeping with the worst spirit of their political conduct towards his countrymen. They had brought the Irish Members together at 12 o'clock on a Saturday, and had kept them for hours with no one to listen to their grievances, and when a number of hon. Members, excited by the rumours in the morning papers, came down to the House, the Prime Minister said—"Let us get rid of this Irish discussion; it can go on at any other time; nobody cares about it; but there is a House for me to glorify the Government, by telling it that the Conference has failed, and that the little game we have been playing for so many months has at length been successful." That conduct capped the insolence with which Her Majesty's Government had treated Ireland again and again throughout the Session, and he hoped his countrymen would look at it in its proper light and draw their own conclusions. They should be told that the Irish Members had been for six hours speaking to empty Benches, and that as soon as the House had begun to fill, Irish questions were to be shelved, in order that the Prime Minister might make a statement on Egyptian affairs.

MR. BIGGAR said, he should not attempt to discuss the question that was then before the Committee; as he thought that the particular point raised in connection with the Constabulary Vote had been pretty well exhausted; but there were other points to be raised in relation to that Vote, which would not be decided by the Division they were about to take. He wished, therefore, to ask the Government whether they would not make the Report of that Vote the First Order some day next week, so that the points he had alluded to and which had not been dealt with, or referred to in the most remote degree might be discussed in a reasonable manner? He had one grievance to call attention to. He did not think the discussion upon it would last a long time; but at the same time it was a practical grievance. He consequently appealed to the Government to arrange that the Report of the Vote might be made the First Order on the day for which it might be fixed, and he would promise that he would not occupy more time than he could possibly avoid.

Mr. GLADSTONE: I do not think I can promise to make this Vote the First Order; but I hope the hon. Member will have a convenient opportunity afforded him of discussing the point he desires to bring forward.

Mr. PARNELL said, the Prime Minister had expressed a desire to be allowed to make a statement in regard to Foreign Affairs, and had suggested that the discussion of the Irish Constabulary Vote should at once be closed, in order that he might be enabled to bring forward that matter, leaving the debate on the Vote to be resumed on the Report. He (Mr. Parnell) should, therefore, defer until the Report the reply he had been desirous of making to the speech of the right hon. Gentleman the Chief Secretary, only saying at the present moment that he regarded that speech as most unsatisfactory. Postponing any further remarks he should have to make until the Report, he supposed the Committee would now go to a Division upon the Vote.

Question put.

The Committee *divided*:—Ayes 33; Noes 90: Majority 57.—(Div. List, No. 205.)

Mr. PARNELL said, he was not in the House when the Prime Minister expressed his desire that the discussion should close, in order to enable him to make that important announcement upon Foreign Affairs which was expected from him that evening; but, he said, upon hearing of it, that he was willing to agree to the arrangement on the understanding that matters in connection with the Vote were discussed upon Report. It should be understood that a fair opportunity should be afforded for the purpose—he would not say such a good opportunity as they now had, at 6 o'clock in the evening; but an opportunity when a fair discussion could be raised. He ventured to submit that it would be a reasonable arrangement to take the Report stage not later than 11 o'clock or half-past.

Mr. GLADSTONE made a gesture of assent.

Mr. HEALY wished to say, without standing in the way of the statement about to be made, that the Chief Secretary had had due Notice of the intention to raise questions in relation to the conduct and treatment of Mr. French. He would not stand between the House and the Prime Minister now. He would only say that the Government must be prepared, on the Report stage, to have these matters fully discussed.

Mr. ARTHUR O'CONNOR said, he also was anxious to bring forward upon this Vote some questions as to the treatment by the police of persons among his own constituents, and the action of subordinate agents of the police in Queen's County. He would endeavour to do this on Report. He waived his right now in deference to the wish of the Prime Minister, upon the understanding, which, so far as he could gather, had been arrived at, otherwise he should have felt it his duty to go into the question of the treatment by individual constables and sub-constables of persons among his own constituents in Queen's County.

Mr. PARNELL said, he was anxious there should be no misunderstanding on the point. Were they to understand that the Report of this Vote would not be taken later than half-past 11?

Mr. GLADSTONE said, he intended to answer the hon. Gentleman to that effect. He could not give an absolute pledge as to the exact time; but, as nearly as possible, he would say it should not be later than, say, half-past 11.

said to have been made by the Minister of Education under Louis Napoleon. He said that when the clock struck a certain hour exactly the same lessons were being repeated in every school in France; and, in the same way, the so-called Board of Education in Ireland, consisting of men alien in every sense of the word to the Irish people, could say that, in spite of all the wishes and aspirations of the Irish population, at a certain hour of the day in every school in Ireland a particular system of education was being enforced. In regard to the police, the right hon. Gentleman the Chief Secretary to the Lord Lieutenant had had the courage to enter into a comparison between the treatment of the police, in the matter of pensions, in the two countries — England and Ireland. In doing that, he had left out of the question the great central fact that in England the Local Authorities had the control of the police, while in Ireland, as had been stated over and over again, they were simply and mainly a military garrison, neither controlled by the Local Authorities, nor wanted by the people. They were not required to keep the peace; they were not needed to preserve order; but were maintained as the only sanction to British rule—the sanction of subsidized bayonets.

Mr. GLADSTONE: I have now to ask the Committee that as the discussion has lasted several hours, this Vote may be agreed to, and any further remarks upon it postponed until the Report, inasmuch as the House is in expectation of a statement upon an important matter as to which delay would be highly inconvenient.

Mr. O'DONNELL said, he did not intend to stand for any length of time between the Committee and the statement about to be made by the Prime Minister; but he would remind the Committee that since 12 o'clock that day and down to within a very few minutes ago, hon. Members on the Irish Benches had been obliged to retail the grievances of their country in connection with the Constabulary Vote to almost empty Benches; but now the House had began to fill they were asked to put aside these Irish questions, in order that the Prime Minister might announce the collapse of the Conference to an anxious and expectant audience. Not a Cabinet Minister had been present during the whole of the discussion on the Irish Constabulary Vote. During most of the time occupied by the exhaustive address by the hon. Member for the City of Cork (Mr. Parnell), the strength of the Liberal Party had varied between six and four Members, including the Representatives of Her Majesty's Government. That was the sort of attention the Imperial Parliament had been in the habit of giving to the statement of Irish grievances in that House; and now, after six hours of discussion carried on before empty Benches, when there was at length an opportunity of having something like a full House to listen to a debate on Irish affairs, the Premier suddenly and confidently came in and asked that the Irish question might be put off until the Report or some other period, in order that he might have the joy and satisfaction of telling his faithful henchmen that he had managed to wriggle out of the Conference. He asserted that the proceeding of the Government that day in interrupting the discussion of an important matter, nnder such circumstances, was a scandal which, however, was entirely in keeping with the worst spirit of their political conduct towards his countrymen. They had brought the Irish Members together at 12 o'clock on a Saturday, and had kept them for hours with no one to listen to their grievances, and when a number of hon. Members, excited by the rumours in the morning papers, came down to the House, the Prime Minister said—"Let us get rid of this Irish discussion; it can go on at any other time; nobody cares about it; but there is a House for me to glorify the Government, by telling it that the Conference has failed, and that the little game we have been playing for so many months has at length been successful." That conduct capped the insolence with which Her Majesty's Government had treated Ireland again and again throughout the Session, and he hoped his countrymen would look at it in its proper light and draw their own conclusions. They should be told that the Irish Members had been for six hours speaking to empty Benches, and that as soon as the House had begun to fill, Irish questions were to be shelved, in order that the Prime Minister might make a statement on Egyptian affairs.

Mr. BIGGAR said, he should not attempt to discuss the question that was

dends, subject to no other diminution than such as the absolute necessities and primary wants of the Government of the country may entail upon them. Lastly, Sir, I have no scruple to state to the House that although I have no such proposal to make now, yet had it been part of the price of a really stable and complete arrangement for securing the financial equilibrium in Egypt, we should then have been prepared, as the House will see when the Protocols are laid before it, to ask Parliament to make use, to a moderate extent, of the credit of this country for the purpose of assisting to bring about so desirable a consummation. Sir, these were our objects. In the hope of meeting the various and serious difficulties of the case which have grown out of the difference in Estimates between the Government of France and the British Government as to the prospective revenues of Egypt, we have successively submitted several plans to the Conference. The whole of these will be presented in the Papers that are immediately to be placed in the hands of Members; but I will now only state so much as is necessary to explain the final issue—points upon which the respective views have been found mutually irreconcilable. The Representatives of France and England, as I have said, differed irreconcilably in their estimate, not of charge, but of receipt. The Representatives of France absolutely refused any diminution of the dividends payable under the Law of Liquidation. The Representatives of England declared and held themselves unable to accept any plan that did not make certain provision for the necessary charges of administration, which are in their nature first charges upon the Revenue. Well, Sir, only when great authorities—and both France and England are countries in which what may be called financial science is considerably developed—when great authorities differ upon a matter of this kind, a prospective matter, it is time alone that can ultimately decide between them. A great responsibility is incurred on the one side and on the other; and it is quite evident that the party which is right ought to gain its end. When we found the existence of this serious difficulty, the question that came before was this—was it possible to devise a plan under which, if we were right, the charges of Government would be sufficiently provided for, and under which, if France were right, the full dividends would be received by the Bondholders? The matter was considered by us with a view to obtaining a plan of that character; and what was done can, I think, be explained to the House as a form that is not otherwise than simple. I can explain it by stating simply the order of charges upon the Egyptian Revenue. We submitted a plan—and this is the plan to which I wish particularly to call the attention of the House, as connected with the final issue—we submitted a plan in which the charges on the Egyptian Revenue were stated in the following order:—In the first place, we proposed that there should be a pre-preference Debt of £8,000,000.

LORD RANDOLPH CHURCHILL: Before any administrative charges?

MR. GLADSTONE: Yes; before any administrative charges. The noble Lord is perhaps not aware that under the Law of Liquidation already special provision is made independently of charges for administration, and we were desirous of confirming this arrangement so far as we safely could, and no further. The plan, therefore, was this. In the first place, there was a pre-preference Debt of £8,000,000; that might have been £8,000,000 raised in cash in order to meet the indemnity claims, and to meet all other claims which are now pressing on the Government of Egppt; or it might have been a loan contracted for £4,500,000 in cash, and the issue of pre-preference Bonds for the remaining £3,500,000.

LORD RANDOLPH CHURCHILL: At what rate of interest?

MR. GLADSTONE: At such rate of interest as it could be raised at in the market. We proposed pre-preference obligations in order that the money might be raised on the most economical terms. The second charge on the Egyptian Revenue was to be the dividends on other Debts, minus a deduction of ½ per cent—a deduction which we had originally proposed—and so we proposed to leave the Debts in their position of preference and anterior to the administrative charges, but minus a deduction of ½ per cent. The third charge was the administrative expense of the Government at a fixed amount, which I may state in round numbers at £5,250,000 in all. It is well to say that I speak of the Egyptian pound; but there is no great difference between that and the pound sterling. There is a good deal of detail in this, of course; but I will not trouble the House with it—it will only bewilder their attention. The fourth charge on the Revenue, after the administrative expenses, was to be the ½ per cent, making up the full dividend on the Debt now due to the Bondholders, and some other items of Debt I need not now more particularly mention. Then, fifthly, there was a provision for the disposal of the surplus, if surplus there should exist. In this way, as we considered, both the objects were gained. If we were right, the expenses of the Government would have been perfectly provided for; and if the French calculations were right, besides providing for the expenses of the Government, there would have been sufficient provision for the payment of full dividends to the Bondholders. We proposed this as a permanent arrangement; but rather than have seen the Conference fail, we should have been prepared to accept this plan for a period of three years only, to be followed by a re-assembling of the Conference, as that would have given a sufficient time for testing its operation, and showing which calculations were most entitled to reliance. Well, to-day—and only this day—the French Representatives presented their final proposals, to which I will call the attention of the House, and the House will kindly compare them with the proposals of the British Government, which I have just described. According to the French proposals, there were certain classes constituting an order, in which charges were imposed upon Egyptian Revenue. In the first class there was set the new loan of which I have spoken, and what is known as the "Privilege Debt." I have not mentioned "Privilege Debt" before, because we did not make an essential distinction between the two kinds of Debt; but the French, in their proposals, made that distinction—consequently, for the first I introduce the term "Privilege Debt." Well, that was the first charge on the Egyptian Revenue; the second charge was to be the other, and principally the Unified Debt. On this the full dividends were to be paid before any of the other charges of administration were satisfied. The third order of charge upon the Revenue was to be the expenditure necessarily connected with the administration; to which the French Plenipotentiary added a fourth, a provision to which, I believe, he attached greater importance and value than we did—that is to say, that after paying all the dividends in that diminution, and after pa ing all the administrative charges, theysurplus Revenue should be freely at the disposal of the Egyptian Government. But, apart from the surplus, it was necessary—and we undoubtedly deemed it pre-eminently necessary—to consider the provision to be made for the case of deficit. I forgot to state to the House at the beginning that our estimate of the Egyptian Revenue was made with all the aid we could obtain, and all the care we could apply to it, and it shows a deficit of between £300,000 and £400,000 a-year; whereas the French are more sanguine in their estimate by a sum of between £600,000 and £700,000. The difference between our plan and the French plan which we are now scrutinizing was that we made provision for a deficit, if it should occur, and it was this. In the case of a deficit, it was to be considered and provided for by joint consultation between the Egyptian Government and the Commission of the Caisse. I may say that the constitution of the Caisse according to the proposal of the French would, we understand, have been altered, and, instead of consisting of the Representatives of four Powers, it would have consisted of the Representatives of seven Powers—namely, the whole of those Powers who met together in the Conference. The Egyptian Government and the Commission of the Caisse were, as I have said, to devise the measures necessary to meet the deficit; but if these measures involved an infringement on the full dividends, in that case it was provided—firstly, that the Caisse could not act except by a unanimous vote; and, secondly, in the event of any difference among the members of the Caisse, the matter was to be referred—as to supplying the deficit—to the seven Powers, Representatives of which were then assembled in Conference, and who, unhappily, have not been able to deal with the question of Egyptian Finance. To this plan I am bound to say, without requiring a very long time for any minute investigation, we took decided objection. As we conceived, the fatal objections were two. Certainly, in the first place, it would have meant, if there be any truth in our computation of Egyptian finance — it would have meant financial confusion in Egypt. For, Sir, upon the existence of a deficit what would have happened? This would have happened. The Egyptian accounts of Revenue and Expenditure are not made up—nor are those of any other Eastern country—to a certain day, as are the accounts of England on the 31st of March. They must be gathered together a long time, and after much inquiry, in order to constitute anything like a real exhibition of Revenue and Expenditure. That having been performed, they were to be referred to the Commission of the Caisse with the Egyptian Government. But the Commission of the Caisse was necessarily, and by its own composition, a hostile tribunal. It would have been their business to examine every minute particular, to see what arrears there were in the collection of Revenue—to see whether it was possible to gather in that Revenue, and institute most elaborate inquiries, requiring an indefinite time; and then there would be the condition that if any single Power objected, no result could be obtained. And the final provision was that there should be a reference to the seven Powers of Europe. It was, in our view, pretty plain that the Powers of Europe, if they had instructed their Representatives upon the Caisse to object to supplying the deficit by deductions from the dividends, would simply repeat their objections when their Representatives met again in Conference. But, Sir, besides the financial objection, we took another objection to this plan, which was quite fatal to it in our eyes—it was the position assigned by this plan to the Commission of the National Debt, or the Commission of the Caisse. There has been in this and, perhaps, in other countries a belief that it was part of our plan to re-create the Dual Control in a form yet more stringent, more savouring of dominion over Egyptian affairs. That was never any part of our plan; but I am bound to say that, in our deliberate conviction, it must been the inevitable consequence of the adoption of the French proposals, and I will take the liberty of stating our objections to it in some words used today by Lord Granville at the Conference, and which will appear upon the Protocol—

> "We do not think that powers of this magnitude should be in any case intrusted to the Commission of the Caisse. We have already proposed to give to that body by the Anglo-French Agreement powers of check and investigation as great as we can justify; but the present proposal is fundamentally different. The additional powers proposed by the French Plenipotentiary would, in our judgment, confer on the Commissioners of the Caisse a mastery over the Government and the affairs of Egypt; and to this we can on no account consent."

Well, Sir, I have now explained, I think, pretty well the manner in which it has come about that irreconcileable difficulties prevented the Conference from arriving at a conclusion; but there are other certain results which have been achieved by the Conference. Amid this wreck of good intentions and much intelligent labour on all sides, it is a great thing that the Powers should be agreed as to the necessary charge upon the Egyptian Government, and substantially as to the loan needful to be contracted in the present exigency; and I must say it is also a great advantage that there should be a total dissipation and destruction of the idea which has prevailed in this country that we should ever have proposed to constitute what, in our view, was an International Control similar in kind to that of the Dual Control, or, as I think in this case, one involving evils considerably beyond it. The view which we take of Egyptian finance was supported in the Conference by Italy and by Turkey; but France, as I have said, was unable to bring her opinions into harmony with ours; and Russia, Germany, and Austria, in those circumstances of difference between England and France, declined to give any opinion. The end of it is, therefore, that the Conference, not having arrived at any result, according to the mode of procedure adopted on some other occasion, has been adjourned without any date being fixed for its reassembling. I have now, Sir, substantially concluded what I have to state to the House. Of course, this failure—this complete failure—of the effort made by us for the satisfactory adjustment of Egyptian Finance, through the action of the United Powers, will entail upon us very serious consideration of the position and of the measures which will be necessary. I need hardly say that I am not about to enter upon these measures without safe and trustworthy conclusions, which cannot be arrived at by the Goverment without further consideration and the lapse of some time. My remaining business is to say that the Protocols will be presented at the very earliest moment, and to explain when that earliest moment will be. The House is aware that it is absolutely necessary to submit draft Protocols to the Plenipotentiaries who have taken part in the Conference. I do not think that will entail any serious delay. My noble Friend the Under Secretary of State for Foreign Affairs will be able to state, in case of need, what has been done. In consequence of Monday being Bank Holiday, there will be some difficulty; but we have endeavoured to confront that difficulty, and to secure rapid progress in the preparation of the Papers on that day. A large number of copies —120, I believe—will be ready on Monday afternoon.

LORD EDMOND FITZMAURICE: Without translation.

MR. GLADSTONE: Yes, without translation; but I hope they will be a sufficient number for practical purposes, and on Tuesday it is hoped that the Papers will be generally distributed.

SIR STAFFORD NORTHCOTE: Will they be ready at the meeting of the House on Monday?

MR. GLADSTONE: Yes. I understand that the Papers on Monday will be ready for the meeting of the House. Well, Sir, there is one other question which will naturally be asked—What is the position of the Anglo-French Agreement? I always told the House that the Anglo-French Agreement was entirely dependent upon the arrival at a substantial result by the Conference; and the consequence is that that Agreement is now in abeyance, and is without any binding effect and force as regards either Power. I must not, however, shrink from saying that Her Majesty's Government continue to value the provisions of that Agreement; and, moreover—although, unfortunately, a difference has arisen upon a matter of computation, with regard to which a difference may most innocently occur—we continue most highly to appreciate the spirit of friendship and conciliation, and far-sighted wisdom which, as we think, was shown by the French Government in negotiating the provisions of that Agreement. I thank the House for the attention with which it has listened to this statement. A full one it could not be. Still, I believe that in outline it is a true and correct one; and if there is any desire to put any question in regard to it, we will endeavour to answer it with the indulgence of the House.

SIR STAFFORD NORTHCOTE: The extreme gravity of the statement which we have just listened to I am sure will be appreciated by the House, and I should be very unwilling to make any comment at this moment on what we have heard. We have been promised information supplementary to that which the Prime Minister has given; but what I wish particularly to inquire is this: We are now approaching the end of the Session; is it intended by the Government to make any proposals to Parliament in the residue of the present Session? We must remember that the Conference was invited to meet on account of what the Government considered the very serious and urgent condition of Egyptian finance. It was hoped by the Government that the result of the meeting of that Conference would be the adoption of a plan which would meet the difficulties which they described as urgent and immediate. Well, unfortunately, the Conference has failed to devise a plan, and what we wish to know is this: How does the Government propose to deal, or will they tell us very soon, if not now, how they propose to deal with those difficulties which the Conference was called together to deal with, and which it has failed to deal with? Or are we to suppose that the House is to separate without any proposal being made on the subject?

MR. GLADSTONE: I think I may say without doubt that we have no proposal of the kind to make to Parliament. I was, perhaps, not sufficiently full in my statement. I said we should have asked Parliament for the use of British credit if a substantial arrangement could have been adopted; I ought to have added that, as no substantial arrangement had been adopted, we do not intend to make any proposal, any request to Parliament for the use of its credit, or any other proposal.

SIR STAFFORD NORTHCOTE: Are we to get no further information as to the state of Egyptian financial affairs?

conceived, the fatal objections were two. Certainly in the first place it would have [illegible] computation of Egyptian finance—it would have [illegible] confusion in Egypt. For Sir, upon the existence of [illegible] what would have happened? This would have happened. The Egyptian [illegible] of Revenue and Expenditure [illegible] are those of any [illegible] country—to a certain day, [illegible] of England on the 31st of March. They must be [illegible] together a long time, and after [illegible] before [illegible] anything like a real statement of Revenue and Expenditure. That having been [illegible] they were to be referred to the [illegible] of the Caisse with the Egyptian Government. But the Com[illegible] Caisse was necessarily and [illegible] composition, a hostile tribunal. It would have been their business [illegible] every favourite part [illegible] there were in the [illegible] Revenue [illegible] who [illegible] possible to get [illegible] that Re[illegible] elaborate [illegible] the condition that [illegible] Powers [illegible] And the final provision was that there should be a refer[illegible] the several Powers of Europe. It was [illegible] view [illegible] plain that the Powers of Europe [illegible] they had instructed their Representatives [illegible] the Caisse [illegible] applying the [illegible] by [illegible] would [illegible] on their Rep[illegible] Conference. But Sir, [illegible] Govern[illegible] [illegible] Egyptian [illegible]. That was never any part of our plan; but I am bound to say that [illegible] conversation at [illegible] the acceptance of the [illegible] of the French proposals, and I [illegible] of [illegible] words [illegible] day by Lord Granville at the Conference, and which will appear upon the Papers:—

"W[illegible]"

Well, Sir, I have now explained I think, pretty well the manner in which it has come about that irreconcilable difficulties prevented the Conference from arriving at a conclusion; but there are other certain results which have been achieved by the Conference. And this [illegible] it is a great thing that the Powers should be agreed as to the necessary charge upon the Egyptian Government, and substantially as to the [illegible] to be contracted [illegible] and I must say it [illegible] advantage that there should be [illegible] and [illegible] which has prevailed [illegible] that we should ever have proposed [illegible] in our view, was [illegible] Dual Control, or as [illegible] involving evils considerably [illegible]. The view which we [illegible] Egyptian finance was supported [illegible] Conference by Italy and by [illegible] France, as I have said, was [illegible] bring her opinions into harmony with ours, and Russia, Germany, and Austria, [illegible] circumstances of [illegible] between England and France [illegible] give any opinion. In [illegible] therefore [illegible] Conference [illegible] have arrived at any result, according to the [illegible] procedure adopted [illegible] has been [illegible] agreed for [illegible] I have now, Sir, [illegible] what I have to state to the House [illegible] the [illegible] of the effect [illegible] of Egyptian finance through the action of the [illegible] Powers will enter upon [illegible] consideration of the [illegible] measures which [illegible] necessary. I need hardly say that I am not about to enter upon

solve itself into Committee of Supply."—(*Mr. Courtney.*)

MR. ARTHUR O'CONNOR rose to Order, and asked the Speaker, as a point of Order, whether, after the Order for Supply had been set up and had been discharged by the Chairman reporting certain Votes, it was competent for a Member of the Goverment to move that the House should resolve itself into Committee of Supply? He did not think that in the whole history of Parliament such a precedent had been established.

MR. HEALY asked whether, in the circumstances, the Resolution passed yesterday extending to Saturdays the Standing Order as to Mondays and Thursdays was now applicable; and, whether Supply not now being the First Order, Motions could be discussed on the Question that the Speaker leave the Chair?

MR. SPEAKER: In reply to the Questions of the two hon. Members, I must state that I consider that the interruption which has taken place to the ordinary course of Business was by reason of an extraordinary counsel with the House itself. ["No, no!" *from the Conservatives and Irish Members.*] The interruption took place with the permission of the House; and I have no hesitation in saying that I shall observe both the spirit and letter of the Motion agreed to by the House on Friday—that on the Question of the House going into Committee of Supply on Saturday, the Speaker shall immediately leave the Chair. I do not see anything in the interruption which has taken place to prevent the House from being in precisely the same position in which it was when it met to-day at 12 o'clock. Under these circumstances, I consider it my duty to leave the Chair without any Question being raised upon it.

LORD RANDOLPH CHURCHILL, with reference to the observation of the Speaker that the interruption of the Business was in consequence of the wish of the House, pointed out that the agreement come to was that the statement of the Prime Minister should be made on the Report of Supply, which should be moved at a certain hour if possible. He thought the Government had taken an unfair advantage of the House in the course that had been pursued to-night.

MR. GLADSTONE replied, that yesterday, when the suggestion was made that the statement should be made on Report, he entirely disapproved of it, because it seemed to him a most violent method of proceeding; but he reserved in his mind what would be the best and least violent method of obtaining the object the noble Lord had in view.

MR. ARTHUR O'CONNOR said, the Motion of the Secretary to the Treasury was a complete and flagrant departure from all the traditions of the House, and it was not justified by a single precedent. Supply had never been suspended except when the Speaker had been called in because disorder had arisen. Most of the Irish Members had gone away, believing that the Order with reference to Supply had been concluded. The Government could see that the Irish Benches were almost completely empty, as they thought Progress had been reported. Now, to ask them to resume the debate when the House was full of English and Scotch Members, and there were only very few Irish Members, was absolutely unfair. [*Interruption, and cries of* "Order!" *from the Ministerial Benches.*]

MR. HEALY: Order! Order! Order!

MR. ARTHUR O'CONNOR complained of the interruption, and said that not one single argument had been advanced from the Treasury Bench in support of such an extraordinary step, and he desired to enter his protest against it.

MR. MONK said, there was no necessity for the Motion just made by the Secretary to the Treasury. [Several MEMBERS: He has made it.] According to the Speaker's ruling he had simply taken the Chair for an important communication to be made by the Prime Minister, and Committee of Supply should be resumed without a Question being put.

MR. SPEAKER: I believe the hon. Gentleman is perfectly correct, and that I might have left the Chair immediately after the statement of the Prime Minister. But the Secretary to the Treasury having made the Motion, I was, of course, bound to put it. As I said before, I consider that the course of Business has been interrupted that a statement might be made on a matter of national concern; and the House ought to be placed in the same position that it was before the interruption occurred.

LORD RANDOLPH CHURCHILL said, the Chairman of Committees had reported to the Speaker the Resolution agreed to in Committee. Therefore, the First Order of the day had terminated. The Second Order was Report of Supply; and before the Motion of the Secretary to the Treasury could be put it was absolutely necessary to go through the Orders of the Day, of which there were 40. It would be setting a precedent which hon. Members opposite would some day bitterly regret if this Motion were agreed to.

MR. SPEAKER: The Chairman could not leave the Chair without reporting to me the proceedings of the Committee. The House had made no Order as to the time at which the Committee should sit again. It may properly proceed as if there had been no interruption. The Question is "That this House do immediately resolve itself into Committee of Supply."

MR. ARTHUR O'CONNOR asked, as a point of Order, whether he could not move, as an Amendment to the Question, that the House should resolve itself into Committee on Monday next?

MR. SPEAKER: Yes; on the question of time, there may be an Amendment.

MR. CALLAN asked why the Prime Minister had asked them to close the Vote for Irish Constabulary purposes except to make a statement——

MR. SPEAKER ruled the hon. Member out of Order.

LORD RANDOLPH CHURCHILL: In order to place myself in Order, I will move, as an Amendment, that this House do resolve itself into Committee of Supply on Monday next. There is nothing so dangerous as setting a precedent of this kind, which on some future occasion may be used by the Government for their own purposes. If Irish Members, and I myself, had supposed that the Government would pursue this unprecedented course, we should certainly have done all in our power to oppose the Prime Minister's proposition. The Government has, by means of a protest, obtained a Vote of £1,500,000 on an abbreviated discussion—and a Vote which they would, in all probability, not have obtained until 12 o'clock at night. I do not believe that there is a more jealous guardian of the rights of Members of the House of Commons than the Prime Minister; and if he will only shake himself free from the evil influences of the Secretary to the Treasury—who apparently recoils from no proceeding, whatever may be its character—and appear in the character of Leader of the House, instead of Leader of the Ministry, he would assent to this course of procedure. If, however, he should persist in this Motion, I do not think he will do much good, for there is nothing that will create more strenuous opposition.

Amendment proposed to leave out the word "immediately," in order to insert the words "upon Monday next,"—(*Lord Randolph Churchill,*) — instead thereof.

Question proposed, "That the word 'immediately' stand part of the Question."

MR. GLADSTONE: I desire only to correct the view taken by the noble Lord, who said this is the most dangerous precedent of which any Government can avail itself. The noble Lord said I availed myself of a pretext to make a statement to the House. What the noble Lord called a pretext is the fact that the House itself, represented by many Gentlemen who spoke, by the silence of all the rest—and, most of all, represented by the noble Lord himself—expressed a very strong desire yesterday that, for the convenience of the House, a statement should be made to-day, and not on Monday, with regard to Egyptian affairs.

LORD RANDOLPH CHURCHILL: On the Report of Supply. [*Cries of* "Order!"]

MR. GLADSTONE: I only wish to observe that the noble Lord's statements as to a pretext having been resorted to are really idle; because what the Government have done they have done in obedience to the impulsion of the House, and without any dissentient voice. [*Cries of* "Without Notice!"] There should, therefore, be no fear of the misuse by the Government of such a precedent for the future for Government purposes. The noble Lord said he wished to have the statement made upon Report; but recollecting that Report of Supply was a recital of the Votes passed by Committee, I considered that that proposal would be the most inconvenient way that could be devised of dealing with the subject. When the House meets upon a Saturday at the close of the Session, it usually sits in Supply to a late hour, and sometimes until Sunday morning; and it was considered by the noble Lord that after disposing of Supply, perhaps at 11 o'clock, an hour before Sunday, we should take this question of the Egyptian Conference. To make the statement at that time on Report of Supply would be most inconvenient to hon. Members, besides which the usual means of publicity will have been completely paralysed until Monday morning. It appears to me that for the House to hear the statement at 6 o'clock was convenient, and that the postponement to 10 or 11 o'clock would have been very inconvenient indeed. I hope that, under these circumstances, and considering the origin of this affair, which was entirely the impulsion of the House itself, and was not suggested by the Government—I hope we may not be prevented from proceeding with Supply. It was well understood, or should have been understood, there was no intention of taking any Irish Votes; and there could not be a more lamentable exhibition, not for the Government, or the Opposition, but for the whole House, than a continual wrangle on this subject.

MR. DAWSON said, he thought the right hon. Gentleman had missed the point they endeavoured to bring out, which was that if they were able to interrupt proceedings of Supply in this way, why was it considered necessary to pass the Constabulary Vote? Why were not the proceedings in Committee merely suspended in order to enable the statement of the Prime Minister to be made, instead of Members being given to understand by their agreeing to a Vote that Supply would be closed for the day?

MR. JUSTIN M'CARTHY asked whether the House would have consented to report Progress if it had been thought that the unprecedented proceeding would be resorted to of setting up Supply again? The fact that Irish Votes were not to be taken did not reconcile the Irish Members at all to this strange and new and startling innovation, which followed so curiously upon the inadvertence of yesterday, for which the Secretary to the Treasury was responsible. He desired only straightforward conduct on the part of the Government, and should certainly resist such an innovation as they proposed.

SIR STAFFORD NORTHCOTE: I am sorry to see the difficulty which has arisen in this matter. I must admit that the circumstances are peculiar; but I think it would be well for the Government to consider how far they are likely to advance Public Business by pressing the Motion. It was generally understood that the Irish Votes were fixed for to-day, and that that would be the only Business; but yesterday, in consequence of the position in which it was known that the Conference stood, the noble Lord the Member for Woodstock (Lord Randolph Churchill) asked whether it would not be possible on Report of Supply for a Minister to make a statement with regard to the Conference. The Chancellor of the Exchequer, I understand, raised an objection to that course of proceeding, stating that it would not be convenient, on Report of Supply, to make such a statement. That objection, however, was overruled; and I certainly understood that Report of Supply would be taken at some period between 6 and 8 o'clock, and that the statement would then be made, provided the Government were in a position to do so. I myself was certainly under the impression that the Prime Minister's statement would be made at the conclusion of Supply. Under the circumstances, and seeing the feeling of the House, I would venture to put it to the Government whether they would be consulting the convenience of the House by the course they propose; and whether, if they persist in it, they will gain any advantage?

SIR WILLIAM HARCOURT said, if there was any intention of continuing the contest upon this question, it would be unseemly to further prolong it. He wished the House, however, to be under no misapprehension. Some hon. Gentlemen on the other side of the House seemed to think the Government intended to take the House by surprise. [*Cheers.*] That was entirely unfounded—there was no such intention. He believed there was no man in the House who did not know the whole afternoon the course which would be taken. ["No, no!"] He should have supposed that it would have been known from the ordinary sources of information. It was quite understood that the Con-

LORD RANDOLPH CHURCHILL said the Chairman of Committees had [illegible] Speaker the House [illegible] The [illegible] Order was Report of Supply, [illegible] Motion of the Secretary to the Treasury [illegible] absolutely necessary to go through the Orders of the Day [illegible] It would be setting a precedent which [illegible] Members [illegible] would [illegible] this Motion were agreed to.

MR. SPEAKER: The [illegible] could not leave the Chair without reporting to the [illegible] of the Chairman. The House had made no Order as to the time at which the Committee should sit again. It may properly proceed as if there had been no interruption. The Question is—"That this House do immediately resolve itself into Committee of Supply."

MR. ARTHUR O'CONNOR asked [illegible] Question, that this House [illegible] resolve itself into Committee [illegible] Monday next?

MR. SPEAKER: Yes, [illegible] the question [illegible] may be an Amendment.

MR. CALLAN [illegible] the Prime Minister had asked [illegible] to close the Votes [illegible] purposes except [illegible] a statement [illegible]

MR. SPEAKER: The hon. Member [illegible] Order.

LORD RANDOLPH CHURCHILL: [illegible] in Order, I will [illegible] an Amendment, that the House [illegible] Committee of Supply on Monday next. There is nothing so dangerous as setting a precedent [illegible] future [illegible] by the Government [illegible] purposes. If [illegible] Members [illegible] had supposed that the Government would pursue this [illegible] we should certainly [illegible] all in our power to oppose the Prime Minister's proposition [illegible] by means of a [illegible] Vote of £1,000,000 [illegible] and a Vote which they would, in all probability, not have [illegible] until 12 o'clock at night. [illegible] there is a more jealous guardian of the rights of Members of the House of Commons than the Prime Minister, and if he will only shake himself free from the evil influence of the Secretary to the Treasury, who apparently [illegible] whatever [illegible] the character of Leader of the House instead of Leader of the Ministry, he will [illegible] If, however, he [illegible] this Motion, I do not think he will do much good, for there is nothing that will create more strenuous opposition.

Amendment proposed, to leave out the word "immediately," in order to insert the words "upon Monday next."—(*Lord Randolph Churchill*,)—instead thereof.

Question proposed, "That the word 'immediately' stand part of the Question."

MR. GLADSTONE: I desire only to [illegible] the view taken by the noble Lord, who said this is the most dangerous precedent which any Government can avail itself. The noble Lord said I availed myself of a pretext to make a statement to the House. What the noble Lord called a pretext is the fact that the House itself, represented by [illegible] represented by the noble Lord himself, expressed a very strong [illegible] yesterday that, for the convenience of the House, a statement should be made to-day, and not on Monday, with regard to Egyptian affairs.

LORD RANDOLPH CHURCHILL: On the Report of Supply. [*Cries of* "Order!"]

MR. GLADSTONE: I only wish to observe that the noble Lord's [illegible] as to a [illegible] having been [illegible] are [illegible] the [illegible] they [illegible] the opinion of the House, [illegible] "Wait till Monday." There [illegible] therefore, be no fear of the use [illegible] by the Government of such a precedent for the future for Government purposes. The noble Lord said he wished to have the statement made upon Report [illegible] Report of Supply was a [illegible] of the Votes passed in Committee, I considered that that proposal would be the most inconvenient way that could be devised of dealing with the

tinguished men that ever adorned that Chair, Mr. Speaker Onslow, said on a memorable occasion that the Forms and Rules of the House were an indispensable protection of the minority, and that it was the duty of every Speaker and Chairman for the time being to enforce those Rules and Forms for their protection. One of the best established Rules of the House was, "That the Orders of the Day be disposed of in the order in which they stand on the Paper." The first Order that day was Supply; the second was Report. Supply having been brought to an end, Report ought to be next taken.

THE SOLICITOR GENERAL (Sir FARRER HERSCHELL) said, now that the Government had yielded what they had been contending for he hoped this discussion would not be prolonged. They would take no further Votes in Supply, but would proceed to the Report. They would accept the proposal that on Monday the House should resolve itself into Committee of Supply.

LORD RANDOLPH CHURCHILL said, he was prepared to withdraw his Amendment, on condition that the Secretary to the Treasury withdrew his Motion.

MR. SPEAKER said, it was necessary to make an Order as to Supply for Monday.

Question put, and *negatived.*

Question, "That the words 'upon Monday next' be there inserted," put, and *agreed to.*

Committee upon *Monday* next.

Resolution to be reported upon *Monday* next.

SUPPLY.—REPORT.

Resolutions [1st August] *reported.*

First and Second Resolutions *postponed.*

Third Resolution *agreed to.*

Fourth Resolution read a second time.

Motion made, and Question proposed, "That this House doth agree with the Committee in the said Resolution."

MR. WARTON moved that the Report be postponed until Monday, as a protest against the manner in which the Vote had been taken in Committee by the Secretary to the Treasury.

Amendment proposed, to leave out from the word "That," to the end of the Question, in order to add the words "the Debate on the Further Consideration of the Resolution be adjourned,"—(*Mr. Warton,*)—instead thereof.

Question put, "That the words proposed to be left out stand part of the Question."

The House *divided:*—Ayes 36; Noes 4: Majority 32.—(Div. List, No. 206.)

Main Question put, and *agreed to.*

Subsequent Resolutions *agreed to.*

Postponed Resolutions to be considered upon *Monday* next.

SIR GEORGE CAMPBELL: As a personal explanation, Mr. Speaker, I wish to say that I voted in the minority, because I thought I was voting that the Report be not adjourned.

House adjourned at a quarter after Eight o'clock till Monday next.

HOUSE OF LORDS,

Monday, 4th August, 1884.

MINUTES.]—PUBLIC BILLS—*First Reading*—Revenue, &c.* (242).

Second Reading—Education (Scotland) Provisional Order* (218); Local Government (Ireland) Provisional Orders (Labourers Act) (No. 8)* (217); Military Pensions and Yeomanry Pay* (232); Chartered Companies* (231); Infants (237), *disch.*; Public Health (Ireland) (Districts)* (238).

Committee—Report—Expiring Laws Continuance* (236).

Report—Cholera Hospitals (Ireland)* (229).

Third Reading—Public Works Loans* (221); Metropolitan Board of Works (Money)* (232), and *passed.*

EGYPT—THE CONFERENCE.

MINISTERIAL STATEMENT.

EARL GRANVILLE: My Lords, I rise for the purpose of laying on the Table of your Lordships' House certain Papers, and I must apologize to your Lordships for their not being in a more perfect state. It has been physically impossible to produce the Protocols with the translations in the time within which we were most anxious to present them. I think, however, that these Papers will give the general information which your Lordships require, and the translations will be ready the day after to-morrow. Your Lordships are aware that the Conference was, at its sitting on Saturday, adjourned without coming to an agreement on the alteration in the Law of Liquidation. It is not necessary for me, on this occasion, to say much in regard to the preliminary Anglo-French Agreement, which has already been submitted to your Lordships. I am aware that it has met in this country with considerable criticism, and even Votes of Censure have been threatened. For my part, I not only believe that the Agreement would have gained by full discussion; but I regret that the Agreement, from a condition made at the time, is not at present binding either on France or on this country. It was negotiated in a statesmanlike and friendly spirit on principles which I shall always consider creditable to the two Governments, securing for each country that which was valuable for each, and on both making concessions which were valuable and just. Charles Fox, when he invented handicapping two racehorses, advised that the owner of each should place a sovereign in the hands of the handicapper. If one owner accepted the award and the other refused, the sovereign went to the owner who accepted; but if both owners accepted, or both owners refused, the sovereigns remained with the handicapper, who, Mr. Fox thought, might be assumed to have come to a fair and a right decision. On the principle which a great statesman applied to a mere pastime, it might equally be argued that when two Governments arrived at an adjustment of a natural difference, which at first obtains the approval of both countries, or which provokes considerable criticism in both, there is an *à priori* probability that the arrangement has not been of a very one-sided character. I am very sorry to say that this sort of justification, whatever it may be worth, for the British negotiators has not been wanting in France. The arrangement was severely criticized by the French Press, and the feelings of the Chamber have been so adverse that it naturally had its influence upon the negotiations. I have here a short Memorandum showing the different proposals that were made to the Conference. Our first proposal was made on the 28th of June. It was that a pre-Preference Loan of £8,000,000 should be guaranteed by England, the interest and Sinking Fund amounting to 4½ per cent; that the interest on each of the existing loans should be reduced by ½ per cent, and the Sinking Funds suspended—we left it to the Congress to decide whether the Domain Loan should be included—that the surplus should go, one-half to the Egyptian Government and the other half to the Sinking Funds, and that the charge for the Army of Occupation should be limited to £300,000 a-year. Then came the French counter-proposal made on a higher estimate of revenue. It was made on the 22nd of July, and was as follows:—That the Sinking Fund should be suspended, but that the rate of interest on all the loans should be maintained except the Suez Canal Loan made by England, from which 1 per cent should be deducted; that the administrative expenses should be fixed at the sum proposed by England; that an inquiry into the land revenue should be undertaken by England, and the result communicated to a Conference in 1886, and that the £8,000,000 loan should be guaranteed by all the Powers. To this, which we rejected, we made two counter-proposals on the 24th of July. One of these was that the new loan should be raised without guarantee, the indemnities being paid in its Stock; that the administrative expenses, as agreed between us and the French, should be the next charge on the Egyptian Revenues; that the third charge should be the interest on the existing debts; that any surplus should be divided equally between the Sinking Funds and the Egyptian Exchequer; and that any deficit should fall on the interest of the loans. The other proposal was that the diminution of interest under our original plan should last only for 10 years, and that the Conference should then meet again, and that we should only guarantee so much of the pre-Preference Loan as would not be required for the indemnities. On the 28th of July we discussed the first of the two proposals, to which the French objected, proposing instead to make the entire interest of all the existing debts the second charge, and the administrative expenses the third. If there should be a surplus the whole should go to the Egyptian Exchequer for 10 years. If there was a deficit the Commission of the Caisse would arrange, in concert with the Egyptian Government, how to meet it; but that no reduction in the interest of the Debt could take place. After discussion, in which we offered to give our proposal a duration of only three years, the French took it *ad referendum*. On the following day, the 29th of July, no answer having been received from the French Government, we made, on a suggestion from Count Nigra, the following amended proposal:—That after the interest on the New Loan, which would form the first charge on the Revenues of Egypt, the next charge should be the interest on all the existing loans, less ½ per cent; that the third charge should be the administrative expenses; that the fourth should be the ½ per cent, so far as the balance would allow, and that if there was any surplus it should be divided between the Sinking Fund and the Egyptian Exchequer; and that this arrangement should be for three years. To this, on the 2nd of August, the French made their final counter-proposal, which we rejected.

"That the New Loan should be made in Privileged Stock, which would be the first charge on the Revenues; that the second charge should be the full interest on the other loans, but that the Sinking Fund should be suspended for three years; that the third charge should be the administrative charges as we had settled them; that any balance should go to the Egyptian Exchequer; that any deficiency should be reported to the Commission of the Caisse, to consist of seven members, who would arrange with the Egyptian Government how to meet it. If this involved a reduction of interest it could only be effected by an unanimous vote of the Commissioners. If they differed, the matter would be referred to the Great Powers; that the inquiry into the land revenue should be undertaken and the result brought before a meeting of the Conference in 1887."

Your Lordships will have perceived that the last proposal of the French Government differed from ours in two respects—first, as to the mode of raising the New Loan on which both Governments were willing to arrive, and might easily have arrived at an agreement; secondly, as to the manner in which the necessary charges of the administration and the interest of the present Debt shall be dealt with. The French plan, in our judgment, would produce a normal deficit of £500,000, or, according to the Egyptian authorities, of £1,000,000 a-year, leaving to the Commission of the Caisse, whose official duty it is to represent the creditors, not the Egyptian debtors, to decide how far, from year to year, this deficiency is to be made good, thus, practically, excluding the remedy of any reduction of the interest unless, after an indefinite lapse of time, the Representatives of the Powers should agree unanimously to it. This would have given to the Caisse, not merely the addition of some useful powers of check and investigation such as was provided for in the Anglo-French Agreement; but would have given to it the complete control of the government and affairs of Egypt. It is a great misfortune that France and England could not come conscientiously to an agreement, especially as if we had done so the other Powers were ready to concur in it. No one can deplore this more than Her Majesty's Government; but I cannot altogether regret, if the disagreement was inevitable, that the Ultimatum of the French Government should be one which I believe your Lordships will unanimously be of opinion it was impossible for us to accept. I hope that this House will understand that, in saying this, I do not pretend to criticize the conduct of France in wishing to defend the rights of her subjects. Even if so large a number of Egyptian securities were not held in this country, I should entirely sympathize with the French Government in the desire that rights secured—though in different circumstances—under International Agreement to individuals should, if it were possible, be maintained. But the view which we desired to place before the Powers, parties to this International Agreement, was that, while Egypt was bound to do her best to meet the claims upon her, it was the duty of all of us to see that Egypt was placed in a position in which she could live. It has been asked whether Her Majesty's Government applied to Germany to mediate. Now, certainly, I thought it my duty to urge strongly upon the Representatives of all the Powers the hope that, in the interests of Egypt, we should receive their support. It was not likely that I should except such a Power as Germany—whose attitude towards us about Egypt has been of a very friendly character—from this appeal, or that I should conceal my belief that her influence in Europe might be of great use to Egypt in this crisis. I did not ask for the mediation of Ger-

general information which your Lordships require, and the translations will be ready the day after to-morrow. Your Lordships are aware that the Conference was, at its sitting on Saturday, adjourned without coming to an agreement on the alteration in the Law of Liquidation. It is not necessary for me, on this occasion, to say much in regard to the preliminary Anglo-French Agreement which has already been submitted to your Lordships. I am aware that it has met in this country with considerable criticism, and even Votes of Censure have been threatened. For my part, I not only believe that the Agreement would have gained by full discussion, but I regret that the Agreement, from a condition made at the time, is not at present binding either on France or on this country. It was negotiated in a statesmanlike and friendly spirit on principles which I shall always consider creditable to the two Governments, securing for each country that which was valuable for each, and on both making concessions which were valuable and just. Charles Fox, when he invented handicapping two racehorses, advised that the owner of each should place a sovereign in the hands of the handicapper. If one owner accepted the award and the other refused, the sovereign went to the owner who accepted; but if both owners accepted, or both owners refused, the sovereigns remained with the handicapper, who, Mr. Fox thought, might be assumed to have come to a fair and right decision. On the principle which a great statesman applied to a minor pastime, it might equally be argued that when two Governments arrived at an adjustment of a natural difference, which at first obtains the approval of both countries, or which provokes considerable criticism in both, there is an *à priori* probability that the arrangement has not been of a very one-sided character. I am very sorry to say that the want of appreciation, whatever it may be worth, for the British negotiators has not been wanting in France. The arrangement was severely criticized by the French Press and the feelings of the Chamber have been so adverse that it naturally had its influence upon the negotiations. I have here a short Memorandum showing the different proposals that were made to the Conference. Our first proposal was made on the 28th of June. It was that a pre-Preference Loan of £8,000,000 should be guaranteed by England, the interest and Sinking Fund amounting to [illegible] per cent; that the interest on each of the existing loans should be reduced by ½ per cent, and the Sinking Funds suspended; we left it to the Congress to decide whether the Domain Loan should be included; that the surplus should go, one half to the Egyptian Government and the other half to the Sinking Funds, and that the charge for the Army of Occupation should be limited to £[illegible],000 a year. Then came the French counter-proposal made on a higher estimate of revenue. It was made on the 22nd of July, and was as follows:—That the Sinking Fund should be suspended, but that the rate of interest on all the loans should be maintained except the Suez Canal Loan made by England, from which 1 per cent should be deducted; that the administrative expenses should be fixed at the sum proposed by England; that an inquiry into the land revenue should be undertaken by England, and the result communicated to a Conference in 1886; and that the £8,000,000 loan should be guaranteed by all the Powers. To this, which we rejected, we made two counter proposals on the [illegible] of July. One of these was that the new Loan should be raised without guarantee, the interest being paid in [illegible] Stock; that the administrative expenses, as agreed between us and the French, should be the next charge on the Egyptian Revenues; that the third charge should be the interest on the existing debts; that any surplus should be divided equally between the Sinking Funds and the Egyptian Exchequer, and that any deficit should fall on the interest of the loans. The other proposal was that the diminution of interest under our original plan should last only for 10 years, and that the Conference should then meet again, and that we should only guarantee so much of the pre-Preference Loan as would not be required for the indemnities. On the [illegible] of July we discussed the first of the two proposals, to which the French objected, proposing instead to make the entire interest of all the existing debts the second charge, and the administrative expenses the third. If there should be a surplus the whole should go to the Egyptian Exchequer for [illegible] years. If there was a deficit the Commission of the Caisse would arrange, in concert with the Egyptian Government, how to meet it; but that no reduction in the interest of the Debt could take place. After discussion, in which we offered to give our proposal a duration of only three years, the French took it *ad referendum*. On the following day, the 29th of July, no answer having been received from the French Government, we made, on a suggestion from Count Nigra, the following amended proposal:—That after the interest on the New Loan, which would form the first charge on the Revenues of Egypt, the next charge should be the interest on all the existing loans, less ½ per cent; that the third charge should be the administrative expenses; that the fourth should be the ½ per cent, so far as the balance would allow, and that if there was any surplus it should be divided between the Sinking Fund and the Egyptian Exchequer; and that this arrangement should be for three years. To this, on the 2nd of August, the French made their final counter-proposal, which we rejected.

"That the New Loan should be made in Privileged Stock, which would be the first charge on the Revenues; that the second charge should be the full interest on the other loans, but that the Sinking Fund should be suspended for three years; that the third charge should be the administrative charges as we had settled them; that any balance should go to the Egyptian Exchequer; that any deficiency should be reported to the Commission of the Caisse, to consist of seven members, who would arrange with the Egyptian Government how to meet it. If this involved a reduction of interest it could only be effected by an unanimous vote of the Commissioners. If they differed, the matter would be referred to the Great Powers; that the inquiry into the land revenue should be undertaken and the result brought before a meeting of the Conference in 1887."

Your Lordships will have perceived that the last proposal of the French Government differed from ours in two respects—first, as to the mode of raising the New Loan on which both Governments were willing to arrive, and might easily have arrived at an agreement; secondly, as to the manner in which the necessary charges of the administration and the interest of the present Debt shall be dealt with. The French plan, in our judgment, would produce a normal deficit of £500,000, or, according to the Egyptian authorities, of £1,000,000 a-year, leaving to the Commission of the Caisse, whose official duty it is to represent the creditors, not the Egyptian debtors, to decide how far, from year to year, this deficiency is to be made good, thus, practically, excluding the remedy of any reduction of the interest unless, after an indefinite lapse of time, the Representatives of the Powers should agree unanimously to it. This would have given to the Caisse, not merely the addition of some useful powers of check and investigation such as was provided for in the Anglo-French Agreement; but would have given to it the complete control of the government and affairs of Egypt. It is a great misfortune that France and England could not come conscientiously to an agreement, especially as if we had done so the other Powers were ready to concur in it. No one can deplore this more than Her Majesty's Government; but I cannot altogether regret, if the disagreement was inevitable, that the Ultimatum of the French Government should be one which I believe your Lordships will unanimously be of opinion it was impossible for us to accept. I hope that this House will understand that, in saying this, I do not pretend to criticize the conduct of France in wishing to defend the rights of her subjects. Even if so large a number of Egyptian securities were not held in this country, I should entirely sympathize with the French Government in the desire that rights secured—though in different circumstances—under International Agreement to individuals should, if it were possible, be maintained. But the view which we desired to place before the Powers, parties to this International Agreement, was that, while Egypt was bound to do her best to meet the claims upon her, it was the duty of all of us to see that Egypt was placed in a position in which she could live. It has been asked whether Her Majesty's Government applied to Germany to mediate. Now, certainly, I thought it my duty to urge strongly upon the Representatives of all the Powers the hope that, in the interests of Egypt, we should receive their support. It was not likely that I should except such a Power as Germany—whose attitude towards us about Egypt has been of a very friendly character—from this appeal, or that I should conceal my belief that her influence in Europe might be of great use to Egypt in this crisis. I did not ask for the mediation of Germany or of any other Power, though I do not see what objection there would have been in doing so if there had been a chance of mediation being acceptable and accepted on a satisfactory basis. I must state how grateful we feel to Italy for the support she has given us, a support which seems to us to be based on a very friendly feeling to this country and on an enlightened interest in the welfare of Egypt. We also appreciate the assistance given us by Turkey, as a proof that our consistent adherence to our word was not without its effect upon the Sovereign of the Ottoman Empire. I must add, that we have no just reason to complain of the neutral attitude of the great military States. Knowing that the decision of the Powers must always be unanimous, and can never be decided by a majority, and perceiving a divergence between two of the Powers, both as to facts and as to principles, it was of course a great temptation to avoid pronouncing an opinion which would not at the time be decisive. Be that as it may, the Conference having adjourned without an Agreement places a great responsibility upon us. We have recovered our perfect freedom of action; but it will require the most careful consideration how we shall use it. Her Majesty's Government have in contemplation a preliminary step which I should hope to be able to describe to-morrow.

THE MARQUESS OF SALISBURY: My Lords, I can only heartily congratulate Her Majesty's Government on having got rid of this Conference. I believe it was founded on a misconception. It was founded on an attribution of a higher international sanction to the provisions of the Law of Liquidation than that law justly deserves, and, Her Majesty's Government having unnecessarily tied their own hands, it required all these dangerous and clumsy expedients for the purpose of untying them again. There was a great danger—a danger which I think the event has proved—that if this Conference had come to a decision, those engagements which appear in the Anglo-French Agreement with respect to the powers of the Caisse would have developed, as we all feared they would, into a Multiple Control. The very readiness shown by the French Government to seize and extend and expand the powers of the Caisse proved the importance which they attached to that organization; and I think Her Majesty's Government took alarm, not quite too late, but very late indeed, when they saw that by giving the power of the purse practically to the Caisse, we gave to them the power of the Government altogether, and it is my pleasure to congratulate Egypt on having escaped from the permanent dominion of the tribunal which was dissolved on Saturday, because those same Powers that met there, and were unable to agree even upon the principles of their action, would have had, if the original Agreement had been carried out, to decide again and again upon questions vital to the conduct of finance, and therefore to the conduct of good government in Egypt; and Egypt would have met in their Conference with the same inability to view her interests or duties from the same point of view that brought the enterprize of Her Majesty's Government to so inauspicious a conclusion upon Saturday. I think that we cannot distrust too much the attempt to manage details by the mechanism of any kind of Multiple International Control. The very circumstances on which the noble Lord has dwelt—that all the decisions of the tribunal must be taken unanimously—is in itself quite sufficient to incapacitate any such machine from any effective government of any country that is confided to it. But, my Lords, I do not wish to criticize at any length the statement of the noble Lord, which, no doubt, is as clear as could be expected under the circumstances which are necessarily more or less complicated. I do not understand the application of the pleasant apologue which he told us from the history of Charles Fox, that if the owners did not agree the handicapper got the money. The owners on this occasion are England and France; but who is the handicapper? Who has got the money on this occasion? Obviously somebody—some very powerful person—somebody who will not trust them—somebody who has got advantages which they have not got. I shall not mention who that is, for I have not the advantage of the noble Earl's assistance to indicate the personage who must be considered as keeping the money on this occasion. But I am afraid that in the future the truth of the noble Earl's apologue will be shown. But, after all, these are matters of the past, and I do not wish to exaggerate their importance. I am sorry that the noble Lord has thought it necessary to renew his adhesion to what I consider are the absolutely extinct provisions of the Anglo-French Convention; but I hope we may believe that, having been thrown, as the Prime Minister said, into abeyance, no authority which can exist can call them back into activity. But I cannot help being very much interested in the last statement of the noble Earl—that he was conscious that a great responsibility rested on Her Majesty's Government, and that he was about to-morrow to state the first step which they were going to take in the discharge of that responsibility. Well, we shall await that announcement with the very greatest interest, because the problem before us is one which, undoubtedly, at first sight, seems to require all the skill of Her Majesty's Government to solve. By the hypothesis on which the Conference was dissolved, the very resources which are at present at the command of the Government of Egypt are insufficient for carrying on the government of the country and paying its debts. It is not a question of there being a difficulty; there is an impossibility. According to the view of Her Majesty's Government, and owing to the manner in which they elected to close the Conference, it is impossible, while paying the Debt, to satisfy, with justice to the Egyptian people, the present exigencies of the Government. Well, but by the acknowledgment of the noble Earl again, they are not able to reduce the interest of the Debt without the consent of the Powers, which they do not possess. They are not able to reduce the cost of the government of Egypt, because that is the ground on which they have dissolved the Conference. The money must be found somewhere, and they cannot get it from the credit or resources of the English Government, because they have taken no Vote of Parliament for that purpose; and, therefore, they are at present in the condition of having found that certain money, by their own most solemn assertions, was indispensably necessary, and having, by assertions equally solemn, ascertained there are no resources from which that money can be drawn. I shall listen with great interest to the account to-morrow how they propose to solve this problem; but a discussion of the Conference itself is premature until the Papers are placed before us.

LORD HOUGHTON: With regard to the Egyptian accounts, I wish to put a Question to my noble Friend the Secretary of State for Foreign Affairs, because, by some misapprehension, a rumour has gone abroad, and it is mentioned by a public print—one of the best informed upon Egyptian affairs—I wish to know whether there is any ground for any suspicion that these accounts are unsatisfactory or inaccurate; and whether the criticisms of the French or any other experts justify such statements?

EARL GRANVILLE: The Question of my noble Friend is a very natural one, because one gentleman referred to is a near relative of my noble Friend. The report was founded upon a misunderstanding or misapprehension. There was no accusation made against the form of the accounts, or the manner in which they were kept. The question as to the difference of opinion was a difference as to the estimates of revenue arising from the Land Tax, and that had nothing to do with the Accountant's office. I am glad to take the opportunity of stating that no two gentlemen could have done their work more efficiently than those upon whom the duties devolved, and their work has been performed very much to their credit with the assistance of a staff of *employés* which has been wonderfully diminished, and which has been almost exclusively confined to the Natives of the country.

CITY OF LONDON—THE BENEFICE OF ST. OLAVE, JEWRY.

QUESTION. OBSERVATIONS.

THE EARL OF MILLTOWN, in rising to ask, Why the benefice of Saint Olave, Jewry, in the City of London, of which the Lord Chancellor is the patron, has been left vacant for two years, notwithstanding the repeated prayers of the parishioners for the appointment of some godly clergyman as rector? said, that on this site there had been a church for over 700 years, and now a scheme had been set on foot to unite the parish to that of St. Margaret's, and to secularize the church. The church was built by Sir Christopher Wren, and hundreds, perhaps thousands, of City worthies lay buried in its vaults. The inhabitants were prepared to use almost any means to prevent the desecration of the dead which the sale of the site would entail. In some cases, no doubt, it was inevitable that this should take place; but the inhabitants of the parish denied that this was the case here. If the scheme were carried out, one church would have to serve for seven parishes. It was true that the congregation had been extremely small; but that had been owing largely to the fact of its rector having been an absentee for many years, and clergymen of neighbouring parishes had found themselves able to fill their churches. The population of the district was increasing, and it was probable that a large amount of dwellings for the working classes would be erected in it. He thought that this was not a time to deprive the City of an interesting relic such as this church. In conclusion, he begged to ask the Question of which he had given Notice.

THE LORD CHANCELLOR, in reply, said, that he would not have permitted a union of those two parishes to take place, if it had not appeared to him that a strong and clear case for it had been made out. The two parishes of St. Margaret and St Olave had happened to be vacant at the same time, and it had been suggested to him that it would be desirable to take the opportunity for their union. The suggestion had come from the Bishop of London, and it had also been supported by persons deeply interested in the welfare of the Church and its efficiency in that part of the City, and who had contributed largely out of their own means towards those objects. The aggregate population of both parishes was about 650. The Church of St Margaret, which was the larger and better in all ways of the two churches, was within a stone's throw of St. Olave's, and in it there was ample accommodation not only for the whole united congregations, but for considerably more people. As to the architecture of St. Olave's Church, opinions might differ; but, from what he had heard, he should by no means think that it was either one of the most interesting or most beautiful of those built after the Great Fire. He had carefully inquired into the matter, and had come to the conclusion that there was a strong case established for the union, provided the necessary consents were obtained. That had been done, according to his own view of the law applicable to the case, which was confirmed by the Law Officers of the Crown. The clergyman whom he had appointed to St Margaret's had undertaken the duty on the understanding that if the union took place he would accept the charge of the united parishes. The whole, or nearly the whole, of the endowments of St. Olave's would be devoted to the erection and endowment of a church in some other district where it was really wanted.

THE BISHOP OF LONDON said, that Parliament had sanctioned the general principle of the Act under which this arrangement had been carried out 24 years ago, and he had only acted in this case upon the principles which Parliament had so sanctioned. This appeared to him to be exactly one of those cases which the Act was intended to meet. The church with which it was proposed to unite this one was within a few minutes' walk of St. Olave, Jewry. When there were at least 30 churches needed in Metropolitan districts which were for the most part unable to provide places of worship for themselves, it was desirable that when a church was no longer required the endowments should be applied in supplying needs which were very great and urgent. At a Vestry representing the united parishes the scheme was approved, with only two dissenting voices.

INFANTS BILL.—(No. 237.)

(*The Lord Fitzgerald.*)

SECOND READING.

Order of the Day for the Second Reading read.

LORD FITZGERALD, in moving that the Bill be now read a second time, said, the principle of the Bill was to recognize the mother's right, in the event of her surviving her husband, to be the guardian of her children either alone, if he had appointed no guardian, or conjointly with any guardian appointed by him. By the Common Law, the father's right to the custody and care of his infant children was fully recognized. It was subsequently, to some extent, affected by statute, especially the Infants Protection Act, 1873, and controlled by the Lord Chancellor, representing the Queen as *Parens Patriæ*, where infants had been made wards of Courts in respect of their property. It was not intended to interfere with that branch of the law as it now existed. By an Act passed in the 12th year of the Reign of Charles II., the father was enabled to appoint guardians of his children, who after his death were clothed with very large powers over the infant children, their education, and their property, to the entire exclusion of the surviving mother. If the father did not appoint guardians, then the mother became guardian for nurture during the period of nurture; but full guardianship could only be obtained through the medium of Chancery. The surviving mother had no power to appoint a guardian to act after her decease. When the Statute of Charles II. was passed, the rights of a married woman and the claims of a mother had but small recognition in the law. Now, with the light of advancing civilization, the situation was entirely altered. The last relics of feudal barbarism in ignoring women's rights were rapidly disappearing. Under that Statute power was given to the father to appoint guardians to act after his death. Great cruelty was too often practised on the surviving mother, and it often happened that, although she was blameless in conduct and of unblemished character, her infant children were taken from her and committed to the charge of strangers during that period of life when they most required that maternal care and maternal love for which there could be no compensation. Their Lordships could not fail to recall to memory, even within the last few years, some instances of the greatest cruelty arising from this state of the law. The great object which the present Bill sought to effect was to redress that crying grievance. Accordingly, the effect of the 2nd clause would be to constitute the surviving mother guardian of her infant children in conjunction with any guardian appointed by the father. The 3rd clause permitted both parents to appoint guardians to act jointly after the decease of the survivor, and enabled the father to appoint a guardian to act with the surviving mother; and by the 4th sub-clause power was given in certain grave cases to the mother to apply to the Court during her husband's lifetime to appoint a guardian to act after her decease in conjunction with her surviving husband. The remainder of the Bill consisted of procedure, but of an important and valuable character. It clothed the Court with new and full powers to take order for the welfare of infants on the application of the mother during the life of the father—

> "Having regard to the welfare of the infant, the conduct of the parents, and the wishes alike of the father and of the mother."

It gave a new jurisdiction to the County Courts, but rendered safe by a right to each party to have the case at once removed to Chancery, coupled with a summary right of appeal from every order made by a County Court Judge. He had only further to add that the Bill did not interfere with the right of the father during his life, or with the rights of property, and left wholly untouched the burning question of religious teaching. He hoped it might be possible to pass the Bill this Session.

Moved, "That the Bill be now read 2ª."—(*The Lord Fitzgerald.*)

Earl Cairns said, this was a Bill which unquestionably made the largest change in the law of this country relating to families that had been seen for the last 200 years. He desired to point out to their Lordships that the Bill had been printed and circulated only on Saturday afternoon, and that on Monday they were asked to assent to the principle by reading the measure a second time. Considering the circumstances in which they were placed at that late period of the Session, he thought this was rather hard on their Lordships. Various Bills had been relinquished on the ground that they would lead to a great deal of debate; and as he was certain this Bill would lead to a considerable discussion he did not think it possible to do otherwise than to refer it to a Select Committee of their Lordships' House. Every sentence of the Bill would require the greatest consideration. He should like to abstain from offering any opinion as to whether he agreed to the necessity for an alteration of the law; he would say nothing about that; but he held a very strong opinion that it would be utterly impossible to pass this Bill in its present shape. The proposals which it made would lead to squabbles on all the families in the country. It proposed to give a complete blank cheque to the County Court Judges to act in all cases where the guardians of the children differed. In conclusion, he implored their Lordships, before they made a change in the law, to appoint a Select Committee to inquire into the matter.

THE LORD CHANCELLOR said, he thought that the principle of the Bill was sound, and that the objections to its provisions were capable of sufficient answers. The existing law in regard to the rights of the mother respecting her children was unjust and unsatisfactory, and ought to be amended in the direction which the Bill proposed to alter it. He contended that the mother had natural rights as strong as those of the father, and there were many things in which she was more competent to decide, especially as to daughters under age. Why should not the natural equality of her rights be recognized, while both parents were living, or if she were the survivor? And, when both were dead, what ground was there, in nature or in reason, for refusing her all voice and power in the selection of those who should then take care of the orphan children, some of whom might be girls of tender years? Was it not fair that the widow should be the guardian, if her husband had appointed no guardians, and if he had, that she should be a joint guardian? As to squabbles, and interference of County Court Judges, he could not conceive why the harmony of any families, in which there were at present no squabbles, should be disturbed by a legal recognition of the mother's natural and moral rights, and, as some Court must have authority, in cases of difference, the poor as well as the rich must be able to go to one. But as the noble and learned Earl opposite (Earl Cairns) considered that it would be impossible to discuss it satisfactorily this Session, it would, of course, be useless to proceed with it.

LORD BRAMWELL expressed his entire concurrence with everything which had been said by the noble and learned Earl opposite (Earl Cairns). The Bill might be made the means of a great deal of mischief. The law with respect to the guardianship of infants needed some amendment; but it was a most difficult and delicate subject, and required the greatest care.

LORD FITZGERALD said, he had hoped that he should have been able to remove all the objections which his noble and learned Friends had raised to the Bill in Committee. He thought he had done no harm in eliciting that discussion; on the contrary, he had assisted in attracting public attention to a great and admitted grievance. In view of the statements of noble and learned Lords, he considered he would best do his duty at present by not pressing the Motion for the second reading of the Bill.

Motion (by leave of the House) *withdrawn.*

Order of the Day for the Second Reading *discharged.*

House adjourned at a quarter past Six o'clock, till To-morrow, a quarter past Ten o'clock.

HOUSE OF COMMONS,

Monday, 4th August, 1884.

MINUTES.] SELECT COMMITTEE — *Report* — Thames River Preservation [No. 321].

SUPPLY — *considered in Committee* — CIVIL SERVICE ESTIMATES: CLASS V.—FOREIGN AND COLONIAL SERVICES, Votes 1 to 6, 8 and 9. CLASS IV.—EDUCATION, SCIENCE AND ART, Votes 2, 3, 8 to 11 inclusive, 13a, 16 and 17.

Resolutions [August 1] *reported.*

PUBLIC BILLS — *Second Reading* — Corrupt Practices (Suspension of Elections) [314].

Re-committed — Report — Considered — Third Reading — Supreme Court of Judicature Amendment [307] and *passed.*

QUESTIONS.

LAND LAW (IRELAND) ACT, 1881—FAIR RENTS—SIR RICHARD WALLACE.

MR. GRAY asked the Chief Secretary to the Lord Lieutenant of Ireland, Whether he is aware that, in the agreements for fair rents settled out of court by Sir Richard Wallace with his tenants, a proviso is inserted binding the tenant, in addition to the stated rent, to pay court leet and all other customary dues; whether this, in some cases, if enforced, would make the new rent higher than the old; whether the agent is in the habit of not enforcing these additional payments, save in cases where tenants may make themselves obnoxious to him; and, whether such agreements are legally binding upon the tenants?

THE SOLICITOR GENERAL FOR IRELAND (Mr. WALKER) (for Mr. TRE-

VELYAN): The Land Commissioners state that in some agreements for fair rents lodged with them from Sir Richard Wallace's estate, it has been stipulated that leet and other customary dues should be paid in addition to the fixed rent. The Commissioners would have preferred that the whole rent should have been stated in one sum; but as the agreements, with the consent of the parties interested, ran in a different form, the Commissioners did not feel justified in rejecting them. They are legally binding in their present form. The Commissioners were informed by Sir Richard Wallace's agent that the leet money on the estate was only 8*d*. from each head tenant, and 4*d*. from each cottier tenant, and there would be this addition to the rent if enforced.

SIR RICHARD WALLACE: I would wish to supplement this Question. It is asked whether the effect of this agreement was to make the new rents higher than the old? My answer is, decidedly not. [*Cries of* "Order, order!"]

MR. GRAY: I rise to Order. I did not ask the hon. Baronet a Question.

MR. SPEAKER: The hon. Baronet is not entitled to answer a Question which has already been answered by a Member of the Government.

SIR RICHARD WALLACE: I wish to make a personal explanation.

MR. SPEAKER: The hon. Baronet can make a personal explanation.

SIR RICHARD WALLACE was understood to say that the new rent could not be higher than the old rent. The amount was too trivial, the leet money being 8*d*. for each head tenant and 4*d*. for each cottier tenant—the agent never made any difference between the tenants. He (Sir Richard Wallace) was convinced that his agent was too straightforward a man to have laid himself open to such an unwarrantable charge.

MR. GRAY: The explanation of the hon. Baronet may have been, no doubt, satisfactory to himself; but I did not hear a word of it.

POOR LAW (IRELAND)—ELY DISPENSARY—USE OF BUILDING FOR PARTY PURPOSES.

MR. HEALY asked the Chief Secretary to the Lord Lieutenant of Ireland, Whether anything has been done in reference to the use of the Ely Dispensary, Derrygonnelly, as an Orange Lodge?

The Solicitor General for Ireland

THE SOLICITOR GENERAL FOR IRELAND (Mr. WALKER) (for Mr. TREVELYAN): The Board of Guardians have appointed another Committee to inquire into the matter, and for that purpose to meet the Committee of Management of the Ely Dispensary on Monday the 18th instant. As this day is so far distant, the District Inspector of the Local Government Board has been instructed to obtain, if possible, information as to the facts of the tenure of the dispensary building.

IRELAND—THE VISIT OF THE LORD LIEUTENANT TO BELFAST—DISPLAY OF FLAGS.

MR. BERESFORD (for Mr. CORRY) asked the Chief Secretary to the Lord Lieutenant of Ireland, Is it a fact that Mr. George H. Thorman, licensed publican, living in Ballymacault, Belfast, had suspended from his windows for ten hours, on the 12th July, a Union Jack and a Stars and Stripes without any interference on the part of the authorities, and that at about eight o'clock the same evening, at the request of a sergeant of Constabulary, he immediately had them removed; but, notwithstanding his prompt action, a summons was issued against him at the suit of Head Constable Reilly; was the summons issued by the directions of or with the consent of the District Inspector of Constabulary; is it a fact that for several years licensed publicans in Belfast have exhibited flags on various occasions without any prohibition or criminal prosecution; is it a fact that, on the occasion of the recent visit of the Lord Lieutenant to Belfast, a publican at the corner of York Street and Donegal Street had suspended several flags, and also had an arch extended from his premises across the latter street, and, if so, was he remonstrated with, or has he been prosecuted for the offence; is it a fact that, on the same occasion, the same, or similar, flags for which Mr. Sherman was summoned were suspended from the police barracks in Ballymacault; and, is it the intention of the Executive that, for the future, loyal publicans in Ireland shall be prohibited from indicating their loyalty by any flag or symbol?

THE SOLICITOR GENERAL FOR IRELAND (Mr. WALKER) (for Mr. TREVELYAN): The facts are stated with substantial accuracy in the Question. In the case of Mr. Sherman, the summons was issued by direction of the District Inspector, who was not at the time aware that the flags had been so promptly removed when objected to by the police. The magistrates, in consideration of this promptitude, did not convict, but adjourned the case for a year—which is tantamount to a dismissal. With regard to the general question, it is right to observe that the display of flags from police stations and public-houses cannot properly be considered as on the same footing. The display of non-Party flag from a police station is not illegal; but from a public-house the display of any flags or emblems, not the usual sign of the house, is. [6 & 7 *Will.* IV. c. 38, s. 8.] The whole case forming the subject of the Question is under the consideration of the Inspector General, and further inquiry is being made into the action of the police, with which the Inspector General is not satisfied.

INLAND NAVIGATION AND DRAINAGE (IRELAND)—DRAINAGE OF THE RIVER BARROW.

MR. ARTHUR O'CONNOR asked the Financial Secretary, If he will lay upon the Table the report of the Surveyor of the Board of Works, Ireland, respecting the drainage of the Barrow, without waiting for the Report of the Valuator; and, whether he can say approximately at what dates the Valuator is expected to finish the district from Monasterevan to Athy, and when he expects to be able to commence with those of Rosenallis, Phillipstown, and Rathangan severally?

MR. COURTNEY: The final Report of the Chief Engineer to the Board of Works cannot be made until the valuation has been completed; but I can undertake to lay a preliminary Report, giving the general facts of the case, with an approximate estimate of the costs, before the House on Thursday next. As regards the valuator's work, we are constantly urging expedition; and we hope that the heaviest part of the work of the entire district will be completed by the end of September next.

EGYPT—THE PRESS LAW.

MR. HEALY asked the Under Secretary of State for Foreign Affairs, Whether, on the demand of the British auhorities or otherwise, Nubar Pasha is engaged in elaborating a Law against the liberty of the press in Egypt; if not, why has Nubar sent a circular to the Consuls General representing the Powers, asking their support in this sense; whether the proposed press measures are mainly directed against *The Bosphore Egyptien*, and *The Pyramides*; and, if it is the fact, as stated in *The Fortnightly Review* for August, in an article on Nubar Pasha, that previously Sir Evelyn Baring refused the demand of Mr. Clifford Lloyd to use his influence with M. Barrière to allow the *Bosphore* to be suppressed?

LORD EDMOND FITZMAURICE: The attention of Her Majesty's Government was called by the Egyptian Government to the difficulties under which they laboured with regard to Press offences, owing to the immunities enjoyed by foreigners under the Capitulations, and to the refusal of some of the Foreign Representatives to co-operate with them in enforcing the Press Laws in the case of newspapers conducted by their co-nationalists. Her Majesty's Representatives at the principal capitals in Europe were instructed last month to bring the matter before the Governments to which they are accredited. There is no ground for the statement in *The Fortnightly Review* quoted by the hon. Member.

LAW AND JUSTICE (IRELAND)—GLIN PETTY SESSIONS—CASE OF DANIEL M'COY.

MR. SYNAN asked the Chief Secretary to the Lord Lieutenant of Ireland, Whether Daniel M'Coy, of Ballyhahill, in the county of Limerick, a member of the late Land League and of the National League was, on the 24th instant, sentenced to a month's imprisonment, upon a charge of being drunk and disorderly, by Captain Hatchell, at Glin Petty Sessions, without the option of a fine, as is usual, and without examining the evidence against the charge; whether on the same occasion he sentenced two other persons for the same offence, which they admitted, to a fine of 2*s.* 6*d.* and 10*s.* respectively; and, whether he will recommend His Excellency the Lord Lieutenant to commute said imprisonment to a fine, or to remit or reduce said sentence, and enable the said Daniel M'Coy to return home to save his harvest?

THE SOLICITOR GENERAL FOR IRELAND (Mr. WALKER) (for Mr. TREVELYAN): Daniel M'Coy was sentenced to a month's imprisonment for being drunk and very disorderly while in charge of a horse and car at Glin, where a number of people were assembled on the occasion of a regatta. The other fines referred to in the Question were imposed for simple cases of drunkenness. There does not appear to be any reason to question the propriety of the exercise of the magistrate's discretion; but it is, of course, open for M'Coy, or any person on his behalf, to appeal to the Lord Lieutenant for a mitigation of the sentence.

THE MAURITIUS.

MR. COLERIDGE KENNARD asked the Under Secretary of State for the Colonies, Is it the intention of the Government to grant the people of Mauritius the same privileges in responsible Government as promised to the people of Jamaica?

MR. EVELYN ASHLEY: The Secretary of State has announced his readiness to sanction the elective principle being introduced into the Legislature of Mauritius, and is awaiting detailed proposals which will then be considered by him. The detailed provisions will be, however, probably somewhat different from those in Jamaica. I would point out that the wording of the Question conveys an inaccurate impression, because in neither case is it intended to introduce responsible government as established in the self-governing Colonies.

COMMISSIONERS OF NATIONAL EDUCATION (IRELAND) — STEWARDSTOWN NATIONAL SCHOOL.

MR. BERESFORD (for Mr. MACARTNEY) asked the Chief Secretary to the Lord Lieutenant of Ireland, Whether he is aware that the Roman Catholic National School, Stewardstown, county Tyrone, has been used for a considerable time as a place of practice by a so-called Nationalist Band; whether this has been done with the knowledge of the Patron and schoolmaster; and, whether it is in accordance with the rules laid down by the Commissioners of National Education?

THE SOLICITOR GENERAL FOR IRELAND (Mr. WALKER) (for Mr. TREVELYAN): Over two months ago, when the Commissioners discovered that the band had been permitted to play in the schoolroom, they at once, on the 30th of May, wrote to the manager—

"Expressing their regret that the manager should have permitted the school-house to be used for purposes leading to serious local controversies, and requesting him to take immediate steps to have the Commissioners' rules faithfully complied with in future."

The manager, on receipt of this letter, assured the Board that the breach of the rules would be entirely discontinued.

ROYAL IRISH CONSTABULARY — DR. MADIGAN, MEDICAL OFFICER.

MR. SYNAN asked the Chief Secretary to the Lord Lieutenant of Ireland, Whether Dr. Madigan of Dromcollagher, in the county of Limerick, was removed as Medical Officer of the Constabulary at Springfield Castle and Clonmore in said county, and another doctor appointed, although the latter lived over eight miles from the stations, and Dr. Madigan was resident within two miles; whether the reason given by the Inspector General was that the stations were not in Dr. Madigan's dispensary district; whether the Constabulary station of Mount Kennedy is in Dr. Madigan's dispensary district, and why another doctor has been appointed medical officer to it; and, whether Dr. Madigan is a Catholic, and the doctors appointed by the Inspector General are Protestants?

THE SOLICITOR GENERAL FOR IRELAND (Mr. WALKER) (for Mr. TREVELYAN): Dr. Madigan was never appointed by the Inspector General to be medical attendant of the Springfield Castle and Clonmore stations. But in 1882, when these stations, which are merely protection posts, were established, he was allowed by the County Inspector to act temporarily in that capacity pending a regular appointment. In conformity with a section of the Code then in force, but afterwards repealed, the appointment was given to the dispensary doctor of the district—Dr. Bolster, who holds a dispensary quite close to the two protection posts. With regard to the Ballykennedy station, it is true that it is in Dr. Madigan's dispensary district; but the section of the Code above referred to, and which gave dispensary doctors a prior claim to these appointments, was cancelled last year, as it was found not to work satisfactorily. The occurred before the Ballykennedy appointment was made, and it was given to Dr. Mahony, who resides about two miles off, instead of Dr. Mulligan, who resides nine [illegible] away. The religious profession of the several gentlemen is as stated in the question, but in no way influenced an appointment.

LAW AND JUSTICE (SCOTLAND)—ISLAND OF LEWIS—CONVICTION FOR ASSAULT.

MR. DICK PEDDIE (for Mr. J. W. BARCLAY) asked the Secretary of State for the Home Department, Whether his attention has been called to the following report of legal proceedings in Lewis:—

[illegible]

whether he is aware that John Ross, who presided as procurator fiscal, is also law agent, or partner of the law agents for the sole proprietrix of Lewis, and chief official for the management of the whole of the Island; and, whether, considering that it is alleged on behalf of the defence that authority was granted to build the house in question, that the warrant granted for its demolition was irregular, he will order a special and independent inquiry into the circumstances of this case and the administration of justice in Lewis?

THE LORD ADVOCATE (Mr. J. B. BALFOUR) (in reply) I have seen the report referred to. I have already stated in answer to previous Questions that Mr. John Ross, Procurator Fiscal, is a member of a firm who are local law agents for the proprietrix of the Island of Lewis, but that he is not factor or land agent for the estate, which I suppose is meant by the expression "chief official for the management of the whole of the Island." I do not find any irregularity in the legal proceedings, or any ground for suggesting that there has been any miscarriage of justice, and I do not see any reason for ordering further inquiry.

REGISTRATION OF VOTERS (IRELAND)—NEW REVISION COURT, MONAGHAN.

MR. HEALY asked Mr. Solicitor General for Ireland, At whose instance was the order appearing in last Gazette made appointing Clones as an additional Revision Court for Monaghan; who suggested the division of the districts given in the Schedule; can he explain why, although continual applications have been made to the Lord Lieutenant for similar facilities in County Dublin, they have always been refused; and, what measures may be taken to procure the additional Courts required for the Metropolitan county?

THE SOLICITOR GENERAL FOR IRELAND (Mr. WALKER) (for Mr. TREVELYAN) The order was made in compliance with a Memorial signed by a large number of the inhabitants of the polling districts of Clones, Newbliss, and Rosslea, and also by the Lieutenant of the county and several magistrates residing in the district. The County Court Judge reported that the change would be a great accommodation to the residents of the district. With regard to the county of Dublin, it appears that on the 21st of August in last year Memorials were received, praying to have additional Revision Courts appointed for the county; and the applicants were informed that, having regard to the late period at which the application was made, and to the fact that the Quarter Sessions had been then fixed by the Recorder, and to the probability of legislation on the subject, it was not then considered advisable to make any change. The matter stands differently now. The subject of the Memorials is now receiving attention, and it is hoped that any changes necessary will be made.

LAW AND JUSTICE (IRELAND)—TYRONE ASSIZES—"QUEEN v. BEATTY."

Colonel KING-HARMAN asked the Chief Secretary to the Lord Lieutenant of Ireland, Whether his attention has been directed to the case of assault entitled the "Queen v. Beatty," tried at the last Tyrone Assizes; whether, on the trial, a complete alibi on behalf of Beatty was proved, and whether the learned Judge who tried the case, after hearing the evidence, directed the jury to acquit Beatty on the ground that there was no evidence to sustain the charge; whether this Beatty is the same person who was returned for trial by Captain Whelan on the charge of the murder of Francis M'Glone, and whether such charge was subsequently withdrawn by the Crown, and the charge of assault on O'Neill, the companion of M'Glone on the night of his death, was the only charge upon which Beatty was tried at the Assizes; whether Francis M'Glone made a deposition before his death, and therein stated that he was so drunk he could not blame any person; whether the coroner's jury which inquired into the death of Francis M'Glone was composed of six Protestants and six Catholics, and returned a verdict that deceased came by his death by brain fever brought on by a blow or fall, but expressly stated that they could place no reliance on the evidence of the witness O'Neill; whether this O'Neill is the same witness upon whose uncorroborated evidence Captain Whelan, R.M., returned Beatty for trial, and whether, on such examination, Captain Whelan refused to hear any evidence tendered on behalf of Beatty, and also refused to admit Beatty to bail; whether the learned Judge on the trial reflected on the magistrate who sent forward such a case, and said he ought to have received evidence tendered before him on behalf of Beatty; and, whether, having regard to the fact that Beatty is a young man of most respectable character, the sole support of his parents, and has been detained in jail without any evidence to warrant such detention for upwards of five months, and has been obliged to pay the expenses of his trial when deprived of the means of livelihood, the Government are prepared to recommend any compensation to him in consequence?

The SOLICITOR GENERAL for IRELAND (Mr. Walker) for (Mr. Trevelyan): It is true that in the assault case the Judge directed the jury to acquit Beatty after hearing the evidence for the defence. This evidence was not before the magistrates who returned him for trial. He is the same person who was returned for trial by Captain Whelan for the murder of Francis M'Glone. That charge was not withdrawn by the Crown; but the Grand Jury ignored the bill for manslaughter, and, consequently, it was for the assault on O'Neill that Beatty was tried. Francis M'Glone made an information before his death, in which he stated that he went into a public-house in Dungannon with Arthur O'Neill, and a strange man, afterwards identified by O'Neill as Beatty, but that he did not remember anything after that, as he was drunk. The Coroner's jury was composed of an equal number of Protestants and Catholics, and they found a verdict that M'Glone died from inflammation of the brain brought on by a fall or a blow. They did not add that no reliance could be placed on the evidence of O'Neill. He was corroborated by several persons as to Beatty having been in the public-house on the occasion; but there was a discrepancy in some points between his evidence and that of other witnesses. When Captain Whelan returned Beatty for trial, he did not refuse to examine witnesses for the defence. On the contrary, he did examine one witness who was about proceeding to America, and Beatty's solicitor said he would reserve his defence for the Assizes. The Government are not aware that the learned Judge who tried the case made any reflection on the magistrate who sent it for trial, or made the statement referred to. The District Inspector, who was in Court, reports that he heard nothing of the kind said. Beatty is not the sole support of his parents, as his father is in service. It is believed that local subscriptions have been made to defray his expenses; but, whether that be so or not, the Crown are not prepared to recommend any claim for compensation.

SUNDAY CLOSING (IRELAND)—ARRESTS FOR DRUNKENNESS, &c.

MR. WARTON asked the Chief Secretary to the Lord Lieutenant of Ireland, in reference to the recent Return [headed "Arrests for Drunkenness, &c, (Irelan)," and numbered 259], at what hour Sunday, for the purposes of that Return, is supposed to begin; and, whether such hour is not that of eight of the clock in the forenoon, or how otherwise?

THE SOLICITOR GENERAL FOR IRELAND (Mr. WALKER) (for Mr. TREVELYAN): For the purposes of the Return, Sunday was calculated as beginning immediately after 12 o'clock on Saturday night and ending at 12 o'clock on Sunday night.

PREVENTION OF CRIME (IRELAND) ACT, 1882—PATRICK FARRY—COMPENSATION MONEY.

COLONEL KING-HARMAN asked the Chief Secretary to the Lord Lieutenan of Ireland, Why it is that Patrick Farry, who was so seriously injured when on Protection Duty at Castle Island in December 1880, as to be obliged to leave the Royal Irish Constabulary, and who was awarded, on the 1st of June last, the sum of £400 compensation under the Crimes Act, to be paid to him in three instalments, the first instalment to be paid to him forthwith, has not been paid one farthing of the money due to him?

THE SOLICITOR GENERAL FOR IRELAND (Mr. WALKER) (for Mr. TREVELYAN): The money cannot be paid until it is collected. The collection of the first instalment in this case has just been completed, with the exception of a few shillings considered irrecoverable. The amount collected—namely, £131 18*s.* 10*d.*, will be paid over to Farry in a few days.

COLONEL KING-HARMAN asked the Chief Secretary to the Lord Lieutenant of Ireland, Why it is that, in cases where compensation money has been awarded by order of the Lord Lieutenant, under the Crimes Act, to persons who have suffered from outrages in Ireland during recent years, the money awarded is not paid over at once to those who may be entitled to it; whether he is aware that great hardships and sufferings are inflicted upon the injured persons, and that the action of the law is brought into contempt by this delay; and, whether the Government will consider, during the Recess, the propriety of paying the sum awarded to injured persons without delay, and in one lump sum?

THE SOLICITOR GENERAL FOR IRELAND (Mr. WALKER) (for Mr. TREVELYAN): The money awarded cannot be paid over at once, as is suggested in this Question. It cannot be paid over till it has been collected. The collectors are members of the Constabulary, and are proceeding with the collection as rapidly as they can; and in any cases where the persons awarded compensation make a proper case for being paid whatever portion of the award has been collected, the Government ascertain the amount from the collectors and pay it over without waiting for the completion of the collection. Where no such application is received, the collection proceeds uninterruptedly until he has received the entire sum or instalments, if the collection be by instalments. The Government has no fund at its disposal out of which it could advance the compensation awarded, which is the only mode by which what is suggested in the final paragraph of this Question could be carried out.

POOR LAW (IRELAND)—ELECTION OF GUARDIANS—BALTINGLASS UNION.

MR. M'COAN asked the Chief Secretary to the Lord Lieutenant of Ireland, Whether, at the late election of a Poor Law guardian at Rathdangan, county Wicklow, Mr. Dagg, the clerk and returning officer of the Baltinglass Union, declared the result of the voting to be 72 valid votes for Cecil and 71 for Kenna; whether, at the subsequent inquiry held by Dr. M'Cabe, by order of the Local Government Board, Cecil was still found to be entitled to 72 votes, but Kenna to only 69, the reduction in his case resulting from new evidence which had not been before the returning officer when he credited him with 71; whether the vote of the Board of Guardians to raise the salary of Mr. Dagg, as clerk of the Union, from £95 to £110 a-year, was supported by guardians representing a valuation of £17,000, and was opposed by only four guardians, representing a valuation of £400; and, whether, in view of the fact that the salary of the late clerk, Mr. Cooke, was £140, and that the Local Government Board objected at the time to the reduction of this amount after his death, ten years ago, the Board will now sanction the small increase of the reduced salary which has been recently voted by so preponderant a majority of the guardians to the present clerk?

THE SOLICITOR GENERAL FOR IRELAND (Mr. WALKER) (for Mr. TREVELYAN): The facts are correctly stated in the first and second paragraphs of the Question. The proposal to raise the clerk's salary from £95 to £110 per annum was carried by a majority of 17 Guardians to four; but the Local Government Board have no Return showing the valuation of the property of these gentlemen. The question of sanctioning the proposed increase is at present under the consideration of the Board.

SOUTH AFRICA—NATAL AND ZULULAND.

MR. DILLWYN asked the Under Secretary of State for the Colonies, Whether Her Majesty's Government have now received any definite information concerning the enrolment in May last, in the Colony of Natal, of a body of Volunteers for military service in Zululand; whether he is aware that this force was organised by means of advertisements in the newspapers and of printed circulars; and, whether he can inform the House why the Natal Government did not take steps to prevent the breach of the Neutrality Laws of the Colony thus threatened?

MR. EVELYN ASHLEY: The enrolment referred to was ostensibly, at any rate, not for military service in Zululand, but for service in the Reserve, "for the protection of the property of White residents and others from Usutu marauders," to use the words of the printed Circular referred to. Sir Henry Bulwer has been informed by the Secretary of State that the issue of such an advertisement was improper, and that the proceeding was clearly an interference with his responsibility for the protection of the Reserve as Special Commissioner for Zululand, and that of Mr. Osborn, as Resident Commissioner; that it had naturally given rise to misapprehension; and that he should take such measures as might prevent its recurrence. I may add that the force collected numbered only 10, and was dispersed in a fortnight.

ARMY—PAY DEPARTMENT—QUARTERMASTERS.

MR. BIGGAR asked the Secretary of State for War, Whether it is true that the Army Quartermasters, who, until lately, were eligible for and frequently appointed to Regimental Paymasterships, have been excluded absolutely and permanently from the Army Pay Department; if so, on what grounds; whether it is the fact that they held these Paymasterships to the advantage of the Public Service; and, whether it is intended to recoup them in the amount which they have lost by being deprived of the appointment of Paymaster, with its substantial advantages in pay and retired pay?

SIR ARTHUR HAYTER: In reply to the first part of the hon. Member's Question, I have to say that since the formation of the Army Pay Department in 1878, the qualification for appointment has been the holding of the rank of captain in the Army. As I stated in reply to the hon. Member's Question on Friday last, the revised Pay Warrant rather facilitates than otherwise the admission of quartermasters into the Pay Department by reducing the qualifying commissioned service as combatant officers from ten to seven years, and admitting lieutenants as well as captains. My answer to the hon. Member's second Question is that some of the quartermasters who were appointed to be paymasters in former times gave very good service; and, in answer to the third, I have to say that it is not intended to recoup the quartermasters, since it cannot be recognized that they have sustained any loss by the recent change in the Regulations for appointments to the Pay Department.

THE ANNUAL ESTIMATES.

SIR ALEXANDER GORDON asked Mr. Chancellor of the Exchequer, If he will give to this House greater facilities for controlling the normal expenditure of the Country by causing all the Annual Estimates to be prepared upon the system adopted in the Naval Estimates for the present year, in which the items of a current year's original Estimate are shown in comparison with the corresponding items of the previous year's original Estimate, by the latter being placed in juxta-position to the former;

the items of a similar nature voted in any Supplementary Estimate for the year being shown separately below the original item, and accounted for in a separate sub-total as in the Navy Estimates. The estimated increase or decrease of any item and any vote being shown as the difference between the original Estimates, and not the difference between the original Estimate of the current year and the total of the original and the Supplementary Estimates of the previous year?

MR. COURTNEY: Perhaps my hon. and gallant Friend will allow me to answer. Directions will be given that, in future, the summer Supplementary Estimates, which are now included in the comparison of the new Estimates with the Estimates for the previous year, shall, in future, be distinctly and separately marked as "Supplementary." It is impossible to include the spring Supplementary Estimates also, as they are not voted at the time the annual Estimates are made up, but it may be said generally of them that they are balanced by savings, and involve no real addition to the Annual Expenditure.

THE CHURCH IN THE COLONIES—GRENADA.

MR. PICTON asked the Under Secretary of State for the Colonies, Whether there has been received at the Colonial Office a Petition to the Colonial Secretary from inhabitants of Grenada, asking for his interference in regard to a vote of £250 for repairing an Anglican parsonage in the town of St. George, such grant having been carried against the votes of a majority of the unofficial members of the Legislative Council, and being a violation of the Act which disestablished the Anglican Church in the Colony; and, whether any, and what, action has been or will be taken in the matter by the Colonial Secretary?

MR. EVELYN ASHLEY: Such a Petition has been received. I already answered a Question as to this on the 2nd of June, and I have little to add. We had already at that date sent a despatch to the Governor asking on what grounds the Colonial Government considered itself bound to undertake the repair of this parsonage? No reply has as yet been received.

EGYPT—OPERATIONS IN THE SOUDAN—THE ROYAL MARINES.

LORD RANDOLPH CHURCHILL (for Sir H. DRUMMOND WOLFF) asked the Secretary to the Admiralty, Whether the Officers and men of the Royal Marines recently employed in the Soudan will receive their gratuities according to the Prize Scale laid down in the Admiralty Instructions in which their corps is included?

MR. CAMPBELL-BANNERMAN: This is not a case of prize money, and we are, therefore, not bound to any prize scale; but the Army Prize Scale will, as in the case of 1882, be followed in distributing the gratuities to the Marines who served with the Army in the Soudan.

GIBRALTAR—THE SANITARY COMMISSION.

MR. ANDERSON asked the Under Secretary of State for the Colonies, If the Governor of Gibraltar has been yet able to induce civilians of position and standing to fill the vacancies in the office of Commissioner; and, if Her Majesty's Government are prepared to rescind some of the changes which have proved objectionable to the civilian population?

MR. EVELYN ASHLEY: Yes, Sir; the Governor of Gibraltar has been instructed to rescind the chief provisions of the law regulating the Sanitary Commission, to which objection was taken by the Commissioners who represented the ratepayers. It is expected that these gentlemen will now resume their functions; but there has not yet been time to receive information to that effect.

LAW AND JUSTICE (IRELAND)—DANIEL MAHONY.

MR. DEASY asked Mr. Solicitor General for Ireland, If it is a fact that the Grand Jury of the Bantry, county Cork, Quarter Sessions found a true bill against a man named Daniel Mahony, who was charged with housebreaking and robbery; whether it is a fact that, through some alleged informality in framing the indictment, the accused was not brought to trial, but liberated unconditionally; and, whether it was in consequence of the said Daniel Mahony having been a crown witness at the Cork Summer Assizes of 1883 that he was set at liberty?

THE SOLICITOR GENERAL FOR IRELAND (Mr. WALKER): Daniel Mahony was committed for trial on a charge of larceny of £10—not housebreaking, as stated in the Question. The informations did not state whether the woman from whom the money was stolen was a married woman. If so, the name of her husband should be given. When the indictment was prepared a blank for the name was left, and, unfortunately, it was afterwards overlooked by the officials, and was not discovered in time. The prosecution fell through on account of this informality; but the charge remains intact, and a fresh bill will be sent up to the next Quarter Sessions. There never was any intention of abandoning the prosecution; and the suggestion that Mahony was set at liberty because he was a Crown witness at the Cork Summer Assizes is wholly without foundation.

SOUTH AFRICA (ZULULAND)—THE RESERVE TERRITORY.

MR. GUY DAWNAY asked the Under Secretary of State for the Colonies, Whether there is any truth in the statement in *The Times* of July 21st, to the effect that—

"The present condition of the Zulu Reserve is described as being deplorable. About 1,000 rebels have collected there, centred in Inkandhla, under Dabulamanzi. These roam about as they please, simply evading the troops when in movement against them, by passing round them. The Usutus seem to consider the Imperial forces to be sent there more for their protection than for that of the loyalists whose numbers are fast diminishing,"

or in that of *The Times* of July 31st, which states that Usutu refugees in Natal have lately attempted to raid into the Reserve; and, in that case, whether he can corroborate the statement of the President of the Board of Trade, that—

"The chiefs with whom we entered into engagements can come into the Reserved Territory, and find security there?"

MR. EVELYN ASHLEY: I must certainly decline to endorse the expression "deplorable" introduced into the hon. Member's Question as applicable to the condition of the Zulu Reserve. Papers about to be presented will, I think, satisfy the hon. Member as to this. The "1,000 rebels" mentioned must be a *réchauffé* of the attack made by the Usutus on Mr. Osborn some time ago, before any steps had been taken to restore order. We have no information of any Usutu attack threatening on the Natal side. There is no reason to doubt that any refugee Chiefs will find effectual protection in the Reserve under the Residents and the troops.

MR. GUY DAWNAY asked whether there was any room in the Reserve Territory to allocate land to any considerable number of refugees?

MR. EVELYN ASHLEY: That is impossible to answer, because what the hon. Member may mean by "considerable" I do not know. If the hon. Member will give me any number I will make inquiries.

ROYAL IRISH CONSTABULARY—CONSTABLE BERNARD KING.

MR. JUSTIN M'CARTHY asked the Chief Secretary to the Lord Lieutenant of Ireland, Whether his attention has been called to the circumstances of the death of Police Constable Bernard King, who was stationed in Larkfield, county Longford, and was doing duty in Granard in that county, on Monday 14th July, on which day, after returning to his station, he suddenly fell ill; whether it is true that he was not visited by a doctor until Sunday July 20th, and was not removed into hospital (where he died) until Tuesday July 22nd; and, whether he will cause some inquiry to be made in order to see if negligence on the part of any one contributed to the police constable's death?

THE SOLICITOR GENERAL FOR IRELAND (Mr. WALKER) (for Mr. TREVELYAN): I am informed that the constable complained of feeling unwell on the 15th July, but appeared on parade as usual on that day and the next. On the 16th he reported himself sick, and he was visited by the doctor on the 17th, 19th, and 20th. He was certified to be suffering from a bilious attack and headache. On the 20th the doctor recommended his removal to hospital, and he was taken there by two of his comrades on the 22nd. He died in hospital on the 25th, of meningitis. The district officer reports that no man could be more carefully looked after than the deceased constable was while in barrack by his comrades and the sergeant's wife, and there is no doubt that he was properly treated in hospital.

There does not appear to be any ground for attributing negligence to anyone.

IRELAND—STATE-AIDED EMIGRATION.

MR. DAWSON asked the Chief Secretary to the Lord Lieutenant of Ireland, Whether he is aware that a woman named Jane Kenny, who had been frequently convicted of robberies, was, with her illegitimate son, sixteen years of age, about to be sent from Limerick Female Prison to Canada; that she was a native of Carlow, and registered in the workhouse there as a Catholic; that she became a Protestant in Limerick; that the Governor of the Limerick Prison wrote letters and sent telegrams, with pre-paid reply, asking Carlow guardians to give money to buy clothes for the son; that, on refusal, the woman returned to Carlow Workhouse and became a Catholic again; whether it was out of the public funds that the expenses of the telegrams were paid, and if public funds were to have been applied to pay the passage money of these people; by whose authority the Governor of Limerick Prison sent this application, and offered to pay the boy's fare to Limerick; and, whether State-aided emigrants sent to Canada are largely drawn from such classes?

THE SOLICITOR GENERAL FOR IRELAND (Mr. WALKER) (for Mr. TREVELYAN): Jane Kenny, when received into Limerick Prison, was registered as a Protestant and a married woman. The Prisons' Board have at their disposal a charitable fund called "Barbara Tuthill's Fund," bequeathed to enable them to assist cases needing aid. Jane Kenny's case was considered a suitable one to assist by means of this fund. It was believed that if she was separated from her old associates the woman would do well. It was therefore proposed to send her to Canada with her son, the fare to be paid out of the charitable fund referred to. The Governor of the Prison, by the authority of the Vice Chairman of the Prisons' Board, wrote to Carlow to ascertain if the Guardians would provide clothes for the boy. One letter was sent at the public expense. It is not the fact that telegrams—pre-paid or otherwise—were sent at the public cost, or that any public expense would have been incurred if the proposal for emigration had been carried through. When the Carlow Guardians refused to provide clothing for the boy, Jane Kenny returned to Carlow. I am not aware whether she then professed herself a Roman Catholic. As I have already intimated, it was not proposed to send this woman out as a State-aided emigrant, and it is not the fact that State-aided emigrants are drawn from such classes.

TREATY OF BERLIN—ARTICLE 44—THE JEWS IN ROUMANIA.

BARON HENRY DE WORMS asked the Under Secretary of State for Foreign Affairs, Whether he is aware that the number of Jews in Roumania rendered destitute by the new edict against hawking is 20,000, and not 2,000, as stated in the Despatch of Her Majesty's Representative, dated Bucharest, June 29; whether he is aware that the Jews and their families thus reduced to destitution by the action of the Roumanian Government are unable to leave Roumania for the purpose of earning their living elsewhere, from the fact that the Roumanian Government will not, even in the case of those who have been domiciled in the Country for generations, grant them the necessary passports, on the ground that they are not Roumanian subjects; whether this action is not a distinct violation of Article 44 of the Treaty of Berlin; whether he is aware that Article 7 of the Roumanian Constitution, made subsequent to, and on the basis of, the understanding by which Roumania was granted her independence by the Great Powers, is used as a means of evading the express stipulations of Article 44 of the Treaty of Berlin; and, whether Her Majesty's Government, as one of the Signatory Powers at the Treaty of Berlin, will alone, or in conjunction with the other Powers, make representations to the Roumanian Government on the subject?

LORD EDMOND FITZMAURICE: In a despatch dated July 21, a copy of which has been supplied to the hon. Member, Her Majesty's Minister at Bucharest intimated that the number of Jews in Roumania affected by the new edict against hawking "is much more considerable than the 2,000 mentioned in his previous despatch." It seems doubtful whether this edict is at variance with Article 44 of the Treaty of Berlin. Inquiry will, however, be made as to the statement that Jews are prevented from leaving Roumania, and until an answer is received I can make no further statement.

LAW AND JUSTICE (IRELAND) — MR. GEORGE BOLTON, A BANKRUPT.

MR. HEALY asked the Chief Secretary to the Lord Lieutenant of Ireland, Whether, as the Report for George Bolton's salary was obtained by accident, he can now announce the decision of the Government?

THE SOLICITOR GENERAL FOR IRELAND (Mr. WALKER) (for Mr. TREVELYAN): The Irish Government had been advised that the Treasury Circular providing for the suspension of a civil servant when he becomes a bankrupt or enters into a composition with his creditors in the Bankruptcy Court does not in its literal terms apply to Mr. Bolton in his character of Crown Solicitor; but the Lord Lieutenant, nevertheless, has come to the decision, considering the admitted financial position of Mr. Bolton and the interest of the Public Service, that he ought to be dealt with by analogy to the Circular, and accordingly it has been decided that Mr. Bolton shall be suspended. The same decision will apply to his position of Solicitor to the Valuation Office.

THE NEW PUBLIC OFFICES—THE ADMIRALTY AND WAR OFFICE.

MR. BARRAN asked, What course the Government propose to take in consequence of the decision of judges on the recent competition for the design for the New Admiralty and War Office; and, whether the building will be commenced at once?

MR. SHAW LEFEVRE: I have informed Messrs. Leeming and Leeming, the authors of the successful design in the recent competition, that, subject to the approval of Parliament, they will be employed as architects for the building of the New Admiralty and War Office, and that the Government will submit a Vote to this House for the commencement of the building. As there is not time for Members to form a judgment on the design in what remains of the present Session, I shall defer submitting a Vote till next year. In the meantime the architects will be in communication with my Department with a view to making such modifications and improvements in the plan as may be suggested to them, so that it may be laid before the House next year in as perfect a shape as possible.

THE WELLINGTON STATUE.

SIR ROBERT PEEL asked the First Commissioner of Works, with reference to the statement made by him some time ago to the noble Lord the Member for North Leicestershire, Whether he can now fully state what arrangements have been made respecting the future site of the equestrian statue of the illustrious Duke?

MR. SHAW LEFEVRE: The removal of the statue of the Duke of Wellington to Aldershot will commence on Thursday next. An Ordnance store will be made ready to receive it there pending the final decision as to the site for its erection, on which the military authorities have to be consulted. The site will probably be the centre of the parade ground in the North Camp. A suitable pedestal will then be erected for it out of the money contributed to the Prince of Wales's Fund. The statue will be put together and erected again by the artificers of the Royal Engineers.

ARMY (INDIA)—QUARTERMASTERS.

MR. T. THORNHILL asked the Under Secretary of State for India, If he can state why Quartermasters of the British Army, serving in India and holding the rank of Captain, have only received the allowances of that rank from October 1st 1882, instead of, as in the case of other grades of non-combatant Officers, from July 1st 1881?

MR. J. K. CROSS: I am not aware what other grades of non-combatant officers are meant; but I may state that the Royal Warrant of 1881 did not accord the Indian allowances of captains to quartermasters in India. These allowances were sanctioned by the Secretary of State for India in Council in September, 1882; and, in accordance with custom, retrospective effect was not given to the Orders which sanctioned them.

MR. BUCHANAN asked the Under Secretary of State for India, Whether the Correspondence between Her Majesty's Government and the Government of India respecting the arrears of non-effective Army charges is now complete, and when it will be laid upon the Table, in accordance with his promise on the 26th of May?

MR. J. K. CROSS: When I answered the hon. Member on May 26, I was in hopes that an agreement would speedily be arrived at regarding the method of paying for the non-effective Army Charges in future. In this, however, some delay has occurred, and I will therefore make no objection to the production of the Correspondence to March 31 last, relating to the payment of the arrears, if the hon. Member will move for it.

CENTRAL ASIA—DELIMITATION OF THE AFGHAN FRONTIER.

MR. ONSLOW asked the First Lord of the Treasury, Under whose protection the Commission recently appointed to fix the Afghan Boundaries will be; will the Amir be represented; if so, by how many officers; what will be the duties of the Commission, and what orders have been given to them; in case of difference of opinion between our officers and the Russian officers, or those of the Amir, to what Government will our officers refer; is the escort to be provided to consist entirely of Native Troops, and, what arrangements have been made for constant communication between our officers and either the Home Government or the Government of India?

MR. GLADSTONE: On inquiry I find that communications are still going on with the Russian Government with regard to these various points, and I am not as yet in a position to give an answer.

MR. ONSLOW: Will the right hon. Gentleman say if it is true that our Mission is to start in October, or, as reported in *The Times*, that it is to be put off to the spring of next year? Perhaps this Mission is one of the most important that has ever been sent out from India; and I hope before the House adjourns we shall have some further information.

MR. GLADSTONE: I agree, Sir, as to the importance of this Commission. All I can say is that I have not heard anything of the suggested postponement.

MR. ONSLOW: I shall put a further Question on the subject next Monday.

MR. BOURKE: I beg to give Notice that on the Appropriation Bill I shall call attention to the whole of this subject.

MR. ONSLOW: That being the case, I will put my Question down for Thursday.

PARLIAMENT—PALACE OF WESTMINSTER—WESTMINSTER HALL.

SIR GEORGE CAMPBELL asked the First Lord of the Treasury, Whether he will use his influence with the First Commissioner of Works to induce him to reserve for Grand Committee Rooms, and other extensions, the ground to the west of Westminster Hall lately occupied by the Law Courts, so that the Hall may be again, as it was originally, the centre of the Palace of Parliament?

MR. CAVENDISH BENTINCK asked whether, having regard to the great objection that existed to the present scheme, and the impossibility of its being properly discussed during the present Session, it was not desirable to postpone the whole question till next Session?

MR. GLADSTONE: I am afraid I must ask the right hon. Gentleman to put that Question down on the Paper. I should not like to give an answer to it before first communicating with the Chancellor of the Exchequer and the First Commissioner of Works. I believe that a certain amount of accommodation, available for one Grand Committee, is included in the plan as it now stands, to which the Government intend to ask the sanction of Parliament. Beyond that I do not think that my right hon. Friend is prepared to go. The hon. Gentleman asks me to use my influence with the First Commissioner of Works. Well, of course, the Treasury has a certain control over the Office of Works; but, at the same time, that Department must be allowed a certain amount of independence and judgment on a matter on which it is more competent than the Treasury to form an opinion.

MR. MITCHELL HENRY: Before the Vote is taken will the First Commissioner of Works allow Members of the House to visit the *locus in quo*?

MR. SHAW LEFEVRE: I will give orders that any hon. Member who desires to see the west front of Westminster Hall shall be admitted within the inclosure at any time to-morrow. Indeed, I shall have great pleasure in personally explaining to any hon. Member what is proposed to be done there between the hours of 3 and 4 o'clock to-morrow.

THE MAGISTRACY (IRELAND) — MR. CLIFFORD LLOYD.

MR. HEALY asked the First Lord of the Treasury, If the Government have come to any decision as to the future employment of Mr. Clifford Lloyd?

MR. GLADSTONE: I am obliged to the hon. Member for having postponed this Question, in order to enable me to communicate with the Lord Lieutenant for Ireland. The hon. Member is aware that Mr. Clifford Lloyd was called on public grounds from an employment in Ireland to employment of a higher grade in Egypt. He will no longer prosecute that employment in Egypt. The Irish Government cannot give any positive pledge that he will not resume his post as Resident Magistrate in Ireland; but they hope to make some more adequate and suitable arrangement.

MR. HEALY asked if the right hon. Gentleman was aware of the statement made by the Secretary to the Treasury a few nights ago, that Mr. Clifford Lloyd would not be appointed in Ireland?

MR. COURTNEY: I think I said he would not be one of the five persons receiving extra pay.

EGYPT—SLAVERY—THE CONVENTION OF 1877.

SIR GEORGE CAMPBELL asked the First Lord of the Treasury, Whether effect is to be given in Egypt Proper to the existing Convention of 17th August 1877, and Khedivial Decree in accordance therewith, under which the buying and selling of human beings is prohibited, under severe penalties, from the 17th of the current month; and, if he will give an assurance that, whether or not the further measures recommended by Lord Dufferin for altogether abolishing slavery be immediately effected, Her Majesty's Government will, as recommended by Lord Dufferin, press the Egyptian Government to give the fullest possible effect in Egypt Proper to the existing Convention and its Annexes?

LORD EDMOND FITZMAURICE: Her Majesty's Government have no reason for doubting the intention of the Khedive to give due effect to his Treaty engagements in regard to Egypt Proper. They lose no opportunity of pressing upon the Egyptian Government the necessity of observing their engagements in regard to the treatment of the question of Slave Trade and Slavery, and I would refer the hon. Member to the despatch of Sir Evelyn Baring, dated February 25, 1884, in Slave Trade No. 2.

THE AUSTRALASIAN COLONIES—CONFEDERATION.

MR. BLAKE asked the First Lord of the Treasury, If, in view of the fact that four out of seven of the Australasian Colonies have agreed to proceed at once to confederate in an Australasian Dominion, and of his statement that no business will be taken in the Autumn Session except the Franchise Bill, it may not be possible to introduce and pass an enabling Bill before the end of this Session, so as to obviate the loss of a whole year, which will otherwise occur in giving effect to the decisions of the Colonial Parliaments? The hon. Member also asked whether the right hon. Gentleman would undertake to introduce a Bill in the Autumn Session?

MR. GLADSTONE: I can give no pledge at the present time with regard to the Autumn Session in deviation from what I have already stated. Of course, what I have stated will not bind the House or the Government in connection with causes at present unforeseen and of a sufficient magnitude to require that we should deviate from the policy already laid down; but at present there is no such cause before us. The Question which is upon the Paper asks whether this important object of enabling the Australasian Colonies to confederate might be accomplished by the introduction of an enabling Bill in the present Session? What I have to say in answer is that it would not be right to introduce such a Bill and then to withdraw it. That would not be respectful to the Colonies, nor would it be likely to be understood in a favourable sense. Neither would it be right to introduce such a Bill if it were to become the subject of differences of opinion; and to continue sitting until a Bill, if it were opposed, could be passed would be contrary to the pledge which the Government have given to the House not to proceed with contentious Business at this period of the Session. But if we could be assured that the House would give its unanimous assent to a Bill for the simply enabling purpose described in the Question, even at this moment I would agree to its introduction.

Mr. BLAKE: Would the right hon. Gentleman be so kind as to test the feeling of the House by introducing a Bill? I think I may promise, on the part of my Friends in this part of the House, that we would not offer any opposition to such a Bill.

Mr. GLADSTONE: My hon. Friend has evidently not observed what I stated. He proposes that I should introduce a Bill to test the feeling of the House. But I observed that it would not be respectful to the Colonies and would not wear a friendly aspect, were I to introduce a Bill and then to withdraw it. Either the Government or the House would be open to some criticism in the Colonies. I understand the hon. Member to speak confidently for the quarter of the House with which he is connected, and so far I am well satisfied. I could not, however, at this moment, as growing out of a Question, inquire from right hon. and hon. Members opposite what their views are; but I think it probable that in the course of the evening they may have the kindness to make their views known to us. If it appears that there exists such a unanimous disposition as would alone justify the introduction of the Bill, Notice of the Bill might be given this evening, and it might be introduced to-morrow.

EGYPT—ARMED STEAMERS ON THE NILE.

Mr. GOURLEY asked the Secretary to the Admiralty, If he can inform the House what number of armed steamers are now engaged in patrol duty on the Nile, above and below the First Cataract, and whether all are under the command of British Naval Officers; further, to inquire if he can state what number of steamers are under the control of General Gordon; and, whether suitable craft are being prepared for the purpose of opening up communications with Dongola, Berber, and Khartoum during the rise of the Nile?

Mr. CAMPBELL-BANNERMAN: There are four steamers engaged in patrol duty on the Nile, and they are all under the command of British naval officers. There is no certain information as to the number of steamers under the control of General Gordon. Certain preparations have been made for passing some steam vessels up the Second Cataract.

EGYPT—POLICY OF HER MAJESTY'S GOVERNMENT.

Sir STAFFORD NORTHCOTE asked the First Lord of the Treasury, Whether he will give the House an opportunity of discussing the policy of the Government, with regard to the affairs of Egypt, on Thursday next?

Mr. GLADSTONE: There is something rather unusual in the form of the Question of the right hon. Gentleman, because I apprehend the different stages of the Appropriation Bill will give the right hon. Gentleman an opportunity of discussing the policy of the Government at his option, and without application or reference to me. But I have another remark to make which is more to the present purpose. When the right hon. Gentleman put a Question to me on Saturday, I put a construction upon it which, perhaps, was not quite accurate. I understood him to ask whether I could then name a day on which I could explain to Parliament the measures which we intended to adopt in Egypt, growing out of the recent failure of the Conference? The consideration of those measures, I had said, would require some time, and I replied accordingly that I could not name a day for that purpose. There is, however, a step of some importance which the Government contemplate, and which I hope to be in a condition to announce to-morrow. I should prefer not answering the Question now put to me until I am in a condition to make that announcement to the House, and I think it might possibly be more for the convenience of the right hon. Baronet and other Gentlemen opposite if that course were followed. I think they would be then able to form a judgment in a manner more satisfactory to themselves as to any course they may think fit to take. I am under the impression that it would, in any case, be thought desirable that Supply should be allowed to terminate before we enter into a discussion of a general character with regard to Egypt.

Sir STAFFORD NORTHCOTE: Of course, I am willing to put the Question to-morrow. Like the right hon. Gentleman, I am anxious to see Supply finished; but, at the same time, I think it much more important that the Egyptian Question should be discussed while it is still fresh.

MR. GLADSTONE: I do not say that it is more important Supply should be finished, but only that it would be more convenient in the first place that Supply should be finished, merely in respect to the economy of time.

ITALY—ROME—THE ENDOWMENTS OF THE PROPAGANDA.

MR. O'DONNELL asked the First Lord of the Treasury, Whether Her Majesty's Government still adhere to the declaration contained in the Despatch of Lord Kimberley to the Governor of Gibraltar, dated the 16th of January 1871, that—

"The deep interest which is felt by many millions of Her Majesty's subjects in the position of the Pope renders all that concerns his personal dignity and independence, and freedom to exercise his spiritual functions, fit subjects for the notice of Her Government. . . . . Her Majesty desires me to state that this subject will continue to receive the careful attention of Her Government;"

whether he is aware that the endowments of the Propaganda, contributed by all the Catholic nations of the world, including a large section of Her Majesty's subjects, are strictly applied in the exercise of the spiritual functions of the Pope in connection with the Catholic missions throughout all regions of the world; and, if he will take, without delay, any steps which may be requisite to prevent any portion of these endowments from being converted by force to the secular uses of the Italian Government?

MR. GLADSTONE: The hon. Member, I think, cannot have been in his place when a former Question on this subject had been answered. So far, at least, as regards the practical part of his inquiry, I may say that, with respect to the despatch of Lord Kimberley, from which the hon. Member has quoted a passage, I cannot admit there is anything in that despatch from which Lord Kimberley would desire to recede at the present time. The character of the endowments to which the hon. Member refers has repeatedly been the subject of description in this House on the part of the Government, and I do not propose to go over the ground again. With respect to any steps that may be requisite to prevent any portion of these endowments from being diverted by force to the secular uses of the Italian Government, I must ask myself whether the matter is one within the legal jurisdiction of the Italian Government. If it be within the legal jurisdiction of the Italian Government—as I have always understood it was—I am not prepared to undertake to interfere with their legal jurisdiction. What Her Majesty's Government has repeatedly said is that they have instructed their Ambassador to be on the watch for any favourable opportunity for exercising an influence in the direction indicated by the hon. Member; but no such opportunity has presented itself to any of the Powers, several of whom are even more interested than the British Crown in the matter.

MR. GRAY asked the Prime Minister whether he would state the Powers which he deemed to be much more interested than England in this question.

MR. GLADSTONE replied that he had not spoken by way of experiment. Certainly, he should imagine that the Powers would be interested in this question in some sort of proportion to the Roman Catholic population. England, no doubt, had a large interest in the matter; but he did not stand upon that distinction.

MR. GRAY said, he had no desire to raise a controversial question upon the right hon. Gentleman's remark; but if the right hon. Gentleman indicated such countries as France, or Austria, or Spain, he would ask him whether he was aware that the funds of the Propaganda were only used for the benefit of missionary countries, and that those Catholic countries were not missionary countries, and had no interest in the funds?

[No reply.]

SUPPLY—RELIEF OF GENERAL GORDON—VOTE OF CREDIT.

SIR WALTER B. BARTTELOT asked the Secretary of State for War, Whether any expedition for the relief of General Gordon is contemplated; and, whether a Railway is to be made from Suakin to Berber or any part of the road to Berber; and, if so, whether a Supplementary Estimate will be presented to the House?

MR. GLADSTONE: It is my intention to-morrow to propose a Vote of Credit to enable Her Majesty's Government to undertake operations for the relief of General Gordon, should they become necessary, and to make certain preparations in respect thereof. I believe there is in the Diplomatic Vote to-night an item which might become the subject of discussion in connection with the state of affairs of the Soudan. If that item of the Vote be chosen for the discussion, I should propose the Vote of Credit to-morrow at such a time as I could, because there is already in contemplation an arrangement for the first Vote to-morrow, and we are also very desirous, if we can, to bring on the Report of the Constabulary Vote. But, perhaps, it might be more convenient to the House, and to Gentlemen opposite, that they should found the discussion on the Vote of Credit, and in that case passing over the subject to-night, I should be ready to propose the Vote of Credit as the first Vote in Supply to-morrow.

MR. JOSEPH COWEN asked whether the proposed Vote of Credit, and the interesting statement which the right hon. Gentleman was to make to-morrow, formed one and the same subject.

MR. GLADSTONE: No; the two things are quite distinct. I did not say that I intended to make a statement of some interest. What I stated was that Her Majesty's Government contemplated a step of some importance, which I hope to be in a condition to announce to-morrow.

MR. LABOUCHERE asked whether that Vote would be a Vote of Credit or a Vote for the Diplomatic Service?

MR. GLADSTONE: It is not a question of a Vote for the Diplomatic Service, but of a Vote of Credit properly so called, and I propose, if the House should deem it a convenient course, to take any discussion that may be raised upon the Vote of Credit to-morrow. In that case, I should propose to take the Vote of Credit as the first Vote to-morrow. If, on the contrary, the discussion were taken to-night, for which there will be abundant justification on the Diplomatic Vote, I should bring on the Vote of Credit whenever I can.

MR. ASHMEAD-BARTLETT: I do not think the House exactly understands what this Vote is. May I ask the right hon. Gentleman whether it is to be a Vote of Credit for a considerable sum to purchase the supplies for an Expedition for the relief of General Gordon? It would be a great advantage to the House to know definitely what is the proposal.

MR. GLADSTONE: I have read to the House the purpose for which the Vote is to be taken.

SIR STAFFORD NORTHCOTE: Will the right hon. Gentleman state it again?

MR. GLADSTONE: It is

"A Vote of Credit to enable Her Majesty's Government to undertake operations for the relief of General Gordon, should they become necessary, and to make certain preparations in respect thereof."

MR. PULESTON: Will the right hon. Gentleman state the amount?

MR. GLADSTONE: I will not enter into any further explanation until I make the Motion.

MR. NEWDEGATE: Does the right hon. Gentleman intend to introduce the Appropriation Bill this week?

MR. GLADSTONE: It is observed in this neighbourhood that I have not the gift of prophecy, and I cannot venture upon a prediction which might possibly tend to defeat itself.

LORD RANDOLPH CHURCHILL: Is there any precedent for taking a Vote of Credit without previous Notice of the amount?

MR. GLADSTONE: I shall give the Notice in the regular form, so that it will appear on the Paper.

MR. BOURKE: I should like to ask, as a Question arising out of the right hon. Gentleman's statement with regard to to-morrow, whether the announcement will involve a Motion on the part of the Government which will give the House an opportunity of judging of the policy of the Government?

MR. GLADSTONE: I cannot give any information about this announcement until I make it. I would have done so to-day, but it was not in my power; I made a great effort on Saturday to communicate the information, and the right hon. Gentleman may rest assured that I shall act on the same principle, and will not lose a moment.

LORD RANDOLPH CHURCHILL: I am afraid I am extremely stupid; but I cannot make out what is to take place to-morrow. All I want to know is when the Vote of Credit will be proposed?

Mr. GLADSTONE: If the discussion on the Soudan and the case of General Gordon should not be taken to-night, then I should be prepared to propose the Vote of Credit as the first Vote in Supply to-morrow. If, on the other hand, the discussion on the Diplomatic Vote were taken to-night, then I should propose the Vote of Credit to-morrow at such an hour as I can bring it on.

Mr. J. LOWTHER: In the event of a discussion being taken to-night, will Government be prepared to make a statement?

Mr. GLADSTONE: No.

Mr. W. E. FORSTER: I believe there is a misconception on another point. I understood my right hon. Friend to state that he would give Notice of the Vote of Credit to-night, and that the amount would be stated at the time.

Mr. GLADSTONE: Yes.

Mr. W. H. SMITH: I should like to ask the Government whether it is intended to propose an appropriation in Ways and Means in regard to the Vote of Credit?

The CHANCELLOR of the EXCHEQUER (Mr. Childers): That is a Question which should be asked when the Vote of Credit is proposed.

Lord RANDOLPH CHURCHILL asked why, if the amount of the Vote was to be laid upon the Table that night, it could not at once be stated to the House?

Mr. GLADSTONE: I have given my Notice in the usual course, and I have said quite as much as is usual in giving Notice.

Sir STAFFORD NORTHCOTE: I would suggest that we had better take the discussion on the Vote of Credit and not on the Diplomatic Vote.

CENTRAL ASIA — DELIMITATION OF THE AFGHAN FRONTIER.

Mr. ONSLOW asked the Under Secretary of State for Foreign Affairs, Whether it was intended that the English Commissioners for the demarcation of Afghanistan should meet the Russian and Afghan Commissioners this year or next?

Lord EDMOND FITZMAURICE replied, that it was very difficult to make partial statements while a matter of this kind was proceeding. He should require Notice of the Question.

Mr. ONSLOW said, he had put Notices on the subject on the Paper already. He now gave Notice that, in future, he should address his Questions to the Prime Minister.

ORDERS OF THE DAY.

—o—

SUPPLY—CIVIL SERVICE ESTIMATES.

Supply—*considered* in Committee.

(In the Committee.)

Class V.—Foreign and Colonial Services.

(1.) Motion made, and Question proposed,

"That a sum, not exceeding £157,975, (including a Supplementary sum of £35,000), be granted to Her Majesty, to complete the sum necessary to defray the Charge which will come in course of payment during the year ending on the 31st day of March 1885, for the Expenses of Her Majesty's Embassies and Missions Abroad."

Sir WILFRID LAWSON said, the Papers had already been laid upon the Table in relation to the prohibition by the Egyptian Government of the landing of Mr. Wilfrid Blunt in Egypt. As those Papers had only been laid upon the Table that day, many hon. Members might not have had an opportunity of reading them. He would therefore state as briefly as he could the nature of their contents, and he would then ask the noble Lord the Under Secretary of State for Foreign Affairs to explain the reason why Her Majesty's Government had taken the course they had in the matter. Mr. Blunt had been before the country for a long time in connection with Egyptian matters. It would be remembered how, in 1882, he had warned the Government of the natural result of their policy in Egypt; and if they had accepted that warning, they would have been in a very much better position than that which they occupied to-day. Indeed, if there was one man to whom more than another the whole of the country and Her Majesty's Government were indebted, it was Mr. Wilfrid Blunt; and there could be no doubt that the political prisoners would have been executed but for the efforts of Mr. Blunt. Mr. Blunt had certainly rendered great service to the Government. Last autumn Mr. Blunt determined to go out to India, and he stopped in Egypt on his way. He did not engage in any political mission there, the political questions in which he had been engaged having been thoroughly threshed out, and Mr. Blunt could do no more in regard to them. He merely called there, and, having called there, he was treated as any other English gentleman would have been by Her Majesty's Representatives, who entertained him and entered into communications with him. He then left Egypt and went to India, and after remaining in India for some time, he returned, but was not allowed to land in Egypt again. All he (Sir Wilfrid Lawson) had now to do was to state the reasons given in the Papers laid before the House that day why Mr. Blunt was not allowed to land. It must be remembered that these reasons had been indorsed and approved by Sir Evelyn Baring and Earl Granville. All that was material as to the action of Egypt in the matter, so far as preventing the landing of an English subject, would be found on pa e 3 of the Papers which gave the letter of Cherif Pasha to Sir Evelyn Baring. That letter opened out the whole business. Cherif Pasha said—

"You are doubtless aware of Mr. Blunt's relations with Arabi and of the campaign undertaken by him in London to cast upon His Highness the odium of the massacres at Alexandria. I have no intention of reverting to past events, but I shall confine myself to acquainting you in a few words with the attitude adopted by Mr. Blunt during his recent stay in Egypt. On his arrival at Cairo he immediately entered into communication with the families of the rebels and with several other persons compromised in the recent events."

Now, he did not suppose that anybody knew there was a law in Egypt, or in England, that nobody was to confer with the families of rebels; but he was informed by Mr. Blunt that all the stories about interviews prolonged far into the night were untrue; that while in Egypt he was in bed regularly by half-past 9 or 10 o'clock; but that on one occasion he had received an invitation to dine with the officials connected with the British Embassy. The next thing stated in the letter was that—

"In his walks in the Bazaar he was continually conversing with the merchants with regard to Arabi."

That was the second charge. The third was that—

"Having learnt that a certain Abdel Rajah was detained in prison as implicated in the matter of the anonymous letters, he presented himself at the Zaptieh for admission to see the prisoner."

What really took place was, that Mr. Blunt asked Sir Evelyn Baring "to obtain permission for him to look over the prison," but receiving no answer, he walked in and saw this man, no one interfering. Certainly there was not much harm in that. Mr. Blunt was next charged as follows:—

"Having met with a refusal on the part of the police officials, Mr. Blunt endeavoured to evade the orders, but not having succeeded he departed, abusing the guards and boasting that he would shortly return with an order from Her Majesty's Representative which would open all doors to him.

Mr. Blunt stated that there was no truth whatever in that charge, that nothing of the kind occurred, and that he spoke to and abused nobody. The fifth charge was—

"Mr. Blunt further employed himself in starting a newspaper, the intended object of which was to create popularity for Arabi, and to weaken the authority of the Khedive. On his being informed that in order to publish a newspaper in Egypt the sanction of the Government must previously be obtained, he is reported to have replied that, if necessary, he would obtain that sanction from London."

Mr. Blunt informed him (Sir Wilfrid Lawson) that he never had such an idea in his mind, and that he never thought of starting a newspaper in Egypt. The sixth charge was—

"You are further aware, my dear Minister, of the ideas he tried to disseminate in the country with regard to the foundation of an Arab Empire, and the imbecility of the present system of government."

Mr. Blunt said that he pleaded guilty to the charge, with the exception of not having advised the foundation of an Arab Empire. He certainly thought the Government of Egypt most imbecile, and had said so on many occasions. The right hon. Member for North Lincolnshire (Mr. J. Lowther), indeed, two of the Members for Lincolnshire, and the Member for Eye (Mr. Ashmead-Bartlett) went up and down this country calling the Members of Her Majesty's Government imbecile, but they were not banished, for nobody cared a bit what they said. As far as he could make out from reading the Papers, these were the sole charges against Mr. Blunt, on account of which he was not allowed to land in Egypt; and he should be much surprised if the Committee were to arrive at the conclusion that this was a proper way to treat a British subject. It was monstrous that a Liberal Government should act in the way the present Government had acted towards Mr. Blunt. He did not suppose that Mr. Blunt was particularly anxious to go to Egypt at the time he was refused permission to land, and he did not think that Mr. Blunt sustained any serious amount of inconvenience. A gross indignity, however, was put upon him, simply because he had told the truth; and the matter threw a flood of light on what was going on in that country. It showed that they were in Egypt for nothing more than to bolster up a system of cruelty and oppression, and to stifle freedom of opinion. Unless the Government could give a better reason than they had yet given for this extraordinary proceeding, as explained in the Papers laid before the House, he should certainly feel disposed to move the reduction of the Vote in order to see whether the Committee would be inclined to join him in protesting against the odious, dangerous, and unjust policy which Her Majesty's Government were encouraging in Egypt. He should like very much to hear what the Government would have to say in defence of the extraordinary course they had taken.

LORD EDMOND FITZMAURICE said, that he was, on the whole, glad that his hon. Friend had called attention to this subject, because it would enable him to bring out the real facts of the matter. Hon. Members would probably have read the Papers which had been presented, and he wished they could have been presented sooner; but, owing to want of time, it had been impossible. It would at once be seen that the whole of the question lay in a nutshell. As to the main facts, there was no dispute. His hon. Friend said humorously that Mr. Blunt had been refused permission to land in Egypt, because on his former visit he had been in the habit of sitting up late at night; but that it was owing to the hospitality kindly extended to him by the members of Her Majesty's Mission, and that sitting up late at night under such circumstances was not likely to do much harm. But he (Lord Edmond Fitzmaurice) could not help thinking the Committee would see, on reading the Papers, that that humorous version of Mr. Blunt's proceedings was scarcely borne out. The whole case, in reality, turned on two things—in the first place, on the right of the Egyptian Government; and, secondly, on the facts stated in the letter of Cherif Pasha to Sir Evelyn Baring on the 8th of October. As to the right of the Egyptian Government, and the legal aspect of the case, there could be no doubt at all. It was a matter of the right of self-preservation, which all Governments at times were obliged to exercise in periods of great difficulty. Occasionally, the exercise of a strict legal right did appear to interfere with that complete liberty which, as a rule, it was the desire of every civilized State to extend, not only to its own subjects, but to those of other nations. Mr. Blunt, exercising his rights, which nobody would question, some time ago did take a leading part in Egyptian affairs; but, having chosen to take a certain line, he must also take the consequences. Mr. Blunt, to use an old proverb, could not claim to "eat his loaf and to have it also." He could not claim to express opinions hostile to the Egyptian Government, or to conspire against them, and then claim their assent and protection. Mr. Blunt claimed that those who had been in active rebellion against the Government were in reality patriots, whose names were held in honour by the country, and when they entered into a conspiracy against a Government of which they disapproved, he seemed to imagine that they ought to be protected by that Government. Now, it was necessary to take a clear line in a question of that kind; no man could be on both sides. He could not claim the protection of the Government, and also to be allowed to enter into agreements and conspiracies against it. His hon. Friend said that Mr. Blunt did admit one charge, and the admission was an exceedingly important one—namely, that, while in Egypt, Mr. Blunt did attempt to disseminate ideas which nobody could deny were hostile to the existence of the Government of that country.

LORD RANDOLPH CHURCHILL asked where that admission was to be found?

LORD EDMOND FITZMAURICE said, it was what the hon. Baronet had said himself. His hon. Friend had controverted Paragraphs 1, 2, 3, 4 and 5

most excellent and intelligent Private Secretaries any Minister ever had the good fortune to possess. He [illegible] communicate to the Prime Minister the result of these interviews, knowing well, for a long time, what great interest the right hon. Gentleman had taken in the affairs of Egypt. Mr Blunt alleged that he never saw the Prime Minister himself. He started on his tour in the month of September, and at that time the Prime Minister was taking that little yachting voyage to Copenhagen, which all remembered. The day before Mr Blunt left for Egypt he received a letter from Mr Hamilton begging him to call upon him. Therefore Mr Hamilton, knowing that Mr Blunt was going to Egypt, sent for Mr Blunt to call and see him before he went. Mr Blunt proceeded to Downing Street, where he found Mr Hamilton installed in the Prime Minister's apartment, and exercising, no doubt, more or less Ministerial authority. Mr Hamilton questioned Mr Blunt very closely as to the proceedings which he intended to take, and gave him to understand that he would be favourably received in Egypt by Sir Evelyn Baring. Mr Hamilton acquainted himself with the whole of Mr Blunt's proposals, for Mr Blunt was not the man to keep anything back; and Mr Blunt then took farewell of Mr Hamilton and departed for Egypt, feeling certain that Mr Hamilton must have communicated all that had passed to the Prime Minister. If there had been anything very objectionable in the course Mr Blunt proposed to pursue he felt certain the Prime Minister, either then and there, or immediately afterwards, the moment he heard of these contemplated proceedings, would have [illegible] Mr Blunt in the strongest possible manner. But nothing of the kind took place, and from that moment to the day Mr Blunt was forbidden to land in Egypt no [illegible] of any sort reached him. Was it probable, then, that the Prime Minister was not aware of Mr Blunt's journey to Egypt, or that he disapproved of it? Mr Blunt having arrived at Cairo at once waited upon Sir Evelyn Baring; and, as hon. Members opposite, who were not particularly prejudiced in favour of English officials in Egypt, might imagine, Sir Evelyn Baring was horrified at Mr Blunt's presence and Mr Blunt's proposals. He did not sympathize with them at all; he put his foot down upon Mr Blunt at once, and declined to give him any assistance in any shape or kind. So much was this the case that Sir Evelyn Baring actually refused to get permission for Mr Blunt to visit a gentleman who was confined in prison in Cairo not upon any charge, but simply upon suspicion. Mr Blunt asked Sir Evelyn Baring to procure him permission to visit this gentleman, and Sir Evelyn Baring peremptorily refused. There was hardly a country in the world in which such a course would have been taken in reference to a prisoner confined only on suspicion, against whom no charge had been brought. In any other country such a man would have been allowed to see his friends; but in Egypt, under the wise and enlightened Administration of Her Majesty's Government, political prisoners did not possess that advantage, and therefore the Representative of the British Government refused permission in Egypt for Mr Blunt to visit a friend who happened to be confined in prison. Mr Blunt, however, saw other friends in Cairo, and ascertained that there was no danger whatever at that moment of any movement being made in favour of the National Party, or even of the discussion of the idea that there was a National Party, and least of all that there was any feeling in favour of the restoration of Arabi Pasha. Having ascertained that through his friends, and without any proceeding which partook of the nature of conspiracy, Mr Blunt left Egypt for India, having nothing more to do. He had gone to Cairo and seen those gentlemen. His journey to Cairo had been suggested in the highest official quarters. He had done nothing wrong. He had asked to see a gentleman who was in prison. He had been rudely refused permission, and he then reverted to his original idea of proceeding to India and of abandoning Egyptian affairs altogether. What followed? Mr Blunt received an intimation that he would not be allowed to land in Egypt on his return. Now, that was very hard treatment indeed, whether the person subjected to it was an Englishman, a Frenchman, a German, an Italian, or the subject of any other country. Surely it was a hard measure of justice to prevent a man from [illegible]

would turn to page 9 of the Papers laid upon the Table, they would find a letter from Mr. Blunt to Earl Granville, dated the 1st of May. At the bottom of that page, in the third paragraph from the bottom, he would invite the attention of the noble Lord to a passage in which Mr. Blunt made these remarks—

"Having abandoned all active interest in Egyptian politics, I was encouraged last September, in the highest official quarter, again to visit Egypt, with a view to consulting with Sir Evelyn Baring as to a possible development there of English policy."

He (Lord Randolph Churchill) thought that passage would provide a much better elucidation of this unfortunate occurrence than that which the noble Lord had endeavoured to give. Many hon. Members would be aware that Mr. Blunt had strong views of the revolution brought about by Arabi and of the future of Egypt. Probably, few Members would be found who would agree with him upon those points; but he did not think there was a man in the House who would be prepared to say that Mr. Blunt was not a gentleman of the highest honour and integrity, although he had come prominently before the public in relation to Egyptian affairs. Although Mr. Blunt held strong opinions, and did not hesitate to put them forward in the strongest possible manner, no one, not even an official of the Government, had ever questioned or treated with suspicion his integrity, veracity, or high honour. Therefore, when he saw a statement of that kind in the Papers laid before the House, that Mr. Blunt had abandoned all active interest in Egyptian politics, and had been encouraged last September, in the highest official quarter, again to visit Egypt, with a view to consulting with Sir Evelyn Baring as to a possible development there of English policy, he had thought it right to put himself in communication with Mr. Blunt, in order to ascertain what was the explanation of that passage. Mr. Blunt informed him that he was visited in September last by a gentleman, notoriously enjoying the friendship and the confidence of the Prime Minister—Mr. Knowles, the editor of *The Nineteenth Century*. That gentleman informed Mr. Blunt that the moment was well chosen for his again revisiting Egypt. He (Lord Randolph Churchill) did not vouch for these statements himself; but Mr. Blunt made them, and nobody yet had questioned the honour or veracity of Mr. Blunt; and he (Lord Randolph Churchill) thought the case was of such a nature that it ought to be put before the House of Commons. Mr. Blunt stated that Mr. Knowles went to him, and suggested that the moment was auspicious for again revisiting Egypt, with a view of ascertaining whether there was any probability of the revival of the National Party, and whether there was any probability of arranging some method by which Arabi Pasha might be restored to his native land. In the interview, as Mr. Blunt states, Mr. Knowles made a very free use of the Prime Minister's name. [Mr. GLADSTONE dissented.] He had no doubt that if the Prime Minister would get up at the Table and deny that statement, the Committee would accept his denial; but, according to the representation of Mr. Blunt, Mr. Knowles made a very free use of the Prime Minister's name. Was that so? [Mr. GLADSTONE dissented.] Mr. Knowles would not have thought proper to make a direct use of the Prime Minister's name without direct authority, and Mr. Knowles was a gentleman who worthily enjoyed the friendship of the Prime Minister, and would not be presumed to use the name of the right hon. Gentleman without authority. Mr. Blunt, who was an enthusiast, took fire at that suggestion that there was a chance of the National Party in Egypt being recognized by the English Government, and he placed himself in communication with no less a person than the Prime Minister's Private Secretary, Mr. Hamilton. Mr. Blunt communicated to Mr. Hamilton what had passed between himself and Mr. Knowles. He stated to Mr. Hamilton that he was encouraged by what had reached him to make a journey to Egypt on his way to India, and he communicated fully to Mr. Hamilton the exact steps he meant to take when he got to Egypt, and the parties with whom he intended to communicate when he arrived there. If he (Lord Randolph Churchill) recollected rightly, Mr. Blunt had two interviews with Mr. Hamilton some time before he started, and unless the Prime Minister contradicted him, he should decline altogether to believe that Mr. Hamilton, who, as everybody knew, was one of the

order that he might not interfere with the calm which had fallen upon all minds, and the perfect tranquillity which reigned throughout the country, in order that an era of peace and concord might be inaugurated. That was in the month of October. Three months later, Cherif Pasha and all his tribe were kicked out of Egypt by Sir Evelyn Baring in order to preserve the tranquillity which reigned throughout the country, and the era of peace and concord which had been entered into. The Prime Minister, to use his own picturesque language, said that he had shattered the Native Government. But it was in order that the Native Government should not be shattered that Mr Blunt was prevented from landing in Egypt. So much, then, for Cherif Pasha. He now came to Nubar Pasha. The noble Lord the Under Secretary of State made a great point of the action of Nubar Pasha. He said that not only Cherif Pasha but Nubar Pasha, a new man, had adopted the same course of action in regard to Mr Blunt. But why was Nubar Pasha put into the Government at Cairo? It was solely because he was likely to be a passive instrument in the hands of Sir Evelyn Baring. Cherif Pasha had at times displayed a little tendency towards [illegible] and to independent [illegible]. Cherif Pasha was [illegible]. As to the statement that he had kept Mr Blunt out of Egypt of his own motion, there might [illegible] attached [illegible] with Nubar Pasha there was [illegible] possibility of that. Nubar Pasha [illegible] excluded Mr Blunt from Egypt in response to the demand of Sir Evelyn Baring. Sir Evelyn Baring wrote to Nubar Pasha to know if he shared the views in regard to Mr Blunt entertained by his Predecessor. Nubar Pasha knew what the views of Cherif Pasha were, [illegible] he knew also [illegible] had [illegible] and [illegible] was not likely to express any disagreement with Sir Evelyn Baring. Therefore, he wrote to say that he [illegible] concurred in the views of Cherif Pasha. He wrote to Sir Evelyn Baring—

"[illegible] Mr [illegible] that [illegible] obliged to their great regret [illegible] Mr Blunt [illegible] arrived at [illegible] Cherif Pasha."

As to the statement of the noble Lord the Under Secretary of State that that made the case worse against Mr Blunt, that argument was really worth nothing at all. The only complaint was that Mr Blunt had been unfairly and unjustly excluded from Egypt. He had already pointed out that there was nothing in the circumstances of Mr Blunt's case to justify his exclusion, and that if there were circumstances about Mr Blunt's visit which did justify it the same measure ought to be applied to hundreds of other persons who were at the present moment in Cairo. The real fact was—and it was the explanation of the whole matter—that Mr Blunt had property in Egypt which he had held for some time, and the Egyptian Government had taken advantage of his absence to plunder it. They had made exorbitant demands upon him for Land Tax and other matters amounting to £105, hoping, no doubt, that in Mr Blunt's absence the matter would not be attended to, and that they would be enabled to retaliate upon Mr Blunt by seizing his property. Fortunately, Mr Blunt had a friend in Cairo who settled the demand. But would it be believed that, owing to the action of Sir Evelyn Baring, Cherif Pasha and Nubar Pasha, Mr Blunt was not only unable to land at Suez, but he was forbidden to see his agent from Cairo [illegible] his property. He was forbidden [illegible] by the British Agent, although he had gone to Cairo originally under the sincere belief that he was acting with the knowledge and approval of the Prime Minister [illegible] Mr Blunt [illegible] harm in Cairo [illegible] return thanks to the discourtesy of Sir Evelyn Baring, he was [illegible] the lowest [illegible] positively [illegible] the rudest manner [illegible] Mr Blunt [illegible] agent was prevented from going on [illegible] with him. [illegible] Mr Blunt's letter to Earl Granville [illegible] stated that [illegible] Mr Blunt [illegible] Mr Blunt [illegible] and the [illegible].

LORD EDMOND FITZMAURICE: What is the date?

LORD RANDOLPH CHURCHILL replied that Mr Blunt's letter was dated May [illegible]. He knew that Sir Evelyn Baring stated that, as far as he was

ing in Egypt against whom no charge whatever had been brought. The hardship and injustice of it became far greater, however, when they considered the circumstances under which Mr. Blunt went to Egypt, and his conduct while there. He came now to the conduct of Cherif Pasha. The noble Lord the Under Secretary of State had informed the Committee that Cherif Pasha had acted upon his own motion. No doubt, the noble Lord fully believed that that was so. Very likely the noble Lord only believed the information furnished to him from certain sources in Egypt; but he (Lord Randolph Churchill) took leave to disbelieve that statement altogether, and to repudiate it as utterly worthless. The Government of Cherif Pasha had no existence except through the action of Sir Evelyn Baring, and nothing would induce him (Lord Randolph Churchill) to believe that Cherif Pasha, of his own motion, dared to forbid the landing of a British subject in Egypt. The idea was too ridiculous to be stated except in the House of Commons. It was said that Cherif Pasha took this course of his own motion, and that he said the return of Mr. Blunt to Egypt would be fatal to the Government. The charges made by Cherif Pasha against Mr. Blunt were extremely amusing. Among other things, he said that Mr. Blunt employed himself in starting a newspaper, the intended object of which was to create popularity for Arabi, and to weaken the authority of the Khedive. That was the first charge. But why was a newspaper started in Cairo to create popularity for Arabi to be prohibited, while the proprietor of a scurrilous journal called *The Bosphore Egyptien* was allowed week by week to appear in Cairo? The reason was that *The Bosphore Egyptien* was kept up in the interest of the French Consul (M. Barrière), and was directed to oppose the best English interests. For that reason Her Majesty's Government were very bold in dealing with a British subject, while they displayed the utmost timidity where the interests of a Foreign Power were concerned. At all events, Her Majesty's Government had adopted a very different policy in regard to *The Bosphore Egyptien* from that which they had adopted in the case of Mr. Blunt. So much for the newspaper question; but he thought it was a point upon which the noble Lord ought to give an explanation to the Committee, to show why there was one measure of justice for a Frenchman and another for an Englishman. There had been some talk about stopping *The Bosphore Egyptien*; but it had, nevertheless, been allowed to go on. Cherif Pasha proceeded, in his charges against Mr. Blunt, to say—

"You are further aware, my dear Minister, of the ideas he tried to disseminate in the country with regard to the foundation of an Arab Empire, and the imbecility of the present system of government."

It would be perceived that Mr. Blunt's great crime lay in the last sentence—the ideas Mr. Blunt tried to disseminate in regard to the imbecility of the present system of government, and that was the reason why Mr. Blunt was to be kept out of Egypt. He wanted to know why *The Times* Correspondent had not also been turned out, because ever since the Egyptian troubles begun he had sounded one trumpet only—namely, the imbecility of the Government, Native and British, unable to decide which was the most imbecile. The imbecility of the Government was not only the talk of the Bazaar, but of everybody in Egypt, the burden of the song in which every foreigner, high and low and rich and poor, joined. All concurred that it was impossible to produce anything except in the shape of disunion. Why was everybody allowed to talk about the imbecility of the Government of Egypt, while Mr. Blunt, who went out in a blameless and harmless capacity, was to be the one exception to the rule, and not to be allowed to criticize a solitary act of the Government? Mr. Blunt, a British subject, had been forbidden by Sir Evelyn Baring to land in Egypt, because he had expressed a strong opinion as to imbecility of the Native Government. Surely this was a nice state of things, under a Liberal British Government and a Liberal Prime Minister. Cherif Pasha says—

"We feel ourselves all the more justified in acting thus in the present case, because, thanks to the calm which has fallen upon all minds, and to the perfect tranquillity which reigns throughout the country, His Highness intends to order the immediate suppression of the Special Commissions and of the Court Martial at Alexandria, in order thus to enter upon an era of peace and concord."

Mr. Blunt was kept out of Egypt in

MR. MITCHELL HENRY said, he had asked himself while listening to the [illegible] whether any hon. Members who had spoken regarded with proper weight the condition of things in Egypt, and had any real desire to ameliorate the condition of that country? If the House of Commons was to be deluded by the speeches to which they had just listened they would imagine that Mr. Wilfrid Blunt, as an Englishman, was one of the most harmless persons [illegible]. Whatever the views of Mr. Blunt might be—and to some extent he had always shared them—(*Cries of* "Oh!")—Yes, he had certainly shared in the desire of Mr. Blunt for the advancement of the Native cause in Egypt; but he had never been able to associate himself with the means Mr. Blunt had adopted in carrying them out. (An hon. MEMBER: What means?) If hon. Gentlemen would allow him to proceed he would endeavour to make his statement as short and as succinct as he could. Mr. Blunt's great offence was this—that his policy had not succeeded, and that Her Majesty's Government had determined not to adopt it; but, on the contrary, had decided to maintain the authority of the present Khedive and to assist him in fulfilling his duties towards Egypt. The Khedive had shown courage that would have been remarkable in any man, but which was peculiar in an Egyptian. He was accused by Mr. Blunt [illegible] which would have degraded [illegible]. It was Mr. Blunt who [illegible] Mr. [illegible] W[illegible] and Lord Randolph Churchill [illegible] bringing forward charges against the Khedive in that House, which he had utterly failed to prove. (*Cries of* "No!") He appealed to the [illegible] of the [illegible] of the House [illegible], which [illegible] the noble Lord's statements [illegible] and [illegible]. Was it [illegible] having been instigated by Mr. Blunt to make [illegible] come forward in the House of Commons and speak of Mr. Blunt as though he were a person who [illegible] mischief and who desired to do no mischief in Egypt. Mr. Blunt's presence in Egypt at a moment when he was [illegible] from a visit to Arabi Pasha in Ceylon could do nothing but injury to the cause of order in Egypt. The Egyptians could never be relieved from oppression by putting them in opposition to the governing power of the country. No doubt, they had been oppressed; but they would not continue to be oppressed as soon as there was a capable Government established in the country. (*Ironical cheers.*) Surely the efforts of the present Government were directed towards the establishment of good order and freedom in the country. It was all very well for hon. Members some of whom had never visited Egypt, to make a jest of this statement; but nations like Egypt were not to be compelled into freedom all at once. Even some Members of the House of Commons, at a critical moment, did not always know how to act with complete propriety. He could only trust that Her Majesty's Government would discourage everybody, whoever he might be, who endeavoured to disseminate opinions which they regarded as inimical to the good government of Egypt, and he hoped that further experience would teach even Members of the House of Commons that well-regulated liberty depended on the observance of good temper. He trusted that, in the present state of affairs in Egypt, having at heart the good of the Egyptian people as well as any hon. Member of that House, the Home Government would assist the Egyptian Government in keeping out of the country, at the present moment, all those who wished to depose the Khedive. (*Cries of* "Oh!")

SIR JOSEPH M'KENNA said, he did not [illegible] whether [illegible] Nubar Pasha was the real agent in the matter was a feature which [illegible] for the judgment of the House. The responsibility would have been [illegible] and the course pursued would have [illegible] if Sir Evelyn Baring [illegible] the chief power in Egypt [illegible] best known [illegible] that Mr. Blunt was [illegible] British subject, who had [illegible] Egypt, but who [illegible] for the very reason that English interests were paramount and must be regarded. Sir Evelyn Baring might, under certain circumstances, have been justified [illegible]. At the same time he could not help thinking that

aware, no pressure had been put on Mr. Beaman to prevent his meeting Mr. Blunt on board the *China;* but the fact remained that Mr. Beaman was prevented from seeing Mr. Blunt, and as the people at Cairo only acted on the authority of Sir Evelyn Baring, he (Lord Randolph Churchill) declined to accept the disclaimer of Sir Evelyn Baring in a matter of this kind. It was a matter which ought to receive the direct attention of the House of Commons, in order to decide whether Her Majesty's subjects had a right to go to Egypt. If all persons who were distasteful to the Egyptian Government were to be excluded from that country he did not know where the matter would end. He knew of no country where such an arbitrary course had been adopted except Russia. [An hon. MEMBER: And Ireland.] He did not know that it was the case in Ireland; but Russia was, he thought, the only country in which such a thing could occur. He believed there were people who had been kicked out of Russia; but it must be borne in mind that this course was taken in Egypt in an era of peace and concord, with perfect tranquillity reigning throughout the country. In order to show how low and miserable a thing a British subject was, it was only necessary to refer to the treatment accorded by the Egyptian Government to Mr. Wilfrid Blunt. He thought that Mr. Blunt was entitled to ample reparation at the hands of the Egyptian Government for the injury which had been done to him.

MR. LABOUCHERE said, he thought that the facts of this case were very remarkable. Without exaggerating them, what were they? Mr. Wilfrid Blunt was a well-known gentleman, who had taken a great interest in Egyptian politics, and who had certain views of his own in regard to them. Mr. Blunt had always stated those views in this country. He went to Ceylon to visit Arabi and other exiles, and he was then told that he would not be allowed to return to Egypt. That decision was taken, not by the desire of Sir Evelyn Baring, but by that of Cherif Pasha, and it was subsequently confirmed by that of Nubar Pasha. It came, therefore, practically to this—if they examined the charges it would be seen that no overt act was complained of on the part of Mr. Blunt. No doubt, spies acccompanied him, who watched him during the night, and told absurd stories of his having been seen talking to certain people; but if hon. Members would carefully examine the despatches they would see that the real reason why Mr. Blunt was not permitted to land in Egypt again was on account of the views he had expressed in his writings in this country in regard to Egyptian policy. What did it amount to? We had really spent a large amount of money for the benefit of Egypt; and we had, therefore, a distinct interest in the good government of the country. If a Frenchman, or a German, or an Austrian were to go to Egypt, was it pretended for a moment that the Egyptian Government would have ventured to prevent him from landing in consequence of anything he might have written in regard to Egypt in his own country, or because he had been to Ceylon and had visited Arabi? Therefore, it came to this—that from the mere fact of our spending money in Egypt, and having an Army there, any Austrian, Frenchman, or German might land, but an Englishman could not land, unless he was in accord with the Egyptian Government as to the way in which the Government should be carried on in that country. If he were to go there during the Recess, with his hon. Friend the Member for Carlisle (Sir Wilfrid Lawson)—[An hon. MEMBER: Go.] "Go," said the hon. Member; but they could not go. If they did, they would certainly be stopped at once. There was nothing Mr. Blunt had said which he and his hon. Friend had not said, and they had even said much more. But if they went to Egypt it would only be to find spies put upon them and to get in difficulties with the Government. Thousands of persons in this country entertained the same views as Mr. Blunt. There was one thing he should like to know definitely. It was no use talking about the authority of the Egyptian Government. It was the authority of Her Majesty's Government. Nothing could be done without our authority; and he wished to know if it had come to this pass in Egypt—that every Englishman was to be stopped from landing whose views did not tally with those of some Nubar or Cherif or other Pasha, who was the dummy, for the time being, of the English Government?

MR. MITCHELL HENRY said, he had asked himself, while listening to the debate, whether some hon. Members who had spoken regarded with proper weight the condition of things in Egypt, and had any real desire to ameliorate the condition of that country? If the House of Commons was to be deluded by the speeches to which they had just listened they would imagine that Mr. Wilfrid Blunt, as an Englishman, was one of the most harmless persons possible. Whatever the views of Mr. Blunt might be—and to some extent he had always shared them—[*Cries of* "Oh!"] Yes; he had certainly shared the desire of Mr. Blunt for the advancement of the Native cause in Egypt; but he had never been able to associate himself with the means Mr. Blunt had adopted in carrying them out. [An hon. MEMBER: What means?] If hon. Gentlemen would allow him to proceed he would endeavour to make his statement as short and as succinct as he could. Mr. Blunt's great offence was this—that his policy had not succeeded, and that Her Majesty's Government had determined not to adopt it; but, on the contrary, had decided to maintain the authority of the present Khedive, and to assist him in fulfilling his duties towards Egypt. The Khedive had shown courage that would have been remarkable in any man, but which was peculiar in an Egyptian. He was accused by Mr. Blunt of many shocking crimes—crimes which would have disgraced a common malefactor. It was Mr. Blunt who instigated the noble Lord the Member for Woodstock (Lord Randolph Churchill) in bringing forward charges against the Khedive in that House, which he had utterly failed to prove. [*Cries of* "No!"] He appealed to the conscience of the nation and to the good sense of the House of Commons, who had come to the conclusion that the noble Lord's statements were reckless and without foundation. Well, the noble Lord, having been instigated by Mr. Blunt to make these statements, now came forward in the House of Commons and spoke of Mr. Blunt as though he were a person who could do no mischief, and who desired to do no mischief in Egypt. Mr. Blunt's presence in Egypt at a moment when he was returning from a visit to Arabi Pasha in Ceylon could do nothing but injury to the cause of order in Egypt. The Egyptians could never be relieved from oppression by putting them in opposition to the governing power of the country. No doubt, they had been oppressed; but they would not continue to be oppressed as soon as there was a capable Government established in the country. [*Ironical cheers.*] Surely the efforts of the present Government were directed towards the establishment of good order and freedom in the country. It was all very well for hon. Members, some of whom had never visited Egypt, to make a jest of this statement; but nations like Egypt were not to be compelled into freedom all at once. Even some Members of the House of Commons, at a critical moment, did not always know how to act with complete propriety. He could only trust that Her Majesty's Government would interrupt everybody, whoever he might be, who endeavoured to disseminate opinions which they regarded as inimical to the good government of Egypt; and he hoped that further experience would teach even Members of the House of Commons that well-regulated liberty depended on the observance of good temper. He trusted that, in the present state of affairs in Egypt, having at heart the good of the Egyptian people as well as any hon. Member of that House, the Home Government would assist the Egyptian Government in keeping out of the country, at the present moment, all those who wished to depose the Khedive. [*Cries of* "Oh!"]

SIR JOSEPH M'KENNA said, he did not think the circumstance whether Cherif Pasha or Nubar Pasha was the real agent in the matter was a feature which called for the judgment of the House. The responsibility would have been the same, and the course pursued would have been quite as justifiable, if Sir Evelyn Baring himself, as the chief power in Egypt, had, for reasons best known to himself, pronounced that Mr. Blunt was a dangerous British subject, who had once been admitted into Egypt, but who ought to be excluded in future. For the very reason that English interests were paramount and must be regarded, Sir Evelyn Baring might, under certain circumstances, have been justified in excluding him. At the same time, he could not help thinking that a grave indignity had been inflicted upon this country and its interests in excluding an Englishman in the position of Mr. Blunt from Egypt at the mere bidding of Cherif Pasha or Nubar Pasha, when such a course would never have been dreamt of in the case of any person entitled to the protection of the French or German Government. He could not undertake to pronounce an opinion whether Mr. Blunt ought to be excluded from Egypt. If he were a bad subject; if he were engaged in fostering rebellion; if he were acting contrary to the policy of the nation which was protecting Egypt, he admitted that under such circumstances it would be justifiable to exclude Mr. Blunt, but not upon the fiction of putting forward creatures such as Cherif Pasha and Nubar Pasha must be conceded to be to bear the responsibility. He held it to be a serious matter, and contrary not only to British but to International Law, that any nation, without assigning a good and proper cause, should endeavour to prevent a British subject passing along the high road of the world from calling at any particular place.

MR. GLADSTONE: After the reference which has been made to me by the noble Lord the Member for Woodstock (Lord Randolph Churchill), I feel it incumbent on me to say a few words. The noble Lord appears to have been led into some error. He thinks that Mr. Blunt ought not to have been excluded from Egypt, and he further thinks it a peculiar hardship that Mr. Blunt should have been excluded from Egypt considering the circumstances under which he went there, those circumstances, according to the noble Lord, being that the journey was suggested by Mr. Knowles, who is a gentleman well known to me, who possesses my confidence, and, therefore, that the visit of Mr. Blunt to Egypt had my approval.

LORD RANDOLPH CHURCHILL: I said that it raised a presumption.

MR. GLADSTONE: The noble Lord now says that the circumstances raised that presumption. The noble Lord connects my name with that of Mr. Knowles, and says that Mr. Knowles led Mr. Blunt to believe that the journey which he recommended would command my approval. Now, so far as Mr. Knowles is concerned, I have had some pleasant intercourse with him, and I hope, under favourable circumstances, to have some more. I am not at all ashamed of the association with Mr. Knowles in which the noble Lord places me; but any account of Mr. Knowles is idle without mentioning the fact that he is editor of *The Nineteenth Century*, and he is no doubt wise, being editor of *The Nineteenth Century*, to make the most of that position. Indeed, he is the editor of it from the crown of his head to the sole of his foot. In every day, and in every hour of his life, whenever you find that Mr. Knowles has had an interview with—be it Mr. Blunt or anybody else—you may rely upon it that the upshot and aim of that interview are wholly *The Nineteenth Century*. I may tell the noble Lord a little more. If Mr. Blunt had gone to Egypt and had satisfactorily executed his purpose, and returned to this country, Mr. Knowles would have gone to him and said that nothing could be more interesting than an article by Mr. Blunt in *The Nineteenth Century*. That is the full explanation of the course taken by Mr. Knowles. At one time I used to see a great deal of Mr. Knowles; but since I came into Office my opportunities have been very limited indeed, and I do not recollect to have exchanged any opinions on Egypt with Mr. Knowles, except, perhaps, a few words of the very slightest importance. I now turn to a more personal matter. As regards Mr. Hamilton, the question is rather more serious, for Mr. Hamilton is not the editor of a magazine, and he has no purely literary purpose in view. I am very glad that the noble Lord, in referring to Mr. Hamilton, did justice to his character as a Private Secretary, and to his claims, which cannot be too highly estimated, upon my gratitude for the services he has rendered to me. It is merely a question of memory between Mr. Hamilton and Mr. Blunt; and although we may presume that both gentlemen are incapable of the slightest wilful misrepresentation, there is a fundamental difference in the account they give. I have in my hand a little memorandum which Mr. Hamilton wrote for me on this subject a couple of months ago; but I never read it until within the last few weeks, when I learned that Mr. Hamilton and Mr. Blunt had been friends. I will not say that they are not personal friends now, but they had been personal friends; and Mr. Hamilton, considering the part Mr. Blunt had taken appeared to me to be nothing at all improbable in the idea that Mr. Blunt's case was correct as it had been given to me, because everybody knows that the sympathies of the Prime Minister are in favour of freedom of nationality; and it occurred to me that as Mr. Blunt went out to Egypt at a very difficult moment indeed, it was not improbable that the Prime Minister, acting as another great man once acted before—Louis XV.—was really bent upon carrying on a little diplomacy on his own account, unknown to Sir Evelyn Baring or Earl Granville. I was certain that his opinions were on the side of the National Party, and I thought I might support them by trying to take a step in the same direction. The right hon. Gentleman has rebuked me for having laughed at the idea of the existence of Native government in Egypt. He said that it was only natural that I should receive such an idea with jeers. If the right hon. Gentleman will recollect, the jeers came from his own side of the House.

MR. GLADSTONE: I beg the noble Lord's pardon. I said it would be natural that jeers should come from certain quarters of the House; but I think I admitted that they came from this side also.

LORD RANDOLPH CHURCHILL: Personally, I have never said a word in favour of the annexation of Egypt; and if I have lately advocated the extension of British power in Egypt, it was because I thought that it was only by such means that a real National Government could ever be established. I think that annexation is to be avoided by every possible means, and I have always hesitated to recommend it; but, at the same time, I have considered it my duty to place the interests of the Egyptian people far and beyond those of the Egyptian Government. These have been my views ever since the Egyptian difficulty began. The Prime Minister I noticed did not defend the exclusion of Mr. Blunt from Egypt, the special feature of that exclusion being the difference of treatment meted out to Mr. Blunt to that meted out to French officials or the subjects of any other nation.

SIR WILFRID LAWSON: As everything that is said by an Englishman in reference to Egypt is liable to be misinterpreted, I want to make one matter quite clear. It is only a small point. What I said in regard to the charge against Mr. Blunt, of having interviews with the rebels, which were prolonged far into the night, was that the only time he was up late at night was an occasion when he was living with the attaché of the British Embassy at a dance party. Upon another point the charges brought against Arabi are certainly not true. He has been charged in this House of having been guilty of the massacres at Alexandria; but when an inquiry was made the Government officials wrote home to say that a very good case for defence might be made out. But now, when the Government of Egypt is attacked, no inquiry into the charges made against the Khedive dare be made. I must say that I regret the course taken by the noble Lord the Member for Woodstock (Lord Randolph Churchill) in bringing up the communications of Mr. Blunt with Mr. Hamilton, because I do not think they have any bearing upon the real question at all. What I wish to say is this—that the noble Lord the Under Secretary of State has put the question upon a very serious footing. He said distinctly that Mr. Blunt having been opposed to the Government of Egypt, and having been a friend of Arabi, and having expressed strong opinions, must take the consequences of those opinions. The Prime Minister appears to take the same line, because he has endorsed the opinions of my hon. Friend near me the despot from Galway (Mr. Mitchell Henry), who says boldly and plainly that we ought to trample out everything that is antagonistic to the Government of Egypt.

MR. MITCHELL HENRY: I did not say anything of the kind.

SIR WILFRID LAWSON: Well, then, what was it that my hon. Friend did say?

MR. MITCHELL HENRY: What I said was that in the interest of those who were charged with the Government of Egypt I desired to keep out a man whose policy had utterly failed, and whose return would simply lead to further difficulties and complications. For that reason I objected to the re-opening by Mr. Blunt of questions that have been settled.

SIR WILFRID LAWSON: Exactly so; except in the opposite sense. Anybody would suppose I had an opinion to prove the utter nullity of any authority now exercised by the Egyptian Government, with a view to the putting forward of that which they really desire—namely, the establishment of British dominion in Egypt. That is perfectly intelligible, and I quite understand all those jeers. I fully accept them, coming from that quarter. They are impartial in their nature. There is a motive power in them which is aimed at the realization of certain views. But the noble Lord just now observed, and observed with perfect truth, that the jeers were not confined to that side of the House. I think my hon. Friend the Member for Carlisle (Sir Wilfrid Lawson) and the hon. Member for Northampton (Mr. Labouchere) joined in those jeers; and I wish to say a serious word to my hon. Friends. Do they wish to realize the prospect of the establishment of British dominion in Egypt? [SIR WILFRID LAWSON: No.] They do not. Then I will only tell them that the words they use, and the jeers they make use of, apply with all the force they possess towards the establishment of that state of things. I have ventured to express that opinion before to my hon. Friend the Member for Carlisle (Sir Wilfrid Lawson). And having some means of forming a judgment, I tell him now, from this Bench, that those who desire the establishment of British dominion in Egypt have no more effective ally than hon. Members who scoff and jeer the statement of my hon. Friend the Member for Galway (Mr. Mitchell Henry), when he says that he desires the maintenance of the authority of the Egyptian Government, and to see it converted into a reality. It is known to the House, and I freely admit that the position of England in Egypt at this moment, and the heavy responsibilities with which she is charged, have required, in our view, that we should assert a title to interpose in matters connected with the government of Egypt where we consider it absolutely necessary in the circumstances in which we stand. But that is not the annihilation of the Egyptian Government. I admit it freely, that if we were acting in a spirit of disparagement towards the Egyptian Government, and that if our object was to undermine their credit and dignity, it would be in our power to do so. But what we seek is to limit our power of interference; and, therefore, I own, it is a matter of grief and astonishment to me, whatever may be the indications which come from other quarters of the House, to hear from Gentlemen like my hon. Friends the Member for Carlisle (Sir Wilfrid Lawson) and the hon. Member for Northampton (Mr. Labouchere), who profess—and I must believe in the sincerity of their professions, notwithstanding appearances and the danger of what they say and do in this House—to entertain a desire that the practical domination of England shall not become permanent in Egypt—it is a matter of grief and astonishment to me to hear the jeers with which they greeted the remarks of my hon. Friend the Member for Galway (Mr. Mitchell Henry). I have thought it necessary to say this, because it is with us a sacred duty to respect, as far as the necessities of our position will permit, the independence and dignity of the Khedive. I admit that it is a qualified independence, and that every opportunity is taken for disparaging that independence; but, still, I affirm that our sole purpose is to maintain that independence and dignity as far as it is in our power to permit of their being maintained. And I must say that we are entitled to look for assistance, and not discouragement, in the prosecution of that object, from my hon. Friends the Member for Carlisle (Sir Wilfrid Lawson) and the hon. Member for Northampton (Mr. Labouchere), and those who think with them on this and other matters, who have at all times professed a warm desire, under the circumstances which have heretofore existed, to limit the scope of English intervention, and to shorten its duration. I may assure them that they can only accomplish that purpose by endeavouring to cherish and foster something like liberty of action on the part of the Khedive, and I confess that I should have expected support and encouragement in that work from that quarter of the House, rather than derision and jeers.

LORD RANDOLPH CHURCHILL: I hope I may be allowed to say a few words by way of explanation. I stated, in the first instance, that I did not put forward the statements of Mr. Blunt as my own. I never have done so. I said that I was here to state Mr. Blunt's case as well as I could; but I never intended to put it forward as my own. But there

wished to join the Mahdi, but who was prevented from doing so by the Egyptian Government, who interfered with his movements in a manner which was certainly quite as liable to excite observation as anything that has been done in the case of Mr. Blunt. The occasion of the interference was when the movements of Mr. O'Kelly were attracting some attention in the House. I was asked a Question about it at the time, and I stated that this French gentleman—a newspaper Correspondent—was proposing to accompany Mr. O'Kelly when he was stopped. Only to-day I stated, in reply to a Question that the Egyptian law, which enables foreigners to act in a certain manner in reference to newspaper articles, was being seriously considered with a view to its alteration. The whole condition of the Press Law in Egypt has attracted the attention of the Egyptian Government; and a Circular upon the subject has, I believe, been addressed to the European Powers. No doubt this has been the result of the impunity which has hitherto enabled foreigners to set at defiance the remonstrances of the Executive Government.

Mr. M'COAN said, he thought the memory of the noble Lord the Under Secretary of State was at fault when he described the case of the French Correspondent as one which was analogous to that of Mr. Blunt. It was the case of a newspaper Correspondent who desired to join the Mahdi in company with Mr. O'Kelly. The Egyptian Government stopped both of them, but did not expel either from Egypt. Consequently there was no parallel whatever between the two cases.

Mr. ASHMEAD-BARTLETT said, the hon. Member for Wicklow (Mr. M'Coan) had anticipated a remark which he was about to make. It was perfectly certain that there was only the most remote analogy between the case of the stopping of Mr. O'Kelly and the French Correspondent at Dongola, and that of Mr. Blunt. The Government, in this instance, had placed themselves in a thoroughly ridiculous position. It was evident, from the statements of the noble Lord the Member for Woodstock (Lord Randolph Churchill)—statements which had been made with great force and truth—that the treatment of Mr. O'Kelly and the Frenchman bore no comparison with that of Mr. Blunt by Sir Evelyn Baring and the Egyptian Government. There was nothing novel, however, in the facts which had been adduced. Parliament was accustomed to see British subjects insulted and trampled on, their interests despised, their rights set at defiance; while foreign subjects, backed up by their own Governments, were allowed any amount of immunity. He wished, however, to call the attention of the Committee to the remarkable inconsistency of the statement of the Prime Minister. The right hon. Gentleman informed the Committee that Mr. Blunt was stopped because his entry into Egypt would be dangerous to the order and peace of that country. He (Mr. Ashmead-Bartlett) desired to say, in the first place, lest the few remarks he had to make might be misunderstood, that he was not a believer in Mr. Blunt's views with regard to Egyptian policy. He thought the noble Lord had well described the views of that gentleman as those of a sentimentalist and an enthusiast; well meaning, no doubt, but mistaken in their aims. But when the Prime Minister gave, as a reason for the interference with the movements of a British subject in Egypt, that that interference was necessary for the protection and safety of the country, he would ask them why on earth they had been so unwilling to send a telegram to that gallant and unfortunate officer, General Hicks, forbidding him to proceed? Such a despatch would have had the effect of saving that officer and his army of 13,000 men, and an immense amount of subsequent ruin and bloodshed. [*A laugh.*] The Prime Minister laughed. He did not know why the right hon. Gentleman should laugh. Perhaps he was about to repeat the statement he had made once before, in reply to the Leader of the Opposition, that he had heard enough of General Hicks. It was perfectly notorious that if that unfortunate officer had acted upon his own views, he would not have started upon his ill-fated expedition; and a single telegram sent to Egypt by Her Majesty's Ministers would have stopped him, with the result of saving his life, and securing the safety of the 13,000 men who accompanied him. Therefore, he (Mr. Ashmead-Bartlett) said that to defend the action of the Government in the case of Mr. Blunt upon the necessities of Egypt, and to refuse intervention on the same ground in the case of General Hicks, was a contradiction of terms. He had placed a Motion on the Paper [illegible] Sir Evelyn Baring. [illegible] Her Majesty's Government under the advice of Sir Evelyn Baring, but the [illegible] Prime Minister [illegible] Her Majesty's Government [illegible]

[illegible]

[illegible] was to be evacuated, and that

orders to that effect had already gone forth. It was unnecessary to remind [illegible] was at [illegible] present [illegible] He believed that Sir Evelyn Baring was largely [illegible] Egypt and [illegible] He had been [illegible] Lord Randolph Churchill as being incapable [illegible] contrary to [illegible] Her Majesty's Government [illegible] Lord [illegible] Her Majesty's Government [illegible]

[illegible]

This policy [illegible] which Sir Evelyn Baring [illegible] Egypt [illegible] British [illegible] Ministry from [illegible] which [illegible] He [illegible] Sir Evelyn Baring [illegible]

[illegible] a reduction in respect

wished to join the Mahdi, but who was prevented from doing so by the Egyptian Government, who interfered with his movements in a manner which was certainly quite as liable to excite observation as anything that has been done in the case of Mr. Blunt. The occasion of the interference was when the movements of Mr. O'Kelly were attracting some attention in the House. I was asked a Question about it at the time, and I stated that this French gentleman —a newspaper Correspondent—was proposing to accompany Mr. O'Kelly when he was stopped. Only to-day I stated, in reply to a Question that the Egyptian law, which enables foreigners to act in a certain manner in reference to newspaper articles, was being seriously considered with a view to its alteration. The whole condition of the Press Law in Egypt has attracted the attention of the Egyptian Government; and a Circular upon the subject has, I believe, been addressed to the European Powers. No doubt this has been the result of the impunity which has hitherto enabled foreigners to set at defiance the remonstrances of the Executive Government.

Mr. M'COAN said, he thought the memory of the noble Lord the Under Secretary of State was at fault when he described the case of the French Correspondent as one which was analogous to that of Mr. Blunt. It was the case of a newspaper Correspondent who desired to join the Mahdi in company with Mr. O'Kelly. The Egyptian Government stopped both of them, but did not expel either from Egypt. Consequently there was no parallel whatever between the two cases.

Mr. ASHMEAD-BARTLETT said, the hon. Member for Wicklow (Mr. M'Coan) had anticipated a remark which he was about to make. It was perfectly certain that there was only the most remote analogy between the case of the stopping of Mr. O'Kelly and the French Correspondent at Dongola, and that of Mr. Blunt. The Government, in this instance, had placed themselves in a thoroughly ridiculous position. It was evident, from the statements of the noble Lord the Member for Woodstock (Lord Randolph Churchill)—statements which had been made with great force and truth—that the treatment of Mr. O'Kelly and the Frenchman bore no comparison with that of Mr. Blunt by Sir Evelyn Baring and the Egyptian Government. There was nothing novel, however, in the facts which had been adduced. Parliament was accustomed to see British subjects insulted and trampled on, their interests despised, their rights set at defiance; while foreign subjects, backed up by their own Governments, were allowed any amount of immunity. He wished, however, to call the attention of the Committee to the remarkable inconsistency of the statement of the Prime Minister. The right hon. Gentleman informed the Committee that Mr. Blunt was stopped because his entry into Egypt would be dangerous to the order and peace of that country. He (Mr. Ashmead-Bartlett) desired to say, in the first place, lest the few remarks he had to make might be misunderstood, that he was not a believer in Mr. Blunt's views with regard to Egyptian policy. He thought the noble Lord had well described the views of that gentleman as those of a sentimentalist and an enthusiast; well meaning, no doubt, but mistaken in their aims. But when the Prime Minister gave, as a reason for the interference with the movements of a British subject in Egypt, that that interference was necessary for the protection and safety of the country, he would ask them why on earth they had been so unwilling to send a telegram to that gallant and unfortunate officer, General Hicks, forbidding him to proceed? Such a despatch would have had the effect of saving that officer and his army of 13,000 men, and an immense amount of subsequent ruin and bloodshed. [*A laugh.*] The Prime Minister laughed. He did not know why the right hon. Gentleman should laugh. Perhaps he was about to repeat the statement he had made once before, in reply to the Leader of the Opposition, that he had heard enough of General Hicks. It was perfectly notorious that if that unfortunate officer had acted upon his own views, he would not have started upon his ill-fated expedition; and a single telegram sent to Egypt by Her Majesty's Ministers would have stopped him, with the result of saving his life, and securing the safety of the 13,000 men who accompanied him. Therefore, he (Mr. Ashmead-Bartlett) said that to defend the action of the Government in the case of Mr. Blunt upon the necessities of Egypt, and to refuse intervention on the same

ment of the Khedive, considering that the action of Mr. Blunt was of a dangerous kind, had endeavoured to prevent him, by warning or otherwise, from coming back to Egypt, it would not have been open to them to take that step; and however much the Government of this country wished the exclusion of Mr. Blunt, they would have entered a protest against the action of the Egyptian Government. Sir Evelyn Baring, believing there was some illegality on the part of the Egyptian Government, telegraphed to Earl Granville for instructions as to the course he was to take; and the answer which he received from the noble Earl was singularly diplomatic; it said nothing, but meant a great deal. "You may abstain," said Earl Granville, "from opposing the action of the Egyptian Government," which was the same as saying—"We do not ask you should [illegible] we think you should take the responsibility of objecting to it." But after that another despatch had been sent by Sir Evelyn Baring to Earl Granville, saying that he proposed to forward a copy of Nubar Pasha's letter to Mr. Blunt, and "I should be glad to receive instructions as to whether the letter met with the approval of Her Majesty's Government." Well, the answer to that was, to his mind, singularly extraordinary. Instead of replying that the action of Nubar Pasha was sanctioned by Her Majesty's Government, Earl Granville said—"I have no proposal to make to you with regard to Mr. Blunt." But, as a matter of fact, Sir Evelyn Baring had made no proposal at all with regard to Mr. Blunt. He would leave that matter to the consideration of the Committee. He maintained that the question [illegible] the exclusion of a British subject by the arbitrary act of a foreign Government, an act which the Attorney General said was always to be regarded with the greatest [illegible] to be guarded against with the greatest care. It was the exclusion of a British subject with the concurrence of Her Majesty's Government, and as such the Committee ought to regard it. The position of the Government in this matter he held to be [illegible] and absurd. He thought the case was even worse than that which he had brought forward in that House on a former occasion. The action of the Government could only compare with their action in the case of the crew of the [illegible] and with their abandonment of General Gordon. It appeared that the Government had failed to recognize the [illegible] principle that a British subject was entitled to the protection of the British Government.

MR. LABOUCHERE asked for some explanation of the law stated by the Attorney General with reference to the exclusion of Mr. Blunt from Egypt. He had always supposed that when a Government acted beyond the law it acted arbitrarily. That was precisely what the Egyptian Government had done in this case. But they had done more than that; they had acted directly contrary to the law. The hon. and learned Gentleman asked—What law? The answer was the Capitulations. By the Capitulations every foreigner had a right to [illegible] in Egypt, to [illegible] there, and to [illegible]. Therefore, if this case had occurred to any other foreigner, that foreigner would only have had to go to his own Government and ask that they should interfere on his behalf in accordance with the Capitulations; and Mr. Blunt had just the same right as any other Englishman to go to the Foreign Office and to ask why in his case the Capitulations were not to be [illegible]. Mr. Blunt had a treaty and legal right to reside in Egypt, and when the Egyptian Government refused to allow him to do so, they acted contrary to law, and in an arbitrary manner.

MR. M'COAN said, he could speak with personal knowledge on this matter. He had a very [illegible] acquaintance with the Capitulations, and he begged to say that the [illegible] Member for the Northampton (Mr. Labouchere) was [illegible] right in his statement [illegible] Capitulations [illegible] were in [illegible] Egypt any Englishman had [illegible] of the country and [illegible].

THE ATTORNEY GENERAL (Sir HENRY JAMES) said, his statement had been, that his recollection of the Capitulations was that every English subject observing the law of the country had a right to remain in the country. Therefore if there were no objection to Mr. Blunt's conduct, he would have a cause of complaint against the Egyptian Go-of the incomes of the Ministers themselves. Sir Evelyn Baring had in this matter played only a subordinate part, taking his cue from Downing Street. He had not dared to initiate that independent policy which ought to have commended itself to his judgment. There was evidence in the Papers that Sir Evelyn Baring recommended that an expedition should be sent to relieve General Gordon as early as March last, although he had previously written against it. The chief charge against Sir Evelyn Baring was, as he had pointed out, that he took his cue from Downing Street. Finally, he asked the Committee to consider the extraordinary reasons given to them for not despatching an expedition to the relief of General Gordon. In drawing attention to this point, as he had already stated, as there was to be a debate on Egyptian affairs, he did not intend to go into the question at large. The reasons, or rather the excuses, put forward by the Government for not taking action in this matter were so unworthy, and he ventured to say so discreditable, that they deserved special attention from hon. Members. The statement had been made by several Ministers that General Gordon had, at a certain moment, changed his policy, and that he had developed a policy of going out of his way to attack the Mahdi. He (Mr. Ashmead-Bartlett) admitted that it might have been wiser if General Gordon had concealed his intention in those periphrastic mystifications which the Government so well knew how to employ for the purpose of concealing their meaning; but General Gordon was a soldier, and said exactly what he meant. That phrase "smash up the Mahdi" meant nothing that was not necessary, in his judgment, to be done for the peace of Egypt. General Gordon, for obvious reasons, actually tolerated slavery; he waited till he was besieged in Khartoum until he took any measures of force. To say that he had changed his policy or attitude was a gross injustice to General Gordon and a perversion of his meaning. He asked Her Majesty's Government what else they were doing but endeavouring to smash up the Mahdi's followers? What were the British Forces doing at Wady Halfa and Assouan, and what were their officers at Suakin and other places doing, but smashing up the tribes which followed the Mahdi? He would not move the reduction of the Vote in view of the larger debate of to-morrow; but he hoped that Members who were anxious to begin to discuss the tactics of the Government with regard to General Gordon would not find that they had been deprived of the opportunity of doing so by the unsatisfactory way in which the Government had arranged the Business of the House. He trusted that the Prime Minister would bear in mind the statement made by him on Saturday, that the Vote for the relief of General Gordon and for the restoration of order in the Soudan would be put down for to-morrow. The right hon. Gentleman had promised that a special Vote for General Gordon would be put on the Paper, distinct from any other Vote which the Government might have to bring forward, in order to pay for the destruction of property at Alexandria, or on account of the other blunders they made in Egypt upon that special Vote. He hoped that a clear statement would be made by Her Majesty's Government as to this question of relief or non-relief of General Gordon.

Baron HENRY DE WORMS said, he was hardly disposed to sympathize with Mr. Blunt; but there were, no doubt, many Members of that House who would agree that his exclusion from Egypt was, at least, very extraordinary. It would be in the recollection of the Committee that some years ago Lord Palmerston introduced into the House a Bill called the Conspiracy Bill, which had for its object to obtain powers for excluding from this country persons deemed to be dangerous conspirators. Now, the measure which had been adopted by the Government of the Khedive, and which had received the direct sanction of Her Majesty's Government, savoured of the nature of that Conspiracy Bill, because the worst that anyone had said of Mr. Blunt was that he was a person who was intriguing against the Government of the Khedive; and for that reason he had been, no doubt, excluded from Egypt, not by the Government of the Khedive; but by the direct action of Her Majesty's Government. He did not know whether any previous speaker had called attention to the details in the Papers laid upon the Table; but they certainly seemed to be worthy of attention. If the Government of the Khedive, considering that the action of Mr. Blunt was of a dangerous kind, had endeavoured to prevent him, by warning or otherwise, from coming back to Egypt, it would not have been open to them to take that step; and however much the Government of this country wished the exclusion of Mr. Blunt, they would have entered a protest against the action of the Egyptian Government. Sir Evelyn Baring, believing there was some illegality on the part of the Egyptian Government, telegraphed to Earl Granville for instructions as to the course he was to take; and the answer which he received from the noble Earl was singularly diplomatic; it said nothing, but meant a great deal. "You may abstain," said Earl Granville, "from opposing the action of the Egyptian Government;" which was the same as saying—"We do not think you should sanction it; but we think you should take the responsibility of objecting to it." But, after that, another despatch had been sent by Sir Evelyn Baring to Earl Granville, saying that he proposed to forward a copy of Nubar Pasha's letter to Mr. Blunt, and should be glad to receive instructions as to whether the letter met with the approval of Her Majesty's Government. Well, the answer to that was in terms equally extraordinary; instead of replying that the action of Nubar Pasha was sanctioned by Her Majesty's Government, Earl Granville said—"Act as you propose in your telegram with regard to Mr. Blunt." But, as a matter of fact, Sir Evelyn Baring had made no proposal at all with regard to Mr. Blunt. He would leave that matter to the consideration of the Committee. He maintained that this question was not merely one as to the exclusion of a British subject by the arbitrary act of a Foreign Government, an act which the Attorney General said was always to be regarded with the greatest suspicion, and to be guarded against with the greatest care—it was the exclusion of a British subject with the concurrence of Her Majesty's Government, and as such the Committee ought to regard it. The position of the Government in this matter he held to be mischievous and absurd. He thought the case was even worse than that which he had brought forward in that House on a former occasion. This action of the Government could only compare with their action in the case of the crew of the *Nisero* and with their abandonment of General Gordon. It appeared that the Government had failed to recognize the Constitutional principle that a British subject was entitled to the protection of the British Government.

MR. LABOUCHERE asked for some explanation of the law stated by the Attorney General with reference to the exclusion of Mr. Blunt from Egypt. He had always supposed that when a Government acted beyond the law it acted arbitrarily. That was precisely what the Egyptian Government had done in this case. But they had done more than that—they had acted directly contrary to the law. The hon. and learned Gentleman asked, What law? The answer was the Capitulations. By the Capitulations every foreigner had a right to land in Egypt, to trade and live there, and to be judged by particular tribunals. Therefore, if this case had occurred to any other foreigner, that foreigner would only have had to go to his own Government and claim that they should interfere in his behalf in accordance with the Capitulations; and Mr. Blunt had just the same right as any other Englishman to go to the Foreign Office, and to ask why in his case the Capitulations were not to be enforced. Mr. Blunt had a Treaty and legal right to land in Egypt; and when the Egyptian Government refused to allow him to do so, they acted contrary to law, and in an arbitrary manner.

MR. M'COAN said, he could speak with personal knowledge on this matter. He had a very intimate acquaintance with the Capitulations; and he begged to say that the hon. Member for Northampton (Mr. Labouchere) was perfectly right in the statement he had just made. He knew that by the Capitulations which were in operation in both Turkey and Egypt any Englishman had full right to land in any part of the latter country, and to live and trade there as long as he liked.

THE ATTORNEY GENERAL (Sir HENRY JAMES) said, his statement had been that his recollection of the Capitulations was that every English subject observing the law of the country had a right to remain in the country. Therefore, if there were no objections to Mr. Blunt's conduct, he would have a cause of complaint against the Egyptian Government, which he could put forward through the Consul General in Egypt. But, as to whether Mr. Blunt had made any complaint, he knew nothing. Nor did he know whether there was sufficient ground for the exclusion of Mr. Blunt, although, as to the principle on which his right to land in Egypt rested, he thought there was no question whatever. Sir Evelyn Baring had consulted Mr. Cookson, the man who in all Egypt was best qualified to advise on the subject; and it was after Mr. Cookson's advice had been received that Sir Evelyn Baring took the course which he had pursued.

LORD RANDOLPH CHURCHILL said, he did not think it right that the Attorney General should hold up Mr. Cookson to cover his deficient knowledge of the law.

LORD EDMOND FITZMAURICE said, that Mr. Cookson had been consulted, and that there was no justification for saying that Mr. Cookson concurred in the view put forward by the hon. Member for Northampton (Mr. Labouchere) and the hon. Member for Wicklow (Mr. M'Coan).

MR. M'COAN asked if the noble Lord would take upon himself the responsibility of saying that Mr. Cookson was of opinion that under the Capitulations Mr. Blunt was not entitled to land in Egypt? He had known that gentleman for many years at Constantinople; he knew the extent of his authority in a question of this kind; and while he might, without presumption, set his own experience against that of Mr. Cookson, he ventured to affirm that Mr. Cookson could never have advised that Mr. Blunt had not a right under the Capitulations to land and attend to his affairs in Egypt. If he could give such advice, he was little fit for the office of Consul and Judge.

LORD EDMOND FITZMAURICE said, he believed that Mr. Cookson had been consulted by Sir Evelyn Baring with regard to the subject generally. Similar powers to those exercised by the Egyptian Government it was well known had been exercised in Turkey, foreigners having been excluded from that country in exactly the same manner as Mr. Blunt had been excluded from Eg p. The position under the Capitulations was that certain rights were given to foreign subjects; but they were contingent upon the rights not being abused. It was improbable that any Government would give a general power to foreigners to land and abuse their laws. No State could exist for any length of time with such a law in operation. There were in Egypt certain well-recognized rights of foreigners who enjoyed the benefit of the Capitulations, on condition that their privileges were not abused. If a man thought he had been unjustly treated he had a right to appeal to his Consul; but the Consul was not under an obligation to extend his protection to foreigners who abused their rights.

MR. BOURKE said, that the case put by the noble Lord was that if a foreigner landed in Turkey or any other country and abused his privileges he was not entitled to protection from his Consul; but that was not the case with Mr. Blunt, who had been prevented from landing, and had, therefore, had no opportunity of abusing his privileges. There could have been no abuse of privileges by Mr. Blunt; and he gathered from the Papers that he was excluded from Egypt not on account of anything he had done there, but for something he had done in England.

BARON HENRY DE WORMS said, it could not have been clear that Mr. Blunt was properly excluded from Egypt, because Sir Evelyn Baring wrote to Earl Granville in these words—

"Can the Egyptian Government, acting through its own officers, prevent an English subject landing in Egypt, or must they act through the Consular authorities? I am unable here to obtain any satisfactory answer to this question, and I beg your Lordship will be so good as to furnish me with instructions as to how I am to act."

If the Capitulations were so clear, Sir Evelyn Baring would have been able to ascertain in Egypt whether Mr. Blunt could land or not.

LORD EDMOND FITZMAURICE: I said Mr. Blunt had no right to plead the Capitulations when he had abused the privileges conferred upon foreigners under them.

SIR GEORGE CAMPBELL said, he thought the subject of Mr. Blunt's exclusion from Egypt had been well threshed out; and, therefore, he would ask a question of the Under Secretary of State for Foreign Affairs on a subject of more importance. He referred to the Slave Trade in Egypt, and he asked the noble Lord whether the execution of the Convention with regard to it was coming into effect on the 17th of August, 1884? He had already addressed a very plain question on this subject to the noble Lord; but the answer which he received had somewhat obscured the position. The proposition of the Earl of Dufferin not only declared that slavery should be prohibited, but that it should be altogether abolished. Sir Evelyn Baring was of a contrary opinion, and he expressed himself to that effect in a despatch which the noble Lord had referred to. But the question he had put to the noble Lord on a former occasion was as to whether it was intended by Her Majesty's Government to press upon the Khedive of Egypt to give effect not to the proposal of the Earl of Dufferin, to which Sir Evelyn Baring was unfavourably inclined, but to the original Convention now standing, and the Decree of the Egyptian Government, by which the trade in human beings would become unlawful, and prohibited under the severest penalties on the 17th of August, 1884. He expressed an earnest hope that the noble Lord, in the answer which he gave to this inquiry, would not throw any doubt on the state in which the law in Egypt would be on that date in reference to slavery. He hoped the noble Lord the Under Secretary of State for Foreign Affairs would be able to assure them that the answer he had previously given did not imply a doubt that the British Government would be less zealous than they would have been if they had not been in Egypt at all. He trusted the noble Lord would be able to assure the Committee that Her Majesty's Government would impress on the Khedive of Egypt the obligation which rested on him, under the Decrees which would come into force on the 17th of the present month. Referring to the subject, the Earl of Dufferin had stated that, with regard to Egypt Proper, under the Convention of seven years ago, the selling of slaves from family to family would cease on the 17th of August, 1884; and then, assuming, as a matter of course, that the Convention would come into effect, the Earl of Dufferin went on to say that we should press the Egyptian Government to inflict the heaviest possible punishment in case of a violation of the Convention. He (Sir George Campbell) had only now to ask the noble Lord if it was intended that the Convention and its Annexes would come into force in Egypt on the 17th of the present month; and if the Government were prepared to press the Khedive of Egypt to give full effect to the Convention? This was a question of the utmost importance in the interests of humanity; by the Convention a great step was taken towards the abolition of slavery. They were now in a position to press the execution of the Convention upon the Khedive with greater authority and power than they would have been were they not in possession of the country; and therefore he hoped the noble Lord would at once tell the Committee that his words were not intended to derogate the authority of this Convention.

MR. ASHMEAD-BARTLETT said, the hon. Gentleman (Sir George Campbell) who had asked the question that night about the subject of slavery, and who had now re-introduced the subject, had done public service in bringing forward this great question of slavery in connection with Egypt; but if the hon. Gentleman expected that Her Majesty's Government were going to do anything to diminish slavery in Egypt, or to do away with it altogether, he would be grievously disappointed. He would be put off with vague phrases and promises. He (Mr. Ashmead-Bartlett) thought the country would notice with surprise what he ventured to call the hypocrisy of two of the Ministers of the Crown, not in that House, who attended the great anti-slavery meeting at the Guildhall the other day, and made fine speeches in favour of the abolition of slavery all over the world, while the Government had been doing their utmost to encourage slavery of the most cruel and abominable kind throughout the whole of the Soudan, and to tolerate it in Egypt. How many thousand persons had been subjected to cruel slavery and outrage in consequence of the conduct of Her Majesty's Government during the past two years? The noble Lord the Under Secretary of State for Foreign Affairs might possibly say these were vague observations; but he would give the strongest possible proof that the policy of Her Majesty's Government, with regard to Egypt and the Soudan, had promoted, and would continue to promote slavery, although Earl Granville and the Earl of Derby attended the Guildhall meetings and

shock to religion in Italy, and directed against religion at large; but they freely acknowledged that Catholics in England and Ireland and elsewhere throughout the British Empire had no claim upon Her Majesty's Government to interfere for the protection of Italian Catholics on a question of Italian national religious institutions; but it was an institution of a totally different description which had been assailed by the Italian Government of late—it was an institution partaking of the international character of the Papacy which had been assailed. The institution of the Propaganda was not, and never had been, merely or mainly concerned with the Catholic religion in Italy and for Italians—it had been mainly concerned with the Catholic religion throughout the world, in the British Empire as much as elsewhere, and, in fact, in the British Empire more than in, perhaps, all the other nations of the world. It was an institution, in the first place, for promoting the missionary enterprize for the conversion of the heathen; and, in the second place, an institution for carrying on, and aiding the carrying on, the Catholic religion in all countries. Its funds had been supplied by the contributions of Catholics throughout the whole world, the endowments were formed, and the securities for their productive investment were taken and established entirely with a view to its international character. The Propaganda was founded, in a geographical sense, on Italian soil, which was now under the established Government of the Sardinian dynasty; but the creation of a temporal Government in Italy in no way took away the international character of the great institution which long preceded the Sardinian dynasty in Italy. It was necessary for the world before the Sardinian dynasty was established, and it was just as necessary for the world to-day; it was an institution which in an especial degree concerned the Catholic subjects of Her Majesty in the British Empire, and that simply arose from the fact of the enormous Colonial Empire ruled by Her Majesty. Throughout India, throughout large portions of the British Empire, in consequence of the historic circumstances at home, millions of Catholics had been and were vastly dependent upon the discharge and full liberty of the teaching functions of their Church—upon the complete liberty of the institution of the Sacred Congregation of the Propaganda. Now, the hon. Member for Clonmel (Mr. A. Moore) brought this question forward in the House on two occasions in February last, and called the attention of Her Majesty's Government to the gravity of the proceedings that were about to take place in Italy; and, in reply, the Prime Minister expressed himself with a certain amount of that large and copious language which, perhaps, was the most useful kind of language for giving expression to opinions that, for one reason or another, it was not desirable too definitely to express. But, at any rate, one promise was made by the Premier on the 18th of February last—namely, that the British Ambassador in Italy would take every opportunity to maintain and support the claims of the Catholic subjects of Her Majesty's Government. On that occasion, the right hon. Gentleman said that—

"Sir John Lumley will be instructed to use his good offices in the matter, in case he should see any opening for that purpose."—(3 *Hansard*, [284] 1200.)

Whether openings for that purpose had occurred or not, there was issued the other day a Decree of the Italian High Court bringing the construction of the Propaganda under the ordinary law with regard to Ecclesiastical Corporations in Ireland. That Decree had been in operation ever since, and at any time since the British Government was aware of the strength of feeling of all Catholics on the subject the British Ambassador could and ought to have made serious representations on the matter. Instead of any representations having been made, the Premier to-day reiterated, but in a somewhat different form, the answer he gave last week, the gist of which was that the British Ambassador had, down to the present, done no single thing whatever towards safeguarding the rights of the Catholics at large, and of British Catholics in particular, on the international question of the international institution of the Propaganda. To-day the language of the Premier certainly displayed an improvement upon his former answers, because to-day he distinctly expressed the opinion that the whole question was an Italian legal question; his answer implied that the whole importance of this institution

such express declaration, while in regard to the positive statement, which he understood the hon. Member had found in the despatch, and which, to a certain extent, had disturbed his mind, all he could say was, speaking from recollection, that there was nothing in the despatch at all to show that there was any desire or intention to suspend the operation of the Khedival Decree. All that Her Majesty's Government could do was to impress on the Egyptian Government to do whatever was possible under the circumstances; and his hon. Friend might be perfectly certain that whatever could be done by the Government towards the abolition of slavery would be done. It was not likely that in the year that this country had been celebrating the jubilee of the abolition of slavery there would be any laxity on the part of Her Majesty's Ministers in using whatever influence they had upon Foreign and Colonial authorities to secure an abolition of those practices, which were so repugnant to every Englishman, no matter to what Party he belonged. He could only express regret that upon such a question as this of slavery the hon. Member for Eye (Mr. Ashmead-Bartlett) was not able to resist the temptation to indulge in a violent attack on the Government. The hon. Gentleman had used the word "hypocrisy"—[Mr. ASHMEAD-BARTLETT: Hear, hear!]—and now he cried "Hear, hear!" Surely, after all, the hon. Member must know that in regard to this question of slavery there was no division of Party at all; and when he accused the Government of hypocrisy in this matter—[Mr. ASHMEAD-BARTLETT: Two Ministers.]—well, two of the most important Ministers—Earl Granville and the Earl of Derby—he could not seriously mean what he said. Earl Granville and the Earl of Derby had both exerted themselves in every way to promote the abolition of slavery. If it were in Order for him so to do, he could with perfect ease show that during the time Earl Granville had presided at the Foreign Office, he had exerted himself in the cause of the abolition of slavery in a way which entitled him to the gratitude of every man.

SIR GEORGE CAMPBELL explained that his mind was not at all disturbed by the despatch of Sir Evelyn Baring; but it was disturbed by the answer which the noble Lord gave him earlier in the evening; and it was somewhat more disturbed by the observations the noble Lord had just addressed to the Committee. The Question he had asked was whether the Convention was to be put in force on the 17th of August or not, and the noble Lord had said Her Majesty's Government would do the best they could in the matter; a plain answer was not returned to a plain question. He merely asked, and he hoped the noble Lord would answer him, "Yes" or "No," was it or was it not the intention of the Government that the Convention solemnly entered into in 1877 was to come into force, as arranged, on the 17th of August?

LORD EDMOND FITZMAURICE: The question is under the consideration of Her Majesty's Government.

MR. O'DONNELL said, he wished to take the advantage of this Vote to call attention to what he considered the singular neglect of Her Majesty's Government and of the Ambassador of Her Majesty's Government in Italy to safeguard to the best of their ability the international rights of the Catholic subjects of Her Majesty involved in the unfounded spoliation of the Propaganda. Now, on a consideration of this question, they must bear in mind two very different and distinct matters—namely, the position of the national Catholic institutions in Italy, and the position of the international Catholic institutions in Italy. Now, to take an example of the former, let them take at once, say, the monastic institutions established in Italy on Italian soil for the special service of Italian people, and supported and endowed out of Italian funds, and for local Italian objects. Like every Catholic, and he hoped like every honest man, no matter what his religious belief might be, he held that the confiscation of national religious institutions was none the less robbery though it might be done according to certain Parliamentary forms. With regard to the national Italian institutions, he could not help thinking that the way in which they had been robbed by the Italian Government was most unjustifiable and iniquitous in the extreme; but the Catholic subjects of Her Majesty made no claim on Her Majesty's Government to interfere in respect to Italian national institutions, even though of a religious character. Their spoliation was considered by Catholics a great shock to religion in Italy, and [illegible] against religion at large; [illegible] freely acknowledged that Cath[illegible] England and Ireland and [illegible] throughout the British Empire [illegible] claim upon Her Majesty's Govern[illegible] to interfere for the protection of It[illegible] Catholics on a question of Italian[illegible] tional religious institutions; but it [illegible] an institution of a totally different de[illegible]scription which had been assailed by the Italian Government of late—it was [illegible] institution partaking of the international character of the Papacy which had been assailed. The institution of the Propaganda was not, and never had been merely or mainly concerned with the Catholic religion in Italy and for Italians—it had been mainly concerned with the Catholic religion throughout the world, in the British Empire as much as elsewhere, and, in fact, in the British Empire more than in, perhaps, all the other nations of the world. It was an institution, in the first place, for promoting the missionary enterprise for the conversion of the heathen; and, in the second place, an institution for carrying on, and aiding the carrying on, the Catholic religion in all countries. Its funds had been supplied by the contributions of Catholics throughout the whole world, the endowments were formed, and the securities for their productive investment were taken and established entirely with a view to its international character. The Propaganda was founded, in a geographical sense, on Italian soil, which was now under the established Government of the Sardinian dynasty; but the creation of a temporal Government in Italy in no way took away the international character of the great institution which long preceded the Sardinian dynasty in Italy. It was necessary for the world before the Sardinian dynasty was established, and it was just as necessary for the world today; it was an institution which in an especial degree concerned the Catholic subjects of Her Majesty in the British Empire, and that simply arose from the fact of the enormous Colonial Empire ruled by Her Majesty. Throughout India, throughout large portions of the British Empire, in consequence of the historic circumstances at home, millions of Catholics had been and were vastly dependent upon the discharge and full liberty of the teaching functions of their

[illegible] of any [illegible] the Pro[illegible] somewhat [illegible] gave [illegible] that the [illegible] to the [illegible] whatever [illegible] rights of the [illegible] British Cath[illegible] international [illegible] tional institu[illegible] To-day the [illegible] certainly displ[illegible] upon his form[illegible] day he distinctly [illegible] that the whole [illegible] legal question; the whole impor[illegible] of universal Catholicism was dependent upon a private local law of one particular nation — namely, the Italian nation. Why, following the view expressed by the Premier to-day, if the Italian High Court chose to bring the Papacy itself, which was undoubtedly a Corporation *sole*, under the law regarding Ecclesiastical Corporations in Italy they could do so. The would just have as much legal claim to come to an opinion of that sort with regard to the Papacy itself, as they would in regard to this necessary and inseparable portion of the Papacy, the institution of the Propaganda. The very first function of the Church was to teach all nations, and the College of the Propaganda was specially an institution for that universal and world-wide purpose; and if the Italian High Court could do what it pleased with the College of the Propaganda, it could, with exactly as much legal right, declare that the Papacy was an Italian Corporation, that the Pope was an Italian Bishop, and the complaints of the Catholic subjects of Her Majesty, against even the most violent interference with the direct spiritual authority of the Pope, might be answered by some future Premier that that was an Italian legal question. That was the position against which Catholics protested, and he begged to remind the Premier that there were no divided counsels in this matter amongst Catholics. The question had been raised by Catholic Members of the House, who sat amongst the usual supporters of Her Majesty's Government; and only a few days ago the Party who followed the hon. Member for the City of Cork (Mr. Parnell) passed, in the most emphatic and solemn way, a request to that hon. Member to bring forward this question on behalf of their Body; so, whether Catholic Members sat on the Opposition or the Ministerial side of the House, there was absolute unanimity upon the gravity of this question affecting Catholic interests throughout the British Empire. He (Mr. O'Donnell) quoted to-day from a despatch which, in reply to a Petition of the Vicar Apostolic at Gibraltar, was sent by the Earl of Kimberley to the Governor at Gibraltar, on the 16th of January, 1871. Just before that date Rome had been seized by the Italian troops, and the Vicar Apostolic at Gibraltar had sent in a Petition to Her Majesty's Government for some assurance with regard to the freedom and security of the Papal functions. The Earl of Kimberley, in his reply, distinctly acknowledged that—

"The deep interest which is felt by many millions of Her Majesty's subjects in the position of the Pope renders all that concerns his personal dignity, and independence, and freedom to exercise his spiritual functions, fit subjects for the notice of Her Majesty's Government, and they have not failed to take such steps as are in their power to afford to the Pope the means of security in case of need."

So far did Her Majesty's Government go in 1871. It was impossible to conceive anything more essential to the freedom to exercise the Pope's spiritual functions than the security of the Propaganda, and the declaration of the British Government in 1871 absolutely and entirely covered the security of the Propaganda. Now, only 13 years after that declaration contained in the despatch of the Earl of Kimberley, they had the Premier stating that this infinitely grave question of the Propaganda was a mere Italian legal question; and, so far from there being any acknowledgment that it was a matter which required the notice of Her Majesty's Government, they were told that during all the months that had passed the British Government had not seen an opportunity for calling any attention whatever to the matter. Of course, he did not wish to use any language to which the Premier might reasonably object; he intended to confine himself strictly to exposing the important facts of the case. At the same time, there was a remarkable difference between the declaration of Her Majesty's Government 13 years ago, that everything affecting the freedom of the Pope to exercise his spiritual authority and functions was of the utmost concern to Her Majesty's Government, and their present declaration that their Ambassador had not found an opportunity of uttering even a word of protest in this most important matter of the Propaganda. There was a vast and, apparently, inexplicable difference between the two declarations. He did not know whether that difference could be at all explained by the course recent delicate negotiations had taken. If he remembered aright, the Premier had admitted that the solitary European Government which supported him in the recent Conference *fiasco* was the Italian Government. ["And the Turkish!"] But the Premier would be the very last man to admit that the Turkish Government could be considered an important European Government. He (Mr. O'Donnell) confined himself to the Italian Government, which, properly speaking, was, after all, the only European Government which could be quoted in that connection. The complaint Catholics had to make was that if the Government of King Humbert claimed to deal with the property of the Propaganda, as a religious Corporation, they might just as legally claim to deal with any other portion of the property administered by the Papacy. He did not go at all into the question of the amount of loss that had been inflicted, or that might be inflicted upon the Propaganda by the measures of the Italian Government. He was content with arguing the question on principle. He found that an Italian High Court, interpreting an Italian local law, had ventured to declare that that Italian local law dealt with the endowments of an institution of universal Catholicism, and he protested against such a declaration. The carrying out of that declaration would be fatal to the freedom of the Catholic Church in all its parts and functions. If the Propaganda could be despoiled at the domination of the High Court, the High Court might put forth an Italian secular claim to all the contents of the storied halls of the Papacy. It was for these reasons that he had taken the opportunity, on the Vote which included the salary of the British Ambassador at Rome, to call attention to what was undoubted neglect on the part of the Government of the Ambassador—he left it to them to settle between themselves whether it was the Government or the Ambassador who was the more at fault in the matter. The Committee could not close their eyes to the fact that a Catholic institution, in no way local, in no way merely national, in no way merely territorial, had been, with the consent of Her Majesty's Government, who were bound to guard the religious interests of all the subjects of Her Majesty, made liable to the application of an Italian local law, and might have its property dealt with in this fashion today and in that fashion to-morrow. When the Government admitted the claim of the Italian Law Court to deal with this universal institution of the Church, they destroyed the value of the declaration which, even as late as 1871, they made to a spokesman of Her Majesty's Catholic subjects that everything that concerned the free exercise of the spiritual functions of the Papacy was, and must remain, a subject for the notice of Her Majesty's Government. He had to propose the omission from the Vote of the item which represented the salary of the British Ambassador at the Court of Rome, who, bound on behalf of his Government to protect the interests of all British subjects, had most glaringly failed to discharge his duty with regard to the Catholic subjects of Her Majesty, in a matter of the most vital importance to their religion. This was a subject in which all parties were interested. Personally, he should be just as emphatic if an institution of universal Protestantism, or a universal missionary enterprize, established and endowed by the contributions of sincere Protestants throughout the world, were ceased or confiscated by a Government, no matter which. Every institution must have some local basis, must be under some roof, and within some walls. This was a question of universal justice—it was a question of universal religion. Nothing more was required by any Catholic subject of Her Majesty than that Her Majesty's Government should maintain the international character of the Propaganda, and distinctly refuse to consider that that international institution was to be confounded with the more local and more national institutions such as local Bishoprics or conventual establishments, against whose spoliation Catholics might justly protest; but which spoliation differed very widely from the grave injury inflicted on the Sacred Institution of the Propaganda.

Motion made, and Question proposed,

"That the Item of £7,000, for the Salary of Her Majesty's Ambassador at Rome, be omitted from the proposed Vote."—(*Mr. O'Donnell.*)

MR. MOORE said, that they, the Catholic subjects of Her Majesty, 10,000,000 in number, had every reason to be thankful to his hon. Friend (Mr. O'Donnell) for having brought this question forward. They had had to be thankful to the hon. Member on other occasions, although, perhaps, his words were not always acceptable in every quarter. This was probably owing to the fact that his words were sometimes armed, like a dart, with barbs, and carried consternation into the ranks of his opponents. He (Mr. Moore), for his own part, could only admire the great ability and great thought the hon. Member always brought to bear on these matters. It was a great matter of regret that no Cabinet Minister thought it worth his while to be present on this occasion; but, no doubt, the noble Lord the Under Secretary of State for Foreign Affairs would give them whatever consolation was in his power; but they had a right, when a question of such importance as this was under discussion, to expect a proper answer from a Cabinet Minister. If there was no prospect of their being favoured with such an answer, it might be necessary for them to move to report Progress. What he (Mr. Moore) wished to say was that in the early part of the Session the Prime Minister pledged himself that Her Majesty's Minister in Rome would use every effort which lay in his power, and would avail himself of every opportunity which presented itself, to exercise influence upon the Italian Government in the interest of the Catholic subjects of the Queen. What they wished to ask now was, whether those good offices had been used, and whether anything had been done to protect or safeguard the interests of British Catholics? Was the noble Lord in a position to lay any Papers on the Table, or to give any information on the subject? He should like to know, in particular, what was going to be done with the property of the Propaganda—was it going to be converted into State bonds, objectionable as they were, or was the "conversion" only an euphemistic phrase by which a more extensive process of confiscation was covered? As he was informed, or, rather, as he had found in the columns of *The Times* one morning, this process of conversion amounted in reality to a process of confiscation. Early in the month of February there appeared in *The Times* details as to how the process of so-called conversion was carried out. The Correspondent wrote—

"The manner of proceeding is this. It was first decided that a special duty for preliminary expenses of 30 per cent, should be imposed on the mass."

That was to keep the lawyers in a good humour—

"To this 30 per cent was added a transfer duty of 4 per cent, from which mortmain property had been exempt, and 6 per cent for land tax, making in all 40 per cent. Then a progressive duty has been imposed for the benefit of the Governmental Ecclesiastical Fund, a duty beginning with 15 per cent on 10,000 francs revenues, and amounting up to 40 or 50 per cent on larger sums."

Well, they could judge whether the term "confiscation" was justified—whether it lay with him to use such a term as a true description of what was taking place in Italy—when they read the remainder of this paragraph. *The Times* Correspondent went on to say—

"The result is that a Bishopric of 40,000 francs has been reduced to 12,500 francs, a second of 50,000 francs to 18,000 francs, and a third of 100,000 francs to 24,000 francs. The Governments interested in the 12,000,000 or 15,000,000 francs of the Propaganda think that this conversion much resembles a confiscation, and wish to be informed on the subject."

Had the Government adopted any means to ascertain what was taking place in Rome in regard to this institution—in which the Irish Members were so deeply interested? Before he left the question of finance he might add that, supposing the transaction he had described took place, these religious bodies would be paid in State paper—paper inscribed "*Nelo gran libro dei debito d'Italia*," whatever that might mean—belonging to the Italian Consolidated Fund. The value of this paper was pretty well known. The Italian people were ground down to the full extent they could possibly bear; and if Italy should at any time be involved in a war, or any internal eruption, the bonds would at once decrease in value 50 or 60 per cent. They were not to be paid in cash, and were to be inscribed in the "Grand Book of the Debt of Italy." A very "grand book" it was! The position of the Irish Members in this matter, and why they claimed the protection of the House of Commons for the Catholics of the country and the protection of the Government to whose Revenue they contributed, was this. They numbered—Her Majesty's Catholic subjects—10,000,000, and the Propaganda was the direct means of communication between these and the Holy See. As a matter of fact, for the spiritual subjects of the Holy See in this country the Propaganda was no missionary institution. It was the absolute and direct medium of communication between the Holy See and its spiritual subjects, and as such had been assured to them by the Memorandum of the 8th of September, 1870, received from M. Blanc, of the Italian Foreign Office, and forwarded to Earl Granville by Sir Augustus Paget. All the ecclesiastical business between the Catholic Bishops of this country and the Holy See was transacted through the Propaganda—and transacted absolutely free of cost to Her Majesty's subjects. Questions of discipline, questions of Church management, and a great many other questions were referred to the Propaganda; and the assistance of lawyers, translators, printers, and skilled experts were obtained through it free of cost. If the property of the Propaganda were confiscated, these costs would in the future be thrown upon Her Majesty's subjects, in distinct violation of their rights and freedom of association with the Holy See. This could not be too clearly understood. Apart entirely from its relations with England and Her Majesty's Roman Catholic subjects in these countries, the Propaganda was also the great focus and centre of missionary enterprize. His hon. Friend (Mr. O'Donnell) had spoken, eloquently enough, of the interest which every civilized nation in the world justly took in this institution; but no country had a greater interest in the preservation of these pioneers of civilization than England, the greatest Mahomedan country—taking into consideration their Eastern Possessions—in the world. The Propaganda sent forth missionaries, and to the valuable services of these men he could testify. He had seen a man broken down in health, worn out with intermittent fever, returning to Rome after a residence of 30 years in equatorial Africa, with the people of King John of Abyssinia. This man had been turned out of the country at a moment's notice, and had been compelled to travel all the way from Abyssinia to Khartoum without equipage or escort of any kind. But the missionary aspect of the question was one which, perhaps, would have less weight with the Foreign Office than that involving the rights and liberties of Her Majesty's subjects. The question was a very plain one. As he had said, for his co-religionists the Propaganda was the Holy See—their direct means of communicating with the Papacy. The Memorandum received from M. Blanc, and forwarded to Earl Granville by Sir Augustus Paget, contained these words—

"The Italian Government guarantees on its territory. (*a*.) The liberty of communication between the Sovereign Pontiff, and Foreign States, clergy, and peoples. (*b*.) The Italian Government engages to preserve all the institutions, offices, and ecclesiastical bodies, and their officials existing at Rome. The Government engages to preserve entire, and without subjecting them to special taxes, all the ecclesiastical properties whose revenues belong to ecclesiastical charges, offices, corporations, institutes, and bodies having their seat at Rome. These Articles would be considered a public bi-lateral contract, and would form the subject of an agreement with the Powers having Catholic subjects."

The Memorandum contained an account of the various negotiations which had taken place as to the settlement of the question of the temporal power, and gave a *résumé* of the points which had been from time to time considered. The terms of the document distinctly, absolutely, and fully covered liberty of communication between Her Majesty's Catholic subjects and the Propaganda. Nothing could be more clear than the promises of the Italian Government to Her Majesty's Government, or the fact that they had guaranteed the security of the property of this institution, and had distinctly declared in the document to which he referred that Her Majesty's subjects should not suffer. And yet that guarantee had been allowed to be set aside, and the obligations solemnly and voluntarily tendered by the Italian Government had been directly infringed. He did not know what answer the noble Lord the Under Secretary of State would be able to give. He was sorry to hear the Prime Minister say that no European or other Power had moved in the matter. He believed the right hon. Gentleman was labouring under some misapprehension on that point. Certainly, there had been a Resolution of Congress, and the American Government had moved in the matter. He also understood that the German Government had been moving; but whether that was so or not it was not so easy for one who was altogether outside the diplomatic world to say. This much was quite certain, that in the Memorandum presented to the Representative of this country in 1870 a distinct arrangement was entered into by which the Italian Government proposed to guarantee the security of the property of the Propaganda and to undertake that it should remain as heretofore one of the ornaments of the country and of the Catholic Church. He hoped and trusted to hear from Her Majesty's Government that at least their interests had been guarded, that the fullest possible information would be given to the Committee on the subject, and that the Committee would be thoroughly reassured that whatever might be contemplated steps would be taken with the object of preventing the revenues of this most ancient College from being confiscated for secular purposes.

Mr. MARUM: I wish to supplement these observations which have already been offered [illegible] the despatch of the Earl of Kimberley, which has been referred to by the hon. Member for Dungarvan (Mr. O'Donnell). I desire to read to the Committee the observations of a former Prime Minister of strong Protestant proclivities and of strong hand—I mean the late Lord Palmerston. They will be found in the Correspondence and the Reports furnished to this House in [illegible] of the Correspondence with Lord Normanby and the Prince Castelcicala, [illegible] [illegible] *Treatise upon International Law* [illegible] and also by Sir Travers Twiss in his work upon the same subject published this very year, 1884 [illegible].

"[illegible] *de facto* [illegible] *de jure* [illegible]"

We ask no intervention as to Italian property or Italian institutions, but only in reference to international property acquired and maintained under the dynasties of absolute Sovereigns *de facto* [illegible] the most ancient and venerable in the world. As Lord Macaulay puts it—

"[illegible] are but of yesterday when compared with the line of Supreme Pontiffs."

This view is set forth in a Rescript issued this year by the Propaganda and signed by Cardinal Simeoni, Prefect of the Institution, and the Archbishop of Tyre, from which I will read an extract with the permission of the Committee:—

"Most Illustrious and Reverend Lord,—Your Lordship is aware of the judgment pronounced [illegible] January last by the Supreme Court [illegible]

"[illegible]"

only but for the good of the entire human race.

"It is, therefore, clearly evident that the above-mentioned judgment does not strike at the property of a particular institution, but injures the capital destined exclusively to the exercise of the Roman Pontiff's Apostolic Ministry of converting the nations to the light of faith and civilization. It causes this injury as well as by exposing the Propaganda to the danger of seeing, some time or other, the total or partial loss of its property, in consequence of eventualities which are not improbable, as also by making the payment of its funds dependent on the will of the parties in power, and therefore a matter of the most deplorable uncertainty, but, above all, depriving it of the free disposal of its capital, a freedom which is absolutely necessary to it, on account of its essential character of initiating religious movements, and of the frequent occasions on which it has to meet the extraordinary needs of divers missions.

"The Holy Father, most deeply grieved by this new and fierce attack on the imprescriptible rights of his Apostolic Office, and foreseeing the sad consequences that will arise from the conversation of the actual patrimony of the Sacred Congregation—a patrimony, moreover, already alienated for the greater part of the Government, *pendente lite*—feels it his duty to provide in the best possible way for the future security of so deserving an institution. To obtain this security he has deigned to command me to declare, as I now do by this circular, that henceforth the administrative seat of the Propaganda for all donations, legacies, and offerings, by which the piety of the faithful may wish to meet its continual and heavy expenditure, is transferred out of Italy. And in order to provide for the greater general convenience it has been decided to establish in different parts of the world Centres or Procurations, where the offerings of the faithful may be put out of all danger, and be at the free and independent disposal of the Sacred Congregation for the benefit of the Missions. These Procurations are indicated in the annexed list, with which, as well as with the present Circular, your Lordship will make all the faithful confided to your care acquainted. I shall send you further instructions when necessary. The Sacred Congregation, however, cherishes a strong hope that this new blow struck at the Church, far from weakening the piety of Catholics, will, on the contrary, stimulate them to meet, with ever-increasing generosity, the needs of the Mission—needs which are becoming day by day more imperative and more numerous.

"In the meantime I pray God to preserve you, &c.

"From the Propaganda, March 15, 1884.

"John Cardinal Simeoni, Prefect,

"D. Archbishop of Tyre, Secretary."

LIST OF PROCURATIONS.

In Europe.

Vienna, Munich, Paris, Madrid, Lisbon } At the Apostolic Nuncatures.

The Hague—With the Apostolic Internuncio.
Belgium—With the Archbishop of Malines.
Malta—With the Agent of the Sacred Congregation.
London—With His Eminence the Cardinal Archbishop.
Dublin—With His Eminence the Cardinal Archbishop.
Constantinople—With the Patriotic Vicar of the Latins.

In Asia.

Bombay, Calcutta, Madras } With the Vicar Apostolic.

In America.

New York—With His Eminence the Cardinal Archbishop.
San Francisco, Quebec, Toronto } With their respective Archbishops.
Rio Janeiro—With the Apostolic Internuncio.
Buenos Ayres, Quito } With the Apostolic Delegate.

In Oceanica.

Sydney—With the Archbishop.

In Africa.

Algiers—With His Eminence the Cardinal Archbishop.

N.B.—Whenever distance prevents the faithful from remitting sums to the above centres, they can address themselves to their own Ordinary.

The Pope, in his last Allocution to the Cardinal, denounced, in vigorous terms, the recent violations of the rights of the Church, demanded the restitution of the Temporal Power, and protested with marked warmth against the judgment given by the Italian Courts concerning the property of the Propaganda. His Holiness said he foresaw fresh attacks upon the Papacy; but he would ever uphold with firmness the rights of the Holy See. The United States' Minister in Rome has telegraphed that the recent judgment of the Italian Court of Appeal, regarding the conversion of the real property of the Propaganda into Rente, does not affect the American College, which, as a building used as a seminary, is expressly exempt from the operation of the judgment. Now, the Pope exercises spiritual jurisdiction over millions of Her Majesty's subjects in her Realm, "upon which the sun never sets," and, as premier Bishop of Christendom, he is even Bishop of Westminster Diocese, wherein Her Majesty resides; and it is absolutely essential for the full and complete exercise of the universal Roman Catholic religion that the institution of the Propaganda be preserved. In fact, the principle of universality is involved, and it is now assailed by the Italian Government, no doubt designed to destroy Catholicism. We call upon Her Majesty's Government to sustain us, and to protect our property in Rome, now being plundered with sacrilegious hand by the rapacious Italian Government to supply an Exchequer, beggared by the oppression of the populations, held down by huge Military and Naval Forces, and ground to powder by taxation. We are not mere volunteers, as the following document exhibits:—

"At a meeting of the Archbishops and Bishops of Ireland, held in Maynooth College, on the 2nd of July, 1884, it was proposed by the Most Rev. Dr. Nulty, Bishop of Meath, seconded by the Most Rev. Dr. Logue, Bishop of Raphoe, and resolved—

"That we request Irish Members of Parliament, of all political Parties, to use their influence with Her Majesty's Government in support of the letter which we have addressed to Mr. Gladstone, requesting him to take all the effective steps in his power to prevent the threatened spoliation of the property of the Propaganda, in which so many of Her Majesty's subjects have a deep interest.

"To E. Mulhallen Marum, Esq., LL.B., M.P., J.P.'"

Now, what is the Italian Government? The arch-brigand, Garibaldi—a political Jack Sheppard — was expelled from Rome by the French nation exercising European police. Yet, upon the same state of facts and International Law, the unscrupulous Count Cavour and the convicted Carbonaro, Panizzi, and his comrades—mere Italian Invincibles—proceeded to usurpation, sacrilege, confiscation, and robbery. No declaration of war was made, or even a Manifesto, which, according to the overwhelming weight of authority, constituted a distinct breach of International Law. In Kent's *Commentaries upon International Law* all the authorities are cited upon this point. Puffendorf, Ermignon, and Vattel are clear upon the subject, and even Grotius and Bynkershock agree that a Manifesto at least is requisite. I am sorry to see that neither the Prime Minister nor a single Minister of the Crown is present—no one left to answer us but an Under Secretary for State—not a single Law Officer—English or Irish—is present to reply to us. This, as my hon. Friend (Mr. Moore), complains, is bad treatment, and shows a foregone conclusion which I protest solemnly against.

LORD EDMOND FITZMAURICE: I am well aware of the interest which the question brought forward by the hon. Member for Dungarvan (Mr. O'Donnell) excites among Her Majesty's Roman Catholic subjects. The document which the hon. Member for Kilkenny (Mr. Marum) referred to as having been circulated among Members of the House shows the importance which Roman Catholics attach to the question. I make this admission, because I feel how totally impossible it is for me to make any additional statement to that which was made at Question time to-day by the Prime Minister. The position of the question is this—that Her Majesty's Ambassador at Rome was instructed to take any opportunity that might offer of making a friendly representation in connection with this subject. It was, however, felt by him—and Her Majesty's Government have no reason to doubt the wisdom of that view—that it would not be wise in him to take the first step; but rather to associate himself with any action that might be taken by one of the Continental Powers—one of those Roman Catholic nations which may be said to be more immediately interested in the question, although, no doubt, it is a question in which Her Majesty's Government, on behalf of Her Majesty's Roman Catholic subjects in every part of the world, are bound to take deep interest. Nevertheless, it has been thought more prudent that the first step should be taken by one of the other Powers; and, as far as Her Majesty's Government have been informed, at this moment, no steps, so far, have been taken. I speak, however, under some disadvantage, because I am aware that to-day, about the time I left the Foreign Office, a despatch had arrived from Her Majesty's Ambassador at Rome; but I have not had an opportunity of reading that despatch, although I have been informed that it gives the views of Her Majesty's Representative, and explains the reasons why he has hitherto not been able to take any step in the matter. It has been suggested, in the conversation which has occurred, that Papers might be laid upon the Table; but, of course, I cannot undertake, without consulting the Secretary of State, to say what Papers can or cannot be laid upon the Table. I will, however, as it will be my duty, communicate to the Secretary of State the wish which has been expressed by hon. Members, that the Correspondence which has taken place upon the question shall be laid, as far as possible, upon the Table.

Mr. MOLLOY: Will the noble Lord be able to give us the contents of the despatch he has referred to, to-morrow?

Lord EDMOND FITZMAURICE: I will do the best I can to give the House all the information that it may be in my power to give. At the same time there are some points which have been raised by the hon. Member for Clonmel (Mr. Moore) which I think I am at liberty to touch upon now. He wants to know whether this is an absolute measure of confiscation, or whether it is merely that the College of the Propaganda is merely to be under the obligation to invest the proceeds of the sale of its lands in the Italian funds? As far as I understand the question there has been no absolute confiscation, but merely a change of investment. I understood hon. Members to indulge in some merriment at the expense of the credit of the Italian Government, and it has been said that the securities in which the College have been required to invest the proceeds of their sales of land are not good investments; but I am bound to say that, so far as I am aware, the credit of the Italian Government has been steadily rising of late years; and if the College of the *Propaganda Fide* is obliged to invest the proceeds of its sales of land in Italian securities, it will have been compelled to invest them in very good securities. As I have said, the commercial credit of the Italian Government has been steadily rising; the Italian Stocks have been increasing in value; Italian paper has reached *par*, and not long ago the Government succeeded in withdrawing their paper currency from circulation, and substituting specie payments. All these things go to the credit of the Italian Government, and they show that the condition of things in Italy is steadily improving. On the other hand, hon. Members say, and it is perfectly true, that in some portions of Italy there has been a heavy taxation upon the land; but if the College of the Propaganda is compelled to sell its landed property, and to invest in the general securities of the Italian Government, it does not appear to me that the change of investment will be very injurious to the College. The word "international" has been freely used in the course of the discussion; but is this institution really international, in the full sense of the word? Has it been fully recognized as an international institution by Treaties and Conventions, and are Institutions to be regarded as international that are only so considered upon notions based rather upon international morality than International Law? Of course, I do not feel myself capable of competing with the hon. Member who spoke last in that knowledge of civil and canonical law, of which he is so great a master. I shrink, therefore, from engaging either in an ecclesiastical argument with the hon. Member. All I will say with reference to the alleged international character of the College of the Propaganda is that I cannot think it is quite correct to say that it is an uncontested fact. No doubt, it has an international character, in one sense—namely, that many nations are interested in it; but the term "international character" is rather a fine-drawn expression. I will not, however, dwell too much upon that point; but all I will say is that I will prefer to wait until I have read the despatch, which, I understand, has arrived to-day, before giving any more definite information. If, after I have read it, I find that I can give hon. Members further information, I can only say that I shall be most happy to do so.

Mr. HEALY said, the matter before the Committee was one of very considerable delicacy; and he scarcely thought it right that it should have been met by the noble Lord by an assertion that he was unable to give satisfactory assurances, because a despatch from Her Majesty's Ambassador had only reached the Foreign Office that day, and he had been unable to read it. At the same time, it was only right to say that the hon. Member for the City of Cork (Mr. Parnell), who had been requested by his Party to bring forward this question, had only been stopped from doing so by reason of a communication which had reached him from very distinguished members of the Catholic Church, who informed him that it was not considered desirable the question should be raised in the House of Commons until further information had been received. The hon. Member for

Dungarvan (Mr. O'Donnell), who was not in possession of that information, and who was not acting with the Party ... [illegible]

... sidered that Her Majesty's Ambassador stood upon a different footing from the ... [illegible]

Minister, and it was that the great Congress of the free Republic of America had taken action in this matter, and that the Government of the next free Government to that of the United States ought not to be behindhand in the representations it was making to the Italian Court. Her Majesty's Government had not chosen to take that course, and, as far as he could gather, the Prime Minister appeared to be totally unacquainted, officially, with the fact that the American Government had made a protest. They knew that the Congress had passed a Resolution in reference to the *Propaganda Fide*, and that, in addition, huge meetings had been held in every city of America on the same important subject. He had read reports of the meetings which had been held in Boston and New York, presided over by the highest dignitaries of those States; and he was amazed that Her Majesty's Government should rely upon the non-action of some of the Continental States, and ignore the fact that the American Government had already taken action. [Mr. GLADSTONE: Is that known?] He had read it in a newspaper, which was the only form in which intelligence of this kind was open to him. He had read in the Irish American Press. He spoke, of course, under the correction of better information in the possession of Her Majesty's Government. But, at all events, he had in print a Resolution passed by the American Congress, and his statement had been confirmed by that of an hon. Member opposite.

MR. COURTNEY: Was the Resolution passed by both Houses?

MR. HEALY said, the Resolution to which he referred was one passed by the House of Representatives. Whether the Congress was represented by one House or not, he knew, was a matter of dispute in America. At all events, the House of Representatives had passed a Resolution. Of course, he knew that the American Senate had to be consulted in regard to Ambassadorial functions; but he had never been able to understand whether one House or both Houses acting together constituted what was called the American Congress. At any rate, the American House of Representatives had entered a Resolution on its Books on the subject; and he believed he was right in stating that the American Minister at Rome had made representations to the Court of Italy in regard to it. But in the Republic of America there were not more than 8,000,000 of Catholics, while in Ireland there were 5,000,000; in England, 9,000,000; and in their Colonial Possessions many millions more. Then, why should a Government like that of America, which professed non-interference in European affairs, in the same way that they rejected European interference in the affairs of America, be left to take the initiative? Why Her Majesty's Government should have been behindhand with that of America he could not understand. He was told that in the opinion of certain highly-informed ecclesiastics of this country it was undesirable that this debate should be raised, and that it was even inexpedient that the fact should be brought out that England had not acted in the matter, because the other Catholic countries had lagged behind. But as that fact had been brought out, however undesirable it might be to bring it out at the present juncture, it became necessary that the whole of the circumstances of the case should be stated. No doubt, it was inexpedient to raise the discussion until the full effect of the attitude of the Italian Government was ascertained; but as the hon. Member for Dungarvan (Mr. O'Donnell) had felt it his duty to raise the question, and had done so on his own individual responsibility, seeing that a debate had arisen, it was only proper, and no individual Member could be blamed for expressing his opinion, that the views of the Irish Members should be expressed in regard to the action of Her Majesty's Government, showing that it did not meet either with their approval or with the general support of the House. If it should prove to be inexpedient for the hon. Member for Dungarvan (Mr. O'Donnell) to have raised the subject, he would have to incur all the responsibility. For his part, he (Mr. Healy) could only say that he regretted extremely that Her Majesty's Government should not have met the matter in a straightforward spirit, prepared to grapple with it firmly. He certainly believed that if Her Majesty's Government had expressed a strong opinion, as representing the views of the Catholics of England, the Italian Government would not have proceeded to the length they had done.

Colonel NOLAN said, he would only detain the Committee for a few minutes; but he agreed with the remarks which had fallen from his hon. Friend the Member for Monaghan (Mr. Healy) that there were now only three Powers in Europe who were Catholic in name—France, Austria, and Spain, and that it would have been dangerous for either of them to have urged this question upon the attention of the Italian Government. The noble Lord the Under Secretary of State for Foreign Affairs said the reason this country had not interposed was that those three Catholic countries had made no sign. No doubt France, Austria, and Spain had always been looked upon as the three great Catholic Powers of Europe; but each of them would be able to give good reasons why she ought not to interfere, and why England might reasonably have been called upon to interpose. It was absurd to ask Austria to interfere to the extent of a strong remonstrance, because it would at once be asked how many men she was prepared to put in the field. The same objection applied to France, because the question would then be whether Italy would remain neutral in the next Franco-German War, which they all hoped might never come off, and, if not, how many troops she could place in the field. Then, again, if either France or Austria were to raise the question, it might have the effect of rousing Catholic feeling in those countries, and it was impossible to say what the consequences might be. Under these circumstances, neither France nor Austria could interfere at the present moment. The same observation did not possibly apply to Spain; but King Alfonso could not forget the part which his Royal Predecessor, King Amadeus, had taken in the establishment of the Italian Government. He would naturally consider the jealousy which existed between the two Royal Families, and the great mischief which might ensue from the interference of Spain. Therefore, in the present state of deadlock among the Roman Catholic Powers of Europe there was every reason why England, as a Protestant Power, might very well take the lead in bringing forward representations on the subject. Half the Roman Catholics of the world subscribed to this Fund, and if there was any International Fund in the world this was one; but the object of the Italian Government was to confiscate it, as similar property had been confiscated in France. Of course, he did not wish the Government to go to war upon this matter; but they might make some strong representation to the Italian Government, and he should be delighted if they gave any indication of any intention to do so.

Mr. DAWSON said, there was a grave and clear distinction between institutions in Rome of an international character, and this Propaganda. Austria and France might interfere with regard to the Austrian or French College; but really Austria had nothing to do with the Propaganda. She was always represented diplomatically during the Temporal Power, and was now represented at Rome; but England and Ireland were not diplomatically represented, and they, therefore, stood in a different category from other countries in respect to the Propaganda. This Fund was largely an Irish fund for sending missionaries from Rome to other countries for the propagation of the Faith. His hon. Friend had said this was not now promoted by any ecclesiastical authorities; but he had received a letter from an Irish Bishop asking him to take part in this discussion, for the Fund was purely Irish money. It was their money sent into Italy just as the bondholders' money sent into Egypt was the money of the bondholders. Although the Fund might be small, this was as important a matter of justice as was the matter of the bondholders' money in Egypt or anywhere else; and he thought it was a pity that the noble Lord (Lord Edmond Fitzmaurice) should state that the Ambassador's despatch was not fully before him, at this moment, when it had been known this matter was likely to be discussed. When there was a vast Department for dealing with foreign affairs, it was a pity that the noble Lord should not be in full possession of the facts, so as to put them before the House; and if it was worth the while of Her Majesty's Ambassador to interfere at all, the information ought not to be kept back till the matter was all over. He would remind the Prime Minister that he himself had always taken great interest in any international or literary institution, and had striven to see justice done to nationalities, and to preserve the interests of literature all over the world.

He had taken very significant action in regard to Monte Casino, in order to prevent the Italian Government, shortly after its assumption of power, from confiscating and sequestrating that great Roman Catholic Library to which the world was so much indebted. This College of the Propaganda was not only a College for preparing priests for missionary work; it was not only a Propaganda of the Faith; but was also a Propaganda of literature and culture. Irish money had been sent out to be invested for these purposes, and distinguished Irish priests had been sent out as ornaments to various British Colonies where millions of Roman Catholics lived under the rule of the Queen. Therefore, he thought there were just and strong reasons for the preservation of Irish interests, and of literature, culture, and education. He remembered that a distinguished Member of the Royal Family had done his utmost to preserve a great Dominican foundation in Rome. These places were the sources of that great learning which Rome possessed, and the influence of that high personage was exercised to prevent that confiscation. If that was so, he should like to know what was the position of this Propaganda, and what would be the result of this sequestration? He thought they were justified in asking the noble Lord what was to be the effect of this action of the Italian Government upon this money subscribed for the Propaganda by Ireland, and upon these foundations in which they had a monetary interest? Why could not the noble Lord state exactly how the matter stood, so that if they could not get a very binding declaration from the Government, the Irish Bishops and the Irish people might at any rate know how the matter rested—what the transfer was, and how far it affected the funds of the Irish people?

MR. JUSTIN M'CARTHY said, he thought his hon. Friend had put very well the point as to the position of this Propaganda. That had been pressed on the Prime Minister's notice that evening in a sort of irregular discussion upon Questions by the hon. Member for Carlow (Mr. Gray). There was a very distinct difference between the case of England in regard to this Fund, and the case of France, or Spain, or Italy. The Prime Minister had stated, in answer to a Question on this subject, that if the Government of Italy were acting in accordance with the Italian Municipal Law, it would be no business of ours to interfere, even though the interests of British subjects were being affected; but some of the incidents and facts of recent history showed that no country recognized such a position. No Foreign Government, even though acting according to its own Municipal Law, was entitled to do wrong, without another Government having the right to interfere in the interest of its own subjects. That position had been established in the case of the Alabama claims. England, of all countries, had a right to require Italy to alter her Municipal Law if it was injurious to our interests, for united Italy was the child of England, which, more than any other nation in the world, made the Italian Kingdom. That had been admitted over and over again by Cavour and by Garibaldi, and he thought the country which made Italy ought to be able to influence Italy. He, therefore, hoped this discussion would be of some use.

MR. GLADSTONE: The hon. and gallant Member for Galway (Colonel Nolan) says he thinks that England might well interfere in this case, as being the custodian of vested interests in general. But if we were to attempt to interfere with the Italian Government on the ground that we had invariably respected the interests and rights of Corporate Bodies, and the Italian Government were to reply by a reference to the case of the Irish Church, I should be puzzled what reply to make; and if the Italian Government were to point to those Irish Members who now urge this interference as among those who voted for and pressed with some warmth for the Disestablishment of the Irish Church, I should have still more difficulty in replying. [An hon. MEMBER: Oh, oh!] I am stating my opinion, and I hope the hon. Member will have some better means of meeting it than by crying "Oh!" I was dealing with the specific plea put forward by the hon. and gallant Member for Galway, who said we ought to interfere in this matter because we are persons who have always maintained the vested rights of Corporate Bodies. That, I think, is a very awkward argument for us to advance. I will refer to another instance. The hon. Member for Longford (Mr.

Justin M'Carthy says he has found an analogy to this case in something which he supposed to have happened growing out of the American War. He thinks that we contended at one time that we could not meet the demands of International Law because our Municipal Law forbade it. I apprehend that it is the duty of every country to make its laws consistent with International Law. This is a case of Municipal Law with regard to which the hon. Member for Longford has not endeavoured to show that there has been any great breach of International Law, and unless there has been a breach of International Law his argument with reference to America falls to the ground. Then, as I understand hon. Members, it is urged that we have a right to hold language to the other to another country—"If your laws are so bad that they [illegible] our citizens, you must alter them." [Mr. Justin M'Carthy: Or compensate them.] I do not think that argument could be maintained. There are a great many bad laws in the world which inflict considerable hardship on individuals. Some of them are perhaps in our own country, and a great many are in foreign countries; but I am not aware that we can go to a foreign country and say that because their laws are bad, and they inflict great loss on some of our citizens, therefore we demand compensation. I do not think such a principle could be maintained. You must show that the persons for whom you demand compensation have been treated contrary to the law of the country in which they reside. [Mr. Healy: Why did you interfere [illegible] of the Egyptian bondholders?] [illegible] We cannot say "Because your laws inflict injury, [illegible] therefore [illegible] after them." All these are [illegible] the real scope of the [illegible]. Now, I wish there to be no misunderstanding, and I am sorry that [illegible] should have arisen from any language of mine, anything of the kind. We have never laid down for one moment as a fixed rule that we [illegible] other countries interfere. I do not at all say that we have adopted any such proposition as that. The conduct of other countries is no [illegible] in point in a case of this kind, but, unquestionably, if there is to be interference, when we have ascertained what is the true state of the case, we [illegible] interfere. That [illegible] I think, at once. The [illegible] said that the American Minister at Rome has interfered, and I [illegible] understood that the hon. Member for Monaghan (Mr. Healy) would be very well [illegible] point by our taking account of what passed in the House of Representatives in reference to this matter. I do not [illegible] that by any general principle of law we [illegible] such a Resolution as was there adopted; but if the American Minister has interfered, that is a fact which is not material as to make [illegible] and I am sure my hon. and learned Friend [illegible] of International Law. My hon. Friend the Member for Carlow (Mr. Dawson) gives me credit for having attempted to interfere in the case of [illegible] property in Italy, the famous [illegible] of Monte Cassino. I certainly [illegible] the expediency of doing anything that could be done for the maintenance of that [illegible] that subject, but that was entirely in the character of a private individual, and it was only by courtesy which I shall always gratefully [illegible] that I was allowed to represent the case to the Italian Government. The interference of a Government is a very different thing, because when a Government interferes it does so as a right, whereas the [illegible] individual, who has no right, is a pure matter of favour and grace [illegible]. What I [illegible] the speeches to-night [illegible] and with [illegible] which [illegible] interference [illegible] kind of interference [illegible] hon. Member for Longford (Mr. Justin M'Carthy) [illegible] the length of threatening or [illegible]. What I suppose he thinks is that something in the nature of an appeal *ad misericordiam* might be made. [Mr. Healy: No. We want nothing founded upon right but something founded upon right, then I do not see why he should be so careful to say he would not insist. I shall be glad to be more fully informed.

MR. JUSTIN M'CARTHY: I said, it would be enough to go on the ground of right, and that there would probably be no necessity for insistance.

MR. GLADSTONE: Then I must ask this. I have not gathered what is the distinct and definite ground of right upon which this claim is to be insisted upon. It is to be an appeal upon the ground of right, and what is the case alleged? The case alleged is, that a large amount of property had been created in Italy, and invested in Italy by means of contributions gathered from, I may say, the whole of Latin Christendom. That is very likely the case, and it is now said that much damage has been suffered from the compulsory conversion to which this property has been subjected. I have not been able to examine the facts—upon which, I think, my noble Friend offered a good argument—but I will assume that the allegations made are warranted, and that the property has been seriously damaged. But does that give a good title as a right for one nation to interfere with the internal legislation of another? Does the fact that this property has been created by contributions from abroad, from Austria, France, and Spain, quite as much as, and, perhaps, a good deal more than, from Ireland—which is always generous, but has not had very ample means—does that give a title to follow the property into the country to which the contributions have been voluntarily sent, and when invested has become subject to the actual laws of the country? There are a vast number of churches in the Colonies which have been founded by funds sent from England—I mean churches in connection with the Established Church in this country—but that does not give any title to us to protest against any legislation dealing with them, because we have chosen to send the money to found them.

MR. O'DONNELL said, that not only was the Propaganda founded in the days of the Temporal Power, but its object was to extend and establish the Catholic Church in all parts of the world.

MR. GLADSTONE: As to the argument derived from the fact that this is an institution of propagation, not having the end and aim of its work in the country where it has its seat, why, that argument applies to all the Missionary Societies in England, and to every Missionary Society in Europe. All these Societies might, on that principle, be allowed to set up pretensions against the legitimate power of the country in which they were established. The hon. Gentleman says that this institution was founded in the days of the Temporal Power of the Popedom. No doubt of it. If you tell me that that is a consideration, and that the hardship of the change effected is a consideration which may, as a matter of feeling and equity, be fairly represented in the way of what I may call an appeal *ad misericordiam*, then we get on ground where some observations on our part might be more practicable; but I must say that the particular institutions which are founded under the shelter of the general Government of a country must accept their fortune under the general law of that country, whereas, to warrant the interference of one Power with another, there must be matter of public law involved. So that I firmly hold to the principle that any argument advanced must be an argument of amity or comity, and that it cannot be made on the ground of law.

MR. HEALY: How about the Egyptian bondholders?

MR. GLADSTONE: Does the hon. Gentleman really think that by his question he has contributed anything to this discussion? Whatever the rights of the bondholders are, they were founded on the express consent of all the Powers of Europe; and, therefore, they have no relation to a case of this kind. I do not pretend to be in possession of the whole of the facts of the case, and I have only put forward a general principle, and likewise laid down certain general lines to which, in my judgment, action in this matter should be confined, if there is to be any chance of success. On the other hand, I must say that it has not been shown that there exists any just title in any quarter to attempt any interference with the Sovereign rights of the Italian State affecting directly the different properties under State control. I hope the hon. Gentleman will be content to look at the matter in that light. I fully admit that the action of other Powers in this case is not a matter for our guidance; but I say that it is absolutely necessary for the security and maintenance of the respective rights of independent Powers that any claim that we may [illegible] should be based on distinct and [illegible] grounds, and not on arguments which would only recoil on those who advanced them.

MR. MOORE said, that the right hon. Gentleman the Prime Minister had spoken of the supporters of this Motion as being amongst those who were foremost in [illegible] the Disestablishment of the Church in Ireland; but he was satisfied that if anyone else had dared to compare the Disestablishment of the Irish Church with the sequestration of the funds of the Propaganda in the presence of the right hon. Gentleman, he would have received a castigation which he would have long remembered. The two cases were entirely distinct; and the present was simply the seizure of the property of [illegible] citizens to [illegible] the revenues of the Italian State. The Under Secretary of State for Foreign Affairs had stated that we [illegible] to take isolated action. But France, Spain, and Austria were [illegible] [illegible] Powers, and they had [illegible] in the Propaganda [illegible] [illegible] the interests of the Church [illegible] [illegible] [illegible]

[illegible]

[illegible] that they [illegible] their ap[illegible].

MR. DAWSON remarked that the Prime Minister had said there was no analogy between the case of the Egyptian bondholders, alluded to by the hon. Member for Monaghan (Mr. Healy), and the case of the Propaganda; but his impression was that there had been a change in the Government of Egypt since the claims of the bondholders were secured. A new Khedive had been set up, and another might be set up to-morrow; but the claims of the bondholders would not lapse on that account. To his mind the cases were parallel.

SIR JOSEPH M'KENNA said, he believed that if the right hon. Gentleman the Prime Minister would put this case before the Italian Government on the ground of public opinion, or on that of equity, he would succeed in protecting these funds. He and his hon. Friends asked no more than that at present. Whether the right existed under International Law to the extent at which it would be possible for the right hon. Gentleman to [illegible] the funds of the Propaganda from the hands of the Italian Government he knew not; but he was satisfied that if the right hon. Gentleman were to exercise those powers of [illegible] which he [illegible] possessed in a higher degree than himself, he would [illegible] in the present case to [illegible] the moral and religious welfare of mankind.

MR. MOLLOY hoped that some means would be found without delay to protect the funds of the Propaganda College.

MR. BIGGAR said, he had listened attentively to the speech of the noble Lord the Under Secretary of State for Foreign Affairs, and [illegible] gathered that the only [illegible] made by him was that [illegible] [illegible] of the Foreign Office. There could be no doubt [illegible] which had [illegible] [illegible] property would be taken by the State, and [illegible] tax would [illegible] at the rate of 15 per [illegible] [illegible] [illegible] than [illegible] Those were [illegible] the hon. Member for [illegible] (Mr. Moore) [illegible] he had thought it entirely [illegible] them. The hon. Member had further shown that the Italian

Government had bound itself not to interfere with property of this kind in the Italian States, and he (Mr. Biggar) thought that that pledge of the Italian Government constituted an exceedingly good standpoint from which to object to this confiscation of the property of Catholics who were scattered all over the world. He maintained that the British Government, as the ruling power in this country, was in duty bound to interfere on behalf of Her Majesty's Catholic subjects at home and abroad; and he might remark that, in comparison with other Powers, England had the reputation of very much neglecting the interests of her subjects in foreign countries. He was informed, on excellent authority, that the other Powers, through their Consuls, had always of late very much more consulted the interests of their subjects than was the case with England. However, he believed the country had some little influence abroad, and he hoped it would be exercised in this case, without resorting to a system of underhand or underground negotiations. It would seem, from the replies of the Government, however, that their intention was, if possible, to shelve the question. He hoped the hon. Member for Dungarvan (Mr. O'Donnell) would divide the Committee on his Amendment.

Mr. O'DONNELL said, the right hon. Gentleman the Prime Minister had stated that when property was invested in a State, subject to the laws of that State, and when a revolution occurred by which a fresh Government was introduced, no objection could be raised to any fate that might befall the investments under the old *régime* when they passed under the new *régime*. But surely it was possible that objections might be raised under the new *régime*. If in any State of Europe or Asia large investments of property had taken place on the faith of the established Government there, and that Government were overthrown by revolution, might not the universal character of the claim embolden the Prime Minister to make the strongest representations to the new Government on behalf of the owners of the property? When the right hon. Gentleman just now extorted cheers from some of his more enthusiastic followers, he had observed that he did not get an universal response to his proposition that the property of the Propaganda College must be subject to every vicissitude and every injustice which the new *régime* might put upon it, without any redress or remonstrance from abroad. There had been a little too much reference to International Law in the course of the discussion, and he thought equity would have been a much better basis on which to argue this question. There was no such thing as law between nation and nation; the term was essentially one of analogy, and it was by playing on it that the Prime Minister had met the objections of Catholic Members on that occasion. He did not, of course, impugn the motives which had induced the hon. Member for the City of Cork (Mr. Parnell) to change his attitude on this question; but it was known that he (Mr. O'Donnell) had for months past intended to bring forward this Motion, and up to that moment not a single protest had been made against it; and only a few days ago he had seen letters from Catholics asking Irish Members to lose no opportunity of bringing forward this matter. Therefore, he was ready to take his share of the responsibility for raising the question in the House of Commons. He contended that Her Majesty's Government, in dealing with the Italian Government, should stand upon the ground of equity, and they might then put their argument into any form they chose. He altogether repudiated that appeal *ad misericordiam*, which the Prime Minister had suggested might be made to the Italian Government, for one which addressed itself to their sense of equity; and he believed that had Her Majesty's Government at first appealed to the Italian Government upon that ground, the complaint he was now urging would not have been made. He was certainly prepared to acquiesce in the suggestion of his hon. Friend the Member for Cavan (Mr. Biggar) to press this Motion to a Division, because the conduct of the British Ambassador, although it was not necessarily the policy of the Government, had certainly not been satisfactory, inasmuch as he had allowed month after month to slip away without rendering any account of his action to the Government at home.

Mr. LYNCH said, he also wished to avail himself of the opportunity afforded by this Vote for entering his protest against the conduct of the Government.

As a Roman Catholic and a Member of that House he felt bound to take this course [illegible] opposition to the Government, and he appealed to hon. Members on the opposite side of the House to support the cause of justice by following his example.

Question put.

The Committee *divided*:—Ayes 2[illegible]; Noes [illegible]: Majority [illegible].—(Div. List, No. 207.)

Original Question again proposed.

MR. PULESTON said, it was now more than a year since an important member of the Diplomatic Service was sent to Mexico as Diplomatic Agent, or in some similar capacity; and it would be satisfactory to the Committee to state what steps had been taken towards [illegible] between this country and Mexico. [illegible]

[illegible]

some arrangement with Mexico, whereby their commercial relations with that country would be placed upon a satisfactory footing.

LORD EDMOND FITZMAURICE said, the question of the hon. Gentleman (Mr. Puleston) was a very natural one; but he was sorry he could not give a definite answer at that moment with regard to the position of the negotiations with Mexico. He hoped, however, he should not have to trespass much longer upon the patience of the hon. Member. When a definite arrangement was made, he would take the earliest opportunity of informing the House. The question had not been lost sight of; the negotiations had been proceeding; and in a short time he sincerely hoped he should be in a position to make a statement on the subject. A very distinguished English Diplomatist had gone to Mexico, and a most distinguished Mexican Diplomatist, M. Mariscal, had visited England; and by that means an important step had been taken towards restoring the diplomatic relations [illegible] unfortunately [illegible]. He agreed with the hon. [illegible] of the [illegible] relations could exist between England and Mexico.

MR. PULESTON [illegible] that he should [illegible] able to make a statement before the end of the present Session.

LORD EDMOND FITZMAURICE: Yes.

MR. MOLLOY said, he would have to trespass for [illegible] which he stated [illegible] of the Vote [illegible]. The item in [illegible] for the cost of [illegible] Mexico [illegible] the Treaty [illegible] King [illegible] the House [illegible] Mexico [illegible] were [illegible] of [illegible] was not an extravagant [illegible] charge. It was not [illegible] a question of amount, he [illegible] would [illegible] the same if [illegible] or £[illegible] which he wished to direct the attention of the

Committee was that, as a result of Admiral Hewett's Mission, they had got a couple of Treaties, which a little examination would show to be absolutely valueless — Treaties from which they could expect no substantial return either politically or philanthropically. The effect of them would be to identify us in the minds of the Soudanese with their worst and most hated enemies. The Abyssinians had always been and still were the bitterest enemies of the whole of the Arab Tribes from Darfour to the Red Sea. By these Treaties we had made common political cause with the savage, miscalled "Christian" mountaineers, and the animosity and hatred with which they were regarded by the Soudanese would, in consequence, be extended to us. Now, as to the value of the Treaties which Admiral Hewett had negotiated. They were two in number. The first had reference to the withdrawal of the garrisons from Kassala and two other places, Amedib and Sanhit, which were so small and so unimportant as not to be found on any map he had been able to consult. By the Third Article of the principal of the two Conventions, King John undertook—

"To facilitate the withdrawal of the troops of His Highness the Khedive from Kassala, Amedib, and Sanhit, through Ethiopia to Massowah."

He (Mr. M'Coan) did not quite understand what was meant by "facilitating the withdrawal of the troops." It might or it might not mean that King John would march a Force to the relief of the garrisons, and protect their retreat to the sea at Massowah; or it might mean that he would give them free transit through Abyssinia. Anyhow, that was the only thing which King John engaged to carry out as an equivalent for what we undertook to give to him. And what was that? We engaged to deliver up to him the large district of Bogos, a district lying immediately to the North of Abyssinia Proper, and within some 60 or 80 miles of the sea at Massowah. Now, the noble Lord (Lord Edmond Fitzmaurice) would, probably, tell the Committee that Bogos was formerly Abyssinian territory, and that its annexation by Egypt was never recognized by Her Majesty's Government, or never, in fact, effectively took place. Anticipating some such a statement as that, he (Mr. M'Coan) ventured to tell the Committee what the history of Bogos was. In the time of Mehemet Ali, it was a sort of "no man's land" between Abyssinia and the Northern parts of the Soudan. It was inhabited then, as now, by a number of perfectly distinct tribes having no tribal unity, and who recognized no common Chief. Mehemet Ali annexed the district and placed troops in it, and it became substantially a part of the Egyptian Soudan. For several years the hold of Mehemet Ali on it was a very shifting one. Sometimes he got taxation from the district, and sometimes he got none; but, at all events, the claims of Egypt upon Bogos were unbroken from the time of Mehemet Ali to that of Ismail. During the last 50 years, not even in the days of King Theodore, or any of the Chiefs who divided with him authority over Abyssinia, had any claim to it ever been made, and it was formally recognized by the Porte as Egyptian territory. In the Reign of the late Khedive, Ismail, the hold of Egypt upon Bogos was tightened. Garrisons were regularly placed in it, taxation was organized and enforced, and it became as much a part of the Egyptian Soudan as Dongola or Khartoum. That had been the territorial condition of Bogos for some 50 or 60 years, yet in Article II. of the Treaty we had, without reference to the Porte at all, taken upon ourselves to hand over the whole of this territory to the present King of Abyssinia. And, at this point, let them consider who the King of Abyssinia was. Up to a few years ago, he was simply one of the three Chiefs exercising authority over the three districts or Provinces into which Abyssinia had been immemorially divided. He was Chief of the Northern Province, and mainly owing to the cannons and rifles left with him by Lord Napier of Magdala, after the defeat of Theodore, he succeeded in subjugating to his own authority the Chiefs of the other two districts. The Negoosa Negust, King of Kings of Ethiopia—this King Johannes—was as barbarous a savage as was to be found South of Cairo, and his people were quite as savage a population as existed in any part of Africa. They continued still, as in Bruce's time, to eat the raw flesh of living animals; and though nominally belonging to the Coptic Church, their treatment of Protestants, or Catholics, or people espousing any other form of the Christian religion, was barbarous in the extreme. A recent Report of the Propaganda recounted a a great number of such atrocities committed by King John. Thus, he had seized Catholic missionaries, and, failing to induce them to abandon Catholicism, had cut off their feet, hands, and legs. Yet this was the King with whom, and on equal terms of civilization and dignity, Admiral Hewett had negotiated two Treaties at a cost of £4,000. He Mr. M'Coan need hardly say that any engagements entered into by such a savage were not worth the paper they were written upon. Nor had any means to insure the carrying out of the Treaties been provided by the appointment of Consuls or Agents, who might supervise their execution. We relied upon the word of this savage, and on no better guarantee had surrendered to him a great district of Egyptian territory. We did not in terms give King John Kassala, but we had in effect said—"We will not give it to you; but we will not prevent you taking it." Practically, therefore, it was understood that King John should seize and hold the Kassala district, one of the most cultivated and civilized and prosperous Provinces in Upper Egypt, and the centre of a thriving trade. With the arms and ammunition he would find in Kassala, Amedib, and Sanhit, his power for evil over the neighbouring tribes would be alarmingly great. Strengthened by these stores, he would be able to work his savage will upon the whole. By conferring such advantages on a savage of this kind we had identified ourselves with him and become, in a sense, responsible for all the barbarities which, thus strengthened, he would commit. Nor was the mischief so done merely temporary. By turning Massowah into a free port for the admission of arms and ammunition, it was made permanent. For many years the struggle of the Khedive of Egypt had been to keep the King of Abyssinia from obtaining military materials in this way. The constant desire of the King had been to get access to the sea for this purpose. Very little pure merchandise passed out of Massowah, and less passed in, but now the passage of one kind of goods would certainly be largely increased by the new Treaty. King John had been for many years one of the largest slave dealers in that part of Africa. Some 20,000 Abyssinian slaves, who were the highest priced slaves in Egypt and Turkey, passed over the Abyssinian Frontier every year, and for each of these King John received a toll of two dollars, so that he made a large revenue from the active pursuit of this abominable traffic. To give philanthropic colour to the Mission, it had been negotiated that—

"His Majesty the Negoos Negust agrees to prohibit to the best of his ability, the buying and selling of slaves within his dominions."

If King John were a model of honour and good faith, such an undertaking might have some value; but, being the savage he was, it had no value whatever, and all the more so, that there would be no Consular Agent on the spot. King John's whole interest would lie in continuing in the future, as in the past, to encourage the traffic in slaves, and we should be absolutely without the means of knowing whether he did so or not. For giving up the district of Bogos, which did not belong to us, and as to which we had not consulted the Sovereign Power at all, and for in effect, also, surrendering the wealthy and prosperous Province of Kassala, with all the Government stores and munitions of war, as well as those in Amedib and Sanhit, we had got, what?—an "Agreement" from this savage to facilitate the retreat of the garrisons, and a promise to discourage the Slave Trade. That was a poor return for £4,000. To his Mr. M'Coan's mind, the most serious part of the business was that it would have been circulated throughout the whole of the Soudan that they had made common cause with this savage King, and that they were as bad as he was. The action we had taken would, he was persuaded, intensify the Moslem animosity and hatred and distrust of us which already existed. Not merely on the ground of policy, but even on the ground of getting the worth of what it cost us, we had made a very bad bargain, and therefore, he begged to move the reduction of the Vote by £4,000.

Motion made, and Question proposed,

"That the Item of £4,000, for Admiral Hewett's Special Mission to Abyssinia, be omitted from the proposed Vote."—(*Mr. M'Coan*.)

Baron HENRY DE WORMS said, he thought the hon. Member (Mr. M'Coan) had done good service in calling the attention of the Committee to this Vote. It might be in the recollection of the Committee that he (Baron Henry De Worms) had, not long ago, brought it under the attention of the Under Secretary of State for Foreign Affairs, and had asked how it was that Kassala, Amedib, and Sanhit had been ceded to Abyssinia? And the answer he had received was that, so far as Articles I. and II. of the Treaty of Adowa were concerned, there was no evidence that Kassala had been ceded. It appeared to him, however, that in Article II. there was every evidence of such being the case. Article II. said—

"On and after the 1st day of September, 1884, corresponding to the 8th day of Maskarram, 1877, the country called Bogos shall be restored to His Majesty the Negoosa Negust; and when the troops of His Highness the Khedive shall have left the garrisons of Kassala, Amedib, and Sanhit, the buildings in the Bogos country which now belong to His Highness the Khedive, together with all the stores and munitions of war which shall then remain in the said buildings, shall be delivered to and become the property of His Majesty the Negoosa Negust."

What was the real meaning of guaranteeing that the garrisons should be withdrawn from Kassala, Amedib, and Sanhit, and should be occupied by the King of Abyssinia? It was a quibble to say that it did not mean the cession of these places to King John. In 1810 these places were taken by Mehemet Ali, and became the property of the Porte. It might be said that the question of the Suzerainty of the Porte arose on the broader question of Egypt itself; but, admitting that, it was still a question whether the Porte ought not to have been consulted before these places were handed over to the King of Abyssinia. So far as he could gather, he believed the Porte never had been consulted. If that were so, it amounted to this—that, in order to bring about an alliance with Abyssinia, they had handed over territory which belonged to somebody else. What was the object of their alliance with the King of Abyssinia? Some time ago, the Government were asked if —as it was rumoured—they intended to enter into an alliance with the King of Abyssinia? These questions were generally met by an absolute denial or an evasive answer. Hon. Members now saw what such denial was worth. There could be no question—there could be no doubt—that there was a most absolute Treaty between the King of Abyssinia and Her Majesty's Government, and that there was the most distinct connection between the cession of the towns of Kassala, Amedib, and Sanhit, and the relief of General Gordon. Then, as the hon. Gentleman very pertinently asked, who had they allied themselves with? They had allied themselves with a nation probably excelling in barbarity the Soudanese themselves, whom they had sought their assistance to overcome. In allying themselves in this manner, they were encouraging a religious feud, because they were employing a nation professing Christianity against a nation of Mussulmans, and they were increasing the difficulties of a situation already rendered difficult enough by their vacillating policy. As the vacillating policy of Her Majesty's Government had materially increased their expenses and their liabilities in that part of the globe, he should support the Motion for the reduction of the Vote.

Sir GEORGE CAMPBELL said, that on this question he could not at all agree with the hon. Member for Wicklow (Mr. M'Coan). He (Sir George Campbell) had never been in the country in question himself; but an opportunity of travelling over it had been afforded recently to a gentleman, who had availed himself of it, and it seemed to him that the journey had borne good fruit. The journey he referred had been made the subject of a book of a very interesting and instructive character. The author was not a partizan, nor had the journey been undertaken in connection with this subject. This writer, Mr. James, had visited the territory in question, and, according to this gentleman's narrative, it possessed a good climate and a large population, principally Christian. There were many Christian missionaries in the country, and Mr. James gave his readers to understand that it was occupied by Egyptian garrisons, who held it as a foreign country; and it appeared to Mr. James that the country was one which might very well be given up to the Abyssinians.

Mr. M'COAN: The Abyssinians never had it.

SIR GEORGE CAMPBELL said, that the Abyssinians had certainly possessed it very recently, or, at any rate, part of it, and he should be very glad to hear of its being included within the borders of Abyssinia. At the same time, he thought the Under Secretary of State for Foreign Affairs should explain precisely what was meant by the territory of Bogos. The Treaty with King John was somewhat obscure on that point, and was calculated to give rise to some misapprehension; and it seemed to him, from a careful study of the document, that it was not intended to include Kassala in the territory of Abyssinia. Mr. James, in his book, explained to the reader the characteristics of the country, and the interesting tribes who occupied it. Kassala was a very civilized place. Not only were there Greek merchants there, but also some manufactures; and it was, in fact, a large and important place. He (Sir George Campbell) was one of those who desired to see political boundaries correspond with ethnological boundaries, and it seemed to him that the whole country occupied by a Christian population should be handed over to the Christians. He would not go beyond that; but if they did go farther, the result would be constant disturbance and prolonged difficulty. He, therefore, hoped that Her Majesty's Government would not encourage the King of Abyssinia to attempt to conquer any territory outside the ethnological boundary. The idea he (Sir George Campbell) had gathered from the circumstantial account of Mr. James, had not been such as was suggested by the hon. Member for Wicklow, for, as he had said, this would seem to be a civilized country. No doubt, they were in a very unpleasant position as to General Gordon, who had got himself into this scrape; and it would be a matter for congratulation if they could get him out of it without unnecessary bloodshed. He should be glad to see General Gordon get out by way of the Blue Nile, or the White Nile, or any other way.

MR. ASHMEAD-BARTLETT agreed with the hon. Member who had spoken from that side of the House (Baron Henry De Worms), that the hon. Member for Wicklow (Mr. M'Coan) had raised a most important question. Of all the barbarous and cruel and pusillanimous acts that Her Majesty's Government had been guilty of in regard to the Soudan, this invasion of the territory of the Arabs by Abyssinian hordes was the worst. Could it be doing right to induce these savages, who hardly deserved the name of Christians, to precipitate themselves upon a people alien in race and religion—a people with whom they had been at feud for generations? To invite them to do this thing in the interest of General Gordon, of civilization, and of the Soudan, was utterly absurd, and an act of sheer barbarity and cruelty. The hon. Member who had just sat down had described the Abyssinians as a civilized people; but they were in reality nothing better than a horde of savages. Possibly, the noble Lord (Lord Edmond Fitzmaurice) might disagree with the hon. Member; but his opinion would have undergone a change if he had read the accounts which had come from the country in question from a correspondent of *The Daily News*, with Admiral Hewett. The noble Lord would have seen, if he had read this gentleman's correspondence, that the Abyssinians were little better than savages; that Sir William Hewett's Mission was, from time to time, placed in very great danger by them; and that their habits and modes of life were filthy and barbarous in the extreme. If these savages had had placed before them merely the task of wresting Kassala from the Arabs, Parliament might have looked upon the enterprize and its success with complacency; but, as a matter of fact, they would have to go through thousands of Arab tribesmen, who had been comparatively friendly to us in the Soudan, to get there. No doubt, fire, sword, rapine, and every sort of savage licence would be inflicted upon these tribes. What was the object of this invasion? As the hon. Member for Wicklow had pointed out, England could gain nothing by it. Then, what was the object of it? Nominally, it was to relieve Kassala. They knew what that meant —the absolute extinction of Kassala and most of its inhabitants. Kassala was a town of 25,000 inhabitants—a town which, according to Sir Samuel Baker, had multiplied three-fold within the past 25 years, a town of considerable prosperity and extensive trade. This town was to be handed over to Abyssinia. It was no use saying that it was not to be handed over to that country. When they invited a savage Monarch to make himself master of a place, and he told them he should retain it, and no one was sent out to act as a check on him, or to control his movements, they were practically giving it to him. The British Government had made themselves responsible for the Soudan. They had driven away an Egyptian Minister who had wanted to restore peace and order in the Soudan; they had massacred 6,000 or 7,000 Arabs there; and now they were sending a horde of 20,000 savages, the natural enemies of the Arabs and the people in possession, to seize upon a large town, and devastate and lay waste the surrounding country without the slightest restraint. If it had been intended that this march should be conducted on civilized principles, and if it had been intended to place some restraint on the King of Abyssinia, the Government would have sent Admiral Hewett, or some of his officers, to accompany the King, in order to prevent wanton bloodshed and useless destruction of property. They had been afraid to do that. Admiral Hewett had been sent on his Mission. He had gone as rapidly as he could, but had been detained on the way six weeks or two months whilst the King was at his bath. He left the King as soon as he could, and hurried away. The Government had left him to make what arrangements he chose, and to do what he liked in the matter. Surely, no course of action could have been more likely to lead to destruction of life and property—useless destruction of life and property. It was not possible to stigmatize this action of the Government in terms sufficiently strong. It was even worse than instigating the Bulgarians to attack the Mussulmen, or the Turks to make war on the Bulgarians, without taking precautions to prevent atrocities, because the Turks were more civilized than these Arabs and Abyssinians. He admitted the responsibility of this country to protect the garrison of Kassala; but it was a responsibility they should bear themselves, and their action should not be to relieve the town of the plague of the Arabs by sending a worse plague in its place. The result of this action was very likely to be, for the moment, to drive the Arab besiegers and the Egyptian garrison into union against the Abyssinian barbarians. It was said that the assistance of the Abyssinians had been invited in the interest of General Gordon; but he (Mr. Ashmead-Bartlett) should have thought no step more disastrous to General Gordon could have been taken. It would create the greatest bitterness and the deepest hostility amongst the Soudanese. It would fill the whole of the Soudanese with the deadliest hatred to the British, when they knew how their country had been ravaged and their people slaughtered and enslaved by these Christian Abyssinians at our instigation. He was curious to hear what the Under Secretary of State for Foreign Affairs would have to say in defence of the action of the Government. He was not surprised at the Prime Minister running away—what could he say; how could he defend the ruin and bloodshed about to take place in the Soudan? That was a very awkward question for one who had talked so loudly and so pretentiously of the rights of peoples and the evils of bloodshed and rapine, at a time when not he himself, but a Minister to whom he was opposed, was in Office. No doubt, that was a very unpleasant subject for the Prime Minister, and it was not to be wondered at that the right hon. Gentleman withdrew from the debate. It would be interesting to hear what the Under Secretary of State for Foreign Affairs had to say in defence of this most cruel, pusillanimous, and unjustifiable outrage on the Mussulman inhabitants of the Soudan.

Lord EDMOND FITZMAURICE: The hon. Gentleman who has just spoken, as the evening draws on, seems to me to become, if possible, more and more extreme in his language. Early in the evening the Government were "base" and "cowardly," but now they are "cruel," "barbarous," and "pusillanimous," and I do not know how many terrible things. They have been committing outrages, and are arranging rapine and massacres. I will not attempt to follow the hon. Member in regard to his vague and general accusations, nor will I attempt to vie with him in the use of strong language. I will simply, at this late hour of the evening, refer to what I am sure he wishes—namely, to the main facts of the case. Now, this Treaty is a very short one. It is a Treaty of Seven Articles, and it may be generally described in this way—that, on the one hand, the King of Abyssinia [illegible] the retreat and withdrawal of [illegible] Egyptian garrisons from [illegible] Slave Trade Treaty. On the other [illegible] Egypt [illegible] Abyssinia [illegible] property of Abyssinia [illegible] First Article of the Treaty [illegible] perhaps the most important [illegible]

[illegible]

Massowah is vital to the [illegible] these regions [illegible] object of Abyssinia [illegible] Massowah, [illegible] arrangement [illegible] very important [illegible] the interests of the [illegible] of these regions [illegible] I agree [illegible] description of the Abyssinians [illegible] we have heard to-night, I should [illegible]

[illegible]

this district of Bogos to Abyssinia? At one time it was Abyssinian territory [illegible] years ago [illegible] Abyssinia.

MR. M[illegible]

LORD EDMOND FITZMAURICE [illegible] condition of warfare [illegible] Egypt [illegible] was certain to [illegible] the King of Abyssinia [illegible] King of Egypt [illegible] First Article of the Treaty [illegible] Massowah [illegible] Third Article of the Treaty [illegible]

[illegible] what the meaning of this Article is. It [illegible] The Egyptian garrisons are to be withdrawn from the places, Kassala, [illegible] King of Abyssinia [illegible] of the Treaty, [illegible] King of Abyssinia [illegible]

MR. ASHMEAD-BARTLETT: He [illegible]

LORD EDMOND FITZMAURICE [illegible]

[illegible] try to [illegible] seem

to think that we ought to have something to say upon every event which takes place abroad, and that we ought to interfere in matters that are not of vital interest to ourselves. What is of importance to us is to secure the withdrawal of the Egyptian garrisons, and, so far as we can, to reduce the causes of dispute between Abyssinia and Egypt. But if it then happen that in consequence of this Treaty, or in consequence of the steps which the King of Abyssinia may take, or may not take, in these regions, some further portion of a territory—the boundary of which has varied from time to time—may have to be ceded to Abyssinia, it is not a matter for this country or for hon. Members to become alarmed about. It is desirable for us to look at these things from a calm and common-sense point of view. I know very well an attempt has been made to paint this question in colours dark and gloomy. We have been accused of letting loose fanatical hordes of fifth-rate Christians on these Mahommedans. We have done nothing of the kind. The descriptions we have had of "barbarous tribes," "Abyssinian savages," and so on, have been grossly exaggerated; and it seems to me that the "horrible barbarity" of the Abyssinians was discovered by some hon. Members opposite about the same time that they first heard of the existence of this Treaty. I am not contending that the civilization of the Abyssinians is a high form of civilization, or that their Christianity is a very noble form of Christianity. I have heard them described as "fifth-rate Christians." The other day I quoted from a work by Dean Stanley on the Eastern Churches, and everyone who refers to that work will see that the Abyssinian form of Christianity is not a very exalted one. But if we desire to improve the condition of Christianity and civilization in that country, the best way to do it is to give the people improved communication with more civilized races; and that we have done by giving them access to Massowah. We have done it also in another way. One of the difficulties that the people has suffered from has been the constant obstacles thrown in their way in regard to the consecration of the Aboonas, or priests, by the Coptic Patriarch. In the Fourth Article of the Treaty the Khedive undertakes that these difficulties shall no longer exist. The Article is—

> "His Highness the Khedive engages to grant all the facilities which His Majesty the Negoosa Negust may require in the matter of appointing Aboonas for Ethiopia."

The Fifth Article does not require any detailed notice. It says—

> "His Majesty the Negoosa Negust and His Highness the Khedive engage to deliver up, the one to the other, any criminal or criminals who may have fled, to escape punishment, from the dominions of the one to the dominions of the other."

The Sixth Article refers all differences to Her Majesty in these terms—

> "His Majesty the Negoosa Negust agrees to refer all differences with His Highness the Khedive which may arise after the signing of this Treaty to Her Britannic Majesty for settlement."

And Article VII. has reference merely to the ratification of the Treaty. There is only one other point which I need mention, and that is what was said by my hon. Friend who has now left the House (Baron Henry De Worms) with reference to the Porte. As I said the other day, it has never been shown that the Bogos territory comes within the territory of the Sultan—I see no reason to withdraw from what I then said. I think it will be seen that this Treaty is one which will not be disadvantageous to the region affected by it. In regard to the suppression of the Slave Trade, there is a good deal to be done by this Treaty with the King of Abyssinia; and I hope that, as the trade of Massowah increases, and as the British Consul who may be stationed there assumes—as he will assume—an important position, it will be found possible, as is the case in other parts of the world, to do much towards stopping that horrible trade which has led to so many of the evils which have been found to exist there.

LORD RANDOLPH CHURCHILL said, that the noble Lord had declared that he was going to be very calm, and he certainly had been, and both dull and prolix in addition. There were several points, not so much of detail as of general principle, which had appeared to him (Lord Randolph Churchill) to be of a very objectionable character. In the first place, as to the First Article of the Treaty. No doubt, everyone in the House was quite ready to concede that it was an excellent thing that Massowah should be open to the Abyssinians. The Second Article, however, was objectionable, because, in that, the British Government had ceded to the King of Abyssinia a territory which they had not the smallest right in the world to cede. That was the real point of the whole matter—that the British Government had taken upon themselves to band over to the King of Abyssinia, who was, undoubtedly, a barbarian, a large territory over which the Abyssinians had no control, and over which the British Government could exercise no sort of authority. He wished to know why such a proceeding, which, undoubtedly, in more civilized parts of the world, would have been repudiated and denounced by the British Government, if adopted by any other Government, had became legitimate, proper, and decent, when adopted by them in this part of Africa? What right had they to give over the Bogos people to the Sovereignty of the King of Abyssinia? It was, at least, 60 or 80 years since the territory had belonged to Abyssinia, if, indeed, it had ever belonged to it. The noble Lord seemed very positive on the point; but he had failed to give hon. Members his sources of information. But supposing that this territory at one time had belonged to the Abyssinians, the fact that it no longer belonged to them, and had ceased to be their property for 50 or 60 years, was a great proof that it should not belong to them, and that the Abyssinians were not fit to hold it or govern it. He protested against the principle of the Second Article of the Treaty, which assumed that the British Government had a right to distribute the Soudan—or rather this territory with this disagreeable name—in the way in which they proposed to distribute it. Then, they came to the question of Kassala, and the territory round it. That was a much more serious matter. It was not denied that the King of Abyssinia intended to annex Kassala, and the British Government meant handing over a country filled with a Mahommedan population to the rule of a man who, in the eyes of the Mahommedans, was a heretical Sovereign. He wished to ask again what right the British Government had to treat this population around Kassala in a different manner to that in which they would treat the population of any other part of the Soudan? The great point of the Government policy in the Soudan was that the people there were struggling to be free. Why were the people at Kassala to be placed in this disgraceful position, that they of all others of the Soudan were not to be allowed to be free, but were to be placed under the rule, not of the Mahdi, but of a *soi disant* Christian? Nothing more odious to the Mahommedan population in that part of the world could be conceived. The noble Lord had given no reason why these people should be treated in a different manner to the people of Darfur. What guarantee was there that the garrisons of Kassala and the places round it would be rescued by the King of Abyssinia? Would they ever know what became of these garrisons. To anyone who had read the accounts of the Mission of Admiral Hewett, it was quite plain they had been drawn entirely from Liberal sources. It was entirely owing to the enterprize of *The Daily News* that they had received such full accounts of the Mission at all, and yet it was clear from those accounts that the Abyssinians were an extremely savage and barbarous race. That was certainly the impression entertained of them at the time of the Abyssinian War. He wished to know what guarantee the Government had that, in return for bringing about the cession of Bogos, the garrisons of Kassala and the other places would ever be liberated, or that they would even be allowed to withdraw? It seemed to him there was no guarantee at all—that the King of Abyssinian might attack them without our having any remedy against him. There was another point which might not have occurred to the noble Lord or to the Foreign Office, but which was very remarkable. The British Government was now engaged in supervising the administration of a thoroughly Mahommedan country, and if the British Government was to have any success whatever in having this arrangement acceded to by Mahommedan subjects in Egypt, it must more or less consult their religious feelings and their religious law. Well, he knew the Mahommedans, as a rule, were not very fond of Christians. There was a deep gulf between Mahommedans and Christians, and where the question of government was concerned, that difference had been found very wide indeed. But, curiously enough, he had been told, on the authority of a very learned man now in England—an Ulema of the University of Cairo—that if there were a set of Christians on the face of the earth whom the Mahommedans loathed and abhorred more than another, it was the Abyssinian Christians. They were forbidden by their religion to make any terms with them, and wars had been going on between them for generations. There had never been any peace between them. This was a principle recognized by all Mahommedans; whether or not it was in the Koran he could not say. The Secretary to the Treasury (Mr. Courtney) looked upon all this with supreme contempt—he was anxious to get to those little niggling Votes which were so dear to his heart and so troublesome to everyone else. To his (Lord Randolph Churchill's) mind, these subjects were not beneath the notice of the Committee, and it was not too much to ask that the Committee should discuss them when they came on for the first time. If the particular question now under debate was so completely beneath the notice of the hon. Gentleman the Secretary to the Treasury, he would recommend him to follow the example of the Prime Minister, and, for the moment, leave the House. This was certain—that if Her Majesty's Government were anxious to affront and displease Mahommedans in Egypt as outrageously as they could, they would do it by concluding a Treaty with Abyssinia. Besides, there was a belief amongst the Arabs, that some day mischief would arise from the Abyssinians. These facts he gave the Committee as he had received them from a learned man from Cairo, whom he himself was inclined to believe. The Government had been most unfortunate in the course they had taken; and he did not know whether the view he had just expounded had been put to the noble Lord or the Foreign Office before. If it had not, it was not altogether unworthy of their notice. It appeared to him that the step the Government had taken had been a singularly ill-advised one, and if the hon. Member for Wicklow divided against the Vote, he (Lord Randolph Churchill) should certainly vote with him.

SIR WILFRID LAWSON said, that the explanation of the noble Lord (Lord Edmond Fitzmaurice), and his defence of the Government, was as strong a case as had yet been made out against them. The noble Lord had admitted that the Abyssinians were not first-rate Christians—that they were fifth-rate Christians.

LORD EDMOND FITZMAURICE: I said someone else described them as such.

SIR WILFRID LAWSON said, that even if they were first-rate Christians, we had no right to put them to this use. He agreed with what had been said by the noble Lord opposite (Lord Randolph Churchill). The hon. Member (Mr. Ashmead-Bartlett) had certainly used strong language, and if these Abyssinians were the brutes and savages he had described them to be, nothing could be worse than their employing them in this business. One of the things he wished to know was this—what was the meaning of this obscure Article of the Treaty—

"His Majesty the Negoosa Negust engages to faciliate the withdrawal of the troops of His Highness the Khedive from Kassala, Amedib, and Sanhit, through Ethiopia to Massowah?"

That was the real point of their inquiry now. Did that mean that these fifth-rate Christians and first-rate savages were to be sent out into the Soudan to lay waste the country and to "assist in getting these Egyptian troops out," or did it not? ["No!"] Then, how were the Abyssinians to assist in getting them out, if troops were not to go there? He could not understand what it all meant. When they went to war it was the custom to do all the harm they could to a country, and these fifth-rate Christians and first-rate savages were just the fellows to follow out that principle to the letter. It seemed to him that they were now in a worse position than they were some time ago. What an outcry there was when they employed the North American Indians against the Americans in the War of Independence! Chatham's most powerful speech was made against it—the speech that they used to learn as schoolboys; and here they were doing the same thing again in the year 1884. He had hoped that, they were getting beyond these horrors. First, they interfered with the freedom of action of a peaceful and laborious people in Egypt; then they went through every species of horror in slaughtering and dispersing the Arabs; and now the noble

Lord the Under Secretary of State for Foreign Affairs made a speech in support of the employment of fifth-rate Christians for this kind of warfare. He should certainly vote for the proposal of the hon. Member for W[illegible].

BARON HENRY DE WORMS said, he wished just to make one remark in answer to an observation of his noble Friend Lord Edmond Fitzmaurice. As he, Baron Henry De Worms, had understood the noble Lord, he had said there was no evidence in the Treaty or the accompanying documents that the King of Abyssinia [illegible] to take Kassala, A[illegible] and [illegible]. [illegible] to him, Baron Henry De Worms, that there was distinct evidence in the case.

LORD EDMOND FITZMAURICE said, the hon. Member was not in the House when he spoke. He had stated that it was not within the four corners of the Treaty.

BARON HENRY DE WORMS said, it was quite clear that Admiral Hewett, who was a party to the Treaty, knew at the time he was [illegible] that it was the intention of the King of Abyssinia to attack Kassala and the other places. In his Report to Earl Granville, in the 12th paragraph, he said—

[illegible] Kassala [illegible] Abyssinia [illegible] their [illegible]

And in a letter to the Secretary to the Admiralty on the [illegible] of June, the Admiral made a statement to the effect that [illegible] King [illegible] Wa[illegible] King [illegible] Kassala [illegible] If [illegible] the hon. Member for W[illegible] Mr. M'Coan had [illegible].

MR. LABOUCHERE protested against [illegible] stirring up war [illegible] Soudan. [illegible] make [illegible] Egypt [illegible] whatever [illegible] Abyssinia [illegible] Prime Minister [illegible] that the independence of the Soudan had been declared, and if that was the [illegible] why should Admiral Hewett go to Abyssinia to employ the people of that country against the Soudanese? There had been a proof given in the first place that the garrison of Kassala wished [illegible] and in the second place that it [illegible] wished [illegible]. They had simply given up the Soudan, and yet in the [illegible] they had made every kind of attack upon it and had sent General Gordon to Khartoum, where he seemed to be passing his time killing and [illegible] the Natives whose [illegible] they sent Admiral Hewett to the King of Abyssinia to prevail on him to make a raid on that country. Why could they not let the Soudan alone, having declared its independence? They had gone on raiding and killing and would probably continue to do so [illegible] [illegible] Embassy to the place, a [illegible] [illegible] Army [illegible], and [illegible] That would [illegible] the House [illegible] against this [illegible] [illegible] wasted [illegible] money [illegible] wicked purpose as the stirring up of war in that part of the world. He hoped the hon. Member (Mr. M'Coan) would divide the Committee.

Question put.

The Committee *divided*:—Ayes 32; Noes 47: Majority 15.—(Div. List, No. 208.)

Original Question again proposed.

SIR GEORGE CAMPBELL said, he had given Notice that he would propose to reduce the Supplementary Vote by £[illegible] expenses connected with Egypt. He had put that Motion on the Paper because he very strongly disapproved of the arrangements made for [illegible] the [illegible] for five years, for he believed that would be most disastrous. But at this period of the Session he [illegible] he should not propose the [illegible].

MR. LABOUCHERE [illegible] separate [illegible] There were [illegible] was perhaps not generally known that there was an [illegible] the Foreign Office, a charge for a chaplain at a Legation or Embassy. But why were they supposed to be [illegible]? Where there was a [illegible] a chaplain [illegible] appointed; but there were several Embassies where there were chaplains and, in some cases, £300 a-year was [illegible] for them.

THE CHAIRMAN: I do not see that any of these Votes relate to chaplains, and the hon. Member will not be in Order in debating any question in regard to them.

MR. LABOUCHERE wished to obtain from the Chair a ruling on a point which was a very important one, and one on which questions were constantly being raised. Were the various items to be taken *seriatim* in such a manner as that if one hon. Member got up and made a proposal upon some item near the end of the Vote, no other hon. Member would afterwards be at liberty to raise any discussion upon any item that stood before it? He was not going to attack the Vote, but only to ask a question. Of course, if the Chairman maintained the ruling that had just been laid down, the matter was at an end; but it certainly was most inconvenient, and it was very desirable that there should be some definite and distinct statement from the Chair upon the subject.

THE CHAIRMAN: The Rule of the House is very precise. It is clearly laid down that, after a Question has been proposed from the Chair for the diminution of any item, no Motion can be made or debate allowed upon any preceding item. The hon. Member, therefore, cannot debate any preceding item. There is no Vote for Chaplains before us now—if there was such an item to come on, the hon. Gentleman would be in Order; but there is not.

Original Question put, and *agreed to.*

(2.) £155,402 (including a Supplementary sum of £2,910), to complete the sum for Consular Services.

CAPTAIN AYLMER wished to call attention to a matter in connection with this Vote. There was a very large sum put down here as fees received during the year 1882-3, amounting altogether to £45,102. That was a very large sum, and it was well worthy of the consideration of the Committee. It was very right that English subjects abroad, requiring the services of a Consul to witness documents, should be charged a fee. He did not attack that principle at all, and he was very glad that the amount was so large; but his opinion was that, considering the fees that were charged, the amount might be very much larger. There was not the least check upon these charges, so far as he could learn. An Englishman abroad, appearing before a Consul for the purpose of signing his name, getting a writ issued, or anything else, had to pay 6*s.*, 7*s.*, or 8*s.*, or whatever was required by the Consular Office, as a fee; but no accounts seemed to be kept of these payments, nor did there seem to be any possible check to secure a thoroughly accurate return. He (Captain Aylmer) himself had had to pay on very many occasions, and the money had always been put in the Consul's pocket, or into that of his clerk, and there was no way in which the Government could check the amount. He had often discussed the matter with gentlemen who were travelling abroad, and the opinion generally entertained, without charging anybody with dishonesty, was that a considerable portion of the money never arrived at the English Exchequer at all. The difficulty could be very easily met by providing that a Consular stamp should be affixed, or something of that sort done; but as matters stood at present, all he could say was, that a man appeared before the Consul, the Consul witnessed the signature, the man paid a fee, the money disappeared in the Consul's pocket, the Consul made no entry and kept no account, and there was no possible check of any sort. Many Consular Offices abroad, where Englishmen had to go to sign important documents, were in a very disgraceful state. Very large sums were set down in the Votes for these Offices—£200 a-year was allowed for the Consular Office chiefly used in Paris; but to get into that Office one had to pass through a dark room without a window, and it was generally hampered with a heap of luggage, which was not at all a right or proper condition for an English Consular Office to be in. That was a state of things that was much complained of.

LORD EDMOND FITZMAURICE said, these Consular Offices were regulated under the terms of an Order in Council. Every Consul or Consular officer who received fees had to make a careful account of the amount received. No doubt, in theory, the method of check might not seem a very perfect one; but the matter was receiving attention. At the same time, he was bound to think that there never had been the least suspicion of any improper conduct on the part of any Consular officer in regard to those fees. However, the sub- [illegible]

CAPTAIN AYLMER said, [illegible] ... "[illegible]" ... Captain Aylmer replied ... "[illegible]" Whereupon the [illegible]

MR. ASHMEAD-BARTLETT said he had hoped [illegible] ... There were several points in connection with [illegible] ... The Prime Minister was asked over and over again last week and the week before [illegible] Votes, but ... Friday. When ... [illegible] ... would feel that it was unreasonable that these Votes should be pressed forward that night. Under these circumstances, and in view of the postponement of the Ministerial Statement, he was [illegible] in asking [illegible]

MR. LABOUCHERE said they were always glad to hear the hon. Member for [illegible] ... [illegible]

MR. ASHMEAD-BARTLETT rose to Order. [illegible] ... hon. Member ... Mr. Ashmead-Bartlett would not be able to refer to any of the preceding Votes.

THE CHAIRMAN: [illegible] ... preceding Votes.

CAPTAIN AYLMER said, he thought it was necessary that the hon. Member for Northampton, under these circumstances, should say whether he intended to move the reduction of the Vote or not.

MR. LABOUCHERE said he did not intend to move the reduction of the Vote. He only wanted to know about the Kertch [illegible] ... Egyptian [illegible] ... know what was going on at Khartoum. Was Mr. Power still there? He would like to hear some details about that.

LORD EDMOND FITZMAURICE said, that with regard to Kertch, an opportunity had been taken of making certain [illegible] in reference to the

Consular Office, and the gentleman referred to by the hon. Member for Northampton, who was an unpaid Vice Consul, had been withdrawn. There would now be a regular Consul there, for Kertch was becoming a very important place. In regard to Khartoum, Mr. Power was merely a temporary Acting Consul, charged with Consular duties.

MR. CALLAN wished to ask the Under Secretary of State for Foreign Affairs for an explanation on one point. He wished to know on what principle these Consular salaries and duties were apportioned? He found that in the Brazils, the Consul at Pernambuco had £800 a-year and £400 for allowances, or £1,200 in all; while the fees received amounted to only £116. In another case, the Consul received £600 a-year in salary and £150 in allowances; while the fees received were £119. But in the Argentine Republic, at Rosario, the Consul received no salary, and the expenses for Office allowances were only £300 a-year; while the fees received amounted in 1882 to £320, and last year to £355. On looking back to the Estimates for previous years, he found that in 1879 the Consul at Rosario received £400 a-year in salary and £200 for expenses and Office allowances. What was the state of trade in Rosario at that time? On looking over the Board of Trade Returns, he found that the shipping from Rosario in 1879 consisted of 42 English vessels with a tonnage of 22,000 tons, and crews, giving the most trouble to the Consuls, of 696; whereas, in the past year, the shipping had increased to 153 vessels, with a tonnage of 109,000 tons. He held in his hand a Return given to him by one of the Ministers of the Republic. It was the Return of one English line going to Rosario—Lambert and Holt's Line—and from that it appeared that in 1878, when there was a Consul at Rosario, with £600 a-year, only 12 ocean steamers went into Rosario; whereas in the present year, up to the 1st of June, 29 steamers of one firm alone went there, and in all, last year, 97 ocean steamers went into the port. Taking the fees received in the Office, it appeared that in 1879 the Consul's duties were so light that only £94 13*s*. was received in fees; whereas, last year, the amount received and returned to the Foreign Office was £355, which was £55 in excess of the salary or allowances for the Consul's Office. In 1878 and 1879, when there was a Consul in existence, with a salary and allowances of £600 a-year, there was only one-fifth of the present tonnage or of the present official duties; but now only £300 a-year was allowed for Office expenses, and there was no salary at all. He was glad to hear that there was a Departmental Commission sitting on the subject, and he wanted to know on what principle the salary was granted—whether by the amount of fees received, the amount of shipping entering the port, or the nature and amount of the general duties performed? If the salary was fixed in reference to any one of these considerations—the tonnage, the number of the crews, the amount of business going into the Office, the amount of the fees received, or the increasing importance of the port—there could be no possible reason why the city of Rosario, which, in 1879, possessed a Consulate, should in the present year, when it had become the second port of the Argentine Republic, be reduced to a Vice Consulate. He hoped some explanation would be given to the Committee as to the principle on which the salaries were allocated, and that immediate steps would be taken to remedy this wholly unjustifiable inequality which ought not to exist. He hoped, now that the attention of the Under Secretary of State for Foreign Affairs had been drawn to the matter, that he would be able to give some consideration to it before the Report.

MR. BRYCE wished to ask the noble Lord the Under Secretary of State for Foreign Affairs about the Consulates in Asia Minor and Armenia, and also as to the allocation of places where Consuls were kept. It was said last winter, that new instructions had been given to Consuls in Asiatic Turkey that they were to bring to the notice of the Government, and especially to the notice of Her Majesty's Ambassador at Constantinople, any oppressions upon the subjects. But the results had been somewhat narrow, and he wanted to know what was the real state of the case? As to the places of these Consular Stations, he found that some Consuls had been withdrawn from Asiatic Turkey where they used to be maintained. That might have been done from motives of economy; but if Consuls were to be withdrawn at all, there were other places from which they might have been withdrawn with more advantage—places where they were less needed than some of those from which they had been withdrawn. The Committee would remember that, immediately after the Anglo-Turkish Convention, the late Government sent Military Consuls to the Armenian Frontier charged with strategic duties. They were to observe the progress of Russia, and to enable us to defend the Frontier of Asiatic Turkey. But he supposed the functions of those Consuls vanished with the Anglo-Turkish Convention itself, which was now relegated to a limbo from which it could never emerge.

MR. ASHMEAD-BARTLETT: Who says so?

MR. BRYCE, continuing, said, these officials never performed military duties, but they did very good work in reporting instances of cruelty and oppression, of scandalous injustice and exactions, sometimes by officials and sometimes by robber tribes. These instances of oppression were sent to Constantinople. Our Ambassador, in many cases, interfered, and in some cases there was very little doubt that some sort of check, though not complete, was imposed upon the conduct of these oppressors. Now, this force of observers had been diminished, and he would suggest to the Government that they would do better to remove their Vice Consuls from places like Broussa and Alexandretta than from places where great oppressions were constantly being exercised, and from which Reports would be of very great value. Since Turkey had done nothing, some good might be done, at any rate, by having Consuls at those places to let them know what was going on, and then the Government would have means of remonstrating with effect. Similar remarks would apply to the case of European Turkey. There were many places where they might have Consuls. They had none at all up at Bosnia, and a conflagration might break out at any moment. They ought to have a British officer in that immense district of country charged with knowing what the condition of the country was. They knew what serious results followed in 1875 and 1876 from the ignorance of this country and of the Government as to the state of European Turkey. The massacres of 1876 took them completely by surprise; but if they had had a proper staff to diffuse the information through the country a very different result might have happened. He wanted to know whether the Government could not transfer the Consuls from places where they were less needed to those places where they were greatly needed?

MR. O'SHEA said, the time had arrived when the remuneration of Consuls and Consular Agents abroad ought, in his opinion, to be inquired into; because there was no doubt that, while some of those gentlemen were well paid, others were under-paid. He would take the case of the Consuls in Spain as an instance. The Vice Consul at Santander received a salary of £100 a year, and an allowance of £280 for Office expenses and rent, which latter amount included £200 for fees, whereas the amount of fees payable to the Government appeared to be only £134. The Committee would be aware that Santander was a very important port, and he could not understand why, having regard to the amount of British commerce represented there, the position of their Representative there should not be advanced from Vice Consul to that of Consul, and why his salary should not be raised proportionately. Again, the Vice Consul at Carthagena, a very important place, where difficult questions relating to shipping often arose, received only £200 and £100 as an allowance for Office expenses and rent. The fact that this Vice Consulate returned the large sum of £620 in fees to the British Government was in itself sufficient to show that this country ought to be well represented there. Then he observed that the Consul General at Havana, who received £1,200 a year as salary and £600 a year for Office expenses and rent, also received from the Spanish Government £11[illegible] a year for house rent as Commissary Judge. He thought it was not right that a Consul should receive any money at all from a Foreign Government. Without going into further detail, he trusted the whole subject would receive the attention of the Foreign Office.

MR. ASHMEAD-BARTLETT said, he had been very much amused at hearing the hon. and learned Member for the Tower Hamlets (Mr. Bryce) protest against what he called outrages in

Turkey in Asia; and, generally, he was entertained with the line which the hon. and learned Member took on that point as one of the supporters, through thick and thin, of the policy of Her Majesty's Government, which had caused far more ruin and loss of life in other Mahomedan countries. ["Order, order!"] He submitted that he was perfectly in Order. Surely it was right to answer the argument of the hon. and learned Member by analogy; but, passing from that subject, he desired to have some information from Her Majesty's Government with regard to the position of the Acting Consul at Khartoum. To use the language of the Under Secretary of State for Foreign Affairs, that gentleman had been in a perilous position for the last four or five months. The last communications from him were dated the 23rd of March and the 7th of April, in the former of which he said—

"We are daily expecting British troops; we cannot believe that we are to be abandoned by the Government; our existence depends on England."

On the 7th of April he said—

"Khartoum is at present the centre of an enormous rebel camp; our store of food and ammunition is rather short; the situation is very critical; we are trying to run a steamer to Berber; but yesterday, owing to the rebel fire, she had to return."

That was the statement of a gentleman who, according to the noble Lord, accepted a very onerous position at great peril to himself, discharged his duties in that position with great advantage to the country, was lauded by a British Minister for having done so, and then, so far as they knew, had been abandoned to his fate. That gentleman was Mr. Power, the Consular Agent of this country at Khartoum. Now, he wished to say, on behalf of Mr. Power, that every statement which had appeared in *The Times*, coming from him as Correspondent, and every statement made by him to the Government, had been entirely borne out by facts; there was no important statement made by Mr. Power, and which had appeared in the public Press, or in the official records, that could be impugned. His accuracy was undoubted, and the statements he had made as coming from General Gordon himself had been proved up to the hilt by subsequent accounts published in the Blue Book. He thought the Prime Minister and the Government owed a public apology to Mr. Power for the language they had at one time used, which threw a doubt upon his accuracy. No one at that moment knew what was going to be done with him, although they might possibly hear something on the subject to-morrow. He wanted to know how long this gentleman was to be left in his perilous position, or whether, having in that position discharged his duties faithfully, he was to be abandoned by the Government? Without detaining the Committee any longer on that subject, he would pass to the position of the Consul at Tamatave. At present he appeared to have been of no advantage to this country. He had been sent out to Madagascar last November; but, so far as it was possible to judge from the answers of the Government on the subject, he had as yet discharged no functions whatever, although he (Mr. Ashmead-Bartlett) was willing to admit that he might have discharged functions of which they had no knowledge. No doubt, it was the fault of the Government rather than of the Consul that nothing was done. Now, the position of this gentleman also was one of considerable danger, because it was understood that the ill-feeling of the French towards the English had much increased of late, the resistance which the Hovas had made being attributed to the action of the British Representative in Madagascar. He wished to know what the Consul there was doing to fulfil his duties? The noble Lord had rather scoffed at the amount of trade which their Representative in Madagascar had to look after; but he could state that the amount of that trade was represented by about £750,000 sterling a-year. ["No, no!"] That was a correct statement; he had made it before, and he should repeat it again and again, until the Government showed that they were alive to the importance of this question. Last year 40 ships, sailing under the British Flag, cleared from one port in the Island alone. The depression which existed in the shipping trade was perfectly well known; and surely hon. Members had a right to complain when an important part of that trade was neglected by Her Majesty's Government. The trade with Madagascar amounted, as he had pointed out, to £750,000 a-year; but it had been almost entirely destroyed, and large numbers of planters and traders had been practically ruined, while nothing was done by the Government to protect British subjects or British interests in the Island. He did not blame the Consul; it was the policy of the Government that was at fault, and, for all they could see, those great interests were being neglected. Therefore, he said that the Committee had a right to claim on this subject from the Government a full explanation. The Government had submitted to loss of territory, they had accepted insults freely from France, they had established themselves in Egypt only to see their influence and whole policy set at nought; and yet they were actually too timorous to protect British interests in Madagascar. Before he assented to the Vote being taken, he should expect to receive a very distinct statement of facts in connection with the position of affairs in Tamatave, a clear statement as to the Government's intentions with regard to Mr. Power, and also an assurance that the Government were at last plucking up heart to take some efforts to put an end to a state of affairs generally so seriously injurious to the interests of Great Britain.

MR. WHITLEY said he had to ask the attention of the Committee and the Government to an important point connected with the position of the British Consul in Madagascar. It appeared, on the statement of commercial men competent to speak on the subject, that English commercial interests in Madagascar were not, and could not be, attended to, owing to the fact that the Consul resided in the interior of the Island, at a great distance from the port. It [illegible] the case that the Consul did not reside within reach of those whose business lay at the port and export trade [illegible] and [illegible] interests in Madagascar [illegible] was a just one. He [illegible] there was a state of war [illegible] British [illegible] that, at the present [illegible] a great deal of risk and [illegible] he was sure they would receive with gratitude an assurance from Her Majesty's Government that their interests would be protected. He understood that it was the intention when the Consul was sent out to the Island, that there should be more than one Representative of British interests there; but the only Representative he knew of was the gentleman who lived in the interior, and who was described by commercial men as being no Representative at all. That was a matter of very serious importance, because he was in a position to assure the noble Lord the Under Secretary of State for Foreign Affairs that there was a great amount of commercial depression. Knowing that to be the case, it was felt most strongly by his constituents that the commercial interests of the country should be protected wheresoever they existed, if it were possible to do so; and they believed that if a more determined position were taken up by the Government that end would be gained. He wanted the noble Lord, who, he believed, was anxious, as far as lay in his power, to protect British interests, to represent at the Foreign Office that a very strong feeling existed with regard to this question amongst commercial men in Liverpool and in other commercial centres.

MR. WARTON asked the attention of the noble Lord, although the point had [illegible] with the hon. Gentleman the Secretary to the Treasury, to the manner in which the accounts relating to the expenditure at Constantinople were stated. He would simply instance, for his purpose, the item for messengers [illegible] and for constables. The salary in each case was put down at so much, and then underneath the amount there was another amount bracketed to the amount above without the slightest information on the face of the Estimate or in any footnote as to what the extra sum was for. Besides, the salaries of the constables at so and so a day were [illegible]. This irregularity showed itself in every item of the Vote, and certainly called for a clear explanation, which he hoped the noble Lord or the hon. Gentleman would be able to furnish to the Committee.

LORD EDMOND FITZMAURICE said he would be glad if he were able to reply on all the points raised since the last Division. The hon. Member for Louth (Mr. Callan) had called his attention to the Consular arrangements at Rosario. He was willing to say that if his hon. Friend put forward a case, and furnished the needful figures and facts, he would look

Muskat. Formerly, the Home Government contributed half the amount for Muscat, and the Indian Government half at Zanzibar. At the same time, the number of Consuls on the Coast had been increased, amongst those appointed being those Consuls whose names and appointments had attracted the attention of the hon. and gallant Member. The arrangement with regard to the Postal Service, which had really been a Slave Trade Service, was no longer renewed as a Postal Service, but as a Slave Trade Service. That was to say, whereas formerly the whole of the money which now appeared under the contract mentioned in this Vote appeared as a Postal arrangement, it had now been taken over by the Foreign Office, because it was, in reality, an arrangement with regard to the Slave Trade. That arrangement, it was believed, would materially contribute to the suppression of the Slave Trade in those regions.

CAPTAIN AYLMER asked where were the headquarters of the four new Consuls? It was said to be on the African mainland; but that was a very wide description. It was important that the public should know where they were stationed.

LORD EDMOND FITZMAURICE replied, that the Coast was divided into four districts, each under the charge of one of these Consuls. The Consuls would not be stationary, but would move about. That was an essential part of the arrangement.

Vote *agreed to.*

(4.) £4,420, to complete the sum for Tonnage Bounties, &c. and Liberated African Department.

(5.) £2,005, to complete the sum for the Suez Canal (British Directors).

(6.) £20,951, to complete the sum for Colonies, Grants in Aid.

(7.) £17,300, to complete the sum for Subsidies to Telegraph Companies.

(8.) £15,000, for Cyprus, Grant in Aid.

MR. MOLLOY said, he would like to know how long this iniquitous charge was to last?

MR. EVELYN ASHLEY said, it would last as long as the deficiency lasted. The deficiency was only £15,000.

MR. MOLLOY said, the Vote asked for was £30,000; but the hon. Gentleman said the deficiency was only £15,000. This was a remnant of the Tory policy, for which the country had now to pay.

MR. COURTNEY said, this was the apparent deficiency in September last; but it was not so large now.

MR. WARTON said, the deficiency was at one time £90,000; but, owing to the increased prosperity of the Island under their rule, there was a prospect of the Island returning a surplus.

Vote *agreed to.*

(9.) £13,832, for Subsidy to Castle Mail Packets Company.

(10.) £284,825, to complete the sum for Science and Art Department.

(11.) £102,133, to complete the sum for British Museum.

MR. WARTON asked whether the authorities would not arrange to let the public see this Museum in the evening?

MR. COURTNEY said, the Trustees of the Museum had considered that matter, but had not seen their way to carry out the suggestion, being very apprehensive as to the risk of fire. They had, however, to some extent, introduced the electric light into the Reading Room.

Vote *agreed to.*

(12.) £8,500 (including a Supplementary sum of £2,500), to complete the sum for University Colleges, Wales.

(13.) £4,252, to complete the sum for Deep Sea Exploring Expedition (Report).

(14.) £255, to complete the sum for Transit of Venus.

MR. WARTON asked whether this Vote was the end of the expenses connected with this matter?

MR. COURTNEY said, he believed it was.

Vote *agreed to.*

(15.) £13,031, to complete the sum for Universities, &c. in Scotland.

(16.) £1,700, to complete the sum for National Gallery, &c. in Scotland.

(17.) £5,000, for Scottish Historical Portrait Gallery.

the capital and Tamatave, which was the cause of his having a permanent residence at the latter place. He trusted these explanations would be satisfactory to the commercial world, and that it would not be thought that the hon. Member for Eye (Mr Ashmead-Bartlett) was correct in saying that he had at any time under-rated the importance of the trade of Madagascar. The hon. Member for Eye had spoken of the trade of Madagascar as being £2,000,000. (Mr. Ashmead-Bartlett: No.) Those were his figures, and he appeared to use them as a convenient mode of expression with regard to trade in other countries; but he did not think the hon. Member opposite (Mr. Whitley), who used his figures more carefully, would be likely to fall into the same error.

Mr. ASHMEAD-BARTLETT said, the noble Lord had repeated a statement with regard to himself after he had denied it. He had never, either inside or outside that House, stated that the trade of Madagascar was £2,000,000, or any other number of millions. The statement of the noble Lord was, therefore, quite inaccurate. He challenged the noble Lord to show that he had ever stated the trade in any part of the world to be £2,000,000, so that the noble Lord had been guilty of a sheer invention, which he seemed anxious to maintain without any proof whatever. Again, the noble Lord was unjust in accusing him of wanting to raise a debate on Madagascar affairs on this Vote. It was of no use telling the Committee that there was a Consul who was going about the Island; their wish was to ascertain what that Consul was doing, and what the Government were doing to restore the £750,000 of trade which had been destroyed by the French operations in Madagascar. What were the Government doing, either of themselves or through their Consul, to get rid of the miserable state of things in the Island, which was causing considerable loss to the community. He should like to hear the opinion of the hon. Member for Liverpool (Mr Whitley), who, at least, knew what he was talking about, on the information which the noble Lord had given him; and he would like to know whether the commercial men concerned in this trade of £750,000 were satisfied with the statement of the noble Lord? He had had a large number of communications from persons interested in this matter, and he thought he should be justified in moving that Progress be reported after the statement of the noble Lord; and, at all events, he had a right to call upon the noble Lord to withdraw the statement that he (Mr. Ashmead-Bartlett) had said the trade of Madagascar was £2,000,000, instead of £750,000, as he had said.

Lord EDMOND FITZMAURICE said, he could give no further information beyond what he had from time to time given. The Foreign Office had received no special information. If the hon Member never said £2,000,000, he would at once accept that explanation and withdraw the statement he had made; but he had made it because he had seen that figure attributed to the hon. Member in various speeches during the Recess.

Mr. ASHMEAD-BARTLETT said, the point he had put with regard to Mr. Power was, whether the Government admitted the substantial accuracy of Mr Power's statements? Considerable blame had been thrown upon Mr. Power; and what he wished to know was, whether the noble Lord had any proof in support of what he had said, or whether he was willing to admit that Mr. Power deserved general credit?

Mr. COURTNEY, replying to the hon and learned Member for Bridport (Mr Warton), explained that it was represented to the Treasury last year that it was necessary to increase the salaries of certain officials in Asia Minor, and they had consented to give an extra amount.

Vote *agreed to*.

(3.) £25,670 (including a Supplementary sum of £11,080), to complete the sum for the Suppression of the Slave Trade.

Captain AYLMER asked for some information in explanation of the large increase in the amount allowed for some places?

Lord EDMOND FITZMAURICE said, he had already answered this question in one of the Egyptian debates in connection with the subject of slavery. Two or three changes had been made. The Home Government would now be responsible for the whole of the arrangements connected with Zanzibar, and the Indian Government for those at

Muskat. Formerly, the Home Government contributed half the amount for Muscat, and the Indian Government half at Zanzibar. At the same time, the number of Consuls on the Coast had been increased, amongst those appointed being those Consuls whose names and appointments had attracted the attention of the hon. and gallant Member. The arrangement with regard to the Postal Service, which had really been a Slave Trade Service, was no longer renewed as a Postal Service, but as a Slave Trade Service. That was to say, whereas formerly the whole of the money which now appeared under the contract mentioned in this Vote appeared as a Postal arrangement, it had now been taken over by the Foreign Office, because it was, in reality, an arrangement with regard to the Slave Trade. That arrangement, it was believed, would materially contribute to the suppression of the Slave Trade in those regions.

CAPTAIN AYLMER asked where were the headquarters of the four new Consuls? It was said to be on the African mainland; but that was a very wide description. It was important that the public should know where they were stationed.

LORD EDMOND FITZMAURICE replied, that the Coast was divided into four districts, each under the charge of one of these Consuls. The Consuls would not be stationary, but would move about. That was an essential part of the arrangement.

Vote *agreed to.*

(4.) £4,420, to complete the sum for Tonnage Bounties, &c. and Liberated African Department.

(5.) £2,005, to complete the sum for the Suez Canal (British Directors).

(6.) £20,951, to complete the sum for Colonies, Grants in Aid.

(7.) £17,300, to complete the sum for Subsidies to Telegraph Companies.

(8.) £15,000, for Cyprus, Grant in Aid.

MR. MOLLOY said, he would like to know how long this iniquitous charge was to last?

MR. EVELYN ASHLEY said, it would last as long as the deficiency lasted. The deficiency was only £15,000.

MR. MOLLOY said, the Vote asked for was £30,000; but the hon. Gentleman said the deficiency was only £15,000. This was a remnant of the Tory policy, for which the country had now to pay.

MR. COURTNEY said, this was the apparent deficiency in September last; but it was not so large now.

MR. WARTON said, the deficiency was at one time £90,000; but, owing to the increased prosperity of the Island under their rule, there was a prospect of the Island returning a surplus.

Vote *agreed to.*

(9.) £13,832, for Subsidy to Castle Mail Packets Company.

(10.) £284,825, to complete the sum for Science and Art Department.

(11.) £102,133, to complete the sum for British Museum.

MR. WARTON asked whether the authorities would not arrange to let the public see this Museum in the evening?

MR. COURTNEY said, the Trustees of the Museum had considered that matter, but had not seen their way to carry out the suggestion, being very apprehensive as to the risk of fire. They had, however, to some extent, introduced the electric light into the Reading Room.

Vote *agreed to.*

(12.) £8,500 (including a Supplementary sum of £2,500), to complete the sum for University Colleges, Wales.

(13.) £4,252, to complete the sum for Deep Sea Exploring Expedition (Report).

(14.) £255, to complete the sum for Transit of Venus.

MR. WARTON asked whether this Vote was the end of the expenses connected with this matter?

MR. COURTNEY said, he believed it was.

Vote *agreed to.*

(15.) £13,031, to complete the sum for Universities, &c. in Scotland.

(16.) £1,700, to complete the sum for National Gallery, &c. in Scotland.

(17.) £5,000, for Scottish Historical Portrait Gallery.

Motion made, and Question proposed,

"That a sum, not exceeding £1,195, be granted to Her Majesty, to complete the sum necessary to defray the Charge which will come in course of payment during the year ending on the 31st day of March 1885, for the Salaries and Expenses of the National School Teachers' Superannuation Office, Dublin."

MR. BIGGAR said, the Irish Members had not caused any serious delay in regard to the Irish Votes; and he thought the Government might consent to postpone this Vote, especially as they had made great progress in the last half hour. This was the night of the Bank Holiday, and it would be exceedingly difficult for Members to get cabs. He begged to move that Progress be reported.

Motion made, and Question proposed, "That the Chairman do report Progress, and ask leave to sit again."—(Mr. Biggar.)

MR. COURTNEY said, he entirely sympathized with the hon. Member with regard to the difficulty of getting cabs; but if the Committee would take this Vote, he did not intend to propose the Vote for the Queen's Colleges.

MR. HEALY said, a number of Irish Members had gone home on the understanding that this Vote would not be taken that night. It seemed to him to be a fatal mistake for them to go home at any time. It had been distinctly understood, as the hon. Member for Queen's County (Mr. Arthur O'Connor) had said, that no other Irish Votes would be taken that night; and therefore he thought the Government ought not to take this Vote now. It would be much better to discuss it in daylight.

MR. COURTNEY said, he thought it would be much better not to discuss it at all.

MR. BIGGAR said, there was no reason to anticipate very much discussion; but the Vote was of a contentious nature.

MR. HEALY asked if the hon. Gentleman would withdraw the Vote if the Irish Members agreed to the Votes for the Endowed Schools Commissioners (Ireland), and the National Gallery (Ireland)?

MR. COURTNEY consented to withdraw the Vote.

Motion, by leave, withdrawn.

Original Question again proposed.

Motion, by leave, withdrawn.

(18.) £470, to complete the sum for the Endowed Schools Commissioners, Ireland.

(19.) £1,441, to complete the sum for the National Gallery of Ireland.

Resolutions to be reported To-morrow.

Committee to sit again To-morrow.

MR. HEALY: If the hon. Gentleman wishes to take the Report of Supply of Saturday I shall not object.

SUPPLY.—REPORT.

Postponed Resolutions [1st August] considered.

MR. HEALY: I should like now to repeat the question I put to the right hon. Gentleman the Chief Secretary the other evening on the subject of visits to prisoners in Irish gaols. Is the existing rule to be done away with, and is the discretionary power to be taken from the Governors of gaols? I put the question to the hon. and learned Gentleman the Solicitor General for Ireland, in the absence of the right hon. Gentleman the Chief Secretary.

THE SOLICITOR GENERAL FOR IRELAND (Mr. WALKER): I have written about this matter, but, as yet, have received no information.

Resolutions agreed to.

CORRUPT PRACTICES (SUSPENSION OF ELECTIONS) BILL.—[BILL 314.]

(Mr. Attorney General, Mr. Solicitor General.)

SECOND READING.

Order for Second Reading read.

Motion made, and Question proposed, "That the Bill be now read a second time."—(Mr. Attorney General.)

MR. WARTON said, he must really object to this Bill being read a second time. In 1880, it would be remembered, there were several Royal Commissions appointed for the purpose of inquiring into electoral corruption. Seven boroughs were affected in the result—boroughs returning two Members each, so that 14 Members were involved. Of these 14 Members, 11 were Liberals, and three Conservatives. Bills had been brought forward in previous Sessions suspending the elections. The reason he opposed the present measure was because it was not a repetition of the Bills of previous years, as it should be. He, in his ignorance, trusting the Attorney General, had assumed that the hon. and learned Member intended to treat the House justly and fairly in this matter; but the hon. and learned Member had moved the second reading by merely formally raising his hat, implying that there was no occasion for him to make any statement. But this Bill was different from others which had been brought in before. He was not going into the Constitutional point, as that would take a long time to argue; but, shortly, he would say he doubted very much whether it was a Constitutional practice to suspend elections in boroughs without knowing what they were going to do with those boroughs. The boroughs might differ in their degrees of guilt—some might deserve disfranchisement, others might deserve partial disfranchisement; whilst it might be found consistent with justice to treat others in a different manner. There had been three Acts passed, one in 1881, another in 1882, and the third in 1883. There had been some excuse for the Act of 1881, as it was not desirable to have the elections taking place in the Recess; but desirable that Parliament should have reserved to it the right of saying, some day after the first meeting of Parliament in 1882, what should be done with the boroughs. But, as year after year slipped by, there was less and less excuse, for the Government had had ample time to deal with the boroughs. Not only could they have dealt with them if they had thought fit, but every year was an increased punishment to the boroughs, as they were all the time deprived of their legislative rights. It was, particularly, a punishment to those boroughs which were not so guilty as the others. They all knew what had happened in the case of Wigan, which now enjoyed its proper number of Representatives. With regard to the terms of the present Bill, he had thought them the same as the terms of the Bills which had preceded this measure until he had come to read them—showing how important it was to carefully scrutinize every Bill brought forward by the Government. He found a very great and important difference between this Bill and those of the three previous years. In every one of the three previous years the provision had been that the suspension was not to go beyond the first seven days of the Sitting of Parliament "next year." The only difference in the three Bills had been the correction in the third—that of 1883—of a slight inelegance of phraseology, which the Attorney General had adhered to as long as he could. The Government, he repeated, had had less and less excuse on account of want of time to make up their minds what to do with the boroughs. Still, they had not made up their minds; and now they were not content with limiting the Bill to the next Session of Parliament—which, ordinarily, would be in 1885—but they inserted these words in the measure—"Until after the expiration of the present Parliament." The Parliament might last until 1887. The present Government, with their usual contempt for the Constitution, had more than once suggested the idea that Parliament might last beyond six years. They might find it convenient to take a seventh Session, otherwise they might find it impossible to pass a complete Reform Bill. The present Parliament had only lasted four years and a-half, so that it was possible for it to go on until April, 1887, meeting two full Sessions after the half Session which it was intended to hold in the Autumn. This extension of time in the Bill was what he bitterly complained of. The measure should be in accordance with previous Bills. What was the motive for extending the period? If they looked at the boroughs affected by the Bill, they would find that their populations went from 14,885—which was the population of Sandwich—to 35,570—the population of Macclesfield — before the General Election. Now, if they allowed an increase of, say, 10 per cent, or even 15 per cent, for the years which had elapsed since the General Election, it was clear that none of the places would have reached a population of 50,000; and it might, therefore, be that the Government intended to disfranchise the boroughs by a side wind—by proposing in the Redistribution Bill, or some other measure, that no place of less than 50,000 inhabitants should return a Member to Parliament, or, it might be, two Members. [*Cries of* "Divide!"]

Notice taken, that 40 Members were not present; House counted, and 40 Members being found present.

MR. WARTON said, that, having made his point, he did not wish to take up any further the time of the House. He would merely move that the Bill be read a second time that day month.

Amendment proposed, to leave out the word "now," in order to add, at the end of the Question, the words "upon this day month."—(*Mr. Warton.*)

Question proposed, "That the word 'now' stand part of the Question."

THE ATTORNEY GENERAL (Sir HENRY JAMES) thought that when the hon. and learned Gentleman had the alteration in the Bill explained to him he would have no objection to the measure. In the previous Bills, the Government had simply prevented the issue of Writs for these boroughs during the Vacation. They had provided that they should not issue until seven days after the re-assembling of Parliament in the next year of meeting. This year, however, Parliament was about to be prorogued under special circumstances; and if the ordinary course had been adopted they would have interfered with the Constitutional right of Parliament to issue a Writ between October and February. If they suspended the right until October only, however, in that month, or in the Autumn Session, they might have to introduce another Bill to suspend the issue of Writs again until seven days after the meeting of the next Session. If they did that, and if a Dissolution were to occur, they would have taken away the right of the boroughs to have any return at all. All they had done had been to alter the phraseology of the measure to suit the circumstances of the present case, and they could not have done other than they had done without violating certain great principles which they were bound to maintain.

CAPTAIN AYLMER objected to the alteration from the principle of the previous Bills. Certain persons very much interested in this subject had been communicated with, and had expressed objection to the change, being of opinion that it would not be wise to go beyond seven days after the next meeting of Parliament. The principle which had been adopted by Parliament all through should be adhered to, and he trusted the Attorney General would alter the Bill accordingly. If he did not, he might experience some difficulty in passing it through Committee.

THE ATTORNEY GENERAL (Sir HENRY JAMES) said, that the persons interested in the boroughs which were not fully represented in the House had been spoken to on the subject, and had willingly accepted the principle of the Bill on its being properly explained. The hon. Member for West Cheshire (Mr. H. Tollemache), for instance, had removed his blocking Notice from the Paper. The boroughs would be safer, and would have greater rights under the Bill in its present form, than under it in any other form. If hon. Members interested in these boroughs were against the principle of the Bill, he would promise to alter it.

Question put.

The House *divided*:—Ayes 50; Noes 2: Majority 48.—(Div. List, No. 209.)

Main Question put, and *agreed to*.

Bill read a second time, and *committed* for *To-morrow*.

YORKSHIRE REGISTRIES BILL.

(*Mr. Dundas, Mr. Stuart-Wortley, Mr. Norwood, Mr. Guy Dawnay, Sir Andrew Fairbairn, Mr. Charles Wilson.*)

[BILL 316.] LORDS' AMENDMENTS.

MR. T. A. DICKSON: I move that the Lords' Amendments to this Bill be considered.

MR. WARTON: Are they printed?

MR. T. A. DICKSON: Yes. The alterations are merely on points of detail, and were put in at the suggestion of the Lord Chancellor.

Motion *agreed to*.

Lords' Amendments *considered*, and *agreed to*.

SUPREME COURT OF JUDICATURE AMENDMENT BILL.—[*Lords*.]

[BILL 307.] CONSIDERATION.

Order for Consideration, as amended, read.

Bill *re-committed* in respect of a New Clause (Abolition of offices of sworn clerks to Examiners in Chancery); *con-*

sidered in Committee, and *reported*; as amended, *considered*; read the third time, and *passed*, with Amendments.

House adjourned at a quarter after Two o'clock.

HOUSE OF LORDS,

Tuesday, *5th August*, 1884.

MINUTES.]—PUBLIC BILLS—*Second Reading*—Prosecution of Offences (233); Criminal Lunatics (239); Superannuation * (235).

Committee—Municipal Elections (Corrupt and Illegal Practices) (212).

Committee—Report—Education (Scotland) Provisional Order * (218); Local Government (Ireland) Provisional Orders (Labourers Act) (No. 8) * (217); Metropolitan Asylums Board (Borrowing Powers) * (234); Military Pensions and Yeomanry Pay * (232); Chartered Companies * (231); Public Health (Ireland) (Districts) * (238).

Report—Canal Boats Act (1877) Amendment * (228).

Third Reading—Prisons * (213); Trusts (Scotland) * (209); Turnpike Acts Continuance * (206); Cholera Hospitals (Ireland) * (229-246); Expiring Laws Continuance (236), and *passed*.

EGYPT—POLICY OF HER MAJESTY'S GOVERNMENT.—QUESTION.

THE MARQUESS OF SALISBURY: May I ask the noble Earl the Secretary of State for Foreign Affairs, Whether it is in his power to give us the information he promised as to the important step which Her Majesty's Government contemplate taking with reference to Egypt?

EARL GRANVILLE: My Lords, I stated yesterday that Her Majesty's Government were fully alive to the responsibility imposed upon them in consequence of the failure of the Conference to come to an agreement. The noble Marquess is quite right in assuming that I expressed a hope that I should be able to state to-day the preliminary step which Her Majesty's Government wish to take in this matter. I have now to state that we have obtained Her Majesty's gracious approval to appoint Lord Northbrook to go to the East in order to report and advise Her Majesty's Government as to the counsels which they should give to the Egyptian Government in the present circumstances, and also with regard to any measures necessary to be taken in connection therewith. I am happy to say that my noble Friend the First Lord of the Admiralty has consented to undertake these duties. I may, perhaps, conveniently add that Sir Evelyn Baring, after the discharge of his duties, both in this country and in Egypt, to the complete satisfaction of Her Majesty's Government, has been strongly advised by his medical adviser to take considerable leave of absence; but, with his usual public spirit, he has agreed to shorten that leave in order that he may accompany Lord Northbrook to Egypt.

MUNICIPAL ELECTIONS (CORRUPT AND ILLEGAL PRACTICES) BILL.

(*The Earl of Northbrook.*)

(NO. 212.) COMMITTEE.

House in Committee (according to order).

Clauses 1 to 4 severally *agreed to*.

Clause 5 (Expense in excess of maximum to be illegal practice).

THE MARQUESS OF SALISBURY said, he rose to appeal to the Government to make some alteration in this clause, the object of which was to prevent undue expenditure in municipal elections. The object of the clause was a very desirable one; but, in order that the clause might work satisfactorily, it would not be wise to press it too far. There were certain matters connected with these elections with regard to which a moderate expenditure would be perfectly legitimate. Thus it was necessary that the names of the candidates should be made known to the electors, and that their views with regard to local policy should be ascertained. It was also necessary that a certain limited amount of money should be expended upon the hire of halls in which speeches could be made. Such matters as these would not involve very large expenses, certainly; but it was necessary that they should be incurred, or the electors would be restricted to the names of those men they knew most about, and thus the freedom of choice would be very considerably diminished. In these circumstances, he thought that the candidates should be allowed to expend a sufficient sum to enable them to bring their views before

Notice taken, that 40 Members were not present; House counted, and 40 Members being found present,

MR. WARTON said, that, having made his point, he did not wish to take up any further the time of the House. He would merely move that the Bill be read a second time that day month.

Amendment proposed, to leave out the word "now," in order to add, at the end of the Question, the words "upon this day month."—(*Mr. Warton.*)

Question proposed, "That the word 'now' stand part of the Question."

THE ATTORNEY GENERAL (Sir HENRY JAMES) thought that when the hon. and learned Gentleman had the alteration in the Bill explained to him he would have no objection to the measure. In the previous Bills, the Government had simply prevented the issue of Writs for these boroughs during the Vacation. They had provided that they should not issue until seven days after the re-assembling of Parliament in the next year of meeting. This year, however, Parliament was about to be prorogued under special circumstances; and if the ordinary course had been adopted they would have interfered with the Constitutional right of Parliament to issue a Writ between October and February. If they suspended the right until October only, however, in that month, or in the Autumn Session, they might have to introduce another Bill to suspend the issue of Writs again until seven days after the meeting of the next Session. If they did that, and if a Dissolution were to occur, they would have taken away the right of the boroughs to have any return at all. All they had done had been to alter the phraseology of the measure to suit the circumstances of the present case; and they could not have done other than they had done without violating certain great principles which they were bound to maintain.

CAPTAIN AYLMER objected to the alteration from the principle of the previous Bills. Certain persons very much interested in this subject had been communicated with, and had expressed objection to the change, being of opinion that it would not be wise to go beyond seven days after the next meeting of Parliament. The principle which had been adopted by Parliament all through should be adhered to, and he trusted the Attorney General would alter the Bill accordingly. If he did not, he might experience some difficulty in passing it through Committee.

THE ATTORNEY GENERAL (Sir HENRY JAMES) said, that the persons interested in the boroughs which were not fully represented in the House had been spoken to on the subject, and had willingly accepted the principle of the Bill on its being properly explained. The hon. Member for West Cheshire (Mr. H. Tollemache), for instance, had removed his blocking Notice from the Paper. The boroughs would be safer, and would have greater rights under the Bill in its present form, than under it in any other form. If hon. Members interested in these boroughs were against the principle of the Bill, he would promise to alter it.

Question put.

The House *divided*:—Ayes 50; Noes 2: Majority 48.—(Div. List, No. 209.)

Main Question put, and *agreed to.*

Bill read a second time, and *committed* for *To-morrow.*

YORKSHIRE REGISTRIES BILL.

(*Mr. Dundas, Mr. Stuart-Wortley, Mr. Norwood, Mr. Guy Dawnay, Sir Andrew Fairbairn, Mr. Charles Wilson.*)

[BILL 316.] LORDS' AMENDMENTS.

MR. T. A. DICKSON: I move that the Lords' Amendments to this Bill be considered.

MR. WARTON: Are they printed?

MR. T. A. DICKSON: Yes. The alterations are merely on points of detail, and were put in at the suggestion of the Lord Chancellor.

Motion *agreed to.*

Lords' Amendments *considered,* and *agreed to.*

SUPREME COURT OF JUDICATURE AMENDMENT BILL [*Lords*].

[BILL 307.] CONSIDERATION.

Order for Consideration, as amended, read.

Bill *re-committed* in respect of a New Clause (Abolition of offices of sworn clerks to Examiners in Chancery); *con-*

important, could not be introduced, because time did not permit of it; and that surely was a reason for making the Bill temporary. On general grounds a Bill of this importance, which did not concern the House of Commons only, and which was produced very late in the year, ought to be passed in such a form as to give every facility for amendment if required.

After Clause 40, *moved* to insert the following clause:—

"This Act shall continue in force to the end of the year one thousand eight hundred and eighty-six, and no longer."—(*The Marquess of Salisbury.*)

THE EARL OF NORTHBROOK said, he was sorry he could not ask their Lordships to accept the Amendment of the noble Marquess. The reason why the Parliamentary Elections Bill was made temporary was because of the jealousy which the House of Commons rightly felt concerning legislation which affected their own Body; and for that reason the Acts of Parliament passed, providing for the trial of Election Petitions, were made temporary, so that they might from time to time consider the expediency of continuing them or not. The same reason did not apply to this Bill. It dealt with the Municipal Corporations Act of 1882, which was not a temporary but a permanent Act; and, therefore, this should also be permanent. The noble Marquess seemed to think some greater power of amendment would be gained by putting in this clause than by excluding it. He did not understand that any additional facilities would be so required; the measure would be as capable of amendment as any other Act of Parliament by a Bill being introduced in the usual way to amend it. It would, moreover, be undesirable to introduce the precedent of making Bills temporary because they came up late in the Session.

THE MARQUESS OF SALISBURY said, that in the 2nd clause of this Bill it was stated that corrupt practices were to mean treating, undue influence, and bribery at elections, which were defined in the 1st Schedule; and in Part I. of that Schedule was incorporated a portion of the Corrupt Practices Act, which was a temporary measure. If, therefore, that Act expired, a certain portion of the present Bill would remain suspended in the air without any meaning. It was true that if the Bill was permanent amending Bills might be introduced; but it required something more even than willingness on the part of the House of Commons to pass amending Bills. The proposal he had made was a much more simple way of settling the question.

THE LORD CHANCELLOR observed, that the noble Marquess appeared to be in error in his judgment as to what would happen if the Corrupt Practices Act were not renewed. A portion of that Act was incorporated into the present Bill for the purposes of definition; and for that purpose it was immaterial whether the Act was re-enacted or lapsed. Neither was it the fact that it would be easier to amend the Bill if made temporary, and afterwards included in an Expiring Laws Continuance Bill, for it would be impossible to engraft Amendments upon it in those circumstances, and an amending Act would have to be introduced, precisely in the same way as if the Bill were not made temporary.

On Question? Their Lordships *divided*:—Contents 39; Not-Contents 37: Majority 2.

Amendment *agreed to*.

Clause *added* accordingly.

The Report of the said Amendment to be received on *Thursday* next.

PROSECUTION OF OFFENCES BILL.

(*The Earl of Dalhousie.*)

(NO. 233.) SECOND READING.

Order of the Day for the Second Reading, read.

THE EARL OF DALHOUSIE, in moving that the Bill be now read a second time, said, that a Committee had been appointed to consider the manner in which the Office of Public Prosecutor was carried on. It had been found that the existing system, which was tentative in its character, required considerable modification. The Public Prosecutor, although he decided what prosecutions should be taken up, took no practical part in their conduct. That duty was performed by the Solicitor to the Treasury, and the Committee had reported that it would be expedient on several grounds—among others on the grounds of expense and efficiency—that the duty of deciding in what cases the State should undertake prosecutions should be united in the same Department as that which carried on those prosecutions. The best possible plan would be to unite in one Office the present Office of Public Prosecutor and the Treasury Solicitor, and to hand both Offices over to the Solicitor to the Treasury, and that was what the Bill proposed to do.

Moved, "That the Bill be now read 2ª."—(*The Earl of Dalhousie*.)

THE EARL OF MILLTOWN remarked that the present Office of Public Prosecutor was somewhat of a sinecure, and had only been created a short time. He wished to know if it was intended to give the holder a retiring allowance?

THE EARL OF DALHOUSIE: There is no provision in the Bill to that effect.

LORD ELLENBOROUGH inquired what penalties were attached to the non performance, by the Chief Constables, of the duty of reporting cases, as required by the Bill?

THE EARL OF LONGFORD said, that such a duty would entail great extra labour, seeing that there were 50,000 or 60,000 cases annually.

THE EARL OF KIMBERLEY said, that the Chief Constables already had to make Reports.

THE EARL OF DALHOUSIE: If the noble Lord Lord Ellenborough had read the Bill, he would have seen that no penalty attached to the non-performance of the duty.

Motion *agreed to*: Bill read 2ª accordingly, and *committed* to a Committee of the Whole House on *Thursday* next.

CRIMINAL LUNATICS BILL.—No 239

(*The Earl of Dalhousie*.)

SECOND READING.

Order of the Day for the Second Reading, read.

THE EARL OF DALHOUSIE, in moving that the Bill be now read a second time, remarked that it was based on the unanimous recommendations of a Departmental Committee, which investigated the subject of criminal lunatics about two years ago. The Bill had been amended by the Standing Committee on Law during its passage through the House of Commons in order to meet the objections raised by an hon. Member belonging to the Party opposite, and, as it now stood, it passed with the unanimous approval of the other House. The main object of the Bill was to provide for the maintenance of criminal lunatics, and also for the maintenance of persons of that class who might, after the expiration of their sentences, become pauper lunatics. The measure also made it clear how the expense of maintaining them was to be borne. The noble Earl concluded by moving that the Bill be read a second time.

Moved, "That the Bill be now read 2ª."—(*The Earl of Dalhousie*.)

THE EARL OF MILLTOWN said, he was willing to admit that the Bill made no change in the existing law, which was somewhat objectionable. One of the clauses of the Bill provided that in cases of prisoners under sentence of death the Secretary of State, if it was represented to him that the prisoner was insane, should appoint two or more medical practitioners, who should report to him in writing as to the mental condition of a prisoner, and the majority of them might certify in writing that the prisoner was insane, and in such cases he was bound to practically reprieve the prisoner and cause him to be sent to a lunatic asylum. As in cases of murder the question of the insanity of the accused was, or might be, always inquired into at the trial, he objected to the clause, for nothing could be more undesirable than that a subsequent investigation of the same subject should be held *in camerâ* by the Secretary of State. Such an investigation might upset the verdict of a jury, with the result that a criminal who richly deserved the extreme penalty of the law would be committed instead to a lunatic asylum. It was easy to get two doctors to certify that any man in the world was insane. They had heard a great deal lately of the way in which a question of sanity or insanity was decided by two medical men; and he, therefore, thought that the evidence of two doctors ought not to be regarded as conclusive. Those who sought to reform the law in this respect desired, not that the evidence of medical practitioners should be rejected, but that it should be tested and weighed, and treated as evidence, not as a final and conclusive judgment. He objected also to that clause of the Bill which provided that those criminal lunatics whose term of sentence had expired, but who still continued insane, were to be treated as pauper lunatics. It seemed rather hard on the ordinary pauper lunatics that these atrocious criminals should be sent to herd among them.

THE EARL OF DALHOUSIE said, that the clause referred to by the noble Earl at the commencement of his remarks was nothing more or less than a re-enactment of the existing law.

Motion *agreed to;* Bill read 2ª accordingly, and *committed* to a Committee of the Whole House on *Thursday* next.

EXPIRING LAWS CONTINUANCE BILL.

(*The Lord Sudeley.*)

(NO. 236.) THIRD READING.

Order of the Day for the Third Reading read.

Moved, "That the Bill be now read 3ª."—(*The Lord Sudeley.*)

LORD DENMAN moved the insertion of a clause proposed on the 23rd of August, 1881, and on the 22nd of August, 1883, only altering "widows and spinsters," to "all women not legally disqualified."

Moved, after Clause 2, to add the following Clause:—

"Provided that the Act 35 & 36 Vict. c. 33, continued as aforesaid, shall be hereby extended so as to admit all women not legally disqualified who have the same qualification as the present electors for counties and boroughs to vote for the election of Members of Parliament for counties and boroughs."—(*The Lord Denman.*)

THE EARL OF REDESDALE (CHAIRMAN of COMMITTEES) said, that such an Amendment would be out of Order, as it was not possible to amend any of the Acts included in the Expiring Laws Continuance Bill.

LORD DENMAN said, that if every expiring law were to be unalterable in a Continuance Bill, a dangerous principle would be established.

Amendment (by leave of the House) *withdrawn.*

Motion *agreed to.*

Bill read 3ª accordingly, and *passed.*

The Earl of Milltown

REPRESENTATION OF THE PEOPLE BILL AND REDISTRIBUTION.

QUESTION. OBSERVATIONS.

THE EARL OF REDESDALE (CHAIRMAN of COMMITTEES), who was very imperfectly heard, was understood to say, in rising to ask, Whether it is the intention of Her Majesty's Government, in accordance with the strongly-expressed wish of this House and the precedents of other Reform Bills, to introduce proper provisions for redistribution in the Representation of the People Bill in the next Session of Parliament? that it would be in the recollection of their Lordships that a fortnight ago he called their attention to the only manner in which the extension of the franchise could be satisfactorily dealt with. On that occasion he had endeavoured, as far as possible, not to say anything of a Party character. He had then suggested that, as had been the case in all former Reform Bills, redistribution should be connected with the Reform Bill itself, and he believed that that was the only reasonable way of dealing with the subject. If the Government wanted to represent the people they must take care how they framed their Redistribution Bill, and see that interests which it was desirable to protect were protected. He was not at all disposed to imagine that noble Lords opposite or the Prime Minister were disinclined to introduce a fair measure, for the reputation and character of the Prime Minister in the future would be largely at stake. His own opinion was that it was desirable that proper provisions for redistribution should be introduced in the Representation of the People Bill itself. It was universally admitted that such a course was desirable and necessary, and such an admission was an admission that one Bill ought to be connected with the other. The matter must be dealt with as a whole; it was objectionable in every way to treat of it in parts, and it was most important that they should have some assurance in regard to the manner in which the Government were about to proceed. It was by the want of this Bill that the whole of the agitation against that House had been occasioned, and everyone must feel that to ask the House to pass one Bill without having the other before it was unjust to that House and inexpedient having regard to the well-being of the country. If that were so, the charges brought against that House were made on nothing less than false pretences, they did a great deal of harm and caused a great deal of discontent towards the Government of the country. It was reasonable that they should have some assurance from the Government, because if they had not been able to make up their minds as to what those terms of redistribution should be, they ought not to complain that their Lordships should have suspected their intentions; and if they had it would be most useful for the Government to make a declaration of their intention now, so that the House might know what it had to meet on reassembling.

THE EARL OF WEMYSS said, he sympathized most heartily with the object of the noble Earl, and if he thought a favourable answer awaited him would not have interposed in the discussion. But, differing, as he did, that an [illegible] answer would be given to the question, he would not think it desirable at present to press the Government to state definitely what course they had decided to take with regard to the Bill. The statements which had been made at conciliation had failed, and they were now at a stage at which, however much it might be deprecated, was not wholly unreasonable. There had been great demonstrations in London, in Manchester, and in Birmingham, on one side; but he was credibly informed that there would be, in the course of this week, a [illegible] at Manchester [illegible] York [illegible] together to support the action of their Lordships' House; therefore it was quite evident that public [illegible] was very [illegible]. Under these circumstances, he believed it was not desirable for the Government to [illegible]. There were [illegible] at which [illegible] reassembled [illegible] consideration by both sides of the position in which they found themselves. The Government might then be inclined to adopt the suggestion of the noble Earl, or some other plan might be devised which it would be not only constitutionally right but patriotic for the Government to follow. Under these circumstances he hoped the noble Earl would not be forcing a declaration from the Government that the Lords against all possibility [illegible].

LORD LAMINGTON said, that the noble Earl on the cross Benches, the Earl of Wemyss, had again played the part of the candid friend of both sides, and [illegible] which was too very black nor white as [illegible] it appeared. Then the Earl had alluded to possible demonstrations in the future, but he, Lord Lamington, must say that those demonstrations, whether on the one side or the other, were very much to be deprecated. This was a question of too much importance to be disposed of in the way suggested by the noble Earl. He, Lord Lamington, was of opinion that the only way to solve the difficulty was by the Government bringing in with the Franchise Bill a Redistribution Bill. He had as much respect for the rights of the House of Commons as for those of that House, and he had reason to have, for he had spent a large portion of his life in the Lower House. But their Lordships' House ought to have a voice, as they had a right of considering the whole scheme. He was also strongly of opinion that this was a question on which the country should be consulted. They should not forget that the Bill was one for the enfranchisement of 2,000,000 of the people, and that the question had been described by a Member of the Government as the greatest that had arisen since the Revolution of 1688. It was said that the question had been decided at the last election; but if that had been so, why, in the name of fortune, did not the Government introduce their Franchise Bill in 1880, 1881, 1882, or 1883? But they did not do so, though they now complained that some 2,000,000 of electors were being kept out of the franchise. This was the first time that he had spoken on the subject; but he must say it was a most extraordinary thing that the Bill should have been delayed for the back end of the Parliament when it was, as the Government said, so absolutely essential. That House ought to have fair time to consider the whole question. This was the time for the Government to say what course they would take and to clear up the matter and prevent this disgraceful agitation going on.

EARL GRANVILLE: I am afraid I cannot boast of being in the position of my noble Friend opposite in not having spoken on this subject before; but I find myself in a very embarrassing dilemma. I am required to meet the wishes of two noble Earls. One noble Earl asks me a question, and very naturally expects me to give an answer to it, while the other noble Earl asks me not to answer it, and gives his reasons for offering that advice. I think, perhaps, that the best course for me to take in this dilemma is a middle course—namely, to say that I have really nothing to add to the statements that have already been made in both Houses upon this subject.

LORD DENMAN: No one is more interested in the question of Reform than I. In 1821, on the transfer proposed from Grampound to Leeds, household suffrage for those paying "scot and lot" was preferred as the more Constitutional franchise, and Lords Althorpe and Milton, Attorney General Scarlett, and Mr. Denman, voted with some others in opposition to Lord John Russell's £10 rental; but neither succeeded. In the same year Mr. Lambton got printed in *Hansard's Debates* his Reform Bill. It contained a blank Schedule for redistribution. In 1859 a suffrage for counties and boroughs, with an equal £10 rental, was proposed. There was also a redistribution of seats. But the Resolution of Lord John Russell, which was almost impracticable, destroyed the Bill on the 31st of March. On the 12th of August I blamed the Ministry—who came in upon Reform—for not having brought in a Bill, and engaged, in the presence of the noble Earl, now Secretary of State for India, to bring in the same Bill, which was capable of any modification and amendment, and I commend the speech of Mr. Disraeli, then Chancellor of the Exchequer, to the consideration of your Lordships. It foretold the delay which occurred between 1859 and 1866. I said I had not latterly agreed to the Amendment of Earl Cairns because I thought it unnecessary, as the Bill of 1859 showed an earnest desire to assimilate the franchise in counties and boroughs. But the question slept for seven years, and in 1866 two Bills were brought in, and the Government went out upon the Redistribution Bill. The present Premier boasted of his measure, which was a very trumpery one, letting in small shopkeepers, and not giving the franchise—as proposed in 1821 for Leeds—to householders, who knew, in the words of the Earl of Malmesbury, in 1867, that they had a Queen. I am against Autumn Sessions, for the one in 1820 for the Bill of Pains and Penalties was a disastrous failure, and the one as to *clôture* failed, for 40 Members might at any time defeat it. My Motion for the second reading after six months appeared to me the best course. There was no time for a Conference, much less for a free Conference, on the Franchise Bill; and the Bill was, as against the House of Lords, quite stereotyped, from the refusal in "another place" of any Amendment. In 1832, my father, on addressing the voters at Nottingham, was greeted with hisses, groans, and imprecations. Halters were exhibited round men's necks, and there were loud shouts of "No Denman!" "Burke him!" "Bristol him!" The same expression is in an interesting work called *A Stroke of an Afghan Knife*. Some culprits said of themselves they were outlaws living with halters round their necks; they must keep together or be slain. At Derby a gentleman proposing the House of Lords was compared to Cæsar, quoting, "Because he was ambitious, I slew him." This proposer was Premier in an amateur debating society in Derby; but when the question of the abolition of the House of Lords was debated, this Premier was in a minority, and had to resign. The present Government, though beaten on the visitation of secret societies by the police of Ireland, and on the Affirmation Bill, refused to resign; and it appears to me that though on each of these occasions they might have called for a Dissolution, yet they would have no right, if again in a minority, to press their advice for Dissolution on the Crown. Three measures were all despatched on the 10th of July, which *The Times* and *The Morning Post* proclaimed beforehand!! Resolutions have no force, and law must prevail.

THE EARL OF REDESDALE (CHAIRMAN of COMMITTEES), said, that the noble Earl opposite had given no answer to his Question, which was, whether it was the intention of the Government to introduce proper provisions for redistribution in the Representation of the People Bill in the next Session of Parliament.

EARL GRANVILLE: In reply to the noble Earl, I may state that it is the intention of the Government to reintroduce the Franchise Bill in the state in which it is now in this House.

THE EARL OF REDESDALE (CHAIRMAN of COMMITTEES): Then all I can say is that if that is the intention of the Government, it amounts to a most deliberate proposal to keep up an unfair and unjust charge against this House, in order, I suppose, to serve some Party purpose. To say that they will bring in again in the same way the Bill which this House has refused this Session to consider because it was an imperfect measure—to say now that they will take care only to introduce the same imperfect measure—is only to invite this House to take the same course it did on the last occasion.

THE LORD CHANCELLOR: It is to be hoped that this House will think better of it [illegible] takes the same course. This matter may be stated in a few words. The Government, who are responsible for the conduct of Business, are of opinion that the proper and only practicable way of accomplishing the two objects in view, both of which they have at heart, is to take the course which they have taken. The House of Commons, by an enormous majority, is of the same opinion; but your Lordships, by a smaller majority, are of a different opinion. When those who entertain the opinion of your Lordships are responsible for the conduct of affairs [illegible] they will act on the opinion [illegible] but as long as we are responsible for the conduct of affairs [illegible] the right [illegible] upon [illegible]

THE MARQUESS OF SALISBURY: The doctrine [illegible] and [illegible] that, as I understand it, is that whenever [illegible] and the House of Commons are agreed, the House of Lords [illegible] to yield. As the House of Commons is always agreed with the Ministry and most from the very nature of [illegible] always be so, we have [illegible] order of things—that there is only one Legislative Body and the whole government of the country, executive and administrative, is in its hands. [illegible] laid down by a Minister of the Crown. I hope your Lordships will never yield; and whatever may be the course you may think it right to take, I hope that you will never allow it to be influenced by the manifest and almost offensive attempt at dictation which the particular procedure selected by the Government indicates.

EARL GRANVILLE: I can only enter my protest against the converse doctrine—that the House of Commons is always to yield whenever the House of Lords thinks differently.

LORD BRABOURNE said, he did not think it wise to apply the word unfair to Her Majesty's Government. He protested, however, against the language used by some of Her Majesty's Ministers out of doors. He wished to draw their Lordships' attention particularly to the language reported in that morning's papers as having been used yesterday by a Cabinet Minister, which, he believed, was much more ill appropriate and much more unfair than anything which had been said that night. That Minister was reported to have said—"The [illegible] are afraid of the franchise. They only wish for redistribution in order to defeat the franchise." When a Cabinet Minister used language of that kind to his fellow-countrymen, it showed that they were only at the beginning of an agitation to which the Government were lending themselves, and of the consequences of which they could have no idea.

THE EARL OF KIMBERLEY said, that the latter part of the speech of the noble Lord [illegible] expectation of [illegible] which the [illegible] sentence might have led him to [illegible]. The right hon. Gentleman, to whose speech the noble Lord had adverted, would, no doubt [illegible] of the [illegible] had been characterized [illegible] taken [illegible]

LORD ELLENBOROUGH said, that if the Government would adjourn Parliament to some time in October, and in the meantime take the necessary steps towards and consider the question of redistribution, then the Franchise Bill, which was not read and the Redistribution Bill could be considered, if not passed together in one Session. Pursuing such a course would show that the Government were [illegible] to dispose of both portions of the question

PUBLIC HEALTH—DRAINAGE OF LONDON.—OBSERVATIONS.

LORD FORBES, in rising to call attention to the drainage of London, referred to the presence of cholera near our shores, and to the desirableness of some steps being taken by the authorities to carry out the best practicable scheme of drainage they could. He appealed to their Lordships to take action in the matter, not only for their own sakes, but particularly for the sake of the toiling masses in London, who were necessarily confined to the City for the greater part of the year, and whose home surroundings scarcely ever changed. At this time of the year, when the wealthier classes were leaving the City for the country, he thought their Lordships could not do anything better than show their sympathy for the large masses of the people who were left behind in the town, by endeavouring to secure for the Metropolis a better system of drainage than it now possessed. The House of Commons had recently formed a small Committee to investigate the subject of the ventilation of that House, and the cause of certain inodorous smells which had been found to prevail in the House for some time previously. The Committee had reported to the effect that the smell was owing to the burning of bricks at Battersea. Their Lordships would remember that during the debate late at night on the Franchise Bill a disagreeable smell had prevailed in their Lordships' Chamber; and, however it might be accounted for, whether from the burning of bricks, or from any other similar cause, he believed the real source of the mischief was the defective drainage of London. He would now call attention to the condition of the Thames. It had been stated on competent authority that the sewage which was poured into the river was beginning to make its way up the river in a sort of permanent form. The state of the Thames in its lower reaches was, n his opinion, simply horrible, and was the result of the present system of drainage, which consisted simply in pouring the sewage into the Thames at a time when the tide was running out; but it had to be remembered that a large portion of the sewage was brought back by the inflow of the tide; and it must be evident to all those who considered the question that this system of drainage, always objectionable, could not, in any sense, be accepted as a solution of the question. It was computed that 164,000,000 gallons of liquid sewage were poured into the river daily, and, in order to deal effectively with such a problem as this, some remedy was certainly needed. He had heard of two schemes by which the sewage of London might be dealt with—the Hendon scheme and the Aylesbury scheme. The Aylesbury Company had made an offer to the Metropolitan Board of Works to take over the sewage of London for the purpose of dealing with it in as innocuous a manner as possible; but that offer had been curtly refused. He thought the refusal of the Metropolitan Board of Works was worthy of their attention, and called, to some extent, for a remonstrance. By the method adopted at Aylesbury, the sewage was deodorized before entering the river, and poured in in a purer state than the River Pollution Commission required. In his opinion, the Aylesbury scheme possessed enormous advantages over any other in dealing with the difficulty felt; and it seemed to him to offer a perfect solution of the question of how the drainage of our large towns should be dealt with.

THE EARL OF DALHOUSIE said, he must compliment the noble Lord on the zeal, ability, and research, which he had brought to bear in the treatment of this question, and also on the ability with which he had called the attention of their Lordships to the question. He was glad to have this opportunity of assuring the noble Lord that Her Majesty's Government were fully alive to the dangers to which he had referred, and that the Metropolitan Board of Works were anxious to bring about some amelioration of the state of things which at present prevailed. The question of the pollution of the lower Thames by sewage from the outfalls at Crossness and other places was first brought under the notice of the Secretary of State on the 19th of January, 1882, by the Port of London Sanitary Authority, who asked the Secretary of State to take (under the Metropolis Local Management Act of 1858, c. 104, s. 31), immediate remedial measures in the matter. On receipt of this complaint the Secretary of State called upon the Corporation Sanitary Committee to furnish the evidence upon which their complaint was based. In reply, the Corporation forwarded a printed Report of their Sanitary Committee containing analyses of samples of the water, and stating that

[illegible] health was [illegible]

This Report was immediately forwarded by the Secretary of State, together with the first letter of the City Corporation, to the Metropolitan Board of Works for observations, February 20, 1882. On the [illegible] of March the Metropolitan Board reported that they had referred the matter to a Sub-Committee for inquiry and report. On the 20th of March the Town Clerk asked, for the information of the Port of London Sanitary Committee, what had been done. He was informed by the Home Office that they were in communication with the Metropolitan Board and his letter and the reply were sent to the Board as a reminder. On the [illegible] of April the Metropolitan Board wrote to say that they [illegible] to make a complete [illegible] as they wished to [illegible] investigations during the [illegible] when the river was [illegible] to be at its worst. But they were already of opinion, so far as they had gone, [illegible] health were [illegible] greatly exaggerated. This reply was communicated to the Port of London Sanitary Authority. A fortnight elapsed and the Secretary of State then wrote, April 18, and [illegible] a definite answer from the Board [illegible] that [illegible] this the Metropolitan Board replied on the [illegible] of May [illegible] Secretary of State did not [illegible] the Metropolitan Board [illegible] He [illegible] with the [illegible] Board [illegible] May [illegible] Metropolitan Board [illegible]

mission was forwarded by the Secretary for presentation to Parliament on the 1st of February 1884. In July the attention of the Secretary of State was called to the state of the river, and he accordingly consulted Lord Bramwell, the Chairman, and asked him for his views. On the 12th of July, the Chairman of the Royal Commission reported that he and the other Commissioners examined the river.

[illegible] Metropolitan [illegible] sewage [illegible]

A very strong letter was thereupon addressed by the Secretary of State to the Chairman of the Metropolitan Board, enclosing a copy of Lord Bramwell's letter. The Secretary of State pointed out that the first Report of the Commission six months before had pointed out that the main cause of the evil was the discharge of the sewage in its crude state without any attempt to render it less offensive by separating the solids [illegible] and he also reminded the Board that when they obtained their powers to deal with the main drainage there was a [illegible] understanding that such deodorization would be provided. The Secretary of State therefore asked to be informed without delay what measures the Board had taken to fulfil those pledges, and threatened that he would be compelled to take action under the statute of 1858. On the 14th of July the Erith Local Board requested the Secretary of State to urge on the Metropolitan Board the importance of deodorization pending the inquiry by the Royal Commission. The Secretary of State said in reply that he was strongly impressed with the danger of the present state of things and forwarded a copy of the correspondence to the Metropolitan Board. On the 21st of July the Metropolitan Board replied that they quite recognized the responsibility devolving upon them, [illegible] for some weeks [illegible] of water [illegible] a high temperature [illegible] produced an exceptional [illegible]. The Board had difficulty in obtaining an immediate supply of deodorizing chemicals, but they had now made arrangements for manufacturing [illegible] Report [illegible] was sent to the

Home Office on the 23rd of July; and, in forwarding it to the Metropolitan Board on the 30th of July, the Secretary of State observed that the responsibility which the Board now admitted had been most imperfectly discharged during the present year and former periods. The existing state of things was neither new nor unprecedented, and yet for two years the Board had been contesting facts which could not be denied; and in the month of June the Board, being unprepared, found it a practical impossibility to deal with the evil for several weeks. The Secretary of State had called for inquiry as to how far the measures taken by the Board since the 10th of July had had the effect of curing or mitigating the evils complained of; and he insisted, in conclusion, on the necessity of placing things on a permanent footing, so as to prevent the possibility of a recurrence of the danger. The Secretary of State consulted the Local Government Board, who said that the letter of the Metropolitan Board did not give sufficiently definite information to enable the Local Government Board to pronounce as to the efficiency of the measures taken, but that, if desired, they would send an engineering inspector to visit and report. To this the Secretary of State assented. On the 28th of July the Local Government Board sent on a complaint from the East and West India Dock Company as to the great increase of sewage in the river, and its foul condition. This letter was sent on to the Metropolitan Board. The Secretary of State had called officially on the Royal Commissioners and on the Sanitary Authority of the Port of London to report on the efficiency of the measures taken by the Metropolitan Board to purify the river, and had also instructed the River Police Authorities to report daily to him as to the state of the river. The latest information he had received testified to a slight improvement. The Papers on the subject would be presented to Parliament to-day.

The Earl of LONGFORD said, he had been pleased to read in the papers of that morning that at the outfall the nuisance was so far abated that they might eat their fish dinner in comfort; but his experience upon a recent annual occasion, well known to their Lordships, when the noble and learned Lord (Lord Bramwell) was one of the party, was quite the reverse.

Lord Forbes

THE NEW PUBLIC OFFICES—DESIGNS FOR THE NEW ADMIRALTY AND WAR OFFICE.—OBSERVATIONS.

Lord LAMINGTON, in rising to call the attention of the House to the designs for the new Public Offices, said, he did not understand whether the agreement entered into with the successful competitors would prevent Parliament from having an opportunity of expressing its opinion of the designs. From what he had seen of the elevation of the new buildings they were not architecturally in harmony with the other Public Offices, and would crowd the space between the Admiralty and Spring Gardens. He thought the Government ought to suspend their action in proceeding with the execution of the plans until they had before them all the particulars of the competition; or, perhaps, it would be better if they were to withdraw their present arrangement, and to enter into a larger scheme for the improvement of the Public Offices.

Lord SUDELEY: The noble Lord who has brought forward this subject (Lord Lamington) has criticized most severely the designs which the judges have selected for the new Offices. He, however, says that he has not seen the plans in Spring Gardens, and only judges from some sketches he has seen in the papers. Now, my Lords, this criticism may be just or it may be unjust; but of this there can be no doubt, that there has never been a competition for public buildings carried out with greater fairness and impartiality. The First Commissioner took great pains, and the selection was made with the names of the competing architects absolutely secret, and the arrangements made precluded the possibility of the names leaking out. The architects, subject to the approval of Parliament, will be Messrs. Leeming and Leeming, nevertheless it does not follow that the actual design will be carried out in its entirety. During the Autumn the design will be considered most carefully, and such modifications will be made as may be found necessary. The noble Lord is afraid that the Horse Guards will be swamped, and he implies that this consideration has not entered into the minds of the judges. I can assure him that this was very carefully weighed. If, however, this is likely to prove the case, it will be very easy to leave out or alter the position of the campanile tower, 260 feet high, and make modifications. As regards the point mentioned by the noble Lord, that the consideration of these Offices ought also to include the widening of Great George Street and the erection of other Public Offices, I will only say that experience of past years has proved the utter impracticability of undertaking any general scheme for the erection of a series of Public Offices. No one is better aware of this than the noble Lord himself, who, when Chairman of the Committee on the subject gave the matter up as hopeless, and the Committee only left the matter to the Government. I trust the noble Lord, before he leaves town, will be able to go to Spring Gardens and see the plans, and I am sure he will come away much more satisfied in his mind as to those designs.

THE EARL OF WEMYSS asked whether the modified or the original designs would be shown on the models?

THE EARL OF KIMBERLEY: The modified designs.

LORD STRATHEDEN AND CAMPBELL thought Government should pause and suspend the execution of their scheme.

EGYPT—THE PORTE AND THE SOUDAN.—QUESTION.

LORD STRATHNAIRN asked Her Majesty's Government, What right, now that the Sovereignty of the Porte over Egypt Proper had been acknowledged, England had to advise the Khedive to abandon the Soudan without obtaining the consent of the Porte?

EARL GRANVILLE: We have never questioned any rights which the Sultan has over Egypt; but, as far as the Egyptians themselves are concerned, they not having an Army or money sufficient to reconquer the Soudan, we advised them not to go on with an undertaking which was impossible.

LORD STRATHNAIRN said, that as the answer of the noble Earl was most unsatisfactory, he should take the earliest opportunity of again calling the attention of their Lordships' House to the subject.

House adjourned at Seven o'clock, to Thursday next, Four o'clock.

HOUSE OF COMMONS,

Tuesday, 5th August, 1884.

MINUTES.]—SUPPLY—*considered in Committee*—RELIEF OF GENERAL GORDON (VOTE OF CREDIT), £300,000—CIVIL SERVICE ESTIMATES—CLASS IV.—EDUCATION, SCIENCE, AND ART, Votes 14, 15, 19—CLASS VI.—NON EFFECTIVE AND CHARITABLE SERVICES, Votes 1 to 9 and 9—CLASS VII.—MISCELLANEOUS, Votes 1, 2.

Resolutions [August 4] *reported.*

PUBLIC BILL—*considered as amended*—*Third Reading*—Cholera, &c. Protection * [303], and *passed.*

QUESTIONS.

IRELAND—NATIONAL SCHOOL, BELFAST—USE OF SCHOOLROOM FOR PARTY PURPOSES.

MR. HEALY asked, Whether it is the fact that on Thursday evenings the Whitehouse National School, Belfast, is used as an Orange band room, and that Party tunes offensive to the Catholics of the village are constantly played; and, whether this is with the sanction of the Commissioners of Education?

THE SOLICITOR GENERAL FOR IRELAND (Mr. WALKER): A temperance band meets every Thursday evening in the Whitehouse schoolroom. By its Rules it is non-political, and the playing of Party tunes is absolutely forbidden, either in the schoolroom or elsewhere. It was upon the pledge of the Members to obey this Rule that the manager, who is a Presbyterian minister, gave the use of the school; and so long as the Rule was observed, the school being non-vested, there was no violation of the Regulations of the Commissioners. It, however, now appears that about the 12th of July the band on some occasions broke that Rule. The Commissioners will not permit this, and are in communication with the manager on the subject.

NAVAL DISCIPLINE ACT, CLAUSE 58.

SIR JOHN HAY asked Mr. Solicitor General, Whether, referring to his statement that—

"The Naval Discipline Act declares that the number of officers composing a Court Martial must not exceed nine, but it need not be more than five,"

is in accordance with Clause 58, sub-section 16, where the officer appointed to preside at the Court is directed to summon all the officers of the rank next in seniority to himself to the number of nine, or such number not less than five is attainable, is complete; and, whether, therefore, a Court Martial constituted of five officers only, where more are present, is a legal Court Martial?

THE SOLICITOR GENERAL (Sir FARRER HERSCHELL), in reply, said, that the statement made by him was, no doubt, that although a Court Martial must not exceed nine and be not less than five, there was no absolute obligation that it should consist of nine. No doubt, under the section to which the right hon. and gallant Gentleman referred, and to which he also referred at the time, all the officers were to be summoned; but the right hon. and gallant Gentleman would find in the Admiralty Instructions a provision that even if the officer who was to preside had been chosen, leave of absence might be given by the officer summoning the Court Martial or the superior officer present to officers who would otherwise be bound to attend. He knew his right hon. and gallant Friend was under the impression that those Instructions referred to proceedings under the Act of 1861, and that the legislation had been changed since; but he would call his attention to the fact that the Act of 1861 was in precisely the same terms as the Act of 1866. Those Instructions were issued in 1862, and had been in force ever since; and, therefore, the provision which he had in his mind when making the statement had been in force since 1862 under the old Act, which was in precisely the same terms as the present.

SIR JOHN HAY asked the Secretary to the Admiralty, If he will state what reason is assigned for selecting an Admiral Superintendent of one of Her Majesty's Dockyards to preside at a Court Martial on the Captain of Her Majesty's ship *Defence*, contrary to the spirit of the Naval Discipline Act, Clause 58, Section 16, when other Flag Officers were available for that duty?

MR. CAMPBELL-BANNERMAN: The section referred to exempts certain officers from the ordinary obligation to serve upon Courts Martial, in order, it may be presumed, to prevent their being disturbed in the discharge of their important duties. But it excepts any occasion on which they may be specially directed to sit by orders from the Admiralty. In this case the Admiral Superintendent was so directed, being the only available Flag Officer at the Port besides the Commander-in-Chief.

CIVIL SERVICE WRITERS—ORDER IN COUNCIL, 1876.

MR. ARTHUR O'CONNOR asked Mr. Chancellor of the Exchequer, If he will, during the Recess, consider the desirability of improving the position of the Civil Service writers by a modification of the Order in Council of 12th February, 1876?

THE CHANCELLOR OF THE EXCHEQUER (Mr. CHILDERS): In reply to the hon. Member, I have to say that the Order in Council to which he refers has nothing to do with writers, except the 19th section, which provides that they are to be paid by piece work, at rates fixed by the Civil Service Commissioners, with the consent of the Head of the Department and of the Treasury. I have not heard that there is any difficulty in obtaining competent writers under this system.

DEFENCES OF THE EMPIRE—COALING STATIONS, &c.

SIR HENRY TYLER asked the Secretary of State for War, with reference to his observations on the projects for the defence of coaling stations and chief mercantile ports of the Empire, Whether he will place upon the Table any Reports or Memoranda by the Responsible Military Advisers?

THE MARQUESS OF HARTINGTON: The Report of the Commission on the Defence of the Coaling Stations and Colonial Possessions abroad was considered a confidential document. There was certainly a great deal in it which it would be extremely inexpedient to make public. He had always regarded the Report of his Advisers as equally confidential. He had not had time to consider whether those Reports, or any part of them, could, without inconvenience or danger, be made public; but he would consider whether any part of those Reports could be presented to the House. With regard to the mercantile ports of the Empire, the Report of Lord Morley's Committee had not yet been fully considered by the War Department. He had received Reports from the Inspector General of Fortifications and the Inspector of Artillery, and those proposals awaited the consideration of the Defence Committee. Until the opinion of that Committee had been received, he could not say whether it would be possible to lay the Report of the Committee or of the Military Authorities before the House?

EGYPT MILITARY OPERATIONS)—REPORT ON THE BOMBARDMENT OF ALEXANDRIA.

SIR HENRY TYLER asked the Secretary of State for War, Whether, in reference to the reports and conclusions which have been communicated to the public through the agency of the Attaché of the United States of America present in Egypt, he will lay upon the Table the Report on the Bombardment of Alexandria, made in accordance with the orders of the Secretary of State?

THE MARQUESS OF HARTINGTON: This Report is of a highly confidential character, and cannot be presented to Parliament.

THE ROYAL IRISH CONSTABULARY—HEAD CONSTABLE IRWIN.

MR. HEALY asked, How many policemen have been promoted within the last three years on the recommendation of ex-Detective Director and County Inspector French; was Head Constable Irwin one of these, was he constantly about Mr. French's office in the Castle, by whose recommendation or instrumentality was he appointed to Wexford, why did he leave Wexford on the 24th June, and remain away nearly a month; after how many years' service is the rank of head constable conferred, how many years had Irwin served, and when he was promoted; and, what records had he?

THE SOLICITOR GENERAL FOR IRELAND (Mr. WALKER): Nine promotions were made within the last three years, all in 1882, on the recommendation of Mr. French. There is no reason to doubt that they were all of them proper promotions. Head Constable Irwin was not promoted on such recommendation. Mr. French had nothing whatever to say to his promotion, nor is it a fact that he was constantly about the Detective Director's Office. He never was employed there, except upon one occasion for a month during a press of business. Upon his promotion to the rank of Head Constable he was allocated to Wexford to fill a vacancy at that station in ordinary course. He was absent on special police duty for a month in the West of Ireland. There is no fixed period of service after which the rank of Head Constable is attained. Irwin had served eight years. He had two first class favourable records, and no unfavourable records.

MR. HEALY: Is it true that he is the youngest Head Constable in the Force?

THE SOLICITOR GENERAL FOR IRELAND (Mr. WALKER): I will inquire.

MR. WILLIAM REDMOND: What vacancy did Mr. Irwin fill up? For I am informed there was only one Head Constable stationed at Wexford for many years.

THE SOLICITOR GENERAL FOR IRELAND (Mr. WALKER): If the hon. Member puts the Question on the Paper I will make inquiries into it.

BRIDGES (IRELAND)—DRUMHERIFF BRIDGE—COUNTIES LEITRIM AND ROSCOMMON.

COLONEL O'BEIRNE asked, Whether it is a fact that the duties of the Drumheriff Bridge Committees, appointed by the grand juries of the counties of Leitrim and Roscommon, were confined to the approval of a plan and specification of a bridge, and the acceptance of tenders and declaration of a contractor for same; if it is not likewise a fact that the county surveyor of Roscommon has objected to Mr. Irwin, the assistant county surveyor of Leitrim, acting as county surveyor for the said county (this office being now vacant), although Mr. Irwin was appointed by the county Leitrim grand jury to inspect and report upon, for approval or otherwise, of all county presentments, and, when necessary, issue summonses in case of default, and that the said Mr. Irwin has in the most emphatic manner condemned the materials made use of by the contractor in the construction of the abutments and piers of Drumheriff Bridge, the specification having been deviated from in many respects; and, if, under these circumstances, and as the best means of safeguarding the interests of the cesspayers of the county Leitrim, will an order be given to enable Mr. Irwin to act pro tem. as county surveyor, or some other steps taken to protect the interests of the cesspayers?

THE SOLICITOR GENERAL FOR IRELAND (Mr. WALKER): It may have been proposed to limit the duties of the Committee, as stated; but the Act of Parliament contemplates the carrying out of the work under the direction and management of the Committee. I am informed that it is a fact that the county surveyor of Roscommon and the assistant surveyor of Leitrim differ in respect of the materials to be made use of by the contractor generally as to the work; and, as was stated in reply to a former Question, the joint Committee of the Grand Juries is the proper tribunal to adjust these differences. It is very questionable whether the Grand Jury of Leitrim had any legal authority to delegate to Mr. Irwin the powers mentioned in the Question. The vacancy in the office of county surveyor will be filled up as soon as the examination required by law before the Civil Service Commissioners can be held. It will be commenced on the 12th instant.

THE MAGISTRACY (IRELAND) — MR. JOHN M'MAHON, OF BALLYBAY, CO. MONAGHAN.

MR. HEALY asked, Whether Lord Dartrey, Lieutenant of Monaghan, has forwarded to the Lord Chancellor the influential memorials and resolutions asking for the appointment of Mr. John J. M'Mahon, of Ballybay, to the Commission of the Peace; and, if so, what decision has been arrived at?

THE SOLICITOR GENERAL FOR IRELAND (Mr. WALKER): The Lord Chancellor informs me that no such memorial was forwarded to him by Lord Dartrey; but that within the last four or five days the name of Mr. M'Mahon was brought to his notice by the Rev. Canon O'Neill, of Ballybay. This application will be duly considered.

LAW AND JUSTICE (IRELAND)—THE CROSSMAGLEN PRISONERS.

MR. HEALY asked, On what grounds have the Government refused to allow Mr. Alfred Webb, T.C., Dublin, to obtain a sight of the so-called Mullabawn and Crossmaglen books, required by him in the preparation of the Memorial to the Lord Lieutenant on behalf of the Crossmaglen prisoners?

THE SOLICITOR GENERAL FOR IRELAND (Mr. WALKER): Mr. Webb applied to be allowed to inspect the books given in evidence in the Crossmaglen trial, alleging as a reason that he was looking into the case of the prisoners. There is no precedent for permission being granted after a trial for any person to examine the documentary evidence used and produced at the trial, and I do not think such a precedent should be established. When a Memorial is presented, the books will be carefully considered, along with all the other circumstances.

MR. HEALY: Would the Government consider this an exceptional case, and allow Mr. Webb a look at the documents?

THE SOLICITOR GENERAL FOR IRELAND (Mr. WALKER): When the Memorial is presented will be the proper time.

MR. HEALY: But Mr. Webb is preparing the Memorial, and how can he prepare it unless he sees the documents?

[No reply.]

POOR LAW (IRELAND)—ELECTION OF GUARDIANS, CARMEEN DIVISION, COOTEHILL UNION—THE INQUIRY —MR. VAUGHAN MONTGOMERY, J.P.

MR. HEALY asked, What decision has been come to by the Law Officers as to the prosecution of Mr. Vaughan Montgomery, J.P.; and, will the Papers be laid before the Lord Chancellor?

THE SOLICITOR GENERAL FOR IRELAND (Mr. WALKER): The Attorney General for Ireland has not notified his final decision in this case, as he is absent in Sligo. It would be premature to make any communication to the Lord Chancellor before he does so.

MR. HEALY said, he would repeat the Question on Thursday.

THE MAGISTRACY (IRELAND)—MR. TIPPING, J.P.

MR. BIGGAR asked, Whether Edward Tipping, of Bellengan, Dundalk, is a Justice of the Peace for the county of Louth; whether it has been brought to the notice of the Lord Chancellor, that Mr. Tipping petitioned the Irish Bankruptcy Court in 1883, offering his creditors five shillings in the pound; and if so, whether the Lord Chancellor proposes to take any action in the matter. [illegible]

THE SOLICITOR GENERAL FOR IRELAND (Mr. WALKER): [illegible] of the Lord Chancellor. [illegible] made that [illegible] arrangement by Mr. [illegible] for a [illegible] Court of Bankruptcy. [illegible] have, however, been [illegible] with the [illegible] creditors. [illegible] will be made on this [illegible]

THE NORTH SEA FISHERIES [illegible]

MR. BIRKBECK asked the Under Secretary of State for Foreign Affairs, Whether [illegible] Her Majesty's Government [illegible] North Sea [illegible] the Netherlands [illegible] North Sea [illegible] agreement [illegible]

LORD EDMOND FITZMAURICE: [illegible] Her Majesty's [illegible] North Sea [illegible] further Question; but if the hon. Member will put it down I will reply to it.

MERCHANT SHIPPING [illegible] QUARANTINE [illegible] AT MADEIRA

MR. CAINE asked the Under Secretary of State for Foreign Affairs, [illegible] Madeira [illegible] British [illegible] Madeira [illegible] Foreign Office is taking any steps to secure such accommodation as may be necessary?

LORD EDMOND FITZMAURICE: Her Majesty's Consul at Madeira has reported [illegible] the hon. Member [illegible] arrangements at Madeira [illegible] defective; [illegible] details [illegible] Earl Granville [illegible] the Board of [illegible] their [illegible] Portuguese [illegible]

SOUTH AFRICA—THE TRANSVAAL [illegible]

MR. GUY DAWNAY asked the President of the Board of Trade, with reference [illegible] far from [illegible] and [illegible] the Natives [illegible] have [illegible] better and [illegible] rule [illegible] Natives [illegible] Transvaal, [illegible] Mr. [illegible] account of [illegible] Natives [illegible] stated that Natives [illegible] Transvaal and [illegible] supposed to have [illegible] what portion of the country?

MR. CHAMBERLAIN, in reply, said, [illegible] the [illegible] Mr. [illegible] account of his interview; but he thought it would be unwise to accept as absolutely conclusive the evidence of the piteous appeals of any Chiefs whatsoever with reference to a matter in which they might be considered to be interested and to have grievances against the Boers. As regarded the second Question, the early history of the Transvaal was contained in the Blue Books before the House; and, so far as his memory served him, it was contained in some of the despatches of the late Sir Bartle Frere. Originally the Transvaal was inhabited by a Bechuana Tribe. This Bechuana Tribe was practically driven out by a tribe of the Zulus. After the Boers had attacked this tribe of Kaffirs and destroyed them, then the Bechuanas in their turn came back and re-migrated in large numbers to the Transvaal. There were now about 750,000 of them. This immigration took place in all parts of the Transvaal, but principally in the North.

CORRUPT PRACTICES (SUSPENSION OF ELECTIONS) BILL.

In reply to Mr. RAIKES,

THE ATTORNEY GENERAL (Sir HENRY JAMES) said, that the Bill was intended to be merely suspensory in its operation.

COLONIAL NAVAL DEFENCE ACT, 1865 —COLONIAL WAR VESSELS.

MR. BLAKE asked the Secretary to the Admiralty, Whether the Government of Victoria had, before the departure of their vessels of war, *Victoria*, *Albert*, and *Childers*, from England on the 14th of February, fulfilled all the requirements of the Admiralty, so as to entitle them to the privileges accorded to Colonial vessels of war, under section three of "The Colonial Naval Defence Act, 1865;" whether the Government of Victoria had also, in accordance with section six of the same Act, placed the said vessels at Her Majesty's disposal; whether the Law Officers of the Crown have advised the Admiralty that such vessels, on being placed at Her Majesty's disposal, are to be deemed to all intents vessels of war of the Royal Navy, and would be entitled to fly the white ensign; whether the Agent General for Victoria was informed on the 13th of February, and was requested to inform the Commandant of the squadron, that the necessary formalities to obtain the Orders in Council having been fulfilled, he might safely proceed on his voyage; whether Orders in Council, under sections three and six of the said Act, were passed at the Council of the 4th of March; whether, on the following day, the 5th of March, the Admiralty requested that the vessels might be ordered to the seat of war at Suakin; and, whether this was not an acceptance of their services?

MR. CAMPBELL-BANNERMAN: I venture to refer my hon. Friend to the answers given regarding the status of the vessels by the Under Secretary of State for the Colonies and myself on the 19th of February last, and to the statement by the First Lord of the Admiralty which appears in the daily newspapers of the 2nd instant. I would only supplement that statement by pointing out that in order that the vessels should have the status, given under Section 6 of "The Colonial Naval Defence Act," they must be not only "placed at Her Majesty's disposal," but "accepted by the Admiralty." The services of these vessels were not accepted, but were declined with an expression of thanks, and with full recognition of the spirit of the offer; and although the Commanding officer was instructed by the Agent General for the Colony, with the concurrence of the Admiralty and Colonial Office, to communicate with Sir William Hewett on his way down the Red Sea, it was hardly anticipated that the Admiral would require the services of the vessels, nor, as a matter of fact, was it found necessary to accept them.

NAVY—DOCKYARD RE-ORGANIZATION —THE NEW SCHEME.

LORD RANDOLPH CHURCHILL (for Sir H. DRUMMOND WOLFF) asked the Secretary to the Admiralty, Whether he will obtain and present to Parliament evidence from the foremen of the yard and assistant constructors selected from them, as regards the effect of the reorganization scheme on their prospects, seeing that they have had no opportunities of making their statements before the Committee?

SIR THOMAS BRASSEY, in reply, said: The witnesses examined by the Committee on Constructors included several officers well acquainted with Dockyard administration. The case of the foremen of the Yard is thoroughly understood at the Admiralty, and further evidence of a formal character is unnecessary. Every desire exists to open the [illegible] promotion to men of the practical [illegible] for which the foremen of the Yards are distinguished. The [illegible] according to their qualifications [illegible] the [illegible] Navy and the professional [illegible] Board.

CONTAGIOUS DISEASES (ANIMALS) [illegible] AND THE [illegible]

Mr. ALBERT GREY asked the Chancellor of the Duchy of Lancaster, Whether [illegible] has been called to the following paragraph which appeared in *The Times* of [illegible]:—

"W[illegible]

"W[illegible]

[illegible]

and [illegible] these [illegible] of [illegible] C[illegible] tag[illegible]

Mr. [illegible] in reply, said [illegible] *The Times* was [illegible] Mr. M[illegible] W[illegible] being [illegible] to

brought through Canada and shipped at a Canadian port. This renders it necessary to ascertain the view of the Canadian Government upon the subject. A communication has therefore been addressed to the Government [illegible] that purpose.

MERCHANT SHIPPING—THE COLLISION IN THE THAMES.

Mr. GOURLEY asked the President of the Board of Trade, If he can give the House [illegible] information regarding [illegible] and loss of [illegible] on Saturday night [illegible] the Thames [illegible] below Gravesend [illegible] steamers, and [illegible] the [illegible] carried [illegible] passenger [illegible]

Mr. CHAMBERLAIN: Until the result of [illegible] is being held [illegible] to express any [illegible] this case. I am informed [illegible] passenger ship has a gross [illegible] and that the total number [illegible] exclusive of the master was [illegible] of whom five were engaged [illegible]

PARLIAMENTARY ELECTIONS—THE NEW REGISTER.

Sir EDWARD WATKIN asked the Secretary of State for the Home Department, Whether, considering that it is [illegible] Register of 1884 [illegible] who were [illegible] Register of 1883, that the Register [illegible] will contain [illegible] new electors according [illegible] the Register of [illegible] over [illegible] per [illegible] will [illegible] the Return [illegible] has been given [illegible] figures [illegible] has been brought [illegible] the Return will [illegible] expense?

Mr. HIBBERT, in reply, said: A [illegible] the two Registers [illegible] in order to ascertain [illegible] several [illegible] the Register [illegible] I [illegible] all gave [illegible] the Local [illegible] many [illegible] have [illegible] have changed their residences, or where the lists are not even alphabetical—probably be impossible. The expense would also be considerable, as the Local Authorities would, no doubt, have to employ extra clerks to make the searches.

EDUCATION DEPARTMENT—AGE OF CHILDREN LEAVING SCHOOL.

MR. W. J. CORBET asked the Vice President of the Committee of Council, If he will give a Return of the average age at which children leave school in England, Scotland, Wales, and Ireland respectively?

MR. MUNDELLA: I am unable to give the Return for which the hon. Member asks; but if he will refer to page 13 of the Report of the Education Department for 1883-4, he will find a paragraph showing the number and the percentage of children in England and Wales who left school after passing the Fourth and Fifth Standards in 1882. The hon. Member will find a similar paragraph as regards Scotland at page 14 of the Report of the Scotch Education Department for 1883-4. From this it appears that 42 per cent of the scholars in Standard IV. leave school after passing it, while 58 per cent of those in Standard V. leave school after passing that Standard. In Scotland 23 per cent of the scholars in Standard IV. leave school after passing it, and 53 per cent of those in Standard V. As the Standard of total exemption in Scotland is Standard V., we may reasonably expect that under the operation of the Act of last year the number of children leaving school before passing that Standard will diminish. The Question, so far as it relates to Ireland, should be addressed to the Chief Secretary for Ireland.

INDIA (MADRAS)—FLOGGING—CASE OF MARIAPPEN.

MR. BIGGAR asked the Under Secretary of State for India, Whether he will cause inquiries to be made into the statement made by Mr. C. Pritchard, barrister-at-law, Salem, to the honourable the Judges of the High Court, Madras, in his Letter to them bearing date 16th February 1884, that a lad named Mariappen, aged 10, was sentenced by Dr. Macleane, district magistrate of Salem, on 26th September 1882, to receive twenty stripes, though on the day previous, viz. 25th September, he, Mr. Pritchard, as counsel for the lad, had procured an adjournment of the case whether he will cause inquiry to be made into Mr. Pritchard's statement, in the same Letter,

"I was somewhat surprised at the superintendent of police rushing into Court, and saying that it was the wish of the district magistrate that the under-trial prisoners should be detained to witness the thrashing of a little boy, the above Mariappen;"

and, whether it is customary that persons not yet convicted should be forced to witness a flogging?

MR. J. K. CROSS: The India Office has no information beyond what may be derived from the newspapers as to the letter referred to in the hon. Member's Question, or the circumstances with which it deals. The letter appears to have been addressed to the Judges of the High Court in January of last year and as that Court has, therefore, had an opportunity of considering the statement which it contains, it does not appear to be necessary to call on the Government of Madras for a Report. I have no reason to believe that it is customary that persons not yet convicted are forced to witness floggings; and Mr. Pritchard, in his letter, expressly states that in this instance the prisoners were not detained to witness the flogging.

EGYPT—THE CONFERENCE—THE MINISTERIAL STATEMENT.

SIR STAFFORD NORTHCOTE asked the noble Marquess the Secretary of State for War, Whether the Prime Minister was likely to be able to make his promised statement before the Orders of the Day were called on?

THE MARQUESS OF HARTINGTON: My right hon. Friend has full intention of making the statement he promised yesterday, and I have every reason to believe that he intended to make it before the Orders of the Day were called on. We have, however, got through the Questions somewhat more rapidly than usual; and as my right hon. Friend is not in his place at present, but will be in a very few minutes, it might be for the convenience of the House that the Speaker should leave the Chair for a few moments, in order to give my right hon. Friend the opportunity of being in his place.

MR. GLADSTONE, who at that moment entered the House, said: I must apologize to the House for the inconve- [illegible]

in any way affect the position of Sir [illegible]

[illegible]

the Earl of Northbrook's [illegible]

[illegible]

the Earl of Northbrook.

MR. GLADSTONE: The precise ap- [illegible]

Northbrook is a matter which I consider as appertaining rather to the form of the Commission given than as one to be determined in substance on the first stage of the affair. I think the function of the Earl of Northbrook would correspond in substance with that which has been generally designated by the title of High Commissioner. I presume that will be the title given to the Earl of Northbrook on the present occasion.

Mr. JOSEPH COWEN: Will Parliament be made acquainted with the Commission and the terms of it, in the same way as it was made acquainted with the terms of the Commission which the right hon. Gentleman himself fulfilled when he went to the Ionian Islands?

Mr. GLADSTONE: Oh, certainly; the terms of the Commission will be laid before Parliament.

Mr. A. J. BALFOUR: As the practical result of the appointment of the Earl of Northbrook will be to produce considerable delay, I think we have a right to ask what are the particular subjects connected with Egypt, about which the Government feel their ignorance, and about which they would like advice? I should like to ask whether it is on the subject of finance that they require further information; or whether it is on the subject of the internal administration of Egypt? I think it must be plain—but perhaps I have no right to make any comment.

Mr. GLADSTONE: I have nothing to add to the statement I have already made. It is quite evident that the inquiry might include finance and internal administration as well—that is to say, we have asked the Earl of Northbrook to report and advise upon the counsel which we ought to offer to the Egyptian Government, and to advise as to any steps which it may be requisite to adopt in connection therewith.

Lord RANDOLPH CHURCHILL said, he supposed that full and complete information with regard to the Egyptian finances would be laid before the House. The information laid before the Conference, the French Representatives contended, was essentially defective.

Mr. GLADSTONE: No information on the internal administration of Egypt has been laid before the Conference.

Lord RANDOLPH CHURCHILL: And on finance?

Mr. GLADSTONE: The information on finance has been communicated to the House, and it will be for the Members of the House to consider whether it is defective or not.

Sir STAFFORD NORTHCOTE: Would the right hon. Gentleman inform the House whether there are any steps connected with Egyptian affairs, financial or other, which the Government contemplate taking before they receive the Earl of Northbrook's advice?

Mr. GLADSTONE: It is impossible for me to bind myself, to give an answer on that subject. It might depend on necessities which might arise spontaneously. I can only say our object is to have the advantage of the Earl of Northbrook's inquiry and advice on the general situation.

Sir STAFFORD NORTHCOTE: The object of my Question is this. Some months ago the Government informed us that the financial affairs of Egypt were in such an urgent state as to demand a Conference at once. That Conference has spent some months in its deliberations, and no result has arisen from them. What I want to know is, whether the Government will take any steps in connection with the financial position of Egypt before Lord Northbrook has been able to report and advise?

Mr. GLADSTONE: I am afraid I must still say that it would be very difficult for me to answer that Question. I admit there is a very urgent state of financial affairs in Egypt; and I can conceive it to be quite possible that application may be made to the Government on the subject, with which they will deal in the best manner they can, pending the inquiry and Report. But undoubtedly it is not our intention to take any step of a definite character which can be avoided, but to reserve the situation, as far as possible, entire until the completion of the inquiry.

Mr. COLERIDGE KENNARD: Has any reference been made, on the part of the Government, to the Ottoman Porte?

Mr. GLADSTONE: That is a question of great importance, on which it is quite impossible for me to enter at the present moment. This and other questions will come within the scope of the Earl of Northbrook's inquiry, and any answer on the point would necessarily be premature.

SIR H. DRUMMOND WOLFF: If the Government has not consulted the Porte, by what right do they send a High Commissioner to make inquiries into the condition of a portion of the Porte's Dominions? When the right hon. Gentleman was sent to the Ionian Islands it was under a Treaty, which enabled us then to appoint such an official.

MR. GLADSTONE: The hon. Member has referred to the case in which I was High Commissioner. I do not wish to point to his assertion with regard to the bearing of the Treaty on which that appointment was made; but he is quite premature, and has mistaken me in saying that we have not consulted the Porte, inasmuch as on that subject I have made no communication whatever to the House.

ORDERS OF THE DAY.

SUPPLY—RELIEF OF GENERAL GORDON (VOTE OF CREDIT).

SUPPLY—*considered* in Committee.

(In the Committee.)

(1.) Motion made, and Question proposed,

"That a sum, not exceeding £300,000, be granted to Her Majesty, beyond the ordinary Grants of Parliament of 1884-5, to enable Her Majesty to undertake operations for the relief of General Gordon, should they become necessary, and to make certain preparations in respect thereof."

MR. GLADSTONE: Sir, the statement which I shall have to make in proposing this Vote of Credit, which you, Sir, have already read from the Chair, will be, I hope, not a very lengthened one, will be simple in its character, and, I trust, not involving any highly contentious matter. The purpose of the Vote of Credit is described in general terms upon the face of the Paper which has been placed in the hands of Members, and I will refer a little more particularly to the basis upon which our proposition rests. Sir, the Committee is well aware that we are under pledges as regards General Gordon to aid him by military means in a certain contingency. Perhaps it may be desirable that I should refer particularly to the nature of those pledges, though I believe they are generally in the recollection of the Committee. They are to be found in telegrams that are in the possession of the House, dated April 23 and May 17, and they are to be found in various declarations made by myself in this House, and by Earl Granville in the other House of Parliament. But, Sir, they are to be found especially—as I am now addressing the House of Commons, and the House of Commons, perhaps, pays the greatest attention to what is addressed by responsible Ministers of the Crown to itself—they are to be found especially in a speech delivered by my noble Friend the Secretary of State for War (the Marquess of Hartington) on the 13th of May, when he dealt more fully with this portion of the subject than any of his Colleagues had done on any previous occasion. I am quoting from *Hansard*, May 13, page 233; and I will, first of all, refer to certain sentences. My noble Friend then stated that, before an expedition for the relief of General Gordon could be ordered or announced, it was necessary to have the clearest proof of its necessity. He stated that such an expedition would not be justified for the purpose of enabling General Gordon to smash or overpower the Mahdi; nor for the purpose of giving a satisfactory Government to the inhabitants of the Soudan; nor for the purpose of enabling the garrisons of the Soudan to march out with the honours of war; and my noble Friend went on to say, in a passage which I will now quote—

"We must be satisfied, as far as it is possible for us to satisfy ourselves, that such an expedition is necessary to secure the safety of General Gordon, and of those for whose safety he has made himself responsible. It is necessary that we should be satisfied that the original view as to the possibility of evacuation is now impossible of execution. General Gordon will not be called upon by the Government to do anything which will be derogatory to his honour or to his character. Those who have trusted themselves in his service, those who have fought for him, who have increased the perils in which they stood before by entering his service, no doubt, General Gordon is responsible for, and cannot desert; but there is no reason to believe that, if escape is possible for him, it is not also possible for those who stand towards him in the relation which I have described."—(3 *Hansard*, [288] 233-4.)

The telegram, which is before the Committee, and which is dated May 17, was conceived in the spirit of those expressions. And now I think I need not enter into any minute description; but I will rather remind the Committee of what has taken place; and, not seeking in any degree either to extend or contract those pledges, I think I may assume that the Committee is fully aware that we have given pledges to aid General Gordon in a certain contingency. Next, I am bound to say that we consider that these pledges, in a general sense, were approved by Parliament. Some may, perhaps, have thought they went too far, and some may have thought they did not go far enough; but, speaking of the general body of the Committee, we are under the belief that these pledges were approved, and that I need not now argue in support of the principle on which they rest, or go back upon a field which we have traversed to a sufficient extent on former occasions. Well, now, Sir, we and the country have been under very considerable embarrassment from the want of direct official communication with General Gordon. That difficulty has beset us, and to no inconsiderable extent perplexed us for a time which is now approaching no less than four months. But, although there has been this want of official communication with General Gordon, yet, in the absence of such communication, there has been a series of reports which has reached us, and which, although they cannot be placed upon a footing with direct and responsible accounts, yet, when taken together, may be held to have considerable importance, and undoubtedly, I think, have acted a good deal more upon the mind of the public, who are so deeply interested in the safety of General Gordon. These reports have not been altogether uniform in their character. For instance, upon a particular occasion—namely, the 4th of July—one of the London journals—and in referring to the London journals I may say that, as far as I am able to judge, all those varied reports have been perfectly impartial, and have not been altered or modified for the purpose of supporting any particular view—at one time the reports in one journal had been more favourable or more unfavourable and at other times the reverse; but in quoting from them generally I quote without the slightest reference to anything, except to the fact that such a telegram has reached this country—well, I think it was on the 4th and 5th of July that reports in *The Daily Telegraph*, which had previously had some reports of a very favourable character, came to convey the darkest view of the case that was brought before us with respect to Khartoum and General Gordon. On the 4th of July we were told that the town had been captured without difficulty by the Mahdi; that no massacre had taken place, however, and that General Gordon was safe, but that he entirely declined to quit the place. On the 5th of July there was also a statement to the effect that Khartoum was in possession of the Mahdi; but when we came to look at the sources we found that the report of the 4th came from the insurgent Army itself, which represented that Khartoum had been captured; and the reports of the 5th of July from what are described as Native sources. But, Sir, speaking generally, such has not been the tenour of the reports that have been received. On the whole, they have—some may think to a very high degree, some may think in a lower degree, and upon that I do not enter at all; but in some degree or other they have converged towards certain points. The points to which they have converged have been what may be termed the safety of General Gordon, in the sense in which that term is applicable to a man who is in a country where fighting is going on, and in a town foreign to him, and likewise to his power to remove from Khartoum, if considerations of honour or prudence, or whatever motives may govern the mind of that heroic man, should dictate such a course. I may just quote in support of what I say two reports, which came from *The Daily News'* Correspondent on the 30th of June. On the 30th of June that journal—and perhaps other journals; but I do not know—that journal gave a report which was brought by certain pilgrims to Suakin, and their report was to the effect that the town of Khartoum was all right on the 23rd of May, and that food was plentiful there. They had also a report of pilgrims who had arrived at Tahkrova, and who gave the very same account which came from another place, that all was well at Khartoum on the 23rd of May, and that food and water were sufficient for its supply. I quote this as an illustration of the way in which reports that are not official or responsible, yet concurring with each other when arriving from different places [illegible] one another to a certain extent. On another day, the 29th of July [illegible] and Reuter's Agency [illegible] Kassala. He reported that he had seen a letter from General Gordon [illegible] and reporting the presence of rebels [illegible]

[illegible]

[illegible] a document with regard to which we can be altogether free from mystery, [illegible] and at first sight [illegible] may be explained by [illegible] Mudir of Dongola [illegible] British Government. But [illegible] I have [illegible]

[illegible]

undertake operations for the relief of General Gordon should they become necessary. Besides that, we hope we shall thus obtain the direct authority of Parliament to certain preparations connected therewith. Well, Sir, these preparations are preparations which are to be explained by the condition and circumstances of Egypt, and the condition of season and climate under which communications may be carried on in that country. They are preparations as distinguished from operations. [*Laughter by* Mr. ASHMEAD-BARTLETT.] Perhaps the hon. Gentleman the Member for Eye (Mr. Ashmead-Bartlett) may have a better mode of description; but I think I convey a tolerably clear idea to the minds of the Committee when I speak of preparations as distinguished from operations. The Vote in itself is rather, perhaps, a Vote of principle than anything else—I mean to say, rather a Vote of principle than the representation of an exact figure. A figure we must present, and we must regulate it by what appear to us to be the dictates of good sense; but it is impossible for us, until this contingency arises—and God forbid it should arise!—a sentiment in which, I hope, we all join—but until this contingency should arise, it would be impossible for us to form an accurate estimate of the demands that may be made upon us. What I look at is the assent of Parliament, such as we conceive it to be, to the pledges—I might even say as regards a great portion of the Committee—but, at least, to those pledges into which we have entered as respects General Gordon, and the authority which we feel was placed in our hands to act according to the dictates of prudence and justice upon those pledges under cover of the Vote which we ask Parliament to give us. With respect to the particular preparations, I think the Committee will feel with me that it would not be for the public interest that I should enter into any explanations whatever. In our opinion, it would be of no advantage even to the object of those who sought information, inasmuch as the information must at present necessarily be partial, and, to a certain extent, therefore, misleading. What we feel is this—it is impossible for us to judge, unless and until the contingency arrives, in what way, by what specific means and form of action, that contingency ought to be met. It is plainly, therefore, our duty to reserve to ourselves, subject to our responsibility to Parliament, a full discretion in the choice of the best, the most prudent, and the most effective methods of proceeding. Any explanations that might now be entered into with respect to preparations would tend to limit that field of action, and, I may also say, it might have other inconvenience in Egypt itself of a character more direct and more immediately bearing on the purpose which, if the occasion arises, we should have in view. I believe I have now stated to the Committee all that it appears necessary to state in order to convey the double purpose of this Vote—the major purpose, to obtain the authority of Parliament, for acting, as circumstances may require, upon our responsibility; and the secondary and subsidiary purpose of taking such steps as may appear to my noble Friend and his advisers, with the sanction of the Cabinet, in the way of military preparation, as prudence may appear to require, when the matter is considered in connection with the peculiarities of Egypt, and what may be required by the seasons of the year, or in order that we may not be taken unawares, should the time come. On these grounds, I hope it will be found by the Committee that there is no novelty of principle in the proposal we now make; that it is simply an attempt on our part to place ourselves in a condition to redeem the honourable engagements under which we have come to Parliament and to the country, in view of circumstances when Parliament itself would have been prorogued, and, therefore, when we should not have had a direct and immediate means of obtaining its authority by the summary method of an immediate application. Under these circumstances, I beg to present the Vote of Credit which has been placed in your hands.

MR. LABOUCHERE said, he did not understand the right hon. Gentleman the Prime Minister to have asserted that universal assent was given to the pledges he had mentioned when they were made in the House. He did not think anyone would contest that when those pledges were given, it was upon the full and distinct understanding that General Gordon was acting in accordance with his instructions, and the orders given to him. But he apprehended, on reading the Papers which everyone had had an opportunity of reading, that General Gordon had not only not fulfilled his instructions, but had acted in complete discord with them. What were those instructions? They were contained in the letter of Earl Granville to Sir Evelyn Baring, and pointed out the best way of effecting the evacuation of the Soudan, and of securing the safety of the garrisons. That was why General Gordon was sent out; but when he arrived in Egypt, without the knowledge of Her Majesty's Government, he accepted the position of Governor General of the Soudan, and started for Khartoum. This fact would be found recorded in the Blue Books a few days later than Earl Granville's letter in a telegram from that noble Earl to Sir Evelyn Baring, to ask if General Gordon had any [illegible] position under the Egyptian [illegible]. General Gordon had then started for Khartoum, and [illegible] what then occurred. He wrote [illegible] to the effect that the people were all entirely in favour of his Mission [illegible]. Then [illegible] that Zebehr Pasha should [illegible] Soudan, and [illegible] Mahdi, the Sultan of Kordofan. But [illegible] the Mahdi [illegible] the position of Sultan [illegible] General Gordon immediately changed his tone and said he would [illegible] the Mahdi. [illegible] from the [illegible] reports received from the Soudan [illegible] Blue Books [illegible] General [illegible] determined [illegible] nate Soudan [illegible] was [illegible] Prime M[illegible] Mr. Lab[illegible] Her Majesty's

Government, who had sent him out, had absolutely recognized the independence of the Soudan. More than that, he told all his followers who wished to leave Khartoum that they could retire, and, according to the Blue Books, everyone who was able to leave did leave at the commencement of General Gordon's Mission, the rest remaining to fight with him. But he believed, at the present moment, that General Gordon was determined [illegible] had got some vague plan in his head, like a sort of Egyptian [illegible] of inducing the Egyptians to retake the Soudan, and of forcing [illegible] reinforcements to support [illegible] in establishing some sort of rule which was not the rule of the Soudanese. Under these circumstances, accepting the pledges in their fullest sense, he had thought they were bound to send an English Army to bring back General Gordon from Khartoum. They had heard from Mr. Stanley, and he was an authority in the matter, that there was nothing easier at present than for Gordon to get away from Khartoum, and to bring away all those who were acting with him. But [illegible] he remained there issuing a species of paper money to be paid for by us or by the Egyptian Government, and sallying forth day after day to destroy what [illegible] General Gordon could [illegible] get away. That [illegible] was not his policy, and he stopped there because he chose to stop there. If Mr. Labouchere did not see why money should be spent and [illegible] General Gordon. He was at [illegible] Governor General of the Soudan, and why was this country to pay for him? It was the Egyptian Government that ought to pay. Egypt had plenty of money, and [illegible] was some [illegible] that an [illegible] was taken away [illegible] Egypt for the bondholders [illegible] in favour of [illegible] were the bondholders [illegible] have [illegible] suggest that the money [illegible] as a matter of kindness to Egypt [illegible] would be very different [illegible] that the taxpayers of Great Britain and Ireland were to pay for [illegible] as they had to pay for this expedition to Suakin. What did they gain from the Suakin Expedition? It cost a number of valuable lives and a large amount of money. The present Vote was only £300,000; but if an expedition for the relief of General Gordon, was undertaken it would cost very much more than £300,000—£300,000 was a mere sop. Parliament would next Session be asked to agree to a Vote of £3,000,000, and would be told that they had already assented to such expenditure by agreeing to the present Vote. The Prime Minister himself stated that it was a Vote of principle; and it was precisely because it was a Vote of principle that he objected to it. The principle was whether they ought, or ought not, to do their best to get General Gordon back? The principle was that they, and not the bondholders, ought to pay for the expedition which had been made necessary owing to the misdeeds of the Egyptians themselves in the Soudan. General Gordon was sent out to bring away the garrisons by peaceful means if he possibly could, and he had had ample opportunities of doing so. He would not detain the Committee further; but he should certainly take the opinion of the Committee upon the Vote.

Sir GEORGE CAMPBELL said, he felt himself to be in a very great dilemma as to the vote which he ought to give. He had no objection to a definite sum of £300,000, or two or three times £300,000, in order to enable Her Majesty's Government to get General Gordon out of Africa, and put him in some safe place from which he would not be likely to break out again; but, as the Prime Minister had just said, this was not a Vote of £300,000, but a Vote of principle, which might involve the necessity of their entering into a campaign in Central Africa, and it was perfectly evident that if they were to enter into a campaign in Central Africa, £300,000 would be a mere drop in the ocean. The Committee might find, when they came back in October, that they had committed themselves to an expedition which might cost £10,000,000 and many thousands of lives. That was the question upon which he wished to have a clear answer, and he was afraid, if he were to be guided by the words of the Prime Minister, the answer would be that they would be committed. At all events, he wanted to know whether, if the Committee voted this sum of £300,000, Her Majesty's Government would agree not to incur any more expenditure than this £300,000 would cover, before Parliament re-assembled in October? If he were to understand that they were only voting to Her Majesty's Government a definite sum, and that no increased expense would be incurred until Parliament was called together again, he would be prepared to assent to the Vote; but he was not prepared to agree to a Vote which would be practically in the nature of a blank cheque, placed in the hands of the Government to be used without restraint. He trusted to the good sense of Her Majesty's Government to prevent a great campaign; but he was unwilling to subject them to the pressure, which he knew they would be subjected to, in regard to undertaking a campaign. Although he believed that General Gordon was very much in fault himself in regard to the position in which he was now placed, still he admitted that they were bound to relieve him if it could be done on reasonable terms. With him (Sir George Campbell) it was very much a matter of amount. Looking at all the circumstances, it seemed to him that there was a danger of entering into an enormous campaign in the deserts of Africa which must necessarily cost them thousands of lives, and in regard to which Mr. Stanley told them that their soldiers would die like flies, while the cost would amount to many millions of money. He could not conscientiously vote for a war of that kind, and certainly not at the present moment, until it was known that General Gordon had exhausted every other means of escaping by way of the Nile, or by the means which Mr. Stanley pointed out. The great difficulty was for General Gordon to take away with him the Egyptians who had trusted him. As to the number of Egyptians who were likely to follow him, there might be many who would prefer to make their own terms with the rebels, instead of going with General Gordon. The experience had hitherto been that whenever an attempt was made by a garrison to come to terms with the enemy, no massacre had followed. But he agreed with some of his hon. Friends below him that General Gordon had entered upon a line of action in which he could not reckon on the military support of the country, and therefore the [illegible] George Campbell would end as he had begun, by saying that, in any case he was ready to vote £[illegible] as a definite sum, but he would not vote for it if it were to commit the country to immeasurable liabilities before Parliament reassembled in the month of October.

MR. BOURKE: I need not say that it is not my intention to oppose this Vote. On the contrary, I believe that it will receive general support on this side of the Committee. But it does appear somewhat hard upon me and my Friends, and especially upon me, to have to support a proposition of this kind. It is five months ago since I ventured to say, in this House that I thought the sending out of General Gordon would probably result in the Government being compelled to send a Force to rescue him. We are now within a measurable distance of that step. But notwithstanding the policy of the Government in sending him upon that Mission, it is our duty, I think, to do our best to rescue General Gordon and those who have stuck to him. The strictures of the hon. Member for Northampton (Mr. Labouchere) on General Gordon are [illegible] undeserved. Notwithstanding the folly of the Government in sending General Gordon, when they were certainly not in a position to know exactly what he would do, [illegible] General Gordon [illegible] the [illegible] as he [illegible] at first that [illegible] was an [illegible] and he [illegible] General Gordon has [illegible] the [illegible] great [illegible] at the same [illegible] I think there are many things which [illegible] Soudan. [illegible] I am quite sure [illegible] pressing [illegible] of [illegible] I [illegible] Mission [illegible] have [illegible]

which he has performed the work he undertook. At the same time I cannot help [illegible] General Gordon's [illegible] that Her Majesty's Government have [illegible] indelible disgrace on England by the way they have treated [illegible]. But that, as I said before, is no reason why we should not assist the Government in relieving General Gordon. These measures which it is now proposed to take ought to have been taken many months ago for his relief, but although they are taken at the last moment, I hope they may not prove to be too late. On the 13th of May the Secretary of State for War mentioned the contingencies that must arise before the Government could take steps for his relief. The Prime Minister [illegible] that any of those contingencies have arisen. On the contrary, he seems to [illegible] that they have not arrived. I should like to know what contingency Her Majesty's Government expected to arrive? What contingency [illegible] the death of General Gordon? [illegible] to be waiting [illegible] contingency arose long ago. But it is clear that General Gordon [illegible] I do not believe that there is any Government in Europe which would have treated its [illegible] in the way [illegible] Her Majesty's Government have treated [illegible]. Nothing [illegible] the conduct of [illegible] in this respect. General Gordon wrote to the Mudir of Dongola [illegible] felt himself deserted by the Government. But although the present Vote is brought forward very tardily and at the last moment, I can assure the Government that I am most happy to give them my most earnest support, and I further think that I may say [illegible] the evils which [illegible] from this Bench, and which [illegible] happen in respect of General Gordon. I am quite sure that any measures which Her Majesty's Government may propose for the [illegible] and the [illegible] will be cheerfully supported by hon. Gentlemen on [illegible]

SIR WILFRID LAWSON: I am not [illegible] of my hon. Friend [illegible] Sir George Campbell [illegible] as [illegible] I am very [illegible] to the Vote

First, of all, I feel bound to consider what was the object with which General Gordon was sent out. There is no doubt about that, because we were told in Her Majesty's Speech from the Throne that General Gordon had been sent out—

"To report on the best means of giving effect to the resolution of the Khedive to withdraw from the interior of the Soudan."

He went out on this Mission entirely at his own risk, knowing the danger and prepared to take the consequences. There is no doubt about that, because the Secretary of State for War distinctly stated that in this House, on the 3rd of April, and explained that—

"General Gordon left this country with a most distinct and clear understanding, repeated over and over again by himself, that the Mission which he was going to undertake was one which he was prepared to undertake with such resources as he might find on the spot; and he distinctly understood that it was not a part of the policy of the Government, in despatching that expedition, to risk having to send a fresh expedition for the relief of Khartoum or any similar garrisons."—(3 *Hansard*, [286] 1115.)

It is quite clear, therefore, that General Gordon went out knowing that he was not to have an Army sent to his rescue under any circumstances. That being the case, and that being the clear intimation given by the Government to the House, I want to know what has happened to induce the Government to change their course of action? What has caused them to come down to the Committee now for an expedition, when they distinctly told the House that no expedition would be sent out for his relief? An expedition must necessarily involve a fearful slaughter of brave men; and what, therefore, has happened to put Her Majesty's Government in a different frame of mind from that in which they were when General Gordon was sent out? Of course, many things have happened. We have been told that General Gordon was obliged to ask for the Suakin Expedition; and although the Government did not give a warm approval to it, they did nothing to express their disapproval of the proposal, and sent out an expedition which committed a fearful amount of slaughter. Another change of policy was that Gordon had sent word home in one of his despatches that he considered it to be his mission to smash the Mahdi. Nothing more unjust than this desire on the part of General Gordon to smash the Mahdi has ever been heard of in modern times. What did General Gordon himself and Baker Pasha say about the Soudan? Both of these eminent authorities have admitted that it was the horrible state of things in the Soudan which made the people rebel. And both have contended that the Soudanese were perfectly justified in doing what they were doing. For that I have even a higher authority than Gordon or Baker—namely, the Prime Minister himself, who described these people, in this House, as "rightly struggling to be free." I, for one, if nobody else does, will certainly vote against this money being spent to carry out this enterprize, if it is only to prevent, at any rate, an attempt on the part of Gordon to smash the Mahdi. Why should Gordon smash the Mahdi? Why should we go about the world smashing people? I thing we have had enough of this smashing business. We smashed Cetewayo; what good came out of it? We smashed Shere Ali and Arabi; and what good came of it all? The country surely must have found by this time that it does not pay, for we suffer most by it ourselves. We are now called upon to vote £300,000 for an enterprize which was commenced and will be continued to smash the Mahdi. Smash him if you like, but that will not get rid of the difficulty. Other Mahdis will spring up like mushrooms. Mushrooms and reformers and rebels spring up because of the sufferings they have to undergo from bad government. Smash the Mahdi, and smash as many of them as you like, and they will spring up again if the bad government be not improved; and all your expenditure will have been in vain. Now, what has happened in this country? Some people say that we ought to rescue Gordon because he is a Christian hero. [Mr. R. N. FOWLER (Lord Mayor): Hear, hear!] The Lord Mayor cheers that. I do not dispute that Gordon is a Christian hero. I dare say Gordon is doing his best, according to his lights, but he has a curious way of showing Christian heroism. The Lord Mayor admired General Gordon's previous career. For myself, I do not see very much to admire in it. First of all, he spent a long time in putting down the Taepings. What right had he to put them down? They were just as good as the Chinese Government, as far as I know. He killed hundreds and thousands of these people.

Then he went to the Soudan, and his [illegible] position there was all a sham for Gordon himself [illegible] slavery [illegible] had [illegible] ever it has been. I don't believe in Christian heroes going about the world [illegible] people's heads off and quoting Scripture as they do it. As for the Vote of £300,000 for putting down the Mahdi, I would rather vote £300,000 [illegible] the Mahdi to put down General Gordon. [illegible] Yes, and I have the Prime Minister to support me there. The Mahdi and his followers have been described by the right hon. Gentleman as people rightly struggling to be free. The Mahdi is the leader of these people, and instead of voting £300,000 to put him down, I say that it is a shame that the Committee should be called upon to vote this money. If Gordon is the Christian hero you talk about, the Government [illegible] by sending out people to be slaughtered for his sake. A Christian hero would rather suffer [illegible] *Laughter.* [illegible] Members laugh; but what [illegible] an Army [illegible] Talk about massacres [illegible] which was that [illegible] took place [illegible] I shall, therefore, vote against the Motion. I support the policy of the Secretary of State for War [illegible] of not sending an expedition [illegible] to which [illegible] agreed [illegible]

MR. ASHMEAD-BARTLETT said, he [illegible]

[illegible]

was sent out to save, put in plain and [illegible] language the position of [illegible] He [illegible] there would be no [illegible] Soudan, and no peace for Egypt [illegible] the Mahdi was smashed up. [illegible] in which every soldier and statesman in Europe would agree [illegible] which Her Majesty's Government in sending out an expedition to Suakin had confirmed, and a statement which the Vote proposed that night completely endorsed. What satisfaction he had derived from the speech of the Prime Minister consisted very much in the fact that the right hon. Gentleman had abstained from repeating that most unfair and unjust charge which, without the slightest evidence, [illegible] from the [illegible] that General Gordon had changed his policy, as [illegible] evinced a desire [illegible] of smashing up the Mahdi. General Gordon went out [illegible] to carry out a pacific [illegible] Government knew perfectly well he had exhausted all the [illegible] in his power. He had [illegible] slavery, and had endeavoured [illegible] Mahdi. Indeed, [illegible] that all his [illegible] Mahdi, and found [illegible] and in [illegible] that he said it was [illegible] military operations. What would the hon. Baronet and [illegible] Members who had used the expression [illegible] the Mahdi, [illegible] General Gordon [illegible] General Gordon do [illegible] was placed? [illegible] Mahdi's fanatic [illegible] certain [illegible] General. But Gordon [illegible] soldiers and [illegible] have [illegible] accomplish [illegible] General Gordon had no [illegible] to secure [illegible] necessary to [illegible] power of the Mahdi. Was [illegible] Committee [illegible] say that General Gordon [illegible] his policy, or was not justified in everything he had done? In the mouth of the Government there might be a great inconsistency in these expressions; but the hon. Baronet, however extraordinary, inconceivable, and almost unimaginable his views on these subjects were, at the same time was, to some extent, consistent in the matter. But for Ministers to cavil at smashing up the Mahdi, and to use it as a charge against General Gordon after they had sent out the fruitless expedition of General Graham to Suakin, which smashed up 6,000 Arabs without any result whatever—for them to reproach General Gordon with this phrase of "smashing up the Mahdi," was not only unjust, but in the last degree inconsistent. He would take up the words of the hon. Baronet, and ask why the Arabs at Dongola and Assouan had not just as much right to struggle for freedom as the Arabs about Khartoum? It was ridiculous to describe these savage fanatics as martyrs—"peoples rightly struggling to be free." These wild Arabs had no appreciation whatever of liberty; their sole idea of freedom was massacre, outrage, and rapine, and they destroyed everything they came across. Hitherto, that had been the inevitable result of their struggle to be free. The Committee had had that night two most extraordinary attempts to hold back information—two most extraordinary attempts at delay. They had been told, on the one hand, that a Cabinet Minister was going out as High Commissioner to deal with the difficulties in regard to Egypt. But Her Majesty's Government had known the difficulties in regard to Egypt for months and years; but they had actually been proposing to Europe a plan to deal with some of these difficulties, without having any alternative policy whatever, Now, face to face with the failure of all their projects, they found themselves obliged to send out a Cabinet Minister to Egypt, in order to get a little more time. The same course was now being pursued in regard to this Gordon Expedition. The Prime Minister, it was true, had asked for a certain Vote of money; but he had taken away much of the effect and all the benefit of that request and of that Vote, by making it seem to the Committee and the country that the old vice of indecision and vacillation still prevailed in the Councils of the Government. The Premier said—"If the necessity arises." When, in the name of Heaven, would the necessity arise if it had not arisen now? What further danger or peril could General Gordon be in, except that which had led to the destruction of the other garrisons of Sinkat and Berber, and the destruction of General Hicks's army? Of course, General Gordon could be in no peril beyond the same kind of peril that had led to the destruction of the other garrisons. If they were to wait until he was *in extremis*, of what advantage would this Vote of Credit be? They were too late to relieve Sinkat, Tokar, or Berber; they brought back General Graham's Force when it might have saved Berber; and now, as far as he understood the statement of the Prime Minister, it was announced that, as far as they could achieve it, the Ministry were going to be too late in trying to relieve Khartoum. How long were British troops to be kept dangling about the Nile, in unhealthy positions in the neighbourhood of Assouan and Dongola? It was known that the Nile would soon begin to fall; that the climate would then become unhealthy, and that British troops, if retained there, would suffer considerable loss. Under such circumstances, would it not be wiser to undertake adequate and sufficient operations at once for the relief of General Gordon, who was undoubtedly expecting assistance from them? The Prime Minister had expressed surprise that General Gordon had addressed himself to the Mudir of Dongola, and not to Her Majesty's Government; but he forgot that General Gordon had told the Government that, as they had abandoned him, he would have nothing more to do with them, but that he would go to work on his own plan, and act upon his own judgment, For that reason, Gordon had sent the message to the Mudir of Dongola, the only person in the neighbourhood who had proved himself to be a man with resolution and courage. General Gordon had declined to have further intercourse with Her Majesty's Government, and nobody could blame him for it. Before he sat down, he wished to say a few words with regard to the fall of Berber and the massacre of its garrison. It was a matter which had several times been brought before the House. The Government were altogether responsible for the massacre, according to the best [illegible]

tish Government to prevent the Egyp- [illegible]

officers, who had received accounts from reliable merchants that entered Berber shortly after the capture, and saw the streets piled up with dead bodies. Major Kitchener had stated that he had not the slightest doubt that Berber was taken by a *coup de main* early in June, and that all the male inhabitants were slaughtered. What steps had Her Majesty's Government taken in regard to the women and children? None whatever. No efforts had been made to rescue them from slavery and a life of misery and degradation. It was well known that the British Ministry did nothing to rescue or ransom the women taken at Sinkat, and subjected to outrage and slavery by Osman Digna's fanatic soldiers. He had not the least doubt that the same fate would befal those who had been captured at Berber, although there were among them the wives and families of Egyptian and even of Europeans merchants. All of them would be subjected to horrible treatment, and, as far as he knew, Her Majesty's Government had made no attempt whatever to rescue them, or purchase their safety. Yet, while this was going on, and while thousands of unoffending people were being massacred in the Soudan owing to the shirking of responsibility by the British Government, they had two Cabinet Ministers going down to the Guildhall, and using very grandiose language about anti-slavery, and professing great abhorrence of the Slave Trade. He would not repeat what was said last night—the word of opprobrium which could alone describe such conduct; but he would leave hon. Members to imagine it. He did not intend to oppose the Vote; but he thought the Government were pursuing a course which was most unsatisfactory with regard to Egypt. The Prime Minister had made use of uncertain and ambiguous phrases — extraordinary phrases about Votes of principle. He should like to know why the Vote of £300,000 was described as "a Vote of principle?" And he should further like to know what was the difference meant by the right hon. Gentlemen between "preparations" and "operations?" [*Cries of* "Oh!" *and* "Divide!"] He did not intend to be intimidated by hon. Members opposite. He admitted that their interruptions were disagreeable; but he was very far from being intimidated by them. If hon. Members wished him to finish quickly, they had better hear him. He supposed that the difference between the "preparations" and "operations" of the Prime Minister was very much like that between "war" and "military operations." He thought they had a right to ask from the Government that they should admit the necessity had arisen not only for preparations, but for efficient operations to be undertaken at once for the relief of General Gordon. Her Majesty's Government were undertaking the work in the slowest and most costly way possible. They were sending out small detachments of troops, and making little snatches at preparation, and were yet doing nothing that would bear actual fruit. The cost, in the long run, would be three-fold to the country if they continued to pursue this kind of half operation, and there would either be no result, or, at any rate, a less satisfactory result than there would be if the Government would undertake at once an adequate expedition. He urged on the Government, before the debate closed, to make some more reassuring statement than that of the Prime Minister's, and to admit that a necessity for immediate action undoubtedly existed.

MR. W. E. FORSTER: The proposed Vote will not require much discussion on the part of the supporters of the Government, or the majority of the Members of the House; but one or two remarks have been made by my hon. Friend on my right (Sir Wilfrid Lawson) to which I desire to make some allusion. As regards those that are to the disparagement of the character of General Gordon, I think General Gordon's character will take care of itself. I have very little doubt as to what will be the opinion of my fellow-countrymen in general, and probably of even the hon. Baronet, when the veil is raised, and the action of General Gordon during the last few months turns out to have been a series of acts of heroism. Let me turn now to one or two facts. The hon. Member for Northampton (Mr. Labouchere) seems to think that General Gordon was not appointed Governor General of the Soudan with the concurrence of Her Majesty's Government. [MR. LABOUCHERE: Hear, hear!] Nothing can be further from the truth. General Gordon was requested to accept from the Khedive the position which was offered to him—the position of Governor General, and to obey any Firman of the Khedive, and he was as much appointed by Her Majesty's Government Governor General of the Soudan as it was possible to be. He was not merely an Envoy; he was sent with responsible duties of importance, and the Government have never in the slightest degree disowned him. It was as the servant of the Government that he undertook these responsibilities. I am very glad indeed that this Vote is proposed. I do not think it was possible for the House to separate without it, and I was exceedingly glad to hear the strongest parts of the speech of the noble Marquess the Secretary of State for War on Thursday last repeated by the Prime Minister. If, however, the Vote had been proposed some weeks or months ago, I think it probable that the very fact of its proposal might have obviated the necessity of the proceedings which are now to be taken. The only further remark I wish to make [illegible] that the Government [illegible] the fact that [illegible] General Gordon [illegible] We have no positive knowledge as to what despatches have been received by General Gordon from Her Majesty's Government. [illegible]

General Gordon has received any communications from the Government those communications are telegrams telling him to [illegible] and if possible [illegible] a settled Government [illegible]

MR. LABOUCHERE: By peaceable means.

MR. W. E. FORSTER: Surely every Member [illegible] have read the Blue Book [illegible] having made the greatest efforts [illegible] about a settled state of things by peaceable means [illegible] When he telegraphed to Sir Evelyn Baring that having tried peaceable means [illegible] going to [illegible] he was not discouraged by the Government. The Government [illegible] to be held to [illegible] Sir Wilfrid Lawson [illegible] absolutely nothing [illegible] departure of the garrisons and [illegible] who would use every [illegible] and would [illegible] abandon [illegible] He was [illegible] attacked by the Mahdi and by the forces of the Mahdi [illegible] with very great [illegible] difficulty [illegible] that we shall [illegible] get the better of his enemies during the summer, there is almost a certainty that he will be in a position of the greatest possible danger, and a fearful calamity might happen if the Government did not send relief.

SIR JOHN HAY remarked, that a rumour had gone abroad that a considerable portion of the Vote was to be spent in subsidizing Abyssinian forces. He sincerely hoped that the Abyssinians were not going to be engaged in any expedition at the cost of Her Majesty's Government; and he therefore trusted that there was no truth in the rumour. He would be glad, however, to hear from the Government what the facts of the matter were. He quite admitted that the Government were entitled to be reticent as to the forces they were about to employ, and the nature of the operations they proposed to undertake—whether by river, by way of Suakin, or by a Southern approach to Khartoum. He fully recognized all that, and he did not ask for any information upon any such point. He thought the Government were right, in a matter concerning warlike operations, to be reticent, and not to afford to other persons the information which would be supplied if they were to answer such questions. But he hoped the Government did not intend to give money to the Abyssinians, for the purpose of getting that savage race to perform duties which they ought to perform themselves. He did not propose to go over the ground which had been so well occupied by the right hon. Member for Bradford (Mr. W. E. Forster) in respect to the conduct and character of General Gordon; but there was one point on which the noble Marquess the Secretary of State for War would, probably, give him some information. It had reference to the services of General Gordon against the Taepings in China. Either the noble Marquess or Sir George Lewis was Secretary of State for War at the time, and Colonel Gordon was at Shoeburyness at the time he received his appointment. He had always understood that it was by the wish of the Government, at the distinct desire of Viscount Palmerston, who communicated direct with Colonel Gordon, that he consented to proceed to China in order to put down the Taeping Rebellion. The hon. Baronet the Member for Carlisle (Sir Wilfrid Lawson) was altogether mistaken in suggesting that General Gordon went out on his own accord. He went out in obedience to the wishes and commands of Her Majesty's Government. He had considered it necessary to say this, because the hon. Baronet seemed to imply that General Gordon had been seeking for distinction in foreign employment, and was not acting by the command of his own Sovereign. That was an entire mistake, and he (Sir John Hay) was able to correct it, because he had full cognizance of the real facts of the case. He hoped to receive an answer from Her Majesty's Government as to the employment of Abyssinian troops.

MR. ARTHUR ARNOLD said, he hardly thought his hon. Friend the Member for Carlisle (Sir Wilfrid Lawson) was serious when he asserted that the Vote was asked for in order to smash the Mahdi. Anyone who had followed the career of General Gordon must admit that there was no officer in the service and pay of the Crown who more fully and completely acknowledged his responsibilities; and he thought the hon. Baronet could have been hardly serious in suggesting that General Gordon went out of his own will to China. Nor could he (Mr. Arnold) agree with the hon. Member for Kirkcaldy (Sir George Campbell) in desiring to make the Vote a definite one. It was, as it had been described by the Prime Minister, a Vote of principle; and the Committee would establish a very bad precedent if they were to consent to tie up the hands of Her Majesty's Government, and allow them to expend the exact amount of this Vote, but nothing more. The hon. Member for Eye (Mr. Ashmead-Bartlett) said that, as this was to be a Vote of principle, Her Majesty's Government no longer asserted that General Gordon had departed from the objects of his Mission. No expression of that sort had fallen from the Prime Minister, nor could there have been, because the facts were plain and palpable to all the world. His right hon. Friend the Member for Bradford (Mr. W. E. Forster) did not seem to be aware of the fact that the last telegram sent to General Gordon by the Government enjoined him to consider measures for his own removal, and the removal of others who had suffered with him, by whatever route he might think best.

MR. W. E. FORSTER said, there was [illegible]

MR. ARTHUR ARNOLD [illegible]

[illegible] at present, what the nature of the pro- [illegible]

THE MARQUESS OF HARTINGTON [illegible]

we should not make such preparations as might be necessary, though he intimated that it would be impossible to say what form our preparations might assume, until we knew whether there would be a necessity for active operations. I cannot agree with my hon. Friend the Member for Northampton (Mr. Labouchere), that General Gordon was disobeying the instructions given him. There is no proof whatever of that, though some rumours which reached us from time to time about General Gordon seemed inconsistent with his instructions, and were difficult to understand, and we asked for explanations. But there was certainly nothing whatever to prove that General Gordon has in any way departed from the original object of his Mission, which was to withdraw by peaceable means, and if not, if he found it necessary, to employ armed force. It is true that we heard lately that General Gordon was engaged in active operations. 'How much of that is true or not, it is impossible to say. But it is quite reasonable, and very probable, that the only means that General Gordon might find for maintaining his own position at Khartoum, and withdrawing the garrison, was to assume offensive operations. My hon. Friend also said that General Gordon was endeavouring to induce Egypt to reconquer the Soudan. Whatever may be the minor inconsistencies of General Gordon, that is a most improbable conclusion. We know that if General Gordon had one conviction stronger than another, it was that the whole Soudan had been brought into its present position by the domination of Egypt. It is probable that General Gordon, before retiring from Khartoum, might desire to establish some settled form of Government. That, in the opinion of Her Majesty's Government, would be exceeding his instructions. ["Oh!"] His Mission, and his primary object, were to evacuate the Soudan. Certainly no instructions were ever given to General Gordon to establish a settled form of Government. At the same time, there is not the slightest doubt that he has undertaken a most beneficial and salutary work. The right hon. Gentleman the Member for King's Lynn (Mr. Bourke) thinks it hard to be called upon to support this Vote, because he opposed the Mission of General Gordon originally, and prophesied that it would involve us in an expedition for relief. I cannot recollect that the right hon. Gentleman indulged in that prediction; but I can well believe that, as the right hon. Gentleman is not inclined to take a favourable view of anything done by Her Majesty's Government, he spoke disapprovingly of the Mission of General Gordon. But, nevertheless, a strong opinion was very generally entertained that it was extremely probable, such was the influence he had shown himself to exercise over the Native races, that he would be better able, than any other man, to secure by his personal influence, unaided by any material force, the withdrawal of the garrisons from the Soudan without bloodshed, and without further loss of life. The right hon. Gentleman also says that General Gordon long ago reproached us with having cast indelible disgrace upon the British name. We discussed those telegrams two months ago, and I have no wish to reopen the question; but what I want to point out is, that General Gordon, as far as the Government know, never addressed any request to them for the assistance of a British Force to rescue him and those with him. He did suggest that if Zebehr was appointed Governor of Khartoum, a small force in connection with that appointment should be despatched to Berber; but he never, to the knowledge of the Government, recommended, or suggested, as part of the requirements for rescuing him, that the despatch of an Army was necessary. Whatever the obligations of the Government to General Gordon, and they are very great and onerous, General Gordon is the last man in the world to suggest the employment of a British Force to insure his own personal safety. The right hon. Gentleman has discussed the probable position of General Gordon. It is very difficult to know what messages General Gordon may have received, and what he has not received. There is every prospect, however, that in a very short time more authentic information will be received about General Gordon, the policy which he is pursuing, and his ability to hold out at Khartoum, or the probability of his withdrawing with that portion of the garrison which is desirous of withdrawing with him. Major Kitchener is, it appears, in communication with tribes apparently not under the influence of the Mahdi, and it is possible that he may by means of negotiations which [illegible] going [illegible] with powerful tribes be able [illegible] Gordon. [illegible] what [illegible] the Government [illegible] the country [illegible] now [illegible] what measures are necessary for the fulfilment of the obligations which they have undertaken.

SIR STAFFORD NORTHCOTE: I [illegible] what has fallen from the hon. Member [illegible] by the hon. Member for Salford (Mr. Arnold). The hon. Member was [illegible] taken [illegible] the speech of the right hon. Gentleman the Member for King's Lynn (Mr. Bourke) [illegible] I [illegible] perfectly [illegible] mistaken [illegible] proper [illegible] the Government [illegible] General Gordon. My right [illegible] the policy of the Government [illegible] regard to General Gordon [illegible] did not think that this was an occasion on which it was desirable to enter into such a discussion. What the Opposition desire to do by supporting the Vote of Credit is to express their sympathy with General Gordon and their desire to rescue him from the position in which he is placed, partly by the [illegible] of the Government and partly [illegible] his own [illegible] Marquess [illegible] the policy of the Government [illegible] We [illegible] and [illegible] Mr. [illegible] I hope we [illegible]

which I hope we are not, to review the whole conduct of the Government in [illegible] General Gordon. I [illegible] that we [illegible] of a [illegible] character [illegible] the Government [illegible] largely responsible for [illegible] in which General Gordon was placed [illegible] the hon. Member for Bradford (Mr. W. E. Forster) has pointed [illegible] taken at an earlier stage [illegible] which they are now taking, and which, if taken sooner, might have prevented the mischief which has happened. But we cordially agree with [illegible] they are now giving [illegible] the [illegible] may be at hand [illegible] We are [illegible] to give [illegible] General Gordon. [illegible] that we [illegible] which the Government [illegible] contingencies that might arise. The noble Marquess spoke of [illegible] great deal of [illegible] already been spent, and we have no information to [illegible] I trust that the Government have formed some plan in their own mind by which they will be able clearly to ascertain what is the exact position of General Gordon, and to afford him support and bring him away. The country ought to be put [illegible] satisfactory state [illegible] of the country [illegible] It was [illegible] troops from the Soudan. We [illegible] that [illegible] garrisons [illegible] Everybody [illegible] garrisons were [illegible] withdrawn [illegible] I am not referring [illegible] speaking from memory, but I say that I [illegible] of

General Gordon that he was endeavouring to restore or provide for a system of peaceful government in th e country which must now be abandoned. It was, however, one of the main objects set before him in his instructions, and his communications with the Government show that he believed it to be his task. The question before the Committee, however, is not the discussion of the general principle of the Government in regard to the Mission of General Gordon. I have no intention of entering into such a discussion. What we have now before us is a proposal that some provision should be made for the rescue of General Gordon, whenever that can be effected. I do not at all complain of the Government for being reticent as to the particular mode they propose to adopt. I think I understood what the Prime Minister meant when he said that this is a Vote of principle. It permits the Government to see that the work is properly carried through, if it can be carried through, for the sum mentioned; but should more extensive operations be necessary for the rescue of General Gordon, Parliament would, of course, feel it necessary to support the Government in the matter. If the work can be carried through for the sum mentioned, of course, it would be highly satisfactory.

Mr. WILLIS said, that looking at this matter, and exercising his own judgment, he thought that General Gordon had failed in the Mission he had undertaken. He had not procured the return of the garrisons, nor had he given up to the Chiefs of the tribes the government of the country as was proposed. General Gordon went out to effect the abandonment of the Soudan which had been governed by intrigue and cruelty; but it appeared by the telegram on page 115 of the Blue Book, that he had changed the whole course of his policy and decided to postpone the evacuation of the district. He desired to have Egyptian and British troops sent to him for the purpose of maintaining himself in the position of Governor General, when, as the right hon. Gentleman the Member for Bradford (Mr. W. E. Forster) must know, he had gone out as Governor General of the Soudan, without the expectation of receiving any assistance in men or money. Even when General Gordon drew up a plan for a successor whom he named, that successor was not to receive either men or money for the purpose of maintaining his position. He contended, therefore, that the Mission of General Gordon had failed, and that it was the duty of the Government to determine that Mission, and to see that no part of the money now asked for should be used for the purpose of maintaining General Gordon in the Soudan. He maintained that General Gordon had by no means proved himself to be a great hero. On the 27th of February, in his Proclamation of that date, he declared to the people that British troops were coming to Khartoum, and he (Mr. Willis) said that General Gordon had no ground whatever for making that statement. Again, he had endeavoured and actually proposed to destroy the troops of the Mahdi, who was endeavouring to relieve the country from the cruelty and oppression under which it had so long suffered. If the right hon. Gentleman at the head of the Government would give the assurance he asked for, that none of the money should be applied to maintain Egyptian, or other rule, in the Soudan, he should offer him the assistance of his vote; but, if not, he should feel it his duty to vote against the Motion before the Committee.

Baron HENRY DE WORMS said, he wished to draw attention to a statement made by the noble Marquess the Secretary of State for War. A few minutes ago, the noble Marquess, whose words he had taken down, said that General Gordon would have been exceeding his instructions in endeavouring to establish an organized Government in Khartoum. Now, he (Baron Henry De Worms) distinctly stated, on the authority of the instructions given by Her Majesty's Government to General Gordon, that those instructions were entirely at variance with the noble Marquess's statement. The instructions to General Gordon contained this passage—

"We trust Your Excellency will take most effective measures to establish an organized Government in the different Provinces of the Soudan, for the maintenance of order and the suppression of the incitement to revolt."

He would ask how those instructions, given to General Gordon when he was sent on his absurd Mission, could be reconciled with the statement just made by the noble Marquess, when he said that

General Gordon would be exceeding his instructions in endeavouring to establish an organized form of Government in Khartoum?

MR. ILLINGWORTH said, it was now four years since the bombardment of Alexandria took place; but the history of events during that period could not have been very gratifying or encouraging to Members in any part of the House. It had been, on the whole, a history of misfortune and vicissitude. He was one of those who, at the outset, deprecated [illegible] in Egypt by means of that bombardment; and he had also voted against the rewards and pensions given to [illegible] others in respect of the naval and military proceedings which took place. It was said that the Committee were not called upon on that occasion to enter into the question of the general [illegible] in that part of the world; but they were asked to support a Vote [illegible] General Gordon. [illegible] the Prime Minister that [illegible] wanted except [illegible] Mr. [illegible] part [illegible] [illegible]

[illegible]

for believing that the despatch had not reached him. It laid down the policy of Her Majesty's Government and called upon him to retire from the Soudan as soon as possible, and to bring away those persons who were [illegible] to leave Khartoum with him. He trusted that that was still the policy of Her Majesty's Government, and that they intended to carry it out. He would only add that he did not regard General Gordon as anything like a safe instrument to be trusted only by the Government in carrying out their work in Egypt. He believed that hereafter it would be found that their interference in that country was altogether unnecessary, and that they might have safeguarded their interests without making themselves responsible for the government of Egypt and getting [illegible] Soudan.

[illegible] MAKINS said, it seemed to be the general wish of hon. Members that the presence of General Gordon [illegible]. The hon. Member [illegible] Campbell [illegible] with regard [illegible]. He implied [illegible] [illegible]

[illegible]

SIR HENRY TYLER [illegible] the [illegible] reason why the [illegible] military expedition to Suakin had no result was because it was not followed up, as it should have been, by the construction of a railway from Suakin to Berber. The line could have been constructed with comparative ease, and the brave Arabs who had been so fruitlessly slaughtered would have been better employed in making the railways than in fighting, and when taken into British pay they would have been its best protection. Had that railway been constructed to Berber, the difficulties of the present position would have been very much lessened; and Her Majesty's Government would, at the same time, have done a good work by opening up the commerce of Central Africa, and conferring a permanent benefit on the world.

Question put.

The Committee *divided*:—Ayes 174; Noes 14: Majority 160.—(Div. List, No. 210.)

SUPPLY—CIVIL SERVICE ESTIMATES.

Class IV.—Education, Science, and Art.

(2.) Motion made, and Question proposed,

"That a sum, not exceeding £452,627, be granted to Her Majesty, to complete the sum necessary to defray the Charge which will come in course of payment during the year ending on the 31st day of March 1885, for the Salaries and Expenses of the Commissioners of National Education in Ireland."

Mr. MOLLOY asked the Secretary to the Treasury to be good enough to state the order in which the Irish Votes would be taken.

Mr. COURTNEY said, the understanding was that if they got through the Vote of Credit at a reasonable time they should go on with Classes VI. and VII.; if they were disposed of by half-past 11 it was intended to take the Constabulary Vote.

Mr. MOLLOY said, that the statement of the Prime Minister was that the Constabulary Vote would not be taken without due Notice.

Mr. BIGGAR said, he was desirous of ascertaining what was to be done with regard to the claims of the teachers in Convent Schools in Ireland. As neither the right hon. Gentleman the Chief Secretary nor the Solicitor General for Ireland, who could speak on behalf of the Irish Government, were present, he should be glad if some Representative of Her Majesty's Government would state whether or not they had, up to the present time, come to any conclusion with regard to the proposal to increase the emoluments of nuns in view of the good work they were doing and had done in times past. Some time ago the attention of the right hon. Gentleman the Chief Secretary had been drawn to this question, when he said that he was formulating a plan by which he proposed to increase those emoluments. It would seem that the right hon. Gentleman had put the matter off; and he (Mr. Biggar) had supposed that when the Vote for Education in Ireland came forward the right hon. Gentleman would have been in a position to state his views on the subject. He hoped that someone on behalf of the Government would state what it was really intended to do. He did not propose to go into all the grievances of which the nuns complained; but it could not be denied that, while they had produced a tangible result by the example which they set to the people, they were under great disadvantages in respect of emoluments inasmuch as they received no pensions and no salaries.

Mr. COURTNEY said, his hon. and learned Friend the Solicitor General for Ireland was not present—a fact which he regretted, because probably he would be able to give some information to the Committee in relation to the views of the Government in this matter. He might say that, in his opinion, no conclusion had been arrived at, because he apprehended that, had the Irish Government decided upon the course they intended to pursue, they would have applied to the Treasury to sanction an order for payment. No application had been made or sanctioned, and, therefore, he concluded that the proposed arrangements of the Irish Government had not reached their final stage; but how far they had gone he was not in a position to state.

Mr. JUSTIN HUNTLY M'CARTHY asked what the Government proposed to do with regard to the question of National School teachers, in view of the Division of Friday night? He need not repeat to the Committee the arguments he had made use of on that occasion, but would simply ask if the Government [illegible] their way to introduce a Supplementary Estimate.

MR. COURTNEY said that would be rather [illegible] procedure. The right [illegible] of Secretary [illegible] the Lord Lieutenant of Ireland had stated [illegible] the other night what were the [illegible] of the Government in this matter, and had said that legislation would [illegible] to deal with it next year.

MR. HEALY said he did not quite catch what the hon. Gentleman had said with regard to next year. [illegible] had [illegible] the right hon. Gentleman the Chief Secretary to say that he would bring in a Bill. He asked whether that was [illegible] intentions of the Government in this matter [illegible]

[illegible]

know whether the Government were going to throw overboard the intentions of [illegible] Government in 187[illegible] [illegible] the National School teachers of Ireland [illegible] the average, as compared with [illegible] England and Scotland [illegible] was now received. A plan had been proposed by the right hon. Gentleman the Chief Secretary to the Lord Lieutenant of Ireland [illegible] plan had failed, and, owing to its failure, the sum of £[illegible] had not been distributed, as it was expected it would have been, among the teachers. That being the [illegible]

[illegible]

supporter except the Solicitor General for Ireland. The opinions of hon. Members who voted in the minority on that occasion were entitled to respect. Were they to be informed, when they brought forward their grievances for redress, that those grievances were to be redressed by the kindly wand of British legislation, and were they afterwards to find themselves left in the lurch? They had that evening already voted £300,000 for the relief of General Gordon; but this was a question of far more importance than the government of the Soudan, which country the Government were going to abandon. When they voted with a light heart sums of money like this, and for such a purpose, were they to be told that it was too late in the Session to do anything tending to improve the state of education in Ireland? He thought that nothing could be more unsatisfactory than the manner in which the Government had met this complaint, after having in view the much larger sum they had obtained from the Committee for a less important purpose.

MR. BERESFORD said, on Friday last he had unfortunately missed the Division, or he should certainly have voted with the minority. He believed that the National School teachers in Ireland were justly dissatisfied with the position in which they found themselves, which had been shown to be unremunerative as compared with the position of teachers in this country. He had been recently speaking with some National School teachers in the North of Ireland, and he could assure the Committee that they were a most deserving class of men, and that the work they had to do they performed in a most efficient manner. He trusted the Government would take their position into consideration, and do something in their behalf.

MR. COURTNEY said, the hon. Member for Monaghan (Mr. Healy) had raised a very ingenious argument to show that the Treasury ought to increase the salaries of National School teachers. The hon. Member had said that the right hon. Gentleman to whom this work was entrusted contemplated, when it was originally introduced, that the Unions should contribute one moiety of the expense; and he contended that, the Unions not having done so, the Treasury should make good the amount to the teachers. It was quite true the Treasury had not disbursed the money; but he was afraid that all he could say in this matter was that, although the local taxation had not been levied, he could not admit that any claim arose upon the Treasury. Then the hon. Gentleman advanced an argument which, in a Parliamentary sense, was even more defective than the ingenious arguments which preceded it. He pointed to the fact that there had been a very narrow Division on Friday night, in which the Government barely escaped defeat. No doubt that was a very important fact; but, at the same time, those Members who resisted that Motion, and those Members who were not present to resist that Motion, must pa some attention to the character of theydemand. What was the demand? It was submitted, in the first place, that the salaries of the school teachers were inadequate. Assuming that to be so—admitting, for the moment, that the salaries were inadequate and insufficient—then the question arose, by whom should the deficiency be made up? Who should be called upon to supply an adequate amount? In comparison with the salaries obtained by school teachers in England and Scotland, no doubt those in Ireland were small. Whether they were relatively less was still a matter open to considerable debate. Undoubtedly they were less in amount; but the proportion of money drawn from the Imperial Exchequer for Ireland was infinitely greater than that drawn for England or Scotland. That being so, the deficiency, it seemed to him, must be made up from local sources, and not at the cost of the Exchequer. Of course, Irish Members would urge that the deficiency should be made up by the Exchequer; and he knew of no part of the country which, in such a case, would not prefer that the Exchequer should make up what was required. He found it so in Wales, and elsewhere. Everyone wanted their deficiencies to be met by the Imperial Exchequer; and it was, therefore, not surprising that the plea for making up the deficiency in this case from the Imperial Exchequer should be supported by all the Irish Members, including the hon. Member for Armagh (Mr. Beresford). Even the hon. Member for Cavan (Mr. Biggar) was willing to join in "looting" the Treasury. He could not admit that the combination of

Irish Members in support of a demand on behalf of the Irish teachers at the expense of the Exchequer was [illegible] consideration of the existing state of things, and when the matter was being considered, regard must be had to the fact that [illegible] greater amount of money was granted for Ireland than for England or Scotland. However, next year his right hon. Friend (Mr. Trevelyan) intended to bring in a Bill which would deal with the whole question of [illegible] education in Ireland, and not the least [illegible] of that Bill would probably be the improvement of the salaries of school teachers.

MR. JUSTIN HUNTLY McCARTHY said, the Secretary to the Treasury had not fairly met the question at issue, and he maintained that if the Government undertook the work of education they [illegible] do it well and thoroughly. It [illegible] insisted upon governing Ireland, it was only fair that they should [illegible] work to be [illegible] properly and [illegible]. Irish Members [illegible] [illegible] England [illegible] which the English Government [illegible] [illegible] Ireland [illegible] [illegible] starving [illegible] [illegible] self [illegible] Irish [illegible] and [illegible] way [illegible] was given [illegible] Imperial Exchequer [illegible] England or Scotland [illegible] English and Scotch teachers were [illegible] that was the reason [illegible] Irish [illegible] were [illegible] their Representatives [illegible] [illegible] [illegible] [illegible]

readily be accepted when it concerned [illegible] case of the Irish National teachers who had suffered a [illegible] and whose interests were quite as [illegible] as those of General [illegible]

MR. MONTAGU SCOTT said, he [illegible] of taking part in [illegible] he must [illegible] present on Friday night [illegible] voted with his hon. Friends below the Gangway, in the same way as the hon. Member for Armagh (Mr. Beresford) would have voted [illegible] had he been present. Then, he would like to know, where [illegible] of the Government have [illegible] gathered [illegible] the hon. Member for [illegible] (Mr. Healy), was that the Irish [illegible] paid [illegible] most [illegible] only an average of [illegible] a year. It was not a question [illegible] money came from. If [illegible] were employed and entrusted [illegible] important function of [illegible] they must be [illegible] starvation [illegible] received. If the Irish Members [illegible] a Division [illegible]

MR. JUSTIN McCARTHY observed, that the Secretary to the Treasury admitted [illegible] did not agree [illegible]. He said the [illegible] deficiency [illegible] and not [illegible] Treasury. [illegible] Government [illegible] a scheme by which the teachers [illegible] larger remuneration [illegible] down, [illegible] now was what should be [illegible] Gentleman said [illegible] of the [illegible] at [illegible] starving [illegible] Government had not [illegible] Session [illegible] year [illegible] year [illegible] a year. While [illegible] preparing their [illegible] they were [illegible] they should take from the Treasury enough money to keep these people from starving; and having done that they would be able, with an easier conscience, to enter upon their larger scheme for paying the teachers without taxing the localities too heavily, and without taking too much from the Treasury.

MR. KENNY said, the Secretary to the Treasury had advanced arguments which had nothing to do with the question, his argument being that the sum allowed for Ireland was larger than the amount granted for either England or Scotland. They all knew that; but the state of things in Ireland was absolutely different from that in the other parts of the Kingdom. In England the Local Authorities had control over these matters; they had compulsory rates, and they had School Boards; but in Ireland that was not so. The Secretary to the Treasury had, in fact, made no defence of this treatment of the Irish teachers. The hon. Gentleman could not deny that the teachers had this grievance; and if the matter was pressed upon him he would have to admit it for the sake of truth as well as for the sake of argument. The amount of money contributed in Ireland locally was very small; but the people in Ireland were not compelled to pay for education, and what was levied was a sort of voluntary rate. In some instances, the Boards of Guardians did not levy a rate; they had no control over the money, and the result was that they took up the Act of 1875 at one time with greater readiness than they did now; and the Act had now practically fallen into disuse. The Secretary to the Treasury seemed to be in great glee over the idea of another Division on this question, evidently believing himself to be safe with the myrmidons whom he had brought down by a four-line Whip to defeat the Irish Members. He remembered that not long ago, when the hon. Member for Waterford asked the hon. Gentleman the Secretary to the Treasury for an interview respecting the granting of some money for certain purposes in Ireland, the hon. Gentleman said he did not want an interview, and the hon. Member could put down what he wanted to say in writing. The Secretary to the Treasury endeavoured to prevent a purely Irish fund being applied to Irish purposes; but in the end he was forced to give way, and now, in regard to this case of the Irish teachers, the best he could say in a speech specially prepared to minimize the claims of the teachers, was that the English teachers only received half as much again as the Irish teachers. Then he endeavoured to make a distinction, and to show that, after all, the Irish teachers were in almost as good a position as the English teachers. When this question was brought forward, the hon. Gentleman calmly said the Irish teachers were as well paid as the English teachers, having regard to the demand for labour, and the current rate of wages in England and in Ireland. But the class from whom these teachers were drawn had now open to it a variety of occupations. Since the Civil Service had been thrown open a large number of Irishmen had gone into the Service, and the result of so many of this class being drawn away was that the teachers, and especially the younger teachers, had to be recruited from a class very inferior to that from which they were drawn 10 or 15 years ago. That was due to the fact that the salaries given to teachers were not equal to the salaries given in the Civil Service, and if this state of things continued the class of Irish teachers was bound to still further depreciate; and whatever the Secretary to the Treasury might say against further grants from the Consolidated Fund, it was certain that unless something was done to improve the class of Irish teachers and the future education in Ireland there would be an end to efficient instruction.

SIR LYON PLAYFAIR said, he thought that all who knew anything about Irish education would agree that the emoluments given to Irish teachers were not such as they would desire to see given to men of efficient training. There were some points, at all events, of common agreement on which Irish Members on the opposite side, and many educationalists on this side would be in common accord. In the first place, the Irish teachers had been and were very efficiently trained. Religious difficulties in Ireland had prevented their getting their training in neutral and common training schools, and the Government—too late, he thought—had perceived that difficulty, and had recently voted a certain amount of money in order that teachers might receive training according to their religious professions and in [illegible]

[illegible]

for, talk of the system of education as they liked, the schools in Ireland [illegible]

[illegible]

I tell you that this compulsory rating must be applied wholly to Roman Catholic education, because 75 per cent of the population of Ireland are Roman Catholics. If you rate the people compulsorily the rates must be applied to Roman Catholic schools." Now, except in incidence, what was the difference between a local tax and an Imperial tax? The difference was only a matter of area and locality. Suppose they applied this principle of the hon. Member for Monaghan to the £720,000 which the State granted for education in Ireland. They would have to remember that out of that £720,000, £620,000 came from Protestant England and Scotland, and would be obliged to apply it to Protestant education. Whether they were taxing for Imperial or for local purposes, the money must be applied for the benefit of the people taxed. The Imperial taxes applied to the whole of the people whatever their religious belief, and local taxes were for the benefit of the whole of the locality on the same principle. In this matter what was he endeavouring to bring about? Hon. Members knew that he had always been and was extremely anxious for advanced education in Ireland. He was dissatisfied with the results obtained. They wanted a development of their National Board, for it had not achieved good results. It had been in existence 50 years, and certainly had not produced the results which were to have been expected. They must, before they could get complete command over their schools, have local rating and Local Boards. He knew the difficulties in the way of bringing about this local rating and establishing these Local Boards. Many would like to establish them; but would the priests like them? No; and if it was attempted to establish them great difficulties would be encountered. But if they could be appointed he did not doubt that they would be productive of great good in enlisting local co-operation. What they wanted in Ireland was Local Boards, and local co-operation in school matters. They should not always look to the Government for increasing aid. Let them get the localities interested in the advance of education, and having secured Local Boards and local management, let them come to the State for increased aid. Let the Government, which tried to advance education, find that ardent local co-operation which it wished to find, and let it discover those local desires for the purposes of education which were so essential, and without which the education and enlightenment of the people could not be satisfactorily advanced. An hon. Member opposite (Mr. Montagu Scott) said that on the Vote the other day they might have defeated the Government. He was sorry if that were so. If he had been present he should have voted with the Government, not because he had the least jealousy of the purposes of education in Ireland. He did not care whether education there was denominational, or mixed; but what he did care for was that the State should only do its part, and that the nation should do its part in order to meet the State. Without that they could not expect to diffuse education over Ireland, which was so essential in order to produce an industrious and useful people.

MR. MARUM said, that as the line of argument taken by the Secretary to the Treasury (Mr. Courtney) and the right hon. Gentleman who had just sat down seemed to be a comparison between the local aid given in England and Scotland and that given in Ireland, he, for his part, should like to draw some comparison between the resources from which the local aid was derived in the two parts of the United Kingdom. The right hon. Gentleman the Chief Secretary had also used as an argument a comparison between the local aid given in England and that given in Ireland. When a complaint was made of the large increase in the cost of the Constabulary in Ireland, the right hon. Gentleman had immediately drawn a comparison between the amount spent on police in the counties of England and the amount spent in the counties of Ireland. He (Mr. Marum) declined to accept that comparison. Let them compare the prosperity of the county of Kilkenny—the population since 1841 had decreased from 202,000 to 99,000, or more than 50 per cent—with the prosperity of any English county. The county contained 508,000 acres, of an annual value of £343,000. Let them compare that with any county in England of the same area. Let them compare the taxation, and then suppose that the two counties were brought into the market, would there be any comparison between either of their relative values capitalized? He might be told that this would give only the fee simple, and that that was unsaleable at that moment in Ireland. He would take the tenancy interest as a test of value then. What comparison could they draw between the English counties and the Irish from a farming point of view? In Ireland they would have to look at the soil, at the state of the labour market, the adaptability of the country to agricultural machinery, and the large and important question of markets. On the latter point alone it would have to be borne in mind that they could get a beast from Canada to Manchester cheaper than they could get one from a Midland county in Ireland to Manchester. He put these matters simply to illustrate his argument. When comparisons were drawn between the local aid given in England and Scotland and that given in Ireland, they must take into consideration [illegible]

[illegible]

agricultural interest of the United Kingdom. The hon. Member for South Leicestershire had twice brought forward, and [illegible] a favourable reception [illegible] that [illegible]

[illegible]

Mr. [illegible] wished to say this with regard to [illegible] of local taxation [illegible] arose, and when a similar Motion was brought forward [illegible] Irish Members [illegible] their [illegible] satisfied [illegible] show that the [illegible] Ireland [illegible]

[illegible]

maintained that, in proportion to her wealth, Ireland contributed more than England to the cost of National education. He asserted that, even if it were not so, it was England's bounden duty to take the whole burden of National education in Ireland on her own shoulders. The wealth of England had been estimated to be, as compared with that of Ireland, as 13 to 1. They paid much more in Ireland for National education in proportion—as compared with England—than 1 to 13. He had heard the Chief Secretary say that the pence contribution of the Irish children was, on an average, 4*s*., and that of the English children 6*s*. Surely 4*s*. was a very large proportion indeed for Irish children to pay, considering the relative wealth of the two countries. Why did England expect that Ireland should pay even a larger proportion, and stand on a level with her in this particular matter? England robbed Ireland of education when she was educating herself—she made education in Ireland penal for several centuries. How much, then, did she owe on that score to the Irish people? She owed a debt she would never be able to repay. England had blinded the eyes of the minds of the Irish people, and now, a few generations later, the people were to be equal in the race of education in England, Scotland, and Ireland. Some time after robbing Ireland of education England was eager to give it to her again—Protestant education. She desired to force that on the Irish people; but they would not have it, and the result was that they were left, in a measure, to pay for education themselves out of their own pockets. Did that not keep up still more the charge, the claim, they had against England on this question of education? Moreover, there remained this fact—that, at the present day—as could be proved by Parliamentary Returns—Ireland was over-taxed, and paid a larger proportion to the Imperial Exchequer than was paid by England. Ireland, not only in the matter of education, but in many other respects, was over-taxed, over-burdened, and oppressed; and yet it was expected that in this matter of education they would be able to put down pound for pound, and penny for penny, in proportion with wealthy and opulent England. Moreover, the population of Ireland was divided. There was a large section of the people hostile to Irish interests and hostile to public education, in so far as it was a really National and Catholic education, and from this section they got no help. This section gave nothing towards the general purposes of education in Ireland; any money they had to spend in that way they preferred to spend on proselytizing insititutions. So that Ireland was placed at a serious disadvantage all along the line in this matter. These circumstances deserved more consideration than they got from the Secretary to the Treasury or from the English Government, Whig or Tory as the case might be. Then he maintained that there was not in the whole world a people who had to so large an extent voluntarily taxed themselves for purposes of education and religion as the Irish people. They had in Ireland to support the whole of their clergy. They had to build their churches, their convents, their monasteries, and to do it all without any charge upon the British Exchequer. The English clergy were paid out of the money of the State; whereas in Ireland there was no claim in that matter against the State. Voluntarily, and of the free hearts of the people, hundreds and thousands of pounds were paid for education, convents, monasteries, churches, and yet no credit was given to Ireland for that by the right hon. Gentleman the Member for the University of Edinburgh (Sir Lyon Playfair). Those facts should not be overlooked in this matter. Moreover, the Irish National Board had never been popular. Some surprise had been expressed that in 50 years a better result had not been produced. Why, it was only quite lately that they had been forcing them to travel in anything like a national groove. For some time this Board was denounced by the guardians of the morals and the faith of the Irish people; and when the Government chose to force on a system of education against the wishes of the people, was it to be wondered at that the operation of that system did not produce such good results as would have been the case under more prosperous circumstances? All those things went to show that on the side of the Irish people there was no fault; but that there was great fault on the side of the Government of England for endeavouring to force an unpopular system of education on a country, and, when their hands were somewhat relaxed in that [illegible]

Convent School. Such was the liberality and sense of fair play and justice which [illegible] he, and so exhortative of good behaviour on the part of the Irish people. But the right hon. Gentleman entirely evaded the question which the Irish Members wished to press on the attention of Parliament. The question was not one of the incidence of local taxation, or local effort in aid of education; but it was the present insufficiency of the payments made to the National School teachers in Ireland. How did the right hon. Gentleman attempt to meet that point? He said the Government had agreed to establish Denominational Training Colleges in Ireland, such as were established in England and Scotland; and he had said that when these Colleges had been at work for some years then they would have a staff of teachers in Ireland who would be able to have a better classification and to earn higher rates of salary, and who, being better qualified, would also earn increased results and enable the children to secure increased attainments. That might be all very true; but it had nothing to do with the salaries of the present teachers. The Training Colleges might hereafter turn out a very efficient staff for teaching purposes; but the existing teachers would not benefit one iota by the higher standard which was to be attained hereafter by their successors. The speech of the right hon. Gentleman entirely evaded the point at issue. No answer had been attempted by the Government—the Government did not make an appearance of concerning itself to understand the Vote. The Secretary to the Treasury sat there, as he was bound by his Office to do, with a volume of the Estimates before him; but he knew nothing about the administration of the Irish Education Department. The hon. Member knew himself that he did not possess the information necessary to enable him to deal properly with this subject. Sitting next the Secretary to the Treasury was the hon. and learned Gentleman the Solicitor General for Ireland. He (Mr. A. O'Connor) wondered what English Members would think if, in place of the right hon. Gentleman the Vice President of the Council (Mr. Mundella), they were to see in charge of the English Education Votes, and directed to expound or defend them, the English Attorney General or the English Solicitor General? Why, English Members would simply refuse to accept the Government Estimate. They would refuse to pass it without a much better explanation and defence than either of those officials would be likely to give. The Solicitor General for Ireland sat on the Front Bench loyally enough to do what service he could in the matter; but it was entirely beyond his province even to explain this Vote and what took place in connection with it from one year's end to another. The hon and learned Gentleman sat there merely, perhaps, because he thought there should be at least one Representative of some portion of the Irish Executive present. Well, he (Mr. A. O'Connor) was bound to say that, under these circumstances, the position of an Irish Member discussing these Irish Votes was not only painful, but cynically painful. It made a man feel that he came to the House simply because it was his duty to do so, and not because it was of any use—that he came simply because Ireland called him, just as he would shoulder a musket if she called upon him to do it. He was unable to do effective work. He met, as representing the Government, a Gentleman who could not be a master of the Estimate he had to propose to the Committee. It seemed to him that this was not treating the Irish Members—it was not treating the people of Ireland—it was not treating the interests of Ireland with that respect which the Government ought to show, bringing on Estimates of such immense consequence to the welfare of the Irish people, without even the Chief Secretary to the Lord Lieutenant being in his place. Well, that being the case, the temptation was strong on one not to say a word on the Vote at all; but simply to refuse assent to it—to divide against it as a whole. Yet one hardly liked to do that, because it would seem that they were not even giving expression to the feelings of dissatisfaction and grievance which they knew to be very strong in the country. He would not weary the Committee by adding to what had been said on the question of the pension and pay of the teachers; but he would ask the hon. and learned Gentleman the Solicitor General for Ireland if he could say what the Irish Government proposed to do, or proposed to submit, with regard to the position of the assistant teachers? They were classed by examination; but whether they came out in the third class, or the second class, [illegible] the first class they could receive [illegible] as [illegible] teachers. That was a grievance which had been repeatedly urged on the attention of the Government, and he had never yet heard that the Government had [illegible] regard to it. [illegible] The Department required schoolmasters [illegible] with books and school apparatus and [illegible] payments [illegible] [illegible]

schools throughout the country. Now, these schools were of two descriptions. Some were called "vested" and [illegible] [illegible] vested [illegible] the Vested Schools, [illegible] vested in the Commissioners of National Education, and others were vested in local Trustees for the purpose of being maintained as National Schools. Now [illegible] vested schools [illegible] the expense of building schools which were vested in the Commissioners, and with regard to schools which were vested in local Trustees, under Rule [illegible] of the Rules [illegible] of this year, the grant [illegible] two-thirds for any [illegible] [illegible]

[illegible] [illegible] treat with even the semblance of fairness a very large proportion of the [illegible] schools [illegible] that this was a [illegible] against a Catholic [illegible] which would be disgraceful [illegible] country.

but which in a country which was itself Catholic was almost incredible. The Resident Commissioner, he was bound to say, had expressed his regret at the state of things; but stated that while the present Rules existed he was unable to give any assistance, and the only way in which assistance could be obtained was by dismissing the monks. The parish priest who gave this information said—

"This, of course, I declined to do, for the monks in question were men who had actually received certificates from the Commissioners themselves as qualified teachers."

He added—

"As a matter of fact, the school, for want of Government assistance, is hardly in a state to justify it in being used as a school."

It was tumbling all to pieces; the priest had no means of building another, and the Commissioners refused to give him aid. This priest went on to say—

"These Rules were made at a time when the Commissioners were hostile to Catholic education, and when it was declared by Archbishop Whateley that Catholic education would be one of the most effectual means of undermining the religious instincts of the people. They wanted to throw an obstacle in the way of the children getting into the hands of religious communities. They are not now so bigoted."

He (Mr. A. O'Connor) hoped that they were not. Up to the year 1855 monks were allowed to teach in the schools and to be classified; but after the year 1855 until very recently they were not allowed to become classified at all. In the days of the late Chief Secretary, the right hon. Gentleman the Member for Bradford (Mr. W. E. Forster), on representations which were made to him, the Rules were changed. so that the members of religious communities were admitted to classification as teachers; but although the grievance was in that way partly removed, and the teachers were allowed to remain, the injustice in reference to grants for buildings was not removed, but it had remained to the present day. The Commissioners themselves were fully aware of the injustice. The Resident Commissioner had written to suggest a mode of evading the Rules; but nothing had been done to alter them. He thought if the Chief Secretary could have been present the Committee might probably have heard something from the right hon. Gentleman about the intention of the Government to alter the Rules, because he had promised to look into the matter when it was brought before him some time ago; but in the absence of the right hon. Gentleman how were they to know what the intentions of the Commissioners were? Then there was another matter upon which, as well, the Chief Secretary might have been of use if he had been present—namely, in regard to the payment made to the nuns as teachers. The nuns in Ireland were unquestionably the best teachers the people had, and that was a fact which had long been recognized by almost every Inspector in every part of the country. The Appendix to the last Report which he had opened casually contained a paragraph stating that in eight Convent Schools the average attendance was 1,347; the teaching staff consisted of 40 nuns and 36 paid masters; the scholars were of a higher class than those in the ordinary schools; and the Inspectors reported that they had no doubt the Convent Schools were the best in the district, far surpassing the ordinary schools in the supply of books, while the class rooms were of a superior class, better kept and regulated; and, considering the higher education of the nuns, there was no doubt that the Roman Catholic children made more rapid progress than those of any other school. A wholesome tone of discipline pervaded all of them, and in many of them the children were learning extra subjects. The same kind of testimony was given by every one of the Inspectors throughout the country. He held in his hand a copy of the Inspector's Report in regard to Kinsale, and it was of such a favourable character that anyone interested in school management would take an interest in reading it. The total number of pupils in the school, according to Mr. Sheehy's Report, was 756; the teaching power was ample. The average attendance was large, and there were 20 teachers giving instruction in literary subjects, and one in industrial pursuits. There were also seven monitresses belonging to the school. He believed that all the ladies who taught in this school were highly qualified as regarded their acquirements, method of teaching, and skill in organization. The Report of the Inspector stated that the lady who had the chief charge of the school and directed the entire education of the children and the training of young nuns was superior to anyone connected with the Middle Schools [illegible] in educational [illegible] [illegible] in Dublin and elsewhere. The Inspector reported [illegible]

[illegible]

lay teachers would have £58, the [illegible] [illegible] £47 [illegible] consideration the very low rate of pay [illegible]

The CHAIRMAN [illegible]

MR. ARTHUR O'CONNOR [illegible]

Motion made, and Question proposed,

"That the Item of £25,568, for Salaries and Wages, be omitted from the proposed Vote."—(*Mr Arthur O'Connor.*)

THE SOLICITOR GENERAL FOR IRELAND (Mr. WALKER) said, the hon. Member for Queen's County (Mr. A. O'Connor), during the course of his speech, appealed to him, and suggested that it was somewhat strange that the right hon. Gentleman the Chief Secretary for Ireland (Mr. Trevelyan) should be absent upon this occasion. The right hon. Gentleman was not absent through any fault of his own; he was anxious and desirous to take part in the discussion of every important Irish question, and to listen to the views of hon. Gentlemen from Ireland, who sat below the Gangway on the Opposition side of the House. Unfortunately, the cause of the right hon. Gentleman's absence was beyond his control. The right hon. Gentleman had been most unremitting in his attention to the Business of his Office, and for a long time he had been suffering from indisposition. He (Mr. Walker) was quite sure that if the hon. Member for Queen's County had known all these circumstances, he would scarcely have attributed to the right hon. Gentleman a desire to purposely absent himself from this discussion. They must remember that the right hon. Gentleman was present the other evening when this subject was before the House, and that he made a very useful contribution to the debate which then took place, embracing in his speech most of the points which had been advanced to-night. He (Mr. Walker) could not allow the observations of the hon. Member to pass by without acquainting the Committee with the real reasons of the absence of his right hon. Friend. Now, everybody admitted that the subject which was now under the consideration of the Committee was a most important one, inasmuch as the cause of education concerned not only the Irish people, but every people. The payment of teachers was a serious branch of the subject, because if teachers were not paid enough it was not alone the teachers themselves, but the cause of education, which suffered. It was admitted that the present system of education in Ireland had failed to produce the results which were, at all events, looked for. Both the late Government and the present Government had agreed that in the improvement of Irish education money was not everything. It had been felt that the cause of education would be promoted all the more by importing amongst the great body of teachers zeal and stimulus, than that education should be supported entirely by the State. It had been felt that every stimulus should be offered to Local Bodies to promote education. The Bill that was introduced by the right hon. Gentleman the Member for East Gloucestershire (Sir Michael Hicks-Beach) failed, it was said, because the voluntary test was offered, and that test had already broken down. The result of the voluntary test was summed up by the right hon. Gentleman the Member for the University of Edinburgh (Sir Lyon Playfair) when he said that £14,726 was the total of the voluntary contributions. The compulsory scheme had been suggested, and it was shadowed forth by his right hon. Friend (Mr. Trevelyan) that, as the compulsory system had been successful both in England and Scotland, it might with advantage be applied to Ireland. It had been argued that if local contributions could be given to the great cause of Irish education, they would supply the zeal and stimulus which certainly were wanting, and that they would also supply one of the demands in the present system which hon. Members had alluded to—namely, that they had not that complete control over education that they desired to have. The greater the local contributions were, the more reason there would be to extend control to the people. For these reasons, it had been thought it would not be at all undesirable to give the system a trial. The hon. Member for Queen's County (Mr. A. O'Connor) called attention to the alteration of the Rules, and had referred to what the Chief Secretary had, on a previous occasion, said upon the subject. He (Mr. Walker) would undertake to communicate with his right hon. Friend on the matter; and he was persuaded that if the right hon. Gentleman had made any promise upon the subject he would fulfil it. There was another matter to which the hon. Member for Queen's County referred, and that was the support which was given to schools conducted under the National system by nuns. He (Mr. Walker) knew something of Ireland, and he entirely agreed with everything that had been said by hon. Members in regard to the schools in charge of nuns. Those ladies had naturally no other object than the proper training of the children confided to their care; and he had seen schools managed by them in a way which would do credit to any managers. No doubt the present educational system was such that the nuns had not derived all the advantages others had. Being religious, they could not conform to the Rules as other persons could. No doubt, when the system sketched out by his right hon. Friend (Mr. Trevelyan) came into force, the position of the nuns of Ireland in charge of National Schools would be greatly improved. He (Mr. Walker) did not expect his contribution to this debate would be of any great advantage; and, therefore, he regretted very much the absence of his right hon. Friend the Chief Secretary. The right hon. Gentleman knew the [illegible] perfectly. He devoted much of his time [illegible] before he went to Ireland, and he had made [illegible] during the years he had been at the Irish Office. [illegible] great [illegible] personal [illegible] Mr. Walker had [illegible] the Chief Secretary [illegible] personal [illegible] which [illegible] have prevented [illegible] being present in the House [illegible].

MR. DAWSON [illegible]

[illegible]

cation in Scotland and that which regulated education in Ireland. Scotland was [illegible] religious, but it was not [illegible] people [illegible] were but a few amongst [illegible] perfectly [illegible] they [illegible] the State [illegible] given. He [illegible] the Scotch Education Act [illegible] that Act Parliamentary grant might be made to the managers of any school which, in the opinion of the Scotch Education Department, efficiently contributed to the secular education of the parish or burgh in which the school was situated. He could not for the life of him see what justice or fair dealing should enable this country to [illegible] with the [illegible] vast majority of the people of Scotland, and with the small [illegible] of Catholic feeling in Scotland, and at the same time refuse to [illegible] sympathy with the feelings of the [illegible] Catholics in Ireland. [illegible] the Member for the University of Edinburgh (Sir Lyon Playfair) on every [illegible] of the Irish people [illegible] Mr. Dawson [illegible]

[illegible] Mr. Dawson [illegible] they were [illegible] Ireland had [illegible] was [illegible] extraordinary [illegible] Ireland was called [illegible] Why the [illegible] poverty [illegible] the Government grant; though they had proved by their results that they had achieved the great object of teaching, they were only allowed a small grant because they could not comply with the regulation, which they did not think convenient to their close order and retirement, which, however, in no way detracted from the character of their instruction. Who supplied their schools, their magnificent convents, and residential places? The Catholic people of Ireland; and yet the right hon. Gentleman forgot all that, and shut out from his vision figures showing these facts. It was a computation which did not exceed the bounds of possibility that within the last 20 years, two decades of the utmost adversity, two decades which would not occur again owing to the legislation of the right hon. Gentleman, the Irish people had, for the purposes of religious instruction, expended out of their poverty £4,000,000 or £5,000,000. The right hon. Gentleman (Sir Lyon Playfair) had said that the religious element was one of great difficulty. It was aroused, certainly, when it was insulted and outraged. The other day he visited a little Catholic school in Carlow. There was not a non-Catholic within 20 miles; but he found that all the religious emblems had been locked up for fear the Inspector, looking in suddenly, should see them. There was a mural slab in the school recounting the worth of a former parish priest, the inscription concluding with the words—"God rest his soul." That slab had to be covered up, because it was against the Rules that such an inscription should be displayed. Those were trifles; but they went to make life miserable, and to make the educational system exceedingly unpalatable to the people. Now, it had been said that the teachers in Ireland were inferior to those in England and Scotland. To say that was very like adding insult to injury. The Irish Members spent hours the other night showing how poorly the Irish teachers were paid, and yet how proficient in their art they were expected to be. They were paid £57 a-year, or only half what the English teacher got; and they were given none of the social position a teacher should be surrounded with. It was to the credit of the right hon. Gentleman the Chief Secretary (Mr. Trevelyan) that he had commenced to stem the torrent of injustice by providing Training Colleges. It was only the other day that there were no Training Colleges in Ireland. There were, however, now; and he thought the right hon. Gentleman the Member for the University of Edinburgh (Sir Lyon Playfair) would acknowledge, when he came to consult the statistics, how badly the teachers were paid. If the teachers had worked under the same conditions as the English teachers, and had then failed to achieve proper results, the right hon. Gentleman might have come forward, and with some ground passed censure upon the condition of Irish education. Now, he (Mr. Dawson) entirely approved of compulsory attendance; but he was of opinion that they would never be able to secure a proper attendance if the religious sentiments of the people were trampled under foot. If Denominational Schools were organized in Ireland a great source of irritation would be removed. As he had said, in Scotland a school was allowed to receive a grant if it contributed its fair share towards the secular education of the parish in which it was situated. That was what he desired to see in Ireland. If there was such a condition of things objections would be removed, and compulsory attendance might be enforced. He had had an opportunity of conversing with many of the Catholic Prelates on the subject, and he was in a position to say that those prelates were not opposed to the compulsory system if it was properly safeguarded, or if they were satisfied as to what they had a right to look after, and what it was their great and holy business to look after—namely, the faith of their flocks. There were in Scotland, and in many places in England, School Attendance Committees, which did not work such great revolutions as School Boards. Attendance Committees were, as a rule, composed of members of the Corporation, clergymen, and others, and he thought that such Committees might with advantage be formed in Ireland; each creed would be represented on the Committee, and, as a consequence, there would be no hardship. It was estimated that there were only 25 per cent of illiterate persons in Ireland. He wished that those persons could read and write; but considering all the impediments in the way of education in Ireland, and all the grievances which were heaped one upon another in the country, the percentage was not very discreditable. He was sorry to have troubled the Committee so long upon this matter; but it was one on which he felt a deep interest, and it was one in which the first step was to be taken to regenerate Ireland. There was a word or two he ought to say upon the unpractical character of the curriculum of the Irish schools. The total pursuit of classical and literary culture, to the [illegible] which would enable the people to be bread-winners, was, in his opinion, a great blot on the Irish educational system. Industrial education was required in England; but it was wanted a thousand times more in Ireland. It was a reproach to say Irish people that they were not skilled in any trade. It, however, there was industrial training in the elementary schools of Ireland, the Irish people sent over to this great country would be able to take their proper part in the industrial [illegible] [illegible]

the hon. and learned Gentleman had had an interview with the Chief Secretary, [illegible] prepared to [illegible] satisfactory statement on [illegible] They were also anxious to know whether any of the [illegible] respecting the Educational system in Ireland were to be [illegible] They were anxious to hear that Ireland did not contribute [illegible] to the support of [illegible] England did, and it was [illegible] that the Board School system in England and Scotland was a [illegible] He thought it would [illegible] that there was very great difference [illegible] the result of the Board School system. A good many Members of the House of Commons [illegible] Board School system in [illegible] had not been by any means a great success; in fact, [illegible]

[illegible]

Mr. [illegible] despite [illegible] Secretary [illegible] General for Ireland (Mr. Walker) [illegible] the very best [illegible] Ireland [illegible] the worst-paid schools, that they should get a small sum of money from the State, and that, at the same time, in very many cases they should get no fees whatever from the pupils. Many of the Convent Schools were nothing more nor less than Charity Schools, the children of which paid no fees, but were given a lunch to encourage them to attend. In the case of such schools it was clearly the duty of the State to give reasonable and fair compensation to the teachers. Another of the charges which had been brought against the Irish people was that they did not contribute to educational purposes as the English and Scotch people did; but he believed that was an entire fallacy. In every diocese in Ireland a very large boarding and day school existed for the children of the well-to-do parents, and these schools received no support from the State. The priest who undertook to superintend the erection of the schools built the schools entirely at the expense of the Catholic people, supplied Professors, and did everything that was required, without making any application whatever to the State. The same applied in a very marked degree to the provision made for the daughters of well-to-do people in Ireland, because a large number of the better class girls were sent as boarders to the different Convent Schools, which schools received no grant from the State. So, in point of fact, the contention of the right hon. Gentleman the Member for the University of Edinburgh (Sir Lyon Playfair) was entirely unworthy of consideration. He believed that the Irish people, in proportion to their means, were very much more liberal in regard to education than the people of England and Scotland. There were no wealthy people in Ireland to pay the expenses of the education of children; but a large number of people were on the verge of pauperism, and therefore it was too bad to complain that the Irish people did not provide sufficient funds for educational purposes. Complaint was made that the Irish teachers were less able to get result fees than the teachers here. It was not, however, so much the result of lack of ability on the part of the teacher that the fees were so small; but it was owing to the fact that the children were not kept at school a sufficient length of time to enable good results to be attained. Taking it all in all, the Government had given the Irish people great cause to complain of the way in which they had dealt with educational matters in Ireland. Complaint was very justly made on the score of the salaries paid to teachers in the position of nuns who taught in Convent Schools for years. The result of the examination of pupils in Convent Schools had been in advance of the National Schools generally; in some years it had been decidedly above the result in the Model Schools of Ireland, upon which a large amount of public money had been spent —spent both on the building of schools and on the payment of teachers. He thought the Government ought to give hon. Members an undertaking that the Chief Secretary (Mr. Trevelyan) would give them a reply with regard to Convent Schools on Report. On a former occasion the right hon. Gentleman had said that the Government did not propose to move a Supplementary Estimate that year for the assistance of Convent Schools; but he (Mr. Biggar) thought that if the Government were not prepared to do that this year, the right hon. Gentleman (Mr. Trevelyan) might very fairly give them his views with regard to what the increase ought to be in future years. The right hon. Gentleman might give them his opinion with regard to the amount of increased salary which ought to be paid to the nuns, and, also, as to the assistance afterwards of building of the schools in which nuns received their pupils.

Mr. DEASY said, he was very glad that his hon. Friend the Member for Cavan (Mr. Biggar), who was so thoroughly well acquainted with the subject, had referred to the question of the payment of nuns. He hoped that the Government would seriously take the question into consideration next Session, when they would, he trusted, be forced to take in hand the general question of National education in Ireland. There could not be any doubt that the nuns laboured under very severe disadvantages from the present system, which debarred them from receiving any remuneration as result fees. He could not conceive why nuns should not be paid by results just as other teachers were. If the pupils of nuns compared favourably with the pupils of other teachers, he could see no valid reason for refusing to them similar remunera-

[illegible] to that which was granted to other teachers. He [illegible] understood [illegible] it was that [illegible] this [illegible] Supplementary Estimate for the payment of National teachers [illegible] not many nights ago that they [illegible] a very long debate upon a Supplementary Estimate for the payment of [illegible] Magistrates in Ireland. Why should not the same rule be applied to National teachers, unless it was that the Government were unwilling to give a penny for the purpose [illegible] thing [illegible] people [illegible]. [illegible] matter [illegible] to mention in connection with this Vote was the training of teachers. He [illegible] to complain of the fact that the Government [illegible] in Ireland to acquire [illegible] knowledge [illegible] culture [illegible] children who attended National Schools [illegible] particularly agricultural [illegible]. Ireland was a [illegible]. It was [illegible] which [illegible] Government [illegible] grapple [illegible] people of Ireland [illegible]. He [illegible] Session [illegible] subject [illegible]. He was persuaded that the Government would [illegible] necessary [illegible] dealing with [illegible] system [illegible] Ireland [illegible] provision for the training [illegible] [illegible] Dr. [illegible] National [illegible] Mr. Justin Huntly McCarthy [illegible] Irish Members [illegible] House [illegible] always [illegible] against them on Irish matters, [illegible] right or wrong; [illegible] entered for [illegible] would have [illegible] Dr. Davis [illegible] repre- [illegible] the Home [illegible] an [illegible] a very [illegible] the Motion [illegible] Mr. Justin Huntly McCarthy), and that the Government [illegible] would have been turned into a [illegible]. [illegible] he was glad that [illegible] Ireland had [illegible] under the Act of 1875 [illegible] in the first place, [illegible] that the rates in Ireland [illegible] for the [illegible], and if [illegible] the ap- [illegible] the remunera- [illegible] unjust to [illegible] ratepayers to contribute to [illegible]. He believed it was then [illegible] another system of [illegible] in addi- [illegible] system which [illegible] people of Ireland would not [illegible] very long. He be- [illegible] in Ireland [illegible] under [illegible] Irish Members would [illegible] improving the [illegible] when the [illegible] itself next Session. They had [illegible] by the right hon. [illegible] Member for the University [illegible] (Sir Lyon Playfair) that [illegible] their [illegible] but the [illegible] days in that [illegible] in having [illegible] the manage- [illegible] affairs. He did [illegible] everything [illegible], and [illegible] that were [illegible] House of Commons [illegible] in the [illegible] therefore not [illegible] Irish people that they [illegible] what they wanted [illegible] not make [illegible] House of [illegible] of the [illegible] they had on [illegible] the [illegible] there was [illegible] and that of the Prime Minister, or anyone who happened to be on the Treasury Bench, who could vote down any proposition they might make. He should be willing, and he was sure that everyone on those Benches would be also willing, to undertake that they would never come into that House with an education question relating to Ireland if they were permitted to live at home, and settle these matters in their own country. These were the reasons why the Irish people did not come up to the standard laid down by the right hon. Gentleman the Member for the University of Edinburgh. It was all very well for Scotchmen to raise this question. Irish Members knew perfectly well that if a majority of Scotch Members decided on doing anything, they had only to represent the matter to the Government, and the Government was quite willing to accede to any demand they might make. But it was altogether a different matter with Irish Members. The opinions of all Irish Representatives had more than once concurred with regard to certain measures being necessary for the country; but when they approached the Government, they found it did not suit them to consider the question, and they were simply told that their views could not be entertained. The hon. Gentleman the Secretary to the Treasury had argued at great length on a large number of statistics, to show that the Irish people ought to contribute as much in Ireland towards National Education as the people contributed in England; and he said that even in the case of Irish Harbours——

MR. COURTNEY: I beg the hon. Member's pardon—I did not mention Ireland. I referred to the Harbours of Scotland.

MR. DEASY said, he accepted the statement of the hon. Gentleman. He thought he had referred to Ireland, because he knew that he never made any but uncomplimentary remarks with regard to Ireland; accordingly, he had taken for granted that nothing uncomplimentary to any country but Ireland could have fallen from the hon. Gentleman. But as he had disclaimed the observation, he should pursue the matter no farther. He would conclude by again pressing on the Government, when they took up this question, as undoubtedly before long they would be compelled to take it up, to seriously consider the question of improving the agricultural training of teachers in Ireland.

MR. KENNY said, that the statement of the right hon. Gentleman the Member for the University of Edinburgh (Sir Lyon Playfair) had left the Committee under the impression that the people of Ireland only contributed locally something like 1 per cent of the amount necessary for the purposes of National Education.

SIR LYON PLAYFAIR: I said 18 per cent in school fees, and 1 per cent in local rates.

MR. KENNY said, he wanted the Committee to understand that 19·6 of the amount necessary to develop National Education in Ireland was subscribed by the Irish people, either by local rates levied by Boards of Guardians, or in fees paid by the school children. That was the actual state of the case; but it seemed to be the impression with many Members of the Committee that the people of Ireland only contributed 1 per cent. It was well to know that there were two good reasons why the people of Ireland could not be expected to pay local rates for National Education. In the first place, there was no law making it compulsory upon anyone in Ireland to levy taxation in support of National Education; and, in the second place, there was no local representative Body which was empowered to deal with and disburse the funds which might be collected. It was purely optional with the Boards of Guardians in Ireland whether they took advantage of the Act of 1875, which was passed by the late Government; and when ratepayers and Boards of Guardians saw that there was no power whatever to control the distribution of the money, it was only natural that the Act should not be taken advantage of, and it was only the fair inference that the amount, which was at first estimated at £30,000 a-year, should have fallen in successive years below the miserable sum of £11,000. He would now refer to the speech of the right hon. Gentleman the Member for the University of Edinburgh. There was no person who had a greater admiration for the manner in which the Scotch people managed their educational affairs than he had; and there was no one more conscious of their shortcomings in other

MR. JUSTIN HUNTLY McCARTHY

There was, of course, a proportion of bi-linguists, in some parts, where, although Irish was the familiar language spoken, it was immaterial which language should be taught them—although, for his own part, he preferred the Gaelic. But where the Gaelic language was alone spoken he contended that instruction should be imparted in the schools in that language.

MR. PATRICK MARTIN said, he wished to call the attention of the Committee to the neglect with which the Government had treated a question of vital importance to the Catholic population in Ireland—that was to say, the mode in which, at the present moment, educational endowments were devoted solely and exclusively to Protestant purposes which ought to be used for the general benefit of the population. Although, perchance, the discussion might have have been more fully raised on the Votes for Endowed Schools which had been passed, yet as he had, from the changes made in the order of the Votes, not been enabled to then raise the discussion, he desired to now make a few observations in respect to the conduct of the Board of Education in taking one of these Endowed Schools under their control. He referred to the Swords Borough School. That school, though the funds by which it was supported were directed to be applied for the educational necessities of the inhabitants without distinction of religion, was, at the present moment, used entirely by Protestants. He had called attention more than once to the gross misapplication of the public funds, which, as shown in the Reports of the Royal Commissioners, had taken place in the management of that school. The Chief Secretary had not attempted to deny the existence of the abuse, or the injustice of the mode in which the revenues of the school were administered. Yet very recently the Board of Education, though there was a National School founded and supported by the Catholics of Swords out of their own resources, had granted to this Endowed School the privileges and rights of a National School, and they were entitled to a supply of school books at a cheap rate. Let him briefly mention that this Swords School, thus entirely devoted to Protestant scholars, was originally founded under a Charter, and supported out of lands granted by Parliament; these were now represented by a capital of £24,000, from which a revenue of about £700 was received. Now, the conditions of the Charter were that the funds of the Trust should be applied generally to the inhabitants of the borough, without distinction, for the purpose of education.

THE DEPUTY CHAIRMAN (Mr. SHAW-LEFEVRE): May I ask the hon. and learned Member what connection there is between this case and the Vote before the Committee?

MR. PATRICK MARTIN said, the question came within this Vote because the money intended by Parliament to be devoted exclusively for the benefit of the poor who required State aid for National Education was, by the Commissioners, applied for the benefit of the Swords School. At least, that was his opinion, subject to the ruling of the Chairman.

THE DEPUTY CHAIRMAN (Mr. SHAW LEFEVRE) said, the Committee were engaged in discussing the item of Salaries and Wages; and he did not, therefore, think the hon. and learned Gentleman was in Order in discussing the supply of school books, by the National Education Commission, to the Swords Borough School.

MR. GRAY asked whether it was not competent to the hon. and learned Gentleman opposite to discuss the question of the Swords Borough School, seeing that it had been taken under the control of the National Education Board, whose salaries were included in this Vote?

THE DEPUTY CHAIRMAN (Mr. SHAW LEFEVRE) said, he understood the hon. and learned Gentleman to say that the relevancy of the question to the Vote under discussion lay in the fact that the books supplied to the school were paid for out of the money voted by Parliament.

MR. PATRICK MARTIN said, he need not state that he should most readily submit to the judgment of the Chairman. The hon. Member for Carlow (Mr. Gray) had pointed out that the salaries of the Commissioners came under this Vote; and he (Mr. Martin) ventured to think he was right in continuing his account of their action with regard to the Swords Borough School. He might remind the Chairman of the wide line of discussion, and the grave and serious questions that had been more than once raised in the House upon the Votes for Diplomatic Salaries. His complaint was that the school was now exclusively a Protestant [illegible] that the revenues were now being used for Protestant purposes [illegible] Ireland.

Mr. COURTNEY: [illegible] understand the hon. and learned Gentleman to say that the only connection between this question and the Vote before the Committee was the fact that certain books were supplied by the Commissioners. Am I correct in so understanding the hon. and learned Gentleman?

Mr. PATRICK MARTIN: [illegible]

[illegible]

Question put.

The Committee *divided*:—Ayes [illegible]; Noes [illegible]: Majority [illegible].—(Div. List, No. [illegible].)

Original Question again proposed.

Mr. HEALY said, he wished again to call attention to the case of Mr. Sheridan, to which he had referred on Friday last. It was well known that Mr. Sheridan [illegible] National School teachers [illegible] a dinner [illegible] drink the health of Her Majesty [illegible] the Lord Lieutenant. [illegible]

[illegible] obliged to do that,

not because they admired Earl Spencer at all, but because they knew they would lose their situations if they did not apologize. Now, he wanted to know whether the Government approved of this system of Circularizing teachers. Was it a practice in this country? Would the Government in this country insist on the health of all the Princes and Princesses, and all the little Princes and Princesses of Wales being drunk at such a dinner? The National School teachers received £57 a-year, and very much loyalty could not be expected for that. If they were to be required to drink the Lord Lieutenant's health at their dinners they ought to receive £10 extra for that purpose.

Mr. COURTNEY said, he was not aware of all the circumstances of this case, except from the hon. Member's speech; but it was obvious that the matter did not turn upon the consideration of any particular Government, or on the individuality of Earl Spencer. Drinking his health was part of the custom, he being the Representative of Her Majesty. He could not conceive that the matter had anything to do with Earl Spencer personally. There seemed to have been some over-susceptibility on the part of Mr. Sheridan, who, he thought, had rather overstrained the matter; but it did not seem to him worth while to pursue the incident any further.

Mr. GRAY said, he thought it important that the Committee should know whether the hon. Gentleman did or did not mean that Mr. Sheridan's Circular was to be acted upon. It was important to have some guide for the future, and it was from that point of view they desired to discuss the matter. It was quite impossible in Ireland to regard any distinguished person occupying the position of Lord Lieutenant simply as the Representative of the Queen. That never had been and never could be. He would remind the Prime Minister that when Earl Spencer was Viceroy in Ireland in 1870, as the Representative of the Queen and of the Government which had just disestablished the Irish Church, he was "Boycotted" by the noblemen and aristocracy of Ireland, who declined to attend his *levées*, or Lady Spencer's drawing rooms—not because they wished to show any disrespect to the Queen, but because they disapproved of the policy he represented. They disapproved of Earl Spencer the politician, and not of Earl Spencer the Viceroy; and they took every opportunity of slighting him. If those noblemen and gentlemen had a perfect right to show their disapproval of the policy which Earl Spencer then represented, surely the same right extended to men occupying a humbler position if they thought proper for any reason to disapprove of the policy of Earl Spencer the statesman and politician in 1884. The action of these teachers was dictated by no feeling of disloyalty, for they drank with all proper marks of respect the health of the Queen; but was it to be made a matter of censure in Ireland that persons thought fit at a banquet not to express approval of the policy of the Viceroy, who, at the same time, was the Representative of the policy of the Government? Were they to be visited with censure for that? This Circular of Mr. Sheridan threatened them with dismissal from their employment; with losing their situations and being reduced to beggary. If it was an offence in Ireland not to drink the Lord Lieutenant's health, why should it not also be an offence not to drink the Chief Secretary's health? The Chief Secretary was supposed to be, and Constitutionally he ought to be, a better Representative of the Constitution than the Viceroy. He held that the Viceroy ought to be the Representative of both Parties, while the Chief Secretary ought to be the Representative of the policy of the Government. Why, then, should people not be threatened with dismissal if they did not drink the health of the Chief Secretary? They might think Earl Spencer's policy had been a curse to the country; and for that reason, and not because of any hostility to him as an individual, they might refuse to drink his health. The Secretary to the Treasury seemed to have held out an indication that some *quasi*-intimation should be given to Mr. Sheridan that he should exhibit no such extreme sensitiveness in the future; and if that was to be taken as an assurance they might let the matter end. This Circular had created the greatest feeling of indignation among the teachers; but so much did they feel themselves under the power of the Board, and so much did they dread the exercise of that power, that they wrote replies which the hon. Member for Monaghan (Mr. Healy) had not charac-

might be school teachers, in such a matter. If I may venture to give an opinion, and always reserving the right to change that opinion on circumstances not now known to me coming to light, I should say that Earl Spencer's wish would be that his health should be drunk freely, or that it should not be drunk at all. At any rate, I should think he would deprecate any interference with individual liberty for the purpose of procuring a compliment which, under such circumstances, and when so procured, would be of little value. That is the impression with which I should be disposed to look upon the matter. I hope that the day may be coming near when the Crown and everything relating to it may be welcomed in Ireland with the heartiest loyalty. I cannot deny there is something in the distinction drawn in the double character of the Lord Lieutenant, who is certainly, on the one hand, the Representative of the Crown—and, in my opinion, the Crown has never been more worthily represented—and, on the other hand, a partizan statesman who identifies himself with those measures of which we may take different views according to the political opinions we may entertain. It will be felt we cannot go further into the matter, not knowing more about the state of the case; and I would, therefore, express a hope that the discussion may not be continued.

MR. T. P. O'CONNOR said, he would not, after what had fallen from the Prime Minister, further pursue the subject. The right hon. Gentleman's statement formed a very satisfactory conclusion to the debate. He (Mr. O'Connor) wished again to call attention to a subject which he was sorry to say he had had to note every year without, apparently, any amendment on the part of the Department. He found that this year, for books and apparatus, a sum of no less than £35,000 was set down, which was an increase of £1,000 on the Estimate of last year. Now, he had called attention over and over again to the character of these books. He did not suppose that any Education Department in the world purchased books, from the standpoint of common sense so imbecile, from the standpoint of literature so worthless, and from the point of view of nationality so insulting, as the Irish Board of Education. Owing to the system adopted in Ireland, the use of these books was practically compulsory, and there was nothing like free trade in the choice of books as there was in England. He knew the Secretary to the Treasury would not be able to give him any assistance in this matter, as he was as innocent of information upon them as he was of the ancient literature of Ireland. No; it was perhaps possible that the hon. Gentleman did know something about the ancient literature of Ireland; but he certainly did not know anything about the National School books of that country. The Irish Members had reason to complain of the manner in which these Irish questions were treated. For the first time for a considerable period they had had an utterance from the Prime Minister on an Irish question, and that utterance had been of a very satisfactory character. He thought if the Prime Minister were to intervene more frequently in Irish matters, they would have more reason to be satisfied with what went on in that country. They brought on Irish subjects, and the right hon. Gentleman the Chief Secretary—owing to an illness which they all regretted and hoped would be soon terminated—was absent from his place. The Solicitor General for Ireland, with a prudent reserve not always practised by Law Officers, confined himself to giving opinions as sparse as lawyers usually gave when they were asked to give them for nothing. The hon. and learned Gentleman chained his tongue, and declined to say anything as to the educational administration of Ireland. The Secretary to the Treasury, being an old journalist, was, of course, able to pick up information with great facility, and was able to give it with that air of omniscience which every leader writer was able to display who was worth anything to a newspaper proprietor. If he (Mr. O'Connor) had been foolish enough to give forth a small share of the large store of knowledge he might have on a particular subject, the hon. Gentleman the Secretary to the Treasury would get up and convince English Members of the Committee, and endeavour to teach him, that his (the Financial Secretary's) knowledge, as compared with his (Mr. O'Connor's), was as an Encyclopædia compared to an A B C or early primer. However, he would not now go fully into the arguments, but would defer his statement to the Report, if he thought it desirable to go into the subject. [illegible] single Member of the Government, and that was what he (Mr. O'Connor) [illegible] the Government [illegible] the knowledge of the right hon. Gentleman the Chief Secretary [illegible] What was the result? Why, that the Prime Minister, the Secretary to the Treasury, and the Solicitor General for Ireland [illegible] attitude which he should have thought [illegible] as they would be ashamed [illegible] affairs. [illegible] Members [illegible] Prime Minister [illegible] Secretary [illegible] have the Prime Minister getting up and declaring that the school books were a disgrace [illegible]

that when the Chief Secretary and the Prime Minister were sitting on the Front Bench, the Prime Minister [illegible] He (Mr. O'Connor) would [illegible] any answer on the subject.

MR. COURTNEY said, he was aware that [illegible] Member had called attention to the subject [illegible] and that he had quoted extracts from the school books, and had [illegible] the House very [illegible] He had an impression, however, that he had seen a statement [illegible] he could not say whether he had dreamt this or whether he had really seen it [illegible]

MR. T. P. O'CONNOR said the hon. Member [illegible] *The Times* newspaper. If [illegible] Ireland [illegible] *The Times* [illegible] nearly every day [illegible] *The Times* [illegible]

MR. GRAY said, that [illegible] Primary Education in Ireland as long ago as the year 1868. That [illegible] on good grounds the complete abolition of these Model Schools, and the utilization of the funds for many other purposes. Like many of the recommendations of other Commissions, however, this recommendation had remained such, and nothing more, up to the present day. The hon. Member for Carlow (Mr. Dawson) had obtained a Return dated 12th of August, 1880, which showed the work of these schools. At that time they were in receipt of £36,086 a-year. The sum seemed now to be somewhat reduced; at any rate, the amount asked for in the Estimate was only £33,543. Probably, if the matter were properly explained, it would be shown that the schools had some other source of income which was not mentioned in the Return, but which would bring the amount up to £36,086. But, whether the exact sum was £33,000 or £36,000, the Committee would agree with him that the sum was a substantial one. It was only right, when the Royal Commission had stated that this sum should not be expended any longer on this particular purpose, that the Secretary to the Treasury—a Gentleman so jealous of the public purse—should give some intimation why, for the past 15 years, he and his Predecessors had asked the House to sanction this expenditure. Now, the Return to which he referred was a Return first giving the cost of the construction of the Model Schools, and this he found to be £160,304. The cost of the staff and maintenance was, as he had stated, given at £36,086; and, besides these figures, the Return gave the number of pupils on the books, and an analysis of them both as to their religion and the occupation of their parents. In 1880 there were only 11,873 pupils on all the books of the Model Schools of Ireland. For these 11,800 pupils, this £160,000 had been spent on buildings—and very splendid buildings they were—and Parliament was called on to vote £36,000 a-year. When they compared the miserable salaries paid for the ordinary National Schools of the country with the enormous Vote—proportionately to the number of scholars educated in the schools—for these Model Schools, it would be seen that there were occasions when the Treasury could not only be liberal out of Imperial funds, but even extravagant, in some Departments in Ireland. They found an explanation when they came to make an analysis of the scholars in the schools, and the occupations of the parents. For reasons into which he need not now enter, the Heads of the Catholic Church in Ireland had long ago declared their complete disapproval of the Model School system, and had warned their clergy and their flocks not to permit Catholic children to attend these schools. He would not go into the reason why the Catholic Church in Ireland adopted that view. Suffice it to say that it had adopted it. The proportion of Catholics and Protestants in Ireland was as 5 to 1; yet out of the total number of 11,873 scholars in the Model Schools—and this was sufficient in itself to condemn them—only 3,198 were Catholics, the rest being Protestants. There were 4,100 belonging to the late Established Church, and 3,641 Presbyterians, the remainder belonging to other Protestant denominations. Thus, while Catholics were an enormous majority of the entire population, they were only a small minority of the scholars educated in these Model Schools. The schools were kept up for the advantage and convenience of a small minority of the population, composed of wealthy persons who had no claim whatever to education at the public expense. When they came to analyze the parentage of the children they were educating gratuitously they found that his statement with regard to their social condition was absolutely verified. Of the 11,873, 344 were agents or managers; and surely an agent or manager, whatever agency or managership he might have, had no claim to have his child educated gratuitously. He was not sure that some of these parents did not pay the nominal sum of 5*s.* a-quarter. Some of the children were educated gratuitously; but in some cases a nominal payment was made. Six were apothecaries, 29 were architects—who were, undoubtedly, professional men—30 were artists, 19 were attorneys, 33 auctioneers, 10 bailiffs, 2 barristers, 86 clergymen—endowed already by the State, and now getting their children educated for nothing—842 were clerks, 72 engineers, 2 fishery proprietors—he should like to know what claim fishery proprietors had to have their children educated for nothing—210 were Government *employés* other than clerks, 258 were grocers, 36 were medical doctors, 284 merchants and tailors,

7 newspaper editors—and as both a newspaper [illegible]

[illegible]

Colonel KING-HARMAN said he [illegible]

Gentleman's figures, but had heard one or two things which were very curious, [illegible]

[illegible]

Mr. GRAY [illegible]

Colonel KING-HARMAN said he had [illegible]

Mr. GRAY said he had [illegible]

Colonel KING-HARMAN [illegible] King-Harman's [illegible] was that [illegible] Ireland [illegible] were aware [illegible] grocers, but here [illegible] drapers, and so on [illegible] England [illegible] and people other than agricultural labourers, journeyman shoemakers, tailors, bricklayers, masons, and so forth, were, perhaps, amongst the most needy men in Ireland, and amongst those who most required State aid in the education of their children. These classes were generally most industrious, and, in intelligence, were far above the agricultural labourer. They were certainly not amongst those who did not require this kind of education. He only mentioned those items he had heard the hon. Member refer to, and which, he maintained, were misleading.

MR. COURTNEY said, that at that time of night, when it was the desire of the Irish Members to enter upon the consideration of other subjects, he did not feel justified in occupying much time in replying to the hon. Member for Carlow (Mr. Gray). This question was one which had been often discussed. The Model Schools, everyone must admit, were institutions which few regarded with satisfaction. Some of them might be fairly described as a success; but there were others which certainly had not been successful; but, as the hon. Member for Carlow must know very well, it was one thing to set up a school and another thing to abolish it. So long as these schools were in existence and maintained a fair average of attendance of scholars, it would be difficult to put an end to them.

MR. ARTHUR O'CONNOR: What is the intention of the Government with regard to them?

MR. COURTNEY said, he was unable to answer that question at that moment. The attendance at present was at least a fair average, sufficient to justify the maintenance of the schools. There was an average attendance of 90 at the smallest Provincial Model School. That was sufficient to justify the maintenance of the school. The larger Model Schools had a very respectable attendance. The schools were there if scholars chose to make use of them; but, as the hon. Gentleman had pointed out, they had come under the ban of the Catholic hierarchy, and for that reason were not attended by as many Catholic pupils as might be expected in proportion to the population. The hon. Member had hinted that many persons availed themselves of this Model School education for their children who were perfectly well able to pay school fees. A great many of the parents did pay school fees according to their means. Three thousand paid 1*s.* 1*d.* per quarter, 4,000 paid 2*s.* 6*d.*, 2,700 paid 5*s.*, and 595 paid 10*s.* That 595, he should think, would cover a good many of those the hon. Member had referred to as hardly eligible for gratuitous education. He should hope, at least, that it would include the newspaper editors and proprietors. Then there were 35 who paid £1 a-quarter. Many of the parents, therefore, the hon. Member had referred to should be exempt from his censure.

MR. KENNY: Does the hon. Member mean that those who pay the highest fees compensate the State for the amount expended on them, or that the average payments compensate the State?

MR. COURTNEY: Of course, not the average.

LORD RANDOLPH CHURCHILL: We all regret sincerely the absence of the right hon. Gentleman the Chief Secretary to the Lord Lieutenant, and particularly the cause of that absence. It is a perfect farce discussing Irish Educational Estimates with no one to take part in the discussion from the Government Bench but the Secretary to the Treasury, for it is plain from his defence that he is hopelessly ignorant of the whole subject of Irish affairs from beginning to end. If he had not been so hopelessly ignorant of these affairs, he could not have concealed from the Committee that these Model Schools are about the greatest imposture which could be kept up in Ireland. The House of Commons—particularly the English portion of it—have always been under the impression that there is a system of mixed education in Ireland, and these Model Schools are very often triumphantly pointed to as a part of the great success of mixed education in Ireland. But the fact is that mixed education does not exist in that country. The education there is thoroughly denominational, and the House of Commons has usually preferred to recognize the fact that it is maintaining in Ireland by grants from the State a system of education as denominational as it can be. Yet these Model Schools are every year trotted out to persuade the House of Commons that there is a system of mixed education existing in Ireland—a system in which Catholics, Presbyterians, and members of the Church of England join together in equal numbers to receive the benefits of education. It happened to me to be concerned in an inquiry into the subject of Irish Education, and I then found that there is no such thing as mixed education in the country. What you find generally in the model schools is this—that there are a great proportion of Protestants attending them. These schools, with the Universities and the elementary schools, are attended by a great proportion of Protestants, and by two or three model Catholics, who are trotted out whenever an inspection takes place to prove that a system of mixed education obtains in Ireland. But, as a matter of fact, you are keeping up these model schools in Ireland solely for the benefit of the Protestant body, and it is undoubtedly a source of great grievance and annoyance to the great body of the Catholic population, and particularly to the great body of the Catholic clergy. The Committee will observe that there are in Ireland 7,800 elementary schools, of which there is scarcely one which is not thoroughly denominational. But in order to keep up the farce of mixed education you sustain, at a cost of [illegible] a year [illegible] over Ireland for the benefit principally of the Protestant population. You spend among [illegible] a year [illegible] for the farce of [illegible] mixed education that you are [illegible] a system of mixed education in Ireland. [illegible]

[illegible]

positive statement from the Government as to what they will do it will be an excellent thing. This is a very sore subject in Ireland. The hon. and gallant Gentleman the Member for the County of Dublin said it was not an advantageous proper thing that the members of the Irish Church should have their children [illegible] model schools.

COLONEL KING-HARMAN: I said [illegible] Irish clergymen were [illegible] by the State, and that was not the fact. I [illegible] statement.

LORD RANDOLPH CHURCHILL: I [illegible] issue with the hon. and gallant Gentleman. I cannot see how he can say that the Irish Church is not endowed by the State. I have an idea that when the Irish Church was disestablished excellent terms were made with the clergy by the State. Nothing will induce me to believe that the terms [illegible] with the State at that time [illegible]. It may [illegible] as the hon. and gallant Gentleman would wish, but it is [illegible] keeping up these model schools [illegible] that [illegible] Ireland [illegible]

[illegible]

mind that this was a matter which had been frequently discussed since the Royal Commission condemned these schools in 1869, he must say it was time, having now arrived at the year 1884, for the Government to at least contemplate the possibility of, at some period or other, making up its mind with regard to the schools, and announcing its decision to the House. As the hon. Gentleman said, when a school was established it was difficult to abolish it; but how many generations were to elapse before the Government would put a stop to this system of education? He should be content if the noble Marquess (the Marquess of Hartington) would state that this time next year the Government would say what decision they had come to with regard to the recommendations of the Royal Commission of 1869. He should be delighted to withdraw his Motion, and to give the Government another 12 months to consider the subject. It was easy to vote them down, no doubt; but he did think the Irish Members had a moral right, in the face of the Report of the Royal Commission and of the Return which had been quoted to the Committee, to insist on the Government telling them that they would give the matter their serious attention. He did not think it was necessary for him to reply to the strictures of the hon. and gallant Gentleman the Member for the County of Dublin (Colonel King-Harman). He had been abundantly dealt with by the noble Lord (Lord Randolph Churchill). He (Mr. Gray) considered that when the Irish Church and the incumbents of benefices in that Church got large sums which, by a special Act of Parliament, they were able to convert into a special fund for that Church, it did constitute an endowment. The clergy of the Disestablished Church in Ireland, whether they were at that time incumbents or not, who now derived benefit from the fund, were now entitled to be considered as endowed by that fund, and were not fit persons for public charity. He was quite aware that the Church had been disestablished in 1869; but he knew, also, that it had not been disendowed. He should be content with the absence of the right hon. Gentleman the Chief Secretary to the Lord Lieutenant if they could have an assurance that between this and next year the Government would take this matter into consideration. On that understanding—if anyone would tell them that the Report of the Commission would be acted on—he should be willing to withdraw his Motion; but if he did not receive such an assurance, and if he was informed that all these wealthy persons, or persons presumed to be wealthy, were to continue to have their children educated by the State, although he should be beaten, he should consider it his duty to go to a Division.

Mr. BIGGAR said, he was not disposed to argue this question, as the hon. Member for Carlow (Mr. Gray) had argued it in a better way than he could. He should like, however, to make an appeal to the Secretary to the Treasury. He (Mr. Biggar) very often blamed the Government for giving large sums of money where it was not required; and, on the other hand, for being exceedingly stingy where they ought to be liberal. This was a case in point. What they did in the matter of Irish education was this. They gave over £3 a-head for all the pupils in these schools, they being the children of a particularly well-off class, and acted in a most stingy manner towards the National School teachers, who had to teach the children of the very poor, and they treated the nuns in a worse way than they did the National School teachers. That was a matter which he thought the Secretary to the Treasury, from a purely English point of view, would do well to take into consideration. This system obtained in almost every Public Office. They saw a great many people who had to do very little work receiving large salaries, whilst those who did nearly all the work received small salaries. As the Secretary to the Treasury represented the Money Department of the State, it seemed to him (Mr. Biggar) that he would be doing a judicious thing by cutting off this £35,000 a-year of National Expenditure.

Mr. COURTNEY said, he had a word or two to say in reply to the appeals which had been made to him. With respect to the general question raised, it had been asked more than once that evening whether the Government would, next Session, take this matter into consideration. Well, it had been already stated that it was the intention of the Government, next Session, to bring in a Bill dealing with the question of education in Ireland, and he had no doubt the model schools would form a part of the subject of legislation. He [illegible] Mr. Courtney would take care that the effect of the discussion that evening was represented to the right hon. Gentleman the Chief Secretary to the Lord Lieutenant, so that the subject would be considered by the Irish Government in connection with the Bill which was to be brought in.

Motion, by leave, *withdrawn.*

Original Question again proposed.

MR. ARTHUR O'CONNOR said, there would be very little chance of reform in the [illegible] system of education in Ireland in the course of next year, and he thought that every one who had listened to the discussion of this Vote must feel that though there might be a hundred and one points in relation to [illegible] which the attention of the Government might reasonably be directed by the Irish Members, it would be very [illegible] than one which the English mind could readily or easily grasp. He would [illegible] that the English [illegible] Members [illegible] the hon. Gentleman the Secretary to the Treasury, [illegible] for their [illegible] rate of [illegible] [illegible] the [illegible] there was one question [illegible] which the English and Scotch Members would [illegible] under [illegible] as well as those who represented the Irish [illegible] and that was the question of [illegible]. He would [illegible] some [illegible] years ago to inquire into the Civil Service of Ireland generally, and they had presented a Report [illegible] that the [illegible] of the civil servants in Ireland should be [illegible] in England [illegible] of [illegible] House of Commons [illegible] that [illegible] of [illegible] in Ireland [illegible] [illegible] classes of civil servants in Ireland he supposed there was no class which was so hard worked and highly [illegible] and, at the same time, [illegible] paid, [illegible] Inspectors of National Schools, and he would ask the attention of the hon. Gentleman the Secretary to the Treasury while he referred to the comparative position of the National Schools in England and those employed in Ireland. In Page [illegible] of the Estimates they would find the details of one Vote, and at Page [illegible] the details of the other. In England, the two senior Inspectors [illegible] at £[illegible] a year, and there were three on the old scale at £700. There were 73 Inspectors at a minimum of £[illegible] which rose by an annual increment of £[illegible] a very substantial advance every third year until it reached a maximum of £[illegible]. There were also [illegible] Inspectors on the old scale whose salaries rose from a [illegible] of £200 to a maximum of £[illegible]. There were 25 Inspectors [illegible] salary of £[illegible] a year [illegible] to a maximum of £[illegible]. The [illegible] Inspectors had been Inspectors' Assistants, after having been [illegible] and they had been appointed [illegible] examination. The [illegible] Inspectors had a minimum salary of £[illegible] [illegible] of £[illegible] [illegible] matter [illegible] to contrast the pay of the Irish Inspectors with that of the English Inspectors. There were in Ireland [illegible] District Inspectors who began with a salary of £[illegible] a year, which rose by an annual increment of £[illegible] and [illegible] £[illegible] to a maximum of £[illegible]. When it was considered that these Inspectors were appointed after a competitive examination the programme of which was [illegible] for [illegible] in the Civil Service [illegible] the same [illegible] as that the qualifications required [illegible] English and Irish Inspectors respectively were [illegible] in proportion to their several salaries. It was [illegible] that [illegible] was [illegible] Irish Inspectors, but [illegible] other [illegible] that none [illegible] of first class [illegible] possessing great bodily strength [illegible] and patience [illegible] their labours. Their duties were a great deal more [illegible] than those of the Inspectors in this country. They had themselves to examine [illegible] for promotion, and classes [illegible] at the [illegible] they were called on to advise the schoolmasters on a hundred different matters, which were dealt with by correspondence with the Education Department of this country, and, upon the whole, it would be very difficult to find a class of public servants on whom so many and such various responsibilities devolved as on this particular class of men employed to inspect the National Schools of Ireland. They began at a minimum salary, which was actually less than that of the English Sub-Inspectors who never passed an examination at all.

MR. MUNDELLA said, surely the hon. Member was misinformed. No Inspector was admitted without a severe examination.

MR. ARTHUR O'CONNOR: But it is only a pass-examination.

MR. MUNDELLA: It is an examination for the Civil Service.

MR. ARTHUR O'CONNOR said, he found he was mistaken, as there was an examination. He should have said they had a pass-examination; but the fact remained that the competition for the post of Inspector in Ireland was very much more stringent than they had to undergo in England, while the English Sub-Inspectors underwent merely a pass-examination. After having acted as schoolmasters they became Assistant Inspectors, and from that position they passed up to Inspectorships. They began at a scale of salary which was £50 higher than that which was given to the District Inspectors in Ireland, where some of the most qualified men who held these appointments went in at a minimum of £250, which was only what was given to a clerk in the upper division of the Civil Service, with an annual increment of £10 a-year up to a maximum salary of £500; whereas, in England, the Sub-Inspectors had a minimum of £300, while in the lowest scale of Inspectors the salary went up to £600 on the old scale and on the new scale to £800 a-year. Considering the qualifications required of these men, the nature of the competition they had to undergo, the duties they were called upon to discharge, and the responsibilities resting upon them, he thought it very unjust towards them that, contrary not only to the Report of the Commission to which he had referred, but contrary also to the Resolution come to by that House on the 4th of July, 1873, the existing scale of remuneration should not have been amended, but should still be maintained. He thought that if ever there was a claim for an increased allowance of pay which was a reasonable one, it was the claim now made on behalf of these Irish Inspectors. They had made application—he did not remember when it was sent in—but it was within his knowledge that they had applied to the Department for an improvement in the terms under which their services were remunerated. He was not aware whether the Government had given any final or favourable reply to that application, neither had he heard any argument which could for a single moment justify the refusal of the claim. He did not know whether the hon. Gentleman the Secretary to the Treasury was prepared to make any statement in regard to this matter; but it was essentially a Treasury question, and if anything had been done or directed, it must necessarily have been reported to him. He hoped, therefore, the hon. Gentleman would be able to give the Committee, not the determination of the Chief Secretary or of the National Education Department, but that which he had come to himself, and he also trusted that the communication he might have to make would be of a satisfactory character.

MR. COURTNEY said, the subject was one he had had under his observation, because it was one of the matters that were referred to the Treasury. He must point out that the comparison the hon. Member had made as between the Inspectors of Schools in England and Ireland, was not quite exact. It was, in fact, inexact in this material circumstance, that more than half, or about half, of the Inspectors of England were in the lowest grade of Inspectors' Assistants. There were 291 Inspectors in England altogether, and of those no fewer than 142 were Inspectors' Assistants, who received salaries of from £150 to £300 per annum.

MR. ARTHUR O'CONNOR said, he had confined his remarks to the Inspectors and Sub-Inspectors.

MR. COURTNEY said, he was aware the hon. Member had confined his remarks to the Inspectors and Sub-Inspectors, and that fact constituted the point of his (Mr. Courtney's) observation. The hon. Member had not considered and compared that part of the organization which related to the large class of Assistants. In England, as he had stated, there were 112 [illegible] Inspectors' Assistants who were doing a lower class of work than the Inspectors and receiving lower salaries, which varied from £[illegible] to £[illegible] a year. Then there were about [illegible] Inspectors and Junior Inspectors running up to the highest grades, the Sub Inspectors receiving salaries of from £[illegible] to £[illegible] a year. Under the scheme of inspection in England there was only a limited number of superior officers and a large number of others occupying inferior positions, while under the system which prevailed in Ireland there was a large number of superior officers and a comparatively limited number of inferior officers, so that what had been done in Ireland had in reality been [illegible] [illegible]

[illegible]

[illegible] KING-HARMAN said [illegible]

[illegible] had amounted to was that, some [illegible] eight pro[illegible] Inspec[illegible] increase the [illegible] Sub Inspectors, but in the [illegible] Inspectors employed in [illegible] were to be compelled to [illegible] salary which was much less [illegible] officers of the same grade in England.

MR. COURTNEY said the pay of an Assistant Inspector in Ireland was not [illegible] that of a Sub Inspector in England.

COLONEL KING-HARMAN said he was speaking of the Assistant Inspectors in England as compared with the Assistant Inspectors in Ireland.

MR. COURTNEY: They are about [illegible]

COLONEL KING-HARMAN said he [illegible] This was [illegible] which he was [illegible] Members [illegible] that [illegible] the House [illegible] to [illegible] Trea[illegible] rather [illegible] and [illegible] re[illegible] of men [illegible] Ireland, [illegible] and, [illegible] to be [illegible] the Trea[illegible] Ireland [illegible] they [illegible] the [illegible] but, [illegible] pay of [illegible] He [illegible] views [illegible] Member for [illegible]

MR. [illegible] said he [illegible] the Trea[illegible] was [illegible] part [illegible] was [illegible] He [illegible] was mistaken in the view he had advanced, probably because of his want of acquaintance with the details of Irish education. It was not fair, in making a comparison between the systems adopted in England and Ireland, to compare the Sub-Inspectors of England with the District Inspectors in Ireland. However much the hon. Gentleman might attempt, by the repetition of certain figures, to obfuscate the minds of hon. Members, the fact remained that the Inspectors of the highest class went up to £900 in England, while the District Inspectors in Ireland did not go up to two-thirds of that sum. In Ireland the highest salary paid to the District Inspectors was £500, while the Inspectors' Assistants in that country received £125 as compared with £150, which was the salary of the Assistant Inspectors in England; while in England they went up to £300, and in Ireland to £200. It was true that the proportion of Assistants was much smaller in Ireland than in England; and what was the consequence? Why, that whereas in England every Inspector received substantial assistance from an Assistant Inspector, in Ireland the Inspectors had only a few days in each year in which they obtained any assistance. Again, in the matter of leave, in England the Inspectors had 42 days' holiday, while the Irish Inspectors had only 29, so that the English officers had 13 days more leave than was accorded to the Irish Inspectors. As a rule, also, he found that the Irish Inspector was a better qualified man than the English Inspector. In Ireland the Inspector had more duties to perform, duties of a more varied character and of greater responsibility than those discharged by the English Inspector. Under these circumstances, it was monstrous that the pay of the Irish Inspector should be only a little more than half the salary given to the English Inspector. The large number of Sub-Inspectors in England increased the advantages of the English Inspectors, while the small number in Ireland operated to the disadvantage of the Irish Inspectors. He hoped the hon. Gentleman the Secretary to the Treasury would look more closely at the figures given in the two sets of Estimates, in which case he might be induced to admit, as the House of Commons had admitted 11 years ago, that, considering the competition which was required in the case of the Irish Inspectorships, the officials in that country were greatly underpaid as compared with the Staff in England.

MR. DICK-PEDDIE said, there could be no doubt as to the superior organization of the Inspection Staff in England and Scotland to that in Ireland. Yet, on examining the Estimates, the Committee would find that the Inspection Department cost more in Ireland in proportion to population than it did in England or Scotland. In England the amount expended was £115,000; in Scotland it was £21,400; in Ireland it was £29,000. If there were a number of underpaid officials in Ireland, it was because there were too many persons employed in the work of inspection. The proper remedy for the present state of things was to make the organization of the Staff in Ireland similar to what it was in England and Scotland. The question, as it appeared to him, was one of readjustment, and not of amount of salaries.

MR. KENNY said, the hon. Gentleman the Secretary to the Treasury had instituted a comparison that was very unfair. He had said that if England had 140 Inspectors and Ireland 66, Ireland had too many. He (Mr. Kenny) was of opinion that the fair course would be to point out that England had 280 Inspectors and Assistant Inspectors, and Ireland only 73 Inspectors and Assistant Inspectors, which gave something like a fair relative proportion. It was perfectly clear, however, that the Inspectors in Ireland were paid a sum considerably less than was paid in England. They knew that the maximum salary to which an Irish Inspector could attain was £600 a-year, while in England an Inspector could rise to a position in which his salary was £900 a-year. No wholesale comparison between England and Ireland would get over this fact, or make it appear that the Irish Inspectors were as well paid as those of England. There was one point on which he should like to hear an answer from the Secretary to the Treasury, and if it should not come within the province of the hon. Gentleman, he hoped it would be answered by some other Member of the Government whose Department it did refer to. He wished to ask whether the Inspectors and Assistant Inspectors in England were compelled to devote their whole time from year's end to year's end to the duties of their offices, or were they allowed to do anything else?

MR. MUNDELLA said, they were compelled to devote the whole of their time to their duties.

MR. KENNY: To devote the whole of their time?

MR. MUNDELLA: Yes.

Vote *agreed to.*

(3.) £1,195, to complete the sum for the Teachers' Pension Office, Ireland.

MR. ARTHUR O'CONNOR said, this was a purely Irish Vote, and dealt with the pensions of Irish schoolmasters; but the Superintendent of the Office was an Englishman. He should be sorry to move a reduction of the Vote, because that gentleman happened to be a personal friend of his own; but he thought it was a very bad system that a purely Irish Vote should be given in charge to a subordinate official in one of the English Public Departments, which had nothing whatever to do with education, except that there was a certain amount, £200 a-year, to Mr. Denham Robinson, the Controller of the War Office, who went over for one or two days to see how things were going on in the Superannuation Office.

MR. COURTNEY said, it was true that Mr. Denham Robinson was the Superintendent referred to, but he had nothing to do with the working of the Office. He was the Actuary of the War Office, and had to revise the Tables under which the scheme was arranged, and from time to time to supervise its working, and see whether the scheme was carrying out financially that for which it was designed.

MR. ARTHUR O'CONNOR: But why should an Englishman stationed in England have to do that?

MR. COURTNEY said, it was an economical arrangement by which the Government employed for the duty required to be done—which did not demand an Actuary's whole time—an official who was devoted to similar work under Government employ.

MR. ARTHUR O'CONNOR asked whether the hon. Gentleman the Secretary to the Treasury was aware that Mr. Denham Robinson's work was more than enough to take up the whole of his time, and that he was allowed extra pay and allowances?

MR. GRAY said, it would be obvious to the Committee that this appointment had the appearance of making a snug berth for Mr. Denham Robinson, who was a War Office official. It was only part of an entire system.

MR. ILLINGWORTH said, this was not an Irish Vote.

Vote *agreed to.*

(4.) £1,250, to complete the sum for the Royal Irish Academy.

CLASS VI.—NON-EFFECTIVE AND CHARITABLE SERVICES.

(5.) Motion made, and Question proposed,

"That a sum, not exceeding £206,929, be granted to Her Majesty, to complete the sum necessary to defray the Charge which will come in course of payment during the year ending on the 31st day of March 1885, for Superannuation and Retired Allowances to Persons formerly employed in the Public Service, and for Compassionate or other Special Allowances and Gratuities awarded by the Commissioners of Her Majesty's Treasury."

MR. ARTHUR O'CONNOR asked the hon. Gentleman the Secretary to the Treasury if this was the Vote which included the allowance for the superannuation of a person of the name of Connellan?

MR. COURTNEY: Yes, Sir.

MR. ARTHUR O'CONNOR asked the amount that was given to Connellan under the Vote?

MR. COURTNEY: £450.

MR. ARTHUR O'CONNOR asked if the hon. Gentleman was aware of the nature of the charges which had been made against this recipient of a Government pension, and whether, in the face of those charges, he still held that this Vote should be passed by the Committee in its integrity without any discussion? Was the hon. Gentleman aware that Connellan had escaped prosecution by removing himself into a foreign country? And, further, he would ask whether the Government had ever had under its consideration the position of this man, and his claim to a pension?

MR. COURTNEY said, it was perfectly true that the pension in question was included in this Vote. That pension had been awarded in 1868. Of course, the hon. Member was aware that, under the Superannuation Act, Civil servants in a certain position were entitled to pensions after attaining a certain age.

In the year 1868 this person was retired at a certain age—that was to say, at the age at which a person had a right to retire. Papers were sent in to the Treasury, which papers being in the required order, a pension was awarded. The circumstances dated so far back that he had no personal cognizance of the steps that were taken at the time; but he believed it was quite true that when Connellan retired, there were accusations of infamous conduct against him. He believed, also, that the matter had been so far inquired into as to ascertain that no warrant was issued against Connellan in England. He was. therefore, a person who, having served his time in the Civil Service, was entitled on that ground to a pension; and however grave might have been his conduct, whatever foundation there might have been for the charges against him, it must be remembered that there had been no warrant against him or conviction for felony, and, therefore, he (Mr. Courtney) apprehended that he had at the time an indefeasible right to a pension, and that it remained indefeasible to that day.

MR. ARTHUR O'CONNOR asked on what Statutes or otherwise the claim was founded?

MR. COURTNEY said, he had already referred to the Superannuation Act, and he believed the right and just view of the law to be, that conviction for felony would have forfeited the pension, and that there having been no conviction for felony the pension could not be taken away. The conclusion he had arrived at was that the Treasury would be liable to an action at law if payment were refused. Of course, if the House of Commons refused to vote the pension, it might be pleaded in defence of such action that Parliament had not placed any money at their disposal for the payment of the amount claimed; but he was not prepared to say whether a Court of Law would hold the plea to be valid. On these simple grounds the Government thought it right to submit a Vote to the House of Commons to meet this expense. They did not see their way to withdraw the pension which was awarded in 1868, which had been regularly paid from that time to the present, and which, there being no conviction for felony against this person, they believed was due as a right now. That was the view he ventured to lay before the Committee. The Committee would exercise their discretion in judging the matter; but in point of law he believed there was no answer to the claim. Whatever course might commend itself to him were he a private Member of that House, he found it impossible, as a Member of the Government, to withdraw the Vote from the Estimate.

MR. HEALY said, he inferred, from the manner in which the hon. Gentleman had answered the questions of the hon. Member for Queen's County (Mr. A. O'Connor) on the subject of Connellan's pension, and from the fact that he had given more information than he usually afforded the House, that the hon. Gentleman had consulted with his Colleagues, who had more experience than he possessed, with reference to this Vote. He inferred also that the hon. Gentleman had received information as to the verdicts which had just been given in Ireland, for he ventured to say that if those verdicts had not been returned, the Committee would have been told that Connellan was one of the most righteous persons in Great Britain, and that it was a shame and a scandal that such charges should be made against him. But he was quite sure, notwithstanding the position which the Government had taken up, that the hon. Gentleman knew a great deal more about Connellan than he had told the Committee. Although, perhaps, he had not gone back to the whole history of the case, having no desire to do so, he knew the facts of the case, and that the facts were as disgraceful as they could possibly be. Lord Carlisle, at the time Lord Lieutenant of Ireland, was the man responsible for all that had taken place. The Government knew that.

MR. COURTNEY: Lord Carlisle was not Lord Lieutenant of Ireland.

MR. HEALY said, that it was his influence which settled the matter. That, at any rate, was the statement made on the subject. [Mr. COURTNEY: No.] Would the Government, then, inform the Committee on what ground Connellan obtained his pension? It appeared that at the time Connellan was stopping at a country house in Devonshire, that he there committed this disgraceful offence, and that the question was submitted to the Government of the day; it was also laid before a jury of honour, or a Court of Honour, which decided—that was to say, the noble Lord he had referred to decided for this jury or Court—that Cornellan would have to resign his official position and leave the country. It was then, and under these circumstances that this pension had been put held up for Cornellan; and because he said that if he were prosecuted and did not get a pension, he would implicate many more persons than himself. It was said that the man Cornwall, now in Kilmainham Gaol, was one of the persons who would have been implicated. This was the case of a man who had been charged with the commission of a gross offence; who, upon that charge being inquired into, was obliged to give up his situation in the Civil Service and to leave the country, who, nevertheless, had been placed on a pension of £400 by the Government of the day, and which successive Governments had continued to him, year after year. Supposing the charge had been one of murder, he asked, would the Government, in the case of a man so accused, who had left the country so quickly that a warrant could not be executed against him, have given him a pension? [illegible]

Were not English Members as much interested in knowing what was proper [illegible] Irish Members? They knew [illegible] Cornellan belonged to; they knew [illegible] the Secretary to the Treasury [illegible] Members [illegible] walk into the Lobby and support the Government in giving a pension [illegible] The hon. Member for Northampton (Mr. Labouchere) [illegible] knew all the circumstances surrounding the dismissal of Cornellan [illegible] that he was getting a large pension from the State, and he would very much like to know whether [illegible] sat on Sundays; but what might be expected from them when it came out that they had voted £450 a-year as a pension to this man? He appealed to Her Majesty's Government not to allow their name to be tarnished by putting upon the Estimates a charge of this kind, and to the supporters of Her Majesty's Government not to go into the Lobby to vote it.

MR. LABOUCHERE said, the result of the inquiry into the charge against this person was that he was invited to give up his official position, and to take his name off the books of the Clubs of which he was a member, with the knowledge that if he did not do so he would take the consequences. He practically admitted the allegation by taking his name off the Club books, and by giving up his official position. He (Mr. Labouchere) believed he went to America. He thought the Government might have acted in the same manner with regard to the pension. Supposing they were not to pay the pension. If they said—"We shall not pay you; we shall do precisely as those gentlemen did who investigated the matter; and if you like to bring an action you will take the consequences, but we shall not on our parts take action against you," he was quite satisfied that would end the matter. But the Government had not done so, and now the Committee was again asked to vote this pension. He believed that if hon. Members had been aware of what they were voting in former years, the Vote would not have been now on the Estimates. His view of the case was that, law or no law, the man ought not to have the pension. The Secretary to the Treasury had spoken of Connellan as a poor pensioner, 77 years of age, who would not live long, and who ought to have the pension as a provision for his old age. In his (Mr. Labouchere's) opinion, that was not exactly the provision that should be made for him—he thought it ought to be something in connection with one of the gaols. But as the pension had now come before the Committee, and as they had to vote on the question, he should divide, on his judgment, against Connellan having one penny of the money.

MR. COURTNEY said, the hon. Member for Monaghan (Mr. Healy) had referred, in the course of his speech, to Lord Carlisle. Since the hon. Member spoke he had made inquiries, and found that Lord Carlisle died in 1864, the pension in question having been awarded in 1868. Now, the hon. Member had also spoken of scrutinizing hon. Members who went into the Lobby to support this pension. He (Mr. Courtney) had put the matter before the Committee as a matter of law and justice, and he conceived, having regard to the principles of law and justice, that Her Majesty's Government would be entirely unworthy of their position, if they were then for the first time, upon no record, upon no conviction, and upon no warrant issued, to refuse the pension. The hon. Member, as he had pointed out, had directed some observations to hon. Members who should vote for the Motion before the Committee. He (Mr. Courtney) said, for himself, that if he were an independent Member of the House he should be ashamed of himself if he were to shrink from voting the pension because the hon. Member for Monaghan was going to intimidate him.

MR. HEALY said, he was not going to intimidate anybody. All the remarks made in that House, he presumed, were addressed to the intelligence of hon. Members, and he trusted no one would be led away by the remarks of the Secretary to the Treasury. He thought, in a matter of this kind, that argument alone should be used, and seeing opposite an hon. Member who was a very faithful supporter of the Government, he would put the case to him. The hon. Member knew that a Vote was going to be put to the Committee which involved a pension to a man accused of an unnatural offence, and he knew that it had never been found out till that evening that this pension was on the Books of the House. He (Mr. Healy) would put it to that Christian Gentleman the hon. Member for Donegal (Dr. Kinnear) to say with what face he could go before his constituents and before the Synod of which he was a member, and admit that he had voted for the pension of this offender being paid by the British taxpayer? He maintained that on this question Members must act on their own individual responsibility. On ordinary questions he would say that the Government were responsible; but in this matter the consciences of private Members were concerned. The Government had more information on this subject than was in possession of the Committee; but now, at all events, they had the fact that Corry Connellan was a man of the [illegible], and that he was getting a pension of £[illegible] a year. The Secretary to the Treasury said there was no warrant against him. But whose fault was that? The Government of the time, and successive Governments, had hushed up the case because of [illegible] aristocratic relations, things of that kind [illegible] but it was little thought that this Corry Connellan on the Estimates was the [illegible] about which there was this old scandal. He hoped the appeal he made would be regarded favourably by hon. Members who were staunch supporters of the Government. The Secretary to the Treasury himself had [illegible] and he would put it to hon. Members and even to the Christian Divine who represented [illegible] that if the pension were refused by the House of Commons the Treasury would have a complete answer [illegible] Mr. [illegible] admitted that it would [illegible].

THE CHAIRMAN: [illegible] hon. Member [illegible] with regard to [illegible] Member [illegible] Order.

MR. HEALY: I apologise at [illegible].

THE CHAIRMAN: The remarks of the hon. Member are characterised by a [illegible] employed here. He has [illegible] hon. Member for [illegible] Christian Divine [illegible].

MR. HEALY said he would withdraw [illegible] Christian [illegible]. He [illegible] was [illegible] House refused to [illegible] was [illegible] Member [illegible] was a [illegible] Government [illegible] Secretary to the Treasury said [illegible] was [illegible] of £[illegible] Secretary to the Treasury [illegible] future years [illegible] the name of Mr. Connellan on the Estimates, as had usually been done [illegible] this year.

MR. [illegible] and [illegible] pressed, [illegible] Mr. [illegible] Her Majesty [illegible].

MR. ARTHUR O'CONNOR said, that with regard to the [illegible] of the Secretary to the Treasury as to the [illegible] Statute, of this [illegible] Pension List, [illegible] of the Act [illegible] That Act was [illegible] the Superannuation Act [illegible] Pay.

[illegible]

There [illegible] the right of either [illegible] Connellan, or any other person, [illegible] a pension for past services.

MR. COURTNEY said [illegible] under the present Act.

MR. ARTHUR O'CONNOR repeated that the Superannuation Act [illegible] was [illegible] Act [illegible] the [illegible] and [illegible] that [illegible] right to [illegible] past services. [illegible] of the Secretary to the Treasury would not [illegible] But [illegible] Secretary to the Treasury was wrong. The hon. Gentleman [illegible] had been [illegible] to draw his pension [illegible] Act [illegible] the Superannuation [illegible] that [illegible] Secretary to the Treasury [illegible] that [illegible] a man was [illegible] the [illegible] pension. Now, he would put it to the Committee whether, if a man was charged with committing treason and fled the country, he would still have a right, under this pretended statutory enactment, to continue to draw his pension? It was perfectly obvious that he would not, and the Treasury would not think of continuing the pension. But there was another point. How was it that if a Civil servant went on to the Pension List, and wished to draw his pension abroad, he had so much difficulty in obtaining permission to have his pension paid to him outside this country? And how was it that this infamous fellow, who was pensioned in 1868, was allowed to go all over the world, the Government not caring where he was, and was allowed to draw his pension through a Dublin bank, he supposed by power of attorney? This man was now in the United Kingdom, and ought to be proceeded against, and nobody knew that better than the occupants of the Treasury Bench. If not, then there was in this case some new departure as to the rule which obtained in this country as to issuing pensions abroad. Why was there this difference between the case of an ordinary Civil servant pensioned in England, and the case of this man? Had the Government, put as it were on the defensive, set their backs against the wall, and declared that, no matter what the charge against this man was, they would continue to defend him as they continued to defend wretches like French? It looked very much like it. He would appeal, then, to independent Members. This man, Corry Connellan, was charged with having committed a detestable offence, which made him utterly unfit to mix in any community of civilized beings; but he was retained on the Pension List, and the Government insisted on maintaining not only that it was equitable, but that he had a statutory right to remain on the Pension List. But they had not produced a single proof or legal argument in support of that contention, and on the strength of the Act 4 & 5 *Will.* IV. he challenged that contention, and would like to hear his argument answered. He trusted that in 24 hours the names of all who voted in the Division would be published throughout the country, so that the public might know who were prepared to support the Government in their proposal to retain this man on the Pension List, infamous as this man was. There was no hiding the character of the Division. Irish Members did not object to anything else in this enormous Vote; but they held that the retention of this man on the Pension List was an outrage on public opinion in Ireland, because when he left Ireland it was supposed that he did not go on the Pension List, but that he received some assistance from the Secret Service Fund, and nobody would have thought that the Government would have the audacity to put him on the Pension List. As an ex-Civil servant, and not because he was a Member of that House, he felt wounded and outraged by the retention of such an infamous character as this man on the Pension List under all the circumstances.

MR. SYDNEY BUXTON said, he could easily understand the impossibility of the Government on their own initiative withdrawing this Vote from the cognizance of the House, and thereby judging the matter for themselves; but the Committee would have no such difficulty in the matter. There seemed to be no question that there were suspicious circumstances in connection with this case. That was not denied; and there also appeared to be no doubt that if this man had not left the country, a warrant would have been issued against him. Under these circumstances, although this alleged offence occurred 16 years ago, and this was the first time it had really been raised in the Committee of the House of Commons, he could not see that there was any reason why the Committee should not discuss the case, and, if they chose, refuse to grant this Vote. Certainly, the fact of its occurring so long ago was no reason for not doing so. It seemed to him that they would be doing no injustice if they refused the Vote. If they granted it, then, without question, Mr. Connellan would draw his pension, and the House of Commons would practically have declared that he was an innocent man; but if they refused the Vote, then, if Mr. Connellan applied for his pension and proved his innocence, there was no question that he would be in the right, and would be able legally to obtain his pension. That the Secretary to the Treasury had already told them; but, on the other hand, if Mr. Connellan was a guilty man, as was alleged, he would not dare to apply for this pension, and the House of Commons would have done its duty in the case. Therefore, in spite of the taunts which the Secretary to the Treasury levelled at those who were going to vote against this pension, he should support the Amendment.

MR. WARTON said, he should be sorry that a single Member's vote should be influenced by taunts from either side of the House, but certainly there had been taunts, and two hon. Members had threatened to take notice of the names of Members who voted in support of the Government. He, at all events, was not to be deterred by taunts; and looking at the matter in a cool, quiet, lawyer-like way, with no emotion or prepossession, he felt it his duty to support this Vote, and on these grounds. In the first place, he did not think the hon. Member for Queen's County (Mr. A. O'Connor) was correct in the interpretation he had put upon the 30th section of the Act 4 & 5 *Will.* IV. He was sure the hon. Member would not quote an Act unfairly; but the hon. Member seemed to think the words of that section implied that no Civil servant was entitled to claim a pension absolutely. Now, that Proviso seemed to him to refer to an original claim for a pension, and to the question whether or not the person's past services warranted, or even appeared to warrant, the granting of a pension at the time. An adverse decision might give the Government a right to refuse a pension; but, whichever way it was decided, the question was then settled once and for all, and the quarterly or annual payments would follow, as a matter of course, on the granting of the pension. As the hon. Member opposite (Mr. S. Buxton) had said, the Committee were now about to declare the guilt or innocence of this man; but, in his opinion, they had nothing to do with either. All they knew was that a certain charge had been made against him; but there was no legal proof that the charge was well-founded; there was no record of a conviction; and, therefore, that was a sufficient answer to the other legal point that a man convicted of felony should lose his pension. Both these legal points fell to the ground; and, therefore, he should be inclined to support the Vote on that ground, and because he could not see that it was the duty of Her Majesty's Government to do anything but stand by this Vote, as they were bound to do, in the usual way.

MR. KENNY asked whether the Secretary to the Treasury could tell the Committee at what period Mr. Connellan fled from Ireland, and what time elapsed between his leaving Ireland to avoid prosecution, and the date when his pension was first made payable to him, because he apprehended that that point might affect the interpretation of the 30th section of the Act 4 & 5 *Will.* IV.?

MR. COURTNEY replied, that the facts were rather difficult to get at; but Mr. Connellan resigned his office in September, 1868, and the pension was granted to him almost immediately afterwards.

MR. HEALY asked why, as the Government had stated that this man was living in the East End of London, he could not receive his money in the ordinary way? Why should the Government take more trouble to see that this man got his pension than they would with regard to any decent man in this country? He was able to get his pension in Australia, or at the Cape of Good Hope, through the machinery of a bank in Dublin into which the Treasury paid it. It was now said that he had turned up in some of his old haunts in London; why, then, could he not get his money in the usual way?

MR. PARNELL said, he thought a pension should be paid to the pensioner personally, for it seemed to him that the Statute did not require that a pension should be paid through a bank, but only required that it should be paid to the person entitled to receive it. Why, then, he would like to know, did the Government not put a literal interpretation on the Statute, and require this man, if he desired to have his pension, to come to the Office for it, and prove his identity? In that way they would be able to see whether Mr. Connellan was or was not so far conscious of his guilt as to be afraid of placing himself within the power of a warrant. It seemed to him that the Government had had ample time to inquire into this matter; and that in order to save the Committee from its present dilemma they ought to have adopted some policy with regard to it. He should be glad to know what further steps the Government intended to take in this matter in the event of his view being correct, that they were bound by Statute to pay a pension personally to the person entitled to receive it? It was manifest that the matter could not be allowed to rest where it now was. Some investigation must be made. Did the Government propose to wait, as they did in the case of French and others, until legal proofs were produced in the Courts of Law as to the guilt of this man; or did they propose to enter into any investigation of the subject? He thought that was a reasonable request, and one upon which the Committee would be disposed to insist, that this matter should be inquired into by the Government, with a view to further action, if it should be found that the allegations made that night, and on other nights, were true. These allegations had not now been made for the first time; but they had never been denied. They were notorious in Ireland, and some action must follow with respect to them on the part of the officials of the Government, who were responsible in such matters. It would be utterly impossible for Parliament to continue to vote a pension to this man under the circumstances which had come out until his character had been cleared. It was not denied that these charges were made against him—that he fled the country under the circumstances which had been related; that he had never come back, and during these 16 years had never appeared in Ireland—where he had always lived up to that time—and had never been heard of by any people who knew him in Ireland. Under all the circumstances, and pending an inquiry, he really did think the Government ought not to ask the Committee to vote this sum of money; and that, without deciding the question whether they would ultimately pay the pension or not, they should withdraw this money from this Vote, and suspend the payment of the pension until they had had time—if they had not already had abundant time—to ascertain their legal position, and the rights of the case.

THE CHANCELLOR OF THE EXCHEQUER (Mr. CHILDERS): This is a question which no man in the House would wish to enter into very fully; but, at the same time, I think that when a matter of this kind has been challenged, it is important to state clearly how in point of law and of right the case stands. If I am rightly informed, the matter stands in this way. In the year 1868 the Government of that day granted a pension, or a superannuation allowance, to an officer in the Irish Civil Service; and at that time, it would appear, from what we have heard to-night, that there then were afloat certain reports, which seemed to have some authority, that that person had been guilty of an abominable offence. That offence, if it was committed, was committed before the pension was granted. The pension was awarded late in the year 1868. I can only assume that those who awarded the pension had no knowledge of these charges; but the pension was so awarded. The hon. Member for Queen's County (Mr. A. O'Connor) says the impression at the time in Ireland was that this person had not received a pension, but had received assistance from the Secret Service Fund. Of this impression I know nothing; but the person referred to did receive a pension, and it was annually paid to him. From the time when it was granted, and every year since, the pension has appeared on the Estimates not only in the lump with other pensions, but as a pension to this person individually. Therefore, so far from the case being that he received Secret Service money, he has been, as everyone who cares to look at the Estimates will see, on the Pension List for some 15 or more years. That being the case, I ask what has happened with respect to this person since the time of the pension being awarded? I am told nothing whatever has happened. There has been no charge made against him, and no warrant has been issued against him; and he stands at this moment, so far as legal proceedings are concerned, innocent of the offence which rumour—and perhaps more than rumour—charged him with. He has been subject to no warrant and to no charge; but there were rumours before he received his pension, and those rumours have lately been revived. The question then arises whether, he being subject to no charge at the present time, his pension is to be stopped; and a clause of an old Act has been quoted, which, I am bound to say, never was understood to have—and, indeed, could not have—the meaning now assigned to it. It merely says that no one shall claim, as a legal right, a superannuation allowance for past services; but that clause embodies a well-known rule, that a pension is an act of grace and not of right. But that has nothing whatever to do with the stoppage of a pension which has already been awarded. That being the position of this person's pension now, that pension is called in question for the first time after the lapse of 16 years. What is the position, and what is the right, of the Government and of Parliament now? It has been suggested whether, inasmuch as this person does not apparently receive his pension *in propria persona*, through a practice which prevails in regard to pensions, but receives it through an agent, complying with the regulations laid down, we are bound to continue to pay this pension through that agency, and whether, under the circumstances, we should require this person to appear at a Government Office, where pensions are paid, to receive the pension in person. As to that, I am bound to say that the Government will consider the point, and the question will be this—whether there is a right—I do not mean a strict legal right, but a right of long-established custom—in the pensioner to receive his pension through some other person, as his agent, or whether it is a matter of mere favour that he so receives it; and, if it is a matter of favour, whether, in a case like this, that favour should be withdrawn, and the pensioner should be required to come and receive the pension in person. For my part, I believe that the Government would do well to make inquiry upon this point, for we are not in a position, at this moment, to say whether this is a matter of favour or not. If, after due inquiry on the part of the Government, it should turn out to be a matter of mere favour, and not of official right or custom, and if it should turn out that this person was not a man to whom any favour should be granted, the favour might be withdrawn. That, however, could not be done without inquiry. If it were only a favour, the Government would certainly feel justified in withdrawing it if it were not deserved.

MR. HEALY said, the offer of the right hon. Gentleman, made on the spur of the moment, presented some points for consideration. On the Report he would again refer to this subject, and ask the Government what they proposed to do. He would now ask whether, if it were decided that Connellan should receive his pension in person, the Scotland Yard Detective Office would be informed of the exact date of the payment, so that steps might be taken to secure the arrest of the man? If a detective officer were at the bank when Mr. Connellan came to receive his pension, the taxpayers would be saved £136 a-year.

THE CHANCELLOR OF THE EXCHEQUER (Mr. CHILDERS): It is absolutely out of my power to answer this question. As to what legal proceedings, if any, might or would be taken, I have no knowledge whatever. I only speak for the Treasury as to this question of favour or of right. If Mr. Connellan receives his pension through an agent as a favour, the favour might, after inquiry, be withdrawn.

MR. PARNELL: I would ask the hon. and learned Gentleman the Solicitor General for Ireland whether he does not think it right, after this debate, to ask the Chief Secretary to direct the Chief of the Detective Department to look into this charge against Mr. Connellan? If I am not mistaken, ample evidence can be obtained at any moment as to the commission of these offences by Connellan some years ago.

THE SOLICITOR GENERAL FOR IRELAND (Mr. WALKER): As I understand the matter, this was an offence committed in England; therefore, the Irish Officials are relieved from responsibility.

MR. HEALY: Are the English Law Officers relieved?

THE SOLICITOR GENERAL FOR IRELAND (Mr. WALKER): I only answered the question put to me.

MR. HEALY: I would take the liberty of asking the same question of the English Law Officers.

Question put, and *negatived*.

Original Question put, and *agreed to*.

(6.) £11,000, to complete the sum for Merchant Seamen's Fund Pensions, &c.

(7.) £461,000, for Pauper Lunatics, England.

(8.) £62,000, to complete the sum for Pauper Lunatics, Scotland.

(9.) £14,500, to complete the sum for Pauper Lunatics, Ireland.

MR. ARTHUR O'CONNOR said, he wished to ask the Government whether, during the Recess, they would cause some inquiry to be made into the subject of the classification of lunatics in workhouses in Ireland? The condition of the imbeciles in Irish workhouses was an absolute disgrace to anything calling itself a civilized Administration. The poor creatures were absolutely without anything like proper guardianship, and the places in which they were confined were not fit for the occupation of human beings. In wet weather the ground was often moist. The rooms were not properly lighted. Moreover, children of from two to six years of age were allowed to play about amongst the imbecile women. The places in which these people were kept, and the manner in which they were treated, was absolutely horrible. Would any Member of the Government say that the matter should have attention?

MR. COURTNEY said, the question had been raised on the Vote for the Irish Local Government Board, and the Chief Secretary had then promised to give it consideration.

Vote *agreed to.*

(10.) £12,747, to complete the sum for Hospitals and Infirmaries, Ireland.

MR. HEALY said, he did not wish to make a charge against any of the Institutions covered by this Vote; but he wished to say that he had heard it stated that the accommodation in the Rotunda Lying-in Hospital, for which £700 was charged, was scarcely what it should be. Would the Government cause an inquiry to be made—would they ascertain whether it was a fact that the students awaiting their turn were without proper accommodation, and had to occupy the same apartments as the women waiting to be confined? If such were the case, it was a lamentable state of things, and women should not be subjected to treatment of that kind. The place for the students should be quite apart; the students should not be interspersed with the patients in the wards. He did not wish to make the smallest charge against the Charity, which was a famous one. The expenditure of a few pounds would remedy the defect of which he complained.

MR. COURTNEY said, the Government would cause the matter to be inquired into.

Vote *agreed to.*

(11.) £48,115, for Friendly Societies Deficiency.

(12.) £2,101, to complete the sum for Miscellaneous Charitable and other Allowances, Great Britain.

(13.) Motion made, and Question proposed,

"That a sum, not exceeding £2,648, be granted to Her Majesty, to complete the sum necessary to defray the Charge which will come in course of payment during the year ending on the 31st day of March 1885, for certain Miscellaneous Charitable and other Allowances in Ireland."

MR. HEALY asked whether the Government would give the Committee some explanation of the following item :—

"F. French Church, Portarlington: Stipend of the Rev. J. R. Triphook, Minister of St. Paul's, otherwise called the French Church, Portarlington; a charge transferred from the Consolidated Fund. (This charge will cease on next vacancy), £43 18*s.* 4*d.*?"

MR. ARTHUR O'CONNOR said, that on this point the late Lord Frederick Cavendish had promised to make arrangements for discontinuing the item on the death of the present incumbent. He (Mr. A. O'Connor) saw an asterisk in the Vote calling attention to the footnote—

"The charges included in these Sub-heads are in course of gradual diminution."

MR. HEALY wished to know the meaning of the item? There was a French Foundation at Portarlington, where, 200 years ago, there had been a Colony of Huguenots. For what reason was this money voted for this French Church?

MR. COURTNEY said, that this Church was founded by an Act of the Irish Parliament in the 41st year of King George III.—just before the Union.

MR. HEALY said, it was most absurd to give a man nearly £44 a-year, because, 200 years ago, a number of Huguenots came over to Ireland from France. In that part of Ireland, French names were frequently met with. it was true; but there was no reason why a French Church should be maintained at the cost of the State. There might be a number of Greek names there, and, if there were, would the State keep up a Church for them? He begged to move the reduction of the Vote by £44.

Motion made, and Question proposed,

"That a sum, not exceeding £2,604, be granted to Her Majesty, to complete the sum necessary to defray the Charge which will come in course of payment during the year ending on the 31st day of March 1885, for certain Miscellaneous Charitable and other Allowances in Ireland."—(*Mr. Healy.*)

Mr. COURTNEY said, he hoped the hon. Member would not think it necessary to press this Motion. They were getting rid of these Votes one by one. In the case of Great Britain, a Vote of this kind had ceased quite recently, and would never appear in the Estimates again. The gentleman in receipt of the salary at Portarlington was a very old man, and when he died there would not be a successor appointed. The present incumbent had been receiving the salary for a long time, and it would be exceedingly hard to stop it now. The charge was not likely to continue very long.

Mr. GRAY agreed that it would be hard to refuse to vote this sum to the rev. gentleman who had been receiving it for so long. Would it not, however, be better, in cases of this kind, instead of waiting for the gradual dropping off of Votes, which it was acknowledged could not be defended in principle, to estimate the value of the life interest, and give it as compensation to the recipient of the income? As the hon. Gentleman the Member for Queen's County (Mr. A. O'Connor) had had an understanding on this subject with the late Lord Frederick Cavendish, he (Mr. Gray) would appeal to the hon. Member for Monaghan not to go to a Division. They might, he thought, be content with the assurance that the arrangement come to with the late noble Lord would be carried out.

Motion, by leave, *withdrawn.*

Mr. DEASY said, he should like to ask a question as to the last item but one—to defray the expense of maintain ing 12 lunatics and idiots formerly supported in the Hardwicke cells of the House of Industry. How were idiots generally paid for and maintained in Ireland?

Mr. COURTNEY said, this item was in respect of idiots who had been sent into the country to escape an epidemic disease. There was a great reduction in the item.

Mr. HEALY said, there was a great deal of money wasted under this Vote and other Votes in Ireland. When these useless Votes dropped out one by one, would it not be as well to devote the money so saved to useful purposes, such as the construction and maintenance of fishery piers?

Original Question put, and *agreed to.*

(14.) £875, for Redemption of Consolidated Fund Allowances.

The CHAIRMAN: Class VII.——

Mr. GRAY: What Class have we arrived at?

The CHAIRMAN: I am now going to put the Votes in Class VII.

Colonel NOLAN: What is their character?

Mr. BIGGAR said, he thought the Committee had not been very stingy to the Government that night, having raised no serious opposition to the Votes in Class VI. It was too hard to ask them now to go on with Class VII., at 10 minutes to 2 in the morning. He would move to report Progress.

Mr. COURTNEY said, there were only two Votes to be taken, and the Committee would find no difficulty in disposing of them.

Class VII.—Miscellaneous.

(15.) £18,776, to complete the sum for Temporary Commissions.

(16.) £4,693, to complete the sum for Miscellaneous Expenses.

The CHAIRMAN: The Question is that I report Progress, and ask leave to sit again.

Mr. ARTHUR O'CONNOR: Before you put that Question, Sir, I should like to ask what was the last Vote but two—we could not catch it in this part of the House at all?

The CHAIRMAN: £875, for Redemption of Consolidated Fund Allowances.

Mr. ARTHUR O'CONNOR: In what Class did that come?

The CHAIRMAN: In Class VI.

Resolutions to be reported *To-morrow.*

Committee to sit again *To-morrow.*

SUPPLY—REPORT.

Resolutions [4th August] *reported.*

First Two Resolutions *agreed to.*

Third Resolution *postponed.*

Fourth and Fifth Resolutions *agreed to.*

Sixth Resolution *postponed.*

Eleven following Resolutions *agreed to.*

"(18.) That a sum, not exceeding £470, be granted to Her Majesty, to complete the sum necessary to defray the Charge which will come in course of payment during the year ending on the 31st day of March 1885, for the Expenses of the Office of the Commissioners of Education in Ireland appointed for the Regulation of Endowed Schools."

MR. ARTHUR O'CONNOR said, this was a Vote which, according to many authorities, was absolutely indefensible. The Commissioners themselves admitted in their Reports that they were unable to discharge this duty—that they had too many other duties to perform, and were not remunerated for this work. They, practically, declined to do it. There were several estates concerned in this matter which the Commissioners complained they had not the means of visiting. The schools were in a state of dilapidation—the Commissioners could not keep them in repair; and in respect of some schools the Commissioners had money which they could not spend. In some cases they had more masters than scholars, and in one place they had a master over 83 years of age. They had no power to combine their resources from different estates, and, from beginning to end, there was not one particle of their administration which could meet with approval or deserved commendation in any way. The Commissioners desired to be relieved of their duties; everything was going to rack and ruin under their hands; their schools were a perfect farce; and a considerable amount of money which, if properly managed, could be turned to great national benefit, was now only an example of how well certain persons knew "how not to do it." Under these circumstances, and considering that the House had to meet again in a few hours, he must urge the Secretary to the Treasury to postpone this Vote. For that purpose, he should move that the debate be adjourned.

MR. COURTNEY agreed to postpone the Vote.

Vote *postponed.*

Subsequent Resolution *agreed to.*

Postponed Resolutions to be taken into Consideration *To-morrow.*

House adjourned at a quarter after Two o'clock.

[INDEX.

LONDON: CORNELIUS BUCK, 22, PATERNOSTER ROW, E.C.

INDEX

TO

HANSARD'S PARLIAMENTARY DEBATES,

VOLUME CCXCI.

EIGHTH VOLUME OF SESSION 1884.

EXPLANATION OF THE ABBREVIATIONS.

In Bills, Read 1°, 2°, 3°, or 1°, 2°, 3°, Read the First, Second, or Third Time.—In Speeches, 1R., 2R., 3R., Speech delivered on the First, Second, or Third Reading.—*Amendt.*, Amendment.—*Res.*, Resolution.—*Comm.*, Committee.—*Re-Comm.*, Re-Committal.—*Rep.*, Report.—*Consid.*, Consideration.—*Adj.*, Adjournment or Adjourned.—*cl.*, Clause.—*add cl.*, Additional Clause.—*neg.*, Negatived.—*M. Q.*, Main Question.—*O. Q.*, Original Question.—*O. M.*, Original Motion.—*P. Q.*, Previous Question.—*R. P.*, Report Progress.—*A.*, Ayes.—*N.*, Noes.—*M.*, Majority.—*1st Div.*, *2nd Div.*, First or Second Division.—*l.*, Lords.—*c.*, Commons.

When in this Index a * is added to the Reading of a Bill, it indicates that no Debate took place upon that stage of the measure.

When in the Text or in the Index a Speech is marked thus *, it indicates that the Speech is reprinted from a Pamphlet or some authorised Report.

When in the Index a † is prefixed to a Name or an Office (the Member having accepted or vacated office during the Session) and to Subjects of Debate thereunder, it indicates that the Speeches on those Subjects were delivered in the speaker's private or official character, as the case may be.

Some subjects of debate have been classified under the following "General Headings:"—ARMY — NAVY — INDIA — IRELAND — SCOTLAND — PARLIAMENT — POOR LAW — POST OFFICE — METROPOLIS — CHURCH OF ENGLAND — EDUCATION — CRIMINAL LAW — LAW AND JUSTICE — TAXATION, under WAYS AND MEANS.

[*cont.*

[*cont.*

[cont.

[*cont.*

[cont.

Great Seal Bill (H. L.)
(*The Lord Chancellor*)
l. Royal Assent *July* 28 [47 & 48 *Vict* c. 30]

***Great Western Railway and Bristol and Portishead Pier and Railway Companies Bill* (*Lords*)**
c. Moved, "That, in the case of the Great Western Railway and Bristol and Portishead Pier and Railway Companies Bill (*Lords*), Standing Orders 211, 236, and 237 be suspended

[*cont.*

[*cont.*

[cont. [cont.

[cont.

[cont.

[cont.

[*cont.*

[cont.

PARLIAMENT—*cont.*
COMMONS—
Committee of Public Accounts—The Secret Service Fund, Questions, Mr. Gray; Answers, Mr. Trevelyan, Sir William Harcourt, Mr. Courtney, Lord Richard Grosvenor *July* 28, 636
Public Bills—Unprinted Bills, Observations, Mr. Warton *Aug* 1, 1412
The House of Lords and the Representation of the People Bill, Notice of Resolution, Mr. Willis; Question, Mr. Newdegate; Answer, Mr. Gladstone *July* 28, 670; Question, Mr. Labouchere; Answer, Mr. Gladstone *July* 29, 872

BUSINESS OF THE HOUSE AND PUBLIC BUSINESS
Royal Courts of Justice Bill, Question, Mr. Whitley; Answer, Mr. Courtney *July* 22, 46;—*Attendance of Ministers*, Question, Lord Eustace Cecil; Answer, Mr. Courtney *July* 25, 492;—*Procedure—House of Lords Bills*, Observations, Mr. Warton; Reply, Mr. Gladstone *July* 25, 522;—*Irish Bills in the House of Lords*, Questions, Mr. Parnell, Mr. O'Donnell; Answers, Mr. Gladstone *July* 28, 663;—*Progress of Public Business*, Question, Lord Randolph Churchill; Answer, Mr. Gladstone *July* 29, 874;—*Burgh Police and Health (Scotland) Bill*, Question, General Sir George Balfour; Answer, The Lord Advocate *July* 31, 1188

PALACE OF WESTMINSTER
House of Commons—Telegraphic News-recording Instrument for Use of Members, Question, Mr. Gray; Answer, Mr. Shaw Lefevre *July* 24, 317
Westminster Hall, Questions, Sir George Campbell, Mr. Cavendish Bentinck, Mr. Mitchell Henry; Answers, Mr. Gladstone, Mr. Shaw Lefevre *Aug* 4, 1578;—*The British Museum*, Question, Mr. Newzam-Nicholson; Answer, Sir John Lubbock *July* 24, 315
Westminster Hall (West Front), Questions, Sir George Campbell, Mr. Dick-Peddie; Answers, Mr. Shaw Lefevre *July* 24, 307; Questions, Mr. Dick-Peddie; Answers, Mr. Shaw Lefevre *July* 31, 1167;—*Site of the Old Law Courts*, Question, Sir George Campbell; Answer, Mr. Gladstone *Aug* 1, 1367

Distribution of the Statutes to Members, Question, Mr. Tomlinson; Answer, Mr. Courtney *July* 31, 1171
Parliamentary Elections—The New Register, Question, Sir Edward Watkin; Answer, Mr. Hibbert *Aug* 5, 1750
"*Remington Perfected Type-Writers*," Question, Mr. Labouchere; Answer, Mr. Shaw Lefevre *July* 31, 1172

Parliament—Business of the House—Committee of Supply—Standing Order 425a
Postponement of Motion, Mr. Gladstone; Questions, Lord Randolph Churchill; Answers, Mr. Gladstone *July* 31, 1188

[*cont.*

Parliament—Business of the House—Committee of Supply—Standing Order 425a—cont.
Moved, "That, for the remainder of the Session, the Standing Order of the 27th of November, 1882, relating to Notices on going into Committee of Supply on Monday and Thursday, be extended to Saturday" (*Mr. Gladstone*) *Aug* 1, 1367; after short debate, Question put; A. 123, N. 23; M. 100 (D. L. 201)

Parliament—Supply — Business of the House
Moved, "That this House will immediately resolve itself into Committee of Supply" (*Mr. Courtney*) *Aug* 2, 1530
After short debate, Amendt. to leave out "immediately," insert "upon Monday next" (*Lord Randolph Churchill*) *v.*; Question proposed, "That 'immediately' &c.;" after further short debate, Question put, and negatived
Question, "That 'upon Monday next' &c." put, and agreed to

Parliament—Standing Orders
Standing Order, No. 1, 2nd Class read *Aug* 1, 1346
Amendt to insert after "street"
"Subway, to be used for the conveyance of passengers, animals, or goods, in carriages, or trucks, drawn or propelled on rails" (*Mr. Holms*); Question proposed, "That those words be there inserted;" after short debate, Question put, and agreed to
Standing Order No. 6 read
Amendt. to add,
"The Notices shall also state what power it is intended to employ for moving carriages or trucks upon the Tramway" (*Mr. Holms*); Question proposed, "That those words be there added;" after short debate, Question put, and agreed to
Remaining Amendts. agreed to
Ordered, That the said Orders be Standing Orders of this House

Parliament — Palace of Westminster—House of Commons—Ventilation of the House
Ordered, That the Committee appointed to inquire into the Ventilation of the House have power to inquire as to the noxious smells which occasionally pervade the House, and into the cause of the same (*Mr. William Henry Smith*) *July* 23
Question, Mr. Thorold Rogers; Answer, Sir William Harcourt *July* 28, 669; Question, Mr. Borlase; Answer, Sir Charles W. Dilke *July* 31, 1188

PARNELL, Mr. C. S., *Cork City*
Ireland—Questions
Magistrates Salaries, 874, 875
Poor Law Guardians, 502
Prevention of Crime Act, 1882—Extra Police, 1364, 1365
Royal Irish Constabulary (Numbers), 870

[*cont.*

[cont.

[cont.

SUPPLY

The Annual Estimates, Question, Sir Alexander Gordon; Answer, Mr. Courtney *Aug* 4, 1868

The Civil Service Estimates—The Foreign Office Vote, Question, Lord Randolph Churchill; Answer, Mr. Gladstone *July* 28, 669

Egypt (Events in the Soudan)—Expedition for Relief of General Gordon—Vote of Credit, Questions, Lord Eustace Cecil, Mr. W. E. Forster, Mr. Labouchere; Answers, The Marquess of Hartington, Lord Edmond Fitzmaurice *July* 24, 320; Questions, Sir Walter B. Barttelot, Mr. Joseph Cowen, Mr. Labouchere, Mr. Ashmead-Bartlett, Sir Stafford Northcote, Mr. Puleston, Mr. Newdegate, Lord Randolph Churchill, Mr. Bourke, Mr. J. Lowther, Mr. W. E. Forster, Mr. W. H. Smith; Answers, Mr. Gladstone, The Chancellor of the Exchequer *Aug* 4, 1584

SUPPLY

Resolutions [July 21] reported *July* 22, 180
Resolutions 1 to 5, inclusive, agreed to
Resolution 6; after short debate, agreed to
Remaining Resolutions agreed to

Considered in Committee *July* 22, 47—Civil Service Estimates—Class II.—Salaries and Expenses of Civil Departments, Votes 37 to 39
Resolutions reported *July* 24, 490
First and Third Resolutions agreed to
Second Resolution postponed

Considered in Committee *July* 23, 199—Civil Service Estimates—Class II.—Salaries and Expenses of Civil Departments, Votes 40 to 42; Class III.—Law and Justice—Votes 1 and 2
Resolutions reported *July* 24

Considered in Committee *July* 24, 343—Civil Service Estimates—Class III.—Law and Justice, Votes 3 to 13
Resolutions reported *July* 25

Considered in Committee *July* 25, 539—Civil Service Estimates—Class III.—Law and Justice, Votes 14 to 19, 21, 23, 25, and 32; Class IV.—Education, Science, and Art, Vote 2
Resolutions reported *July* 28

Considered in Committee *July* 28, 671—Army Estimates, Votes 15 to 25; Navy Estimates, Votes 12 to 17
Resolutions reported *July* 29

Considered in Committee *July* 29, 876—Civil Service Estimates—Class III.—Law and Justice, Votes 24 and 20; Committee—R.P.

Considered in Committee *July* 30, 1050—Civil Service Estimates — Class V.—Foreign and Colonial Services, Vote 7
Resolution reported *July* 31

Considered in Committee *July* 31, 1190—Civil Service Estimates—Class III.—Law and Justice, Votes 20, 22, 24, 26, and 28
Resolutions reported *Aug* 1

Considered in Committee *Aug* 1, 1413—Civil Service Estimates—Class III.—Law and Justice, Votes 27, 30, and 31; Class IV.—Education, Science, and Art, Votes 4 to 7

[*cont.*

Supply—*cont.*

Resolutions reported *Aug* 2, 1539
First and Second Resolutions postponed
Third Resolution agreed to
Fourth Resolution; after debate, agreed to
Subsequent Resolutions agreed to
Postponed Resolutions considered *Aug* 4, 1710; after short debate, agreed to

Considered in Committee *Aug* 2, 1438—Civil Service Estimates—Class III.—Law and Justice, Vote 29
Resolution reported *Aug* 7

Considered in Committee *Aug* 4, 1588—Civil Service Estimates—Class V.—Foreign and Colonial Services, Votes 1 to 6, 8 and 9; Class IV.—Education, Science, and Art, Votes 2, 3, 8 to 13, 13a, 16, and 17
Resolutions reported *Aug* 5, 1890
Third and Sixth Resolutions postponed
Other Thirteen Resolutions agreed to

Considered in Committee *Aug* 5, 1757—Relief of General Gordon (Vote of Credit), £300,000; Civil Service Estimates — Class IV.—Education, Science, and Art, Votes 14, 15, and 19; Class VI.—Non-Effective and Charitable Services, Votes 1 to 9 and 9a; Class VII.—Miscellaneous, Votes 1 and 2
Resolutions reported *Aug* 7

Supreme Court of Judicature Amendment Bill [H.L.]
(*Mr. Herbert Gladstone*)

c. Read 1°* *July* 24 [Bill 307]
Read 2°* *July* 28
Committee—R.P. *July* 29, 1013
Committee; Report *Aug* 1, 1432
Bill re-committed; Committee; Report; Considered; read 3° *Aug* 4, 1714

Supreme Court of Judicature (Chancery Examiners' Office [Compensation]
c. Resolution considered in Committee, and agreed to *Aug* 1, 1436
Resolution reported *Aug* 4

Switzerland—The "Salvationists"
Question, Sir Robert Peel; Answer, Lord Edmond Fitzmaurice *July* 31, 1175

Synan, Mr. E. J., *Limerick Co.*
Ireland—Questions
Law and Justice—Glin Petty Sessions—Case of Daniel M'Coy, 1558
Prevention of Crime Act, 1882—Extra Police at Limerick, 652
Royal Irish Constabulary—Dr. Madigan, Medical Officer, 1560
Supply—Irish Land Commission, 1868
Police in Counties and Boroughs in England and Wales, &c. 418

Talbot, Mr. J. G., *Oxford University*
Education Department — Over-Pressure in Board Schools, 1859
School Accommodation, 1857
Egypt, Defence of—Expenses—Supplementary Estimate, 501
Supply—National Gallery, 1428

[*cont.*

END OF VOLUME CCXCI., AND EIGHTH VOLUME OF SESSION 1884.

LONDON: CORNELIUS BUCK, 22, PATERNOSTER ROW, E.C.